ANNOTATED LEADING CASES OF

INTERNATIONAL CRIMINAL TRIBUNALS

VOLUME II:

THE INTERNATIONAL CRIMINAL TRIBUNAL

FOR RWANDA 1994-1999

André KLIP and Göran SLUITER (eds.)

Intersentia • Hart • Verlag Österreich

Please cite as: ICTR, Sentence, *Prosecutor v. Serughago*, Case No. ICTR-98-39-S, T.Ch. I, 5 February 1999, Klip/Sluiter/ALC-II-823.

Annotated Leading Cases of International Criminal Tribunals
André Klip and Göran Sluiter (eds.)
Cover illustration: Tom Van Delm

© 2001   Intersentia
         Hart Publishing
         Verlag Österreich
         Antwerp – Groningen – Oxford – Vienna
http:// www.intersentia.be

ISBN 90-5095-135-X
D/2001/7849/10
NUGI 698

TABLE OF CONTENTS

Part 4 Judgement and Sentencing

10. Judgement

11. Judgement and Sentence

12. Judgement, Sentence and Plea of Guilty

PREFACE

This is the second volume in the series "Annotated Leading Cases of International Criminal Tribunals". It contains decisions of the International Criminal Tribunal for Rwanda (ICTR). The ICTR has jurisdiction over the tragedy that took place in Rwanda in 1994. Estimates are that in excess of half a million persons were killed over a period of just a few months. The systematic planning and commission of the genocide triggered the establishment of the ICTR by the Security Council by Resolution 955 (1994), adopted on 8 November 1994. The ICTR has its seat in Arusha, Tanzania. The annex to the Resolution contains the Statute of the Tribunal. In many respects the ICTR Statute is identical to that of the Yugoslav Tribunal, which had been established one year earlier. Still, there are a few important differences between the two Statutes. One concerns the subject matter jurisdiction of the Tribunals. Whereas the ICTR has, according to Article 4 of the ICTR Statute, jurisdiction over violations of Article 3 common to the four "Geneva Conventions" (1949), the ICTY has a more expanded jurisdiction over grave breaches of these conventions (Article 2) and over violations of the laws or customs of war (Article 3), which do not appear in the ICTR Statute. A more procedural difference between the two Tribunals is that the ICTR does not have a separate Appeals Chamber. According to Article 12 (2) of the ICTR Statute, the Appeals Chamber of the ICTY also serves as the appellate body for the ICTR. Furthermore, the two Tribunals share one Prosecutor.

It cannot be denied that the ICTR suffered from a difficult start. This included serious problems in the organisation and management of the Tribunal. An internal United Nations inquiry, under the supervision of under Secretary-General Paschke, revealed evidence of general mismanagement within the Tribunal. Other problems concerned the large geographical distance between Arusha, Kigali and The Hague and limited courtroom facilities. In spite of these problems, the ICTR has managed to produce interesting case law, that begs for wider dessimination.

This volume bears many similarities to the previous one. The reader will again find the full text of the decision, identical to the written original text as issued by the Press and Information Office of the ICTR, including individual opinions. We could only include the full text of a significant number of decisions by reducing the original format of the decision considerably. Still, we wanted the reader to be able to identify the page of the original text, which can be found throughout the text in brackets [ ]. Just as with the first volume, we have incorporated *corrigenda* issued by the Tribunal. Another important similarity with the previous volume involves the inclusion of commentaries of competent scholars to one or more decisions. Exceptionally, a decision has been commented upon by two scholars.
This volume covers the most important case law of the ICTR in the first five years of its existence. It includes all important decisions issued before 31 December 1999.

This volume, however, also differs in some respects from the previous one. The reader will find an index at the end of the book. Volume III of the series, dealing with ICTY case law, will contain a cumulative index for Volumes I and III. Another difference is that we have given considerable more scope for discussion of the cases to our commentators. This has enabled them to elaborate in greater detail on (more) aspects of a decision. Another difference, by definition, relates to the selection of decisions. The different selection and the different context in which the ICTR operates, have also resulted in minor changes in the classification of the case law. We have classified the decisions under four different thematic Parts. This is one fewer than in the previous volume because the ICTR has never resorted - fortunately- to the so-called Rule 61 procedure.

Part 1 deals with preliminary matters and covers decisions of the ICTR before the actual proceedings have commenced. Just as in the first volume, it contains a decision on jurisdiction, the Kanyabashi case. What is new are a number of decisions on the form of the indictment. Given the importance of this issue for subsequent proceedings, we have found it necessary to incorporate some of these decisions in the cases of Nsabimana, Bagambiki, Ruggiu and Kabiligi and Ntabakuze.

Part 2 concentrates on relations to national jurisdictions. It includes matters of co-operation, but is broader in scope than the heading in the first volume: "cooperation with national authorities". This Part includes three decisions on deferral requests. Deferral includes a dimension of co-operation, but also deals with the fair administration of justice. The importance of deferral for the effective functioning of the ICTR is self-evident. We have included three deferral decisions, because they each amount to the commencement of important prosecutions by the ICTR. The second group of decisions in this Part have been categorised under the heading "Decisions relating to the release of Ntuyahaga". The release of accused Ntuyahaga has resulted in interesting case law, part of which raises issues of State co-operation.

Part 3 covers a wide variety of decisions, which all raise so-called procedural matters. This is, of course, a potentially broad category. The first group of decisions under this heading relate to the arrest and transfer to the custody of the Tribunal of accused persons. Although these decisions also raise aspects of State co-operation, the primary significance of these decisions, in our view, lies in the presence of the accused before the ICTR, which is indispensable for the progress of the trial. Two decisions deal with the arrest of Barayagwiza. Since this volume does not contain decisions issued after 31 December 1999, we have not incorporated the final decision of the Appeals Chamber pertaining to the arrest of Barayagwiza; this decision will appear in a subsequent volume.

Under this heading the reader will also find a substantial number of decisions dealing with evidentiary issues, divided into those relating to witnesses and those relating to disclosure in the broadest meaning of the term.

Seven decisions relating to witnesses have been included. They all deal with attempts to obtain testimonial evidence, by ordering or facilitating the appearance of witnesses at trial. Given the importance of testimonial evidence for the functioning of the *ad hoc* Tribunals, these decisions have been included.

Disclosure of evidence has given rise to difficult evidentiary questions, in an international context. The associated issues are of importance for shaping the law of criminal procedure of the ICTR; therefore we have included some of these decisions. An essential condition for a fair trial is the free choice of counsel. The way the accused before the ICTR (seek to) effectuate their right to counsel has given rise to interesting decisions in the Ntakirutimana and Akayesu cases, which have both been published.

Finally, we have included in this part four decisions which concentrate on the right of the accused to appeal and the scope of such appeals. In particular, as more and more prosecutions and trials take place, these become important issues for the Tribunal. Whereas the accused has to be given access to a meaningful exercise of the right of appeal, the Appeals Chamber should not be unduly overburdened with elaborate appeals.

Part 4 covers all Judgements and Sentencing Judgements issued by the ICTR in the first five years of its existence. We have divided this Part into three sub-headings. The first contains only judgements, establishing the guilt or innocence of the accused, the Akayesu judgement. We have then included a sub-heading relating to Judgement and Sentencing judgement. This is the result of a change in the Rules of the Tribunals according to which the establishment of guilt and the accompanying sentence need to be pronounced in one decision. This was the case in the Kayishema and Ruzindana decision and in the Rutaganda decision. The Kayishema and Ruzindana case is accompanied by two separate commentaries. Given the importance of the issue of cumulative charging, demonstrated by a Separate Opinion of Judge Khan on this matter, we believe it necessary and appropriate to provide for a separate commentary on this issue.

Finally, Part 4 contains a sub-category including sentencing judgements. These include a sentencing judgement issued some time after the establishment of the guilt of the accused, in the Akayesu case. In addition, there are two sentencing judgements following a plea of guilty by the accused, in the Kambanda and Serushago cases. We have also included the decision relating to the plea of guilty in the Serushago case.

This being the second volume of Annotated Leading Cases of International Criminal Tribunals, we have already planned publication of the third and fourth volumes containing important decisions of the ICTY in the coming two years. We will also follow other legal developments. In a future we may therefore also see volumes with decisions of the international criminal court and of the Special Court for Sierra Leone.

We owe acknowledgments to many persons without whom we could not have completed this second volume. These include our publisher Intersentia, and particularly Hans Kluwer and Lieve Rampelbergh, our student-assistants Linda Couwenberg and Dominique Donkersloot, who assisted with the corrections of the texts and the Netherlands School of Human Rights Research that greatly facilitated our work. Steven Freeland from the University of New South Wales, Australia, offered tremendous help by correcting our English. Last but not least, we wish to thank the distinguished authors for their commentaries to the decisions.

We hope that this volume may contribute to the dessimination of the important work of the ICTR and that it will provide access to its decisions to practitioners, as well as to academics.

André Klip and Göran Sluiter
Utrecht, October 2000

UNITED NATIONS NATIONS UNIES

International Criminal Tribunal for Rwanda
Trial Chamber 2

Before: Judge William H. Sekule, Presiding Judge OR: ENG
Judge Tafazzal H. Khan
Judge Navanethem Pillay

Registrar: Mr. Frederik Harhoff

Decision of: 18 June 1997

THE PROSECUTOR

versus

JOSEPH KANYABASHI

Case No. ICTR-96-15-T

DECISION ON THE DEFENCE MOTION ON JURISDICTION

Office of the Prosecutor:
  Mr. Yacob Haile-Mariam

Counsel for the Defence:
  Mr. Evans Monari
  Mr. Michel Marchand

[page 2] THE TRIBUNAL,

SITTING AS Trial Chamber 2 of the International Criminal Tribunal for Rwanda ("the Tribunal"), composed of Judge William H. Sekule as Presiding Judge, Judge Tafazzal H. Khan and Judge Navanethem Pillay;

CONSIDERING the indictment submitted by the Prosecutor against Joseph Kanyabashi pursuant to Rule 47 of the Rules of Procedure and Evidence ("the Rules") and confirmed by Judge Yakov A. Ostrovsky on 15 July 1996 on the basis that there existed sufficient evidence to provide reasonable grounds for believing that he has committed genocide, conspiracy to commit genocide, crimes against humanity and serious violations of Article 3 common to the Geneva Conventions and Additional Protocol II thereto;

TAKING NOTE of the transfer of the accused from Belgium to the Tribunal's Detention Facilities on 8 November 1996 and his initial appearance on 29 November 1996 before this Chamber;

BEING NOW SEIZED OF the preliminary motion filed by the Defence Counsel on 17 April 1997 pursuant to Rule 73(A)(i) of the Rules, challenging the jurisdiction of the Tribunal;

HAVING ALSO RECEIVED the Prosecutor's response, filed on 22 May 1997, to the Defence Counsel's motion;

HAVING HEARD the parties at the hearing of the Defence Counsel's motion and the Prosecutor's response, held on 26 May 1997;

CONSIDERING the provisions of the UN Charter, the Statute of the Tribunal and the Rules, in particular Rules 72 and 73;

TAKING INTO CONSIDERATION the decision of 10 August 1995 of the Trial Chamber of the International Criminal Tribunal for the Former Yugoslavia in Case No. IT-94-1-T, The Prosecutor versus Duško Tadić; and the decision of 2 October 1995 rendered by the Appeals Chamber of the International Criminal Tribunal for the Former Yugoslavia in Case No. IT-94-1-AR72, on appeal of the said decision of the Trail Chamber.

AFTER HAVING DELIBERATED:

1.   The Defence Counsel submitted his preliminary motion pursuant to Rule 73(A)(i) of the Rules 139 days after the initial appearance of the accused. By so doing, he manifestly exceeded the time-limit prescribed in Rule 73(B) of the Rules, which stipulates that preliminary motions by the accused shall be brought within sixty (60) days after the initial appearance, and in any case before the hearing on the merits. Rule 73(C) of the Rules further lays down that failure to apply within this time-limit shall constitute a waiver of the right, unless the Trial Chamber grants relief to hear the preliminary motion upon good cause being shown by the Defence Counsel.**[page 3]**

2.   The Trial Chamber, therefore, must first examine whether there are reasonable grounds for proceeding with the examination of this preliminary motion.

A.   On the Consequence of the Defence Counsel's Failure to Submit his Preliminary Motion Within Sixty Days After the Initial Appearance Of the Accused.

3.   Rule 72(B) of the Rules allows the Prosecution as well as the Defence to file preliminary motions and further establishes that the Trial Chamber shall dispose thereof *in limine litis*. The purpose of this requirement, evidently, is to ensure that all basic questions and fundamental objections raised by the parties against the competence, the proceedings and the functions of the Tribunal are properly addressed and dealt with before the beginning of the trial on its merits.

4.   Rule 73(A) identifies some of the preliminary motions which must, for reasons of expediency, be raised and disposed of before the beginning of the trial on the merits, such as objections against the jurisdiction of the Tribunal or against defects in the indictment. Rule 73(B), accordingly, specifies that such motions must be filed within sixty (60) days after the initial appearance in order to ensure their consideration well in advance of the trial. Rule 73(C) goes on to establish that failure to meet the time-limit shall constitute a waiver of the right to submit such preliminary motions. If, however, the Defence shows good cause, the Trial Chamber might grant relief from this waiver. These Rules are clear and leave no room for misunderstanding.

5.   The Trial Chamber notes, however, that the Defence motion was filed out of time, and was surprised that neither the Defence nor the Prosecutor made any reference to this fact when the preliminary motion was heard by the Trial Chamber. Defence Counsel did not file any request for a waiver and did not provide the Trial Chamber with any explanation for his failure to respect the prescribed time-limit. The Prosecutor, on her part, did not object to hearing this motion.

6.   Notwithstanding the fact that some of the questions raised by the Defence Counsel have already been addressed in the decision rendered on 2 October 1995 by the Appeals Chamber for the Former Yugoslavia, the Trial Chamber finds that, in view of the issues raised regarding the establishment of this Tribunal, its jurisdiction and its independence and in the interests of justice, that the Defence Counsel's motion deserves a hearing and full consideration. The Trial Chamber, therefore, grants relief from the waiver *suo motu* and will thus proceed with the examination of the Defence Counsel's preliminary motion.

B.   On the Substance of the Preliminary Motion

7.   In his preliminary motion, the Defence Counsel raised a number of challenges concerning the jurisdiction of the Tribunal. These challenges can be adequately condensed into the following five principal objections:

(i)   That the sovereignty of States, in particular that of the Republic of Rwanda, was violated by the fact that the Tribunal was not established by a treaty through the General Assembly;

(ii)   that the Security Council lacked competence to establish an ad-hoc Tribunal under Chapter VII of the UN Charter;[page 4]

(iii)   that the primacy of the Tribunal's jurisdiction over national courts was unjustified and violated the principle of *jus de non evocando*;

(iv)   that the Tribunal cannot have jurisdiction over individuals directly under international law; and

(v)   that the Tribunal is not and cannot be impartial and independent;

8.   The Prosecutor responded that the basic arguments in the Defence Counsel's motion were addressed by the Trial Chamber and, in particular, by the Appeals Chamber of the International Criminal Tribunal for the Former Yugoslavia in the Tadić-case. The Trial Chamber notes that, in terms of Article 12(2) of the Statute, the two Tribunals share the same Judges of their Appeals Chambers and have adopted largely similar Rules of Procedure and Evidence for the purpose of providing uniformity in the jurisprudence of the two Tribunals. The Trial Chamber, respects the persuasive authority of the decision of the Appeals Chamber of the International Criminal Tribunal for the Former Yugoslavia and has taken careful note of the decision rendered by the Appeals Chamber in the Tadic case.

B.1.   On the Defence Counsel's Objection that the Sovereignty of States, in Particular that of the Republic of Rwanda, Was Violated by the Fact that the Tribunal Was Not Established by a Treaty Through the General Assembly.

9.   The Defence Counsel submitted in his written and oral submissions that the Tribunal should and in fact could only have been established by an international treaty upon recommendation of the General Assembly, which would have permitted the member States of the United Nations to express their

approval or disapproval of the establishment of an ad-hoc Tribunal. The Defence Counsel argued that by leaving the establishment of the Tribunal to the Security Council through a Resolution under Chapter VII of the UN Charter, the United Nations not only encroached upon the sovereignty of the Republic of Rwanda, and other Member States, but also frustrated the endeavours of its General Assembly to establish a permanent criminal court. The Tribunal, in the Defence Counsel's view, was therefore not lawfully established.

10.   The Prosecutor, in response to this first objection raised by Defence Counsel, rejected the notion that the Tribunal was unlawfully established and contended that, since there was a need for an effective and expeditious implementation of the decision to establish the Tribunal, the treaty approach would have been ineffective because of the considerable time required for the establishment of an instrument and for its entry into force.

11.   The Trial Chamber finds that two issues need to be addressed. One is whether the accused as an individual has *locus standi* to raise a plea of infringement of the sovereignty of States, in particular that of the Republic of Rwanda, and the other is whether the sovereignty of the Republic of Rwanda and other Member States were in fact violated in the present case.

12.   As regards the first of these questions, the Appeals Chamber held in the Tadić-case that **[page 5]**

"To bar an accused from raising such a plea is tantamount to deciding that, in this day and age, an international court could not, in a criminal matter where the liberty of an accused is at stake, examine a plea raising the issue of violation of State sovereignty."

The Trial Chamber agrees with this conclusion and accepts that the accused in the present case can raise the plea of State sovereignty. In any event, it is the individual and not the State who has been subjected to the jurisdiction of the Tribunal.

13.   As regards the second question whether the sovereignty of the Republic of Rwanda has been violated by the Security Council's decision to establish the Tribunal, the Trial Chamber notes that membership of the United Nations entail certain limitations upon the sovereignty of the member States. This is true in particular by virtue of the fact that all member States, pursuant to Article 25 of the UN Charter, have agreed to accept and carry out the decisions of the Security Council in accordance with the Charter. For instance, the use of force against a State sanctioned by the Security Council in accordance with Article 41 of the UN Charter is one clear example of limitations upon sovereignty of the State in question which can be imposed by the United Nations.

14.   The Trial Chamber notes, furthermore, that the establishment of the ICTR was called for by the Government of Rwanda itself, which maintained that an international criminal tribunal could assist in prosecuting those responsible for acts of genocide and crimes against humanity and in this way promote the restoration of peace and reconciliation in Rwanda. The Ambassador of Rwanda, during the discussion and adoption of Resolution 955 in the Security Council on 8 November 1994 declared that:

"The tribunal will help national reconciliation and the construction of a new society based on social justice and respect for the fundamental rights of the human person, all of which will be possible only if those responsible for the Rwandese tragedy are brought to justice."

15.   Against this background, the Trial Chamber is of the view that the Security Council's establishment of the Tribunal through a Resolution under Chapter VII of the UN Charter and with the participation of the Government of Rwanda, rather than by a treaty adopted by the Member States under the auspices of the General Assembly, did not violate the sovereignty of the Republic of Rwanda and that of the Member States of the United Nations.

16.   The Defence Counsel further argued that the establishment of the Tribunal through a resolution of the Security Council effectively undermined the General Assembly's initiative to set up a permanent international Criminal Court. The Trial Chamber, however, mindful of the fact that such a tribunal may well be created by an international treaty, finds that this question has no bearing on the jurisdiction of this Tribunal and must therefore, be rejected.

B.2. On the Defence Counsel's Objections that the Security Council Lacked Competence to Establish an *ad-hoc* Tribunal under Chapter VII of the UN Charter

17.   The second main issue addressed by the Defence relates to the interpretation and delimitation of Chapter VII of the UN Charter and more specifically to the contents and boundaries of the authority of the Security Council.

18.   In his written and oral submissions, the Defence Counsel argued that the establishment of the Tribunal by the Security Council was ill-founded for five basic reasons: **[page 6]**

(i)   that the conflict in Rwanda did not pose any treat to international peace and security;

(ii)   that there was no international conflict to warrant any action by the Security Council;

(iii)   that the Security Council thus could not act within Chapter VII of the UN Charter;

(iv)   that the establishment of an ad-hoc tribunal was never a measure contemplated by Article 41 of the UN Charter; and finally

(v)   that the Security Council has no authority to deal with the protection of Human Rights.

The Trial Chamber will now examine each of these contentions in turn.

19.   *"The conflict in Rwanda dit not pose any threat to international peace and security".*

On several occasions, e.g. in Congo, Somalia and Liberia, the Security Council has established that incidents such as sudden migration of refugees across the borders to neighbouring countries and extension or diffusion of an internal armed conflict into foreign territory may constitute a threat to international peace and security. This, might happen, in particular where the areas immediately affected have exhausted their resources. The reports submitted by the Special Rapporteur for Rwanda of the United Nations Commission on Human Rights (see Doc. S/1994/1157) and also by the Commission of Experts appointed by the Secretary General (see Doc. S/1994/1125) concluded that the conflict in Rwanda as well as the stream of refugees had created a highly volatile situation in some of the neighbouring regions. As a matter of fact, this conclusion was subsequently shared by the Security Council and formed the basis for the adoption of Security Council's resolution 955 (1994) of 8 November 1994.

20.   Although bound by the provisions in Chapter VII of the UN Charter and in particular Article 39 of the Charter, the Security Council has a wide margin of discretion in deciding when and where there exists a threat to international peace and security. By their very nature, however, such discretionary assessments are not justiciable since they involve the consideration of a number of social, political and circumstantial factors which cannot be weighed and balanced objectively by this Trial Chamber.

21.   While it is true that the conflict in Rwanda was internal in the sense that it emerged from inherent tensions between the two major groups forming the population within the territory of Rwanda and otherwise did not involve the direct participation of armed forces belonging to any other State, the Trial Chamber cannot accept the Defence Counsel's notion that the conflict did not pose any threat to international peace and security. The question of, whether or not the conflict posed a threat to international peace and security is a matter to be decided exclusively by the Security Council. The Trial Chamber nevertheless takes judicial notice of the fact that the conflict in Rwanda created a massive wave of refugees, many of whom were armed, into the neighbouring countries which by itself entailed a considerable risk of serious destabilisation of the local areas in the host countries where the refugees had settled. The demographical composition of the population in certain neighbouring regions outside the territory of Rwanda, furthermore, showed features which suggest that the conflict in Rwanda might eventually spread to some or all of these neighbouring regions. **[page 7]**

22.   The Trial Chamber concludes that there is no merit in the Defence Counsel's argument that the conflict in Rwanda did not pose any threat to international peace and security and holds that this was a matter to be decided exclusively by the Security Council.

23. ***"There was no international conflict to warrant any action by the Security Council."***

The Defence Counsel further contends that there was no international conflict to warrant any action by the Security Council. This argument has been partly addressed in the preceding paragraphs in the sense that *if* the Security Council had decided that the conflict in Rwanda did in fact pose a threat to international peace and security, this conflict would thereby fall within the ambit of the Security Council's powers to restore and maintain international peace and security pursuant to the provisions in Chapter VII of the UN Charter.

24. The Security Council's authority to take such action, furthermore, exists independently of whether or not the conflict was deemed to be international in character. The decisive pre-requisite for the Security Council's prerogative under Article 39 and 41 of the UN Charter is not whether there *exists* an *international* conflict, but whether the conflict at hand entails a threat to international peace and security. Internal conflicts, too, may well have international implications which can justify Security Council action. The Trial Chamber holds that there is no basis for the Defence Counsel's submission that the Security Council's competence to act rested on a pre-existing international conflict.

25. ***"The Security Council could not act within Chapter VII of the UN Charter."***

During his oral submission, the Defence Counsel further added that the Security Council was not competent to act in the case of the conflict in Rwanda because international peace and security had already been re-established by the time the Security Council decided to create the Tribunal.

26. The Trial Chamber observes, once again, that this argument entails a finding of fact based on evidence and that, in any case, the question of whether or not the Security Council was justified in taking actions under Chapter VII when it did, is a matter to be determined by the Security Council itself. The Trial Chamber notes, in particular, that cessation of the atrocities of the conflict does not necessarily imply that international peace and security had been restored, because peace and security cannot be said to be re-established adequately without justice being done. In the Trial Chamber's view, the achievement of international peace and security required that swift international action be taken by the Security Council to bring to justice those responsible for the atrocities in the conflict.

27. ***"The establishment of an ad-hoc tribunal was never a measure contemplated by Article 41 of the UN Charter."***

The thrust of this argument lies in the contention that the establishment of an ad-hoc Tribunal to prosecute perpetrators of genocide and violations of international humanitarian law is not a measure contemplated by the provisions of Chapter VII of the UN Charter. While it is true that establishment of judicial bodies is not directly mentioned in Article 41 of the UN Charter as a measure to be considered in the restoration and maintenance of peace, it clearly falls within the ambit of measures to satisfy this goal. The list of actions contained in Article 41 is clearly not exhaustive but indicates some examples of the measures which the Security Council might eventually decide to impose on States in order to remedy a conflict or an imminent threat to international peace and security. This is also the view of the Appeals Chamber in the Tardic-case. **[page 8]**

28. ***"The Security Council has no authority to deal with the protection of Human Rights"***

Finally, the Defence Counsel holds that the international protection of Human Rights is embedded in particular international instruments such as the global International Covenants on Civil and Political Rights & Social, Economic and Cultural Rights and in the regional conventions on Human Rights for Europe and Africa, all of which have established particular international institutions entrusted with the task of protecting the body of international Human Rights. The Defence Counsel claims, therefore, that the protection of Human Rights is not a matter for the Security Council.

29. The Trial Chamber cannot accept the Defence Counsel's argument that the existence of specialized institutions for the protection of Human Rights precludes the Security Council from taking action against violation of this body of law. Rather to the contrary, the protection of international Human Rights is the responsibility of all United Nations organs, the Security Council included, without any limitation, in conformity with the UN Charter.

B.3. **On the Defence Counsel's Objections Against the Primacy of the Tribunal's Jurisdiction Over National Courts And Against Violation of the Principle of *Jus de non Evocando.***

30.   Although the Defence Counsel did not explicitly challenge the primacy of the Tribunal's jurisdiction over national courts, this objection is implied in the Defence Counsel's contention that establishment of the Tribunal violated the principle of *jus de non evocando.*

31.   This principle, originally derived from constitutional law in civil law jurisdictions, establishes that persons accused of certain crimes should retain their right to be tried before the regular domestic criminal Courts rather than by politically founded ad-hoc criminal tribunals which, in times of emergency, may fail to provide impartial justice. As stated by the Appeals Chamber in the Tadić-case: "As a matter of fact and of law the principle advocated by the Appellant aims at one very specific goal: to avoid the creation of special or extraordinary courts designed to try political offences in times of social unrest without guarantees of a fair trial." In the Trial Chamber's opinion, however, the Tribunal is far from being an institution designed for the purpose of removing, for political reasons, certain criminal offenders from fair and impartial justice and have them prosecuted for political crimes before prejudiced arbitrators.

32.   It is true that the Tribunal has primacy over domestic criminal Courts and may at any stage request national Courts to defer to the competence of the Tribunal pursuant to article 8 of the Statute of the Tribunal, according to which the Tribunal may request that national Courts defer to the competence of the Tribunal at any stage of their proceedings. The Tribunal's primacy over national Courts is also reflected in the principle of *non bis in idem* as laid down in Article 9 of the Statute and in Article 28 of the Statute which establishes that States shall comply without undue delay with any request for assistance or an order issued by a Trial Chamber. The primacy thereby entrenched for the Tribunal, however, is exclusively derived from the fact that the Tribunal is established under Chapter VII of the UN Charter, which in turn enables the Tribunal to issue directly binding international legal orders and requests to States, irrespective of their consent. Failure of States to comply with such legally binding orders and requests may, under certain conditions, be reported by the President of the Tribunal to the Security Council for further action. **[page 9]** The Trial Chamber concludes, therefore, that the principle of *jus de non evocando* has not been violated.

B.4. **On the Defence Counsel's Objections Against the Tribunal's Jurisdiction over Individuals Directly under International Law.**

33.   The Defence Counsel further contends that bestowing the Tribunal with jurisdiction over individuals is inconsistent with the UN Charter, for the reason that the Security Council has no authority over individuals, and that only States can pose threats to international peace and security.

34.   The Prosecution responded to this contention by citing the Nüremberg Trials which, in the Prosecution's view, established that individuals who have committed crimes under international law can be held criminally responsible directly under international law. The Prosecutor further contended that attribution of individual criminal responsibility is a fundamental expression of the need for enforcement action by the Security Council. It is indeed difficult to separate the individual from the State, as the duties and rights of States are only duties and rights of the individuals who compose them, and as international criminal law, like other branches of law, deals with the regulation of human conduct. It is to individuals, not the abstract, that international law applies, and it is against individuals that it should provide sanctions. In the words of the Deputy Prosecutor in the trial against *Frank Hans* in 1946:

> "It seems intolerable to every sensitized human being that the men who put their good will at disposition of the State entity in order to make use of the power and material resources of this entity to slaughter, as they have done, millions of human beings in the execution of a policy long since determined, should be assured of immunity. The principle of State sovereignty which might protect these men is only a mask; this mask removed, the man's responsibility reappears."

35.   The Trial Chamber recalls that the question of direct individual criminal responsibility under international law is and has been a controversial issue within and between various legal systems for

several decades and that the Nüremberg trials in particular have been interpreted differently in respect of the position of the individual as a subject under international law. By establishing the two International Criminal Tribunals for the Former Yugoslavia and Rwanda, however, the Security Council explicitly extended international legal obligations and criminal responsibilities directly to individuals for violations of international humanitarian law. In doing so, the Security Council provided an important innovation of international law, but there is nothing in the Defence Counsel's motion to suggest that this extension of the applicability of international law against individuals was not justified or called for by the circumstances, notably the seriousness, the magnitude and the gravity of the crimes committed during the conflict.

36.   In his submissions, furthermore, the Defence Counsel referred to a number of other areas of conflicts and incidents in which the Security Council took no action to establish an international criminal tribunal, e.g. Congo, Somalia and Liberia, and the Defence Counsel seems to infer from the lack of such action in these cases that individual criminal responsibility should not be taken in the case of the conflict in Rwanda. The Trial Chamber, however, disagrees entirely with this perception. The fact that the Security Council, for previously prevailing geo-strategic and international political reasons, was unable in the past to take adequate measures to bring to justice the **[page 10]** perpetrators of crimes against international humanitarian law is not an acceptable argument against introducing measures to punish serious violations of international humanitarian law when this becomes an option under international law. The Trial Chamber, thus, cannot accept the Defence Counsel's objections against the Tribunal's jurisdiction over individuals.

B.5. On the Defence Counsel's Objections Based on the Allegation that the Tribunal is not Impartial and Independent.

37.   The Defense Motion asserted that the Tribunal was set up by the Security Council, a political body and as such the Tribunal is just another appendage of an international organ of policing and coercion, devoid of independence.

38.   The Prosecutor, in response, challenged the claim in the Defense Motion that the Tribunal cannot act both as a subsidiary organ of the Security Council and as an independent Judicial body. He stated that although the ICTY and the ICTR share certain aspects of personnel, materials and means of operation, the Tribunal for Rwanda is a separate Tribunal with its own Statute, its own sphere of jurisdiction and its own rules of operation and as such it has legal independence.

39.   This Trial Chamber is of the view that criminal courts worldwide are the creation of legislatures which are eminently political bodies. This was an observation also made by the Trial Chamber in the Tadić-case. To support this view, the Trial Chamber in that case relied on *Effect of Awards of Compensation made by the United Nations Administrative Tribunal* (1954) I.C.J. 47, 53; Advisory Opinion of 13 July), which specifically held that a political organ of the United Nations, in that case the General Assembly, could and had created "an independent and truly judicial body." Likewise, the Security Council could create such a body using its wide discretion under Chapter VII.

40.   This independence is, for example, demonstrated by the fact that the Tribunal is not bound by national rules of evidence as stated under rule 89 A of the Rules of Procedure and Evidence. The Tribunal is free to apply those Rules of Evidence which best favor a fair determination of the matter before it as stipulated in rule 89(B) of the Rules.

41.   Further, the judges of the Tribunal exercise their *judicial* duties independently and freely and are under oath to act honorably, faithfully, impartially and conscientiously as stipulated in rule 14 of the Rules. Judges do not account to the Security Council for their judicial functions.

42.   In this Trial Chamber's view, the personal independence of the judges of the Tribunal and the integrity of the Tribunal are underscored by Article 12 (1) of the Statute of the Tribunal which states that persons of high moral character, integrity, impartiality, who possess adequate qualifications to become

judges in their respective countries and having widespread experience in criminal law, international law including international humanitarian law and human rights law, shall be elected.

43.   This Trial Chamber also subscribes to a view which was expressed by the Appeals Chamber in the Tadic case that when determining whether a tribunal has been 'established by law', consideration should be made to the setting up of an organ in keeping with the proper international standards providing all the guarantees of fairness and justice. **[page 11]**

44.   Under the Statute and the Rules of Procedure and Evidence, the Tribunal will ensure that the accused receives a fair trial. This principle of fair trial is further entrenched in Article 20 which embodies the major principles for the provision of a fair trial, *inter alia*, the principles of public hearing and subject to cross examination. The rights of the accused are also set out such as the right to counsel, presumption of innocence until the contrary is proved beyond a reasonable doubt, privilege against self-incrimination and the right to adequate time for the preparation of his/her case. These guarantees are further included in rules 62, 63 and 78 of the Rules. The rights of the accused enumerated above are based upon Article 14 of the International Covenant on Civil and Political Rights and are similar to those found in Article 6 of the European Convention on Human Rights.

45.   Defence Counsel argued that the obligation imposed on the Tribunal to report to the Security Council derogates its independence as a judicial organ. The Prosecutor contended that this obligation was discretionary. In fact it is mandatory. In Article 34 of the Statute, the Tribunal is duty bound to do this annually. This requirement is not only a link between it and the Security Council but it is also a channel of communication to the International community, which has an interest in the issues being addressed and the right to be informed of the activities of the Tribunal. In the Chamber's view, the Tribunal's obligation to report progress to the Security Council is purely administrative and not a judicial act and therefore does not in any way impinge upon the impartiality and independence of its judicial decision.

46.   The Defence Counsel further contended that African jurisprudence and Human Rights Covenants were overlooked in the setting up of the Tribunal. This contention cannot be correct because the important instruments on human rights in Africa, including the Charter of the Organization of African Unity (O.A.U.) and the African Charter On Human Rights ("the African Charter") were indirectly included in the law applicable to the Tribunal. Articles 3 and 7 of the African Charter on Human and People's Rights, for example, contain rights which are similar to those guaranteed in the Statute.

47.   The Defence Counsel argued that the impartiality of the Tribunal has not been demonstrated for the reason that there has been selective prosecution only of persons belonging to the Hutu ethnic group.

48.   In his response, the Prosecutor dismissed these allegations and stated that indictments have been issued against leading perpetrators of the genocide and that subject to the availability of evidence, he intended to prosecute Hutu and Tutsi "extremists". The use of the word "extremists" is inaccurate and unfortunate, in view of Article 1 of the statute.

49.   The Trial Chamber simply reiterates that, pursuant to Article 1 of the Statute, all persons who are suspected of having committed crimes falling within the jurisdiction of the Tribunal are liable to prosecution.

50.   The Trial Chamber is not persuaded by the arguments advanced by the Defence Counsel that the Tribunal is not impartial and independent and accordingly rejects this contention. **[page 13]**

FOR THESE REASONS,

DECIDES to dismiss the motion submitted by the Defence Counsel challenging the jurisdiction of the Tribunal.

Arusha, 18 June 1997.

William H. Sekule   T.H. Khan   Navanethem Pillay
Presiding Judge   Judge   Judge

Pronounced in open Court on the 3rd of July 1997

WH Sekule
Presiding Judge

On 2 October 1995 the Appeals Chamber of the ICTY rendered its ground breaking judgement on jurisdiction in the Tadić case.[1] Almost 2 years later Trial Chamber 2 of the ICTR is faced in the case against Kanyabashi with an analogous challenge to its jurisdiction.[2] In the light of the Tadić judgement it is not at all surprising that the Trial Chamber rejects the challenge and affirms its jurisdiction: the reference to the former judgement in preambular paragraph 8 and the expression of respect for "the persuasive authority of the decision of the Appeals Chamber of the International Criminal Tribunal" (par. 8) make it clear from the outset that Trial Chamber 2 does not intend to deviate from the appellate jurisprudence of the ICTY. This explains the relative brevity of the Kanyabashi decision. Quite apart from the merits of the Tadić judgement in substance, the acceptance of that decision as a quasi-precedent[3] is desirable as a matter of judicial policy. Still, the decision of Trial Chamber 2 in Kanyabashi is not simply a copy of the jurisdiction judgement in Tadić. On closer reading one cannot fail to note that, in some respects, the ICTR in Kanyabashi places slightly different emphasis in its decision than did the ICTY in Tadić.

The Trial Chamber allows the accused to raise the plea of an infringement of State sovereignty by the establishment of the ICTR. It confirms the statement in Tadić that an international criminal court must allow the individual to make such a plea (par. 12). The judges in both Tadić and in Kanyabashi are certainly well advised to confine their statements to the level of international criminal jurisdiction. It is difficult, however, to find a particular distinguishing reason which justifies not transposing these statements to the level of national criminal jurisdiction as well. It is thus very likely that ICTY/ ICTR jurisprudence on the State sovereignty point will be relied upon to question the application of the doctrine of *male captus bene detentus* in national *fora* – a doctrine which is based on the idea that the individual cannot invoke the violation of State sovereignty.

In substance, the Trial Chamber rejects the State sovereignty objection primarily by reference to articles 25 and 41 of the UN Charter (par. 13). This reference is correct and in itself sufficient to deny a violation of Rwanda's sovereignty. As the ICTY did in Tadić,[4] the Trial Chamber tries to infer the existence of the consent of the State(s) concerned as an additional basis. This is a dubious argument given the eventual negative vote by Rwanda on the establishment of the ICTR.[5] Interestingly, the Trial Chamber does not refer to the principle of universal jurisdiction as did the ICTY in Tadić at this juncture.[6] This should not, however, be construed as a deviation from Tadić; most probably the reliance on universal jurisdiction was simply not considered necessary in the light of the Tribunal's firm legal basis under Chapter VII of the UN Charter.

---

[1]   ALC-I-33 *et seq.* with comment by H. Fischer at 140 *et seq.* The literature on this judicial milestone has been growing steadily since; for more detailed case studies see *inter alia* G. Aldrich, Jurisdiction of the International Criminal Tribunal for the Former Yugoslavia, 90 American Journal of International Law 1996, p. 64; J. E. Alvarez, Nuremberg Revisited: The Tadić Case, 7 European Journal of International Law 1996, p. 245; C. Greenwood, International Humanitarian Law and the *Tadić* Case, 7 European Journal of International Law 1996, p. 265; C. Kreß, Friedenssicherungsrecht und Konfliktsvölkerrecht auf der Schwelle zur Postmoderne: Das Urteil des Internationalen Straftribunals für das ehemalige Jugoslawien (Appeals Chamber) im Fall Tadić vom 2. Oktober 1995, Europäische Grundrechte Zeitschrift 1996, p. 638; T. Meron, The Continuing Role for Custom in the Formation of International Humanitarian Law, 90 American Journal of International Law 1996, p. 238; G. P. Politakis, Enforcing Humanitarian Law: The Decision of the Appeals Chamber on the *Dusko Tadić* Case (Jurisdiction), 52 Zeitschrift für öffentliches Recht 1997, p. 283; P. Rowe, The International Criminal Tribunal for Yugoslavia: The Decision of the Appeals Chamber on the Interlocutory Appeal on Jurisdiction in the Tadić case, 45 International and Comparative Law Quarterly 1996, p. 691; M. Sassoli, La première décision de la chambre d'appel du Tribunal Pénal pour l'ex Yuogoslavie: Tadić (Compétence), 100 Revue générale de droit international public 1996, p. 101; G. R. Watson, The Humanitarian Law of the Yugoslavia War Crimes Tribunal: Jurisdiction in Prosecutor v. Tadić, 36 Virginia Journal of International Law 1996, p. 687.

[2]   For a first brief summary of the Kanyabashi decision see V. Morris, 92 American Journal of International Law 1998, p. 66.

[3]   The Trial Chamber does not seem to consider this judgement as a precedent in the technical sense. In ICTY, Judgement, *Prosecutor v. Zlatko Aleksovski*, IT-95-14/1-A, A.Ch., 24 March 2000, par. 89 *et seq.* the Appeals Chamber of the ICTY has attributed the legal effect of precedent to its own judgements. In light of the institutional linkage between ICTY and ICTR at the appellate level much can be said for extending this effect so as to operate for both *ad hoc* Tribunals.

[4]   The ICTY Appeals Chamber pointed to the willingness of Bosnia and Germany to co-operate with the Tribunal (note 1, par. 56; ALC-I-54).

[5]   For an account of the position of Rwanda's government on the establishment of the ICTR, see P. Akhavan, 90 American Journal of International Law 1996, p. 504 *et seq.*

[6]   Note 1, par. 57 *et seq.*; ALC-I-54 *et seq.*

The analysis of this legal basis is the object of the following paragraphs (19 to 29).[7] On this point, the decision in Kanyabashi – understandably – is much less elaborate than Tadić (the latter being the first comprehensive judicial analysis of the Security Council powers under Chapter VII of the UN Charter).[8] The crucial question in Kanyabashi is whether the Security Council has the power to intervene in the internal Rwandan conflict by setting up an international criminal tribunal. More interesting than the positive answer to this question *in casu* are some elements of the Chamber's reasoning. The Chamber states that the question whether a conflict poses a threat to international peace and security "is a matter to be decided exclusively by the Security Council" (par. 21). The same sort of ultimate decision making power is accorded to the Security Council with respect to the question whether a particular coercive measure taken under Chapter VII is necessary to restore peace and security (par. 26). This position deviates from Tadić – and in the present writer's view deplorably so. Tadić marks a very significant contribution to the promotion of the rule of law in international affairs in determining that the discretion of the Security Council under article 39 of the UN Charter – wide as it certainly is – has its limits.[9] While denying the existence of such limits, the Chamber in Kanyabashi still seeks – *obiter* from its own point of view – to justify the Security Council's exercise of discretion in the case of Rwanda. Hereby it makes two noteworthy statements. Whereas the Appeals Chamber stated in Tadić that internal armed conflicts may come within the scope of the term "threat to peace" in article 39 of the UN Charter[10] without qualifying such internal armed conflicts further, the Trial Chamber in Kanyabashi places emphasis on the cross-border repercussions of the Rwandan conflict (cf. especially par. 21). This can be read as a slightly more cautious interpretation of article 39 of the UN Charter. With respect to the question at what point in time an international criminal *ad hoc* tribunal may no longer be necessary under article 39 of the UN Charter the Chamber holds that an adequate restoration of peace and security presupposes that justice be done (par. 26). This is both an important and a laudable – though unfortunately not altogether uncontroversial – statement about the interplay between justice and peace.

The last part of the Kanyabashi decision which deserves close attention is the reasoning on the criminal responsibility of individuals under international law (para. 33 *et seq.*). In Tadić it has been acknowledged – on the basis of a careful analysis of international practice – that individuals may be held criminally responsible under customary international law not only for war crimes in the traditional sense but also for crimes committed in internal armed conflict.[11] The Appeals Chamber has summed up the scope of that criminal responsibility in the following words[12]: "Customary law imposes criminal liability for serious violations of common Article 3, as supplemented by other general principles and rules on the protection of victims of internal armed conflict, and for breaching certain fundamental principles and rules regarding means and methods of combat in civil strife." The reference to "other general principles and rules on the protection of victims of internal armed conflict" was meant to point to "the core" of Additional Protocol 2 to the Geneva Conventions.[13] As Article 4 of the ICTR Statute brings all of Additional Protocol 2 under the Tribunal's jurisdiction one would have expected Kanyabashi to elaborate on the general statement in Tadić and to hereby provide a further clarification of the international criminal law of the internal armed conflict. The decision, however, does not provide this clarification. Interestingly, no reference at all is made to Tadić at this point and the whole issue is not discussed in the context of the customary process of "criminalizing internal atrocities". Instead, the Trial Chamber in Kanyabashi calls the Security Council's approach as embodied in both the ICTY and the ICTR Statutes "an important innovation of international law" and simply holds that there is nothing to "suggest that this extension of the applicability of international law against individuals was not justified or called for by the circumstances, notably the seriousness, the magnitude and the gravity of the crimes committed during

---

[7]   The Trial Chamber does not touch further upon the issue whether a Security Council based *ad hoc* Tribunal is entitled to scrutinize the legality of its legal basis. In *Tadić* the Appeals Chamber had affirmed such power as part of its inherent *Kompetenz-Kompetenz* (note 1., par. 14 *et seq.*; ALC-I-39 *et seq.*).

[8]   For an evaluation of this very important part of the Tadić judgement see C. Kreß, note 1, ALC-I-501 *et seq.*

[9]   Note 1, par. 28 *et seq.*; ALC-I-43 *et seq.*

[10]   Note 1, par. 30; ALC-I-44 *et seq.*

[11]   Note 1, par. 96 *et seq.*; ALC-I-69 *et seq.*

[12]   Note 1, par. 134; ALC-I-81.

[13]   Note 1, par. 98 and 117; ALC-I-70 and 76.

the conflict" (par. 35). This reasoning is surprising. It reads as if the Security Council, by enacting the ICTR Statute, had made use of a legislative power. Clearly, the Security Council has played a very significant role in the aforementioned customary process and this role has been rightly recognized in Tadić.[14] But it is difficult to see how the Security Council could have "innovated" the law simply by enacting the Statutes of ICTY and ICTR without infringing even a not too strictly conceived *nullum crimen* principle.[15] The "seriousness" of the crimes in itself certainly does not constitute a sufficient explanation. Thus Kanyabashi should have explored further the customary route which has been identified by Tadić. It is certainly not illegitimate to entertain some doubts as to whether the result of such customary analysis would have been to affirm the customary nature of all of Additional Protocol 2 at the time when the crimes had been committed.[16] Be that as it may: to have refrained from an analysis of customary international law constitutes the main weakness of the decision.

Claus Kreß

---

[14]   Note 1, par. 133; ALC-I-81.

[15]   R. S. Lee, The Rwanda Tribunal, 9 Leiden Journal of International Law 1996, p. 54, categorically states: "It is not within the competence of the Security Council to legislate or to create new international law".

[16]   For an excellent presentation of the relevant material see M. Cottier, Völkerstrafrechtliche Verantwortlichkeit für Kriegsverbrechen in internen Konflikten, in: I. Erberich *et al.,* ed., Friede und Recht, Stuttgart etc. 1998; for the position taken by the ICTR in Judgement, *Prosecutor v. Akayesu,* ICTR-96-4-T, 2 September 1998, par. 615, see in this volume p. 518.

UNITED NATIONS   NATIONS UNIES

International Criminal Tribunal for Rwanda
Tribunal pénal international pour le Rwanda

TRIAL CHAMBER II

Before: **Judge William H. Sekule**   ORG: ENG.
                       Judge Yakov A. Ostrovsky
                       Judge Tafazzal H. Khan

Registry: **Mr. John Kiyeyeu**

Date of hearing: **9 July 1998**

THE PROSECUTOR

versus

SYLVAIN NSABIMANA

Case No. ICTR-97-29A-T

DECISION ON THE DEFENCE MOTION FOR THE AMENDMENT OF THE INDICTMENT, WITHDRAWAL OF CERTAIN CHARGES AND PROTECTIVE MEASURES FOR WITNESSES

The Office of the Prosecutor:
    Mr. Frederic Ossogo

Counsel for the Defence:
    Mr. Charles Tchakounte Patie

[page 2] THE INTERNATIONAL CRIMINAL TRIBUNAL FOR RWANDA ("the Tribunal"),

SITTING AS Trial Chamber II, composed of Judge William H. Sekule, Presiding, Judge Yakov A. Ostrovsky and Judge Tafazzal H. Khan ("the Trial Chamber");

CONSIDERING the indictment submitted by the Prosecutor dated 14 October 1997 against Sylvain Nsabimana which was confirmed by a decision of this Tribunal rendered on 16 October 1997 by Judge Aspegren ("the confirming Judge");

CONSIDERING the initial appearance of the accused Sylvain Nsabimana which took place on 24 October 1997;

BEING SEIZED OF a defence motion filed on 25 April 1998 based upon rule 72 of Rules of Procedure and Evidence ("the Rules") in which the Defence seeks to amend the indictment on the basis of defect in form and seeks to dismiss certain charges as well as seeking protective measures for the defence witnesses;

NOTING the Prosecutor's response to the motion filed on 7 July 1998;

CONSIDERING rules 72 and 73 of the Rules pertaining to preliminary motions and motions generally, respectively;

TAKING INTO ACCOUNT Article 19(1) and 21 of the Statute of the Tribunal ("the Statute") and rule 75 of the Rules dealing with protective measures;

CONSIDERING Articles 17(4) and 18 of the Statute and rules 5, 47, 55 of the Rules;

CONSIDERING the decision rendered on 24 November 1997 by Trial Chamber I on the preliminary motion filed by the defence based on defects in the form of the indictment in the *Prosecutor vs Ferdinand Nahimana* (Case No. ICTR-96-11-T);

HAVING heard arguments of the parties on 9 July 1998.

ARGUMENTS BY THE PARTIES

Defence Submissions

A. Regarding Amendment to the Indictment Due to Defects in Form

The Defence Counsel stated that the indictment does not meet the require legal standards. He submitted:

(a)   that there existed vagueness in the concise statement of facts such as the dates regarding the appointment of the accused as the Prefect of Butare, the massacres in **[page 3]** Butare, the Tutsi refuge in the *Ecole Evangeliste du Rwanda* ("E.E.R."), the beating up of the Tutsi as well as the killing of the Tutsi by the Interahamwe as referred to in paragraphs 3.5, 3.13 and 3.14 of the concise statement of facts respectively;

(b)   that it was unclear which ethnic group was killed or how the accused facilitated murder;

(c)   that there was insufficient information to prove the allegation that the accused was indifferent when the massacres occurred (paragraph 3.13);

(d)   that there were some ambiguous phrases used such as: "relatively calm" in paragraph 3.9, and "during the events referred to in this indictment" and reference to the words "facilitation" and "encouraged" in paragraph 3.12, "incitement" in paragraph 3.13 and reference to the phrase "who were either beaten up or killed by soldiers or taken to the neighbouring forest where many of them were executed" in paragraph 3.14";

(e)   that the information regarding the manner in which the accused is alleged to have incited the population to commit the massacres in paragraph 3.13 of the statement and how he encouraged the killers in paragraph 3.12 lacked clarity;

(f)   that the role of the accused in planning the massacres referred in paragraph 4 of the statement needed some elaboration;

(g)   that the information on the acts of omission were insufficient such as the inadequate facts to explain why the accused failed to take any measures or why the accused did not punish his subordinates and whether the accused had the power and means to punish his subordinates.

B. Dismissal of The Counts

On this issue, the Defence Counsel submitted:

(a)   that the counts are vague. For example, that there is lack of evidence in the statement to support the counts, particularly, counts 1 and 2 that there is no evidence to show that the accused incited the massacres in count 1 (Genocide) nor is there evidence to show that he planned the massacres or that the subordinates were ready to incite the population. There is also no indication of omissions referred to in count 2 of the indictment and the relationship between the facts and the counts is not established yet the facts should correspond with the crimes charged against the accused;

(b)   that counts 3 and 4 of the indictment should be withdrawn because the two counts dealing with crimes against humanity (murder) and crimes against humanity (extermination) in Article 3 of the Statute emanate from the same facts, that is, as part of "widespread or systematic attack against a civilian population." **[page 4]**

C. Regarding Protective measures for the Defence Witnesses

The Defence Counsel, referring to Article 21 of the Statute and to rules 69, 72, 73 and 75 of the Rules, made general submissions on the protection of the Defence witnesses. He stated further:

(a)   that the potential witnesses, just as in all other cases before this Tribunal, will face harm to their person and are endangered in person and property. He referred to the assassination of Mr. Seth Sendanshonga in May 1998 in Nairobi, Kenya, who was a potential witness for the Defence, as an example of the danger facing the potential witnesses;

(b)   that the Trial Chamber should take judicial notice of the danger posed to the potential witnesses pursuant to rule 94 of the Rules since it was common knowledge that witnesses are scattered worldwide, always fleeing and continuously being threatened;

(c)   that the witnesses should be allowed to move freely in order to testify before the Tribunal and that they should be guaranteed a safe return to the countries in which they have been residing;

(d)   that the Defence should be permitted to use pseudonyms and witnesses should not appear in open court;

(e)   that pursuant to rule 34 of the Rules, the Trial Chamber should direct the Registrar to contact the potential witnesses in Burundi, Canada, The United kingdom, Mozambique, Italy, Rwanda, Kenya, Cameroon Côte D'Voire, Senegal, Tanzania and Austria, among others.

Submissions of the Prosecutor:

The Prosecutor observed that the written text submitted by the Defence was based upon rule 72 of the Rules whereas the oral submission included rule 50 of the Rules. He then contended as follows:

(a)   that it is only the Prosecutor who could request that an indictment be amended and not the Defence;

(b)   that according to the 24 November 1997 decision of Trial Chamber I in the case of *The Prosecutor vs Ferdinand Nahimana* (ICTR-96-11-T) in which it was stated that what the accused required to know are the circumstances in which he committed the acts and that pursuant to rule 47 of the Rules, which requires that the indictment have concise facts, the prosecution has satisfied that requirement if the indictment and all the supporting materials are read together;

(c)   that with respect to the vagueness of the periods within which the accused is alleged to have committed the crimes mentioned in the indictment, it is difficult to specify the periods and the exact nature of the massive crimes given the situation in which the events in Rwanda occurred; **[page 5]**

(d)   that reference to the period between "1 January and 31 December 1994" was only indicative of the temporal jurisdiction of the Tribunal and that the dates given, such as 19 April 1994, correspond to those given to the Prosecutor by the witnesses in their statements;

(e)   that the phrase "relatively calm" in paragraph 3.9 of the statement shows that the situation in Butare was not absolutely calm and is just comparative to other places in Rwanda at the time;

(f)   that it is not a requirement that certain words should be used in the concise statement of facts hence the use of the word "facilitation" is in order provided that in the counts the language of the Statute is used;

(g)   that the Prosecutor could not give a precise date as to when the Tutsi were "either beaten up or killed by soldiers or taken to neighbouring forest where many of them were executed" in paragraph 3.14 of the statement because the acts did not occur once but took place on a regular basis;

(h)   that the counts in 1 and 2 of the indictment have been set out according to the requirements of Article 3 of the Statute;

(i)   that it would not be proper to withdrawal counts 3 and 4 of the indictment because 'murder' and 'extermination' are different crimes;

(j)   that raising the issue of the accumulation of counts is premature because according to the *Nahimana* and *Ntagerura* decisions, the issues of accumulation of counts are for the court to examine at the end of the trial;

(k)   that the Defence motion on protective measures for their witnesses should be dismissed because it is defective since it did not provide specific information about the witnesses, namely, the number and categorization of witnesses and the basis for the application;

(l)   that rule 94 of the Rules cannot be applied without referring to any report or affidavits or other supporting documents.

Rejoinder by The Defence:

In reply, the Defence stated:

(a)   that rules 50, 51, 72 and 73 of the Rules apply to both parties hence the Tribunal should guarantee the rights of the accused;

(b)   that the Prosecutor should have referred to the supporting materials when the confirming judge was considering the indictment and not after its confirmation, and that any reference to witness statements is premature since the evidence is not yet **[page 6]** before the Trial Chamber;

(c)   that he maintains his objections to the current form of the indictment as stated earlier.

DELIBERATIONS:

The findings of the Trial Chamber are set out below.

As the substance of the issues raised in the Defence motion are to a large extent similar to the preliminary motion filed on 17 April 1997, by the Defence in the *Prosecutor vs Ferdinand Nahimana* (Case No. ICTR-96-11-T), the Trial Chamber's present deliberations concerning the objections against the form of the indictment will take into account Tribunal's decision of 24 November 1997 in that case.

As a general observation, the Trial Chamber holds that the accused must be able to recognize the circumstances and the actions attributed to him in the indictment and the concise statement of facts. In other words, the accused must be made to understand how and when his actions under the particular circumstances, constituted one or more crimes covered by the Tribunal's jurisdiction. Furthermore, the Trial Chamber interpretes the phrase "concise statement of the facts" in rule 47 to mean "a brief statement of facts but comprehensive in expression." as defined in the case *Nahimana* (supra).

On the defects in the indictment, the Trial Chamber has noted the imprecise dates and is also aware of the difficulties the Prosecutor is facing in providing precise dates but is of the view that there is a need for further clarification.

On the issue of vagueness of counts in the indictment, Article 20(4)(a) of the Statute stipulates that the accused must be informed promptly and in detail in a language he or she understands of the nature and cause of charges against him or her. This is provided for under rule 47(B) of the Rules which requires that the indictment shall set forth the name and particulars of the suspect and a concise statement of the facts of the case and of the crime with which the suspect is charged.

The Trial Chamber has read the concise statement of facts in this indictment. We underscore the need to have the precise statement of facts correspond to and explain the specific charges. The Prosecutor should also ensure that the facts used as a basis for the charges are clear enough so that the accused will not have to refer to the witness statements.

As a general rule, indictments are expected to be drafted in a precise manner. In the instant case, the accused is entitled to further information so that he can prepare his defence effectively and efficiently. Specifically, the Prosecutor should provide additional information to indicate the manner in which the accused is linked to the alleged acts that form the basis of the counts. It is our view that, generally, the indictment has provided some link between the concise statement of facts and the counts but in some cases, more detailed information is required to make the charges clearer.

To that end, the Prosecutor should give further explanation of the words "facilitated", and "encouraged" in paragraph 3.12 of the statement of concise facts to enable the accused to sufficiently **[page 7]** understand the counts brought against him without having to wait for the discovery of the witness statements.

With regard to the time periods mentioned in the concise statement of facts, we note that the period "1 January-31 December 1994" is *ratione temporis* of the Tribunal's jurisdiction.

Additionally, we are conscious that the period mentioned may not be as precise as the defence may wish, but given the particular circumstances of the conflict in Rwanda and the alleged crimes, it could be difficult to determine the exact times when the acts alleged in concise facts occurred. It is our opinion, therefore, that the time frames mentioned are sufficiently precise to enable the accused to know the acts for which he is charged in the indictment.

31

Regarding the motion on protective measures for the defence witnesses, it is our view that the substance of the motion is insufficient as it has only listed the countries in which the witnesses reside. The Defence Counsel has not specified precise information about the witnesses neither has he stated the actual problems faced by the witnesses wherever they are. He has not even indicated whether the potential witnesses have expressed a desire to secure the Tribunal's protection.

The relevant provisions of rule 75 of the Rules which provide the conditions for considering such applications have not been observed. Hence, in this regard, the Trial Chamber cannot, pursuant to rule 94 of the Rules, take judicial notice of the problems facing the potential witnesses. However, in the case of *The Prosecutor vs Joseph Kanyabashi* (ICTR-96-15-T), the Trial Chamber, in its decision of 25 November 1997, stated that there is always a need for substantiation of requests for the protection of witnesses. Therefore, in the instant case, the relief sought should, *inter alia*, specify both the legal and factual basis upon which the measures sought are based.

FOR THESE REASONS,

THE TRIBUNAL

1.   **DIRECTS** the Prosecutor, to amend the following parts of the indictment within thirty days and implement the following changes:

(i)   elaborate on the following words and phrases: "facilitated," "encouraged," "during the events referred to in this indictment" in paragraph 3.12 of the statement of concise facts;

(ii)   explain further the acts which are attributed to the soldiers in paragraph 3.14 of the concise statement of facts;

(iii)   indicate briefly how, in paragraph 3.13 of the concise statement of facts, the population was "incited" to massacre the Tutsi;

(iv)   specify the role of the accused in planning the events under paragraph 4.

2.   **INVITES** the Defence to file a fresh motion, if they so wish, providing both the factual and [page 8] legal basis for its application on the protection of its witnesses.

3.   **DISMISSES** the defence motion on all other points.

Arusha, 24 September 1998.

William H. Sekule   Yakov A. Ostrovsky   Tafazzal Hossaine Khan
Presiding Judge   Judge   Judge

UNITED NATIONS   NATIONS UNIES

International Criminal Tribunal for Rwanda

TRIAL CHAMBER II

OR: ENG

Before: Judge William H. Sekule, Presiding
              Judge Yakov Ostrovsky
              Judge Tafazzal H. Khan

Registrar: Dr. Agwu Ukiwe Okali

Decision of: 21 May 1999

THE PROSECUTOR

v.

SYLVAIN NSABIMANA and
ALPHONSE NTEZIRYAYO

Case No. ICTR-97-29-I

DECISION ON THE PROSECUTOR'S URGENT MOTION FOR STAY OF
EXECUTION OF DECISION OF 24 SEPTEMBER 1998
&
DECISION ON NSABIMANA'S MOTION FOR WITHDRAWAL OF THE
INDICTMENT AND IMMEDIATE RELEASE

The Office of the Prosecutor:
    Japhet Daniel Mono
    Celine Tonye

Counsel for Sylvain Nsabimana:
    Josette Kadji
    Charles Tchacounte Patie

Counsel for Alphonse Nteziryayo
    Titinga Frédéric Pacere

[page 2] THE INTERNATIONAL CRIMINAL TRIBUNAL FOR RWANDA (TRIBUNAL),

SITTING as Trial Chamber II, composed of Presiding Judge William H. Sekule, Judge Yakov Ostrovsky and Judge Tafazzal H. Khan;

CONSIDERING the Statute of the Tribunal (Statute) and the Rules of Evidence and Procedure (Rules);

CONSIDERING the Indictment of 14 October 1997 against Sylvain Nsabimana (Nsabimana) and Alphone Nteziryayo (Nteziryayo), confirmed on 16 October 1997 by Judge Lennart Aspegren;

NOTING the 16 October 1997 decision under Rule 54 to issue separate case numbers for the two Accused, the resultant confusion, and that one case should exist, *The Prosecutor v. Sylvain Nsabimana and Alphonse Nteziryayo*, Case No. ICTR-97-29-I;

CONSIDERING Nsabimana's initial appearance on 24 October 1997 and not guilty pleas to all five counts;

CONSIDERING Nsabimana's motion to sever, set a date for status conference, and return of personal effects of 19 November 1997;

CONSIDERING Nsabimana's motion for the amendment of the indictment, withdrawal of certain charges and protective measures for witnesses of 23 April 1998 (English translation filed 9 July 1998);

CONSIDERING Nsabimana's request to the Prosecutor on 12 June 1998 for amendment of the Indictment;

CONSIDERING this Chamber's *"Decision on the Defence Motion for Orders to Sever Proceedings, Set a Date for a Status Conference and for the Return of Personal Effects"* of 8 July 1998, which included denying severance;

CONSIDERING Nteziryayo's initial appearance on 17 August 1998 and not guilty pleas to all six counts;

NOTING that the Prosecution's motion of 17 August 1998 to join this case, with that of Elie Ndayambaje, Joseph Kanyabashi, Pauline Nyiramasuhuko and Arsene Shalom Ntahobali, is still pending before this Chamber;

NOTING the Appeals Chamber decision of 3 June 1999 in *The Prosecutor v. Joseph Kanyabashi* (Case No. ICTR-96-15-1) and the rulings regarding joinder;

CONSIDERING the Prosecution's motion of 18 August 1998 entitled *"Prosecutor's Request for Leave to File an Amended Indictment"* to which was attached, as Annex A, a new proposed amended Indictment. **[page 3]**

CONSIDERING Nteziryayo's *"Brief in Response of the Accused Against the Prosecutor's Requests for Leave to Amend the 14 October 1997 Indictment Confirmed on 16 October 1997"* (English translation filed 10 November 1998);

NOTING that the Prosecution's motion to amend is still pending before this Chamber;

NOTING the Appeals Chamber decision of 3 June 1999 *in the Prosecutor v. Joseph Kanyabashi* (Case No. ICTR-96-15-1) regarding leave to amend an Indictment;

CONSIDERING this Chamber's *"Decision on the Defence Motion for the Amendment of the Indictment, Withdrawal of Certain Charges and Protective Measures for Witnesses"* of 24 September 1998 (decision of 24 September 1998);

CONSIDERING the Prosecution's Urgent Motion (Urgent Motion) of 28 September 1998;

CONSIDERING the Prosecutor's *"Indictment (as modified during the confirmation process)"* of 18 November 1998, which purportedly incorporated the "the corrections demanded by the Confirming Judge during the confirmation hearing on 16 October 1997";

CONSIDERING Nsabimana's motion entitled *"Defence Motion for the Withdrawal of Any Indictment against the Accused and for His Consequent Immediate Release"* of 25 January 1999 (dated 10 January 1999) (English translation filed 30 March 1999);

CONSIDERING the Prosecutor's brief in response of 6 April 1999;

CONSIDERING in particular paragraph 31 of the Prosecutor's brief in response of 6 April 1999 which states that "the Tribunal could defer decision on the requests for amendments, [and] joinder of cases...";

CONSIDERING the parties' submissions at the hearing held on 21 April 1999 on Nsabimana's motion entitled *"Defence Motion for the Withdrawal of Any Indictment against the Accused and for His Consequent Immediate Release"* of 25 January 1999;

CONSIDERING this Chamber's oral decision on 21 April 1999 denying Nsabimana's motion entitled *"Defence Motion for the Withdrawal of Any Indictment against the Accused and for His Consequent Immediate Release"* of 25 January 1999;

CONSIDERING the parties' submissions at the hearing held on 18 May 1999 on the Prosecution's Urgent Motion (Urgent Motion) of 28 September 1998;

NOW DECIDES the Prosecution's Urgent Motion (Urgent Motion) of 28 September 1998;

NOW REITERATES in writing the decision of 21 April 1999 on Nsabimana's Motion for withdrawal of the Indictment and immediate release of 30 March 1999. **[page 4]**

LEGAL BASIS FOR URGENT MOTION

1.   On 28 September 1998, the Prosecution filed the Urgent Motion under Rule 54, moving for a stay of execution of this Chamber's decision of 24 September 1998. Rule 54 provides, in part, that a Trial Chamber may issue an order as may be necessary for the purposes of the preparation or conduct of the trial.

2.   The Defence contented, at the hearing, that the Prosecutor's urgent motion was not well founded or, in other words, inadmissible under Rule 54. The Defence also contended that the Prosecution was seeking to circumvent Rule 72(D) in that a stay of execution amounted to an unauthorised appeal of a decision.

3.   This Chamber finds that the motion for a stay of execution of a Trial Chamber's decision in this case falls within the purview of Rule 54. This Chamber also finds that Rule 72(D)'s prohibition of certain appeals does not preclude a party from moving for a stay of execution of a decision. Thus, under Rule 54, there exists a legal basis for a motion for stay of execution, and this Chamber finds the Urgent Motion admissible.

THE EFFECT OF THIS CHAMBER'S NOT GRANTING THE URGENT MOTION

4.   Having found that the Prosecutor's Urgent Motion is admissible, this Chamber now analyses the effect or legal significance of this Chamber's not granting to date the Prosecutor's motion for stay of execution of the decision of 24 September 1998. This Chamber notes that the Urgent Motion (of 28 September 1998) was not heard until 18 May 1999 and not decided until today, more than eight months after filing.[1] Thus, the Indictment confirmed 16 October 1997 constitutes the current charging document; and to date, this Chamber has not granted any stay, and the decision of 24 September 1998 remains in effect.

---

[1]   This Chamber notes various causes of this long delay. The Registry's failure to notify the Chamber of the Urgent Motion and schedule a timely hearing contributed to the delay.

5.   In fact, at the hearing on 18 May 1999, the Prosecution stated that "it is clear that the Court Order [of 24 September 1998] is still intact and has not been complied with" (Eng. transcript, at 6) and that the Prosecution had the capacity to comply immediately. (*Ibid.* at 22.) The Prosecution's representations make it difficult to understand, in the absence of this Chamber's granting the Urgent Motion, why the Prosecution failed to comply with the decision of 24 September 1998. The Prosecution's inaction is tantamount to the assertion that the mere filing of its Urgent Motion relieved them of the duty to comply. This is not so.

6.   The Prosecution asserted, in motions and at the hearing, several reasons for making the Urgent Motion. First, the Prosecution sought to avoid duplication of work, namely amending the Indictment in accordance with the decision of 24 September 1998 and again amending the Indictment in accordance with the Prosecution's pending motion to amend. In other words, if this Chamber granted the Prosecution's motion to amend the Indictment (of 18 August 1998), this would supersede this Chamber's decision of 24 September 1998. Second, the Prosecution sought to secure sufficient time to comply with the decision of 24 September 1998. Third, the proposed amended Indictment "may well have addressed the orders of the Chamber in its decision of 24 September 1998." (Urgent Motion, at para. 2(ii).) **[page 5]**

7.   This Chamber finds that the failure to hold a timely hearing on the Urgent Motion does <u>not</u> relieve the Prosecution from complying with previous Tribunal orders. Thus, an order of the Tribunal must stand and have effect unless the Tribunal issues a superseding order. Here, the Prosecution, for many months, has failed to comply with this Chamber's decision of 24 September 1998, which ordered relatively simple amendments.

8.   This Chamber finds the Prosecutor's reasons for the Urgent Motion and non-compliance with the decision of 24 September 1998 to be not particularly compelling. This Chamber further finds that compliance with the decision of 24 September 1998 would have caused <u>no legal prejudice</u> to the Prosecution's case.

9.   When faced with a situation requiring either: (1) the possible duplication of work; or (2) non-compliance with this Chamber's decision, this Chamber hopes that in the future the Prosecution will elect to do the former.

10.   This Chamber also notes that the Prosecution may have had a remedy to its purported predicament. For example, the Prosecution could have renewed its urgent motion, contacted the Registry to confirm the scheduling of a hearing, or made a separate motion for urgent review of its motion to amend (of 18 August 1998).

11.   The Prosecution, in the alternative (should this Chamber deny the Urgent Motion) moved "that the period of 30 days be enlarged so that we comply with the Order immediately." (Hearing of 18 May 1999, Eng. Transcript, at 23.)

DEFENCE MOTION FOR WITHDRAWAL OF INDICTMENT AND RELEASE

12.   Nsabimana filed a motion entitled *"Defence Motion for the Withdrawal of Any Indictment against the Accused and for His Consequent Immediate Release"* on 25 January 1999 (dated 10 January 1999) (English translation filed 30 March 1999). Nsabimana alleges that the Prosecutor has failed to comply with this Chamber's decision of 24 September 1998, that there are further defects in the Indictment, and seeks withdrawal of the indictment and immediate release, under Rules 51 and 73. This Chamber heard the motion on 21 April 1999.

13.   The Prosecution, in its brief in response, asserts that under Rule 51 the power to withdraw an indictment is exclusive to the Prosecutor, and, thus, Nsabimana's motion is inadmissible. The Prosecution does not state what constitutes the appropriate remedy for non-compliance with the decision of 24 September 1998.

14. At the hearing of 21 April 1999, this Chamber orally denied the defence motion and found that there is "no legal grounds to grant that order." (Eng. Transcript, at 60.)

15. This Chamber already has found that the Prosecution was not in compliance, but finds that immediate compliance with the decision of 24 September 1998 will satisfy the court as to any alleged remaining defects. This Chamber finds that Rule 51 does not provide Nsabimana a remedy, nor does his purported Rule 73 motion warrant withdrawal and release. Regarding an appropriate remedy for non-compliance, this Chamber admonishes the Prosecution for its non-compliance. **[page 6]**

FOR THESE REASONS,

AFTER HAVING DELIVERATED,

THE TRIBUNAL

ORDERS the Prosecutor to comply with this Chamber's decision of 24 September 1998 (ordering the Prosecutor to amend the existing Indictment in certain respects) within fourteen (14) days of the date of the filing of this decision in the original English;

DENIES the Prosecutor's Urgent Motion (filed 28 September 1998) for a stay of execution of this Chamber's decision of 24 September 1998 as requested, because interests of justice require compliance;

ORDERS the Prosecutor to make the corrections to the Indictment as instructed by the confirming Judge on 16 October 1997, but only where such corrections do not conflict with the decision of 24 September 1998;

DENIES Nsabimana's motion for the withdrawal of the indictment and immediate release;

ADMONISHES the Prosecution for failing to comply with this Chamber's decision of 24 September 1998.

DIRECTS the Registry, under Rule 54, to re-number this case, *"The Prosecutor v. Sylvain Nsabimana and Alphonse Nteziryayo,"* as one single case, Case No. ICTR-97-29-I, and create a single index.

Arusha, 21 May 1999.

William H. Sekule   Yakov Ostrovsky   Tafazzal H. Khan
Judge, Presiding   Judge   Judge

UNITED NATIONS   NATIONS UNIES

International Criminal Tribunal for Rwanda
Tribunal pénal international pour le Rwanda

Trial Chamber II

OR: ENG

Before: Judge William H. Sekule, Presiding
            Judge Yakov A. Ostrovsky
            Judge Tafazzal Hossain Khan

Registry: Mr. John M. Kiyeyeu

            24.9.1998

THE PROSECUTOR

versus

EMANNUEL BAGAMBIKI
SAMUEL IMANISHIMWE
YUSSIF MUNYAKAZI

Case No. ICTR-97-36-(I)

DECISION ON THE DEFENCE MOTION ON DEFECTS IN
THE FORM OF THE INDICTMENT

For the Prosecution:
    Mr. William Egbe

For the Defence:
    Ms. Marie Louise Mbida Kanse Tah
    Mr. Georges So'O

[page 2] The International Criminal Tribunal for Rwanda (the "Tribunal"),

SITTING AS Trial Chamber II, composed of Judge William H. Sekule, Presiding, Judge Yakov A. Ostrovsky and Judge Tafazzal H. Khan, (the "Trial Chamber");

CONSIDERING the indictment filed on 9 October 1997 by the Prosecutor against Emmanuel Bagambiki, Samuel Imanishimwe and Yusuf Munyakazi pursuant to article 17 of the Statute of the Tribunal ("the Statute");

CONSIDERING FURTHER the indictment against Samuel Imanishimwe ("the accused") which was confirmed by Judge Lennart Aspegren on 10 October 1997;

TAKING NOTE of the initial appearance of the accused which took place on 27 November 1997;

HAVING BEEN SEIZED of a preliminary motion filed by the Defence on 24 March 1998, ("Defence Motion") contending that due to defects in the form of the indictment, against the accused, the Prosecutor should be ordered to "redefine the facts;"

HAVING RECEIVED the Prosecutor's written reply ("Prosecutor's Reply"), filed on 24 March 1998, in which she submitted that the Defence Motion should be dismissed as the indictment complies with the Statute and the Rules of Evidence and Procedure ("the Rules");

HAVING HEARD the parties during an open session of 26 March 1998.

AFTER HAVING DELIBERATED:

1.   In its written motion and at the hearing the Defence argued that the Prosecutor is obliged to state precise facts of the crime or crimes with which the accused is charged in the indictment. If this obligation is not met, the Defence contended, the accused's right to be "informed, in detail, of the nature and cause of the charge against him," as guaranteed under article 20(4)(a) of the Statute, would be violated. (Defence Motion, p. 3).

2.   Additionally, the Defence averred that the indictment was drafted in a vague manner and supported by insufficient and questionable documentation. The Defence further argued that the accused and others were inappropriately charged with the same crimes. Therefore, the Defence claimed that the Prosecutor should be ordered to further clarify the facts, without which it could not prepare an adequate defence.

3.   The Prosecutor's representative responded that first, the Defence Motion joined two issues, which could not be addressed by the Trial Chamber simultaneously. He stated that the claims in the instant motion, that the evidence against the accused is insufficient to support the charges and that there is a lack of a concise statement of facts, were essentially arguments that there were defects in the merits and defects in the form of the indictment, respectively, which constitute distinctly different issues. At this stage of the proceedings, the Prosecution claimed, the Trial "Chamber is bound to examine and dispose of issues relating to defects in [the] form" of the indictment only. (Prosecutor's Reply, para. 37.) Defects in the merits are questions that should be addressed, as evidentiary questions, once the trial begins. **[page 3]**

4.   Next, the Prosecution claimed that in the indictment a concise statement of facts was provided along with the crimes charged. The said indictment was then disclosed to the Defence on 8 October 1997, giving him sufficient notice to prepare for trial. Therefore, the Prosecution submitted that the only question remaining for the Trial Chamber to resolve is whether the time frame, within which the alleged crimes were committed, were sufficiently described.

On the Defects in the Form of the Indictment Due to an Insufficient Concise Statement of the Facts Against the Accused

5.   As a preliminary matter, the Trial Chamber notes that at this stage of the proceedings, issues concerning the merits of the indictment are not yet ripe for consideration. Therefore, we will limit the

scope of the analysis in this decision to the possible defects in the form of the indictment only. Rule 72(B) of the Rules contains a non-exhaustive list of pre-trial motions which the accused may bring forth prior to the commencement of the trial on the merits. Sub-section (ii) of this rule provides the accused with the right to object to the form of the indictment. Thus, the Trial Chamber recognizes the right of the accused to bring forth such objections.

6.   The Statute, through article 20(4)(a), guarantees the accused the right "To be informed promptly, and in detail, in a language he or she understands of the nature and cause of the charges against him." In addition, rule 47(B) of the Rules states "The indictment shall set forth the name and particulars of the suspect and a *concise statement of the facts* of the case and of the crime with which the suspect is charged ..." (Emphasis added.) The Trial Chamber notes that neither the Statute nor the Rules define the phrase "concise statement of facts."

7.   Although the Rules do not define the phrase "concise statement of the facts," as provided in rule 47, there is sufficient persuasive precedent, in the decisions of this Tribunal as well as the decisions of the International Criminal Tribunal for the Former Yugoslavia, to guide the Trial Chamber in reaching a decision with regard to this matter. The Trial Chamber recalls the decision of 24 November 1997, in the case of the *Prosecutor v. Ferdinand Nahimana* (ICTR-96-11-T), where the Tribunal interpreted the phrase in question to mean "a brief statement of facts but comprehensive in expression." (Para. 20.) With this interpretation as a foundation, the Trial Chamber will address the objections raised by the Defence in the instant motion.

8.   The Defence claims that counts 7, 8, 9, 10 and 13 are drafted and presented in such a manner that "it [is] impossible for the Tribunal to know which facts correspond with which crimes" due to "the wide range of facts and the disorderly definition of the identical facts." (Defence Motion, Para. 7.) Although it is true that in all of the abovementioned counts the Prosecutor refers to paragraphs 3.17, 3.18, 3.20, 3.25 and 3.30, of the concise statement of facts, it is clear that more than one crime may arise out of the same act or set of acts. Therefore, the Trial Chamber observes that no difficulties arise from the use of overlapping facts.

If the intention of the Defence was to raise the principle of *non-bis-in idem*, that is, the inappropriate accumulation of charges, then the Trail Chamber again must refer to the *Nahimana* decision, *supra*, (paras. 35 – 37) in which the Tribunal held that this question also could not be addressed at this stage of the proceedings.

9.   The Defence submitted that counts 11, 12 and 19 of the indictment were vaguely drafted, in terms of the facts and the law, but only provided the Trial Chamber with details of this objection to **[page 4]** count 12 at the oral presentation of this motion. The Defence states that count 12 of the indictment charges the accused with crimes against humanity under article 3(f) of the Statute, (torture as a part of a widespread and systematic attack against any civilian population) and was based on paragraphs 3.24 and 3.25 of the concise statement of facts, of which the former did not appear to refer to any acts of torture. It would be reasonable to read paragraph 3.24 however, as a foundation for paragraph 3.25, which in fact does include allegations of torture at the Cyangugu Barracks. Thus, the Trial Chamber is of the opinion that there is no need for further clarification of that particular count.

10.   The Trial Chamber has reviewed also counts 11 and 19 of the indictment. It appears that count 11 (crimes against humanity) provides the accused with information that would enable him to establish a link between his acts, that is allegedly imprisoning civilians, and the criminal charges brought against him by the Prosecutor. In particular paragraph 3.22 of the concise statement of facts states that "refugees [escorted there by the accused] could not leave the stadium which was guarded by gendarmes." The accused allegedly exercised *de facto* authority over the said gendarmes. Therefore, we find that the information provided in count 11 is sufficient to allow the accused to begin to prepare his defence.

11.   Count 19 charges the accused persons and others with conspiracy to commit genocide. Paragraphs 3.12 through 3.30 of the statement of facts are articulated in such a way that the Prosecutor's intent to join the accused with Emmanuel Bagambiki and Yussuf Munyakazi, in their alleged criminal acts and omissions, is intelligible. However, the Trial Chamber notes that in paragraph 3.14 reference to

the phrase "*held a large number* of meetings among themselves, *or* with others ...," without supplying further details, renders this paragraph vague and by extension count 19 inadequately supported. (Emphasis added.)

FOR ALL THE FORGOING REASONS THE TRIAL CHAMBER:

ORDERS the Prosecution to clarify paragraph 3.14 of the concise statement of facts by providing further information with regard to the alleged meetings referred to in that paragraph. Specifically, the Prosecution should present details, such as the approximate dates, locations and the purpose of these meetings, so far as possible, and also clarify whether the accused persons and others named in the indictment were the only persons present at these meetings or if others, not named in the indictment, were present also.

DISMISSES the Defence Motion on all other points.

Arusha, 24 September 1998.

Yakov A. Ostrovsky   Tafazzal Hossain Khan
Judge   Judge

Judge Sekule appends a separate opinion, on the issue of count 19, to this decision.

UNITED NATIONS   NATIONS UNIES

International Criminal Tribunal for Rwanda
Tribunal pénal international pour le Rwanda

TRIAL CHAMBER II

OR: ENG

Before: **Judge William H. Sekule, Presiding**
              Judge Yakov A. Ostrovsky
              Judge Tafazzal Hossain Khan

Registry: **Mr. John M. Kiyeyeu**

THE PROSECUTOR

versus

EMMANUEL BAGAMBIKI,
SAMUEL IMANISHIMWE
AND
YUSUF MUNYAKAZI

Case No. ICTR-97-36-I

**SEPARATE OPINION OF JUDGE SEKULE ON THE DECISION OF THE DEFENCE
MOTION ON DEFECTS IN THE FORM OF THE INDICTMENT**

The Office of the Prosecutor:
    Mr. William T. Egbe

Counsel for Samuel Imanishimwe
    Ms. Marie Louise Mbida Kanse Tah
    Mr. Georges So'o

[page 2] I have carefully considered the issues presented in the Defence motion and opine as follows:

With regard to count 19:

I do not agree with the inclusion of persons who are specifically named but not formally charged ("named others") within count 19. I reiterate the observations I made regarding count 19 in another separate opinion in this case. The pertinent portion of my opinion read as follows;

My reasons for agreeing with the Defence motion as it concerns the removal of the named others are as follows:

First, as a matter of law, the conspiracy to commit genocide charge mentioned in count 19 is complete as it already includes three persons. Accordingly, in the instant case, there is no legal need to specifically name others when the phrase "and others" would suffice.

Second, there may be prejudice to the accused due to evidence which may be adduced during the trial which pertains to the named others but implicates the accused. In this scenario, the Defence may not be able to challenge this evidence because the pertinent matters may be within the particular knowledge of the named others, who are not present or represented. Indeed, one of the named others may be the pivotal conspirator.

Third, the inclusion of the named others in count 19 presents a serious risk of prejudice to them because evidence will need to be adduced by the Prosecution to show the alleged linkage between the named others and the accused. Obviously, the named others will not be represented by counsel at the trial and, therefore, they will not have the opportunity to contest evidence which implicates them in conspiracy. To include the named others in count 19 may violate the spirit of Article 20(4)(d) of the Statute which requires that the trial of an accused should be in his or her presence.

For the above reasons, in that decision I opined that the named others in count 19 should be deleted. Regarding the present motion, I reiterate the above opinion. Furthermore, any call for additional information in paragraph 3.14 or the relevant concise statement of facts should *specifically apply to the persons charged.*

Regarding all other issues:

I share and endorse the majority opinion.

Arusha, 24 September 1998.

William H. Sekule
Presiding Judge

International Criminal Tribunal for Rwanda
Tribunal Pénal International pour le Rwanda

Before: Judge Laïty Kama, Presiding   Original: English
              Judge Navanethem Pillay
              Judge Tafazzal H. Khan

Registry: Ms. Marianne Ben Salimo

Decision of: 24 May 1999

THE PROSECUTOR

vs

GEORGES HENRI YVON JOSEPH RUGGIU

Case No. ICTR-97-32-T

DECISION ON DEFENCE PRELIMINARY MOTION ON DEFECTS IN
THE FORM OF THE INDICTMENT

The Office of the Prosecutor:
    Mr. Leonard Asira Nguthi
    Mr. William T. Egbe

Counsel for the Accused:
    Mr. Mohammed Aouini
    Mr. Jean-Louis Gilissen

[page 2]THE INTERNATIONAL CRIMINAL TRIBUNAL FOR RWANDA (the "Tribunal"),

SITTING as Trial Chamber I, composed of Judge Laïty Kama, presiding, Judge Navanethem Pillay and Judge Tafazzal H. Khan;

CONSIDERING the indictment against Georges Henri Yvon Joseph Ruggiu dated 9 October 1997 and confirmed on the same day pursuant to Article 18 of the Statute of the Tribunal (the "Statute") and Rule 47 of the Rules of Procedure and Evidence (the "Rules");

CONSIDERING the preliminary motion and supporting brief filed by the Defence, pursuant to Rule 72(B)(ii) of the Rules, as well as the Prosecutor's response thereto;

HAVING HEARD the parties at a hearing on 23 April 1999;

CONSIDERING the provisions of Article 17 and 20 of the Statute and Rule 47 of the Rules.

Submissions by the parties

The Defence

1.   Defence Counsel submitted that the indictment against the accused is defective *inter alia* for the following reasons:

1.1 the concise statement of facts contained in the indictment does not conform to the provisions of Article 17 of the Statute and Rule 47 of Rules because it does not specify the acts the accused is alleged to have committed that form the factual ingredients of the offences for which the accused is indicted;

1.2 the concise statement of facts is vague and imprecise and it refers to phrases such as "the events referred to in this indictment" instead of identifying and explaining these events;

1.3 the period or time frame the offences were allegedly committed by the accused are vague and it lacks the minimum level of accuracy required to enable the accused to know the criminal acts alleged in the indictment;

1.4 the charges in the indictment lack the required precision because it does not provide the accused with accurate information to enable him to establish a link between the alleged acts and the charges against him. The accused is therefore unable to relate one or more of the several alleged acts to the offence of direct and public incitement to commit genocide or to the offence of a crime against humanity, as charged in Counts one and two of the indictment.

2.   The Defence Counsel further submitted that a defective indictment against the accused is a violation of Article 17 of the Statute and Rule 47 of the Rules. It is also a violation of the accused's right to a fair trial, pursuant to Article 14 of the International Covenant on Civil and **[page 3]** Political Rights. In light of these submissions, the Defence Counsel prayed that the Tribunal declare the indictment against the accused, null and void, and further order the termination of all subsequent criminal proceedings against the accused.

The Prosecutor

3.   The prosecutor made the following submissions in response to Defence Motion :

3.1. the indictment against the accused gives him sufficient information to enable him to prepare a defence to the charges preferred against him;

3.2. the indictment sufficiently informs the accused of the nature of the offences with which he is charged and the facts supporting those charges. If further details are required by the accuded, they could be found in the supporting material;

3.3. the description of the time frames and the geographical references in the counts sufficiently place in time the acts and the crimes with which the accused is charged;

4.   The Prosecutor further submitted that the Defence, by way of this motion, is requesting further particulars to the allegations and charges in the indictment. This request, according to the Prosecutor, falls outside the ambit of the provisions of Rule 72 (B) (ii) of the Rules.

AFTER HAVING DELIBERATED

An interpretation of the relevant provisions of the Statute and the Rules.

5.   Article 17(4) of the Statute of the Tribunal (the "Statute") states that once the Prosecutor has established that a *prima facie* case exists against the accused, she shall prepare an indictment containing a concise statement of facts and the crime or crimes with which the accused is being charged.

6.   Rule 47(A) of the Rules states that if the Prosecutor is satisfied that there is sufficient evidence to provide reasonable grounds for believing that a suspect has committed a crime she shall prepare and forward an indictment for confirmation.

7.   The Tribunal refers to its decision of 25 November 1997, in the case of "Prosecutor versus Gérard Ntakirutimana" (ICTR-96-17-T). In this case the term *"prima facie"* as envisaged in Article 17(4) of the Statute was defined as sufficient information which justifies a reasonable suspicion that the suspect did in fact commit the crime or crimes for which he is charged and the term "sufficient evidence" in Rule 47(A) of the rules was interpreted to mean essential facts, that when supported by evidence, could result in a conviction. This did not mean conclusive evidence or evidence beyond a reasonable doubt.

8.   Furthermore, Article 20(4)(a) of the Statute stipulates that the accused must be informed in detail of the nature and cause of the charge or charges against him. Rule 47(B) of the Rules states that an indictment shall contain the name and particulars of the suspect, a concise statement **[page 4]** of the facts of the case and the crime or crimes for which the accused is charged.

9.   The Tribunal, after having considered the provisions of Articles 17(4) and 20(4)(a) of the Statute and Rules 47(A) and (B) of the Rules, finds that the indictment at the time of its confirmation, must set out a *prima facie* case against the accused and the allegations therein must constitute an offence within the jurisdiction of the Tribunal. The indictment must also identify the suspect and inform him or her in a clear and concise manner the nature of the charges against him or her and the facts on which they are based.

Two decisions rendered by the ICTY

10.   The Tribunal notes two decisions by the International Criminal Tribunal for the former Yugoslavia (the "ICTY")

11.   In the case of "Prosecutor versus Duško Tadić" (IT-94-I-T), the ICTY, in its decision of 14 November 1995, found that Rule 47(B) of the Rules had been complied with since the indictment identified the accused, stated paragraph by paragraph the facts of each offence and specified clearly the particular provisions of international humanitarian law that have been violated. The ICTY in this case also found that paragraph 4 of the indictment lacked the necessary degree of specificity in that it did not provide the accused with any specific or concise statement of facts of the case and of the crimes with which he is charged.

12.   In the case "Prosecutor versus Zejnil Delalic and others" (IT-96-21-T), the ICTY in its decision of 26 April 1996, stated that the principal function of the indictment is to notify the accused in a summary manner as to the nature of the crimes of which he is charged and to present the factual basis for the accusations.

A review of the indictment

On the concise statement of facts

13.   The Tribunal maintains that although it is prudent to read the indictment together with the supporting material, which will assist in the amplification of the allegations and charges against the

accused, the indictment, when read on its own, must be able to inform the accused, with sufficient clarity, of the nature and cause of the charge or charges against him.

14. The Tribunal recognises the accused's right to be informed promptly, of the nature and cause of the charge or charges against him, as guaranteed in Article 20(4)(a) of the Statute. In most cases, the indictment is the first document served on the accused at the time of his arrest and this document must therefore satisfy this guarantee, as envisaged in Article 20(4)(a) of the Statute. The concise statement of facts in the indictment, although brief in nature, must be sufficiently detailed to assist the accused in understanding the charges against him.

15. The Tribunal notes that the concise statement of facts in the indictment must allege, with sufficient precision and clarity, the factual allegations the Prosecutor is relying on to support the count or counts with which the accused is charged in the indictment. These factual allegations, if proved beyond reasonable doubt, by evidence tendered at the trial of the accused, could result **[page 5]** in a conviction of the accused. It is further noted that, this concise statement of facts must consist of a body of allegations, although brief in nature, must be comprehensive, to include each and every element that constitute the offence or offences as charged.

16. Referring to the concise statement of facts and the two counts in the indictment of the accused in this case, the Tribunal notes that both Counts 1 and 2 rely on events as alleged in paragraphs 3.7 and 3.8 of the concise statement of facts. Whilst there appears to be sufficient information in these two paragraphs to enable a reasonable person to understand the allegations with respect to Count 1, that is the charge of direct and public incitement to commit genocide, as stipulated in Article 2(3)(c) of the Statute, this is not the case for Count 2, which charges the accused for a crime against humanity (persecution), pursuant to Article 3(h) of the Statute. It is necessary to allege how the accused, by way of radio broadcasts, persecuted Tutsi, certain Hutu and Belgians. The Prosecutor is therefore called upon to clarify the allegations in paragraph 3.8 of the indictment, by furnishing more information that illustrates the *nexus* between the alleged broadcasts, on the one hand and the alleged persecution on the other.

On the period or time frame

17. The Tribunal notes that the indictment does not specify with sufficient clarity and precision the temporal context in which the alleged acts were committed. Paragraph 3.1 of the indictment refers to the period between "January 1 and December 31 of 1994". Paragraph 3.6 of the indictment refers to the periods "1993", "better half of 1993", and "the end of 1994". Paragraph 3.7 refers to "between or about the month of January 1994, until in or about the month of July 1994," The Prosecutor is called upon to provide a more specific time frame of the allegations in the indictment. **[page 6]**

FOR THESE REASONS THE TRIBUNAL,

ORDERS the Prosecutor to either withdraw the charges against the accused or, alternatively, amend the indictment by:

(i) clarifying the allegations in paragraph 3.8 of the indictment, with respect to Count 2;

(ii) furnishing sufficient details of the time periods referred to in the allegations as contained in the concise statement of facts;

INVITES the Prosecutor, in the event of her electing to amend the indictment against the accused, to effect the aforementioned amendments within 30 days from the date of this order;

DISMISSES the defence motion in every other respect.

Arusha, 24 May 1999

Judge Laïty Kama	Navanethem Pillay	Tafazzal H. Khan
Presiding Judge	Judge	Judge

International Criminal Tribunal for Rwanda
Tribunal pénal international pour le Rwanda

TRIAL CHAMBER II

OR: ENG

Before: Judge William H. Sekule, Presiding
             Judge Lloyd George Williams
             Judge Pavel Dolenc

Registry: John Kiyeyeu

Decision of: 8 October 1999

THE PROSECUTOR

v.

GRATIEN KABILIGI &
ALOYS NTABAKUZE

Case No. ICTR-97-34-I
Case No. ICTR-97-30-I

_____

DECISION ON THE PROSECUTOR'S MOTION TO AMEND THE INDICTMENT

_____

The Office of the Prosecutor:
    David Spencer
    Frédéric Ossogo
    Holo Makwaia

Counsel for Gratien Kabiligi:
    Jean Yaovi Degli

Counsel for Aloys Ntabakuze:
    Clemente Monterosso

[page 2] INTRODUCTION

1.   **THE INTERNATIONAL CRIMINAL TRIBUNAL FOR RWANDA** (Tribunal),

SITTING as Trial Chamber II, composed of William H. Sekule, Presiding, Judge Lloyd George Williams and Judge Pavel Dolenc, as specially designated by the President of the Tribunal;

BEING SEIZED OF the "Prosecutor's Request for Leave to File an Amended Indictment" (Motion) filed 31 July 1998 in the case of *The Prosecutor v. Gratien Kabiligi and Aloys Ntabakuze* (Case No. ICTR-97-34-1 and ICTR-97-30-I), and the "proposed amended indictment"

BEING SEIZED OF the other related motions of the parties, including:

      a.   The "Prosecution Motion for a Temporary Stay of Execution of the Decision of 5 October 1998 Relating to the Defects in the Form of the Indictment" (Prosecution Motion for Stay) filed 21 June 1999;

      b.   Ntabakuze's "Motion for the Inadmissibility of Prosecution's Request for Leave to File an Amended Indictment" (Reply) filed in English on 24 September 1998;

      c.   Kabiligi's "Motion Challenging the Composition of the Trial Chamber and its Jurisdiction" (Motion Challenging Composition) filed in English on 9 July 1999;

      d.   Kabiligi's "Request Filed by the Defence Counsel for Disclosure of Materials" (Disclosure Motion) filed in English on 25 November 1998;

      e.   Kabiligi's "Additional Defence Brief in Reply to the Prosecutor's Motion and Brief to Amend the Indictment and for Joinder, as well as an Objection Based on Lack of Jurisdiction" (Objection to Jurisdiction) filed in English on 11 June 1999.

CONSIDERS the written submissions of the parties, including:

      a.   Kabiligi's "Submissions in Reply to the Prosecutor's Motions for Joinder and Amendment of the Indictment" filed in English on 22 July 1999, regarding the submissions relating to amendment;

      b.   Ntabakuze's "Defence Response to the Prosecutor's Motion Requesting Leave to Amend the Indictment" (one of two translations) filed in English on 12 August 1999;

      c.   Kabiligi's "Defence Brief on the Merits, in Response to the Prosecutor's Request for Leave to Amend the Indictment" (Brief on the Merits) filed in English on 12 August 1999;

      d.   The "Defence Brief in Reply to the Prosecutor's Motion Seeking a Stay in the Execution of the Decision of 5 October 1998 on Defects in the Form of the Indictment" filed in English on 6 August 1999; **[page 3]**

      e.   The "Prosecutor's Reply to the Defence Motion for an Order Ruling Inadmissible the Prosecutor's Motion for Joinder of Accused" (one of two translations) filed in English on 29 September 1998;

      f.   Kabiligi's "Brief in Reply to the Prosecutor's Response to Defence Motion for Disclosure of *Annexure 'B'*" filed in English on 11 August 1999.

      g.   The "Prosecutor's Brief in Response to the Request by the Defence for Disclosure of Annex B to the Motion to Amend the Indictment" filed in English on 21 December 1998;

      h.   The "Prosecutor's Brief in Reply to the Response by Counsel for the Accused Gratien Kabiligi to the Prosecutor's Request for Leave to File an Amended Indictment and Motion for Joinder of Trials" filed in English on 15 March 1999, regarding the submissions relating to amendment;

2.   The Trial Chamber has considered all of the written and oral submissions of each of the parties on the issues raised.

3.   The Trial Chamber notes particularly Rules 50, 66, and 69 of the Rules of Procedure and Evidence (Rules) and the Statute of the International Criminal Tribunal for Rwanda (Statute).

4.   The Trial Chamber heard the parties at an *inter partes* hearing on 11 August 1999.

5.   The Trial Chamber, in an oral decision, granted the Motion on 13 August 1999.

6.   The Trial Chamber now files its written decision on the Motion.

SUBMISSIONS OF THE PROSECUTION

Amendment of the Indictment

7.   The Prosecution submits that the bases for the Motion include: incorporating new evidence gathered after the confirmation of the indictment; to represent the full culpability of the accused, and; bringing the indictment in line with current jurisprudence and internal charging policies.

8.   The Prosecution submits that this Trial Chamber need not review supporting material to grant the Motion, relying on the decision of Trial Chamber I in *Prosecutor v. Nyiramasuhuko and Ntahobali*, at para. 13 (Decision on the Status of the Hearings for the Amendment of the Indictments and for Disclosure of Supporting Material, 30 Sept. 1998).

9.   In response to the defence contention, the Prosecution submits that Rule 50 governs this Motion and Rule 47 does not apply. The Prosecution submits that discussion here is not to verify if the counts are supported by factual evidence, whose probative value should be examined by the Trial Chamber. Accordingly, the Trial Chamber will have an opportunity to review the evidence at trial. The Prosecution asserts that the massive amounts of documentation in her **[page 4]** possession impede presenting supporting material for the Motion.

10.   The Prosecution notes that it filed under seal the supporting material for the proposed amended indictment with the Registry.

11.   At the hearing, the Prosecution withdrew its prayer of paragraph 7(b) (paragraph 8(b) in the French version) of the Motion. This particular prayer sought to have a single judge review the supporting material for the Motion. The Prosecution withdrew this prayer based on the contention that the Trial Chamber, not a single judge, had jurisdiction over the Motion, relying on the decisions in *Prosecutor v. Musema*, ICTR-96-13-T, at paras. 3, 4 (Decision on the Prosecutor's Request for Leave to Amend the Indictment, 6 May 1998) and *Prosecutor v. Akayesu*, ICTR-96-4-T, at p. 2 (Leave to Amend the Indictment, 17 June 1997).

Delay and Prejudice

12.   The Prosecution submits that the proposed amended indictment will not prejudice or infringe the rights of the accused to a fair trial. *See* Brief in Support of the Prosecutor's Request for Leave to File an Amended Indictment, at paras. 17-45. At the hearing, the Prosecution conceded that granting the amendment would delay the trial of Kabiligi and Ntabakuze.

Substitution of the Indictment

13.   At the hearing, the Prosecution submitted that the proposed amended indictment does not amount to a "substitution" of the indictment. The charges in the proposed amended indictment are substantially similar and it contains nothing "new or unusual." English Transcript at p. 108.

Annex B

14.   The Prosecution submits that the interests of witness protection are paramount and seeks to prevent the disclosure of Annex B. At the hearing, the Prosecution orally moved for the non-disclosure of Annex B. The Prosecution submitted that the Trial Chamber should postpone disclosure of Annex B, which contains the supporting material for the proposed amended indictment, and deny the defence motions for disclosure.

15.   The Prosecution filed Annex B, the supporting materials, with the Registry under seal on 31 July 1998.

Identification of "Others"

16.   At the hearing, with respect to Count 1, the Prosecution orally moved to add the names Théoneste Bagosora and Anatole Nsengiyumva to the proposed amended indictment after the words "conspired with."

Cumulative or Alternative Charges

17.   The Prosecution submits that the proposed amended indictment does not charge the accused with crimes in a cumulative manner. **[page 5]**

Form of the Indictment – Historical Background

18.   The Prosecution submits that the historical background section of the proposed amended indictment is necessary and provides context. Further, the decision in *Akayesu* is precedent for the historical background.

Rule 53bis

19.   The Prosecution submits that Rule 53*bis* applies in the case at bench. Further, the Prosecution submits that the Tribunal adopted Rule 53*bis* at the June 1998 Plenary of the Tribunal, but due to an administrative oversight it failed to incorporate it into the amended version of the Rules which was distributed. In the alternative, Rule 50 alone provides a sufficient basis for this Trial Chamber to rule.

Compliance with Decision of 5 October 1998

20.   The Prosecution submits that the filing of this Motion on 31 July 1998 constitutes compliance with the Decision of 5 October 1998. Namely paragraphs 5.5 through 5.8 and 5.10 through 5.12 of the proposed amended indictment provide the ordered clarification. The Prosecution submits that there is "no violation of the court's order," but apologized to the Trial Chamber merely for not having filed in a timely manner the Prosecution Motion for Stay. English Transcript, at p. 112.

SUBMISSIONS OF THE DEFENCE

Amendment of the Indictment

21.   Ntabakuze, in his Reply, first objected to the amendment of the indictment and moved that the Trial Chamber rule the Prosecution's Motion inadmissible on the grounds that it "runs foul of the requirement to dispose of preliminary motions *in limine litis* and would render it more difficult for the Trial Chamber to hear the case of the accused." *See* Reply, at p. 3.

22.   Kabiligi, in his Motion Challenging Composition, objected to the previous composition of the former Trial Chamber II. *See also* Defence Objection to Jurisdiction.

23.   The Defence submits that the Trial Chamber cannot authorise amendments to indictments without first being satisfied that there is evidence not in relation to the culpability of the accused but sufficient to support a case against the accused. The Defence submits that the Trial Chamber should have to apply this same standard of proof to the Prosecution both at the stage of confirmation of an indictment (under Rule 47), and under the Rule 50 procedure pertaining to amendment of indictments. The Defence submits that any other approach as regards the standards of proof required would be illogical considering Articles 19 and 20 of the Statute.

24.   The Defence submits that Rule 50 implicitly requires the Trial Chamber to review the supporting material or other evidence for the Motion. **[page 6]**

25.   The Defence submits that the Trial Chamber must deny the Motion for several reasons. The Defence asserts that there exists no factual or legal basis for the Motion and that it relies on mere

allegation, not proof. The Defence submits that granting the Motion would violate the presumption of innocence and Articles 19 and 20 of the Statute.

26. The Defence submits that the new charge of conspiracy to commit genocide has different elements and requires new evidence.

27. The Defence submits that the decision relied upon by the Prosecution (*Prosecutor v. Nyiramasuhuko, supra*), for the proposition that the Trial Chamber need not review supporting material, is not valid legal authority because the Appeals Chamber on 3 June 1999 in effect overturned that decision. *See Kanyabashi v. Prosecutor*, ICTR-96-15-A, at para. 15 (Decision on the Defence Motion for Interlocutory Appeal on the Jurisdiction of Trial Chamber I, 3 June 1999).

28. The Defence submits that the Prosecution, in its original prayer, sought "confirmation" of the amended indictment in paragraph 7(b) of the Motion (paragraph 8(b) of the French version), but withdrew it, and thus deprived the Defence of the procedural safeguard of a review of the supporting materials.

29. The Defence submits that the supporting material for the Motion is not new. The Defence further asserts, based on the information available to it to date, that there is no factual basis for the Motion, particularly the conspiracy and rape charges.

Delay and Prejudice

30. The Defence submits that granting the Motion will prejudice the accused, including causing undue delay in their preparations and trial. The Defence submits that the Trial Chamber should not grant a motion to amend two years after the filing of the original indictment. In other words, there is no justification for the delay and the Prosecution has not diligently prosecuted this case.

31. The Defence also submits that the proposed amended indictment names individuals that are still at large. Thus, if authorities apprehend these individuals and bring them to the Tribunal, joining such individuals to this case will cause further delay.

Substitution of the Indictment

32. The Defence submits that the proposed amended indictment amounts to a substitution of indictments, thereby circumventing the confirmation procedure. In other words, the Motion amounts to the filing of a wholly new indictment and the Prosecution should have sought confirmation of this new indictment and should have sought to withdraw the previous indictment under Rule 51.

33. The Defence objects to the increased size of the proposed amended indictment, asserting that the indictment has quintupled in size or increased from ten to fifty-five pages. **[page 7]**

Annex B

34. The Defence submits that the Trial Chamber has a duty to review the evidence that supports the Motion, namely Annex B, and allow the Defence to see Annex B for a full, adversarial or *inter partes* hearing on the merits of the Motion. The Defence moves for disclosure of Annex B and whatever supporting material that serves as the basis of the Motion. *See* Disclosure Motion.

35. At the hearing, the Defence submitted that it would be "fully satisfied" if it had a redacted version of Annex B, and that the Prosecution has had more than one year to make such redactions. English Transcript, at pp. 34, 117, 120.

Cumulative or Alternative Charges

36. The Defence submits that the proposed amended indictment includes concurrent or overlapping charges. The Defence objects to Counts 2 and 3 being charged cumulatively rather than alternatively.

Form of the Indictment – Historical Background

37. The Defence submits that sixty percent of the proposed amended indictment, particularly the historical background portion, is irrelevant, not related to either accused, and prejudicial. The Defence,

objecting to the form of the proposed amended indictment, moved to have the irrelevant portions deleted, including on the grounds that the irrelevant portions violate the Rule 47(C) requirement for a concise statement of facts.

Rule 53bis

38.   The Defence submits that Rule 53*bis* does not apply because it was not in force at the time of the filing of the Motion. Further, Rule 50 is baseless because it made reference to Rule 53*bis* which was non-existent.

Compliance with Decision of 5 October 1998

39.   The Defence submits that the Prosecution has failed to comply with the oral decision of May 1998 and the written Decision of 5 October 1998 in which the Trial Chamber ordered the Prosecution to clarify paragraphs 2.11 and 2.12. of the original indictment.

DELIBERATIONS

Admissibility of the Motion and Composition of the Trial Chamber

40.   With regard to the issue of the admissibility of the Motion raised by the Defence Reply, the Trial Chamber finds that the written decision of 5 October 1998 negates the defence claim that the Trial Chamber cannot rule on the Motion because of the lack of an earlier decision (*litispendence*). Thus, the Trial Chamber finds that this defence motion is moot. **[page 8]**

41.   The composition of the Trial Chamber is not an issue in this Motion because the Appeals Chamber decided this matter on 3 June 1999. The Defence conceded this point and did not object to the present composition of the Trial Chamber at the hearing on 11 August 1999. The Trial Chamber, therefore, finds that the Defence Motion Challenging Composition and, the Defence Objection to Jurisdiction are no longer live issues.

Amendment of the Indictment

42.   With regard to the standard of proof for amendment under Rule 50, the Trial Chamber finds that it need not be satisfied that a *prima facie* case exists against the accused for the new charges, however, the Prosecutor does need to demonstrate that there are sufficient grounds both in fact and law to allow the amendments. Consequently, the Trial Chamber has considered the Prosecutor's request, the brief thereto and the submissions developed by the Prosecutor during the hearing. *See Prosecutor v. Kanyabashi*, ICTR-06-15-T, at para. 19 (Reasons for the Decision on the Prosecutor's Request for Leave to Amend the Indictment, dated 12 August 1999).

43.   However, it is abundantly clear from a reading of Rule 50 that, apart from the procedure to be followed after the confirming process with respect to the amendment of an indictment, this Rule does not lay down any specific standard of proof for the amendment of an indictment. Therefore, on a strict interpretation of this Rule, it is a matter of the discretion of the Trial Chamber whether or not it allows an amendment of an indictment.

44.   The case of *Kanyabashi v. Prosecutor*, ICTR-96-15-A (Decision on the Defence Motion for Interlocutory Appeal on the Jurisdiction of Trial Chamber I, 3 June 1999) mentioned above, merely decided the issue of the composition of the Trial Chamber and did not consider the merits of the case, with respect to leave to amend the indictment.

45.   The Trial Chamber, having considered the Prosecution's submissions, the request and supporting brief, the written and oral submissions of both parties, is satisfied that the Prosecution has shown sufficient grounds, both in fact and in law, to justify the amendments to the indictment against the accused.

Delay and Prejudice

46.   The Trial Chamber is of course at all times mindful to ensure full respect of the right of the accused to be tried without undue delay as stipulated in Article 20(4)(c) of the Statute. In considering the question of undue delay, the Tribunal cannot be held responsible for delays occurring before the accused is brought under its jurisdiction. The issue which presently concerns the Chamber is twofold, whether the Prosecution acted with undue delay in submitting the request and whether the amendments if so granted will cause any resulting undue delay in the trial of the accused. *See Prosecutor v. Kanyabashi*, ICTR-06-15-T, at para. 23 (Reasons for the Decision on the Prosecutor's Request for Leave to Amend the Indictment, dated 12 August 1999).

47.   The Appeals Chamber found that consideration of the issue of delay must include the "special features of each case." *Prosecutor v. Kovacevic*, IT-97-24-AR73, at para. 30 (Decision Stating Reasons for Appeals Chamber's Order of 29 May 1998, 2 July 1999). **[page 9]**

48.   In *Barker v. Wingo*, 407 U.S. 514, 530 (22 June 1972), the United States Supreme Court, dealing with the issue of delay and speedy trial found that a "balancing test necessarily compels courts to approach speedy trial cases on an ad hoc basis. We can do little more than identify some of the factors which courts should assess in determining whether a particular defendant has been deprived of his right. Though some might express them in different ways, we identify four such factors: length of delay, the reason for the delay, the defendant's assertion of his right, and prejudice to the defendant."

49.   In *O'Flaherty v. Attorney General of St. Christopher and Nevis and Others*, 38 West Indian Reports 146 (1986), the High Court of Justice of the Federation of Saint Christopher and Nevis examined the issue of delay and held that "[t]here is no formula as to what constitutes unreasonable delay, there is no inflexible rule, each case has to be looked at in the light of its own circumstances and the balancing of the conduct of the applicant and that of the respondent and the existing facilities."

50.   In the case at bench, the Trial Chamber finds that there has been no factual demonstration that the proposed amendments to the indictment will give rise to undue delay. The accused were arrested in July 1997. *See* Brief in Support of the Prosecutor's Request for Leave to File an Amended Indictment, at para. 42. In line with international jurisprudence, the length of this delay does not rise to the bevel that warrants denying the Motion. *See also Kovacevic, supra*, at para 31. The Trial Chamber finds justifiable the Prosecution's explanation that the delay of filing the Motion on 31 July 1998 included time required to sift through new evidence. Moreover, the additional time that the amendment will occasion and the time required to prepare for this complex case is not likely to prejudice the rights of the accused.

51.   The Trial Chamber finds that the proposed amendments, if granted, will not cause any prejudice to the accused which cannot be cured by the provisions of the Rules.

Substitution of the Indictment

52.   In *Kovacevic*, the Trial Chamber accepted the defence objection that the size of the amendment expanded the indictment from eight to eighteen pages and that the "proposed amendment ... is so substantial as to amount to a substitution of a new indictment" *Prosecutor v. Kovacevic*, IT-97-24-AR73, at para. 22 (Decision Stating Reasons for Appeals Chamber's Order of 29 May 1998, 2 July 1999). The Appeals Chamber, however, reversed the Trial Chamber's denial of the amendment and held that the increased size of the amendment is but one factor to be taken into account. *Ibid.* at para. 24.

53.   The Trial Chamber finds that the amendments proposed by the Prosecution do not amount to a substitution of the indictment.

Annex B

54.   The Trial Chamber finds that Annex B will be disclosed to the Defence, pursuant to Rule 66(A)(ii), unless the Prosecution applies for relief from the obligation to disclose, pursuant to Rule 66(C), Rule 53 or Rule 69. The Trial Chamber has not reviewed Annex B. The Trial Chamber finds the Defence Disclosure Motion to be without merit. **[page 10]**

Identification of "Others"

55.   The Trial Chamber notes the submissions of the Defence with respect to the vagueness of the word "others" in Count 1 of the proposed amended indictment. The Trial Chamber orders that the Prosecution identify the "others" mentioned in the charge, if their identity is known, without prejudice to the right of the Prosecution to move for non-disclosure where permitted by the Rules. If the identity of the "others" is unknown, the Trial Chamber finds that the Prosecution must specify this fact in the indictment by using the term "other persons."

Cumulative or Alternative Charges

56.   With respect to Count 2 and Count 3 of the proposed amended indictment, the Trial Chamber notes that Counts 2 and 3 rely on the exact same paragraphs of the concise statement of facts of the indictment.

57.   The Trial Chamber holds that it is more appropriate to address the issue of cumulative or alternative counts at trial, when determining the relevant facts and law.

Form of the Indictment – Historical Background

58.   The Trial Chamber notes that it is the practice of the Prosecution to provide a significant amount of contextual information. Though the Trial Chamber itself would prefer a more concise indictment, it does not find it necessary at this time to order large-scale deletions in the proposed amended indictment.

Rule 53bis

59.   The Trial Chamber notes that the Tribunal adopted Rule 53*bis* at the June 1998 Plenary of the Tribunal, but due to an administrative oversight it was not incorporated in the amended Rules which were published.

60.   The Trial Chamber finds that Rule 50 is valid and provides a sufficient basis for this decision. The Trial Chamber does not rely on Rule 53*bis* in deciding the Motion.

61.   Any reference to Rule 53*bis* is not applicable to the Motion, as already indicated by the Trial Chamber. In any event, this would not affect the validity of Rule 50, but would only be applicable to such portion of Rule 50 in which reference to Rule 53*bis* is made.

Compliance with Decision of 5 October 1998

62.   The Trial Chamber notes that to date it has not granted the Prosecution's stay, nor did the Prosecution comply with the decision of 5 October 1998. Here, the "Prosecution Motion for a Temporary Stay of Execution of the Decision of 5 October 1998 Relating to the Defects in the Form of the Indictment" was filed 21 June 1999, more than eight months after the decision.

63.   As this Trial Chamber stated previously, "an order of the Tribunal must stand and have **[page 11]** effect unless the Tribunal issues a superseding order. Here, the Prosecution for many months, has failed to comply with this Chamber's decision [of 5 October 1998] . . . , which ordered relatively simple amendments." *Prosecutor v. Nsabimana and Nteziryayo*, ICTR-97-29-I, at para. 7 (Decision on the Prosecutor's Urgent Motion for Stay of Execution, 17 June 1999). "The Prosecution's inaction is tantamount to the assertion that the mere filing of its [motion for stay] . . . relieved them of any duty to comply. This is not so." *Ibid.* at para. 5.

64.   The Trial Chamber expresses its serious concern about the Prosecution's non-compliance and apparent practice of not complying with decisions by merely filing a motion for stay of execution. An order, unless vacated, is binding and must be carried out. The Trial Chamber admonishes the Prosecution for its non-compliance.

65.   The Trial Chamber, however, finds that the granting of the Motion and the proposed amended indictment now supersede the order of 5 October 1998. This is without prejudice to any possible defence motion on alleged defects in the form of the indictment.

CONCLUSION

66.   **AFTER HAVING DELIBERATED**, the Trial Chamber **GRANTS** leave to the Prosecution to amend the indictment against Gratien Kabiligi and Aloys Ntabakuze as set out in the proposed amended indictment, including:

a. the addition of Conspiracy to Commit Genocide proscribed by Article 2(3)(b) of the Statute;

b. the addition of the words "Théoneste Bagosora, Anatole Nsengiyumva, and" to Count 1 of the proposed amended indictment, after the words "conspired with,"

c. the clarification of the word "others" in Count 1 in the proposed amended indictment by replacing the word "others" with named individuals if they are known, or "other persons" if they are unknown, as stated above;

d. the addition of a count of Crime Against Humanity (Extermination) proscribed by Article 3(b) of the Statute;

e. the addition of a count of Crime Against Humanity (Rape) proscribed by Article 3(g) of the Statute;

f. the addition of a count of Crime Against Humanity (Persecution) proscribed by Article 3(h) of the Statute;

g. the addition of a count of Serious Violation of Article 3 common to the Geneva Conventions and Additional Protocol II (Outrages Upon Personal Dignity) proscribed by Article 4(e) of the Statute; **[page 12]**

67.   The Trial Chamber **ORDERS** that the amended indictment, reflecting the amendments so ordered, be filed with the Registry and served on the accused forthwith.

68.   The Trial Chamber **REMINDS** the Prosecutor of her obligations under Rule 66(A)(ii) of the Rules of Procedure and Evidence.

69.   The Trial Chamber **DISMISSES** the "Prosecution Motion for a Temporary Stay of Execution of the Decision of 5 October 1998 Relating to the Defects in the Form of the Indictment" as moot.

70.   The Trial Chamber **DISMISSES** Ntabakuze's "Motion for the Inadmissibility of Prosecution's Request for Leave to File an Amended Indictment" as moot.

71.   The Trial Chamber **DENIES** Kabiligi's "Motion Challenging the Composition of the Trial Chamber and its Jurisdiction."

72.   The Trial Chamber **DENIES** Kabiligi's "Additional Defence Brief in Reply to the Prosecutor's Motion and Brief to Amend the Indictment and for Joinder, as well as an Objection Based on Lack of Jurisdiction."

73.   The Trial Chamber **DENIES** Kabiligi's "Request Filed by the Defence Counsel for Disclosure of Materials."

74.   The Trial Chamber **DENIES** the oral motion of the defence to strike the historical background section and other portions of the indictment.

75.   Judge Dolenc attaches to this Decision, his Separate and Concurring Opinion.

Arusha, 8 October 1999.

William H. Sekule   Lloyd George Williams
Judge, Presiding   Judge

UNITED NATIONS   NATIONS UNIES

International Criminal Tribunal for Rwanda

TRIAL CHAMBER II

OR: ENG

Before:	Judge William H. Sekule, Presiding
	Judge Lloyd George Williams
	Judge Pavel Dolenc
Registry:	John M. Kiyeyeu
Decision of:	8 October 1999

THE PROSECUTOR

v.

GRATIEN KABILIGI &
ALOYS NTABAKUZE

Case No. ICTR-97-34-I
Case No. ICTR-97-30-I

SEPARATE AND CONCURRING OPINION OF JUDGE DOLENC

DECISION ON THE PROSECUTOR'S MOTION TO AMEND THE INDICTMENT

The Office of the Prosecutor:
    David Spencer
    Frédéric Ossogo
    Holo Makwaia

Counsel for Gratien Kabiligi:
    Jean Yaovi Degli

Counsel for Aloys Ntabakuze:
    Clemente Monterosso

[page 1] I.   INTRODUCTION

1.   By designation of the President of the International Criminal Tribunal for Rwanda (Tribunal), I, Judge Pavel Dolenc, have the honour of sitting in the former Trail Chamber II.

2.   I concur with the decision of the majority of the Trial Chamber (Majority Decision) to grant the "Prosecutor's Request for Leave to File an Amended Indictment" (Motion) and deny the other related motions. I, however, submit this Separate and Concurring Opinion (Opinion) because I have a different opinion from that of the majority on the question of whether a Trial Chamber need review the supporting material for new charges and what standard of proof the Trial Chamber should apply in a review process.

3.   The Majority Decision holds that the Trial Chamber need not review the supporting material for new charges (at para. 42; Transcript of oral decision, at 4) and introduces a new standard of proof for amending an indictment (at paras. 40-42; Transcript of oral decision, at 5). I do not agree with these holdings.

4.   I also believe that the issue of the "substitution" of the indictment warrants further discussion. On the issue of the substitution of the indictment, the Majority Decision (at paras. 52, 53) relies only on a short citation of the decisions of the International Criminal Tribunal for the former Yugoslavia (ICTY) Trial and Appeals Chambers in *Prosecutor v. Kovacevic* (IT-97-24-AR73).

5.   I submit this Opinion to present my understanding of the Statute of the International Criminal Tribunal for Rwanda (Statute) and the Rules of Procedure and Evidence (Rules) governing the procedure for amending an indictment. I think that some observations are not superfluous, particularly because this area of the law is not well settled. The Rule on amendment is silent regarding the standard of review, the practice is unsettled, and the views of the Judges, Prosecutors, and Defence Counsel are divergent.

6.   Part II of this Opinion presents the relevant provisions of the Statute and Rules. Part III discusses the amendment of an indictment in general, the four different options in deciding motions to amend, disqualification, and an apparent dilemma. Part IV offers additional reasoning on the issue of the substitution of the indictment. Part V concludes that a Trial Chamber, under Rule 50, after an initial threshold, generally should review supporting material or other evidence to satisfy itself of the existence of a prima facie case for any new charges or amendments, and that the Trial Chamber should conduct such a review.

II.   RELEVANT PROVISIONS

7.   **Rule 15(C)** (Disqualification) reads:

(C) The Judge of a Trail Chamber who reviews an indictment against an accused, pursuant to Article 18 of the Statute and Rules 47 and 61, shall not sit as a member of the Trial Chamber for the trial of that accused. **[page 2]**

8.   **Rule 47(E) and (F)** (Submission of the Indictment by the Prosecutor) read:

(E) The reviewing Judge shall examine each of the counts in the indictment, and any supporting materials the Prosecutor may provide, to determine, applying the standard set forth in Article 18 of the Statute, whether a case exists against the suspect.
(F) The reviewing Judge may:
(i) request the Prosecutor to present additional material in support of any or all counts, or to take any further measures which appear appropriate;
(ii) confirm each count;
(iii) dismiss each count; or
(iv) adjourn the review so as to give the Prosecutor the opportunity to modify the Indictment.

9.   **Article 18** of the Statute (Review of the Indictment) reads:

1. The Judge of the Trial Chamber to whom the indictment has been transmitted shall review it. If satisfied that a prima facie case has been established by the Prosecutor, he or she shall confirm the indictment. If not so satisfied, the indictment shall be dismissed.

2. Upon confirmation of an indictment, the Judge may, at the request of the Prosecutor, issue such orders and warrants for the arrest, detention, surrender or transfer of persons, and any other orders as may be required for the conduct of trial.

10.   **Rule 50(A) and (B)** (Amendment of the Indictment) read:

(A) The Prosecutor may amend an indictment, without prior leave, at any time before its confirmation, but thereafter, until the initial appearance of the accused before a Trial Chamber pursuant to Rule 62, only with leave of the Judge who confirmed it but, in exceptional circumstances, by leave of a Judge assigned by the President. At or after such initial appearance, an amendment of an indictment may only be made by leave granted by that Trial Chamber pursuant to Rule 73. If leave to amend is granted, Rule 47(G) and Rule 53 *bis* apply *mutatis mutandis* to the amended indictment.

(B) If the amended indictment includes new charges and the accused has already appeared before a Trial Chamber in accordance with Rule 62, a further appearance shall be held as soon as practicable to enable the accused to enter a plea on the new charges.

11.   ICTY **Rule 50(A)** (Amendment of Indictment) reads:

(A)   The Prosecutor may amend an indictment:

(i)   at any time before its confirmation, without leave;

(ii)   thereafter, and until the commencement of the presentation of evidence in terms of Rule 85, with leave of the Judge who confirmed the indictment, or a Judge assigned by the President; or

(iii) after the commencement of the presentation of evidence, with leave of the Trial Chamber hearing the case, after having heard the parties. **[page 3]**

If leave to amend is granted, the amended indictment shall be reviewed by the Judge or Trial Chamber granting leave. Rule 47(G) and Rule 53 *bis* apply *mutatis mutandis* to the amended indictment.

12.   **Rule 73*bis*** (B) (Pre-Trial Conference) reads, in part:

"At the Pre-Trial Conference, the Trial Chamber ... may order the Prosecutor ... to file ... a summary of facts on which each witness will testify...."

13.   **Rule 73*ter*** (B) (Pre-Defence Conference) reads, in part:

"At that Conference, the Trial Chamber ... may order that the defence ... file ... a summary of the facts on which each witness will testify...."

III.   DISCUSSION

A.   Notion of Amendment

14.   Neither the Statute nor the Rules have any provisions that expressly limit the scope of amendment. The Statute and Rules do not provide any subsequent prima facie test of amendments despite the fact that such amendments can include broadened charges or new charges against the same person or against new suspects. Notably, Rule 50 does not provide a standard of review.

15.   Some interpret this lacuna to mean that the Judges do not review the evidence for motions to amend and Prosecutors need not present supporting material for new changes. Under such an interpretation, the question of disqualification of Judges who are dealing with motion for leave the amendment does not arise. I interpret this lacuna differently.

16.   There is no need for review of supporting material if a motion to amend is not based on new evidence. The Prosecutor might make such a motion (not based on new evidence) to comply with an order to provide greater specificity in the form of the indictment, harmonise the indictment to current jurisprudence, clarify, correct, specify, or divide counts (to separate individual and superior responsibility). The practice of the Tribunal is varied, but all such changes to the indictment have been called "amendment."

17.   A Confirming Judge or Trial Chamber can order amendments to correct the errors and defects of charges, to modify or to add some additional elements, to improve unclear, ambiguous, imperfect, uncertain or non-concrete charges. Such amendments do not need additional supporting material and, consequently, no review by a Trial Chamber.

18.   The Prosecutor, however, may seek to add charges (charges that were dismissed from the previous indictment or that are completely new) or broaden existing charges with new aggravating circumstances or with new suspects. In this case, such amendments rely on new or additional support material and require review by a Trial Chamber. **[page 4]**

19.   Rule 50(B) provides that upon granting a motion to amend an indictment adding new charges, the Trial Chamber must hold "a further appearance ... to enable the accused to enter a plea on the new charges." (emphasis added). First, this language implies that there is a different procedure for new charges. Second, this language implies that there is no need for any different procedure for "other" amendments, or those that are not related to new charges.

20.   Under objective criteria, "new charges" could mean that the amendment includes the same accused with new charges, or the same accused with the same charges but the scope of the charge is new. Under subjective criteria, new charges could mean that the amendment includes new accused persons.

21.   One dictionary defines amendment as: "[t]o change or modify for the better. To alter by modification, deletion, or addition." Black's Law Dictionary 81 (6th ed. 1990). Another defines amendment as: "make minor changes (in a text or piece of legislation or other ruling) in order to make it fairer or more accurate, or to reflect changing circumstances." The New Oxford Dictionary of English 53 (1998).

22.   Some of the difficulty in deciding this issue of amendment of indictments lies in the use of the words "charges" and "counts." The Statute and Rules appear to use the terms interchangeably. According to one dictionary, a charge means "[i]n a criminal case, the specific crime the defendant is accused of committing" Black's Law Dictionary 233 (6th ed. 1990). The same dictionary, however, states that, "'[c]ount' and 'charge' when used relative to allegations in an indictment or information are synonymous." *Ibid.* at 348.

23.   With regard to amendment, generally there exist two scenarios. In the first scenario, the Prosecutor finds new evidence. The new evidence is memorialised in new supporting material. The supporting material supports new allegations, which the Prosecutor will incorporate into a new proposed amended indictment, which will include a new concise statement of facts and new counts. The Prosecutor moves to amend, and the Trial Chamber may review the supporting material to determine the existence of a prima facie case and rule on the motion. In the second scenario, the Prosecutor has no new evidence, no new supporting material, and no new allegations, but moves to amend the indictment for other reasons. The Trial Chamber need not review supporting material in this second scenario.

24.   Thus, the Trial Chamber must have discretion to decide if there need be a review of the supporting material.

   B.   A Judge is Disqualified Upon Reviewing Supporting Material

25.   Under Rule 15(C), a Confirming Judge who reviews supporting material at an *ex parte* hearing is disqualified from sitting at trial on the same case. Rule 15(C) is a procedural safeguard for the accused that attempts to ensure that the three Judges hearing his case will not have seen, reviewed, or in any way even appear to be biased by the supporting material.

26.   This disqualification may represent one of the apparent reasons for the Trial Chambers' reluctance to review supporting material to grant leave to amend an indictment. The concern is that the disqualification under Rule 15(C) might apply by analogy to any **[page 5]** Judge that reviews supporting material or other evidence under Rule 50. It appears to me, however, that Rule 15(C) applies strictly to a Confirming Judge and does not apply to any other stage of the proceedings, including a motion to amend.

C.   Four Options for Deciding a Motion to Amend

27.   Such an expansive and unwarranted interpretation of Rule 15(C) creates a dilemma in deciding a motion to amend. The Trial Chamber must choose between four options: (1) denying a motion because no prima facie case is proved without presenting supporting material; (2) granting the motion without having reviewed the supporting material; (3) remanding the case to a Confirming Judge to review the supporting material and make a finding on the existence or not of a prima facie case, or; (4) granting or denying a motion after deciding whether or not to review supporting material.

28.   I am of the opinion that the fourth option is the correct one. This is despite the fact that such a procedure possibly might invite an objection or appeal on the grounds of an alleged Rule 15(C) violation. I am of the opinion that such an objection or appeal is without merit. I think that the Trial Chamber should grant or deny a motion to amend after reviewing new supporting material or other new evidence for new charges. An analysis of each of the four options from which a Trial Chamber must choose follows.

1. Denying a motion because no prima facie case is proved

29.   The first option of denying a motion to amend because no prima facie case is proved is the most unacceptable. This option, in effect, would mean denying all motions to amend. That is, the Trial Chamber could grant no amendment because it insists on reviewing supporting material but then insists that such a review would disqualify the Judges. Such a procedure defies logic and violates the spirit of Rule 50.

2. Granting a motion without reviewing the supporting material

30.   The second option is that of granting a motion to amend without reviewing supporting material. Some contend that the language of Rule 50 does not trigger any need to review supporting material or other evidence to determine the existence of a prima facie case for an amendment. Indeed, the words prima facie do not appear in Rule 50. The problem, however, is that Rule 50 gives the Trial Chamber the authority to "grant leave," but does not provide the criteria or standard of proof on which to make such a decision. This constitutes a lacuna.

31.   Trial Chamber I held that a Trial Chamber need not review supporting material (nor remand the case to a Confirming Judge) to grant leave to amend an indictment. "A Trial Chamber seized with an application for leave to amend an indictment under Rule 50 against an accused who has already been indicted, has no cause to enquire into a *prima facie* basis for the charge." *Prosecutor v. Nyiramasuhuko & Ntahobali*, ICTR-97-21-I, at para. 13 (Decision on the Status of the Hearings for the Amendment of the Indictments and for Disclosure of Supporting Material, 30 september 1998 (emphasis added) (ruling on four cases). **[page 6]**

32.   The Prosecutor has cited the *Nyiramasuhuko* decision in several cases as authority for the proposition that a Trial Chamber need not review supporting material in deciding a motion to amend under Rule 50.

33.   This decision asserts that a Trial Chamber can decide a motion to amend based only on the representations of the parties and need not satisfy itself as to the existence of a prima facie case for new counts. Several of my learned colleagues share this view, and several very recent written and oral decisions also reflect this view. *See Prosecutor v. Ndayambaje*, ICTR-96-8-I, at para. 15 (Decision on the Prosecutor's Request for Leave to File an Amended Indictment, 2 September 1999) (holding that a "Trial Chamber seized with a motion, requesting leave to amend an indictment pursuant to Rule 50, against an accused who has already been indicted, has no cause to inquire into a *prima facie* basis for proposed

amendments to the indictment"); *Prosecutor v. Nsengiyumva*, ICTR-96-12-I, at para. 9 (Decision on the Prosecutor's Request for Leave to File an Amended Indictment (2 September 1999) (same); *Prosecutor v. Nsabimana & Nteziryayo*, ICTR-97-29-I, at 4 (Decision on Prosecutor's Request for Leave to File an Amended Indictment, 10 September 1999) (same); *Prosecutor v. Bagosora*, ICTR-96-7-I, at 5-6 (Decision on the Prosecutor's Request for Leave to Amend the Indictment, 23 September 1999) (same); *Prosecutor v. Kanyabashi*, ICTR-96-15-I, at paras. 17-21 (Reasons for the Decision on the Prosecutor's Request for Leave to Amend the Indictment, 13 September 1999) (same); *Prosecutor v. Nyiramasuhuko & Ntahobali*, ICTR-97-21-I, at paras. 17-18 (Decision on the Prosecutor's Request for Leave to Amend the Indictment, 6 September 1999) (same).

34.   In the case at bench, the Prosecutor shares this view, and submits that the *Nyiramasuhuko* decision is controlling. The Defence disagrees, objects to the Motion, and urges the Trial Chamber to order disclosure and consider supporting or other evidence material (even if redacted) to determine the merit of the Motion.

35.   In several recent motions to amend, including that in the case at bench, the Prosecutor prayed for the Trial Chamber to remand the motion to the Confirming Judge. The Prosecutor in its prayer, first moved to amend, then moved to "[d]esignate a single Judge to review the amended indictment pursuant to Rule 47." *Prosecutor v. Kabiligi & Ntabakuze*, ICTR-97-34-I, ICTR-97-30-I, at para. 8(b) (Prosecutor's Request for Leave to File an Amended Indictment) (filed 31 July 1998); *Prosecutor v. Bagosora*, ICTR-96-7-T, at para 7(b) (Prosecutor's Request for Leave to File an Amended Indictment) (filed 31 July 1998); *Prosecutor v. Nsengiyumva*, ICTR-96-12-T, at para 7(b) (Prosecutor's Request for Leave to File an Amended Indictment) (filed 31 July 1998).

36.   At the hearing in the case at bench (as in others) the Prosecutor, relying on the *Nyiramasuhuko* decision, withdrew this prayer, asserting that the Trial Chamber had jurisdiction and did not need to review the supporting material. *See* Transcript of Hearing of 11 August 1999, at 10,82.

37.   If, however, a Trail Chamber seized of a case need not review the supporting material (for a motion to amend the indictment) in the case of new charges, this means that the Prosecutor has not proved a prima facie case. This, in turn, creates a loophole through which the Prosecutor can circumvent the confirmation process. The Prosecutor could move to **[page 7]** amend an indictment, including adding new charges, for which she knows she cannot establish a prima facie case.

38.   With such a loophole, the Prosecutor could charge in an indictment only one count and later file a motion to amend with an unlimited number of charges that are not supported by supporting material establishing a prima facie case. This type of filing would seem to be contrary to the principle of a fair trial, violating particularly the spirit and purpose of the provisions of the Article 18(1) of the Statute and of the Rule 47(E) that only a confirmed charge should be grounds for trial.

39.   Under this option, a Trial Chamber is placed in a position where it can only accept at face value the Prosecutor's representations that there exists a prima facie case. To make a finding of fact, with regard to the merit of a motion to amend new charges, a Trial Chamber must review something, new supporting material or other new evidence.

40.   In the case at bench, the Majority Decision (at para. 42) introduces a new standard of proof for new charges, in addition to the prima facie test for review of the indictment, namely, that "the Prosecutor does need to demonstrate that there are sufficient grounds both in fact and law to allow the amendments." The Majority Decision holds that this new standard of proof does not require the Trial Chamber to review the supporting material relating to new charges.

41.   In my opinion, such an emergency exit from an awkward situation is not justified. This situation is caused by the legal lacunae in Rule 50, which does not lay down any specific standard of proof for amendments. Consequently, the only possible inference is that Majority Decision holds that the mere submissions of the Prosecutor are treated as a proof in order to demonstrate sufficient factual grounds to allow the amendments. This position conflicts with the basic requirement in Article 18(1) of the Statute and Rule 47(E) that only reviewed and confirmed charges should be grounds for trial. Indeed, this

precondition for trial must be applied in proceedings for amendments not directly on the basis of Rule 50, but by analogy with Rule 47(E) just because of the respective lacunae in Rule 50. In my opinion, an application of Rule 47(E) by analogy also is well founded under Article 32(b) of the Vienna Convention on the Law of Treaties because the alternative leads to a result which is manifestly unreasonable.

42.   The introduction of a new standard of proof in the process to amend an indictment has no support in any provision of the Statute, Rules, or, I believe, in national jurisdictions that require a judicial review of charges.

43.   The Majority Decision holding that the mere submission of a party demonstrates sufficient factual grounds for alleged facts is not correct. The establishment of factual grounds, regardless of the standard of proof, is an evidentiary matter, not a matter of mere allegation. **[page 8]**

3. Remanding the motion to a Confirming Judge for review

44.   Some contend that remanding the motion to amend the indictment to the Confirming or "reviewing" Judge represents the best procedure to determine the merit of the motion and if a prima facie case exists for an amendment. This procedure would be analogous to that of Rule 47(E) and would avoid any objection or appeal based on an expansive interpretation of Rule 15(C). Remanding the motion, however, appears illogical to me because a Trial Chamber would decide the issue of a motion to amend the indictment without knowing if a prima facie case exists or if the Confirming or reviewing Judge will grant or deny the new charges. This also places a single Confirming Judge in a awkward position of greater authority than a Trial Chamber. Remanding also may hinder judicial economy if the motion must "yo-yo", or go back and forth, between the Trial Chamber and Confirming or reviewing Judge.

45.   ICTY Rule 50 is different form ICTR Rule 50. At the ICTY, if the Prosecutor files a motion to amend *before the presentation of evidence*, the Trial Chamber must remand the motion to the Confirming Judge for purpose of determining if there exists a prima facie case, similar to the procedure under Rule 47. The ICTY procedure under Rule 50, that expressly directs either a Confirming Judge or the Trial Chamber (*after* the presentation of evidence) to review supporting material in determining a motion to amend, supports the notion that such a review is an important step which the Tribunal should not bypass. The ICTY procedure also supports the notion that the same body reviews the supporting material and decides a motion to amend.

46.   In *Kovacevic*, the Appeals Chamber, though not specifically on this point, reversed an ICTY Trial Chamber's denial of the Prosecutor's motion to amend fourteen new charges. *Prosecutor v. Kovacevic*, IT-97-24-AR73, at para. 38 (Decision Stating Reasons for Appeals Chamber's Order of 29 May 1998) (2 July 1998). For purpose of remand, the Appeals Chamber found that the Prosecutor had not yet established a prima facie case for the fourteen new charges. "The Appeals Chamber has not hereby determined whether a <u>prima facie case has been established in relation to the charges added</u> in the Amended Indictment, as required for its confirmation." *Ibid.* (emphasis added). Thus, this case may stand for the rule that the Prosecutor must prove that there exists a prima facie case for new charges that she seeks to amend.

47.   In at least two other ICTY cases, both *Prosecutor v. Meakic and Others* and *Prosecutor v. Sikirica and Others*, the Trial Chamber held that under ICTY Rule 50 the Prosecutor should refer its applications to amend the indictment to the Judge who confirmed the indictment or to any other reviewing Judge designated by the President. *Prosecutor v. Meakic and Others*, IT-95-4-PT, *Prosecutor v. Sikirica and Others*, IT-95-8-PT, at 2 (Decision on the Prosecutor's Motion for Leave to Amend the Indictment, 26 August 1998) (deciding both cases). Though these decisions show the difference between the two Tribunal's Rules regarding amendment, the decision to remand motions to amend to the Confirming Judge highlight the need for scrutiny of the substance behind the motion for amendment. *See also Prosecutor v. Kvocha et al*, IT-98-30 (Order Granting Leave to File an Amended Indictment and Confirming the Amended Indictment, 9 November 1998); *Prosecutor v. Kolundzija*, IT-95-8-I and IT-98-30-PT (Decision Rejecting the Prosecutor's **[page 9]** Request for Leave to Amend Indictments, 6 July 1999); *Prosecutor v. Sikirica et al*, IT-95-8-PT (Decision on the Prosecutor's Motion for Leave to Amend the Indictment, 29 July 1998).

> 4. Granting or denying the motion after deciding whether or not to review supporting material

48. The fourth option is granting or denying a motion to amend after deciding whether or not to review the supporting material. A Trial Chamber should review the supporting material or other evidence for the new charges, and the Judges should not be disqualified on this ground. This option seems the most acceptable to me.

49. Under Rule 50, a Trial Chamber should hear the motion for leave to amend the indictment, under a three-step process. First, the Trial Chamber should satisfy itself of the initial threshold (i.e. considering the parties' submissions regarding jurisdiction, admissibility, rationale, timeliness, any possible delay or prejudice, etc.). Second, the Trial Chamber should decide if it is necessary to review the supporting material or other evidence. Third, if having decided that a review is necessary, the Trial Chamber should review the new supporting material to determine if the Prosecutor has established a prima facie case for each amendment, and on that basis grant or deny a motion to amend.

50. The case law of the ICTR, namely three decisions, support the proposition that the Trial Chamber should review supporting material in deciding a motion to amend. The first two decisions, however, relate to motions to amend made after the commencement of trial, and the third relates more to the jurisdiction of the Trial Chamber, as opposed to a Confirming Judge, to hear the motion to amend. These decisions appear to be more on point than that in *Nyiramasuhuko*.

51. In *Musema*, the Prosecutor during trial moved to amend the indictment to add one new charge and amend others, relying on evidence in the form of witness testimony already before the Trial Chamber and new supporting material in the form of witness statements. *Prosecutor v. Musema*, ICTR-96-13-T, at paras. 3, 4 (Decision on the Prosecutor's Request for Leave to Amend the Indictment, 6 May 1999). Trial Chamber I "considered the evidence presented by the Prosecutor in support of her motion" and found "that a *prima facie* case has been established by the Prosecutor with respect to the new counts and grants leave to file the amended indictment. *Ibid.* at para. 19 (emphasis added). Thus, the Trial Chamber hearing the motion reviewed evidence already before it and new supporting material, satisfied itself as to the factual merit of the motion, and did not mention the possibility of disqualification. The Trial Chamber, in ruling on the Defence submission that only the Confirming Judge could hear the motion, found no need to remand the matter to the Confirming Judge, and found that Rule 50 makes "the Trial Chamber competent to entertain the motion." *Ibid.* at para. 13.

52. In *Akayesu*, the Prosecutor during trial moved to amend the indictment to add three new charges, and "submitted evidentiary [and supporting] material in support of his motion." *Prosecutor v. Akayesu*, ICTR-96-4-T, at 2 (Leave to Amend the Indictment, 17 June 1997). Trial Chamber I granted the motion after having considered the evidence already before it and "the accompanying evidentiary material." *Ibid.* at 3. The Trial Chamber found the **[page 10]** motion to be "well-founded." *Ibid.* The Trial Chamber did not discuss the possibility of disqualification, nor did it specifically make any findings related to whether the Prosecutor had established a prima facie case on the new charges. *Ibid.* The review of the new material, however, demonstrates that the Trial Chamber in *Akayesu* sought to satisfy itself as the factual merit of the motion to amend.

53. In *Bagosora and 28 Others*, the Prosecutor sought confirmation of an indictment, which included adding one new charge to the cases against eleven (out of twenty-nine) accused persons whom already had made an initial appearance before a Trial Chamber. *Prosecutor v. Bagosora and 28 Others*, ICTR-98-37-I, at 1, 10 (Dismissal of Indictment, 31 March 1998). Judge Khan dismissed the entire indictment against all twenty-nine accused persons without an examination of the merits of the charges. *Ibid.* at 12. In so ruling, Judge Khan found that adding one new charge (in relation to eleven accused persons) amounted to a motion for leave to amend the (existing) indictments, and such motions properly lie before the Trial Chamber. *Ibid.* at 10. "Thus, the logical course to follow for the Prosecutor [to seek to amend an indictment] would be to approach the appropriate Trial Chamber in accordance with [R]ule 50." *Ibid.* This decision supports the position that after initial appearance, the Trial Chamber hears a motion for

leave to amend, and the Confirming Judge does not participate further. This decision, however, is silent on the issue of the standard of review of a motion to amend.

D.   *Ex parte or inter partes* hearing

54.   I am inclined to believe that the Trial Chamber generally should perform a review of supporting material for an amendment at an *inter partes* hearing. I also can foresee a situation, however, well before the commencement of trial, where the Trial Chamber could grant a Prosecutor's motion for such a review to take place at an *ex parte* hearing. The Trial Chamber should have the flexibility and discretion to order an *ex parte* or *inter partes* hearing to review the supporting material or other evidence, including ordering the redaction of sensitive information and assignment of pseudonyms.

55.   The decision on holding an *ex parte* or *inter partes* hearing should consider the stage of the proceedings; whether the motion is to take place early in the proceedings, during pretrial, or during trial. The Trial Chamber must respect the right of the accused to a fair trial in making this determination.

E.   *Review of Supporting Material Does Not Disqualify the Trial Chamber*

56.   There are several reasons why a Trial Chamber's review of supporting material or other evidence in order to decide a motion to amend does not disqualify any of its members from sitting at trial.

57.   The question is whether disqualification under Rule 15(C) (that the Confirming Judge who reviews supporting material under Rule 47 cannot sit at trial) applies <u>by analogy</u> to the Trial Chamber that reviews supporting material or other evidence for a motion for leave to amend the indictment under Rule 50. I think it does not. **[page 11]**

58.   The provisions on disqualification of Judges are an exception to the general presumption of the impartiality of Judges, under Article 12(1) and (3) of the Statute and Rule 14(A). One principle of the interpretation of laws requires that exceptions be construed *stricti sensu*; therefore, the Tribunal should apply strictly the provision on disqualification of Judges. This means that <u>only</u> the Confirming Judge is disqualified, but Judges of a Trial Chamber, who review supporting material or other evidence for purposes of deciding a motion for leave for amendment, are not disqualified from trial.

59.   Supporting material for establishing a prima facie case for new charges merely must meet a low standard of proof and need not be the same evidence produced at trial. For these reasons, I think that prior knowledge of supporting material does not have the significance of unfair prejudice for the accused despite Rule 15(C). The position that the Trial Chamber Judges should rely on the Prosecutor's mere representations and not verify the existence of a prima facie case for new charge violates the presumption of innocence, the essence of the judicial function, and gives the Prosecutor an unjustifiably favourable position. This may be contrary to Article 20(1) of the Statute. That is, if the accused is presumed innocent, including of all new charges in a proposed indictment, some initial, low threshold, showing is required to overcome this presumption.

60.   Disqualification of a Judge is presumed if he: took part in the investigation; served in other proceedings against an accused; was a counsel; was a witness; was affected by the alleged crime, or; is related to the parties (*index inhabilis*). The competent authority might order the withdrawal of a Judge if other circumstances raise a suspicion as to his impartiality (*index suspectus*).

61.   Whether such an analogy applies may depend on the relationship between the review of the indictment under Rule 47 and the decision on the motion for leave to amend the indictment under Rule 50.

62.   The purpose of the confirmation of an indictment is "to sift meritorious from a nonmeritorious cases." Daniel D.N. Nsereko, *Rules of Procedure and Evidence for the Tribunal for the Former Yugoslavia*, 5 Criminal Law Forum 528 (1994). The confirmation is "a safeguard against unreasonable or unwarranted action on the part of the prosecution." Morris & Scharf, The International Criminal Tribunal for Rwanda 478 (1997). Thus, the confirmation of indictment is a mechanism to ensure fair procedure in accordance with the Rule 47(E). This mechanism should apply to <u>each count</u> of the indictment (the

"Judge shall examine each of the counts in the indictment ...") to prevent the suspect from being charged with even one charge that is not based on a finding of prima facie evidence.

63.   The Confirming Judge examines supporting material and this is the reason for disqualification. The jurisprudence of the Tribunals, however, shows that the review of the indictment also includes other considerations, e.g., litispendence on previous confirmed charges. I presume that he could dismiss charges also on *non bis in idem* grounds, or because of death or incurable mental disease of the suspect. **[page 12]**

64.   What is the legal significance of the act of confirmation? Has it the significance of making an indictment legally valid (a constitutive effect), or is it only approbation of the Prosecutor's representation of the existence of a prima facie case (a declaratory effect)?

65.   In an adversarial criminal procedure system, the trial and subsequent judgement can take place only on the basis of a valid indictment. If the confirmation has constitutive effect, unconfirmed charges are "null and void" and, consequently, also those proceedings and decisions of the Tribunal, which are based on said null and void indictment, are invalid. The Tribunal should pay careful attention to such defects of the indictment, *proprio motu*, at every moment of procedure.

66.   Such a constitutive-effect approach seems wrong to me. If the Trial Chamber finds an accused person guilty – beyond a reasonable doubt – it is illogical to declare all the proceedings and the judgment "null and void" for lack of an earlier prima facie showing. The same argument also applies to the charges that were dismissed under Article 18(1) of the Statute and Rule 47(F)(iii) and renewed as amendment.

67.   On the other hand, if the Trial Chamber acquits after trial based on a "null and void" indictment, a question of *non bis in idem* can arise. That is, if there existed no valid procedure and judgement, the Prosecutor could file a new indictment for the same charges against the same accused person.

68.   I am of the opinion, therefore, that the confirmation only has a declaratory effect and does not affect the legal validity of the indictment. Although unconfirmed charges are valid grounds for criminal procedure before the Tribunal and for its judgement in spite of provisions of the Article 18(1) of the Statute and Rule 47. Of course, procedures based on unconfirmed counts breach these provisions, but since this error has no impact on the validity and correctness of the judgement, it cannot constitute grounds for appeal in the sense of provision of the Article 24(1)(a) of the Statute.

69.   It appears that the same idea led the drafters of the Statute. The first paragraph of Article 18 of the Statute reads that "the Judge of the trial chamber to whom the indictment has been transmitted ..." shall review the indictment and confirm or dismiss it. The definitive articles "the Judge" and "the chamber" reveal that the Confirming or reviewing Judge should not be disqualified from trial, most likely because the material supporting the indictment are not supposed to be of such significance as to justify any disqualification.

70.   Article 14 of the Statute reads that ICTR shall adopt for itself the Rules of the ICTY with such changes as deemed necessary. Therefore, changes to the ICTY Rules should be based on good cause to be necessary.

71.   ICTY Rule 50(A) requires that the amended indictment be reviewed using the same standard of proof as the confirmation of the first indictment. ICTR Rule 50 has not followed that provision, and without good reason. It seems to me, therefore, that ICTR Rule 50 is contrary to said provision of the Statute. **[page 13]**

72.   Review of an indictment also is common in civil law systems of criminal procedure. Usually the reviewing Judge is the same as the presiding Judge of the Trial Chamber. He verifies that the indictment complies with the law (regarding form, constituents, and contents). If he finds any defects, he sends it to the Prosecutor for correction. If he is satisfaid with the indictment, he causes it to be served on the suspect without any further act of confirmation. For example, in Slovenia the reviewing Judge is not disqualified from the trial, on the contrary, he presides over the Trial Chamber. Indeed, the suspect may object to the indictment and the Judges who hear his motion are disqualified from sitting in the Trial

Chamber because they may hear and decide questions of fact, including a defence of contradictory evidence.

73.   Accordingly, confirmation of the charges plays a relatively minor role and should not constitute grounds for disqualification of reviewing Judges. Also some other decisions of the Judges are based on a Prosecutor's investigative evidence, but without disqualification. Nevertheless, Rule 15 sets out this ground for disqualification, and the Tribunal must respect this, but it should not extend his ground by analogy to disqualify Judges in some similar procedural situations.

F.   Waiver

74.   The defence may waive the Trial Chamber's review of supporting material or other evidence if it does not object to the motion to amend. That is, the Trial Chamber may grant the amendment or order the filing of a new indictment, if the defence does not object to the Prosecutor's motion to amend or otherwise waives such review. *See Prosecutor v. Semanza*, ICTR-97-20-I, at 2 (Decision on the "Motion by the Office of the Prosecutor for Leave to Amend the Indictment") (2 September 1999).

75.   One might consider waiver to be like a fifth option, allowing the Trial Chamber to grant a motion to amend without reviewing supporting material. In the case at bench, Counsel for both accused persons have objected to the Motion. Waiver is inapplicable here.

G.   Disqualification and Eliminating Rule 15(C)

76.   Eliminating Rule 15(C) represents one step toward settling this area of the law. The plain meaning of Article 18 of the Statute and other practical considerations favour eliminating Rule 15(C).

77.   The plain meaning of Article 18 supports the elimination of Rule 15(C). The plain meaning of Article 18 of the Statute indicates that it is one of the Judges of the Trial Chamber (that will try the case) that confirms the indictment. Article 18(1) seems to indicate that a case goes to a Trial Chamber, for confirmation, and then trial in the same Trial Chamber. Article 18(2) further supports this view because the Confirming Judge can make orders "for the conduct of trial." The alternative thesis is that a Confirming Judge in one Trial Chamber is making orders for the conduct of trial in another Trial Chamber, and is, therefore, illogical.

78.   There are other practical reasons for eliminating Rule 15(C). It is the practice of the ICTR that the Judges of the Trial Chamber review supporting material before trial, i.e. at the **[page 14]** Pre-Trial Conference (under Rule 73 *bis*) and at the Pre-Defence Conference (under Rule 73 *ter*). Under these Rules, the Trial Chamber may review "a summary of the facts on which each witness will testify." This fact alone obviates any purpose for the distinction made by Rule 15(C) and precludes any such application by analogy to a Trial Chamber reviewing supporting material or other evidence for a motion to amend. Thus, Rule 15(C) goes beyond the plain meaning of Article 18, and the purported procedural safeguard that it affords is impractical and unnecessary. The Tribunal should eliminate Rule 15(C).

IV.   SUBSTITUTION OF THE INDICTMENT

79.   The Defence submits that the requested amended indictment amounts to a substitution of the previous indictment because of the numerous new charges, allegedly based on new evidence, and other changes, including the increased length of the document (fifty-one pages instead of the previous eleven pages). The Majority Decision (at para. 52) cites the holding of the Trial Chamber in the *Kovacevic* case that the "proposed amendments is so substantial as to amount to a substitution of a new indictment" and the holding of the Appeals Chamber that reversed the decision in the same case that "the increased size of the indictment is but one factor to be taken into account." The Majority Decision (at para. 53) then concludes "that the amendments proposed by the Prosecution do not amount to a substitution of the indictment."

80.   My interpretation of these decisions is that the Trial Chamber could deny the proposed amended indictment if it amounts to a substitution of the previous indictment, considering among other reasons,

the increased size of the amendments. It is difficult to say if my understanding of these decisions is correct because the reasoning contained in the decisions is very cursory, but if it is so, I disagree with them.

81.   I think, contrary to the submission of the defence and the apparent view of the Majority Decision, that the alleged substitution of the indictment in the present case (and in similar instances of "amended indictments") has no impact on the admissibility of such amendments. A proposed amended indictment is an act of the Prosecution, an instrument of accusation, and when granted, it in fact replaces, substitutes for the previous indictment without the latter being withdrawn. If it were not so, the Trial Chamber would have to consider and decide upon both, or even more, of the indictments on the trial.

82.   I agree with the Defence contention that the amended indictment would substitute for the previous indictment. It appears that in similar situations, the Prosecution never has withdrawn the previous indictment at the ICTR and the ICTY. Rather, the previous indictment ipso facto became moot. This practice can invoke legal difficulties. Also this form of amendments most likely does not correspond with plain meaning of the word "amendment" and with the wording of the Rule 50(A) where it reads that Prosecutor may _amend_ the indictment and not to replace it. Further, this form of amendment creates problems, such as difficulties as: establishing what changes in the concise statements of facts amount new charges, especially if changes are based on new evidence; limiting a further appearance and pleading only for new charges, and; limiting preliminary motions for the new charges or for new amended indictment as a whole. Nevertheless, the form of amendments is not prescribed and cannot be obstacle for granting the amendments. **[page 15]**

83.   Obviously the problem is not in form but in substance, since the defence objects to the _amount_ of amendments, that means the quantity and quality of changes. But neither the Statute nor the Rules have any provisions on this issue. There are no criteria to assess when the amendments amount to a substitution of the indictment and what are the consequences if it is so. Consequently, the amount of amendments is not legal hindrance for granting the amended indictment. Therefore, in my opinion, the decision depends exclusively on the discretionary right of a Trial Chamber taking into consideration if such an amended indictment is justified under the circumstances of each particular case and not on accession whether the proposed amended indictment amounts to a substitution of the previous one. However, in my opinion, the Majority Decision should substantiate its finding with additional arguments to be persuasive to the parties.

V.   CONCLUSION

84.   The Trial Chamber, in deciding a Prosecutor's motion to amend the indictment under Rule 50, should hear the motion for leave to amend the indictment, under a three-step process. First, the Trial Chamber should satisfy itself of the initial threshold of the motion (i.e. submissions on jurisdiction, admissibility, rationale, timeliness, any possible delay or prejudice, etc.). Second, the Trial Chamber should decide if it is necessary to review the supporting material or other evidence. Third, if having decided that a review is necessary, the Trial Chamber should review the new supporting material to determine if the Prosecutor has established a prima facie case for the amendment, and on that basis grant or deny the motion.

85.   If the Prosecutor has no new supporting material and her motion to amend is not for purposes of adding new counts based on new evidence, the Trial Chamber could decide the motion based on the submissions of the parties alone.

86.   I am inclined to believe that the Trial Chamber generally should perform a review of supporting material at an _inter partes_ hearing. I, however, also can foresee a situation – well before the commencement of trial – where the Trial Chamber should grant a Prosecutor's motion for such a review to take place at _an ex parte_ hearing. The Trial Chamber should have the flexibility and discretion to order an _inter partes_ or _ex parte_ hearing to review the supporting material or other evidence, including ordering redaction and pseudonyms.

87.   I am of the opinion that Rule 15(C) does not bar a Trial Chamber from reviewing supporting material or other evidence at a hearing on a motion to amend the indictment. It is in light of my interpretation of Article 18 of the Statute, other Rules, and the practice of the Tribunal that I am in favor of eliminating Rule 15(C) at the next Plenary.

88.   In my view, substitution of the indictment does not constitute sufficient legal grounds to deny a motion to amend. **[page 16]**

89.   In the case at bench, I **CONCUR** in granting the Motion and denying the other related motions. I, however, think that the Trial Chamber generally should review the Prosecutor's supporting material or other evidence to determine if there exists a prima facie case for her motion to amend new charges.

Arusha, 8 October 1999.

Pavel Dolenc
Judge

Relevant Human Rights Standards

Rule 47(C) of the Rules of Procedure provides that "The indictment shall set forth the name and particulars of the suspect, and a concise statement of the facts of the case and of the crime with which the suspect is charged."

Under Article 17, paragraph 4 of the Statute the indictment is to contain "a concise statement of the facts and the crime or crimes with which the accused is charged". International human rights law provides limited guidance as to these provisions should be interpreted.

Article 20, paragraph 4 (*a*) of the Statute reflects Article 14, paragraph 3 (*a*) of the International Covenant on Civil and Political Rights "In the determination of any criminal charge against him, everyone shall be entitled to the following minimum guarantees, in full equality:

(a)   To be informed promptly and in detail in a language which he understands of the nature and cause of the charge against him;

Article 6, paragraph 3 (*a*) of the European Convention on Human Rights differs slightly: in the English text, the word "charge" is replaced by "accusation." In French, "accusation" appears in both instruments. The United Nations Human Rights Committee has not yet addressed the precise issue of how specific a charge must be in an indictment or the equivalent, under Article 14, paragraph 3 (*a*).[1] The relevance of general principles adopted by the European Court of Human Rights in relation to Article 6, paragraph 3 (*a*) was recognised by the Appeals Chamber of the ICTY in *Prosecutor v. Kovacevic*.[2]

Article 6, paragraph 3(*a*) of the European Convention must be assessed in light of the more general right to a fair hearing (Article 6, paragraph 1), as the European Court of Human Rights noted in *Pélissier & Sassi v. France*:[3]

> "52. . . . The Court considers that in criminal matters the provision of full, detailed information concerning the charges against a defendant, and consequently the legal characterisation that the court might adopt in the matter, is an essential prerequisite for ensuring that the proceedings are fair. [Citations omitted]"

Article 6, paragraphs 3 (a) and 3 (b) are also connected; the right to be informed of the nature and cause of an accusation is allied to the right to prepare a defence.[4] In *Pélissier & Sassi v. France* the Court observed that:

> "51. . . . [Article 6 paragraph 3 (a) points] to the need for special attention to be paid to the notification of the "accusation" to the defendant. Particulars of the offence play a crucial role in the criminal process, in that it is from the moment of their service that the suspect is formally put on written notice of the factual and legal basis of the charges against him . . . Article 6 § 3 (a) of the Convention affords the defendant the right to be informed not only of the "cause" of the accusation, that is to say the acts he is alleged to have committed and on which the accusation is based, but also the legal characterisation given to those acts. That information should, as the Commission rightly stated, be detailed. [Citation omitted.]"

There is an important distinction between Article 6, paragraph 3 (a), and Rule 47(C):

> "53. Article 6 § 3 (a) *does not impose any special formal requirement as to the manner* in which the accused is to be informed of the nature and cause of the accusation against him . . . [*ibid.* Citation omitted]"

---

[1]   See *e.g. Leehong v. Jamaica*, Communication No. 613/1995, CCPR/C/66/D/613/1995 (13 July 1999,) par. 9.4; *McLawrence v. Jamaica*, Communication No. 702/1996, CCPR/C/60/D/702/1996 (18 July 1997,) par. 5.19; *Williams v. Jamaica*, Communication No. 561/1993, CCPR/C/59/D/561/1993 (8 April 1997), par. 9.2.)

[2]   ICTY, Decision Stating Reasons for Appeals Chamber's Order of 29 May 1998, *Prosecutor v. Kovacevic*, Case No. IT-97-24-AR73, 2 July 1998 par. 30.

[3]   European Court of Human Rights, *Pélissier & Sassi v. France*, 25 March 1999, 25444/94.

[4]   *Ibid.*, par. 54.

The Court considers whether, in light of the proceedings as a whole, the accused can reasonably claim to have been unaware of the factual ingredients and legal characterisation of the charges.[5] The Tribunals, however, have ruled that lack of specificity in an indictment cannot be "cured" by, for example, pre-trial discovery to the defence of supporting material. The ICTR observed in *Prosecutor v. Nyiramashuko* that: "Whilst it is essential to read the indictment together with the supporting material, the indictment on its own must be able to present clear and concise charges against the accused, to enable the accused to understand the charges. This is particularly important since the accused does not have the benefit of the supporting material at his initial appearance.[6] This principle is applied by both the Tribunals.[7]

Article 6, paragraph 3(*a*) is breached if a defendant has not been adequately notified of the legal characterisation of the charge – even if adequate notice has been given of the facts alleged. In *Pélissier & Sassi v. France*, it was held that the adequate steps had not been taken to notify the accused that they might be convicted of "aiding and abetting criminal bankruptcy" rather than "criminal bankruptcy", which were, at the material time, two distinct offences.[8] This confirms the Commission's decision in *Chichlian & Ekindjian v. France*.[9]

The Form of the Indictment and the Requirement of "Fair Warning"

The Tribunal (Trial Chamber II) observed in *Prosecutor v. Bagambiki, Imanishimwe & Munyakazi*, that

> "7.   Although the Rules do not define the phrase "concise statement of facts," as provided in rule 47, there is sufficient persuasive precedent, in the decisions of this Tribunal as well as the decisions of the International Criminal Tribunal for the Former Yugoslavia, to guide the Trial Chamber . . ."[10]

In *Prosecutor v. Nsabimana* Trial Chamber II commented that:

> "As a general observation, the Trial Chamber holds that the accused must be able to recognise the circumstances and the actions attributed to him in the indictment and the concise statement of the facts. In other words, the accused must be made to understand how and when his actions under particular circumstances, constituted one or more crimes covered by the Tribunal's jurisdiction. Furthermore, the Trial Chamber interprets the phrase "concise statement of the facts" in rule 47 to mean "a brief statement of facts but comprehensive in expression" as defined in the case *Nahimana* [Case No. ICTR-96-11-T, decision of 24th November 1997]."[11]

Both Trial Chambers took this approach in the other cases under review, relying on the Nahimana (supra) decision in Bagambiki (supra) and in Ruggiu (supra).

The case law of the International Criminal Tribunal for the Former Yugoslavia – referred to in Bagambiki (supra) – is an important source of persuasive authority.[12] More recent cases have explored, in particular, the degree to which Rule 47(C) is to be interpreted as analogous to national standards, as opposed to an autonomous provision, whose interpretation must be tailored to the particular nature of the cases over which both Tribunals have jurisdiction. In *Krnojelac (supra)* Trial Chamber II observed that

---

[5]   See *Gea Catalan v. Spain*, Application No. 19160/91, 26 January 1995, par. 28 and 29 and *De Salvador Torres v. Spain*, Application No. 21525/93, 26 September 1996, par. 30 to 33.

[6]   Decision on the Preliminary Motion by Defence Counsel on Defects in the Form of the Indictment, *Prosecutor v. Nyiramashuko*, Case ICTR-97-21-I, 4 September 1998, par. 13.

[7]   ICTR, Decision on the Defence Preliminary Motion on the Form of the Indictment, *Prosecutor v. Ruggiu*, Case No. ICTR-97-32-T, 24 May 1999, par. 13 and ICTY, Decision on the Defence Preliminary Motion on the Form of the Indictment, *Prosecutor v. Krnojelac*, Case No. IT-97-25-PT, 24 February 1999, par. 12 to 16.

[8]   European Court of Human Rights, *Pélissier & Sassi v. France*, 25 March 1999, 25444/94, par. 55 to 63.

[9]   European Commission on Human Rights, *Chichlian & Ekindjian v. France*, 16 March 1989, Series A, No. 162-B, par. 65.

[10]   ICTR, Decision on the Defence Motion on Defects in the Form of the Indictment, *Prosecutor v. Bagambiki, Imanishimwe & Munyakazi*,Case No. ICTR-97-36-(I), 24 September 1998.

[11]   Decision on the Defence Motion for the Amendment of the Indictment, Withdrawal of Certain Charges and Protective Measures for Witnesses, *Prosecutor v. Nsabimana*, Case No. ICTR-97-29A-T, 24 September 1998.

[12]   e.g. *Prosecutor v. Tadic*, Case No. IT-94-1-T,14 November 1995; *Prosecutor v. Delalic et al.*, case No. IT-96-21-T, 26 June 1996; *Prosecutor v. Blaskic*, Case No. IT-95-14-T, 4 April 1997.

The extent of the prosecutor's obligation to give particulars in an indictment is to ensure that the accused has a "concise statement of the facts" upon which reliance is placed to establish the offences charged but only to the extent that such statement enables the accused to be informed of the "nature and cause of the charge against him" and in "adequate time [. . .] for the preparation of his defence." An indictment must contain information as to the identity of the victim, the place and approximate date of the alleged offence and the means by which the offence was committed." (Para. 12, footnotes omitted)

Article 18 and Rule 47 give effect to two of the basic guarantees contained in Article 21 of the Statute, namely that the accused should "be informed promptly and in detail in a language which he understands of the nature and cause of the charge against him" (par. 4(*a*)) and should "have adequate time and facilities for the preparation of his defence and to communicate with counsel of his own choosing" (par. 4(*b*).) The Tribunal went on, in footnote 19, to refer to "the particularity with which a criminal offence must be pleaded in common law jurisdictions," citing a number of relevant Australian and English decisions. The indictment failed to provide sufficient information in relation to the relevant details of several counts, and required amendment (Par. 36 to 63)

In Prosecutor v. Kvočka the Trial Chamber accepted the standard laid down in Krnojelac (supra), but with important qualifications:

"16. While allusions to the practice in civil- and common-law jurisdictions are helpful, the sole determinant of the law applied by the International Tribunal is its Statutes and Rules; moreover, the influence of domestic criminal practice on the work of the International Tribunal must take due account of the very real differences between a domestic criminal jurisdiction and the system administered by the International Tribunal.

17. The Trial Chamber finds that as a general rule, the degree of particularity required in indictments before the International Tribunal is different from, and perhaps not as high as, the particularity required in domestic criminal law jurisdictions. The mandate of the International Tribunal under Article 1 of its Statute is to "prosecute persons responsible for serious violations of international humanitarian law . . . in accordance with the provisions of the present Statute". The massive scale of the crimes with which the International Tribunal has to deal makes it impracticable to require a high degree of specificity in such matters as the identity of the victims and the dates for the commission of the crimes – at any rate, the degree of specificity may not be as high as that called for in domestic jurisdictions. However, there may be cases in which more specific information can be provided as to the time, the place, the identity of victims and the means by which the crime was perpetrated; in those cases, the Prosecution should be required to provide such information."[13]

As in Krnojelac (supra), the Tribunal concluded that the indictment did not comply with Rule 47(C) in a number of respects (*e.g.*, Par. 19, 26, 32.). The ICTR adopted a broadly similar approach in Nsabimana:

"We are conscious that the time period mentioned may not be as precise as the defence may wish, but given the particular circumstances of the conflict in Rwanda and the alleged crimes, it could be difficult to determine the exact times when the acts alleged in concise facts occurred. It is our opinion, therefore that the time frames mentioned are sufficiently precise to enable the accused to know the acts for which he is charged in the indictment."

The ICTY also observed in Kvočka (supra) that the same issue arises in relation to the identity of victims:

"[T]he degree of detail that is required [regarding victims of the crimes alleged] presents a special difficulty, and it is in this area that the contrast between a domestic criminal law system and an international criminal law tribunal is most pronounced. There can be little doubt but that the identity of the victim is information that is valuable to the Defence in the preparation of their

---

[13]   Decision on Defence Preliminary Motions on the Form of the Indictment *Prosecutor v. Kvocka & Ors*, Case No. IT-98-30-T, 12 April 1999.

cases. But the massive scale of the crimes alleged before this International Tribunal does not allow for the specific naming of victims. However, if the Prosecution is in a position to do so, it should. (par. 23)."

Application of Rule 47(C) in the cases under review

In Nsabimana (supra) the Tribunal was of the view that, despite the difficulties facing the Prosecutor in doing so, more precise dates were needed to clarify the statement of facts. On the issue of vagueness, the Tribunal observed as follows:

> "We underscore the need to have the precise statement of facts correspond to and explain the specific charges. The Prosecutor should also ensure that the facts used as a basis for the charges are clear enough so that the accused will not have to refer to the witness statements.

The Prosecutor was required to indicate the manner in which the accused was linked to the alleged acts forming the basis of the counts – more detailed information was required to make some charges clearer. For example, the words "facilitated" and "encouraged" in paragraph 3.12 should be further explained, to enable the accused sufficiently to understand the counts brought against him, without having to wait for discovery of the witness statements. Reference has already been made to the Tribunal's decision on the time frames mentioned in the original indictment.

In its decision of 21st May 1999, the Tribunal denied the Prosecutor's urgent motion for a stay of execution on the decision of the earlier decision. It also ordered the Prosecutor to comply with that decision, within a further fourteen days, rejecting the Prosecutor's contention that either the mere filing of a motion for a stay, or the failure to hold a timely hearing on that motion, in any way relieved the Prosecutor from her duty of compliance. The Tribunal admonished the Prosecutor for this failure to comply, especially as compliance would have caused no legal prejudice to her case. However, the accused's motion for the withdrawal of the indictment and immediate release was denied – immediate compliance with the earlier order would cure any alleged remaining defects. The Tribunal commented again on the duty of the Prosecutor to comply with its orders in Kabiligi (infra, at par. 63).

In Bagambiki (supra) the Tribunal (Trial Chamber II) found that the information in the indictment met the standard of "a brief statement of facts but comprehensive in expression," except in one respect. Count 19 (conspiracy to commit genocide) was inadequately supported; the inclusion of the phrase "*held a large number of meetings* among themselves [i.e. the co-accused], *or* with others . . .*" rendered that aspect of the count vague, no further details being supplied. (Par. 11. The Tribunal's emphasis.) The Prosecutor was ordered to provide, so far as possible, details – such as the approximate dates, locations and the purpose – of these meetings, and to clarify whether the accused and others named in the indictment were the only persons present at these meetings or if others, not named, were also present. Judge Sekule gave a separate opinion, re-iterating his observations at any earlier stage in the case, that all reference to "others," whether named or otherwise, in Count 19 should be deleted.

In Kabiligi (infra) the Tribunal ordered a similar amendment of the reference to "others" in Count 1 of the amended indictment. If the identity of these persons was known, they should be identified – without prejudice to the right of the Prosecutor to move for non-disclosure. If their identity was unknown, then the indictment must refer to them as "other persons" (*ibid.*, par. 55.)

In Ruggiu (supra) the Tribunal (Trial Chamber I) found that the indictment against the accused did inform the accused "with sufficient clarity, of the nature and cause of the charge or charges against him" (par. 13) in relation to Count 1 (direct and public incitement to commit genocide) but not in relation to Count 2 (persecution). In relation to Count 2, the Prosecutor was required to clarify how the accused, by way of the alleged radio broadcasts, persecuted Tutsi, certain Hutu and Belgians. (Par. 16) The Prosecutor was also required to provide a more specific time frame in relation to allegations than was contained in the original indictment. (Par. 17)

Amendments to Indictments: the Function of the Trial Chamber

There is disagreement over the basis on which the Trial Chamber should grant leave, under Rule 50, for amendment of an indictment, after the initial appearance of the accused before it. The prevailing view, with which Judge Dolenc disagrees, is that the Trial Chamber should consider whether or not to grant leave, without deciding whether a *prima facie* case has been established, for example, for new charges. This was re-affirmed in Trial Chamber II's decision in *Prosecutor v. Kabiligi & Ntabakuze:*

> "42. With regard to the standard of proof for amendment under Rule 50, the Trial Chamber finds that it need not be satisfied that a *prima facie* case exists against the accused for the new charges, however, the Prosecutor does need to demonstrate that there are *sufficient grounds both in fact and in law to allow the amendments* . . . [Emphasis supplied. Citation omitted.]"[14]

The Trial Chamber was satisfied that the Prosecutor had satisfied this standard.

The Trial Chamber accepted, however, that amendments should not be allowed if they amounted to substitution of a new indictment. Relying on the decision of the ICTY Appeals Chamber in Kovacevic (supra), the Tribunal concluded that an increase in size of an indictment is only one factor in deciding whether or not proposed amendments amount to a substitution of a new indictment.

In his separate and concurring opinion, Judge Dolenc disagreed with the majority on both issues. Article 18 of the Statute, in conjunction with Rules 47(E) and (F) of the Rules of Procedure, provides that the indictment should contain only counts which have been examined and confirmed by a reviewing Judge, he or she being satisfied that the supporting materials presented by the Prosecutor have established a *prima facie* case. ("[T]he spirit and purpose of . . . Article 18(1) . . . is that only a confirmed charge should be grounds for trial." Par. 38.) To adopt the majority's view in a case where the amendments propose to add new counts or to broaden the scope of existing ones, creates "a loophole through which the Prosecutor can circumvent the confirmation process. The Prosecutor could amend an indictment, including adding new charges, for which she knows she cannot establish a prima facie case." (Par. 37)

Judge Dolenc also pointed out that the procedure contained in the Rules of Procedure of the ICTY differs from that of the ICTR – before the commencement of the presentation of evidence, the Trial Chamber must remand a motion to amend to the confirming Judge or to another Judge assigned by the President (Rule 50(A), Rules of Procedure (ICTY).) This procedure requires that a *prima facie* case be established in relation to additional or extended charges (Par. 45 to 47) In Judge Dolenc's view, however, remittal of the determination of a *prima facie* case to a confirming Judge would not be the correct solution in the context of the ICTR (Par. 44.)

Under Rule 15(C), a judge of the Trial Chamber who reviews an indictment pursuant to Article 18 and Rules 47 and 61 shall not sit as a member of the Trial Chamber for the trial of that accused. Judge Dolenc considered that this is a specific procedural requirement, not a fundamental principle, that there is no legal obstacle to the same judges deciding whether there is or is not a *prima facie* case to warrant an amendment and sitting as members of the Trial Chamber for the trial. (Par. 25 to 27, 56 to 73) Judge Dolenc's remarks on this aspect of the case appear to contradict somewhat his earlier emphasis on the importance of the confirmation process (" 68 . . . the confirmation only has a declaratory effect and does not affect the legal validity of the indictment. . . . 73 . . . confirmation of the charges plays a relatively minor role . . . "). However, in Judge Dolenc's view there was no objection, in principle, to allowing substitution of the original indictment by a new one. (Paras. 79 to 83)

The Statute of the ICC explicitly provides that "if the prosecutor seeks to add new charges or to substitute more serious charges, a hearing . . . to confirm those charges must be held" – but in the context of a clear separation between the functions of the Pre-Trial Chamber and the Trial Chamber of the ICC, up to the commencement of the trial itself (Statute of the International Criminal Court, Article 61,

---

[14]   Decision on the Prosecutor's Motion to Amend the Indictment, *Prosecutor v. Kabiligi & Ntabakuze,* Cases No. ICTR-97-34-I and ICTR-97-30-I, 8 October 1999.

paragraph 9) Under Article 40, paragraph 4, "under no circumstances shall a judge who has participated in the pre-trial phase of a case be eligible to sit on the Trial Chamber hearing that case."

It is the absence of a systematic division between a Pre-Trial Chamber and a Trial Chamber, that creates the procedural dilemma highlighted by the Kabiligi decision.

Conclusion

The procedure of the International Tribunals consciously adopts one of the principal features of the accusatorial system of criminal procedure found in countries of the common law tradition – namely that a formal indictment, detailing the material facts alleged and the legal character of the offences charged is an essential foundation of a criminal trial. It also incorporates a feature found in many of those systems – that the indictment must be confirmed by a reviewing judge, not on the basis of a preliminary investigation of the facts of the case, but on the basis of an examination as to whether the indictment, together with the material supporting it discloses a *prima facie* case.

These broad similarities have been noted by a number of the U.S. commentators on the International Tribunals.[15] In particular, the close similarity between Rule 47(C) and Rule 7(c) of the U.S. Federal Rules of Criminal Procedure has been pointed out. The same author holds that the failure of the ICTY – in the Tadić case – to observe U.S. standards in relation to the specificity of indictments and the permissible variance between a count and a conviction being a basis for concluding that this was an "error" by the Tribunal, albeit a "harmless" one.[16]

However, it would be better to give provisions such as Rule 47(C) an autonomous interpretation, both because of the factors mentioned in Kvocka (*supra*) and Nsabimana (*supra*) and because the nature of a trial before the Tribunals differs considerably from a jury trial in a common law jurisdiction. Instead, it would be more fruitful to pursue the lines of development opened up by international human rights law – particularly as, in cases such as Pélissier & Sassi v. France (*supra*), the relevant standards are progressively becoming clearer and more specific.

John O'Dowd

---

[15]   (*e.g.* J.E. Alvarez, Rush to closure: Lessons of the Tadic Judgment, 96 Michigan Law Review, June 1998, at p. 2039; Michael P. Scharf, Trial and Error: an Assessment of the First Judgment of the Yugoslavia War Crimes Tribunal, 30 New York University Journal of International Law and Politics, Fall 97/ Winter 98, at pp. 170 to 172.

[16]   Scharf, *op. cit.*, pp. 183 to 187 and 199 to 200.

UNITED NATIONS   **NATIONS UNIES**

INTERNATIONAL CRIMINAL TRIBUNAL FOR RWANDA

Case No. ICTR-95-5-D   THE TRIAL CHAMBER 1

12.03.1996

**DECISION ON THE FORMAL REQUEST FOR DEFERRAL
PRESENTED BY THE PROSECUTOR**

IN TRIAL CHAMBER I OF THE
INTERNATIONAL CRIMINAL
TRIBUNAL FOR RWANDA

Case Number: ICTR-96-5-D
And
IN THE MATTER OF:
AN APPLICATION
BY THE PROSECUTOR
FOR A FORMAL REQUEST FOR
DEFERRAL BY SWITZERLAND
And
IN THE MATTER OF:
ALFRED MUSEMA

DECISION OF THE TRIAL CHAMBER ON THE APPLICATION BY THE PROSECUTOR FOR A FORMAL REQUEST FOR DEFERRAL TO THE COMPETENCE OF THE INTERNATIONAL CRIMINAL TRIBUNAL FOR RWANDA IN THE MATTER OF ALFRED MUSEMA (PURSUANT TO RULES 9 AND 10 OF THE RULES OF PROCEDURE AND EVIDENCE)

Considering the Application dated 4 March 1996 ("the Application"), filed by the Prosecutor of the International Criminal Tribunal for Rwanda ("the International Tribunal"),

Noting that Trial Chamber 1 has been designated by the President of the International Tribunal pursuant to Rule 9 of the Rules of Procedure and Evidence ("the Rules") of the International Tribunal to answer the Application, **[page 2]**

Having heard the Prosecutor at a public sitting held in Arusha on 11 March 1996.

Taking into account the documents submitted by the Representative of the Prosecutor at the public sitting on 11 March 1996, and in particular the correspondence from the Swiss judicial authorities and addressed to the Prosecutor,

I. – The Application

1.   This is an application by the Prosecutor of the International Criminal Tribunal for Rwanda, made pursuant to article 8 (2) of the Statute of the International Criminal Tribunal for the Prosecution of Persons Responsible for Genocide and other Serious Violations of International Humanitarian Law Committed in the Territory of Rwanda and Rwandan citizens responsible for such acts or violations committed in the territory of neighbouring States, between 1 January 1994 and 31 December 1994, and in accordance with Rule 9 (iii) of the Rules of Procedure and Evidence, seeking an order from the Trial Chamber in relation to investigations and criminal proceedings being conducted by Switzerland respecting serious violations of International Humanitarian Law committed in the Prefecture of Kibuye in the territory of Rwanda between April 1994 and July 1994, and allegedly involving Alfred Musema, for a formal request to be made to the Government of Switzerland for its courts to defer to the competence of the Tribunal.

2.   Pursuant to Rule 10 of the Rules, the Prosecutor has requested the Trial Chamber to issue a formal request to Switzerland in the following terms:

    a) The courts of Switzerland defer to the competence of the Tribunal in regard to all investigations and all criminal proceedings in respect of Alfred Musema.

    b) In regards to all such investigations and criminal proceedings of Alfred Musema, the Tribunal requests that Switzerland forward to the Tribunal the results of said investigations, criminal proceedings, copies of the courts' records and judgements concerning Alfred Musema, if any.

    c) The reasons advanced by the Prosecutor in support of his proposal are:

1) National investigations have been instituted against Alfred Musema by Switzerland for crimes alleged to have taken place in the Prefecture of Kibuye and elsewhere in Rwanda. **[page 3]**

2) The Prosecutor has been conducting in the Prefecture of Kibuye investigations into crimes within the jurisdiction of the Tribunal and in which Alfred Musema is a suspect.

3) The national investigations instituted by Switzerland closely relate to, or otherwise involve, significant factual and legal questions which may have implications for investigations or prosecutions before the Tribunal.

3.   In his application the Prosecutor has furnished facts which, in brief, are that in February 1995 Switzerland decided to commence investigations in relation to Alfred Musema, which involve investigations into allegations of murder and incitement to murder Tutsis and moderate Hutus. Alfred Musema, who was the Director of the tea factory in Gisovu, prefecture of Kibuye, was arrested by the Swiss authorities on 11 February 1995, in the territory of Switzerland, following a warrant of arrest issued by the examining magistrate investigating the case. Alfred Musema is being detained in Switzerland. The *Tribunal de division suisse* ruled that he be kept in custody, a decision which has been confirmed monthly in accordance with the applicable provisions of Swiss law (Articles 56 and ff. of the Martial Criminal Procedure); the latest such decision extends the detention period to 25 March 1996. He is suspected of having committed crimes punishable under Swiss law (Articles 2, Chapter 9 and 109, Martial Criminal Code), including crimes which amount to serious violations of the Geneva Conventions of 12 August 1949 and the Additional Protocols of 8 June 1977. The Swiss examining magistrate has conducted investigations in various countries, including the Republic of Rwanda.

4.   The Prosecutor has further stated that he has been investigating allegations of serious violations of international humanitarian law that occurred in the territory of the Republic of Rwanda including massacres perpetrated between April 1994 and July 1994 in the same Prefecture of Kibuye, in which Alfred Musema was allegedly involved. The Prosecutor's investigations include interviews of witnesses and the collection of documents in order to determine the truth of the allegations that the massacres, in particular in the Prefecture of Kibuye, were planned and resulted in the serial murder of a large number of people protected under international law. To the extent that his investigations essentially target people in a position of authority, the Prosecutor is of the opinion that Alfred Musema's alleged criminal responsibility might be preponderant. Indeed, Alfred Musema was the Director of the tea factory in Gisovu (Prefecture of Kibuye). He is alleged to have taken advantage of his position as a Director to aid and abet the execution of serious violations of international humanitarian law. More specifically, he is alleged to have been seen repeatedly on the massacre site known as Bisesero, Prefecture of Kibuye. He is alleged to have given instructions to the killers and to have directed the attacks. Several witnesses have stated that they saw him fire on the assembled civilians. Moreover, vehicles from his factory were allegedly used to transport the killers to the massacre site. His employees and drivers were also regularly present. **[page 4]**

5.   The Prosecutor has submitted that in order to develop the ongoing investigations, he must collect further essential evidence and obtain full access to the statements, documents and other findings of the investigations conducted by Switzerland in relation to Alfred Musema. According to the Prosecutor, if Switzerland continues investigations which are similar to his, a number of confusions and complications might occur. It could turn out to be detrimental to investigations before the Tribunal, in particular in relation to testimonies. It is indeed to be feared that witnesses might become reluctant to appear before successive investigators and would no longer be willing to cooperate fully and effectively in the questioning. Testimonies might thus lose credibility as the number of questionings in different conditions increases, whereas some other witnesses might even be exposed to threats and see their lives put in danger.

II. – The analysis

6.   Article 7 of the Statute of the International Tribunal extends its jurisdiction to the prosecution of persons responsible for serious violations of international humanitarian law committed in the territory of Rwanda and Rwandan citizens responsible for such violations committed in the territory of neighbouring States, between 1 January 1994 and 31 December 1994. Article 8 of the Statute states that:

> "1.   The International Tribunal for Rwanda and national courts shall have concurrent jurisdiction to prosecute persons for serious violations of international humanitarian law committed in the territory of Rwanda and Rwandan citizens for such violations committed in the territory of neighbouring States, between 1 January 1994 and 31 December 1994.
>
> 2.   The International Tribunal for Rwanda shall have primacy over the national courts of all States. At any stage of the procedure, the International Tribunal for Rwanda may formally request national courts to defer to its competence in accordance with the present Statute and the Rules of Procedure and Evidence of the International Tribunal for Rwanda."

Such primacy, however, can only be exercised if a formal request is addressed to the national court to defer to the competence of the International Tribunal. The Rules specify the modalities for exercising this right. **[page 5]**

> Rule 9 of the Rules states that:
>
> "Where it appears to the Prosecutor that in any such investigations or criminal proceedings instituted in the courts of any State:
> (i)   (...)
> (ii)   (...)
> (iii)   what is in issue is closely related to, or otherwise involves, significant factual or legal questions which may have implications for investigations or prosecutions before the Tribunal, (...).

8.   In order to meet the conditions for a deferral, the Prosecutor therefore must demonstrate:

> a) that national investigations or criminal proceedings have been instituted against said Alfred Musema by the Government of Switzerland respecting crimes which come under the jurisdiction of the International Tribunal;
>
> b) that investigations are being conducted by the Prosecutor on serious violations of international humanitarian law allegedly committed in the territory of Rwanda or in the territory of neighbouring States between 1 January 1994 and 31 December 1994, in particular in the Prefecture of Kibuye, by several persons, including Alfred Musema;
>
> c) that these investigations or criminal proceedings are closely related and otherwise involve factual or legal questions which may have implications for the Prosecutor's investigations or prosecutions.

9.   The Prosecutor states, and this is confirmed by a letter dated 22 February 1996 addressed to the Prosecutor by Major Claude Nicati, the Swiss Examining Magistrate responsible for the case, that an investigation has been instituted against said Alfred Musema in Switzerland, and that said Alfred Musema has been arrested by the Swiss authorities in compliance of a warrant of arrest issued by the Examining Magistrate responsible for the case, and that he is still in custody.

10.   The Prosecutor indicates that his Office is investigating allegations of serious violations of international humanitarian law committed in the territory of the Republic of Rwanda, including the massacres executed between April and July 1994 in the Prefecture of Kibuye, and allegedly involving Alfred Musema.

11.   The Prosecutor is of the opinion that the International Tribunal is the appropriate jurisdiction to examine the case of Alfred Musema, taking into account the seriousness of the factual charges and of the legal questions which are bound to be raised in connection with the case before it. **[page 6]**

12.   The Prosecutor rightly observes that Article 9.2 of the Tribunal's Statute, concerning the principle of *non bis in idem*, sets limits to the subsequent prosecution by the Tribunal of persons who have been tried by a national court for acts constituting serious violations of international humanitarian law. As Swiss criminal legislation does not contain any provision concerning genocide or crimes against humanity, Alfred Musema has only been prosecuted by the Swiss courts for charges related to serious violations of the Geneva Conventions and of the Additional Protocols. Thus, should the Prosecutor subsequently wish to qualify the charges against Alfred Musema as genocide or crimes against humanity, Article 9 of the Statute would preclude any prosecution for such charges if a decision has already been made by the Swiss national courts.

13.   The Prosecutor considers, not without reason, that the continuation of parallel investigations by the Swiss courts and the International Tribunal might be detrimental to the investigations, including the testimonies. As they are repeated, testimonies can lose their credibility, not to mention the risk of causing the witnesses to be distrustful; moreover the witnesses might be traumatised and even threatened of bodily harm.

14.   The Swiss Government has already expressed its willingness to cooperate with the International Tribunal. Such willingness is demonstrated by the decision by the *Conseil federal suisse*, of 20 March 1995, to implement on their own Resolution 955 of the Security Council of the United Nations. Consequently, a federal decree was adopted on 21 December 1995, governing the cooperation with the International tribunal and enabling the Swiss courts to defer to the competence of the International Tribunal and to order provisional measures to maintain the status quo on the order of the International Tribunal. At the hearing on 11 March 1996, the Prosecutor has submitted copies of these two documents from the Swiss Government to Trial Chamber I.

15.   In the light of the foregoing, the Judges of the Trial Chamber are of the opinion that the request for deferral by the Swiss authorities in the case of Alfred Musema meets the conditions set forth in Rule 9 of the Rules of Procedure and Evidence, and that such request should be favourably received. **[page 7]**

III. – The Decision

THE TRIAL CHAMBER
BASED ON THE FOREGOING DETERMINES AS FOLLOWS

Considering all the matters before it and addressed in the public hearing,

Taking into account the provisions of Article 8 (2) of the Statute, and

Considering the requirements contained in Rule 9(iii) of the Rules,

the Trial Chamber consisting of Judge Laïty Kama, as Presiding Judge, Judge Lennart Aspergren and Judge Navanethem Pillay, being seized of the Application made by the Prosecutor,

HEREBY GRANTS the said Application,

FORMALLY REQUESTS the Swiss federal Government to defer to the International Tribunal all investigations and criminal proceedings currently being conducted in its national courts against Alfred Musema,

INVITES the Swiss Government to take all necessary steps, both legislative and administrative, to comply with this formal request and to notify the Registrar of the International Tribunal of the steps taken to comply with this formal request,

REQUESTS that the Government of Switzerland forward to the International Tribunal the results of its investigations and criminal proceedings and a copy of the court's records and the judgement, if already delivered,

REQUESTS that the Government of Switzerland continue to detain Alfred Musema until an indictment is established and confirmed and a warrant of arrest is issued against him by the International Tribunal, **[page 8]**

The Trial Chamber requests the Registrar of the International Tribunal to notify the Government of Switzerland of this Decision and Order.

Dated this 12th day of March 1996
Arusha

Laïty Kama   Lennart Aspergren   Navanethem Pillay
President   Judge   Judge

UNITED NATIONS   NATIONS UNIES

INTERNATIONAL CRIMINAL TRIBUNAL FOR RWANDA

Case No. ICTR-96-6-D   THE TRIAL CHAMBER 1

12-3-1996

DECISION ON THE FORMAL REQUEST FOR DEFERRAL
PRESENTED BY THE PROSECUTOR

IN TRIAL CHAMBER I OF THE
INTERNATIONAL CRIMINAL
TRIBUNAL FOR RWANDA

Case Number: ICTR-96-6-D
And
IN THE MATTER OF:
AN APPLICATION
BY THE PROSECUTOR
FOR A FORMAL REQUEST FOR
DEFERRAL BY THE KINGDOM OF
BELGIUM
And
IN THE MATTER OF:
RADIO TELEVISION LIBRE DES MILLE
COLLINES SARL

DECISION OF THE TRIAL CHAMBER ON THE APPLICATION BY THE PROSECTOR FOR A FORMAL REQUEST FOR DEFERRAL TO THE COMPETENCE OF THE INTERNATIONAL CRIMINAL TRIBUNAL FOR RWANDA IN THE MATTER OF RADIO TELEVISION LIBRE DES MILLE COLLINES SARL (PURSUANT TO RULES 9 AND 10 OF THE RULES OF PROCEDURE AND EVIDENCE)

Considering the Application dated 10 March 1996 ("the Application"), filed by the Prosecutor of the International Criminal Tribunal for Rwanda ("the International Tribunal"),

Noting that Trial Chamber 1 has been designated by the President of the International Tribunal pursuant to Rule 9 of the Rules of Procedure and Evidence ("the Rules") of the International Tribunal to answer the Application, **[page 2]**

Having heard the Prosecutor at a public hearing held in Arusha on 11 March 1996,

I – The Application

1.   The application by the Prosecutor of the International Criminal Tribunal for Rwanda, made pursuant to article 8 (2) of the Statute of the International Criminal Tribunal for the Prosecution of Persons Responsible for Genocide and other Serious Violations of International Humanitarian Law Committed in the Territory of Rwanda and Rwandan citizens responsible for Genocide and other such violations committed in the territory of neighbouring States, between 1 January 1994 and 31 December 1994, and in accordance with Rule 9 (iii) of the Rules of Procedure and Evidence, seeking an order from the Trial Chamber in relation to investigations and criminal proceedings being conducted by the Kingdom of Belgium regarding serious violations of International Humanitarian Law committed in the territory of the Republic of Rwanda between 1 January and 31 December 1994 by persons associated with the private radio station Radio Television Libre des Mille Collines sarl ("RTLM"), for a formal request to be made to the Kingdom of Belgium for its courts to defer to the competence of the Tribunal.

2.   Pursuant to Rule 10 of the Rules, the Prosecutor has requested the Trial Chamber for issuing a formal request to the Kingdom of Belgium in the following terms:

   a) The courts of Belgium defer to the competence of the Tribunal in regard to all investigations and all criminal proceedings concerning the activities of Radio Television Libre des Mille Collines sarl as well as all persons associated with RTLM.

   b) In addition, in regards to all such investigations and criminal proceedings the Tribunal requests that the Kingdom of Belgium forward to the Tribunal the results of said investigations, criminal proceedings, copies of the courts' records and judgements concerning the activities of Radio Television Libre des Mille Collines sarl as well as persons associated with RTLM. **[page 3]**

c) The Prosecutor advanced the following reason in support of his proposal:

1) Investigations have been instituted by the Kingdom of Belgium concerning the activities of Radio Television Libre des Mille Collines sarl as well as persons associated with RTLM for alleged serious violations of international humanitarian law in Rwanda.

2) The Prosecutor is currently conducting investigations on the activities of Radio Television Libre des Mille Collines sarl as well as on persons allegedly responsible for crimes committed through the utilisation of RTLM which fall within the jurisdiction of the Tribunal.

3) The investigations instituted by the Kingdom of Belgium involve factual and legal questions which may have implications for investigations or prosecutions before the Tribunal.

3. In support of his application the Prosecutor has furnished facts which, in brief, are that in March 1995. The Kingdom of Belgium decided to commence investigations in relation to the activities of Radio Television Libre des Mille Collines sarl as well as on persons associated with RTLM who allegedly committed crimes within the jurisdiction of the Tribunal through the use of RTLM. These investigations have enabled the Kingdom of Belgium to collect six or seven binders of materials concerning RTLM at the request of the Belgian examining magistrate in charge of the case.

4. The Prosecutor has further stated that he is currently investigating allegations of serious violations of international humanitarian law that allegedly occurred in the territory of the Republic of Rwanda including the broadcasts which allegedly incited genocide and violence in 1994. The Prosecutor is particularly investigating RTLM broadcasts, its management, its financing, its journalists and its broadcasters. The investigations are targeting the collection of materials including but not limited to recordings of RTLM **[page 4]** broadcasts, the activities of RTLM officials, the activities of RTLM journalists and broadcasters.

5. The Prosecutor has submitted that, in order to develop the ongoing investigations, he must collect additional essential evidence and obtain full access to the statements, documents and other findings of the investigations. He submits furthermore that if the Kingdom of Belgium continues investigations which are similar to his own, this situation might be cause for confusion and complications. There may also be repercussions for the investigations before the Tribunal particularly concerning the collection of witness statements. It is thus feared that some of the witnesses might be reluctant to appear before successive investigators, and would no longer be willing to cooperate fully and effectively during questioning. Some might even be exposed to threats and see their lives put in danger. **[page 5]**

II – Analysis

6. Article 7 of the Statute of the International Tribunal extends its jurisdiction to the prosecution of persons responsible for serious violations of international humanitarian law committed in the territory of Rwanda and Rwandan citizens responsible for such violations committed in the territory of neighbouring States, between 1 January 1994 and 31 December 1994. Article 8 of the Statute states that:

"1. The International Tribunal for Rwanda and national courts shall have concurrent jurisdiction to prosecute persons for serious violations of international humanitarian law committed in the territory of Rwanda and Rwandan citizens for such violations committed in the territory of neighbouring States, between 1 January 1994 and 31 December 1994.

2. The International Tribunal for Rwanda shall have primacy over the national courts of all States. At any stage of the procedure, the International Tribunal for Rwanda may formally request national courts to defer to its competence in accordance with the present Statute and the Rules of Procedure and Evidence of the International Tribunal for Rwanda."

Such primacy, however, can only be exercised if a formal request is addressed to the national court to defer to the competence of the International Tribunal. The Rules specify the modalities for exercising this right.

7.   Rule 9 of the Rules states that:

"Where it appears to the Prosecutor that in any such investigations or criminal proceedings instituted in the courts of any State:
(i)   (...)
(ii)   (...)
(iii)   what is in issue is closely related to, or otherwise involves, significant factual or legal questions which may have implications for investigations or prosecutions before the Tribunal,
(...). **[page 6]**

8.   In order to meet the conditions for a deferral, the Prosecutor therefore must demonstrate:

a) that national investigations or criminal proceedings have been instituted by the Kingdom of Belgium concerning RTLM and persons associated with RTLM;

b) that an investigation is being conducted on serious violations of international humanitarian law allegedly committed in the territory of Rwanda or in the territory of neighbouring States between 1 January 1994 and 31 December 1994, in particular those regarding RTLM broadcasts and person associated with this radio station;

c) that these investigations or criminal proceedings are closely related to, or otherwise involve, factual or legal questions which may have implications for the Prosecutor's investigations or prosecutions.

9.   The Prosecutor states that an investigation has been instituted by the Kingdom of Belgium concerning RTLM and the persons who allegedly committed crimes within the jurisdiction of the RTLM through the operation of RTLM.

10.   The Prosecutor indicates that his Office is investigating the activities of RTLM and those persons allegedly responsible for crimes within the jurisdiction of the International Tribunal.

11.   The Prosecutor rightly observes that Article 9. 2 of the Statute of the Tribunal, concerning the principle of *non bis in idem*, sets limits to the subsequent prosecution by the Tribunal of persons who have been tried by a national court for acts constituting serious violations of international humanitarian law. As Belgian criminal legislation does not contain any provision concerning genocide or crimes against humanity, the persons prosecuted for such acts by the Belgian courts cannot be charged with acts relative to genocide or crimes against humanity. Therefore, Article 9 of the Statute would preclude any prosecution for such charges if a decision has already been made by the Belgian national courts.

12.   The Prosecutor considers that continuing parallel investigations by the Belgian courts and the International **[page 7]** Tribunal might be detrimental to the investigations. Repeated hearings of witnesses should indeed be avoided, so as not to create mistrust and confusion in the testimonies, which would affect their credibility. This would also allow to avoid disturbing further witnesses who have already had a trauma, and submit them to possible threats.

13.   The Prosecutor request indicates that the Kingdom of Belgium is not opposed to deferring its investigations on individuals involved in RTLM to the competence of the Tribunal.

14.   In view of the above, the Judges of the Trial Chamber submit that the request for deferral by the Belgian authorities in the case of RTLM satisfies the conditions required by Article 9 of the Rules of Procedure and Evidence and thus reserve a favourable ruling on this matter.

III – The Decision

THE TRIAL CHAMBER

BASED ON THE FOREGOING DETERMINES AS FOLLOWS:

Considering all the matters before it and addressed in the public hearing,

Taking into account the provisions of Article 8 (2) of the Statute, and

Considering the requirements contained in Rule 9 (iii) of the Rules,

the Trial Chamber consisting of Judge Laïty Kama, as Presiding Judge, Judge Lennart Aspergren and Judge Navanethem Pillay, being seized of the Application made by the Prosecutor,

HEREBY GRANTS the said Application,

FORMALLY REQUESTS the Government of the Kingdom of Belgium to defer to the International Tribunal all investigations and criminal proceedings currently being conducted concerning the activities of RTLM as well as persons involved in the case of RTLM.

INVITES the Government of the Kingdom of Belgium to take all necessary steps, both legislative and administrative, to comply with this formal request and to notify the Registrar of the **[page 8]** International Tribunal of the steps taken to comply with this formal request,

REQUESTS that the Government of the Kingdom of Belgium forward to the International Tribunal the results of its investigations and criminal proceedings and a copy of the court's records and the judgement, if already delivered,

The Trial Chamber instructs the Registrar of the International Tribunal to notify the Kingdom of Belgium of this Decision and Order.

Dated this 12th day of March 1996
Arusha

Laïty Kama	Lennart Aspergren	Nananethem Pillay
President	Judge	Judge

UNITED NATIONS **NATIONS UNIES**

INTERNATIONAL CRIMINAL TRIBUNAL FOR RWANDA

Case No. ICTR-96-7-D

TRIAL CHAMBER 1

17-5-1996

**DECISION ON THE APPLICATION BY THE PROSECUTOR
FOR A FORMAL REQUEST FOR DEFERRAL**

IN TRIAL CHAMBER I OF THE
INTERNATIONAL CRIMINAL TRIBUNAL
FOR RWANDA

Case Number: ICTR-96-7-D
And
IN THE MATTER OF:
AN APPLICATION
BY THE PROSECUTOR
FOR A FORMAL REQUEST FOR
DEFERRAL BY THE KINGDOM OF
BELGIUM

AND

IN THE MATTER OF:
THÉONESTE BAGOSORA

DECISION OF THE TRIAL CHAMBER ON THE APPLICATION BY THE PROSECUTOR FOR A FORMAL REQUEST FOR DEFERRAL TO THE COMPETENCE OF THE INTERNATIONAL CRIMINAL TRIBUNAL FOR RWANDA IN THE MATTER OF THÉONESTE BAGOSORA (PURSUANT TO RULES 9 AND 10 OF THE RULES OF PROCEDURE AND EVIDENCE)

Considering the Request dated 15 May 1996 ("the Request"), filed by the Prosecutor of the International Criminal Tribunal for Rwanda ("the International Tribunal"),

Noting that Trial Chamber 1 has been designated by the President of the International Tribunal pursuant to Rule 9 of the Rules of Procedure and Evidence ("the Rules") of the International Tribunal to answer the Application.

Having heard the Prosecutor at a public sitting held in Arusha on 16 May 1996, **[page 2]**

I – The Request

1.   This is an application by the Prosecutor of the International Criminal Tribunal for Rwanda, made pursuant to article 8 (2) of the Statute of the International Criminal Tribunal for the Prosecution of Persons Responsible for Genocide and other Serious Violations of International Humanitarian Law Committed in the Territory of Rwanda and Rwandan citizens responsible for such acts or violations committed in the territory of neighbouring States, between 1 January 1994 and 31 December 1994, and in accordance with Rule 9 (iii) of the Rules of Procedure and Evidence. seeking an order from the Trial Chamber in relation to investigations and criminal proceedings being conducted by the Kingdom of Belgium respecting serious violations of International Humanitarian Law committed in the Prefecture of Kibuye in the territory of Rwanda between April 1994 and July 1994 by Théoneste Bagosora. for a formal request to be made to the Kingdom of Belgium for its courts to defer to the competence of the Tribunal.

2.   Pursuant to Rule 10 of the Rules, the Prosecutor has requested the Trial Chamber to issue a formal request to the Kingdom of Belgium in the following terms:

   a) The courts of Belgium defer to the competence of the Tribunal in regard to all investigations and all criminal proceedings in respect of Théoneste Bagosora,

   b) In regards to all such investigations and criminal proceedings of Théoneste Bagosora, the Tribunal requests that the Kingdom of Belgium forward to the Tribunal the results of said investigations, criminal proceedings, copies of the courts' records and judgements concerning Théoneste Bagosora, if any.

   c) The reasons advanced by the Prosecutor in support of his proposal are:

1) Investigations have been instituted against Théoneste Bagosora by the Kingdom of Belgium for murder and violations of the Geneva Conventions of 12 August 1949 and of Additional Protocols I and II of 8 June 1977, which were allegedly committed in the territory of Rwanda during 1994.

2) The Prosecutor has been conducting investigations into crimes allegedly committed by Théoneste Bagosora which fall within the jurisdiction of the Tribunal. **[page 3]**

3) The national investigations instituted by the Kingdom of Belgium closely relate to, or otherwise involve, significant factual and legal questions which have implications for investigations or prosecutions before the Tribunal.

3.   In his request the Prosecutor has furnished facts which, in brief, are that as early as 8 April 1994, the Belgian military office opened an investigation against Colonel Théoneste Bagosora, Director of the Cabinet of the Ministry of Defense under the regime of former President Habyarimana. The belgian civilian courts carried on the investigation, pursuant to an order from the Tribunal of First Instance in Brussels, dated 24 April 1995. The Examining Magistrate, Judge D. Vandermeersch, issued an international warrant of arrest for Colonel Théoneste Bagosora on 29 May 1995. On 9 March 1996, Colonel Théoneste Bagosora was apprehended by the Cameroonian authorities. To this day, he is still being held by the Cameroonian authorities, pending a decision on his extradition.

4.   The current investigations of the Kingdom of Belgium against Colonel Théoneste Bagosora involve allegations of murder and crimes of international law which constitute serious violations of the Geneva Conventions of 12 August 1949 and of additional Protocols I and II of 8 June 1977. Théoneste Bagosora is alleged, <u>inter alia</u>, to have been directly responsible for the massacres which followed the attack against President Habyarimana on 6 April 1994, and for the murder, on 7 April 1994, of 10 soldiers from the belgian contingent of the United Nations Assistance Mission to Rwanda.

5.   The Prosecutor has submitted that in order to develop the ongoing investigations, he must collect further essential evidence and obtain full access to the statements, documents and other findings of the investigations conducted by the Kingdom of Belgium in relation to Théoneste Bagosora. In his investigations, the Prosecutor is collecting evidence in order to determine the merits of the allegations that the massacres were planned and led to the mass murder of a great many victims who were protected under international law. The investigations by the Prosecutor focus mainly on persons in position of authority, who were responsible for serious violations of international humanitarian law. To the extent that the investigations relate to persons in positions of authority, Colonel Théoneste Bagosora's alleged criminal responsibility seems most important. Indeed, Théoneste Bagosora, born in 1941 in Gicyie commune, was successively Second in Command of the *École Supérieure Militaire* in Kigali, Commander of the military camp in Kanombe and Director of the Cabinet of the Ministry of Defense, a position he continued to hold during the April 1994 events, though he had already retired in September 1993. A native of the same region as former President Habyarimana, he had become one of his close associates and participated in the Arusha accords as a military advisor. The aim of the Prosecutor's investigations is to assess Théoneste Bagosora's responsibility for the events and massacres which followed the attack on the presidential plane on 6 April. It is stated in the request that within six hours of the attack against the presidential plane on 6 April 1994, while the massacres were starting in Rwanda, Théoneste Bagosora allegedly assumed de facto control of the army and the country. The aim of the Prosecutor's investigations is therefore to assess Théoneste Bagosora's responsibility for said massacres.

6.   According to the Prosecutor, if the Kingdom of Belgium continues investigations which are similar to his investigations, a number of confusions and complications **[page 4]** might occur. It could turn out to be detrimental to investigations before the Tribunal, in particular in relation to testimonies. It is indeed to be feared that witnesses might become reluctant to appear before successive investigators and would no longer be willing to cooperate fully and effectively in the questioning. Testimonies might thus lose credibility as the number of questionings in different conditions increases, whereas some other witnesses might even be exposed to threats and see their lives put in danger.

II – Analysis of the merits of the request

7. Article 7 of the Statute of the International Tribunal extends its jurisdiction to the prosecution of persons responsible for serious violations of international humanitarian law committed in the territory of Rwanda and Rwandan citizens responsible for such violations committed in the territory of neighbouring States, between 1 January 1994 and 31 December 1994.

Article 8 of the 3 Statute states that:

"1.   The International Tribunal for Rwanda and national courts shall have concurrent jurisdiction to prosecute persons for serious violations of international humanitarian law committed in the territory of Rwanda and Rwandan citizens for such violations committed in the territory of neighbouring States, between 1 January 1994 and 31 December 1994.

2. The International Tribunal for Rwanda shall have primacy over the national courts of all States. At any stage of the procedure, the International Tribunal for Rwanda may formally request national courts to defer to its competence in accordance with the present Statute and the Rules of Procedure and Evidence of the International Tribunal for Rwanda."

Such primacy, however, can only be exercised if a formal request is addressed to the national court to defer to the competence of the International Tribunal. The Rules specify the modalities for exercising this right. **[page 5]**

Rule 9 of the Rules states that:

"Where it appears to the Prosecutor that in any such investigations or criminal proceedings instituted in the courts of any State:
(i)   (...)
(ii)   (...)
(iii)   what is in issue is closely related to, or otherwise involves, significant factual or legal questions which may have implications for investigations or prosecutions before the Tribunal,
(...).

9.   In order to meet the conditions for a deferral, the Prosecutor therefore must demonstrate:

a) that national investigations or criminal proceedings have been instituted against said Théoneste Bagosora by the Kingdom of Belgium respecting crimes which come under the jurisdiction of the International Tribunal;

b) that investigations are being conducted by the Prosecutor on serious violations of international humanitarian law allegedly committed in the territory of Rwanda or in the territory of neighbouring States between 1 January 1994 and 31 December 1994, in particular in respect of violations allegedly committed by Théoneste Bagosora;

c) that these investigations or criminal proceedings are closely related and otherwise involve significant factual or legal questions which may have implications for the Prosecutor's investigations or prosecutions.

10.   The Prosecutor states that an investigation has been instituted by the Kingdom of Belgium in respect of acts allegedly committed by Théoneste Bagosora, which might also come within the jurisdiction of the Tribunal. This is supported by documents provided by the Prosecutor in support of his case, including: the order for an investigation against Théoneste Bagosora, under the charges of murder and serious violations of the Geneva Conventions of 12 August 1949 and of additional Protocols I and II of 8 June 1977, issued by the Prosecutor of the King of Belgium on 21 April 1995, the Order of 24 April 1995 issued by the President of the Tribunal of First Instance of Brussels nominating an Examining Magistrate to pursue the case, and the international warrant of arrest issued on 29 May 1995 by the belgian Examining Magistrate responsible for the case against Théoneste Bagosora.

11.   The Prosecutor indicates that his Office is investigating the crimes allegedly committed by Théoneste Bagosora.

12. The Prosecutor considers, not without reason, that the continuation of parallel investigations by the belgian courts and the International Tribunal might be detrimental to the investigations, including the testimonies. As they are repeated, testimonies can indeed lose their credibility, not to mention the risk of causing the witnesses to be distrustful; moreover the witnesses might be traumatised and even threatened of bodily harm. **[page 6]**

13. Moreover, the Prosecutor rightly observes that Article 9.2 of the Tribunal's Statute, concerning the principle of *non bis in idem*, sets limits to the subsequent prosecution by the Tribunal of persons who have been tried by a national court for acts constituting serious violations of international humanitarian law. And, in the case of Théoneste Bagosora, as belgian law does not contain any provision concerning genocide or crimes against humanity, it was only for murder and serious violations of the Geneva Conventions of 12 August 1949 and Additional Protocols I and II of 8 June 1977 that the belgian authorities were able to prosecute him, given the facts that he is charged with. Therefore, should the Prosecutor subsequently wish to prosecute Théoneste Bagosora for the same facts, characterising them as genocide and crimes against humanity, he would not be able to do so, if Théoneste Bagosora had already been tried by belgian jurisdictions.

14. Finally and in addition, according to the Prosecutor's request the Kingdom of Belgium has always been cooperative and it is expected that the latter would not be reluctant to accede to this request. Moreover, at the hearing on 16 May 1996, the representative of the Prosecutor stated that, in a telephone conversation with the authorities of the belgian Ministry of Justice, the Government of the Kingdom of Belgium indicated its goodwill and its willingness to comply fully with the decisions of the International Tribunal, including in the case concerning Théoneste Bagosora. The representative of the Prosecutor has confirmed that to that end, a law was enacted on 22 March 1996 by the Kingdom of Belgium.

15. In the light of the foregoing, the Judges of the Trial Chamber are of the opinion that the request for deferral by the belgian judicial authorities in the case of Théoneste Bagosora complies the provisions of Rule 9 of the Rules of Procedure and Evidence, and that such request should be favourably received. **[page 7]**

III – The Decision

THE TRIAL CHAMBER

BASED ON THE FOREGOING DETERMINES AS FOLLOWS:

Considering all the matters before it and addressed in the public hearing,

Taking into account the provisions of Article 8 (2) of the Statute, and

Considering the requirements contained in Rule 9(iii) of the Rules,

the Trial Chamber consisting of Judge Laïty Kama, as Presiding Judge, Judge Lennart Aspegren and Judge Navanethem Pillay, being seized of the Request made by the Prosecutor,

HEREBY GRANTS the said Request,

FORMALLY REQUESTS the Government of the Kingdom of Belgium to defer to the International Tribunal all investigations and criminal proceedings currently being conducted against Théoneste Bagosora,

INVITES the Government of the Kingdom of Belgium to take all necessary steps, both legislative and administrative, to comply with this formal request and to notify the Registrar of the International Tribunal of the steps taken to comply with this formal request,

REQUESTS that the Government of the Kingdom of Belgium forward to the International Tribunal the results of its investigations and criminal proceedings and a copy of the court's records and the judgement, if already delivered,

The Trial Chamber requests the Registrar of the International Tribunal to notify the Government of the Kingdom of Belgium of this Decision.

Dated this 17th day of May 1996
Arusha

Laïty Kama	Lennart Aspegren	Navanethem Pillay
President	Judge	Judge

According to Article 7 of the Statute, the ICTR has jurisdiction to prosecute those persons responsible for serious violations of international humanitarian law committed in the territory of Rwanda, and Rwandan citizens responsible for such violations committed in the territory of neighborouring States, between 1 January 1994 and 31 December 1994.

Since national courts may have concurrent jurisdiction for these crimes, it was necessary to establish a system to solve positive conflicts of jurisdiction between the Tribunal and those States. In this respect several questions arise. The most fundamental issue is to determine the best place to hold the trial.[1] Is it before the courts of the State where the alleged crimes have been committed or the courts of the State of which the defendant is a national? Or is it better to prosecute before a supranational court?

Although it has been argued that the best place for the trial is the state *locus delicti*[2] and that a deferral of a case to an international tribunal violates the principle of *jus de non evocando,*[3] the Statutes and the decisions of the ICTY and the ICTR leave no room for interpretation.[4]

The ICTR Statute states explicitly that the Tribunal has primacy over the national courts of all States.[5] Under the Statute, the Tribunal is in a hierarchical relation with States. In contrast to the co-operation between States and the ICC, there is a vertical relationship between the ICTR and the states.[6] According to Article 8, paragraph 2 of the Statute, the ICTR may formally request national courts to defer to its competence in accordance with both the Statute and the Rules of Procedures and Evidence.

Unlike the ICC, whose Statute is a treaty to be ratified by States so that its position is complementary and dependent on the free co-operation of national authorities, the ICTY and the ICTR were established by a Security Council Resolution which obliges all states to co-operate fully with the International Tribunal and its organs.

The question of the territorial extent of the primacy of the ICTR is particularly illustrated in the annotated Musema case. In this case the ICTR Trial Chamber decided to go beyond the ambit of the United Nations and formally requested a non UN State (Switzerland) to defer to the Tribunal all investigations and criminal proceedings being conducted in relation to the activities of Alfred Musema. Since Switzerland has been willing to co-operate with the *ad hoc* Tribunals and in 1995 created a legal basis for close co-operation between its legal authorities and the ICTY and the ICTR, the ICTR's request for deferral was granted.[7]

Nevertheless on other levels, the primacy of the ICTR over the national courts is not absolute. Article 9, paragraph 2 of the Statute sets limits on the subsequent prosecution by the Tribunal of persons who have been tried before a national court for acts constituting serious violations of international humanitarian

---

[1] Regarding the question of the 'best' place to prosecute see T. Vander Beken, Forumkeuze in het internationaal strafrecht. De verdeling van misdrijven met aanknopingspunten in meerdere staten, Antwerp-Apeldoorn, Maklu, 1999, 486 pages and H.D. Wolswijk, Locus delicti en rechtsmacht, Deventer-Utrecht, Gouda Quint-Willem Pompe Instituut, 1998, 353 pages.

[2] Radovan Karadžić, who has been indicted twice by the ICTY, had proposed that he be tried in his homecountry. See B.S. Brown, Primacy or Complementarity: Reconciling the Jurisdiction of National Courts and International Criminal Tribunals, 1998, 23 Yale Journal of International Law, p. 384.

[3] ICTY, Decision on the Defence Motion on Jurisdiction, *Prosecutor v. Tadić*, Case No. IT-94-1-T, T.Ch.II, ALC-I-21.

[4] However, even members of the Security Council did raise arguments purporting to limit the scope of the Tribunal's primacy. The United Kingdom stated that the primacy of the ICTY relates primarily to the courts of the former Yugoslavia, and that in relation to "elsewere it will only be in the kinds of exceptional circumstances outlined in Article 10, paragraph 2, that primacy should be applicable". The Russian Federation considered that deferral "is not a duty automatically to refer proceedings to the Tribunal on such a matter. A refusal to refer the case naturally has to be justified. We take it that this provision will be reflected in the rules of procedure and the rules of evidence of the Tribunal." (cited in B.S. Brown, o.c., at p. 399, footnote 69)

[5] Note that the Article 9, paragraph 2 of the ICTY Statute is less explicit and only refers to '*primacy over national courts'*. See B.S. Brown, o.c., p. 402.

[6] ICTY, Judgement on the Request of the Republic Croatia for Review of the Decision of Trial Chamber II of 18 July 1997, *Prosecutor v. Blaškić*, Case No. IT-95-14-AR108*bis*, 29 October 1997, ALC-I-263.

[7] Regarding the Swiss position see Bulletin officiel de l'Assemblée fédérale, 1998, V, 2330-2331 and J. van Wijnkoop, regarding the prosecution of alleged war criminals in Switzerland, see the Presentation given at the annual Seminar on the Law of Armed Conflicts, Geneva, October 1997, 5-6 (electronic copy http://www.vbs.admin.ch/internet/GST/KVR/e/rr/active.htm)

law (the principle of *non-bis-in-idem*).[8] These limitations are subject to situations where the act for which the person was tried was characterised as an ordinary crime or the national court proceedings were not impartial or independent or were designed to shield the accused from international criminal responsibility, or the case was not diligently prosecuted.

According to Rule 9 of the Rules of Procedure and Evidence, deferral for the purpose of investigation by the ICTR can be applied, depending *inter alia* upon the seriousness of the alleged offences, the status of the accused at the time of the alleged offences or the general importance of the legal questions involved in the case.

But what does this mean in practice? Since it is impossible to bring every case that is connected with the atrocities in Rwanda before the Tribunal, choices have to be made. Therefore the Tribunal must focus on the principal perpetrators in a way that it can serve as a catalyst for actions by the States themselves. Deferral should only be used in cases concerning real leaders and where the international community must demonstrate its commitment to international justice through the prosecution of perpetrators of crimes against humanitarian law.[9]

In the three annotated decisions of the ICTR, the Prosecutor formally requested deferral by Belgium to the competence of the Tribunal (the Bagosora and the Radio Télévision Libre Mille Collines cases) and by Switzerland (the Musema case) pursuant to Rules 9 and 10 of the Rules of Procedure and Evidence. In each of these cases the Trial Chamber granted the application made by the Prosecutor and formally requested that Belgium and Switzerland defer to the Tribunal all investigations and criminal proceedings currently being conducted in relation to the activities of the persons involved.

The Prosecutor put forward similar arguments in relation to her application in each of the cases. She indicated that national investigations and criminal proceedings had been instituted by Belgium and Switzerland respectively, that an investigation was being conducted regarding the persons involved in serious violations of international humanitarian law allegedly committed in the territory of Rwanda or in the neighbouring states between 1 January 1994 and 3 December 1994, that these investigations and criminal proceedings were closely related to, or otherwise involved in factual or legal questions which may have implications for the Prosecutor's own investigations or prosecutions and that there were no *non-bis-in-idem* problems.

In addition, the Prosecutor argued that continuing parallel investigations by the national courts and the ITCR might be detrimental to the investigations, and that repeated hearings of witnesses should be avoided, so as not to create mistrust and confusion in their testimonies, which would possibly affect their credibility. According to the Prosecutor a deferral would also avoid further distress to witnesses who have had already experienced significant trauma, as well as submitting them to possible threats or bodily harm. Finally, the Prosecutor argued that the States concerned were willing to co-operate with the Tribunal or were not opposing to deferring their investigations.

Although the arguments of the Prosecutor and the decisions of the Trial Chamber to defer criminal investigations and proceedings to the ICTR may seem clear, there may be one particular legal question to address. In the case of Radio Télévision Mille Collines (RTLM), the Prosecutor as well as the Trial Chamber, not only requested the deferral of all investigations and criminal proceedings then being

---

[8]   In the Tadić-case the defence tried to challenge the primacy of the ICTY with a motion based on *non-bis-in-idem*. The defence argued that the prosecution of Tadić had already reached the final stage in a State (Germany), so that Tadić could not be tried (again) before the ICTY. Since the proceedings in Germany had not progressed to the point of the actual trial as the term is used in the Statute, the ICTY decided that there was no issue of *non bis in idem* and rejected the motion. See ICTY, Decision on the defence motion on the principle of *non-bis-in-idem*, *Prosecutor v. Tadić*, Case No. IT-94-1-T, 14 November 1995, ALC-I-146, with a commentary by Otto Lagodny; A. Klip, International Prosecutors, in T. Vander Beken and M. Kilchling, The Role of the Public Prosecutor in the European Criminal Justice Systems, Brussels, 2000, 145.
[9]   This assumption has been used as an argument in favour of the defence. In a case where the Belgian judicial authorities had arrested a citizen of Rwanda in order to prosecute him for crimes for which the ICTR was also competent, the Belgian court rejected an argument by the defence that the mere fact that the ICTR did not request for deferral, indicated that the case was less serious (Court Brussels, 22 July 1996, Journal des Procès, 310, 20 September 1996, p. 28-31).

conducted in relation to persons involved in the case of RTLM, but also those concerning the legal entity RTLM itself. As a result deferral was requested in respect of investigations and proceedings against legal persons, which seems to conflict with Article 5 of the Statute ("The ICTR shall have jurisdiction over natural persons..."). The decision of the Belgian Court of Cassation in this case does not refer to this issue, instead only identifying three persons and deferring their cases to the ICTR.[10] Apart from this, the most interesting aspects of the deferral discussion are to be found at the national level, where compliance with ICTR decisions is not without its problems.[11]

In 1996, a law was enacted in Belgium to enable compliance with the decisions of the ICTR and ICTY.[12] Article 6 of this Act states that the Belgian Court of Cassation may decide to defer a case to the Tribunal if requested by the Tribunal and if it concerns a crime that is within the competence of the Tribunal. The Court of Cassation shall take this decision only after the person concerned has been heard and if it is confident that there is no *error in personae.*

The application of this provision gave rise to interesting questions and discussions regarding the issue of deferral. One of them is the question as to how the Belgian Court is able to determine any possible *error in personae* if the concerned person is not actually present in Belgium. According to the preparatory documents of the Act, the Court has to determine whether there is in reality a link between the person and the crimes on which the jurisdiction of the Tribunal is based.[13] The result is that the Belgian Court can check the jurisdictional claims of the International Tribunal, although this Tribunal is hierarchically superior. Furthermore, according to the Belgian Act, a case can only be deferred after verification by the Belgian judiciary that the *ad hoc* Tribunal is competent *rationae materiae* to try the alleged crime. It is clear that, if such a verification would lead to the conclusion that the Tribunal is not competent, the principle of the primacy of the Tribunals would be undermined. To date, such conflicts have not arisen and judicial decisions remain conservative. In the Bagosora case, where the suspect was in Cameroon at the relevant time – the Court of Cassation invoked *force majeure* to justify the fact that the person concerned was not heard and chose to limit itself to the (simple) consideration that the ICTR was competent *rationae materiae, rationae personae,* and *ratione loci.*

A decision to defer a case to the International Tribunal not only creates problems for national courts, but also raises questions with regard to the legal position of persons involved in the procedure. For the defendant it has already been shown that arguments based on the *jus de non evocando* are not in line with the concept of primacy, and therefore have not been accepted. Decisions to defer, however, can also have a large impact on the legal position of the victim since the effectiveness of his claim is often dependent of the decision of the criminal trial. Although Article 23, paragraph 3 of the Statute makes reference to the possibility that the Trial Chamber may order the return of any property and proceeds acquired by criminal conduct, including these acquired under duress, to the rightful owners the victims do not have any right to be represented at the trial before the Tribunal. Nevertheless, it should be possible at least to take victims' interests into account when states decide upon a request for deferral.[14]

These brief comments illustrate that decisions regarding the deferral of cases, although covered in formal wording touch upon fundamental questions related to the choice of international criminal tribunals. It is

---

[10] Court of Cassation, 9 oktober 1996, Prosecutor general at the Court of Cassation v. Nahimana, Revue de droit pénal et de criminologie, 1997, p. 1076.

[11] For comparable problems regarding the transfer of cases to the ICTR see e.g. G. Sluiter, To Cooperate or not to Cooperate?: The Case of the Failed Transfer of Ntakirutimana to the Rwanda Tribunal, Leiden Journal of International Law, 1998, p. 383-395.

[12] Act of 22 March 1996 on the recognition of and the co-operation with the ICTY and the ICTR, Moniteur Belge, 27 April 1996. In relation to this Act see D. Vandermeersch, La loi du 22 mars 1996 relative à la reconnaissance du Tribunal international pour l'Ex-Yougoslavie et du Tribunal international pour le Rwanda et à la coopération avec ces Tribunaux, Revue de droit pénal et de criminologie, 1996, p. 855-908.

[13] Marie-Anne Swartenbroekx, Dessaisissement d'un juge d'instruction belge en faveur du Tribunal pénal pour le Rwanda, in Revue du droit des étrangers, 1996, p. 379.

[14] According to Belgian law, this is not possible. See M.-A. Swartenbroekx, o.c. p. 381.

clear that the rule of primacy does not exclude basic discussions on sovereignty issues and on the legal position of the persons involved.

Tom Vander Beken

International Criminal Tribunal for Rwanda
Tribunal Pénal International pour le Rwanda

TRIAL CHAMBER I

OR: FR

Before: Judge Navanethem Pillay, Presiding
             Judge Lennart Aspegren
             Judge Laïty Kama

Registry: Ms Prisca Nyambe

Decision of: 18 March 1999

THE PROSECUTOR

versus

BERNARD NTUYAHAGA

Case No. ICTR-98-40-T

DECISION ON THE PROSECUTOR'S MOTION
TO WITHDRAW THE INDICTMENT

Office of the Prosecutor:
    Mr. Mohamed Othman
    Mr. James Stewart

Counsel for the Defence:
    Mr. Georges Komlavi Amegadjie

Amicus Curiae:
    The Government of the Kingdom of Belgium, represented by Mr. Éric David

[page 2] THE INTERNATIONAL CRIMINAL TRIBUNAL FOR RWANDA ("THE TRIBUNAL"),

SITTING as Trial Chamber I of the Tribunal, composed of Judge Navanethem Pillay, presiding, Judge Lennart Aspegren and Judge Laïty Kama;

CONSIDERING a motion dated 23 February 1999, whereby the Prosecutor, acting pursuant to Rule 51 of the Rules of Procedure and Evidence ("the Rules"), sought leave to withdraw the indictment against the accused Bernard Ntuyahaga ("the accused");

CONSIDERING the addendum to said motion, filed on 10 March 1999, whereby the Prosecutor additionally requested that the Chamber order the release of the accused Bernard Ntuyahaga from the Tribunal's custody to the authorities of the United Republic of Tanzania;

CONSIDERING the indictment dated 26 September 1998 submitted by the Prosecutor in accordance with Rule 47 of the Rules and considering the Decision on the review of said indictment rendered by Judge Yakov A. Ostrovsky on 29 September 1998 and the subsequent corrigenda filed thereon on 30 September 1998 and 2 October 1998;

CONSIDERING that by the aforementioned Decision, Judge Ostrovsky dismissed counts 1, 2 and 4 of the indictment, ordered the Prosecutor to join counts 3 and 5 and confirmed count 3;

CONSIDERING that the indictment as confirmed by Judge Ostrovsky thus comprises a single count of crime against humanity (murder), as stipulated in Article 3(a) of the Statute of the Tribunal ("the Statute"), and that it alleges that the accused is criminally responsible for the murder of Mrs. Agathe Uwilingiyimana, then Prime Minister of Rwanda, and ten Belgian soldiers United Nations Assistance Mission for Rwanda ("UNAMIR"), which murders were allegedly committed as part of a widespread or systematic attack against a civilian population on national or political grounds;

CONSIDERING that the accused pleaded not guilty to the said count during his initial appearance before this Chamber on 13 November 1998;

CONSIDERING the Defence Brief in reply and counter claims dated 12 march 1999, whereby it is argued, *inter alia*, that the motion of the Prosecutor for withdrawal of the indictment is inadmissible, that the motion is not well founded, and that the Chamber should dismiss it; further the Defence claimed that a finding should be made on the innocence of the accused, and that he should therefore be acquitted and released;

CONSIDERING that the Government of the Kingdom of Belgium requested leave of the Chamber to appear as an Amicus Curiae ("the Belgian Government") so as to make submissions on the motion of the Prosecutor to withdraw the indictment, and that by Decision of 8 March 1999, taken pursuant to Rule 74 of the Rules, the Government of the Kingdom of Belgium was granted leave to appear;

HAVING HEARD the representatives of the Prosecutor, the Defence and the Belgian Government during the public hearing held on 16 March 1999; **[page 3]**

WHEREAS, at the commencement of the said hearing, the representative of the Prosecutor presented in *limine litis* an oral motion, on the basis of Rule 73 of the Rules, requesting the Tribunal to dismiss the Advisory brief on the motion of the Prosecutor for withdrawal of the indictment, filed by the Registrar for the attention of the Judges on 15 March 1999, on the grounds that the Registrar is not party to the proceedings and therefore cannot legally present such a brief;

WHEREAS during the said hearing the Chamber ruled that the Registrar had no *locus standi* in the present matter and the Judges therefore had not considered the Registrar's Advisory brief;

AFTER HAVING DELIBERATED,

WHEREAS the Chamber considers it appropriate to examine the question of the withdrawal of the indictment, the counter claims of the Defence, and the eventual implications of the withdrawal of an indictment;

1. On the withdrawal of the indictment:

WHEREAS in support of her motion for leave to withdraw the said indictment, the Prosecutor argued in the main as follows:

(i)   withdrawal of the indictment would promote the exercise of concurrent jurisdiction as provided for under Article 8(1) of the Statute by allowing national courts to prosecute the accused;

(ii)   the judicial proceedings instituted by the Prosecutor should be within the framework of a global policy aimed at shedding light on the events that occurred in Rwanda in 1994 and highlighting the complete landscape of the criminal acts perpetrated at the time, and that such objective would not be achieved through the prosecution of a single count indictment the factual elements of which relate solely to the murders of the former Prime Minister and ten UNAMIR Belgian soldiers;

(iii)   the Decision on review of the indictment has narrowed the scope of prosecution and deprived the Prosecutor of the opportunity to execute her strategy of prosecuting the accused for the totality of his criminal involvement;

(iv)   The Kingdom of Belgium has instituted proceedings against the persons implicated in the murder of the ten UNAMIR Belgian soldiers; **[page 4]**

Concerning, firstly, the submission of the Prosecutor that withdrawal of the indictment would promote the exercise of concurrent jurisdiction as provided for under Article 8(1) of the Statute by allowing national courts to prosecute the accused;

WHEREAS the Chamber notes that this submission of the Prosecutor is supported by the Belgian Government, who consider that the activities of the Tribunal and national jurisdictions are complementary and that the need to criminally punish for the atrocities perpetrated in Rwanda in 1994 implies that the Tribunal cooperates with States in proceedings against those responsible for the atrocities;

WHEREAS, according to the Belgian Government, the cooperation provided for by the Security Council of the United Nations in the Statute, whereby all States must fully cooperate with the Tribunal, implies necessarily a reciprocal cooperation of the Tribunal with States, although this is not expressly provided for in the Statute or the Rules, the Tribunal can co-operate with States and thus facilitate the due process of Justice;

WHEREAS the Chamber, although it accepts the submissions of the Prosecutor and the Belgian Government inasmuch as the Tribunal does not have exclusive jurisdiction over crimes included in its mandate and that its criminal proceedings are complementary to those of national jurisdictions, it wishes to underscore that, in its opinion, and as submitted by the Defence, the principle of concurrent jurisdiction as provided in paragraph (1) of Article 8 of the Statute, which recognizes the complementary nature of the judicial work performed by the Tribunal and national courts, must be read together with the provisions of paragraph 2 of said Article 8, which confers upon the Tribunal primacy over the national courts of all States;

WHEREAS the primacy of the Tribunal is also recognized under Article 9 of the Statute which, in accordance with the *non bis in idem* principle, provides that no person shall be tried by a national court for acts for which he has already been tried by the Tribunal, even if in the circumstances provided for under paragraph 2 of Article 9, a person who has been tried before a national court may be subsequently tried by the Tribunal;

WHEREAS, consequently, once proceedings are instituted before the Tribunal against a person, the Tribunal has primacy over any other national court;

WHEREAS, in support of its submissions, the Belgian Government quoted the provisions of Rule 11*bis* of the Rules of Procedure and Evidence of the International Criminal Tribunal for the former Yugoslavia (the "ICTY");

WHEREAS, on this matter, the Chamber notes, on the one hand, that such provisions do not exist in the Tribunal's Rules;

WHEREAS the Chamber notes, on the other hand, that the scope of cooperation that the ICTY can give to national autorities, pursuant to said Rule 11bis of the ICTY Rules, is limited twofold, firstly by the fact that the ICTY only cooperates with the State in which the accused was arrested, and secondly, by the fact that sub-rule (C) of said Rule provides that: **[page 5]**

> "At any time after the making of an order under this Rule and before the accused is convicted or acquitted by a national court, the Trial Chamber may, upon the Prosecutor's application and after affording an opportunity to the authorities of the State concerned to be heard, rescind the order and issue a formal request for deferral under Rule 10";

WHEREAS, in any case, and without making a finding on the submission of the Belgian Government that the Tribunal's Rules be modified, the Chamber holds that, even if the Rules of the Tribunal contained provisions akin to those of Rule 11*bis* of the Rules of Procedure and Evidence of the ICTY, these provisions would not be applicable in the present matter, as the Tribunal is not aware that the authorities of the United Republic of Tanzania, which arrested Bernard Ntuyahaga, would be willing to continue the proceedings within their own jurisdiction for crimes alleged in the indictment;

WHEREAS, finally, the Chamber is of the opinion that the primacy recognized by the Statute is clear inasmuch as the Tribunal may request any national jurisdiction to defer investigations or ongoing proceedings, whereas the reverse, namely the deferral of investigations and proceedings by the Tribunal to any national jurisdiction, is not provided for;

WHEREAS, in the,.present matter, an indictment having been confirmed and the initial appearance of the accused having taken place, the Chamber concludes that the question of concurrent jurisdiction cannot be invoked by the Prosecutor in support of a request for withdrawal of an indictment;

WHEREAS, that said, the Tribunal wishes to emphasize, in line with the General Assembly and the Security Council of the United Nations, that it encourages all States, in application of the principle of universal jurisdiction, to prosecute and judge those responsible for serious crimes such as genocide, crimes against humanity and other grave violations of international humanitarian law;

WHEREAS thereupon, the Tribunal wishes particularly to thank the Kingdom of Belgium for the interest it has shown in the activities of the Tribunal and the support it has always given;

WHEREAS the Tribunal understands and empathises with the citizens of the Kingdom of Belgium, in particular the families of the ten UNAMIR Belgian soldiers, to see justice done;

As to the argument whereby the withdrawal of the indictment would be justified because the objective of the Prosecutor is to shed light on the events that occurred in Rwanda in 1994 and highlighting the complete landscape of the criminal acts perpetrated at the time, and that such objective would not be achieved through the prosecution of a single count indictment the factual elements of which relate solely to the murders of the former Prime Minister and ten UNAMIR Belgian soldiers;

WHEREAS the Chamber recalls that, although under Articles 17 and 18 of the Statute it is incumbent upon the Prosecutor to prepare an indictment, the reviewing Judge has unfettered discretion, and decides, on the basis of the evidence, whether to confirm or dismiss each count; **[page 6]**

WHEREAS, furthermore, under Rule 47 (I) of the Rules, the dismissal of a count shall not preclude the Prosecutor from subsequently bringing an amended indictment based on the acts underlying the dismissed count if supported by additional evidence;

WHEREAS, in any case, the Chamber stresses that it is the sole duty of the Prosecutor to devise the prosecution strategy and therefore to decide, even before instituting any proceedings, whether such action serves the interests of her mandate as Prosecutor;

WHEREAS, moreover, the Chamber is of the opinion that it is not within its purview to consider the question as to whether or not the prosecution of a person on a single count relating to the murders of the former Prime Minister and ten Belgian soldiers enables the Prosecutor to "shed light on the events that occurred in Rwanda in 1994";

WHEREAS, before the Chamber, all accused persons are presumed innocent and are equal before the law, and no distinction or ranking may be made among them on the basis of the number of counts with which they are charged;

In fine, as to the motion of the Prosecutor

WHEREAS the Chamber recalls that the Prosecutor has sole responsibility for prosecutions and thus the decision on whether or not to proceed in any given matter rests with the Prosecutor, and that she has the right, at any stage of the proceedings, to apply for leave to withdraw an indictment in accordance with the provisions of Rule 51 (A) of the Rules, which reads as follows:

> "The Prosecutor may withdraw an indictment, without prior leave, at any time before its confirmation, but thereafter, until the initial appearance of the accused before a Trial Chamber pursuant to Rule 62, only with leave of the Judge who confirmed it but, in exceptional circumstances, by leave of a Judge assigned by the President. At or after such initial appearance an indictment may only be withdrawn by leave granted by that Trial Chamber pursuant to Rule 73";

WHEREAS the Chamber, contrary to the submissions of the Defence, finds that the Prosecutor's motion is well founded;

2. On the requests of the Defence

WHEREAS the Defence Council submitted in the Brief in reply, dated 12 March 1999, that the Prosecutor has not respected her obligation to disclose evidentiary materials pursuant to Rule 66 of the Rules and that, according to the Defence, it is therefore obvious that the Prosecutor does not to this day have any evidence to sustain her allegations against the accused;

WHEREAS consequently, according to the Defence Counsel, it is incumbent on the Chamber to find the motion of the Prosecutor inadmissible and not well founded, and for the accused to be declared innocent, to be acquitted and released;

WHEREAS during the hearing, the Prosecutor, in answer to the Defence, replied that to present a motion to be granted leave to withdraw the indictment does not in any way signify the absence **[page 7]** of charges against the accused, which would lead to his acquittal;

WHEREAS, furthermore, if the need arose, the Prosecutor is ready to continue the proceedings;

WHEREAS, in any case, the Chamber reminds the Defence that, in accordance with Rule 98*bis* of the Rules, an acquittal can only be considered at the stage where the Prosecutor has presented all her evidence, and the Chamber finds that the evidence is insufficient to sustain a conviction on any one count;

The Chamber therefore finds the Defence request is premature and dismisses it;

3. As to the implications of the withdrawal of an indictment:

WHEREAS the Chamber holds that the withdrawal of an indictment is tantamount to a termination of proceedings and, consequently, entails the immediate and unconditional release of the accused;

WHEREAS thereupon, pursuant to the general principles of law, a person who is no longer under indictment may not be deprived of his or her freedom and must therefore be released immediately if he or she is not held for any other cause;

WHEREAS, however, the Prosecutor has requested the Chamber, were it to authorise the withdrawal of the indictment, to order the release of the accused Bernard Ntuyahaga from the Tribunal's custody to the authorities of the United Republic of Tanzania;

WHEREAS the said request is supported by the Belgian Government;

WHEREAS the Prosecutor argued that the Chamber has the competence to make such an order on the basis of the provisions of Rules 40*bis* and 65 of the Rules;

WHEREAS, as submitted by the Defence, the Chamber is of the opinion that the Prosecutor errs in law when she argues that the Chamber can avail itself in this matter of the provisions of Rule 40*bis* and 65 of the Rules;

WHEREAS Rule 65 of the Rules deals with provisional release, being applicable only when a person is still an accused before the Tribunal and who, consequently, will be called to appear before it, a procedure which is fundamentally different from the release of an individual who is no longer under indictment;

WHEREAS the provisions of Rule 40*bis* (H) of the Rules are not applicable in the present matter as they pertain to the release of suspects provisionally detained by the Tribunal; **[page 8]**

WHEREAS, in any case, the Chamber is of the opinion that, pursuant to the provisions of the Statute and the Rules, it does not have jurisdiction to order the release of a person who is no longer under indictment into the custody of any given State, including the Host State, the United Republic of Tanzania;

FOR THESE REASONS,

THE TRIBUNAL

GRANTS the Prosecutor leave to withdraw the indictment against Bernard Ntuyahaga;

ORDERS in the absence of any other charge against him, the immediate release of Bernard Ntuyahaga from the Tribunal's Detention Facilities;

INSTRUCTS the Registrar to take all the necessary measures to execute the present Decision, if need be with the cooperation of the authorities of the Host State, the United Republic of Tanzania.

Arush, 18 March 1999.

Navanethem Pillay	Lennart Aspegren	Laïty Kama
Presiding Judge	Judge	Judge

International Criminal Tribunal for Rwanda
Tribunal Pénal International pour le Rwanda

DECISION BY THE REGISTRAR IN EXECUTION OF THE DECISIONS BY TRIAL CHAMBER I ORDERING THE RELEASE OF MR BERNARD NTUYAHAGA

[page 2] THE REGISTRAR of the International Criminal Tribunal for Rwanda (hereinafter "the Tribunal"),

CONSIDERING the Decision on the Prosecutor's motion to withdraw the Indictment, which Decision was rendered by Trial Chamber I of the Tribunal on 18 March 1999 in the matter of the Prosecutor versus Bernard Ntuyahaga (Case No. ICTR-98-40-T);

CONSIDERING the correspondence dated 25 March 1999 from Honourable Judge Navanethem Pillay, Presiding Judge of Trial Chamber I in the matter of the Prosecutor versus Bernard Ntuyahaga, in reply to the extremely urgent motion for an immediate stay of execution of the Decision rendered by Trial Chamber I on 18 March 1999 in the matter of "Bernard Ntuyahaga versus the Prosecutor of the ICTR";

CONSIDERING Article 16 of the Statute of the Tribunal adopted on 8 November 1994 by Resolution 955 (1994) of the United Nations Security Council, as amended on 30 April 1998 by Resolution 1165 (1998) of the same organ;

CONSIDERING the correspondence dated 27 March 1999 addressed to the Registrar of the Tribunal by Mr. Bernard Ntuyahaga and his counsel, Mr. Georges Komlavi Amegadjie;

WHEREAS in its Decision mentioned *supra* Trial Chamber I

> **"ORDERS...,** the immediate release of Bernard Ntuyahaga form the Tribunal's Detention Facilities;
> [and]
> **INSTRUCTS** the Registrar to take all the necessary measures to execute the present Decision, if need be with the cooperation of the authorities of the Host State, the United Republic of Tanzania;"

WHEREAS in her correspondence mentioned *supra* Honourable Judge Navanethem Pillay notified the Registrar as follows:

> "After having consulted with my colleagues, the Judges of Trial Chamber I, Judge Lennart Aspegren and Judge Laïty Kama, I wish to reiterate that the Decision of 18 March 1999 had immediate effect.
>
> The Defence motion of 22 March 1999, which calls for Trial Chamber I to stay the execution of its Decision of 18 March 1999, thus asking the Chamber to review its own Decision, is inadmissible, and cannot be considered by the Trial Chamber.
>
> It should be noted that, in the execution of the Chamber's Decision, the Registrar shall take into account considerations that may arise, notably factors pertaining to the security of Bernard Ntuyahaga.
>
> Consequently, kindly inform the Defence Counsel of the status of the motion filed by him."
> **[page 3]**

WHEREAS in his correspondence mentioned *supra* Mr. Ntuyahaga expressed the wish to be released in Dar es Salaam, in the United Republic of Tanzania,

WHEREAS it is therefore necessary to execute immediately the Decisions of Trial Chamber I and to release Mr. Bernard Ntuyahaga.

INSTRUCTS the Commanding Officer *ad interim* of the United Nations Detention Facility to put Mr. Bernard Ntuyahaga at the disposal of the Chief of the Security and Safety Section of the Tribunal on 29 March 1999;

INSTRUCTS the Chief of the Security and Safety Section of the Tribunal to take the necessary measures for the conveyance of Mr. Bernard Ntuyahaga to Dar es Salaam on 29 March 1999.

Done in Arusha, on the 29th day of March 1999

Agwu Ukiwe Okali

Registrar

International Criminal Tribunal for Rwanda
Tribunal Pénal International pour le Rwanda

OR: FR.

DECLARATION ON A POINT OF LAW

BY

**JUDGE LAÏTY KAMA, PRESIDENT OF THE TRIBUNAL,
JUDGE LENNART ASPEGREN AND
JUDGE NAVANETHEM PILLAY**

[page 1] 1. Trial Chamber I of the International Criminal Tribunal for Rwanda, composed of Judge Navanethem Pillay, presiding, Judge Lennart Aspegren and Judge Laïty Kama, rendered on 18 March 1999 a decision in the matter of "The Prosecutor versus Bernard Ntuyahaga" (Case no. ICTR 98-40-T) wherein it:

>   (i)   granted the Prosecutor leave to withdraw the indictment against Bernard Ntuyahaga;

>   (ii)   ordered in the absence of any other charge against him, the immediate release of Bernard Ntuyahaga form the Tribunal's Detention Facilities; and

>   (iii) instructed the Registrar to take all the necessary measures to execute the present Decision, if need be with the cooperation of the authorities of the Host State, the United Republic of Tanzania.

2.   In light of said Decision, Defence Counsel for Mr. Bernard Ntuyahaga, Mr. Georges Komlavi Amegadjie, filed a motion on 22 March 1999, seeking a stay of execution of the abovementioned Decision. On 25 March 1999, Presiding Judge Pillay sent a letter to the Registrar, Mr. Agwu U. Okali, to the effect that the case "The Prosecutor versus Bernard Ntuyahaga" is closed before the Chamber, that the Defence motion was inadmissible and that the Decision rendered by the Chamber on 18 March 1999 had immediate effect; in the execution of said Decision, the Registrar was to take into account any considerations that may arise, notably factors pertaining to the security of Bernard Ntuyahaga.

3.   Some days thereafter, the Registrar informed the Judges of Trial Chamber I that he had carried out their instructions to him through, namely, a "Decision by the Registrar in execution of the Decisions rendered by Trial Chamber I ordering the release of Mr. Bernard Ntuyahaga", dated 29 March 1999. In this Decision, the Registrar instructed the Commanding Officer of the Detention Facility to release Mr. Ntuyahaga to the Chief of the Security and Safety Section on 29 March 1999, and instructed the latter to escort Mr. Ntuyahaga on the same day to Dar es Salaam, United Republic of Tanzania. **[page 2]**

4.   On 31 March 1999, the Prosecutor, Ms Louise Arbour, filed a motion submitting that the Registrar of the Tribunal, Mr. Agwu U. Okali, had issued to Mr. Bernard Ntuyahaga a document entitled "Safe Conduct" and dated 29 March 1999, covering the period 29 March to 13 April 1999, by which the Registrar:

>   "Request Member States of the United Nations, other States, International Organizations and all other persons to whom it may concern, to accord safe conduct to Bernard Ntuyahaga and extend to him any necessary cooperation to enable him to move freely in or transit through, without let or hindrance, any country to his final destination, in accordance with the relevant provisions of International Law."

In her motion, the Prosecutor requested the Chamber to rescind the said safe conduct on the grounds, firstly, that neither the provisions of the Statute nor those of the Rules of Procedure and Evidence permit the Registrar to issue such a document and, secondly, that neither the Statute nor the Rules nor International Law impose on States and international organizations the obligation to comply with a Safe Conduct document issued by the Registrar.

5.   The Judges learned of the document entitled "Safe Conduct" through the motion filed by the Prosecutor. At the request of the President of the Tribunal, a copy of the so-called "Safe Conduct" document was delivered by the Registry to Trial Chamber I on 12 April 1999.

6.   By an inter-office memorandum dated 12 April 1999, the President invited the Registrar to submit to him any comments that he may have in response to the aforementioned motion filed by the Prosecutor. The Registrar sent a Reply dated 12 April 1999 to the President, in which he argues in the main the following:

>   (i)   the Trial Chamber cannot admit the Prosecutor's motion because the case is closed before it;

>   (ii)   the Prosecutor's motion was moot because the safe conduct no longer had any merit, the authorities of the United Republic of Tanzania having taken Bernard Ntuyahaga into custody;

(iii)   the Safe Conduct document issued by the Registrar was consistent with the Trial Chamber's Decision of 18 March 1999 and the letter of 25 March 1999 and was therefore valid.

7.   The Judges wish to emphasize, first of all, that the motion submitted to them by the Prosecutor, whereas said Chamber had already clearly ruled that the case "The Prosecutor versus Bernard Ntuyahaga" is closed before it, is *ipso facto* inadmissible.

8.   In addition, the Judges wish to make the following three comments on the matter:

(i)   The Prosecutor sought from the Chamber leave to withdraw the indictment and has thus terminated proceedings against Mr. Bernard Ntuyahaga. Therefore, she no longer has standing to file a motion in the matter "The Prosecutor versus Bernard Ntuyahaga", which matter is unquestionably closed;

(ii)   The document entitled "Safe Conduct" issued by the Registrar in favour of Mr. **[page 3]** Bernard Ntuyahaga has in no way prejudiced the Prosecutor, since she had sought leave to withdraw the indictment;

(iii)   Since Mr. Ntuyahaga has been arrested by the authorities of the United Republic of Tanzania during the period of validity of the document entitled "Safe Conduct" issued to him by the Registrar, it appears that the authorities of the United Republic of Tanzania attached no weight to the document issued by the Registrar. Consequently, it is clear that the Prosecutor's motion seeking annulment of said document is clearly moot.

9.   However, in light of the significance of the issue raised by the Prosecutor as to whether the Registrar has authority under the provisions of the Statute and the Rules of Procedure and Evidence to issue a document granting safe conduct, the Judges have decided to issue this declaration in order to clarify any ambiguity there may be, in particular, to the status of the document entitled "Safe Conduct" issued by the Registrar on 29 March 1999.

10.   The Judges note that in his document entitled "Safe Conduct", the Registrar indicated that said document was issued:

"(...) pursuant tot the authority vested in him by the Tribunal's Statute and Rules of Procedure and Evidence, and in furtherance of the execution of said Decision of 18 March 1999."

11.   First of all, as concerns the provisions of both the Statute of the Tribunal and the Rules of Procedure and Evidence, the Judges agree with the Prosecutor that none of the provisions grant the Registrar the authority to issue a safe conduct. The Judges observe in this respect that the Registrar himself did not refer to the specific conferring such authority upon him and that, in his Reply dated 12 April 1999, he failed to offer a response to the Prosecutor on the matter.

12.   Notwithstanding the above, the Judges note paragraph 2 of Security Council resolution 955 of 8 November 1994, which provides that the Security Council decides:

"(...) that all States shall cooperate fully with the International Tribunal and its organs (...)".

The Judges note that the Security Council dit, indeed, make ample provision for States to cooperate with the organs of the Tribunal, including its Registry, but they are of the opinion that such a provision in no way confers upon the Registrar the authority to seek the cooperation of States in matters not explicitly provided for in the Statute or in the Rules of Procedure and Evidence which provisions provide that the Registrar acts under the direction of a Judge or a Chamber. Indeed, the Judges hold that the Registrar has power to seek the cooperation of States only in the exercise of the functions specifically assigned to him under the Statute and the Rules of Procedure and Evidence, such as the transmittal of a warrant of arrest or a request for transfer duly issued by a Judge at the request of the Prosecutor.

13.   The Judges, nothing that neither the provisions of said Security Council resolution, nor those of the Statute, nor those of the Rules of Procedure and Evidence empower the Registrar to issue a safe conduct, thus find that the Registrar, by so doing, acted *ultra vires.*

14.   With respect to the Registrar's contention that he issued the document entitled "Safe **[page 4]** Conduct":

"(...) in furtherance of the execution of the Tribunal's Decision of 18 March 1999".

the Judges note that the Decision rendered by Trial Chamber I on 18 March 1999 clearly:

"Instructs the Registrar to take all the necessary measures to execute the present Decision, if need be with the cooperation of the authorities of the Host State, the United Republic of Tanzania."

In accordance with said ruling, the Registrar has valid grounds to take all necessary measures to execute the Decision by the Chamber, that is, to execute the order to release Bernard Ntuyahaga immediately from the Tribunal's Detention Facility and to set him free. The Registrar acted specifically to this end by issuing the document signed on 29 March 1999 by which he issued various instructions to the Commanding Officer of the Detention Facility and the Chief of the Security and Safety Section of the Tribunal. However, neither the Chamber's Decision of 18 March 1999, nor the letter of 25 March 1999 from the Presiding Judge to the Registrar, empowered the latter to issue a safe conduct to Bernard Ntuyahaga.

15.   In his Reply to the Prosecutor's motion, the Registrar, first of all, in paragraph 23, submitted that the issuance of a Safe Conduct document was part of the "necessary measures" he was instructed to take in order to execute said Decision by the Chamber and went on to assert in paragraph 29 that the Chamber's Decision did not expressly preclude him from issuing such a document. The Judges will only declare in this regard that issuing a Safe Conduct document goes beyond the scope of measures necessary to effect release, even though the Judges had requested the Registrar to take into account considerations that may arise, notably factors relating to the security of Bernard Ntuyahaga. Clearly, the instructions given by the Chamber were in no way a licence to the Registrar to exceed the powers ordinarily vested in him under the Statute and the Rules of Procedure and Evidence. Consequently, and granted that the Decision of 18 March 1999 or the letter of 25 March could have led the Registrar, in good faith, to consider affording certain guarantees to Bernard Ntuyahaga, the Judges are of the view that the Registrar therefore should have definitely consulted the Chamber. The Judges hold that, in instant case, "The Prosecutor versus Bernard Ntuyahaga", it was incumbent upon the parties, particularly the Defence, where necessary, to seek relief measures, if any, from the Trial Chamber for Bernard Ntuyahaga. The Registrar when seized of such a request, should have transmitted it to the Trial Chamber or, at least, informed it about it.

16.   Indeed, the Judges are of the opinion that, under the provisions of the Statute and the Rules of Procedure and Evidence and in light of case-law developed by the International Criminal Tribunal for the Former Yugoslavia, only a Trial Chamber could be empowered to issue a safe conduct, as held by the Trial Chamber of the International Criminal Tribunal for the Former Yugoslavia, presided over by Judge Gabrielle Kirk McDonald, in the decision rendered on 22 October 1997 in the matter "The Prosecutor versus Mile Mrksic, Miroslav Radic, Veselin Sljivancanin and Slavko Dokmanovic" (Case No. IT-95-13a-PT).

17.   In light of the foregoing, the undersigned Judges, anxious that the issuance by the Registrar of a document entitled "Safe Conduct" does not set a precedent and mindful of the need for the Tribunal to ensure proper respect and compliance for the law, declare the following: **[page 5]**

(i)   neither the provisions of Security Council resolutions, nor those of the Statute, nor those of the Rules of Procedure and Evidence, nor any instructions rendered by the Trial Chamber, empower the Registrar to issue the document entitled "Safe Conduct", dated 29 March 1999, and which he delivered to Mr. Bernard Ntuyahaga; by so doing, the Registrar acted *ultra vires*;

(ii)   consequently, the document entitled "Safe Conduct" is null and void;

(iii)   this declaration is public and the Registrar is instructed to immediately and formally notify it to the Prosecutor of the Tribunal, to Mr. Bernard Ntuyahaga, to his Counsel, Mr. Georges Komlavi Amegadjie, to the Government of the United Republic of Tanzania, the Host State of the Tribunal, and to the Government of the Kingdom of Belgium, which appeared as *Amicus Curiae* in the matter "The Prosecutor versus Bernard Ntuyahaga."

Arusha, 22 April 1999,

Laïty Kama	Lennart Aspegren	Navanethem Pillay
President	Judge	Judge

Concurrent jurisdiction

The Prosecutor offered a number of reasons for the motion of withdrawal of the indictment, which is tantamount to a termination of the proceedings. The most important was that in the Decision on the Review of Indictment, Judge Ostrovsky dismissed a substantive part of the indictment, because of insufficient proof.[1] This made it for the Prosecutor less attractive to continue an energy and time-consuming prosecution. Another essential consideration was that Belgium was prepared to take over the proceedings, because Belgium had instituted proceedings against persons, including Ntuyuhaga, implicated in the murder of ten UNAMIR soldiers.[2] The Prosecutor saw in this case an excellent application in practice of the principle of concurrent jurisdiction, as provided for in Article 8 (1) of the ICTR Statute.[3]

The Trial Chamber, however, refused to cooperate in a transfer of Ntuyahaga to Belgium. Belgium more or less adopted the view that concurrent jurisdiction between national jurisdictions and the ICTR implies the possibility of reciprocal cooperation, though only States have a duty to cooperate and even if it is not explicitly provided for in the Statute or RPE. The Trial Chamber addressed the matter in a rather formalistic manner, ruling that it simply lacked the power under its Statute and RPE to defer investigations and proceedings to the national level. Rule 11bis of the ICTY RPE indicates a trend to a more effective division of labour between the ICTY and national jurisdictions, and could serve as a possible basis for such deferral.[4] The Trial Chamber, however, established that no such Rule was part of the ICTR RPE and denied this Rule legal effect for the ICTR. If this is the ICTR approach to every ICTY Rule that has not yet been adopted by the ICTR there is reason for concern.[5] One of the objectives of

---

[1]   Decision on the review of the indictment, *Prosecutor v. Ntuyahaga*, Case No. ICTR-98-40-I, 29 September 1998.

[2]   The death of ten Belgian UNAMIR soldiers caused the withdrawal of the Belgian battalion from UNAMIR; see Special report of the Secretary-General on UNAMIR, containing a summary of the developing crisis in Rwanda and proposing three options for the role of the United Nations in Rwanda, U.N. Doc. S/1994/470, 20 April 1994.

[3]   The establishment of the ICTR is, just as the establishment of the ICTY, based on the assumption that both the ICTR and States, in particular Rwanda, will prosecute genocide suspects. The "principle of concurrent jurisdiction" has been underlined by the U.N. Security Council in Resolution 978 (1995) and by the U.N. General Assembly in Resolution 200 (1995); see V. Morris and M.P. Scharf, The International Criminal Tribunal for Rwanda, 1995, p. 305 – 312. The application in practice of "concurrent jurisdiction" between the ICTR and Rwanda has been subject to criticism, in that the "minor perpetrators" stand trial in Rwanda under inferior conditions (denial of fair trial and possibility of death penalty) than the "major perpetrators" appearing before the ICTR; see on this issue M.H. Morris, The Trials of Concurrent Jurisdiction: The Case of Rwanda, 7 Duke Journal of Comparative & International Law 1997, p. 349 – 374.

[4]   Rule 11bis of the ICTY RPE provides as follows:
Suspension of Indictment in case of Proceedings before National Courts
(A)   Where, on application by the Prosecutor or *proprio motu*, it appears to the Trial Chamber that
       (i) the authorities of the State in which an accused was arrested are prepared to prosecute the accused in their own courts; and
       (ii) it is appropriate in the circumstances for the courts of that State to exercise jurisdiction over the accused,
       the Trial Chamber, after affording the opportunity to an accused already in the custody of the Tribunal to be heard, may order that the indictment against the accused be suspended, pending the proceedings before the national courts.
(B)   If an order is made under this Rule:
       (i) the accused, if in the custody of the Tribunal, shall be transferred to the authorities of the State concerned;
       (ii) the Prosecutor may transmit to the authorities of the State concerned such information relating to the case as the Prosecutor considers appropriate;
       (iii) the Prosecutor may direct trial observers to monitor proceedings before the national courts on the Prosecutor's behalf.
(c)   At any time after the making of an order under this Rule and before the accused is convicted or acquitted by a national court, the Trial Chamber may, upon the Prosecutor's application and after affording an opportunity to the authorities of the State concerned to be heard, rescind the order and issue a formal request for deferral under Rule 10.
(D)   If an order under this Rule is rescinded by the Trial Chamber, the Trial Chamber may formally request the State concerned to transfer the accused to the seat of the Tribunal, and the State shall comply without undue delay in accordance with Article 29 of the Statute. The Trial Chamber or a Judge may also issue a warrant for the arrest of the accused.

[5]   There is a certain discrepancy between the ICTY and ICTR Rules of Procedure. The ICTY Rules, have after an increasing number of amendments, taken a different shape on certain points than the ICTR Rules, which have followed the initial amendments, but not (yet) the most recent ones.

Article 14 of the ICTR Statute, explicitly pointing to the ICTY RPE as a source for the ICTR RPE, is in fact to provide for harmonisation of the legal framework of the two Tribunals.[6]

Even if Rule 11bis were applicable to the ICTR, the Trial Chamber further argues, this would be of no avail in this case, because it only envisages deferral of the case and transfer of the accused to the State were he was arrested. Ntuyuhaga was arrested in and transferred by Tanzania, which had not shown any interest in prosecution of Ntuyahaga. The scope of application touches upon a crucial issue, which has not been addressed by the Trial Chamber. Does the rule of speciality, familiar to extradition between States, apply to the transfer of an accused by a State to the ICTR or ICTY?[7] This question was not addressed in the legal frameworks of the *ad hoc* Tribunals, but it came to the fore during the negotiations on the ICC Statute. It has been argued in that context that the special character of the relationship between States and an international criminal tribunal does not require the application of a rule of speciality.[8] Although a rule of speciality was inserted in the Rome Statute as a result of a compromise, it was argued that in the "more vertical" framework of the *ad hoc* Tribunals the rule does not apply.[9] The decision of the Trial Chamber in this case may be considered an indication to the contrary.[10] A possible application of the rule of speciality by the ad hoc Tribunals is then not based on national sovereignty interests, but on the rights and interests of the surrendered person.

Another element of concurrent jurisdiction is the legal effect of a conviction or acquittal by the ICTR for the national level, and *vice versa*. The ICTR Statute contains a provision stating that "[n]o person shall be tried before a national court for acts constituting serious violations of international humanitarian law under the present Statute, for which he or she has already been tried by the International Tribunal for Rwanda."[11] This non-bis-in-idem regulation attaches, contrary to most national provisions, trans-jurisdictional effect to convictions or acquittals of the ICTR.[12] This provision explains the motion of the Defence for an acquittal. An acquittal of Ntuyahaga with respect to the alleged murder of Belgian UNAMIR soldiers would constitute a bar to subsequent prosecution in Belgium for the same offences.[13] The Trial Chamber rightly pointed out that such a conclusion would be premature, because evidence had not yet been presented. The withdrawal of the indictment thus only results in the termination of the proceedings which enables each State to institute proceedings for the offences set out in the indictment of the Prosecutor.

The question arises as to whether this decision constitutes a bar to other forms of cooperation by the ICTR – or ICTY – to national jurisdictions, such as the provision of evidence. A strict application of the Statute would deny such power, because none of the ICTR organs have been vested with the power to provide assistance to national jurisdictions. Still, the Prosecutor has at several occasions indicated her readiness to assist domestic jurisdictions which pursue, in good faith, charges of serious violations of international humanitarian law.[14] It can be expected that this kind of assistance is in no way hampered by

---

[6]   See V. Morris and M.P. Scharf, The International Criminal Tribunal for Rwanda, 1995, p. 413. Such "harmonisation" is further guaranteed by a common Appeals Chamber for the two Tribunals.

[7]   The rule of speciality means that a person shall only be proceeded against by the requesting jurisdiction for the conduct which specifically furnished the grounds for his or her surrender. From this also follows a prohibition for re-extradition of the person to another jurisdiction.

[8]   See the contribution of Wilkitzki with respect to Article 101 of the ICC Statute; P. Wilkitzki, in: O. Triffterer (ed.), Commentary on the Rome Statute (1999), Article 101, margin Nos. 1 – 9.

[9]   See *ibid.*

[10]   Also Rule 11bis of the ICTY RPE is drafted in such a fashion that the speciality rule is fully respected, since the ICTY may only defer a case and transfer a suspect to the State where he was arrested; see *supra* note 4. See also page 4 of Decision on the Prosecutor's Motion to Withdraw the Indictment, *Prosecutor v. Ntuyahaga*, Tr. Ch. I, Case No. ICTR-98-40-T, 18 March 1999.

[11]   Article 9, paragraph 1 of the ICTR Statute.

[12]   For the scope of application of non-bis-in-idem in the context of the ICTY, see Decision on the Defence Motion on the Principle of Non-Bis-In-Idem, *Prosecutor v. Tadić*, Tr. Ch., Case No. IT-94-1-T, 14 November 1995, commented by Lagodny in ALC-I-154.

[13]   It would constitute a bar to prosecution in each UN Member State; since Article 9, paragraph 1 has only effect for UN Members, non-Member States would not be barred under international law from instituting proceedings for same offences.

[14]   See *e.g.* Statement by the Prosecutor following the Withdrawal of the Charges against 14 Accused, press release CC/PIU/314-E, The Hague, 8 May 1998.

this decision. Still, it would have been preferable to regulate such matters in the RPE, along the lines of Article 93, paragraph 10 of the ICC Statute.

Internal division of powers

The implications of the withdrawal of the indictment, being the immediate and unconditional release of the accused, led to a debate on the internal division of powers, in particular the powers of the ICTR Registrar set against the powers of the Judges and Chambers. The facts that provoked this debate are quite remarkable and need to be summarised here.

The Trial Chamber ordered the immediate release from Ntuyahaga. It denied the request of the Prosecutor to order the release of Ntuyahaga into the custody of Tanzania, because Ntuyahaga was no longer under indictment. The Registrar was then instructed by the Trial Chamber to take all the necessary measures to execute this decision, if need be with the cooperation of the host-State, Tanzania. The Registrar issued a decision on 1 April 1999, in execution of this decision. From the decision of the Registrar, it appears that according to correspondence between the Registrar and Presiding Trial Chamber Judge Pillay, the Registrar should in executing the Trial Chamber decision "take into account considerations that may arise, notably factors pertaining to the security of Bernard Ntuyahaga". The Registrar must have understood "security" in a broad sense, because he provided Ntuyahaga with a "safe conduct" document, by which he requested all UN Member States, other States and international organisations to accord safe conduct to Ntuyahaga and extend to him any necessary cooperation to enable him to move freely in or transit through, without let or hindrance, any country to his final destination, in accordance with the relevant provisions of international law.

The Prosecutor submitted this "safe conduct" document to the Trial Chamber and requested it to rescind it. However, since the case of Ntuyahaga was closed, the motion was held inadmissible. Nevertheless, the Judges would like to comment on the matter and clarify certain issues. This prompted the issuance of a unique "declaration on a point of law" by the three members of the Ntuyahaga Trial Chamber.

Before embarking upon the content of this declaration, the question of its legal status arises. Its sole purpose is, as the Judges put it, "(...) to clarify any ambiguity there may be, in particular, to the status of the document entitled "Safe Conduct" issued by the Registrar on 29 March 1999".[15] It should therefore be considered as an "authoritative interpretation" in this respect. There is, however, one direct legal consequence: the "safe conduct", as issued by the Registrar, is declared null and void.[16] In that sense, the declaration thus exceeds the character of a mere authoritative interpretation.

The Judges deal with two issues, which are, although closely related, not fully identical. First, does the Registrar have the power to issue a safe conduct document? Second, may he independently solicit State cooperation? The second question will be dealt with under the next heading.

The Judges of the Ntuyahaga Trial Chamber attempt to clearly indicate that the power to issue a safe conduct order is strictly reserved to the Judges. A safe conduct order limits the powers of the ICTR and national prosecutors to instigate proceedings and is as such reserved to the judiciary. The problem is, of course, that this power is not regulated in the legal framework of the ICTR, and this power has thus not been attributed to neither the Judges nor the Registrar. But the Judges rightly referred to ICTY case-law, according to which only a Trial Chamber could be empowered to issue a safe conduct.[17] The arguments of the Registrar do not contradict this, but emphasise that he was empowered to issue this safe conduct, because, according to him, the Trial Chamber instructed him to do so. The Judges refute this view, but they in my view fail to acknowledge that their instructions to the Registrar were clearly vague and could be interpreted in different ways. Indeed, the instruction by the Trial Chamber "to take all necessary measures to execute" its decision, and the subsequent exchange of letters with Judge Pillay, may have led the Registrar to believe that Ntuyahaga should not be arrested again at the national level for the offences

---

[15]   Paragraph 9 of the Declaration.

[16]   *Id.*, para. 17.

[17]   Strangely, they only mention the decision rendered in *Prosecutor v. Mrkšić and others*, Case No. IT-95-13a-PT, 22 October 1997 and not the Decision on the Defence Motions to Summon and Protect Defence Witnesses, and on the Giving of Evidence by Video-Link, *Prosecutor v. Tadić*, Case No. IT-94-1-T, T.Ch. II, 25 June 1996, which is still the landmark decision on safe-conduct.

set out in the indictment. In this respect, the Judges should have been more critical regarding their own formulation of the decision and "instructions" to the Registrar.

This is not to say that the Registrar was not at fault. The Judges correctly held that he was acting *ultra vires* and he should have consulted the Judges, if he believed, acting in good faith that the decision purported to offer certain post-release guarantees to Ntuyahaga.[18] One can detect a certain irritation with the Judges. They were definitely "not amused" to find out about the safe conduct order only through the Prosecution motion.[19]

There is another reason as to why the Registrar should have known that he was acting *ultra vires*. In the Tadić case, the ICTY Trial Chamber has clearly ruled that safe conduct orders by the Tribunal can only have internal effect in the sense that national authorities cannot be requested to offer safe conduct.[20] This decision should at least have made the Registrar doubt the legality of his actions and submit his doubts to the Judges.

The declaration of the Judges, although some self-criticism would be in place, is certainly a useful one. The main practical objective of the declaration was to avoid the creation of a precedent for the Registry. And the Judges have succeeded in that respect. However, the declaration hopefully provokes a more general debate on the powers of the ad hoc Tribunals and in particular the division of these powers between the principal organs. There is still some uncertainty in this respect. For example, may the Prosecutor request States to execute a search for evidence in a private home, or is only a Judge or Chamber, pursuant to Article 18 of the ICTR Statute, empowered to do so, by issuing a search warrant? The declaration provides a guiding principle in answering such questions. The Judges are clearly vested with the authoritative interpretation of the content and extent of the powers of all the organs. In case of doubt on their powers, the Registrar and Prosecutor should submit the matter to the Judges or consult with them.

State cooperation

The next issue raised by the Declaration is whether the Registrar can solicit independently State cooperation. The "safe conduct document" in fact included a broad request to UN Member States, other States, international organisations and all other persons to enable Ntuyahaga to move freely and not to arrest him.

The major difficulty here is of course Article 28 of the ICTR Statute and paragraph 2 of Security Resolution 955; both oblige a State to cooperate with the ICTR, *including all its organs*. Does this mean each organ of the ICTR has the power to request assistance from States and other subjects of international law? No, this depends on the attribution of powers in the Statute and the Rules of Procedure and Evidence. Generally, it can be said that if an organ has been endowed with specific powers, it may solicit State cooperation if this is necessary for an effective exercise of these powers. In this respect, the Judges in their declaration rightfully submit that "(…) the Registrar has power to seek the cooperation of States only in the exercise of the functions specifically assigned to him under the Statute and the Rules of Procedure and Evidence (…)".[21] They then mention as examples the transmittal of a warrant of arrest or a request for transfer duly issued by a Judge at the request of the Prosecutor.[22] These examples are somewhat unfortunate, because in these situations the Registrar merely solicits State cooperation on behalf of the Judge or Chamber. In fact, it is the Judge or Chamber, it can be argued, who have been vested with the power to request these forms of assistance.[23] This might create the impression that the Registrar cannot independently solicit State cooperation at all, but this is not true. For example, in the field of the protection of victims and witness the Registrar has been vested with autonomous powers and

---

[18]   See paragraph 17 of the declaration.

[19]   See paragraph 5 of the declaration.

[20]   Decision on the Defence Motions to Summon and Protect Defence Witnesses, and on the Giving of Evidence by Video-Link, *Prosecutor v. Tadić*, Case No. IT-94-1-T, T.Ch.II, 25 June 1996; for a critical comment see André Klip in ALC-I-225.

[21]   Paragraph 12 of the Declaration.

[22]   *Ibid.*

[23]   No-one will support the view that the Registrar could by himself order a person's arrest or transfer.

has in this field, legitimately, sought State cooperation.[24] This would have been a better example of the Registrar's power to solicit State cooperation.

The Judges in their declaration rightly held that the Registrar by issuing a safe conduct and requesting State cooperation acted *ultra vires* to the Statute and Rules of Procedure and Evidence. However, they failed to address the question as to what this means for State cooperation. How should States respond to requests for assistance which they believe to be *ultra vires*?

The reaction of Tanzania to the request by the Registrar was apparently one of complete disregard. As it is mentioned in the Declaration: "Since Mr. Ntuyahaga has been arrested by the authorities of the United Republic of Tanzania during the period of validity of the document entitled "Safe Conduct" issued to him by the Registrar, it appears that the authorities of the United Republic of Tanzania attached no weight to the document issued by the Registrar."[25] Although the views of Tanzania and the Judges converge on the lawfulness of the safe conduct document and request for assistance, the reaction of Tanzania should be condemned. It is unfortunate the Judges fail to do so, and it is to be hoped that no precedent is set.

The obligations of Tanzania under the Security Council Resolution and the Statute to cooperate concern requests of the Registrar as well. In case the Registrar acts *ultra vires* in requesting a certain type of assistance, the lawfulness of the request is not automatically affected as far as a State's duty to give effect to the request is concerned.[26] There exists a presumption of validity. In this respect it should be noted, that the Registrar, acting in good faith pursuant to the instructions of the Trial Chamber and its Presiding Judge, may had reason to believe the lawfulness of his safe conduct document and accompanying requests to States.[27] It is therefore also difficult to qualify his actions as manifestly *ultra vires*.[28]

It is a matter for concern that Tanzania apparently unilaterally declared the request for assistance *ultra vires* and set it aside. In general, when States unilaterally interpret the lawfulness of a request for assistance by one of the ad hoc Tribunals, this could seriously hamper the Tribunals to function effectively.[29] It is with good reason that other States, such as the Federal Republic of Yugoslavia, have received great criticism for unilaterally pronouncing on the legality (of certain acts) of the ICTY.

What Tanzania should have done when it was confronted with the request of the Registrar, was entering into contact with the ICTR, in particular the President. The Judges of the ICTR are the authoritative interpreters of the extent of the powers of all the organs, and the extent of the duty to cooperate incumbent upon States. Not only would they have declared the safe conduct null and void, as they did in this declaration, but they would have done so at an earlier stage. Such consultation thus also serves a useful purpose as far as legal certainty is concerned.

Göran Sluiter

---

[24]   One could think in particular of requests to States for relocation of witnesses within their territory.

[25]   Paragraph 8 of the Declaration.

[26]   See on this complicated issue K. Doehring, Unlawful Resolutions of the Security Council and their Legal Consequences, in Max Planck Yearbook of United Nations Law, Vol. 1, 1997 [J.A. Frowein, R. Wolfrum, *eds.*], p. 91 – 109. Although this article is concerned with Security Council resolutions, it is nevertheless of relevance here, because requests for cooperation may be equated with "the application of an enforcement measure under Chapter VII of the Charter of the United Nations" (Report of the UN Secretary-General pursuant to paragraph 2 of Security Council Resolution 808 (1993), presented 3 May 1993, U.N. Doc. S/25704).

[27]   Generally, States will confide in the organs of the *ad hoc* Tribunals as far as the legality of their actions is concerned; they are of course in a better position to judge this than States.

[28]   The – controversial – concept of "manifestly ultra vires" is sometimes used to indicate that acts which are manifestly ultra vires are void *ab initio* and as such are incapable of creating binding obligations for States; see E. Osieke, The Legal Validity of Ultra Vires Decisions of International Organizations, 77 American Journal of International Law 1983, p. 249.

[29]   In this respect, regard should be had to one of the findings of the ICTY – and ICTR – Appeals Chamber in the Blaškić subpoena case, where it held with respect to the right of a State to withhold national security sensitive documents that "[t]o admit that a State holding such documents may unilaterally assert national security claims and refuse to surrender those documents could lead to the stultification of international criminal proceedings (...) The very *raison d'être* of the International Tribunal would then be undermined"; Judgement on the Request of the Republic of Croatia for Review of the Decision of Trial Chamber II of 18 July 1997, Prosecutor v. Blaškić, Case No. IT-95-14, A.Ch. 29 October 1997, par. 65.

International Criminal Tribunal for Rwanda
Tribunal pénal international pour le Rwanda

TRIAL CHAMBER II

OR: Eng.

Before: **Judge William H. Sekule, Presiding**
            Judge Yakov A. Ostrovsky
            Judge Tafazzal Hossain Khan

Registry: **Mr. John M. Kiyeyeu**

           7.11.98

THE PROSECUTOR

versus

JEAN-BOSCO BARAYAGWIZA

Case No. ICTR-97-19-I

DECISION ON THE EXTREMELY URGENT MOTION BY THE DEFENCE FOR ORDERS TO REVIEW AND/OR NULLIFY THE ARREST AND PROVISIONAL DETENTION OF THE SUSPECT

The Office of the Prosecutor:
    Mr. James T. Egbe, Trial Attorney
    Mr. Mathias Marcussen, Legal Advisor

Counsel for the Accused:
    Mr. Justry P.L. Nyaberi, Lead Counsel

---

*   Editor's note: the editors have incorporated in this decision the corrigendum of 24 November 1998 (Decision on the Extremely Urgent Motion by the Defence for Orders to Review and/or Nullify the Arrest and Provisional Detention of the Suspect/Corr., *Prosecutor v. Barayagwiza*, Case No. ICTR-97-19-I, T. Ch. II, 24 November 1998).

[page 2] THE INTERNATIONAL CRIMINAL TRIBUNAL FOR RWANDA (the "Tribunal"),

SITTING AS Trial Chamber II, composed of Judge William H. Sekule, Presiding, Judge Yakov A. Ostrovsky and Judge Tafazzal H. Khan (the "Trial Chamber");

CONSIDERING the indictment filed on 22 October 1997 by the Prosecutor against Jean-Bosco Barayagwiza pursuant to Article 17 of the Statute of the Tribunal ("the Statute") and rule 47 of the Rules of Procedure and Evidence of the Tribunal ("the Rules"), which was confirmed by Judge Lennart Aspegren on 23 October 1997;

CONSIDERING THAT the initial appearance of Jean-Bosco Barayagwiza took place on 23 February 1998;

BEING NOW SEIZED OF a motion filed by the Defence Counsel on 19 February 1998, entitled Extremely Urgent Motion by the Defence for Orders for Review and/or Nullify the Arrest and Provisional Detention of the Suspect (hereinafter the "Motion");

HAVING HEARD the arguments of the parties on 11 September 1998.

PLEADINGS BY PARTIES

Defence Submissions

In the Motion, the Defence submit;

1. That the accused rights, liberties and freedoms under article 20 of the Statute have been violated because: the provisional detention was a miscarriage of justice under rule 5 (Non-compliance with Rules); the Prosecutor's request for provisional detention was unprocedural and unwarranted; rule 40(*bis*) (Transfer and Provisional Detention of Suspects) was not satisfied regarding the provisional detention; and there was no justification for the arrest or provisional detention.

2. Rule 40 (*bis*) breaches the provisions of articles 17, 18 and 19 of the Statute.

3. The provisional charges were illegal.

The Defence requests the Trial Chamber to declare;

1. The arrest and provisional detention unlawful, null and void.

2. The entire proceedings are a nullity.

3. The accused be set free.

4. In the alternative, that the accused be released on bail pending further hearing.

Prosecutor's Response

1. Even if there was a defect in the procedure, then that defect is now cured and the accused is **[page 3]** before this Tribunal on a proper legal basis.

2. There is nothing in the Statute or Rules that allows the relief sought.

3. The Defence submission is based upon a faulty procedural analysis.

4. Rule 40 (*bis*) is valid legislation.

5. The Defence has failed to show exceptional circumstances to justify release under rule 65.

Chronology of Events:

Because much of the dispute between the parties is based on the chronology of events since the arrest of the accused, and the authority under which the accused was subject at particular stages of his detention, the Trial Chamber provides an outline below.

In relation to the events the <u>Defence</u> contend:

On 15 April 1996, the accused was detained in Cameroon *at the behest of the Prosecutor.*
On 15 October 1996, the Prosecutor withdrew her case against accused.

On 23 January 1997, other suspects detained with accused were transferred (according to the Defence, this shows discrimination by the Prosecutor).

On 21 February 1997, the accused is released by Cameroonian court. The accused is re-arrested at the behest of the Prosecutor who referred to rule 40 (provisional detention).

On 6 May 1997, the accused first received reasons for detention from Prosecution.

On 22 October 1997, an indictment is submitted to ICTR Judge.

On 23 October 1997, the indictment is confirmed.

Therefore, the defence contends the accused was detained at the behest of the Prosecutor for 20 months prior to transfer with no formal indictment.

In relation to the events the Prosecution contend:

On 15 April 1996, the accused is detained *at the behest of the Rwandan and Belgian governments.*

On 21 February 1997, the accused released by Cameroonian court after rejecting request for extradition by the Rwandan government. The decision did not mention the ICTR as a party.

On March 3 1997, the Prosecutor, pursuant to rule 40 (*bis*), requests the transfer of accused to Arusha.

On 22 October 1997, the indictment is submitted to ICTR Judge.

On 23 October 1997, the indictment is confirmed.

On 19 November 1997, the accused is transferred to Arusha.

On 23 February 1998, the accused has his initial appearance.

Although the Cameroonian authorities were very slow to respond to the transfer request however, this was out of the Prosecutor's control. **[page 4]**

DELIBERATIONS

In their entirety, the Defence and Prosecution submissions raise a number of questions relating to the interpretation of the Statute and Rules and the Trial Chamber's power to grant certain relief. However, if the Trial Chamber finds that the Defence has failed to prove violation of the accused rights, then the Trial Chamber need not address the jurisprudential questions which flow from such a violation.

Chronology of Events:

The Trial Chamber considers that there are two fundamental stages during which the Defence must show a violation of the accused rights under the jurisdiction of the Tribunal:

1.   *The period between the arrest on 15 April 1996 and the transfer request on 3 March 1997.*

The Defence claims that the accused was initially arrested at the request of the Prosecution. The Prosecution claims that the accused was initially detained at the behest of the Rwandan and Belgian governments. The Defence has provided no evidence to support its version. Conversely, a letter dated 15 October 1996 from the Prosecutor to the accused indicates that the Prosecution version is correct in stating that "Cameroonian authorities arrested 12 individuals from Rwanda on the basis of international warrants of arrest issued by the Public Prosecutor's Offices in Kigali and Belgium." (Defence exhibit at p. 8). The Defence did not challenge the accuracy of this document in its written motion and failed to substantiate its objection to this factual assertion during the hearing. The Defence objected during the Prosecution submission which relied upon this document. However, despite being invited to address the matter in reply, it failed to do so (Transcript at p. 60). In the absence of any other evidence, the Trial Chamber accepts that the accused was arrested at the behest of the Rwandan and Belgian governments.

The Defence has provided no evidence to support its contention that the accused *remained* in detention due to a request by the Prosecutor while he was in Cameroon prior to 21 February 1997. Although it is clear that for a certain period the Prosecutor was interested in investigating the accused. On the 17 April 1996 she requested that provisional measures under rule 40 be taken in relation the accused along with thirteen others, but, on the 16 May 1996 the Prosecutor informed Cameroon that she only wished to pursue the case against four of the detainees. The accused was not one of the four. This period is not undue delay, particularly considering that, in any event, the accused was being held at the request of the Rwandan and Belgian governments. On 21 February 1997, the Prosecution made a request under rule 40 for the provisional detention of the accused. (Defence exhibit, letter dated 16 May 1997 from James Stewart of Prosecution to President Kama). For these reasons the Trial Chamber finds that the Defence failed to show that the accused was kept in custody because of the Prosecutor, on the basis of a rule 40 request or for any other reason, before 21 February 1997.

It is the view of the Trial Chamber that detention under rule 40 for a period between 21 February 1997 and 3 March 1997, when the Tribunal made a rule 40 (*bis*) request, does not violate the rights of the accused under rule 40. [page 5]

2.   *The period between 3 March 1997 and the actual transfer of the accused on 19 November 1997.*

The Tribunal issued a request under rule 40 (*bis*) on 3 March 1997 requesting the Cameroonian authorities to proceed with the transfer of the accused to the Tribunal's Detention Facilities. (Decision Confirming the Indictment dated 23 October 1997, Defence exhibit at p. 46). The maximum time periods for provisional detention provided for under rule 40 (*bis*) take effect from *the day after the accused is transferred.* At the end of the maximum time periods provided for under rule 40 (*bis*), if the indictment has not been confirmed and an arrest warrant signed, the suspect shall be released or delivered to the authorities of the State to which the request was initially made. In the instant case the indictment of the accused was confirmed before the accused was even transferred. Accordingly, in relation to the time periods for provisional detention, there has been no violation of the defendant's rights under rule 40 (*bis*).

What the Prosecution did, if anything, after the rule 40 (*bis*) request was made in order to ensure that the accused was transferred is unclear. No credible evidence has been adduced. In any event, once the transfer request has been made the matter rests with the State authority to comply. In the instant case the Cameroonian government did not transfer the accused until November 1997. This cannot amount to a breach of the Rules by the Prosecution. Furthermore, as accepted by the Defence, there are no Rules which provide a remedy for a provisionally detained person before the host country has transferred him prior to the indictment and the warrant for arrest (Motion at p. 4).

It is regrettable that the Prosecution did not submit an indictment until 22 October 1997. However, the indictment has now been confirmed and the accused is legally before the Tribunal. In any event, under rule 40 (*bis*) the time in which the indictment must be submitted does not start to run until the day after the accused is transferred. Again, in the instant case the indictment of the accused was confirmed before the accused was even transferred.

For the above reasons, the Trial Chamber finds that the Defence has not shown that the Prosecution violated the rights of the accused due to the length of detention or delay in transferring the accused.

Other Legal Issues

1.   *Was provisional detention justified?*

The Defence suggests that the provisional charges of conspiracy to commit genocide, direct and public incitement to commit genocide, and crimes against humanity, were totally different in form and nature from the confirmed indictment and, therefore, the provisional charges were unnecessary and illegal. This position is without merit. The Defence is wrong to claim that the provisional charges were *totally different in form and nature.* The fact that the indictment contained different information merely reflects the process of investigation and Prosecutorial discretion. Evidently, the Prosecution satisfied Honourable Judge Aspegren that there was a reliable and consistent body of material which tends to show that the suspect may have committed a crime over which the Tribunal has jurisdiction. Accordingly, the Defence has not shown that the provisional charges submitted by the Prosecution were merely aimed at keeping the suspect in custody indefinitely. [page 6]

2.   *Did the Prosecutor discriminate against the accused?*

The Defence assert that the accused was intentionally discriminated against because the Prosecution transferred some accused from Cameroon but left others there. This position is without merit. The Prosecutor may exercise her valid discretion regarding persons against whom she wishes to proceed. The Defence has adduced no evidence which illustrates an act of the Prosecution which could be considered outside the realms of Prosecutorial discretion.

3.   *Is rule 40 (bis) valid?*

Rule 40 (*bis*) is valid; it does not contradict articles 17-20 but compliments them. Nowhere in articles 17-20 is it mandated that an indictment must be confirmed before a suspect can be provisionally detained. Rule 40 (*bis*) was properly created during a plenary session as provided under article 14 of the Statute and rule 6 of the Rules. Further, although rule 40 (*bis*) is a complex and flexible rule, the Defence did not pinpoint which sections of rule 40 (*bis*) it considers to be *ultra vires*, or which parts of articles 17-20 are violated by rule 40 (*bis*).

FOR ALL THE ABOVE REASONS, THIS TRIAL CHAMBER

DISMISSES the Defence motion.

Arusha, 17 November 1998

William H. Sekule
Presiding Judge

Yakov A. Ostrovsky
Judge

Tafazzal H. Khan
Judge

International Criminal Tribunal for the Prosecution of Persons Responsible for Genocide and Other Serious Violations of International Humanitarian Law Committed in the Territory of Rwanda and Rwandan Citizens responsible for genocide and other such violations committed in the territory of neighbouring States between 1 January and 31 December 1994	Case No:	ICTR-97-19-AR72
	Date:	3 November 1999
	Original:	English

IN THE APPEALS CHAMBER

Before: **Judge Gabrielle Kirk McDonald, Presiding**
                    Judge Mohamed Shahabuddeen
                    Judge Lal Chand Vohrah
                    Judge Wang Tieya
                    Judge Rafael Nieto-Navia

Registrar: **Mr. Agwu U. Okali**

Decision of: **3 November 1999**

JEAN-BOSCO BARAYAGWIZA

v.

THE PROSECUTOR

DECISION

Counsel for the Appellant:
    Mr. Justry P.L. Nyaberi

The Office of the Prosecutor:
    Mr. Mohamed C. Othman
    Mr. N. Sankara Menon
    Mr. Mathias Marcussen

Index

[page 3] I. INTRODUCTION

1.   The Appeals Chamber of the International Criminal Tribunal for the Prosecution of Persons Responsible for Genocide and Other Serious Violations of International Humanitarian Law Committed in the Territory of Rwanda and Rwandan Citizens responsible for genocide and other such violations committed in the territory of neighbouring States, between 1 January and 31 December 1994 ("the Appeals Chamber" and "The Tribunal" respectively) is seized of an appeal lodged by Jean-Bosco Barayagwiza ("the Appellant") against the "Decision on the Extremely Urgent Motion by the Defence for Orders to Review and/or Nullify the Arrest and Provisional Detention of the Suspect" of Trial Chamber II of 17 November 1998 ("the Decision")[1]. By Order dated 5 February 1999, the appeal was held admissible[2]. On 19 October 1999, the Appellant filed a Notice to Appeal seeking to disqualify certain Judges of the Trial Chamber from sitting on his case ("19 October 1999 Notice of Appeal"). On 26 October 1999, the Appellant filed an additional Notice of Appeal concerning a request of the Prosecutor to amend the indictment against the Appellant ("26 October 1999 Notice of Appeal").

2.   There are several areas of contention between the parties. The primary dispute concerns the arrest and detention of the Appellant during a nineteen-month period between 15 April 1996, when he was initially detained, and 19 November 1997, when he was transferred to the Tribunal's detention unit pursuant to Rule 40*bis* of the Tribunal's Rules of Procedure and Evidence ("the Rules")[3]. The secondary areas of dispute concern: 1) the Appellant's right to be informed promptly of the charges against him; 2) the Appellant's right to challenge the legality of his arrest and detention; 3) the delay between the Tribunal's request for the transfer of the Appellant form Cameroon and his actual transfer; 4) the length of the Appellant's provisional detention; and 5) the delay between the Appellant's arrival at the Tribunal's detention unit and his initial appearance. **[page 4]**

3. The accused made his initial appearance before Trial Chamber II on 23 February 1998. On 24 February 1998, the Appellant filed a motion seeking to nullify his arrest and detention[4]. Trial Chamber II heard the oral arguments of the parties on 11 September 1998 and rendered its Decision on 17 November 1998[5].

4.   The dispute between the parties initially concerns the issue of under what authority the accused was detained. Therefore, the sequence of events since the arrest of the accused on 15 April 1996, including the lengthy procedural history of the case, merits detailed recitation. Consequently, we begin with the following chronology[6].

5.   On 15 April 1996, the authorities of Cameroon arrested and detained the Appellant and several other suspects[7] on suspicion of having committed genocide and crimes against humanity in Rwanda in 1994[8]. On 17 April 1996, the Prosecutor requested that provisional measures pursuant to Rule 40 be

---

[1]   Prosecutor v. Barayagwiza, *Decision on the Extremely Urgent Motion by the Defence for Orders to Review and/or Nullify the Arrest and Provisional Detention of the Suspect* ("Decision"), Case No. ICTR-97-19-1, undated but filed on 17 November 1998. See also Prosecutor v. Barayagwiza, *Corrigendum*, Case No. ICTR-97-19-1, 24 November 1998.

[2]   Prosecutor v. Barayagwiza, *Decision and Scheduling Order* ("*5 February 1999 Scheduling Order*"), Case No. ICTR-97-19-AR72, 5 February 1999.

[3]   In the interim, the indictment was confirmed on 23 October 1997. Not all of this nineteen-month period of provisional detention is attributable to the Tribunal, as will be discussed, *infra*.

[4]   Prosecutor v. Barayagwiza, *Extremely Urgent Motion by the Defence for Orders for Review and/or Nullify the Arrest and Provisional Detention of the Suspect* ("*Extremely Urgent Motion*"), Case No. ICTR-97-19-1, dated 19 February 1998, filed 24 February 1998.

[5]   See footnote 1. The Prosecutor did not file a Response to the *Extremely Urgent Motion*. Prosecutor v. Barayagwiza, *Transcript*, 11 September 1997 at p. 8.

[6]   Appendix A contains most of the information that follows in the form of a timeline.

[7]   It is unclear from the record precisely how many individuals were arrested, but it was between 12 and 14, including the Appellant.

[8]   *Decision* at p. 4. The Appellant asserts in the *Extremely Urgent Motion* that he was arrested and detained at the behest of the Prosecutor, while the Prosecutor claimed that the Cameroon authorities arrested and detained the Appellant at the behest of the Belgian and Rwandan authorities. See Prosecutor v. Barayagwiza, *Prosecutor's Provisional Memorial (Pursuant to the Scheduling Order of the Appeal Chamber made on 5 February 1999) ("Prosecutor's Provisional Memorial")*, Case No. ICTR-

taken in relation to the Appellant[9]. On 6 May 1996, the Prosecutor asked Cameroon for a three-week extension of the detention of all the suspects, including the Appellant[10]. However, on 16 May 1996, the Prosecutor informed Cameroon **[page 5]** that she only intended to pursue prosecutions against four of the detainees, *excluding* the Appellant[11].

6.   The Appellant asserts that on 31 May 1996, the Court of Appeal of Cameroon adjourned *sine die* consideration of Rwanda's extradition request, pursuant to a request to adjourn by the Deputy Director of Public Prosecution of the Court of Appeal of the Centre Province, Cameroon[12]. The Appellant claims that in making this request, the Deputy Director of Public Prosecution relied on Article 8(2) of the Statute[13].

7.   On 15 October 1996, responding to a letter from the Appellant complaining about his detention in Cameroon, the Prosecutor informed the Appellant that Cameroon was not holding him at her behest[14]. Shortly thereafter, the Court of Appeal of Cameroon recommenced the hearing on Rwanda's extradition request for the remaining suspects, including the Appellant. On 21 February 1997, the Court of Appeal of Cameroon rejected the Rwandan extradition request and ordered the release of the suspects, including the Appellant[15]. The same day, the Prosecutor made a request pursuant to Rule 40 for the provisional detention of the Appellant and the Appellant was immediately re-arrested pursuant to this Order[16]. The Prosecutor then requested an Order for arrest and transfer pursuant to Rule 40*bis* on 24 February 1997[17] and on 3 March 1997, Judge Aspegren signed an Order to that effect[18]. The Appellant was not transferred pursuant to this Order, however, **[page 6]** until 19 November 1997[19].

97-19-1, dated 16 February 1999, filed 23 February 1999 at para. 3. The Trial Chamber found that there was no evidence supporting the Appellant's claim and held that he had been arrested and detained on the basis of requests from Rwanda and Belgium. *Decision* at p. 4. We note, however, that although the record makes references to the disposition of the Rwandan extradition request, there is no such reference to the disposition of the Belgian extradition request. The Appellant asserts that Belgium never made such an extradition request and that only Rwanda had requested his extradition. See <u>Prosecutor v. Barayagwiza</u>, *Rejoinder to the Prosecutor's Provisional Memorial filed on 22 February 1999 ("Rejoinder")*, Case No. ICTR-97-19-72(A), 11 March 1999 (English version filed 9 July 1999), at para. 3. For our purposes, it is unnecessary to consider the disposition of the Belgian extradition request – if indeed there was one.

[9]   *Decision* at p. 4.

[10]   See 15 October 1996 letter from the Prosecutor to the Appellant (and others), attached as Annex 1 ("*15 October 1996 letter*") to <u>Prosecutor v. Barayagwiza</u>, *The Appellant's Reply to Prosecutor's Response Pursuant to the Scheduling Order of 3rd June 1999 ("Appellant's Reply")*, Case No. ICTR-96-19-A, 2 July 1999.

[11]   *Decision* at p. 4.

[12]   <u>Prosecutor v. Barayagwiza</u>, *Amended Version of Appellant's Brief ("Amended Brief")*, Case No. ICTR-97-19-72, dated 23 February 1999, English Version filed 13 April 1999 at p. 2, para. 7.

[13]   *ibid.*

[14]   *See 15 October 1996 letter.* See also *Prosecutor's Provisional Memorial* at para. 6.

[15]   *Ibid.* at para. 7.

[16]   <u>Prosecutor v. Barayagwiza</u>, *Prosecutor's Response Pursuant to Scheduling Order of 3 June 1999 ("Prosecutor's Response")*, Case No. ICTR-96-19-A, 22 June 1999, at para. 10. See also Annexes 2, 3 and 4 attached thereto. It is unclear from the record what exactly transpired between 21 February 1997, when the Cameroon Court of Appeal ordered the Appellant's release, and 24 February 1997, when the Appellant was rearrested pursuant to the Tribunal's Rule 40 Order. However, the Appeals Chamber takes judicial notice of the fact that 21 February 1997 was a Friday and 24 February 1997 was a Monday. Moreover, the record does not seem to include the Rule 40 request or the resulting Order. However, in a letter to the Registrar requesting the transfer and provisional detention of the Appellant, the Prosecutor states: "Until Friday last week, the two suspects concerned were in detention in the Republic of Cameroon pursuant to a request for extradition by the Republic of Rwanda. On Friday 21 February 1997, a Cameroon court ordered their immediate release following a refusal of the extradition request. However, *I was able to secure a continuation of their detention by means of a request to the Republic of Cameroon under Rule 40'*. See Annex 3 to *Prosecutor's Response* (emphasis added).

[17]   *Ibid.*

[18]   *Ibid.* The Rule 40*bis* Order was filed on 4 March 1997. See <u>Prosecutor v. Barayagwiza</u> *Ordonnance aux fins de transfert et de placement en detention provisoire (Article 40bis)*("*Rule 40bis Order*"), Case No. ICTR-97-19-DP, 3 March 1997, attached as Annex 5 to *Prosecutor's Response. The Rule 40bis Order* states at p. 4: "THE TRIBUNAL, in accordance with Rule 40*bis* of the Rules... REQUESTS the Prosecutor to submit the indictment against Jean Bosco Barayagwiza before the expiration of the said 30-day limit of the provisional detention". See *Prosecutor's Response*, Annex 5. The Appellant also asserts that he was not shown any authentic documents relating to his arrest and detention until 6 May 1997. *Amended Brief*, at p. 4. However, the Appellant also acknowledges that on 10 March 1997, the Deputy Director of Prosecutions of the Court of Appeal of the Centre Province of Cameroon showed him "photocopies of documents supposed to have been sent by the ICTR for [his] transfer and detention". *Ibid.*

[19]   *Decision* at pp. 3, 5.

8.   While awaiting transfer, the Appellant filed a *writ of habeas corpus* on 29 September 1997[20]. The Trial Chamber never considered this application[21].

9.   The President of Cameroon issued a Presidential Decree on 21 October 1997, authorising the transfer of the Appellant to the Tribunal's detention unit[22]. On 22 October 1997, the Prosecutor submitted the indictment for confirmation, and on 23 October 1997, Judge Aspegren confirmed the indictment[23], and issued a Warrant of Arrest and Order for Surrender addressed to the Government of Cameroon[24]. The Appellant was not transferred to the Tribunal's detention unit, however, until 19 November 1997 and his initial appearance did not take place until 23 February 1998[25].

9.   On 24 February 1998, the Appellant filed the Extremely Urgent Motion seeking to have his arrest and detention nullified[26]. The arguments of the parties were heard on 11 September 1998[27]. Trial Chamber II, in its Decision of 17 November 1998, dismissed the Extremely Urgent Motion *in toto*. In rejecting the arguments put forward by the Appellant in the Extremely Urgent Motion, the Trial Chamber made several findings. First, the Trial **[page 7]** Chamber held that the Appellant was initially arrested at the behest of Rwanda and Belgium and not at the behest of the Prosecutor[28]. Second, the Trial Chamber found that the period of detention under Rule 40 from 21 February until 3 March 1997 did not violate the Appellant's rights under Rule 40[29]. Third, the Trial Chamber found that the Appellant had failed to show that the Prosecutor had violated the rights of the Appellant with respect to the length of his provisional detention or the delay in transferring the Appellant to the Tribunal's detention unit[30]. Fourth, the Trial Chamber held that Rule 40*bis* does not apply until the actual transfer of the suspect to the Tribunal's detention unit[31]. Fifth, the Trial Chamber concluded that the provisional detention of the Appellant was legally justified[32]. Sixth, the Trial Chamber found that when the Prosecutor opted to proceed against some of the individuals detained with the Appellant, but excluding the Appellant, the Prosecutor was exercising prosecutorial discretion and was not discriminating against the Appellant[33]. Finally, the Trial Chamber held that Rule 40*bis* is valid and does not contradict any provisions of the Statute[34]. On 4 December 1998, the Appellant filed a Notice of Appeal against the Decision[35] and ten days later the Prosecution filed its Response[36].

---

[20]   This *writ* was not addressed to a specific Trial Chamber. Prosecutor v. Barayagwiza, *Extremely Urgent Motion by the Counsel for the Suspect for Orders for Immediate Release of Jean Bosco Barayagwiza*, Case No. 97-19-I, 29 September 1997. Attached as Annex 12 to *Appellant's Reply*.

[21]   See discussion at section IV.B.3., *infra*.

[22]   See Annex 5 to *Appellant's Reply*.

[23]   *Decision* at pp. 2, 5. In noting the delay between the Rule 40*bis* Order filed on 4 March 1997 and the submission of the indictment for confirmation on 22 October 1997, the Trial Chamber stated: "It is regrettable that the Prosecution did not submit an indictment until 22 October 1997". *Ibid.* at p. 5.

[24]   See Annex 4 to *Prosecutor's Response*.

[25]   *Decision* at p. 2. One other event occurring *prior* to the Appellant's initial appearance is worthy of note. On 11 March 1997, the Appellant made an application for Defence Counsel to be assigned to him. According to the Prosecutor, the Appellant was not assigned Defence Counsel until 5 December 1997. See *Prosecutor's Response*, at para. 19 and Annexes 6 and 7 attached thereto. Notwithstanding the fact that the Appellant was not formally assigned Defence Counsel until 5 December 1997, 16 days after his transfer to the Tribunal's detention unit, there are documents in the record that bear the name and signature of the Appellant's Counsel, Mr. Justry P.L. Nyaberi, prior to that date. It is unclear from the record under what authority Mr. Nyaberi was acting prior to his formal assignment as the Appellant's Counsel on 5 December 1997.

[26]   *Extremely Urgent Motion*. See also footnote 5, *supra*.

[27]   *Decision* at p. 2. See also footnote 5, *supra*.

[28]   *Ibid.* at p. 4.

[29]   *Ibid.*

[30]   *Ibid.* at p. 5.

[31]   *Ibid.*

[32]   *Ibid.*

[33]   *Ibid.* at p. 6.

[34]   *Ibid.*

[35]   Prosecutor v. Barayagwiza, *Notification of Appeal of Decision of Trial Chamber II, Case No. ICTR-97-19-1*, dated 27 November 1998, filed 4 December 1998. The Appeals Chamber deemed the Appellant's Notice of Appeal to be filed in a timely manner in the *5 February 1999 Scheduling Order*.

[36]   Prosecutor v. Barayagwiza, *Prosecutor's Response to Defence's Appeal of the Decision of Trial Chamber II on the Extremely Urgent Motion by the Defence for Orders to Review and/or Nullify the Arrest and Provisional Detention of the Suspect (17 November 1998)*, Case No. ICTR-97-19-1, 14 December 1998. Both parties subsequently filed briefs. See Prosecutor

11. The Appeals Chamber considered the Appellant's appeal and found that the Decision dismissed an objection based on the lack of personal jurisdiction over the accused and, therefore, an appeal lies as of right under Sub-rule 72(D). Consequently, a Decision and Scheduling Order was issued on 5 February 1999[37], and the parties submitted additional **[page 8]** briefs[38]. Notwithstanding these additional submissions by the parties, however, the Appeals Chamber determined that additional information was required to decide the appeal. Consequently, a Scheduling Order was filed on 3 June 1999[39], directing the Prosecutor[40] to specifically address the following six questions and provide documentation in support thereof:

1) Whether the Appellant was held in Cameroon for any period between 21 February 1997 and 19 November 1997 at the request of the Tribunal, and if so, what effect did this detention have in relation to personal jurisdiction.

2) Whether the Appellant was held in Cameroon for any period between 23 February 1998 and 11 September 1998 at the request of the Tribunal, and if so, what effect did this detention have in regard to personal jurisdiction.

3) The reason for any delay between the request for transfer and the actual transfer.

4) The reason for any delay between the transfer of the Appellant to the Tribunal and his initial appearance.

5) The reason for any delay between the initial appearance of the Appellant and the hearing on the Appellant's urgent motion.

6) The disposition of the *writ of habeas corpus* that the Appellant asserts that he filed on 2 October 1997[41].

12. The Prosecutor filed her Response to the 3 June 1999 Scheduling Order on 22 June 1999[42], and the Appellant filed his Reply on 2 July 1999[43]. The submissions of the parties in response to these questions are set forth in section II.C., *infra*. **[page 9]**

---

v. Barayagwiza, *Memorandum of Appeal*, Case No. ICTR-97-19-1, dated 27 November 1998, filed 10 December 1998; Prosecutor v. Barayagwiza, *Prosecutor's Motion to Reject the Defence Appeal of the Decision of Trial Chamber II ("Prosecutor's Motion")*, Case No. ICTR-97-19-I, 18 December 1998; Prosecutor v. Barayagwiza, *The Defence Memorial in Support of the Accused Person's Appeal of the Decision of Trial Chamber II on the Extremely Urgent Motion by the Defence for Orders to Review and/or Nullify the Arrest and Provisional Detention of the Accused ("Defence Memorial")*, Case No. ICTR-97-19-1, 2 February 1999; and Prosecutor v. Barayagwiza, *Rejoinder to the Prosecutor's Response to the Defence's Appeal ("Rejoinder")*, Case No. ICTR-97-19-1, dated 17 December 1998, filed 4 April 1999.

37   5 February 1999 *Scheduling Order*.

38   Prosecutor v. Barayagwiza, *Defence Written Brief in Compliance of the "Decision and Scheduling Order" of the Appeals Chamber dated 5 February 1999 ("Defence Written Brief")*, Case No. ICTR-97-19-1, 18 February 1999; *Amended Brief; and Prosecutor's Provisional Memorial.*

39   Barayagwiza v. The Prosecutor, *Scheduling Order ("3 June 1999 Scheduling Order")*, Case No. ICTR-97-19A, 3 June 1999.

40   Pursuant to the *3 June 1999 Scheduling Order*, the Appellant was given an opportunity to respond to the Prosecutor's submission.

41   *3 June 1999 Scheduling Order* at pp. 3-4. Although the Appellant asserted that he filed the *writ of habeas corpus* on 2 October 1997, the document was actually filed (as evidenced by the ICTR date-stamp) on 29 September 1997.

42   *Prosecutor's Response.*

43   *Appellant's Reply.*

II. THE APPEAL

A. The Appellant

13.   As noted *supra*[44], the Appellant has submitted numerous documents for consideration with respect to his arrest and detention. The main arguments as advanced by the Appellant are consolidated and briefly summarised below.

14.   First, the Appellant asserts that the Trial Chamber erred in constructing a "Chronology of Events" without a proper basis or finding. According to the Appellant, the Trial Chamber further erred in dividing the events into arbitrary categories with the consequence that the Trial Chamber considered the events in a fragmented form. This resulted in a failure to perceive the events in their totality[45].

15.   Second, the Appellant claims that the Trial Chamber erred in holding that the Appellant failed to provide evidence supporting his version of the arrest and detention. Thus, the Appellant contends, it was error for the Trial Chamber to conclude that the Appellant was arrested at the behest of the Rwandan and Belgian governments. Further, because the Trial Chamber found that the Appellant was detained at the behest of the Rwandan and Belgian authorities, the Trial Chamber erroneously held that the Defence had failed to show that the Prosecutor was responsible for the Appellant's being held in custody by the Cameroon authorities from 15 April 1996 until 21 February 1997[46].

16.   Third, the Appellant contends that the Trial Chamber erred in holding that the detention under Rule 40 between 21 February 1997 and 3 March 1997, when the Rule 40*bis* request was approved, does not constitute a violation of the Appellant's rights under Rule 40. Further, the Trial Chamber erred in holding that there is no remedy for a provisionally detained person before the detaining State has transferred him prior to the indictment and warrant for arrest[47]. **[page 10]**

17.   Fourth, the Appellant argues that the Trial Chamber erred in failing to declare that there was a breach of the Appellant's rights as a result of the Prosecutor's delay in presenting the indictment for confirmation by the Judge. Furthermore, the Appellant contends that the Trial Chamber erred in holding that the Appellant failed to show that the Prosecutor violated his rights due to the length of the detention or delay in transferring the Appellant. Similarly, the Appellant contends that the Trial Chamber erred in holding that the provisional charges and detention of the Appellant were justified under the circumstances[48].

18.   Fifth, with respect to the effect of the detention on the Tribunal's jurisdiction[49], the Appellant sets forth three arguments. The Appellant's first argument is that the overall length of his detention, which was 22 months[50], was unreasonable, and therefore, unlawful. Consequently, the Tribunal no longer has personal jurisdiction over the accused[51]. The Appellant next asserts that the pre-transfer detention of the accused was "very oppressive, torturous and discriminative"[52]. As a result, the Appellant asserts that he

---

[44]   See, e.g., *Extremely Urgent Motion; Memorandum of Appeal; Defence Memorial; Amended Brief; Defence Written Brief; Rejoinder and Appellant's Reply*. In total, the Appellant raises more than 20 issues, most of which are repetitive or irrelevant.

[45]   *Defence Memorial* at p. 6, paras. 3-5.

[46]   *Ibid.* at pp. 6-7, paras. 6-11.

[47]   *Ibid.* at p. 8, paras. 15-17.

[48]   *Ibid.* at pp. 8-9, paras. 18-20.

[49]   The *5 February 1999 Scheduling Order* had specifically found that the Decision dismissed an objection based on the lack of personal jurisdiction over the accused and therefore, an appeal lies of right under Sub-rule 72(D). The *5 February 1999 Scheduling Order* requested the parties to brief the issue of whether the Appellant was unlawfully in the custody of the Tribunal before his transfer to the detention unit. However, in his submission pursuant to the *5 February 1999 Scheduling Order*, the *Defence Written Brief*, the Appellant closely linked his relief sought, immediate release from confinement, with the issue of personal jurisdiction. Consequently, this line of argument is briefly summarised.

[50]   From his arrest on 15 April 1996 until his initial appearance on 23 February 1998.

[51]   *Defence Written Brief* at paras. 12, 16.

[52]   *Ibid.* at para. 18.

is entitled to unconditional release[53]. Finally; the Appellant contends that his detention cannot be justified on the grounds of urgency. In this regard, the length of time the Appellant was provisionally detained without benefit of formal charges amounts to a "monstrous degree of prosecutorial indiscretion and apathy"[54].

19.   In conclusion, the Appellant requests the Appeals Chamber to quash the Trial Chamber Decision and unconditionally release the Appellant[55]. **[page 11]**

B. The Prosecutor

20.   In responding to the Appellant's arguments, the Prosecutor relies on three primary counter-arguments, which will be summarised. First, the Prosecutor submits that the Appellant was not in the custody of the Tribunal before his transfer on 19 November 1997, and consequently, no event taking place prior to that date violates the Statute or the Rules. The Prosecutor contends that her request under Rule 40 or Rule 40*bis* for the detention and transfer of the accused has no impact on this conclusion[56].

21.   In support of this argument, the Prosecutor contends that the Appellant was detained on 15 April 1996 at the instance of the Rwandan and Belgian governments[57]. Although the Prosecutor made a request on 17 April 1996 to Cameroon for provisional measures[58], the Prosecutor asserts that this request was "only superimposed on the pre-existing request of Rwanda and Belgium" for the detention of the Appellant[59].

22.   The Prosecutor further argues that the Tribunal does not have custody of a person pursuant to Rule 40*bis* until such person has actually been physically transferred to the Tribunal's detention unit. Although an Order pursuant to Rule 40*bis* was filed directing Cameroon to transfer the Appellant on 4 March 1997, the Appellant was not actually transferred until 19 November 1997. Consequently, the responsibility of the Prosecutor for any delay in bringing the Appellant to trial commences only after the Tribunal established custody of the Appellant on 19 November 1997[60].

23.   The Prosecutor argues that custody involves "care and control" and since the Appellant was not under the "care and control" of the Tribunal prior to his transfer, the Prosecutor is not responsible for any delay resulting from Cameroon's failure to promptly transfer the Appellant[61]. Furthermore, the Prosecutor asserts that Article 28 of the Statute strikes a delicate balance of distributing obligations between the Tribunal and States[62]. Under this arrangement, "neither entity is an agent or, *alter ego*, of the other: and the actions of the one **[page 12]** may not be imputed on the other just because they were carrying out duties apportioned to them under the Statute"[63].

24.   The Prosecutor acknowledges that although the "delay in this transfer is indeed long, there is no factual basis to impute the fault of it to the ICTR Prosecutor"[64]. She summarises this line of argument by concluding that since the Appellant was not in the custody of the Tribunal before his transfer to the Tribunal's detention unit on 19 November 1997, it follows that the legality of the detention of the Appellant while in the custody of Cameroon is a matter for the laws of Cameroon, and beyond the competence of the Appeals Chamber[65].

---

53   *Ibid.*
54   *Ibid.* at para. 22.
55   *Ibid.* at para. 25.
56   See *Prosecutor's Provisional Memorial* at paras. 26-39.
57   *Ibid.* at para. 27.
58   *Decision* at p. 4.
59   *Prosecutor's Provisional Memorial* at para. 29.
60   *Ibid.* at paras. 30-31.
61   *Ibid.* at paras. 35-36, citing to *Black's Law Dictionary.*
62   *Prosecutor's Provisional Memorial* at para. 37.
63   *Ibid.*
64   *Ibid.* at para. 31.
65   *Ibid.* at para. 39.

25.   The second principal argument of the Prosecution is that the Prosecutor's failure to request Cameroon to transfer the Appellant on 16 May 1996[66] does not give the Appellant "prescriptive claims against the Prosecutor's eventual prosecution"[67]. The thrust of this contention seeks to counter the argument[68] that the Prosecutor is somehow estopped from prosecuting the Appellant as the result of correspondence between the Prosecutor and both Cameroon[69] and the Appellant himself[70].

26.   The Prosecutor asserts that simply because at a certain stage of the investigation she communicated to the Appellant that she was not proceeding against him, this cannot have the effect of creating statutory or other limitations against prosecution for genocide and other serious violations of international humanitarian law[71]. Moreover, the Prosecutor argues that she cannot be barred from proceeding against an accused simply because she did not proceed with the prosecution at the first available opportunity[72]. Finally, the Prosecutor claims that her "abstention from proceeding against the Appellant-Defendant before 3 March 1997 was **[page 13]** due to on-going investigation"[73].

27.   The third central argument of the Prosecutor is that any violations suffered by the Appellant prior to his transfer to the Tribunal's detention unit have been cured by subsequent proceedings before the Tribunal, presumably the confirmation of the Appellant's indictment and his initial appearance[74].

28.   In conclusion, the Prosecution argues that there is no provision within the Statute that provides for the issuance of the order sought by the Appellant, and, in any event, the remedy sought by the Appellant is not warranted in the circumstances. In the event the Appeals Chamber finds a violation of the Appellant's rights, the Prosecutor suggests that the following remedies would be proper: 1) an Order for the expeditious trial of the Appellant; and/or 2) credit for the period of undue delay as part of the sentence, if the Appellant is found guilty, pursuant to Rule 101(D)[75].

C.   Arguments of the Parties Pursuant to the 3 June 1999 Scheduling Order

29.   With respect to the specific questions addressed to the Prosecutor in the 3 June 1999 Scheduling Order, the parties submitted the following answers.

1)   Whether the Appellant was held in Cameroon for any period between 21 February 1997 and 19 November 1997 at the request of the Tribunal, and if so, what effect did this detention have in relation to personal jurisdiction.

30.   On 21 February 1997, following the Decision of the Cameroon Court of Appeal to release the Appellant, the Prosecutor submitted a Rule 40 Request to detain the Appellant for the benefit of the Tribunal. Further, the Prosecutor submits that following the issuance of the Rule 40*bis* Order on 4 March 1997, Cameroon was obligated, pursuant to Article 28, to implement the Prosecutor's request. However, because the Tribunal did not have custody of the Appellant until his transfer on 19 November 1997, the Prosecutor contends that the Tribunal "could not regulate the conditions of detention or other matters regarding the **[page 14]** confinement of the accused"[76]. Nevertheless, the Prosecutor argues that between

---

[66]   On this day, four of the suspects arrested and detained with the Appellant were transferred to the Tribunal's detention unit pursuant to a request by the Prosecutor. See *Decision* at p. 4.

[67]   *Prosecutor's Provisional Memorial* at paras. 40-49.

[68]   A review of the record shows that this argument does not seem to be directly raised by the Appellant.

[69]   See text at para. 7, *supra*.

[70]   In a letter dated 15 October 1996, the Prosecutor communicated to the Appellant that she was not proceeding against him at that time. See text at footnote 14 and *Prosecutor's Provisional Memorial* at para. 40.

[71]   *Prosecutor's Provisional Memorial* at para. 41.

[72]   *Ibid.* at para. 42.

[73]   *Ibid.* at para. 43.

[74]   *Ibid.* at para. 44. The Prosecutor does not specify which subsequent proceedings cured the alleged violations.

[75]   *Ibid.* at para. 45.

[76]   *Prosecutor's Response* at para. 12.

21 February 1997 and 19 November 1997, 'there existed what could be described as joined or concurrent personal jurisdiction over the Appellant, the personal jurisdiction being shared between the Tribunal and Cameroon"[77].

31.   The Appellant contends that Cameroon was holding him at the behest of the Prosecutor during this entire period[78]. Furthermore, the Appellant argues that "[t]he only Cameroonian law applicable to him was the law concerning the extradition"[79]. Consequently, he argues that the issue of concurrent or joint personal jurisdiction by both the Tribunal and Cameroon is "fallacious, misleading and unacceptable"[80]. In addition, he asserts that, read in conjunction, Articles 19 and 28 of the Statute confer obligations upon the Detaining State only when the appropriate documents are supplied[81]. Since the Warrant of Arrest and Order for Surrender[82] was not signed by Judge Aspegren until 23 October 1997, the Appellant contends that his detention prior to that date was illegal, given that he was being held after 21 February 1997 on the basis of the Prosecutor's Rule 40 request[83].

2)   **Whether the Appellant was held in Cameroon for any period between 23 February 1998 and 11 September 1998 at the request of the Tribunal, and if so, what effect did this detention have in regard to personal jurisdiction.**

32.   The parties are in agreement that the Appellant was transferred to the Tribunal's detention unit on 19 November 1997, and consequently was not held by Cameroon at any period after that date[84]. **[page 15]**

3) The reason for any delay between the request for transfer and the actual transfer.

33.   The Prosecutor fails to give any reason for this delay. Rather, without further comment, the Prosecutor attributes to Cameroon the period of delay[85] between the request for transfer and the actual transfer[86].

34.   The Appellant contends that the Prosecutor "forgot about the matter and didn't really bother about the actual transfer of the suspect"[87]. He argues that since Cameroon had been holding him pursuant to the Tribunal's Rule 40*bis* Order, Cameroon had no further interest in him, other than to transfer him to the custody of the Tribunal. In support of his contentions in this regard, the Appellant advances several arguments. First, the Prosecutor did not submit the indictment for confirmation before the expiration of the 30-day limit of the provisional detention as requested by Judge Aspegren in the Rule 40*bis* Order[88]. Second, the Appellant asserts that the Prosecutor didn't make any contact with the authorities of Cameroon to provide for the transfer of the Appellant pursuant to the Rule 40*bis* Order. Third, the Prosecutor did not ensure that the Appellant's right to appear promptly before a Judge of the Tribunal was respected. Fourth, following the Rule 40*bis* Order, the Appellant claims, "[t]he Prosecutor didn't

---

[77]   *Ibid.* at para. 13.
[78]   *Appellant's Reply* at paras. 6-10. He also asserts that he was being held at the behest of the Prosecutor from 17 April 1996, when the first Rule 40 request relating to the Appellant was issued, until 15 October 1996, when the Prosecutor sent a letter to the Appellant, in which the Prosecutor informed him that she no longer had any interest in his detention. *Ibid.* at para. 6. See *15 October 1996 letter.*
[79]   *Ibid.* at para. 8.
[80]   *Ibid.*
[81]   *Ibid.* at para. 9.
[82]   Prosecutor v. Barayagwiza, *Warrant of Arrest and Order for Surrender ("Arrest Warrant")*, 23 October 1997, attached as Annex 4 to the *Appellant's Reply.*
[83]   *Appellant's Reply* at para. 9.
[84]   *Prosecutor' Response* at para. 14; *Appellant's Reply* at para. 11.
[85]   The delay, from 4 March 1997 until 19 November 1997, totaled 260 days.
[86]   *Prosecutor's Response* at para. 15. In a meager attempt to bolster this claim, the Prosecutor submits that long delays occurred in the transfer of other accused from Cameroon to the Tribunal's detention unit. See *Ibid.* at para. 16.
[87]   *Appellant's Reply* at para. 12.
[88]   See footnote 18, *supra.*

make any follow-up and didn't even show any interest"[89]. Fifth, the Appellant contends that the triggering mechanism in prompting his transfer was his filing of a *writ of habeas corpus*[90]. In conclusion, the Appellant rhetorically questions the Prosecutor, "How can she expect the Cameroonian authorities to be more interested [in his case] than her?" [sic][91]. **[page 16]**

4) The reason for any delay between the transfer of the Appellant to the Tribunal and his initial appearance.

35.   The Prosecutor contends that the Trial Chamber and the Registry have responsibility for scheduling the initial appearance of accused persons[92].

36.   While the Appellant acknowledges that the Registrar bears some responsibility for the delay[93], he argues that the Prosecutor "plays a big role in initiating of hearings" and plays a "key part in the process"[94]. The Appellant contends that the Prosecutor took no action to bring him before the Trial Chamber as quickly as possible. On the contrary, the Appellant asserts that the Prosecutor delayed seeking confirmation of the indictment and "caused the removal of the Defence's motion for Habeas Corpus from the hearing list on 31 October 1997 thus delaying further the appearance of the suspect before the Judges"[95].

5)   The reason for any delay between the initial appearance of the Appellant and the hearing on the Appellant's urgent motion.

37.   With respect to the delay between the initial appearance and the hearing on the Urgent Motion, the Prosecutor again disclaims any responsibility for scheduling matters, arguing that the Registry, in consultation with the Trial Chambers, maintains the docket[96]. The hearing on the Urgent Motion was originally docketed[97] for 14 May 1998[98]. However, on 12 May 1998, Counsel for the Appellant informed the Registry that he was not able to appear and defend his client at that time, because he had not been assigned co-counsel as he had requested and because the Tribunal had not paid his fees[99]. Consequently, the hearing was re-scheduled for 11 September 1998. **[page 17]**

6) The disposition of the *writ of habeas corpus* that the Appellant asserts that he filed on 2 October 1997[100].

38.   With respect to the disposition of the *writ of habeas corpus* filed by the Appellant on 2 October 1997[101], the Prosecutor replied as follows:

> 24.   The Prosecutor respectfully submits that following the filing of the *habeas corpus* on 2 October 1997 the President wrote the Appellant by letter of 8 October 1997, informing

---

[89]   *Appellant's Reply* at para. 12.

[90]   *Ibid.*

[91]   *Ibid.*

[92]   *Prosecutor's Response* at para. 17. In this regard, it should be noted that the delay between the Appellant's transfer, on 19 November 1997, and his initial appearance, on 23 February 1998, totaled 96 days. Moreover, the Prosecutor seems to rely on the fact that a Judicial Holiday from 15 December 1997 until 15 January 1998 should excuse delay in scheduling the Appellant's initial appearance during that 31 day period. See *Ibid.* at para. 20.

[93]   *Appellant's Reply* at para. 15.

[94]   *Ibid.* at para. 14.

[95]   *Ibid.*

[96]   *Prosecutor's Response* at para. 21.

[97]   Prosecutor v. Barayagwiza, *Scheduling Order*, Case No. ICTR-97-19-T, 9 March 1998.

[98]   This was 79 days after the Appellant's initial appearance.

[99]   See *Appellant's Reply* at paras. 16-17 and Annexes 6, 7, 8 and 9 thereto.

[100]   See footnote 41 with regard to the date.

[101]   *Ibid.*

him that the Office of the Prosecutor had informed him that an indictment would be ready shortly.

25.   The Prosecutor is not aware of any other disposition of the *writ of habeas corpus*[102].

39.   In fact, the letter[103] referred to was written on 8 September 1997 – prior to the filing of the *writ of habeas corpus* – and the Appellant contends that it was precisely this letter which prompted him to file the *writ of habeas corpus*. Moreover, the Appellant asserts that he was informed that the hearing on the *writ of habeas corpus* was to be held on 31 October 1997[104]. However, directly contradicting the claim of the Prosecutor, the Appellant asserts that "the Registry without the consent of the Defence removed the hearing of the motion from the calendar only because the Prosecution promised to issue the indictment soon"[105]. Moreover, the Appellant claims that the indictment was filed and confirmed on 22 October 1997 and 23 October 1997, respectively, in order to pre-empt the hearing on the *writ of habeas corpus*[106]. The Appellant is of the view that the *writ of habeas corpus* is still pending, since the Trial Chamber has not heard it, notwithstanding the fact that it was filed on 29 September 1997. **[page 18]**

III.   APPLICABLE AND AUTHORITATIVE PROVISIONS

40.   The relevant parts of the applicable Articles of the Statute, Rules of the Tribunal and international human rights treaties are set forth below for ease of reference. The Report of the U.N. Secretary-General[107] establishes the sources of law for the Tribunal. The International Covenant on Civil and Political Rights is part of general international law and is applied on that basis. Regional human rights treaties, such as the European Convention on Human Rights and the American Convention on Human Rights, and the jurisprudence developed thereunder, are persuasive authority which may be of assistance in applying and interpreting the Tribunal's applicable law. Thus, they are not binding of their own accord on the Tribunal. They are, however, authoritative as evidence of international custom.

A.   The Statute

Article 8
Concurrent Jurisdiction

1.   The International Tribunal for Rwanda and national courts shall have concurrent jurisdiction to prosecute persons for serious violations of international humanitarian law committed in the territory of Rwanda and Rwandan citizens for such violations committed in the territory of neighbouring States, between 1 January 1994 and 31 December 1994.

---

[102]   *Prosecutor's Response* at paras. 24-25.

[103]   *Prosecutor's Response*, Annex 12. The letter from President Kama to the Appellant's Counsel is five sentences long, and substantively consists of the following: "I acknowledge receipt of your letter dated 1 September 1997 concerning the detention of Mr. Jean Bosco Barayagwiza by Cameroonian authorities, and I take note of the fact that the situation is indeed a matter for concern. I have already reminded the Prosecutor of the need to establish as soon as possible an indictment against Mr. Jean Bosco Barayagwiza, if she still intends to prosecute him. Only recently, Mr. Bernard Muna, the Deputy Prosecutor, reassured me that an indictment against Mr. Jean Bosco Barayagwiza should soon be submitted to a Judge for review. Such being the case, I recognise your right to submit to the Tribunal a motion in due form on this matter. The motion will then be referred to one of the Tribunal's Chambers for consideration."

[104]   *Appellant's Reply* at para. 18.

[105]   *Ibid.*

[106]   *Ibid.* at para. 21.

[107]   Report of the Secretary-General Pursuant to Paragraph 5 of Security Council Resolution 955 (1994), U.N. Doc. S/1995/134 at paras. 11-12. See also Report of the Secretary-General Pursuant to Paragraph 2 of Security Council Resolution 808, U.N. Doc. S/25704 and Add. 1 (22 February 1993), establishing the International Criminal Tribunal for the former Yugoslavia at paras. 33-35.

2.   The International Tribunal for Rwanda shall have primacy over the national courts of all States. At any stage of the procedure, the International Tribunal for Rwanda may formally request national courts to defer to its competence in accordance with the present Statute and Rules of Procedure and Evidence of the International Tribunal for Rwanda.

Article 17
Investigation and Preparation of Indictment

1.   [...]

2.   The Prosecutor shall have the power to question suspects, victims and witnesses, to collect evidence and to conduct on-site investigations. In carrying out these tasks, the Prosecutor may, as appropriate, seek the assistance of the State authorities concerned.

3.   [...] **[page 19]**

4.   Upon a determination that a prima facie case exists, the Prosecutor shall prepare an Indictment containing a concise statement of the facts and the crime or crimes with which the accused is charged under the present Statute. The Indictment shall be transmitted to a Judge of the Trial Chamber.

Article 20
Rights of the accused

1.   [...]

2.   [...]

3.   [...]

4.   In the determination of any charge against the accused pursuant to the present statute, the accused shall be entitled to the following minimum guarantees, in full equality:

  (a)   To be informed promptly and in detail in a language in which he or she understands of the nature and cause of the charge against him or her;

  (b)   [...]

  (c)   To be tried without undue delay;

  (d)   [...]

  (e)   [...]

  (f)   [...]

  (g)   [...]

Article 24
Appellate Proceedings

1.   [...]

2.   The Appeals Chamber may affirm, reverse or revise the decisions taken by the Trial Chambers.

Article 28
Cooperation and Judicial Assistance

1.   States shall cooperate with the International Tribunal for Rwanda in the investigation and prosecution of persons accused of committing serious violations of international humanitarian law. **[page 20]**

2.   States shall comply without undue delay with any request for assistance or an order issued by a Trial Chamber, including, but not limited to:

(a)   The identification and location of persons;

(b)   [...]

(c)   [...]

(d)   The arrest or detention of persons;

(e)   The surrender or transfer of the accused to the International Tribunal for Rwanda.

B. The Rules

Rule 2
Definitions

[...]

Accused: A person against whom one or more counts in an indictment have been confirmed in accordance with Rule 47.

[...]

Suspect: A person concerning whom the Prosecutor possesses reliable information which tends to show that he may have committed a crime over which the Tribunal has jurisdiction.

[...]

Rule 40
Provisional Measures

(A)   In case of urgency, the Prosecutor may request any State:

(i)   to arrest a suspect and place him in custody;

(ii)   to seize all physical evidence;

(iii)   to take all necessary measures to prevent the escape of a suspect or an accused, injury to or intimidation of a victim or witness, or the destruction of evidence.

The state concerned shall comply forthwith, in accordance with Article 28 of the Statute.

(B)   Upon showing that a major impediment does not allow the State to keep the suspect in custody or to take all necessary measures to prevent his escape, the Prosecutor may apply to a Judge designated by the President for an order to transfer the suspect to the **[page 21]** seat of the Tribunal or to such other place as the Bureau may decide, and to detain him provisionally. After consultation with the Prosecutor and the Registrar, the transfer shall be arranged between the State authorities concerned, the authorities of the host Country of the Tribunal and the Registrar.

(C)   In the cases referred to in paragraph B, the suspect shall, from the moment of his transfer, enjoy all the rights provided for in Rule 42, and may apply for review to a Trial Chamber of the Tribunal. The Chamber, after hearing the Prosecutor, shall rule upon the application.

(D)   The suspect shall be released if (i) the Chamber so rules, or (ii) the Prosecutor fails to issue an indictment within twenty days of the transfer.

Rule 40*bis*
Transfer and Provisional Detention of Suspects

(A)   In the conduct of an investigation, the Prosecutor may transmit to the Registrar, for an order by a Judge assigned pursuant to Rule 28[108], a request for the transfer to and provisional detention of a suspect in the premises of the detention unit of the Tribunal. This request shall indicate the

---

[108]   Rule 28 governs Duty Judges.

grounds upon which the request is made and, unless the Prosecutor wishes only to question the suspect, shall include a provisional charge and a summary of the material upon which the Prosecutor relies.

(B)   The Judge shall order the transfer and provisional detention of the suspect if the following conditions are met:

(i)   the Prosecutor has requested a State to arrest the suspect and to place him in custody, in accordance with Rule 40, or the suspect is otherwise detained by a State;

(ii)   after hearing the Prosecutor, the Judge considers that there is a reliable and consistent body of material which tends to show that the suspect may have committed a crime over which the Tribunal has jurisdiction; and

(iii) the Judge considers provisional detention to be a necessary measure to prevent the escape of the suspect, physical or mental injury to or intimidation of a victim or witness or the destruction of evidence, or to be otherwise necessary for the conduct of the investigation.

(C)   The provisional detention of the suspect may be ordered for a period not exceeding 30 days from the day after the transfer of the suspect to the detention unit of the Tribunal.

(D)   The order for the transfer and provisional detention of the suspect shall be signed by the Judge and bear the seal of the Tribunal. The order shall set forth the basis of the request made by the Prosecutor under Sub-Rule (A), including the provisional charge, and shall state the Judge's grounds for making the order, having regard to Sub-Rule (B). The order shall also specify the initial time limit for the provisional detention of the suspect, **[page 22]** and be accompanied by a statement of the rights of a suspect, as specified in this Rule and in Rules 42[109] and 43[110].

(E)   As soon as possible, copies of the order and of the request by the Prosecutor are served upon the suspect and his counsel by the Registrar.

(F)   At the end of the period of detention, at the Prosecutor's request indicating the grounds upon which it is made and if warranted by the needs of the investigation, the Judge who made the initial order, or another Judge of the same Trial Chamber, may decide, subsequent to an *inter partes* hearing, to extend the provisional detention for a period not exceeding 30 days.

(G)   At the end of that extension, at the Prosecutor's request indicating the grounds upon which it is made and if warranted by special circumstances, the Judge who made the initial order, or another Judge of the same Trial Chamber, may decide, subsequent to an *inter partes* hearing, to extend the detention for a further period not exceeding 30 days.

(H)   The total period of provisional detention shall in no case exceed 90 days, at the end of which, in the event the indictment has not been confirmed and an arrest warrant signed, the suspect shall be released or, if appropriate, be delivered to the authorities of the State to which the request was initially made.

(I)   The provisions in Rules 55(B) to 59 shall apply *mutatis mutandis* to the execution of the order for the transfer and provisional detention of the suspect.

(J)   After his transfer to the seat of the Tribunal, the suspect, assisted by his counsel, shall be brought, without delay, before the Judge who made the initial order, or another Judge of the same Trial Chamber, who shall ensure that his rights are respected.

(K)   During detention, the Prosecutor, the suspect or his counsel may submit to the Trial Chamber of which the Judge who made the initial order is a member, all applications relative to the propriety of provisional detention or to the suspect's release.

---

[109]   Rule 42 governs the Rights of Suspects during Investigation.
[110]   Rule 43 governs Recording Questioning of Suspects.

(L)   Without prejudice to Sub-Rules (C) to (H), the Rules relating to the detention on remand of accused persons shall apply *mutatis mutandis* to the provisional detention of persons under this Rule.

Rule 58
National Extradition Provisions

The obligations laid down in Article 28 of the Statute shall prevail over any legal impediment to the surrender or transfer of the accused or of a witness to the Tribunal which may exist under the national law or extradition treaties of the State concerned. **[page 23]**

Rule 62
Initial Appearance of Accused

Upon his transfer to the Tribunal, the accused shall be brought before a Trial Chamber without delay, and shall be formally charged. The Trial Chamber shall:

  (i)   satisfy itself that the right of the accused to counsel is respected;

  (ii)   read or have the indictment read to the accused in a language he speaks and understands, and satisfy itself that the accused understands the indictment;

  (iii) call upon the accused to enter a plea of guilty or not guilty on each count; should the accused fail to do so, enter a plea of not guilty on his behalf;

  (iv)   in case of a plea of not guilty, instruct the Registrar to set a date for trial.

Rule 72
Preliminary Motions

(A)   Preliminary motions by either party shall be brought within sixty days following disclosure by the Prosecutor to the Defence of all material envisaged by Rule 66(A)(I)[111], and in any case before the hearing on the merits.

(B)   Preliminary motions by the accused are:

  i)   objections based on lack of jurisdiction;

  ii)   [...]

  iii)   [...]

  iv)   [...]

(C)   The Trial Chamber shall dispose of preliminary motions *in limine litis*.

(D)   Decisions on preliminary motions are without interlocutory appeal, save in the case of dismissal of an objection based on lack of jurisdiction, where an appeal will lie as of right.

(E)   Notice of Appeal envisaged in Sub-Rule (D) shall be filed within seven days from the impugned decision.

(F)   Failure to comply with the time-limits prescribed in this Rule shall constitute a waiver of the rights. The Trial Chamber may, however, grant relief from the waiver upon showing good cause. **[page 24]**

---

[111]   Rule 66 governs disclosure of materials by the Prosecutor, including all supporting material which accompanied the indictment when confirmation was sought and all prior statements obtained by the Prosecutor from the accused.

C. International Covenant on Civil and Political Rights[112]

Article 9

1.   Everyone has the right to liberty and security of person. No one shall be subjected to arbitrary arrest or detention. No one shall be deprived of his liberty except on such grounds and in accordance with such procedures as are established by law.

2.   Anyone who is arrested shall be informed, at the time of his arrest, of the reasons for his arrest and shall be promptly informed of any charges against him.

3.   Anyone arrested or detained on a criminal charge shall be brought promptly before a judge or other officer authorised by law to exercise judicial power and shall be entitled to trial within a reasonable time or to release. It shall not be a general rule that persons awaiting trial shall be detained in custody, but release may be subject to guarantees to appear for trial, at any other stage of the judicial proceedings, and, should occasion arise, for execution of the judgment.

4.   Anyone who is deprived of his liberty by arrest or detention shall be entitled to take proceedings before a court, in order that that court may decide without delay on the lawfulness of his detention and order his release if the detention is not lawful.

Article 14

1.   [...]

2.   [...]

3.   In the determination of any criminal charges against him, everyone shall be entitled to the following minimum guarantees, in full equality:

   (a)   To be informed promptly and in detail in a language which he understands of the nature and cause of the charge against him;

   (b)   [...]

   (c)   [...]

   (d)   [...]

   (e)   [...]

   (f)   [...]

   (g)   [...]

4.   [...]

5.   [...]

6.   [...]

7.   [...] **[page 25]**

D. European Convention on Human Rights[113]

Article 5

1.   Everyone has the right to liberty and security of person. No one shall be deprived of his liberty save in the following cases and in accordance with a procedure prescribed by law;

---

[112]   999 UNTS 171 (16 December 1966)("ICCPR").
[113]   213 UNTS 221 (4 November 1950)("ECHR").

(a)　[...]

(b)　[...]

(c)　the lawful arrest or detention of a person effected for the purpose of bringing him before the competent legal authority on reasonable suspicion of having committed an offence or when it is reasonably considered necessary to prevent his committing an offence or fleeing after having done so;

(d)　[...]

(e)　[...]

(f)　the lawful arrest or detention of a person against whom action is being taken with a view to deportation or extradition.

2.　Everyone who is arrested shall be informed promptly, in a language which he understands, of the reasons for his arrest and of any charge against him.

3.　Everyone arrested or detained in accordance with the provisions of paragraph 1(c) of this Article shall be brought before a judge or other officer authorised by law to exercise judicial power and shall be entitled to trial within a reasonable time or to release pending trial. Release may be conditioned by guarantees to appear for trial.

4.　Everyone who is deprived of his liberty by arrest or detention shall be entitled to take proceedings by which the lawfulness of his detention shall be decided speedily by a court and his release ordered if the detention is not lawful.

Article 6

1.　[...]

2.　[...]

3.　Everyone charged with a criminal offence has the following minimum rights:

(a)　to be informed promptly, in a language which he understands and in detail, of the nature and cause of the accusation against him; **[page 26]**

(b)　[...]

(c)　[...]

(d)　[...]

(e)　[...]

E. American Convention on Human Rights[114]

Article 7

1.　[...]

2.　[...]

3.　No one shall be subject to arbitrary arrest or detention.

4.　Anyone who is detained shall be informed of the reasons for his detention and shall be promptly notified of the charge or charges against him.

---

[114]　1144 UNTS 123 (22 November 1969)("ACHR").

5. Any person detained shall be brought promptly before judge or other law officer authorized by law to exercise judicial power and shall be entitled to trial within a reasonable time or to be released without prejudice to the continuation of the proceedings. His release may be subject to guarantees to assure his appearance for trial.

6. Anyone who is deprived of his liberty shall be entitled to recourse to a competent court, in order that the court may decide without delay on the lawfulness of his arrest or detention and order his release if the arrest or detention is unlawful. In states Parties whose law provides that anyone who believes himself to be threatened with deprivation of his liberty is entitled to recourse to a competent court in order that it may decide on the lawfulness of such threat, this remedy may not be restricted or abolished. The interested party or another person in his behalf is entitled to seek these remedies.

7. [...]

Article 8

1. Every person has the right to a hearing, with due guarantees and within a reasonable time, by a competent, independent, and impartial tribunal, previously established by law, in the substantiation of any accusation of a criminal nature made against him or for the determination of his rights and obligations of a civil, labor, fiscal, or any other nature.

2. Every person accused of a criminal offense has the right to be presumed innocent so long as his guilt has not been proven according to law. During the proceedings, every person is entitled, with full equality, to the following minimum guarantees:

    (a) [...]

    (b) prior notification in detail to the accused of the charges against him; **[page 27]**

    (c) [...]

    (d) [...]

    (e) [...]

    (f) [...]

    (g) [...]

    (h) [...]

3. [...]

4. [...]

5. [...] **[page 28]**

IV. DISCUSSION

A. Were the rights of the Appellant violated?

1. Status of the Appellant

41. Before discussing the alleged violations of the Appellant's rights, it is important to establish his status following his arrest and during his provisional detention[115]. Rule 2 sets forth definitions of certain

---

[115]   This is particularly important because the individual's rights, including the permissible length of pre-trial detention, vary based on whether the individual is a suspect or an accused.

terms used in the Rules[116]. The indictment against the Appellant was not confirmed until 23 October 1997. Pursuant to the definitions of "accused" and "suspect" set forth in Rule 2, the Appeals Chamber finds that the Appellant was a "suspect" from his arrest on 15 April 1996 until the indictment was confirmed on 23 October 1997. After 23 October 1997, the Appellant's status changed and he became an "accused"[117].

2. The right to be promptly charged under Rule 40*bis*

42.   Unlike national systems, which have police forces to effectuate the arrest of suspects, the Tribunal lacks any such enforcement agency. Consequently, in the absence of the suspect's voluntary surrender, the Tribunal must rely on the international community for the arrest and provisional detention of suspects. The Statute and Rules of the Tribunal establish a system[118] whereby States may provisionally detain suspects at the behest of the Tribunal pending transfer to the Tribunal's detention unit.

43.   In the present case, there are two relevant periods of time under which Cameroon was clearly holding the Appellant at the behest of the Tribunal. Cameroon arrested the Appellant pursuant to the Rwandan and Belgian extradition requests[119] on 15 April 1996. Two days later, the Prosecutor made her first Rule 40 request for provisional detention of the Appellant. On 6 May 1996, the nineteenth day of the Appellant's provisional detention pursuant to Rule **[page 29]** 40, the Prosecutor requested the Cameroon authorities to extend the Appellant's detention for an additional three weeks[120]. On 16 May 1996, however, the Prosecutor informed Cameroon that she was no longer interested in pursuing a case against the Appellant at "that stage"[121]. Thus, the first period runs from 17 April 1996 until 16 May 1996 – a period of 29 days[122], or nine days longer than allowed under Rule 40. This first period will be discussed, *infra*, at sub-section IV.B.2.

44.   The second period during which Cameroon detained the Appellant for the Tribunal commenced on 4 March 1997[123] and continued until the Appellant's transfer to the Tribunal's detention unit on 19 November 1997. On 21 February 1997, the Cameroon Court rejected Rwanda's extradition request and ordered the release of the Appellant[124]. However, on the same day, while the Appellant was still in custody, the Prosecutor again made a request pursuant to Rule 40 for the provisional detention of the

---

[116]   The definitions set forth in Rule 2 are in accord with the statutory and case law of most legal systems of the international community.

[117]   See also Rule 47(H)(ii), which provides: "Upon confirmation of any or all counts in the indictment, the suspect shall have the status of the accused".

[118]   See Article 20 of the Statute and Rules 40 and 40*bis*.

[119]   See footnote 8, *supra*.

[120]   *15 October 1996 letter*.

[121]   *Decision* at p. 4. See also *15 October 1996 letter*.

[122]   There is reason to believe, however, that the first period actually continued to run until 15 October 1996. On 15 October 1996, the Prosecutor, in a letter to the Appellant and several other detainees, informed them that Cameroon was not holding them at her behest. See Annex 1 to *Appellant's Reply* and *Prosecutor's Provisional Memorial* at para. 6. She stated in this letter that she had informed the Cameroon authorities on 16 May 1996 that at that "stage" she only wished to proceed against 4 of the individuals then being held by Cameroon. The Cameroon authorities apparently did not consider the Tribunal's request for the Appellant to end on 16 May 1996. This is demonstrated by the fact that on 31 May 1996, the Deputy Director of Public Prosecution of the Cameroon Centre Province Court of Appeal requested the adjournment of the Court's consideration of the Rwandan extradition request on the grounds that the Tribunal had primacy under Article 8(2) of the Statute. See *Amended Brief* at p. 2, para. 7. The Prosecutor has not directed the Appeals Chamber to any evidence refuting this assertion of the Appellant. As a result of the Cameroon Prosecutor's arguments, the Cameroon Court of Appeal adjourned consideration of the Rwanda extradition request. This adjournment continued until shortly after the 15 October 1996 letter. A copy of this letter was sent to the Cameroon authorities, and after they received this letter, the Rwandan extradition hearing apparently resumed, culminating in a decision of 21 February 1997, in which the Cameroon Court denied the Rwandan extradition request. See the following paragraph. However, we will use the 16 May 1996 date as the date on which the first period ended, since that date is most favourable to the Prosecutor, as the Respondent in this appeal.

[123]   The Prosecutor made her second Rule 40 request on 21 February 1997, following the decision of the Cameroon Court of Appeal with respect to the Rwandan extradition request. However, we are using the date on which the Rule 40*bis* Order was filed as the starting date for the second period of detention.

[124]   *Decision* at pp. 3-4.

Appellant. This request was followed by the Rule 40*bis* request, which resulted in the Rule 40*bis* Order of Judge Aspegren dated 3 March 1997, and filed on 4 March 1997. This Order comprised, *inter alia*, four components. First, it ordered the transfer of the Appellant to the Tribunal's detention unit. Second, it ordered the provisional detention in the Tribunal's detention unit of the Appellant for a maximum period of thirty days. Third, it requested the Cameroon authorities to comply with the transfer order and to maintain the Appellant in custody until the actual transfer. Fourth, it **[page 30]** requested the Prosecutor to submit the indictment against the Appellant prior to the expiration of the 30-day provisional detention[125].

45.   However, notwithstanding the 4 March 1997 Rule 40*bis* Order, the record reflects that the Tribunal took no further action until 22 October 1997. On that day, the Deputy Prosecutor, Mr. Bernard Muna (who had spent much of his professional career working in the Cameroon legal community prior to joining the Office of the Prosecutor) submitted the indictment against the Appellant for confirmation. Judge Aspegren confirmed the indictment against the Appellant the next day and simultaneously issued a Warrant of Arrest and Order for Surrender addressed to the Government of Cameroon on 23 October 1997[126]. However, the Appellant was not transferred to the Tribunal's detention unit until 19 November 1997. Thus, Cameroon held the Appellant at the behest of the Tribunal from 4 March 1997 until his transfer on 19 November 1997. At the time the indictment was confirmed, the Appellant had been in custody for 233 days, more than 7 months, from the date the Rule 40*bis* Order was filed.

46.   It is important that Rule 40 and Rule 40*bis* be read together. It is equally important in interpreting these provisions that the Appeals Chamber follow the principle of "effective interpretation", a well-established principle under international law[127]. Interpreting Rule 40 and Rule 40*bis* together, we conclude that both Rules must be read restrictively. Rule 40 permits the Prosecutor to request any State, in the event of urgency, to arrest a suspect and place him in custody. The purpose of Rule 40*bis* is to restrict the length of time a suspect **[page 31]** may be detained without being indicted. We cannot accept that the Prosecutor, acting alone under Rule 40, has an unlimited power to keep a suspect under provisional detention in a State, when Rule 40*bis* places time limits on such detention if the suspect is detained at the Tribunal's detention unit. Rather, the principle of effective interpretation mandates that these Rules be read together and that they be restrictively interpreted.

47.   Although both Rule 40 and Rule 40*bis* apply to the provisional detention of suspects, there are important differences between the two Rules. For example, the time limits under which the Prosecutor must issue an indictment vary depending upon which Rule forms the basis of the provisional detention. Pursuant to Rule 40(D)(ii), the suspect must be released if the Prosecutor fails to issue an indictment within 20 days of the transfer of the suspect to the Tribunal's detention unit, while Rule 40*bis*(H) allows the Prosecutor 90 days to issue an indictment. However, the remedy for failure to issue the indictment in the proscribed period of time is the same under both Rules: *release of the suspect.*

---

[125]   *Rule 40bis Order.*

[126]   *Warrant of Arrest and Order for Surrender*, 23 October 1997, attached as Annex 4 to *Prosecutor's Response.*

[127]   This principle is also known by the Latin phrase *ut res magis valeat quam pereat*. See Cayuga Indians Claims, Annual Digest and Reports of Public International Law Cases (H. Lauterpacht, ed.), 1925-1926, No. 271. See also Timor Island, The Hague Court Reports (1916); Corfu Channel, 1949 ICJ Reports 24; Free Zones of Upper Savoy and the District of Gex, (second phase), PCIJ Series A, No. 24 at p. 17. This principle is embodied in Article 31(1) of the Vienna Convention on the Law of Treaties, 23 May 1969, 1155 U.N.T.S. 331:
"A treaty shall be interpreted in good faith in accordance with the ordinary meaning to be given to the terms of the treaty in their context and in the light of its, object and purpose". Although neither the Statute nor the Rules are treaties, the Appeals Chamber and the Trial Chambers of the Tribunal and the International Criminal Tribunal for the former Yugoslavia have had recourse to Article 31(1) of the Vienna Convention in interpreting the Statutes of the Tribunals. Other cases where Trial Chambers of the International Tribunal or the ICTY have had recourse to Article 31 in interpreting the provisions of the Statutes include: Prosecutor v. Théoneste Bagosora and 28 Others, *Decision on the Admissibility of the Prosecutor's Appeal from the Decision of a Confirming Judge Dismissing an Indictment Against Théoneste Bagosora and 28 Others*, Case No. ICTR-98-37-A, 8 June 1998 at pp. 12-13; Prosecutor v. Tadić, *Decision on the Prosecutor's Motion, Protective Measures for Victims and Witnesses*, Case No. IT-94-I-T, 10 August 1995 at p. 10; Prosecutor v. Erdemović, *Judgement*, Case No. IT-96-22-A, 7 October 1997 at p. 3; and Prosecutor v. Delalić and Others, Case No. IT-96-21-T, 16 November 1998, at pp. 396-397. See also Prosecutor v. Kanyabashi, *Joint and Separate Opinion of Judge McDonald and Judge Vohrah*, Case No. ICTR-96-15-A, 3 June 1999 at para. 15.

48.   The Prosecutor may apply for Rule 40*bis* measures "in the conduct of an investigation"[128]. Rule 40*bis* applies only if the Prosecutor has previously requested provisional measures pursuant to Rule 40 or if the suspect is otherwise already being detained by the State to whom the Rule 40*bis* request is made[129]. The Rule 40*bis* request, which is made to a Judge assigned pursuant to Rule 28, must include a provisional charge and a summary of the material upon which the Prosecutor relies[130].

49.   The Judge must make two findings before a Rule 40*bis* order is issued. First, there must be a reliable and consistent body of material that tends to show that the suspect may have committed an offence within the Tribunal's jurisdiction[131]. Second, the Judge must find that provisional detention is a necessary measure to `prevent the escape of the suspect, physical or mental injury to or intimidation of a victim or witness or the destruction of evidence, or to be otherwise necessary for the conduct of the investigation"[132]. **[page 32]**

50.   Pursuant to Rule 40*bis*(C), the provisional detention of the suspect may be ordered for an initial period of thirty days[133]. This initial thirty-day period begins to run from the "day after the transfer of the suspect to the detention unit of the Tribunal"[134]. Two additional thirty-day period extensions are permissible. At the end of the first thirty-day period, the Prosecutor must show that an extension is warranted by the needs of the investigation in order to have the provisional detention extended[135]. At the end of the second thirty-day period, the Prosecutor must demonstrate that special circumstances warrant the continued provisional detention of the suspect for the final thirty-day period to be granted[136]. In no event shall the total period of provisional detention of a suspect exceed ninety days[137]. At the end of this cumulative ninety-day period, the suspect must be released[138] if the indictment has not been confirmed and an arrest warrant signed[139].

51.   The Statute and Rules of the Tribunal envision a system whereby the suspect is provided a copy of the Prosecutor's request, including provisional charges, in conjunction with the Rule 40*bis* Order[140]. He is also served a copy of the confirmed indictment with the Warrant of Arrest[141], and pursuant to Rule 62(ii) he is to be orally informed of the charges against him at the initial appearance[142]. In the present case, 6 days elapsed between the filing of the Rule 40*bis* Order on 4 March 1997 and the date on which the Appellant apparently was shown a copy of the Rule 40*bis* Order[143]. Additionally, 27 days elapsed between the confirmation of the indictment against the Appellant on 23 October 1998 and the service of a copy of the indictment upon the Appellant on 19 November 1998.

52.   The Trial Chamber found that the Appellant was initially arrested at the behest of Rwanda and Belgium, a point the Prosecutor reiterates in this appeal, contending that the Prosecutor's request was merely "superimposed" on the existing requests of those States. However, the Prosecutor fails to acknowledge that on 16 May 1996, she requested a three-**[page 33]**week extension of the provisional detention of the Appellant. The Appeals Chamber finds the Appellant was detained at the request of the Prosecutor from 17 April 1996 through 16 May 1996. This detention – for 29 days – violated the 20-day limitation in Rule 40.

---

[128]   Rule 40*bis*(A). Rule 40, by comparison, applies only in case of urgency. See Rule 40(A).
[129]   Rule 40*bis*(B)(i).
[130]   Rule 40*bis*(A).
[131]   Rule 40*bis*(B)(ii).
[132]   Rule 40*bis*(B)(iii).
[133]   Rule 40*bis*(C).
[134]   *Ibid.*
[135]   Rule 40*bis*(F).
[136]   Rule 40*bis*(G).
[137]   Rule 40*bis*(H).
[138]   Or, if appropriate, delivered to the authorities of the State to which the Rule 40*bis* request was initially made. *Ibid.*
[139]   *Ibid.*
[140]   Rule 40*bis*(E).
[141]   Rule 55(B)(ii).
[142]   Rule 62(ii).
[143]   See footnote 18.

53.   The Prosecutor also successfully argued before the Trial Chamber that Rule 40*bis* is inapplicable, since its operative provisions do not apply until after the transfer of the suspect to the Tribunal's detention unit[144]. It is clear, however, that the purpose of Rule 40 and Rule 40*bis* is to limit the time that a suspect may be provisionally detained without the issuance of an indictment. This comports with international human rights standards. Moreover, if the time limits set forth in Rule 40(D) and Rule 40*bis*(H) are not complied with, those rules mandate that the suspect must be released.

54.   Although the Appellant was not physically transferred to the Tribunal's detention unit until 19 November 1997, he had been detained since 21 February 1997 solely at the behest of the Prosecutor. The Appeals Chamber considers that if the Appellant were in the constructive custody[145] of the Tribunal after the Rule 40*bis* Order was filed on 4 March 1997, the provisions of that Rule would apply. In order to determine if the period of time that the Appellant spent in Cameroon at the behest of the Tribunal is attributable to the Tribunal for purposes of Rule 40*bis*, it is necessary to analyse the relationship between Cameroon and the Tribunal with respect to the detention of the Appellant. In fact, the Prosecutor has acknowledged that between 21 February 1997 and 19 November 1997, "there existed what could be described as joined or concurrent personal jurisdiction over the Appellant, the personal jurisdiction being shared between the Tribunal and Cameroon"[146].

55.   The Tribunal issued a valid request pursuant to Rule 40 for provisional detention, and shortly thereafter, pursuant to Rule 40*bis*, for the transfer of the Appellant. These requests were honoured by Cameroon, and *but for* those requests, the Appellant would have been **[page 34]** released on 21 February 1997, when the Cameroon Court of Appeal denied the Rwandan extradition request and ordered the immediate release of the Appellant.

56.   Thus, the Appellant's situation is analogous to the "detainer" process, whereby a special type of warrant (known as a "detainer" or "hold order") is filed against a person *already in custody* to ensure that he will be available to the demanding authority upon completion of the present term of confinement[147]. A "detainer" is a device whereby the requesting State can obtain the custody of the detainee upon his release from the detaining State. The U.S. Supreme Court has stated that, "[I]n such a case, the State holding the prisoner in immediate confinement acts as agent for the demanding State..."[148]. Moreover, that court has held that since the detaining state acts as an agent for the demanding state pursuant to the detainer, the petitioner is in custody for purposes of filing a *writ of habeas corpus* pursuant to U.S. law[149]. Thus, the court reached the conclusion that the accused is in the constructive custody of the requesting State and that the detaining State acts as agent for the requesting state for purposes of *habeas corpus* challenges[150]. In the present case, the relationship between the Tribunal and Cameroon is even stronger, on the basis of the international obligations imposed on States by the Security Council under Article 28 of the Statute.

57.   Other cases have held that a defendant sentenced to concurrent terms in separate jurisdictions is in the constructive custody of the second jurisdiction after the first jurisdiction has imposed sentence on him. For example, In the Matter of Eric Grier, Peritioner v. Walter J. Flood, as Warden of the Nassau County Jail, Respondent[151], the court concluded that "*constructive custody attached before any sentence*

---

[144]   See *Decision* at p. 5.

[145]   Constructive custody has been referred to as "having power and control over the body". See Re Moina, 1 QB 241, 3 All ER 525 (Court of Appeal, Queen's Bench 1959). A court in the Philippines has even held, in the context of a bail hearing, that a petitioner was in the constructive custody of the courts when he was physically incapacitated in a hospital less than one kilometre from the police station and the police had not attempted to serve an arrest warrant on him, despite the fact that they were aware of his whereabouts. See Miguel P. Panderanga v. Court of Appeals and People of the Philippines, (Philippines Supreme Court, 1995) 1995 Philippines S. Ct. LEXIS 3495.

[146]   *Prosecutor's Response* at para. 13.

[147]   See Shelton, *Unconstitutional Uncertainty: A Study of the Use of Detainers*, 1 U.Mich.J.L.Ref. 119 (1968).

[148]   Braden v. 30th Judicial Circuit Court of Kentucky, 410 U.S. 484 (1973) at 498-499.

[149]   *Ibid.*

[150]   *Ibid.*

[151]   In the Matter of Eric Grier, Peritioner v. Walter J. Flood, as Warden of the Nassau County Jail, Respondent, 375 N.Y.S. 2d 506 (Sup Ct of N.Y. 1975). In this case, the court stated, "In the interests of justice he should get credit toward both sentences for all the time he is in custody, either actual or constructive". *Ibid.*, at p. 508.

was imposed[152]. In Ex p. Hampton M. Newell[153], the court ruled that although the petitioner was in the physical custody of the federal authorities, he was in the constructive custody of the State of Texas on the basis of a detainer that Texas had filed against him[154]. **[page 35]**

58.   The Prosecutor relies, in part, on a definition of custody ("care and control") from an oft-cited law dictionary[155]. However, this same law dictionary also defines custody as "the detainer of a man's person by virtue of lawful process or authority"[156], Thus, even using the Prosecutor's authority, custody can be taken to mean the detention of an individual pursuant to lawful authority even in the absence of physical control. It would follow, therefore, that notwithstanding a lack of physical control, the Appellant *was* in the Tribunal's custody *if* he were being detained pursuant to "lawful process or authority" of the Tribunal. Or, as a Singapore court noted in Re Onkar Shrian[157], "[T]hat the person bailed is in the eye of the law, for many purposes, esteemed to be as much in the prison of the court by which he is bailed, as if he were in the actual custody of the proper gaoler"[158].

59.   The Prosecutor has also relied on In the Matter of Surrender of Elizaphan Ntakirutimana[159] in support of the proposition that under international law, an order by the Tribunal for the transfer of an individual does not give the Tribunal custody over such a person until the physical transfer has taken place[160]. Reliance on this case is misguided in two respects. First, the U.S. Fifth Circuit Court of Appeals recently upheld a District Court ruling that reversed the Decision of the Magistrate that Ntakirutimana could not be extradited[161]. Second, notwithstanding the reversal, Ntakirutimana had challenged the transfer process and is thus clearly distinguishable from the facts in the present case. There is no evidence here that either the Appellant sought to challenge his transfer to the Tribunal, or that Cameroon **[page 36]** was unwilling to transfer him. On the contrary, the Deputy Prosecutor of the Cameroon Centre Province Court of Appeal, appearing at the Rwandan extradition hearing on 31 May 1996, argued that the Tribunal had primacy and, thus, convinced that Court to defer to the Tribunal[162]. Moreover, as noted above[163], the President of Cameroon signed a decree order to transfer the Appellant prior to the signing of the Warrant of Arrest and Order for Surrender by Judge Aspegren on 23 October 1997. These facts indicate that Cameroon was willing to transfer the Appellant.

60.   The co-operation of Cameroon is consistent with its obligation to the Tribunal. The Statute and Rules mandate that States must comply with a request of the Tribunal for the surrender or transfer of the

---

[152]   *Ibid.* at p. 509 (emphasis added).
[153]   Ex p.Hampton M. Newell, 582 S.W. 2d 835, (Ct of Crim App of Texas 1979).
[154]   *Ibid.* at p. 836.
[155]   See discussion at para. 23, *supra.*
[156]   *Black's Law Dictionary*, 6th Ed. at p. 384.
[157]   Re Onkar Shrian, 1 MLJ 28 (Singapore High Court 1970).
[158]   *Ibid.*, citing to 3 Hawkins' Pleas of the Crown, 7th Ed. at p. 186. Another court has held that "constructive custody" includes a fairly broad category of situations in which the prisoner is not within the physical custody of the authorities. *"[C]ustody includes without limitation actual custody ... and constructive custody of prisoners and juveniles ... temporarily outside the institution whether for the purpose of work, school, medical case, a leave granted [by statute], a temporary leave of furlough granted to a juvenile or otherwise."* Wisconsin v. Sevelin, Case No. 96-0729-CR (Wisconsin Court of Appeals 1996), citing to State v. Gilbert, 115 Wis.2d 371, 378-79, 340 N.W.2d 511, 515 (Wisconsin Supreme Court 1983) (italics in original).
[159]   In the Matter of Surrender of Elizaphan Ntakirutimana, 988 F.Supp. 1038, 1997 U.S. Dist. LEXIS 20714 (S.D. Tex. 1997).
[160]   *Provisional Memorial* at para. 37.
[161]   In the Matter of Surrender of Elizaphan Ntakirutimana, ___ F.Supp. ___, 1998 U.S. Dist. LEXIS 22173, 1998 WL 655708 (S.D. TX 1998). In overruling the Magistrate Judge, Judge John D. Rainey issued the following order: "Therefore, the Court hereby certifies to the Secretary of State that Ntakirutimana be arrested and detained within this judicial district while awaiting his surrender to the proper authorities. Any transfer of Ntakirutimana, however, should be abated for thirty days in order to provide Ntakirutimana's counsel an opportunity to file any *habeas corpus*". *Ibid.* at p. 61. On 5 August 1999, the U.S. Fifth Circuit Court of Appeals upheld the District Court decision, and lifted the stay on the extradition. See Elizaphan Ntakirutimana v. Janet Reno, Madeleine Albright and Juan Garza, 184 F.3rd 419, 1999 U.S. App. LEXIS 18253 (5th Cir. 1999).
[162]   See footnote 122.
[163]   See text at footnote 22.

accused to the Tribunal[164]. This obligation on Member States of the United Nations is mandatory, since the Tribunal was established pursuant to Chapter VII of the Charter of the United Nations[165].

61. Thus, the Appeals Chamber finds that, under the facts of this case, Cameroon was holding the Appellant in constructive custody for the Tribunal by virtue of the Tribunal's lawful process or authority. In the present case, the Prosecutor specifically requested Cameroon to detain and transfer the Appellant[166]. The Statute of the Tribunal obligated Cameroon to detain the Appellant for the benefit of the Prosecutor[167]. The Prosecutor has admitted that it had personal jurisdiction over the Appellant after the Rule 40*bis* Order was issued. That Order also asserts personal and subject matter jurisdiction: This finding does not mean, however, that the Tribunal was responsible for each and every aspect of the Appellant's detention, but only for the decision to place and maintain the Appellant in custody. However, as will be discussed below, this limitation imposed on the Tribunal is consistent with international law. Even if the appellant was not in the constructive custody of the Tribunal, the principles governing the provisional detention of suspects should apply. **[page 37]**

62. The Appeals Chamber recognises that international standards view provisional (or pretrial) detention as an exception, rather than the rule[168]. However, in light of the gravity of the charges faced by accused persons before the Tribunal, provisional detention is often warranted, so long as the provisions of Rule 40 and Rule 40*bis* are adhered to. The issue, therefore, is whether the length of time the Appellant spent in provisional detention, prior to the confirmation of his indictment, violates established international legal norms for provisional detention of suspects.

63. It is well-established under international human rights law that pre-trial detention of suspects is lawful[169], as long as such pre-trial detention does not extend beyond a reasonable period of time[170]. The U.N. Human Rights Committee, in interpreting Article 9(2) of the ICCPR, has developed considerable jurisprudence with respect to the permissible length of time that a suspect may be detained without being

---

[164]   See Article 28(2)(e) and Rules 40 and 40*bis*.

[165]   Prosecutor v. Tadić, *Decision on the Defence Motion for Interlocutory Appeal on Jurisdiction*, Case No. IT94-1-AR72, 2 October 1995) at paras. 9-48.

[166]   See *Decision* at p. 4.

[167]   See Article 28(2)(d) of the Statute.

[168]   See, for example, ICCPR Article 9(3). The Appeals Chamber also takes judicial notice of the fact that pretrial detention is not the norm throughout many civil law jurisdictions and is more commonly utilised in common law jurisdictions. Islamic law also has an aversion to pre-trial detention of accused persons: "The system (with which most Westerners are familiar) of the pretrial detention of accused persons, or their release on bail or promise to appear for trial, is generally not recognized under Islamic law. Most Islamic jurists agree that the accused should be at large prior to trial, since a mere accusation of guilt is not sufficient to justify the *Ta'azir* punishment of incarceration". M. Lippman, S. McConville and M. Yerushalmi, Islamic Criminal Law and Procedure (New York: Praeger) at p. 62.

[169]   Prosecutor v. Delalić, *Decision on Motion for Provisional Release filed by the Accused Zejnil Delalić*, Case No. IT-96-21-T, Trial Chamber II, 25 September 1996 at para. 21 and the cases cited therein.

[170]   See, for example, Article 9(2) of the ICCPR, ECHR Article 5(2), ACHR Article 7(4), U.N. Human Rights Committee General Comment 8 and Committee of Ministers of the Council of Europe Resolution 65(11). See also Stömüller v. Austria, A Series 9 (ECtHR 1969) at p. 40. The domestic criminal procedure codes of many States specify the length of permissible detention for suspects during the investigation phase. See, for example, Articles 24 and 25 of the Indonesian Code of Criminal Procedure. Pursuant to Article 24, an investigator may order the detention of a suspect for up to a maximum of 60 days for purposes of pre-trial investigation. Pursuant to Article 25, a public prosecutor may order the detention of a suspect for a maximum of 55 days. See LawBook on The Code of Criminal Procedure (Act No. 8/1981), Department of Information, Republic of Indonesia. See also Article 208 of the Japanese Code of Criminal Procedure which provides that the maximum period of detention prior to being formally charged is 10 days, which may be extended to an absolute maximum of 28 days in the most exceptional circumstances. See B.J. George, Jr., "Rights of the Criminally Accused", 53 Law and Contemporary Problems, Nos. 1-2 (Winter and Spring 1990) at pp. 89-90. See also Article 10 of the Brazilian Code of Criminal Procedure, Decree-Law No. 3.689 of 3 October 1941, that limits the detention of suspects for investigative purposes to 10 days (as compared with 30 days for detained accused). Article 92(1) of the Chinese Criminal Procedure Law provides that once a suspect has been arrested, the period of time the suspect may remain in pre-trial detention while the police carry out their investigation is generally limited to two months. However, in "complicated cases", this period can be extended up to a maximum of seven months. See Wang Chenguang and Zhang Xianchu, Introduction to Chinese Law (Hong Kong: Sweet and Maxwell Asia, 1997) at § 5.09. See also "Opening to Reform? An Analysis of China's Revised Criminal Procedure Law," Lawyers Committee for Human Rights, October 1996 at pp. 25-28.

charged. For example, in <u>Glenford Campbell v. Jamaica</u>[171], the suspect was detained for 45 days without being formally charged. **[page 38]**

In holding this delay to be a violation of ICCPR Article 9(2), the Committee stated the following:

> [T]he Committee finds that the author was not "promptly" informed of the charges against him: one of the most important reasons for the requirement of "prompt" information on a criminal charge is to enable a detained individual to request a prompt decision on the lawfulness of his or her detention by a competent judicial authority. A delay from 12 December 1984 to 26 January 1985 does not meet the requirement of article 9, paragraph 2[172].

64. Similar findings have been made in other cases involving alleged violations of ICCPR Article 9(2). For example, in <u>Moriana Hernández Valentini de Bazzano</u>[173], a period of eight months between the commencement of detention and filing of formal charges was held to violate ICCPR Article 9(2). In <u>Monja Jaona</u>[174], a period of eight months under which the suspect was placed under house arrest without being formally charged was found to be a violation of ICCPR Article 9(2). In <u>Alba Pietraroia</u>[175], the petitioner was detained for seven months without being formally charged and the Committee held that this detention violated ICCPR Article 9(2). Finally, in <u>Leopoldo Buffo Carballal</u>[176], a delay of one year between arrest and formal filing of charges was held to be a violation of ICCPR Article 9(2).

65. The Appeals Chamber also notes that the delay in indicting the Appellant apparently caused concern for President Kama. In a letter sent to the Appellant's Counsel on 8 September 1997, President Kama:

> I have already reminded the Prosecutor of the need to establish as soon as possible an indictment against Mr. Jean Bosco Barayagwiza, if she still intends to prosecute him. Only recently, Mr. Bernard Muna, the Deputy Prosecutor, reassured me that an indictment against Mr. Jean Bosco Barayagwiza should soon be submitted to a Judge for review[177].

However, even at that point the 90-day period had expired. **[page 39]**

66. Additionally, the Trial Chamber, in its Decision dismissing the Extremely Urgent Motion, stated, "It is regrettable that the Prosecution did not submit an indictment until 22 October 1997"[178]. Moreover, even the Prosecutor acknowledged that the delay in indicting the Appellant was not justified. During the oral argument on the Appellant's Extremely Urgent Motion on 11 September 1998, Mr. James Stewart, appearing for the Prosecutor, acknowledged that the Appellant could or should have been indicted earlier:

> Now, I will say this, and I have to be frank with you, the president of this tribunal – and this is reflected in one of the letters that was sent to the accused – was anxious for the prosecutor to

---

[171]   Glenford Campbell v. Jamaica, Communication No. 248/1987, <u>Official Records of the Human Rights Committee 1991/1992</u>, CCPR/11/Add. 1 Volume ii, United Nations 1995, at p. 383.

[172]   *Ibid* at p. 386, para. 6.3.

[173]   Moriana Hernández Valentini de Bazzano Communication No. 5/1977, 15 August 1979, reprinted in U.N. Human Rights Committee, *Selected Decisions under the Optional Protocol (second to sixteenth sessions)*, CCPR/C/OP/1, United Nations 1985, at p. 40.

[174]   Monja Jaona, Communication No: 132/1982, 1 April 1985, reprinted in U.N. Human Rights Committee, *Selected Decisions under the Optional Protocol, vol. 2 (seventeenth to thirty-second sessions)*, CCPR/C/OP/2, United Nations 1990, at p. 161.

[175]   Alba Pietraroia, Communication No. 44/1979, 27 March 1981, reprinted in U.N. Human Rights Committee, *Selected Decisions under the Optional Protocol (second to sixteenth sessions)*, CCPR/C/OP/1, United Nations 1985, at p. 76.

[176]   Leopoldo Buffo Carballal, Communication No. 33/1978, 27 March 1981, reprinted in U.N. Human Rights Committee, *Selected Decisions under the Optional Protocol (second to sixteenth sessions)*, CCPR/C/OP/1, United Nations 1985, at p. 63.

[177]   *Prosecutor's Response*, Annex 12.

[178]   *Decision* at p. 5.

produce an indictment, if we were going to indict this man, and it may have been that *the indictment was, was not produced as early as it could have been or should have been ...*[179]

67.   In conclusion, we hold that the length of time that the Appellant was detained in Cameroon at the behest of the Tribunal without being indicted violates Rule 40*bis* and established human rights jurisprudence governing detention of suspects. The delay in indicting the Appellant violated the 90-day rule as set forth in Rule 40*bis*. In the present appeal, Judge Aspregren issued the Rule 40*bis* Order with the proviso that the indictment be presented for confirmation within 30 days (the Rule permits for two 30-day extensions). In doing so, he invoked Sub-rule 40*bis*, thereby making an assertion of jurisdiction over the Appellant. The Prosecutor agrees that there was "joined or concurrent jurisdiction" over the Appellant[180]. Sub-rule 40*bis*(H) provides explicitly that the suspect shall be released or, if appropriate, be delivered to the authorities of the State to which the request was initially made if the indictment is not issued within 90 days. This limitation on the detention of suspects is consistent with established human rights jurisprudence.

3. The delay between the transfer of the Appellant and his initial appearance

68.   In the present case, the Appellant was transferred to the Tribunal on 19 November 1997. However, his initial appearance was not held until 23 February 1998 – some 96 days *after* his transfer. At the outset of this analysis the Appeals Chamber rejects the Prosecutor's contention that a 31-day holiday recess, between 15 December 1997 and 15 January 1998, could somehow justify this delay. The Appellant should have had his initial appearance well **[page 40]** before the holiday recess even commenced and did not have it until over one month after the end of the recess.

69.   The issue, therefore, is whether the 96-day period between the Appellant's transfer and initial appearance violates the statutory requirement that the initial appearance is held without delay. There is no evidence that the Appellant was afforded an opportunity to appear before an independent Judge during the period of the provisional detention and the Appellant contends that he was denied this opportunity. Consequently, it is even more important for the protection of his rights that his initial appearance was held without delay.

70.   Rule 62, which is predicated on Articles 19 and 20 of the statute, provides that an accused shall be brought before the assigned Trial Chamber and formally charged *without delay* upon his transfer to the seat of the Tribunal. In determining if the length of time between the Appellant's transfer and his initial appearance was unduly lengthy, we note that the right of the accused to be promptly brought before a judicial authority and formally charged ensures that the accused will have the opportunity to mount an effective defence. The international instruments have not established specific time limits for the initial appearance of detainees, relying rather on a requirement that a person should "be brought promptly before a Judge" following arrest[181]. The U.N. Human Rights Committee has interpreted "promptly" within the context of "more precise" standards found in the criminal procedure codes of most States. Such delays must not, however, exceed a few days[182]. Thus, in Kelly v. Jamaica[183], the U.N. Human

---

[179]   Prosecutor v. Barayagwiza, *Transcript*, 11 September 1998 at p. 72 (emphasis added).

[180]   *Prosecutor's Response* at para. 13.

[181]   ICCPR Article 9(3). See also ICCPR Articles 9(2) and 14(3)(a); ECHR Articles 5(1)-(4) and 6(3); and ACHR Articles 7(3)-(6).

[182]   See International Human Rights Instruments, Compilation of General Comments and General Recommendations Adopted by Human Rights Treaty Bodies, U.D. Doc. HRI/GEN/Rev. 1 (1992), at p. 9, cited in M.C. Bassiouni and P. Manikas, The Law of the International Criminal Tribunal for the Former Yugoslavia, (Irvington-on-Hudson: Transnational, 1996) at p. 913, footnote 86.

[183]   Kelly v. Jamaica, Communication No. 253/1987. However, the Committee has found that a period of 50 hours without being promptly brought before a Judge did not violate ICCPR Article 9(3). Portorreal v. The Dominican Republic, Communication No. 188/1984, reprinted in CCPR/C/OP/2 at p. 214. See also M.C. Bassiouni and P. Manikas, The Law of the International Criminal Tribunal for the Former Yugoslavia; *op. cit.*, at p. 913. The major human rights treaties make a distinction between what could be considered pre-trial or investigatory rights and rights that arise at or during trial. Thus, ICCPR Article 9, ECHR Article 5 and ACHR Articles 7(3)-7(6) embrace pre-trial or investigatory rights, while ICCPR Article 14, ECHR Article 6 and ACHR Article 8 cover trial rights. A comparison of ICCPR Article 9(2) and ICCPR Article 14(3)(a) show a striking

Rights Committee held that a detention of five weeks before being brought before a Judge violated Article 9(3). **[page 41]**

71.   Based on the plain meaning of the phrase, "without delay", the Appeals Chamber finds that a 96-day delay between the transfer of the Appellant to the Tribunal's detention unit and his initial appearance to be a violation of his fundamental rights as expressed by Articles 19 and 20, internationally-recognised human rights standards and Rule 62. Moreover, we find that the Appellant's right to be promptly indicted under Rule 40*bis* to have been violated. Although we find that these violations do not result in the Tribunal losing jurisdiction over the Appellant, we nevertheless reaffirm that the issues raised by the Appellant certainly fall within the ambit of Rule 72[184].

72.   In the Tadić Interlocutory Appeal Decision[185], the Appeals Chamber set forth several policy arguments for why a liberal approach to admitting interlocutory appeals is warranted. The Appeals Chamber there stated:

> Such a fundamental matter as the jurisdiction of the International Tribunal should not be kept for decision at the end of a potentially lengthy, emotional and expensive trial. All the grounds of contestation relied upon by Appellant result, in final analysis, in an assessment of the legal capability of the International Tribunal to try his case. What is this, if not in the end a question of jurisdiction? And what body is legally authorized to pass on that issue, if not the Appeals Chamber of the International Tribunal? Indeed – this is by no means conclusive, but interesting nevertheless: *were not those questions to be dealt with in limine litis, they could obviously be raised on an appeal on the merits. Would the higher interest of justice be served by a decision in favour of the accused, after the latter had undergone what would then have to be branded as an unwarranted trial.* After all, in a court of law, common sense ought to be honoured not only when facts are weighed, but equally when laws are surveyed and the proper rule is selected. In the present case, the jurisdiction of this Chamber to hear and dispose of the Appellant's interlocutory appeal is indisputable[186]. **[page 42]**

We find that the challenge to jurisdiction raised by the Appellant is consistent with the logic underlying the decision reached in the Tadić case[187]. Given that the Appeals Chamber is of the opinion that to proceed with the trial of the Appellant would amount to an act of injustice, we see no purpose in denying the Appellant's appeal, forcing him to undergo a lengthy and costly trial, only to have him raise, once again the very issues currently pending before this Chamber. Moreover, in the event the Appellant was to be acquitted after trial we can foresee no effective remedy for the violation of his rights. Therefore, on the basis of these findings, the Appeals Chamber will decline to exercise jurisdiction over the Appellant, on the basis of the abuse of process doctrine, as discussed in the following Sub-section.

---

similarity between those provisions with respect to the right of the individual to be promptly informed of the charges. The same is true of ECHR Article 5(2), ECHR Article 6(3) and ACHR Article 8(2)(b). An examination of the jurisprudence under the international human rights treaties shows that delays of as little as ten days between the arrest and the providing of the information required pursuant to ECHR Article 5(2) have been held to violate the "promptness" requirement of ECHR Article 5(2). See Van Der Leer v. Netherlands, A Series 170-A, (ECtHR 1990), at para. 31. See also Glenford Campbell v. Jamaica, Communication No. 248/1987, in which the Human Rights Committee held that a delay of 45 days between detention and the presentation of formal charges violated Article 9(2) of the ICCPR. We note, however, that the right to be informed promptly at the trial stage of the proceedings is governed by ICCPR Article 14(3)(a) and ECHR Article 6(3), which are the fair trial provisions of those treaties and relate to accused persons. The pre-trial or investigatory due process provisions of ICCPR and ECHR, Article 9(2) and Article 5(3), respectively, were the provisions relied on in Glenford Campbell and Van Der Leer. We see no reason why the logic underlying those decisions is invalid solely on the basis that the individual concerned is an accused, rather than a suspect.

[184]   See 5 February 1999 Scheduling Order, in which the Appeals Chamber found that the Trial Chamber's Decision "dismissed an objection based on the lack of personal jurisdiction over the accused and, therefore, an appeal lies as of right under Sub-rule 72(D)".

[185]   Prosecutor v. Tadić, *Decision on the Defence Motion for Interlocutory Appeal on Jurisdiction*, Case No. IT94-1-AR72, 2 October 1995.

[186]   *Ibid.* at para. 6 (emphasis added).

[187]   The Appeals Chamber notes that at the time of the Tadić appeal, ICTY Rule 72 and ICTR Rule 72 were identical in that both allowed an appeal based on "an objection based on lack of jurisdiction".

B. The Abuse of Process Doctrine

1. In general

73.   The Appeals Chamber now considers, in light of the abuse of process doctrine[188] the Appellant's allegations concerning three additional issues: 1) the right to be promptly informed of the charges during the first period of detention; 2) the alleged failure of the Trial Chamber to resolve the *writ of habeas corpus* filed by the Appellant; and 3) the Appellant's assertions that the Prosecutor did not diligently prosecute her case against him. These assertions will be considered. Before addressing these issues, however, several points need to be emphasised in the context of the following analysis. First and foremost, this analysis focuses on the alleged violations of the Appellant's rights and is not primarily concerned with the entity responsible for the alleged violation(s). As will be discussed, it is clear that there are overlapping areas of responsibility between the three organs of the Tribunal and as a result, it is conceivable that more than one organ could be responsible for the violations of the Appellant's rights. However, even if fault is shared between the three organs of the Tribunal – or is the result of the actions of a third party, such as Cameroon – it would undermine the integrity of the judicial process to proceed. Furthermore, it would be unfair for the Appellant to stand trial on these charges if his rights were egregiously violated. Thus, **[page 43]** under the abuse of process doctrine, it is irrelevant which entity or entities were responsible for the alleged violations of the Appellant's rights. Second, we stress that the circumstances set forth in this analysis must be read as a whole. Third, none of the findings made in this sub-section of the Decision, in isolation, are necessarily dispositive of this issue. That is, it is the combination of these factors – and not any single finding herein – that lead us to the conclusion we reach in this sub-section. In other words, the application of the abuse of process doctrine is case-specific and limited to the egregious circumstances presented by this case. Fourth, because the Prosecutor initiates the proceedings of the Tribunal, her special responsibility in prosecuting cases will be examined in sub-section 4, *infra*.

74.   Under the doctrine of "abuse of process", proceedings that have been lawfully initiated may be terminated after an indictment has been issued if improper or illegal procedures are employed in pursuing an otherwise lawful process. The House of Lords summarised the abuse of process doctrine as follows:

> [P]roceedings may be stayed in the exercise of the judge's discretion not only where a fair trial is impossible, but also where it would be contrary to the public interest in the integrity of the criminal justice system that a trial should take place[189].

It is important to stress that the abuse of process doctrine may be invoked as a matter of discretion. It is a process by which Judges may decline to exercise the court's jurisdiction in cases where to exercise that jurisdiction in light of serious and egregious violations of the accused's rights would prove detrimental to the court's integrity.

75.   The application of this doctrine has resulted in dismissal of charges with prejudice in a number of cases, particularly where the court finds that to proceed on the charges in light of egregious violations of the accused's rights would cause serious harm to the integrity of the judicial process. One of the leading cases in which the doctrine of abuse of process was applied is R. v. Horseferry Road Magistrates' Court *ex parte* Bennett[190]. In that case, the House of Lords stayed the prosecution and ordered the release of the accused, stating that:

---

[188]   "Abuse of process" is distinguished from "malicious prosecution" in that abuse of process results from improper use of regularly issued process, while malicious prosecution refers to wrongfully issued process. See Lobel v. Trade Bank of New York, 229 N.Y.S. 778, 781, 132 Misc. 643. See also Andrew L-T Choo, "Halting Criminal Prosecutions: The Abuse of Process Doctrine Revisited", [1995] Crim. L.R. 864 and the cases cited therein. See also § 347 of the New Zealand Crimes Act of 1961. Under that provision, a Judge may order that, if lawful process has been abused, no indictment be presented or that other appropriate steps be taken for proceedings to be terminated at any stage of the proceedings.

[189]   R. Latif: R. Shahzad, 1 All ER 353 (House of Lords 1996).

[190]   R. v. Horseferry Road Magistrates' Court, *ex parte* Bennett, [1994] 1 AC 42, 95 I.L.R. 380 (House of Lords 1993).

[A] court has a discretion to stay any criminal proceedings on the ground that to try those proceedings will amount to an abuse of its own process either (1) because it will be impossible (usually by reason of delay) to give the accused a **[page 44]** fair trial or (2) *because it offends the court's sense of justice and propriety to be asked to try the accused in the circumstances of a particular case*[191].

The abuse of doctrine has been applied in several cases. For example, in <u>Bell v. DPP of Jamaica</u>[192], the Privy Council held that under the abuse of process doctrine courts have an inherent power to decline to adjudicate a case which would be oppressive as the result of unreasonable delay. In making this determination, the court set forth four guidelines for determining whether a delay would deprive the accused of a fair trial:

(1)   the length of the delay;

(2)   the prosecution's reasons to justify the delay;

(3)   the accused's efforts to assert his rights; and

(4)   the prejudice caused to the accused[193].

Regarding the issue of prejudice, in <u>R. v. Oxford City Justices, *ex parte* Smith (D.K.B.)</u>[194], the court applied the abuse of process doctrine in dismissing a case on the grounds that a two-year delay between the commission of the offence and the issuing of a summons was unconscionable, stating:

In the present case it seems to me that the delay which I have described was not only quite unjustified and quite unnecessary due to inefficiency, but it was a delay of such length that it could rightly be said to be unconscionable. That is by no means the end of the matter. It seems to me also that the delay here was of such a length that it is quite impossible to say that there was no prejudice to the applicant in the continuance of the case[195].

In <u>R. v. Hartley</u>[196], the Wellington Court of Appeal relied on the abuse of process doctrine in quashing a conviction that rested on an unlawful arrest and the illegally obtained confession that followed.

76.   Closely related to the abuse of process doctrine is the notion of supervisory powers. It is generally recognised that courts have supervisory powers that may be utilised in the interests of justice, regardless of a specific violation. The U.S. Supreme Court has stated that courts have a "duty of establishing and maintaining civilized standards of procedure and **[page 45]** evidence" as an inherent function of the court's role in supervising the judicial system and process[197]. As Judge Noonan of the U.S. Ninth Circuit Court of Appeals has stated:

This court has inherent supervisory powers to dismiss prosecutions in order to deter illegal conduct. The "illegality" deterred by exercise of our supervisory power need not be related to a constitutional or statutory violation[198].

The use of such supervisory powers serves three functions: to provide a remedy for the violation of the accused's rights; to deter future misconduct; and to enhance the integrity of the judicial process[199].

---

[191]   [1994] 1 AC 42, at p. 74; 95 I.L.R. at p. 406 (emphasis added).

[192]   Bell v. DPP of Jamaica, [1985] AC 937.

[193]   *Ibid.*

[194]   R. v. Oxford City Justices, *ex parte* Smith (D.K.B.), 75 Cr App R 200 (Divisional Court 1982).

[195]   *Ibid.* at p. 206.

[196]   R. v. Hartley, 2 N.Z.L.R. 199 (Court of Appeal, Wellington, 1978).

[197]   McNabb v. U.S., 318 US 332 (1943) at p. 340.

[198]   U.S. v. Matta-Ballesteros, 71 F.3rd 754 (9th Cir. 1994) at p. 774, citing (in part) to U.S. v. Hasting, 461 U.S. 499, 505 (1983) (Noonan, J. concurring).

[199]   In U.S. v. Hasting, the U.S. Supreme Court stated: "[G]uided by considerations of justice, and in the exercise of supervisory powers, federal courts may, within limits, formulate procedural rules not specifically required by the Constitution or the Congress. The purposes underlying use of the supervisory powers are threefold: to implement a remedy for violation of recognized rights; to preserve judicial integrity by ensuring that a conviction rests on appropriate considerations validly before the jury; and finally, as a remedy designed to deter illegal conduct". See U.S. v. Hasting, 461 U.S. 499, 505 (1983) and the cases cited therein.

77.   As noted above, the abuse of process doctrine may be relied on in two distinct situations: (1) where delay has made a fair trial for the accused impossible; and (2) where in the circumstances of a particular case, proceeding with the trial of the accused would contravene the court's sense of justice, due to pre-trial impropriety or misconduct. Considering the lengthy delay in the Appellant's case, "it is quite impossible to say that there was no prejudice to the applicant in the continuance of the case"[200]. The following discussion, therefore, focuses on whether it would offend the Tribunal's sense of justice to proceed to the trial of the accused.

2.   The right to be promptly informed of the charges during the first period of detention

78.   In the present case, the Appellant makes several assertions regarding the precise date he was informed of the charges[201]. However, using the earliest date, we conclude that the Appellant was informed of the charges on 10 March 1997 when the Cameroon Deputy Prosecutor showed him a copy of the Rule 40*bis* Order[202]. This was approximately 11 months after he was initially detained pursuant to the *first* Rule 40 request. **[page 46]**

79.   Rule 40*bis* requires the detaining State to promptly inform the *suspect* of the charges under which he is arrested and detained[203]. Thus, the issue is when does the right to be promptly informed of the charges attach to suspects before the Tribunal[204]. Existing international norms guarantee such a right, and suspects held at the behest of the Tribunal pursuant to Rule 40*bis* are entitled, at a bare minimum, to the protections afforded under these international instruments[205], as well as under the rule itself. Consequently, we turn our analysis to these international standards.

80.   International standards require that a suspect who is arrested be informed promptly of the reasons for his arrest and the charges against him[206]. The right to be promptly informed of the charges serves two

---

[200]   R. v. Oxford City Justices, *ex parte* Smith (D.K.B.), *op. cit.* footnote 194.

[201]   See footnote 18.

[202]   *Ibid.*

[203]   Although Rule 40*bis*(A) requires the Prosecutor to include a provisional charge with the materials submitted to the Judge in requesting the Order pursuant to Rule 40*bis*. Rule 40*bis*(E) requires the Registrar to serve on the suspect and counsel copies of the Rule 40*bis* order and the Prosecutor's request thereof "as soon as possible".

[204]   Pursuant to Rule 40*bis*(E), copies of the provisional charges and Rule 40*bis* Order must be provided to the suspect as soon as possible. As discussed *supra.*, at Sub-section IV.A.2., the Appellant was apparently shown a copy of the Rule 40*bis* Order and supporting materials on 10 March 1997 – 6 days after the Order was signed. However, the focus of the inquiry here is the determination of when the Appellant was actually notified of the general nature of the charges during the period of time prior to the Rule 40*bis* Order – that is, whether he was informed of the general nature of the charges at any time *after* the initial Rule 40 request on 17 April 1996, but *before* the filing of the Rule 40*bis* Order.

[205]   We also note in this regard that the Appeals Chamber in <u>Prosecutor v. Tadić</u>, *Decision on the Defence Motion for Interlocutory Appeal on Jurisdiction*, IT-94-1-AR72, 2 October 1995, at para. 46, pronounced that, "The fair trial guarantees in Article 14 of the International Covenant on Civil and Political Rights have been adopted almost verbatim in Article 21 of the Statute". Although the Appeals Chamber in <u>Tadić</u> referred to Article 21 of the Statute of the International Criminal Tribunal for the former Yugoslavia, that article is verbatim to Article 20 of the Statute of the Tribunal. We also see no reason to conclude that the protections afforded to suspects under Article 9 of the ICCPR do not also apply to suspects brought before the Tribunal.

[206]   See Article 9(2) of the ICCPR, Article 5(2) of the ECHR and Article 7(4) of the ACHR. The domestic criminal procedure codes of most States have similar provisions. See, for example, Article 5(3) of the Malaysian Constitution: "Where a person is arrested he shall be informed as soon as may be of the grounds of his arrest and shall be allowed to consult and be defended by a legal practitioner of his choice". See also § 84 of the Thai Penal Code of 1956, which provides: "The official or private person making the arrest shall immediately take the person arrested to the office of the administrative or police official and, on arrival, shall produce and read to him the warrant of arrest, if any, and shall notify him of the cause of arrest". See also Article 9(3) of the Constitution of Singapore, which provides, "An arrested person has a right to be informed, as soon as may be, of the grounds of his arrest". Article 34 of the 1947 Constitution of Japan requires that persons under arrest or detention be immediately informed of the charges lodged against them. See B.J. George, Jr., "Rights of the Criminally Accused", *op. cit.* at footnote 170. Moreover, Article 61 of the Japanese Code of Criminal Procedure (1980), provides as follows: "The accused shall not be placed under detention before the court has informed the accused of the charge and has heard his statement regarding it. However, this shall not apply to the cases where the accused has escaped". Section 25(3)(b) of the South African Constitution (1993) states that the accused has the right to be informed with "sufficient particularity of the charge" against him. Section 17(2) of the Zimbabwean Emergency Powers (Maintenance of Law and Order) Regulations, Statutory Instrument No. 458 of 1983, provides that a person subjected to pre-trial detention be informed of the charges as soon as "reasonably practicable after the commencement of his detention, and in any case not later than seven days thereafter, in a language that he understands of the reasons for his detention".

functions. First, it counterbalances the interest of the prosecuting authority in seeking continued detention of the suspect. In this respect, the suspect needs to be promptly informed of the charges against him in order to challenge his detention, **[page 47]** particularly in situations where the prosecuting authority is relying on the serious nature of the charges in arguing for the continued detention of the suspect. Second, the right to be promptly informed gives the suspect the information he requires in order to prepare his defence[207]. The focus of the analysis in this Sub-section is on the first of these two functions. At the outset of this analysis, it is important to stress that there are two distinct periods when the right to be informed of the charges are applicable. The first period is when the suspect is initially arrested and detained[208]. The second period is at the initial appearance of the accused[209] after the indictment has been confirmed and the accused is in the Tribunal's custody. For purposes of the discussion in this Sub-section, only the first period is relevant.

81.   The requirement that a suspect be promptly informed of the charges against him following arrest provides the "elementary safeguard that any person arrested should know why he is deprived of his liberty"[210]. The right to be promptly informed at this preliminary stage is also important because it affords the arrested suspect the opportunity to deny the offence and obtain his release prior to the initiation of trial proceedings[211].

82.   International human rights jurisprudence has developed norms to ensure that this right is respected. For example, the suspect must be notified "in simple, non-technical language that he can understand, the essential legal and factual grounds for his arrest, so as to be able, as he sees fit, to apply to a court to challenge its lawfulness..."[212]. However, there is no requirement that the suspect be informed in any particular way[213]. Thus, at this initial stage, there is no requirement that the suspect be given a copy of the arrest warrant or any other document setting forth the charges against him; in fact, there is no requirement at this stage that the suspect be notified in writing at all[214], so long as the suspect is informed promptly. **[page 48]**

83.   The European Court of Human Rights has held that the required information need not be given in its entirety by the arresting officer at the "moment of the arrest", provided that the suspect is informed of the legal grounds of his arrest within a sufficient time after the arrest[215]. Moreover, the information may be divulged to the suspect in stages, as long as the required information is provided promptly[216]. Whether this requirement is complied with requires a factual determination and is, therefore, case-specific[217]. Consequently, we will briefly survey the jurisprudence of the Human Rights Committee and the European Court of Human Rights in interpreting the promptness requirement of Article 9(2) of the ICCPR, Article 5(2) of the ECHR and Article 7 of the ACHR.

84.   As pointed out above[218], the Human Rights Committee held in Glenford Campbell v. Jamaica[219], that detention without the benefit of being informed of the charges for 45 days constituted a violation of

---

[207]   Consequently, the charges to be provided to the accused at this second stage must be "more specific and more detailed" than that provided at the initial arresting stage. See Nielsen v. Denmark No. 343/57, 2 *Yearbook on the European Court of Human Rights* 412 at p. 462 (1959); GSM v. Austria No. 9614/81, 34 DR 119 (1983).

[208]   See Rule 55, which governs execution of arrest warrants on accused, and which requires the arresting State to provide the arrested accused with a copy of the warrant for arrest and indictment. See also Article 9(2) of the ICCPR, Article 5(2) of the ECHR and Article 7(4) of the ACHR.

[209]   See Articles 19(2) and 19(3) of the Statute and Rule 62. See also ICCPR Article 14(3)(a), ECHR Article 6(3)(a) and Article 8(2)(b) of the ACHR.

[210]   Fox, Campbell and Hartley v. UK, A Series 182 (ECtHR 1990) at para. 40.

[211]   X v. United Kingdom, No. 801077, 16 DR 101 at p. 114 (1979).

[212]   *Ibid.*

[213]   X v. Netherlands, No. 1211/61, 5 *Yearbook on the European Convention on Human Rights* 224 at 228 (1962).

[214]   *Ibid.*

[215]   Fox, Campbell and Hartley v. United Kingdom, *op. cit.* footnote 210 at para. 40.

[216]   *Ibid.*

[217]   *Ibid.* See also X v. Denmark, No. 882879, 30 DR 93 (1982).

[218]   See text at footnote 171, *supra.*

[219]   Glenford Campbell v. Jamaica, *op. cit.* footnote 171 at p. 383. See also the cases cited in footnotes 173-176, *supra.*

Article 9(2) of the ICCPR[220]. Under the jurisprudence of the European Court of Human Rights, intervals of up to 24 hours between the arrest and providing the information as required pursuant to ECHR Article 5(2) have been held to be lawful[221]. However, a delay of ten days between the arrest and informing the suspect of the charges has been held to run afoul of Article 5(2)[222].

85.   In the present case, the Appellant was detained for a total period of 11 months before he was informed of the general nature of the charges that the Prosecutor was pursuing against him. While we acknowledge that only 35 days out of the 11-month total are clearly attributable to the Tribunal (the periods from 17 April-16 May 1996 and 4-10 March 1997), the fact remains that the Appellant spent an inordinate amount of time in provisional detention without knowledge of the general nature of the charges against him. At this juncture, it is irrelevant that only a small portion of that total period of provisional detention is **[page 49]** attributable to the Tribunal, since it is the Tribunal – and not any other entity – that is currently adjudicating the Appellant's claims. Regardless of which other parties may be responsible, the inescapable conclusion is that the Appellant's right to be promptly informed of the charges against him was violated.

86.   As noted above[223] in Bell v. DPP of Jamaica, the abuse of process doctrine was applied where unreasonable delay would have resulted in an oppressive result had the case gone to trial. Applying the guidelines set forth in that case convinces us that the abuse of process doctrine is applicable under the facts of this case. The Appellant was detained for 11 months without being notified of the charges against him. The Prosecutor has offered no satisfactory justifications for this delay. The numerous letters attached to one of the Appellant's submissions[224] point to the fact that the Appellant was in continuous communication with all three organs of the Tribunal in an attempt to assert his rights. Moreover, we find that the effect of the Appellant's pre-trial detention was prejudicial[225].

3.   The failure to resolve the *writ of habeas corpus* in a timely manner

87.   The next issue concerns the failure of the Trial Chamber to resolve the Appellant's *writ of habeas corpus* filed on 29 September 1997[226]. The Prosecutor asserts that *after* the Appellant filed the *writ of habeas corpus*, the President of the Tribunal wrote a letter to the **[page 50]** Appellant[227] informing the

---

[220]   Mr. Campbell was initially arrested on suspicion of murder on 12 December 1984. He was charged with larceny on 25 January 1985 and with murder on 12 March 1985. Throughout the period in question, he remained in detention. *Ibid.*

[221]   X v. Denmark; No. 673074, 1 Digest 457 (1975). See also Fox, Campbell and Hartley v. United Kingdom, *op. cit.* footnote 210 at paras. 40-43 (interval of up to seven hours between the arrests and the giving of al the information required by Article 5(2) were found to meet the requirement of "promptness") and Delcourt v. Belgium, No. 2689/65, 10 *Yearbook on the European Convention on Human Rights* (1967) 238 at pp. 252 and 272.

[222]   Van der Leer v. Netherlands, A Series 170-A (ECtHR 1990) at para. 31.

[223]   See para. 75, *supra.*

[224]   See Annexes 2, 11, 13-20 to *Appellant's Reply.*

[225]   See, for example, Prosecutor v. Barayagwiza, *Transcript*, 11 September 1998, at pp. 39-40, in which the Appellant's Counsel argued, *inter alia*, that "[I]n the Cameroonian prison there was no food. In the Cameroonian prison there was no medical attention. Our client, who is the accused person, had a family. The accused person, your Lordships, had a small business which he was carrying on in Cameroon to feed his family. Indeed, as of the time our client was the accused person, was transferred to this Tribunal he was only 59 kilos. His health had deteriorated from more than 70 kilos because of the conditions which he met in the Cameroonian prison".

Moreover, we find the words of Justice Powell in this respect convincing:

> We have discussed previously the societal disadvantages of lengthy pre-trial incarceration, but obviously the disadvantages for the accused who cannot obtain his release are even more serious. The time spent in jail awaiting trial has a detrimental impact on the individual. It often means loss of a job; it disrupts family life; and it enforces idleness. Most jails offer little or no recreational or rehabilitative programs. The time spent in jail is simply dead time. Moreover, if a defendant is locked up, he is hindered in his ability to gather evidence, contact witnesses, or otherwise prepare his defense. Imposing those consequences on anyone who has not yet been convicted is serious. It is especially unfortunate to impose them on those persons who are ultimately found to be innocent.

Barker v. Wingo, 407 US 514, 92 S.Ct. 2182 (1972), at p. 532-533.

[226]   Regarding the date the *writ* was filed, see footnote 41.

[227]   *Prosecutor's Response*, Annex 12. See footnote 103.

Appellant that the Prosecutor would be submitting an indictment shortly[228]. In fact, the President's letter is dated *8 September 1997*, and the Appellant claims that the *writ* was filed on the basis of this letter from the President[229]. Moreover, the Appellant asserts that he was informed that the hearing on the *writ of habeas corpus* was to be held on 31 October 1997[230]. The Appellant asserts that "the Registry without the consent of the Defence removed the hearing of the motion from the calendar only because the Prosecution promised to issue the indictment soon"[231]. The Appellant also claims that the indictment was filed and confirmed on 22 October 1997 and 23 October 1997, respectively, in order to pre-empt the hearing on the *writ of habeas corpus*[232]. These assertions by the Appellant are, of course, impossible for him to prove, absent an admission by the Prosecutor. We note, however, that the Prosecutor has not directed the Appeals Chamber to any evidence to the contrary, and that the Appellant was never afforded an opportunity to be heard on the *writ of habeas corpus*.

88.   Although neither the Statute nor the Rules specifically address *writs of habeas corpus* as such, the notion that a detained individual shall have recourse to an independent judicial officer for review of the detaining authority's acts is well-established by the Statute and Rules[233]. Moreover, this is a fundamental right and is enshrined in international human rights norms, including Article 8 of the Universal Declaration of Human Rights[234], Article 9(4) of the ICCPR, Article 5(4) of the ECHR and Article 7(6) of the ACHR. The Inter-American Court of Human Rights has defined the *writ of habeas corpus* as:

> [A] judicial remedy designed to protect personal freedom or physical integrity against arbitrary decisions by means of a judicial decree ordering the appropriate authorities to bring the detained person before a judge so that the lawfulness of the detention may be determined and, if appropriate, the release of the detainee be ordered[235]. **[page 51]**

Thus, this right allows the detainee to have the legality of the detention reviewed by the judiciary.

89.   The European Court of Human Rights has held that the detaining State must provide recourse to an independent judiciary in all cases, whether the detention was justified or not[236]. Under the jurisprudence of that Court, therefore, a *writ of habeas corpus* must be heard, even though the detention is eventually found to be lawful under the ECHR[237]. Thus, the right to be heard on the *writ* is an entirely separate issue from the underlying legality of the initial detention. In the present case, the Appellant's right was violated by the Trial Chamber because the *writ* was filed but was not heard.

90.   The Appeals Chamber is troubled that the Appellant has not been given a hearing on his *writ of habeas corpus*. The fact that the indictment of the Appellant has been confirmed and that he has had his

---

[228]   *Prosecutor's Response* at paras. 24-25.

[229]   *Appellant's Reply* at para. 18.

[230]   *Ibid.*

[231]   *Ibid.*

[232]   *Ibid.* at para. 21.

[233]   See, for example, Articles 19 and 20 of the Statute and Rule 40*bis*(J).

[234]   Article 8 reads: "Everyone has the right to an effective remedy by the competent national tribunals for acts violating the fundamental rights granted him by the constitution or by law".

[235]   Habeas Corpus in Emergency Situations (Arts. 27(2) 25(1) and 7(6) of the American Convention on Human Rights, Advisory Opinion OC-8/87, 30 January 1987, Inter-Am.Ct.H.R. (Ser. A) No. 8 (1987) at para. 33.

[236]   See Winterwerp v. Netherlands, A Series 33 (ECtHR 1973) where the European Court stressed that it is essential that a detained person have access to a Court and the right to be heard on the issue of the provisional detention. Some commentators have argued that the theory underlying Article 5(4) of the ECHR is that a judicial remedy should be available to review the legality of an administrative act of detention only. Thus, if the detention is ordered by a "court", Article 5(4) is redundant, since the detention order in that situation is "incorporated" into the court's order. See D.J. Harris, M. O'Boyle and C. Warbrick, Law of the Euopean Convention on Human Rights (Butterworth's 1995) at p. 151. Be that as it may, we do not consider that a Rule 40*bis* Order of a single Judge of the Tribunal constitutes an "order by a court". In this context, such an order is tantamount to administrative detention.

[237]   De Wilde, Ooms and Versyp v. Belgium, No. 1, A Series 12 (ECtHR 1970) at para. 73. In that case, the European Court held that Article 5(4) had been violated, even though Article 5(1) had not. Thus, although Article 5(1) and Article 5(4) contain separate requirements, it is possible to find a violation of one provision without finding that the other had been violated. See also Van Der Leer v. Netherlands, A Series 170-A (ECtHR 1990) and Koendjbiharie v. Netherlands, A Series 185-B (ECtHR 1990).

initial appearance does not excuse the failure to resolve the *writ*[238]. The Appellant submits that as far as he is concerned the *writ of habeas corpus* is still pending. The Appeals Chamber finds that the *writ of habeas corpus* is rendered moot by this Decision. Nevertheless, the failure to provide the Appellant a hearing on this writ violated his right to challenge the legality of his continued detention in Cameroon during the two periods when he was held at the behest of the Tribunal and the belated issuance of the indictment did not nullify that violation. **[page 52]**

4. The duty of prosecutorial due diligence

91.   Article 19(1) of the Statute of the Tribunal provides that the Trial Chambers shall ensure that accused persons appearing before the Tribunal are guaranteed a fair and expeditious trial. However, the Prosecutor, has certain responsibilities in this regard as well. For example, the Prosecutor is responsible for, *inter alia*: conducting investigations, including questioning suspects[239]; seeking provisional measures and the arrest and transfer of suspects[240]; protecting the rights of suspect, by ensuring that the suspect understands those rights[241]; submitting indictments for confirmation[242]; amending indictments prior to confirmation[243]; withdrawing indictments prior to confirmation[244]; and, of course, for actually prosecuting the case against the accused.

92.   Because the Prosecutor has the authority to commence the entire legal process, through investigation and submission of an indictment for confirmation, the Prosecutor has been likened to the "engine" driving the work of the Tribunal. Or, as one court has stated, "[T]he ultimate responsibility for bringing a defendant to trial rests on the Government and not on the defendant"[245]. Consequently, once the Prosecutor has set this process in motion, she is under a duty to ensure that, within the scope of her authority, the case proceeds to trial in a way that respects the rights of the accused. In this regard, we note that some courts have stated that 'mere delay' which gives rise to prejudice and unfairness might by itself amount to an abuse of process[246]. For example, in R. Grays Justices ex p. Graham, the Queen's Bench stated in *obiter dicta* that:

> [P]rolonged delay in starting or conducting criminal proceedings may be an abuse of process when the substantial delay was caused by the improper use of procedure or inefficiency on the part of the prosecution and the accused has neither caused nor contributed to the delay[247]. **[page 53]**

93.   The Prosecutor has asserted that her 'abstention from proceeding against the Appellant-Defendant before 3 March 1997 was due to on-going investigation,[248]. The Prosecutor further argues that she should not be barred from proceeding against the Appellant simply because she did not proceed against the Appellant at the first available opportunity[249]. In putting forth this argument, the Prosecutor relies on

---

[238]   In this regard, we note that *had* the Appellant been released from provisional detention while the *writ* was pending – a situation not applicable under the facts of this case – the need to resolve the *writ* would have been obviated. See Fox, Campbell and Hartley v. UK, A Series 182 (ECtHR 1990) where the applicants sought *habeas corpus* the day after their arrest but were released within 24 hours, before their application was heard. Because the applicants had been released prior to the hearing on the writ, the Court declined to determine whether Article 5(4) of the European Convention on Human Rights (which governs *habeas corpus*) had been complied with.

[239]   See Article 15(1) of the Statute and Rule 39.

[240]   Rules 40 and 40*bis*.

[241]   Rule 42.

[242]   Rule 47.

[243]   Rule 50.

[244]   Rule 51.

[245]   United States v. Judge, 425 F.Supp. 499 at p. 504, citing to United States v. Fay, 505 F.2d 1037 (1st Cir 1976) at p. 1040.

[246]   See R. v. Bow Street Stipendiary Magistrate, ex p. DPP; R v. Bow Street Stipendiary Magistrate, ex p. Cherry, 91 Cr App Rep 283, 154 JP 237, (Queen's Bench 1989), where the court held that in criminal proceedings, mere delay which gave rise to prejudice and unfairness may by itself amount to an abuse of process, and in some circumstances, prejudice would be presumed from substantial delay. In the absence of such a presumption, where there was such substantial delay, it would be for the prosecution to justify it.

[247]   R. v. Grays Justices ex p. Graham, 1 QB 1239, 3 All ER 653, 3 WLR 596, 75 Cr. App. Rep. 229 (1982).

[248]   *Provisional Memorial* at para. 43.

[249]   *Ibid.* at para. 42.

Judge Shahabuddeen's Separate Opinion from the <u>Kovačević</u> Decision[250]. In that Separate Opinion, Judge Shahabuddeen referred to <u>United States v. Lovasco</u>[251], a leading United States case on pre-indictment delay, wherein the Court stated:

> [T]he Due Process Clause does not permit courts to abort criminal prosecutions simply because they disagree with a prosecutor's judgement as to when to seek an indictment. Judges are not free, in defining 'due process', to impose on law enforcement officers our 'personal and private notions' of fairness and to 'disregard the limits that bind judges in their judicial function' . ... Our task is more circumscribed. We are to determine only whether the action complained of – here, compelling respondent to stand trial after the Government delayed indictment to investigate further – violates ... "fundamental conceptions of justice..." which "define the community's sense of fair play and decency"...[252]

The Court continued:

> It should be equally obvious that prosecutors are under no duty to file charges as soon as probable cause exists but before they are satisfied they will be able to establish the suspect's guilt beyond a reasonable doubt[253].

94. The facts in <u>Lovasco</u> are clearly distinguishable from those of the Appellant's case, and, therefore, we do not find the Supreme Court's reasoning persuasive. In <u>Lovasco</u>, the respondent was subjected to an 18-month delay between the alleged commission of the offences and the filing of the indictment. However, Mr. Lovasco had not been arrested during the 18-month delay and was not in custody during that period when the police were conducting their investigation. We also note that in <u>United States v. Scott</u>, in a dissent filed by four of the Court's nine Justices, (including Justice Marshall, the author of the <u>Lovasco</u> **[page 54]** decision), the <u>Lovasco</u> holding regarding pre-indictment delay was characterised as a "disfavored doctrine"[254].

95. Moreover, in the <u>Kovačević</u> Decision[255] relied upon by the Prosecutor[256], the Appeals Chamber held that that the Rules provide a mechanism whereby the Prosecutor may seek to amend the indictment[257]. Pursuant to Rule 50(A), the following scheme for amending indictments is available to the Prosecutor. The Prosecutor may amend an indictment, without prior leave, at any time before the indictment is confirmed. After the indictment is confirmed, but prior to the initial appearance of the accused, the indictment may be amended only with the leave of the Judge who confirmed it. At or after the initial appearance of the accused, the indictment may be amended only with leave of the Trial Chamber seized of the case. The Prosecutor thus has the ability to amend indictments based on the results of her investigations. Therefore, the Prosecutor's argument that investigatory delay at the pre-indictment stage does not violate the rights of a suspect who is in provisional detention is without merit. Rule 40bis clearly requires issuance of the indictment within 90 days and the amendment process is available in situations where additional information becomes available to the Prosecutor.

96. Although a suspect or accused before the Tribunal is transferred, and not extradited, extradition procedures offer analogies that are useful to this analysis. In the context of extradition, several cases from the United States confirm that the prosecuting authority has a due diligence obligation with respect

---

[250] <u>Prosecutor v. Kovačević</u>, *Decision Stating Reasons for Appeals Chamber's Order of 29 May 1998*, and *Separate Opinion of Judge Mohamed Shahabuddeen*, Case No. IT-97-24-AR73, 2, July 1998.

[251] <u>United States v. Lovasco</u>, 431 U.S. 783, 97 S.Ct. 2044 (1977).

[252] *Ibid.* at p. 790.

[253] *Ibid.* at p. 791.

[254] <u>United States v. Scott</u>, 437 U.S. 82 (1978)(*diss. op.* Brennan, J.).

[255] <u>Prosecutor v. Kovačević</u>, *Decision Stating Reasons for Appeals Chamber's Order of 29 May 1998*, and *Separate Opinion of Judge Mohamed Shahabuddeen, op. cit.* at footnote 243.

[256] *Provisional Memorial* at para. 42.

[257] See Rule 50.

to accused awaiting extradition[258]. For example, in Smith v. Hooey, the Supreme Court found that the Government had a 'constitutional duty to make a diligent, good-faith effort to bring [the defendant] before the court for trial'[259]. In **[page 55]** United States v. McConahy[260], the court held that the Government's obligation to provide a speedy resolution of pending charges is not relieved unless the accused fails to demand that an effort be made to return him and the prosecuting authorities have made a diligent, good faith effort to have him returned and are unsuccessful, or can show that such an effort would prove futile. We note that the Appellant made several inquiries of Tribunal officials regarding his status[261]. It is also clear from the record that the Prosecutor made no efforts to have the Appellant transferred to the Tribunal's detention unit until after he filed the *writ of habeas corpus*. Similarly, the Prosecutor has made no showing that such efforts would have been futile. There is nothing in the record that indicates that Cameroon was not willing to transfer the Appellant. Rather, it appears that the Appellant was simply forgotten about.

97. Moreover, conventional law and the legislation of many national systems incorporate provisions for the protection of individuals detained pending transfer to the requesting State[262]. We also note in this regard that the European Convention on Extradition provides that provisional detention may be terminated after as few as 18 days if the requesting State has not provided the proper documents to the requested State[263]. In no case may the provisional detention extend beyond 40 days from the date of arrest[264]. **[page 56]**

98. Setting aside for the moment the Prosecutor's contention that Cameroon was solely responsible for the delay in transferring the Appellant, the only plausible conclusion is that the Prosecutor failed in her duty to take the steps necessary to have the Appellant transferred in a timely fashion. The Appellant has claimed that the Prosecutor simply forgot about his case, a claim that is, of course, impossible for the Appellant to prove. However, we note that after the Appellant raised this claim, the Prosecutor failed to rebut it in any form, relying solely on the argument that it was Cameroon's failure to transfer the

---

[258] For example, in United States v. Pomeroy, 822 F.2d 718 (8th Cir. 1987), the court noted that, '[V]arious cases have placed an obligation on the Government to seek extradition of an accused incarcerated in a foreign state when a treaty exists under which the accused could be extradited'. *Ibid.*, at p. 720. In United States v. Saltzmann, 548 F.2d 395 (2nd Cir. 1976), the defendant was a foreign resident and claimed indigency. The Government failed to inform him that his transportation costs to the United States would be furnished at no cost to him. The defendant asserted that the resulting six-month delay and possible prejudice to his defence warranted dismissal of the indictment. The court agreed. In United States v. Judge, 425 F. Supp. 499 (D. Mass. 1976), the accused challenged an indictment, based on his right to a speedy trial. Although the Government was aware of the accused's address in Ecuador, the Government made no effort to inform the accused of the charges for four years. Upon his arrival in the U.S., he was arrested. The court dismissed the indictment on the grounds that the accused was ignorant of the indictment and had suffered prejudice as a result of the delay.

[259] Smith v. Hooey, 393 U.S. 374, 89 S.Ct. 575 (1969) at p. 383.

[260] United States v. McConahy, 505 F.2d 770 (7th Cir. 1974).

[261] See Annexes 2, 11, 13-20 to *Appellant's Reply*.

[262] For example, Article 18(4) of the European Convention on Extradition (1957), European Treaty Series, No. 24. See also Article 18 of the French Extradition Act, which provides that the detainee must be automatically freed if agents of the requesting State have not taken custody of him within thirty days of the judicial order. Similarly, under United Kingdom law, discharge of the detainee is allowed after the expiration of one month from the date the warrant for return is made, unless an application for judicial review has been made. United Kingdom Extradition Act (1989) §6(2)(b). In other States, if the executive authorises the surrender, the requesting State has a prescribed period within which to collect the detainee and failure to do so will usually result in the right of the detainee to petition for his release. For example, see United Kingdom Extradition Act (1989) §§ 12, 13, and 16; Australian Extradition Act (1988) §§ 22-26; Swiss Statute on International Judicial Assistance in Criminal Matters (1991 as amended 9 December 1996) Articles 57 and 61; see also the U.S. Code § 3188, which allows the detainee to be discharged from custody after two months have elapsed, unless sufficient cause is shown for the delay. In the context of inter-state extradition within the United States, the Supreme Court of Ohio has held that, if no agent of the requesting State 'appears within 6 months from the time of arrest, the prisoner may be discharged'. See Ex p. Hiram P. McKnight, 28 N.E. 1034 (Sup. Ct. Ohio 1891) at pp. 1036-1037. Finally, bilateral extradition treaties may include similar provisions. For example, Article XII(2) of the Treaty on Extradition between Japan and the United States of America (3 March 1978), provides as follows: 'If an order to surrender has been issued by the competent authority of the requested Party and the requesting Party fails to receive the person sought within such time as may be stipulated by the laws of the requested Party, it may set him at liberty and may subsequently refuse to extradite that person for the same offense. The requesting Party shall promptly remove the person received from the territory of the requested Party'. *Ibid.*, reprinted in The Japanese Annual of International Law, No. 23, 1979-1980 at p. 41.

[263] European Convention on Extradition (1957), European Treaty Series, No. 24, Article 16(4).

[264] *Ibid.*

Appellant that resulted in this delay. The Prosecutor provided no evidence that she contacted the authorities in Cameroon in an attempt to get them to comply with the Rule 40*bis* Order[265]. Further, in the 3 June 1999 Scheduling Order, the Appeals Chamber directed the Prosecutor to answer certain questions and provide supporting documentation, including an explanation for the delay between the request for transfer and the actual transfer[266]. Notwithstanding this Order, the Prosecutor provided no evidence that she contacted the Registry or Chambers in an effort to determine what was causing the delay.

99.   While it is undoubtedly true, as the Prosecutor submits, that the Registry and Chambers have the primary responsibility for scheduling the initial appearance of the accused, this does not relieve the Prosecutor of some responsibility for ensuring that the accused is brought before a Trial Chamber 'without delay' upon his transfer to the Tribunal. In the present case, the Appellant was transferred to the Tribunal on 19 November 1997. However, his initial appearance was not held until 23 February 1998 – some 96 days *after* his transfer, in violation of his right to an initial appearance 'without delay'[267]. There is no evidence that the Prosecutor took any steps to encourage the Registry or Chambers to place the Appellant's initial appearance on the docket. Prudent steps in this regard can be demonstrated through written requests to the Registry and Chambers to docket the initial appearance. The Prosecutor has made no such showing and the only logical conclusion to be drawn from this failure to provide such evidence is that the Prosecutor failed in her duty to diligently prosecute this case. **[page 57]**

C. Conclusions

100.   Based on the foregoing analysis, we conclude that the Appellant was in the constructive custody of the Tribunal from 4 March 1997 until his transfer to the Tribunal's detention unit on 19 November 1997. However, international human rights standards comport with the requirements of Rule 40*bis*. Thus, even if he was not in the constructive custody of the Tribunal, the period of provisional detention was impermissibly lengthy. Pursuant to that Rule, the indictment against the Appellant had to be confirmed within 90 days from 4 March 1997. However, the indictment was not confirmed in this case until 23 October 1997. We find, therefore, that the Appellant's right to be promptly charged pursuant to international standards as reflected in Rule 40bis was violated. Moreover, we find that the Appellant's right to an initial appearance, without delay upon his transfer to the Tribunal's detention unit under Rule 62, was violated.

101.   Moreover, we find that the facts of this case justify the invocation of the abuse of process doctrine. Thus, we find that the violations referred to in paragraph 101 above, the delay in informing the Appellant of the general nature of the charges between the initial Rule 40 request on 17 April 1996 and when he was actually shown a copy of the Rule 40*bis* Order on 10 March 1997 violated his right to be promptly informed. Also, we find that the failure to resolve the Appellant's *writ of habeas corpus* in a timely manner violated his right to challenge the legality of his continued detention. Finally, we find that the Prosecutor has failed with respect to her obligation to prosecute the case with due diligence.

D. The Remedy

102.   In light of the above findings, the only remaining issue is to determine the appropriate remedy for the violation of the rights of the Appellant. The Prosecutor has argued that the Appellant is entitled to either an order requiring an expeditious trial or credit for any time provisionally served pursuant to Rule 101(D). The Appellant seeks unconditional immediate release. **[page 58]**

---

[265]   In this regard, we reiterate that it is only possible to conclude from the record that the Appellant was transferred pursuant to the *Rule 40bis Request*, and not the *Warrant of Arrest and Order for Surrender*, since the Presidential Decree was signed before the *Warrant of Arrest and Order for Surrender*.
[266]   See Sub-section I.C., *supra*.
[267]   See Rule 62. Moreover, Article 20(4)(c) of the Statute guarantees the accused a trial 'without undue delay'.

103.   With respect to the first of the Prosecutor's suggestions, the Appeals Chamber notes that an order for the Appellant to be expeditiously tried would be superfluous as a remedy. The Appellant is already entitled to an expedited trial pursuant to Article 19(1) of the Statute. With respect to the second suggestion, the Appeals Chamber is unconvinced that Rule 101(D) can adequately protect the Appellant and provide an adequate remedy for the violations of his rights. How does Rule 101 (D) offer any remedy to the Appellant in the event he is acquitted?

104.   We turn, therefore, to the remedy proposed by the Appellant. Article 20(3) states one of the most basic rights of all individuals: the right to be presumed innocent until proven guilty. In the present case, the Appellant has been in provisional detention since 15 April 1996 – more than three years. During that time, he spent 11 months in illegal provisional detention at the behest of the Tribunal without the benefits, rights and protections afforded by being formally charged. He submitted a *writ of habeas corpus* seeking to be released from this confinement – and was never afforded an opportunity to be heard on this *writ*. Even after he was formally charged, he spent an additional 3 months awaiting his initial appearance, and several more months before he could be heard on his motion to have his arrest and detention nullified.

105.   The Statute of the Tribunal does not include specific provisions akin to speedy trial statutes existing in some national jurisdictions[268]. However, the underlying premise of the **[page 59]** Statute and Rules are that the accused is entitled to a fair and expeditious trial[269]. The importance of a speedy disposition of the case benefits both the accused and society, as has been recognised by national courts:

> The criminal defendant's interest in prompt disposition of his case is apparent and requires little comment. Unnecessary delay may make a fair trial impossible. If the accused is imprisoned awaiting trial, lengthy detention eats at the heart of a system founded on the presumption of innocence. ... Moreover, we cannot emphasize sufficiently that the public has a strong interest in

---

[268]   See, for example, the U.S. Speedy Trial Act of 1974 (As Amended), 18 USC §§ 3161-3174. See also U.S. Federal Rules of Criminal Procedure, Rule 48(b), which permits for dismissal for unnecessary delay in bringing a defendant to trial. In United States v. Correia, 531 F.2d 1095 (1st Cir. 1976), the court held that Rule 48(b) is an independent of the right to a speedy trial, and is not limited to those situations in which the Sixth Amendment right to a speedy trial has been violated. *Ibid.*, at p. 1099. See also the U.S. Second Circuit Rules Regarding Prompt Disposition of Criminal Cases, Rule 4, that provides: 'In all cases the Government must be ready for trial within six months from the date of arrest, service of summons, detention, or the filing of a complaint or of a formal charge upon which the defendant is to be tried (other than a sealed indictment), whichever is earliest. If the Government is not ready for trial within such time, or within the periods as extended by the District Court for good cause under Rule 5, and if the defendant is charged only with non-capital offenses, then, upon application of the defendant or upon motion of the District Court, after opportunity for argument, the charge shall be dismissed'. Cited in United States v. Saltzman, 548 F.2d 395 (2d Cir. 1976) at p. 400. Other States do not set forth specific time limits within which trials must get underway, but nevertheless guarantee against delays in the proceedings. For example, in Barker v. Wingo, 407 U.S. 514, 92 S.Ct. 2182 (1972), the U.S. Supreme Court set forth the following four factors that are to be taken into consideration in analysing a claim that the accused's right to a speedy trial have been violated:

> 1)   the length of the delay;
> 2)   the reason for the delay;
> 3)   the defendant's assertion of his right; and
> 4)   prejudice to the defendant.

Ibid. at p. 530. The Court acknowledged that this approach requires a balancing act, in which the conduct of both the prosecutor and the defence are weighed, and which compels courts to approach speedy trial cases on an ad hoc basis: *Ibid.* In R. v. Smith, 2 S.C.R. 1120 (1989), the Canadian Supreme Court enunciated a similar test to be taken into account in deciding whether a criminal trial is being held within a reasonable period of time:

> 1)   the length of the delay;
> 2)   the reasons for the delay;
> 3)   any waivers of time periods; and
> 4)   whether there was any prejudice to the accused.

Ibid at p. 1131. In addition, the Constitutional Court of the Slovak Republic has determined that expeditious proceedings and hearings without unnecessary delays are required and that three criteria are relevant in analysing assertions that the trial has not proceeded expeditiously:

> 1)   the legal and factual complexity of the case being heard;
> 2)   cooperation of the parties; and
> 3)   the procedures used by the court or other body. .

See Finding of the Constitutional Court of the Slovak Republic, File Ref. II, US 74/97, No. 28/98, 7 July 1998.

[269]   Article 19(1).

prompt trials. As the vivid experience of a witness fades into the shadow of a distant memory, the reliability of a criminal proceeding may become seriously impaired. This is a substantial price to pay for a society that prides itself on fair trials[270].

106. The crimes for which the Appellant is charged are very serious. However, in this case the fundamental rights of the Appellant were repeatedly violated. What may be worse, it appears that the Prosecutor's failure to prosecute this case was tantamount to negligence. We find this conduct to be egregious and, in light of the numerous violations, conclude that the only remedy available for such prosecutorial inaction and the resultant denial of his rights is to release the Appellant and dismiss the charges against him. This finding is consistent with Rule 40*bis*(H), which requires release if the suspect is not charged within 90 days of the commencement of the provisional detention and Rule 40(D) which requires release if the Prosecutor fails to issue an indictment within 20 days after the transfer of the suspect. Furthermore, this limitation on the period of provisional detention is consistent with international human rights jurisprudence. Finally, this decision is also consistent with **[page 60]** national legislation dealing with due process violations that violate the right of the accused to a prompt resolution of his case[271].

107. Considering the express provisions of Rule 40*bis*(H), and in light of the Rwandan extradition request for the Appellant and the denial of that request by the court in Cameroon, the Appeals Chamber concludes that it is appropriate for the Appellant to be delivered to the authorities of Cameroon, the State to which the Rule 40*bis* request was initially made.

108. The Appeals Chamber further finds that this dismissal and release must be with prejudice to the Prosecutor. Such a finding is consistent with the jurisprudence of many national systems[272]. Furthermore, violations of the right to a speedy disposition of criminal charges have resulted in dismissals with prejudice in Canada[273], the Philippines[274], the United States[275] and Zimbabwe[276]. As troubling as this disposition may be to some, the Appeals Chamber believes that to proceed with the Appellant's trial when such violations have been committed, would cause irreparable damage to the integrity of the judicial process. Moreover, we find that it is the only effective remedy for the cumulative breaches of the **[page 61]** accused's rights. Finally, this disposition may very well deter the commission of such serious violations in the future.

---

[270] United States v. Saltzman, 548 F.2d 395 (2d Cir. 1976) at pp. 399-400.

[271] For example, pursuant to §3162 of the U.S. Speedy Trial Act of 1974 (as amended), *op cit.* footnote 268, the charges against the accused must be dismissed or otherwise dropped for failure to provide the accused with a speedy trial.

[272] See discussion at Sub-section IV.B.1. and the cases cited therein.

[273] See R. v. Askov, 2 R.C.S. 1199 (1990), wherein the Canadian Supreme Court held that a permanent stay of the proceedings is the only possible remedy for failure to bring an accused to trial promptly.

[274] See People of the Philippines v. Alberto Opida y Quiambao and Virailio Marcelo, 1986 Philippine Supreme Court LEXIS 2598, where the Court unanimously ordered the release of the accused from pre-trial confinement as a result of the violation of their constitutional right to a speedy trial. Having found that the appellants' constitutional right to a speedy trial was violated, the Court stated:

[W]e now declare that they should not be detained in jail a minute longer. While this is not to say that the accused are not guilty, it does mean that, because their constitutional rights have been violated, their guilt, if it exists, has not been established beyond reasonable doubt and so cannot be pronounced.

In a concurring opinion, Chief Justice Teehankee wrote:

The Court stands as the guarantor of the constitutional and human rights of all persons within its jurisdiction and must see to it that the rights are respected and enforced. It is settled in this jurisdiction that once a deprivation of a constitutional right is shown to exist, the Court that rendered the judgment or before whom the case is pending is ousted of jurisdiction and habeas corpus is the appropriate remedy to assail the legality of the detention. So accused persons deprived of the constitutional right of a speedy trial have been set free.

[275] See Strunk v. United States, 412 U.S. 434, 440, 93 S.Ct. 2260 (1973), wherein the United States Supreme Court, having found the Appellant's right to a speedy trial violated, ordered the District Court Judgment of conviction set aside, the sentence vacated and the indictment dismissed.

[276] See In re Shadreck Siygni Mlambo, Zimbabwe Supreme Court Judgment 221/91, cited in A.R. Gubbay in, 'Human Rights in Criminal Justice Proceedings: The Zimbabwean Experience', in M. Cherif Bassiouni and Ziyad Motala, The Protection of Human Rights in African Criminal Proceedings (Dordrecht: Kluwer, 1995) at pp. 307, 316-317. In this case, the Zimbabwean Supreme Court determined that a four-and-one-half year delay between arrest and commencement of the proceedings violated the accused's right to a speedy trial. In making this determination, the Court relied on the analysis set forth by the U.S. Supreme Court in Barker v. Wingo, 407 U.S. 514 (1972).

109. We reiterate that what makes this case so egregious is the combination of delays that seemed to occur at virtually every stage of the Appellant's case. The failure to hear the *writ of habeas corpus*, the delay in hearing the Extremely Urgent Motion, the prolonged detention of the Appellant without an indictment and the cumulative effect of these violations leave us with no acceptable option but to order the dismissal of the charges with prejudice and the Appellant's immediate release from custody. We fear that if we were to dismiss the charges without prejudice, the Appellant would be subject to immediate re-arrest and his ordeal would begin anew[277]. Were we to dismiss the indictment without prejudice, the strict 90-day limit set forth in Rule 90*bis*(H) could be thwarted by repeated release and re-arrest, thereby giving the Prosecutor a potentially unlimited period of time to prepare and submit an indictment for confirmation. Surely, such a 'revolving door' policy cannot be what was envisioned by Rule 40*bis*. Rather, as pointed out above[278], the Rules and jurisprudence of the Tribunal permit the Prosecutor to seek to amend the indictment if additional information becomes available. In light of this possibility, the 90-day rule set forth in Rule 40*bis* must be complied with.

110. Rule 40*bis*(H) states that in the event that the indictment has not been confirmed and an arrest warrant signed within 90 of the provisional detention of the suspect, the 'suspect shall be released'. The word used in this Sub-rule, 'shall', is imperative and it is certainly not intended to permit the Prosecutor to file a new indictment and re-arrest the suspect. Applying the principle of effective interpretation, we conclude that the charges against the Appellant must be dismissed with prejudice to the Prosecutor. Moreover, to order the release of the Appellant without prejudice – particularly in light of what we are certain would be his immediate re-arrest – could be seen as having cured the prior illegal detention. That would open the door for the Prosecutor to argue (assuming *arguendo* the eventual conviction of the Appellant) that the Appellant would not then be entitled to credit for that period of detention pursuant to Rule 101(D)[279], on the grounds that the release was the remedy for the violation of **[page 62]** his rights. The net result of this could be to place the Appellant in a worse position than he would have been in had he not raised this appeal. This would effectively result in the Appellant being punished for exercising his right to bring this appeal.

111. The words of the Zimbabwean Court in the Mlambo[280] case are illustrative. In ordering the dismissal of the charges and release of the accused, the Zimbabwean Court held:

> The charges against the applicant are far from trivial and there can be no doubt that it would be in the best interests of society to proceed with the trial of those who are charged with the commission of serious crimes. Yet, that trial can only be undertaken if the guarantee under ...the Constitution has not been infringed. In this case it has been grievously infringed and the unfortunate result is that a hearing cannot be allowed to take place. To find otherwise would render meaningless a right enshrined in the Constitution as the supreme law of the land'[281].

We find the forceful words of U.S. Supreme Court Justice Brandeis compelling in this case:

> Decency, security and liberty alike demand that government officials shall be subjected to the same rules of conduct that are commands to the citizen. In a government of laws, existence of the government will be imperilled if it fails to observe the law scrupulously. Our Government is the potent, the omnipresent teacher. For good or for ill, it teaches the whole people by its example. Crime is contagious. If the Government becomes a lawbreaker, it breeds contempt for law; it invites every man to become a law unto himself: it invites anarchy. To declare that in the

---

[277] We note in this regard, that in arguing in opposition to the Extremely Urgent Motion, Mr. James Stewart, appearing for the Prosecutor, stated the following: 'If the accused Barayagwiza is released, what happens then? Do we start all over again?' Prosecutor v. Barayagwiza, *Transcript*, 11 September 1998 at p. 54.

[278] See discussion at para. 95, *supra*.

[279] In this regard, we note that at several points during the oral arguments on the *Extremely Urgent Motion*, Mr. James Stewart, appearing for the Prosecutor, argued (without conceding the point) that if there were any defective procedures attendant to the arrest, indictment or transfer of the Appellant, those defects had been cured by the Appellant's initial appearance before the Trial Chamber. See Prosecutor v. Barayagwiza, *Transcript*, 11 September 1998 at pp. 49, 50 and 71.

[280] In re Shadreck Siyapi Mlambo, *op. cit.* footnote 276.

[281] *Ibid.*

administration of the criminal law the end justifies the means – to declare that the Government may commit crimes in order to secure the conviction of a private criminal – would bring terrible retribution. Against that pernicious doctrine this Court should resolutely set its face[282].

112. The Tribunal – an institution whose primary purpose is to ensure that justice is done must not place its imprimatur on such violations. To allow the Appellant to be tried on the charges for which he was belatedly indicted would be a travesty of justice. Nothing less than the integrity of the Tribunal is at stake in this case. Loss of public confidence in the Tribunal, as a court valuing human rights of all individuals – including those charged with unthinkable crimes – would be among the most serious consequences of allowing the Appellant to stand trial in the face of such violations of his rights. As difficult as this conclusion may be for **[page 63]** some to accept, it is the proper role of an independent judiciary to halt this prosecution, so that no further injustice results. **[page 65]**

V. DISPOSITION

113. For the foregoing reasons, THE APPEALS CHAMBER hereby:

Unanimously,

(1) ALLOWS the Appeal, and in light of this disposition considers it unnecessary to decide the 19 October 1999 Notice of Appeal or the 26 October 1999 Notice of Appeal;

Unanimously,

(2) DISMISSES THE INDICTMENT with prejudice to the prosecutor;

Unanimously,

(3) DISMISSES THE INDICTMENT with prejudice to the Prosecutor;

By a vote of four to one, with Judge Shahabuddeen dissenting,

(4) DIRECTS the Registrar to make the necessary arrangements for the delivery of the Appellant to the Authorities of Cameroon.

Judge Shahabuddeen appends a Separate Opinion to this Decision.

Judge Nieto-Navia appends a Declaration to this Decision.

Done in both English and French, the English text being authoritative.

Gabrielle Kirk McDonald	Mohamed Shahabuddeen	Lal Chand Vohrah
Presiding		

Wang Tieya	Rafael Nieto-Navia

Dated this third day of November 1999

At The Hague,

The Netherlands **[page 65]**

---

[282] Olmstead v. United States, 277 U.S. 438 (1928), at p. 485 (Brandeis, J. dissenting). See also the dissenting opinion of Justice Holmes in Olmstead where he stated: 'For my part I think it is a less evil that some criminals should escape than that the Government should play an ignoble part'. *Ibid.* at p. 470.

Appendix A

Chronology of Events

15 April 1996:	Cameroon arrests twelve to fourteen Rwandans on the basis of international arrest warrants. The accused was among those arrested. The parties disagree with respect to the question of under whose authority the accused was detained. The Appellant asserts he was arrested by Cameroon on the basis of a request from the Prosecutor, while the Prosecutor contends that the Appellant was arrested on the basis of international arrest warrants emanating from the Rwandan and Belgian authorities.
17 April 1996:	The Prosecutor requests that provisional measures under Rule 40 be taken in relation to the Appellant.
6 May 1996:	The Prosecutor seeks a three-week extension for the detention of the Appellant in Cameroon.
16 May 1996:	The Prosecutor informs Cameroon that she seeks to transfer and hold in provisional detention under Rule 40*bis* four of the individuals detained by Cameroon, *excluding* the Appellant.
31 May 1996:	The Court of Appeal in Cameroon issues a Decision to adjourn *sine die* consideration of the Rwandan extradition proceedings concerning the Appellant as the result of a request by the Cameroonian Deputy Director of Public Prosecution. In support of his request, the Deputy Director cites Article 8(2) of the ICTR Statute.
15 October 1996:	The Prosecutor sends the Appellant a letter indicating that Cameroon is not holding the Appellant at her behest.
21 February 1997:	The Cameroon court rejects Rwanda's extradition request for the Appellant. The court orders the Appellant's release, but he is immediately re-arrested at the behest of the Prosecutor pursuant to Rule 40. This is the second request under Rule 40 for the provisional detention of the Appellant.
24 February 1997:	Pursuant to Rule 40bis, the Prosecutor requests the transfer of the accused to Arusha. **[page 66]**
4 March 1997:	An Order pursuant to Rule 40*bis* (signed by Judge Aspegren on 3 March 1997), is filed. This Order requires Cameroon to arrest and transfer the Appellant to the Tribunal's detention unit.
10 March 1997:	The Appellant is shown a copy of the Rule 40*bis* Order, including the general nature of the charges against him.
29 September 1997:	The Appellant files a *writ of habeas corpus*.
21 October 1997:	The. President of Cameroon signs a decree ordering the Appellant's transfer to the Tribunal's detention unit.
22 October 1997:	The Prosecutor submits the indictment for confirmation.
23 October 1997:	Judge Aspegren confirms the indictment against the Appellant and issues a Warrant of Arrest and Order for Surrender to Cameroon.
19 November 1997:	The Appellant is transferred to Arusha.
23 February 1998:	The Appellant makes his initial appearance.
24 February 1998:	The Appellant files the Extremely Urgent Motion seeking to nullify the arrest.

11 September 1998:	The Trial Chamber hears the arguments of the parties on the Motion.
17 November 1998:	The Trial Chamber dismisses the Extremely Urgent Motion *in toto*.
27 November 1998:	The Appellant notified the Appeals Chamber of his intention to appeal, claiming that he did not receive the Decision until 27 November 1998. On that same day, he signs his Notice of Appeal.

International Criminal Tribunal for the Prosecution of Persons Responsible for Genocide and Other Serious Violations of International Humanitarian Law Committed in the Territory of Rwanda and Rwandan Citizens responsible for genocide and other such violations committed in the territory of neighbouring States between 1 January and 31 December 1994	Case No.	ICTR-97-19-AR72
	Date:	3 November 1999
	Original:	English

IN THE APPEALS CHAMBER

Before: **Judge Gabrielle Kirk McDonald, Presiding**
Judge Mohamed Shahabuddeen
Judge Lal Chand Vohrah
Judge Wang Tieya
Judge Rafael Nieto-Navia

Registrar: **Mr. Agwu U. Okali**

Decision of: **3 November 1999**

JEAN-BOSCO BARAYAGWIZA

v.

THE PROSECUTOR

SEPARATE OPINION OF JUDGE SHAHABUDDEEN

Counsel for the Appellant:
      Mr. Justry P.L. Nyaberi

The Office of the Prosecutor:
      Mr. Mohamed C. Othman
      Mr. N. Sankara Menon
      Mr. Mathias Marcussen

[page 1] SEPERATE OPINION OF JUDGE SHAHABUDDEEN

Preliminary

I agree with the Appeals Chamber that the appellant should be released and the indictment dismissed. But I do so only on the ground of delay between the time which elapsed between the appellant's transfer to the detention unit of the Tribunal on 19 November 1997 and the time of his initial appearance before the Trial Chamber on 23 February 1998. With regard to pre-transfer delay, I am not able to support the decision of the Appeals Chamber ("Decision"). As, in these respects, matters of some importance are involved, I should like to explain my position below. But it will be convenient to say something in the first place on the branch on which I agree with the Decision.

1. Post-transfer delay

The appeal is from the Trial Chamber's decision of 17 November 1998 on the appellant's Urgent Motion of 24 February 1998 (dated 19 February 1998). So far as concerns delay between transfer and initial appearance, paragraphs 2 and 9 of the Urgent Motion spoke of the appellant's "continued provisional detention". That would include the period following on transfer. This was made clear in Annexure DM2 to that motion. Under the heading "Violations of my Rights" and the subheading "Summary on detention time", this annexure stated the following: "**98 days** of detention after transfer and before initial appearance (19 November 97 – 23 February 98)" (emphasis as in the original).

At the time of his transfer, the appellant had already been indicted. He was then no longer a suspect and liable to be treated under the scheme of Rule 40*bis* of the Rules of Procedure and Evidence of the Tribunal ("Rules"); he was now an accused within the meaning of Rule 62 of the Rules. The delay of 98 days was in breach of the requirement of **[page 2]** Rule 62 that, upon "his transfer to the Tribunal, the accused shall be brought before a Trial Chamber without delay ..."[1].

That requirement of promptitude, which corresponds to standard international norms, was imposed by a specific provision having the force of law. That provision (Rule 62) is susceptible of the interpretation that non-compliance would result in loss of jurisdiction, on the view that jurisdiction was granted by the Statute to the Tribunal subject to defeasance for non-observance of certain fundamental principles stated or implied by the Statute, one of which was later reflected in that provision of the Rules. A different view seems to be taken in paragraph 71 of the Decision, which suggests that "delay between the transfer ... and ... initial appearance" does "not result in the Tribunal losing jurisdiction...". If jurisdiction continued, it is not easy to see how the appeal could be allowed under Rule 72(D). The appeal, under that Rule, is "in the case of dismissal of an objection based on lack of jurisdiction. The appeal invites the Appeals Chamber to uphold the objection based on lack of jurisdiction. It is difficult to appreciate how the Appeals Chamber can uphold an objection based on lack of jurisdiction if it finds that there was jurisdiction. My own respectful view is that, if there is impermissible delay, jurisdiction is lost and the Rule thereupon becomes applicable.

Matters to be taken into account in evaluating whether that consequence follows from a breach of the requirement of promptitude include the seriousness of the offences with which the accused is charged. Here the offences were serious. But the requirement of promptitude was fundamental, and its breach was also grave, the delay extending to a little over three months. On balance, I respectfully agree with the Appeals Chamber that the administration of justice by the Tribunal would suffer from proceeding with the case notwithstanding the delay. **[page 3]**

To be fair to the Trial Chamber, it has, however, to be pointed out that the oral arguments before it were devoted to the question of pre-transfer delay. As is shown by the transcript of the proceedings relating to the appellant's Urgent Motion, no issue was presented as to delay between transfer and initial appearance. The Trial Chamber was not given any reason to believe that there was such an issue.

---

[1] A similar requirement to be brought before the Judge would apply under Rule 40*bis*(J) even if the appellant was still a suspect.

Also, apart from the fact that the point was not raised orally before the Trial Chamber, it did not form part of the grounds of appeal. Twenty-two grounds of appeal were listed by the appellant in his Memorandum of Appeal of 27 November 1998 (filed on 10 December 1998); none of these grounds referred to delay between transfer and initial appearance. That can be seen from the summary of the appellant's arguments as presented in paragraphs 14-18 of the Decision of the Appeals Chamber, as well as from the summary of the Prosecutor's responding arguments, as presented in paragraphs 20-28 of that Decision. It does not appear that the Prosecutor thought that she was being called upon to meet an argument about delay between transfer and initial appearance. On the contrary, and obviously without thinking that there was such an issue, the Prosecutor was relying, *inter alia*, on the initial appearance to "cure" any previous defect. (Decision, para. 27).

That the appellant's appeal concerned pre-transfer delay is clear from paragraph 25 (the last paragraph) of the Defence Written Brief of 15 February 1999 (filed on 18 February 1999). There counsel for the appellant said:

" ... the upshot of our submissions is that the Appellant was unlawfully held in Cameroon for about 21 months thereby robbing the Trial Chamber II of personal jurisdiction over him. His detention prior to his transfer to the Tribunal's detention unit was manifestly illegal and unlawful; it was long, arbitrary, tortuous and oppressive. He ought to be discharged unconditionally. Trial Chamber II's **[page 4]** decision was wholly unacceptable and we urge the Appeals Chamber to quash it and set the Appellant free".

Thus, what the appellant was seeking to do in the appeal was to challenge the decision of the Trial Chamber on his claim that his arrest and detention were illegal by reason of matters occurring before his transfer. The question of delay between transfer and initial appearance was not presented to the Appeals Chamber in the appellant's early appeal papers. The appellant has only activated the point in response to the recent query about it which was made by the Appeals Chamber on 3 June 1999.

It is also the case that the appellant is not on record as objecting to the Trial Chamber, which took his initial appearance, that there was lack of jurisdiction on the ground of delay between transfer and initial appearance. That is where the objection should naturally have been made.

Nevertheless, the delay was mentioned in the Urgent Motion, even though only clearly stated in an annexure. I consequently agree with the Appeals Chamber that the appellant is entitled to redress for it, but, in the circumstances mentioned above, I would exempt the Trial Chamber whose decision is under appeal from any significant responsibility.

*

I do not, however, agree with the fourth item of the disposition in the Decision, under which the Appeals Chamber "DIRECTS the Registrar to make the necessary arrangements for the delivery of the Appellant to the Authorities of Cameroon".

That direction means that custody is extended until "delivery of the Appellant to the Authorities of Cameroon" is effected – i.e., what is extended is the very custody which the Appeals Chamber says is invalid and because of which invalidity, in item three of the disposition, it orders the "IMMEDIATE RELEASE of the Appellant". If Cameroon does not accept delivery, custody by the Tribunal is indefinitely prolonged. If Cameroon accepts delivery, at the point of time at which Cameroon does so the appellant is in the custody of **[page 5]** Cameroon. I do not think that the fact that the delivery is to be made on the basis of "necessary arrangements" affects the matter.

If this is not a problem, it must be because it is considered that Cameroon has a duty to accept delivery of the appellant, or that, at any rate, Cameroon has some legal basis for doing so. Has it?

A possible argument is that the direction to the Registrar to make the necessary arrangements for the delivery of the appellant to the authorities of Cameroon can be supported by Cameroon's obligation to cooperate with the Tribunal. But also possible is an opposing argument that a state's obligation to cooperate with the Tribunal does not extend to assisting the Tribunal to correct its own errors. Whatever may be the strength of the latter argument, Cameroon can at any rate contend that, even if its duty to cooperate can be so extended, there should be reasonable limits to that duty and that those limits would be exceeded if it were to be required to accept delivery of the appellant in this case.

No doubt, Cameroon was at fault in not transferring the appellant to Arusha as speedily as it should have done in compliance with Judge Aspegren's order of 4 March 1997. Nevertheless, with full knowledge of that, the Tribunal did later issue an indictment and arrest warrant for the appellant. Thus, the Tribunal really wanted to have the appellant transferred to Arusha. This being so, and Cameroon having eventually made the transfer, why should it be under a duty to take back the appellant from the Tribunal?

The direction in which these arguments lie finds support from another quarter. In paragraph 107 of its Decision, the Appeals Chamber relies on Rule 40*bis*(H) of the Rules. For the reasons mentioned below, I do not think that that Rule applied; but, on the assumption that it did, the principle of the provision may be consulted.

Rule 40*bis*(H) of the Rules provides that, if an indictment has not been confirmed and an arrest warrant signed within a maximum period of 90 days after transfer, "the suspect shall be released or, if appropriate, be delivered to the authorities of the State to which the request **[page 6]** was initially made". In determining when it is "appropriate" to deliver custody of the suspect to the requested state, it is useful to bear in mind that the Rule applies where, *inter alia*, "the Prosecutor has requested a State to arrest the suspect and to place him in custody, in accordance with Rule 40, or the suspect is otherwise detained by a State" (Rule 40*bis*(B)(i)) In the present case, immediately before his transfer from Cameroon to Arusha, the appellant could not be described as "otherwise detained by" Cameroon; he was then indeed detained by Cameroon, but solely at the request of the Tribunal. That being so, Cameroon would have no independent legal basis for asserting custody over the appellant if he was returned. It is, therefore, difficult to see how it could be "appropriate" to direct the Registrar to arrange for the "delivery" of the appellant to Cameroon, with the implication that at the point of delivery the appellant reverts to the custody of Cameroon.

The Appeals Chamber considers the criterion of appropriateness by saying:

> "Considering the express provisions of Rule 40*bis*(H), and in light of the Rwandan extradition request for the Appellant and the denial of that request by the court in Cameroon, the Appeals Chamber concludes that it is appropriate for the Appellant to be delivered to the authorities of Cameroon, the State to which the Rule 40*bis* request was initially made". (Decision, para. 107).

With respect, I do not appreciate how the dismissal of the extradition request justifies the conclusion "that it is appropriate for the Appellant to be delivered to the authorities of Cameroon, the State to which the Rule 40*bis* request was initially made". The extradition request was dismissed on 21 February 1997. The appellant was transferred to Arusha on 19 November 1997, that is to say, nine months later. Immediately before the transfer, he was being held by Cameroon but, as observed above, solely at the request of the Tribunal; Cameroon had no other basis for holding him. The Tribunal cannot now give Cameroon a basis which Cameroon does not otherwise have. Therefore it could not be "appropriate" for the Tribunal to require Cameroon to receive delivery of the Appellant from the Tribunal. **[page 7]**

For these reasongs, I should have thought that the order was to set the appellant at liberty and to direct the Registrar to provide him with reasonable facilities to leave Tanzania, if he so wishes.

2. The issue is whether there was lack of jurisdiction

As to the case concerning pre-transfer delay, it is useful to bear in mind that this is not an appeal from a final decision; it is an interlocutory appeal. The competence of the Appeals Chamber in a matter of this kind derives from the Rules. Rule 72(D) of the Rules provides that "[d]ecisions on preliminary motions are without interlocutory appeal, save in the case of dismissal of an objection based on lack of jurisdiction, where an appeal will lie as of right". It has not been contested that the appellant's Urgent Motion was a preliminary motion[2].

---

[2]   Rule 72(A) states that "Preliminary motions ... shall be brought (i) within sixty days following the disclosure by the Prosecutor to the Defence of all the material envisaged by Rule 66(A)(i), ...". The latter requires the Prosecutor to disclose certain material to the Defence "within 30 days of the initial appearance ...". Though dated 19 February 1998, the Urgent Motion was filed on 24 February 1998, i.e, a day after the initial appearance. It is assumed that the material required to be disclosed by

The Appeals Chamber may interpret the position of an accused person in a preliminary motion before a Trial Chamber as amounting to an objection based on lack of jurisdiction. If there was such an objection, a dismissal of it would give him a right of appeal. But whether the appeal succeeds depends on whether the Appeals Chamber is satisfied not merely that such an objection was made, but also that it was sound – that is to say, that there was indeed a lack of jurisdiction in the fundamental sense which I believe is contemplated by Rule 72(D). In effect, there is, in my respectful view, a distinction between saying that an objection was based on lack of jurisdiction and saying that there was in fact a lack of jurisdiction as asserted in the objection[3].

In this case, on 5 February 1999 the Appeals Chamber held that there was a dismissal of "an objection based on lack of jurisdiction", so that an appeal lay as of right. What it now **[page 8]** has to determine is whether there was in fact a "lack of jurisdiction". So, did the Trial Chamber lack jurisdiction within the meaning of Rule 72(D) of the Rules by reason of any delay occurring during the pre-transfer period? I do not think so.

I shall try to explain my reasons in relation to the appellant's complaints concerning the furnishing of reasons for his arrest, non-compliance with the requirements of Rule 40*bis* of the Rules, the delay in transferring him from Cameroon to the Tribunal's detention unit in Arusha, and the non-hearing of his habeas corpus motion.

3. The question of non-disclosure of reasons for arrest

As to the appellant's complaint of non-disclosure of the reasons for his arrest, I agree with the Appeals Chamber's finding "that the Appellant was informed of the charges on 10 March 1997 when the Cameroon Deputy Prosecutor showed him a copy of the Rule 40*bis* Order". (Decision, para. 78). What the Appeals Chamber says is that this "was approximately 11 months after he was initially detained pursuant to the *first* Rule 40 request" (*ibid.*), and that "the Appellant was detained for a total period of 11 months before he was informed of the general nature of the charges that the Prosecutor was pursuing against him". (Decision, para. 85). It would not be correct to suggest, as these statements by themselves do, that during the whole of the 11-month period the appellant was being held at the instance of the Tribunal. And, indeed, the Appeals Chamber acknowledges "that only 35 days out of the 11-month total are clearly attributable to the Tribunal". (Ibid.). Nevertheless, the larger period seems to have influenced its finding "that the abuse of process doctrine is applicable under the facts of this case", that finding being immediately followed by the statement that the "Appellant was detained for 11 months without being notified of the charges against him" (Decision, para. 86) and being preceded, in paragraph 85 of the Decision, by the statement that at "this juncture, it is irrelevant that only a small portion of that total period of provisional detention is attributable to the Tribunal ...". **[page 9]**

The exact period attribuable to the Tribunal may be unclear; it was probably 40-46 days. The total consisted of two custodial periods which were initiated by requests from the Prosecutor to Cameroon. The first period began on 17 April 1996 and ended 29 days later on 16 May 1996. The second began nine months later, on 21 February 1997. It ended either 11 days later, on 4 March 1997, when there was filed a transfer order made by Judge Aspegren on 3 March 1997 (hereinafter referred to as Judge Aspegren's order of 4 March 1997), or, at the latest, on 10 March 1997, when a photocopy of the transfer order was shown to the appellant. During the first and longer of these two periods, and for some time both before and after it, the appellant was in fact being held by Cameroon under legal process not commenced by the Prosecutor. That does not say that the appellant was not also being held pursuant to the Prosecutor's request, but it is a fact worth noticing.

*

---

the prosecution under Rule 66(A)(i) was disclosed. In any case, the question whether the Urgent Motion was a preliminary motion has been foreclosed by the fact that the Appeals Chamber has held that the appeal is admissible, as is mentioned below.

[3]   I sought to address the matter in a dissenting opinion in *Prosecutor v. Kanyabashi*, ICTR, Appeals Chamber, 3 June 1999.

Even if the two periods of custody initiated by the Prosecutor (separated by a nine-month gap and totalling 40-46 days) were for any reason legally defective (as to which I express no opinion), I do not see that this circumstance by itself prevented the Trial Chamber from subsequently exercising jurisdiction pursuant to Judge Aspegren's order of 4 March 1997. Speaking of the period of detention from 17 April 1996 to 16 May 1996, the Appeals Chamber said, "This detention – for 29 days – violated the 20-day limitation in Rule 40." (Decision, para. 52). But the Appeals Chamber did not go on to determine that that holding of invalidity as to that period of detention by itself operated to invalidate any subsequent period of detention. Accordingly, the question of non-disclosure need only be considered with respect to the period of detention covered by Judge Aspegren's order of 4 March 1997. By comparison, it seems that the Appeals Chamber considered the question of non-disclosure in relation to the 11-month period from 17 April 1996 to 10 March 1997, holding that "the delay in informing the Appellant of the general nature of the charges between the initial Rule 40 request on 17 April 1996 and when he was actually shown a copy of the Rule 40*bis* Order on **[page 10]** 10 March 1997 violated his right to be promptly informed" (Decision, para 101). In any event, as the Appeals Chamber otherwise recognised, not all of that period could be attributed to the Tribunal. As to Judge Aspegren's second order made on 23 October 1997 in consideration of Article 19(2) of the Statute and Rules 54 to 61 of the Rules, it is not my impression that a question of non-disclosure of reasons has been raised in connection with this.

The question, then, is whether there was undue delay between the commencement of custody after the making of Judge Aspegren's order of 4 March 1997 and 10 March 1997 when a photocopy, or facsimile, of the order was shown to the appellant, that is to say, a period of six days. The appellant was at the time being held pursuant to the Prosecutor's request of 21 February 1997, that request and the consequential detention being explicitly referred to in Judge Aspegren's order of 4 March 1997. In the light of Rule 40*bis*(B)(i), the intent of that Rule may be understood to be that an order made under the Rule would replace any existing period of detention effected at the request of the Prosecutor not from the time the order was made but from the time when the order was put into operation: otherwise there could be a gap. Thus, after 4 March 1997 it is difficult to appreciate why there should be any question of the appellant being first held and then only being later shown a copy of the Judge's order. So far as that order is concerned, it is reasonable to regard the appellant as being held on the date on which he was shown a copy of the order, namely, on 10 March 1997. However, assuming that there was a gap between these events, it seems to me that, in the peculiar circumstances in which the Tribunal is functioning, the jurisprudence of the European Court of Human Rights and the Human Rights Committee on the question of what period of delay is inadmissible does not require me to consider the gap as excessive.

*

In parenthesis, it may be added that the appellant's complaint was that a photocopy of the Rule 40*bis* order which he was shown on 10 March 1997 was not a certified copy; he was **[page 11]** only shown a certified copy on 6 May 1997. If the photocopy was sufficient, he does not seem to be complaining of any delay in showing it to him on 10 March 1997. What would be applicable at that time would be the principle of Article 9(2) of the International Covenant on Civil and Political Rights. However, it is well understood, as I think is recognised in paragraph 82 of the Decision, that that provision (unlike Article 14(3)(a) of the Covenant) does not require communication of detailed charges or formalities; it is sufficient if the authorities give enough information (whether in writing or orally) to the arrested person of the substance of the allegation on the basis of which he was arrested so as to enable him to challenge the legality of the curtailment of his liberty on that basis, apart from also enabling him to begin the preparation of his defence. In this case, what was required was done.

Also, the appellant challenged the validity of Rule 40*bis* of the Rules as being in excess of the rule-making power conferred on the judges by Article 14 of the Statute. The challenge was correctly dismissed by the Trial Chamber. So too was his argument that, because of Article 19(2) of the Statute, he could only be arrested on the basis of a confirmed indictment. It is useful to mention these issues because they seemed to be connected in the appellant's mind with his arguments about non-disclosure of reasons.

4. The provisions of Rule 40bis did not apply to pre-transfer detention

The question which the foregoing leaves is whether there were other factors which impaired the legality of what may be regarded as a third custodial period commencing with Judge Aspegren's order of 4 March 1997 and ending with the transfer of the appellant to the detention unit of the Tribunal on 19 November 1997. The appellant says, and the Appeals Chamber agrees, that there was non-compliance with Rule 40bis of the Rules in relation to his detention in Cameroon at the instance of the Tribunal. I am not persuaded. A preliminary issue is whether the provisions of that Rule apply to pre-transfer custody. **[page 12]**

I understand the Appeals Chamber to be taking the view that the appellant was "in the constructive custody of the Tribunal after the Rule 40*bis* Order was filed on 4 March 1997" (footnote omitted); on this basis, it considers that "the provisions of that Rule would apply" to the pre-transfer detention. (Decision, para. 54). With respect, to hold that "the provisions of that Rule would apply" before the transfer conflicts with the clear meaning of the Rule that the procedural guarantees which it provides begin to operate only as from the time of transfer to the detention unit of the Tribunal. This meaning of the Rule conforms with the holding of the Appeals Chamber that the "initial thirty-day period begins to run from the 'day after the transfer of the suspect to the detention unit of the Tribunal'". (Ibid., para. 50).

The text of Rule 40*bis* need not be reproduced here; it is set out in the Decision and may be consulted there. It is enough to say that the body of the Rule corresponds to its title, which reads, "Transfer and Provisional Detention of Suspects". The Rule is speaking to the question of the mode of authorising a transfer of a suspect to the detention unit of the Tribunal in Arusha and to the question of the conditions under which he is to be provisionally detained after his transfer to that unit; it is not addressed to the conditions applicable to pretransfer detention. The references in Rule 40*bis*(F) and (G) to an extension of time being granted "subsequent to an *inter partes* hearing" are at least consistent with the view that the protective procedures of Rule 40*bis* apply only after the transfer of the suspect to Arusha. The Rule assumes that there would always be an interval between arrest in the requested state and transfer to Arusha but that the time stipulated by the Rule would nevertheless begin to run only as from transfer. That assumption is overlooked by an interpretation which says that "the provisions of that Rule would apply" to pre-transfer detention and that accordingly the time stipulated by the Rule is to begin to run from the time of arrest in the requested state and not from the time of transfer to Arusha. If time is to begin to run from the time of arrest in the requested state, it cannot also begin to run from the time of transfer to Arusha. The plain **[page 13]** meaning of the text that the latter should be the case will therefore stand amended by force of judicial decree. That is not possible.

The Appeals Chamber draws attention to the circumstance that "the Prosecutor has acknowledged that between 21 February 1997 and 19 November 1997, 'there existed what could be described as joined or concurrent personal jurisdiction over the Appellant, the personal jurisdiction being shared between the Tribunal and Cameroon'". (Decision, para. 54). Jurisdiction is not necessarily custody, actual or constructive. The reality of the control exercised by Cameroon over the appellant is evidenced by the circumstance that effect to Judge Aspegren's transfer order of 4 March 1997 was given by an order made by the President of Cameroon on 21 October 1997, whereby the President authorised the transfer ("est autorise, le transfert ..."): in effect, without the active participation of Cameroon, there could be no transfer.

The necessity, unremarkable enough, for the active participation of the requested state is not denied by *Ntakirutimana v. Attorney-General of the United States* (cited in paragraph 59 of the Decision). In that case, the appellate court of the requested state ruled in favour of the transfer of an accused whose surrender had been requested by the Tribunal. There is nothing in the appellate decision which shows that a requested state does not have exclusive custody of the accused person until transfer, or that, at any point of time before that stage, it would tolerate any assertion of authority by the Tribunal over the custody of the accused.

But, even if jurisdiction were necessarily the same as custody, I do not see how that suffices to found the Appeals Chamber's holding that "the provisions of [Rule 40*bis*] would apply" to the pre-transfer period of detention. (Decision, para. 54). Whether this is so or not depends on the terms of the Rule. The terms of the Rule limit its safeguards to post-transfer detention.

The maxim *ut res magis valeat quam pereat* may be thought supportive of the interpretation placed on Rule 40*bis* by the Appeals Chamber, which invokes it in paragraph **[page 14]** 46 and footnote 127 of the Decision. However, it seems to me that the maxim, in the sense of "effective interpretation", is directed to the adoption of an interpretation which would give effect to the substantial purpose of the text; it is not directed to changing the substance of the purpose of the text. The latter is legislation, not interpretation[4]. Here the substantial purpose of the text is to ensure release if no indictment has been filed after a maximum period of provisional detention by the Tribunal following on transfer to the detention unit of the Tribunal in Arusha. That purpose is substantially changed if the procedure prescribed by the text is made to apply also to the materially different matter of pre-transfer detention in the requested state.

Within reasonable limits, the principle of the maxim in question is a good servant, and it has of course been repeatedly used in international law[5]; outside of reasonable limits, it is a bad master, colliding, for example, with statements to the effect that the duty of the court is to interpret and not to revise a treaty or to rewrite it or to reconstruct it[6]. The maxim cannot be applied in a way which overlooks a distinction between the general sentiment inspiring a provision and the actual purpose of the provision[7]. In this case, the general sentiment underlying Rule 40*bis* was unquestionably a concern with the liberty of a suspect; it does not follow that the specific procedure laid down by the Rule was directed to ensuring his liberty in all circumstances in which his liberty might be in question.

Judge Aspegren, correctly, did not understand Rule 40*bis* in the way in which the Rule has been interpreted by the Appeals Chamber, namely, that "the provisions of that Rule **[page 15]** would apply" to pre-transfer detention. The operative provisions of his order of 4 March 1997 stated as follows:

"Orders the transfer of the suspect Jean Bosco Barayagwiza to the Tribunal's dominion;

Orders the provisional detention of Jean Bosco Barayagwiza in the Tribunal's Detention Facilities for a maximum period of thirty days from the day after his transfer;

Respectfully requests the Cameroonian Government to comply with the Tribunal's order for transfer, and to keep Jean Bosco Barayagwiza in custody until he is handed over to the Tribunal for transfer and detention under the authority of the Tribunal;

Requests the Prosecutor to submit the indictment against Jean Bosco Barayagwiza before the expiration of the said 30-day limit of the provisional detention;

Requests the Registrar of the Tribunal to notify the Cameroonian Government and to inform the Rwandan Government of this decision"

Judge Aspegren's order visualised that the transfer would be made to the detention unit of the Tribunal in Arusha; that, pending transfer, Cameroon would hold the suspect in custody; and that, within 30 days of the transfer, the Prosecutor would submit an indictment against him[8]. In the event, Cameroon did not make the requested transfer until 19 November 1997. It is not easy to see how this delay operated

---

[4]   An example of the proper functioning of the maxim is provided by the decision in a case in which a statutory provision "which empowered justices to suspend, in case of sickness, the order of removal of any pauper who should be 'brought before them for the purpose of being removed,' was construed as authorising such suspension without the actual bringing up of the pauper before the justices, as the literal construction would have defeated the humane object of the enactment". (See Sir Peter Benson Maxwell, *The Interpretation of Statutes*, 9th ed., p. 244, citing *R. v. Everdon* (1807), 9 East. 101). There the substantial purpose of the statute – to suspend a removal order in case of sickness – was not changed; what the interpretation did was to say that the prescribed mechanism for giving effect to that purpose was not exhaustive.

[5]   See, for example *The Territorial Dispute (Libyan Arab Jamahiriya/Chad), I.C.J. Reports 1994*, p. 25, para. 51.

[6]   See, inter alia, *Acquisition of Polish Nationality, P.C.I.J., Ser. B, No. 7, p. 20; The Peace Treaties, I.C.J. Reports 1950, p. 229; and Aerial Incident of 27 July 1955, I.C.J. Reports 1959*, p. 183, Judge Sir Hersch Lauterpacht, dissenting.

[7]   In *Nuclear Tests (New Zealand v. France), I.C.J. Reports 1995*, p.313, I happened likewise to think that a distinction could be drawn between general motivation and specific solution.

[8]   The judge was thus giving the prosecution less time to present an indictment than could be allowed under Rule 40*bis*. A question, into which I do not enter without the benefit of argument, is whether he could competently do so having regard to the circumstance that such a requirement is not specified as one of the conditions which, if satisfied, ground a mandatory duty of the judge to issue an order. The judge could refuse to extend time after the first maximum period of 30 days; but could he at the beginning of the process impose a requirement to file an indictment within that time? Possibly, a term to similar effect could be imposed as a condition of renewal of the period, but that is another question.

to impose a reading on Judge Aspegren's order of 4 March 1997 so as to require the Prosecutor to submit an indictment within 30 days of the date of the order, instead of 30 days of the date of the transfer as the Judge plainly intended. The indictment was both submitted and confirmed even before the accused was transferred to the Tribunal's detention unit and therefore even before the 30-day period **[page 16]** specified in the Judge's order had begun to run. By contrast, the Appeals Chamber held that the "delay in indicting the Appellant violated the 90-day rule as set forth in Rule 40*bis*". (Decision, para. 67). That was so only if the interpretation of the Appeals Chamber as to when time begins to run under that Rule is correct.

If a suspect is held by a requested state under a Rule 40*bis* order for an unreasonable time, the answer is not to square the circle and to force upon the Rule a meaning which it cannot bear, but to move before the issuing judge or a Trial Chamber for relief as suggested in the second and third of three courses mentioned in section 5 below. These courses need not rest on any theory of constructive custody. Constructive custody or no constructive custody, if the suspect is being made to suffer as a result of process issuing out of the Tribunal, the Tribunal has competence to correct the injustice by terminating the process which leads to that result. But that does not mean that "the provisions of [Rule 40*bis*] would apply" to pre-transfer detention.

In my view, under Rule 40*bis*(C) time begins to run only from the transfer of the suspect to the detention unit of the Tribunal. On that basis, the safeguard steps prescribed by the provision were not violated.

*

I have considered an alternative interpretation of the Decision of the Appeals Chamber. This is that, while the *provisions* of Rule 40*bis* did not themselves apply to the pre-transfer period, the *principle* of those provisions applied on the basis that the appellant was in the constructive custody of the Tribunal and therefore entitled to the protection of the purpose of the Rule, which was largely to secure the release of an arrested person if a confirmed indictment was not presented against him within a maximum of 90 days. Granted, for the purposes of argument, the applicability of the theory of constructive custody, the suggested interpretation really rests on the idea of abuse of process. However, as will be later **[page 17]** argued, that concept assumes the continued existence of jurisdiction, with the result that an entitlement to release by reason of that concept could not be said to rest on lack of jurisdiction within the meaning of Rule 72(D) of the Rules under which the appeal is being entertained. The point, in its more general aspect, is dealt with in section 8 below.

5. The delay in making a transfer from Cameroon to Arusha

The appellant's main contention lies in his complaint that the Tribunal was responsible for failing to ensure that he was transferred by Cameroon to the Tribunal's detention unit as speedily as possible in accordance with Judge Aspegren's order of 4 March 1997; the appellant was not transferred until 19 November 1997. The Appeals Chamber takes he view that the Tribunal was responsible on the ground that the appellant was in the constructive custody of the Tribunal while he was held in Cameroon at the Tribunal's request, a view which, as I understand it, is premised on there being a relationship of agent and principal as between Cameroon and the Tribunal. (See para. 56 of the Decision, where references are made to "agent" as used in United States case-law). With respect, I am not persuaded that that was the relationship or that there was any relationship giving rise to constructive custody.

I favour the submission of the Prosecutor that Cameroon and the Tribunal are not the *alter ego* of each other. What the Security Council did was to apportion responsibilities to states and to the Tribunal on the basis of there being a legal obligation on the part of states to cooperate with the Tribunal – an obligation deriving immediately from the Statute of the Tribunal and ultimately from the Charter of the United Nations. A state which is cooperating with the Tribunal is discharging its own responsibilities and not those of the Tribunal.

The obligation of a state to cooperate with the Tribunal may be triggered in different ways; however triggered, the obligation remains that of the state. The trigger could be an order of a judge requesting the state to hold the suspect and to transfer him to the detention **[page 18]** unit of the

Tribunal. The order of the judge of the Tribunal is but the condition precedent to the activation of the obligation of the state under the Statute; it does not create a relationship of agent and principal as between the state and the Tribunal or put the Tribunal in constructive custody of the suspect for the purpose of fixing it with responsibility for the acts or omissions of the state. If, for example, the state were to hold the suspect in unacceptable physical conditions, the responsibility would be that of the state, not of the Tribunal. The state and the Tribunal are each separately responsible for their own acts or omissions.

Arguing for a different view, the Decision of the Appeals Chamber refers to what is substantially United States internal extradition law. Generally valuable as is that respected body of law, I am not confident of the utility of any analogies which it furnishes, in this particular field, on the subject of principal and agent, or on the subject of constructive custody, or on the subject of detainer process. Internal extradition in the United States "is founded on, and controlled by, the Constitution of the United States and effectuating federal statutes"; it is not "governed by the same principles as are applicable to international extradition"; the proceedings are "sui generis". (See 35 *Corpus Juris Secundum*, p. 381). True, as it was put in a dissenting opinion in a United States case, "The Tribunal is not a sovereign nation". (*Ntakirutimana v. Attorney-General of the United States, supra*, Judge DeMoss, dissenting). But neither is it a state within a federal-type arrangement. The legislation and jurisprudence of a particular state as to relations between components of the state offer limited guidance on relations between the Tribunal and states which are sovereign on the international plane. These latter relations are regulated by the unique system devised by the Statute of the Tribunal; they are not based on the internal distribution of power among the units of a state, however those units are designated.

But the foregoing does not mean that there is nothing that the Tribunal can or should do. The Tribunal has an obligation to consider the situation if in fact delay is caused by the state. Three possibilities may be considered: **[page 19]**

The first possibility arises under Article 28 of the Statute and the corresponding provisions of Rule 7*bis* of the Rules, relating to the duty of states to cooperate with the Tribunal[9]. Under those provisions, the President of the Tribunal may report the conduct of a non-cooperating state to the Security Council. The remedy thus provided is a powerful one; but it may come too late so far as the suspect is concerned. More pertinently, it does not result from the kind of decision that would ground an appeal.

A second possibility is this. The view can be taken that the power of a judge to issue an order for custody arid transfer includes by necessary implication power to rescind the order in proper cases. Whether or not recourse was made to the reporting provisions mentioned above, if, on a report from the Registrar or the Prosecutor or on an application made by or on behalf of the suspect, the judge, after an appropriate hearing, was satisfied that the suspect was kept too long in custody and was consequently suffering unjustly because of the process of the Tribunal, the judge could, in my opinion, competently rescind the order and thus set the suspect at liberty so far as the Tribunal was concerned. He could do so on the footing that any authority given by him to the state to hold the suspect in custody pending transfer incorporated an implicit condition that the authority was to be exercised by the state within a reasonable time (as is implied, in the case of an accused, by Rule 59(B) of the Rules), and that, accordingly, the judge retained competence to consider whether the condition had been breached. No question of constructive custody need be involved.

But a decision of that kind would not be a decision on a preliminary motion within the meaning of Rule 72(D) of the Rules, and there could be no question of an appeal. Even if such a decision were one on a preliminary motion, appellate intervention would really rest on the doctrine of abuse of process, the question being whether the proceedings should be stayed in the light of the delay in giving effect to the process of the Tribunal. As argued below, the **[page 20]** application of this doctrine would not result in a finding of lack of jurisdiction so as to entitle the Appeals Chamber to give a remedy under Rule 72(D) of the Rules.

---

[9]   The reporting provisions of Rule 59 of the Rules seem to be restricted to the case of an accused, as distinguished from a suspect.

A third possibility remains. It may be said that the statutory power of the Prosecutor to investigate and to prosecute was impliedly conditioned by a duty of due diligence, which in turn required her to be active on the question of compliance by Cameroon with the judge's transfer order. I respectfully agree with the Appeals Chamber in considering that that is right; after all, it is the Prosecutor who wanted the suspect to be transferred for purposes of continuing investigations relating to the same suspect. It follows that failure to discharge the duty to monitor the situation could ground a release by the judge. The appellant says that he was simply "forgotten" by the Prosecutor. The evidence does not go all that way, but it goes far enough to recall that there "is as a rule no difficulty encountered by doing nothing or little"[10]. The trouble is that doing nothing or little in this case was not allowed.

But, again, a decision of that kind would not be a decision on a preliminary motion. Even if the decision could be regarded as one made on a preliminary motion, appellate intervention would really rest on the doctrine of abuse of process, the question being whether the proceedings should be stayed in the light of the delay produced by the neglect. As argued below, that doctrine would not ground an interlocutory appeal on the basis of lack of jurisdiction.

Thus, in none of the three cases can the Appeals Chamber intervene.

6. The failure to hear the appellant's habeas corpus motion

Now for the question of the appellant's habeas corpus motion of 29 September 1997 (filed on 2 October 1997). In paragraph 90 of its Decision, the Appeals Chamber found that "the failure to provide the Appellant a hearing on this *writ* violated his right to challenge the legality of his continued detention in Cameroon during the two periods when he was held at **[page 21]** the behest of the Tribunal...". But for the fact that its actual decision rendered the point moot, it is evident that the Appeals Chamber would have ordered a hearing of the habeas corpus motion on the basis that it is "still pending", as asserted by the appellant, in which case the question of release would fall to be decided both in the present proceedings and in the habeas corpus motion.

I am not persuaded that an issue relating to the hearing of the habeas corpus motion is before the Appeals Chamber. This is because none of the twelve prayers addressed to the Trial Chamber in the Appellant's Urgent Motion of 24 February 1998 referred to the habeas corpus motion, complained of non-hearing of it, or sought a hearing of it. It has to be remembered that the appeal is from the decision of the Trial Chamber on that Urgent Motion.

The Trial Chamber was not asked by the appellant to determine an objection based on lack of jurisdiction arising from the non-hearing of the habeas corpus motion. The Trial Chamber's summary of the issues presented to it by the defence, as set out in its written decision, shows that it did not consider that it had such an objection before it. That is supported by the transcript of the oral arguments before the Trial Chamber. As is seen below, defence counsel mentioned the habeas corpus motion in the course of his oral arguments before the Trial Chamber, but he did not, in my view, do so on the basis that the motion was still outstanding and should be heard. Interestingly too, none of the twenty-two errors alleged in the appellant's Memorandum of Appeal of 27 November 1998 (filed on 10 December 1998) complained about the Trial Chamber's decision in so far as the habeas corpus motion was concerned.

It is not correct to tax the Trial Chamber with not dealing with an issue which it was not asked to determine. Nor, subject to narrow exceptions, can it be right for the Appeals Chamber to pass on an issue which was not argued before the Trial Chamber and on which the latter has not expressed its views, either as to the facts or as to the law. The jurisdiction of the Appeals Chamber is limited to matters which formed part of an objection based on lack **[page 22]** of jurisdiction which was dismissed by the Trial Chamber. No such objection was dismissed by the Trial Chamber so far as concerns the non-hearing of the habeas corpus motion. Consequently, the Appeals Chamber is without jurisdiction to deal with the point.

---

[10]   *Admissibility of Hearings of Petitioners by the Committee on South West Africa, Advisory Opinion, I.C.J.Reports 1956,* p. 23 at p. 53, Judge Sir Hersch Lauterpacht, separate opinion.

Further, I do not consider that a hearing of the habeas corpus motion by any Chamber is still required. The Appeals Chamber can draw a reasonable inference that, at the time, defence counsel himself took the view that the filing of the indictment made a hearing pointless. In the Trial Chamber, defence counsel said that "these [documents relating to the indictment] were meant [presumably by the Prosecutor] to pre-empt the argument of our application for habeas corpus". (Transcript of oral arguments in the Trial Chamber, 11 September 1998, pp. 84-85). Defence counsel did not say that he himself did not share the view that the filing of the indictment would pre-empt the argument of the application for habeas corpus; I think that at the time he thought that it would.

And why would he think so? Because of the nature of the orders requested in the habeas corpus motion. These, as set out in that motion, were as follows:

"1. An order for Habeas Corpus requiring that the suspect Jean Bosco Barayagwiza be produced before the tribunal.

2. An order requiring the immediate release of Jean Bosco Barayagwiza who is currently in prison custody in Yaounde, Cameroon.

3. An order requiring that in the alternative and if for any lawful reason the suspect, Jean Bosco Barayagwiza cannot be released, he be indicted and transferred to the tribunal's seat in Arusha within 30 days or such reasonable time as this Honourable Tribunal may set.

4. An order requiring that in the meantime, the suspect Jean Bosco Barayagwiza be accorded medical attention by the tribunal and that the tribunal do provide him with food and other basic needs." **[page 23]**

Thus, in the alternative to his immediate release, what the appellant sought was an indictment and transfer to the Tribunal's seat in Arusha. In these respects, the position later changed in favour of the very position desired by the appellant: an indictment was filed and he was transferred to Arusha. A principal part of the prayers of his motion thereby became *sans objet*. Further, after the transfer he could no longer ask for medical attention and food – the complaint was directed to the period while he was in Cameroon. What was left was a demand for his release. But since this demand was taken over by his Urgent Motion of 24 February 1998, it cannot credibly be accepted that the original habeas corpus request was regarded by counsel for the appellant as "still pending" so as to result in duplicated applications before the Trial Chamber on the same point. Habeas corpus is of course a great writ; but that does not settle everything. If, in this case, the motion for the writ is not "still pending", it simply cannot be considered, with the result that there is no need to review cases in which, although a matter has become moot, the fundamental importance of the issues involved may justify a pronouncement[11].

The appellant suggests that the Prosecutor somehow managed to arrange for the removal of the case from its place in the hearing list, on which, so he was informed, it was due to be heard on 31 October 1997. The appellant has no proof of that. What he could say, but what he does not say, is whether he later sought to get the Registrar to put back the case for hearing or in any way to protest to him about the alleged removal of the case from the calendar. There is no evidence that he did.

The appellant did not tell the Trial Chamber which took his initial appearance on 23 February 1998 that his habeas corpus motion was "still pending". The "applications" to which his counsel then referred were, in my opinion, different motions. Counsel mentioned "two motions". (Transcript of the initial appearance proceedings, 23 February 1998, p.16). One was a motion to quash the whole indictment on the basis of alleged defects of form. **[page 24]** (Ibid., p 18) The other was a motion "to review and or nullify the arrest and provisional detention of the accused person". (Ibid., p.17). That referred to the Urgent Motion which is the subject of this appeal. This Urgent Motion was dated 19 February 1998 although bearing a filing date of 24 February 1998; somehow, though not yet filed, reference was made to it at the hearing on 23 February 1998. In my understanding, the habeas corpus motion of 29 September 1997 (filed on 2 October 1997) was not referred to in the oral proceedings on 23 February 1998.

---

[11]   See, in this latter respect, 5 *Corpus Juris Secundum*, para. 1354(1).

The appellant is saying now (29 June 1999) that "the motion is still pending"[12]. But he is saying that to the Appeals Chamber in response to the Appeals Chamber's inquiry of 3 June 1999 as to the "disposition of the writ of Habeas Corpus that the Appellant asserts that he filed on 2nd October 1997". What he is saying now he did not say before. Paragraph 9 of his "Duplique" of 18 December 1998 (filed on 28 December 1998) did say that the habeas corpus motion was never heard; but the appellant said that to the Appeals Chamber and not to the Trial Chamber, and then only by way of stating an alleged consequence of the Prosecutor being precipitated by the filing of the habeas corpus motion into filing the indictment[13]. He did not claim that the habeas corpus "motion is still pending" and demand a speedy hearing. That simple statement was never made in his voluminous previous pleadings. I have given reasons why he did not make it and why he could not make it.

Finally, if, contrary to the foregoing, the habeas corpus motion is "still pending" as is now asserted by the appellant, any delay in hearing it would merely ground action to stay further proceedings on the basis of the doctrine of abuse of process. As argued below, the Appeals Chamber is not competent to grant relief on that basis in an interlocutory appeal. At this stage, the Appeals Chamber must take the view that the matter was one for the relevant Trial Chamber alone. **[page 25]**

7. *The delay in hearing the Urgent Motion*

Among the things which led to its decision, the Appeals Chamber mentions "the delay in hearing the Extremely Urgent Motion" (Decision, para. 109), that is to say, the Urgent Motion which is the subject of this appeal. So the Appeals Chamber is finding that there was such delay and that such delay is a ground of its decision.

The Urgent Motion was filed on 24 February 1998, but determined only on 17 November 1998. The facts show that, except for the first eleven weeks, the time was taken up by the appellant in settling a dispute concerning arrangements for his legal representation. (See annex 10 to Prosecutor's Response, filed on 22 June 1999, being a letter from defence counsel dated 12 May 1998). For this reason, the focus should be on the first eleven weeks.

The delay of eleven weeks was noticeable, but the material before the Appeals Chamber does not enable any conclusions to be safely drawn as to the reasons. In the case of this appeal – an appeal from the decision of the Trial Chamber on the same motion – forty-seven weeks have already gone by; that there is a good explanation does not efface the fact that much time has passed. From the factual point of view, I do not believe that the Appeals Chamber is in a good position to link its decision to the time taken to hear the Urgent Motion.

From the jurisdictional point of view, there is also a problem. It is evident that any delay in hearing the Urgent Motion could not have formed part of the matters put to the Trial Chamber in the same motion as material to justify an objection based on lack of jurisdiction. Since the appeal is from the decision of the Trial Chamber on the matters which were put to it in support of the Urgent Motion, it follows that the Appeals Chamber has no competence to consider any delay in hearing the Urgent Motion. **[page 26]**

8. *If there was abuse of proces, this did not lead to a lack of jurisdiction on the part of the Tribunal*

This section assumes that there was abuse of process in relation to pre-transfer detention but considers whether this led to a "lack of jurisdiction" within the meaning of Rule 72(D) of the Rules so as to enable the Appeals Chamber to act under that provision.

The appellant fell prima facie within the jurisdictional provisions of the Statute. A possible argument is that to prosecute him notwithstanding the alleged breaches of his human rights amounted to an abuse of process, that such abuse of process deprived the Trial Chamber of jurisdiction, and that consequently there was a "lack of jurisdiction" within the meaning of Rule 72(D). Does the doctrine of

---

[12]   Para. 22 of the Appellant's Reply to the Prosecutor's Response Pursuant to the Scheduling Order of 3rd June 1999.
[13]   See also the heading of section VII of the amended version of Appellant's Brief dated 15 February 1999, corrected 23 February 1999, where he says that there was "Refusal to hear the Motion of Habeas Corpus".

abuse of process support the proposition? In particular, assuming that there were breaches of the appellant's human rights so as to attract the application of the doctrine, did the doctrine lead to a lack of jurisdiction?

Cases on the subject of abuse of process assume that the trial court had jurisdiction, or indeed that a fair trial was perfectly possible in exercise of that very jurisdiction, but are directed to the different question whether, in its discretion, the court should have permitted that jurisdiction to be exercised having regard to the public interest in maintaining the integrity of the criminal justice system free of affronts to the public conscience. (*R. v. Latif and Shahzad*, [1996] 1 WLR 104, HL, at p. 112, Lord Steyn; and see *R. v. Mullen, The Times*, 15 February 1999 (CA)). In a leading case of 1994, Lord Griffiths made this clear when he said that the question was "whether assuming the court has jurisdiction, it has a discretion to refuse to try the accused". (*R. v. Horseferry Road Magistrates' Court, ex parte Bennett*, 95 ILR 398, HL, at p. 390). In the words of Lord Lowry, "it is not jurisdiction which is in issue but the exercise of a discretion to stay proceedings ...". (Ibid., p. 408). Referring to another case, he said, "While that (magistrates') court had *jurisdiction* to entertain committal proceedings, the High Court decided that to permit the criminal proceedings against the accused to continue would be an abuse of process of the court (of **[page 27]** trial)". (Ibid, p. 411, original italics). In other words, the legal machinery had the capacity to turn, but the particular circumstances made it unjust to allow it to be put in motion.

Other cases, some from different countries, could be cited; but, in my opinion, even with any variations they may show, they do not overthrow the basic position taken in *Bennett* as to the distinction, in the doctrine of abuse of process, between the existence of jurisdiction and a stay of its exercise. I am reinforced in this view by paragraph 74 of the Decision of the Appeals Chamber, stating:

> "It is important to stress that the abuse of process doctrine may be invoked as a matter of discretion. It is a process by which Judges may decline to exercise the court's jurisdiction in cases where to exercise that jurisdiction in light of serious and egregious violations of the accused's rights would prove detrimental to the court's integrity."

I interpret this to mean that the Appeals Chamber recognises that the doctrine of abuse of process goes to discretion, and does not touch jurisdiction. Where I differ is as to the consequences on the appellate process of the Tribunal of this distinction. Abjuring the rigidity of the law but not shunning its rigour, it appears to me that, since the concept of abuse of process assumes the continuing existence of the normal trial jurisdiction and does not remove it, where the concept is applied it cannot logically lead to the conclusion that there was a "lack of jurisdiction."

To come back to the pre-transfer detention in this case, if there were any breaches of human rights this could raise a question whether the jurisdiction of the Tribunal should be exercised; but this would not result in "lack of jurisdiction" within the meaning of Rule 72(D) of the Rules. It is to the actual terms of that Rule that the discussion must turn when considering the application of the doctrine. The reference in the Rule to "jurisdiction" seems to be a reference to "jurisdiction" as prescribed by the Statute. In the case of failure to comply with a fundamental principle, such as that which requires an accused person to be promptly **[page 28]** put before the Trial Chamber the Statute itself can be interpreted to mean that there is loss of personal jurisdiction. However, I would hesitate to give any larger meaning to the reference to "jurisdiction" in Rule 72(D). More particularly, as set out in the Statute, the ingredients of "jurisdiction" do not exclude a case in which there is jurisdiction in fact and in law, but in which it would be an abuse of process for that jurisdiction to be exercised. The existence of jurisdiction has to be separated from its exercise.

In effect, if there were any breaches of the appellant's human rights in respect of the pre-transfer detention, this did not lead to "lack of jurisdiction" within the meaning of Rule 72(D) of the Rules. It may be that the Appeals Chamber can indeed consider whether there has been an abuse of process, but not in an interlocutory appeal under that Rule.

9. Limits on the competence of the Appeals Chamber

That last remark leads to an observation or two on the scope of the jurisdiction of the Appeals Chamber. The Decision of the Appeals Chamber states that "courts have supervisory powers that may be utilised in the interests of justice, regardless of a specific violation". (Decision, para.76). The Decision makes it clear that these supervisory powers can be exercised as between an appellate court and the court appealed from. The idea is a useful one. But, in applying it in the case of the International Criminal Tribunal for Rwanda, caution is appropriate to the nature and structure of the Tribunal.

Without questioning its validity, it may be observed that the system of interlocutory appeals, as introduced by the Rules, goes somewhat beyond the strict international requirement relating to a right of appeal[14]. This does not relieve the Appeals Chamber of its duty to exercise with vigour any jurisdiction which it has; but it at least serves to emphasise the point that, however robustly the Appeals Chamber does so, it has to confine itself within the framework of the scheme under which it is empowered to act. **[page 29]**

To hold that the interlocutory appellate provisions of Rule 72(D) of the Rules cover a case relating to pre-transfer delay involves a stretching of that provision. That stretching can only be justified on the view that the Appeals Chamber may act as if it were endowed with inherent authority to supervise all the activities of an inferior court. I believe that the Appeals Chamber will accept that it does not have that power; that it does not have overall surveillance or general oversight of the workings of a Trial Chamber as if the latter were an inferior court as understood in some systems; that it may not intervene on the basis that it has competence to do so wherever it is disposed to take the view that something was done. For to do so would amount to an impermissible amendment of Article 24 of the Statute of the Tribunal and an unlawful expansion of the province of action thereunder assigned to the Appeals Chamber.

The first instance jurisdiction of the Tribunal has been confided to the Trial Chambers. Save where it can clearly be demonstrated that the Appeals Chamber has power to intervene, the process is to be administered by the Trial Chambers – errors or no errors. They are the judiciary too. Even a final court of appeal makes errors, as witness cases in which it overrules its own previous decisions. The reason, if one were needed, is that it "is common knowledge that courts of law and other tribunals, however praiseworthy their intentions may be, are not infallible"[15].Their fallibility is part of the entire system; it has to be accepted. A system of appeals may provide a remedy; but it is necessarily limited. And the limits must be observed if the system is not to collapse. In one jurisdiction, it was once estimated that about 33 per cent of all appeals succeeded, whether from the lower courts to an intermediate court of appeal or from the latter to the final court of appeal. Thus, there was "no reason for believing that if there was a higher tribunal still the proportion of successful appeals to it would not reach at least that figure"[16]. **[page 30]**

With that sobering thought in mind, it seems to me that the Appeals Chamber cannot, in an interlocutory appeal, give a remedy simply because it considers that there were breaches of the appellant's human rights. It can do so only if such breaches deprived the Trial Chamber of jurisdiction. In this case, with the exception of post-transfer delay (which rested on a specific Rule of fundamental importance), they did not.

10. Conclusion

In an opinion which I appended to the decision in *Prosecutor v. Kovacevic* (ICTY, Appeals Chamber, 2 July 1998) I referred to *United States v. Lovasco*, 431 U.S. 783(1977). Recalling that opinion, paragraph 94 of the Decision of the Appeals Chamber in this case refers to *United States v. Scott* (437 U.S. 82 (1978) and states that, in that case, in "a dissent filed by four of the Court's nine Justices,

---

[14]   Cf. Article 14(5) of the ICCPR, reading, "Everyone convicted of a crime shall have the right to his conviction and sentence being reviewed by a higher tribunal according to law".
[15]   *Effect of Awards of Compensation made by the United Nations Administrative Tribunal, Advisory Opinion, I.C.J. Reports 1954*, p. 47, at p. 86, Judge Hackworth, dissenting.
[16]   Lord Justice Atkin, "Appeal in English Law" (1927-29), 3 Camb. L.J. 1, at p. 9.

(including Justice Marshall, the author of the <u>Lovasco</u> decision), the <u>Lovasco</u> holding regarding pre-indictment delay was characterised as a 'disfavoured doctrine'".

That, no doubt, is a possible interpretation of what the minority in *Scott* held. It may, however, be of some interest to note that what the minority in *Scott* actually said was that the decision in *Scott* itself "may be limited to disfavoured doctrines like pre-accusation delay. See generally United States v. Lovasco, 431 U.S. 783(1977)". That is all that the minority in *Scott* said on the question of *Lovasco*. For myself, I understand the minority in *Scott* to be referring the reader "generally" to *Lovasco* for information about "disfavoured doctrines like pre-accusation delay", and not to be saying that the specific holding in *Lovasco* regarding the pre-indictment delay in that case could be characterised as a "disfavoured doctrine".

More particularly, I am inclined to the view that the general if brief remark of the minority in *Scott* was not intended to cast doubt on the particular *Lovasco* holding (which was material to the issue in *Kovacevic*) that "prosecutors are under no duty to file charges as soon as probable cause exists but before they are satisfied that they will be able to establish **[page 31]** the suspect's guilt beyond a reasonable doubt". I should not think that the minority in *Scott* (inclusive of Justice Marshall who authored that statement) intended to question it; the majority did not. The statement looks to me like good law.

On the other hand, I would indeed have a difficulty with *Lovasco* if it was promoting the idea that any kind of pre-accusation delay, however extravagant, could be disregarded on the ground of prosecutorial discretion. But I doubt that it was really doing so; I note that it recognised that a "tactical" delay would be impermissible. That there should be some limitation on pre-accusation delay makes sense. However, for the reasons given above, I do not consider that it is competent for the Appeals Chamber to consider whether any limitation was breached in the circumstances of this case.

Accordingly, I regret my inability to support the Decision of the Appeals Chamber so far as pre-transfer delay is concerned. I agree with the Decision with respect to the threemonth delay between transfer and initial appearance. For the reasons mentioned above, I do not, however, agree with item 4 of the disposition, directing "the Registrar to make the necessary arrangements for the delivery of the Appellant to the Authorities of Cameroon"; the appellant should be simply set at liberty and provided with reasonable facilities to leave Tanzania, if he so wishes. On this basis, and subject to these qualifications, I would also allow the appeal. **[page 32]**

Done in both English and French, the English text being authoritative.

Mohamed Shahabuddeen

Dated this 3rd day of November 1999

At the Hague

The Netherlands

DECLARATION OF JUDGE NIETO-NAVIA

I wish to clarify my position with respect to the fourth dispositive paragraph. According to Rule 40*bis*, the Appellant "shall be released or, *if appropriate*, be delivered to the authorities of the State to which the request was initially made" (emphasis added). I am not convinced that it is appropriate to direct the Registrar to make the necessary arrangements to deliver the Appellant to the Cameroonian authorities. The Appeals Chamber found that the Appellant was detained by Cameroon since 21 February 1997 "solely at the behest of the Prosecutor"[1]. 'The Chamber further found that the "Appellant would have been released on 21 February 1997, when the Cameroon Court of Appeal denied the Rwandan extradition request and ordered the immediate release of the Appellant" *but for* the Tribunal's "valid request pursuant to Rule 40 for provisional detention, and shortly thereafter, pursuant to Rule 40*bis*, for the transfer of the Appellant"[2]. Therefore, Cameroon is under no legal obligation to accept the Appellant unless they wish to proceed with his prosecution. Under these circumstances, the Registrar should obtain the views of the Cameroonian authorities, and deliver the Appellant to them only if appropriate.

Rafael Nieto-Navia

Judge

---

[1] Jean Bosco Barayagwiza v. The Prosecutor, *Decision*, Appeal Chamber, Case No.: ICTR-97-19-AR72, para 54
[2] *Ibid.*, para. 55.

OR: ENG

Before: Judge Lloyd George Williams, Presiding
                 Judge Yakov Ostrovsky
                 Judge Pavel Dolenc

Registrar: Dr. Agwu Ukiwe Okali

Decision of: 6 October 1999

THE PROSECUTOR

v.

LAURENT SEMANZA

Case No. ICTR-97-20-I

DECISION ON THE "MOTION TO SET ASIDE THE ARREST AND
DETENTION OF LAURENT SEMANZA AS UNLAWFUL"

The office of the Prosecutor:
    David Spencer
    Frédéric Ossogo

Counsel for Laurent Semanza:
    André Dumont

[page 2] 1. **The International Criminal Tribunal for Rwanda** (Tribunal), sitting today as Trial Chamber III, composed of Presiding Judge Lloyd George Williams, Judge Yakov Ostrovsky, and Judge Pavel Dolenc, decide the "Motion to Set Aside the Arrest and Detention of Laurent Semanza as Unlawful" (Motion).

BACKGROUND

2.   On or about 26 March 1996, authorities in Cameroon arrested Mr. Laurent Semanza (Semanza), pursuant to an international arrest warrant issued by the Rwandan Attorney General's Office.

3.   On 17 April 1996, the Prosecutor issued a request for provisional measures in respect of the accused, along with 11 other persons.

4.   On 6 May 1996, the Prosecutor requested the Cameroon authorities to extend the detention of Semanza for three months.

5.   On 16 May 1996, the Prosecutor expressed the intention to proceed against four of the twelve persons against whom provisional measures had been sought. Semanza was not one of these four persons.

6.   On 21 February 1997, the Court of Appeal of the Centre (Criminal Chamber) in Yaoundé (Cameroon) ordered the release of Semanza, having found inadmissible the Rwandan extradition request.

7.   On 21 February 1997, the Prosecutor issued a new request to the authorities in Cameroon for the provisional arrest of Semanza.

8.   On 24 February 1997, the Prosecutor requested the Tribunal to order the transfer and provisional detention of Semanza, pursuant to rule 40*bis* of the Rules of Procedure and Evidence (Rules).

9.   On 3 March 1997, Judge Aspegren presided over an *ex parte* hearing on the request of the Prosecution for a Rule 40*bis* order.

10.   On 4 March 1997, Judge Aspegren filed an "Order for Transfer and Provisional Detention" (40*bis* Order).

11.   On 17 October 1997, the Prosecutor filed an indictment against Semanza.

12.   On 23 October 1997, Judge Aspegren confirmed the indictment.

13.   On 11 November 1997, authorities transferred Semanza from Cameroon to the custody of the Tribunal.

14.   On 16 February 1998, Semanza made his initial appearance before the Tribunal and pleaded not guilty to the seven counts contained in the indictment. **[page 3]**

15.   On 31 May 1998, the Prosecutor filed a motion for leave to amend the indictment (to add seven new counts) under Rule 50.

16.   On 18 June 1999, Trial Chamber II granted the Prosecution motion by an oral decision. The Trial Chamber filed the written decision on 2 September 1999.

17.   On 24 June 1999, Semanza made a further appearance on the first amended indictment pursuant to Rule 50(B) and entered a plea of not guilty to all counts. Following the taking of the pleas, the Prosecution orally moved for leave of the Trial Chamber to correct minor translation discrepancies between the English and French versions of the first amended indictment. The Trial Chamber, in an oral decision, granted the Prosecutor's motion.

18.   On 2 July 1999, the Prosecutor filed the second amended indictment (the current charging document) to comply with the decision of 24 June 1999 to correct the minor translation discrepancies.

19.   On 16 August 1999, the Defence filed the Motion.

20.   On 2 September 1999, the Prosecutor filed its Response to the Motion.

21.   On 22 September 1999, the Defence filed its Brief in support of the Motion.

22.   On 23 September 1999, the Trial Chamber heard the parties at a hearing on the Motion.

SUBMISSIONS OF THE PARTIES

Submissions of the Defence

23.   The Defence argues that the detention of the accused is unlawful and unjustifiable on the following grounds:

   (a)   the accused did not receive a formal indictment stating the charges against him before his transfer, and therefore was unable to prepare his defence;
   (b)   the provisional detention of the accused violated the rights of the accused under Article 20 of the Statute and Rule 40;
   (c)   the extension of the detention in the absence of judicial control was arbitrary and an abuse of the rights of the accused;
   (d)   the accused has been discriminated against, as compared to others arrested in Cameroon;
   (e)   the Prosecution failed to comply with Rule 40*bis* and the 40*bis* Order to file an indictment within thirty days, by 2 April 1997.

24.   The Defence argues that there was a violation of Rules 5, 66(A) and 72 because the Defence did not receive copies of all documents in French. **[page 4]**

25.   The Defence submits that the legal proceedings in Cameroon bar any trial of Semanza by the Tribunal under of the principle of *non bis in idem*, as laid down in Article 9(2)(b) of the Statute.

26.   The Motion prays that the Trial Chamber find Semanza's "arrest and his pre-trial detention void *ab initio.*" Motion, at 4.

Submissions of the Prosecution

27.   The Prosecution argues that the Trial Chamber should deny the Motion because Semanza's detention is lawful under the Statute and Rules. The Prosecution submits that the Tribunal did not extend arbitrarily Semanza's detention in violation of Rule 5, as the Defence contends, and that the Prosecutor does not have judicial control *stricto senso* over detention within a sovereign State.

28.   The Prosecutor submits that *non bis in idem* principle of Article 9(2)(b) is not applicable as the accused was the subject of extradition proceedings, not a criminal trial, in Cameroon, and the two proceedings are fundamentally different.

FINDINGS OF THE TRIAL CHAMBER

Semanza's Detention Before His Transfer to the Custody of the Tribunal

29.   The Trial Chamber finds that the Defence failed to distinguish clearly between the periods of detention before and after Semanza's transfer to the custody of the Tribunal.

30.   With regard to an accused person detained by a sovereign State before his transfer to the custody of the Tribunal, the Trial Chamber notes the decision in *Prosecutor v. Ntagerura*, ICTR-96-10-I, at para. 37 (Decision on the Preliminary Motion Filed by the Defence Based on Defects in the Form of the Indictment, 1 December 1997) in which Trial Chamber II refused "to terminate and nullify the proceedings before it as a consequence of acts of State over which it has no knowledge or control." *See also Prosecutor v. Barayagwiza*, Case ICTR-97-19-I, at 5 (Decision on the Extremely Urgent Motion by the Defence for Orders to Review and/or Nullify the Arrest and Provisional Detention of the Suspect,

17 November 1997). In other words, an accused, before this transfer to the custody of the Tribunal, has no remedy under the Statute and Rules for the detention and acts by sovereign States over which the Tribunal does not exercise control.

31.   The Trial Chamber, therefore, holds that it is not for the Tribunal to consider alleged violations of Semanza's rights before his transfer to the custody of the Tribunal. **[page 5]**

Semanza's Detention After His Transfer to the Custody of the Tribunal

32.   With regard to the defence claim that Tribunal proceedings against Semanza violate the principle of *non bis in idem*, as laid down in Article 9 and Rule 13, the Trial Chamber finds that the extradition proceedings in Cameroon did not constitute a trial on the merits. Thus, trial of Semanza before the Tribunal does not infringe Article 9 or Rule 13.

33.   The Trial Chamber finds that any deadline as to the issuance of the indictment that Judge Aspegren may have suggested at the *ex parte* hearing on the Rule 40*bis* Order was not legally binding on the Prosecutor. The matter of issuance and confirmation of indictments is governed by the Rules.

34.   Rule 40(D) requires the issuance of an indictment *within twenty days of the suspect's transfer* to the custody of the Tribunal. Pursuant to Rule 40*bis*, the indictment must be confirmed before the expiration of the provisional detention period that runs for *thirty days from the day after the transfer* of the suspect to the Tribunal.

35.   In the case at bench, the indictment was issued and confirmed *before* the transfer of Semanza into the custody of the Tribunal. Therefore, the provisions of Rules 40 and 40*bis* were in no way contravened.

36.   The Trial Chamber consequently finds that the Defence has failed to show any violation of the provisions of the Statute and the Rules with regard to Semanza's detention after his transfer to the custody of the Tribunal.

CONCLUSION

37.   For the reasons given, the Trial Chamber **DENIES** the Defence Motion to Set Aside the Arrest and Detention of Laurent Semanza as Unlawful.

Arusha, 6 October 1999.

Lloyd George Williams	Yakov Ostrovsky	Pavel Dolenc
Judge, Presiding	Judge	Judge

The proceedings

On 17 November 1998, Trial Chamber II of the ICTR dismissed Barayagwiza's motion for orders to review and nullify his arrest and provisional detention.[1] He lodged an appeal with the Appeals Chamber, in accordance with Rule 72 of the Rules of Procedure and Evidence (RPE) of the ICTR. The Appeals Chamber allowed the Appeal on 3 November 1999. It found that the fundamental rights of the Appellant had been repeatedly violated and the Prosecutor's failure to prosecute the case was tantamount to negligence. Consequently, it dismissed the indictment against Barayagwiza and ordered his immediate release. In his Separate Opinion, Judge Shahabuddeen disagreed with the majority on most of the issues. In his opinion, only the Appellant's right to an initial appearance without delay had been violated. However, he agreed with the majority that the indictment should be dismissed.

However, the Appellant was not set free immediately after the Decision, the Prosecutor having submitted a motion for review in accordance with Rule 120 of the RPE. That motion was successful. On 31 March 2000, the Appeals Chamber reviewed its earlier Decision of 3 November 1999 in the light of new facts presented by the Prosecutor. It arrived at the conclusion that, although the rights of the Appellant had been violated, these violations did not justify the dismissal of the indictment. It, therefore, rejected the Appellant's application for release and decided that he was instead entitled to other remedies as a result of the violation of his rights.

Some basic facts

A useful "Chronology of Events" can be found in Appendix A attached to the Appeals Chamber's decision of 3 November 1999. On the basis of this, one may distinguish four different periods of detention of the Appellant. The *first period* started on 17 April 1996 with the Prosecutor's request to Cameroon to take provisional measures against the Appellant and ends on 16 May 1996, the day on which the Prosecutor informed Cameroon that she did not seek his transfer to the seat of the Tribunal. During this period, the Appellant was deprived of his liberty on the basis of both a Rwandan request for his extradition and the Prosecutor's request pursuant to Rule 40 of the RPE. This period lasted twenty nine days. The *second period* ran from 16 May 1996 to 21 February 1997. During that period, Cameroon held the Appellant and deprived him of his liberty solely on the basis of Rwanda's extradition request. This period lasted some nine months. It ended with Cameroon's refusal to extradite the Appellant to Rwanda. The *third period* started on 21 February 1997, when the Appellant was re-arrested at the Prosecutor's request and ended with his transfer to the seat of the Tribunal on 19 November 1997. The Appellant was deprived of his liberty on the basis of Rule 40 from 21 February to 4 March 1997, and thereafter, according to the Appeals Chamber, on the basis of Rule 40 *bis*. In total, this period lasted almost eight months. The *fourth period* started on 19 November 1997 with the arrival of the Appellant at the seat of the Tribunal. On 23 February 1998, some ninety six days later, he made his initial appearance before the Tribunal.

Arrest, detention, and transfer in the Rules of Procedure and Evidence

Originally, the Rules of Procedure and Evidence of both the ICTY and the ICTR provided only for the arrest and transfer of accused persons. It follows from the Statutes of the Tribunals that an accused is a person against whom a *prima facie* case has been established and an indictment has been confirmed. Pursuant to Rule 47, an indictment containing the charges against that person may be confirmed if there is sufficient evidence to provide reasonable grounds for believing that he has committed a crime within the jurisdiction of the Tribunal. The same Rule provides that, upon confirmation of the indictment by a Judge, that Judge may issue an arrest warrant. In this system, an indictment always precedes the arrest of a person for the purpose of his transfer to the Tribunal. Among other things, Rule 55 of the RPE of both Tribunals is concerned with the execution of arrest warrants. In this respect, the RPE of the ICTY are more detailed those of the ICTR. Rule 55(E) of the ICTY's RPE, for instance, expressly provides that, at the time of his arrest, the indictment and a statement of his rights must be read to the accused. Rule 55(C) of the ICTR's RPE, on the other hand, merely states that the arrest warrant and a statement of his rights

---

[1]   For the text of the Decision see *supra* p. 123., as well for a similar decision in the case of Semanza.

must be served upon the accused. It does not specifically require that this is done at the time of his arrest. Both sets of Rules provide no time limits in relation to the duration of the accused's detention either before or after he has been transferred to the Tribunal. In addition, Rule 40 confers upon the Prosecutor the power to request any State to arrest a suspect " provisionally". A suspect is a person who has not yet been indicted. Rule 2 defines him as a person about whom the Prosecutor possesses reliable information which tends to show that the person may have committed a crime within the jurisdiction of the Tribunal. States must comply with such requests. However, the Prosecutor did not have the power to request the transfer of the suspect to the Tribunal. Transfer could only be effected on the basis of an indictment followed by an arrest warrant. One may finally note that Rule 40 did not limit the time a suspect could be deprived of his liberty by the requested State and made no mention of any rights of the arrested person.

Soon after the two Tribunals started their work, they discovered that the original system of the RPE in the matter of arrest and transfer created difficulties. Both Tribunals were confronted with situations in which persons suspected of having committed crimes under their Statutes were arrested by States and the question of their transfer to the Tribunals arose before they could be indicted. In February 1996, the Bosnian government arrested general Djukić and colonel Kršmanović on suspicion of having committed international crimes. Although not indicted, they were transferred to the ICTY. The arrest of twelve to fourteen persons, among them the Appellant, by Cameroon at the request of Rwanda in April 1996 is another important event. Both Tribunals decided to revise their Rules of Procedure and Evidence with a view to providing an explicit basis for the transfer of suspects to the Tribunals and their subsequent provisional detention. As a result, they both adopted a new Rule 40 *bis.* The two new Rules differ in some respects, although these are more in form than in substance.

Rule 40 *bis* of the Rwanda Tribunal's RPE, adopted on 15 May 1996, provides for the transfer and provisional detention of a suspect on the order of a Judge. The Judge may, at the request of the Prosecutor, order transfer and provisional detention in the premises of the Tribunal of a person arrested by a State at the request of the Prosecutor pursuant to Rule 40, or who is otherwise detained in that State. Pursuant to sub-rule (C), provisional detention may be ordered for a period not exceeding thirty days from the signing of the provisional detention order. It may, however, be prolonged for two further periods of thirty days each. According to sub-rule (H), the total period of detention shall in no case exceed ninety days, at the end of which, in the event the indictment has not been confirmed and an arrest warrant signed, the suspect must be released. Sub-rule (E) requires that copies of the order and the Prosecutor's request be served upon the suspect and his counsel as soon as possible. As far as the rights of the suspect are concerned, while he or she still remains in the requested State, the provisions of Rule 55 (B) to 59 *bis* apply *mutatis mutandis* to the execution of the order pursuant to sub-rule (I). This seems to imply that, at the time of his arrest, the suspect must be served with the order and a statement of his rights must be read to him.

Sub-rule (C) was found to create special difficulties due to the fact that the total period of ninety days might run out before the suspect was transferred to the Tribunal.[2] The sub-rule was therefore revised, so that provisional detention may be ordered for a period not exceeding thirty days after the transfer of the suspect. It is the revised sub-rule that is at issue in this case.

Unlike the ICTY, the ICTR also decided to make amendments to Rule 40 with a view to enabling the transfer of suspects to the Tribunal. New sub-rules (B) and (C) have been added. They empower a Judge to order the transfer of a suspect and his subsequent provisional detention if the requested State has made it clear that it is unable to keep the person under provisional detention or to prevent his escape. In this situation, the suspect may, after transfer, be provisionally detained for a maximum of twenty days. The person must be released if the Prosecutor fails to issue an indictment within this period. The amended sub-rule apply in this case, with respect to Barayagwiza's detention in Cameroon in 1996 and 1997. The question of whether, and to what extent Rules 40 and 40 *bis* overlap are beyond the scope of this commentary.

---

[2]   See John Jones, The Practice of the International Criminal Tribunals for the Former Yugoslavia and Rwanda, Ardsley NY 1999, 564.

Violations of the Appellant's rights under the Statute and the RPE

The initial appearance

The most obvious violation of the Appellant's rights under the Statute and the RPE was the delay in bringing him before the competent Trial Chamber after his arrival at the seat of the Tribunal. The issue was discussed by the Appeals Chamber in paragraphs 68-71. Pursuant to Rule 62 of the RPE the accused was to be brought before the Trial Chamber "without delay". Rule 62 makes clear that the initial appearance of the accused, which constituted the beginning of the trial stage, was an important moment in the proceedings against the accused. Among other things, he would then be formally charged and would be called upon to enter a plea. Although the Rule does not mention it, the reference in paragraph 70 of the Appeals Chamber's Decision to Article 9(3) of the ICCPR made it clear that the initial appearance might also have been the proper moment to consider whether the accused should remain in detention. In the case of the Appellant, no less than ninety six days passed before his initial appearance.

The indictment

As discussed in paragraphs 42-67, the Appeals Chamber also arrived at the conclusion that the Appellant's right to be promptly indicted under Rules 40 and 40 *bis* had been violated. In its view, this occurred on two different occasions, the first time being in 1996, when he was held in custody in Cameroon at the request of the Rwandan authorities as well as at the request of the Prosecutor. According to the Appeals Chamber, Rule 40 required the Prosecutor to indict the Appellant within twenty days after she made her request for him to be deatined by the authorities of Cameroon, failing which the Appellant would have to be released (paragraph 52). In addition, the Appeals Chamber concentrated on the violation of Rule 40 *bis*, which occurred after Judge Aspegren's order for the Appellant's transfer and provisional detention was filed on 4 March 1997. In this situation, Rule 40 *bis* required confirmation of the indictment within ninety days at the latest, failing which the suspect must be released. However, the indictment was actually confirmed on 23 October 1997, more than seven months after the order was filed (paragraph 67). On both occasions, the Appellant remained in custody after expiration of the relevant period.

A literal reading of both Rules does not, however, warrant the conclusions reached by the Appeals Chamber. It is obvious from their text that the relevant time periods start to run from the moment a suspect has been transferred to the Tribunal and not at an earlier moment. If that is the proper interpretation of the Rules, no violation of the Appellant's rights under Rules 40 and 40 *bis* had in fact occurred. This is the approach adopted by Judge Shahabuddeen, who, in his Separate Opinion, speaks of the plain meaning of Rule 40 *bis*. His interpretation finds additional support in the fact that the text of Rule 40 *bis* has since been revised to replace the phrase 'from the signing of the provisional detention order' in sub-rule (C) by the phrase 'from the date of transfer'.

Despite this, however, the Appeals Chamber was clearly worried by the consequences a literal interpretation of the Rules might entail. In its view, this would mean that a suspect could held in provisional detention in a State for an indefinite period, while there would be no incentive for the Prosecutor to indict him. Borrowing the concept of 'constructive custody' from the case law of United States courts on interstate extradition, it therefore construed Rules 40 and 40 *bis* as requiring that an indictment be confirmed within twenty, or ninety, days respectively after the arrest of a person by a State at the request of the Prosecutor or the Tribunal, failing which the person must be released by that State.

The potential consequences of a literal interpretation are worrying indeed. No doubt, the system favoured by the Appeals Chamber appears entirely reasonable. However, this does not alter the fact that, to quote Judge Shahabuddeen, the interpretation chosen by the Appeals Chamber was "directed to changing the substance of the purpose of the text" and amounted to legislation rather than interpretation. Legislation that the Prosecutor could not foresee. One may also wonder whether other solutions which would not automatically involve the suspect having to be released after a fixed period of time could have been found to protect the suspect against unwarranted delays while remaining in custody in a State at the behest of the Prosecutor or the Tribunal. Article 20 of the ICTR Statute, which is concerned with the rights of the accused, provides an excellent basis for finding adequate and proper solutions. I will return to this matter when discussing the question of whether the Prosecutor did in fact diligently prosecute the case against the Appellant and the significance and effect of international human rights standards.

Information with regard to the reasons for arrest

At paragraphs 78-86, the Appeals Chamber considered whether the Appellant's right under the Statute and the RPE to be promptly informed of the reasons for his arrest and of any charges against him had been respected. It concluded that the Appellant had been informed of these matters on 10 March 1997 when a copy of Judge Aspegren's Rule 40 *bis* order of 4 March 1997 was shown to him. In its view, however, that information should already have been given within a short time after the Prosecutor made her Rule 40 request to the Cameroon authorities in April 1996. There was, thus, a delay of some eleven months, an obvious violation of Appellant's rights. It is not entirely clear on what statutory basis the reasoning of the Appeals Chamber rests. In paragraph 79, the Chamber seemed to take Rule 40 *bis* as its starting point but then quickly turned to a discussion of general human rights standards without referring back to the Rule.

Here again, Judge Shahabuddeen dissented. In his Opinion, he made a distinction between two periods: the period 17 April 1996 – 16 May 1996 on the one hand and 21 February 1997 – 10 March 1997 on the other. While he did not venture an opinion on the question of whether the rights of the Appellant had been violated during the first period, he concluded that there was no excessive delay in informing the Appellant during the second period, since not more than seven days had passed before the Appellant was informed of the charges contained in Judge Aspegren's order.

As indicated above, Rule 55(C) of the ICTR RPE requires that the indictment and a statement of rights be served upon an accused. It does not provide that this has to be done at the moment of the accused's arrest. One may, however, suppose that these documents must be served upon the accused either at the moment of his arrest or within a short time after his arrest. Pursuant to Rule 40 *bis*(I), the provision of Rule55(C) apply *mutatis mutandis* to the execution of orders for the transfer and provisional detention of a suspect. Rule 40 does not mention a duty to serve the Prosecutor's request upon the suspect. On the basis of the facts established by the Appeals Chamber, there are sufficient reasons to believe that the Appellant was not promptly informed of the reasons for his arrest in relation to the Prosecutor's request of 17 April 1996. However, the majority fails to explain how a person's right, under the Statute and the RPE, to be informed of the formal charges can be violated before that person has actually been charged in accordance with the relevant provisions. Since the provisional charge against the Applicant was confirmed on 4 March 1997, how could the Prosecutor have informed him of its substance some eleven months earlier? As far as Judge Shahabuddeen's approach is concerned, while he may have been right in assuming that there was no excessive delay in informing the Appellant of the charge, it does not automatically follow that the Appellant was also promptly informed of the reasons for his arrest. As Judge Shahabuddeen observed, the Appellant was re-arrested by Cameroon at the request of the Prosecutor on 21 February 1997. He was informed of the reasons for his arrest on 10 March 1997. A delay of almost three weeks may well be considered excessive. I will also return to this matter when discussing international human rights standards.

The writ of habeas corpus

Another issue examined by the Appeals Chamber concerned the failure of the Trial Chamber to resolve Appellant's writ of *habeas corpus* in a timely manner. The writ was filed on 29 September 1997 while the Appellant was still in Cameroon. According to the Appeals Chamber, the Trial Chamber did not hear submissions by the Appellant in relation to this writ. His initial appearance before the Trial Chamber did not excuse its failure to resolve the writ. Judge Shahabuddeen disagreed with the majority for a variety of reasons, all of them related to the facts of the case.

The Appeals Chamber interpreted the Statute as giving a general right to persons detained at the behest of the Prosecutor or the Tribunal to "have recourse to an independent judicial officer for review of the detaining authority's acts" (paragraph 88). This represents a right that does not depend on the place where a person has been arrested or is being deprived of his liberty. This aspect of the decision is important and should certainly be welcomed. One has to keep in mind that, pursuant to the statutes of the

ICTY and the ICTR, States are under an unconditional obligation to comply with requests or orders of the Prosecutor or the Tribunal for the arrest or provisional detention of a person. In these circumstances, recourse of the arrested person to national courts of the requested State would virtually never constitute an effective remedy. The decision of the Appeals Chamber fills a gap that might otherwise have serious negative consequences for the protection of individual rights. While the Chamber concentrated on Rule 40 *bis* orders, what it said is also highly relevant where Rule 40 requests are concerned.

Prosecutorial due diligence

At paragraphs 91-98, the Appeals Chamber determined whether the Prosecutor took the steps necessary to have the Appellant transferred in a timely fashion. The Appellant awaited his transfer from 24 February 1997, when he was re-arrested by Cameroon at the request of the Prosecutor, until 19 November 1997, when he was finally transferred to Arusha. The Appeals Chamber noted that the Prosecutor failed to rebut in any form Appellant's claim that he was simply forgotten. It therefore found that the Prosecutor did not pay sufficient respect to Appellant's right under Article 19, paragraph 1 of the ICTR Statute to a fair and expeditious trial. For support of its view it referred to the case law of United States courts concerning international and interstate extradition as well as to a number of extradition treaties and extradition laws. Moreover, at paragraph 99 the Appeals Chamber found that the Prosecutor made no efforts to ensure Appellant's timely initial appearance after transfer. In his Separate Opinion, Judge Shahabuddeen was inclined to share the majority's view that there were unwarranted delays in transferring the Appellant. However, in his view these could not form the basis of an interlocutory appeal.

The delays in transferring the Appellant are worrying indeed. Transfer is a process involving both the Tribunal and the requested State. As the Appeals Chamber rightly observed, the fact that the requested State has to make the decision as to whether a person will be transferred does not absolve the Prosecutor from any responsibility. In his Separate Opinion, Judge Shahabuddeen discussed various possibilities open to the Prosecutor and the Tribunal to promote the timely transfer of a suspect or an accused. The duty of the Prosecutor in this respect may not only be derived from Article 19, paragraph 1 of the Statute but perhaps also from Article 20, paragraph 4 (c), which guarantees the right of the accused to be tried without delay.

Violations of international human rights standards

The general approach of the Appeals Chamber

The Appeals Chamber repeatedly referred to international human rights law. It used expressions such as "established international legal norms", "international standards", "established human rights jurisprudence", "internationally-recognized human rights standards", "existing international norms", and "international human rights standards". In its discussion of these international standards, the Appeals Chamber concentrated primarily on the text of the International Covenant on Civil and Political Rights and the European Convention for the Protection of Human Rights and Fundamental Freedoms, as well as case law developed by international bodies relating to these conventions. In general there are two ways in which the Appeals Chamber applied international human rights standards. Sometimes they are invoked as a means to interpret provisions in the ICTR Statute or in its Rules of Procedure and Evidence. On other occasions, they provide a direct basis for the Appeals Chamber's decision, without any (explicit) reference being made to provisions in the Statute or the RPE. The overall approach of the Appeals Chamber is aptly summarized in footnote 205, where it is said that the Chamber saw "no reason to conclude that the protections afforded to suspects under Article 9 of the ICCPR do not also apply to suspects brought before the Tribunal".

I will not comment on the theoretical aspects of the Appeals Chamber's general approach; suffice to say that I welcome its approach. Persons suspected or accused of international crimes should be no less entitled to respect for their basic individual rights than any other suspects or accused. Moreover, both *ad hoc* Tribunals inevitably provide role models for national systems of criminal justice. Lack of respect for individual rights could, therefore, have negative consequences that transcend the limited framework of the Tribunals. The forceful way in which the Appeals Chamber asserted the rights of the individual is in marked contrast to the first hesitating steps in this area of human rights law made by the Trial Chamber of the ICTY in the 1995 case of *Prosecutor v. Duško Tadić*. In that decision, it was held that the unique nature of the international tribunal and the exceptional circumstances in which it has to operate might prevent it from applying international human rights standards without any reservations or restrictions.[3] The approach of the Appeals Chamber in *Jean Bosco Barayagwiza v. Prosecutor* is all the more welcome because the Chamber had to venture into a field where rules contained in the ICTR Statute and RPE show a number of gaps and deficiencies. This is mainly due to the fact that there is no specific Article in the Statute with regard to the right to liberty and security of a person. While Article 20 of the Statute, guaranteeing the right to a fair hearing, is largely copied from Article 14 of the ICCPR, there is no similar Article in the Statute applying the terms of Article 9 of the ICCPR.

On the other hand, the approach of the Appeals Chamber does raise some questions. There is a marked tendency in the Decision to equate international human rights standards with standards laid down in the Statute and the RPE, and *vice versa*. This is particularly apparent in the Chamber's inclination to give to legal terms and expressions in human rights conventions the same meaning as apparently similar terms and expressions in the Statute and RPE. As a result, the significance of international human rights standards for the case of the Appellant is sometimes underestimated and sometimes overestimated. In trying to explain this criticism, I will start with a discussion of the meaning of the term 'charge' in human rights conventions.

The 'charge' in human rights conventions

The term 'charge' is frequently used in both Articles 9 and 14 of the ICCPR and Articles 5 and 6 of the ECHR. Since the rights of persons under these provisions largely depend upon whether or not they have been charged, the meaning to be attributed to the concept of 'charge' is of fundamental importance. The European Court of Human Rights has in particular rendered many decisions in which it concerned itself with the meaning of this concept. There are good reasons to believe that its case law is also of relevance for interpretation of the relevant ICCPR provisions.[4]

Both Article 9 of the ICCPR and Article 6 of the ECHR guarantee a fair trial for a person against whom a criminal charge is pending. The concept of 'charge' in these provisions is an autonomous one; its meaning does not depend on the meaning of similar terms in national laws. In this respect, the European Court has defined a charge as "the official notification to an individual by the competent authority that he has committed a criminal offence".[5] The prime example of an official notification is, of course, an indictment. But an official accusation brought against a person during pre-trial investigations may also constitute a charge even though it often has a provisional character. Moreover, other steps may also constitute a charge within the meaning of Article 14 of the ICCPR and Article 6 of the ECHR. In *Foti v. Italy*, the European Court defined these steps as "other measures which carry the implication of such an allegation and which likewise substantially affect the situation of the suspect".[6] Thus, for instance, the arrest of a person on suspicion of having committed a criminal offence, or the search of his home, are measures amounting to a criminal charge.[7] According to the European Commission, a request for the arrest of a person made to another State within the framework of extradition proceedings may also constitute a criminal charge.[8]

A person confronted with a charge may claim all the rights accorded under Article 14 of the ICCPR or Article 6 of the ECHR. For the purpose of the present discussion it is sufficient to mention the right to be promptly informed of the nature and cause of the accusation against the accused as well as the right to be tried without undue delay. The right to be informed of the nature and cause of the charge serves the

---

[3]   ICTY, Decision on the Prosecutor's Motion Requesting Protective Measures for Victims and Witnesses, *Prosecutor v. Tadić*, Case No. IT-94-1-T, T. Ch., 10 August 1995, ALC-I-155, par. 27-28.
[4]   Cf. Manfred Nowak, U.N. Covenant on Civil and Political Rights; CCPR Commentary, Kehl-Strasbourg-Arlington 1993, 243-244.
[5]   See, for instance, European Court of Human Rights, *Eckle v. Germany*, 15 July 1992, Series A-51.
[6]   European Court of Human Rights, *Foti v. Italy*, 10 December 1982, Series A-56.
[7]   See, for instance, *Foti v. Italy* and *Eckle v. Germany* noted above.
[8]   See its report in European Court of Human Rights, *Vallon v. Italy*, 3 June 1985, Series A-95, at 18-19.

purpose of enabling the accused to prepare a defence. Neither the ICCPR nor the ECHR contain a provision fixing the period within which a person who has been charged in one way or another must be formally indicted. However, they do require that the competent authorities proceed with the case without undue delay.

The term 'charge' also fulfils an important function in Article 9 of the ICCPR and Article 5 of the ECHR. A person arrested on suspicion of having committed one or more criminal offences must be informed of the reasons for the arrest as well as any charges. At this stage of a criminal investigation, information about the charges will often be summary and primarily serve to enable that person to have the lawfulness of his arrest reviewed by a court, rather than to prepare a defence. Moreover, the person arrested or detained on suspicion of having committed a criminal offence must be brought promptly before a judge or other officer authorized by law to exercise judicial powers and is entitled to a trial within reasonable time or to be released.

The initial appearance

Even though the Appeals Chamber held that the delay in bringing the Appellant before the competent Trial Chamber did not only violate Rule 62 of the RPE but also established human rights standards. As the Appeals Chamber correctly observed, the requirement of promptness in bringing an arrested person before a judge or other officer exercising judicial functions, which is included in both Article 9, paragraph 3 of the ICCPR and Article 5, paragraph 1 (c) of the ECHR, must be understood to involve not more than a few days.

The indictment

At paragraph 67 of its Decision, the Appeals Chamber arrived at the conclusion that the delay in formally indicting the Appellant did not only violate Rule 40 *bis* of the RPE but also established human rights jurisprudence. In this and the preceding paragraphs, the Appeals Chamber appears to assume that a suspect and an accused have a right under human rights conventions to be charged without delay after having been arrested. However, Articles 9, paragraph 2 and 14, paragraph 3 (a) of the ICCPR and Articles 5, paragraph 2 and 6, paragraph 3 (a) of the ECHR respectively are concerned with a different matter: the right of a person to be promptly informed of any charges against him. The same is true for the five Communications of the United Nations Human Rights Committee to which the Appeals Chamber referred at paragraphs 63 and 64. Even if one were to follow the Appeals Chamber in its interpretation of both conventions, it is not clear why violation of the Rule would automatically constitute a violation of international human rights standards. The Appellant was provisionally charged in Judge Aspegren's order of 4 March 1997. That order, issued within two weeks after Appellant's re-arrest by Cameroon at the Prosecutor's request, may itself amount to a criminal charge within the meaning of Articles 9 and 14 of the ICCPR and Articles 5 and 6 of the ECHR. The fact that an indictment was not confirmed within ninety days after the order does not automatically violate international human rights standards, since the ICCPR and the ECHR do not specify fixed timetables for replacing provisional charges with final ones. The difficulty with the Appeals Chamber's approach is that it seems to equate a charge within the meaning of human rights conventions to an indictment within the meaning of the ICTR Statute. Meanwhile, it may well be that unwarranted delays in indicting a person charged with having committed a criminal offence do violate that person's right under human rights conventions to be tried without delay. However, that is another matter.

Information with regard to the reasons for arrest

Article 9, paragraph 2 of the ICCPR and Article 5, paragraph 2 of the ECHR require that a person arrested on suspicion of having committed a criminal offence be informed, at the time of the arrest, of the reasons for his arrest and be promptly informed of any charges against him. Moreover, a general obligation to inform a suspect or an accused of the charge against him is laid down in Article 14, paragraph 3 (a) of the ICCPR and Article 6, paragraph 3 (a) of the ECHR. As has been noted above, the arrest of a person may itself amount to a criminal charge within the meaning of these provisions, and the same is true for a request to arrest a person within the framework of extradition proceedings.

In discussing the relevance of Article 9, paragraph 2 of the ICCPR and Article 5, paragraph 2 of the ECHR, both the majority and Judge Shahabuddeen concentrated on delays in informing the Appellant of Judge's Aspegren's order of 4 March 1997 for his arrest and provisional detention, confirming the provisional charge against the Appellant. They appear to tacitly assume that the term 'charge' in human rights conventions has the same meaning as the term 'charge' in the ICTR Statute and RPE. This leads to an under-estimation of the importance of international human rights standards in the case.

Pursuant to these standards, the Appellant should have been promptly informed of the reasons for his arrest and of 'any charges' against him after the Prosecutor's request of 17 April 1996, made on the basis of Rule 40, was executed by the competent authorities of Cameroon. It is highly likely from the facts of the case as established by the Appeals Chamber that, at this stage, the Appellant received no information at all. In this respect, it is wholly irrelevant whether or not, and when, a Judge of the ICTR ordered the transfer and provisional arrest. From the perspective of international human rights standards, one of the worrying aspects of Rule 40 is that it is silent on the matter. The rights of the suspect specified in Rule 42 only apply when a suspect is to be questioned by the Prosecutor. Similarly, the Appellant should have been promptly informed of the reasons for his arrest and the 'charges' against him after his re-arrest by Cameroon on 24 February 1997 at the Prosecutor's request. In this respect, it is immaterial whether or not the Appellant was promptly informed of Judge's Aspegren's order of 4 March 1997. Even if one were to consider this was the case, the fact remains that the Appellant received the relevant information only on 10 March 1997, almost three weeks after his arrest. The delay was excessive.

Article 9, paragraph 4 of the ICCPR and Article 5, paragraph 4 of the ECHR require that a court order the release of the person deprived of his liberty where that person's detention is not lawful. The most important reason for releasing a person is that the grounds for depriving him of his liberty are insufficient or non-existent. However, both provisions also require the person's release even where there are sufficient reasons for his arrest and detention but where these measures have not been effected "in accordance with such procedures as are established by law". The term 'law' includes the procedural requirements laid down in the two conventions themselves. Therefore, a failure to promptly inform the person of the reasons for his arrest and of any charges against him makes his detention illegal. The Appeals Chamber arrived at the same conclusion at paragraphs 85 and 104 of its Decision.

The Appeals Chamber then examined how long the Appellant has spent in illegal provisional detention at the behest of the Tribunal. It determined that this amounted to eleven months, covering the whole period from 17 April 1996 to 10 March 1997. This also included the time during which the Appellant was deprived of his liberty in Cameroon pursuant solely to Rwanda's extradition request, which lasted approximately nine months. In this respect, the Chamber noted that only thirty five days of the eleven month total are clearly attributable to the Tribunal. However, it went on to observe that: "At this juncture, it is irrelevant that only a small portion of that total period of provisional detention is attributable to the Tribunal, since it is the Tribunal – and not any other entity – that is currently adjudicating the Appellant's claims".

The Appeals Chamber's reasoning is hard to follow. Since its Decision did not make any mention of a debate between the parties as to the propriety of Appellant's detention on the basis of the Rwandan request, one may assume that, in itself, there was nothing wrong with it. In my opinion, the failure of the Prosecutor to promptly inform the Appellant of the reasons for having him arrested at the behest of the Tribunal before and after he was detained solely on the basis of Rwanda's request did not in any way vitiate the legality of that detention. Consequently, there can be no question of attributing its illegality to the Tribunal or any other entity.

The writ of habeas corpus

Article 9, paragraph 4 of the ICCPR and Article 5, paragraph 4 of the ECHR grant the right to every person deprived of his liberty to have the lawfulness of his detention examined by an independent court. Since international extradition proceedings always involve two States the question arises as to which of those States' courts should the arrested person turn for relief – the courts of the requested State or those of the requesting State. Normally, the person requested will turn to the courts of the requested State.

Usually, extradition law leaves a large discretion to the authorities of that State to arrest a person, although that discretion may be restricted by the relevant extradition treaty. There are therefore good reasons for offering the arrested person a judicial remedy against his arrest. This is well illustrated by Article 5, paragraphs 1 (f) and 4 of the ECHR. Unlike Article 9 of the ICCPR, these provisions explicitly mention the right of the person arrested on the basis of an extradition request to turn to the courts of the requested State for relief. Meanwhile, one cannot ignore that the very basis for his arrest lies in an extradition request. That request will be accompanied by a warrant for his arrest, usually issued by a court of the requesting State. Pursuant to the national law of most States, the person arrested may turn to that court with an application to reconsider its decision. In the case law on the ECHR, a request for the arrest of a person is considered to amount to a "criminal charge". As a consequence, Article 5, paragraphs 1(c) and 4, accord him the right to address a writ of *habeas corpus* to a court in the requesting State, even if that court had previously issued an order for his arrest. This is not, as the Appeals Chamber concluded, because the initial order was "tantamount to adminstrative detention"[9] but rather because the arrested person will not yet have had the opportunity to have been heard by the court ordering his arrest.

The situation under the Statutes of the *ad hoc* international tribunals is fundamentally different from that in international extradition law. Pursuant to the Statutes, States have an unconditional obligation to comply with orders and requests. Under these circumstances, it is doubtful whether the examination of a writ of *habeas corpus* by the courts of the requested State could be considered to be an effective remedy. As the Appeals Chamber noted in a different context, the situation under the statutes is more reminiscent of United States interstate extradition law, which leaves virtually no room for the competent authorities of the requested State to refuse to comply with orders of the courts of the requesting state.

Prosecutorial due diligence

On the basis of the facts established by it, the Appeals Chamber held that the Prosecutor failed to show due diligence in prosecuting the Appellant without undue delay, especially where the latter's transfer was concerned. On this issue, the Chamber is on solid grounds. In particular, the European Court of Human Rights has rendered a number of judgments on the matter of undue delay in extradition proceedings. Its most recent and most important judgment is that in the case of *Quinn v. France*, in which it held that France, acting pursuant to a Swiss extradition request, violated Article 5, paragraph 1 (c) of the ECHR by not conducting extradition proceedings with due diligence.[10] More relevant for the case of Appellant is that, in *Vallon v. Italy*, the European Commission of Human Rights found that Italy failed to exercise appropriate due diligence in pursuing an extradition request addressed to another European State.[11] That the requesting party has responsibilities in this regard is confirmed in the case law of many national courts, among them the Supreme Court of the United States, to which the Appeals Chamber refered. Meanwhile, the prevailing approach is that one has to distinguish between delays caused by the requested State and by the requesting State. Here again, the legal situation under the Statute differs considerably from international extradition law. Theoretically, proceedings for deciding on requests for the transfer of a suspect or an accused should be swift, since the requested State is, as a matter of principle, obliged to comply with these requests. However, as is demonstrated by the practice of the ICTY, some States seem to take an extraordinary amount of time to reach a decision. In these situations, it is the responsibility of the tribunal to intervene and exert pressure upon the reluctant State.

Conclusions

At paragraph 100 of its Decision, the Appeals Chamber concluded that the rights of the Appellant under the Statute had been violated in several respects. Moreover, human rights standards had been ignored on a number of occasions. The Appeals Chamber also held that there had been an abuse of process on the

---

9   Paragraph 89, footnote 236.
10   European Court of Human Rights, *Quinn v. France*, 22 March 1995, Series A-311. In an earlier case against Belgium no violation was held to have occurred; see European Court of Human Rights, *Kolompar v. Belgium*, 24 September 1992, Series A-235-C.
11   See *supra* note 8.

part of the Prosecutor. On the other hand, Judge Shahabudeen arrived at the conclusion that only Rule 62 has been violated.

I have attempted to explain that not all criticisms of the Appeals Chamber are justified. In my opinion, there was no violation of "the Appellant's right to be promptly charged pursuant to international standards as reflected in Rule 40 *bis*". Neither the ICCPR nor the ECHR recognise such a right. They accord the person the right to be promptly informed of the "charges". That, however, is an entirely different matter. As far as Rule 40 *bis* is concerned, I share Judge Shahabuddeen's opinion that, in the circumstances of Appellant's case, the Rule did not oblige the Prosecutor to have an indictment confirmed within ninety days after Appellant's re-arrest in Cameroon. It is also hard to understand how the Appellant's right under the ICTR Statute and RPE to be promptly informed of a formal charge could have been violated before he was actually charged in accordance with the relevant provisions. On the other hand, it is obvious that the Appellant's right to be promptly informed of the reasons for his arrest and of any 'charges' against him in accordance with international human rights standards had been violated, and more often than the Appeals Chamber assumed. Finally, I strongly disagree with the Appeals Chamber as to how long the Appellant spent in illegal detention in Cameroon at the behest of the Tribunal. In sum, the violations of Appellant's rights, although serious, were considerably less egregious and numerous than the Appeals Chamber believed.

Remedies

On the basis of the Appeals Chamber's findings, the question arose as to what remedies should be determined for the violation of Appellant's rights. Paragraphs 101-112 of the Decision are devoted to this matter. After having discussed several possibilities, the Chamber concluded that dismissal of the case and release of the Appellant was the only acceptable option. This certainly is a very bold and courageous step, considering the fact that the Appellant was accused of conspiracy to commit genocide. However, the Appeals Chamber was of the opinion that the integrity of the Tribunal permitted no other choice. One wonders how it would have decided the case if it would have instead reached the conclusions I have expressed above.

Dismissal of criminal cases as a result of official misconduct is a remedy accepted by the courts of many States. There is, of course, considerable variation in the way national legal systems make use of that remedy. Among other things, the choice will depend on the availability of other effective remedies for correcting the wrongs done to the accused. Usually, a relevant consideration is also whether unlawful conduct on the part of law officers shows an intent to prejudice the rights of the accused or instead constituted negligence. One may note that the Prosecutor's conduct in the case of the Appellant fell in the second category. To date, international human rights conventions and the subsequent case law of international bodies have had surprisingly little to say about the dismissal of criminal cases as a remedy for the violation of human rights. Meanwhile, both Article 9 of the ICCPR and Article 5 of the ECHR make it imperative that a person be released if his detention was unlawful. I take it for granted that, in the case of more serious violations of these Articles, the nature of this particular remedy rules out any possibility of re-arresting the suspect or the accused. Another remedy which is accepted in the case law of international bodies concerning these two Articles has been the reduction of the sentence in the situation of a conviction, not to be confused with the usual deduction from the sentence imposed of the time already spent in provisional detention. Finally, the two Articles provide that a person wrongfully arrested or detained shall have an enforceable right to compensation, a right that is of particular importance when a person has been acquitted. Of course, recourse can also be had to a combination of different remedies. My own assessment of the legal situation in the case of the Appellant leads me to believe that a combination of these remedies would have been an appropriate solution.

The Decision of 31 March 2000

Not surprisingly, the decision of the Appeals Chamber provoked vehement negative reaction in some circles. For instance, Rwanda decided a few days later to suspend its co-operation with the ICTR. The Prosecutor submitted a motion for review on the basis of Rule 120. As the Decision on this motion could not be included in this Volume, I will resist the temptation to comment further. Instead, I only mention the findings and the conclusion.

On the basis of new information before it, the Appeals Chamber has now found that the Appellant was already aware of the general nature of the charges against him by 3 May 1996 at the latest. New information has also led it to assume that the delay in transferring the Appellant to the seat of the tribunal could not be attributed to the Prosecutor. On the contrary, they were due to Cameroon's attitude, while the Prosecutor had actually made efforts to speed up the process. Finally, the Appeals Chamber found that the initial appearance of the Appellant had been deferred with the consent of his counsel. In the opinion of the Appeals Chamber, these new facts diminished "the role played by the failings of the Prosecutor as well as the intensity of the violation of the rights of the Appellant". The Appeals Chamber has consequently reviewed its decision and rejected the application of the Appellant to be released. It has further decided that, should the Appellant be found not guilty, he should receive financial compensation for the violation of his rights. On the other hand, if he were to be found guilty, his sentence should be reduced to take account of these violations.

Bert Swart

UNITED NATIONS   NATIONS UNIES

International Criminal Tribunal for Rwanda
Tribunal pénal international pour le Rwanda

TRIAL CHAMBER 2

OR: ENG

Before: Judge William H. Sekule, Presiding Judge
Judge Yakov Ostrovsky
Judge Tafazzal Hossain Khan

Registry: Ms. Prisca Nyambe

Decision of: 6 October 1997

THE PROSECUTOR

VERSUS

CLÉMENT KAYISHEMA AND
OBED RUZINDANA

Case No. ICTR-95-1-T

DECISION ON THE MOTION FOR THE PROTECTION
OF DEFENCE WITNESSES

The Office of the Prosecutor:
   Mr. Jonah Rahetlah
   Ms. Brenda Sue Thornton

Counsel for the Accused:
   Mr. Philippe Morriceau (Clément Kayishema)
   Mr. Pascal Besnier (Obed Ruzindana)

[page 2] International Criminal Tribunal for Rwanda, (the "Tribunal"),

SITTING AS Trial Chamber 2 ("the Trial Chamber"), composed of Judge William H. Sekule, Presiding Judge, Judge Yakov Ostrovsky and Judge Tafazzal Hossain Khan;

CONSIDERING the indictment submitted by the Prosecutor on 22 November 1995 against Clément Kayishema and Obed Ruzindana and confirmed on 28 November 1995 by Judge Navanethem Pillay pursuant to Rule 47 of the Rules of Procedure and Evidence (the "Rules"), on the basis that there was sufficient evidence to provide reasonable grounds for believing they had committed genocide, conspiracy to commit genocide, crimes against humanity and violations of Article 3 common to the 1949 Geneva Conventions and Additional Protocol II thereto;

CONSIDERING the initial appearance of Obed Ruzindana which took place on 29 October 1996;

CONSIDERING ALSO THAT on 13 December 1996 the Prosecutor filed a motion before Trial Chamber I requesting the court to issue an order for protective measures in respect of the Prosecution witness against Obed Ruzindana which was granted by Trial Chamber I in its Decision of 4 March 1997;

BEING NOW SEIZED OF a Preliminary motion filed by the Defence Counsel on 9 July 1997, pursuant to Rule 75 of the Rules in which he generally seeks protective measures for potential witnesses for Obed Ruzindana but specifically seeks the non-disclosure of the identity of defence witnesses to the public and media;

CONSIDERING the provisions of Articles 19 and 21 of the Tribunal's Statute and Rules 69 and 75 of the Rules regarding the protection of victims and witnesses;

CONSIDERING the Prosecutor's written response to the Defence Counsel's motion dated 29 September 1997;

HAVING HEARD the oral submissions by the parties on 30 September 1997;

AFTER HAVING DELIBERATED:

WHEREAS the Defence in its motion for the protection of potential witnesses for Obed Ruzindana has requested this Trial Chamber to order for the non-disclosure of the identities of the defence witnesses as well as for other related reliefs;

WHEREAS the Defence Counsel has requested for various protective measures for all of its witnesses scattered in several countries such as the Republics of Kenya, Rwanda and Tanzania;

WHEREAS the Defence Counsel submitted that most of the defence witnesses are Hutu by ethnicity and are unwilling to testify openly in favour of the accused or any person charged for crimes falling within the jurisdiction of the Tribunal owing to the fear of being implicated in the **[page 3]** genocide which occurred in Rwanda in 1994 and of possible reprisals against the witnesses upon their return to Rwanda after having testified;

WHEREAS, in support of this motion, the Defence Counsel has relied upon and has invited the Trial Chamber to consider the Report of the U.N. on the Human Rights Situation in Rwanda No. E/CN/4/1997/61 of January 1997 as submitted by the U.N. Human Rights Commission's Special Rapporteur, Mr René Degni-Ségui as well as an article entitled "The Security in Rwanda" reported in a bi-monthly magazine called "DIALOGUE" No. 195 for the month of May to June 1997, p. 103 both of which illustrate that the security situation in Rwanda is unstable and dangerous;

WHEREAS ALSO the Defence Counsel relied upon a document filed by the Office of The Prosecutor (the "OTP") namely an Affidavit of Mr Oyvind Olsen, the Commander of Investigations in the OTP in Kigali dated 24 March 1997 in which it is stated that killings have occurred in Rwanda and in Kibuye Prefecture as a result of either party disputes or of revenge attacks directed at the returning refugees allegedly accused of having participated in genocide acts;

WHEREAS FURTHER Commander Olsen in the above mentioned affidavit states that Kibuye Prefecture has been designated by the U.N. as being in phase IV indicating that visits are only possible for U.N. staff members under armed escorts by the Rwandan Patriotic Army;

CONSIDERING THAT the Defence Counsel cited the case of The Prosecutor Vs. Elie Ndayambaje ICTR-96-8-T in which Mr Tchoungang, the Defence Counsel in that case supported his motion for protective measures for the defence witnesses by referring to the NAKI Operation where potential defence witnesses located in the Republic of Kenya were faced by threats of deportation to Rwanda thereby putting their lives in danger;

CONSIDERING ALSO THAT, in further substantiation of his motion, the Defence Counsel has submitted that potential defence witnesses would be difficult to trace and has cited an article in the "Guardian" newspaper published in Tanzania dated 22 September 1997 showing that the Government of the Republic of Tanzania plans to resettle all refugees, who were living outside established settlements, in one place;

WHEREAS the Prosecutor contended that the Trial Chamber could not exercise its discretion to grant the measures sought by the defence in paragraph 15 of the defence motion without proof of genuine fear of personal safety of specific witnesses;

GIVEN THE FACT THAT the Prosecutor in her response specifically opposed the measure mentioned in paragraph 18 due to its vagueness and its unspecific nature;

WHEREAS FURTHER the Prosecution, while objecting to the Defence Counsel's submission that witnesses for the defence may be fearful of being charged for complicity in the crimes for which the accused is charged, submitted that pursuant to Rule 75 of the Rules protective measures are limited to physical and material security and not to the fear of being prosecuted; **[page 4]**

CONSIDERING THAT the Prosecution agreed with the Defence Counsel's submission on non-disclosure of witnesses but implored the Trial Chamber not to grant the request in totality but instead to limit the disclosure to the mentioning of the fact that an individual is a witness which measure should also be extended to Prosecution witnesses; and furthermore, that such limitation should exclude the immediate team of the Prosecutor, some designated Counsels and some members of the public to enable it to collect information to contradict any accusations that may be raised by the defence;

WHEREAS the Defence Counsel while responding to the preceding argument contended that it was untenable because the issue of being an individual *per se* and that of being a witness are so interlinked that they cannot be separated and that furthermore, the Trial Chamber has never ordered such a measure for the Prosecution;

A. On the matter of the request for the non-disclosure of the identity of witnesses to the public and the media

WHEREAS measures for the non-disclosure of the identity of witnesses to the public and the media are provided for in Rule 75(B);

WHEREAS in the present situation these measures are even more warranted by the many concordant reports, issued by various sources, which describe the particularly volatile situation at present in Rwanda and in the neighbouring countries where those persons who may have, in one way or another, borne witness to the events of 1994, are found today;

MINDFUL OF Security Council Resolution 955 (1994) establishing the Tribunal and Article 28 of the Statute under which the Trial Chamber can request the cooperation and assistance of relevant Governments which in this case are the Governments of the Republics of Kenya, Tanzania and Rwanda;

CONSIDERING similar motions in the cases of The Prosecutor versus Georges Anderson Rutaganda ICTR-96-3-T, decided on 6 March 1997 and The Prosecutor versus Elie Ndayambaje ICTR-96-8-T decided on 8 September 1997, in which the Trial Chamber solicited the cooperation of States, UN organisations including the United Nations High Commissioner for Refugees (the "UNHCR") and any other organisation;

The Trial Chamber is therefore of the opinion that, regarding the non-disclosure of the identity of the defence witnesses, it is appropriate to grant the reliefs requested by the Defence as indicated below;

B. On the issue of the request for the temporary non-disclosure of the identity of defence witnesses to the Prosecution until such time as they are under the protection of the Tribunal and on the issue of fear of reprisals on return to Rwanda

WHEREAS reports and submissions on the security situation in Rwanda and the neighbouring countries have been produced with regard to the security situation in Rwanda; **[page 5]**

The Trial Chamber observes that a situation such as the one referred to above would pose a risk to potential defence witnesses and substantially prejudice the rights of the accused to conduct a proper defence;

This Trial Chamber is also of the considered opinion that once defence witnesses have been put under the protection of the Tribunal, the Defence should disclose the identity of its witness in sufficient time prior to the trial to allow the Prosecution to rebut any evidence that its witnesses may raise;

C. On fear of criminal prosecution

WHEREAS the Prosecution has emphasised the need for the Defence Counsel to substantiate the relief sought;

TAKING NOTE THAT by virtue of Article 21 of the Statute and in order to ensure a fair trial to the accused, the Trial Chamber is obliged to take steps to provide appropriate and possible measures to protect witnesses;

WHEREAS Rule 75 provides, *inter alia*, that a Judge or a Chamber may *proprio motu* or at the request of either party, or of the victim or witnesses concerned, or the Victims and Witnesses Unit (the "VWU"), order appropriate measures for the protection of victims and witnesses, provided that these measures are consistent with the rights of the accused;

WHEREAS this Trial Chamber is conscious of the fact that protective measures for witnesses should not hinder due process or be used as a way of providing immunity to the witnesses against possible prosecution;

WHEREAS the Trial Chamber is of the opinion that the Defence Counsel in his oral submissions has provided the relevant base in support of his request;

The Trial Chamber, therefore, is inclined to hold that protective measures should not extend to providing immunity from criminal prosecution by any appropriate authority;

D. On the issue of being accorded measures similar to those granted to the Prosecution

WHEREAS the Defence Counsel has argued that measures similar to those granted to the Prosecution should be accorded to the defence;

WHEREAS the Prosecutor in her written and oral response cited Article 19 of the Statute, Rules 75 and 69 of the Rules as grounds for according the defence a fair and equitable trial by granting protective measures similar to those accorded to the Prosecution witnesses;

BEARING IN MIND THAT the Prosecution has partially supported the Defence's request and that the measures sought by the defence are pertinent for justice to be achieved, this Trial Chamber recognises that pursuant to Article 20 (1) of the Tribunal's Statute all parties are equal **[page 6]** before the Tribunal;

MINDFUL OF its previous decisions on this issue as cited above, in which protective measures have been granted to the Prosecution witnesses, this Trial Chamber is of the view that, to the extent possible, defence witnesses should be accorded protective measures similar to those provided for Prosecution witnesses;

CONSIDERING THAT the Prosecution may need to contact any of the defence witnesses, the Trial Chamber is of the considered opinion that under Rule 75 it can *proprio motu* allow the Prosecution to make such contact upon prior notice to the defence;

NOW THEREFORE THE TRIAL CHAMBER ORDERS:

(I)   that the Defence Counsel furnishes particulars of the witnesses to the VWU, thereby enabling it to initiate appropriate steps to implement the protective measures mentioned below so that the presence of the witnesses and their safety is ensured.

(ii)   that pursuant to Security Resolution 955 (1994) and Article 28 of the Statute, the Registrar should solicit the assistance and cooperation of the Governments of the Republics of Kenya, Tanzania, Rwanda as well as the UNHCR and should take all possible measures to ensure the availability of the witnesses to testify before the Tribunal.

(iii)   the names, addresses, whereabouts of the defence witnesses and any other information identifying them shall not be disclosed to the Prosecution, until further order.

(iv)   the names, addresses, whereabouts of the defence witnesses and any other information identifying the witnesses shall be kept under the seal of the Tribunal and not included in any of the public records of the Tribunal.

(v)   the names, addresses, whereabouts of the defence witnesses and any other information identifying them shall not be disclosed to the public or the media.

(vi)   the Office of the Prosecutor shall not reveal to anyone except its immediate team, the names, addresses, whereabouts of the defence witnesses and any other information identifying them once such information has been revealed to it by the Defence.

(vii)   the public and the media shall not take photographs, make audio and video recordings or sketches of the defence witnesses who are under the protection of the Tribunal, without its authorisation.

(viii)   the Defence shall be permitted to designate pseudonyms for each of its witnesses for use during any communication *inter partes* and to the public as well as in the official proceedings of the Tribunal. **[page 7]**

The Prosecution and its representatives who are acting pursuant to their instructions shall notify the Defence Counsel of any request for contacting the defence witnesses, and the Defence Counsel shall make arrangements for such contacts.

Pursuant to Rule 75 of the Rules, the Defence is at liberty to request a Judge or Trial Chamber, at any time, to amend or add to any of the protective measures for its witnesses as abovementioned.

Arusha, 6 October 1997

William H. Sekule,   Yakov Ostrovsky   Tafazzal Hossain Khan

Presiding Judge   Judge   Judge

UNITED NATIONS   NATIONS UNIES

International Criminal Tribunal for Rwanda
Tribunal pénal international pour le Rwanda

CHAMBRE I – CHAMBER I

OR: FR.

Before: **Judge Laïty Kama, Presiding Judge**
             Judge Lennart Aspegren
             Judge Navanethem Pillay

Registry: **Mr. Frederik Harhoff**

Decision of: **19 November 1997**

THE PROSECUTOR

VERSUS

JEAN-PAUL AKAYESU

Case No. ICTR-96-4-T

DECISION ON THE MOTION TO SUBPOENA A WITNESS

Office of the Prosecutor:
    Mr. Pierre-Richard Prosper
    Ms. Sara Darehshori

Counsel for the Defence:
    Mr. Nicolas Tiangaye
    Mr. Patrice Monthé

[page 2] THE INTERNATIONAL CRIMINAL TRIBUNAL FOR RWANDA (the "TRIBUNAL"),

SITTING as Trial Chamber I, composed of Judge Laïty Kama, Presiding Judge, Judge Lennart Aspegren and Judge Navanethem Pillay;

HAVING RECEIVED from the Defence a motion dated 11 November 1997 and filed the same day, requesting the Tribunal to subpoena Major-General Roméo Dallaire, a Canadian national and former Commander-in-Chief of the United Nations Assistance Mission in Rwanda (UNAMIR), as a witness for the defence in the case of the Prosecutor versus Jean-Paul AKAYESU;

HAVING TAKEN COGNIZANCE of a brief in reply by the Prosecutor on 12 November 1997 informing the Chamber that she had no objection to the motion by the Defence requesting the appearance of General Dallaire;

HAVING HEARD the parties during the hearing held on 19 November 1997;

AFTER HAVING DELIBERATED,

WHEREAS under the terms of Rule 54 of the Rules of Procedure and Evidence ("the Rules") *"At the request of either party or proprio motu, a Judge or a Trial Chamber may issue such orders, summonses, subpoenas, warrants and transfer orders as may be necessary for the purposes of an investigation or for the preparation or conduct of the trial,"*;

WHEREAS the Defence filed a motion on 11 November 1997 for General Dallaire to be subpoenaed in the case of the Prosecutor versus Jean-Paul Akayesu;

WHEREAS in the said motion, the Defence explained that by its Resolution 872 of 5 October 1993, the United Nations Security Council created UNAMIR; that General Dallaire was appointed Commander-in-Chief of this multinational force; that the United Nations peacekeeping troops were in Rwanda when the massacres began following the attack that costs the lives of President Juvénal Habyarimana and his Burundian counterpart, Cyprien Ntaryamira; that hearing General Dallaire would serve to enlighten the Defence on the Rwandan tragedy;

WHEREAS in support of its motion, the Defence produced copies of two letters dated 9 April 1997, written by Mr. Paul Szasz (Acting Director and Deputy to the Under-Secretary-General, Office of the Legal Counsel) and addressed to the Defence, and by Mr. Hans Corell (Under-Secretary-General for Legal Affairs, The Legal Counsel) and addressed to Mr. Robert R. Fowler (Permanent Representative of Canada to the United Nations in New York) respectively; **[page 3]**

WHEREAS the said letters show that the Secretary-General of the United Nations would not object to General Dallaire testifying as a witness, subject to the immunity he enjoyed at the time of the events insofar as he was officially representing the United Nations: WHEREAS, however, the United Nations could waive the immunity if the Tribunal ordered General Dallaire to appear as a witness;

WHEREAS the Prosecutor, in response to the Defence motion, submitted a short brief informing the Chamber that she was not opposed to this request made by the Defence and confirmed this position during the hearing of 19 November 1997;

WHEREAS the Tribunal, seeking to ensure full respect of the rights of the accused to a proper defence, is of the opinion that the request submitted by the Defence is justified and that the said request should be granted;

FOR THESE REASONS,

THE TRIBUNAL

DECLARES the motion by the Defence to be admissible and well-founded;

SUMMONS Major-General Roméo Dallaire to appear as a witness for the defence in the ongoing legal proceedings against Jean-Paul Akayesu;

REQUESTS the Secretary-General of the United Nations, consequently, to waive the immunity he enjoys by virtue of his position as former Commander-in-Chief of UNAMIR.

Arusha, 19 November 1997

Laïty Kama	Lennart Aspegren	Navanethem Pillay
Presiding Judge	Judge	Judge

UNITED NATIONS   NATIONS UNIES

International Criminal Tribunal for Rwanda

Trial Chamber 2

OR: ENG

Before: Judge William H. Sekule, Presiding Judge
              Judge Tafazzal H. Khan
              Judge Navanethem Pillay

Registrar: Ms. Prisca Nyambe

Decision of: 25 November 1997

THE PROSECUTOR

versus

JOSEPH KANYABASHI

Case No. ICTR-96-15-T

DECISION ON THE PROTECTIVE MEASURES FOR DEFENCE WITNESSES AND THEIR FAMILIES

Office of the Prosecutor:
   Mr. Udo Gehring
   Mr. Holo Makwaia

Counsel for the Defence:
   Mr. Michel Marchand

[page 2] THE TRIBUNAL,

SITTING AS Trial Chamber 2 of the International Criminal Tribunal for Rwanda ("the Tribunal"), composed of Judge William H. Sekule, Presiding, Judge Tafazzal H. Khan and Judge Navanethem Pillay;

CONSIDERING the indictment submitted by the Prosecutor against Joseph Kanyabashi pursuant to Rule 47 of the Rules of Procedure and Evidence ("the Rules") and confirmed by Judge Yakov A. Ostrovsky on 15 July 1996 on the basis that there existed sufficient evidence to provide reasonable grounds for believing that he has committed genocide, complicity in genocide, crimes against humanity and violations of Article 3 common to the Geneva Conventions and Additional Protocol II thereto;

TAKING NOTE of the transfer of the accused from Belgium to the Tribunal's Detention Facilities on 8 November 1996 and his initial appearance on 29 November 1996 before this Chamber;

CONSIDERING THAT on 18 December 1996 the Prosecutor filed a motion before Trial Chamber I requesting the court to issue an order for protective measures in respect of the Prosecution witnesses against Joseph Kanyabashi which was granted by the Trial Chamber in its Decision of 6 March 1997;

CONSIDERING THAT on 9 September 1997, the accused Joseph Kanyabashi in a letter dated 20 August 1997, filed his request for the assignment of another Lead Counsel which was granted by the Trial Chamber on 29 October when the Defence Counsel was allowed to withdraw form the case;

CONSIDERING ALSO THAT on 27 May 1997 the former lead Defence Counsel submitted a motion for the protection of defence witnesses and their families which was scheduled for hearing on 29 October but was postponed to enable the present Defence Counsel to submit a new motion in this respect to the Trial Chamber;

BEING NOW SEIZED OF a Preliminary motion filed by the Defence Counsel on 4 November 1997, pursuant to Rule 75 of the Rules in which he seeks protective measures for potential defence witnesses whereby the witnesses' identities would not be divulged to the public and the media (measures 5-6 and 8) and to the Prosecutor (measure 4); and miscellaneous and general measures (measures 1,2,3, 7 and 9);

WHEREAS the Defence Counsel has in his motion mentioned that there was potential defence witnesses scattered in several countries such as Europe, North America, the Republics of the former Congo-Zaire and Kenya but has in his oral motion limited his request for protective measures only to potential defence witnesses located in Kenya; **[page 3]**

CONSIDERING the provisions of Articles 19, 20 and 21 of the Tribunal's Statute (hereinafter referred to as "the Statute") and Rules 69 and 75 of the Rules regarding the protection of victims and witnesses;

CONSIDERING the written response filed by the Prosecutor on 16 July 1997;

TAKING INTO ACCOUNT the oral submissions made by the parties on 5 November 1997;

PLEADINGS OF THE PARTIES:

A. THE DEFENCE

The Defence submitted as follows:

(i)   that the protective measures sought in respect of its potential witnesses are necessary to allay fears of the witnesses that they or their family members may be subjected to repatriation to Rwanda and their unwillingness to testify before the Tribunal unless their protection is secure;

(ii)   that although the defence had identified twenty (20) potential defence witnesses in the former Congo-Zaire, it is currently impossible to locate them because they have been displaced by invading forces and the defence has received information to the effect that two (2) of the witnesses have been killed and that the others are also feared to be dead;

(iii) that the authorities in the Republic of Rwanda and the Democratic Republic of Congo permitted the disappearance and death of the above mentioned potential defence witnesses;

(iv) that six of the potential defence witnesses who are in the Republic of Kenya also have families living in both Kenya and Rwanda with at least one family member being imprisoned in Rwanda and as such the witnesses are unwilling to come forth to testify before the Tribunal owing to the apparent threat to their lives and that of their families.

In support of the motion and to illustrate the precarious situation of potential defence witnesses particularly those located in the Republic of Kenya, the Defence Counsel relied upon several documents, *inter alia*, an article in the Washington Post newspaper entitled "Rwandans led Revolt in Congo" written by John Pomfret and dated 9 July 1997; the July report of an organisation called "The Physicians for Human Rights" and the Garreton Report of the Human Rights Commission UNO dated 2 April 1997; a report of the Joint Mission UNO dated 2 July 1997 and several reports of Amnesty International dated 12 August 1996, January and 25 September 1997; **[page 4]**

B. THE PROSECUTION

In her written response, the Prosecutor generally conceded to the grant of measures 5-8 of the defence motion and noted that the Defence was relying upon Article 21 of the Statute and rules 72 and 75 of the Rules;

The Prosecutor made several contentions as shown below:

(i) that Measure 4 was unnecessary and measures 1 and 9 were vague and superfluous because those measures simply re-state the mandate of the Tribunal to protect witnesses through the Registry and the Victims and Witnesses Protection Unit (hereafter referred to as the VWPU) both of which are prohibited from revealing the names of witnesses placed under the protection of the Tribunal by its order.

(ii) that the Defence Counsel's submission on the fear or threat of arrest of potential witnesses for the defence was mere speculation on the part of the defence since no details were provided to explain the imminent arrest of the potential defence witnesses and their families;

(iii) that in the event that the said witnesses were deported to Rwanda or elsewhere those States would have to cooperate with the Tribunal pursuant to Article 28 of the Statutes and would surrender those people before the Trial Chamber if the Tribunal so requested.

(iv) that in respect of measure 2 for the Defence to request for refugee status and such other related status from the Tribunal was beyond the scope of the relief sought by the Defence since the power to grant refugee status rests exclusively with the State in which the applicant is seeking refuge, in this case, the Republic of Kenya and as such the Tribunal could not justify its interference in the sovereignty of the Republic of Kenya;

(v) that under Article 28 of the Statute, the obligation of a State is to assist the Tribunal in the investigation and prosecution of persons responsible for violating international humanitarian law through a fair trial respecting the interests of the accused, the victims and the witnesses as provided for in Article 21 of the Statute, rule 40 A (iii) and rule 75;

(vi) that in the alternative if the Tribunal found that it has jurisdiction under rule 75 of the Rules to request States to accord potential witnesses the necessary asylum or such other status, the motion does not give sufficient information to enable the Trial Chamber to make any judgement on the merit of the request;

(vii) that pursuant to rule 67 of the Rules and considering the case of **The Prosecutor v. Delilac et al Case No. IT-94-I-T** decided by the ICTY, there is no reciprocal obligation requiring the Defence to disclose to the Prosecution the witnesses it intends to call at the trial unless the witness would

221

be pleading the defence of alibi or a special defence under rule 67(B) **[page 5]** and (C) of the Rules;

(viii) that since under Article 15 of the Statute the Prosecutor is empowered to prosecute persons who have committed crimes falling within the Tribunal's jurisdiction, the Defence should be ordered to provide to the Prosecutor basic and rudimentary information about the defence witnesses to enable her to fulfil her mandate by according her an opportunity to impeach defence witnesses so as to establish their veracity, truth and credibility;

C.   DEFENCE'S REJOINDER:

(i)   The Defence Counsel while agreeing that despite the lack of a statutory reciprocal obligation placed upon the Defence, it was not forbidden for the Defence to disclose to the Prosecutor the identities of its potential witnesses but that it might pose a risk to the Defence.

(ii)   The Defence Counsel requested the Trial Chamber to follow its previous decisions and order that there should be no such disclosure to the Prosecution until a further order has been made by the Trial Chamber;

(ii)   The Defence Counsel, however, disagreed with the Prosecutor's submission in respect of measures 2-3 and stated that he preferred to have recourse to the Trial Chamber which had all the powers rather than seek the assistance of the UNHCR which has been criticized for being inefficient.

DELIBERATIONS

A. Regarding the matter of confidentiality: the request for the non -disclosure of the identity of witnesses to the public and the media

The Trial Chamber takes cognizance of the fact that in the present situation the request for the non - disclosure of the identity of witnesses to the media is warranted by the many concordant reports issued by various sources which describe the particularly volatile situation at present in Rwanda and in the neighbouring countries where those persons, who may have in one way or the other borne witness to the events of 1994, are found today. Hence, divulging the identity of the witnesses may prove dangerous and detrimental to them.

The Trial Chamber takes judicial notice of similar motions decided in the cases of **The Prosecutor v. Georges Anderson Rutaganda ICTR-96-3-T**, decided on 6 March 1997 and **The Prosecutor v. Elie Ndayambaje ICTR-96-8-T** decided on 8 September 1997 in which the Tribunal has solicited the cooperation of States, UN organizations including the United Nations High Commissioner for Refugees (the "UNHCR") and other organizations. **[page 6]**

The Trial Chamber is therefore of the considered opinion that it is appropriate to grant the reliefs sought by the Defence as indicated below.

B. On the issue of repatriation to Rwanda and the fear of reprisals on return to Rwanda

The Trial Chamber considers Article 21 of the Tribunal's Statute and rule 75 of the Rules which obliges it to take the necessary steps to provide appropriate measures to protect witnesses in order to ensure a fair trial.

The Trial Chamber is of the view that there is need for the defence to substantiate its request for the relief sought and is not inclined to agree with the submission of the Prosecution on this point that no legal basis has been laid. On the facts presented, the Chamber is of the view that the Defence has provided such a basis.

The Trial Chamber has considered the various reports and submissions on the security situation in Rwanda and the neighbouring countries that have been produced and observes that situations described in the annexes to the Defence motion may well pose a risk to potential defence witnesses and may prejudice the rights of the accused in conducting a proper defence.

The Trial Chamber is, however, of the view that the granting of refugees status falls within the ambit of domestic law, in this case under Kenyan Law and Kenyan Authorities hold the sovereign right to prosecute criminal offenders within their territory.

The Trial Chamber holds that protective measures should not extend to providing immunity from criminal prosecution by any appropriate authority;

C. On the matter of anonymity: the request for the temporary non -disclosure of the identity of defence witnesses to the Prosecution until such time as they are put under the protection of the Tribunal

The Trial Chamber has given serious consideration to the provisions of rules 66 and 67 of the Rules and finds that whilst rules 66 and 69 of the Rules make it obligatory for the Prosecution to disclose to the Defence the evidence that it will be relying upon, there is no reciprocal obligation placed upon the Defence to disclose to the Prosecution the witnesses it would be calling, except in cases where the defence of alibi or a special defence would be relied on by the Defence.

In this regard, the Chamber agrees with the Prosecutor's interpretation of rule 67 of the Rules. However, it is the Trial Chamber's view that a fair trail calls for each party to be accorded an opportunity to cross-examine each other's witnesses so as to establish the relevant facts and the truth;

The Trial Chamber is, therefore, of the considered opinion that for a fair trial to take place, once defence witnesses have been placed under the protection of the Tribunal, the Defence may disclose **[page 7]** the identity of its witnesses in sufficient time prior to the trial to allow the Prosecution to prepare its case for rebuttal.

D. On the matter of granting protective measures similar to those already granted to the Prosecution

The Trial Chamber has noted the submission made by the Defence Counsel in his written text of the motion to the effect that measures similar to those granted to the Prosecution witnesses should be granted to the Defence.

The Trial Chamber considers the provisions of Articles 19(1), 20 and 21 of the Statute and rule 75 of the Rules as grounds for ensuring that a fair and equitable trial takes place through the equal treatment of both parties as provided in Article 20(1) of the Statute which in this case entitles the Defence to be granted similar protective measures for its witnesses.

It is the view of the Trial Chamber, therefore, that where there is a need for the Prosecution to contact some Defence witnesses, then under rule 75, it can *proprio motu* allow the Prosecutor to make such contact upon prior notice to the Defence.

The Trial Chamber is mindful of its previous decisions on this issue in which it granted protective measures to the Prosecution witnesses and hence is of the view that to the extent possible, the defence witnesses in this case should be accorded similar protective measures as stipulated below.

FOR ALL THE ABOVE REASONS THE TRIAL CHAMBER ORDERS AS FOLLOWS:

(i) That the Defence Counsel shall furnish the VWU with the particulars pertaining to its witnesses, and the VWU shall then take appropriate protective measures as laid down below to ensure the presence of the witnesses and their safety.

(ii) That pursuant to Security Council Resolution 955/94 and Article 28 of the Statute, the Tribunal authorises the Registrar to solicit for the assistance of the Republic of Kenya and the UNHCR and after receiving the information concerning the witnesses from the Defence Counsel, the Registrar shall take all possible measures to ensure their availability to the Tribunal in cooperation with the Government of the Republic of Kenya.

(iii) That subject to rule 67 of the Rules, the names, addresses, whereabouts of the defence witnesses and other identifying information of the Defence witnesses, shall not be disclosed to the Prosecution, until further order. **[page 8]**

(iv) That the names, addresses, whereabouts of the defence witnesses and other identifying information of the Defence witnesses shall be kept under the seal of the Tribunal and not included in any of the public records of the Tribunal.

(v) That in cases where such names, addresses, whereabouts of the defence witnesses and other identifying information about the defence witnesses that appear in the Tribunal's public records, this information shall be expunged from the Tribunal's public records.

(vi) That the names, addresses, whereabouts of the defence witnesses and other identifying information of the defence witnesses shall not be disclosed to the public and the media.

(vii) That the public and the media shall not take photographs, make audio and video recordings or sketching of the defence witnesses who are under the protection of the Tribunal, without its authorisation.

(viii) That the Prosecution and its representatives who are acting pursuant to their instructions shall notify the Defence Counsel of any request for contacting the defence witnesses, and the Defence Counsel shall make arrangements for such contacts.

(ix) That the Defence shall be permitted to designate pseudonyms for each of its witnesses for use in the proceedings of the Tribunal, during any communication *inter partes* and to the public as well as in the official proceedings of the Tribunal.

(x) That pursuant to Rule 75 of the Rules, the defence is at liberty to request a Judge or Trial Chamber, at any time, to amend or add to any of the abovementioned protective measures for the defence witnesses.

Dated at Arusha, Tanzania this 25th Day of November 1997 **[page 9]**

William Sekule,	Tafazzal Hossain Khan	Navanethem Pillay
Presiding Judge	Judge	Judge

UNITED NATIONS   NATIONS UNIES

International Criminal Tribunal for Rwanda
Tribunal pénal international pour le Rwanda

CHAMBER I – CHAMBRE I

OR: FR

Before: Judge Laïty Kama, Presiding Judge
               Judge Lennart Aspegren
               Judge Navanethem Pillay

Registry: Mr. Lars Plum
               Mr. John M. Kiyeyeu

Decision of: 17 February 1998

THE PROSECUTOR

VERSUS

JEAN-PAUL AKAYESU

Case No. ICTR-96-4-T

DECISION ON A MOTION FOR SUMMONSES AND
PROTECTION OF WITNESSES CALLED BY THE DEFENCE

Office of the Prosecutor:
    Mr. Pierre-Richard Prosper
    Mr. James Stewart

Counsel for the Defence:
    Mr. Nicolas Tiangaye

[page 2]THE INTERNATIONAL CRIMINAL TRIBUNAL FOR RWANDA (the "TRIBUNAL"),

SITTING as Trial Chamber I, composed of Judge Laïty Kama, Presiding Judge, and of Judge Lennart Aspegren and Judge Navanethem Pillay;

HAVING RECEIVED from the Defence a motion dated 2 December 1997 (the "motion") for the appearance and protection of two Defence witnesses, Jean Kambanda and Pauline Nyiramasuhuko, who have both been indicted by the Prosecutor before the Tribunal in cases nos. ICTR-97-23-I and ICTR-97-21-I respectively, and are currently detained by the Tribunal awaiting trial;

HAVING RECEIVED the Prosecutor's response, dated 12 February 1998, in which she does not object to the appearance and argues, on the contrary, that an accused may be obliged by a sovereign decision of the Tribunal to testify, even if the witness is opposed to testifying;

HAVING ALSO RECEIVED a response to the motion, dated 3 February 1998, from Ms. Nicole Bergevin, Counsel for Pauline Nyiramasuhuko, in which the Counsel informs the Tribunal of the refusal of the said accused to testify;

HAVING BEEN NOTIFIED by the Registry of the Tribunal that Jean Kambanda had received a copy of the motion and had stated that he did not wish to be represented at the hearing to consider the motion or to respond to the motion;

HAVING HEARD the Parties, as well as Ms Bergevin, during the hearing held to that effect on 13 February 1998;

AFTER HAVING DELIBERATED,

WHEREAS, in support of its motion, the Defence argued that hearing the said two accused would enlighten the Tribunal on events that took place in Taba Commune which have a direct bearing on the charges brought by the Prosecutor against Jean-Paul Akayesu and that, consequently, these testimonies would be useful for the discovery of the truth;

Whereas the Tribunal is of the opinion that each time it decides whether or not to call an accused on exceptional basis to testify in a case other than his or her own trial, the relevance and probative value of the evidence required from the accused should be weighed against the prejudice that the obligation to appear as a witness could possibly cause the accused;

WHEREAS although the provisions of Rule 90 (E) of the Rules of Procedure and Evidence of the Tribunal (the "Rules") provide that a witness may object to making any statement which might tend to incriminate him, the fact remains that the Chamber may, however, compel the witness to answer the question and that testimony compelled in this way could be used as evidence during subsequent prosecution for perjury, as provided for in Rule 91 of the Rules; **[page 3]**

Whereas, as regards an accused, the Tribunal is of the opinion that compelling him or her to appear as a witness could perhaps violate his or her fundamental right not to be forced to testify against himself or herself or to confess guilt, a right which is recognized under the provisions of Article 20 (4)(g) of the Statute of the Tribunal, and also under those of Article 14 (3)(g) of the 1966 International Covenant on Civil and Political Rights;

WHEREAS, accordingly, the Tribunal considers that in this case there is a risk that the appearance of the two accused as witnesses could cause prejudice to them;

FOR THESE REASONS

THE TRIBUNAL

DISMISSES the motion filed by the Defence for the appearance of the said two accused as witnesses.

Rendered on 17 February 1998,

Signed in Arusha on 23 February 1998.

Laïty Kama	Lennart Aspegren	Navanethem Pillay
Presiding Judge	Judge	Judge

UNITED NATIONS   NATIONS UNIES

International Criminal Tribunal for Rwanda
Tribunal pénal international pour le Rwanda

CHAMBER I – CHAMBRE I

OR: ENG

Before: Judge Laïty Kama, Presiding Judge
               Judge Lennart Aspegren
               Judge Navanethem Pillay

Registry: Mr. Antoine K.M. Mindua

Decision of: 26 March 1998

THE PROSECUTOR

VERSUS

GEORGES ANDERSON NDERUBUMWE RUTAGANDA

Case No. ICTR-96-3-T

———————————————

DECISION ON THE URGENT MOTION FILED BY THE DEFENCE FOR THE
IMMEDIATE TRANSFER AND APPEARANCE OF A DETAINED WITNESS,
FRODUALD KARAMIRA

———————————————

The Office of the Prosecutor:
    Mr. James Stewart
    Mr. Udo Gehring

Counsel for the Accused:
    Ms. Tiphaine Dickson

[page 2]THE INTERNATIONAL CRIMINAL TRIBUNAL FOR RWANDA (the "TRIBUNAL"),

SITTING as Trial Chamber I, composed of Judge Laïty Kama as Presiding Judge, Judge Lennart Aspegren and Judge Navanethem Pillay;

HAVING BEEN SEIZED by the Defence Counsel's motion of 20 February 1998, filed pursuant to Rule 90*bis* of the Rules of Procedure and Evidence (the "Rules"), requesting an order for the immediate transfer and appearance of Froduald Karamira as a witness for the defence in the trial of Georges Anderson Rutaganda (the "accused");

NOTING that Froduald Karamira is believed to be currently detained in Kigali Central Prison, Rwanda;

CONSIDERING THAT the Prosecutor opposed Defence Counsel's motion in a response dated 2 March 1998;

HAVING HEARD the Prosecutor and the Defence Counsel at a hearing on 27 February 1997;

AFTER HAVING DELIBERATED,

1.   The Defence Counsel submitted that the testimony of Froduald Karamira is crucial to the case of the accused for the following reasons:

(a) He will be able to confirm or invalidate the statement in this case by the expert witness Professor Filip Reyntjens, concerning the conversations they allegedly had in April 1994;

(b) He will be able to confirm or invalidate the existence of orders and links between the Interahamwe organisation and outside elements, in particular, Colonels Théoneste Bagosora and Tharcisse Rehzaho;

(c) He will be able to provide direct testimony on the meaning and nature of the speech commonly referred to as "Power" which he delivered on 23 October 1993 at the Nyamirambo stadium in Kigali, which prosecution witnesses have already testified to;

(d) He will be able to provide direct testimony on the events that took place in Kigali in 1994;

(e) He will be able to provide direct testimony on the signing of an agreement between the Rwandan opposition parties and the RPF in Brussels in June 1992; **[page 3]**

(f) He will be able to provide the Tribunal with any information relating to the Interahamwe and their evolution; and

(g) He will be able to testify to all the facts concerning Georges Rutaganda.

2.   Defence Counsel averred:

a) that Froduald Karamira was sentenced to death on 14 February 1997 by the Rwandan Criminal Court in Kigali for crimes of Genocide, that he has exhausted all avenues of recourse before the Rwandan Courts and that his presence is no longer required for any criminal proceedings in Rwanda;

b) that Froduald Karamira is not facing a prison term, but the death penalty. Therefore, his transfer to the ICTR Detention Facility is not likely to extend the period of his detention; and

c) that Froduald Karamira must be transferred immediately to the ICTR Detention Facility, given his imminent execution.

3.   The Prosecutor, in opposing the defence motion, submitted that the Defence:

(a) has failed to demonstrate that the conditions under Rule 90bis(B) of the Rules have been met;

(b) has given no indication that Froduald Karamira wishes to testify;

(c) has given no indication that Froduald Karamira may have any evidence relating to the conduct of the accused and that this would help the accused in his defence.

4.   The Prosecutor also submitted that in the event of the Tribunal deciding that Froduald Karamira is an essential witness for the defence, it may consider other mechanisms for obtaining his testimony. One such mechanism is proved for in Rule 71 of the Rules.

5.   The Tribunal notes that Article 20(4)(e) of the Statute of the Tribunal affords the accused the right to obtain the attendance and examination of witnesses on his behalf under the same conditions as witnesses against him. **[page 4]**

6.   The Tribunal recalls that Rule 90*bis* (B) of the Rules states that:

"The transfer order shall be issued by a Judge or Trial Chamber only after prior verification that the following conditions have been met:

(i)   the presence of the detained witness is not required for any criminal proceedings in progress in the territory of the requested State during the period the witness is required by the Tribunal;

(ii)   transfer of the witness does not extend the period of his detention as foreseen by the requested State;".

7.   The Tribunal refers to its previous decision in the case of Jean-Paul Akayesu (ICTR-96-4-T), dated 31 October 1997, wherein a letter from the Rwandan Minister of Justice had served to verify that the conditions as set out in Rule 90*bis*(B) have been complied with.

8.   The Tribunal notes that subsequent to the hearing on 27 February 1998, the Defence had furnished copies of a document with no proper seal, stamp or any other form of authentication. Although this was irregular, the Tribunal nevertheless considered the contents of this document. This document indicated that Froduald Karamira had been convicted and sentenced to death for crimes of genocide by a Kigali court of the first instance, a specialized Trial Chamber, and that he was denied appeal by the Kigali Court of Appeal.

9.   The Tribunal nevertheless notes that this document tendered by the Defence does not in itself, confirm that Froduald Karamira has exhausted all post appeal avenues available to him within the Rwandan criminal code, such as pardon or commutation of sentence. It also notes that, the Defence has failed to show that conditions provided for under Rule 90 *bis* of the Rules, particularly its paragraph (i), have been complied with.

10.   Furthermore, the Tribunal notes that the Defence has also failed to present evidence, indicating that Froduald Karamira would consent to testify for the defence. **[page 5]**

11.   Consequently, the Tribunal finds that since the conditions set forth under Rule 90 *bis* (B) of the Rules have not been complied with, it is proper, as the case stands, to dismiss the Defence motion for the immediate transfer and appearance of Froduald Karamira.

FOR ALL THE ABOVE REASONS,

THE TRIBUNAL

DISMISSES the Defence motion for the immediate transfer and appearance of Froduald Karamira as a witness for the defence in this case.

Arusha, 26 March 1998

Laïty Kama	Lennart Aspegren	Navanethem Pillay
Presiding Judge	Judge	Judge

International Criminal Tribunal for the Prosecution of Persons Responsible for Genocide and Other Serious Violations of International Humanitarian Law Committed in the Territory of Rwanda and Rwandan Citizens responsible for genocide and other such violations committed in the territory of neighbouring States between 1 January and 31 December 1994

Case No.   ICTR-96-3-A

Date: 8 June 1998

Original: ENGLISH

IN THE APPEALS CHAMBER

Before: **Judge Gabrielle Kirk McDonald (Presiding)**
             Judge Mohamed Shahabuddeen
             Judge Lal Chand Vohrah
             Judge Wang Tieya
             Judge Rafael Nieto-Navia

Registry: **Mr. Agwu U. Okali**

Decision of: **8 June 1998**

PROSECUTOR

v.

GEORGES ANDERSON NDERUBUMWE RUTAGANDA

DECISION ON APPEALS AGAINST THE DECISIONS BY TRIAL CHAMBER I REJECTING THE DEFENCE MOTIONS TO DIRECT THE PROSECUTOR TO INVESTIGATE THE MATTER OF FALSE TESTIMONY BY WITNESSES "E" AND "CC"

The office of the Prosecutor:
    Mr. James Stewart
    Mr. Pierre-Richard Prosper
    Mr. Udo Gehring
    Mr. Holo Makwaia

Counsel for the Accused:
    Ms. Tiphanie Dickson

[page 2] I. INTRODUCTION

1.   Pending before the Appeals Chamber of the International Criminal Tribunal for the Prosecution of Persons Responsible for Genocide and Other Serious Violations of International Humanitarian Law Committed in the Territory of Rwanda and Rwandan Citizens Responsible for Genocide and Other Such Violations Committed in the Territory of Neighbouring States, between 1 January 1994 and 31 December 1994 ("ICTR") is a Notice of Appeal Against the Decision of Trial Chamber I Dismissing the Defence Motion for an Order to the Prosecutor to Investigate A Case of False Testimony (Witness "CC"), filed on 19 March 1998, and a Notice of Appeal Against the Decision of Trial Chamber I Dismissing the Defence Motion for An Order to Prosecutor to Investigate A Case of False Testimony (Witness "E"), filed on 23 March ("Notices of Appeal").

2.   The Notices of Appeal are brought pursuant to Sub-rule 108 (B) of the Rules of Procedure and Evidence of the ICTR ("ICTR Rules" or "Rules"). They concern the Decision on the Defence Motion to Direct the Prosecutor to Investigate the matter of False Testimony by Witness "CC" filed on 26 March 1998 and the Decision on the Defence Motion to Direct the Prosecutor to Investigate the Matter of False Testimony by witness "E" filed on 27 March 1998 ("Trial Chamber Decisions") and are, therefore, considered together by the Appeals Chamber in this Decision. **[page 3]**

II. APPLICABLE PROVISIONS

3.   The applicable provisions of the Statute and Rules of the ICTR that are relevant to the Decision of the Appeals Chamber are as follows:

Article 24

Appellate Proceedings

1.   The Appeals Chamber shall hear appeals from persons convicted by the Trial Chambers or from the Prosecutor on the following grounds:

   a) An error on a question of law invalidating the decision; or

   b) An error of fact which has occasioned a miscarriage of justice.

2.   The Appeals Chamber may affirm, reverse or revise the decisions taken by the Trial Chambers.

Rule 72

Preliminary Motions

(A)   Preliminary motions by either party shall be brought within sixty days following disclosure by the Prosecutor to the Defence of all the material envisaged by Rule 66(A)(i), and in any case before the hearing on the merits.

(B)   Preliminary motions by the accused shall include:

   i)   objections based on lack of jurisdiction;

   ii)   objections based on defects in the form of the indictment; **[page 4]**

   iii)   applications for severance of crimes joined in one indictment under Rule 49, or for separate trials under Rule 82(B);

   iv)   objections based on the denial of request for assignment of counsel.

(C)   The Trial Chamber shall dispose of preliminary motions in limine litis.

(D)   Decisions on preliminary motions are without interlocutory appeal, save in the case of dismissal of an objection based on lack of jurisdiction, where an appeal will lie as of right.

(E)   Notice of appeal envisaged in Sub-Rule (D) shall be filed within seven days from the impugned decision.

(F)   Failure to comply with the time-limits prescribed in this Rule shall constitute a waiver of the rights. The Trial Chamber may, however, grant relief from the waiver upon showing good cause.

Rule 73

Motions

(A)   Subject to Rule 72, either party may move before a Trial Chamber for appropriate ruling or relief after the initial appearance of the accused. Such motions may be written or oral, at the discretion of the Trial Chamber.

(B)   Decisions rendered on such motions are without interlocutory appeal. **[page 5]**

Rule 77

Contempt of the Tribunal

(A)   Subject to the provisions of Rule 90(E), a witness who refuses or fails contumaciously to answer a question relevant to the issue before a Chamber may be found in contempt of the Tribunal.

The Chamber may impose a fine not exceeding USD 10,000 or a term of imprisonment not exceeding six months.

(B)   The Chamber may, however, relieve the witness of the duty to answer, for reasons which it deems appropriate.

(C)   Any person who attempts to interfere with or intimidate a witness may be found guilty of contempt and sentenced in accordance with Sub-rule (A).

(D)   Any judgement rendered under this Rule shall be subject to appeal.

(E)   Payment of a fine shall be made to the Registrar to be held in a separate account.

Rule 91

False testimony Under Solemn Declaration

(A)   A Chamber, on its own initiative or at the request of a party, may warn a witness of the duty to tell the truth and the consequences that may result from a failure to do so. **[page 6]**

(B)   If a Chamber has strong grounds for believing that a witness may have knowingly and wilfully given false testimony, or at the request of a party, the Chamber may direct the Prosecutor to investigate the matter with a view to the preparation and submission of an indictment for false testimony.

(C)   The Rules of Procedure and Evidence in Parts Four to Eight shall apply mutatis mutandis to proceedings under this Rule.

(D)   The maximum penalty for false testimony under solemn declaration shall be a fine of USD 10,000 or a term of imprisonment of twelve months, or both. The payment or any fine imposed shall be made to the Registrar to be held in the account referred to in Rule 77(E).

Rule 108

Notice of Appeal

(A)   Subject to Sub-rule (B), a party seeking to appeal a judgment or sentence shall, not more than thirty days from the date on which the judgement or sentence was pronounced, file with the Registrar and serve upon the other parties a written notice of appeal, setting forth the grounds.

(B)   Such delay shall be fixed at fifteen days in the case of an appeal from a judgement dismissing an objection based on a lack of jurisdiction or a decision rendered under Rule 77 or Rule 91. **[page 7]**

Rule 117

Expedited Appeals Procedure

(A)   An appeal under Rule 108(B) shall be heard expeditiously on the basis of the original record of the Trial Chamber and without the necessity of any written brief.

(B)   All delays and other procedural requirements shall be fixed by an order of the President issued on an application by one of the parties, or proprio motu should no such application have been made without fifteen days after the filing of the notice of appeal. **[page 8]**

III. PROCEDURAL HISTORY

4.   On 10 September 1997, the Defence ("Appellant") filed the Defence Motion for Orders to Direct the Prosecutor to Investigate a Case of False Testimony in reference to the alleged false testimony of witness "E", who testified for the Office of the Prosecutor ("Respondent"). The motion was founded on Sub-rule 91(B) of the Rules which provides that a party may request that the Trial Chamber direct the Prosecutor to investigate allegations of perjury with a view toward preparation and submission of an indictment for false testimony.

5.   On 8 October 1997, the Appellant presented to Trial Chamber I a similar verbal motion with regard to the testimony of witness "CC" which was followed on 2 March 1998 by the Defence Motion to Direct the Prosecutor to Investigate the Matter of False Testimony.

6.   Trial Chamber I heard arguments from the parties on 6 March 1998. The Trial Chamber Decisions rejecting both motions were delivered orally on 10 March 1998 and written Decisions regarding Witnesses "CC" and "E" were filed with the Registry on 26 and 27 March 1998 respectively. The Appellant filed the Notices of Appeals pursuant to Sub-rule 108(B) of the Rules on 19 and 23 March 1998, respectively.

7.   The Appellant additionally filed a motion on 23 March 1998 requesting that the President of the Tribunal, *inter alia*, fix the delays and procedural requirements for an expedited appeal pursuant to Rule 117(B) of the Rules and suspend hearings until such time as the recordings and transcripts required for the appeals were made available to the Appellant. Although Sub-rule 117(A) provides that it is not necessary to submit briefs, the Appellant requested permission to submit a statement of the grounds for the Notices of Appeal because of the importance of the issues presented.

8.   On 24 March 1998, the President rendered a Decision on the Expedited Appeals Procedure following the Motion by the Defence filed with the Registry on **[page 9]** the same day, finding that although not all of the requests in the Appellant's motion were directly linked to the expedited appeals procedure, but came more generally under the ambit of judicial administration, the requested transcripts would be made available to the Appellant to ensure the right of the Appellant to prepare a proper appeal file.[1] The Appellant's request for suspension of hearings in the Trial Chamber was denied because "on the one hand, the expedited appeals procedure does not require the forwarding of the complete case file to the Appeals Chamber, and, on the other hand, because the decision appealed against cannot affect the continuation of the trial."[2] The President granted leave to the Appellant to file written briefs in support of the Notices of Appeal.

9.   In the Trial Chamber Decisions, the Trial Chamber found that if a motion is brought by a party pursuant to Rule 91(B) of the Rules, the onus is on the moving party "to convince the Chamber that there exist strong grounds for believing that a witness has knowingly and wilfully given false testimony."[3] The Trial Chamber held that the Appellant failed to meet this burden.

10.   Moreover, the Trial Chamber held that:

---

[1]   President's Decision on the Expedited Appeals Procedure Following the Motion by the Defence, on 24 March 1998, *The Prosecutor v. Georges Anderson Nderubumwe Rutaganda*, Case No. ICTR-96-3-T, at para. 2.

[2]   *Ibid.*, para 3.

[3]   Decision on the Defence Motion to Direct the Prosecutor to Investigate the Matter of False Testimony by Witness "E", *The Prosecutor v. Georges Anderson Nderubumwe Rutaganda*, Case No. ICTR-96-3-T, 27 March 1998 at 3 and Decision on the Defence Motion to Direct the Prosecutor to Investigate the Matter of False Testimony by Witness "CC", *The Prosecutor v. Georges Anderson Nderubumwe Rutaganda*, Case No. ICTR-96-3-T, 26 March 1998 ("Trial Chamber Decision") at 3.

"in the context of the ongoing trials before the Tribunal, inaccuracies and other possible contradictions could be raised during the overall evaluation of credibility upon the final determination of the probative value of the evidence presented at trial."[4] **[page 10]**

11.   On 14 April 1998, the Appellant filed written briefs[5]in support of the Notices of Appeals pursuant to Sub-rule 108(B) of the Rules. On 12 May 1998, the Respondent filed the Respondent's Brief on Appeal Against the Decision on the Defence Motion to Direct the Prosecutor to Investigate the Matter of Alleged False Testimony by Witness "E" and the Respondent's Brief on Appeal Against the Decision on the Defence Motion to Direct the Prosecutor to Investigate the Matter of Alleged False Testimony by Witness "CC" ("Prosecution Responses").

12.   The Appellant and Respondent have filed other written exchanges[6]. These do not, however, go to the issue now being considered as to whether there is an **[page 11]** appealable decision in this case. Consequently, for the purpose of deciding that issue, it will not be necessary to consider those exchanges. **[page 12]**

---

[4]   *Ibid.*, at p.4 and p. 4, respectively.

[5]   Appeal Against the Decision by Trial Chamber I in the Matter of Witness "CC", *The Prosecutor v. Georges Anderson Nderubumwe Rutaganda*, Case No. ICTR-96-3-T, 14 April 1998; Appeal Against the Decision by Trial Chamber I in the Matter of Witness "E", *The Prosecutor v. Georges Anderson Nderubumwe Rutaganda*, Case No. ICTR-96-3-T, 14 April 1998.

[6]   Motion to Declare Inadmissible the Brief in Reply Filed by the Office of the Prosecutor – Appeal Against the Decision Rendered by Trial Chamber I Dismissing the Defence Motion to to Direct the Prosecutor to Investigate a Matter of False Testimony by Witness "CC", *The Prosecutor v. Georges Anderson Nderubumwe Rutaganda*, Case No. ICTR-96-3-T, 19 May 1998; Motion to Declare Inadmissible the Brief in Reply Filed by the Office of the Prosecutor – Appeal Against the Decision Rendered by Trial Chamber I Dismissing the Defence Motion to to Direct the Prosecutor to Investigate a Matter of False Testimony by Witness "E", *The Prosecutor v. Georges Anderson Nderubumwe Rutaganda*, Case No. ICTR-96-3-T, 19 May 1998; Reply by the Respondent to the Motion to Declare Inadmissible the Brief in Reply Filed by the Office of the Prosecutor (Witness "CC"), *The Prosecutor v. Georges Anderson Nderubumwe Rutaganda*, Case No. ICTR-96-3-T, 21 May 1998; Reply by the Respondent to the Motion to Declare Inadmissable the Brief in reply Filed by the Office of the Prosecutor (Witness "E"), *The Prosecutor v. Georges Anderson Nderubumwe Rutaganda*, Case No. ICTR-96-3-T, 21 May 1998; Appellant's Brief in Response to Respondent's Brief on the Motion to Declare Inadmissible the Brief in Reply Filed by the Office of the Prosecutor – Appeal Against the Decision by Chamber I to Dismiss Defence Motion to Direct the Prosecutor to Investigate the Matter of False Testimony by Witness "CC", *The Prosecutor v. Georges Anderson Nderubumwe Rutaganda*, Case No. ICTR-96-3-T, 22 May 1998; Appellant's Brief in Response to Respondent's Brief on the Motion to Declare Inadmissible the Brief in Reply Filed by the Office of the Prosecutor – Appeal Against the Decision by Chamber I to Dismiss Defence Motion to Direct the Prosecutor to Investigate the Matter of False Testimony by Witness "E", *The Prosecutor v. Georges Anderson Nderubumwe Rutaganda*, Case No. ICTR-96-3-T, 22 May 1998; Response of the Prosecutor (Respondent) to the Amended Motion of the Defence (Appellant) Filed on May 22, 1998 Concerning the Admissibility of the Respondent's Brief Dated and Filed May 12, 1998, in the Matter of the Appeal Against the Decision on the Defence Motion to Direct the Prosecutor to Investigate the Matter of Alleged False Testimony by Witness "CC", *The Prosecutor v. Georges Anderson Nderubumwe Rutaganda*, Case No. ICTR-96-3-T, 26 May 1998; Response of the Prosecutor (Resopndent) to the Amended Motion of the Defence (Appellant) Filed on May 22, 1998 Concerning the Admissability of the Respondent's Brief Dated and Filed May 12, 1998, in the Matter of the Appeal Against the Decision on the Defence Motion to Direct the Prosecutor to Investigate the Matter of Alleged False Testimony by Witness "E", *The Prosecutor v. Georges Anderson Nderubumwe Rutaganda*, Case No. ICTR-96-3-T, 26 May 1998; Amended Motion to Declare Inadmissible the Brief in reply Filed by the Office of the Prosecutor – Appeal Against the Decision Rendered by Trial Chamber I Dismissing the Defence Motion to Direct the Prosecutor to Investigate a Matter of False Testimony by Witness "CC", *The Prosecutor v. Georges Anderson Nderubumwe Rutaganda*, Case No. ICTR-96-3-T, 29 May 1998; Amended Motion to declare Inadmissible the Brief in Reply Filed by the Office of the Prosecutor – Appeal Against the Decision Rendered by Trial Chamber I Dismissing the Defence Motion to Direct the Prosecutor to Investigate the Matter of Alleged False Testimony by Witness "E", *The Prosecutor v. Georges Anderson Nderubumwe Rutaganda*, Case No. ICTR-96-3-T, 29 May 1998; Response of the Prosecutor (Resopndent) to the Amended Motion of the Defence (Appellant) Filed on May 29, 1998 Concerning the Admissability of the Respondent's Brief Dated and Filed May 12, 1998, in the Matter of the Appeal Against the Decision on the Defence Motion to Direct the Prosecutor to Investigate the Matter of Alleged False Testimony by Witness "CC", *The Prosecutor v. Georges Anderson Nderubumwe Rutaganda*, Case No. ICTR-96-3-T, 1 June 1998; Response of the Prosecutor (Respondent) to the Amended Motion of the Defence (Appellant) Filed on May 29, 1998 Concerning the Admissibility of the Respondent's Brief Dated and Filed May 12, 1998, in the Matter of the Appeal Against the Decision on the Defence Motion to Direct the Prosecutor to Investigate the Matter of Alleged False Testimony by Witness "E", *The Prosecutor v. Georges Anderson Nderubumwe Rutaganda*, Case No. ICTR-96-3-T, 1 June 1998.

IV. SUBMISSIONS OF THE PARTIES

1. The Appellant

13.   The Appellant contends that the Trial Chamber "erred in law" and "erred in fact".

14.   The Appellant asserts that the legal standard established by the Trial Chamber Decisions is improper for it holds the moving party to the same burden of proof as that which would be placed on the Prosecution if it had to prove that a witness was guilty of having given false testimony. Further, this burden of proof is even higher than that required of the Prosecution when it is seeking confirmation of an indictment pursuant to Rule 47.

15.   The Appellant also argues that the Trial Chamber erred in fact by finding that it merely raised doubts about the truthfulness of Witness "CC"'s answers.

2. The Respondent

16.   The Respondent contends that the Trial Chamber's standard of proof required for purposes of Sub-rule 91(B) was reasonable and appropriate. The Respondent argues that the standard of proof under that Sub-rule should be higher than the "reasonable grounds" standard of proof under Rule 47 of the Rules.

17.   Further, the Respondent submits that the evidence tendered by the Appellant in support of its motion pursuant to Sub-rule 91(B) failed to meet the standard of proof articulated by the Trial Chamber. Indeed, it contends that it was insufficient to satisfy even the more lenient standard of proof required under Rule 47. **[page 13]**

18.   The Respondent notes that the language of Sub-rule 91(B) is permissive by providing that "the Chamber *may* direct the Prosecutor to investigate" (emphasis added). Accordingly, the Respondent argues that even where the Trial Chamber identifies strong grounds for believing that a witness has "knowingly and willfully given false testimony", the decision to direct an investigation into the matter lies within the Trial Chamber's firm discretion. The Trial Chamber 's discretion should only be disturbed on appeal where its exercise thereof constitutes a "serious, manifest error."[7] **[page 14]**

V. DISCUSSION

19.   The submissions of the parties are concerned for the most part with the standard of proof required to show reasonable grounds that a witness wilfully and knowingly gave false testimony. However, the Appeals Chamber considers that the seminal issue which must first be determined is whether the Notices of Appeal concern a matter that may be appealed.

20.   The Appeals Chamber finds that neither the Statute nor the Rules of the ICTR allow for an appeal from the Trial Chamber Decisions. In the instant matter, therefore, the Appeals Chamber will not address the issues of fact and law regarding the standard necessary to establish "strong grounds for believing that a witness may have knowingly and wilfully given false testimony" under Rule 91.

21.   The instant appeals are filed pursuant to Sub-rule 108 (B). However, the starting point in considering whether the Appeals may be maintained is Article 24 of the Statute of the ICTR. That statutory provision gives the Appeals Chamber authority to hear appeals from "*persons convicted* by the Trial Chamber or from the Prosecutor" (emphasis added). Clearly, the Appellant does not fall into either category.

22.   However, even in instances when a person is not appealing from a conviction, the Appeals Chamber has jurisdiction to hear certain matters which are interlocutory in nature. Rule 72 explicitly

---

[7]   Prosecution Responses at para. 4.

allows for an appeal from a judgement dismissing an objection based on lack of jurisdiction. The Appeals Chamber of the International Criminal Tribunal for the former Yugoslavia ("ICTY") in *The Prosecutor v. Dusko Tadić* [8] ("Tadić Appeals Decision") has upheld the legality of an appeal in these circumstances. It interpreted Rule 72 of the Rules of Procedure and Evidence of the ICTY ("ICTY Rules") which was then identical to ICTR Rule 72 and allowed an **[page 15]** interlocutory appeal from a dismissal based on lack of jurisdiction. The Appeals Chamber stated:

> "Such a fundamental matter as the jurisdiction of the International Tribunal should not be kept for decision at the end of a potentially lengthy, emotional and expensive trial... Would the higher interest of justice be served by a decision in favour of the accused, after the latter had undergone what would then have to be branded as an unwarranted trial. After all, in a court of law, common sense ought to be honoured not only when facts are weighed, but equally when laws are surveyed and the proper rule is selected. In the present case, the jurisdiction of this Chamber to hear and dispose of Appellant's interlocutory appeal is indisputable."[9]

23.   Contrary to the challenges made in the Tadić Appeals Decision, the challenges made in the Appeals *can* be addressed prior to the completion of the trial and, thus, are not in a category of interlocutory decisions for which an appeal is appropriate. This is supported by the Trial Chamber's finding that "inaccuracies and other possible contradictions could eventually be raised during the overall evaluation of credibility upon the final determination of the probative value of the evidence presented at trial."[10] This finding comports with the evaluative process inherent in an ongoing trial before the ICTR, and indeed before the ICTY, where the judgement on the guilt or innocence of an accused is reached only after the receipt of all of the evidence.

24.   The Appellant filed the Notices of Appeal pursuant to Sub-rule 108(B). That Rule, however, prescribes only the time-limit for the filing of a Notice of Appeal in certain circumstances: dismissals of an objection based on lack of jurisdiction (Rule 72) or decisions rendered under Rule 77 or Rule 91. Sub-rule 108(B) does not of itself create a right of appeal. Appealable determinations envisaged by Sub-rule 108(B) do not include the Trial Chamber Decisions which are the subject of the Notices of Appeal. **[page 16]**

25.   Sub-rule 108(B) also refers to Rule 77 which allows a Trial Chamber to impose a fine or a term of imprisonment upon a person found to be in contempt of the Tribunal. This Rule provides explicitly that a judgement rendered under this Rule shall be subject to appeal. Allowing an appeal from a contempt conviction is entirely consistent with the Statute of the ICTR. In such circumstances, the Appeals Chamber would have authority because of the express provision in Article 24 for appeals by "persons convicted". Sub-rule 108(B) then specifies the time-limit for filing the appeal.

26.   Rule 91 is similar to Rule 77 for it provides for a penalty in the form of a fine or a term of imprisonment for the giving of false testimony. Unlike Rule 77, however, this Rule does not state explicitly that a judgement rendered shall be subject to appeal. Implicitly, however, there would be a right of appeal by a person found guilty of giving false testimony, for he or she would be a "person convicted" within the meaning of Article 24 of the Statute of the ICTR. Once again, reference to Sub-rule 108(B) is appropriate only for ascertaining the time-limit for the submission of the appeal.

27.   The instant appeals are not bought by a person convicted of false testimony. Rather, as they are submitted prior to the entry of the judgement, they are interlocutory in nature. However, as noted above, Sub-rule 72(D) does not allow for appeals from interlocutory decisions "save in the case of dismissal of an objection based on lack of jurisdiction". Further, the only other ICTR Rule relating to motions, Sub-rule 73(B), provides that "decisions rendered on such motions are without interlocutory appeal."

---

[8]   Decision on the Defence Motion for Interlocutory Apeal on Jurisdiction, The Prosecutor v. Tadić, Case No. IT-94-1, A.C., 2 Oct. 1995.

[9]   *Ibid.*, at 4.

[10]   *Supra* n. 5.

28.   Finally, although Sub-rule 91(B) allows a party to request that the Trial Chamber direct the Prosecution to investigate an accusation of false testimony, the Appellant has not demonstrated any prejudice caused by the Trial Chamber Decisions refusing to direct the Prosecutor to investigate witnesses "E" and "CC". A credibility determination may be based, but does not necessarily depend, on a judicial finding that a witness has given false testimony. The testimony of a witness may lack credibility even if it does not amount to false testimony within the meaning of Rule 91. Thus, an **[page 17]** investigation for false testimony is ancillary to the proceedings and does not impact on the accused's right to a fair trial. **[page 18]**

VI. DISPOSITION

THE APPEALS CHAMBER, for the foregoing reasons, unanimously:

REJECTS the Defence's Notice of Appeal Against the Decision of Trial Chamber I Dismissing the Defence Motion for an Order to the Prosecutor to Investigate A Case of False Testimony (Witness "CC");

REJECTS the Defence's Notice of Appeal Against the Decision of Trial Chamber I Dismissing the Defence Motion for An Order to Prosecutor to Investigate A Case of False Testimony (Witness "E").

Done in English and French, the English text being authoritative.

Gabrielle Kirk McDonald

Presiding Judge

Judge Shahabuddeen appends a Declaration to this Decision.

Dated this eighth day of June 1998,

At Arusha,

Tanzania.

International Criminal Tribunal for the Prosecution of Persons Responsible for Genocide and Other Serious Violations of International Humanitarian Law Committed in the Territory of Rwanda and Rwandan Citizens responsible for genocide and other such violations committed in the territory of neighbouring States between 1 January and 31 December 1994	Case No. ICTR-96-3-A Date: 8 June 1998 Original: ENGLISH

IN THE APPEALS CHAMBER

Before: **Judge Gabrielle Krik McDonald (Presiding)**
                  Judge Mohamed Shahabuddeen
                  Judge Lal Chand Vohrah
                  Judge Wang Tieya
                  Judge Rafael Nieto-Navia

Registry: **Mr. Agwu U. Okali**

Decision of: **8 June 1998**

PROSECUTOR

v.

GEORGES ANDERSON NDERUBUMWE RUTAGANDA

DECLARATION OF JUDGE MOHAMED SHAHABUDDEEN ON THE ADMISSIBILITY OF APPEALS AGAINST THE DECISIONS BY TRIAL CHAMBER I REJECTING THE DEFENCE MOTIONS TO DIRECT THE PROSECUTOR TO INVESTIGATE THE MATTER OF FALSE TESTIMONY BY WITNESSES "E" AND "CC"

The Office of the Prosecutor:
    Mr. James Stewart
    Mr. Pierre-Richard Prosper
    Mr. Udo Gehring
    Mr. Holo Makwaia

Counsel for the Accused:
    Ms. Tiphanie Dickson

[page 2] My agreement with the Decision to reject the Notices of Appeal rests on Article 24 of the Statute. In one way or another –permissible ways not now explored– a right of appeal has to be traceable to that provision. In this case, such a right is not so traceable.

Done in English and French, the English text being authoritative.

Judge Mohamed Shahabuddeen

Dated this eighth day of June 1998,

At Arushana,

Tanzania.

International Criminal Tribunal for Rwanda
Tribunal pénal international pour le Rwanda

OR: ENG.

TRIAL CHAMBER II

Before:	**Judge William H. Sekule, Presiding**
	Judge Yakov A. Ostrovsky
	Judge Tafazzal Hossain Khan
Registry:	**Mr. John M. Kiyeyeu**

THE PROSECUTOR

versus

ANDRÉ NTAGERURA

Case No. ICTR-96-10A-I

―――――――――――――――

DECISION ON THE DEFENCE MOTION FOR THE PROTECTION OF WITNESSES

―――――――――――――――

The Office of the Prosecutor:
   Mr. Frederic Ossogo

Counsel for the Accused:
    Fakhy N'Fa Kaba Konate
    Benoit Henry

[page 2] THE INTERNATIONAL CRIMINAL TRIBUNAL FOR RWANDA ("the Tribunal"),

SITTING AS Trial Chamber II, composed of Judge William H. Sekule, Presiding, Judge Yakov A. Ostrovsky and Judge Tafazzal Hossain Khan ("the Trial Chamber");

CONSIDERING the indictment issued by the prosecutor on 9 August 1996 against André Ntagerura pursuant to rule 47 of the Rules of Procedure and Evidence ("the Rules") on the basis that there was sufficient evidence to provide reasonable grounds for believing that he has committed genocide, conspiracy to commit genocide, crimes against humanity and violations of Article 3 common to the 1949 Geneva Conventions and Additional Protocol II thereto;

CONSIDERING the decision confirming the indictment, signed by Judge Lennart Aspegren on 10 August 1996;

HAVING NOW BEEN SEIZED of a preliminary motion filed by the defence on 21 November 1997 pursuant to the provisions of Article 21 of the Statute and rule 69 and 75 of the Rules seeking an order for protective measures for witnesses to the crimes alleged in the indictment;

CONSIDERING the response to the aforementioned motion by the Prosecutor filed on 15 July 1997, by which the Prosecutor argues that the measures sought should be considered in light of Article 20 of the Statute and rule 66 of the Rules in that, the rights of the parties provided under the said Article and rule should not be violated;

TAKING INTO ACCOUNT the supplementary motion argued by the defence, which was granted by the Chamber after having not been objected to by the prosecutor;

CONSIDERING the provisions regarding the protection of victims and witnesses in Articles 19 and 21 of the Statute of the Tribunal and in rules 69 and 75 of the Rules;

HAVING HEARD the parties on 13 May 1998;

THE DEFENCE ARGUED:

(A) That based on fears expressed by many potential and declared defence witnesses, most of whom are Hutu, the trial Chamber should grant protective measures sought hereunder to defence witnesses;

(B) That the defence witnesses fear that they may be accused of complicity in the crimes committed in Rwanda in 1994, unless they are protected before coming to testify,

(C) That, the protective measures sought are necessary to facilitate the procurement of travel documents for the witnesses who must travel to the seat of the Tribunal to give evidence; **[page 3]**

(D) That witnesses fears are founded in light of information regarding the security situation in Rwanda as deposed by M.H. Olsen, a security officer attached to the Office of the Prosecutor ("the OTP") in his affidavit dated 27 March 1997, which information compelled the Prosecutor to seek for similar protective measures for her witnesses in all on going cases before the Tribunal;

(E) That the Cyangugu area where most of the potential witnesses come from is known to be unsafe and is a high risk area classified as phase 4 by the United Nations;

(F) That, not withstanding the above reasons which justify granting protective measures, Article 21 of the Statute and rule 75 of the Rules among others, recognise the necessity of the protective measures sought as evidenced in a number of decisions of this Tribunal and those of the International Criminal Tribunal For the Former Yugoslavia, making the granting of protective measures to witnesses a well established practice and a proven necessity;

(G) That in granting the order sought, the Chamber should have regard to Security Council Resolution 955 of 1994 which requires all states to cooperate with the International Criminal Tribunal for Rwanda in among other things, ensuring protection of witnesses;

For the Protection of Witnesses, the Defence Requests the trial Chamber to Specifically Order That;

(A) The names, addresses and other identifying information concerning defence witnesses, as well as their whereabouts shall be sealed and not be included in any Tribunal records;

(B) The names and addresses of defence witnesses as well as their whereabouts and all other identifying information concerning these witnesses shall not be disclosed to the media and or to the public;

(C) There shall be no photographing, audio or video recording or sketching of witnesses, without leave of the Trial Chamber, or of the defence;

(D) The OTP shall not reveal to any one the names, addresses and other identifying information concerning witnesses which may, if necessary, be revealed to it by the Defence;

(E) The names, addresses and all other identifying information concerning the defence witnesses, as well as their whereabouts, if need be, shall not be disclosed to the prosecution, until it is established that the Witnesses and Victims Support Unit of the Tribunal has taken all the necessary measures for the protection of the said witnesses. Failing which, the defence shall be authorised to disclose especially to the prosecutor, and only if need be, only the redacted versions of the documents, prescribed by rule 67(C);

(F) The defence shall use pseudonyms for each witness that it will call to testify whenever referring to such witnesses in Tribunal proceedings and/or communications and discussions between the parties to the trial and the public; **[page 4]**

(G) the defence witness should be afforded protection by the Witness and Victims Support Unit in the same conditions as prosecution witnesses;

(H) (1) defence witnesses shall benefit from immunity from prosecution in relation to the statement they make under oath vis-a-vis the office of the Prosecutor and other national courts;

(2) this immunity from Prosecution shall be exercised on the territory of Tanzania as well as on the territories of various states which lie between the country of residence of the defence witness and the Head Quarters of ICTR during both their travel to the ICTR and their return;

(3) host countries in whose territory witnesses reside are requested to abstain from extraditing or repatriating forcefully such witnesses to Rwanda, or any other country, against their will or choice;

(I) Host governments that accept defence witnesses are requested to cooperate with the Registry of ICTR with a view to establishing, for such witnesses, temporary travel documents such as passports and *laisser passers*, which would permit them to travel to and from Arusha, or to any other place which may be necessary for the purposes of their testimony;

(J) The Registrar and his staff who are responsible for witnesses and victims support should be requested to contact the UNHCR and all governments hosting defence witnesses so that appropriate measures can be taken for their protection throughout the procedure, before, during, and after the trial;

(K) The defence should be authorised to disclose to the Registrar the names and addresses of witnesses which should remain under seal and serve only to facilitate the efforts of the Registry with a view to putting in place the protective and assistance measures;

(L) The defence should be informed about and associated with all the stages of negotiations and of the implementations of protective and assistance measures which are undertaken by the Registry;

(M) Prohibit the Prosecutor and all other members of her office from sharing, discussing, revealing or disclosing directly or indirectly, to any person natural or legal, and to all governments, in particular the government of Rwanda, any information and indication which would allow defence witnesses to be identified or located;

(N) The prosecutor should, upon reasonable notice to the Defence Counsel, submit a written request to the Chamber, or to one of its Judges, to contact any of the defence witnesses subject to protective measures; and that, at the direction of the Chambers, or a Judge there of, and with the consent of the witness or his relative, the defence counsel, together with the Witness and Victims Support Unit will take the necessary measures to facilitate such contact; **[page 5]**

Measures sought shall not affect rights of the defence to apply to the Trial Chamber for additional or amendment of the protective measures;

THE PROSECUTOR RESPONDED AS HEREUNDER:

That considering the relevant provisions in the Statute and the Rules, the Prosecutor has no objection to measures sought by the defence as appearing in items no A,B,C,D,E,F,G,I,K,L and N of the defence motion;

That the contents of the above paragraph not withstanding, the Prosecutor contended:

(a) that the defence motion is not based on convincing supporting material and does not indicate among other things, whether the witnesses for whom the protective measures are sought originate from or are living within or outside Rwanda neither does the motion give particulars or their numbers, or their immigration status;

(b) that following legal precedents of this very Tribunal on this matter, the Chamber is supposed to be satisfied that witnesses for whom protective measures are sought face real fear for their safety and of their family and that, the fear should be based on an objective basis;

(c) that pursuant to rule 67 (A)(i) and (ii), the defence must notify the prosecutor of the names of the witnesses on whom the accused intends to rely to establish the defence of alibi and any other special defence plea; which disclosure is necessary in order to enable the prosecutor to prepare her rebuttal;

(d) that granting the protective measures without due consideration to rule 67 will infringe the prosecutors rights;

(e) that measure H sought by the Prosecutor cannot be granted as sought as it is violative of Article 1 of the Statute which gives powers to the Tribunal to prosecute all those who committed crimes stipulated in the Statute;

(f) that the contents of paragraph (e) above notwithstanding, the request sought cannot be granted for want of further details on the status of the witnesses, as immunity from prosecution is governed by international conventions, notably;
      The Geneva Convention of 28 July 1951 on the Status of Refugees,
      The Vienna Convention of 18 April 1961 on Diplomatic Relations,
      The Vienna Convention of 24 April 1963 on Consular Relations;

(g) that the above conventions notwithstanding, even where the earmarked defence witnesses have refugee, diplomatic or consular status, granting them immunity will still be violative of Article 1 and in particular Article 15 of the statute which grants powers to the Prosecutor to conduct investigation **[page 6]** independently as a separate organ of the Tribunal;

(h) that under Rule 91 of the Rules, the Chamber has power to direct the Prosecutor in case of false testimony under oath, to investigate the matter with a view to preparing and submitting an indictment for false testimony;

(i) Article 1 of the Statute and rule 91(b) of the Rules will be violated if the Chamber will grant the immunity sought by the defence;

(j) that although the Tribunal has primacy over national jurisdictions, the latter cannot be forced *ex officio* to grant immunity from arrest to witnesses which, in the case of Tanzania, will be violative of the agreement signed on 31 August 1995 between the United Nations and the Government of the United Republic of Tanzania;

DELIBERATIONS

(i) WHEREAS generally, measures for the non-disclosure of the identity of victims and witnesses to the public and the media as provided for by the general provisions of rule 69(A) of the Rules, and also more specifically by rule 75(B) of the Rules are not objected to by the Prosecutor;

(ii) WHEREAS it is imperative in view of the security situation in Rwanda and the general need founded on law, to protect witnesses wherever they are;

(iii) MINDFUL of protective measures granted to witnesses under Rule 90(E) which provide that witnesses have the right to object to making any incriminating statement and where the Chamber deems it fit to compel the witness to answer any question, the testimony compelled in this way shall not be used as evidence in a subsequent prosecution against the witness for any offence before the Tribunal other than perjury;

(iv) NOTING that the only type of immunity which falls within the jurisdiction of this Tribunal is the kind provided for under rule 90(E) whereby witness will not be prosecuted by this Tribunal for giving compelled evidence which may incriminate them, excluding perjury;

(v) TAKING INTO ACCOUNT that, with regard to defence request no. L, procedures already exists by which the Witness and Victims Services Unit informs the defence counsel of its activities and the results thereof, rendering it unnecessary to grant this portion of the said request;

(vi) MINDFUL of the fact that based on the defence supporting material and in the circumstances of this motion, there are reasons for defence witnesses to have real fear for their lives and that of members of their immediate family;

(vii) TAKING INTO ACCOUNT the fact that there must be a limit to the number of people related to the witness who will be protected; **[page 7]**

(vii) TAKING INTO ACCOUNT previous decisions on protective measures for witnesses in particular decisions in the case of *The Prosecutor vs Anatole Nsengiyumva* (ICTR-96-12-T), *The Prosecutor vs Georges Rutaganda* (ICTR-96-10-T), *The Prosecutor vs Clement Kayishema and Obed Ruzindana* (ICTR-95-1-T) and *The Prosecutor vs Ferdinand Nahimana* (ICTR-96-11-T) which decisions emphasise that protection to witnesses must be granted only where real fear exist;

FOR THESE REASONS, THE TRIAL CHAMBER

DECIDES as follows:

(1) **Grants** measures sought as appearing in items no. A,B,C,D,E,F,G,I,K and N of the defence motion as appearing herein above which measures were not objected to by the prosecutor; and that protective measures granted shall extend to the witnesses, spouses and members of their immediate families only;

(2) The Chamber in light of rule 90(E) **refrains** from granting immunity from prosecution by national jurisdiction in respect of defence witnesses testimony, for want of jurisdiction, *inter alia*;

(3) That States and other international organisations are **called upon** to cooperate in the implementation of, among other things, these protective measures;

Arusha, 24 August 1998.

William H. Sekule	Yakov A. Ostrovsky	Tafazzal H. Khan
Presiding Judge	Judge	Judge

This annotation addresses seven decisions of the ICTR relating to witnesses. These decisions are considered in groups related to the issues they raise. Four of the decisions involve the issue of protective measures for defense witnesses, three involve the issue of obtaining the appearance of witnesses called by the defense, and one involves the issue of false testimony by a prosecution witness.

Protective Measures and Witness Immunity

Witness testimony is of particular importance in the trials before the Rwanda Tribunal due to the absence of the kind of detailed documentary evidence or paper trail that was available in the trial of the major war criminals before the Nuremberg Tribunal. In order to facilitate witness testimony, Rule 75 of the Rwanda Tribunal's Rules of Procedure and Evidence permit a Trial Chamber, at the request of either party, the witness concerned, or the Victims and Witness Unit, to provide a range of measures for the protection of victims and witnesses.

In light of the widespread criticism of the decision of the ICTY to permit anonymous testimony as a protective measure in the Tadić case,[1] the Rwanda Tribunal has consistently required the Prosecutor to disclose to the defense the identity of witnesses before the commencement of trial and within a time frame that will enable the defense to prepare for cross examination.[2] Moreover, the Rwanda Tribunal has ruled that the Prosecutor may not even temporarily withhold such information from the defense at the pretrial phase without first obtaining an order to that effect from the Trial Chamber.[3] The cases described below are the first to involve Defense requests for witness protection.

In the Decision on the Motions for the Protection of Defence Witnesses, *Prosecutor v. Kayishema and Ruzindana*, Case No. ICTR-95-1-T, 6 October 1997, the defense requested that the Trial Chamber order the non-disclosure of the identity of defense witnesses to the public and media throughout the trial, and to the Prosecution until such time as the witnesses are under the protection of the Tribunal. The defense based its motion on the fact that most of its witnesses were Rwandan Hutus, who were presently located in Kenya, Rwanda, and Tanzania, and were unwilling to testify openly before the ICTR owing to the fear of being implicated in the genocide which occurred in Rwanda in 1994 and of possible reprisals against the witnesses upon their return to Rwanda after having testified. The Prosecutor countered that the Trial Chamber could not exercise its discretion to grant the measures sought by the defense without proof of genuine fear of threat to the personal safety of specific witnesses. According to the Prosecutor, the Defense motion was too vague and unspecific to grant. In addition, the Prosecution argued that fear of being prosecuted is not a legitimate basis upon which to issue protective measures.

The Trial Chamber granted the Defence request for protective measures on the basis of "the many concordant reports, issued by various sources, which describe the particularly volatile situation at present in Rwanda and in the neighboring countries where those persons who may have, in one way or another, borne witness to the events of 1994, are found today." In light of these reports about the general situation, the Trial Chamber did not require a particularized finding with respect to the threat to each witness. By suggesting that in the context of the present volatile situation in the Great Lakes region of Central Africa, protective measures are *per se* warranted, this precedent will render it easier for both the

---

[1]   ALC-I-190-192; Richard May and Marieke Wierda, Trends in International Criminal Evidence: Nuremberg, Tokyo, The Hague and Arusha, 37 Columbia Journal of Transnational Law 1999, p. 725; Sarah Stapleton, Ensuring a Fair Trial in the International Criminal Court: Statutory Interpretation and the Impermissibility of Derogation, 31 New York University Journal of International Law and Politics 1999, p. 535; Natasha A. Affolder, Tadić, the Anonymous Witness and the Sources of International Procedural Law, 19 Michigan Journal of International Law 1998, p.445; Mercedeh Momeni, Balancing the Procedural Rights of the Accused Against a Mandate to Protect Victims and Witnesses: An Examination of the Anonymity Rules of the International Criminal Tribunal for the Former Yugoslavia, 41 Howard Law Journal 1997, p.155; Monroe Leigh, Witness Anonymity is Inconsistent with Due Process, 91 American Journal of International Law 1997, p.80.

[2]   See e.g., Decision on the Preliminary Motion Submitted by the Prosecutor for Protective Measures for Witnesses, *Prosecutor v. Rutaganda*, Case No. ICTR-96-3-T, 26 September 1996; Decision on the Motion Filed by the Prosecutor on the Protection of Victims and Witnesses, *Prosecutor v. Kayishema*, Case No. ICTR-95-1-T, 6 November 1996; Decision on the Motions Filed by the Prosecutor on the Protection of Victims and Witnesses, *Prosecutor v. Ruzindana*, Case Nos. ICTR-95-1-T, and ICTR-96-10-T, 31 January 1997 and 4 March 1997; Decision on the Motion Filed by the Prosecutor on the Protection of Victims and Witnesses, *Prosecutor v. Ndayambaje*, Case No. ICTR-96-8-T, 11 March 1997.

[3]   Decision on the Motion filed by the Prosecutor on the Protection of Victims and Witnesses, *Prosecutor v. Kayishema*, Case No. ICTR-95-1-T, 6 November 1996.

prosecution and the defense to obtain protective measures for their witnesses in other cases before the ICTR. However, this decision, which has the effect of preventing the public and media from viewing the testimony of most witnesses before the ICTR, may also have the effect of undermining the principle of a public trial. It has long been recognized that the public viewing of criminal trial proceedings is necessary to ensure not only that justice is achieved, but that justice is seen to be achieved.[4] As the U.S. Supreme Court has stated, "To work effectively, it is important that society's criminal process satisfy the appearance of justice, and the appearance of justice can best be provided by allowing people to observe it."[5] This is particularly important for the Rwanda Tribunal since it was established by the Security Council with a view toward promoting peace and reconciliation in Rwanda. To be consistent with the relevant international standards,[6] the principle of conducting criminal trial proceedings which are open to the public and the press should be respected in the absence of clear and overwhelming particularized grounds for closing the proceedings with respect to each witness. The Kayishema decision is likely to be subject to criticism for giving insufficient weight to this principle.

Since the defense witnesses feared retaliation, as well as potential prosecution, the Trial Chamber in Kayishema did not find it necessary to address whether fear of prosecution in itself was a sufficient basis for protective measures. However, the Trial Chamber indicated that the protective measures "should not be used as a way of providing immunity to the witnesses against possible prosecution." The issue of immunity arose in a slightly different context in the Decision on the Defense Motion for the Protection of Witnesses, *Prosecutor v. Ntagerura*, Case No. ICTR-96-10A-I, 24 August 1998. In that case, the Defense requested an order giving defense witnesses immunity from prosecution in relation to any statement they make under oath in an ICTR proceeding vis-a-vis other national courts. The Prosecutor argued that, although the Tribunal has primacy over national jurisdictions, it cannot force national jurisdictions to forego prosecutions where the Tribunal is not prosecuting the case. The Trial Chamber agreed with the Prosecutor, and decided to "refrain[] from granting immunity from prosecution by national jurisdiction in respect of defence witnesses testimony, for want of jurisdiction."

A related issue was raised in the Decision on the Protective Measures for Defence Witnesses and Their Families, *Prosecutor v. Kanyabashi*, Case No. ICTR-96-15-T, 25 November 1997, where the Defense requested that the Tribunal grant refugee status, as part of the protective measures necessary for Rwanda Hutu witnesses presently located in Kenya. The Defense argued that these witnesses are unwilling to testify for fear that they would subsequently be refused re-entry and consequently repatriated to Rwanda, where their lives would be in danger. The Prosecutor argued in response that the power to grant refugee status rested exclusively with the State in which the applicant seeks refuge; consequently the Tribunal could not justify its interference in the sovereignty of the Republic of Kenya. Taking cognizance of various reports about the volatile situation in Rwanda, the Trial Chamber agreed that the risk of repatriation of witnesses to Rwanda and the associated threat to their safety was more than mere speculation. However, the Trial Chamber declined to grant the relief requested because "the granting of refugee status falls within the ambit of domestic law, in this case under Kenyan Law and Kenyan Authorities hold the sovereign right to prosecute criminal offenders within their territory." Instead, the Trial Chamber ordered that the defence witnesses be granted measures similar to those granted to the Prosecution witnesses to protect their identity. The question of granting immunity to witnesses has been a difficult one for both the ICTY and the ICTR. The question first arose in relation to the ICTY during the preparation of its Rules of Procedure in 1994. The consideration of this question by the judges of the ICTY has influenced the jurisprudence of the ICTR. The United States had proposed a provision for the ICTY Rules that would have allowed the Prosecutor to grant suspects either full or limited testimonial immunity in order to induce alleged perpetrators to testify against higher level officials.[7] This was one of the most controversial issues considered in connection with the preparation of the rules. After debating

---

[4]   See European Court of Human Rights, *Sutter v. Switzerland*, 22 February 1984, Series A-74, par. 26.
[5]   Richmond Newspapers, Inc. v. Virginia, 448 U.S. 555 (1980).
[6]   International Covenant on Civil and Political Rights, 19 Dec. 1966, 999 U.N.T.S. 171.
[7]   Suggestions Made by the Government of the United States of America: Rules of Procedure and Evidence for the International Tribunal for the Prosecution of Persons Responsible for Serious Violations of International Humanitarian Law Committed in the Former Yugoslavia, Rule 22, U.N. Doc. IT/14 (1993), reprinted in 2 Virginia Morris and Michael P. Scharf, An Insider's Guide to the International Criminal Tribunal for the Former Yugoslavia 509, 539 (1995).

the question in plenary, the judges were still divided. A compromise was reached in which the cooperation of a suspect in the prosecution of another case could constitute a mitigating factor that would justify the imposition of a lesser penalty if the suspect were later convicted of a crime. In his statement concerning the adoption of the Rules, Judge Antonio Cassese, the President of the ICTY, explained:

"The question of the grant of immunity from prosecution to a potential witness has also generated considerable debate. Those in favour contend that it will be difficult enough for us to obtain evidence against a suspect and so we should do everything possible to encourage direct testimony. They argue that this is especially true if the testimony serves to establish criminal responsibility of those higher up the chain of command. Consequently, arrangements such as plea bargaining could also be considered in an attempt to secure other convictions. However, we always have to keep in mind that this Tribunal is not a municipal criminal court but one that is charged with the task of trying persons accused of the gravest possible of all crimes. The persons appearing before us will be charged with genocide, torture, murder, sexual assault, wanton destruction, persecution and other inhumane acts. After due reflection, we have decided that no one should be immune from prosecution for crimes such as these, no matter how useful their testimony may otherwise be. This will apply to both testimonial and use immunity. The degree of cooperation received from an accused will, however, be taken into account as a mitigating factor in sentencing."[8]

The ICTR's decisions in the Kayishema and Ruzindana case, the Ntagerura case, and the Kanyabashi case, as described above, reflect deference to the policy against granting immunity for witness testimony articulated by Judge Cassese. However, there has been some erosion of the absolute prohibition envisioned by Judge Cassese. First, where a witness objects to making any statement on the grounds of its potentially self-incriminating nature, Rule 90(E) permits the Trial Chamber to compel the witness to answer the question while excluding the use of the compelled testimony against the witness for any offense other than perjury. This type of immunity is frequently referred to as "use immunity." Second, under the authority of Article 29, paragraph 4 of the ICTR Statute, the Convention on the Privileges and Immunities of the United Nations,[9] and the precedent of the ICTY, the ICTR can grant "safe conduct" to defense witnesses who fear that they would be arrested and prosecuted for war crimes while temporarily in the host state of the Tribunal or any transit states.[10] Third, the Office of the Prosecutor has announced a policy of *nolle prosequi*, set forth in Regulation No. 1 of 1994 (amended 17 May 1995), under which the Prosecutor can decide to refrain from indicting a suspect in return for testimony against another offender if certain criteria were met.[11] In addition, since Rule 50 of the ICTR Rules provides the Prosecutor the discretion to amend or withdraw an indictment without leave at any time before its confirmation, the prosecutor could conceivably agree to drop various charges against a suspect in return for testimony prior to submitting the indictment for confirmation. Technically, this does not transgress Judge Cassese's policy of non-immunity for persons charged with international crimes since the Rules of Procedure define "accused" as "a person against whom an indictment has been submitted to the designated trial chamber judge for confirmation."

The question of granting refugee status for witnesses raises the same type of concerns as grants of immunity. As far back as 1968, the U.N. General Assembly affirmed that the grant of asylum to those accused of genocide, war crimes, or crimes against humanity was impermissible under international law. Article 1, paragraph 2 of the Declaration on Territorial Asylum states that "The right to seek and to enjoy asylum may not be invoked by any person with respect to whom there are serious reasons for considering that he has committed a crime against peace, a war crime or a crime against humanity...."[12] In addition, Article 7 of the Principles of International Co-operation in the Detention, Arrest, Extradition and Punishment of Persons Guilty of War Crimes and Crimes against Humanity provides that "states shall

---

[8]   See U.N. Doc. IT/29, at 5 (1994), reprinted in 2 Virginia Morris and Michael P. Scharf, An Insider's Guide to the International Criminal Tribunal for the Former Yugoslavia 649, 652 (1995).

[9]   Convention on the Privileges and Immunities of the United Nations, 13 Feb. 1946, 1 U.N.T.S. 15 (1946).

[10]   See 1 Virginia Morris and Michael P. Scharf, The International Criminal Tribunal for Rwanda 672-673 (1998).

[11]   See 1 Virginia Morris and Michael P. Scharf, The International Criminal Tribunal for Rwanda 285 n.1026 (1998).

[12]   Declaration of Territorial Asylum, G.A. Res. 2312, U.N. GAOR, 22nd Sess., Supp. No. 16, at 81, U.N. Doc. A/6716 (1968).

not grant asylum to any person with respect to whom there are serious reasons for considering that he has committed a crime against peace, a war crime or a crime against humanity."[13] Moreover, the international conventions governing refugee status deny such status to persons reasonably suspected of committing serious non-political crimes or human rights abuses.[14] Thus, the U.N. High Commissioner for Refugees sent a circular letter dated 23 September 1996 to all Permanent Missions to the United Nations at Geneva and New York informing them that it would not grant refugee status to Rwanda Tribunal indictees and encouraging States to take similar measures.[15] In this regard, no distinction was made between lower level offenders whose testimony might be important in the trial of higher level offenders.

In addition, states have no international legal obligation to grant asylum; the issue firmly remains a matter of sovereignty under national jurisdiction. State practice regularly refuses asylum to persons who have found protection elsewhere. As a result, States might refuse the return of refugee witnesses after they have testified before the ICTR without violating any international legal obligations. A refusal of re-entry would not constitute expulsion or illegal return since the witnesses would already be outside state territory and under the protection of the Tribunal.[16]

Under Article 8, paragraph 2 of the ICTR Statute and Rules 101 and 126, the ICTR's primacy over national courts permits the ICTR to require national courts to defer to its competence to try an accused. In addition, the principle of *non bis in idem* incorporated in Article 9 of the ICTR Statute prohibits the prosecution by national courts of persons who have already been tried by the ICTY. These provisions were seen as necessary to prevent multiple prosecutions for the same offense (and the embarrassing possibility of differing verdicts) by both the Tribunal and national authorities. These provisions apply only to persons tried by the ICTR; they do not provide the ICTR with authority to shield witnesses from prosecution through grants of immunity or refugee status.

Obtaining Appearance of Defense Witnesses

In issuing summons for the appearance of witnesses on request of the defence, the Trial Chamber compensates for the limited powers and possibilities of the defence in collecting evidence. Where the defence receives no cooperation from national authorities, Tribunal requests have to be complied with. Thus, the Trial Chamber fulfills a prerequisite for a fair trial.[17]

In the Decision on the Motion to Subpoena a Witness, *Prosecutor v. Akayesu*, Case No. ICTR-96-4-T, 19 November 1997, the Defence requested the Tribunal to subpoena Major-General Romeo Dallaire, a Canadian national and former Commander-in-Chief of the United Nations Assistance Mission in Rwanda, as a witness for the defense.[18] The Prosecutor did not oppose the request, but the motion raised a novel question about the immunity of United Nations officials that had not before been addressed by the ICTR.

The Trial Chamber placed great importance on the letter by the U.N. Legal Counsel Hans Corell, indicating that the Secretary-General would not object to General Daillaire testifying as a witness before the ICTR and was willing to waive his official immunity to enable him to do so. The Trial Chamber therefore granted the motion, summonsing Daillaire to appear as a witness for the Defense, and requested the Secretary-General to waive the immunity he enjoys by virtue of his position as former Commander-in-Chief of UNAMIR. As precedent for this action, the ICTR could have looked to the Rule 61 proceeding conducted by the ICTY in the case against Ivica Rajić, in which the witnesses included

---

[13]   G.A. Res. 3074, U.N. GAOR, 28th Sess., Supp. No. 30, at 78, U.N. Doc. A/9030 (1974).

[14]   Convention Relating to the Status of Refugees, April 22, 1954, 189 U.N.T.S. 150, Art. 1, 32, 33.

[15]   The text of the UNHCR circular letter is reproduced in 1 Virginia Morris and Michael P. Scharf, The International Criminal Tribunal for Rwanda (1998), at 496-497 n.1668.

[16]   Philip Matthew Ingeneri, Memorandum Prepared for the Office of the Prosecutor of the International Criminal Tribunal for Rwanda, New England School of Law International War Crimes Project, May 15, 1998, at 8.

[17]   ALC-I-225.

[18]   In early 1994, Major General Dallaire sent a cable to the United Nations Headquarters warning that the Hutu hardliners were laying the groundwork for a systematic campaign to kill Tutsis. Dallaire made repeated requests for reinforcements and for authorization to use force to seize the Hutus weapons caches. See 1 Virginia Morris and Michael P. Scharf, The International Criminal Tribunal for Rwanda 53 (1998).

United Nations Protection Force (UNPROFOR) personnel who were stationed in the area of Stupni Do when it was attacked by Serb forces.[19]

Under the Convention on the Privileges and Immunities of the United Nations,[20] Dellaire was immune from having to appear in national judicial proceedings relating to his official acts because of his status as an expert on mission. The privileges and immunities granted to such persons are granted in the interests of the United Nations and not for the personal benefit of the individuals themselves. Consequently, the Secretary-General has the right and the duty to waive the immunity of any official in any case where, in his opinion, the immunity would impede the course of justice and can be waived without prejudice to the interests of the United Nations pursuant to Article V, Section 20 of the Convention on Privileges and Immunities. The authority to waive the privileges and immunities of United Nations officials and staff members resides in the Secretary-General as the chief administrative officer of the Organization. The Akayesu case raises the interesting hypothetical question of whether the ICTR could have ordered Dellaire to appear if the Secretary-General had declined to waive his immunity. It is not clear that the Convention on Privileges and Immunities would apply to proceedings before an international body, and in any event, as a subsidiary body of the Security Council endowed with enforcement powers under Chapter VII of the U.N. Charter, theoretically the ICTR could have overridden Delaire's immunity even without the Secretary-General's consent.

The Decision on the Urgent Motion Filed by the Defence for the Immediate Transfer and Appearance of a Detained Witness, Froduald Karamira, *Prosecutor v. Rutaganda*, Case No. ICTR-96-3-T, 26 March 1998 involved a Defense request for an order for the immediate transfer and appearance of Froduald Karamira, who had been convicted of Genocide in a Rwandan national court and was awaiting his execution. Although the ICTR had approved (and the Rwandan Government had agreed to) similar transfers of witnesses in the case of Jean-Paul Akayesu,[21] the Trial Chamber denied Rutaganda's motion on the ground that the Defense had not strictly complied with Rule 90bis (B) because (i) the Defense had failed to show that Karamira was not needed for criminal proceedings in progress in Rwanda since there might be post-appeal avenues available to him within the Rwandan criminal code such as pardon or commutation of sentence; and (ii) the Defense had failed to present evidence indicating that Froduald Karamira would consent to testify for the defense as required by Rule 90bis (B). This narrow reading of the requirements of Rule 90bis may make it harder for defendants to obtain witnesses from among the thousands of persons imprisoned in Rwanda in relation to national criminal investigations and prosecutions concerning the 1994 genocide.

The Decision on a Motion for Summonses and Protection of Witnesses Called by the Defence, *Prosecutor v. Akayesu*, Case No. ICTR-96-4-T, 17 February 1998 involved a Defense request for the appearance of two witnesses, Jean Kambanda and Pauline Nyiramasuhuko, who had been indicted by the ICTR and were in ICTR custody awaiting their trial. In a controversial ruling, the Trial Chamber denied the motion on the ground that there was a risk that the appearance of the two accused as witnesses could cause prejudice to them. The Trial Chamber noted that Rule 90(E) permits a witness to object to making any statement which might tend to incriminate him, but permits the Trial Chamber to nevertheless compel the witness to answer the question contingent on a grant of testimonial immunity with respect to prosecution before the ICTR. Such testimony can, however, be used as evidence during subsequent prosecution for perjury under Rule 91. In light of the risk of prosecution for perjury, the Trial Chamber felt that compelling the two witnesses to appear for the Defense could perhaps violate their fundamental right not to be forced to testify against themself or to confess guilt. Thus, the Trial Chamber inexplicably elevated the witnesses interest in avoiding prosecution for perjury (with the maximum sentence of twelve months imprisonment) over the interests of Akayesu to obtain their potentially exculpatory testimony in his trial for genocide (with the maximum sentence of life imprisonment).

---

[19]   Third Annual Report of the International Tribunal for the Prosecution of Persons Responsible for Serious Violations of International Humanitarian Law Committed in the Territory of the Former Yugoslavia since 1991, at para 59, U.N. Doc. A/51/292-S/1996/665 (1996).

[20]   Convention on the Privileges and Immunities of the United Nations, 13 Feb. 1946, 1 U.N.T.S. 15 (1946).

[21]   U.N. Press Release ICTR-INFO-9-2-091, 3 Nov. 1997.

False Testimony by a Prosecution Witness – Interlocutory Appeal

The Decision on Appeals against the Decision by Trial Chamber I rejecting the Defence Motions to Direct the Prosecutor to Investigate the Matter of False Testimony by Witnesses "E" and "CC," *Prosecutor v. Rutaganda,* Case No. ICTR-96-3-T, 8 June 1998, concerned the question of when an interlocutory appeal is permissible. During his trial, Defendant Rutaganda filed a motion to require the Prosecutor to investigate allegations of perjury concerning two of the Prosecution witnesses. The Trial Chamber dismissed the motion on the ground that the Defense had failed to meet its burden of proving "that there exist strong grounds for believing that a witness has knowingly and wilfully given false testimony" as required under Rule 91(B).[22] Arguing that the Trial Chamber applied an erroneous standard of proof, the Defense sought an interlocutory appeal to the Appeals Chamber. The Appeals Chamber rejected the appeal without examining the merits on the ground that the matter was not appealable until after the conclusion of the trial.

The Rwanda Tribunal's Rules permit interlocutory appeal for just three types of Trial Chamber decisions: (1) a judgment dismissing an objection based on lack of jurisdiction under Rule 72(B)(i); (2) a judgment concerning a person who was charged with contempt of the Rwanda Tribunal under Rule 77; and (3) a judgment concerning a person who was charged with giving false testimony under solemn declaration under Rule 91. A Trial Chamber decision dismissing a motion to require the Prosecutor to investigate allegations of perjury do not fall within any of these categories.

Although Rutaganda's interlocutory appeal involved the issue of false testimony, it is to be contrasted with the third category of permissible interlocutory appeals involving the conviction of a third party of perjury. In the situation of a third party convicted of perjury, there is no reason to require the third party to wait until the end of the trial of the accused to appeal a decision relating to false testimony which does not relate to the merits of the case. Considerations of judicial efficiency do not apply to these unrelated decisions. Furthermore, it would be unjust to require the third party to wait until the conclusion of the trial which may take many months and even exceed the maximum term of imprisonment (twelve months) for the offense of false testimony.[23]

The Appeals Chamber had substantial reasons for resisting an expansion of the situations permitting interlocutory appeals. Interlocutory appeals can significantly delay and therefore greatly increase the cost of the trial proceeding. Moreover, the consolidated appeal of all issues relating to the trial at its conclusion contributes to the efficient administration of justice. On the other hand, as the United States Government pointed out in its comments on the Rules of Procedure promulgated in 1994 by the ICTY, "with no mechanism for resolving disputes prior to final judgment, critical legal rulings made by the trial chamber which are thereafter reversed may occasion the need to take substantial additional testimony." The United States thus proposed "that a provision should be inserted to permit interlocutory appeal at the discretion of the appeals chamber."[24] By making the right of interlocutory appeal within the discretion of the appeals chamber, the danger of excessive interlocutory appeals would be eliminated. Such a proposal has been under consideration by the ICTR, but has not been adopted.

Michael Scharf

---

[22]   This decision was consistent with the Trial Chamber's decision in the Akayesu case, ICTR-96-4-T, 2329-2326, in which the Trial Chamber held that mere contradictions and inconsistencies in a witness's testimony, without more, did not establish that the witness had "knowingly and wilfully given false testimony." The Chamber went on to add that the question of inexactitudes and other contradictions in witness statements was more appropriately dealt with as a question of the witness's credibility, which would be assessed at the end of the trial. See John R.W.D. Jones, The Practice of the International Criminal Tribunals for the Former Yugoslavia and Rwanda (2nd ed., 2000), p. 627.

[23]   See 1 Virginia Morris and Michael P. Scharf, The International Criminal Tribunal for Rwanda 554-555 (1998).

[24]   U.S. Comments on Rules Adopted by the Tribunal (May 2, 1994), quoted in 1 Virginia Morris and Michael P. Scharf, The International Criminal Tribunal for Rwanda 555-556 n.1845 (1998).

UNITED NATIONS   NATIONS UNIES

International Criminal Tribunal for Rwanda

TRIAL CHAMBER II

OR: ENG

Before: Judge Yakov A. Ostrovsky, Presiding
             Judge William H. Sekule
             Judge Navanethem Pillay

Registry: Mr. John Kiyeyeu

Decision of: 16 April 1998

THE PROSECUTOR

VERSUS

ELIE NDAYAMBAJE

Case No. ICTR-96-8-T.

DECISION ON THE DEFENCE MOTION OF UTMOST URGENCY TO RESOLVE ALL
DIFFICULTIES POSED BY THE FILE PROCESSING AND, IN PARTICULAR, ISSUES OF
EVIDENCE DISCLOSURE, JUDICIAL CALENDAR AND NON-ENFORCEMENT OF
DECISIONS OF THE TRIAL CHAMBER IN THE NDAYAMBAJE CASE

The Office of the Prosecutor:
    Mr. James K. Stewart
    Mr. Chile Eboe-Osuji
    Mr. Robert Petit

The Counsel for the Accused:
    Mr. Charles Tchoungang

[page 1] The International Criminal Tribunal for Rwanda,

SITTING AS Trial Chamber II ("the Trial Chamber"), composed of Judge Yakov A. Ostrovsky, Presiding, Judge William H. Sekule, and Judge Navanethem Pillay;

NOTING the indictment filed on 17 June 1996, by the Prosecutor against Elie Ndayambaje, pursuant to Rule 47 of the Rules of Evidence and Procedure ("the Rules"), charging him with genocide, conspiracy to commit genocide, crimes against humanity and violations of Article 3 common to the 1949 Geneva Conventions and the 1977 Additional Protocol II thereto;

HAVING CONSIDERED the decision confirming this indictment, signed by Judge Tafazzal H. Khan on 21 June 1996;

BEING MINDFUL OF the initial appearance of the accused which took place on 29 November 1996;

CONSIDERING the motion of utmost urgency filed by the Defence on 17 February 1998, to resolve administrative and procedural difficulties, seeking disclosure of the complete Belgian file; permission to approach the Belgian government if necessary; clarification of witness protection measures, and sanctions against the Prosecution and the Victims and Witnesses Unit;

REMINDED of the fact that this motion was set for hearing on 3 March 1998 initially, but due to the non-appearance of Defence Counsel, the matter was postponed at the request of the Defence Counsel to a date, namely 11 March 1998;

NOTING the written response by the Prosecutor filed on 27 February 1998, requesting that the motion be dismissed and that Defence Counsel be warned officially, for the "offensive and abusive" language of his filed motion,

FURTHER NOTING the Prosecutor's oral submissions for pecuniary sanctions against Defence Counsel for his nonattendance on 3 March 1998, which was later withdrawn in writing;

HAVING HEARD the parties in open session on 11 March 1998, after a delay occasioned by the late appearance of Defence Counsel,

The Defence Counsel requested the following measures:

1.   An order directing the Office of the Prosecutor ("the OTP") to disclose the complete Belgian file, examined by Judge D. Vandermeersch, accompanied by translation of documents from Flemish into English or French, within twenty days of the rendering of this decision, stating that it was his belief that a full review of the file would lead him to find exculpatory materials. He further stated that the question of which portion of these files may be relevant to the defence of his client should be a matter for decision by the Defence and not the Prosecution. **[page 2]**

2.   Furthermore, Defence Counsel requested the Trial Chamber's authorization to approach the authorities of the Kingdom of Belgium for a copy of said file, should the OTP fail to comply in the allotted time.

3.   Defence Counsel argued that the Trial Chamber's decision of 8 September 1997, on the protection of defence witnesses, had not as yet been implemented by the Victims and Witness Unit ("VWU" or "the Unit"). He stated that he had provided witness information under seal to the VWU, but that to date, no conclusive measures had been taken to protect these witnesses, particularly those residing in Kenya. Defence Counsel sought an order for compliance by the VWU within 20 days of the date of decision.

4.   Finally, the Defence Counsel contended that the Prosecutor's failure to disclose all the contents of the Belgian file amounted to non-compliance with the Trial Chamber's order of disclosure, wherefore Defence Counsel requested sanctions against the Prosecutor.

5.   A further request made by the Defence Counsel for the adoption of pre-established calendar to avoid uncertainties and delays, was abandoned by him at the hearing in view of the fact that a date for trial has been fixed.

The Prosecution responded:

1.   The defence motion should be dismissed, in its entirety, on both procedural and substantive grounds.

A) Procedurally, the Prosecution argued that the orders requested by the Defence must be based on fact and supported by evidence. Because all factual allegations made by the Defence were submitted without supporting documentation or correspondences and because the Prosecution disputed each allegation, the motion should be dismissed.

B) The substantive grounds argument was supported by production of excerpts from various cases, including *Prosecutor v. Delalić, et al.* (IT-96-21-T) 26 September 1996. In *Delalić,* the International Criminal Tribunal for the Former Yugoslavia held that the Defence "... must make a *prima facie* showing of materiality and that the requested evidence is in the custody or control of the Prosecutor." (para. 9). Therefore, it was ruled that it would be inappropriate for the Trial Chamber to intervene until such time that the requesting party would specify its needs for certain documents. (para. 10).

The Prosecution further stated that it would be logistically impossible for them to physically disclose the entire file, due to its enormity and because it concerned this particular accused only minimally. Moreover, the file contains names of protected witnesses. The Prosecution asked the Trial Chamber to note that 129 witness statements (PV's) have already been disclosed to the Defence from the Belgian file.

2.   With regard to the issue of translation, the Prosecution contended that less than twenty percent of the contested documents were in Flemish. The Prosecution sought clarification of the obligation to have documents translated. **[page 3]**

3.   The Prosecution objected to the use of offensive language such as "procedural guerrilla strategy" and "taking extraordinary liberties with the imperative decisions of this Trial Chamber," in the instant motion and called for an official warning pursuant to Rule 46 of the Rules.

4.   Subsequent to the hearing and by a communication to the Registrar, the Prosecutor withdrew his request for financial sanction against the Defence Counsel.

The Representative of The Victims and Witness Unit explained at the hearing that:

1.   On a number of occasions the VWU had been in contact with Defence Counsel pursuant to this Chamber's 8 September 1997 order and that the Unit's procedures have been explained to him.

2.   The Office of the Registrar was prepared to assist the Defence Counsel and take all possible measures to ensure cooperation between the Tribunal and the government of the Republic of Kenya as well as the United Nations High Commission for Refugees for witness protection purposes, once the VWU received the needed information concerning the witnesses.

The Defence Counsel has produced a list of witnesses under seal, but had denied the VWU access to the list until such time as the negotiations with the Kenyan government were concluded. This obstructed deliberations as the Kenyan authorities were reluctant to provide blanket assistance to unknown individuals.

3.   The VWU orally requested that the Trial Chamber take note

a) of their on-going negotiations with the Kenyan government and

b) that Defence Counsel is in default of the witness protection decision of the Trial Chamber, *supra*, by withholding the particulars of the potentially protected witnesses and

c) that the VWU is prevented from implementing the order of the Trial Chamber, as long as Defence Counsel withholds disclosure of the witnesses particulars and imposes conditions of his own.

DELIBERATIONS:

I. On the issue of disclosure of the entire Belgian file, the Trial Chamber notes the following:

1.   Rule 66 of the Rules provides two criteria for discovery of documents: materiality to the preparation of the defence and intended use by the Prosecution as evidenced at trial. The Prosecution has stated that they have disclosed relevant materials from the Belgian file, on this basis. The Defence has laid no foundation in fact or in law to warrant a disclosure of the complete Belgian file, in disregard of the said stipulations.

Furthermore, the Trial Chamber notes the Prosecution's statement that the Belgian file is comprised of thousands of pages and covers not only the accused and other accused, indicted by **[page 4]** the Tribunal, but various other parties and events unrelated to this case. Not only is it highly impractical to discover the entire file, but it might be prejudicial to the rights of other persons to do so. We remind the Prosecution however, of its obligation under Rule 68 to disclose exculpatory evidence, should such information be discovered during the course of further investigations.

2.   With regard to translation of the pertinent documents, we find nothing in the Rules which indicates that the OTP is under a direct duty to provide the Defence with translation services. They are however, responsible to initiate the translation process with regard to *any document which they intend to use*. It is then that, in accordance with Rule 3(E) of the Rules and this Trial Chamber's previous rulings, the Registrar becomes the responsible party for making arrangements for translations.

Therefore, it is open to both the Prosecutor and Defence Counsel to approach the Registry with requests for translation of materials to be used from the Belgian file. The Defence may approach the Registry to have translated any documents from the said file, which fall within the scope of this order. The ultimate responsibility for translation of documents rests with the Registry.

3.   Finally, with regard to the Defence request for authorization to approach the legal authorities in Belgium for access to the above mentioned files, no such authorization is necessary. Therefore, should Defence Counsel so desire, he may contact the appropriate officials in the Belgian government, in the course of preparing his case.

II. With regard to witness protection issues raised by the Defence:

The Trial Chamber is of the view that the VWU is not in default of the Witness Protection order, as alleged by the Defence Counsel and holds that the conduct of the Defence Counsel by imposing new conditions extraneous to the decision may not only be hindering the work of the VWU, but also violates the integrity of the decision of the Chamber.

If Defence Counsel intends to use Tribunal resources to protect his witnesses, as he is so entitled under Rule 75, he *must* provide the VWU with the necessary information it needs to assist in the preparation of the case in the case in an appropriate manner, without imposing additional conditions which would cause undue burdens on the Unit.

III. On the issue of requests for sanctions against the parties:

1)   The **Defence** has called for sanctions against the Prosecution for non-compliance with all previous orders on disclosure. The Chamber is of the view that the question of sanctions do not arise in the instant case, as the Prosecution has complied with its disclosure obligations under the Rules.

2)   The **Prosecutor** has also requested that punitive measures be imposed against Defence Counsel, in its written submissions, for the use of offensive and abusive language.

The Chamber notes that Defence Counsel's failure to attend the session of 3 March 1998, without proper explanation and his dilatory attendance at the session of 11 March 1998, caused delays and inconvenience for the Chamber and also notes that the choice of certain language used by Counsel is unfortunate and reprehensible. The Chamber however, does not see the need to proceed further except to remind Counsel to conduct himself professionally. **[page 5]**

FOR THE REASONS STATED ABOVE THE TRIAL CHAMBER:

(1)   **Dismisses** the Defence motion for an order directing the Prosecutor to disclose the complete Belgian file.

(2)   **Dismisses** the Defence motion for an order for compliance by the VWU of the Witness Protection Order of 8 September 1997.

(3)   **Dismisses** the orders for sanctions requested by the Prosecution and Defence.

Done in Arusha, this 16th day of April 1998.

Yakov A. Ostrovsky   William H. Sekule   Navanethem Pillay

Presiding Judge   Judge   Judge

UNITED NATIONS   NATIONS UNIES

International Criminal Tribunal for Rwanda
Tribunal pénal international pour le Rwanda

TRIAL CHAMBER II

OR: ENG

Before: Judge William H. Sekule, Presiding Judge
             Judge Yakov A. Ostrovsky
             Judge Tafazzal H. Khan

Registry: Mr. John Kiyeyeu

             15.6.1998

THE PROSECUTOR

VERSUS

CLEMENT KAYISHEMA
OBED RUZINDANA
Case No. ICTR-95-1-T

DECISION ON THE JOINT DEFENCE MOTION REQUESTING THE INTERPRETATION OF RULES 67 OF THE RULES

The Office of the Prosecutor:
    Mr. Jonah Rahetlah
    Ms. Brenda-Sue Thornton
    Ms. Holo Makwaia

The Counsel for the Accused:
    Mr. Andre Ferran (Counsel For Clement Kayishema)
    Mr. Pascal Besnier (Counsel for Obed Ruzindana)

[page 2] SITTING AS Trial Chamber II of the International Criminal Tribunal for Rwanda ("the Tribunal"), composed of Judge William H. Sekule, Presiding, Judge Yakov A. Ostrovsky and Judge Tafazzal H. Khan;

CONSIDERING that in the instant case, the initial appearance of the accused Clement Kayishema took place on 31 May 1996 and that of the accused Obed Ruzindana on 29 October 1996; and hearing on merits commenced on 11 April 1997;

NOTING THAT the Prosecutor closed her case on 13 March 1998;

CONSIDERING THAT the Tribunal is currently hearing the evidence for the Defence;

BEING SEIZED of the Prosecutor's motion of 12 March 1998 requesting the Trial Chamber to interpret the notion of "defence of alibi" and "special defence" as stipulated in Rule 67 of the Rules of Procedure and Evidence (the "Rules");

TAKING INTO CONSIDERATION THAT by virtue of a letter dated 21 April 1998, the Defence Counsel for Obed Ruzindana had complied with the requirements of rule 67 of the Rules and submitted to the Prosecutor a list of the witnesses who would be deposed on behalf of the accused for the defence of alibi;

MINDFUL OF the imperative need to adhere to the provisions of the Statute of the Tribunal ("the Statute") and the Rules made thereunder;

TAKING INTO ACCOUNT the provisions of rule 67 of the Rules;

HAVING HEARD both parties on 12 May 1998;

PLEADINGS BY THE PARTIES:

A.   Counsel for Clement Kayishema

The Defence Counsel submitted that the Defence was already prepared as to what arguments to use to fight the claims made by the Prosecution witnesses but he went on to state:

(a)   that until the Prosecution closed their case, the defence did not know what they would use to counter the claims made by the Prosecution hence they could not decide [page 3] whether they would use the defence of alibi or other special defences;

(b)   that if the literal interpretation of rule 67 of the Rules was considered, it would be violative of the rights of the accused;

(c)   that Defence is not in a position to know whether to plead defence of alibi and given that lack of clarity of the phrase "defence of alibi" and "special defence"; the Defence would not use either of the defences. However, there was still a need to interpret the phrases "defence of alibi" and "special defence";

(d)   that the Defence was in disagreement with the Prosecutor's submission that the Defence could only use the defence of alibi or special defence and no other;

(e)   that the Defence was caught up in problems of disturbances prevailing in Africa hence it would be difficult to find people who would testify under oath that they saw the accused somewhere different from what the Prosecutor alleged;

(f)   that the Defence should, however, be permitted to plead the defence of alibi by induction, that is, just by implication;

(g)   that the Defence was also not sure whether it would be possible to have a mixed defence for one site;

B.   Counsel for Mr. Obed Ruzindana

The Defence Counsel submitted:

(a)   that since the Defence of Dr. Kayishema was different from the Defence of Mr. Ruzindana, each party could use all evidence at disposal;

(b)   that although in March 1997 the Defence of Mr. Ruzindana has stated that they would use the defence of alibi in its broadest terms and had also confirmed this fact in their written statement to the Prosecutor in April 1998, they were not sure what was meant by the phrases "defence of alibi" and "special defence";

(c)   that according to their interpretation, the phrase "defence of alibi" excludes insanity and superior orders;

(d)   that since both the Prosecutor and the Defence had provided their definitions of phrase "defence of alibi", it was necessary for the Trial Chamber also to provide its **[page 4]** own definition;

Response by the Prosecutor

The Prosecutor commented on the Defence submission pertaining to the selection of defence and stated:

(a)   that rule 67 did not oblige the Defence to use the defence of alibi or a special defence as the only defences but they could use any evidence available to them. However, if the Defence intended to use the defence of alibi or special defence, they were obliged to disclose to the Prosecution;

(b)   that if one considered rule 67(A)(ii) of the Rules, it was clear that in any event, the phrases "defence of alibi" and the "special defence" are common criminal law terms which do not need any interpretation;

(c)   that the concomitant use of the defence of alibi and that of special defence was in order and the Defence could use any or both of those defences at one crime site or several sites but subject to disclosure to the Prosecutor as per rule 67 of the Rules;

(d)   that rule 67(A)(ii)(a) of the Rules provides the context and the particular situation that might arise so the Defence could not claim that the defence of the accused was frustrated;

(e)   that given that rules were unambiguous, the Defence Counsel for Dr. Kayishema should explain why they have not collected their evidence;

(f)   that each party should provide its own interpretation of the Rules the way they understood them and then, the Trial Chamber could only affirm or not affirm a given definition;

(g)   that even if rule 67 of the Rules was not clear, the Defence should have requested an interpretation prior to the commencement of the trial.

Reply by the Defence Counsel for Dr. Clement Kayishema

The Defence Counsel disagreed with the Prosecutor's contention that rule 67 of the Rules was clear and reiterated the difficulties the Defence was facing as well as the need to have **[page 5]** rule 67 interpreted in order to assist in the search for truth. The Defence Counsel further submitted that the parties were operating in a legal and particular context and were all undergoing a learning process in respect to international law, particularly with regard to serious crimes;

There was no response by Counsel for Mr. Obed Ruzindana.

Deliberations

This Trial Chamber has noted the arguments of both parties and is of the view that it cannot define rule 67 of the Rules in an abstract form without a specific problem to address.

It is also the view of the Trial Chamber that the Rules pertaining to the defence of alibi and special defence as provided in rule 67 of the Rules contain in themselves the definition envisaged by the drafters of the Rules.

FOR ALL THE ABOVE REASONS

This Trial Chamber, therefore, DISMISSES the defence motion.

Signed at Arusha, 15 June 1998

William H. Sekule	Yakov A. Ostrovsky	Tafazzal H. Khan
Presiding Judge	Judge	Judge

International Criminal Tribunal for Rwanda
Tribunal pénal international pour le Rwanda

TRIAL CHAMBER II

OR: ENG

Before: Judge William H. Sekule, Presiding Judge
Judge Yakov A. Ostrovsky
Judge Tafazzal H. Khan

Registry: Mr. John Kiyeyeu

THE PROSECUTOR

VERSUS

THÉONESTE BAGOSORA

Case No. ICTR-96-7-T

DECISION ON THE DEFENCE MOTION FOR PRE-DETERMINATION OF RULES OF EVIDENCE

For the Office of the Prosecution:
Mr. James Stewart
Mr. Chile Eboe-Osuji
Mr. Frederick Ossogo

For the Defendant Bagosora:
Mr. Jacques Larochelle
Mr. Raphael Constant

[page 2] THE INTERNATIONAL CRIMINAL TRIBUNAL FOR RWANDA ("the TRIBUNAL"),

SITTING as Trial Chamber II, composed of Judge William H. Sekule, Presiding, Judge Yakov A. Ostrovsky and Judge Tafazzal H. Khan ("the Trial Chamber");

CONSIDERING the indictment against Théoneste Bagosora (the accused), which was confirmed by Judge Lennart Aspegren on 10 August 1996 pursuant to rule 47(D) of the Rules of Procedure and Evidence ("the Rules") on the basis that there was sufficient evidence to provide reasonable grounds for indicting him for Genocide, Crimes Against Humanity, violations of common Article 3 to the 1949 Geneva Conventions, and of the 1997 Additional Protocol II thereto;

FURTHER CONSIDERING THAT pursuant to rule 62 of the Rules the initial appearance of Théoneste Bagosora was held on 7 March 1977 when he pleaded not guilty to all the counts of the indictment;

CONSIDERING THAT the trial of the accused was scheduled to begin on 12 March 1998 but was postponed by a decision of this Trial Chamber on 17 March 1998 until a joint indictment, including Théoneste Bagosora, submitted by the Prosecutor on 6 March 1998, had been decided upon by the confirming Judge;

BEING NOW SEIZED OF a Defence Motion filed on 16 February 1998, based on Articles 19 and 20 of the Statute of the Tribunal ("the Statute") requesting the Trial Chamber to predetermine the rules of evidence applicable to the instant case in order that the accused may be accorded a fair and just trial;

CONSIDERING the written response filed by the Prosecutor on 16 February 1998;

HAVING HEARD the oral arguments of the parties on 13 March 1998;

PLEADINGS BY THE PARTIES

The Defence:

The Defence Counsel referring to the Canadian case of *Smith vs. Queen 75 C.C.C. (3D) 257*, advanced several arguments in support of his contention that the minimum rules of evidence should be predetermined and contended:

  (i)   that although pursuant to rule 89(B) of the Rules, a Trial Chamber may apply those rules of evidence which will best favour a fair determination of the matter before it, these rules are not set out in detail, hence the need for a further analysis;

  (ii) that furthermore, "rules" are general principles which are certain and determined, that is, they are known before hand by both parties and must be applied in an impartial **[page 3]** manner by all the parties in order to achieve an equitable and fair trial for the accused;

  (iii) that the said rules of evidence should be consonant with the spirit of the Statute, general principles of law and the spirit of the Rules;

  (iv) that if one considered some aspects of evidence, such as the requirement of oral testimony as opposed to written depositions, the need to prove a case beyond reasonable doubt, the order of presentation of evidence, the right of rebuttal by the Prosecution, the provision for examination-in chief, cross-examination and re-examination, they are all common law principles, hence it could be argued that the spirit of the rules of evidence is predominantly the spirit of common law;

The Prosecutor:

The Prosecutor referred to several legal texts, *inter alia*, Rosanne, *The Law and Practice of The International Court* (1985) (pp. 608-611), Bin Cheng *General Principles of Law as Applied by International Courts and Tribunals* (1983) (pp. 299-230), and submitted as follows:

(i)   that the sources of the Rules are clear and that pursuant to Article 14 of the Statute and rule 89(A) of the Rules, the Trial Chamber shall not be bound by national rules of evidence;

(ii)   that pursuant to Article 19 of the Statute, the spirit of the Statute is to ensure the conduct of a fair and expeditious trial giving full respect for the rights of the accused and due regard for the protection of the victims and witnesses;

(iii)   that in deciding on the applicability of any particular rule of evidence, the Trial Chamber is permitted to be flexible provided that it applies those rules which best favour a fair determination of the matters before it and as long as those rules are consonant with the spirit of the Statute and the general principles of law;

(iv)   that the flexibility afforded to the Trial Chamber would reduce the chances of the Trial Chamber having to declare a point as *non liquet*, that is, the position of not being able to decide a point because the predetermined rules of evidence do not provide a clear answer to the point in issue;

(v)   that although international law borrows its rules and institutions from domestic systems of law, this is not done by means of importing private law institutions "lock, stock, and barrel" (Lord MacNair's words in the *South West Africa Case, I.C.J. Reports 1950 p. 148-9*), ready made, fully equipped with a set of rules;

(vi)   that this particular accused has no special interest in having the rules of evidence predetermined for his trial in face of the provisions of the Statute and the Rules because other trials have proceeded without such determination and moreover, there **[page 4]** because other trials have proceeded without such determination and moreover, there were other accused who would appear before the Tribunal in future for whom the system would not accommodate separate negotiation;

(vii)   that with regard to the indictment of the accused, the Prosecutor has met the requisite legal obligations under articles 17 and 20(4)(a) of the Statute as well as under rule 47 of the Rules. Hence, the accused has been given ample information to enable him to reasonably understand how and when his actions constituted one or more of the crimes under the Statute;

RESPONSE BY THE DEFENCE:

In response to the Prosecutor's submission, the Defence Counsel submitted:

(i)   that as Counsel, who are entrusted with defending an accused facing very serious crimes, they were unsure of how to proceed and reiterated the need to have the Rules clearly spelt out to enable them defend the accused appropriately;

(ii)   that even if the earlier trials proceeded without rules, that fact could not estop them from requesting that such rules be formulated;

(iii)   that there was no precedent to which they could refer because the Nuremberg Trials, which they could emulate, took place in 1945 and were completely different from the instant trials and as such they were inapplicable;

(iv)   that international law *per se* was not applicable but rather those Rules dealing with individuals vis-a-vis States.

DELIBERATIONS:

It is the view of this Chamber that the Defence motion has raised a new issue, namely, the predetermination of the rules. However, in the face of the fact that the Tribunal has already adopted the

Rules to be applied and considering that several trials have already taken place under the said Rules, the Trial Chamber has carefully considered the arguments advanced by the parties and makes the following observations:

A. With Respect to Fair and Expeditious Trial

The Trial Chamber is fully conscious that the rights of the accused at all stages of the trial should be observed. The Trial Chamber, at the same time, recognizes its obligation to ensure a fair and expeditious trial as stipulated in Articles 19(1) and 20(4)(c) of the Statute. Adherence to these principles does not necessarily call for the predetermination of the rules of evidence as contended by the Defence for reasons outlined below. **[page 5]**

B.   With Regard to Predetermination of The Rules of Evidence

This Trial Chamber observes that under rule 89(A) of the Rules, the functions of the Tribunal are such that it is not bound by any particular legal system. The basic rule is to allow flexibility and efficacy in order to permit the development of the law and not to have pre-determined Rules. This flexibility is permitted under rule 89(B) of the Rules which empowers the Trial Chamber to determine given evidential issues in the best way possible and to arrive at a fair and just decision under given circumstances.

Furthermore, the view of this Trial Chamber is that flexibility is of importance in an International Tribunal such as this one. The Rules adopted by the Tribunal, pursuant to Article 14 of the Statute, are broader than either the common or civil law systems and they reflect an international amalgamated system without necessarily adopting a single national system of evidence.

The Tribunal has had occasion to apply this flexibility in cases it had already handled, namely, *The Prosecutor vs. Jean Paul Akayesu (ICTR-96-4-T), The Prosecutor vs. Rutaganda (ICTR-96-3-T)* and *The Prosecutor vs. Clement Kayishema and Obed Ruzindana (ICTR-95-I-T)*.

In this regard, this Trial Chamber particularly recalls its decision of 17 April 1997 in *The Prosecutor vs. Clement Kayishema and Obed Ruzindana (ICTR-95-I-T)* concerning the probative value of evidence. In that case, the Defence Counsel objected to some portions of the oral testimony of witness A as being contradictory to that witness's earlier written statement. The Trial Chamber directed that should any issue arise concerning evidence, each party was at liberty to raise an objection on a case by case basis.

Incidentally, it may be mentioned that similar Rules have been adopted by our sister Tribunal, the International Criminal Tribunal for the former Yugoslavia ("ICTY"). Our Rules are, as it were, a replica of those Rules and until now, our Tribunal has not faced any insurmountable difficulty.

The Defence has stated that some principles as enumerated earlier have been adopted from the common law system. Besides this general observation, the learned Counsel for the Defence, could not point out any major deficiency in the existing Rules. Assuming, but not conceding, that those principles have been adopted from the common law system, this fact alone is not a valid ground for predetermination of the Rules because those principles are efficacious and have evolved in the course of time and long experience.

It is, therefore, the opinion of this Chamber that the submissions of the Defence regarding predetermination of the Rules cannot be accepted.

C.   With Regard to The Formulation of Rules of Evidence under The Statute

Apart from case law that emerges in judicial proceedings as a result of judicial interpretation of the law, Judges do not make rules. As a general principle of law, this Trial Chamber, therefore, does not have the mandate to make rules in the manner requested by the Defence because according to Article 14 of the Statute and rule 6 of the Rules, this is a function of the Plenary of the Tribunal. **[page 6]**

FOR ALL THE ABOVE REASONS

The Trial Chamber **DISMISSES** the Defence motion.

SIGNED at Arusha this 8th Day of July 1998

Judge William H. Sekule,   Yakov A. Ostrovsky   Tafazzal H. Khan

Presiding Judge   Judge   Judge

International Criminal Tribunal for Rwanda
Tribunal pénal international pour le Rwanda

CHAMBER I – CHAMBRE I

OR: ENG

Before: Judge Laïty Kama, Presiding Judge
              Judge Lennart Aspegren
              Judge Navanethem Pillay

Registry: Mr. K.M. Mindua

Decision of: 4 September 1998

THE PROSECUTOR

VERSUS

GEORGES ANDERSON NDERUBEMWE RUTAGANDA

Case No. ICTR-96-3-T

DECISION ON THE DEFENCE MOTION FOR DISCLOSURE OF EVIDENCE

The Office of the Prosecutor:
  Mr. James Stewart
  Mr. Udo Gehring

Counsel for the Accused:
  Ms. Tiphaine Dickson

[page 2] THE INTERNATIONAL CRIMINAL TRIBUNAL FOR RWANDA (the "TRIBUNAL"),

SITTING as Trial Chamber I, composed of Judge Laïty Kama as Presiding Judge, Judge Lennart Aspegren and Judge Navanethem Pillay;

HAVING BEEN SEIZED by the Defence Counsel's motion of 30 October 1997, pursuant to Rules 66, 67, 68 and 70 of the Rules of Procedure and Evidence (the "Rules"), requesting an order for disclosure in certain specific instances and other relief such as, the adjournment of the proceedings until full disclosure has been made to the Defence, the prohibition of the Prosecutor from calling witnesses whose identity and corresponding documentary evidence have not been disclosed and the imposition of a fine on the Prosecutor as a form of sanction for the late disclosure of evidence and the identities of the witnesses.

NOTING that the Defence Counsel filed a written notice of amendment to her motion, dated 2 March 1998, withdrawing her averments in paragraphs 54 to 65; 72 to 76; and 109 to 111 of the said motion;

CONSIDERING that the Prosecutor opposed Defence Counsel's motion in a written response dated 5 February 1998;

HAVING HEARD the parties at a hearing on 2 March 1998;

CONSIDERING THE DEFENCE COUNSEL'S SUBMISSIONS,

1.   The Defence Counsel, in paragraphs 8, 19, 20, 22, 38, 40, 49, 80, 85, 89, 112, 119, 122, 136 and 142 of her written motion made a number of requests in respect of disclosure of material, which material Defence Counsel alleges is in the Prosecutor's possession or under her control. The Defence Counsel requested the Prosecutor to:

(1.1) furnish Defence Counsel with an inventory of the evidence in her possession, except for evidence governed by Rule 70 of the Rules; the Prosecutor must also indicate which evidence she does not intend to disclose and reasons for her refusal to do so;

(1.2) indicate to the Defence which witnesses she does not intend to call to the stand when she complies with her obligation in respect of disclosure;

(1.3) disclose to the Defence names of all the prosecution witnesses hearing pseudonyms and a final list of expert witnesses the Prosecutor intends to call, as well as their résumés and written reports;

(1.4) disclose to the Defence unredacted copies of the witness statements, including those who have testified, in accordance with the Tribunal's witness protection order of 26 September 1996; **[page 3]**

(1.5) disclose to the Defence any exculpatory evidence in the possession of the Prosecutor or of which she is aware, including the names and addresses of exculpatory witnesses;

(1.6) disclose to the Defence the identities of the members of UNAMIR that were present when the accused allegedly made a speech, as mentioned in the statement of witness X;

(1.7) disclose to the Defence the series of documents concerning the distribution of weapons to the civilian population, as mentioned in the *Rapport du groupe ad hoc Rwanda à la commission des affaires étrangères*;

(1.8) furnish the Defence with a French translation of the passages, excerpts, letters or other documents written in the Flemish language, as contained in the *Rapport du groupe ad hoc Rwanda à la commission des affaires étrangères*;

(1.9) furnish the Defence with all protocols or agreements made between the Tribunal or if applicable, the Officer of the Prosecutor) and the Government of Rwanda, regarding the conditions of movement of witnesses and the exhumation of bodies on Rwandan soil;

(1.10) furnish the Defence with the dates on which the searches, excavations, exhumations or other any other activity that may have taken place on the accused's property, a list of the persons present, an inventory of the goods seized, as well as the chain of possession of such goods;

(1.11) disclose to the Defence any document, report of expert opinion concerning the Interahamwe;

(1.12) disclose to the Defence copies of documents the prosecution witnesses intend to refer to when giving evidence;

(1.13) disclose to the Defence the interview or summary notes of the meeting between General Roméo Dallaire and Mr. Luc Côté; and

(1.14) disclose to the Defence the results of the investigation concerning the circumstances of the attack on the plane carrying the President Habyarimana on 6 April 1994;

2. The Defence Counsel requested in paragraphs 32, 40, 44, 49, 66, 69, 77, 80, 89, 99, 107, 115, 125, 129 and 133 of her written motion, that the Prosecutor make immediate disclosure of the following information once she receives confirmation of its existence;

(2.1) any tape, cassettes or notes made during the collection of statements from prosecution witnesses who have testified or who will testify in the trial of the accused; **[page 4]**

(2.2) any exculpatory evidence, including the names and addresses of exculpatory witnesses;

(2.3) the dates and places of the meetings, held by Mr. Esdras Mpamo and the minutes thereof, as described in the written statement of witness "EE";

(2.4) the identities of the members of UNAMIR that were present when the accused allegedly gave a speech, as described in the written statement of witness "X";

(2.5) all relevant evidence concerning a commercial transaction, as described in the written statement of witness "N";

(2.6) the exact location, date and minutes of a meeting held by the MRND, near the Massango communal office, as described in the statement of witness "C";

(2.7) the identification of the editorial staff of the newspaper "Le FLAMBEAU" on 17/12/1993;

(2.8) a series of documents referred to in the *Le Rapport du groupe ad hoc Rwanda à la commission des affaires étrangères*;

(2.9) all protocols or agreements made between the Tribunal and the government of Rwanda;

(2.10) tapes and transcripts of all speeches to which the Prosecutor intends to refer to, including those which may be referred to by prosecution witnesses;

(2.11) the questions put to each witness when their statements were taken;

(2.12) any map, diagram, communication, telex or any other document which may indicate the RPF positions in Kicukigo secteur, between 7 and 16 April 1994;

(2.13) medical reports for the witnesses in respect of whom the Prosecutor intends to exhibit their wounds;

(2.14) any statement or report given by prosecution witnesses to the police or judicial authority, concerning the events of 1994;

(2.15) details of the criminal records of prosecution witnesses, if applicable;

(2.16) the interview or summary notes of the meeting between Mr. Luc Côté and General Dallaire; and **[page 5]**

(2.17) the results of the investigation of the plane crash, carrying the late President Habyarimana on 6 April 1994.

3.   The Defence Counsel submitted that in the event of the Prosecutor not being in possession or not having any knowledge of the information requested, the Prosecutor must be obliged to conduct a reasonable search to confirm the existence of this information.

CONSIDERING THE PROSECUTOR'S SUBMISSIONS,

4.   The Prosecutor's submissions to Defence Counsel's various requests for disclosure are:

(4.1) Disclosure was made in respect of the 15 witnesses who have to date testified. Approximately 25 witnesses remain to be heard to complete the prosecution case and complete disclosure has been made in respect of all but 4 of these witnesses. In respect of two of these four witnesses partial disclosure has been made. In respect of the third witness, the Prosecutor is presently trying to identify and locate a Rwandan Journalist responsible for video footage of Interahamwe activities and the Prosecutor is therefore not in a position to make full and complete disclosure in respect of this witness. In respect of the fourth witness, the Prosecutor has filed a motion requesting the Chamber's permission in delaying disclosure of the identity and statement of the witness, for reason of safety to the witness and the witnesses family and also for the purpose of safeguarding on-going investigations;

(4.2) All other Defence requests in respect of paragraphs 20, 22, 38, 40 and 49 of Defence motion have been fulfilled;

(4.3) In respect of paragraph 80 of the Defence motion; relating to certain documents concerning the activities of the militia, the Prosecutor was unsuccessful in obtaining these documents;

(4.4) In respect of paragraph 112 of the Defence motion; enquiries have been made with Dr Haglund who stated that the dates, places and persons present at the Amgar Garage exhumations are identified in his report which was communicated to the Defence. Dr Haglund is also unaware of any other searches made at the Amgar Garage property, besides the preparation of sketches made by crime scene analyst, Pierre Heuts. The sketches, photographs and video tape made by Pierre Heuts, were entered as evidence, when he testified as the first witness in the Trial;

(4.5) The defence request in respect of paragraph 119 of Defence motion is broad and unfocused and therefore falls outside the scope of the relevant rules of disclosure. Expert witness, Professor Reyntjens testified that the interahamwe were the spearhead of the genocide. There is also a great deal of evidence on the record to establish the widespread and pervasive involvement of the interahamwe in the events of April to July 1994, notably in Kigali. A mass of witness statements unrelated to the case of the accused, acquired by the Prosecutor make reference to **[page 6]** the interahamwe. The Defence has failed to show why it is material to the defence to have access to this mass of documentation.

5.   The Prosecutor further submitted that:

(5.1) she has complied with the Rules in respect of disclosure and has obeyed the decision of the Tribunal in respect of witness protection measures;

(5.2) she cannot supply what is not in her custody or control and the Office of the Prosecutor should not function as an investigative agency for the Defence;

(5.3) unless she proposes to use documents as evidence at the trial of the accused, she is not obliged to translate them into English or French, for the purposes of disclosure or inspection;

(5.4) she is mindful of her obligation to disclose to the Defence exculpatory evidence, pursuant to Rule 68 of the Rules, and her interpretation and understanding of this rule is that it imposes an obligation on her to provide information, that is, to alert the Defence to the existence of evidence known to the Prosecutor which in any tends to suggest the innocence or mitigate the guilt of the accused, or may affect the credibility of prosecution evidence. Nevertheless disclosure of evidence that may mitigate the guilt of the accused has already been made to the Defence.

AFTER HAVING DELIBERATED,

6.   The Tribunal notes that in terms of Rule 66(A)(i) and (ii) of the Rules, the Prosecutor is obliged *firstly*, to make available to the Defence, within 30 days of the initial appearance of the accused, copies of the supporting material which accompanied the indictment when the indictment was confirmed, as well as all prior statements made by the accused to the Prosecutor and *secondly*, to make available to the Defence copies of all statements of prosecution witnesses that will be called to testify at the trial of the accused, no later than sixty days before the commencement of the trial. This obligation is subject to the provisions of Rules 53 and 69. The Prosecutor may, pursuant to Rule 69(A), apply to a Trial Chamber to order the non-disclosure of the identity of a victim or witness, where the person may be in danger or at risk, until the person is brought under the protection of the Tribunal.

7.   The Tribunal notes that pursuant to Rule 66(B) of the Rules, the Prosecutor, upon a request from the Defence, shall permit the Defence to inspect any books, documents, photographs or tangible objects in her custody or control, subject to any one of the following three conditions been met:

(i) the inspection of any of these items must be material to the preparation of the accused's defence;

(ii) the items must be intended to be used by the Prosecutor as evidence at the trial of the accused;
[page 7]
(iii) the items were obtained from or belonged to the accused.

Furthermore, pursuant to Rule 68, the Prosecutor has an obligation to disclose to the Defence the existence of evidence known to the Prosecutor, which may suggest the innocence of the accused, mitigate the guilt of the accused or affect the credibility of prosecution evidence.

8.   The Tribunal notes that it has in this case, rendered a decision on 26 September 1996, granting protective measures to prosecution witnesses, pursuant to Rule 69(A). In this decision it was ordered that the names, addresses and other identifying information of the witnesses shall not be disclosed to the Defence until such time the witnesses are brought under the protection of the Witnesses and Victims Protection Unit.

9.   The Tribunal accepts the Prosecutor's oral and written submission, that she had made to the Defence full and complete disclosure of all exculpatory evidence, pursuant to Rule 68.

10.   The Tribunal notes that the Prosecutor has not made full and complete disclosure in respect of four witnesses, namely Dominic Cunningham-Reid, Nick Huges, a Rwandan journalist responsible for the video footage taken in Kigali on the alleged activities of the Interahamwe and a witness who is subject to a witness protection order pursuant to Rule 69(A), referred to by the pseudonym JJ.

11.   The Tribunal notes that the Prosecutor has filed a motion dated 9 December 1997, seeking an order to delay the disclosure of the identity and statements of witness JJ to the Defence. The hearing of this motion is pending.

12.   The Tribunal notes that the other three witnesses are not subject to any orders pursuant to Rules 53 and 69 and full disclosure in respect of these three witnesses ought to have been made, pursuant to Rule 66(A)(ii). **[page 8]**

FOR THESE REASONS, THE TRIBUNAL:

ORDERS that the Prosecutor make immediate disclosure, pursuant to Rule 66(A)(ii) of the Rules, in respect of the three witnesses Dominic Cunningham-Reid, Nick Hughes and the Rwandan journalist in question;

DISMISSES Defence Counsel's motion in every other respect.

Arusha, 4 September 1998

Laïty Kama	Lennart Aspegren	Navanethem Pillay
Presiding Judge	Judge	Judge

UNITED NATIONS   NATIONS UNIES

International Criminal Tribunal for Rwanda
Tribunal pénal international pour le Rwanda

CHAMBER II

OR: ENG

Before: **Judge William H. Sekule, Presiding**
           Judge Yakov A. Ostrovsky
           Judge Tafazzal H. Khan

Registry: **John M. Kiyeyeu**

Decision signed: **7 December 1998**

THE PROSECUTOR

VERSUS

THEONÉSTE BAGOSORA

Case No. ICTR-96-7-T

DECISION ON THE DEFENCE MOTION FOR INADMISSIBILITY OF DISCLOSURE BASED ON THE DECISION OF 11 JUNE 1998

The Office of the Prosecutor:
  Mr. Frederic Ossogo

Counsel for the Defence:
  Mr. Raphaël Constant

[page 1] THE INTERNATIONAL CRIMINAL TRIBUNAL FOR RWANDA ("the TRIBUNAL"),

SITTING as Trial Chamber II, composed of Judge William H. Sekule, Presiding Judge Yakov A. Ostrovsky, and Judge Tafazzal H. Khan ("the Trial Chamber");

CONSIDERING the indictment against Théoneste Bagosora ("the accused") indicting him for Genocide, Crimes Against Humanity, violations of Article 3 common to the 1949 Geneva Conventions, and the Additional Protocol II of 1977 thereto which was confirmed by Judge Lennart Aspegren on 10 August 1996 pursuant to rule 47 (D) of the Rules of Procedure and evidence ("the Rules");

FURTHER CONSIDERING that on 7 March 1997, the initial appearance of the accused took place pursuant to rule 62 of the Rules when he pleaded not guilty to all counts of the indictment;

BEING seized of a defence motion filed on 10 September 1998, based on rule 66(A)(ii) of the Rules, requesting the Trial Chamber to consider as inadmissible the Prosecution motions filed on 31 July 1998 regarding the amendment of the instant indictment and joinder of trials of several accused persons, including the accused, on the ground that the Prosecutor did not comply with prior disclosure orders of 27 November 1997 and 11 June 1998 respectively;

CONSIDERING the Prosecutor's written response filed on 15 October 1998 in which she maintained that the requests made by the Defence were without merit both in law and in content;

CONSIDERING the provisions of rule 66(A)(ii) of the Rules regarding discolsure of material by the Prosecutor and rule 73 *bis* on Pre-Trial Conferences prior to the commencement of trials;

TAKING INTO ACCOUNT that the motion on joint trials of the accused and amendment of the indictment, filed on 31 July 1998, has been placed before a reconstituted Trial Chamber;

TAKING INTO CONSIDERATION that, currently, the date of hearing of this case on its merits has not been finalized due to various pending procedural matters that have arisen in this case;

HAVING HEARD the parties on 15 October 1998.

ARGUMENTS OF THE PARTIES

The Defence: The Defence Counsel had in written brief requested that the above mentioned amendment and joint trials motions be ruled inadmissible on the ground that the Prosecutor did not comply with the Trial Chamber's decision of 11 June 1998 to disclose by 30 April 1998. However, in his oral submission, the Defence Counsel noted that his motion had been overtaken by events and was, therefore, purely academic and theoretical.

He consequently narrowed the scope of his argument and concentrated on the issue of non adherence by the Prosecutor to the decisions of the Trial Chamber. He argued that any disclosure after 30 April 1998 should be deemed inadmissible based upon the decision of the Trial Chamber. Furthermore, he contended that when the Trial Chamber made the decision of 11 June 1998, it had intended at this point in the proceedings, to start the trial between 20 to 27 September 1998. Hence, no more disclosures should be made by the Prosecutor. In any event, the Prosecutor has not sought extension of time within which to disclose further documents. **[page 2]**

The Prosecution: In response, the Prosecutor contended that she had actually disclosed a good portion of documents, about 306 documents including many witness statements, *albeit*, belatedly. Moreover, her non-compliance with the Trial Chamber's decision was not intentional for the following reasons. First, the decision was retroactive and the Prosecutor was notified about it on 26 June 1998. Second, given the complexity of the case, the logistical constraints and the need to arrive at the truth, the Prosecutor could not meet the deadlines set by the Trial Chamber. Notwithstanding all those factors, the Prosecutor submitted that she intended to complete disclosure, at the appropriate time.

Rejoinder by The Defence: The Defence Counsel conceded that disclosure was made to the accused in May, August and October 1998, but he still maintained that these disclosures were belated as stated earlier and emphasized that the Prosecutor should have observed her commitment to disclose by 30 April 1998. Moreover, the Prosecutor should have adhered to the order of the Trial Chamber.

DELIBERATIONS

1.   At the outset, during the hearing, the Trial Chamber informed the parties that it would not entertain any discussion regarding the motions concerning the amendment of the indictment and the proposed joint trials motion pending before the reconstituted Trial Chamber II. We in fact found that the submissions made by the parties, in that regard, were irrelevant completely to the issues at hand. The Trial Chamber finds the parties' blatant disrespect of its order reproachable.

2.   As regards the Defence's request to the Trial Chamber to rule all disclosure provided by the Prosecution after the 30 April 1998 inadmissible, we are of the view that such a request is not grounded in law. There are no provisions either in the Statute or the Rules to grant such a request. The Trial Chamber, therefore, must dismiss the Defence request.

3.   We, however, note that during the audience of 12 March 1998, the Prosecutor put forth the suggestion that she needed an extension of time for the completion of her disclosure obligations, provided for in rule 66(A)(ii) of the Rules and committed herself to complete the disclosure by 30 April 1998. The Defence insisted on an earlier date but the Trial Chamber accepted the Prosecutor's request. However, the Prosecutor failed to adhere to Trial Chamber's decision to meet the deadline, which she herself had proposed. Indeed, this is not the first time that she has disregarded an order of this Trial Chamber without satisfactory explanation. We find this pattern of non compliance deplorable.

4.   It is important to note that, with regard to the issue of disclosure, the Prosecutor has disregarded not only the Decision of the Trial Chamber of 11 June 1998 but also the decisions of 27 November 1997 and 17 March 1998, pursuant to which the completion of disclosure could not have been delayed. Moreover, during 1998 alone, the dates for the commencement of the hearing of the case on its merits had been set by the Judges on two occasions (12 March and 15-20 September 1998) and in accordance with rule 66(A)(ii) of the Rules, disclosure should have been completed no later than 60 days before these dates.

5.   The Trial Chamber is cognizant of the amendment and joinder motions filed on 31 July 1998. Without prejudice to those proceedings, the existing indictment is still in force and the previous non-disclosure is not justified. Under such circumstances, the issue of disclosure should no longer be an obstacle to the commencement of the hearing of the case on its merits. **[page 3]**

FOR ALL THE FOREGOING REASONS, THE TRIAL CHAMBER

1.   **DISMISSES** the Defence motion.

2.   **DEPLORES** the Prosecution's previous non compliance with the Rules and Decisions of the Trial Chamber which could undermine the fair and expedient administration of justice.

Arusha, 7 December 1998

Judge William H. Sekule   Judge Yakov Ostrovsky

Presiding Judge   Judge

Judge Khan appends a separate Declaration to this Decision.

UNITED NATIONS   NATIONS UNIES

International Criminal Tribunal for Rwanda
Tribunal pénal international pour le Rwanda

CHAMBER II

OR: ENG

Before: Judge William H. Sekule, Presiding
            Judge Yakov A. Ostrovsky
            Judge Tafazzal H. Khan

Registry: John M. Kiyeyeu

Decision: 7 December 1998

THE PROSECUTOR
VERSUS
THEONÉSTE BAGOSORA
Case No. ICTR-96-7-T

DECISION ON THE DEFENCE MOTION FOR INADMISSIBILITY OF DISCLOSURE BASED ON THE DECISION OF 11 JUNE 1998 JUDGE TAFAZZAL H. KHAN'S SEPARATE DECLARATION

The Office of the Prosecutor:
    Mr. Frederic Ossogo

Counsel for the Defence:
    Mr. Raphaël Constant

[page 1] While I agree with the majority opinion that this motion should be rejected, I wish to add some comments concerning the approach taken by both the Prosecution and by the Defence. This Defence motion was filed on 1 September 1998 under the existing indictment confirmed on 10 August 1996, with the broad heading "Defence Motion for Inadmissibility Based on the Decision of 11 June 1998" (the "motion").

Subject Matter and Scope of the Motion:

The gist of the Defence allegations on which the motion is based is that the disclosures made by the Prosecution after 30 April 1998, the deadline set by the Chamber for disclosure of materials by the Prosecutor to the Defence, are inadmissible because the Prosecution did not obtain an extension of time from that date. The defence, however, admits receiving disclosure in installments during the months of May and August and on the 14 October 1998. Precisely on the basis of these brief facts, the legality or otherwise of the relief sought in the motion may be addressed. However, learned counsel for both parties indulged in arguments far beyond the scope of the motion. Furthermore, notwithstanding repeated reminders made by the Presiding Judge to be brief and to confine their submissions to matters relevant to the instant motion, both Counsel were excessively verbose. This resulted in a transcript which ran into eighty pages for this procedurally outdated and relatively routine motion.

Regarding the Prosecution:

The Prosecution failed to comply with the Chamber's direction that disclosure be completed by April 30 1998. This date was not only a time extension from the original disclosure date ordered on 27 November 1997, but was also a date that the Prosecution itself had requested. Although the Defence suggested an earlier date for disclosure, the Chamber accepted the Prosecution's request at the time of hearing. Accordingly, it was not proper for the learned counsel to submit that he was unaware of the disclosure date prior to the Chamber's written decision stating the same, as an excuse for belated disclosure. If the Prosecution was unable to comply with the order it should have returned before the Chamber to request further time.

Breach of Chamber's Order – Defence Grievance:

In its oral submissions the Defence requested the Chamber to rule all disclosure provided by the Prosecution after 30 April 1998, inadmissible. When called upon to identify the specific Rule(s) upon which he relied, the learned counsel candidly conceded that there were none. Indeed there is no Rule which expressly renders belated disclosure automatically inadmissible at this stage. The learned counsel for the Defence then posed the question as to what action the Chamber could take against the Prosecution for non-compliance with the order for disclosure. In other words, should the Prosecution continue to violate Chamber's order with impunity. I think this is a legitimate question which merits an answer. In my opinion it is implicit that when the Chamber is **[page 2]** empowered by the Rules to make appropriate rulings, in this case pursuant to rule 73 of the Rules, it follows that the Chamber also had implied power to enforce those rulings; and this enforcement power may even include rejection of belatedly disclosed material if the situation so demands. The virtue of applying such power will depend on the facts and circumstances of the particular controversy when it is brought before the Chamber. In my opinion, in the facts and circumstances of the present case, it is not in the interests of justice to reject the belated disclosure.

Regarding the Defence Prayers:

The prayers contained in the motion appear to be unusual and out of context. So far as I understand the first prayer in the written motion, I find it unacceptable. The Defence motion prays, firstly, that the Tribunal,

Rule that, under the circumstances, the Tribunal cannot hear the two motions filed belatedly.

I reject the above prayer outright as it is outside the scope of the motion. Although this motion has been over taken by procedural events, even in the "special context" in which it was filed, the above prayer was unjustified. The Defence did not explain how the belated disclosure adversely affects the hearing of the Prosecution motions for joinder and for amendment filed on 31 July 1998.

Further, despite the Defence's request for draconian measures, it has not supported its prayer with any provision either of the Statute or of the Rules. To expect this Chamber to grant such an extreme request without providing legal basis thereof is, in itself, objectionable.

The Defence motion prays, secondly, that the Tribunal,

Instruct the Prosecutor to take proceedings in the proper court.

This prayer is incomprehensible. Which proceedings? Which proper court? If, by this, the Defence is suggesting that the Prosecution should come before the Chamber to request a further extension when it is unable to meet the set dead lines, then I understand this prayer. If, however, the Defence is again referring to the prosecutor's motions for amendment and for joinder, then I find this prayer ridiculous and express my utter displeasure that a Counsel of high standing would burden this Chamber with such frivolity. **[page 3]**

It is desirable in interlocutory motions, that parties confine themselves to prayers which realistically reflect their particular objection(s) and refrain from introducing extraneous matters.

Conclusion:

As has become its habit, the Prosecution filed its written response to the Defence motion on the day of the hearing, 15 October 1998. This Chamber has previously requested that parties file the written response in a timely manner. These requests were, seemingly, to no avail.

It is well known and hardly needs mention that the Prosecutor has been entrusted with enormous responsibility by the Statute and the Rules relating to the trial and pre-trial proceedings, in addition to conduct of investigations. Therefore, it is expected that the members of the Office of the Prosecutor be diligent in scrupulously discharging their legal obligations to the Defence in accordance with the Rules and guidance of the Chambers and, thereby, ensure that the image of the Prosecutor is not tarnished. Indeed, this is not the first time that the Prosecution has disregarded an order of the Chamber; many of our previous urging and exhortations in this regard have fallen on deaf ears. I find this practice unacceptable.

With the above comments, I dismiss the Defence motion.

7 December 1998.

Judge Tafazzal H. Khan

Article 6 of the European Convention on Human Rights provides for the right to a fair trial. It is a fundamental aspect of the right to a fair trial that criminal proceedings should be adversarial and that there should be equality of arms between the Prosecution and Defence. The right to an adversarial trial means, in a criminal case, that both Prosecution and Defence must be given the opportunity to have knowledge of, and comment on the observations filed and the evidence adduced by the other party.[1] In addition article 6, paragraph 1 requires that the Prosecution should "disclose to the Defence all material evidence for or against the accused (…)".[2] Non-compliance with this obligation could lead to a breach of the rights of the Defence. The disclosure of evidence to the accused constitutes an essential part of these rights in criminal proceedings and one can find this right in both civil law and common law systems.[3] In the United Kingdom, for instance, the Prosecution is under the obligation to disclose to both the judge and the Defence, all the evidence on which any charges are based, as part of the so-called "transfer-procedure".[4] The Rules of Procedure and Evidence of the International Criminal Tribunals for the former Yugoslavia (ICTY) and Rwanda (ICTR) also contain an obligation for the Prosecution to disclose its evidence to the Defence.[5]

Disclosure by the Prosecutor

Rule 66(A) of the ICTR Rules imposes on the Prosecution two obligations. Firstly, the Prosecutor must, within 30 days of the initial appearance of the accused, provide to the Defence copies of the supporting material which accompanied the indictment, as well as all prior statements obtained by the Prosecutor from the accused. This phrase has been interpreted to mean "all statements made by the accused during questioning in any type of judicial proceedings which may be in the possession of the Prosecutor."[6] Secondly, the Prosecutor is obliged to provide to the Defence, no later than 60 days before the date set for trial, copies of the statements of all witnesses whom the Prosecutor intends to call to testify at trial. This obligation has been emphasised by Trial Chamber I of the ICTY in its Decision on the Production of Discovery Materials, of 27 January 1997 in the Blaškić case, in which it stated that every previous statements of all Prosecution witness, in whatever form, must be disclosed to the Defence.[7]

In addition to these disclosure obligations in Rule 66(A), the Defence can request to inspect any books, documents, photographs and tangible objects in the custody or control of the Prosecutor which (1) are material to the preparation of the Defence, or (2) are intended for use by the Prosecutor as evidence at trial, or (3) were obtained from or belonged to the accused (Rule 66(B) of the ICTR Rules). In the Ndayambaje case, the ICTR emphasised that Rule 66 provides two criteria for disclosure: (1) materiality to the preparation of the Defence, and (2) intended use by the Prosecution as evidence at trial.[8] The Trial Chamber also refers to the Celibici case, in which it was held that the Defence must demonstrate "a *prima facie* basis as to the materiality and that the requested evidence is in the custody or control of the Prosecutor."[9]

The Rules are unclear as to the exact understanding of the word "material". In the Celibici case the Trial Chamber of the ICTY did not provide a definition of "materiality", but pointed out that there was

---

[1]   See European Court of Human Rights, *Brandstetter v. Austria*, 28 August 1991, Series A-211, par. 66-67.

[2]   European Court of Human Rights, *Edwards v. United Kingdom*, 16 December 1992, Series A-247B, par. 34.

[3]   See Van den Wyngaert (ed.), Criminal Procedure Systems in the European Community, London, Butterworths, 1993, 408p.

[4]   May, R., Criminal Evidence, London, Sweet & Maxwell, 1995, p.381. See Magistrates' Courts Act 1980, s.5 as substituted by the Criminal Justice and Public Order Act 1994, s.44(2).

[5]   It should be noted that virtually all disclosure-rules of the ICTY and the ICTR (Rules 66-70) are identical.

[6]   ICTY, Decision on the Defence Motion for Sanctions for the Prosecutor's Failure to Comply with Sub-Rule 66(A) of the Rules, *Prosecutor v. Blaškić*, Case No. IT-95-14-T, 21 July 1998, as cited by R.May and M. Wierda, Trends in International Criminal Evidence: Nuremburg, Tokyo, The Hague, and Arusha, 37 Columbia Journal of Transnational Law, 1999, p.758.

[7]   ICTY, Decision on the Production of Discovery Materials, *Prosecutor v. Blaškić*, Case No. IT-95-14-PT, 27 January 1997, par. 38.

[8]   ICTR, Decision on the Defence Motion of Utmost Urgency to Resolve all Difficulties Posed by the File Processing and, in Particular, Issues of Evidence Disclosure, Judicial Calendar and Non-Enforcement of Decisions of the Trial Chamber in the Ndayambaje Case, *Prosecutor v. Ndayambaje*, ICTR-96-8-T, 16 April 1998.

[9]   *Ibidem.*

substantial similarity between Rule 66[10] and the American and British "disclosure-rules".[11] As a result, American and British case law serve as a guideline for the determination of the concept of "materiality". According to this case law, information is material if it has "more than an abstract logical relationship to the issues"; the information must be "significantly helpful to an understanding of important inculpatory or exculpatory evidence"; there must be "a strong indication that the information will play an important role in uncovering admissible evidence, aiding witness preparation, corroborating testimony, or assisting impeachment or rebuttal". It is the Prosecutor who – in the initial stage – decides what information in his custody or control is relevant to the Defence. In case of a dispute between Prosecution and Defence, the Trial Chamber has to resolve the matter.[12]

The Prosecution must also disclose the identity of witnesses in sufficient time prior to trial to allow adequate preparation of the Defence. This has been deduced from Rule 69(C) of the ICTR Rules.[13] In the Celibici case, Trial Chamber II of the ICTY decided that the term "identity" has a significance which goes beyond the mere provision of the names of the witnesses. To identify witnesses, it is necessary for the Defence to know further particulars about them, which in turn to satisfies the right of the accused to an adequate preparation of his Defence. "Substantial identifying information would appear to be the sex of each witness, his or her date of birth, the names of his or her parents, his or her place of origin and the town or village where he or she resided at the time relevant to the charges."[14] The term "identity" does not necessarily include the present addresses of the witnesses.[15] The Trial Chamber acknowledged that "the basic right of the accused to examine witnesses, read in conjunction with the right to have adequate time for the preparation of his defence, envisages more than a blind confrontation in the courtroom. A proper in-court examination depends upon a prior out of court investigation."[16] The Tribunal does not allow "trial by ambush"[17], and it has been stated that "the Rules support the idea that all the names of Prosecution witnesses must be disclosed at the same time in a comprehensive document which thus permits the Defence to have a clear and cohesive view of the Prosecution's strategy to make the appropriate preparations."[18]

Finally, the Prosecutor is under the obligation to disclose to the Defence all "exculpatory evidence". Rule 68 of the ICTR Rules states that "the Prosecutor shall, as soon as practicable, disclose to the Defence the existence of evidence known to the Prosecutor which in any way tends to suggest the innocence or mitigate the guilt of the accused or may affect the credibility of Prosecution evidence." This obligation to disclose exculpatory evidence to the Defence, has recently been refined in the United Kingdom, as a result of some well-known "miscarriage of justice". The failure by the police to disclose to the Prosecution or the Defence certain evidence in favour of the Defence was a reason for the quashing the convictions in the case of the Maguire Seven, the Birmingham Six and Judith Ward. In the case of the Maguire Seven, for example, the results of certain tests carried out by the Forensic Science Service, with results favourable to the defendants, were not notified to the Defence.[19] As a result the Criminal Procedure and Investigations Act 1996 contains an explicit obligation for the Prosecutor to disclose to the accused "any Prosecution material which (…) in the Prosecutor's opinion might undermine the case for the Prosecution against the accused."[20]

---

[10]   Rule 66 of the ICTY Rules and Rule 66 of the ICTR Rules are identical, as are most of the disclosure rules. See *supra*, note 5.

[11]   See ICTY, Decision on the Motion by the Accused Zejnil Delalić for the Disclosure of Evidence, *Delalić et al.*, IT-96-21, 26 September 1996.

[12]   *Ibidem.*

[13]   See ICTY, Decision on the Defence Motion to Compel the Discovery of Identity and Location of Witnesses, *Prosecutor v. Delalić et al.*, Case No. IT-96-21, 18 March 1997. See also *supra*, note 5.

[14]   *Ibid.*, par. 20.

[15]   *Ibid.*

[16]   *Ibid.*, par. 19.

[17]   May and Wierda, *supra* note 6 at p. 758.

[18]   ICTY, Decision on the Production of Discovery Materials, *Prosecutor v. Blaškić*, Case No. IT-95-14-PT, 27 January 1997.

[19]   A. Ashworth, The Criminal Process. An Evaluative Study, Oxford, Clarendon Press, 1994, p. 73.

[20]   Criminal Procedure and Investigations Act 1996, s. 3(1)(a).

As in the United Kingdom, it is provided in the Rules of Procedure and Evidence of both Tribunals that the Prosecutor decides which evidence is "exculpatory". If the Defence requests particular material, the Prosecutor should indicate whether the material is in its possession, whether it contains exculpatory information, and whether its confidentiality should be protected. It is not enough for the Prosecution to declare that it recognises its obligations under the rule and that it has complied with them.[21] On the other hand, there exists no general right of the Defence to browse through Prosecution files, without activating a reciprocal right to disclose (cf. *infra*). The Defence, therefore, must demonstrate a *prima facie* basis why the Trial Chamber should evaluate the exculpatory nature of the material requested.[22]

The term "exculpatory" must be read in a strict sense: it does not follow from the fact that evidence is not inculpatory that it is exculpatory and therefore must be disclosed. In the Celibici case, for example, the Trial Chamber held that evidence of violations of humanitarian law by the victims of the accused, was not exculpatory. "It is clear that prior violations of the laws and customs of war can never be considered as an excuse for later violations of such laws and customs. This would lead to a further escalation of criminal violence."[23]

Emphasising the substantial importance of the obligation to disclosure exculpatory evidence, this requirement has been incorporated in the Rome Statute for the future International Criminal Court (ICC). Article 67, paragraph 2 of the Rome Statute obliges the Prosecutor to disclose to the Defence evidence in its possession or control which it believes "shows or tends to show the innocence of the accused, or to mitigate the guilt of the accused, or which may effect the credibility of Prosecution evidence."

Notwithstanding these rather clear obligations of disclosure for the Prosecution, the Rules are remarkably silent regarding possible sanctions when the Prosecution does not comply with them. This question has been dealt with in the Bagasora case, where the Defence requested the Trial Chamber to declare inadmissible all evidence which the Prosecution had handed over to the Defence after 30 April 1998 – the final date for the Prosecutor to comply with its disclosure obligations. The Trial Chamber held, however, that "there are no provisions either in the Statute or the Rules to grant such a request."[24] In his Separate Opinion Judge Taffazzel H. Khan also observes that the Rules do not contain a provision which expressly renders belated disclosure automatically inadmissible. Nevertheless, Judge Khan does not preclude the possibility that the Trial Chamber may reject belatedly disclosed material: "In my opinion it is implicit that when the Chamber is empowered by the Rules to make appropriate rulings (...), it follows that the Chamber also has implied power to enforce those rulings; and this enforcement power may even include rejection of belatedly disclosed material if the situation so demands."[25] The ICTY has also determined that exclusion of evidence is a possible sanction when the Prosecution does not comply (in time) with its disclosure obligations. In the Celibici case the Trial Chamber stated that "it is part of the duties of the Trial Chamber, according to Article 20 of the Statute, to ensure that a trial is fair and expeditious. It is, therefore, within the competence of the Trial Chamber to exclude any piece of evidence sought to be introduced by the Prosecution, if indeed it seeks to do so, without having given the Defence the opportunity to examine that piece of evidence beforehand and thereby enable it to prepare a proper Defence."[26] This power was based upon Sub-rule 89(D) of the ICTY Rules, which provides for

---

[21]   ICTY, Decision on the Production of Discovery Materials, *Prosecutor v. Blaškić*, Case No. IT-95-14-PT, 27 January 1997, as cited by May and Wierda, *supra* note 17, at 759.
[22]   *Ibid.* See also ICTY, Decision on the Request of the Accused Hazim Delalić Pursuant to Rule 68 for Exculpatory Information, *Prosecutor v. Delalić et al.*, Case No. IT-96-21, 24 June 1997, par. 13.
[23]   ICTY, Decision on the Request of the Accused Hazim Delalić Pursuant to Rule 68 for Exculpatory Information, *Prosecutor v. Delalić et al.*, Case No. IT-96-21, 24 June 1997, par. 17.
[24]   ICTR, Decision on the Motion for Inadmissibility of Disclosure based on the Decision of 11 June 1998, *Prosecutor v. Bagosora*, Case No. ICTR-96-7, 7 December 1998.
[25]   ICTR, Decision on the Motion for Inadmissibility of Disclosure based on the Decision of 11 June 1998, Separate Opinion of Judge Tafazzal H. Khan, *Prosecutor v. Bagosora*, Case No. ICTR-96-7, 7 December 1998.
[26]   ICTY, Decision on Motion by the Defendants on the Production of Evidence by the Prosecution, *Prosecutor v. Delalić et al.*, Case No. IT-96-21, 8 September 1997, par. 9.

the exclusion of evidence if its probative value is substantially outweighed by the need to ensure a fair trial.[27]

Exclusion of evidence is, however, the "*ultimum remedium*". There exist other – less far-reaching – methods to ensure the fairness of the proceedings. The Rules are sufficiently flexible. This has been emphasised in another decision in the Bagosora case: "This Trial Chamber observes that under rule 89(A) of the Rules, the functions of the Tribunal are such that it is not bound by any particular legal system. The basic rule is to allow flexibility and efficacy in order to permit the development of the law and not to have pre-determined Rules. This flexibility is permitted under rule 89(B) of the Rules which empowers the Trial Chamber to determine given evidential issues in the best way possible and to arrive at a fair and just decision under given circumstances."[28] The Trial Chamber, therefore, can freely decide what probative value it attaches to each piece of evidence. The pieces which are "infected" must not be excluded automatically, but can be granted less probative value than "pure" pieces of evidence.

In some cases the Prosecutor can be relieved of its duty to disclose evidence. Rule 66(C) of the ICTR Rules provides for an *in camera* procedure before the Trial Chamber where disclosure of information or materials may (1) prejudice further or ongoing investigations, or (2) be contrary to the public interest, or, (3) affect the security interests of any State. In such cases the Trial Chamber can relieve the Prosecutor from these disclosure obligations. Furthermore, the Trial Chamber can, according to Rule 69, decide to keep the identity of threatened witnesses (temporarily) secret. Finally, Rule 70 of the ICTR Rules enumerates documents which do not have to be disclosed, for instance internal documents prepared in the course of preparation of a case.[29] Rule 70(B) also protects confidential sources which generate Prosecution evidence. These exceptions must, however, be interpreted in a strict sense. In its Decision on the Prosecution and Defence Motions Dated 25 January 1999 and 25 March 1999 Respectively, the Trial Chamber in the *Blaškić* case held that the Prosecution's disclosure obligations pursuant to Rules 66 and 68,[30] and the exculpatory character of confidential Defence documents, take precedence over their confidential nature insofar as the protection of witnesses is maintained or increased.[31]

In the United Kingdom there also exist exceptions to disclosure obligations of the Prosecution. In a recent judgement, the European Court of Human Rights had to evaluate the British system. The European Court acknowledged that the entitlement to disclosure of relevant evidence is not an absolute right. "In any criminal proceedings there may be competing interests, such as national security or the need to protect witnesses at risk of reprisals or keep secret police methods of investigation of crime, which must be weighted against the rights of the accused. In some cases it may be necessary to withhold certain evidence from the Defence so as to preserve the fundamental rights of another individual or to safeguard an important public interest."[32] The Court, however, stipulated two conditions: (1) the measures restricting the rights of the Defence must be strictly necessary, and (2) any difficulties caused to the Defence by a limitation on its rights must be sufficiently counterbalanced by the procedures followed by the judicial authorities. The Court seemed to prefer an *ex parte* procedure before the trial judge: "The fact that the need for disclosure was at all times under assessment by the trial judge provided a further, important, safeguard in that it was his duty to monitor throughout the trial the fairness or otherwise of the evidence being withheld."[33]

---

[27] See also May and Wierda, *supra* note 6, at p. 755-756. It should be noted that there is a difference between Rule 89 of ICTY Rules, and Rule 89 of the ICTR Rules. Sub-rule 89(D) does not appear in the latter.

[28] ICTR, Decision on the Defence Motion for Pre-Determination of Rules of Evidence, *Prosecutor v. Bagosora*, Case No. ICTR-96-7, 8 July 1998.

[29] In the Blaškić case the Trial Chamber held that a war diary and a military log did not constitute internal documents in the sense of Sub-rule 70(A) of the Rules, and that they therefore must be disclosed to the Prosecutor. See ICTY, Order for the Production of Documents Used to Prepare for Testimony of, *Prosecutor v. Blaškić*, Case No. IT-95-14, 22 April 1999.

[30] See *supra*, note 5.

[31] ICTY, Decision on the Prosecution and Defence Motions Dated 25 January 1999 and 25 March 1999 Respectively, *Prosecutor v. Blaskić*, Case No. IT-95-14, 22 April 1999.

[32] European Court of Human Rights, *Fitt v. United Kingdom*, 16 February 2000, par. 45. See also European Court of Human Rights, *Jasper v. United Kingdom*, 16 February 2000.

[33] *Ibid.*, par. 49. See also European Court of Human Rights, *Rowe and Davis v. United Kingdom*, 16 February 2000.

The disclosure obligation of the Prosecution does not include an obligation to provide for translation of the evidence. Only those documents which the Prosecution intends to use at trial must be translated. In that case, the Prosecution must hand over the documents to the Registrar, who is responsible for a proper translation.[34]

Finally it must be noted that the disclosure obligations of the Prosecutor (and the Defence) are of a continuing nature. If either party discovers additional evidence or material which should have been produced earlier pursuant to the Rules, that party is obliged to promptly notify the other party and the Trial Chamber of its existence (Sub-rule 67(D) of the ICTR Rules). A request to set a time limit on the disclosure of evidence cannot, therefore, be granted.[35]

Disclosure by the Defence

The Defence has also some disclosure obligations. Rule 67 of the ICTR Rules states that the Defence must notify the Prosecution if it intends to enter the defence of alibi or "any special defence, including that of diminished or lack of mental responsibility". Moreover, the Defence must disclose to the Prosecutor all evidence upon which the alibi or "special defence" is based. In the Kayishema and Ruzindana case, the Trial Chamber was asked to give a definition of both terms. The Trial Chamber, however, denied the request. According to the Trial Chamber, Rule 67 was clear enough in itself and did not require any further interpretation.[36] Rule 67 defines "alibi" as the defence in which the accused claims to have been present – at the time of the alleged crime – at a place other than that of the crime (Sub-rule 67(A)(ii)(a)). The requirement upon the Defence to disclose its intention to rely upon the defence of alibi reflects the well-established practice in the common law jurisdictions around the world.[37] It is a necessary requirement in order to allow the Prosecution to adequately prepare its case.[38]

Contrary to "alibi", "special defence" is not strictly defined in the Rules. The Rules only indicate that the defence of "diminished or lack of mental responsibility" must be regarded as a "special defence". The Rules do not define "diminished or lack of mental responsibility", or indicate possible other "special defences".[39] In the Kayishema and Ruzindana case, the Prosecution pointed out that "special defence" is a "common criminal law term" and, therefore, requires no further interpretation.[40] For a better understanding of the meaning of "special defence", one should look at national criminal (common) law. In the United Kingdom, for instance, "special defences" are those "which apply in the case of particular crimes",[41] for instance provocation in the case of a charge of murder.[42] "Diminished or lack of mental responsibility" is not a "special defence" in the United Kingdom, but a "general defence" i.e. "a defence which applies in the case of crimes generally". The choice of words in the Rules is therefore unfortunate. The drafters of the Rules probably did not intend to limit the scope of "special defence" to those defences that only apply in the case of particular crimes. The Statutes of both Tribunals, as it happens, do not contain any particular crime-related defences. Therefore, it would be better to conform to the Rome Statute, Article 31, paragraph 1 of which contains a list of "special defences": (1) diminished or lack of

---

[34]   ICTR, Decision on the Defence Motion of Utmost Urgency to Resolve all Difficulties Posed by the File Processing and, in Particular, Issues of Evidence Disclosure, Judicial Calendar and Non-Enforcement of Decisions of the Trial Chamber in the Ndayambaje Case, *Prosecutor v. Ndayambaje*, Case No. ICTR-96-8, 16 April 1998.

[35]   ICTY, Decision on the Applications Filed by the Defence for the Accused Zejnil Delalić and Esad Landzo on 14 February 1997 and 18 February Respectively, *Prosecutor v. Delalić et al.*, Case No. IT-96-21, 21 February 1997, par. 14.

[36]   ICTR, Decision on the joint Defence Motion Requesting the Interpretation of Rules 67 of the Rules, *Prosecutor v. Kayishema and Ruzindana*, Case No. ICTR-95-1, 15 June 1998.

[37]   See for example Criminal Justice Act 1967 (England), s.11. Similar legislation exists in Canada, as well as in certain states of the United States and Australia.

[38]   See ICTR, Judgement, *Prosecutor v. Kayishema and Ruzindana*, Case No. ICTR-95-1, 21 May 1999, par. 233.

[39]   In the Celibici case too, the Trial Chamber noticed that the Rules do not provide for a definition of "special defence". The Trial Chamber stated that "the most favourable meaning for the accused that can be read into sub-Rule 67(A)(ii)(b) is that a special defence is one apart from the general defence open to accused persons and is peculiar to the accused in the circumstances of a given case". The words "special defence" are therefore not limited to defences relating to lack of mental capacity. See ICTY, Judgement, *Prosecutor v. Delalić et al.*, Case No. IT-96-21, 16 November 1998, par. 1157.

[40]   See *supra*, note 36.

[41]   See Smith and Hogan, Criminal Law, London, Butterworths, 1992, p. 187.

[42]   *Ibid.*, 351.

mental responsibility, (2) intoxication, (3) private defence, (4) duress, (5) mistake of fact or mistake of law, and (6) superior orders and prescription of law.[43] The ICC Statute defines each defence.[44]

When giving notification of a special defence, the Defence must disclose the names and addresses of witnesses and any other evidence upon which the accused intends to rely to establish the special defence. This has been emphasised in the Celibici case: "The provisions of Sub-rule 67(A)(ii) impose a clear and unambiguous obligation on the Defence to disclose the names and addresses of all witnesses which they intend to call to testify in relation to the defence of alibi and any special defence (…). Where the language of a Rule is unequivocal, it is not open to either of the parties to challenge their duties thereunder."[45]

As stated above, the Prosecution must disclose to the Defence all documents which are material, if the Defence makes such a request. If such a request is made, the Prosecutor then in turn becomes entitled to inspect a similar, although not as extensive, range of material, namely "books, documents, photographs and tangible objects, which are within the custody or control of the Defence and which it intends to use as evidence at the trial" (Rule 67(C) of the ICTR Rules). This material does not extend, contrary to sub-Rule 66(B), to that which is "material to the preparation" of the Prosecution case. The Defence has no obligation to disclose incriminating evidence.[46]

The precise scope of this obligation has been discussed in the Celibici case. After the Prosecution had disclosed to the Defence a list of all documents which it intended to use at trial, the Prosecution asked the Defence for a similar list. The Defence, however, denied the request. The Trial Chamber stated that "the rationale of Sub-rule 67 is not (…) to oblige the Defence to expose to the Prosecution exactly which documents it will use at trial. As previously set out (…), the Defence is not required to give a list of witnesses to the Prosecution. Neither is it obliged to give a list of those documents which it intends to use at trial. There is no reciprocal obligation placed on the Defence due to the fact that the Prosecution has provided the Defence with such a list of documents."[47] This decision risks rendering as meaningless the disclosure obligations of Prosecution (Rule 66(B) of the ICTR Rules) and Defence (Rule 67(C)). When the parties are not obliged to specify which documents and other pieces of evidence they intend to use at trial, they can restrict themselves to "overwhelm" the other party with all the pieces in their custody or control. It would be better to follow the Prosecutor's opinion in this case: "it is in the interests of justice and necessary for the purposes of the conduct of the trial for the Defence to specify and disclose to the Prosecution as soon as possible all the documents that it intends to use as evidence."[48]

It should be noted that the Defence is never under the obligation to disclose witness statements, even in the case of alibi or special defence.[49] This as a result of the basic adversarial principle that the accused is under no duty to afford assistance to the Prosecution, a principle reflected in many common law and Continental systems. Judge Vohrah in his Separate Opinion held that imposing such an obligation would be contrary to the principle of "equality of arms", a principle intended "to elevate the Defence to the level of the Prosecution".[50] It should also be noted, however, that since the Trial Chamber's decision in Tadić, the Rules of the ICTY and ICTR have been changed. Rule 73*ter* of the ICTR Rules now permits a

---

[43]   Preparatory Commission for the International Criminal Court, Draft Rules of Procedure and Evidence (10 April 2000), PCNICC/2000/L.1/Rev.1/Add.1, Rule 5.30 *juncto* Article 31, paragraph 1 Rome Statute. See also Draft Rule 5.31.

[44]   See Articles 31, paragraph 1, 32 and 33 of the Rome Statute.

[45]   ICTY, Decision on the Motion to Compel the Disclosure of the Addresses of the Witnesses, *Prosecutor v. Delalić et al.*, Case No. IT-96-21, 13 June 1997, par. 11.

[46]   D.D. Ntanda Nsereko, Rules of Procedure and Evidence of the International Tribunal for the Former Yugoslavia, 5 Criminal Law Forum 1994, p.536.

[47]   ICTY, Decision on Motion to Specify the Documents Disclosed by the Prosecutor that Delalić's Defence Intends to use as Evidence, *Prosecutor v. Delalić et al.*, Case No. IT-96-21-T, 8 September 1997, par. 7. See also *supra*, note 5.

[48]   *Ibid.*, para. 4.

[49]   ICTY, Decision on Prosecution Motion for Production of Defence Witness Statements, Separate Opinion of Judge Stephen on Prosecution Motion for Production of Defence Witness Statements, *Prosecutor v. Tadić*, Case No. IT-94-1, 27 November 1996.

[50]   ICTY, Decision on Prosecution Motion for Production of Defence Witness Statements, Separate Opinion of Judge Vohrah on Prosecution Motion for Production of Defence Witness Statements, *Prosecutor v. Tadić*, Case No. IT-94-1, 27 November 1996.

Trial Chamber to order the Defence, prior to the commencement of the presentation of its case but after close of the case for the Prosecution, to file a list of witnesses which it intends to call with a summary of the facts in relation to which each witness will testify.[51]

What if the Defence fails to fulfil its disclosure obligations? As made clear above there are two situations in which the Defence has an obligation to disclose: (1) the "special defence" disclosure, and (2) the "reciprocal disclosure". In both cases the Rules do not contain any explicit sanction in the case of non-compliance. Sub-rule 67(B) of the ICTR Rules only states that failure of the Defence to give notice of a "special defence" does not limit the right of the accused to rely on that defence. This Rule leaves, at first sight, little scope for effective sanctions. Nevertheless, the Trial Chamber held in the Kayishema and Ruzindana case, that where good cause is not shown for the application of rule 67(B), the Trial Chamber is entitled to take into account this failure when weighing the credibility of the defence of alibi and/or any special defence presented.[52] The Defence is allowed, but its non-disclosure can be "credited" when determining the probative value of the evidence.

A second possible sanction is to allow the evidence of the accused himself, but exclude all other evidence as to the special defence. In the Kupreskic et al. case, the Trial Chamber held that if counsel does not file an appropriate alibi notice under Rule 67(A)(ii)(a), the evidence of other witnesses as to alibi is "liable to be excluded by the Trial Chamber".[53]

In case of non-compliance with the "reciprocal disclosure" obligations, the Rules also do not provide for an explicit sanction. Here, the judges are completely free to impose an effective sanction; Rule 67(B) of the ICTR Rules is not applicable. As with possible sanctions directed towards the Prosecution in case of non-compliance, "infected" pieces of evidence can be given less probative value, or even – as an "*ultimum remedium*" – completely excluded. These possibilities are based upon Rule 89.

Finally, it should be noted that the disclosure obligations of the Defence are also of a continuing nature. Rule 67(D) of the ICTR Rules applies both to the Prosecution and the Defence.

Tom Ongena

---

[51]   See May and Wierda, *supra* note 6, at 761.
[52]   ICTR, Decision on the Prosecution Motion for a Ruling on the Defence Continued Non Compliance with Rule 67(A)(ii) and with the Written and Oral Orders of the Trial Chamber, *Prosecutor v. Kayishema and Ruzindana*, Case No. ICTR-95-1, 3 September 1998.
[53]   ICTY, Decision, *Prosecutor v. Kupreškić et al.*, Case No. IT-95-16, 11 January 1999.

UNITED NATIONS NATIONS UNIES

International Criminal Tribunal for Rwanda
Tribunal pénal international pour le Rwanda

CHAMBRE I – CHAMBER I

OR: FR

Before: Judge Laïty Kama, Presiding Judge
Judge Yakov A. Ostrovsky
Judge Lennart Aspegren

Registry: Mr. Frederik Harhoff

Decision of: 11 June 1997

THE PROSECUTOR

VERSUS

GÉRARD NTAKIRUTIMANA

Case No. ICTR-96-10-T
Case No. ICTR-96-17-T

DECISION ON THE MOTIONS OF THE ACCUSED FOR
REPLACEMENT OF ASSIGNED COUNSEL/Corr.

The Office of the Prosecutor:
Mr. Jonah Rahetlah
Ms. Elizabeth Ann Farr
Ms. Brenda Sue Thornton

Counsel for the Accused:
Mr. N.K. Loomu-Ojare

[page 2] THE TRIBUNAL,

SITTING as Trial Chamber I of the International Criminal Tribunal for Rwanda (the "Tribunal"), composed of Judge Laïty Kama as Presiding Judge, Judge Yakov Ostrovsky and Judge Lennart Aspegren;

WHEREAS, through numerous letters addressed to the President of the Tribunal, the accused Gérard Ntakirutimana is requesting that the counsel assigned to him by the Registrar on 10 March 1997, in the person of Mr. N. K. Loomu-Ojare of the Tanganyika Bar Association, be replaced on the grounds of having lost confidence in said counsel, and subsequently that the Registrar assign to him a particular counsel of his choice;

WHEREAS, on this last point, he cites the provisions of Article 20 (4) of the Statute of the Tribunal (the "Statute"), which supposedly entitles him, though indigent, to freely choose his counsel, and submits that the Registrar should never have imposed Mr. Loomu-Ojare on him;

WHEREAS it should be recalled that this is the second request made by the accused for replacement of counsel;

WHEREAS in fact, during a hearing on this matter on 4 March 1997, taking into account the crisis situation that had developed between the accused Gérard Ntakirutimana and his counsel at the time, Ms. Ghislaine Moïse-Bazie of the Côte d'Ivoire Bar Association, who had asked to be withdrawn from the case, the Tribunal considered that there existed, on that occasion, an exceptional case as a condition for the change of assigned counsel, as required by Article 19 (D) of the Directive on Assignment of Defence Counsel (the "Directive"), and, for that reason, decided to withdraw Ms. Moïse-Bazie and instructed the Registrar to immediately assign a new counsel to the accused;

WHEREAS it was therefore at the instruction of the Tribunal that the Registrar assigned Mr. N. K. Loomu-Ojare to replace Ms. Moïse-Bazie;

WHEREAS it is, however, worth pointing out that it was at a time when the accused was fearing his imminent arrest by the Côte d'Ivoire authorities, at the request of the Prosecutor of the Tribunal, that he instructed Ms. Moïse-Bazie, to represent him at his own expense, particularly during his detention in Côte d'Ivoire, Ms. Moïse-Bazie having even declared that she had received the sum of CFA 500,000 in legal fees from the accused and his family;

WHEREAS it was later that Ms. Moïse-Bazie requested that her name be placed on the Registrar's list of counsel eligible for assignment and that request was granted;

WHEREAS it would therefore be inaccurate to state that the accused Mr. Gérard Ntakirutimana has chosen his counsel from the list previously established by the Registrar, since, for practical reasons, the Registrar had limited himself to confirming that Ms. Moïse-Bazie had been instructed by the accused, who in the meantime had declared himself to be indigent; **[page 3]**

TAKING INTO ACCOUNT the rights of the accused, as set forth in Article 14(3)(d) of the International Covenant on Civil and Political Rights (the "Covenant"), in Article 20(4)(d) of the Statute, in Article 7(1)(c) of the African Charter on Human and People's Rights (the "African Charter") and in Article 6(3)(c) of the European Convention for the Protection of Human Rights and Fundamental Freedoms (the "European Convention");

AFTER HAVING DELIBERATED,

WHEREAS the Tribunal considers that the correspondence and oral arguments of the accused Gérard Ntakirutimana raise two important issues:
- firstly, the existence of an exceptional case as a condition for the replacement of counsel, upon the decision of a Chamber, at the request of an accused; and
- secondly, consequences of indigence in relation to the choice of counsel.

A.   On the replacement of Mr. Loomu-Ojare upon the decision of the Chamber

WHEREAS, in accordance with Article 19 (D) of the Directive, only in exceptional cases may the assigned counsel be replaced, upon a decision by a Chamber, at the request of the accused;

WHEREAS, in support of his request for the replacement of his current counsel, the accused essentially claimed, at the hearing convened on 8 May 1997 to that end, that he no longer had confidence in said counsel, solely on the ground that Mr. Loomu-Ojare was a Tanzanian national and that the United Republic of Tanzania maintained special ties with the present Government of the Republic of Rwanda;

WHEREAS, while objecting to the allegations by the accused, Mr. Loomu-Ojare asserted, at the same hearing, that, as a lawyer and in accordance with the professional code of ethics of his Bar, he was totally independent of the Tanzanian Government, and was committed to the defence of Gérard Ntakirutimana;

WHEREAS with regard to Mr. Loomu-Ojare, the Tribunal has had occasion to confirm for itself that he has always conscientiously striven to provide effective legal representation for the accused;

WHEREAS, consequently, the Tribunal is not far from believing that the accused's request for change of counsel is motivated solely by his desire to be assigned a particular counsel, and not because of any loss of confidence vis-à-vis Mr. Loomu-Ojare;

WHEREAS an exceptional case, as required by Article 19 of the Directive, to permit a change of counsel therefore does not exist, and thence the accused's request should not be granted;

B.   Consequences of indigence in relation to the choice of counsel

WHEREAS, at the above-mentioned hearing of 8 May 1997, the accused Gérard Ntakirutimana, on the basis of the provisions of Article 20(4) of the Statute, submitted that any accused, even if indigent, has the right to choose his own counsel and cannot have one imposed upon him, as the Registrar did when he assigned Mr. Loomo-Ojare to him without his prior accord; **[page 4]**

WHEREAS Article 20(4) of the Statute, which does, actually, simply reiterate Article 14 of the Covenant, stipulates:

> "In the determination of any charge against the accused pursuant to the present Statute, the accused shall be entitled to the following minimum guarantees, in full equality:
> (...)
> (b) To have adequate time and facilities for the preparation of his or her defence and to communicate with counsel of his or her own choosing;
> (...)
> (d) To be tried in his or her presence, and to defend himself or herself in person or through legal assistance of his or her own choosing; to be informed, if he or she does not have legal assistance, of this right; and to have legal assistance assigned to him or her, in any case where the interests of justice so require, and without payment by him or her in any such case if he or she does not have sufficient means to pay for it;
> (...)"

WHEREAS it seems that the formula used for the indigent accused, which is the right "to have legal assistance assigned to [him], ..., and without payment by [him] in any such case if [he] does not have sufficient means to pay for it", involves a party other than the accused in the choice of assigned Defence counsel;

WHEREAS, according to Rule 45 of the Rules of Procedure and Evidence (the "Rules") and Article 13 of the Directive, it is the Registrar who is vested with such power;

WHEREAS, this being the case, the question is whether, in so doing, the Registrar is necessarily bound to consider the choice made by the indigent accused;

WHEREAS, on this question, the Tribunal points out that Article 20(4) of the Statute outlines two situations:

- the first situation requires that, where the accused has the means to pay for counsel, the accused may choose whomever he or she wishes;

- the second situation is precisely that of the accused Gerard Ntakirutimana who declared himself to be indigent and was so recognized by the Registrar; in this case, it is for the Registrar to assign him counsel who will be remunerated form the funds allocated by the Tribunal for this purpose;

WHEREAS the Registrar shall assign him a counsel whose name is on the list of counsel eligible for assignment, as drawn up by his office, pursuant to Rule 45 of the Rules and Article 13 of the Directive;

WHEREAS this means that the Registrar cannot be expected to fulfill another obligation, that would be to always follow the wishes of the indigent accused with regard to the choice of counsel, furthermore, while in the present case, the accused Gerard Ntakirutimana had requested, when the Tribunal heard his request on 8 May 1997, that the Registrar assign him a particular counsel whose name was not even on the Registrar's list; **[page 5]**

WHEREAS the Tribunal reads Article 20(4) in the same manner as the Human Rights Committee, the supervisory and interpretation body of the Covenant, established in accordance with Article 28, when it reads Article 14(3)(d) of the said Covenant;

WHEREAS, indeed, in several of its findings, the Human Rights Committee has had to reiterate that the said Article 14 does not entitle the accused to choose Defence counsel assigned to him without payment by him;

WHEREAS, thus, in the cases <u>Little v. Jamaica</u>, [Communication No. 330/1988 UN Doc. CCPR/C/50/D330/1988 (1994)] and <u>Osbourne Wright and Eric Harvey v. Jamaica</u> [Communication No. 459/1991, UN Doc. CCPR/C/55/D/459/1991 (1995)] the Human Rights Committee declared, on the one hand, that Article 14(3)(d) of the Covenant did not entitle the accused to choose counsel provided to him or her without payment by him or her and, on the other, that the counsel must ensure the effective representation of the accused in the interests of justice;

WHEREAS, furthermore, the European Commission on Human Rights also arrived at such an interpretation and adopted a similar position with regard to Article 6(3)(c) of the European Convention, by declaring, in the case <u>F. v. Swiss Confederation</u> (Decision of 9 May 1989, Application No. 12152/86) that Article 6(3)(c) of the European Convention did not guarantee the accused the right to choose the assigned counsel, nor even the right to be consulted on this matter by the court, which must nevertheless ensure that the Defence of the accused is effective;

WHEREAS the European Court of Human Rights, on its part, in the case <u>Croissant v. Germany</u> [62/1991/314/385 (1992)] confirmed the right of an accused to be defended by a counsel of his or her own choosing, while emphasizing that certain limitations apply where free legal representation is concerned; the right of an accused to be defended by counsel of his or her own choosing can therefore not be considered *per se* to be absolute; and while affirming that national courts must certainly take into account the preferences of the accused, such preferences may not be followed when there are relevant and sufficient grounds for maintaining that it was necessary in the interests of justice;

WHEREAS, the principle having thus been set out that the final decision for the assignment of counsel and of the choice of such counsel rests with the Registrar, the Tribunal submits nonetheless that, mindful to ensure that the indigent accused receives the most efficient defence possible in the context of a fair trial, and convinced of the importance to adopt a progressive practice in this area, an indigent accused should be offered the possibility of designating the counsel of his or her choice from the list drawn up by the Registrar for this purpose, pusuant to Rule 45 of the Rules and Article 13 of the Directive, the Registrar having to take into consideration the wishes of the accused, unless the Registrar has reasonable and valid grounds not to grant the request of the accused. **[page 6]**

FOR THESE REASONS

THE TRIBUNAL, by two votes to one,

DECLARES that, in this case, no exceptional case exists to justify the replacement of Mr. N. K. Loomu-Ojare, as requested by the accused Gérard Ntakirutimana;

DECIDES, consequently, not to grant the request made by the accused Gérard Ntakirutimana for Mr. Loomu-Ojare to be replaced;

DECLARES that Article 20(4) of the Statute cannot be interpreted as giving the indigent accused the absolute right to be assigned the legal representation of his or her choice;

DECLARES, nonetheless that, mindful to ensure that the indigent accused receives the most efficient defence possible in the context of a fair trial, and convinced of the importance to adopt a progressive practice in this area, an indigent accused should be offered the possibility of designating the counsel of his or her choice from the list drawn up by the Registrar for this purpose, the Registrar having to take into consideration the wishes of the accused, unless the Registrar has reasonable and valid grounds not to grant the request of the accused.

Arusha, 11 June 1997

Laïty Kama   Lennart Aspegren

Presiding Judge   Judge

Judge Yakov Ostrovsky's separate opinion is attached to the Decision of Trial Chamber I.

UNITED NATIONS   NATIONS UNIES

International Criminal Tribunal for Rwanda
Tribunal pénal international pour le Rwanda

CHAMBRE I – CHAMBER I

OR: ENG.

Before: Judge Laïty Kama, Presiding Judge
             Judge Yakov Ostrovsky
             Judge Lennart Aspegren

Registry: Mr. Frederik Harhoff

Decision of: 11 June 1997

THE PROSECUTOR

VERSUS

GÉRARD NTAKIRUTIMANA

Case No. ICTR-96-10-T
Case No. ICTR-96-17-T

SEPARATE AND DISSENTING OPINION OF JUDGE YAKOV OSTROVSKY ON THE
REQUEST OF THE ACCUSED FOR CHANGE OF ASSIGNED COUNSEL

The Office of the Prosecutor:
    Mr. Jonah Rahetlah
    Ms. Elizabeth Ann Farr
    Ms. Brenda Sue Thornton

Counsel for the Accused:
    Mr. N.K. Loomu-Ojare

[page 2]1. I have carefully considered the factual and legal analysis, and the decision taken by my two learned colleagues in the instant case. However, I respectfully differ with their interpretation of Article 20 (4) (d) of the Statute of the International Criminal Tribunal for Rwanda (the "Statute").

2. Article 20 (4) (d) of the Statute stipulates:

> "To be tried in his or her presence, and to defend himself or herself in person or through legal assistance of his or her own choosing; to be informed, if he or she does not have legal assistance, of this right; and to have legal assistance assigned to him or her, in any case where the interests of justice so require, without payment by him or her in any such case if he or she does not have sufficient means to pay for it."

3. The abovementioned provision is a reproduction of the Article 14 (3) (d) of the International Covenant on Civil and Political Rights (the "Covenant").

4. The interpretation of this provision in the abovementioned documents cannot be the same. There is a substantial difference between these two documents. The Covenant is dealing with the domestic legal systems applicable in the Member States. The Statute provides for the situation related to rights of the accused before the International Tribunal.

5. In the case of International Tribunal, the right of the accused to choose his or her defence counsel and right of the Registrar to assign the defence counsel are not absolute. The cooperation between the Registrar and the accused is essential to have mutual confidence between the accused and his or her counsel, in order to render effective defence. It is of crucial importance to take the necessary measures to ensure a fair trial, in view of the circumstances under which this Tribunal was created and working. **[page 3]**

6. In conformity with Article 20 (4) (d) of the Statute, Rule 45 of the Rules of Procedure and Evidence (the "Rules") and Article 13 of the Directive on Assignment of Defence Counsel (the "Directive"), the Registrar assigns a defence counsel to the indigent accused. But the accused has the right to choose his or her defence counsel from the list drawn up by the Registrar in accordance with Rules 44 and 45 of the Rules.

The Registrar may refuse to assign a counsel to the accused of his or her choice if there are reasonable grounds for doing so. But in the light of Article 20 (4) (d) of the Statute, the Registrar cannot impose his or her decision about the assignment of a defence counsel on the accused without taking into account his or her opinion.

7. The assignment of Mr. N.K. Loomu-Ojare, as a defence counsel was made without consulting the accused, and his right to choose his defence counsel was not respected. Consequently, a situation was created in which the accused is alleged to have no confidence in his currently assigned counsel.

8. On the basis of abovementioned reasons, the instant case should be considered as exceptional in accordance with Article 19 (D) of the Directive.

9. Therefore, I am of view that there is a sufficient legal basis to accept the request of the accused and replace his current defence counsel in the interests of justice.

Arusha, 11 June 1997   Yakov Ostrovsky

                                                            Judge

International Criminal Tribunal for the Prosecution of Persons Responsible for Genocide and Other Serious Violations of International Humanitarian Law Committed in the Territory of Rwanda and Rwandan Citizens responsible for genocide and other such violations committed in the territory of neighbouring States between 1 January and 31 December 1994	Case No.: ICTR-96-4-A Date: 27 July 1999 Original: English

IN THE APPEALS CHAMBER

Before: **Judge Gabrielle Kirk McDonald, Presiding**
                Judge Mohamed Shahabuddeen
                Judge Lal Chand Vohrah
                Judge Wang Tieya
                Judge Rafael Nieto-Navia

Registrar: **Mr. Agwu U. Okali**

Decision of: **27 July 1999**

JEAN-PAUL AKAYESU

v.

THE PROSECUTOR

DECISION RELATING TO THE ASSIGNMENT OF COUNSEL

The Office of the Prosecutor:
     Mr. Bernard Muna
     Mr. Mohamed C. Othman
     Mr. Mathias Marcussen

Accused:
     Jean-Paul Akayesu

[page 2] THE APPEALS CHAMBER of the International Criminal Tribunal for the Prosecution of Persons Responsible for Genocide and Other Serious Violations of International Humanitarian Law Committed in the Territory of Rwanda and Rwandan Citizens responsible for genocide and other such violations committed in the territory of neighbouring States, between 1 January and 31 December 1994 ("Appeals Chamber" and "Tribunal" respectively),

NOTING the Judgement in *The Prosecutor v. Jean-Paul Akayesu*, Case No. ICTR-96-4-T, rendered by Trial Chamber I on 2 September 1998;

NOTING the "Motion for Judicial Review under Section 19 of the Statute and Rules 73 and 105 of the Rules of Procedure and Evidence Urgent Motion for Oral Hearing", filed on 20 January 1999 ("Motion");

NOTING the "Scheduling Order" of the Appeals Chamber filed on 31 March 1999;

NOTING the "Décision portant maintien de Me Giacomo Barletta Caldarera aux intérêts de M. Jean-Paul Akayesu", filed on 31 March 1999;

NOTING the "Registry's Brief in Reply to the Motion", filed on 12 April 1999;

NOTING the "Appelant's Reply to the Registrar's Arguments" dated 23 April 1999, and filed on 28 April 1999;

NOTING the "Petition for Interventions as Amicus Curiae, of the International Criminal Defence Attorneys Association (Rule 74 of the *Rules of Procedure and Evidence*)", filed on 28 April 1999 ("the Petition");

NOTING the "Réplique de Jean-Paul Akayesu sur la Décision du Greffier datée le 24 mars 1999 pour maintenir la commission de Me Giacomo", filed on 4 May 1999;

NOTING the Directive on the Assignment of Counsel, as amended on 8 June 1998, which provides for a right of recourse against a decision not to assign counsel, but does not extend this right of recourse in relation to an appeal before the Appeals Chamber; **[page 3]**

CONSIDERING, however, that, in respect of a decision to assign or not so assign counsel to represent an Appellant before the Appeals Chamber, a right of recourse to the Appeals Chamber is required for the effective exercise of the Appellant's rights under Article 20(4) of the Statute of the Tribunal and has been allowed by the Appeals Chamber of the International Criminal Tribunal for the Former Yugoslavia in the *Order on the Motion to Withdraw as Counsel due to a Conflict of Interest*, IT-96-21-A (24 June 1999) and the *Order Regarding Esad Landžo's Request for Removal of John Ackerman as Counsel on Appeal for Zejnil Delalić*, IT-96-21-A (6 May 1999);

CONSIDERING that the practice of the Tribunal has been to provide a list of approved counsel from which an accused may choose and that Mr. John Philpot was included in this list by the Registrar upon the insistence of the Appellant that he desired that Mr. Philpot be assigned to him, and considering further that the Registrar thereby gave the Appellant a legitimate expectation that Mr. Philpot would be assigned to represent him before the Tribunal;

NOTING that the Appellant has dismissed prior counsel assigned to him and that this is the sixth counsel appointed by the Appellant;

NOTING that the requirements of the Tribunal's Code of Conduct, Directive on the Assignment of Defence Counsel and the Rules of Procedure and Evidence of the Tribunal apply to Counsel assigned to the Appellant;

DIRECTS the Registrar to assign Mr. Philpot as lead counsel, effective 22 September 1998, the date on which the Registry placed Mr. Philpot on the list of approved counsel;

FURTHER DIRECTS the Registrar to reimburse Mr. Philpot in accordance with the Directive on the Assignment of Defence Counsel for any eligible work performed since 22 September 1998 in relation to the Appellant's appeal;

DECIDES that the Appellant and the Prosecution as Cross-Appellant shall comply with the following briefing schedule on the merits of the present case, pursuant to Rules 111 to 113; **[page 4]**

(1)   The Appellant and the Cross-Appellant shall file their briefs by 25 October 1999;

(2)   The Respondent and the Cross-Respondent shall file their briefs by 22 November 1999;

(2)   Briefs in reply may be filed by 6 December 1999;

FURTHER DECIDES, in light of this Decision, to reject the Petition.

Done in both English and French, the English text being authoritative.

Gabrielle Kirk McDonald
Presiding Judge

Dated this twenty-seventh day of July 1999

At The Hague,

The Netherlands.

The right of a defendant to be represented by counsel of his or her own choosing is even more important in international courts than it is in domestic jurisdictions, for several reasons. The choice is also more complicated. Unlike domestic systems, there is no specialist "bar" at the Tribunals – ie a body of counsel educated and trained in the (tradition of the) procedural and substantive law to be applied by the Tribunals.

Nationalistic, ethnic and political considerations may play an important role in the degree of confidence that defendants feel they can place in their counsel, since the alleged offences often are motivated to a considerable extent by these concerns. Even though they do not in any way justify or excuse the offences, defendants cannot be blamed for incorporating these feelings into their choice of counsel. Despite advantages that such a choice may give a defendant, it is not inconceivable that the methods of choice in fact endanger the administration of justice and even the interests of the defendant himself. A further important consideration to the choice of counsel may be the absence of language barriers, notwithstanding the availability of good interpretation services.

Despite its importance, the right to choose counsel is not, however, considered as absolute. Defendants who pay counsel themselves face implicit restrictions. Rules 3 (C) and (D) of the Rules of Procedure and Evidence require counsel to speak one of the official languages of the Tribunal, unless special permission is given to use another language.[1] The defendant generally is not entitled to receive translations of all documents relevant to his case.[2] Thus, even if counsel is permitted in oral argument to use a language other than one of the normal working languages, he may not on his own be capable of fulfilling all duties required of defence counsel. Apart from this limitation the choice seems only to be restricted by the professional qualification of counsel: Rule 44 requires that he is admitted to the practice of law in a state or is a University professor of law.[3] Counsel who are shown to be no longer fit to appear before the Tribunal as a result of their flagrant misbehaviour may be denied the right of standing. This also represents a limitation on the right of a defendant to choose counsel.[4]

Those counsel assigned to indigent defendants require further qualifications. Taking into account Rules 3 (C) and (D)[5] it is not surprising that, in order to be put on the list of available counsel maintained by the Registrar, Rule 45(A) requires them to speak one of the official languages of the Tribunal. However, the requirement of 10 years relevant experience is not self-explanatory. This requirement was originally lacking in Rule 45 ICTY. Most probably as a result of unfortunate experiences, the judges of the ICTY have recently adopted a similar additional requirement in Rule 45(B): counsel must have shown "that they possess reasonable experience in criminal and/or international law". The mere fact that lawyers are admitted to practice in another country does not automatically make them suitable candidates for fulfilling the very demanding task of acting as defence counsel before a Tribunal. Although this may be similarly true for counsel engaged by defendants themselves, remuneration of counsel by the Tribunal creates a responsibility to prevent the waste of public funds. This rather vague criterion of reasonable experience allows the possibility of abuse of power by the Registrar, though there is no indication that this has been the case thus far.

Apart from counsel either engaged by a suspect or an accused or assigned by the Registrar, the ICTR Rules also make reference to the Duty Counsel. He is based in the proximity of the Tribunal and the

---

[1]   This implicit limitation on the choice of counsel was used as an argument by the defendant in the Delalić case of the ICTY, Decision on Defence Application for Forwarding the Documents in the Language of the Accused, *Prosecutor v. Delalić/ Mucić/ Delić/ Landžo*, Case No. IT-96-21-T, 25 September 1996.

[2]   See the decision referred to in footnote 1.

[3]   An example of the acceptance of University Professors as defence counsel is found e.g. in Germany (§ 138 Abs 1 StPO)

[4]   See for the ICTY, Decision on the Request of the Accused Radomir Kovać to Allow Mr. Milan Vujin to Appear as Co-Counsel Acting Pro Bono, *Prosecutor v. Kunarac/ Kovac* Case Nos. IT-96-23-PT and IT-96-23/1-PT, 14 March 2000, in relation to ICTY, Judgment on Allegations of Contempt against Prior Counsel Milan Vujin, *Prosecutor v. Tadić*, Case No. IT-94-1-AR-77 A.Ch., 31 January 2000.

[5]   This requirement is repeated in art. 13 of the Directive on the Assignment of Defence Counsel. However since 1996 Rule 45(B) ICTY provides for the assignment of counsel who do not speak either of the working languages in particular circumstances.

detention facility and may be called to represent a suspect or an accused temporarily until the latter has engaged counsel or counsel is assigned to him.

In domestic systems free legal aid is usually dependent upon the seriousness of the case. The procedure set out in Rule 45 does not, however, envisage this as a criterion for the decision to assign counsel. It focusses instead on the indigence of the defendant. Once this has been established, the Registrar assigns counsel. Rule 45(A) ICTY currently begins with the words: "Whenever the interests of justice so demand, counsel shall be assigned to suspects or accused who lack the means ...". The difference in wording is important. The adoption of Rule 45(A) reflects a change in the system of assignment of Counsel. In its original version the Directive on the Assignment of Defence Counsel of the ICTY provided only for the assignment of one counsel. Since the present art. 16 (C),(D),(E) and (F)[6] introduced the assignment of co-counsel, there is a good reason to consider whether an assignment (which includes the assignment of co-counsel) is demanded by the interests of justice. It is in my opinion not intended that any defendant is without representation by counsel before the Tribunal (unless he chooses to defend himself). This criterion of the "interest of justice" is also relevant in cases where the defendant does not meet the indigence requirement or if he fails to request or obtain the assignment of counsel. The Registrar may then decide in the interest of justice to assign counsel (Directive ICTR art. 10bis, ICTY art. 11bis).

The annotated decisions and opinion mainly deal with the extent to which the right to be represented by counsel of the defendant's choice may be limited by circumstances where counsel is to be assigned due to the indigence of the defendant.[7] On the one hand the Trial Chamber and the Appeals Chamber stress the importance of the fair trial requirement such that an indigent defendant receives the most efficient defence possible, which presupposes a mutual confidence between defendant and counsel. On the other hand the public funding of defence counsel for indigent defendants and the interests of the criminal justice system may justify wider restrictions than those which apply when the defendant himself engages counsel.

Both decisions and the dissenting opinion show that the defendant has a right to be consulted by the Registrar prior to the assignment of counsel. He may express his wishes as to which counsel on the list maintained by the Registrar under Rule 45(A) he would prefer. In practice, if the counsel of preference does not initially appear on that list, he may be subsequently included on it if he meets the requirements of Rule 45(A).[8] The preference of the defendant should be taken into account when assigning counsel. Yet, the Statute, the Rules of Procedure and Evidence as well as the Directive on the Assignment of Defence Counsel contain no explicit provisions on either the issue of consultation with the defendant or of acceding to his preference. Although the right of the defendant to be consulted is accepted by the majority of the Trial Chamber in the Decision on the motion of the accused Gérard Ntakirutimana, thus limiting the risk that the choice of counsel by the Registrar is simply imposed upon him, a failure to consult with the defendant brings with it no consequences. The Chamber denies the request for replacement of Mr N.K. Loomu-Ojare, the counsel assigned to the defendant in the absence of any consultation. In his dissenting opinion judge Ostrovsky finds this failure to consult unacceptable and therefore considers the case as exceptional under art. 19(D) of the Directive, thus mandating the replacement of counsel as requested. But, in his view even this might not automatically result in the assignment of the defendant's choice of counsel, since judge Ostrovsky also acknowledges the right of the Registrar to refuse the assignment of the defendant's choice if there are reasonable reasons for so doing. In this regard judge Ostrovsky appears to differ from the majority only as far as the necessity to "repair" the initial failure is concerned. However the majority decision might also be understood as containing implicit and negative judgements as to the truthfulness and the relevance of the reasons

---

[6] Similar Provisions are found in the ICTR Directive Article 15 (C)(D)(E)(F).

[7] In many domestic systems the principle of free choice of counsel is respected even when counsel is assigned by the competent authorities. See, for example, the English Legal Aid Act 1988, s.32 and § 142 Abs. 1 of the German Code of Criminal Procedure (StPO).

[8] The amendment of Rule 45(C) ICTY (July 2000) now makes this step unnecessary, since it also empowers the Registrar to assign counsel regardless of whether his name appears on the list so long as he fulfils at least the requirements of Rule 44.

underlying the request for replacement of counsel (the nationality of counsel and a resulting fear of lack of independence). That issue touches upon the core of the right to choose counsel.

In the Decision relating to the Assignment of Counsel in the Akayesu-case the Appeals Chamber only briefly mentions art. 20, paragraph 4 of the Statute in the context of a procedural matter. It then describes the practice of the Tribunal to which it appears to attribute a normative effect. This practice includes the ability of the defendant to choose one of the counsel appearing on the list. It does not mention the authority of the Registrar to refuse the assignment of the preferred counsel. This may be understandable in this particular case since the Appeals Chamber takes into account the fact that Mr John Philpot was included on the list by the Registrar only at the insistence of the defendant. This indicates that there were no reasonable grounds for refusing the assignment of Mr Philpot. The Appeals Chamber considers the listing of Mr Philpot as giving rise to a legitimate expectation by the defendant that mr Philpot would be assigned to represent him before the Tribunal.

The decisions and opinion significantly contribute to the development of the law of the Tribunals. The right of an indigent defendant to have counsel assigned to him is clearly linked with the right of a defendant to be represented by counsel of his or her choosing. It is in the interests of a fair administration of justice that there is mutual confidence between the defendant and his or her counsel. The rules seem to prescribe that, at a minimum, assignment of the counsel of choice is granted unless there are reasonable and valid grounds not to do so.

The decision on the motions for replacement of the assigned counsel does not appear to be completely in accordance with this rule. However, the fact that the decision related not to the initial assignment of counsel, but to his replacement, may have been the reason that the stricter criteria of art 19(D) overshadowed the criteria to be applied at the initial assignment. The decision of the Appeals Chamber on the other hand seems not to make any distinction in this respect, since it also related to a replacement of counsel. This is remarkable given that the assignment of Mr Philpot made him the sixth counsel for the defendant. One can only specualte as to the result had the Appeals Chamber heard the motion of Mr Gérard Ntakirutimana.

The reasoning as to the relevant law is not well explained by the Appeals Chamber. The question remains open as to whether the Registrar is entitled not to follow the 'choice' of the defendant and what criteria would apply in these circumstances. The emphasis placed on the effective exercise of the defendant's rights under Article 20, paragraph 4 of the Statute, which are designed to ensure mutual confidence between the defendant and his or her counsel, makes it unlikely that reasons of a practical nature would normally justify the refusal to assign counsel chosen by the defendant.

Paragraph 4 of Article 20 of the Statute specifies the fundamental right of the defendant to be represented by counsel of his own choosing and to have counsel assigned if he or she cannot afford to directly engage one. The provision is generally regarded as a mirror of art 6 European Convention on Human Rights and art 14 of the International Covenant on Civil and Political Rights. In the case law of the European Commission and the European Court of Human Rights, the link between the right of the defendant to choose counsel and to have counsel assigned without payment has been dealt with several times. Initially, the European Commission denied a defendant who relied on legal aid the right to choose counsel to be assigned to him and even the right to be consulted.[9] In the Pakelli-case[10] the Court paid specific attention to the textual difference between the English and the French version of Article 6, paragraph 3 (c) European Convention of Human Rights. Where the English text separated the right to choose counsel and the right to be given free legal assistance by the word "*or*", the French text connected these rights by the word "*and*". The Court concluded that the French text better served the object and purpose of the paragraph.[11] In the ICTR and ICTY Statutes both the French and English text use the word "*and*", thus

---

[9]   See European Commission of Human Rights, *X v. Federal Republic of Germany*, Application 6946/75, 6 Decisions and Reports 1977 p. 119.
[10]   European Court of Human Rights, *Pakelli v. Federal Republic of Germany*, 25 April 1983, Series A-64.
[11]   The American Convention on Human Rights deals with both rights in different subparagraphs (Art. 8, subsections 2d and 2e) and therefore does not provide great assistance in interpreting art. 20, paragraph 4 of the Statute.

linking the the right to choose counsel with the right to have the legal assistance for those who cannot pay for it.

The right of indigent defendants to be represented by counsel of their choice is not expressly stipulated in the decisions. Where the decision of the Trial Chamber and the dissenting opinion of judge Ostrovsky seem to accept only a right to be consulted and an obligation to take the choice of the defendant into account, the decision of the Appeals Chamber comes closer to specifying an obligation to respect the choice of the defendant. It is difficult, however, to determine the extent to which the Appeals Chamber was guided, in giving normative effect to the practice of the Tribunal, by a textual analysis of Article 20, paragraph 4 of the Statute similar to interpretation given to Article 6, paragraph 3 (c) of the European Convention by the European Court. If in the Akayesu case the Appeals Chamber intended to acknowledge the right of an indigent defendant to choose counsel, the particular circumstances of that case do not give rise to any conclusions as to the limits of that right. In practice it might not make a significant difference whether the choice of the defendant is to be respected in principle while allowing exceptions to be made, or to take into account the wishes of the defendant unless there are reasonable and valid grounds not to follow the choice of the accused.

In interpreting the decisions and opinion one cannot disregard amendments adopted to the Rules of Procedure and Evidence and the Directive for the Assignment of Defence Counsel. These indicate a growing awareness as to the meaning of 'the most efficient defence possible' and support what the judges, especially those in the Appeals Chamber, seem to be seeking: progressive practical application of Article 20, paragraph 4 of the Statute.

Alphons Orie

International Criminal Tribunal for the
Prosecution of Persons Responsible for
Genocide and Other Serious Violations of
International Humanitarian Law Committed
in the Territory of Rwanda and Rwandan
Citizens responsible for genocide and other
such violations committed in the territory of
neighbouring States between 1 January and
31 December 1994

Case No: ICTR-98-37-A

Date: 8 June 1998

Original: English

IN THE APPEALS CHAMBER

Before: **Judge Gabrielle Kirk McDonald (Presiding)**
Judge Mohamed Shahabuddeen
Judge Lal Chand Vohrah
Judge Wang Tieya
Judge Rafael Nieto-Navia

Registrar: Mr. Agwu U. Okali

Decision of: 8 June 1998

PROSECUTOR

v.

THÉONESTE BAGOSORA AND 28 OTHERS

DECISION ON THE ADMISSIBILITY OF THE PROSECUTOR'S APPEAL FROM THE DECISION OF A CONFIRMING JUDGE DISMISSING AN INDICTMENT AGAINST THÉONESTE BAGOSORA AND 28 OTHERS

The Prosecutor:
    Louise Arbour
    Bernard A. Muna

[page 2] I. INTRODUCTION

1. The Appeals Chamber of the International Criminal Tribunal for the Prosecution of Persons Responsible for Genocide and Other Serious Violations of International Humanitarian Law Committed in the Territory of Rwanda and Rwandan Citizens Responsible for Genocide and Other Such Violations Committed in the Territory of Neighbouring States between 1 January and 31 December 1994 ("ICTR"), hereby issues its decision with respect to the Prosecutor's *ex partie* Notice of Appeal, filed on 6 April 1998[1] ("Notice of Appeal"), seeking to appeal from the Decision of Judge Tafazzal Hossain Khan[2], ("Decision"), dismissing an indictment against Théoneste Bagosora and 28 Others, filed on 31 March 1998 ("Indictment").

2. In her Notice of Appeal, the Prosecutor requests the Appeals Chamber to provide appropriate relief by quashing Judge Khan's Decision, declaring him competent to review the Indictment and remanding for a review of the Indictment on the merits.

3. This Appeals Chamber decision will also dispose of two additional motions filed by two individuals named in the Indictment. On 23 April 1998, Counsel for Anatole Nsengiyumva filed a motion seeking leave for the applicant to be joined as a party in the Appeal, or alternatively, leave to appear before the Appeals Chamber as *amicus curiae* and make submissions on, *inter alia*, whether an appeal lies from the Decision and whether the Appeals Chamber is competent to hear it, whether parties affected by such an appeal should be excluded from the proceedings, and whether such an appeal could be disposed of *ex parte*.[3] Counsel for Théoneste Bagosora filed on 1 May 1998, a motion arguing that the present appeal was inadmissible and seeking leave **[page 3]** to be heard by the Appeals Chamber on the matter.[4] In separate orders of 29 April and 26 May 1998, the Appeals Chamber stayed consideration of the motions pending determination of whether an appeal lies from the Decision.[5] **[page 4]**

II. LEGAL AND FACTUAL BACKGROUND

1. Procedural History

4. On 6 March 1998, pursuant to Article 17 of the Statute of the ICTR ("Statute") and Rule 47 of the Rules of Procedure and Evidence of the ICTR ("Rules"), the Prosecutor submitted to Judge Khan for review the Indictment, charging the indictees with the commission of various offences within Articles 2, 3 and 4 of the Statute. Sixteen of those individuals were the subjects of indictments pending before the ICTR.

5. On 31 March 1998, Judge Khan ("Confirming Judge") issued his Decision. He found that before reviewing the merits of the Indictment, he had first to determine two issues of jurisdiction, namely whether the Prosecutor could submit the Indictment, and whether a confirming judge had jurisdiction to confirm it under Article 18 of the Statute and Rule 47 of the Rules. He divided the twenty-nine individuals charged into three groups: the "First Group" of eleven persons who had been previously indicted and had made initial appearances and entered pleas before Trial Chambers of the ICTR pursuant

---

[1] Notice of Appeal (Article 24 and Rule 108), *The Prosecutor v. Théoneste Bagosora and 28 Others*, Case No. ICTR 98-37-I, 3 April 1998.

[2] Dismissal Of Indictment, *The Prosecutor v. Théoneste Bagosoro and 28 Others*, Case No. ICTR 98-37-I, 31 March 1998.

[3] Motion by the Defence for Leave and/or Orders to be Enjoined in or be Invited as Amicus Curiae in an Appeal by the Prosecutor, *The Prosecutor v. Théoneste Bagosoro and 28 Others*, Case No. ICTR 98-37-I, 23 April 1998.

[4] "Preliminary Motion regarding an appeal lodged by the Prosecutor against a decision of 30 March 1998 by Judge Tafazzal Hossein KHAN" [*sic*] *The Prosecutor v. Théoneste Bagosoro and 28 Others*, Case No. ICTR 98-37-I, 1 May 1998.

[5] Order on Motion by the Defence in the Matter of Prosecutor v. Anatole Nsengiyumva Seeking Orders for Joinder or Leave to Appear as Amicus Curiae in an Appeal *The Prosecutor v. Théoneste Bagosora and 28 Others*, Case No. ICTR 98-37-I, 29 April 1998; Order on Motion by the Defence in the Matter of Prosecutor v. Théoneste Bagosora *The Prosecutor v. Théoneste Bagosoro and 28 Others*, Case No. ICTR 98-37-I, 26 May 1998.

to Rule 62 of the Rules; the "Second Group" of five persons previously indicted who remained at liberty, and the "Third Group" of thirteen persons who had not been indicted and who at liberty. The Appeals Chamber will use the same terms to refer to these different categories of indictees.

6.   The Confirming Judge considered that the charges contained in the Indictment related to substantially the same facts and offences alleged in the Indictments already existing against the First and Second Groups ("First Group Indictments" and "Second Group Indictements"). Only one new crime, conspiracy to commit genocide, was added to those contained in the First and Second Group Indictments.[6] He rejected, therefore, the Prosecutor's argument that the Indictment should be reviewed under Rule 47 and found that the proper course to follow would be for the Prosecutor to seek leave to amend the First and Second group Indictments under Rule 50, or to withdraw them **[page 5]** pursuant to Rule 51 and resubmit the Indictment for consideration, or to follow the procedure in Rule 72, governing the submission of preliminary motions. In his view, the use of the procedure provided by Rule 47 would be an unwarranted usurpation of the jurisdiction of the Trial Chambers seized of the First Group Indictments and would circumvent the express provisions of the Rules that guarantee the right of the Defence to be heard. He further held that the submission of the Indictment for confirmation was a wrongful attempt on the part of the Prosecutor to join the accused in the three Groups, seeking to impinge on the jurisdiction of the Trial Chambers and contravene the rights of the accused of the First Group to a fair and expeditious trial without undue delay.[7] The Confirming Judge, therefore, declined jurisdiction over the First Group.

7.   In respect of the Second Group, the Confirming Judge found that as the accused had been previously indicted but had not yet made initial appearances, jurisdiction lay with the Judges who had confirmed the Second Group Indictments ("Confirming Judges"). He, therefore, declined jurisdiction over the Second Group.

8.   As to the Third Group, the Confirming Judge held that he was competent to review the Indictment but that consideration for the rights of the accused in the First Group militated against joining them with the Third Group in the Indictment. Noting the Prosecutor's unwillingness to sever the Indictment, he declined to review the substantive elements of the Indictment, also in relation to the Third Group.[8]

9.   The Confirming Judge, therefore, dismissed the Indictment and, at the request of the Prosecutor, ordered its non-disclosure in the interests of protecting future prosecutorial investigations.

10.   In her Notice of Appeal, the Prosecutor listed twenty grounds of appeal and reserved the right to enter such further grounds as the Appeals Chamber may permit. **[page 6]**

11.   The Prosecutor, citing the nature and the importance of the proceedings, sought an expedited, *ex parte* hearing on the matter and requested the Appeals Chamber to order the stay of any trial proceedings in relation to the First and Second Group Indictments.

12.   In an *Ex Parte* Scheduling Order of 23 April 1998, the Appeals Chamber ordered the Prosecutor to submit within seven days a brief addressing the question of whether an appeal lies from the Decision. The Chamber further ordered that the matter would be resolved expeditiously thereafter without oral argument and denied the request to stay proceedings.[9]

13.   The Prosecutor filed her appellate brief[10] ("Appellant's Brief") on 30 April 1998. In the Appellant's Brief the Prosecutor asserts a number of grounds as justifying admission of the appeal and requests the

---

6   Decision at p.10.
7   Decision at pp. 10 and 11 "...the mandatory Rules for joinder of the accused...the only legal procedure...".
8   Decision at pp. 11-12.
9   *Ex Parte* Scheduling Order, *The Prosecutor v. Théoneste Bagosoro and 28 Others*, Case No. ICTR 98-37-I, 23 April 1998.
10   Appellant's Brief by the Prosecutor in Support of the Admissibility of the Appeal of the Dismissal by Judge Khan of the Indictment against Bagosora and 28 Others of 31 March 1998 *The Prosecutor v. Théoneste Bagosoro and 28 Others*, Case No. ICTR 98-37-I, 30 April 1998.

Appeals Chamber to schedule a date for the submission of a brief on the merits and a date for oral arguments on the appeal. **[page 7]**

2. The Notice of Appeal

14.   The Notice of Appeal is based on the Prosecutor's contention that the Indictment represents a critical component of a new Prosecutorial strategy. It is argued, therefore, that the dismissal of the Indictment by the Confirming Judge prejudices the ability of the Prosecutor to discharge her mandate under the Statute, which prejudice has a similar consequential impact on the ICTR.

15.   In support of her submission that the Decision hinders her in the performance of her statutory functions, the Prosecutor lists twenty grounds of appeal and reserved the right to enter such further grounds as the Appeals Chamber may permit. The Appeals Chamber considers that many of these grounds overlap or are insufficiently distinguished to constitute separate foundations for an appeal from the Decision.

16.   The Appeals Chamber will summarise the Prosecutor's grounds below.

17.   The Prosecutor contends that the Confirming Judge made various errors of fact and of law by declining jurisdiction to consider the Indictment and by thereafter dismissing the Indictment. The Prosecutor considers as errors of law, *inter alia*, the findings that the Trial Chambers and Confirming Judges had jurisdiction over, respectively, the First and Second Groups,[11] the holding that the submission of the Indictment constituted an infringement of such jurisdiction[12] and that the Prosecutor should properly have proceeded under Rules 50, 51 or 72 of the Rules,[13] the finding that an individual could be charged only once with the same offences arising from the same or substantially the same facts,[14] and the holding that an accused in the First Group has a right to be heard on the amendment of an indictment.[15]

18.   The Prosecutor submits that the Confirming Judge failed to consider sufficiently the grounds for the employment of the *ex parte* procedure under Rule 47 **[page 8]** and that he considered factors extraneous to his jurisdiction under Rule 47, thereby further erring in law.[16]

19.   In addition, the Prosecutor submits that the Confirming Judge erred in law and in fact by, *inter alia*, holding that the Indictment contained only one substantial new charge[17] and made errors of fact occasioning a miscarriage of justice by finding that the submission of the Indictment under Rule 47 and the form of the Indictment were intended to circumvent or deny the rights of the accused[18]. **[page 9]**

3. Applicable Provisions

20.   The Notice of Appeal is filed pursuant to Article 24 of the Statute and Rule 108 of the Rules. Article 24 provides:

Article 24

Appellate Proceedings

1. The Appeals Chamber shall hear appeals from persons convicted by the Trial Chambers or from the Prosecutor on the following grounds:

---

11   *Ibid.*, at pp. 2-3, paras. 4, 7.
12   *Ibid.*, paras. 5, 8.
13   *Ibid.*, paras. 3, 10, 11, 12.
14   *Ibid.*, paras. 12,13.
15   *Ibid.*, at p.4, para. 17.
16   *Ibid.*, at p.4, paras. 16, 20.
17   *Ibid.*, at p.3, para. 14.
18   *Ibid.*, at p.3, paras. 6 and 9.

a) an error on a question of law invalidating the decision; or

b) an error of fact which has occasioned a miscarriage of justice.

2. The Appeals Chamber may affirm, reverse or revise the decisions taken by the Trial Chambers.

21. Rule 108 provides:

Rule 108

Notice of Appeal

(A)   Subject to Sub-rule (B), a party seeking to appeal a judgement or sentence shall, not more than thirty days from the date on which the judgement or sentence was pronounced, file with the Registrar and serve upon the other parties a written notice of appeal, setting forth the grounds.

(B)   Such delay shall be fixed at fifteen days in case of an appeal from a judgement dismissing an objection based on lack of jurisdiction or a decision rendered under Rule 77 or Rule 91. **[page 10]**

22. Particular reference is made in the Appellant's Brief to Sub-rule 15(A), which provides:

Rule 15

Disqualification of Judges

(A) A Judge may not sit on a trial or appeal in any case in which he has a personal interest or concerning which he has or has had any association which might affect his impartiality. He shall in any such circumstance withdraw from that case. Where the Judge withdraws from the Trial Chamber, the President shall assign another Trial Chamber Judge to sit in his place. Where a Judge withdraws from the Appeals Chamber, the Presiding Judge of that Chamber shall assign another Judge to sit in his place. **[page 11]**

III. DISCUSSION

23.   In the Appellant's Brief, the Prosecutor argues that an appeal from the Decision lies as of right, a contention that is essentially founded on two propositions. Based on a broad reading of Article 24 of the Statute, it is argued that an appeal is allowed in the instant case. It is further submitted that the Appeals Chamber has an inherent right to entertain the appeal.[19] The Appeals Chamber will employ this framework in considering the arguments advanced by the Prosecutor in the Appellant's Brief.

1.   A Liberal Interpretation of Article 24 of the Statute

24.   In support of her first proposition, that Article 24 is sufficiently broad to encompass appeals such as the instant case, the Prosecutor submits that her mandate justifies a liberal reading of Article 24. It is then argued that such a reading would overcome the limitations on the right of appeal contained in the express terms of Article 24. These two elements will be addressed sequentially.

a. A broad reading of Article 24 is justified

25.   The Prosecutor contends that the ICTR Statute must be interpreted liberally in light of its objects and purposes and in accordance with Article 31 of the *Vienna Convention on the Law of Treaties*,[20] such a construction being merited by the context in which the Statute was adopted and the objectives of the

---

[19]   *Supra*, n. 10 at para. 10.
[20]   Vienna Convention on the Law of Treaties, 23 May 1969, 1155 *United Nations Treaty Series* 331.

establishment of the ICTR.[21] It is submitted that the "grave implications" of the Decision on the Prosecutor's ability to discharge her mandate under the Statute jeopardises the achievement of those **[page 12]** objectives and is thus in contradiction to the purposes of the ICTR. It is argued that the Decision thereby constitutes a miscarriage of justice.[22]

26.   The Prosecutor argues, moreover, that Article 1 of the Statute itself supports a broad right of appeal. Article 1 states that the "the ICTR shall have the power to prosecute persons responsible for serious violations of international humanitarian law committed in the territory of Rwanda and Rwandan citizens responsible for such violations committed in the territory of neighbouring States" within the relevant timeframe.[23] The Prosecutor asserts that the term "prosecute" involves not only actions by the Office of the Prosecutor, but also encompasses the activities by the judicial organ of the ICTR, contending that the Appeals Chamber, as an organ of the ICTR, must enjoy "the full complement of jurisdiction conferred on the Tribunal as an institution", except where there is clear expression in the Statute to the contrary.[24]

27.   The Appeals Chamber finds these arguments devoid of merit. The execution of the Prosecutor's mandate is clearly not adversely affected by the Decision, as the Rules provide a variety of remedies to cure the effects of the dismissal of the Indictment. The Appeals Chamber considers that the dismissal of the Indictment is, therefore, not an obstacle to the achievement of the mandate of the ICTR and rejects the contention that it constitutes a miscarriage of justice.

28.   The Appeals Chamber agrees with the Prosecutor on the applicability, *mutatis mutandis*, of the *Vienna Convention on the Law of Treaties* to the Statute. The relevant part of Article 31 reads as follows:

> A treaty shall be interpreted in good faith in accordance with *the ordinary meaning* to be given to the terms of the treaty in their context and in the light of its object and purpose (emphasis added).[25] **[page 13]**

29.   The Appeals Chamber considers that, in the instant case, it is not necessary to engage in an interpretation of the *object and purpose* of the Statute of the ICTR. In the instant case, the Appeals Chamber finds that it cannot abandon the *ordinary meaning of the terms* of those provisions. Rather, it may only interpret them in light of such an ordinary meaning.

30.   With respect to the jurisdiction of the Appeals Chamber, it is axiomatic that the Statute delimits the jurisdiction of the organs of the ICTR. Article 15 of the Statute states that the Prosecutor "shall be responsible for...prosecution" within the terms of Article 1 of the Statute, while Articles 17 and 18 stipulate the procedure for initiating investigations and prosecutions. By the ordinary meaning of the terms in Article 1 of the Statute, therefore, it is the Prosecutor who is charged with responsibility for prosecuting persons charged with criminal offences. Moreover, it is clear from the Statute, *inter alia*, Articles 18 and 19 and 21 through 25, that the involvement of the Trial and Appeals Chambers in prosecutions is limited to an adjudicatory one. The parameters of this function are determined by reference to the aforementioned provisions of the Statute, which are intended to establish a means of balancing the mandate and the discretion of the Prosecutor with the need to ensure respect for the rights of the accused. Although an organ of the ICTR, the Prosecutor is considered to be a party. In relation to the Prosecutor, therefore, the judiciary fulfills a role analogous to the checks and balances necessary to maintain the separation of powers in most national systems. Accordingly, the competence of the Chambers and the Prosecutor form distinct and independent components of the ICTR's jurisdiction under Article 1, rather than encompassing the full ambit of the institution's mandate to prosecute.

31.   In raising this question, the Prosecutor essentially contends that the jurisdiction of the Trial and Appeals Chambers of the ICTR may be construed as being defined by reference to the manner in which

---

[21]   *Supra* n. 10 at paras. 11-13.
[22]   *Ibid.*, at paras. 39-43.
[23]   *Ibid.*, at paras. 44-45.
[24]   *Ibid.*, at paras. 44-50.
[25]   *Supra n. 20*, Article 31 (1).

the Prosecutor elects to discharge her mandate. In addition to finding that it is without legal foundation, the Appeals Chamber is of the view that such a submission deserves further comment. The Appeals Chamber considers that the implication of such a contention can only be that it will have jurisdiction over a matter where such jurisdiction is considered by the Prosecutor to be **[page 14]** necessary to the execution of her statutory functions. The Appeals Chamber finds that such a perception of its competence is not only legally flawed, but places a construction on the relationship between the Chambers and the Prosecutor that offends against the most fundamental principles which guarantee the independence of both organs. Following the establishment of the ICTR by the Security Council of the United Nations, the Prosecutor enjoys sole discretion in the execution of her mandate. Similarly, it is the sole prerogative of the Trial and Appeals Chambers, by applying the Statute and the Rules, to determine the limits of their own competence.

32.   The logical consequence of the interpretation advanced in the Appellant's Brief would be that where the Trial or Appeals Chambers refused to grant any relief requested by the Prosecutor, the Chambers would thereby be obstructing her mandate. Clearly such a proposition is untenable, both in law and in policy. It is axiomatic that justice must be done and must be seen to be done. Thus, a predicate of the effective discharge of the ICTR's mandate is an impartial dispensation of justice. The Prosecutor's construction of the competence of the Chambers, rather than fulfilling that objective, would imperil its very achievement.

33.   The Prosecutor's arguments for a teleological interpretation of the Statute, therefore, do not support such a broad interpretation of Article 24. Nevertheless, in view of the Prosecutor's submissions concerning the critical nature of the Indictment, the Appeals Chamber considers it appropriate to review the contentions concerning that provision.

b.   The present appeal implicitly falls within Article 24 of the Statute

34.   In the view of the Prosecutor, the language of Article 24 provides the Prosecutor with a general right of appeal from decisions of Trial Chambers, such a right being unlimited and unqualified.[26] It is claimed that the general nature of the right **[page 15]** derives from the non-exhaustive phrasing of Article 24,[27] which, it is asserted, is devoid of any language which would qualify the circumstances under which the Prosecutor may appeal decisions originating from the Trial Chamber.[28] Article 24, it is said, provides that the Appeals Chamber may hear appeals against decisions taken by the Trial Chambers from "persons convicted by the Trial Chambers[29] or from "the Prosecutor" *simpliciter*. However, this reading of Article 24, which would grant the Prosecutor an unfettered right of appeal, while that of the accused is limited, would violate the principle of equality of arms. Indeed, the principle of equality of arms requires that the parties enjoy corresponding rights of appeal.

35.   Consistent with this principle, the Appeals Chamber finds that, in the instant case, where the matter affects the right of the accused, the Prosecutor can have no greater power of appeal than accused persons.

36.   While this finding is in itself sufficient to dispose of the Prosecutor's Notice of Appeal, in the interests of justice, the Appeals Chamber will consider the Prosecutor's remaining arguments.

37.   Following the argument that Article 24 of the Statute grants an unlimited right of appeal, the Prosecutor construes the terms of that provision as implicitly allowing an appeal in the instant case. It is argued that a dismissal of an indictment under Rule 47 constitutes a final decision within the meaning of Article 24, as the Decision, by placing in peril the Prosecutor's strategy for the achievement of her mandate, has an effect analogous to a decision finally disposing of a matter. In the view of the Appeals

---

26   *Supra n. 10* at paras. 16, 17.
27   *Ibid.*, at para. 21.
28   *Ibid.*, at paras. 14 - 18.
29   *Ibid.*, at para. 28.

Chamber, however, the Rules provide ample recourse for the Prosecutor. Accordingly, the Appeals Chamber finds the Prosecutor's argument in this regard to be unfounded.

38.   Further, the Prosecutor argues that a single judge is subject to the jurisdiction of the Appeals Chamber in the same manner as Trial Chambers, and that, therefore, **[page 16]** decisions of a single judge may be appealed under Article 24.[30] The Prosecutor argues that under Articles 10 and 18 of the Statute, a single judge is an integral part of the Trial Chamber and that the Rules implicitly envisage appeals from decisions of a single judge, as they provide that Trial Chambers and single judges shall have concurrent jurisdiction in certain circumstances.[31] While it is true that a single judge acting under Article 18 of the Statute and Rule 47 is always a member of a Trial Chamber, he is not acting as such during the review proceedings under these provisions. Rather, he is acting solely in his own capacity as a confirming judge.

39.   The Prosecutor contends, moreover, that the ICTR and the International Criminal Tribunal for former Yugoslavia ("ICTY") have expanded the scope of appellate jurisdiction beyond that expressly conferred by the Statute of either Tribunal. The Prosecutor cites Sub-rule 72(B)(ii) of the ICTY Rules which provides for appeals against decisions on preliminary motions other than those based on lack of jurisdiction[32] and Sub-Rule 73(B) which provides for appeals against decisions on motions other than preliminary motions.[33]Such Rules, however, do not appear in the ICTR Rules. It is obvious that the Appeals Chamber of the ICTR can apply only the Rules of the ICTR.

40.   It is further argued in the Appellant's Brief that this is a general trend of adopting Rules concerning appellate jurisdiction which is consistent with developments in international law that assertedly grant a right of appeal against decisions which raise questions of jurisdiction or of admissibility.[34] The Prosecutor contends that the Decision, by declining jurisdiction, raises such a question and should, therefore, be appealable. All of the examples cited by the Prosecutor, however, allow an appeal by both parties. Indeed, the Appeals Chamber notes that even in the proposed provision of the Draft Statute for the International Criminal Court[35] relating to appeal from the confirmation or the denial of an indictment, the introductory paragraph stipulates that **[page 17]** *"either party* may appeal any of the following interlocutory decisions" (emphasis added). Moreover, the Prosecutor's reliance on this particular example should be viewed in the overall context of that provision, which is merely a draft proposal.

41.   Even if this was not sufficiently compelling to dispose of this leg of the Prosecutor's argument, the Appeals Chamber would refer to its earlier findings that the ICTR Rules contain provisions to cure any perceived adverse effects of the Decision on the Prosecutor.

42.   Notwithstanding its finding that no appeal lies in this matter, the Appeals Chamber considers that to interpret Article 24 of the Statute in a manner consistent with the submissions of the Prosecutor would broaden the scope of the right of the Prosecutor to appeal to a dimension that was not envisaged by the drafters of the Statute or the Rules. Accordingly, the Chamber rejects the Prosecutor's proposition that the present appeal would lie under a broad construction of Article 24 of the Statute.

2.   *An Inherent Right of Appeal*

43.   The Prosecutor's alternative argument, that the appeal may be entertained pursuant to an inherent right of appeal, is founded on two contentions.

---

[30]   *Ibid.*, at paras 41, 42.
[31]   *Ibid.*, at paras. 24-26.
[32]   *Ibid.*, at para. 33.
[33]   Ibid., para. 36.
[34]   *Ibid.*, at para. 37.
[35]   Proposed Article 73 bis, Draft Statute for the International Criminal Court, cited as A/AC.249/1998/CRP.14, 1 April 1998 (excerpts), Cited in *Ibid.*, at para. 37.

a. What is not prohibited is permitted

44.   The Prosecutor asserts that there are no provisions in the Statute or Rules which preclude an appeal against the Decision. In her view, Article 24 does not exclude appeals which fall outside of the express provisions of its text, as "nothing in the Statute or the Rules expressly excludes the jurisdiction of the Appeals Chamber to **[page 18]** hear such an appeal."[36] In support of this thesis, the Prosecutor asserts that there is established in the practice of international courts and tribunals a principle that "what is not specifically prevented by the rules may be applied by the Court".[37] Thus, it is argued, where the ICTR Statute is silent, with respect to a particular competence, such competence may, nevertheless, be exercised.

45.   The Appeals Chamber regards as unhelpful the reliance by the Prosecutor upon this principle. Clearly, the ICTR may apply what is not specifically prohibited by the Rules only where this would be consistent with the objects and purposes of the Statute. Such is not a circumstance presented by the instant appeal.

b. The practice of courts in national jurisdictions

46.   The Prosecutor submits that an inherent right of appeal may be founded on the practice of courts in national jurisdictions. It is argued that a survey of national law indicates the existence of a general principle of law that, in the absence of an express provision to the contrary, a right of appeal generally lies from the decisions of a lower court.[38] The Prosecutor cites provisions from the Codes of Criminal Procedure of the civil law jurisdictions of France, Senegal and Germany, where decisions of lower courts dismissing an indictment may always be appealed to a superior court,[39] and the remedies of *mandamus* and *certiorari* in the common law jurisdictions of the United States and the United Kingdom.[40]

47.   In the view of the Prosecutor, the Appeals Chamber may extrapolate an analogue of such rules to find jurisdiction in the instant appeal. The Prosecutor argues that general principles of law may be applied by international courts, citing, *inter alia,* **[page 19]** Article 38 of the Statute of the International Court of Justice and the jurisprudence of the ICTY.[41]

48.   The Appeals Chamber notes, however, that each of the rules cited by the Prosecutor is based on an explicit statutory provision in the national jurisdiction concerned. The Appeals Chamber, therefore, finds them inapplicable in the instant matter.

49.   The *obiter dicta* of Judge Sidhwa in his Separate Opinion on the Defence Motion for Interlocutory Appeal on Jurisdiction in the *Tadić* case are instructive, but not dispositive, in respect of the Prosecutor's overall assertion of her inherent right of appeal. Judge Sidhwa stated:

> "The law relating to appeals in most national jurisdictions is that no appeal lies unless conferred by statute. The right to appeal a decision is part of substantive law and can only be granted by the law-making body by specific enactment. Where the provision for an appeal or some form of review by a higher forum is not regulated by the statute under which an order is passed, there is usually some omnibus statute providing for appeals in such cases. The courts have no inherent powers to create appellate provisions or acquire jurisdiction where none is granted."[42]

---

[36]   *Ibid.*, at para. 42.
[37]   *Ibid.*, at para. 32, citing Application of the Genocide Convention (Provisional Measures) Order of 13 September 1993, (1993) *I.C.J. Reports,* at p. 396, and *Corfu Channel Case* (Preliminary Objection), (1948), *I.C.J. Reports,* at p.28.
[38]   *Ibid.*, at para. 51.
[39]   *Ibid.*, at paras. 53-57.
[40]   *Ibid.*
[41]   *Ibid.*, at paras. 59-62.
[42]   Separate Opinion of Judge Sidhwa on the Defence Motion for Interlocutory Appeal on Jurisdiction, *The Prosecutor v. Dusko Tadić,* Case No. IT-94-1-AR72, 2 October 1995, para. 6

50. The Appeals Chamber finds that the contentions of the Prosecutor, which would allow her the sole right of appeal, do not establish that it is competent to assert an inherent power of jurisdiction for this Notice of Appeal.

51. In addition to its findings on the substantive arguments concerning Article 24 that are adduced by the Prosecutor, the Appeals Chamber finds that the other principal provision relied upon by the Prosecutor in submitting her Notice of Appeal, Rule 108, does not apply in the case at issue. Rule 108 prescribes only the time-limit for the filing of a Notice of Appeal; it does not create a right of appeal. Moreover, it addresses **[page 20]** specific situations, namely where a party is seeking to appeal a "judgement or sentence" or "a judgement dismissing an objection based on lack of jurisdiction or a decision rendered under Rule 77 or Rule 91". Rule 108 does not apply to a decision of a single judge acting under Rule 47.

52. In concluding her submissions in the Appellant Brief, the Prosecutor argues that the Appeals Chamber is the correct forum to hear the present appeal, referring to Article 24 of the Statute and Part Six (Rules 73 – 106) and Sub-Rule 15(A) of the Rules. Considering its findings, the Appeals Chamber considers it unnecessary to address these contentions.

53. The Appeals Chamber, thus, rejects the Prosecutor's application for leave to appeal the Decision. **[page 21]**

IV. DISPOSITION

THE APPEALS CHAMBER, for the foregoing reasons, unanimously;

REJECTS the Prosecutor's Notice of Appeal from Judge Khan's Decision dismissing the Indictment against Théoneste Bagosora and 28 others,

REJECTS the motions filed, respectively by the accused Anatole Nsengiyumva and the accused Théoneste Bagosora, there being no ground to further consider the said motions.

Done in English and French, the English text being authoritative.

Gabrielle Kirk McDonald
Presiding Judge

Judge Shahabuddeen appends a Declaration to this Decision.

Dated this eighth day of June 1998,

At Arusha,

Tanzania

International Criminal Tribunal for the Prosecution of Persons Responsible for Genocide and Other Serious Violations of International Humanitarian Law Committed in the Territory of Rwanda and Rwandan Citizens responsible for genocide and other such violations committed in the territory of neighbouring States between 1 January and 31 December 1994	Case No.: ICTR-98-37-A Date: 8 June 1998 Original: English

IN THE APPEALS CHAMBER

Before: **Judge Gabrielle Kirk McDonald (Presiding)**
             Judge Mohamed Shahabuddeen
             Judge Lal Chand Vohrah
             Judge Wang Tieya
             Judge Rafael Nieto-Navia

Registrar: Mr. Agwu U. Okali

Decision of: **8 June 1998**

PROSECUTOR

v.

THÉONESTE BAGOSORA AND 28 OTHERS

DECLARATION OF JUDGE MOHAMED SHAHABUDDEEN ON THE ADMISSIBILITY OF THE PROSECUTOR'S APPEAL FROM THE DECISION OF A CONFIRMING JUDGE DISMISSING AN INDICTMENT AGAINST THÉONESTE BAGOSORA AND 28 OTHERS

The Prosecutor:
    Louise Arbour
    Bernard A. Muna

[page 2] My reason, which I think is sufficient, for agreeing with the decision to reject the Prosecutor's Notice of Appeal is that, as a matter of construction, Article 24 of the Statute does not, in my opinion, visualise an appeal being made when there is no case in existence between the Prosecutor and an accused. The Decision of the Reviewing Judge, which is sought to be appealed from, was not made in such a case; it was concerned with the prior question whether there should be such a case.

Done in English and French, the English version being authoritative.

Judge Mohamed Shahabuddeen

Dated this eighth day of June 1998,

At Arusha,

Tanzania

International Criminal Tribunal for the Prosecution of Persons Responsible for Genocide and Other Serious Violations of International Humanitarian Law Committed in the Territory of Rwanda and Rwandan Citizens responsible for genocide and other such violations committed in the territory of neighbouring States between 1 January and 31 December 1994	Case No.:	ICTR-96-12-A
	Date:	3 June 1999
	Original:	English

IN THE APPEALS CHAMBER

Before: Judge Gabrielle Kirk McDonald, Presiding
            Judge Mohamed Shahabuddeen
            Judge Lal Chand Vohrah
            Judge Wang Tieya
            Judge Rafael Nieto-Navia

Registrar: Mr. Agwu U. Okali

Decision of: 3 June 1999

ANATOLE NSENGIYUMVA

v.

THE PROSECUTOR

_____

DECISION ON APPEAL AGAINST ORAL DECISION OF TRIAL CHAMBER II OF 28 SEPTEMBER 1998

_____

Counsel for the Appellant:
    Mr. Kennedy Ogetto
    Mr. Gershom Otachi Bw'oamwa

The Office of the Prosecutor:
    Mr. David Spencer
    Mr. Frédéric Ossogo
    Mr. Chile Eboe-Osuji
    Mr. Luc Cote
    Ms. Josee D'aoust

[page 2] I. INTRODUCTION

1.   The Appeals Chamber of the International Criminal Tribunal for the Prosecution of Persons Responsible for Genocide and Other Serious Violations of International Humanitarian Law Committed in the Territory of Rwanda and Rwandan Citizens Responsible for Genocide and Other Such Violations Committed in the Territory of Neighbouring States, between 1 January 1994 and 31 December 1994 ("the International Tribunal") is seized of an appeal lodged by Defence Counsel for the accused Anatole Nsengiyumva ("the Appellant") against an oral decision rendered by Trial Chamber II composed of Judge Sekule (Presiding), Judge Kama and Judge Khan on 28 September 1998 ("the Decision").[1] By the Decision, Trial Chamber II denied the Appellant's motion contesting the jurisdiction of that Trial Chamber to hear the Prosecutor's Request for Leave to file an Amended Indictment ("the Leave Request") in respect of the Appellant and the Prosecutor's Motion for Joinder, which proposed to join the Appellant with three other accused ("the Joinder Motion").

2.   Anatole Nsengiyumva was arrested in Cameroon on 27 March 1996 and Judge Ostrovsky confirmed the indictment against him on 12 July 1996.[2] Anatole Nsengiyumva was transferred to the International Tribunal's detention unit on 23 January 1997 and made his initial appearance on 19 February 1997 before Trial Chamber I, composed of Judge Kama (Presiding), Judge Sekule and Judge Pillay. The Appellant submits in this appeal that Trial Chamber I has exclusive jurisdiction over his case and that the composition of a Trial Chamber cannot be altered. The President of the International Tribunal, acting pursuant to Article 13 of the Statute of the International Tribunal ("the Statute"), assigned Judge Sekule (Presiding), Judge Kama and Judge Khan to Trial Chamber II, which became seized of the Leave Request and the Joinder Motion both of which were filed on 31 July 1998. Both motions were set down to be heard on 28 September 1998 before Trial Chamber II. At this hearing, the Appellant contested the Trial Chamber's competence to hear the Leave Request and the Joinder Motion, on the grounds that his case had all along been before Trial Chamber I and that, in any event, the re-composition of Trial Chamber II was unlawful. **[page 3]**

3.   Subsequent to the oral dismissal by Trial Chamber II of the Appellant's objection to that Trial Chamber's competence, the Appellant filed a Notice of Appeal on 5 October 1998, entitled "Notice of Appeal (Article 24 Rule 108)". This Notice of Appeal was followed by the "Prosecutor's Response and Challenge to the Admissibility of the Accused's Notice of Appeal" and the "Motion in Appeal on Jurisdiction, Prosecutor's Motion for an Expedited Appeal Procedure Pursuant to Articles 14 and 28(2) of the *Statute* of the ICTR and Rules 117 and 108 of the *Rules of Procedure and Evidence* as Amended", filed on 21 October 1998.

4.   Thereafter, the Appeals Chamber directed the parties to submit written briefs within the time-limit indicated in a Scheduling Order of 18 December 1998. The Appellant filed his "Brief Submitted in Accordance With the Order of the Appeals Chamber Made on 18th December 1998" on 31 December 1998. The English translation of the Prosecutor's Brief was filed on 3 March 1999 and carries the title "Supplementary Brief in Reply by the Prosecutor Regarding the Admissibility of the Notice of Appeal Filed by the Accused Anatole Nsengiyumva Against the Decision of Trial Chamber II Rendered on 28 September 1998 on the Request for Leave to Amend Indictment and Motion for Joinder of the Accused".

II. The Appeal

A. The Appellant

5.   The Appellant requests that the Appeals Chamber provide appropriate relief by 1) quashing the Decision; 2) declaring Trial Chamber II, composed of Judge Sekule, Judge Kama and Judge Khan, to be without jurisdiction to entertain the Leave Request and the Joinder Motion; and 3) remitting the matter to

---

[1]   Transcripts of motion hearing on 28 Sept. 1998 in the case of, *inter alia*, Prosecutor v. Nsengiyumva, Case No.: ICTR-96-12-I, p. 32.

[2]   *Indictment*, Prosecutor v. Nsengiyumva, Case No.: ICTR-96-12-I.

Trial Chamber I "duly constituted".[3] The grounds of appeal invoked by the Appellant can be summarised as follows. The Appellant argues that Trial Chamber II lacks jurisdiction over his case, and consequently the appeal is from an objection based on lack of jurisdiction within the meaning of Sub-rule 72(D) of the **[page 4]** Rules of Procedure and Evidence ("the Rules"). He contends that it follows from Article 13 of the Statute that the composition of the two Trial Chambers cannot be altered. Only Trial Chamber I, composed of Judge Kama, Judge Aspegren and Judge Pillay, and Trial Chamber II, composed of Judge Sekule, Judge Khan and Judge Ostrovsky, constitute the proper Trial Chambers of the Tribunal, to which the jurisdiction to hear cases belongs exclusively. Consequently, Trial Chamber II was not lawfully composed and is not competent to conduct proceedings in any case.[4]

6.   As a second ground of appeal, the Appellant argues that pursuant to Article 19 of the Statute and Sub-rule 50(A) of the Rules, the Trial Chamber before which an accused enters a plea has exclusive jurisdiction to hear his case and that the entering of a plea is a stage which marks the commencement of trial. In consequence, after an accused has pleaded before a Trial Chamber, his case cannot be transferred to another Trial Chamber. Trial Chamber II, therefore, is not competent to hear the Leave Request and the Joinder Motion, even if it is considered to have been lawfully composed.[5]

B. The Prosecution

7. In response, the Prosecution asks that the Appeals Chamber reject the appeal since no right of appeal lies from the Decision. In the event the Appeals Chamber finds the appeal to be admissible, the Prosecution requests that it dismiss the appeal and confirm the competence of Trial Chamber II to hear the Leave Request and the Joinder Motion. The main submissions of the Prosecution may be summarised as follows. The Prosecutor submits that the elements relating to the jurisdiction of the Tribunal are set out in Articles 1 to 7 of the Statute, all of which apply to the Tribunal as a whole and are not restricted to the separate Trial Chambers. In this regard, the Prosecutor argues that neither the Statute nor the Rules make the assignment of a case to a Trial Chamber or the composition of a Trial Chamber a jurisdictional issue. Hence, the subject-matter of the appeal does not involve a question of jurisdiction but one of procedure.[6] **[page 5]**

8.   The Prosecutor is of the view that even if the question submitted for review were one of jurisdiction, there is nevertheless no merit to the appeal given that Article 13 of the Statute enables the President to assign and reassign judges to the Trial Chambers as the administration of justice requires.[7] Moreover, as evidenced by an analysis of Article 19 of the Statute and, *inter alia*, Rules 62, 66, 67, Sub-rule 69(C) and Rule 73*bis* of the Rules, the proceedings before the Tribunal involve different stages, specifically pre-trial, trial and appeal, and trial does not commence at the time of entering a plea.[8] However, even if trials were deemed to commence upon the entering of a plea, the rule against changing the composition of a Trial Chamber does not come into operation until the commencement of the presentation of evidence on the merits of the case.[9]

III. Applicable Provisions

9.   The relevant parts of the applicable provisions of the Statute and the Rules are set out below.

---

[3]   Brief Submitted in Accordance with the Order of the Appeals Chamber Made on 18th December 1998 ("Appellant's Brief"), p. 21.

[4]   *Ibid.*, paras. 6 to 9.

[5]   *Ibid.*, paras. 10 to 13.

[6]   Prosecutor's Response and Challenge to the Admissibility of the Accused's Notice of Appeal, paras. 14 to 18.

[7]   *Ibid.*, para. 59.

[8]   *Ibid.*, paras. 38 to 47.

[9]   *Ibid.*, paras. 50 to 56.

A. The Statute

Article 10
Organisation of the International Tribunal for Rwanda

The International Tribunal for Rwanda shall consist of the following organs:

a) The Chambers, comprising three Trial Chambers and an Appeals Chamber;
b) The Prosecutor;
c) A Registry.

Article 11
Composition of the Chambers [page 6]

Chambers shall be composed of fourteen independent judges, no two of whom may be nationals of the same State, who shall serve as follows:

a) Three judges shall serve in each of the Trial Chambers:
b) Five judges shall serve in the Appeals Chamber.

Article 13
Officers and members of the Chambers

1. The Judges of the International Tribunal for Rwanda shall elect a President.
2. After consultation with the judges of the International Tribunal for Rwanda, the President shall assign the judges to the Trial Chambers. A judge shall serve only in the Chamber to which he or she was assigned.
3. The judges of each Trial Chamber shall elect a Presiding Judge, who shall conduct all of the proceedings of that Trial Chamber as a whole.

Article 14
Rules of procedure and evidence

The Judges of the International Tribunal for Rwanda shall adopt, for the purpose of proceedings before the International Tribunal for Rwanda, the rules of procedure and evidence for the conduct of the pre-trial phase of the proceedings, trials and appeals, the admission of evidence, the protection of victims and witnesses and other appropriate matters of the International Tribunal for Rwanda with such changes as they deem necessary.

Article 19
Commencement and Conduct of Trial Proceedings

1. [...]

2. [...]

3. The Trial Chamber shall read the Indictment, satisfy itself that the rights of the accused are respected, confirm that the accused understands the Indictment, and instruct the accused to enter a plea. The Trial Chamber shall then set a date for trial.

4. [...] [page 7]

Appellate Proceedings

1. The Appeals Chamber shall hear appeals from persons convicted by the Trial Chambers or from the Prosecutor on the following grounds:

a) An error on a question of law invalidating the decision, or
b) An error of fact which has occasioned a miscarriage of justice.

2. The Appeals Chamber may affirm, reverse or revise the decisions taken by the Trial Chambers.

B. The Rules

Rule 15
Disqualification of Judges

(A) A Judge may not sit at a trial or appeal in any case, in which he has a personal interest or concerning which he has or has had any association, which might affect his impartiality. He shall in any such circumstance withdraw from that case. Where the Judge withdraws from the Trial Chamber, the President shall assign another Trial Chamber Judge to sit in his place. Where a Judge withdraws from the Appeals Chamber, the Presiding Judge of that Chamber shall assign another Judge to sit in his place.

(B) Any party may apply to the Presiding Judge of a Chamber for the disqualification of a Judge of that Chamber from a trial or appeal upon the above grounds. After the Presiding Judge has conferred with the Judge in question, the Bureau if necessary, shall determine the matter. If the Bureau upholds the application, the President shall assign another Judge to sit in place of the disqualified Judge.

(C) The Judge of a Trial Chamber who reviews an indictment against an accused, pursuant to Article 18 of the Statute and Rules 47 and 61, shall not sit as a member of the Trial Chamber for the trial of that accused.

(D) [...]

(E) If a Judge is, for any reason, unable to continue sitting in a part-heard case, the Presiding Judge may, if that inability seems likely to be of short duration, adjourn the proceedings, otherwise he shall report to the President who may assign another Judge to the case and order either a rehearing or continuation of the proceedings from that point.

However, after the opening statements provided for in Rule 84, or the beginning of the presentation of evidence pursuant to Rule 85, the continuation of the proceedings can only be ordered with the consent of the accused. **[page 8]**

(F) In case of illness or an unfilled vacancy or in any other exceptional circumstances, the President may authorise a Chamber to conduct routine matters, such as the delivery of decisions, in the absence of one or more members.

Rule 19
Functions of the President

The President shall preside at all plenary meetings of the Tribunal, co-ordinate the work of the Chambers and supervise the activities of the Registry as well as the exercise of all the other functions conferred on him by the Statute and the Rules.

Rule 27
Rotation of the Judges

(A) Judges shall rotate on a regular basis between the Trial Chambers. Rotation shall take into account the efficient disposal of cases.

(B) The Judges shall take their places in their assigned Chamber as soon as the President thinks it convenient, having regard to the disposal of pending cases.

(C) The President may at any time temporarily assign a member of one Trial Chamber to another Trial Chamber.

Rule 48
Joinder of Accused

Persons accused of the same or different crimes committed in the course of the same transaction may be jointly charged and tried.

Rule 50
Amendment of Indictment

(A) The Prosecutor may amend an indictment, without prior leave, at any time before its confirmation, but thereafter, until the initial appearance of the accused before a Trial Chamber pursuant to Rule 62, only with leave of the Judge who confirmed it but, in exceptional circumstances, by leave of a Judge assigned by the President. At or after such initial appearance, an amendment of an indictment may only be made by leave granted by that Trial Chamber pursuant to Rule 73. If leave to amend is granted, Rule 47(G) and Rule 53*bis* apply *mutatis mutandis* to the amended indictment. **[page 9]**

(B) [...]

(C) [...]

Rule 62
Initial Appearance of Accused

Upon his transfer to the Tribunal, the accused shall be brought before a Trial Chamber without delay, and shall be formally charged. The Trial Chamber shall:

(i) [...]

(ii) [...]

(iii) [...]

(iv) in the case of a plea of not guilty, instruct the Registrar to set a date for trial;

(v) [...]

(vi) [...]

Rule 72
Preliminary Motions

(A) Preliminary motions by either party shall be brought within sixty days following disclosure by the Prosecutor to the Defence of all the material envisaged by Rule 66(A)(I), and in any case before the hearing on the merits.

(B) Preliminary motions by the accused are:

i) objections based on lack of jurisdiction
ii) objections based on defects in the form of the indictment;
iii) applications for severance of crimes joined in one indictment under Rule 49, or for separate trials under Rule 82(B)
iv) objections based on the denial of request for assignment of counsel.

The Trial Chamber shall dispose of preliminary motions *in limine litis.*

(C) Decisions on preliminary motions are without interlocutory appeal save in the case of dismissal of an objection based on lack of jurisdiction, where an appeal will lie as a matter of right.

(D) Notice of appeal envisaged in Sub-rule (D) shall be filed within seven days from the impugned decision. **[page 10]**

(E) Failure to comply with the time limits prescribed in this Rule shall constitute a waiver of the rights. The Trial Chamber may, however, grant relief from the waiver upon showing good cause.

Rule 117
Expedited Appeals Procedure

(A)   An appeal under Rule 108(B) shall be heard expeditiously on the basis of the original record of the Trial Chamber and without the necessity of any brief.

(B)   All delays and other procedural requirements shall be fixed by an order of the President issued on an application by one of the parties, or *proprio motu* should no such application have been made within fifteen days after the filing of the notice of appeal.

(C)   Rules 109 to 114 shall not apply to such appeals. **[page 11]**

IV. DISCUSSION

10.   In answering the main questions which have been raised by the present appeal, namely, whether a right of appeal lies from the Decision, and if so, whether Trial Chamber II was competent to hear the Leave Request and the Joinder Motion, the members of the Appeals Chamber differ on a number of issues both as to reasoning and as to result. Consequently, the views of each member of the Appeals Chamber on the particular issues are set out in detail in Opinions appended to this decision.

11.   The Appeals Chamber, for the reasons set out in the Joint and Separate Opinion of Judge McDonald and Judge Vohrah, and, in part, the Joint Separate and Concurring Opinion of Judge Wang and Judge Nieto-Navia and, also in part, the Dissenting Opinion of Judge Shahabuddeen, finds that the appeal is admissible since a right of appeal lies from the Decision pursuant to Sub-rule 72(D) of the Rules.

12.   The Appeals Chamber, for the reasons set out in the Joint and Separate Opinion of Judge McDonald and Judge Vohrah and the Joint Separate and Concurring Opinion of Judge Wang and Judge Nieto-Navia, finds that based on a textual interpretation of Sub-rule 50(A), Trial Chamber I is the only Trial Chamber competent to adjudicate the Leave Request. Judge Shahabuddeen reserves his views, considering that on this point the appeal is not admissible.

13.   The Appeals Chamber, for the reasons set out in the Joint and Separate Opinion of Judge McDonald and Judge Vohrah, the Joint Separate and Concurring Opinion of Judge Wang and Judge Nieto-Navia and the Dissenting Opinion of Judge Shahabuddeen, finds that Trial Chamber II is competent to adjudicate the Joinder Motion.

14.   Accordingly, the Appeals Chamber, by majority, finds that the appeal should be allowed in respect of the Leave Request and, unanimously, finds that the appeal should be dismissed in respect of the Joinder Motion. **[page 12]**

IV. DISPOSITION

THE APPEALS CHAMBER, by a majority of four to one, with Judge Shahabuddeen dissenting, **ALLOWS** the Appeal relating to the Leave Request, and **REMITS** it to Trial Chamber I. **THE APPEALS CHAMBER UNANIMOUSLY DISMISSES** the appeal relating to the Joinder Motion.

Done in both English and French, the English text being authoritative.

Gabrielle Kirk McDonald

Presiding Judge

Judge McDonald and Judge Vohrah append a Joint and Separate Opinion.

Judge Wang and Judge Nieto-Navia append a Joint Separate and Concurring Opinion.

Judge Shahabuddeen appends a Dissenting Opinion.

Dated this third day of June 1999

At Arusha

Tanzania

International Criminal Tribunal for the
Prosecution of Persons Responsible for
Genocide and Other Serious Violations of
International Humanitarian Law Committed
in the Territory of Rwanda and Rwandan
Citizens responsible for genocide and other
such violations committed in the territory of
neighbouring States between 1 January and
31 December 1994

Case No.:   ICTR-96-12-A

Date: 3 June 1999

Original: English

IN THE APPEALS CHAMBER

Before: **Judge Gabrielle Kirk McDonald, Presiding**
                Judge Mohamed Shahabuddeen
                Judge Lal Chand Vohrah
                Judge Wang Tieya
                Judge Rafael Nieto-Navia

Registrar: **Mr. Agwu U. Okali**

Decision of: **3 June 1999**

ANATOLE NSENGIYUMVA

v.

THE PROSECUTOR

JOINT AND SEPARATE OPINION OF JUDGE McDONALD AND JUDGE VOHRAH

Counsel for the Appellant:
    Mr. Kennedy Ogetto
    Mr. Gershom Otachi Bw'oamwa

The Office of the Prosecutor:
    Mr. David Spencer
    Mr. Frédéric Ossogo
    Mr. Chile Eboe-Osuji
    Mr. Luc Cote
    Ms. Josee D'aoust

(*)   Editors'note: the editors have incorporated in this separate opinion the corrigendum of 4 June 1999 (Joint and
        Separate Opinion of Judge McDonald and Judge Vohrah/Corr., *Nsengiyumva v. Prosecutor*, Case No. ICTR-
        96-12-A, A.Ch., 4 June 1999)

[page 2] I. INTRODUCTION

1.   The preliminary question which has to be decided in this appeal is whether a right of appeal lies from the Decision. If so, the issue of whether Trial Chamber II is competent to adjudicate the Leave Request and the Joinder Motion would have to be resolved, necessitating a discussion concerning the circumstances under which a Trial Chamber may be re-composed and to what extent, if any, the Trial Chamber that conducts the initial appearance of an accused has exclusive jurisdiction over his case.

II. DISCUSSION

A. Is the appeal from a dismissal of an objection based on lack of jurisdiction within the meaning of Sub-rule 72(D)

2.   In the Scheduling Order of 18 December 1998,[1] the Appeals Chamber directed the parties to submit briefs on the following issues: (a) Whether the appeal is from dismissal of an objection based on lack of jurisdiction within the meaning of Sub-rule 72(D); and (b) if it is: (i) whether the Trial Chamber is competent to hear the Prosecutor's applications; and (ii) is so, whether the Trial Chamber was lawfully composed.

3.   Sub-rule 72(D) provides that preliminary motions are without interlocutory appeal except in the case of dismissal of an objection based on lack of jurisdiction. In the appeal, the jurisdiction of Trial Chamber II to hear the Leave Request and the Joinder Motion is challenged. Having had his initial appearance before Trial Chamber I, the Appellant objects to the competence of any Trial Chamber other than Trial Chamber I to consider the Leave Request and the Joinder Motion on the grounds that the composition of the Trial Chambers cannot be altered and that cases cannot be transferred from one Trial Chamber to another.

4.   The challenge to the competence of Trial Chamber II to entertain the Leave Request and the Joinder Motion raises the issue as to whether the dismissal of the Appellant's objection to the exercise of its jurisdiction is appealable pursuant to Sub-rule 72(D), and whether Trial [page 3] Chamber II, as re-composed, has jurisdiction to adjudicate the Leave Request and the Joinder Motion.

5.   The jurisdiction of a tribunal concerns its right and power to hear to determine a judicial proceeding. Articles 1 through 7 of the Statute establish the competence of the International Tribunal as a whole, with respect to subject-matter, personal, territorial and temporal (*ratione materiae, ratione personae, ratione loci* and *ratione temporis*) jurisdiction. However, the jurisdiction of the Tribunal is exercised by the Trial Chambers. Consequently, if the competence and the legality of the composition of a Trial Chamber are challenged, it raises the issue of the power of that Trial Chamber to exercise the jurisdiction that the Tribunal possesses.

6.   Since we hold that the appeal relates to a dismissal of an objection based on lack of jurisdiction within the meaning of Sub-rule 72(D), the next issue to be addressed is whether Trial Chamber II was lawfully constituted and thus competent to exercise jurisdiction.

B. Whether Trial Chamber II was unlawfully constituted, and was, therefore, not competent to exercise jurisdiction

7.   The first issue is whether Trial Chamber II as re-composed is competent to decide the Leave Request and the Joinder Motion. A determination of this issue requires an evaluation of the procedural background of the Leave Request and the Joinder Motion.

8.   Relying on evidence freshly discovered in July 1997, pointing to a conspiracy involving the Appellant and other accused, the Prosecutor submitted on 6 March 1998, an indictment before Judge

---

[1]   *Scheduling Order, Prosecutor v. Nsengiyumva*, Case No.: ICTR 96-12-I, App. Ch., 18 Dec. 1998.

Khan for review. In that indictment, the Prosecutor charged twenty-nine individuals with offences substantially related to the same facts. On 31 March 1998, Judge Khan conducted *ex parte* proceedings under Rule 47 and divided the twenty-nine accused into three groups. The first group, consisting of eleven persons including the Appellant, had already been previously indicted and entered pleas at their initial appearances. The second group of five persons had been previously indicted but remained at liberty. The third group consisted of thirteen persons who had not been indicted and who were at liberty. **[page 4]** In the indictment, the Prosecutor had added a new charge of conspiracy against persons in the first and second groups. The learned Judge rejected the Prosecutor's submission that the indictment should be reviewed under the *ex parte* provision of Rule 47 of the Rules. He held that the Prosecutor must first seek leave to amend the original indictments under Rule 50 of the Rules with respect to the persons in the first and second groups, or to withdraw these persons from the indictment and resubmit the indictment, or to follow the procedure in Rule 72 governing preliminary motions.[2] In the event, Judge Khan declined to exercise jurisdiction over all the three groups of persons, having regard especially to the rights of the accused, and accordingly he dismissed the indictment.[3]

9.   On 6 April 1998, the Prosecutor appealed against Judge Khan's decision pursuant to Rule 108 of the Rules setting forth various grounds of appeal. On 8 June 1998, this Appeals Chamber rejected the Prosecutor's Application for Leave to Appeal, finding that a right of appeal did not lie from Judge Khan's decision under the Statute and the Rules.[4]

10.   Consequently, the Prosecutor proceeded on four separate original indictments against the following four accused; Anatole Nsengiyumva; Theoneste Bagosora; Gratien Kabiligi; and Aloys Ntabakuze. Pursuant to Rule 50 of the Rules, the Prosecutor sought leave to amend the respective indictments for the purposes of (i) adding new charges against the Appellant; (ii) expanding certain existing counts; (iii) adding relevant counts to the allegations; and (iv) bringing the present indictments into conformity with the jurisprudence of the Tribunal and current trial practices.[5] Through another motion, the Prosecutor also sought to join the four accused in one and the same case.[6] The discussion as to which Trial Chamber is to consider the Leave Request and, if granted, which Trial Chamber is to rule on the Joinder Motion is dealt with hereafter. **[page 5]**

11.   The Appellant contends that Article 13 of the Statute prohibits the alteration of the composition of the Trial Chambers. A close reading of the Rules and the Statute, however, does not support this contention. Pursuant to Rule 19, the President is directed to coordinate the work of the Chambers. Sub-rule 27(A) provides for the rotation of Judges while taking into account the efficient disposal of cases. Rule 27(B) allows the President to assign Judges to particular Trial Chambers, having regard to the disposal of pending cases, while Sub-rule 27(C) allows for the temporary assignment of a Judge from one Trial Chamber to another Trial Chamber. Sub-rule 15(E) allows the President to assign another Judge to a case if one of the originally assigned Judges is unable, for any reason, to continue sitting in a part-heard case.

12.   These Rules fully comport with the Statute, which as the Tribunal's constitutive document, sets forth the fundamental structure of the institution and addresses the important administrative criteria for the Tribunal's proper functioning. Articles 10, 11 and 13 explain the basic organisation of the Tribunal, the composition of the Chambers, and the means by which officers and members of the Chambers are selected. Article 10 provides that the Tribunal shall be comprised of three organs, including the Trial and Appeals Chambers. Article 11, subparagraph (A), provides that the Trial Chamber shall consist of three Judges. The plain meaning of this provision is that a Trial Chambers is only competent if it comprised

---

[2]   *Dismissal of Indictment,* <u>Prosecutor v. Bagosora and 28 Others</u>, Case No.: ICTR-98-97-I, 31 March 1998, at p.6.
[3]   *Ibid.,* at p. 12.
[4]   *Decision on the Admissibility of the Prosecutor's Appeal from the Decision of a Confirming Judge Dismissing an Indictment Against Theoneste Bagosoro and 28 Others,* <u>Prosecutor v. Bagosora and 28 Others</u>, Case No.: ICTR-98-37-A, 8 June 1998.
[5]   *Prosecutor's Request for Leave to File an Amended Indictment and Brief in Support of Prosecutor's Request for Leave to File an Amended Indictment,* <u>Prosecutor v. Nsengiyumva</u>, Case No.: ICTR-96-12-I.
[6]   *Prosecutor's Motion for Joinder of Accused and Brief in Support of Prosecutor's Motion for Joinder of Accused,* <u>Prosecutor v. Bagosora</u>, Case No.: ICTR-96-7; <u>Prosecutor v. Kabiligi</u>, Case No.: ICTR-97-34; <u>Prosecutor v. Ntabakuze</u>, Case No.: ICTR-97-30; <u>Prosecutor v. Nsengiyumva</u>, Case No.: ICTR-96-12.

three Judges. Article 13(2) directs the President to assign Judges to the Trial Chambers and proscribes a Judge from serving on a Chamber to which he or she was not assigned.

13.   Article 14 of the Statute explicitly directed the Judges to draft the Rules. The Rules were crafted to flesh out and provide substance to the Statute. Rule 15 governs the disqualification of Judges and provides in Sub-rule 15(A) that a Judge may withdraw from a case in which he/she has or has had any association which might affect his/her impartiality and that, in such circumstances, the President shall assign another Judge to sit in his/her place. Such a situation would result in a re-composition of that Trial Chamber. Sub-rule 15(B) allows for the disqualification of a Judge, thereby enabling the re-composition of that **[page 6]** Trial Chamber.[7] Sub-rule 15(E) enables the Presiding Judge to change the composition of the Trial Chamber by assigning another Judge to the case and to order either a rehearing or the continuation of the proceedings where a Judge is unable to continue sitting in a part-heard case.[8]

14.   The President of the International Tribunal is charged with administrative tasks conferred upon him/her by the Statute and the Rules. In interpreting the Statute and the Rules which implement the Statute, Trial Chambers of both the International Tribunal and the International Criminal Tribunal for the former Yugoslavia ("the ICTY"), as well as the Appeals Chamber have consistently resorted to the Vienna Convention of the Law of Treaties ("the Vienna Convention"), for the interpretation of the Statute.[9] Although the Statute is not a treaty, it is a *sui generis* international legal instrument resembling a treaty. Adopted by the Security Council, an organ to which Member States of the United Nations have vested legal responsibility, the Statute shares with treaties fundamental similarities. Because the Vienna Convention codifies logical and practical norms which are consistent with domestic law, it is applicable under customary international law to international instruments which are not treaties. Thus, recourse by analogy is appropriate to Article 31(1) of the Vienna Convention in interpreting the provisions of the Statute. Article 31(1) states that "[a] treaty shall be interpreted in good faith in accordance with the ordinary meaning to be given to the terms of the treaty in their context and in the light of its object and purpose."

15.   The overarching object and purpose of the Statute is ensuring a fair and expeditious trial for the accused. The Trial Chambers are re-composed to ensure that this very aim is achieved. Thus, the contextual interpretation of the provisions of the Statute, and by extension, of the Rules implementing the Statute, should meet that object and purpose. For **[page 7]** example, as noted above, Sub-rule 15(E) authorises the President to assign a new Judge to a Chamber to replace one who is disqualified or otherwise unable to sit in a part-heard case. The Statute, in setting forth the organisational structure of the Chambers, is silent on this point. Rather, the Statute leaves to the Judges the responsibility of drafting rules for the conduct of the proceedings.[10] The Rules that allow for a re-composition meet this purpose. To interpret silence as a prohibition would frustrate this object and purpose of the Statute.

16.   Thus, the assignment of a Judge to a Trial Chamber is not "frozen in time". Altered circumstances such as the resignation, serious illness, death or disqualification of a Judge, or the need for rotation to best co-ordinate the work of the Chambers may demand the recomposition of a Trial Chamber. An interpretation of the Statute that would find a requirement that Judges serve forever in the Chamber to which they are assigned, despite disqualification, illness, death or resignation of a Judge of that Chamber, would lead to an absurd result. Further, it would defeat the object and purpose of the Statute to ensure that an accused has a fair and expeditious trial.

17.   Acting pursuant to his mandate under Article 13 of the Statute, President Kama assigned Judge Sekule (presiding), Judge Khan and himself to Trial Chamber II to hear the Leave Request and the

---

[7]   See *Decision on the Application for the Disqualification of Judges Jorda and Riad*, Prosecutor v. Kordic and Cerkez, Case No.: IT-95-14/2-PT, 8 Oct. 1998.

[8]   However, after the opening statement and the beginning of the presentation of the evidence, a situation not applicable to this case, the proceedings can be ordered to continue only with the consent of the accused.

[9]   Other cases were ICTY Trial Chambers have had recourse to Article 31 in interpreting the provisions of the Statutes include: *Decision on the Prosecutor's Motion, Protective Measures for Victims and Witnesses*, Prosecutor v. Tadi}, Case No.: IT-94-I-T, 10 Aug. 1995, at p. 10; *Judgement*, Prosecutor v. Erdemovi}, Case No.: IT-96-22-A, 7 Oct. 1997, at p. 3; *Decision on the Admissibility of the Prosecutor's Appeal from the Decision of a Confirming Judge Dismissing an Indictment Against Théoneste Bagosora and 28 Others*, Prosecutor v. Théoneste Bagosora and 28 Others, op. cit., note 4 at pp. 12-13.

[10]   See Article 14 of the Statute.

Joinder Motion. The composition of this Trial Chamber reveals President Kama's administrative foresight since the indictments against the four accused who are the objects of the Joinder Motion had been confirmed by Judge Ostrovsky, who confirmed the indictment against the Appellant, and Judge Aspegren, who confirmed the indictments against the other three accused. Sub-rule 15(C) disqualifies a Judge who reviews an indictment against an accused to sit as a member of the Trial Chamber for the trial of the same accused. A Trial Chamber composed of Judges who would not be subject to disqualification should the Leave Request or the Joinder Motion be granted could *only* include three out of the following four Judges: Judge Kama, Judge Sekule, Judge Khan or Judge Pillay, as the International Tribunal at the time was composed of only six Judges. We find that this constitutes an exceptional circumstance which justifies the re-composition of the Trial Chamber. **[page 8]**

18.   In our view, the Statute and the Rules confer upon the President the authority to replace Judges and to re-compose Trial Chambers, in exceptional circumstances, to ensure the attainment of the object and purpose of the Statute and to avoid any absurd result. The alternative would be the discontinuance of trials and the violation of the accused's fundamental rights. The composition and re-composition of Trial Chambers by the President is a judicial administrative function, pursuant to the Statute and the Rules, formulated for the efficient judicial administrative operation of the Tribunal.

C.   Whether the Trial Chamber that conducts the initial appearance has exclusive jurisdiction over the case

1. Whether the Initial Appearance Constitutes the Commencement of Trial

19.   The Appellant asserts that once an accused has made an initial appearance before a Trial Chamber, that Chamber has exclusive jurisdiction over his case on the ground that his initial appearance marks the beginning of trial.[11] We find that in the present case, the Appellant's trial had not commenced for the purpose of deciding whether Trial Chamber I has exclusive jurisdiction over his case. The following discussion will suffice to show that the Appellant's assertion in this regard is unfounded.

20.   In making his assertion, the Appellant relies on the Decision in <u>Prosecutor v. Bagosora and 28 Others</u>.[12] In that case, Judge Khan concluded that a trial commences at the time of the initial appearance, when the accused enters his plea on the charges involving the alleged crimes for which he has been brought before the Tribunal.[13] Article 19 of the Statute directs the Trial Chamber to "set a date for trial" after the accused enters a plea of not guilty. Sub-rule 62(iv), governing the Initial Appearance of an accused, provides for the same result. Clearly, an event could not have occurred if the Statute and the Rules require that a date be set for the commencement of that event. **[page 9]**

21. Further, the provisions of Sub-rule 15(E) clearly provide that a case is considered to be "part-heard" after the opening statement or the presentation of the evidence, neither of which has occurred in this case.[14] Moreover, although Sub-rule 15(E) enables the President to change the composition of the Trial Chamber even in the event of a part-heard case, after the opening statement or the commencement of the presentation of evidence, the proceedings can continue only with the consent of the accused.

22.   We also note that Sub-rule 73*bis*(A), which was adopted after the <u>Bagosora Decision</u>, provides that the Trial Chamber shall hold a Pre-trial Conference prior to the commencement of trial. No Pre-Trial Conference has yet been held in the Appellant's case.

23.   Read together, these provisions lead to the inescapable conclusion that the initial appearance of the Appellant does *not* mark the commencement of his trial. Therefore, Trial Chamber I does not have

---

[11]   *Appellant's Brief* at paras. 10 to 13.

[12]   See *supra* note 2.

[13]   *Appellant's Brief*, para. 12.

[14]   Sub-rule 15(E) governs the disqualification of Judges involving cases which are "partheard." Under the first sentence of that Sub-rule, the President may assign another Judge to replace a Judge who is unable, for any reason, to continue sitting in a part heard case. Such an assignment is permissible even in the absence of the accused's consent. Pursuant to the second sentence of that Sub-rule, however, after the opening statement or the beginning of the presentation of evidence, the proceedings can be continued only with the consent of the accused.

exclusive jurisdiction over his case. We now turn to address the specific disposition of the Leave Request and the Joinder Motion.

2. Whether the Prosecutor's Request for Leave to File an Amended Indictment is Properly Before Trial Chamber II

24.   The Prosecutor submitted the Leave Request to Trial Chamber I, composed of Judge Kama, Judge Pillay and Judge Aspegren. The Appellant's initial appearance has previously been held before Trial Chamber I although, at that time, that Chamber was composed of Judge Kama, Judge Sekule and Judge Pillay. Thus, the composition of Trial Chamber I itself had been altered. However, the Leave Request, was set down for hearing before Trial Chamber II which was also seized of the Joinder Motion.[15] **[page 10]**

25.   Rule 50 contains three stages during which the Prosecutor can amend an indictment.[16] Only one of these three stages is relevant to the disposition of this appeal. The relevant portion of Sub-rule 50(A), provides that "[a]t or after such initial appearance, an amendment of an indictment may only be made by leave granted by *that* Trial Chamber pursuant to Rule 73." (Empasis addedd.)

26.   In referring the Leave Request and the Joinder Motion to the same Trial Chamber, President Kama relied on three grounds: 1) the need for flexibility; 2) the need to avoid assigning the Leave Request and the Joinder Motion to a Chamber where one or more Judges would be disqualified; and 3) the need to resolve both issues simultaneously due to the linkage between the Leave Request and the Joinder Motion.

27.   Relying on Article 31(1) of the Vienna Convention,[17] we find that a need for flexibility alone cannot justify departure from the plain language of the Rules. We also find that no recourse to supplementary means of interpretation is necessary since this approach is resorted to only when the language of a provision is ambiguous.[18] The language of Sub-rule 50(A) is plain and unambiguous. Here, it is clear in the ordinary meaning of the language of that provision that an indictment can be amended after initial appearance of the accused *only by the Trial Chamber before which the initial appearance took place*, in this case Trial **[page 11]** Chamber I. Accordingly, the Leave Request must be returned to Trial Chamber I, as the only competent Trial Chamber to adjudicate this matter.

28.   In fact, there was no need for flexibility except with respect to the Joinder Motion. As will be discussed hereunder, this motion does not run afoul of any explicit Rule that directs its presentation to a particular Chamber, and consequently, different considerations obtain.

---

[15]   The Prosecutor addressed the Joinder Motion to neither a numbered Trial Chamber nor to specific Judges.

[16]   With respect to the procedures for amending indictments, there are slight differences between the Rules of the International Tribunal and the ICTY. Sub-rule 50(A) of the Rules of the ICTY states:

Rule 50

Amendment of Indictment

(A)   The Prosecutor may amend an Indictment:

> (i)   at any time before its confirmation, without leave;
>
> (ii)   thereafter, and until the commencement of the presentation of evidence in terms of Rule 85, with leave of the Judges who confirmed the Indictment, *or a Judge assigned by the President*;
> or
>
> (iii)   after the commencement of the presentation of evidence, with leave of the Trial Chamber hearing the case, after having heard the parties.

(Emphasis added). Notwithstanding the different language used in the two rules, as reflected in the emphasised phrase, we find that an "exceptional circumstance" as set forth in ICTR Sub-rule 50(A) includes circumstances present in this case. The language "hearing the case" contained in ICTY Sub-rule 50(A)(iii) clearly indicates that the trial has begun.

[17]   Article 31(1) of the Vienna Convention states: "A treaty shall be interpreted in good faith in accordance with the ordinary meaning to be given to the terms of the treaty in their context and in the light of its object and purpose." See also Article 31 and 32 of that same Convention.

[18]   See Vienna Convention on the Law of Treaties, 23 May 1969, 1155 U.N.T.S. 331, Articles 31-32. See also <u>Prosecutor v. Erdemovi]</u>, *Judgement*, Case No.: IT-96-22-A, A. Ch., 7 Oct. 1997, *Joint Separate Opinion of Judge McDonald and Judge Vohrah*, at para. 3.

29.   With respect to the issue of the potential disqualification of Judges as it relates to the Leave Request, we find that President Kama's concerns in this regard were not justified. There was no realistic concern for potential disqualification of Judges with respect to the Leave Request.

30.   Regarding the issue of the linkage between the Leave Request and the Joinder Motion, this became so only *after* President Kama re-composed Trial Chamber II and directed that both motions be heard by that Trial Chamber. The Leave Request could and should have properly been presented to, and decided by, the Judges to whom the Prosecutor had addressed the Leave Request since those Judges did not face the disqualification problem.

2. Whether the Joinder Motion is Properly Before Trial Chamber II

31.   Rule 48 of the Rules provides for persons accused of the same or different crimes committed in the course of the same transaction to be jointly charged and tried. Rule 49 of the Rules of the ICTY is identical to Rule 48 of the Rules of the International Tribunal and they both appear to have been drawn from the "same transaction" test found in the federal system of the United States of America. The "same transaction test" provides for offences to be joined if they are "based on the same act or transaction or on two or more acts or transactions connected together or constituting parts of a common scheme or plan."[19] It is **[page 12]** well accepted in some common law jurisdictions that joining accused in one indictment where the "same transaction" test is met can be initiated by the prosecutor or by an order of the court if justice so requires. Where possible public interest and the concern for judicial economy would require joint offences to be tried together. The jurisprudence of the ICTY clearly permits joint trials and points to the existence of specific elements to justify joinder.[20] However, the requirements necessary to be fulfilled before joinder can be granted are not in issue as we are concerned here only with determining the particular Trial Chamber competent to hear the Joinder Motion.

32.   This is not to suggest that the Leave Request and the Joinder Motion should be heard together. We find that there is no justification substantiated by the Statute and the Rules which support the view that the two motions must be heard in the same proceedings before the same Trial Chamber. In any event, there is no Rule that requires the Leave Request and the Joinder Motion to be considered in "direct relation" to each other. For the reasons set out above, we hold that the Leave Request must be returned to Trial Chamber I for determination as to whether it should be granted and that the Joinder Motion may remain with Trial Chamber II for determination on its merits.

33.   In the result,[21] we hold that Trial Chamber II is not unlawfully constituted and that it is competent to exercise jurisdiction over the Joinder Motion.

C. Our conclusions

34.   For the foregoing reasons, we find that

(1)   The appeal is admissible pursuant to Sub-rule 72(D) of the Rules since the Appellant has raised an issue relating to a lack of jurisdiction of the re-composed Trial Chamber II; **[page 13]**

(2)   The re-composition of a Trial Chamber by the President is an administrative decision that does not offend the provisions of the Statute or the Rules;

(3)   Based on the textual interpretation of Sub-rule 50(A), Trial Chamber I is the only Trial Chamber competent to adjudicate the Leave Request; and

(4)   Trial Chamber II is competent to adjudicate the Joinder Motion.

---

[19]   *Criminal Procedure*, Second ed., Wayne R. LaFave and Jerold H. Israel, at p. 761, citing Fed.R.Crim.P 8(a). See also *Decision Stating Reasons for Appeals Chamber's Order of 29 May 1998 and Separate Opinion of Judge Shahabuddeen*, Prosecutor v. Kovacevic, Case No.: IT-97-24-AR73, App. Ch., 2 July 1998, at p. 3.

[20]   See, for example, *Decision on Motion for Joinder of Accused and Concurrent Presentation of Evidence*, Prosecutor v. Kovacevic, Case No.: IT-97-24-PT, T.Ch. II, 14 May 1998.

[21]   See discussion at pp. 3-7, supra.

35.   Consequently, we would allow the appeal in respect of the Leave Request and remit it to Trial Chamber I for adjudication and we would dismiss the appeal in respect of the Joinder Motion.

Done in both English and French, the English text being authoritative.

Gabrielle Kirk McDonald   Lal Chand Vohrah

Dated this third day of June 1999
At Arusha
Tanzania

International Criminal Tribunal for the Prosecution of Persons Responsible for Genocide and Other Serious Violations of International Humanitarian Law Committed in the Territory of Rwanda and Rwandan Citizens responsible for genocide and other such violations committed in the territory of neighbouring States between 1 January and 31 December 1994	Case No.: ICTR-96-12-A Date: 3 June 1999 Original: English

IN THE APPEALS CHAMBER

Before: **Judge Gabrielle Kirk McDonald, Presiding**
Judge Mohamed Shahabuddeen
Judge Lal Chand Vohrah
Judge Wang Tieya
Judge Rafael Nieto-Navia

Registrar: **Mr. Agwu U. Okali**

Decision of: **3 June 1999**

ANATOLE NSENGIYUMVA

v.

THE PROSECUTOR

JOINT SEPARATE AND CONCURRING OPINION OF JUDGE WANG TIEYA AND JUDGE RAFAEL NIETO-NAVIA

Counsel for the Appellant:
Mr. Kennedy Ogetto
Mr. Gershom Otachi Bw'oamwa

The Office of the Prosecutor:
Mr. David Spencer
Mr. Frédéric Ossogo
Mr. Chile Eboe-Osuji
Mr. Luc Cote
Ms. Josee D'aoust

We join our fellow Judges, Judge McDonald and Judge Vohrah, in the Decision disposing of the interlocutory appeal from Mr. Anatole Nsengiyumva ("Appellant") concerning his challenge to the jurisdiction of Trial Chamber II, as recomposed, to hear the Prosecutor's Motion for Joinder ("Joinder Motion") and the Prosecutor's Request for Leave to File an Amended Indictment in respect of the Appellant ("Request"), to the extent that the appeal is held admissible under Rule 72 and upheld on the merits, resulting in the Request being remitted to Trial Chamber I, being the proper Chamber under sub-Rule 50 (A), for decision. We respectfully append a separate and concurring opinion setting forth different reasoning for this conclusion. Since the present case resembles the appeal of *Kanyabashi v. Prosecutor* (Case No. ICTR-96-15-A) in terms of the issues raised for consideration by the Appeals Chamber, except for the ground of lack of independence and impartiality which was not pleaded here, our reasoning in the opinion delivered in *Kanyabashi* stands for this appeal as well.

Done in both English and French, the English text being authoritative.

Wang Tieya   Rafael Nieto-Navia

Dated this third day of June 1999
At Arusha,
Tanzania.

International Criminal Tribunal for the
Prosecution of Persons Responsible for
Genocide and Other Serious Violations of
International Humanitarian Law Committed
in the Territory of Rwanda and Rwandan
Citizens responsible for genocide and other
such violations committed in the territory of
neighbouring States between 1 January and
31 December 1994

Case No.:   ICTR-96-12-A

Date: 3 June 1999

Original: English

IN THE APPEALS CHAMBER

Before: **Judge Gabrielle Kirk McDonald, Presiding**
              Judge Mohamed Shahabuddeen
              Judge Lal Chand Vohrah
              Judge Wang Tieya
              Judge Rafael Nieto-Navia

Registrar: Mr. Agwu U. Okali

Decision of: 3 June 1999

ANATOLE NSENGIYUMVA

v.

THE PROSECUTOR

DISSENTING OPINION OF JUDGE SHAHABUDDEEN

Counsel for the Appellant:
    Mr. Kennedy Ogetto
    Mr. Gershom Otachi Bw'oamwa

The Office of the Prosecutor:
    Mr. David Spencer
    Mr. Frédéric Ossogo
    Mr. Chile Eboe-Osuji
    Mr. Luc Cote
    Ms. Josee D'aoust

[page 1] I respectfully dissent from the decision of the Appeals Chamber. The substance of my reasons is given in an opinion which I have appended to the judgement of the Chamber in the case of *Joseph Kanyabashi v. The Prosecutor*, decided today. As in that case, I have reached the conclusion that the appeal, as an interlocutory appeal, should be dismissed.

There are two points which I should add. The first is that the present case does not raise any question of judicial independence and impartiality. Consequently, my remarks on these points in *Kanyabashi's* case do not apply.

The second point is that, as in *Kanyabashi's* case, the sole ground on which the Appeals Chamber has allowed the present appeal is that, in its view, the procedure for granting leave to make amendments to an indictments, as laid down by Rule 50(A) of the Rules, was not complied with.

But, as in *Kanyabashi's* case, this point was not the subject of objection by the appellant at any stage during the hearing of the matter by Trial Chamber II. His concern was with the alleged illegality of the recomposition of that Trial Chamber and the alleged exclusive competence of Trial Chamber I to handle the whole of the case on the strength of the fact that it took the initial appearance.

This was how the matter was understood by Trial Chamber II: in no part of its oral judgement, delivered immediately after the oral arguments on 28 September 1998, did it pass upon the point concerning the specific amendment procedure prescribed by Rule 50(A) of the Rules or in any way refer to it. What the Presiding Judge spoke of was "the two motions filed by the defence on the issue of the recomposition of the Trial Chamber or, rather, the challenge to the recomposition of Trial Chamber". (Transcript, 28 September 1998, pages 29 – 30).

Nor was any such point, about the specific amendment procedure prescribed by Rule 50(A) of the Rules, raised by the appellant in his Notice of Appeal of 2 October 1998. **[page 3]**

An objection of non-compliance with the amendment procedure prescribed by Rule 50(A) of the Rules would be "an objection based on lack of jurisdiction" within the meaning of Rule 72(D) of the Rules, but, one not having been made to Trial Chamber II, it could not be said that the Trial Chamber dismissed such an objection. Since there is no right of interlocutory appeal unless there is a "dismissal of an objection based on lack of jurisdiction", the appeal is not competent and falls to be dismissed.

Done in English and French, the English text being authoritative.

Mohamed Shahabuddeen

Dated this third day of June 1999
At Arusha
Tanzania

International Criminal Tribunal for the Prosecution of Persons Responsible for Genocide and Other Serious Violations of International Humanitarian Law Committed in the Territory of Rwanda and Rwandan Citizens responsible for genocide and other such violations committed in the territory of neighbouring States between 1 January and 31 December 1994	Case No.:	ICTR-98-40-A
	Date:	3 June 1999
	Original:	English

IN THE APPEALS CHAMBER

Before: **Judge Gabrielle Kirk McDonald, Presiding**
Judge Mohamed Shahabuddeen
Judge Lal Chand Vohrah
Judge Wang Tieya
Judge Rafael Nieto-Navia

Registrar: **Mr. Agwu U. Okali**

Decision of: **3 June 1999**

BERNARD NTUYAHAGA

v.

THE PROSECUTOR

DECISION REJECTING NOTICE OF APPEAL

Counsel for the Appellant:
    Mr. Georges Komlavi Amegadjie

The Office of the Prosecutor:
    Mr. Mohamed Othman
    Mr. James Stewart.

[page 2] THE APPEALS CHAMBER of the International Criminal Tribunal for the Prosecution of Persons Responsible for Genocide and Other Serious Violations of International Humanitarian Law Committed in the Territory of Rwanda and Rwandan Citizens responsible for genocide and other such violations committed in the territory of neighboring States, between 1 January and 31 December 1994 ("the Appeals Chamber" and "the Tribunal" respectively);

NOTING the "Decision on the Prosecutor's Motion to Withdraw the Indictment", "the Decision" of 18 March 1999, in which Trial Chamber I granted the "Prosecutor's Motion Under Rules 51 and 73 to Withdraw the Indictment Against the Accused", and ordered the immediate release of the Accused;

NOTING the "Notice of Appeal", filed by Appellant on 22 March 1999, and the "Requete en extreme urgence aux fins de sursis a l'execution immediate de la Decision rendue par la premiere Chambre de premiere instance le 18 March 1999 dans l'affaire "Bernard Ntuyahaga contre le Procureur du TPIR", filed on 23 March 1999 English verson filed 29 April 1999;

NOTING the "Prosecutor's Response to "Defence's Notice of Appeal of Trial Chamber's Decision of 18 March 1999", filed 15 April 1999;

CONSIDERING Article 24 of the Statute and in particular Sub-rule 72(D) of the Rules of Procedure and Evidence of the Tribunal which provide for right of appeal by persons convicted by the Trial Chamber or on an interlocutory appeal challenging lack of jurisdiction of a Trial Chamber;

NOTING that the Trial Chamber did not convict the Appellant within the meaning of Article 24(1) of the Statute;

FURTHER NOTING that the Appellant is not challenging the jurisdiction of the Trial Chamber under Sub-rule 72(D) of the Rules, in which case an appeal could lie as of right;

FINDING, accordingly, that there is no right of appeal against the Decision; **[page 3]**

HEREBY REJECTS the Notice of Appeal.

Done in both English and French, the English text being authoritative.

Gabrielle Kirk McDonald

Presiding Judge

Judge Shahabuddeen appends a Dissenting Opinion

Dated this third day of June 1999
At Arusha
Tanzania

International Criminal Tribunal for the	Case No.:	ICTR-98-40-A
Prosecution of Persons Responsible for		
Genocide and Other Serious Violations of	Date:	3 June 1999
International Humanitarian Law Committed		
in the Territory of Rwanda and Rwandan		
Citizens responsible for genocide and other	Original:	English
such violations committed in the territory of		
neighbouring States between 1 January and		
31 December 1994		

IN THE APPEALS CHAMBER

Before: **Judge Gabrielle Kirk McDonald, Presiding**
             Judge Mohamed Shahabuddeen
             Judge Lal Chand Vohrah
             Judge Wang Tieya
             Judge Rafael Nieto-Navia

Registrar: **Mr. Agwu U. Okali**

Decision of: **3 June 1999**

BERNARD NTUYAHAGA

v.

THE PROSECUTOR

DISSENTING OPINION OF JUDGE SHAHABUDDEEN

Counsel for the Appellant:
    Mr. Georges Komlavi Amegadjie

The Office of the Prosecutor:
    Mr. Mohamed C. Othman
    Mr. James Stewart

[page 2] The Presiding Judge of Trial Chamber I was recorded as saying:

[w]e understand very clearly your opinion. You oppose the withdraw and you are actually asking for a verdict of innocence and acquittal.[1]

Whether the requested acquittal was legally possible does not affect the fact that the substance of the matter was that the appellant was, on a fair interpretation, objecting to the jurisdiction of the Trial Chamber to grant leave for the withdrawal of the indictment; in his view, its only power was to record a verdict of acquittal. The importance of the right which he claimed is obvious, regard being had to the possibility of raising *ne bis in idem* in bar to any subsequent prosecutions.

I think the appellant fell to be considered as making a preliminary objection within the meaning of Rule 72(B)(i) of the Rues and that he has a right of interlocutory appeal under paragraph (D) of that rule. Accordingly, I respectfully dissent from the decision of the Appeals Chamber.

Mohamed Shahabuddeen

Judge

Dated this third day of June 1999 at

Arusha

Tanzania

[Seal of the Tribunal]

---

[1]   Unofficial transcripts, 16 March 1999, p. 83.

International Criminal Tribunal for the Prosecution of Persons Responsible for Genocide and Other Serious Violations of International Humanitarian Law Committed in the Territory of Rwanda and Rwandan Citizens responsible for genocide and other such violations committed in the territory of neighbouring States between 1 January and 31 December 1994	Case No.: ICTR-96-15-A
	Date: 3 June 1999
	Original: English

IN THE APPEALS CHAMBER

Before: **Judge Gabrielle Kirk McDonald, Presiding**
                  Judge Mohamed Shahabuddeen
                  Judge Lal Chand Vohrah
                  Judge Wang Tieya
                  Judge Rafael Nieto-Navia

Registrar: **Mr. Agwu U. Okali**

Decision of: **3 June 1999**

JOSEPH KANYABASHI

v.

THE PROSECUTOR

DECISION ON THE DEFENCE MOTION FOR INTERLOCUTORY APPEAL ON THE JURISDICTION OF TRIAL CHAMBER I

Counsel for the Appellant:
        Mr. Michel Marchand
        Mr. Michel Boyer

The Office of the Prosecutor:
        Mr. David Spencer
        Mr. Ibukunolu Babajide
        Mr. Chile Eboe-Osuji
        Mr. Robert Petit

[page 2] I. INTRODUCTION

1. The Appeals Chamber of the International Criminal Tribunal for the Prosecution of Persons Responsible for Genocide and Other Serious Violations of International Humanitarian Law Committed in the Territory of Rwanda and Rwandan Citizens Responsible for Genocide and Other Such Violations Committed in the Territory of Neighbouring States, between 1 January 1994 and 31 December 1994 ("the International Tribunal") is seized of an appeal lodged by Joseph Kanyabashi ("the Appellant") against an oral decision rendered by Trial Chamber I composed of Judge Kama (Presiding), Judge Sekule and Judge Pillay on 24 September 1998 ("the Decision"). By the Decision, Trial Chamber I denied the Appellant's motion contesting the jurisdiction of that Trial Chamber to hear the Prosecutor's Request for Leave to File an Amended Indictment ("the Leave Request") in respect of the Appellant and the Prosecutor's Motion for Joinder, which proposed to join the Appellant with five other accused ("the Joinder Motion").

2. The Appellant was arrested in Belgium on 28 June 1995. Judge Ostrovsky confirmed the Indictment against him on 15 July 1996. The initial appearance of the Appellant took place before Trial Chamber II, composed of Judge Khan (Presiding), Judge Aspegren and Judge Pillay on 29 November 1996. The Appellant submits in this appeal that his initial appearance before Trial Chamber II marked the commencement of his trial, and consequently, Trial Chamber II has exclusive jurisdiction over his case. The President of the International Tribunal, acting pursuant to Article 13 of the Statute of the International Tribunal ("the Statute"), assigned Judge Kama (Presiding), Judge Pillay and Judge Sekule to Trial Chamber I, which became seized of the Leave Request and the Joinder Motion, both of which were filed on 18 August 1998. Both motions were set down to be heard on 24 September 1998 before Trial Chamber I. At this hearing, the Appellant contested the Trial Chamber's jurisdiction to preside over the hearing of the Leave Request and the Joinder Motion, on the grounds that his initial appearance had taken place before Trial Chamber II and that the re-composition of Trial Chamber I was unlawful.

3. Subsequent to the oral dismissal by Trial Chamber I of the Appellant's objection, the Appellant filed a Notice of Appeal on 30 September 1998, entitled "Appeal Relating to the [page 3] Lack of Jurisdiction, Rules 108(B) and 117 of the Rules of Procedure and Evidence". This Notice of Appeal was followed by the "Prosecutor's Response and Challenge to the Admissibility of the Defendant's Notice of Appeal" and the "Prosecutor's Motion for an Expedited Appeal Procedure Pursuant to Articles 14 and 24(2) of the Statute of the International Tribunal and Rules 117 and 108 of the Rules of Procedure and Evidence as Amended", filed on 15 October 1998.

4. Thereafter, the Appeals Chamber directed the Parties to submit written briefs within the time-limits indicated in the "Scheduling Order" of 18 December 1998 ("the Order"), filed on 21 December 1998. The "Prosecutor's Brief Pursuant to the Scheduling Order of the Appeals Chamber" was filed on 30 December 1998. The English translation of the Appellant's Brief was filed on 17 February 1999 and carries the same title as that of his Notice of Appeal ("Appeal Relating to the Lack of Jurisdiction, Rules 108(B) and 117 of the Rules of Procedure and Evidence").

II. The Appeal

A. The Appellant

5. The Appellant requests that the Appeals Chamber provide appropriate relief by: 1) ordering the re-composed Trial Chamber I to stay the hearing of the Leave Request and the Joinder Motion; 2) ruling that the re-composed Trial Chamber I has no jurisdiction to hear the Leave Request and the Joinder Motion; 3) quashing the Decision; 4) ordering the Leave Request to be referred to Trial Chamber II for disposition; and 5) ordering Trial Chamber II to convene a hearing, as soon as possible, in order to quash the Leave Request.

6. The grounds of appeal invoked by the Appellant in his brief can be summarised as follows. The Appellant argues that Trial Chamber I lacks jurisdiction over his case, and consequently the appeal is from an objection based on lack of jurisdiction within the meaning of Sub-rule 72(D). He contends that

under Articles 10, 11 and 13 of the Statute, the **[page 4]** composition of a Trial Chamber cannot be altered once the Accused has made his initial appearance before that Trial Chamber, a stage marking the commencement of trial.[1]

7.   As a second ground of appeal, the Appellant contends that even if Trial Chamber I had jurisdiction in its original composition, its re-composition breached Article 13 of the Statute, thereby rendering that Trial Chamber incompetent. According to the Appellant's interpretation of the Statute and the Rules, the re-composition of a Trial Chamber is prohibited except in exceptional cases, a situation not in issue in the present circumstances. The Appellant argues that the Trial Chamber was re-composed only for the purpose of hearing the Joinder Motion, a function not directly relevant to hearing the Leave Request, which was in issue. The re-composition of Trial Chamber I solely to serve that purpose indicates that this Trial Chamber, as re-composed, was not independent and impartial.[2]

8.   As a third ground of appeal, the Appellant submits that even if the Prosecutor's contention that the trial commences at the time of hearing the first witness were found to be persuasive, the Appellant's right to be tried by independent and impartial judges was violated. According to the Appellant, the violation resulted from a decision by the President of the International Tribunal, Judge Kama, to re-compose Trial Chamber I, then composed of Judge Kama, Judge Pillay and Judge Aspegren. President Kama substituted Judge Sekule for Judge Aspegren, resulting in Trial Chamber I being composed of Judge Kama, Judge Pillay and Judge Sekule.[3]

9.   Finally, the Appellant submits that the right to be heard by an independent and impartial Trial Chamber is fundamental. Therefore, in his view, the enjoyment of this right is directly related to the authority and ability to adjudicate, raising the issue of jurisdiction.[4] The Appellant additionally submits that the change in the composition of Trial Chamber I was not justified by exceptional circumstances, as provided for under Rules 15 and 27 of the **[page 5]** Rules, particularly since the Presiding Judge offered no compelling reason justifying that change. The Appellant argues that "the change in the composition of the Chamber was dictated by factors that prove that the re-composed Trial Chamber I was not independent and impartial"[5] and that such a situation gives rise to serious doubt as to the independence and impartiality of that Chamber.[6]

B.   The Prosecutor

10.   The Prosecutor contends that the lack of independence and impartiality of which the Appellant complains are not matters of jurisdiction and are, therefore, not the proper subject of an interlocutory appeal.[7] In this regard, the Prosecutor argues that neither the Statute nor the Rules make the assignment of a case to a Trial Chamber or the composition of a Trial Chamber a jurisdictional issue.[8] The Prosecutor submits that the assignment of Judges to the Chambers is an administrative matter falling within the authority of the President and is unrelated to the elements of the Tribunal's jurisdiction. Consistent with this line of argument, the Prosecutor also contends that jurisdiction is not affected by the particular Trial Chamber which happens to exercise the Tribunal's authority over a particular case.[9]

---

[1]   Prosecutor v. Kanyabashi, *Appeal Relating to the Lack of Jurisdiction, Rules 108(B) and 117 of the Rules of Procedure and Evidence*, Case No. ICTR 96-15-I, 14 October 1998, at paras. 27-29 (*"Appellant's 14 October 1998 Brief"*). In The Prosecutor v. Théoneste Bagosora and 28 Others, *Dismissal of Indictment*, Case No. ICTR-98-37-I, 31 March 1998, Judge Khan ruled that the initial appearance of the accused before a Trial Chamber marks the beginning of his trial (at p. 8).

[2]   *Appellant's 14 October 1998 Brief*, at paras. 39-46.

[3]   Ibid., at paras. 35-38.

[4]   Ibid., at para. 58.

[5]   Ibid., at para. 46.

[6]   Ibid., at paras. 104-106.

[7]   Prosecutor v. Kanyabashi, *Prosecutor's Brief Pursuant to the Scheduling Order of the Appeals Chamber*, Case No. ICTR 96-15-I, 30 December 1998, at p. 2.

[8]   Prosecutor v. Kanyabashi, *Prosecutor's Motion for an Expedited Appeal Procedure Pursuant to Article 14 and 24(2) of the Statute of the ICTR and Rules 117 and 108 of the Rules of Procedure and Evidence as Amended*, Case No. ICTR 96-15-I, 15 October 1998, at p. 4.

[9]   Ibid., at para. 32.

11.   The Prosecutor is, further, of the view that even if the question submitted for review were one of jurisdiction, there is nevertheless no merit to the appeal, given that trials before the International Tribunal do not commence at the initial appearance of the accused. Moreover, even if trials were deemed to commence at the time of taking the plea, the rule against variation of the bench would not come into effect until the commencement of the presentation of evidence on the merits of the case.[10] Finally, Article 13(2) of the Statute, on which the Appellant relies in his appeal, contains the very provision, which authorises the President to assign and reassign Judges to the Trial Chambers as the administration of justice requires. **[page 6]**

III. Applicable Provisions

12.   The relevant parts of the applicable Articles of the Statute and Rules of the Rules are set out below.

A. The Statute

Article 10
Organisation of the International Tribunal for Rwanda

The International Tribunal for Rwanda shall consist of the following organs:

   a) The Chambers, comprising three Trial Chambers and an Appeals Chamber;
   b) The Prosecutor;
   c) A Registry.

Article 11
Composition of the Chambers

Chambers shall be composed of fourteen independent judges, no two of whom may be nationals of the same State, who shall serve as follows:

   a) Three judges shall serve in each of the Trial Chambers;
   b) Five judges shall serve in the Appeals Chamber.

Article 13
Officers and members of the Chambers

1.   The Judges of the International Tribunal for Rwanda shall elect a President. **[page 7]**

2.   After consultation with the judges of the International Tribunal for Rwanda, the President shall assign the judges to the Trial Chambers. A judge shall serve only in the Chamber to which he or she was assigned.

3.   The judges of each Trial Chamber shall elect a Presiding Judge, who shall conduct all of the proceedings of that Trial Chamber as a whole.

Article 14
Rules of procedure and evidence

The Judges of the International Tribunal for Rwanda shall adopt, for the purpose of proceedings before the International Tribunal for Rwanda, the rules of procedure and evidence for the conduct of the pre-trial phase of the proceedings, trials and appeals, the admission of evidence, the protection of victims and witnesses and other appropriate matters of the International Tribunal for Rwanda with such changes as they deem necessary.

Article 19
Commencement and Conduct of Trial Proceedings

---

[10]   Ibid., at paras. 52-53.

1.   [...]

2.   [...]

3.   The Trial Chamber shall read the Indictment, satisfy itself that the rights of the accused are respected, confirm that the accused understands the Indictment, and instruct the accused to enter a plea. The Trial Chamber shall then set a date for trial.

4.   [...]

Article 24
Appellate Proceedings

1.   The Appeals Chamber shall hear appeals from persons convicted by the Trial Chambers or from the Prosecutor on the following grounds:

   a) An error on a question of law invalidating the decision, or
   b) An error of fact which has occasioned a miscarriage of justice.

2.   The Appeals Chamber may affirm, reverse or revise the decisions taken by the Trial Chambers.
   [page 8]

B. The Rules

Rule 15
Disqualification of Judges

(A)   A Judge may not sit at a trial or appeal in any case, in which he has a personal interest or concerning which he has or has had any association, which might affect his impartiality. He shall in any such circumstance withdraw from the case. Where the Judge withdraws from the Trial Chamber, the President shall assign another Trial Chamber Judge to sit in his place. Where a Judge withdraws from the Appeals Chamber, the Presiding Judge of that Chamber shall assign another Judge to sit in his place.

(B)   Any party may apply to the Presiding Judge of a Chamber for the disqualification of a Judge of that Chamber from a trial or appeal upon the above grounds. After the Presiding Judge has conferred with the Judge in question, the Bureau if necessary, shall determine the matter. If the Bureau upholds the application, the President shall assign another Judge to sit in place of the disqualified Judge.

(C)   The Judge of a Trial Chamber who reviews an indictment against an accused, pursuant to Article 18 of the Statute and Rules 47 and 61, shall not sit as a member of the Trial Chamber for the trial of that accused.

(D)   [...]

(E)   If a Judge is, for any reason, unable to continue sitting in a part-heard case, the Presiding Judge may, if that inability seems likely to be of short duration, adjourn the proceedings, otherwise he shall report to the President who may assign another Judge to the case and order either a rehearing or continuation of the proceedings from that point.

   However, after the opening statements provided for in Rule 84, or the beginning of the presentation of evidence pursuant to Rule 85, the continuation of the proceedings can only be ordered with the consent of the accused.

(F)   In case of illness or an unfilled vacancy or in any other exceptional circumstances, the President may authorise a Chamber to conduct routine matters, such as the delivery of decisions, in the absence of one or more members.

Rule 19
Functions of the President

The President shall preside at all plenary meetings of the Tribunal, co-ordinate the work of the Chambers and supervise the activities of the Registry as well as the exercise of all the other functions conferred on him by the Statute and the Rules. **[page 9]**

Rule 27
Rotation of the Judges

(A) Judges shall rotate on a regular basis between the Trial Chambers. Rotation shall take into account the efficient disposal of cases.

(B) The Judges shall take their places in their assigned Chamber as soon as the President thinks it convenient, having regard to the disposal of pending cases.

(C) The President may at any time temporarily assign a member of one Trial Chamber to another Trial Chamber.

Rule 48
Joinder of Accused

Persons accused of the same or different crimes committed in the course of the same transaction may be jointly charged and tried.

Rule 50
Amendment of Indictment

(A) The Prosecutor may amend an indictment, without prior leave, at any time before its confirmation, but thereafter, until the initial appearance of the accused before a Trial Chamber pursuant to Rule 62, only with leave of the Judge who confirmed it but, in exceptional circumstances, by leave of a Judge assigned by the President. At or after such initial appearance, an amendment of an indictment may only be made by leave granted by that Trial Chamber pursuant to Rule 73. If leave to amend is granted, Rule 47(G) and Rule 53 *bis* apply *mutatis mutandis* to the amended indictment.

(B) [...]

(C) [...]

Rule 62
Initial Appearance of Accused

Upon his transfer to the Tribunal, the accused shall be brought before a Trial Chamber without delay, and shall be formally charged. The Trial Chamber shall:

(i) [...]

(ii) [...]

(iii) [...] **[page 10]**

(iv) in the case of a plea of not guilty, instruct the Registrar to set a date for trial;

(v) [...]

(vi) [...]

Rule 72
Preliminary Motions

(A) Preliminary motions by either party shall be brought within sixty days following disclosure by the Prosecutor to the Defence of all the material envisaged by Rule 66(A)(I), and in any case before the hearing on the merits.

(B) Preliminary motions by the accused are:

i) objections based on lack of jurisdiction
ii) objections based on defects in the form of the indictment;

iii) applications for severance of crimes joined in ons indictment under Rule 49, or for separate trials under Rule 82(B)

iv) objections based on the denial of request for assignment of counsel.

The Trial Chamber shall dispose of preliminary motions *in limine litis*.

(C) Decisions on preliminary motions are without interlocutory appeal save in the case of dismissal of an objection based on lack of jurisdiction, where an appeal will lie as a matter of right.

(D) Notice of appeal envisaged in Sub-rule (D) shall be filed within seven days from the impugned decision.

(E) Failure to comply with the time limits prescribed in this Rule shall constitute a waiver of the rights. The Trial Chamber may, however, grant relief from the waiver upon showing good cause.

Rule 117
Expedited Appeals Procedure

(A) An appeal under Rule 108(B) shall be heard expeditiously on the basis of the original record of the Trial Chamber and without the necessity of any brief.

(B) All delays and other procedural requirements shall be fixed by an order of the President issued on an application by one of the parties, or *proprio motu* should no such application have been made within fifteen days after the filing of the notice of appeal. **[page 11]**

(C) Rules 109 to 114 shall not apply to such appeals.

IV. DISCUSSION

13. In answering the main questions which have been raised by the present appeal, namely, whether a right of appeal lies from the Decision, and if so, whether Trial Chamber II was competent to hear the Leave Request and the Joinder Motion, the members of the Appeals Chamber differ on a number of issues both as to reasoning and as to result. Consequently, the views of each member of the Appeals Chamber on the particular issues are set out in detail in Opinions, which are appended to this decision.

14. The Appeals Chamber, for the reasons set out in the Joint and Separate Opinion of Judge McDonald and Judge Vohrah, and, in part, the Joint Separate and Concurring Opinion of Judge Wang and Judge Nieto-Navia, and, in part, the Dissenting Opinion of Judge Shahabuddeen, finds that the appeal is admissible since a right of appeal lies from the Decision pursuant to Sub-rule 72(D) of the Rules.

15. The Appeals Chamber, for the reasons set out in the Joint and Separate Opinion of Judge McDonald and Judge Vohrah and the Joint Separate and Concurring Opinion of Judge Wang and Judge Nieto-Navia, finds that based on a textual interpretation of Sub-rule 50(A), Trial Chamber II is the only Trial Chamber competent to adjudicate the Leave Request. Judge Shahabuddeen reserves his views, considering that on this point the appeal is not admissible.

16. The Appeals Chamber, for the reason set out in the Joint and Separate Opinion of Judge McDonald and Judge Vohrah, the Joint Separate and Concurring Opinion of Judge Wang and Judge Nieto-Navia and the Dissenting Opinion of Judge Shahabuddeen finds that Trial Chamber I is competent to adjudicate the Joinder Motion.

17. Accordingly, the Appeals Chamber by majority finds that the appeal should be allowed in respect of the Leave Request, and, unanimously, finds that the appeal should be dismissed in respect of the Joinder Motion. **[page 12]**

V. DISPOSITION

THE APPEALS CHAMBER, by a majority of four to one, with Judge Shahabuddeen dissenting, **ALLOWS** the Appeal relating to the Leave Request and **REMITS** it to Trial Chamber II. **THE APPEALS CHAMBER UNANIMOUSLY DISMISSES** the appeal relating to the Joinder Motion.

Done in both English and French, the English text being authoritative.

Gabrielle Kirk McDonald
Presiding Judge

Judge McDonald and Judge Vohrah append a Joint Separate Opinion.

Judge Wang and Judge Nieto-Navia append a Joint Separate Opinion.

Judge Shahabuddeen appends a Dissenting Opinion.

Dated this third day of June 1999
At Arusha,
Tanzania.

International Criminal Tribunal for the Prosecution of Persons Responsible for Genocide and Other Serious Violations of International Humanitarian Law Committed in the Territory of Rwanda and Rwandan Citizens responsible for genocide and other such violations committed in the territory of neighbouring States between 1 January and 31 December 1994	Case No.: ICTR-96-15-A Date: 3 June 1999 Original: English

IN THE APPEALS CHAMBER

Before: **Judge Gabrielle Kirk McDonald, Presiding**
                Judge Mohamed Shahabuddeen
                Judge Lal Chand Vohrah
                Judge Wang Tieya
                Judge Rafael Nieto-Navia

Registrar: **Mr. Agwu U. Okali**

Decision of: **3 June 1999**

JOSEPH KANYABASHI

v.

THE PROSECUTOR

JOINT AND SEPARATE OPINION OF JUDGE McDONALD AND JUDGE VOHRAH

Counsel for the Appellant:
     Mr. Michel Marchand
     Mr. Michel Boyer

The Office of the Prosecutor:
     Mr. David Spencer
     Mr. Ibukunolu Babajide
     Mr. Chile Eboe-Osuji
     Mr. Robert Petit

[page 2] I. INTRODUCTION

1.   The issues for consideration in this appeal have been set forth in the Decision of the Appeals Chamber on the Defence Motion for Interlocutory Appeal on the Jurisdiction of Trial Chamber I.

II. DISCUSSION

A. Is the appeal from a dismissal of an objection based on lack of jurisdiction within the meaning of Sub-rule 72(D)

2.   In the Scheduling Order of 18 December 1998[1], the Appeals Chamber directed the parties to submit briefs on the following issues: (a) Whether the appeal is from dismissal of an objection based on lack of jurisdiction within the meaning of Sub-rule 72(D); and (b) if it is: (i) whether the Trial Chamber is competent to hear the Prosecutor's applications; and (ii) if so, whether the Trial Chamber was lawfully composed.

3.   Sub-rule 72(D) provides that preliminary motions are without interlocutory appeal except in the case of dismissal of an objection based on lack of jurisdiction. In the appeal the jurisdiction of Trial Chamber I to hear the hearing of the two Prosecution motions is challenged. Having had his initial appearance before Trial Chamber II, the Appellant objects to the competence of any Trial Chamber other than Trial Chamber II to consider the Leave Request and the Joinder Motion on the grounds that the composition of the Trial Chambers cannot be altered. Also, it is asserted that Sub-rule 50(A) requires the submission of the Leave Request to Trial Chamber II, which conducted his initial appearance. Further, he claims that Trial Chamber I lacks jurisdiction because President Kama was not acting independently and impartially in re-composing Trial Chamber I. The challenge to the competence of Trial Chamber I to entertain the Leave Request and the Joinder Motion raises the issue as to whether the dismissal by Trial Chamber I of the Appellant's objection to the exercise of its jurisdiction is appealable pursuant to Sub-rule 72(D), and whether Trial Chamber I, as re-composed, has jurisdiction to adjudicate the Leave Request and the Joinder Motion. **[page 3]**

4.   The jurisdiction of a tribunal concerns its right and power to hear the determine a judicial proceeding. Articles 1 through 7 of the Statute of the International Tribunal establish the competence of the International Tribunal as a whole, with respect to subject matter, personal, territorial and temporal (*ratione materiae, ratione personae, ratione loci* and *ratione temporis*) jurisdiction. However, the jurisdiction of the Tribunal is exercised by the Trial Chambers. Consequently, if the competence and the legality of the composition of the Trial Chamber are challenged, it raises the issue of the power of that Trial Chamber to exercise the jurisdiction that the Tribunal possesses.

5.   Since we hold that the appeal relates to a dismissal of an objection based on lack of jurisdiction within the meaning of Sub-rule 72(D), the next issue to be addressed is whether Trial Chamber I was lawfully composed and thus competent to exercise jurisdiction.

B. Whether Trial Chamber I was unlawfully composed, and was, therefore, not competent to exercise jurisdiction

6.   The first issue is whether Trial Chamber I as re-composed is the proper Trial Chamber to decide the Leave Request and the Joinder Motion. A determination of this issue requires an evaluation of the procedural background of the Leave Request and the Joinder Motion.

7.   Relying on evidence freshly discovered in July 1997, pointing to a conspiracy involving the Appellant and other accused, the Prosecutor submitted on 6 March 1998, an Indictment before Judge Khan for review. In the Indictment, the Prosecutor charged twenty-nine individuals with offences

---

[1]   Prosecutor v. Kanyabashi, *Scheduling Order*, Case No. ICTR 96-15-I, App. Ch., 18 December 1998.

substantially related to the same facts. On 31 March 1998, Judge Khan conducted *ex parte* proceedings under Rule 47 and divided the twenty-nine accused into three groups. The first group, consisting of eleven persons including the Appellant, had already been previously indicted and entered pleas at their initial appearances. The second group of five persons had been previously indicted but remained at liberty. The third group consisted of thirteen persons who had not been indicted and who were at liberty. In the Amended Indictment, the Prosecutor had added a new charge of **[page 4]** conspiracy against persons in the first and second groups. Judge Khan rejected the Prosecutor's submission that the Indictment should be reviewed under the *ex parte* provision of Rule 47 of the Rules. Judge Khan held that the Prosecutor must first seek leave to amend the Indictment under Rule 50 of the Rules with respect to the persons in the first and second groups, or to withdraw these persons from the Indictment and resubmit the Indictment, or to follow the procedure in Rule 72 governing preliminary motions. Judge Khan, the confirming Judge, declined to exercise jurisdiction over all three groups of persons, based on a consideration for the rights of the accused, and consequently he dismissed the Indictment.[2]

8.   On 6 April 1998, the Prosecutor appealed against Judge Khan's Decision pursuant to Rule 108 of the Rules setting forth various grounds of appeal. On 8 June 1998, this Appeals Chamber rejected the Prosecutor's Application for Leave to Appeal Judge Khan's Decision[3], finding that a right of appeal did not lie from Judge Khan's Decision under the Statute and the Rules.

9.   Consequently, the Prosecutor proceeded on four separate original Indictments against the six named accused: one Indictment against Pauline Nyramasuhuko and Arsène Shalom Ntahobali; another against Sylvain Nsabimana and Alphonse Nteziryayo; another against Elie Ndajambaje; and one against the Appellant. Pursuant to Rule 50 of the Rules, the Prosecutor sought Leave to Amend the respective Indictments for the purposes of (i) adding new charges against the Appellant; (ii) expanding certain existing counts; (iii) adding relevant counts to the allegations; and (iv) bringing the current Indictment into conformity with the Jurisprudence of the Tribunal and current trial practices.[4] Through another motion, the Prosecutor also sought to join the six accused in the same case.[5]The discussion **[page 5]** concerning which Trial Chamber is to consider the Leave Request and, if granted, which Trial Chamber is to rule on the Joinder Motion is set forth below.

10.   The Appellant contends that the composition of the Trial Chambers is static and that once a Judge is assigned to a Trial Chamber he/she may not be re-assigned absent exceptional circumstances.[6] The Appellants asserts Trial Chamber may be re-composed only in accordance with Rule 15 and Rule 27, and that in the instant case, the reasons set forth by Trial Chamber I in dismissing the Appellant's objection, failed to meet the requirements established by those Rules.

11.   A close reading of the Rules does not support the Appellant's assertions. Pursuant to Rule 19, the President is directed to co-ordinate the work of the Chambers. Sub-rule 27(A) provides for the rotation of Judges while taking into account the efficient disposal of cases. Sub-rule 27(B) allows the President to assign Judges to particular Trial Chambers, having regard to the disposal of pending cases, while Sub-rule 27(C) allows for the temporary assigment of a Judge from one Trial Chamber to another Trial

---

[2]   Prosecutor v. Théoneste Bagosora and 28 Others, *Dismissal of Indictment*, Case No. ICTR-98-37-I, 31 March 1998, at p. 12. See also Prosecutor v. Théoneste Bagosora and 28 Others, *Decision on the Admissibility of the Prosecutor's Appeal from the Decision of a Confirming Judge Dismissing an Indictment Against Théoneste Bagosora and 28 Others*, Case No. ICTR-98-37-A, 8 June 1998.

[3]   Prosecutor v. Théoneste Bagosora and 28 Others, *Decision on the Admissibility of the Prosecutor's Appeal from the Decision of a Confirming Judge Dismissing an Indictment Against Théoneste Bagosora and 28 Others*, Case No. ICTR-98-37-A, 8 June 1998.

[4]   Prosecutor v. Kanyabashi, *Prosecutor's Request for Leave to File an Amended Indictment*, Case No. ICTR-96-15-T, 17 August 1998.

[5]   Prosecutor v. Nyramasuhuko and Ntahobali, *Prosecutor's Motion for Joinder of Accused*, Case No. ICTR-97-21-I, 17 August 1998; Prosecutor v. Nsabimana and Nteziryayo, *Prosecutor's Motion for Joinder of Accused*, Case No. ICTR-97-29A and B-I, 17 August 1998; Prosecutor v. Kanyabashi, *Prosecutor's Motion for Joinder of Accused*, Case No. ICTR 96-15-T, 17 August 1998; Prosecutor v. Ndajambaye, *Prosecuto's Motion for Joinder of Accused* Case No. ICTR-96-8-T, 17 August 1998.

[6]   See Prosecutor v. Kanyabashi, Case No. ICTR-96-15-I, *Appellant's Brief: Appeal Relating to an Objection Based on Lack of Jurisdiction Rules 108(B) and 117 of the Rules of Procedure and Evidence*, (hereinafter, *Appellant's 18 December 1998 Brief*), 18 December 1998, at paras. 104-106.

Chamber. Sub-rule 15(E) allows the President to assign another Judge to a case in the event one of the originally assigned Judges is unable, for any reason, to continue sitting in a part-heard case. In announcing the Trial Chamber's Decision on the Appellant's Motion, Judge Kama made reference to these rules:

> [I]n application of Rule 27, the A, B and C and Rule 15(E), the President has the power at any point in time when the needs of administration of justice requires (sic) to assign provisionally a Judge to a given Chamber[7].

12.   These Rules fully comport with the Statute. The Appellant raises several arguments based on the Statute. First, he relies on Article 10, Article 19(1) and Article 22 to advance his argument for judicial independence.[8] Second, the Appellant relies on Article 11 and **[page 6]** Article 12, in asserting that the Statute requires judicial independence not only from external influences, but also judicial independence among the Trial Chambers.[9] Third, the Appellant asserts that Article 13 of the Statute, which requires a Judge to sit only on the Trial Chamber to which he or she was assigned, prohibits re-composition of the Trial Chambers.[10] Fourth, he asserts that Article 13 indicates that the Security Council, in ratifying the Statute, intended to "make the Chamber function in a stable manner while providing for flexibility whenever necessary for the proper administration of justice"[11].

13.   The Statute, as the International Tribunal's consitutive document, sets forth the fundamental structure of the institution and addresses the important administrative criteria for the Tribunal's proper functioning. Articles 10, 11 en 13 explain the basic organisation of the Tribunal, the composition of the Chambers, and the means by which officers and members of the Chambers are selected. Article 10 provides that the International Tribunal shall be comprised of three organs, including the Trial and Appeals Chambers. Article 11(A) provides that the Trial Chambers shall consist of three Judges. The plain meaning of this provision is that the Trial Chambers are only competent if there are three Judges assigned to them. Article 13(2) directs the President to assign Judges to the Trial Chambers and proscribes a Judge from serving on a Chamber to which he or she was not assigned.

14.   Article 14 of the Statute explicitly directed the Judges to draft the Rules. The Rules were crafted to flesh out and provide substance to the Statute. Rule 15 governs the disqualification of Judges and provides in Sub-rule 15(A) that a Judge may withdraw from a case in which he/she has or has had any association which might affect his/her impartiality and that in such circumstances, the President shall assign another Judge to sit in his/her place. Such a situation would result in re-composition of that Trial Chamber. Sub-rule 15(B) allows for disqualification of a Judge, thereby enabling the re-composition of that Trial Chamber.[12] Sub-rule 15(E) enables the President to change the composition of the Trial Chamber by assigning another Judge to the case and to order either a rehearing or the **[page 7]** continuation of the proceedings where a Judge is unable to continue sitting in a part-heard case.[13]

15.   The President of the International Tribunal is charged with administrative tasks conferred upon him/her by the Statute and the Rules. In interpreting the Statute, and the Rules which implement the Statute, Trial Chambers of both the International Tribunal and the International Criminal Tribunal for the former Yugoslavia (hereinafter "ICTY"), as well as the Appeals Chamber have consistently resorted to the Vienna Convention of the Law of Treaties ("the Vienna Convention")[14], for the interpretation of the

---

[7]   Prosecutor v. Kanyabashi, Trial transcript, 24 September 1998, at p. 29.

[8]   Ibid., at paras. 91-94.

[9]   *Appellant's 18 December 1998 Brief* at paras. 102-104.

[10]   Ibid., at para. 98 and Prosecutor v. Kanyabashi, *Appeal Relating to the Lack of Jurisdiction, Rules 108(B) and 117 of the Rules of Procedure and Evidence*, Case No. ICTR 96-15-I, 14 October 1998, ("*Appellant's 14 October 1998 Brief*"), at para. 40.

[11]   *Appellant's 14 October 1998 Brief* at para. 40.

[12]   See Prosecutor v. Kordic and Cerkez, *Decision on the Application for the Disqualification of Judges Jorda and Riad*, Case No. IT-95-14/2-PT, 8 October 1998.

[13]   However, after the opening statement or the beginning of the presentation of the evidence, a situation not applicable to this case, the proceedings can be ordered to continue only with the consent of the accused.

[14]   Vienna Convention on the Law of Treaties, 23 May 1969, 1155 U.N.T.S. 331.

Statute.[15] Although the Statute is not a treaty, it is a *sui generis* international legal instrument resembling a treaty. Adopted by the Security Council, an organ to which Member States of the United Nations have vested legal responsibility, the Statute shares with treaties fundamental similarities. Because the Vienna Convention cofidies logical and practical norms that are consistent with domestic law, it is applicable under customary international law to international instruments which are not treaties. Thus, recourse by analogy is appropriate to Article 31(1) of the Vienna Convention in interpreting the provisions of the Statute. Article 31(1) states that "[a] treaty shall be interpreted in good faith in accordance with the ordinary meaning to be given to the terms of the treaty in their context and in the light of its objects and purpose."

16. The overarching object and purpose of the Statute in ensuring a fair and expeditious trial for the accused. The Trial Chambers are re-composed to ensure the attainment of this object and purpose. Thus, the contextual interpretation of the provisions of the Statute, and by extension, of the Rules implementing the Statute, should meet that object and purpose. For example, as noted above, Sub-rules 15(E) authorises the President to assign a new Judge to a Chamber to replace one who is disqualified or was otherwise unable to sit in a part-heard case. The Statute, in setting forth the organisational structure of the Chambers, is **[page 8]** silent on this point. Rather, the Statute leaves to the Judges the responsibility for drafting rules for the conduct of the proceedings.[16] The Rules that allow for a re-composition meet this pupose. To interpret silence as a prohibition would frustrate this object and purpose of the Statute.

17. Thus, the assignment of a Judge to a Trial Chamber is not "frozen in time". Altered circumstances such as the resignation, serious illness, death, or disqualification of a Judge, or the need for rotation to best co-ordinate the work of the Chambers may demand the re-composition of a Trial Chamber. An interpretation of the Statute that would find a requirement that Judges serve forever in the Chamber to which they are assigned, despite the disqualification, illness, death or resignation of a Judge of that Chamber, would lead to an absurd result. Further, it would defeat the object and purpose of the Statute to ensure that an accused has a fair and expeditious trial.

18. Acting pursuant to his mandate under Article 13 of the Statute, President Kama assigned Judge Pillay, Judge Sekule and himself to Trial Chamber I to hear the Leave Request and the Joinder Motion. The composition of this Trial Chamber reveals President Kama's administrative foresight since the Indictments against the six accused who are the object of the Joinder Motion had been confirmed by the following Judges: Khan, Aspegren and Ostrovsky. Sub-rule 15(C) disqualifies a Judge who reviews an indictment against an accused to sit as a member of the Trial Chamber for the Trial of the same accused. A Trial Chamber composed of Judges who would not be subject to disqualification should the Leave Request or the Joinder Motion be granted could *only* include Judge Kama, Judge Sekule and Judge Pillay, as the International Tribunal as the time was composed of only six Judges. Contrary to the Appellant's contention, we find that this constitutes an exceptional circumstance.

19. The Statute and the Rules confer upon the President the authority to replace Judges and to re-compose Trial Chambers, in exceptional circumstances, circumstances including the disqualification, resignation[17], serious injury or death of a Judge, in order to ensure the attainment of the object and purpose of the Statute and to avoid any absurd result. The **[page 9]** alternative would be the discontinuance of trials and the violation of the accused's fundamental rights. The composition and re-

---

[15] Other cases where Trial Chambers of the International Tribunal or the ICTY have had recourse to Article 31 in interpreting the provisions of the Statutes include: Prosecutor v. Théoneste Bagosora and 28 Others, *Decision on the Admissibility of the Prosecutor's Appeal from the Decision of a Confirming Judge Dismissing an Indictment Against Théoneste Bagosora and 28 Others*, op. cit., note 1 at pp. 12-13; Prosecutor v. Tadić, *Decision on the Prosecutor's Motion, Protectie Measures for Victims and Witnesses*, Case No. IT-94-1-T, 10 August 1995, at p. 10; Prosecutor v. Erdemovic, *Judgement*, Case No. IT-96-22-A, 7 October 1997, at p. 3; and Prosecutor v. Delalic and Others, Case No. IT-96-21-T, 16 November 1998, at pp. 396-397.

[16] See Article 14.

[17] Sub-rule 15(C), for example, clearly states that a Judge who reviewed an Indictment against an accused pursuant to Article 18 and Rules 47 and 61, is disqualified to sit as a member of the Trial Chamber for the trial of that accused. It was precisely for this reason that President Kama re-composed the Trial Chamber.

composition of Trial Chambers by the President is a judicial administrative function, pursuant to the Statute and Rules, formulated for the efficient judicial administrative operation of the Tribunal.

C. Whether the Trial Chamber that conducts the initial appearance has exclusive jurisdiction over the case

1. Whether the Initial Appearance Constitutes the Commencement of Trial

20.   The Appellant also asserts that once an accused has made an initial appearance before a Trial Chamber that Chamber has exclusive jurisdiction over his case, on the ground that his initial appearance marks the beginning of trial.[18] In paragraph 29 of the Appellant's 17 February 1999 Brief, Appellant asserts:

> [A] suspect acquires the status of accused when he enters his plea during his initial appearance before the Trial Chamber. It is only then that he becomes an accused and his case begins in earnest.

We find that in the present case, the Appellant's trial had *not* commenced for the purpose of concluding that Trial Chamber II has exclusive jurisdiction over his case. The following discussion will suffice to show that the Appellant's assertion in this regard is unfounded.

21.   In making this assertion, the Appellant relies on the Decision in <u>Prosecutor v. Bagosora and 28 Others</u>[19]. In that case, Judge Khan concluded that a trial commences at the time of the initial appearance, when the accused enters pleas on the charges involving the **[page 10]** crimes for which he has been brought before the Tribunal.[20] Article 19 of the Statute of the International Tribunal directs the Trial Chamber to "set a date for trial" after the accused enters a plea of not guilty. Sub-rule 62(iv), governing the Initial Appearance of the Accused, provides for the same result. Clearly, an event could not have occurred if the Statute and Rules require that a date be set for the commencement of that event.

22.   Further, the provisions of Sub-rule 15(E) clearly provide that a case is considered to be "part-heard" after the opening statement or the presentation of the evidence, neither of which has occurred in this case[21]. Moreover, although Sub-rule 15(E) enables the President to change the composition of the Trial Chamber even in the event of a part-heard case, after the opening statement or the commencement of the presentation of evidence, the proceedings can continue only with consent of the accused.

23.   We also note that Sub-rule 73*bis*(A), which was adopted after the <u>Bagosora</u> Decision, provides that the Trial Chamber shall hold a Pre-trial Conference prior to the commencement of the trial. No Pre-Trial Conference has yet been in the Appellant's case.

24.   Read together, these provisions lead to the inescapable conclusion that the initial appearance of the Appellant does *not* mark the commencement of his trial. Therefore, Trial Chamber II does not have exclusive jurisdiction over his case. We turn now to address the specific disposition of the Leave Request and the Joinder Motion.

2. Whether the Leave Request is Properly Before Trial Chamber II

---

[18]   *Appellant's 17 February 1999 Brief* at paras. 24-29; para. 43.

[19]   <u>Prosecutor v. Théoneste Bagosora and 28 Others</u>, *Dismissal of Indictment*, Case No. ICTR-98-37-I, 31 March 1998 at p. 9. See also <u>Prosecutor v. Théoneste Bagosora and 28 Others</u>, *Decision on the Admissibility of the Prosecutor's Appeal from the Decision of a Confirming Judge Dismissing an Indictment Against Theoneste Bagosora and 28 Others*, Case No. ICTR-98-37-A, 8 June 1998.

[20]   *Appellant's 17 February 1999 Brief* at para. 25, citing <u>Prosecutor v. Théoneste Bagosora and 28 Others, op cit.</u>, p. 9.

[21]   Sub-rule 15(E) governs the Disqualification of Judges involving cases which are "partheard". Under the first sentence of that Sub-rule, the President may assign another Judge to replace a Judge who is unable, for any reason, to continue sitting in a part heard case. Such an assignment is permissible even in the absence of the accused's consent. Pursuant to the second sentence of that Sub-rule, however, after the opening statement or the beginning of the presentation of evidence, the proceedings can be continued only with the consent of the accused.

25.   The Prosecutor submitted the Leave Request to Trial Chamber II, composed of Judge Sekule, Judge Khan and Judge Pillay. The Appellant's initial appearance had previously been held before Trial Chamber II although, at that time, Trial Chamber II was composed of Judge Khan, Judge Aspegren and Judge Pillay. Thus, the composition of Trial Chamber II had been **[page 11]** itself altered, a fact which the Appellant does not challenge. However, the Leave Request was set for hearing before Trial Chamber I which was seized of the Joinder Motion[22]. The Appellant asserted before the Trial Chamber that the Leave Request should have been heard by Trial Chamber II. In making this assertiion, Counsel for the Appellant relied on Article 13(2) on the Statute and the <u>Bagosora</u> Decision:

> [I]n light of the statute and also in light of the previous decisions that I have just referred to, Kanyabashi argues that the motion for amendment must be heard by Chamber II which is the Chamber before which the initial appearance of the accused was made[23]

26.   Rule 50 contains three stages during which the Prosecutor can amend an Indictment[24]. Only one of these three stages is relevant to the disposition of this appeal. The relevant portion of Sub-rule 50(A), provides that, "At or after such initial appearance, an amendment of an indictment may only be made by leave granted by *that* Trial Chamber pursuant to Rule 73." (Emphasis added.)

27.   In referring the Leave Request and the Joinder Motion to the same Trial Chamber, President Kama relied on three grounds: 1) the need for flexibility; 2) the need to avoid **[page 12]** assigning the Leave Request and the Joinder Motion to a Chamber where one or more Judges would be disqualified; and 3) the need to resolve both issues simultaneously, due to the linkage between the Leave Request and the Joinder Motion. Regarding the need for flexibility, Judge Kama stated:

> Article 13 of the Statute does not disallow flexibility in the composition of the Chamber. ...[A]s an illustration of this flexibility, the Chamber had as evidence what was referred to as Chamber II... It's not the normal composition of Chamber II because the two Judges had been assigned to Chamber I, and this is prove [sic] of the flexibility that the Tribunal and the Chamber is exercising[25].

With respect to avoiding referral to a Chamber where one or more Judges would be disqualified, Judge Kama said:

> ...[I]t cannot be otherwise when we know that the present Tribunal is composed of only six Judges making up two Trial Chambers and that for one reason or another one or other Judge may be unable to be present. ...[W]e belief [sic] that for the proper administration of justice and also for a fair trial, it was not responsible that Judges who have been disqualified be able to sit in a Chamber which are considering amendments for, amendments of Indictments and Motions for Joinder and it

---

[22]   The Prosecutor addressed the Joinder Motion to neither a numbered Trial Chamber nor to specific Judges.

[23]   <u>Prosecutor v. Kanyabashi</u>, Case No. ICTR-96-15-I, Trial transcript, 24 September 1998, at p.10.

[24]   With respect to the procedures for amending Indictments, there are slight differences between the Statutes of the International Tribunal and the ICTY. Sub-rule 50(A) of the ICTY states:

Rule 50
Amendment of Indictment

(A)   The Prosecutor may amend an Indictment:

    (i)   at any time before its confirmation, without leave;

    (ii)   thereafter, and until the commencement of the presentation of evidence in terms of Rule 85, with leave of the Judge who confirmed the Indictment, *or a Judge assigned by the President*;
        or

    (iii)   after the commencement of the presentation of evidence, with leave of the Trial Chamber hearing the case, after having heard the parties.

(Emphasis added). Notwithstanding the different language used in the two rules, as reflected in the emphasized phrase, we find that an "exceptional circumstance" as set forth in ICTR Sub-rule 50(A) includes circumstances present in this case. The language "hearing the case" contained in ICTY Sub-rule 50(A)(iii) clearly indicates that the trial has begun.

[25]   <u>Prosecutor v. Kanyabashi</u>, Case No. ICTR-96-15-I, Trial transcript, 24 September 1998, at pp. 28-29.

is for this reason that the Chamber was composed as you know, taking into account that the other Judges had been pre-disqualified for having confirmed an Indictment[26].

With respect to the issue of the linkage between the Leave Request and the Joinder Motion, Judge Kama indicated that:

> ...[T]he amendments which should be considered today, this consideration should be in direct relation with the Joinder Motion presented by the Prosecutor. The Motions are for the amendment of Indictments and for Joinder of accused[27].

28.   Relying on Article 31(1) of the Vienna Convention[28], we find that a need for flexibility alone cannot justify departure from the plain language of the Rules. We also find that no **[page 13]** recourse to supplementary means of interpretation is necessary since this approach is resorted to only when the language of the provision is ambiguous[29]. The language of Sub-rule 50(A) is plain and unambiguous. Here, it is clear in the ordinary meaning of the language of Sub-rule 50(A) that an indictment can be amended after initial appearance of the accused *only by the Trial Chamber before which the initial appearance took place*, in this case Trial Chamber II. Accordingly, the Leave Request must be returned to Trial Chamber II, as the only competent Trial Chamber to adjudicate this matter.

29.   In fact, there was no need for flexibility except with respect to the Joinder Motion. As will be discussed in the next section, this motion does not run afoul of any explicit Rule that directs its presentation to a certain Chamber and, consequently different considerations obtain.

30.   With respect to the issue of the potential disqualification of Judges as it relates to the Leave Request, we find that President Kama's concerns in this regard were not justified. There was no realistic concern for potential disqualification of Judges with respect to the Leave Request.

31.   Regarding the issue of the linkage between the Leave Request and the Joinder Motion, this became so only *after* President Kama re-composed Trial Chamber I and directed that both motions be heard by that Trial Chamber. The Leave Request could and should have properly been presented to, and decided by, the Judges to whom the Prosecutor addressed the Leave Request since those Judges did not face the disqualification problem.

2.   Whether the Joinder Motion is Properly Before Trial Chamber I

32.   Rule 48 of the Rules provides for persons accused of the same or different crimes committed in the course of the same transaction to be jointly charged and tried. Rule 49 of the Rules of the ICTY is identical to Rule 48 of the Rules of the International Tribunal and they both appear to have been drawn from the "same transaction" test found in the federal **[page 14]** system of the United States of America. The "same transaction test" provides for offences to be joined if they are "based on the same act or transaction or on two or more acts or transactions connected together or constituting parts of a common scheme or plan."[30] It is well accepted in some common law jurisdictions that joining accused in one indictment where the "same transaction" test is met can be initiated by the prosecutor or by an order of the court if justice so requires. The public interest clearly dictates that joint offences may be tried together. The jurisprudence of the ICTY clearly permits joint trials and points to the existence of specific elements to justify joinder and joint trials[31]. However, the requirements necessary to be fulfilled before

---

[26]   Ibid., at pp. 28-30.

[27]   Ibid., at pp. 29-30.

[28]   See discussion, supra., at para. 15.

[29]   See Vienna Convention, Articles 31-32. See also *Prosecutor v. Erdemovic, Judgement and Joint Separate Opinion of Judge McDonald and Judge Vohrah*, Case No. IT-96-22-A, A. Ch., 7 October 1997, at para. 3.

[30]   Criminal Procedure, Second ed., Wayne R. LaFave and Jerold H. Israel, at p. 761, citing Fed.R.Crim.P 8(a). See also *Prosecutor v. Kovacevic, Decision Stating Reasons for Appeals Chamber's Order of 29 May 1998 and Separate Opinion of Judge Shahabuddeen*, Case No. IT-97-24-AR73, 2 July 1998, at p. 3.

[31]   See, for example, *Prosecutor v. Kovacevic, Decision on Motion for Joinder of Accused and Concurrent Presentation of Evidence*, Case No. IT-97-24-PT, 14 May 1998.

joinder can be granted are not in issue since we are concerned here only with determining the particular Trial Chamber competent to hear the Joinder Motion.

33.   This is not to suggest that the Leave Request and the Joinder Motion should be heard together. We find that there is no justification substantiated by the Statute and the Rules which support the view that the two motions must be heard in the same proceeding before the same Trial Chamber. In any event, there is no Rule that requires the Leave Request and the Joinder Motion to be considered in "direct relation" to each other. For the reasons set out above, we hold that the Leave Request must be returned to Trial Chamber II for determination as to whether it should be granted and that the Joinder Motion may remain with Trial Chamber I for determination on its merits.

34.   In the result,[32], we hold that Trial Chamber I is not unlawfully composed and that it is competent to exercise jurisdiction over the Joinder Motion. However, where, as in this case, the challenge from the Appellant is based on allegations that the re-composition gives rise to a lack of independence and impartiality resulting in the violation of the Appellant's fundamental rights to a fair trial, such a concern, notwithstanding our finding that the Trial Chamber was properly composed, warrants examination. **[page 15]**

D.   Does Trial Chamber I as re-composed cause the appearance of a lack of independence and impartiality violating a fundamental right of the Appellant

1.   The principle of independence and impartiality of a Tribunal

35.   The concepts of independence and impartiality are distinct from one another. Independence connotes freedom from external pressures and interference. Impartiality is characterised by objectivity in balancing the legitimate interests at play. Nevertheless, the two concepts are linked insofar as they both give rise to and nurture trust and confidence through an absence of bias, prejudice and partisanship.

36.   Article 20 of the Statute of the International Tribunal and Article 21 of the Statute of the ICTY are in large measure identical to Article 14 of the International Covenant on Civil and Political Rights. Subparagraph (1) of that provision guarantees to an accused the right to an independent and impartial tribunal. However, neither of the two Statutes of the Tribunals specifically refers to the right of a trial by an independent and impartial tribunal. The absence of such reference is not of substantial consequence, since the principles of independence and impartiality are inherent in the notions of fairness and due process duly specified in both Statutes.

37.   Thus, the right of an accused to a trial by an independent and impartial tribunal is of such fundamental value that the claim by the Appellant of a lack of independence and impartiality on the part of Trial Chamber I requires careful analysis.

2.   The Appellant's arguments that the re-composed Trial Chamber I lacked independence and impartiality

38.   A lack of independence or impartiality is plainly incompatible with judicial functions, and a showing by the Appellant as to the lack of independence and impartiality on the part of Trial Chamber I would necessarily result in a violation of his fundamental right to a fair trial. **[page 16]**

39.   The Appellant refers to various international instruments and cites four cases from the European Court of Human Rights ("the European Court") to support his view that a test of appearance is to be applied in evaluating both the independence and impartiality of judges. However, the cases cited by the Appellant concern situations in which the function of the Judges was found to be inconsistent with the

---

[32]   See discussion at pp. 3-8, supra.

nature of other offices they held, creating legitimate doubt as to the appearance of a lack of independence and impartiality.[33]

40.   In assessing the existence of impartiality for purposes of Article 6(1) of the European Convention for the Protection of Human Rights and Fundamental Freedoms, the European Court has consistently applied a test comprising objective and subjective prongs. While the subjective prong serves the purpose of enabling the Court to ascertain the personal conviction of a particular judge in a given case, the objective test helps in the examination by the Court of the guarantees offered by the judge to exclude any legitimate doubt with respect to his/her independence and impartiality.[34] **[page 17]**

41.   As to the subjective prong, the Appellant alleges that Judge Kama's comment during the hearings wherein he stated that "...the amendments which should be considered today, this consideration should be in direct relation with the Joinder Motion presented by the Prosecutor" indicated personal bias in favour of the Prosecution. The personal impartiality of a judge must be presumed until proof to the contrary. In this particular case, Judge Kama's statement does not support a finding of his personal conviction indicating an appearance of subjective bias towards the Prosecution.

42.   Under the objective test, a judge's lack of independence and impartiality is determined, quite apart from the judge's personal conduct, on ascertainable facts which may not only raise doubt as to the lack of independence and impartiality of a judge but could give the appearance of such a lack of independence and impartiality. The determinative factor under this test is whether the doubt can be held to be objectively justified. A change in the composition of the Trial Chamber *per se*, added to the decision on the part of Judge Kama to place before Trial Chamber I both of the Prosecutor's motions, cannot give rise to an objective fear of lack of independence, contradicting the content of the dictum "justice must not only be done; it must also be seen to be done".

43.   The Appellant's contention that it is not necessary that he prove an actual lack of independence or an interest or bias on the part of the Presiding Judge, or that he demonstrate the existence of specific damage is without merit. Sould a finding of an appearance of lack of independence and impartiality be established on the basis of the Appellant's arguments, such a ruling would result in the disqualification of any Judge with respect to whom a moving party alleges, without proof, a lack of independence and impartiality. The Appellant wrongfully assumed that he does not carry the burden to prove the lack of independence and impartiality on the part of the Presiding Judge or the Trial Chamber. The independence and impartiality of the Judges appointed to the Chambers are to be presumed until contrary

---

[33]   The Appellant cites the following cases: The Delcourt Case, Eur. Court, H.R. Judgment of 17 January 1970, Series A, Vol. 11, at pp. 17-19, where the Court held that although the presence of a member of the Procureur général's department at the deliberations of the Cour de Cassation may allow doubts to arise about the satisfactory nature of the system in dispute, they do not however amount to proof of a violation of the right to a fair hearing; Piersack v. Belgium, Eur. Court. H.R., Judgment of 1 October 1982, Series A, Vol. 53, at p. 12, para. 30, where the Court found that an individual, after holding office in the public prosecutor's department an office whose nature is such that he may have to deal with a given matter in the course of his duties, he cannot subsequently sit in the same case as a judge, the public is entitled to fear that he does not offer sufficient guarantees of impartiality; Sramek v. Austria, Eur. Court. H.R., Judgment of 22 October 1982, Series A, No. 84, at p. 20, where the Court found that where a member of a Tribunal is in a subordinate position, in terms of his duties and the organisation of his service vis-à-vis one of the parties to the case, litigants may entertain legitimate doubt about that persons' independence; The Belilos Case, Eur. Court. H.R. Judgment 29 April 1988, Series A, Vol. 132, at pp. 30-31, where the Court found that where the Police Board of Vaud, Switzerland, its single member being appointed by the municipality, is given a judicial function and the proceedings before it are such as to enable an accused to present his defense, the ordinary citizen will tend to see him as a member of the police force, subordinate to his superiors and loyal to his colleagues and such a situation may undermine confidence in the courts.

[34]   See among other authorities: De Cubber v. Belgium, Eur. Court. H.R. Judgment of 26 October 1984, Series A, Vol. 86, at pp. 13-14; Thorgeir Thorgeirssdn v. Iceland, Eur. Court. H.R. Judgment of 25 June 1992, Series A, vol. 239, at para. 49; Fey v. Austria, Eur. Court. H.R. Judgment of 24 February 1993, Series A Vol. 255-A, at para.28; Hauschildt v. Denmark, Eur. Court. H.R. Judgment of 26 September 1988, Series A Vol. 154, at para. 56; Saraiva de Carvalho v. Portugal, Eur. Court. H.R. Judgment of 22 April 1994, Series A Vol. 286-B, at para. 35; The Holm Case, Eur. Court. H.R. Judgment of 25 November 1993, Series A Vol. 279A, at para. 33; Nortier v. Netherlands, Eur. Court. H.R. Judgment of 24 August 1993, Series A, Vol. 267, at paras. 33-36; Piersack v. Belgium, Eur. Court. H.R. Judgment of 1 October 1982, Series A Vol. 53, at para. 27; The Delcourt Case, Eur. Court. H.R. Judgment of 17 January 1970, Series A Vol. 11, at para. 31; Bulut v. Austria, Eur. Court. H.R. Judgment of 22 February 1996, Reports 1996-II, at para. 31; Thomann v. Switzerland, Eur. Court. H.R. Judgment of 1997, 24 EHRR 553, at para. 30.

proof is established.[35] A showing that there exist circumstances likely to give rise to fear or apprehension of lack of independence and impartiality is not enough, in the absence of **[page 18]** substantive grounds supporting legitimate fears that the independence and impartiality of Trial Chamber I could be compromised[36]

44.   President Kama assigned Judges Sekule and Pillay and himself to Trial Chamber I and thereafter directed the Joinder Motion and the Leave Request to that Trial Chamber. In so doing, President Kama evinced his concern for ensuring the smooth administrative functioning of the Chambers since only these particular Judges had not reviewed any Indictment of the accused sought to be joined for trial. This justification is reflected in his comment during the proceedings on the Prosecutor's motions where he stated:

> [W]e belief [sic] that for the proper administration of justice and also far a fair trial, it was not responsible that Judges who have been disqualified be able to sit in a Chamber which are [sic] considering amendments for indictments [sic] and Motions for Joinder.[37]

45.   We fail to see how the statement made by Judge Kama, his decision to re-compose Trial Chamber I, or his decision to place both the Leave Request and the Joinder Motion for joint consideration before the re-composed Trial Chamber I, indicates any pre-determined judgement to grant the Joinder Motion prior to the hearing. We find that President Kama's administrative decision in the assignment of the Judges does not constitute a departure from the Rules, conforms with the independence and freedom from external influences which are necessary in the administration of justice, is justified in the present circumstances and does not support the Appellant's contention that the re-composition of the Trial Chamber gives the appearance of a lack of independence and impartiality. Additionally, the decision to re-compose Trial Chamber I demonstrates President Kama's objectivity in balancing the **[page 19]** legitimate interest of the fundamental rights of the accused to have a fair and expeditious trial before Judges who were not subject to disqualification by the indictment review process while ensuring the efficient assignment of Judges to all of the cases before the Tribunal. Although we find that the assignment of the Leave Request to Trial Chamber I was improper, that alone does not demonstrate any lack of independence or impartiality.

E. Our Conclusions

46.   For the foregoing reasons, we find that

        (1)   The appeal is admissible pursuant to Sub-rule 72(D) of the Rules, since the Appellant has raised an issue relating to a lack of jurisdiction of the re-composed Trial Chamber I;

        (2)   The re-composition of a Trial Chamber by the President is an administrative decision that does not offend the provisions of the Statute or the Rules;

        (3)   Based on the textual interpretation of Sub-rule 50(A), Trial Chamber II is the only Trial Chamber competent to adjudicate the Leave Request;

        (4)   Trial Chamber II is competent to adjudicate the Joinder Motion; and

---

[35]   See, for example, <u>Le Compte Van Leuven and De Meyere v. Belgium</u>, Judgement of 23 June 1981, Series A, No. 43, at p. 25, para. 58. In <u>R.D.S. v. The Queen</u>, Supreme Court of Canada, 1997 Can. Sup. Ct., Lexis, at p. 5. Through Judge Cory, the Court found that a high standard has to be met for a finding of a reasonable apprehension of bias on the part of a Judge.

[36]   In advancing his arguments, the Appellant has failed to take into consideration the fact that the Prosecutor addressed the Leave Request not to a numbered Trial Chamber, but to the following specific Judges: Judge Sekule, Judge Khan and Judge Pillay. These are the same Judges before whom the Appellant had his initial appearance. It follows that if the Prosecutor had intended to influence Judge Kama, Judge Sekule and Judge Pillay, (assigned to Trial Chamber I as re-composed) she would have addressed the motion to them by name. As regards the Joinder Motion, the Prosecutor did not address this motion to a specific Trial Chamber, nor did she include the names of the Judges who would preside over the hearing of this motion.

[37]   <u>Elie Ndayambaje and Others</u>, *Proceedings on Motions Against Composition of Chamber, Motion for Amendment of Indictment and Joinder,* Case No. ICTR-96-8-T, 24 September 1998, at p. 30. As discussed above, of the six Judges appointed to the International Tribunal, only Judge Kama, Judge Sekule and Judge Pillay had not reviewed indictments against the accused who are the subject to the Prosecutor's motions. In any event, only these Judges could sit on the Trial Chamber conducting the trial of the Appellant and the five additional accused if the Joinder Motion is granted.

(5)   The Appellant has failed to show that President Kama was not acting independently and impartially when he re-composed Trial Chamber I.

47.   Consequently, we would allow the appeal in respect of the Leave Request and remit it to Trial Chamber II for adjudication and dismiss the appeal in respect of the Joinder Motion. Further, we would dismiss the appeal with regard to the assertions that President Kama was not acting impartially and independently in referring the Leave Request and the Joinder Motion for adjudication. **[page 20]**

Done in both English and French, the English text being authoritative.

Gabrielle Kirk McDonald   Lal Chand Vohrah

Dated this third day of June 1999
At Arusha,
Tanzania.

International Criminal Tribunal for the Prosecution of Persons Responsible for Genocide and Other Serious Violations of International Humanitarian Law Committed in the Territory of Rwanda and Rwandan Citizens responsible for genocide and other such violations committed in the territory of neighbouring States between 1 January and 31 December 1994	Case No.: ICTR-96-15-A Date: 3 June 1999 Original: English

IN THE APPEALS CHAMBER

Before: **Judge Gabrielle Kirk McDonald, Presiding**
Judge Mohamed Shahabuddeen
Judge Lal Chand Vohrah
Judge Wang Tieya
Judge Rafael Nieto-Navia

Registrar: **Mr. Agwu U. Okali**

Decision of: **3 June 1999**

JOSEPH KANYABASHI

v.

THE PROSECUTOR

JOINT SEPARATE AND CONCURRING OPINION OF JUDGE WANG TIEYA AND JUDGE RAFAEL NIETO-NAVIA

Counsel for the Appellant:
   Michel Marchand
   Michel Boyer

The Office of the Prosecutor:
   Frédéric Ossogo
   Robert Petit
   Chile Eboe-Osuji
   Ibukunolu Babajide
   Mathias Marcussen

[page 2] 1. We join our fellow Judges, Judge McDonald and Judge Vohrah, in the Decision disposing of the interlocutory appeal from Mr. Joseph Kanyabashi ("the Appellant") ("the Decision") concerning his challenge to the jurisdiction of Trial Chamber I, as recomposed, to hear the "Prosecutor's Motion for Joinder of Accused" ("the Joinder Motion") and the "Prosecutor's Request for Leave to File an Amended Indictment in respect of, inter alia, the Appellant" ("the Request"), to the extent that the appeal is held admissible under Rule 72, and upheld on the merits, resulting in the Request's being remitted to Trial Chamber II, being the proper Chamber under sub-Rule 50(A), for decision. In view of the Joint Separate Opinion of Judge McDonald and Judge Vohrah ("the Opinion"), we maintain that any Trial Chamber can hear the Joinder Motion after the Request is disposed of. We respectfully append a separate and concurring opinion setting forth different reasoning for this conclusion.

2. It is necessary for us to append a separate opinion because, in our view, in our reading of sub-Rule 72(D) of the Rules of Procedure and Evidence of the Tribunal ("the Rules"), the Appeals Chamber must first resolve the preliminary issue and decide that an objection does indeed go to jurisdiction before the Chamber can proceed to consider its merits. Therefore, a showing of non-compliance with the Statute and/or the Rules alone is inadequate to establish a right of appeal under the provision. The Appellant must demonstrate that that non-compliance renders the Tribunal incompetent to adjudicate his case. We are not saying that the preliminary stage can be completely divorced from the merits phase. What we would like to emphasise is that an appeal under Rule 72 cannot be upheld unless there has been a prior determination that its basis is jurisdictional. We are of the view that at the preliminary stage, the Appellant need not prove that his objection falls squarely within the meaning of jurisdiction. Establishing a *prima facie* case suffices.

3. We find that only the second of the four grounds of appeal as argued by the Appellant is admissible under sub-rule 72 (B)(i). We hold the appeal on the second ground to be upheld. Without recounting the factual background, which is set out in the Decision, our reasons for this opinion follow.

4. The Appellant argues, as his first ground of appeal, that his initial appearance before Trial Chamber II marked the commencement of his trial, and therefore, that is the Chamber with exclusive jurisdiction over his case. The Opinion has taken a close look at the provisions of the Statute and the Rules to conclude that trial does not commence with the initial **[page 3]** appearance. We respectfully add that, in our view, at issue is not when trial begins, but rather whether the initial appearance of the accused renders a particular Trial Chamber seized of a case to the exclusion of any other Chamber. Therefore, we need not decide when trial begins to resolve this issue. It is clear from Article 19 (3) of the Statute and Rule 62 that the exclusive jurisdiction, if any, of a particular Trial Chamber over a case does not vest with the initial appearance of the accused. The fact is that Rule 62 does not stipulate that the President shall forthwith assign a case to a Trial Chamber upon the transfer of an accused to the seat of the International Tribunal for Rwanda ("the Tribunal"). Furthermore, only rarely do the Rules require a case to be dealt with by a specific Trial Chamber, thereby indicating that there are a very limited number of situations where the authority or power to hear a case lies with a specific Chamber, and none other. The obvious example is the provision of sub-Rule 50 (A). It may be arguable that, in the practice of the Tribunal, exclusive jurisdiction over a case occurs after the opening statements, or the beginning of the presentation of evidence. But this proposition would not be based on any explicit provision of the Statute or Rules. It is implicit in Article 20 of the Statute which guarantees the right of an accused to a fair trial. Moreover, the case under appeal here has not reached that stage where the proposition may reasonably be invoked. Therefore, the jurisdiction, if any, of Trial Chamber I over the present case could not be affected by the Appellant's initial appearance before Trial Chamber II. Consequently, his challenge on this ground fails to make a jurisdictional objection.

5. The second ground of appeal in *Kanyabashi* relates to the interpretation of sub-Rule 50 (A). We concur with the Opinion on Rule 48 which provides that persons accused of the same or different crimes committed in the course of the same transaction may be jointly charged and tried.

6. We respectfully add that there is no difficulty for us to accept that Rule 48 lays down the condition that a joinder motion is meant to be a request for jointly charging and trying several accused. We tend to think that permission for joint charging under that rule does not necessarily require the bringing of a new, substitute indictment in lieu of the existing ones, because by adding names to one of the existing indictments which concern the same facts or transactions, the case may become a joint trial of several

accused on different charges found in one single indictment, subject to, of course, any request for amendment. This proposition may, as some may opine, create a disequilibrium, because the accused whose indictment is **[page 4]** selected for amendment before being joined by charges against other accused, who are mentioned together with him in a separate, joinder motion, may complain about non-compliance with sub-Rule 50 (A),[1] while the other accused may not, due to the fact that their status as co-accused would be one imported into this case by way of the Joinder Motion if the latter is granted. However, this inequitable situation is somewhat more advanced than the stage which the dispute in the present appeal seems to have reached. We note that the Request was filed on 17 August 1998 before Trial Chamber II comprising Judges Sekule, presiding, Khan and Pillay, this composition of the Chamber differing from that before which the Appellant made his initial appearance. We take note of this fact because the Request was placed before the same Chamber before which the initial appearance was conducted, although the composition of the Chamber had changed. It may not be stretching reason to say that "that Trial Chamber", as required by sub-Rule 50 (A), means a particularly numbered Chamber which may, however, be composed of different Judges on account of other provisions of the Rules. On the contrary, the Joinder Motion, also filed on 17 August 1998, did not specify the Trial Chamber to which it was to be presented. No objection based on jurisdiction could have arisen if the Request remained before Trial Chamber II.

7.   We also note that the presiding Judge of Trial Chamber I stressed the close link between the Joinder Motion and the Request. This is an approach which appears to have ignored the issue of which process should appropriately come for consideration by that Chamber. If, as we stated above, the Request remained before Trial Chamber II, there would only be the Joinder Motion pending before Trial Chamber I. Since Rule 48 does not stipulate which Trial Chamber should hear joinder motions, we have no objection to the hearing of this one by Trial Chamber I. What we fail to comprehend is why this motion was heard together with the Request, since the latter had already come before the other Chamber, thus giving rise to the complaint of non-compliance with sub-Rule 50 (A). In fact, it is not difficult to see the Joinder Motion and the Request as separate matters. Unlike new counts to be added by way of amendment – if leave be granted, that is – the existing counts against the various accused are by no means identical because the factual allegations underlying them are quite different. Otherwise, there would have been a joinder motion long before. **[page 5]**

8.   As the facts on the basis of which the various existing indictments were drawn clearly differ, we would infer that the reason for the Joinder Motion was the late discovery in July 1997 of new evidence allegedly pointing to a conspiracy involving the several accused, including the Appellant. To have the amendments of the indictments considered, together with the Joinder motion, at that moment[2] would certainly prolong the proceedings against the several accused, including the Appellant who made his initial appearance in November 1996 because the new Chamber would have to become familiar with the materials that had already been proffered to the Chamber of initial appearance.

9.   Whether non-compliance with sub-Rule 50 (A) may detract from jurisdiction is the issue the deliberation of which persuades us to allow the appeal. We consider that Trial Chamber I lacks jurisdiction to hear the Request. This consideration is chiefly based on our interpretation of sub-Rule 50 (A) which states:

> The Prosecutor may amend an indictment, without prior leave, at any time before its confirmation, but thereafter, until the initial appearance of the accused before a Trial Chamber pursuant to Rule 62, only with leave of the Judge who confirmed it but, in exceptional circumstances, by leave of a Judge assigned by the President. At or after such initial appearance, an amendment of an indictment may only be made by leave granted by that Trial Chamber pursuant to Rule 73. If leave to amend is granted, Rule 47 (G) and Rule 53 bis apply *mutatis mutandis* to the amended indictment. (emphasis added)

---

[1]   There is another way of dealing with questions of non-compliance, which is provided for under Rule 5. However, the condition for Rule 5 to apply would be an objection based on non-compliance raised before the relevant Trial Chamber, as distinct from one based on lack of jurisdiction. This condition was not, however, met in relation to the present appeal.

[2]   The Request was brought on 17 August 1998.

10.   The starting point would be our interpretative approach. We rely on the Appeals Chamber's Decision in *Prosecutor v. Théoneste Bagasora and 28 Others*, where the Chamber agreed with the Prosecution that Article 31 of the Vienna Convention on the law of Treaties of 1969 applies, *mutatis mutandis*, in the interpretation of the Statute.[3] The Rules are devised by the Judges pursuant to Article 14 of the Statute which provides: **[page 6]**

> The judges of the International Tribunal for Rwanda shall adopt, for the purpose of proceedings before the International Tribunal for Rwanda, the rules of procedure and evidence for the conduct of the pre-trial phase of the proceedings, trials and appeals, the admission of evidence, the protection of victims and witnesses and other appropriate matters of the International Tribunal for the former Yugoslavia with such changes as they deem necessary.

11.   The Rules were obviously drafted in conformity with the controlling terms of the Statute. The two documents serve identical purposes and objects underlying the mandate of the Tribunal. It would therefore be appropriate to apply identical rules of interpretation to both, namely, rules of the Vienna Convention on the Law of Treaties, with allowance being given to the distinct characteristics of the Rules, which we concede are not a treaty in the traditional sense of that term. On the other hand, the rules of the Vienna Convention, and Article 31 in particular, reflect customary rules of interpretation which originate from principles found in systems of municipal law "expressive of common sense and of normal grammatical usage".[4] As the interpretation of a provision of any legal instrument is to establish the meaning which is intended by the parties making it, we see no obstacle to applying in the interpretation of sub-Rule 50(A) the rules of the Vienna Convention which contain logical and practical norms consistent with the domestic law and practice of States. This view is buttressed by the fact that the Statute and the Rules are international documents which may be interpreted constructively according to the general rule of interpretation of treaties which are a particular type of such documents. The Statute is an instrument relying on the UN Charter, itself being a treaty, for validity, and the Rules are a derivation of the Statute.

12.   The general rule of interpretation of treaties, found in Article 31 of the Vienna Convention, provides that:

> 1. A treaty shall be interpreted in good faith in accordance with the ordinary meaning to be given to the terms of the treaty in their context and in the light of its object and purpose **[page 7]**
>
> ...
>
> 4. A special meaning shall be given to a term if it is established that the parties so intended.

Article 32, entitled "Supplementary means of interpretation", states that:

> Recourse may be had to supplementary means of interpretation, including the preparatory work of the treaty and the circumstances of its conclusion, in order to confirm the meaning resulting from the application of article 31, or to determine the meaning when the interpretation according to article 31:
> (a)   leaves the meaning ambiguous or obscure; or
> (b)   leads to a result which is manifestly absurd or unreasonable.

13.   It is clear that the Vienna Convention has adopted the textual and the teleological approach of interpretation. Interpretation has to be made "in good faith in accordance with the ordinary meaning to be given to the terms of the treaty in their context and in the light of its object and purpose" except where the treaty itself establishes a specific meaning for a word. A word or a provision is supposed to reflect the final, authentic intention of the parties. As a general rule, the interpreter cannot abandon the plain

---

[3]   Case No. ICTR-98-37-A, 8 June 1998, para.28. Also see *Prosecutor v. Dusko Tadić* (Case No. ICTY-94-I-T), *Decision on the Prosecutor's Motion Requesting Protective Measures for Victims and Witnesses*, 10 August 1995, paras. 17-18; *Prosecutor v. Dra en Erdemović* (Case No. ICTY-96-22-A), Joint Separate Opinion of Judges McDonald and Vohrah, para.3.

[4]   Sir. R. Jennings and Sir A. Watts (eds.), *Oppenheim's International Law* (9th edn., Longman, London and New York, 1996), vol.1, Parts 2-4, s.631, p.1270. Cf. also *Case concerning the Territorial Dispute* (Libya/Chad), ICJ Rep. (1994), p.6, Judgement of 3 February 1994, para.41, and its statement on the customary status of Article 31 has been endorsed in *Case concerning Maritime Delimitation and Territotial Questions between Qatar and Bahrain*, Qatar v. Bahrain (Jurisdiction and Admissibility), ICJ Rep. (1995), p.6, Judgement of 15 February 1995, para.33.

textual meaning of a word or phrase, although the object and purpose of a treaty and the context of its terms are, of course, aids to its interpretation. Recourse to supplementary means is for the purpose of confirming the meaning resulting from the application of Article 31, or of determining the meaning where the interpretation according to Article 31 suggests more than one meaning or where it leads to a result that is manifestly absurd or unreasonable. The general rule of interpretation of treaties thus requires that the interpreters must give words, which are clear, plain and unambiguous their normal meaning, disregarding the literal meaning only in very exceptional circumstances.

14.   In our view, the contentious point in this appeal is the interpretation of sub-Rule 50 (A) which contains the phrase "that Trial Chamber (la Chambre)[5] pursuant to Rule 73". The Rules of the ICTY say in Rule 50 (A)(iii): "with leave of the Trial Chamber hearing the case, after having heard the parties". Does the sub-Rule restrict to a particular Trial Chamber the power to grant leave to the Prosecutor to amend an indictment? The structure of the sub-Rule is quite simple: the Prosecutor may amend an indictment at any time before its confirmation, without seeking leave; after its confirmation but before the initial appearance, with leave of **[page 8]** the confirming Judge; and after such initial appearance, with leave of the Trial Chamber before which the initial appearance was made. Therefore, the provision speaks very clearly about which Trial Chamber may consider requests for leave to amend indictments at the stage of post-initial appearance, and cannot reasonably give rise to different interpretations. The word "that" or "la" should not offer any complication: it means what it means in normal language. What the rule seeks is the assurance that the confirming Judge or the Trial Chamber duly seized of an indictment decides on its amendment, so as to comply with the objects and purposes of the Rules and the Statute to avoid unnecessary delays of trial and to avoid the confusion caused by passing a case back and forth between the confirming Judge and a Trial Chamber. This latter applies *a foriori* to the present case where two Trial Chambers are involved in the matter of amending the indictment against the Appellant. There would be no absurd or unreasonable result from our interpretation of sub-Rule 50 (A) in relation to the present appeal. But such result would occur if the Joinder Motion and the Request along with other like requests, were to be combined for consideration because the problem of the disqualification of Judges under Rule 15 would arise in relation to the hearing of the Joinder Motion, but not in respect of the Request. If in a future case, our interpretation could result in any unreasonable consequences because of the operation of Rule 15 leading to disqualification, the objects and purposes of the Statute and the Rules shall prevail. Having said this, there is no need to look further to supplementary means for the interpretation of the sub-Rule. We would find that the appeal on the second ground is admissible and should be allowed.

15.   The Appellant claims, as the third ground of appeal, that even if Trial Chamber I in its original composition had jurisdiction, the change in its composition breached Articles 10, 11 and 13 of the Statute, thereby rendering Trial Chamber I, as recomposed, incompetent. It is the Appellant's position that Articles 10, 11 and 13 fix the composition of a Trial Chamber; consequently, he posits that any variation therefrom is unlawful and renders the recomposed Chamber incompetent. The issue raised by the Appellant is two-pronged: (1) was Trial Chamber I, as recomposed, lawfully composed under the Statute? (2) if not, did its unlawful composition render it incompetent? There is the sense that to render a Trial Chamber incompetent means to deprive it of the right to exercise its jurisdiction. So the Appellant is in effect arguing that the breach of Articles 10, 11 and 13 divests Trial Chamber I of the right to exercise the jurisdiction it is presumed to have over the present case. **[page 9]**

16.   Articles 10, 11 and 13 serve to establish the two Trial Chambers and allocate three Judges to sit in each of them. The last sentence of Article 13 (2) provides that "A judge shall serve only in the Chamber to which he or she was assigned." In our view, the plain meaning of this provision does not preclude a Judge from sitting occasionaly on a case in a Chamber different than that to which he or she was assigned, provided that the accused's right to a fair trial is not prejudiced (see paragraphs 21 and 22 below).

---

[5]   In the French text, the wording is "la chambre de premiere instance".

17. This ground more suitably appertains to the Joinder Motion than does the Request, since, as stated above in relation to the second ground of appeal, the matter of amending indictments falls within the purview of sub-Rule 50 (A) which only insists on a particular Trial Chamber, but not one with a fixed composition.[6] There is no need for a lengthy discussion of this ground, following our reasoning regarding the second ground, because as long as the Request is separated from the Joinder Motion, under the Statute and Rules, the latter can be dealt with by the recomposed Trial Chamber I or another Trial Chamber. We hold therefore, that the third ground does not serve to found the present appeal. However, it may still deserve some attention for its association with a different inquiry as to whether the matter of re-composition goes to jurisdiction in respect of cases coming, or to come, before the Tribunal.

18. The Appellant seems to have drawn a distinction between a possession of jurisdiction and a possession of the right to exercise jurisdiction. He alleges that Trial Chamber I had jurisdiction but lost the competence or right to exercise it because of its unlawful composition. Therefore, in the context of the Rules, the matter of composition relates to the issue of jurisdiction only in a negative way. Would it not follow, then, that if there is no provision in the Statute or the Rules prohibiting re-composition, then the re-composition ground does not affect the jurisdiction of Trial Chamber I? Following this logic, the argument on the third ground does not go to jurisdiction. **[page 10]**

19. We respectfully submit that the matter of composition is in no way concerned with the jurisdiction of a Trial Chamber. We take the view that the third ground is not admissible under Rule 72. Article 13 and Rules 15 and 27 are all concerned with judicial administration, reflecting considerations of efficiency and judicial economy, themselves being formulated in the interests of fair and expeditious trials, unless action taken thereunder detracts from the jurisdiction of the Tribunal or violates a fundamental right of the accused. There is no such concern in this appeal, as no objection to the jurisdiction of the Tribunal has been made out. In fact, a contravention of sub-Rule 50 (A) did occur, but it affects only the power of Trial Chamber I over the Request, and has been dealt with as a separate ground of appeal, as distinct from the third.

20. Questions relating to judicial administration, such as the seisin of a court at a certain level, would have been regulated in a municipal law context by statutory instruments. The statutory instrument for the Tribunal, the Statute, delegates the power of regulating such matters to the Judges in plenary, and they have duly drafted the Rules and amended them time and again in accordance with the Statute of the Tribunal, as stated above in relation to the second ground of appeal. Therefore, the Rules represent, as it were, an interpretation of the provisions of the Statute. If there is no outright conflict of terms between the two documents, the Judges are to be presumed to have the liberty to amend and improve on the Rules in consideration of any unusual problems which arise in practice but are not covered by the existing Rules. While the Judges may have that liberty, certain general principles of law, recognised by all major legal systems but not explicitly provided for by the Statute, would always, we submit, assume precedence over the need to incorporate in the Rules a new practice that may appear to the Judges to be useful. This is the case with the principle of recusal in the interests of fair trails, which though not articulated in the Statute, finds expression in Rule 15.

21. Under Article 13 (2), a Judge can only be assigned to sit in one of the three Trial Chambers at a time. However, in many instances, a Judge needs to seek recusal from cases allocated to his/her Chamber because of a prior association which might appear to taint **[page 11]** his/her independence or impartiality. This is not an uncommon situation because all Judges confirm indictments. There is no doubt that the procedure of recusal under Rule 15 is of general importance to the work of the Tribunal as an impartial, independent judicial body. On the other hand, the Tribunal may, by reason of this procedure intended to guarantee the right of the accused to a fair trial in consistence with the spirit and objects of Articles 19 and 20 of the Statute, often find itself in the uncomfortable situation where there are many accused in pre-trial detention awaiting trial and a scarcity of Trial Chambers and Judges to deal with the cases. For instance, at the time the Joinder Motion and the Request were heard, there were only two Trial Chambers

---

[6] This had been conceded by the Appellant: "Appeal relating to the Lack of Jurisdiction (Rules 108 (B) and 117 of the Rules of Procedure and Evidence)", 14 October 1998, para.37.

and six Judges.[7] Under these circumstances, and in the interests of fairness to the accused, the President of the Tribunal must be allowed some leeway to recompose Trial Chambers to enable trials to proceed; otherwise, the work of the Tribunal would grind to a halt. We dread therefore that a strictly literal interpretation of Article 13(2) to the exclusion of the provisions of Rules 15 and 27 would lead to what is termed in Article 32 of the Vienna Convention on the Law of Treaties as an "unreasonable" result. We really cannot accept the practice that a trial on a certain indictment may be conducted before a Trial Chamber, a member of which is the Judge who confirmed the indictment, simply because s/he Judge was assigned to that Chamber when s/he was sworn in.

22.   What follows from above is a presumption that judicial necessity may have been the reason underlying Rules 15 and 27. It is in this light that the matter of judicial administration may be best appreciated. In the case of the Tribunal, judicial necessity as a principle is even more important given the very limited number of Judges available to adjudicate cases. It may not be unlikely that, because of the accepted procedure of recusal and these numerous challenges to compositions or re-compositions, the Tribunal will soon find cases unsusceptible to adjudication for there being no available Judges. That would be a bizarre situation where the Tribunal may find itself empowered to adjudicate, but powerless to empanel a Trial Chamber to do so. In the practice of the Tribunal, to allow jurisdictional challenges to be based on re-composition is, ultimately, to allow the parties to question the validity of the portion of the Rules regarding judicial administration. If this is a matter of jurisdiction, whose and which jurisdiction would be questioned: that of the relevant Trial **[page 12]** Chamber to follow the Rules or the Plenary Meeting of the Judges to design and amend the Rules? Is it not true that the validity of the Rules has already been confirmed by Article 14 of the Statute which delegates to the Judges the power to adopt and amend the Rules, provided that they do not contradict the Statute or undermine the objects and purposes of the Tribunal?

23.   Accordingly, a question regarding re-composition pursuant to the Rules does not amount to a potentially jurisdictional challenge within the meaning of sub-Rule 72(B)(i). It follows that the third ground must therefore be deemed inadmissible. With respect to the substantive question as to whether Trial Chamber I was lawfully composed, we simply hold that no provision in the Statute or Rules prohibits changing the composition of a Trial Chamber at the stage of the proceedings against the Appellant, where he has made an initial appearance before a Trial Chamber but the presentation of evidence has not commenced. As the re-composition of Trial Chamber I at the stage of the proceedings against the Appellant is not inconsistent with the Statute and the Rules, we do not need to consider the Appellant's further submissions on why the unlawful composition of the Chamber rendered it incompetent.

24.   With regard to the fourth ground of appeal in *Kanyabashi*, namely, the question of independence and impartially allegedly posed by the re-composition of Trial Chamber I to hear the Request and the Joinder Motion together,[8] we respectfully offer different reasoning from the Opinion.

25.   It may be helpful, above all, to rehearse the submissions of the Appellant with respect to the fourth ground of appeal. It is first noted that the ground consists of two limbs, being judicial independence and impartiality. As tot the first limb, the basic proposition of the Appellant is that a change to the composition of a Trial Chamber would constitute a breach of the Statute of the Tribunal, except in exceptional circumstances as provided for by Rules 15 **[page 13]** and 27 of the Rules.[9] Trial Chamber I is said to have changed its composition without offering a compelling reason to the parties, because, according to the Appellant, Rules 15 and 27 did not apply in this matter. The Appellant then argues that the change in composition was effected at the behest of the President and the Tribunal, including the Office of the Prosecutor.[10] Relying on international and national practice regarding the separation of powers, the Appellant submits that there is a reasonable doubt as to the independence of Trial Chamber I,

---

[7]   The situation has improved since the UN Security Council by Resolution 1165 (1998), 30 April 1998, established a third Trial Chamber for the Tribunal. The new judges were sworn in to office on 22 February 1999.
[8]   *Appellant's Brief*, paras. 104, 138.
[9]   Ibid., para.104.
[10]   Ibid., paras.107-109.

as recomposed, to hear the Request. On the second limb, the Appellant claims that by taking over the Request from Trial Chamber II for consideration, together with order indictments also sought to be amended. Trial Chamber I "appears to have formed its opinion in advance, by favouring the Prosecutor",[11] given that the Joinder Motion for a joint trial on those indictments has already been pending before it. The Appellant reads this action of Trial Chamber I as proof that the Trial Chamber has prejudged on the Joinder Motion before it is heard *inter partes*.[12]

26.   First of all, we would like to affirm that the Chambers of the International Tribunal must act independently and impartially in the exercise of their judicial function, and that this independence and impartiality must not only be done, but also be seen to be done. Even an appearance of partiality or bias on the part of the Chambers would dangerously undermine the authority of the Tribunal, and render ineffective their efforts to fulfil the mandate of the Tribunal to dispense justice in accordance with the Statute and the Rules. One caveat is that the appearance may be perceived by any party to a case, subject, of course, to proof of the existence of the appearance of bias to the satisfaction of the Judges of the Trial Chamber hearing the case. An allegation without sufficient proof does not suffice.

27.   Secondly, we would emphasise that the fourth ground of appeal is raised by the Appellant as a corollary to the objection to Trial Chamber I's re-composition, which constitutes the third ground for this appeal. However, during the proceedings before Trial Chamber I on 24 September 1998, the fourth ground, unlike the third, was not raised by the **[page 14]** Appellant as an independent, preliminary objection based on lack of jurisdiction which was dismissed by Trial Chamber I then and there. Given that the present appeal is interlocutory in nature, there is no other basis to found it than that provided by sub-Rule 72 (B) (i) and (D). Consequently, we find that the fourth ground does not meet the terms of those provisions. It follows that the fourth ground can be dismissed for failing to reasonably put in question the Tribunal's jurisdiction.

28.   However, thirdly, assuming for the moment that the fourth ground could be validly raised to found an interlocutory appeal in general, it has not been the case in the present appeal, because the question of independence or impartiality was considered by the Appellant to be consequential upon that of re-composition. Since the re-composition of Trial Chamber I is not in our view jurisdictional, this fourth ground also cannot go to jurisdiction. It is indeed questionable whether it is appropriate to treat it separately from the third ground concerning re-composition, given that the former is alleged through the manifestation of the latter to involve a contravention of the Statute and the Rules, thus creating the impression of being predisposed to certain requests of the Prosecution before hearing them. It would suffice for the purpose of the present analysis to emphasise that the matter of re-composition has been found not to be jurisdictional, and that insofar as the present case may involve inquiry into whether Trial Chamber I was legally constituted, the re-composition of Trial Chamber I was effected on a sound legal basis, not at the behest of a third party intervening with the judicial function of that Chamber. Any suggestion that Trial Chamber I was composed in spite of the provisions of the Statute and the Rules has not been proved. It does follow that an act of a Trial Chamber performed in accordance with the Statute and the Rules could give rise to an appearance of partiality or bias, unless the complaint concerned is a challenge to the validity of the Rules themselves, which is not the case here. However, even supposing that such a complaint could have been made in the context of his appeal, it would be dubious to regard it as a matter falling within the jurisdiction of the Appeals Chamber, as distinct from the powers of the Plenary Meeting of the Judges of the Tribunal to amend the Rules. It would follow that even this complaint cannot be jurisdictional.

29.   Fourthly, as the re-composition of a Trial Chamber does not necessarily put into doubt the impartiality or independence of the Trial Chamber, especially where it is warranted by the **[page 15]** Statute and the Rules, the Appellant has not shown that the fourth ground could serve as an independent ground for interlocutory appeal. For this we turn to the claim of the Appellant that Trial Chamber I prejudged the Joinder Motion agreeing to hear it with the Prosecution requests to amend the several

---

[11]   Ibid., para.140.
[12]   Ibid., para.147.

indictments, thus creating the appearance of partiality. Because the Appellant alleges that dealing with the amendment requests would predispose the Chamber toward granting the Joinder Motion. Reference is made to our discussion on the second ground of appeal, which shows that the placing of the Request before the recomposed Trial Chamber I contravened the requirement of sub-Rule 50 (A). However, it does not necessarily follow that by jointly considering the several indictments for amendment, with account having been taken of the terms of Rules 15 and 27, Trial Chamber I would necessarily prejudge the matter of the joinder of trials on those indictments before the hearing on the Joinder Motion. After all, its decision on the motion could be in favour of the Appellant. In fact, if the concern of the Appellant is that a joint trial would prejudice his rights to a fair and expeditious trial under the Statute, based on the information we have received through the Briefs of the parties in the present appeal, there is no question of even a consolidation of the several indictments, much less of an attempt to substitute a single indictment for them, given both processes are capable of prolonging the trial proceedings.

30.   We would however go so far as to state that even a prejudgement manifesting partiality does not necessarily lead to a finding of lack of jurisdiction. An impartial judicial institution may lack jurisdiction over certain types of case in a constitutional sense. Conversely, having been conferred by statute with this jurisdiction, it may at some point in the exercise of it appear to be lacking impartiality. In the latter case, the natural course of remedy would be the lodging of an appeal against a decision of a lower court which appeared to be partial in making the decision. But this recourse to interlocutory appeal does not retroactively deprive the lower court of its jurisdiction over the case *ab initio*. An appellate court may treat the issue of partiality as a legal error invalidating the decision under appeal, but cannot proceed to question the *existence* of the jurisdiction of the lower court, as opposed to the *way* in which the jurisdiction has been exercised by the lower court. In respect of the present appeal, the above proposition is certainly applicable to the extent that a claim of partiality on the part of Trial Chamber I does not deprive it of jurisdiction, if any. **[page 16]**

31.   Lastly, it may be arguable that lack of independence or impartiality may affect the rights of the accused to a fair trial as guaranteed by Articles 19 and 20 of the Statute.[13] However, the remedy in such circumstances would be to appeal against the judgement following a trial. It is to be stressed at this juncture that the independence and impartiality of the Chambers and the Judges are to be presumed in any event, unless allegations against them are proved, this being said to affirm that a Chamber can and will redress any complaint of partiality raised and proved by either or both of the parties to a certain case before it.

32.   To sum up, we would state that the claim in the present appeal by the Appellant of lack of independence or impartiality on the part of the recomposed Trial Chamber I does not constitute an objection based on lack of jurisdiction within the meaning of sub-Rule 72 (B) (i) and (D) giving rise to the exercise of his right of interlocutory appeal, and that even assuming that the claim could be validly raised as a ground of interlocutory appeal, it was brought in the present appeal as part of the complaint over the re-composition of Trial Chamber I, an issue which in itself is not jurisdictional. Alternatively, we find that since the Appellant has not shown that the fourth ground is necessarily connected with the third ground, there is no convincing argument by the Appellant to justify that it may serve as an independent basis for interlocutory appeal within the purview of the Statute and the Rules.

CONCLUSION

33.   For the foregoing reasons, we would dispose of the appeal by accepting it on the second ground, which we find to constitute an objection based on lack of jurisdiction within the meaning of sub-Rule 72 (B) (i) and (D), and dismissing the other three grounds for failing to meet the requirement of sub-Rule 72 (B) (i). Accordingly, we would remit the Request to the Trial Chamber stipulated by sub-Rule 50 (A), being Trial Chamber II. We note that since the Request was severed in accordance with the relief sought, the Joinder Motion can be heard by any of the Trial Chambers. **[page 17]**

---

[13]   Ibid., para.108. Also, see n.4, supra, paras.43, 50, 55-56.

Done in both English and French, the English text being authoritative.

Wang Tieya   Rafael Nieto-Navia

Dated this third day of June 1999
At Arusha,
Tanzania

International Criminal Tribunal for the
Prosecution of Persons Responsible for
Genocide and Other Serious Violations of
International Humanitarian Law Committed
in the Territory of Rwanda and Rwandan
Citizens responsible for genocide and other
such violations committed in the territory of
neighbouring States between 1 January and
31 December 1994

Case No.:   ICTR-96-15-A

Date: 3 June 1999

Original: English

IN THE APPEALS CHAMBER

Before: **Judge Gabrielle Kirk McDonald, Presiding**
                 Judge Mohamed Shahabuddeen
                 Judge Lal Chand Vohrah
                 Judge Wang Tieya
                 Judge Rafael Nieto-Navia

Registrar: Mr. Agwu U. Okali

Decision of: 3 June 1999

JOSEPH KANYABASHI

v.

THE PROSECUTOR

DISSENTING OPINION OF JUDGE SHAHABUDDEEN

The Office of the Prosecutor:
    Mr. David Spencer
    Mr. Frédéric Ossogo
    Mr. Robert Petit
    Mr. Chile Eboe-Osuji
    Mr. Ibukunolu Babajide
    Mr. Mathias Marcussen

Counsel for the Appellant:
    Mr. Michel Marchand, Lead Counsel
    Mr. Michel Boyer, Co-Counsel

[page 1] *Preliminary*

The appellant asked the Appeals Chamber to "rule that the reconstituted Trial Chamber I has no jurisdiction to hear and quash the motions for an amended indictment and joinder of trials". It is clear, however, that his chief objection was to the motion for leave to amend being heard by Trial Chamber I. In his view, that motion could be heard only by Trial Chamber II. Accordingly, he asked for an "Order that the motion to amend the Appellant's indictment be referred to Trial Chamber II which has jurisdiction".[1] He did not ask for a similar order of referral in respect of the motion for joinder; presumably, he would be content with this remaining with Trial Chamber I, provided that the motion for leave to amend was transferred to Trial Chamber II.

In respect of the motion for leave to amend, the appeal has been allowed. In respect of the motion for joinder, the appeal has been dismissed; but this is of no practical importance to the appellant. The result of the appeal gives him the substance of what he sought.

Though agreeing with some of its aspects, I respectfully differ from the decision of the Appeals Chamber to allow the appeal in respect of the motion for leave to amend. To explain my dissent, I turn to the issues arising in the case. These may, for present purposes, be summarised as follows:

First, the initial appearance having been held before Trial Chamber II, in the course of which the appellant pleaded "not guilty", did that Trial Chamber have exclusive jurisdiction in the case as a whole, with the consequence that Trial Chamber I had no jurisdiction to hear the motions for amendment and joinder?

Second, did the fact that the initial appearance was held before Trial Chamber II also mean that, under Rule 50(A) of the Rules, that Trial Chamber had exclusive jurisdiction to grant **[page 2]** leave to make the requested amendments to the indictment, with the consequence that Trial Chamber I had no jurisdiction to grant such leave?

Third, even if Trial Chamber I had jurisdiction, was it constituted as required by Articles 10, 11 and 13 of the Statute, and, if it was not, could it exercise its jurisdiction?

Fourth, even if Trial Chamber I had jurisdiction, did its recomposition mean that it could not act independently or impartially, as it was required to do by the Statute, with the consequence that it could not exercise its jurisdiction?

I propose to examine these issues, first, on the question whether they give rise to a right of interlocutory appeal, and, second, if they do, on the substance of the appeal.

I.   WHETHER THE APPELLANT HAS A RIGHT OF INTERLOCUTORY APPEAL

This question turns on whether the appeal is "in the case of dismissal of an objection based on lack of jurisdiction" within the meaning of Rule 72(D) of the Rules, that being the only ground on which an interlocutory appeal may be brought from a decision on a preliminary motion. The Appeals Chamber has answered this in the affirmative. It has done so in a global way. For the purposes of what follows, it will be useful to differentiate in relation to the specific issues summarised above. Thus considered, the case discloses a right of interlocutory appeal on two of those issues, but not on the others.

*

The traditional view of jurisdiction is that it comprises jurisdiction *ratione materiae*, jurisdiction *ratione personae*, jurisdiction *ratione loci* and jurisdiction *ratione temporis*. The prosecution submits that none of these four heads comprehends the appellant's objections, and that accordingly he did not make an objection based on lack of jurisdiction. **[page 3]**

---

[1]   Appeal Relating to the Lack of Jurisdiction, dated 30 September 1998, operative paras.

In support of the position taken by the prosecution, there may be cited the well-known proposition that jurisdiction "is the power of a court to decide a matter in controversy and presupposes the existence of a duly constituted court with control over the subject matter and the parties".[2] That, at any rate in domestic law, precludes a court, *qua* court, from challenging its own existence[3]; but I do not understand it to mean that the determination of a question of jurisdiction may not include the determination of an issue as to whether a particular court, for a reason peculiar to itself, has power to deal with a case of a type which would ordinarily be within the jurisdiction of courts of the same category.

For these reasons, the correctness of the prosecution's submission is not so clear to me. There are two aspects to each of the four standard elements of jurisdiction. Thus, jurisdiction of the subject matter, a rough translation of jurisdiction *ratione materiae*, has been defined as the "power of a particular court to hear the type of case that is then before it"[4]. That suggests that two branches are involved – the power of the *particular* court, and the type of case.

It is not necessary to deal with the second branch of jurisdiction; the appellant does not question that the two motions are among the type of things that could be dealt with by a Trial Chamber. He is raising the first branch of jurisdiction; he is saying that, for various reasons, a particular Trial Chamber lacked power to deal with them. How should this submission be dealt with in relation to the four issues summarised above?

*

As to the first issue, the argument here was that jurisdiction resided only with the Trial Chamber before which the initial appearance was held. In this case, the initial appearance was **[page 4]** held before Trial Chamber II. It followed that Trial Chamber I had no jurisdiction. The appellant's objection to that effect was an objection as to lack of jurisdiction. Accordingly, on the first issue, I consider that the appeal is admissible as an interlocutory appeal under Rule 72 (D) of the Rules.

As to the second issue, concerning non-compliance with the amendment procedure prescribed by Rule 50 (A) of the Rules, this would clearly be an objection to jurisdiction.

However, this issue was not raised by the appellant before Trial Chamber I. It was first raised in the course of the subsequent appeal proceedings. And it was not the appellant who then raised it.[5] It was the prosecution which did so. In the course of its written arguments on appeal, the prosecution said:

> "It is the Prosecutor's bounding duty to assist the Appeals Chamber in matters of law, procedure and fact. This duty involves bringing to the attention and notice of the Appeals Chamber the exact position of the law, procedure and evidence even in circumstances where the point of law, procedure and evidence appears adverse to the Prosecutor's contention. In this regard, the Prosecutor wishes to bring to the attention of the Appeals Chamber the provisions of Rule 50. Sub-rule 50(A) provides in part thus": [the text of the provision being then set out].[6]

That posture was in keeping with the traditions of domestic law. It is good to know that the prosecution has taken those traditions into an international court.

Of more immediate significance is the circumstance that the appellant did not rebut the implication of the Prosecutor's statement that the point about the amendment procedure prescribed by Rule 50(A) was new. His counsel did submit to Trial Chamber I that "the competent Chamber to rule ... on the motion on the amendment ... is Chamber II...".[7] But, as **[page 5]** he explained, that "was the Chamber to

---

2   *Black's Law Dictionary, With Pronunciation*, 6th ed. (Minnesota, 1990), p.853, citing *Pinner v. Pinner*, 33 N.C. App. 204, 234 S.E. 2d 633.

3   For the reasons which it gave, the Appeals Chamber of the International Criminal Tribunal for the former Yugoslavia in effect held that that restraint does not apply in the case of an international court. See *Prosecutor v. Dusko Tadić* (1994-1995) I ICTY JR 357. That holding is not being considered here.

4   *Black's Law Dictionary, With Pronunciation, 6th ed.* (Minnesota, 1990), p. 854.

5   See the Appeal Relating to the Lack of Jurisdiction, 30 September 1998.

6   Prosecutor's Brief Pursuant to the Scheduling Order of the Appeals Chamber, 30 December 1998, section 2A.

7   Transcript, 24 September 1998, p. 7.

which the matter was referred". The argument rested on the original assignment of the matter to Trial Chamber II, on the fact that the initial appearance, inclusive of the "not guilty" plea, had been held before that Chamber, and on the alleged illegality of the composition of Trial Chamber I. Reliance was not placed on the argument of non-compliance with the specific amendment procedure laid down by Rule 50(A) of the Rules.[8]

The oral decision of Trial Chamber I, which was delivered immediately after the oral arguments, did not, in my opinion, manifest an understanding that the appellant was raising a question of non-compliance with the specific amendment procedure prescribed by Rule 50(A) of the Rules; the decision nowhere adverted to the point and, accordingly, the views on it of that Trial Chamber are not available to the Appeals Chamber.[9] Immediately after delivery of the oral decision, it should have been open to the appellant to object that the Trial Chamber had neglected to deal with an argument on the amendment procedure specified by Rule 50(A) of the Rules. The appellant did not do so. Nor did he in his later submissions in the appeal contend that Trial Chamber I failed to consider an argument on the point. What he contended on appeal was that "Rule 50 of the Rules of Procedure and Evidence...confirms this interpretation", i.e., that a trial begins with the plea.[10] That proposition, *besides being made on appeal and not at the hearing before Trial Chamber I*, did not assert that there was a breach of the specific amendment procedure prescribed by Rule 50(A) of the Rules or that Trial Chamber I had failed to consider any such argument.

In view of those circumstances, it would strain belief now to make the belated argument that a submission that there was non-compliance with the amendment procedure prescribed by Rule 50(A) of the Rules was implied by the other arguments which were in fact presented by the appellant to Trial Chamber I. It did not necessarily follow from the appellant's other arguments before Trial Chamber I that he was also submitting to that Trial Chamber that Rule 50(A) **[page 6]** required the amendments to be made by the Trial Chamber which took the initial appearance. Rightly, an argument based on implication has not been made by the appellant. If it were made, it would not hold.

A similar approach seems to have been taken on another point by Judge Wang and Judge Nieto-Navia in their joint separate and concurring opinion. They emphasised that the fourth ground of appeal (relating to independence and impartiality) was raised (in the appeal) "as a corollary" to the objection to Trial Chamber I's recomposition. Notwithstanding the "corollary", they observed that "during the proceedings before Trial Chamber I on 24 September 1998, the fourth ground, unlike the third, was not raised by the Appellant as an independent, preliminary objection based on lack of jurisdiction which was dismissed by Trial Chamber I then and there". The position thus taken is consistent with the fact that, in the companion case of *Anatole Nsengiyumva v. Prosecutor*, decided today, the Appeals Chamber did not take the view that an argument about independence and impartiality was implied by the argument about the composition of the Trial Chamber.

Without entering into the question how far a liberal interpretation of provisions relating to interlocutory appeals in criminal matters is permissible, I would note that there is a distinction between a liberal interpretation and a misinterpretation. There would be a misinterpretation of the provisions governing interlocutory appeals to say that the appellant may be treated as having made an objection to jurisdiction based on non-compliance with the specific amendment procedure prescribed by Rule 50(A) of the Rules.

Reviewing the material, I consider that it would be artificial to say that Trial Chamber I dismissed an objection by the appellant based on non-compliance with the specific amendment procedure prescribed by Rule 50(A) of the Rules. On this point, the appeal is not admissible as an interlocutory appeal under Rule 72(D) and falls to be dismissed. **[page 7]**

---

[8] See also Motion by the Accused Challenging the Jurisdiction of the Trial Chamber seized of the Prosecutor's Request for Leave to File an Amended Indictment and Motion for Joinder of the Accused, 18 September 1998; and Response of the Accused to the Prosecutor's Motion for Joinder of Accused, 18 September 1998.

[9] See transcript, 24 September 1998, pp. 28-31.

[10] Appellant's Brief, 16 December 1998, para. 26. And see, *ibid.*, paras. 37 and 38.

As to the third issue, concerning the composition of Trial Chamber I, it has been held, in one legal system, that a "court may lack *"jurisdiction"* to hear and determine a particular action or application because (i) of the *composition* of the court (for example, the bias of the judge)."[11] (emphasis added). The meaning of that is that the biased judge should not have sat. Here too, the substance of the appellant's argument is that some judges should not have sat; they having sat and not others in their place, the composition of the bench was affected. When there is an error in the composition of the bench, the court is not properly constituted. And where the court is not properly constituted, it cannot exercise its jurisdiction. Authority for that view can be found in some national legal systems.[12]

I think it is also possible to extract some support from the jurisprudence of the International Court of Justice for the proposition that an error in the composition of a judicial, or quasi-judicial, body goes to jurisdiction. The differences between that court and this Tribunal obviously counsel care in using the jurisprudence of the former; but, equally obviously, those differences do not prohibit recourse to that jurisprudence on relevant matters, more particularly having regard to the fact that both institutions are international judicial bodies.

In the *Mortished* case, a panel of the Administrative Tribunal of the United Nations sat with four members, whereas the authorised complement was three. The fourth member was an alternate member; he should only have participated in the judgement in place of another member. Because of the special configuration of the request for an advisory opinion which was made in that case, the Court took the view that further consideration of the point was not called for. (*I.C.J. Reports 1982*, pp. 340-342, paras. 33-35). The sense of the Court on the matter was nevertheless clear. It could not have differed materially from the observation of Judge El-Khani, dissenting, that "it is incomprehensible, and even unlawful, for an alternate to "replace" a full member of the Tribunal who is present, otherwise the Tribunal would have a composition **[page 8]** of four and not three members, which would be a violation of Article 3, paragraph 1, of its Statute." (*Ibid.*, p. 449).

Also arising in that case was a question concerning the composition of the Committee on Applications for Review of Administrative Tribunal Judgements. Subject to possible misunderstanding as to what actually happened, it appears that, in his own absence, the chairman of the Committee designated a non-member of the Committee to act as chairman in his place. The Court referred to the replacement as "[o]ne of the most important irregularities in the procedure adopted by the Committee ...", and considered the particular irregularity to be "fundamental to the whole question of the present reference to this Court" (*Ibid.*, pp. 342-343, paras. 38-39). "Despite the irregularities" the Court "nevertheless" felt called upon to "accept the task of assisting the United Nations Organisation" by giving the requested advisory opinion. (*Ibid.*, p. 347, para. 45). That the Court took this course does not detract from the seriousness with which it regarded the particular irregularity, and not the least for the reason that it considered that the Committee was quasi-judicial in character: in the instant case, the bodies concerned were judicial. In his dissenting opinion, Judge El-Khani said that the "Committee ... does not appear to have been legally constituted". (*Ibid.*, p. 450).

In my opinion, the jurisprudence shows that an error in the composition of a tribunal can go to the jurisdiction of the tribunal. Accordingly, on the third issue, the appeal is admissible as an interlocutory appeal under Rule 72 (D) of the Rules.

As to the fourth issue, concerning the impartiality and independence of Trial Chamber I, a like position is suggested on the basis of the foregoing and other references. Thus, in another case it was held that "[i]f actual or apprehended bias arises from a judge's words or conduct, then the judge has *exceeded* his or her *jurisdiction*"[13] (emphasis added). Bias would, of course, **[page 9]** go to impartiality. Lack of

---

[11]   *Oscroft v. Benabo* [1967] 2 All ER 548 at 557, CA, per Diplock L.J.

[12]   *R. v. Inner London Quarter Sessions, ex parte D'Souza* [1970] 1 All ER, [1970] 1 WLR 376. And see *de Smith's Judicial Review of Administrative Action*, 4th ed. (London, 1980), pp. 111 and 115.

[13]   *R.D.S. v. The Queen*, Supreme Court of Canada, 1997 Can. Sup. Ct., Lexis 83, judgment of Cory J., para. 99. In English law, there is authority for the view that a tribunal, having jurisdiction over a matter in the first instance, might exceed its jurisdiction by breaking the rules of natural justice. See *de Smith's Judicial Review of Administrative Action*, 4th ed. (London, 1980), p. 113, citing *Anisminic Ltd. v. Foreign Compensation Commission* [1969] 2 AC 147, HL, at pp. 171, 195, 207, 215.

independence, though different from impartiality, is not always clearly distinguishable form the latter[14] and would lead to a similar excess of jurisdiction, if not total want of it. In my view, it does not matter whether lack of jurisdiction existed *ab initio* or came about subsequent to the commencement of the proceedings; in either case, there would be a "lack of jurisdiction" within the meaning of Rule 72(D) of the Rules.

But this point was not raised before Trial Chamber I. It is sought now to be tacked on as an inference to be drawn from the recomposition of the Trial Chamber and the placing of all the motions before that Trial Chamber. No doubt, the composition of a court can give rise to doubt about its impartiality[15]; but in this case, as explained above, that inference was not put to the Trial Chamber. The Notice of Appeal, dated 30 September 1998, talks at length of independence and impartiality. So does the Appellant's Brief dated 16 December 1998, containing copious references to those subjects. None of this was put to Trial Chamber I. The oral arguments there never once used the words "impartiality" or "independence". If an objection as to lack of independence and impartiality could have been put to the impugned court while sitting but was not, it is considered waived and should not be permitted to be later raised save in exceptional circumstances.[16] There are no such circumstances in this case.

Accordingly, I think the appeal should be dismissed so far as this point is concerned. In this respect, I support the position taken by Judge Wang and Judge Nieto-Navia in their point separate and concurring opinion.

*

Subject to what has been said above about the second and fourth issues not having been raised before Trial Chamber I, it has also to be borne in mind that the appellant's propositions about the absence of jurisdiction need not be shown to be correct to justify the conclusion that **[page 10]** he was making an objection based on lack of jurisdiction; it is enough if they were reasonably arguable. If they were reasonably arguable, he would have a right of appeal; whether the Appeals Chamber would ultimately uphold any of those propositions at the appeal is a different matter.

The distinction between a claim which is "fondée" on a treaty and a claim which is "bien fondée" on a treaty comes to mind. In the *Ambatielos case (I.C.J. Reports 1953*, p. 10, at p. 12), the International Court of Justice was construing the words "in so far as this claim is based on the Treaty of 1886", as used in the operative part of its judgement of 1 July 1952. In its view, those words were "intended to indicate the character which the Ambatielos claim must possess in order that it may be the subject of arbitration in accordance with the Declaration of 1926 [between Great Brittain and Greece]. They do not mean that the Ambatielos claim must be found by the Court to be validly based on the Treaty of 1886". (*Ibid.*, p. 16).

In the *Unesco* case, of 1956, the International Court of Justice was likewise considering the statutory duty of the Administrative Tribunal of the International Labour Organisation "to hear complaints alleging non-observance, in substance or in form, of the terms of appointment of officials". Referring to the *Ambatielos* case, it observed: ""Complaints alleging" is a wider expression than "complaints based on". The latter may be interpreted as meaning that the object of such a complaint must be legally well-founded. Yet the Court, when confronted with the words "claims ... based on the provisions" of a treaty, considered that these words "cannot be understood as meaning claims actually supportable under that Treaty" (*Ambatielos case, Merits: Obligation to arbitrate, I.C.J. Reports 1953*, p. 17). This is particularly true in the case of the more flexible expression "complaints alleging"".[17]

It does not appear that in the *Unesco* case the Court abandoned the position taken by it in the *Ambatielos* case. Thus, in the *Unesco* case, the Court went on to say that "Article II, paragraph 5

---

[14]   See P. van Dijk et al (eds.), *Theory and Practice of the European Convention of Human Rights* (The Hague, 1998), p. 451.
[15]   *Ibid.*, p. 454.
[16]   See *de Smith's Judicial Review of Administrative Action*, 4th ed. (London, 1980), p. 275; the *Bulut Case*, E.C.H.R., 1996-II, Vol. 5, para. 34; and *In re Pinochet*, 15 January 1999, H.L., U.K., per Lord Browne-Wilkinson.
[17]   *Judgements of the Administrative Tribunal of the International Labour Organisation Upon Complains Made against the United Nations Educational, Scientific and Cultural Organization, I.C.J. Reports 1956*, pp. 88-89.

[containing the phrase "complaints alleging"] does not mean that a mere verbal reference to certain terms or provisions would suffice to establish the jurisdiction of the **[page 11]** Administrative Tribunal. A mere allegation by the complainant cannot be sufficient to cause the Tribunal to accept it for the purpose of examining the complaint" (*I.C.J. Reports 1956*, p. 89). It cited a passage from the *Ambatielos* case to the effect that "it is not enough for the claimant Government to establish a remote connection between the facts of the case and the Treaty" invoked, although balancing this by another citation to the effect that "it is not necessary for that Government to show ... that an alleged treaty violation has an unassailable legal basis ...". (*Ibid.*). I do not consider that the essential principles which these cases laid down have been varied by the later case concerning *Oil Platforms (Islamic Republic of Iran v. United States) Preliminary Objection (I.C.J. Reports 1996*, p. 803).

In this case, to uphold the appellant's right of appeal, the Appeals Chamber has to find that an arguable relationship existed between the appellant's objection and relevant provisions of the Statute and the Rules, read in the light of any applicable jurisprudence; a mere remote connection would not suffice. (*Unesco case, supra,* at p. 89). Where these criteria met?

Without anticipating too much at this stage, it appears to me that the appellant can reasonably relate his submissions to the provisions of the Statute and the Rules and that he can do so in relation to all of the issues summarised above. However, as has been noted, the second and fourth issues were not argued before Trial Chamber I. So far as those issues are concerned, the appellant made no objection as to jurisdiction before the Trial Chamber, and accordingly he has no right of interlocutory appeal in relation to them. He does, however, have a right of interlocutory appeal on the other two issues.

For convenience, I shall consider all four issues below. **[page 12]**

II. WHETHER THE INITIAL APPEARANCE BEFORE TRIAL CHAMBER II MEANT THAT TRIAL CHAMBER I COULD NOT HEAR THE MOTIONS

As to the first of the four issues summarised above, the appellant submits that the trial began with the initial appearance before Trial Chamber II, when he pleaded "not guilty", and that thereafter that Trial Chamber had exclusive jurisdiction in the case as a whole. I agree with the rejection by the Appeals Chamber of the submission but propose to explain my point of view below.

The prosecution agrees that Trial Chamber I could not hear the motions after the trial had begun in Trial Chamber II but questions whether the trial had begun with the initial appearance. It points out that, although the motions were presented to Trial Chamber I after the initial appearance in Trial Chamber II, the hearing in Trial Chamber I took place before the presentation of evidence had begun in Trial Chamber II. By reason of that fact, it argues that the trial had not yet begun in Trial Chamber II.

When a trial begins may depend on the particular regime in force; and, under the same regime, it may begin for one purpose but not for another. Thus, for the purpose of the statutory requirement that a "trial" shall be fair, few would deny that a "trial" could be regarded as having begun before the presentation of evidence has commenced; and this, I think, is the meaning of the term in Rule 15(C) of the Rules which provides that a judge of a Trial Chamber who reviews an indictment against an accused "shall not sit as a member of the Trial Chamber for the *trial* of that accused" (emphasis added). But whether a trial has begun for other purposes could be another matter.

As is shown by Rule 62 of the Rules, the substantial object of the initial appearance is to take the plea of the accused. In this case the accused pleaded "not guilty". I take the general rule to be that a "not guilty" plea does not mark the commencement of a trial but merely establishes the need for a trial.[18] It seems that the Statute has adopted the general rule; thus, **[page 13]** Article 19(3) stipulates that, the accused having pleaded, the "Trial Chamber shall then set the date for trial". This statutory division between the plea stage and the trial stage finds reflection in Rule 62 of the Rules, among others.

---

[18] See, in one jurisdiction, *Quazi v. Director of Public Prosecutions*, 152 J.P. 385, [1988] Crim. L.R. 529, D.C.

I have considered the decision of Judge Khan in *The Prosecutor versus Théoneste Bagosora and 28 others*[19] to the effect that a trial commences with the plea. That may be right in certain situations; but, if it was put forward as a principle of universal validity, I would respectfully demur. In this case, I consider that the trial had not yet begun in Trial Chamber II when the motions were presented to Trial Chamber I. Accordingly, so far as this head of argument is concerned, Trial Chamber I was lawfully seized of the motions.

III.   WHETHER LEAVE TO MAKE THE AMENDMENTS COULD BE GIVEN ONLY BY TRIAL CHAMBER II

As to the second of the four issues summarised above, the question is whether the right to grant leave to amend the indictment was exclusively possessed by Trial Chamber II as a result of Rule 50 (A) of the Rules. I have expressed the view above that the appellant made no objection on this point before Trial Chamber I and that he accordingly has no right of interlocutory appeal under Rule 72(D) of the Rules. On this point, the appeal should be dismissed. I would reserve my views on the substance of the contention, particularly in the light of questions which merit further reflection, including those mentioned below.

To appreciate the situation it is necessary to step back a little and to look into the antecedents of the case. They involved the existence of a prosecutorial problem of common occurrence and the need to find a sensible solution for it in the case of the Tribunal, consistently with governing legal criteria relating to a fair trial. Unless such a solution can be found, the Tribunal becomes incapable of dealing with the factual situation which called it into being and of responding meaningfully to the expectations of the international community. **[page 14]**

On the basis of such material as it has, the prosecution may lay a charge against an accused for a particular offence. As investigations proceed – and the Prosecutor in this case has a continuing duty to investigate – new information may suggest that the accused should be charged for additional offences. The information may also suggest that another person, or other persons, should be made in answer with the original accused in respect of some or all of the charges in a single set of proceedings. How is this to be done?

At the level of details, domestic procedures vary. However, one method – it is not the only one[20] – is this: where, in the light of other evidence, the prosecution desires to join fresh persons with a person who is already charged on an indictment, a common practice is to bring a new indictment against them all, and for the court to stay action on the old indictment or to require the prosecution to elect on which indictment it wishes to proceed.[21]

In substance, this was what the Prosecutor sought to do in this case. She brought a composite indictment against the appellant and 28 others embracing substantially the same matter as that presented in an original indictment against him, along with a count for conspiracy. Judge Khan, however, took the view, *inter alia*, that he had no jurisdiction to confirm the new indictment unless the Prosecutor, with leave of the Trial Chamber hearing the case, first withdrew the original indictment, under Rule 51 of the Rules, and did likewise in respect of several others against whom indictments were also pending.[22]

The Prosecutor did not do so[23], doubtless fearing the creation of a vacuum between withdrawal of the old indictment and conjectural confirmation of the new, with accompanying risk of release of the accused and others in the interval. As the Prosecutor did not do so, Judge **[page 15]** Khan dismissed her

---

[19]   Case No. ICTR-98-37-I of 31 March 1998.
[20]   Alternatively, one of the existing separate indictments might be selected for amendments, inclusive of the addition of the names of the other accused and consequential textual changes; the other indictments being discontinued with leave. See the standard text of *Archbold, Criminal Pleading, Evidence and Practice* (London, 1999), paras. 1-165, 1-218, and 1-220.
[21]   *Archbold, supra*, para. 1-220.
[22]   See his decision of 31 March 1998, paras. 6 and 8, and p. 11.
[23]   *Ibid.*, para. 6.

application for confirmation of the new indictment. It seems that he thought that it was legally not possible to have two overlapping indictments on the file. If that was what he thought, the books show that it is not unusual in some jurisdictions for two indictments to be in existence at the same time against the same person for the same offence or offences based on the same facts, the prosecution of course being permitted to proceed only on one.[24]

The Prosecutor, having failed in her motion before Judge Khan, now sought, by another means but only in relation to six of the accused, to secure her objective of ensuring that they were tried in the same proceedings, without incurring the risk of having the accused meanwhile set at liberty. She would no longer seek to substitute a single indictment against all of the accused. She would rest on the separate original indictments against them, one indictment being against two accused, a second indictment being against another two, a third indictment being against the fifth (the appellant), and a fourth indictment being against the sixth. However, in a motion to amend, she would seek leave to amend each indictment, *inter alia*, by the addition of new charges. Then, as I understand it, in a motion for an order of "joinder of ... the cases" (filed together with the motion to amend but ordered by the Trial Chamber to be heard later), she would ask to hold one trial on all of the indictments. The separate indictments, having been amended, would remain; they would merely be tried together. There would not be a new single substitute indictment. In effect, what was sought was consolidation of hearings on separate indictments, as distinguished form joinder *stricto sensu*, the difference being referred to below.

In some common law areas, two ore more indictments may be tried together if the offences, and the accused if there is more than one, could have been joined in a single indictment.[25] Legislation may be used to regulate the procedure but is not always necessary to authorise it, a court being regarded as having inherent power to adopt that course if the interests of justice so require. The jurisprudence refers to that as a case of consolidation, an idea which is perhaps more customary in civil proceedings, and, possibly for this reason, not so far, I believe, **[page 16]** the subject of observation in the case law either of the International Criminal Tribunal for Rwanda or of the International Criminal for the former Yugoslavia.

As distinguished from consolidation, there is joinder *stricto sensu*, in which two or more accused are charged jointly in the same indictment. This is based on the traditional common law rule that a trial is to be limited to one indictment and what "[w]here two or more indictments are tried together the trial is a nullity.[26]

Which of these two approaches is contemplated by Rule 48 of the Rules? As is mentioned in the decision of the Appeals Chamber, that Rule states that persons "accused of the same or different crimes committed in the course of the same transaction may be jointly charged and tried".

One interpretation of the Rule is that persons who satisfy the stated test may be "jointly ... tried" only if they have been "jointly charged ...", thus reflecting the traditional common law rule relating to joinder *stricto sensu*. Another interpretation is that the provision also embraces the possibility that such persons may be "jointly ... tried" even if they have not been "jointly charged ...", reflecting the principle of consolidation. The prosecution has proceeded on the basis of this latter and wider interpretation, Trial Chamber I has implicitly accepted it, and the Appeals Chamber has now effectively adopted it. The former interpretation is attractive; but not sufficiently so to justify non-acceptance of the adoption of the latter by the Appeals Chamber, and more particularly so in view of the inherent authority on the basis of which courts in some jurisdictions order consolidation.

*

The question which remains, but on which I would reserve my views, is this: where the prosecution seeks leave to amend an indictment as a step in achieving consolidation but does

---

[24]   *Archbold, supra,* paras. 1-208, 1-218, 1-220.
[25]   See *McElroy v. United States,* 164 U.S.76, citing section 1024 of the Revised Statutes; and see Wayne R. La Fave and Jerold H. Israel, Criminal Procedure, 2nd ed. (Minnesota, 1992), p. 772, para. 17.3(a).
[26]   *Archbold, supra,* para. 7-292.

so **[page 17]** after initial appearance, is it the case that the motion for leave to amend can be heard only by the Trial Chamber before which the initial appearance was held?

The plain meaning of Rule 50(A) of the Rules does indeed require leave to be granted by the Trial Chamber which took the initial appearance where amendments are sought to be made to an indictment after the initial appearance. But is there another question as to what are the situations to which the requirement is directed? Is the "plain meaning" of the provision plain enough on this point? Considerations of convenience aside, do the object and purpose of the provision suggest that the provision was directed to a situation in which what was desired was to amend an indictment on the basis that the prosecution would continue only as against the person or persons originally accused? Or, was it also directed to a case in which the substance of what was sought was to require the accused to answer with a new set of accused on basically, if not wholly, similar charges? Could it be that this second situation is a qualitatively different one not within the contemplation of Rule 50 (A) of the Rules, and to which that Rule is in consequence not applicable? Was that perhaps the reasoning behind the observation by President Kama, speaking independently of any submission on that Rule, that the motions for leave to amend were linked to the mention for joinder?

There is, of course, no Rule which requires a Trial Chamber to hear an application for leave to amend an indictment together with an application for joinder of accused persons as a combined operation. That is a consideration; but, in assessing how decisive it is, there may be need to take account of the inherent competence of a judicial body, whether civil or criminal, to regulate its own procedure in the event of silence in the written rules[27], so as to assure the exercise of such jurisdiction as it has, and to fulfil itself, properly and effectively, as a court of law.[28] Without that residual competence, no court can function completely. It is the case that Article 19(1) of the Statute provides that "Trial Chambers shall ensure ... that proceedings are conducted in accordance with the rules of procedure and evidence...". But, where "the rules of **[page 18]** procedure and evidence" do not provide, can it be argued that nothing in that provision of the Statute was intended to denude a Trial Chamber of that residual competence if it could be exercised consistently with the requirement for trials to be fair and expeditious? That, indeed, that residual competence was impliedly granted to the Tribunal by the Statute when it empowered the Tribunal to hold trials?

The Appeals Chamber may be right in deciding that the motion for leave to amend could only be heard by the Trial Chamber which took the initial appearance. But I do not consider that it was either necessary or competent to decide the point if I am right in thinking that the appeal should be dismissed, so far as Rule 50(A) is concerned, on the ground that no objection as to jurisdiction was made before Trial Chamber I on the basis of non-compliance with the specific amendment procedure prescribed by that provision. Accordingly, I would reserve my views on what I believe are some of the questions which arise.

IV. WHETHER THE RECOMPOSITION OF TRIAL CHAMBER I WAS LAWFUL.

The third of the four issues summarised above concerns the recomposition of Trial Chamber I. I support the decision of the Appeals Chamber that the recomposition did not involve an invalidity. But my approach may be different.

I would not found the decision on the argument by the prosecution that "[a]ssignment to the Chambers is an administrative matter within the purview of the President. It simply has nothing to do with the elements of the Tribunal's jurisdiction".[29] Though within the same system – as is often the case in domestic arrangements – the two Trial Chambers could be regarded as separate courts. It is said, in a work of authority, that "... where there is no assignment whatever, a judge of one court who is not a

---

[27] An analogy, in non-criminal proceedings, is provided by *Qatar v. Bahrain, I.C.J. Reports 1994*, p. 112, attention being invited to the separate opinion of Judge Schwebel at p. 130, and to the dissenting opinion of Judge Oda at p. 134, about the decision of the Court to split the jurisdictional phase of the case without regulatory authority.

[28] See *Halsbury's Laws of England*, 4th ed., Vol. 37, para. 14.

[29] Prosecutor's Response and Challenge to the Admissibility of the Defendant's Notice of Appeal, para. 32.

judge, *ex officio* or otherwise, of another court until he is assigned thereto cannot perform judicial acts in the latter court or hold a term thereof".[30] I take that to mean that an assignment, where one is required, goes to the competence of a judge to exercise the jurisdiction of the court. Of course, the function of assigning is an **[page 19]** administrative activity as opposed to a judicial one. But it is an administrative activity which is authorised by statute, and it can have legal effects. These effects go to the competence of a judge to exercise the jurisdiction of the Tribunal. Unless assigned by the President to a Trial Chamber, no judge can exercise any part of the jurisdiction of the Tribunal.

On the other hand, if a provision of the Statute has the effect of precluding a judge from sitting in both Trial Chambers (there were only two at the time), the administrative character of the President's power of assignment cannot be invoked to lift the ban. The President's power of assignment has to be exercised consistently with the Statute.

In this respect, the last sentence of Article 13(2) of the Statute is specific; it says that a "judge shall serve only in the Chamber to which he or she was assigned". That command – a command issuing from the Statute itself – makes no sense if the judge could be simultaneously assigned by the President to both Trial Chambers and could thus serve in both. The structure of the Statute shows that, of six judges, three were to be assigned to one of two Trial Chambers and the remaining three to the other. An assignment of a judge to one Trial Chamber may be rescinded and a new one made. But, so far as that provision is concerned, the provision did not visualise that a judge could, by dual assignments, be a member of both Trial Chambers at the same time.

This conclusion could produce obvious difficulties: it would exclude the possibility of making needed substitute and temporary appointments. If that happens, the Tribunal cannot function. What is the answer?

The answer is to be found in the view that the overriding statutory duty of the Tribunal to hold trials that are fair and expeditious would necessitate the making of substitute or temporary assignments from time to time, recusation being an obvious example of a situation calling for such a remedy; that, for such purposes, the Statute therefore impliedly authorises the rule-making body to make rules providing for substitute or temporary assignments; and that the apparent conflict between this implied authorisation by the Statute of dual assignments and the prohibition of dual assignments by Article 13(2) of the Statute is to be resolved by construing **[page 20]** the latter as being referable to substantive assignments only, and not also to provisional ones. To reach this conclusion, it is not necessary to call on the administrative character of the President's power of assignment or to deny that dual assignments are forbidden by Article 13(2) of the Statute, as they plainly are.

Accordingly, the prohibition set out in the last sentence of Article 13(2) of the Statute does not apply to substitute or temporary assignments. What I am not able to support is the idea that the administrative character of the power to assign somehow enables the President to make a dual assignment in spite of that provision. The President may make a dual assignment, but the situations in which he may do so are not controlled by that provision and are not subject to the prohibition which it imposes.

This is because Article 13(2) is, in my view, addressed to substantive assignments, not to provisional ones. With respect, President Kama saw the distinction correctly when, referring to Rule 15(E) and Rule 27(A), (B) and (C) of the Rules, he said that, under these provisions, "the President has the power at any point of time when the needs of administration of justice require to assign *provisionally* a judge to a given chamber".[31] Those provisional assignments are not assignments within the meaning of Article 13(2).

*

---

[30] See *Corpus Juris Secundum* (Minnesota, 1990), Vol. 21, para. 123, p. 142.

[31] Transcript, 24 September 1998, p. 29 (emphasis added).

For the purposes of this opinion, little turns on the question what principles of interpretation apply to the Statute. However, as the matter has been mentioned, I would offer a respectful word.

A Chamber of the Tribunal, seeking to apply the Statute, may obviously be faced with the task of interpreting it. The Statute prescribes no principles of interpretation. It may therefore be understood as authorising the Tribunal to interpret it in accordance with reason. But reason, which could sometimes be understood differently by each party concerned, suggests that some **[page 21]** known body of principles of interpretation should be sought. In deciding what these should be, the Tribunal will naturally have regard to the character of the Statute.

The Statute is not municipal legislation. And notwithstanding the treaty character of the Charter under which it was made, there could be difficulty in the argument that it is a "treaty" within the meaning of the definition of that term as set out in Article 2(1)(a) of the Vienna Convention on the Law of Treaties 1969. It is, however, an international document proximate in nature to a treaty, having been promulgated by the Security Council acting on behalf of the member States of the United Nations. That proximity to a treaty will justify recourse being had, on an analogical basis, to principles of treaty interpretation. These will include, as has been held in the jurisprudence both of the International Criminal Tribunal for the former Yugoslavia and of the International Criminal Tribunal for Rwanda, the principles set out in that Convention.[32] As is recalled by the decision of the Appeals Chamber, the leading interpretative principle of the Convention is that a "treaty" shall be interpreted in good faith and in accordance with the ordinary meaning to be given to the terms of the treaty in their context and in the light of its object and purpose". (Article 31(1)).

There is another route leading to a substantially similar result. *Serbian Loans, P.C.I.J., Series A, No. 20,* concerned the interpretation of certain loan contracts between a State and private persons or lenders. The Permanent Court of International Justice regarded the contracts as not being treaties between States (*ibid*, p. 40). It applied "elementary principles of interpretation" (*ibid.*, p. 30), and established their meaning "on a reasonable construction" (*ibid.*, p. 40). In the companion case of the *Brazilian Loans, P.C.I.J., Series A, No. 21,* the court spoke of "a familiar rule for the construction of instruments that, where they are found to be ambiguous, they should be taken *contra proferentem*" (*ibid.*, p. 114). In effect, the court applied the body of principles of interpretation generally accepted in domestic jurisdictions, I consider **[page 22]** that that body of generally accepted principles results today in substantially the same general principles of interpretation as are referred to above.

*

For completeness, it is convenient to make a closing reference to a possible argument. The argument, though not made in this case, was made, by the prosecution, in the companion case of *Anatole Nsengiyumva v. Prosecutor*[33], decided today. Based on the use of chambers in the International Court of Justice, the contention seems to be that, if certain chambers were validly constituted in that court, the recomposition of Trial Chamber I was also valid. I have reached the same conclusion, but without the assistance of that argument.

Unlike the Tribunal, the jurisdiction of the International Court of Justice is ordinarily exercised by all of its judges sitting *en banc.* The court had certain chambers, but these were not in question. A new and special type of chamber was established by a rule of court of relatively recent vintage. Four of these chambers, called *ad hoc* chambers, were appointed in the eight-year period between 1979 and 1987, the last judgement of such a chamber being rendered in 1994. No *ad hoc* chambers have been appointed

---

[32] See *Decision on the Prosecutor's Motion requesting Protective Measures for Victims and Witnesses,* in *Tadić,* (1994-1995) I ICTY JR 125 at 141. In the later case of *Prosecutor v. Bagosora,* ICTR-98-37-A, of 8 June 1998, para. 28, the Appeals Chamber of the International Criminal Tribunal for Rwanda said that it agreed "with the Prosecutor on the applicability, *mutatis mutandis,* of the *Vienna Convention on the Law of Treaties* to the Statute". The convention is, in may respects, a consolidation of constumary international law. See, inter alia, *Gabcikovo-Nagymaros Project, I.C.J. Reports 1997,* paras. 46, 99 and 104.

[33] Supplementary Brief in Reply by the Prosecutor Regarding the Admissibility of the Notice of Appeal filed by the Accused Anatole Nsengiyumva, against the Decision of Trial Chamber II Rendered on 28 September 1998 on the Request for Leave to Amend Indictment and Motion for Joinder of the Accused, dated 30 December 1998, para. 39.

since 1987. Legal advisers of potential litigant states may be canvassing the chances of a determined attack being successfully repelled.

What happened was that, in the meantime, argument had been made in and out of the court that the rule of court effectively sought to authorise the election by the court of the members of such a chamber in accordance with the wishes of the parties; that this, in substance, collided with a fundamental principle on which the court, as a permanent court, was created, namely, that, with the exception of judges *ad hoc*, the members of the court would not be chosen by the parties; and that the appointment of such chambers was consequently invalid. **[page 23]**

It can be contended, as it has been contended, that the fact that the full court appointed such chambers meant that the court rejected that argument. But that would be because the court rejected the premise of the argument that elections of members of the chambers were made in accordance with the wishes of the parties. Thus, the question was one of evaluation of the facts, not of the applicability of a principle.

Here, by contrast, the question is not one of evaluation of the facts, but of the applicability of a principle to the facts. Did the prohibition of a dual assignment apply to the admitted facts? I am not confident that the situation concerning chambers at the International Court of Justice helps to answer that question one way or another.

It does not appear to me that the position regarding *ad hoc* chambers is helpful to the analysis which is now required. I think that the appropriate analysis is that set out above. In accordance with that analysis, and without recourse to other possible lines of inquiry, I support the holding of the Appeals Chamber that the recomposition of Trial Chamber I was not prohibited.

V. WHETHER THERE WAS LACK OF INDEPENDENCE AND IMPARTIALITY

As to the last of the four issues, the appellant pleads his "fears about the independence and impartiality of the Chamber".[34] As mentioned above, I support the view of Judge Wang and Judge Nieto-Navia that this contention was not made to Trial Chamber I. The point is inadmissible and the appeal on it, as an interlocutory appeal, should be dismissed.

Even if that is wrong, the result should be the same. It is not necessary to cite authority for the importance of the qualities of independence and impartiality in a judge. But I agree with the decision of the Appeals Chamber that they were not wanting in this case. **[page 24]**

It is generally recognised that, if there is an appearance of lack of independence and impartiality, the appellate court will not inquire into whether there was any actual prejudice. Trial Chamber I spoke of "prejudice", stating that "there is no particular prejudice, as we have seen",[35] and this has been criticised by the appellant.[36] It has to be noted, however, that, in doing so, Trial Chamber I, as it seems to me, had in mind not the specific question of judicial independence and impartiality (which was not argued), but ordinary non-compliance with the Rules, the position being that, under Rule 5, a complaint of non-compliance with the Rules has to show that "material prejudice" resulted from the non-compliance.[37]

Neither the prosecution nor the defence, who both spoke of "prejudice", related that concept to judicial independence and impartiality.[38] Before Trial Chamber I, they were both talking of the appellant's claim to a right to a hearing before Trial Chamber II as a matter of the statutory organisation of the Tribunal, and not as a matter resting on the specific issues of "judicial independence and impartiality." These words were not used in the proceedings before Trial Chamber I.

---

[34]   Appeal Relating to the Lack of Jurisdiction, dated 30 September 1998, para. 24.
[35]   Transcript, 24 September 1998, p. 31.
[36]   Appellant's Brief, 16 December 1998, para. 121.
[37]   See, later, Prosecutor's Response and Challenge to the Admissibility of the Defendant's Notice of Appeal, 15 October 1998, para. 19.
[38]   Transcript, 24 September 1998, pp. 18, 19, 20 and 21.

As to whether there is an appearance of lack of independence and impartiality, this question is not to be answered by asking whether there is a real danger or likelihood of lack of independence and impartiality. The issue is one of public confidence in the system of administering justice. But it is not the case that that issue is to be judged by the views of the hypersensitive and the uninformed. The test is whether the events in question give rise to a reasonable apprehension or suspicion on the part of a fair-minded and informed member of the public that the judge was not impartial.[39] **[page 25]**

On that basis, it is not possible to appreciate how there could be an appearance of lack of independence and impartiality arising from the circumstance that the normal composition of Trial Chamber I was changed. It is artificial to say that a fair-minded member of the public who had taken reasonable steps to inform himself of the material facts would have had any reasonable suspicion that there could be a lack of independence and impartiality.

In addition, it may be noted that the allegations concerning lack of independence and impartiality metamorphose the argument that the recomposition of Trial Chamber I gave rise to invalidity. Thus, counsel for the appellant submitted that "... a change in the composition of the Chamber directly gives rise to a fear of lack of independence"[40]. The appellant also pleaded the circumstance that the motions for leave to amend were placed together with the motion for joinder before Trial Chamber I. It seems clear to me, however, that the ultimate foundation of the contention of lack of independence and impartiality was the fact of recomposition of Trial Chamber I. The alleged invalidity in the recomposition of the Chamber is the premise. For the reasons given above, the premise is not correct.

Consequently, the conclusion does not follow that the dismissal by Trial Chamber I of the appellant's motion challenging the recomposition of the Chamber shows that the appellant has "serious reasons to nurture fears about the independence and impartiality of the Chamber".

CONCLUSION

On the ground on which the Appeals Chamber has upheld the case of the appellant, that ground is, for the reasons given above, inadmissible, the point in question, concerning non-compliance with the amendment procedure prescribed by Rule 50 (A) of the Rules, not having been argued before Trial Chamber I and no decision dismissing an objection to jurisdiction on the basis of that argument having been in consequence made by that Chamber. **[page 26]**

It is not correct that the Appeals Chamber should be deciding issues of this kind without the assistance and benefit of the views of the Trial Chamber from the decision of which the appeal is sought to be brought. The specific question of there being a need to comply with the amendment procedure required by Rule 50(A) of the Rules not having been argued before Trial Chamber I, the views of that Trial Chamber on that question have not been expressed and are not available to the Appeals Chamber.

For the reasons given above, I would dismiss the appeal in its entirety.

---

[39]   *Webb and Hay v. The Queen*, (1994) 81 C.L.R. 41 (High Court of Australia). In paragraph 5 of his opinion in Webb's case, Dean J. compared the main tests thus: "The substance of the House of Lords test is "a real danger of bias". The substance of this Court's test is "a reasonable apprehension of bias". The reference point of the House of Lords test is the appellate court itself or, where the question arises at first instance, the trial judge. The reference point of this Court's test is the fair-minded informed lay observer". See also *R.D.S. v. The Queen*, 1997 Can. Sup. Ct., Lexis 83. Compare the House of Lords decision in *Re Pinochet Ugarte*, The Times, 18 January 1999, in which Lord Browne-Wilkinson, giving the leading speech, said that "it is unnecessary to determine whether the test of apparent bias laid down in Reg. v. Gough [1993] A.C. 646 ("is there in the view of Case No. ICTR-96-15-A the court a real danger that the judge was biased?") needs to be reviewed in the light of subsequent decisions". A similar result is reached through the jurisprudence of the European Court of Human Rights, cited in the judgement of the Appeals Chamber in this case and, in substance, previously relied on by the Bureau of the International Criminal Tribunal for the former Yugoslavia in *Prosecutor v. Delalic*, 4 September 1998.

[40]   Appellant's Brief, 16 December 1998, para. 104. See also, *ibid*, para. 142.

Done in English and French, the English text being authoritative.

Mohamed Shahabuddeen

Dated this third day of June 1999
At Arusha,
Tanzania.

Introduction

Appellate proceedings form a constitutive part of national legal systems in criminal cases.[1] In international criminal proceedings this has not necessarily been the case. The Charters of the international war crimes Tribunals of Nuremberg[2] and Tokyo[3] did not provide for a right to appeal to a higher authority. Unlike their predecessors, the ICTY and the ICTR do provide for appellate proceedings. The Secretary-General of the United Nations, when proposing the ICTY Statute, stressed the importance of the right to appeal: 'such a right is a fundamental element of individual civil and political rights and has *inter alia*, been incorporated in the International Convenant on Civil and Political Rights. For this reason, the Secretary-General proposed that there should be an Appeals Chamber'.[4] This Appeals Chamber also sits in appellate proceedings at the ICTR. An appeal process is also provided for in the Rome Statute establishing an International Criminal Court,[5] with Articles 81 to 83 providing for the right of appeal against decisions of the Pre-Trial or Trial Chamber.[6]

The cases at issue

In the cases at issue, two principle questions were raised. Firstly, what is the scope and extent of the right of interlocutory appeal provided for in Rule 72(B).[7] As "lack of jurisdiction" is the sole ground of interlocutory appeal this raises the question as to how 'jurisdiction' should be interpreted. Secondly, does a right of appeal exist outside the express provisions of the Statute and the Rules by virtue of the principle of natural justice? Before discussing the relevant submissions of the Appeal Chamber judges on these points, a closer look will be taken at the cases in which these questions were raised.

The issues at the heart of three of the four cases were the Prosecutorial strategy of joining trials and judicial efficiency, as well as the right of the accused to appeal in respect of either of these points. In *Bagosora and 28 others*, the Prosecutor brought a composite indictment against the appellant and 28 others embracing substantially the same matters as had been included in the original indictment against him, in addition to a count alleging conspiracy. However, when asked to review the new indictment Judge Kahn, dismissed it. He refused to confirm the indictment in respect of two groups of individuals. The first group of persons had been previously indicted and had already made initial appearances and had entered pleas. The second group had been indicted but remained at liberty. Judge Kahn took the view that he had no jurisdiction over either group, as they had already been assigned to a Trial Chamber which retained jurisdiction. Furthermore, he contended that in relation to the first group, other procedures could

---

[1]   See Article 14, paragraph 5 of the International Convention on Civil and Political Rights (ICCPR): 'Everyone convicted of a crime shall have the right to his conviction and sentence being reviewed by a higher tribunal acoording to law'.

[2]   Article XXVI of the Statute of the International Military Tribunal: 'The Judgment of the Tribunal as to the guilt or the innocence of any Defendant shall give the reasons on which it is based, and shall be final and not subject to review', L. Friedman (ed.), *The Law of War. A documentary history,* Vol. I, p. 892.

[3]   Article XVII of the Charter of the International Military Tribunal for the Far East: 'The judgment will be announced in open court and will give the reasons on which it is based. The record of the trial will be transmitted directly to the Supreme Commander for the Allied Powers for his action thereon. A sentence will be carried out in accordance with the order of the Supreme Commander for the Allied Power, who may at any time reduce or otherwise alter the sentence except to increase its severity', in L. Friedman (ed.), The Law of War. A documentary history, Vol. I, p. 901.

[4]   Report of the Secretary-General pursuant to paragraph 2 of Security Council Resolution 808 (1993), U.N. Doc. S/25704, par. 116, Virginia Morris and Michael P. Scharf, 2 The International Criminal Tribunal for Rwanda, p. 525.

[5]   Adopted on 17 July 1998, 37 International Legal Materials 1998, p. 999.

[6]   Christopher Staker, 'Part 8: Appeal and Revision', in: Otto Triffterer (ed.) Commentary on the Rome Statute of the International Criminal Court : observers' notes, article by article, Baden-Baden, 1999, p. 1015-1035.

[7]   Rule 72 RPE:

    (...) (B) Preliminary motions by the accused are:

       i)   Objections based on lack of jurisdiction;

       ii) Objections based on defects in the form of the indictment;

       iii) Applications for severance of crimes joined in one indictment under Rule 49, or for separate trials under Rule 82 (B);

       iv) objections based on the denial of request for assignment of counsel.

    (C) The Trial Chamber shall dispose of preliminary motions *in limine litis.*

    (D) Decisions on preliminary motions are without interlocutory appeal, save in the case of dismissal of an objection based on lack of jurisdiction, where an appeal will lie as of right. (...)

be followed to achieve the same result. Moreover he thought it would constitute a circumvention of the amendement procedure of Rule 50, and a contravention the rights of the accused, if the procedure of Rule 47 (joinder) would be followed in relation to that group. Judge Khan did, however, declare himself competent to review the indictment of a third group which had not yet been indicted and remained at liberty.[8] The Prosecutor appealed against the dismissal, but the Appeals Chamber refused the Prosecutor's leave to appeal, finding that a right of appeal did not lie from the decision under the Statute and the Rules. The Prosecutor then decided to refrain from relying on one indictment against all the accused, choosing instead to rely on separate original indictments and to seek to amend by motion each separate indictment by the addition of new charges. Then, in a motion for joinder, it would then ask to hold one trial on all of the indictments; the separate indictments would remain, they would merely be tried together.

President Kama, exercising his power under the Statute and Rules, decided to refer the two motions to one Trial Chamber in order to resolve both issues simultaneously. This served the need for flexibility and the linkages between both motions justified this decision. For this purpose, and to avoid disqualification of one or more of the judges, he decided to alter the composition of the Trial Chambers considering the Prosecutor's request for leave to file an amended indictment ('the leave request') and the joinder motion. As the ICTR was at the time composed of only six judges, it was not possible to establish a Trial Chamber in which no member had been involved in either of two earlier cases which had reviewed the indictment. That would entail disqualification under Rule 15(C).[9] Two of the accused, Kanyabashi and Nsengiyuma, contested the competence of this re-composed Trial Chamber.[10] Having had their initial appearance before a specific Trial Chamber, the appellants objected to the competence of any other Trial Chamber to consider the leave request and the joinder motion. They based their objections on the claim that the composition of a Trial Chamber cannot be altered, that Rule 50(A)[11] requires that the leave request should be submitted to the Trial Chamber which had conducted the initial appearance, and that the initial appearance marked the commencement of proceedings and, consequently, that the Trial Chamber had exclusive jurisdiction. The appeal was dismissed. Both appellants sought to quash the decision of the re-composed Trial Chamber, declaring it to be without jurisdiction to entertain the leave request and the joinder motion.

The Appeals Chamber directed the parties in both cases to submit briefs on the following issues: whether the challenge to the competence of the re-composed Trial Chamber to entertain both motions was based on lack of jurisdiction within the meaning of ICTR Rule 72(D):[12] and if it was, whether a Trial Chamber is competent to hear the leave request and the joinder motion, and if so, whether the re-composed Trial Chamber was lawfully re-composed.[13] The Appeals Chamber was divided in answering the contentions put before it. The judges differed as to reasoning and result. Judge Shahabuddeen dissented from the line of argument set out in the Joint and Separate Opinion of Judge McDonald and Judge Vohrah. Judges Nieto-Navia and Wang Tieya concurred in result but based on another reasoning.

---

[8]   ICTR, Decision on the Admissability of the Prosecutor's Appeal from the Decision of a Confirming Judge Dismissing an Indictment against Théonoste Bagosora and 28 Others, *Prosecutor v. Théonoste Bagosora and 28 Others,* Case No. ICTR-98-37-A, A.Ch., 8 June 1998, par. 5, p. 4.

[9]   Rule 15 (C) ICTR Statute: "The Judge who reviews an indictment against an accused, pursuant to Article 18 of the Statute and Rule 47 or 61, shall not be disqualified from sitting as a member of a Trial Chamber for the trial of that accused. "

[10]   Trial Chamber II in the case of Nsengiyuma and Trial Chamber I in the case of Kanyabashi.

[11]   Rule 50(A): "The Prosecutor may amend an indictment, without prior leave, at any time before its confirmation, but thereafter, until the initial appearance before a Trial Chamber pursuant to Rule 62, only with leave of the Judge who confirmed it but, in exceptional circumstances, by leave of the Judge assigned by the President. At or after such initial appearance an amendment of an indictment may only be made by leave granted by a Trial Chamber pursuant to Rule 73. (...)."

[12]   See note 7.

[13]   ICTR, Decision on Appeal Against Oral Decision of Trial Chamber II of 28 September 1998, Joint and Separate Opinion of Judge McDonald and Judge Vohrah, *Nsengiyumva v. Prosecutor,* Case No. ICTR-96-12-A, A.Ch., 3 June 1999, par. 2, p. 2; ICTR, Decision on the Defence Motion for Interlocutroy Appeal on the Jurisdiction of Trial Chamber I, Joint and Separate Opinion of Judge McDonald and Judge Vohrah, *Kanyabashi v. Prosecutor,* Case No. ICTR-96-15-A, A.Ch., 3 June 1999, para. 2, p. 2.

Interlocutory Appeal

The right of appeal in both the ICTR and ICTY Statutes is encapsulated in identical wording. Article 24 of the former and Article 25 of the latter provide for an appeal on two grounds, an error of law and an error of fact.[14] The ICTR and ICTY Statutes do not define the concept of 'appeal' as to form or extent. Unlike national legal systems, the Statutes of the Tribunals provide for a single avenue of appeal to a higher authority. This appeal combines the different forms that exist on the national level.[15] The relief granted by the Appeals Chamber extends to affirmation, reversal or revision of the decisions of a Trial Chamber. Appeal against an acquittal is allowed under the Statute, although 'the Statute was not intended to authorize the Appeals Chamber to reverse an acquittal by the court of first instance and enter a conviction at the appellate level'.[16]

The right of appeal is conferred upon persons convicted by the Trial Chamber and upon the Prosecutor. This seems to suggest that in the case of the Defence there is no possibility of interlocutory appeal. Nevertheless, both Tribunals allow for interlocutory appeal in the Rules of Procedure and Evidence.[17] The ICTY Rules were amended for the purpose of providing for interlocutory appeal based on 'lack of jurisdiction'. This provision was included in Rule 72(D) of the ICTR Rules of Procedure and Evidence. The ICTY Rules also provide for additional grounds for an interlocutory appeal. Apart from an interlocutory appeal relating to jurisdiction, Rule 72(B)(ii) of the ICTY Rules incorporates a system of applying to a panel of three judges for leave to appeal on grounds other than jurisdiction.[18] This Rule has been interpreted in such a way that it provides a 'filter mechanism' for the 'purpose of rejecting abusive interlocutory appeals while promptly admitting admissable interlocutory appeals'.[19] When it was applied for the first time, the three-member bench of the Appeals Chamber proceeded to lay down a cumulative, three-fold test for the grant of leave to appeal.[20]

Jurisdiction

Jurisdiction has been said to be 'an expression which is used in a variety of senses and takes its colours from its context'.[21] The discussion regarding leave to appeal under Rule 72(D) in the cases under consideration demonstrates that this proposition is true. Much of the disagreement arose from the

---

[14] Article 24 ICTR Statute :'1. The Appeals Chamber shall hear appeals from persons convicted by the Trial Chambers or from the Prosecutor on the following grounds:
(a) an error on a question of law invalidating the decision; or
(b) an error of fact which has occasioned a miscarriage of justice.
2. The Appeals Chamber may affirm, reverse or revise the decisions taken by the Trial Chambers'.

[15] In civil law systems there is a distinction between what in French is called *appel*, relating to questions of both fact and law, and *cassation*, relating to fundamental issues of law and normally the form of appeal to the court of highest instance in such systems, See Ch. Van den Wyngaert (ed.), Criminal Procedure Systems in the European Community, London, 1993.

[16] Virginia Morris and Michael P. Scharf, 1 The International Criminal Tribunal for the Former Yugoslavia . A Documentary History and Analysis, p. 295.

[17] The ICTY Statute and Rules did not originally provide for interlocutory appeals. However, when it became clear that the validity of the establishment of the ICTY by the Security Council would be challenged, it was concluded that this issue had to be dealt with as a preliminary matter and could not await final judgment. *See*, ICTY, Decision on the Defence Motion for Interlocutory Appeal on Jurisdiction, *Prosecutor v. Tadić*, Case No. IT-94-1-AR72, A.Ch., 2 October 1995.

[18] Rule 72(B) ICTY Decisions on preliminary motions are without interlocutory appeal save
(i) in the case of motions challenging jurisdiction, where an appeal by either parties lies as of right;
(ii) in other cases where leave to appeal is, upon good cause being shown, granted by a bench of three Judges of the Appeals Chamber'.

[19] ICTY, *Prosecutor v. Delalić et al*, Case No. IT-96-21-AR72.4, A. Ch., 22 November 1996, p. 7, par. 21.

[20] (1) Does the application relate to one of the issues covered by Rule 73 (A)(ii), (iii), (iv) or (v)? (2) Is the application frivolous, vexatious, manifestly ill-founded, an abuse of the process of the court or so vague and imprecise as to be unsusceptible of any serious consideration? (3) Does the application show a serious cause, namely does it either show a grave error in the decision which could cause substantial prejudice to the accused or is detrimental to the interests of justice or raise issues which are not only of general importance but are also directly relevant to the future development of trial proceedings, in that the decision by the Appeals Chamber would seriously impact upon further proceedings before the Trial Chamber? ICTY, Decision on Application for Leave to Appeal (Separate Trials), *Prosecutor v. Delalić et al.*, Case No. IT-96-21-AR72, A.Ch.B. 14 October 1996; See John R.W.D. Jones, The Practice of the International Criminal Tribunals for the Former Yugoslavia and Rwanda, (2nd ed.) New York, 2000, p. 366.

[21] *Anisminic Ltd. v. Foreign Compensation Commission* [1968] 2 Q.B. 862, 889.

ambiguous meaning of 'jurisdiction'. In international law, jurisdiction is understood as referring to 'powers exercised by a state over persons, property, or events'.[22] These powers can be divided into legislative jurisdiction, enforcement jurisdiction and adjudicative jurisdiction. The latter jurisdiction is determined by national law. International law only limits it by confining it to the discretion of states, as for instance in relation to diplomatic immunity. Adjudicative jurisdiction comprises four components: personal (*ratione personae*), territorial (*ratione loci*), temporal *(ratione temporis)* and a subject-matter (*ratione materiae*) element. In this sense jurisdiction is to be understood as an area over which authority can be exercised. In municipal law jurisdiction has a broader meaning. Apart from the four elements of adjudicative jurisdiction, it comprises another aspect, namely 'the power of a court to decide a matter in controversy'.[23] Adjudicative jurisdiction is to be understood as the authority to decide. In some national legal systems this is referred to as 'competence',[24] while other systems refer to both forms of jurisdiction as 'competence'.[25] The submissions made by the Prosecutor, the appellants and the judges pre-suppose different interpretations of the concept of jurisdiction. To gain a better understanding of these interpretations and of the role 'jurisdiction' played in the cases at issue, it is appropriate to take a closer look at the 'jurisdiction debate' that has taken place under English law.

Pure theory and different interpretations of jurisdiction: the parties

Under English common law, the concept of jurisdiction was developed from the earliest times as the key element in supervisory control, exercised by common law courts with general jurisdiction over inferior courts with only a limited jurisdiction.[26] A distinction was drawn between acts done outside the jurisdiction, which could be impeached by the common law courts, and acts done within jurisdiction, which could not be impeached and over which no 'common law control' could be extended.[27] This distinction remained valid for centuries. In practice, however, in order to be able to intervene on a more frequent basis, the common law courts considered almost all findings by inferior courts as jurisdictional. As reaction against this, a theory of the concept of jurisdiction was established, which itself lead to a narrower interpretation of jurisdiction and consequently, to a more limited scope of judicial review.[28] According to this 'pure' theory of jurisdiction, 'objections on the ground of defect of jurisdiction may be founded on the character and constitution of the inferior Court, the nature of the subject-matter of the inquiry, or the absence of some preliminary proceeding which was necessary to give jurisdiction to the Court'.[29] It follows from this that a court does not exceed its jurisdiction by deciding upon an incorrect legal or factual basis, as long as it had the power, ie jurisdiction, to determine the particular issue.

The Prosecutor, in opposing the appeal in Kanyabashi and Nsengiyumva, advocated a narrow interpretation of 'jurisdiction'. To its mind the Tribunal's jurisdiction related to only the four forms of adjudicative jurisdiction: personal, territorial, temporal and subject matter jurisdiction, as laid down in Articles 1 through 7 of the Statute. These articles applied to the Tribunal as a whole, and was not restricted to separate Trial Chambers. As none of these four forms of jurisdiction was affected by the re-composition of the Trial Chamber, the Prosecutor submitted that the Joinder Motion did not relate to

---

[22]   P. Malanczuk, Akehurst's Modern Introduction to International Law, 7th ed. (London, 1997), p. 109.

[23]   Black's Law Dictionary, With Pronunciation, 6th ed. (Minnesota, 1990), p. 853 citing *Pinner v. Pinner*, 33 N.C. App. 204, 234 S.E. 2d 633B3 p. 3.

[24]   The Dutch legal system distinguishes between 'absolute competence' referring to the authority to try certain type of cases (articles 44 and 56 of the Code on Judicial Organization) and 'relative competence' (article 2 of the Code of Criminal Procedure) referring to a certain geographic area.

[25]   Jean Pradel, Droit Pénal Comparé (Paris, 1995), p. 394-362.

[26]   For instance, statutory tribunals of limited jurisdiction with respect to place, persons or subject-matter; *see* J.M. Evans, De Smith's Judicial Review of Administrative Act, 4th ed., London 1980, p. 110.

[27]   J.M. Evans, De Smith's Judicial Review of Administrative Act, 4th ed., London 1980, p. 18-110.

[28]   'This theory may be stated as follows. Jurisdiction means authority to decide. Whenever a judicial tribunal is empowered or required to inquire into a question of law or fact for the purpose of giving a decision on it, its findings thereon cannot be impeached collateraly or on an application for certiorari but are binding until reversed on appeal. "Where a court has jurisdiction to entertain an application, it does not lose its jurisdiction by coming to a wrong conclusion, whether it was wrong in law or in fact.' in: J.M. Evans, De Smith's Judicial Review of Administrative Act, 4th ed., London 1980, p. 110, citing *R. v. Central Criminal Court JJ.* (1886) 17 Q.B.D. 598, 602.

[29]   *Colonial Bank of Australia Ltd. v. Willan* (1874) L.R. 5 P.C. 417, 418.

jurisdiction and was therefore not subject to appeal. The Prosecutor's argument that neither the Statute nor the Rules made the assignment of a case or the composition of a Trial Chamber a jurisdictional matter, seems to follow from this. To its mind the subject matter of the appeal did not involve a question of jurisdiction, but rather one of procedure.[30]

In this it has overlooked the fact that the concept also relates to the procedural power of a court, in English law referred to as jurisdiction. The appellants claimed that Rule 50(A) conferred jurisdiction upon the Trial Chamber holding the initial appearance to hear the leave request. The re-assignment of the case to another Trial Chamber was therefore taken to constitute a violation of this Rule and to go to the issue of jurisdiction. In that sense they relied upon the other interpretation of jurisdiction; as an authority to decide. Accordingly, the joinder motion and the leave request were thought to be subject to appeal as an interlocutory issue.

Pragamatism and principle: the judges

Returning to the English debate, it is instructive to see how the "pure" theory was thought by some to lead to a serious reduction of jurisdictional control. The opponents of this theory were not interested in defining the concept of jurisdiction through a coherent theory. In their view for jurisdiction to be a tool of supervisory control, it should not be restricted by a definition.[31] The House of Lords made it clear in the *Anisminic* decision that under certain circumstances, supervisory control over inferior tribunals also extends to errors made within the tribunal's jurisdiction, for example when there was a breach of natural justice.[32] Consequently the distinction between errors going to jurisdiction and errors within jurisdiction disappeared. However, while the American courts abandoned this distinction openly, English courts continued to pay it lip-service because of its historical roots.[33] This resulted in an incoherent and contradictory body of law which can only be fully understood by a detailed review of the authorities, an investigation that falls outside the scope of this commentary.[34]

The majority of the Appeal Chamber in the Nsengiyumva case was of the view that the request for leave was a jurisdictional matter and the decision was itself subject to appeal. This is because sub-rule 50(A) clearly states that the Trial Chamber before which the initial appearance took place is the only competent Trial Chamber to subsequently amend an indictment. Accordingly, this sub-rule confers the power upon a certain Trial Chamber to hear a case.[35] This viewpoint concurred with that of Judge Shahabuddeen and the appellants; that jurisdiction also entailed authority to decide, conferred upon the court by its Statute and/or Rules of Procedure and Evidence. As to re-composition, the majority of the Judges followed the Prosecutor's argument that 'assignment to the Chambers is an administrative matter within the purview of the President. It simply has nothing to do with jurisdiction'. The appellants, however, arguing for a textual interpretation to Article 13, paragraph 2 of the Statute[36] claimed that this provision should be

---

[30]   ICTR, Decision on Appeal against Oral Decision of Trial Chamber II of 28 September 1998, *Nsengiyumva v. Prosecutor*, Case No. ICTR-96-12-A, A. Ch. 3 June 1999 , par. 7, p. 4; referring to Prosecutor's Response and Challenge to the Admissability of the Accused's Notice of Appeal, par. 14-18.

[31]   J.M. Evans, *De Smith's Judicial Review of Administrative Act*, 4th ed., London 1980, p. 111.

[32]   In the *Anisminic Ltd. v. Foreign Compensation Commission* the House of Lords decided that a judicial tribunal having jurisdiction over a matter in the first instance, might exceed it by breaking the rules of natural justice, applying a wrong legal test or basing its judgement on legally irrelevent considerations. One has to bear in mind that the decision of the House of Lords in the *Anisminic* case was a 'dramatic climax to five years of litigation over a matter which an Act of Parliament expressly forbids to be questioned in any court of law'. In the *Anisminic* case there was a 'no-certiorari' clause forbidding a court from setting aside a decision based upon clear legal error that is non-jurisdictional. The recent extension of the principle of review by certiorari and statutory rights of appeal have made jurisdictional control over administrative tribunals less important. Under these circumstances a decision like in the *Anisminic* case is unlikely. See *Anisminic Ltd. v. Foreign Compensation Commission*, [1969] 2 AC 147, HL, H.W.R. Wade, Constitutional and Administrative Aspects of the Anisminic Case', 85 *L.Q.R.* 198, 198.

[33]   J.M. Evans, *De Smith's Judicial Review of Administrative Act*, 4th ed., London 1980, p. 115.

[34]   J.M. Evans, *De Smith's Judicial Review of Administrative Act*, 4th ed., London 1980, p. 115-119.

[35]   ICTR, Decision on Appeal against Oral Decision of Trial Chamber II of 28 September 1998, *Nsengiyumva v. Prosecutor*, Case No. ICTR-96-12-A, A.Ch., 3 June 1999, par. 12. ICTR, Decision on the Defence Motion for Interlocutory Appeal on the Jurisdiction of Trial Chamber, *Kanyabashi v. Prosecutor*, Case No. ICTR-96-15-A, A.Ch., 3 June 1999, par. 15.

[36]   Article 13, paragraph 2 ICTR Statute: 'After consultation with the judges of the International Criminal Tribunal for Rwanda, the President shall assign the Judges to the Trial Chambers. A judge shall serve only in the chamber to which he or she was assigned'.

understood as a prohibition and therefore fell outside the scope of the administrative judicial powers of the President. Adopting a teleological interpretation, the judges declined this literal understanding of Article 13 on the basis that it would lead to 'unreasonable results'. As to the joinder motion, however, it was decided that re-composition was merely an 'administrative matter' and therefore did not go to jurisdiction. Accordingly the decision relating to the joinder motion was not considered appealable. Due to the limited number of Judges available to hear cases, and the object and purpose of the Statute to ensure an expeditious trial, this was determined to be admissible.[37] Under exceptional circumstances the President 'must be allowed some leeway' to exercise his judicial administrative function in matters such as the re-composition of a Trial Chamber.[38] This leeway, however, finds its limitations in unequivocally worded provisions such as sub-rule 50(A).

In his dissenting opinion, Judge Shahabuddeen stated that non-compliance with the amendment-procedure of sub-rule 50(A) was 'clearly an objection to jurisdiction'.[39] This was because, to his mind, sub-rule 50(A) confers upon a Trial Chamber the power to hear a case.[40] In criticizing the Prosecutor's narrow definition of jurisdiction, which referred only to the four adjudicative jurisdiction elements, he understood jurisdiction to also include the: "power of a particular court to hear the type of case that is then before it"[41] and 'That suggests that two branches are involved – the *power* of the particilar court, and the *type of case*'.[42] (emphasis added) . He agreed with the appellants that an error in the compostion of a court can go to jurisdiction. To support the latter contention he embarked on a short survey of international and national jurisprudence.[43] Referring to the English legal debate, he understood jurisdiction to include the authority to decide and to relate to the constitution and procedural rules of a court. Judge Shahabuddeen agreed with the majority that Article 13, paragraph 2 of the Statute did not prohibit the re-composition of a Trial Chamber. In his view these assignments were to be regarded as temporary and 'substitute assignments' that did not fall under Article 13, paragraph 2. He disagreed with the other members of the Appeals Chamber who felt that assignments under Article 13, paragraph 2 merely constituted an administrative measure. In his view 'assignment (…) goes to competence of a judge to exercise the jurisdiction of a court. Of course, the function of assigning is an administrative activity opposed to a judicial one. But it is an administrative activity which is authorised by statute, and it can have legal effects. These effects go to the competence of a judge to exercise the jurisdiction of the Tribunal'.[44]

It seems to follow from the discussion above that the majority of the Judges took a more pragmatic view in interpreting the silence of the Rules and the Statute with respect to re-composition. They declined to pronounce a definitive opinion as to whether re-composition was a jurisdictional issue or not. This pragmatic approach can also be found in the following decision. In *Bernard Ntuyahaga v. Prosecutor* the appellant filed an interlocutory appeal, based on sub-rule 72 (D), objecting to the decision of the Trial

---

[37]   At the time of the hearing of the Joinder Motion and the Request for Leave, there were only two Trial Chambers and six Judges. UNSC Res. 1165 (1998), 30 April 1998 established a third Trial Chamber. The new Judges were sworn into office on 22 February 1999.

[38]   Exceptional circumstances include sub-rule 15 (C), see *supra* note 9, ICTR, Joint and Separate Opinion of Judge McDonald and Judge Vohrah, *Kanyabashi v. Prosecutor*, Case No. ICTR-96-15-A, A.Ch., 3 June 1999, p. 8.

[39]   , ICTR, Dissenting Opinion of Judge Shahabuddeen, *Kanyabashi v. Prosecutor*, Case No. ICTR-96-15-A, A.Ch., 3 June 1999, p. 6.

[40]   He observed, however, that in objecting to the jurisdiction of the Trial Chamber, the appellants did not base their arguments on sub-rule 50(A) of the RPE. It was the Prosecution which did so. Consequently he dismissed the appeal on that point, B3, p. 4. See also par. V.

[41]   Black's Law Dictionary, With Pronunciation, 6th ed. (Minnesota, 1990), p. 853 citing *Pinner v. Pinner*, 33 N.C. App. 204, 234 S.E. 2d 633.

[42]   ICTR, Dissenting Opinion of Judge Shahabuddeen, *Kanyabashi v. Prosecutor*, Case No. ICTR-96-15-A, A.Ch., 3 June 1999, p. 3.

[43]   However, the reference to the dissenting opinion of Judge El-Khani of the ICJ in the Mortished case, where a panel of only three, instead of four was authorised to sit, does not seem to support this. What this opinion does show is that an 'irregularity' in the composition of a quasi-judicial body can lead to decision not to take an advisory opinion to the United Nations Organisation. It does not, however, link composition to jurisdiction and therefore does not support Judge Shahabuddeen's contention that the jurisprudence of the ICJ supports his views.

[44]   ICTR, Dissenting Opinion of Judge Shahabuddeen, *Kanyabashi v. Prosecutor*, Case No. ICTR-96-15-A, A.Ch., 3 June 1999, p. 18-19.

Chamber to grant leave for withdrawal of the indictment. His argument was that the Statute and Rules only conferred upon a Trial Chamber the power to issue a verdict of acquittal. Without the need for further argument, the majority of the Appeals Chamber deemed the decision not appealable because the objection did not challenge the Trial Chambers jurisdiction under 'sub-rule 72(D). Judge Shahabudeen, however, pointed out in his dissenting opinion that 'the substance of the matter was that the appellant was, on a fair interpretation, objecting to the jurisdiction of the Trial Chamber to grant leave for the withdrawal of the indictment'.[45] He referred to jurisdiction as the authority to decide. This was how the Appeals Chamber and Judge Shahabuddeen understood it in the Kayishema and Nsengiyumva cases. Here, however, an appeal was considered inappropriate. A verdict in the present case would have barred the possibility of a new prosecution as the accused could raise *ne bis in idem* .[46] The president of the Trial Chamber was aware of this when noting that the appellant was 'actually asking for a verdict of innocence and acquittal.'[47] It might fairly be concluded that the concept of jurisdiction is as broad as the Appeals Chamber wants it to be in any particular cicrumstance, ensuring pragmatic results rather than jurisprudential certainty.

Inherent right of appeal

The debate in the Bagosora decision concentrated on another aspect of appellate proceedings at the ICTR; that is, the scope of Article 24 of the Statute. This raises the question as to whether Article 24 is broad enough to include appeals on various grounds. If not, can an appeal, for which neither the Statute nor the Rules expressly provide, be based on the inherent power of a court to create appellate proceedings? The last question was answered in the negative before the ICTY. Judge Sidhwa's Separate Opinion on the Defence for Interlocutory Appeal on Jurisdiction in Tadić stated that "The courts have no inherent power to create appellate provisions or acquire jurisdiction where none is granted'.[48] Other ICTY related decisions support that proposition. It seems to flow from this that when the Rules or the Statute do not provide for appellate proceedings, no appeal lies.[49] However the decision of the Appeals Chamber in Bagosora and 28 others is less definitive on this point.

The Prosecutor in Bagosora and 28 others appealed against the decision of Judge Khan which dismissed the indictment. However, no such appeal was expressly provided for in the Statute and the Rules. The contention of the Prosecutor, that an appeal from the decision lies as of right, was founded on two approaches. Firstly that a broad reading of Article 24 warranted the conclusion that there was a right to appeal to the dismissal of an indictment; secondly, that there was an 'inherent' right of appeal.[50] As to the first argument, the Prosecutor suggested that the Statute must be interpreted liberally in the light of its objects and purposes. Moreover it claimed that its mandate justified a liberal reading of Article 24. To its mind this was supported by the wording of Article 1 of the ICTR Statute: 'The ICTR shall have the power to prosecute persons responsible for serious violations of international humanitarian law committed in the territory of Rwanda and Rwandan citizens responsible for such violations committed in the territory of neighbouring States'. The Prosecutor asserted that 'prosecute' included not only

---

[45]   ICTR, Dissenting Opinion of Judge Shahabuddeen, *Bernard Ntuyahaga v. Prosecutor*, Case No. ICTR-98-40-A, A.Ch., 3 June 1999, p. 2.

[46]   ICTR, Dissenting Opinion of Judge Shahabuddeen, *Bernard Ntuyahaga v. Prosecutor*, Case No. ICTR-98-40-A, A.Ch., 3 June 1999, p. 2.

[47]   *Idem*, referring to the unofficial transcripts, 16 March 1999, p. 83.

[48]   ICTR, Decision on the Admissibility of the Prosecutor's Appeal from the Decision of a Confirming Judge Dismissing an Indictment against Théonoste Bagosora and 28 Others, *Prosecutor v. Théonoste Bagosora and 28 Others*, Case No. ICTR-98-37-A, A.Ch., 8 June 1998, p. 19, citing: ICTY, Decision on the Defence Motion for Interlocutory Appeal on Jurisdiction, *Prosecutor v. Tadić*, Case No. IT-94-1-AR72, A. Ch., 2 October 1995, ALC-I- 33.

[49]   ICTY, Decision on Application for Leave to Appeal, *Dragan Opacić*, Case No. IT-95-7-Misc.1, Bench of the Appeals Chamber, 3 June 1997; Decision on the Admissibility of the Request for Review by the Republic of Croatia of an Interlocutory Appeal of a Trial Chamber and Scheduling Order, *Prosecutor v. Blaškić*, Case No. IT-95-14-AR108bis, App. Ch., 28 October 1998, John R.W.D. Jones, The Practice of the International Criminal Tribunals for the Former Yugoslavia and Rwanda, (2nd. ed.), New York 2000, p.365.

[50]   ICTR, Decision on the Admissibility of the Prosecutor's Appeal from the Decision of a Confirming Judge Dismissing an Indictment against Théonoste Bagosora and 28 Others, *Prosecutor v. Théonoste Bagosora and 28 Others*, Case No. ICTR-98-37-A, A.Ch., 8 June 1998, p. 11-20.

prosecutorial activity, but also judicial activity, and that both the Office of the Prosecutor and the Judiciary are organs of the ICTR. Accordingly, the Appeals Chamber must enjoy 'the full complement of jurisdiction conferred on the Tribunal as an institution, except where there is clear expression in the Statute to the contrary'.[51] Article 24 must therefore be read in a broad way and the decision to dismiss the indictment must therefore be taken to constitute a 'miscarriage of justice'.[52] The Appeals Chamber, this time unanimously, deemed these arguments void of merit and stressed that the competence of the Chambers and the Prosecutor form distinct and independent components of the ICTR's jurisdiction under Article 1.[53] Moreover, the judges understood the reasoning of the Prosecutor to imply an unlimited right of appeal for the Prosecutor and not for the defence. This would seriously violate the principle of equality of arms and basic principles of natural justice and was therefore deemed undesirable. The judges further rejected the Prosecutor's contention that the dismissal of an indictment could be regarded as a final decision. As other remedies were available to the Prosecutor under the ICTR Rules to cure perceived adverse effects of the decision, this argument was put aside.

Arguing that there existed an inherent right of appeal, the Prosecutor relied on the principle that what is not prohibited is permitted. This proposition was, however, dismissed as inapplicable in the case at issue. The judges concluded that it would only apply when it was not inconsistent with the perceived object and purpose of the Statute. The Prosecutor's contention that there exists a general principle of law establishing an inherent right of appeal, was rejected because the Appeals Chamber found that '(...) the contentions of the Prosecutor, which would allow her the sole right of appeal, do not establish that it is competent to assert an inherent power of jurisdiction for this Notice of Appeal'.[54] Unlike cases emanating of the ICTY, the Appeals Chamber at the ICTR is less clear as to a determination of whether or not an inherent right of appeal exists, either as a constituent of natural justice or as a result of a liberal interpretation of the Statute. When examining the question as to whether there is any possibility of appealing a decision where no such appeal is provided for either in the Statute or the Rules, it appears that where a party has no other remedy as to a decision and and appeal would be consistent with the principle of equality of arms, the possibility of an appeal is not entirely precluded by the ICTR.[55]

Scope of appeal

In appellate proceedings before the ICTY and the ICTR questions of both fact and law may be (re)considered, whereas an appeal can also extend to fundamental issues of law. The jurisprudence of the Appeals Chamber, however, shows that an appeal should not amount to a retrial and that 'The appeal process of the International Tribunal is not designed for the purpose of allowing parties to remedy their own failings or oversights during trial or sentencing'[56] and 'an appeal does not involve a trial *de novo* (...). The corrective nature of that [appeal] procedure alone suggests that there is some limitation to any evidentiary material sought to be presented to the Appeals Chamber; otherwise the unrestricted admission of such material would amount to a fresh trial'.[57] In accordance with this approach, three of the Appeals Chamber judges in the cases under consideration refused to allow objections advanced for the first time by the defence only on appeal.[58] Judge Shahabuddeen, in his dissenting opinion in

[51]   ICTR, Decision on the Admissibility of the Prosecutor's Appeal from the Decision of a Confirming Judge Dismissing an Indictment against Théonoste Bagosora and 28 Others, *Prosecutor v. Théonoste Bagosora and 28 Others*, Case No. ICTR-98-37-A, A.Ch., 8 June 1998, p. 12.

[52]   See note 15.

[53]   ICTR, Decision on the Admissibility of the Prosecutor's Appeal from the Decision of a Confirming Judge Dismissing an Indictment against Théonoste Bagosora and 28 Others, *Prosecutor v. Théonoste Bagosora and 28 Others*, Case No. ICTR-98-37-A, A.Ch., 8 June 1998, p. 13.

[54]   *Idem*, p. 19.

[55]   See Staker, *supra* note 6, p. 1026-1027.

[56]   ICTY, Judgement, *Prosecutor v. Erdemović*, Case No. IT-96-22-A, A.Ch., 7 October 1997, ALC-I-544, par. 15.

[57]   See Staker, *supra* note 6, p. 1023, citing. Decison on Appellant's Motion for the Extension of the Time-Limit and admission of Additional Evidence, *Prosecutor v. Tadić* Case No. IT-94-1-A, A.Ch., 15 Oct. 1998, par. 41 and 42.

[58]   This is in line with earlier decisions of the Appeals Chamber before the ICTY, See Staker, p. 1024 referring to Decision Stating Reasons for Appeals Chamber's Order of 29 May 1998, *Prosecutor v. Kovačević*, Case No. IT-97-24-AR73, A. Ch., 15 October 1998, par. 32-33; Decision on Prosecutor's Appeal on Admissibility of Evidence, *Prosecutor v. Aleksovski*, Case No. IT-95-14/1-AR-73, A. Ch. 16 February 1999, par. 20.

Kanyabashi and Nsengiyuma, took the view that the appellants did not object to jurisdiction based on non-compliance with the amendment procedure of sub-Rule 50 (A), as this was not put forward as an objection before the Trial Chamber. Stressing the distinction between a liberal interpretation and a misinterpretation of provisions relating to interlocutory appeals, he claimed that it would be a 'misinterpretation of the provisions governing interlocutory appeals to say that the appellant may be treated as having made an objection to jurisdiction based on non-compliance with the specific amendment procedure prescribed by Rule 50(A) of the Rules'.[59] Judge Wang Tieya and Judge Nieto-Navia adopted a similar reasoning in their joint separate and concurring opinion. In their views, the objection as to the alleged bias of the judges related to an objection on re-composition of the Trial Chamber. It was not put forward before the Trial Chamber as an independent preliminary objection.[60] Even though the above mentioned submissions did not directly lead to a dismissal of the appeal in respect of the joinder motion, they indicate that the onus is on the appellant to persuade the Appeals Chamber of an error in proceedings. The appeal process at the two *ad hoc* Tribunals is not an opportunity to re-litigate matters.

New Rules

At the Seventh Plenary Meeting in February 2000, after the cases at issue were decided, the ICTR judges amended Rule 72, adding three sub-rules: 72(G), (H) and (I) of which the latter two are of particular interest:

"Rule 72
(H) For purposes of Rule 72(B)(i) and (D) an objection based on lack of jurisdiction refers exclusively to a motion which challenges an indictment on the ground that it does not relate to:
(i) any of the persons indicated in Articles 1, 5, 6 and 8 of the Statute;
(ii) the territories indicated in Articles 1, 7 and 8 of the Statute;
(iii) the period indicated in Articles 1, 7, and 8 of the Statute, or
(iv) any of the violations indicated in Articles 2, 3, 4 and 6 of the Statute.

(I) An appeal brought under Rule 72 (D) may not be proceeded with if a bench of three Judges of the Appeals Chamber, assigned by the presiding Judge of the Appeals Chamber, decides that the appeal is not capable of satisfying the requirements of paragraph (H), in which case the appeal shall be dismissed."

The new Rule 72(H) excludes the possibility of basing an interlocutory appeal on lack of jurisdiction as it had been interpreted by the Prosecutor. For the purposes of interlocutory appeal, this interpretation was considered by the judges to be too narrow, and has become irrelevant since the amendment of Rule 72. A preliminary motion or interlocutory appeal cannot now be based on that interpretation of jurisdiction. Rule 72(I) is the result of a suggestion made by Judge Wang and Judge Nieto-Navia in their joint separate and concurring opinion in Kanyabashi and Nsengiyumva. They took the view that the question of jurisdiction should be dealt with as a preliminary issue before a Trial Chamber can consider the merits. For this purpose, Rule 72(I) provides for a system of leave to appeal granted by a bench of three Appeal Chamber judges.

Another Rule was amended at the Seventh Plenary Session. Rule 15(C) on disqualification of judges now reads:

"Rule15:
"C) The Judge who reviews an indictment against an accused, pursuant to Article 18 of the Statute and Rule 47 or 61, shall not be disqualified from sitting as a member of a Trial Chamber for the trial of that accused."

---

[59]   ICTR, Dissenting Opinion of Judge Shahabuddeen, *Kanyabashi v. Prosecutor*, Case No. ICTR-96-15-A, A.Ch., 3 June 1999, p. 6.
[60]   ICTR, Joint Separate and Concurring Opinion of Judge Wang Tieya and Judge Nieto-Navia, *Kanyabashi v. Prosecutor*, Case No. ICTR-96-15-A, A.Ch., 3 June 1999, p. 13-14.

One of the reasons for President Kama to re-compose the Trial Chambers was to avoid disqualification of judges. Under the amended Rule 15 (C), disqualification of a reviewing judge can no longer be an objection. This means that a further 're-composition discussion', such as those referred to above, is unlikely. Bearing in mind that the 're-composition discussion' caused a considerable delay in trial proceedings while the judges of the Rwanda Tribunal formulated a policy of judicial efficiency, the amendments to Rules 15 and 72 can be seen as a product of the lengthy discussion that arose out of the Bagosora and 28 others decision.

Conclusion

The discussion in the cases at issue is important for the functioning of the ICTR to the extent that a disagreement relating to the scope and content of the right of interlocutory appeal amounted to a debate on jurisdiction being the sole ground of appeal. The significance of the decisions lies in the fact that the discussion on jurisdiction produced a negative definition of the concept. All the Appeals Chamber judges dispensed with the narrow concept of jurisdiction put forward by the Prosecutor. In this way they were clear as to how jurisdiction for the purposes of interlocutory appeal should not be interpreted. They seemed to have thought, as in Tadić at the ICTY, that interpreting jurisdiction in such a way would limit the possibility that Rule 72(D) would undermine the administration of justice.[61] Interestingly enough, interlocutory appeals based on this narrow interpretation are now excluded by a recent amendment to the ICTR Rules of Procedure and Evidence. Rejecting the narrow interpretation of jurisdiction does not necessarily mean a broadening of the scope of interlocutory appeal. On the contrary, three factors point in the opposite direction. Firstly, three of the judges took the view that objections that are not raised before a Trial Chamber cannot then be advanced for the first time on appeal. Secondly, the right of appeal is subject to a pragmatic approach prompted by reasons of judicial efficiency and expediency. Thirdly, the incorporation of the leave to appeal system in Rule 72(I) can lead to a 'filter-mechanism' restricting the right of interlocutory appeal. Bearing in mind that the interlocutory jurisdiction of the ICTR is more circumscribed than that of the ICTY, the jurisprudence of the Appeals Chamber, while appearing to pursue judicial efficiency rather than a broadening the right of appeal, leads one to wonder if this will eventually lead to a stricter right of interlocutory appeal at the ICTR. This would be an undesirable development, in particular when one recalls that one of the purposes of establishing one Appeals Chamber for both Tribunals was to make the law uniform. It remains to be seen how jurisprudence on the right to appeal will develop. The fact that the Appeals Chamber in Bagosora and 28 others did not categorically exclude the possibility of an inherent right of appeal, like it did at the ICTY, might make up for this imbalance. Moreover, as was decided in the Erdemović case, the Appeals Chamber can raise matters *proprio motu* 'pursuant to its inherent powers as an appellate body once seised of an appeal lodged by either party pursuant to Article 25 of the Statute'.[62]

Elies van Sliedregt

---

[61]   ICTY, Decision on the Defence Motion for Interlocutory Appeal on Jurisdiction, *Prosecutor v. Tadić*, Case No. IT-94-1-AR72, A. Ch., 2 October 1995, par. 6, ALC-I- 33.
[62]   ICTY, Judgement, *Prosecutor v. Erdemović*, Case No. IT-96-22-A, A. Ch., 7 October 1997, ALC-I-544.

UNITED NATIONS   NATIONS UNIES

International Criminal Tribunal for Rwanda
Tribunal pénal international pour le Rwanda

CHAMBER I – CHAMBRE I

OR: ENG

Before: **Judge Laïty Kama, Presiding**
                Judge Lennart Aspegren
                Judge Navanethem Pillay

Decision of: **2 September 1998**

THE PROSECUTOR

VERSUS

JEAN-PAUL AKAYESU

Case No. ICTR-96-4-T

———————————————

JUDGEMENT

———————————————

The Office of the Prosecutor:
    Mr. Pierre-Richard Prosper

Counsel for the Accused:
    Mr. Nicolas Tiangaye
    Mr. Patrice Monthé

[page 2] List of Contents

1. INTRODUCTION

1.1. The International Tribunal

1.   This judgment is rendered by Trial Chamber I of the International Tribunal for the prosecution of persons responsible for genocide and other serious violations of international humanitarian law committed in the territory of Rwanda and Rwandan citizens responsible for genocide and other such violations committed in the territory of neighbouring States, between 1 January and 31 December 1994 (the "Tribunal"). The judgment follows the indictment and trial of Jean Paul Akayesu, a Rwandan citizen who was bourgmestre of Taba commune, Prefecture of Gitarama, in Rwanda, at the time the crimes alleged in the indictment were perpetrated.

2.   The Tribunal was established by the United Nations Security Council by its resolution 955 of 8 November 1994.[1] After having reviewed various official United Nations reports[2] which indicated that acts of genocide and other systematic, widespread and flagrant violations of international humanitarian law had been committed in Rwanda, the Security Council concluded that the situation in Rwanda in 1994 constituted a threat to international peace and security within the meaning of Chapter VII of the United Nations Charter. Determined to put an end to such crimes and "convinced that...the prosecution of persons responsible for such acts and violations ... would contribute to the process of national reconciliation and to the restoration and maintenance of peace", the Security Council, acting under the said Chapter VII established the Tribunal.[3] Resolution 955 charges all States with a duty to cooperate fully with the Tribunal and **[page 6]** its organs in accordance with the Statute of the Tribunal (the "Statute"), and to take any measures necessary under their domestic law to implement the provisions of the Statute, including compliance with requests for assistance or orders issued by the Tribunal. Subsequently, by its resolution 978 of 27 February 1995, the Security Council "urge[d] the States to arrest and detain, in accordance with their national law and relevant standards of international law, pending prosecution by the International Tribunal for Rwanda or by the appropriate national authorities, persons found within their territory against whom there is sufficient evidence that they were responsible for acts within the jurisdiction of the International Tribunal for Rwanda".[4]

3.   The Tribunal is governed by its Statute, annexed to the Security Council Resolution 955, and by its Rules of Procedure and Evidence (the "Rules"), adopted by the Judges on 5 July 1995 and amended subsequently.[5] The two Trial Chambers and the Appeals Chamber of the Tribunal are composed of eleven Judges in all, three sitting in each Trial Chamber and five in the Appeals Chamber. They are elected by the United Nations General Assembly and represent, in accordance with Article 12(3) (c) of the Statute, the principal legal systems of the world. The Statute stipulates that the members of the Appeals Chamber of the other special international criminal tribunal, namely the Tribunal for the prosecution of persons responsible for serious violations of international humanitarian law committed in the territory of the former Yugoslavia since 1991 ("the Tribunal for the former Yugoslavia"), shall also serve as members of the Appeals Chamber of the Tribunal for Rwanda.

4.   Under the Statute, the Tribunal has the power to prosecute persons responsible for serious violations of international human law committed in the territory of Rwanda and Rwandan citizens responsible for genocide and other such violations committed in the territory of neighbouring States, between 1 January and 31 December 1994. According to Articles 2 to 4 of the Statute relating to its *ratione materiae* jurisdiction, the Tribunal has the power to prosecute persons who committed genocide

---

[1]   UN Document S/RES/955 of 8 November 1994

[2]   Preliminary Report of the Commission of Experts established pursuant to Security Council resolution 935 (1994) (UN Document S/1994/1125), Final Report of the Commission of Experts established pursuant to Security Council Resolution 935 (1994) (Document S/1994/1405) and Reports of the Special Rapporteur for Rwanda of the United Nations Commission of Human Rights (Document S/1994/1157, annexes I and II).

[3]   The establishment of a special international tribunal was also requested by the Government of Rwanda (UN Document S/1994/1115). However, its representative at the Security Council later voted against resolution 955.

[4]   S/RES/978 of 27 February 1995, operative paragraph 1

[5]   The Rules were successively amended on 12 January 1996, 15 May 1996, 4 July 1996, 5 June 1997 and 8 June 1998.

as defined in Article 2 of the Statute, persons responsible for crimes against humanity as defined in Article 3 of the Statute and persons responsible for serious **[page 7]** violations of Article 3 Common to the Geneva Conventions of 12 August 1949 on the protection of victims of war[6], and of Additional Protocol II thereto of 8 June 1977, a crime defined in Article 4 of the Statute[7]. Article 8 of the Statute provides that the Tribunal has concurrent jurisdiction with national courts over which it, however, has primacy.

5.   The Statute stipulates that the Prosecutor, who acts as a separate organ of the Tribunal, is responsible for the investigation and prosecution of the perpetrators of such violations. Upon determination that a prima facie case exists to proceed against a suspect, the Prosecutor shall prepare an indictment containing a concise statement of the facts and the crime or crimes with which the accused is charged. Thereafter, he or she shall transmit the indictment to a Trial Judge for review and, if need be, confirmation. Under the Statute, the Prosecutor of the Tribunal for the former Yugoslavia shall also serve as the Prosecutor of the Tribunal for Rwanda. However, the two Tribunals maintain separate Offices of the Prosecutor and Deputy Prosecutors. The Prosecutor of the Tribunal for Rwanda is assisted by a team of investigators, trial attorneys and senior trial attorneys, who are based in Kigali, Rwanda. These officials travel to Arusha whenever they are expected to plead a case before the Tribunal. **[page 8]**

1.2. The Indictment

6.   The Indictment against Jean-Paul Akayesu was submitted by the Prosecutor on 13 February 1996 and was confirmed on 16 February 1996. It was amended during the trial, in June 1997, with the addition of three counts (13 to 15) and three paragraphs (10A, 12A and 12B). The Amended Indictment is here set out in full:

"The Prosecutor of the International Criminal Tribunal for Rwanda, pursuant to his authority under Article 17 of the Statute of the Tribunal, charges:

JEAN PAUL AKAYESU

with **GENOCIDE, CRIMES AGAINST HUMANITY** and **VIOLATIONS OF ARTICLE 3 COMMON TO THE GENEVA CONVENTIONS**, as set forth below:

Background

1.   On April 6, 1994, a plane carrying President Juvénal Habyarimana of Rwanda and President Cyprien Ntaryamira of Burundi crashed at Kigali airport, killing all on board. Following the deaths of the two Presidents, widespread killings, having both political and ethnic dimensions, began in Kigali and spread to other parts of Rwanda.

2.   Rwanda is divided into 11 prefectures, each of which is governed by a prefect. The prefectures are further subdivided into communes which are placed under the authority of bourgmestres. The bourgmestre of each commune is appointed by the President of the Republic, upon the recommendation of the Minister of the Interior. In Rwanda, the bourgmestre is the most powerful figure in the commune.

---

[6]   Geneva Convention for the Amelioration of the Condition of the Wounded and Sick in Armed Forces in the Field, 12 August 1949, United Nations Treaty Series, vol. 75, No.970 ("Geneva Convention I"); Geneva Convention for the Amelioration of the Condition of the Wounded, Sick and Shipwrecked Members of Armed Forces at Sea, 12 August 1949, *ibid* No.971 ("Geneva Convention II"); Geneva Convention relative to the Treatment of Prisoners of War, 12 August 1949, *ibid*, No.972 ("Geneva Convention III"); Geneva Convention relative to the Protection of Civilian Persons in Time of War, 12 August 1949, *ibid* No.973 ("Geneva Convention IV").
[7]   Protocol Additional...relating to the Protection of Victims of Non-International Armed Conflicts (Protocol II), 8 June 1977, United Nations Treaty Series, vol. 1125, No. 17513

His *de facto* authority in the area is significantly greater than **[page 9]** that which is conferred upon him *de jure*.

The Accused

3.   **Jean Paul AKAYESU** born in 1953 in Murehe sector, Taba commune, served as bourgmestre of that commune from April 1993 until June 1994. Prior to his appointment as bourgmestre, he was a teacher and school inspector in Taba.

4.   As bourgmestre, **Jean Paul AKAYESU** was charged with the performance of executive functions and the maintenance of public order within his commune, subject to the authority of the prefect. He had exclusive control over the communal police, as well as any gendarmes put at the disposition of the commune. He was responsible for the execution of laws and regulations and the administration of justice, also subject only to the prefect's authority.

General Allegations

5.   Unless otherwise specified, all acts and omissions set forth in this indictment took place between 1 January 1994 and 31 December 1994, in the commune of Taba, prefecture of Gitarama, territory of Rwanda.

6.   In each paragraph charging genocide, a crime recognized by Article 2 of the Statute of the Tribunal, the alleged acts or omissions were committed with intent to destroy, in whole or in part, a national, ethnic or racial group.

7.   The victims in each paragraph charging genocide were members of a national, ethnic, racial of religious group.

8.   In each paragraph charging crimes against humanity, crimes recognized by Article 3 of the Tribunal Statute, the alleged acts or omissions were committed as part of a widespread or systematic attack against a civilian population on national, political, ethnic or racial grounds. **[page 10]**

9.   At all times relevant to this indictment, a state of international armed conflict existed in Rwanda.

10.   The victims referred to in this indictment were, at all relevant times, persons not taking an active part in the hostilities.

10A. In this indictment, acts of sexual violence include forcible sexual penetration of the vagina, anus or oral cavity by a penis and/or of the vagina or anus by some other object, and sexual abuse, such as forced nudity.

11.   The accused is individually responsible for the crimes alleged in this indictment. Under Article 6(1) of the Statute of the Tribunal, individual criminal responsibility is attributable to one who plans, instigates, orders, commits or otherwise aids and abets in the planning, preparation or execution of any of the crimes referred to in Articles 2 to 4 of the Statute of the Tribunal.

Charges

12.   As bourgmestre, **Jean Paul AKAYESU** was responsible for maintaining law and public order in his commune. At least 2000 Tutsis were killed in Taba between April 7 and the end of June, 1994, while he was still in power. The killings in Taba were openly committed and so widespread that, as bourgmestre, **Jean Paul AKAYESU** must have known about them. Although he had the authority and responsibility to do so, **Jean Paul AKAYESU** never attempted to prevent the killing of Tutsis in the commune in any way or called for assistance from regional or national authorities to quell the violence.

12A. Between April 7 and the end of June, 1994, hundreds of civilians (hereinafter "displaced civilians") sought refuge at the bureau communal. The majority of these displaced civilians were Tutsi. While seeking refuge at the bureau communal, female displaced civilians were regularly taken by armed local militia and/or communal police and subjected to sexual violence, and/or beaten on or near the bureau communal premises. Displaced civilians were also murdered frequently on or near the bureau communal premises. Many women were forced to endure multiple acts of sexual violence which were at times committed by more than one assailant. [page 11] These acts of sexual violence were generally accompanied by explicit threats of death or bodily harm. The female displaced civilians lived in constant fear and their physical and psychological health deteriorated as a result of the sexual violence and beatings and killings.

12B. **Jean Paul AKAYESU** knew that the acts of sexual violence, beatings and murders were being committed and was at times present during their commission. **Jean Paul AKAYESU** facilitated the commission of the sexual violence, beatings and murders by allowing the sexual violence and beatings and murders to occur on or near the bureau communal premises. By virtue of his presence during the commission of the sexual violence, beatings and murders and by failing to prevent the sexual violence, beatings and murders, **Jean Paul AKAYESU** encouraged these activities.

13. On or about 19 April 1994, before dawn, in Gishyeshye sector, Taba commune, a group of men, one of whom was named Francois Ndimubanzi, killed a local teacher, Sylvere Karera, because he was accused of associating with the Rwandan Patriotic Front ("RPF") and plotting to kill Hutus. Even though at least one of the perpetrators was turned over to **Jean Paul AKAYESU**, he failed to take measures to have him arrested.

14. The morning of April 19, 1994, following the murder of Sylvere Karera, **Jean Paul AKAYESU** led a meeting in Gishyeshye sector at which he sanctioned the death of Sylvere Karera and urged the population to eliminate accomplices of the RPF, which was understood by those present to mean Tutsis. Over 100 people were present at the meeting. The killing of Tutsis in Taba began shortly after the meeting.

15. At the same meeting in Gishyeshye sector on April 19, 1994, **Jean Paul AKAYESU** named at least three prominent Tutsis – Ephrem Karangwa, Juvénal Rukundakuvuga and Emmanuel Sempabwa – who had to be killed because of their alleged relationships with the RPF. Later that day, Juvénal Rukundakuvuga was killed in Kanyinya. Within the next few days, Emmanuel Sempabwa was clubbed to death in front of the Taba *bureau communal*.

16. **Jean Paul AKAYESU**, on or about April 19, 1994, conducted house-to-house searches [page 12] in Taba. During these searches, residents, including Victim V, were interrogated and beaten with rifles and sticks in the presence of **Jean Paul AKAYESU**. **Jean Paul AKAYESU** personally threatened to kill the husband and child of Victim U if she did not provide him with information about the activities of the Tutsis he was seeking.

17. On or about April 19, 1994, **Jean Paul AKAYESU** ordered the interrogation and beating of Victim X in an effort to learn the whereabouts of Ephrem Karangwa. During the beating, Victim X's fingers were broken as he tried to shield himself from blows with a metal stick.

18. On or about April 19, 1994, the men who, on **Jean Paul AKAYESU**'s instructions, were searching for Ephrem Karangwa destroyed Ephrem Karangwa's house and burned down his mother's house. They then went to search the house of Ephrem Karangwa's brother-in-law in Musambira commune and found Ephrem Karangwa's three brothers there. The three brothers – Simon Mutijima, Thaddée Uwanyiligira and Jean Chrysostome Gakuba – tried to escape, but **Jean Paul AKAYESU** blew his whistle to alert local residents to the attempted escape and ordered the people to capture the brothers. After the brothers were captured, **Jean Paul AKAYESU** ordered and participated in the killings of the three brothers.

19. On or about April 19, 1994, **Jean Paul AKAYESU** took 8 detained men from the Taba *bureau communal* and ordered militia members to kill them. The militia killed them with clubs, machetes, small axes and sticks. The victims had fled from Runda commune and had been held by **Jean Paul AKAYESU**.

20.   On or about April 19, 1994, **Jean Paul AKAYESU** ordered the local people and militia to kill intellectual and influential people. Five teachers from the secondary school of Taba were killed on his instructions. The victims were Theogene, Phoebe Uwineze and her fiance (whose name is unknown), Tharcisse Twizeyumuremye and Samuel. The local people and militia killed them with machetes and agricultural tools in front of the Taba *bureau communal*.

21.   On or about April 20, 1994, **Jean Paul AKAYESU** and some communal police went to the house of Victim Y, a 68 year old woman. **Jean Paul AKAYESU** interrogated her about **[page 13]** the whereabouts of the wife of a university teacher. During the questioning, under **Jean Paul AKAYESU**'s supervision, the communal police hit Victim Y with a gun and sticks. They bound her arms and legs and repeatedly kicked her in the chest. **Jean Paul AKAYESU** threatened to kill her if she failed to provide the information he sought.

22.   Later that night, on or about April 20, 1994, **Jean Paul AKAYESU** picked up Victim W in Taba and interrogated her also about the whereabouts of the wife of the university teacher. When she stated she did not known, he forced her to lay on the road in front of his car and threatened to drive over her.

23.   Thereafter, on or about April 20, 1994, **Jean Paul AKAYESU** picked up Victim Z in Taba and interrogated him. During the interrogation, men under **Jean Paul AKAYESU**'s authority forced Victims Z and Y to beat each other and used a piece of Victim Y's dress to strangle Victim Z.

Counts 1-3

(Genocide)

(Crimes against Humanity)

By his acts in relation to the events described in paragraphs 12-23, **Jean Paul AKAYESU** is criminally responsible for:

COUNT 1: **GENOCIDE**, punishable by Article 2(3)(a) of the Statute of the Tribunal;

COUNT 2: Complicity in **GENOCIDE**, punishable by Article 2(3)(e) of the Statute of the Tribunal; and

COUNT 3: **CRIMES AGAINST HUMANITY** (extermination), punishable by Article 3(b) of the Statute of the Tribunal. **[page 14]**

Count 4

(Incitement to Commit Genocide)

By his acts in relation to the events described in paragraphs 14 and 15, **Jean Paul AKAYESU** is criminally responsible for:

COUNT 4: Direct and Public Incitement to Commit **GENOCIDE**, punishable by Article 2(3)(c) of the Statute of the Tribunal.

Counts 5-6

(Crimes Against Humanity)

(Violations of Article 3 common to the Geneva Conventions).

By his acts in relation the murders of Juvénal Rukundakuvuga, Emmanuel Sempabwa, Simon Mutijima, Thaddée Uwanyiligira and Jean Chrysostome Gakuba, as described in paragraphs 15 and 18, **Jean Paul AKAYESU** committed:

COUNT 5:   **CRIMES AGAINST HUMANITY** (murder) punishable by Article 3(a) of the Statute of the Tribunal; and

COUNT 6:   **VIOLATIONS OF ARTICLE 3 COMMON TO THE GENEVA CONVENTIONS,** as incorporated by Article 4(a)(murder) of the Statute of the Tribunal.

Count 7-8

(Crimes Against Humanity)

(Violations of Article 3 common to the Geneva Conventions)

By his acts in relation the murders of 8 detained men in front of the *bureau communal* as described in paragraph 19, **Jean Paul AKAYESU** committed: **[page 15]**

COUNT 7:   **CRIMES AGAINST HUMANITY** (murder) punishable by Article 3(a) of the Statute of the Tribunal; and

COUNT 8:   **VIOLATIONS OF ARTICLE 3 COMMON TO THE GENEVA CONVENTIONS,** as incorporated by Article 4(a)(murder) of the Statute of the Tribunal.

Counts 9-10

(Crimes Against Humanity)

(Violations of Article 3 common to the Geneva Conventions)

By his acts in relation to the murders of 5 teachers in front of the *bureau communal* as described in paragraph 20, **Jean Paul AKAYESU** committed:

COUNT 9:   **CRIMES AGAINST HUMANITY** (murder) punishable by Article 3(a) of the Statute of the Tribunal; and

COUNT 10:   **VIOLATIONS OF ARTICLE 3 COMMON TO THE GENEVA CONVENTIONS,** as incorporated by Article 4(a)(murder) of the Statute of the Tribunal.

Counts 11-12

(Crimes Against Humanity)

(Violations of Article 3 common to the Geneva Conventions)

By his acts in relation to the beatings of U, V, W, X, Y and Z as described in paragraphs 16, 17, 21, 22 and 23, **Jean Paul AKAYESU** committed:

COUNT 11:   **CRIMES AGAINST HUMANITY** (torture), punishable by Article 3(f) of the Statute of the Tribunal; and **[page 16]**

COUNT 12:   **VIOLATIONS OF ARTICLE 3 COMMON TO THE GENEVA CONVENTIONS,** as incorporated by Article 4(a)(cruel treatment) of the Statute of the Tribunal.

In addition and/or in the alternative to his individual responsibility under Article 6(1) of the Statute of the Tribunal, the accused, is individually responsible under Article 6(3) of the Statute of the Tribunal for the crimes alleged in Counts 13 through 15. Under Article 6(3), an individual is criminally responsible as a superior for acts of a subordinate if he or she knew or had reason to know that the subordinate was about to commit such acts or had done so and the superior failed to take the necessary and reasonable measures to prevent such acts or to punish the perpetrators thereof.

Counts 13-15

(Crimes Against Humanity)

(Violations of Article 3 common to the Geneva Conventions)

By his acts in relation to the events at the bureau communal, as described in paragraphs 12(A) and 12(B), **Jean Paul AKAYESU** committed:

COUNT 13: **CRIMES AGAINST HUMANITY** (rape), punishable by Article 3(g) of the Statute of the Tribunal; and

COUNT 14: **CRIMES AGAINST HUMANITY**, (other inhumane acts), punishable by Article 3(i) of the Statute of the Tribunal; and

COUNT 15: **VIOLATIONS OF ARTICLE 3 COMMON TO THE GENEVA CONVENTIONS AND OF ARTICLE 4(2)(e) OF ADDITIONAL PROTOCOL 2**, as incorporated by Article 4(e)(outrages upon personal dignity, in particular rape, degrading and humiliating treatment and indecent assault) of the Statute of the Tribunal. **[page 17]**

(Signed)

Louise Arbour

Prosecutor

[page 18] 1.3. Jurisdiction of the Tribunal

7.   The subject-matter jurisdiction of the ICTR is set out in Articles 2,3 and 4 of the Statute:

Article 2: Genocide

1.   The International Tribunal for Rwanda shall have the power to prosecute persons committing genocide as defined in paragraph 2 of this article or of committing any of the other acts enumerated in paragraph 3 of this article.

2.   Genocide means any of the following acts committed with intent to destroy, in whole or in part, a national, ethnical, racial or religious group, as such:

    a) Killing members of the group;
    b) Causing serious bodily or mental harm to members of the group;
    c) Deliberately inflicting on the group conditions of life calculated to bring about its physical destruction in whole or in part;
    d) Imposing measures intended to prevent births within the group;
    e) Forcibly transferring children of the group to another group.

3.   The following acts shall be punishable:

    a) Genocide;
    b) Conspiracy to commit genocide;
    c) Direct and public incitement to commit genocide;
    d) Attempt to commit genocide;
    e) Complicity in genocide. **[page 19]**

Article 3: Crimes against Humanity

The International Tribunal for Rwanda shall have the power to prosecute persons responsible for the following crimes when committed as part of a widespread or systematic attack against any civilian population on national, political, ethnic, racial or religious grounds:

a) Murder;
b) Extermination;
c) Enslavement;
d) Deportation;
e) Imprisonment;
f) Torture;
g) Rape;
h) Persecutions on political, racial and religious grounds;
i) Other inhumane acts.

Article 4: Violations of Article 3 common to the Geneva Conventions and of Additional Protocol II

The International Tribunal for Rwanda shall have the power to prosecute persons committing or ordering to be committed serious violations of Article 3 common to the Geneva Conventions of 12 August 1949 for the Protection of War Victims, and of Additional Protocol II thereto of 8 June 1977. These violations shall include, but shall not be limited to:

a) Violence to life, health and physical or mental well-being of persons, in particular murder as well as cruel treatment such as torture, mutilation or any form of corporal punishment;
b) Collective punishments;
c) Taking of hostages; **[page 20]**
d) Acts of terrorism;
e) Outrages upon personal dignity, in particular humiliating and degrading treatment, rape, enforced prostitution and any form of indecent assault;
f) Pillage;
g) The passing of sentences and the carrying out of executions without previous judgment pronounced by a regularly constituted court, affording all the judicial guarantees which are recognised as indispensable by civilised peoples;
h) Threats to commit any of the foregoing acts.

8.   In addition, Article 6 states the principle of individual criminal responsibility:

Article 6: Individual Criminal Responsibility

1.   A person who planned, instigated, ordered, committed or otherwise aided and abetted in the planning, preparation or execution of a crime referred to in articles 2 to 4 of the present Statute, shall be individually responsible for the crime.

2.   The official position of any accused person, whether as Head of State or Government or as a responsible Government official, shall not relieve such person of criminal responsibility nor mitigate punishment.

3.   The fact that any of the acts referred to in articles 2 to 4 of the present Statute was committed by a subordinate does not relieve his or her superior of criminal responsibility if he or she knew or had reason to know that the subordinate was about to commit such acts or had done so and the superior failed to take the necessary and reasonable measures to prevent such acts or to punish the perpetrators thereof.

4.   The fact that an accused person acted pursuant to an order of a Government or of a superior shall not relieve him or her of criminal **[page 21]** responsibility, but may be considered in mitigation of punishment if the International Tribunal for Rwanda determines that justice so requires. **[page 22]**

1.4. The Trial

1.4.1. Procedural Background

9.   Jean-Paul Akayesu was arrested in Zambia on 10 October 1995. On 22 November 1995, the Prosecutor of the Tribunal, pursuant to Rule 40 of the Rules, requested the Zambian authorities to keep Akayesu in detention for a period of 90 days, while awaiting the completion of the investigation.

10.   On 13 February 1996, the then Prosecutor, Richard Goldstone[8], submitted an Indictment against Akayesu, which was subsequently amended on 17 June 1997. It contains a total of 15 counts covering genocide, crimes against humanity and violations of Article 3 Common to the 1949 Geneva Conventions and Additional Protocol II of 1977 thereto. More specifically, Akayesu was individually charged with genocide, complicity in genocide, direct and public incitement to commit genocide, extermination, murder, torture, cruel treatment, rape, other inhumane acts and outrages upon personal dignity, which he allegedly committed in Taba commune of which he was the bourgmestre at the time of the alleged acts.

11.   The Indictment was confirmed and an arrest warrant, accompanied by an order for continued detention, was issued by Judge William H. Sekule on 16 February 1996. The following week, the Indictment was submitted by the Registrar to the Zambian authorities, to be served upon the Accused. Akayesu was transferred to the Detention Facilities of the Tribunal in Arusha on 26 May 1996, where he is still detained awaiting judgment.

12.   The initial appearance of the Accused, pursuant to Rule 62 of the Rules, took place on 30 May 1996 in the presence of his counsel before Trial Chamber I, composed of Judge Laïty Kama, presiding, Judge Lennart Aspegren and Judge Navanethem Pillay. The prosecution team, **[page 23]** led by Honoré Rakotomanana[9], Deputy Prosecutor of the Tribunal, was composed of Yacob Haile-Mariam, Mohamed Chande Othman and Pierre-Richard Prosper[10]. The Accused pleaded not guilty to all the counts against him. On the same date, the Chamber ordered the continued detention of the Accused while awaiting his trial[11]. Simultaneous interpretation in French and English, and where necessary Kinyarwanda, was provided at the hearings.

13.   The Accused having been found indigent by the Tribunal, in accordance with the provisions of the Directive on Assignment of Defence Counsel[12], the Registrar of the Tribunal assigned Johan Scheers as defence counsel for the Accused and counsel's fees were paid by the Tribunal. By a decision of 31 October 1996, the Chamber directed the Registrar of the Tribunal to withdraw the assignment of Johan Scheers as defence counsel for Akayesu, pursuant to Article 19 of the Directive on Assignment of Defence Counsel, and to immediately assign Michael Karnavas as the new defence counsel for the Accused. In the same decision, the Chamber postponed the trial until 9 January 1997, at the request of the Accused[13]. On 20 November 1996, the Chamber granted a request for a further change of defence counsel filed by the Accused on 11 November 1996, pursuant to Article 19 of the Directive. On 9 January 1997, the Registrar assigned Nicolas Tiangaye and Patrice Monthé, who served as defence counsel for the Accused until the end of the trial. On 16 January 1997, the Chamber rejected a third motion for change **[page 24]** of defence counsel filed by the Accused on 9 January 1997[14]. The decision of 16 January 1997 also put an end to the interim measures adopted by the Chamber on 13 January 1997, temporarily authorizing the Accused to cross-examine the witnesses himself, along with his two counsel.

---

[8]   On 1 October 1996, Louise Arbour succeeded Richard Goldstone as Prosecutor of the Tribunal.

[9]   On 26 April 1997, Bernard Acho Muna succeeded Honoré Rakotomanana as Deputy Prosecutor of the Tribunal.

[10]   Besides the people already mentioned, the Prosecutor was represented during the trial by Patricia Viseur Sellers, James K. Stewart, Luc Côté, Sara Dareshori and Rosette Muzigo-Morrison.

[11]   Decision: Order for Continued Detention Awaiting Trial, *The Prosecutor v. Jean-Paul Akayesu*, Case No. ICTR-96-4-T, Trial Chamber I, 30 May 1996.

[12]   ICTR/2/L.2

[13]   Decision Concerning a Replacement of an Assigned Counsel and Postponement of the Trial, *The Prosecutor v. Jean-Paul Akayesu*, Case No. ICTR-96-4-T, 31 October 1996.

[14]   Decision on the Request of the Accused for Replacement of Assigned Counsel, *The Prosecutor v. Jean-Paul Akayesu*, Case No. ICTR-96-4-T, Trial Chamber I, 16 January 1997.

14.   On 27 May 1996, the then counsel for the Accused, Johan Scheers, filed a preliminary motion under Rule 73 of the Rules[15], requesting the Chamber to (i) rule that the criminal proceedings were inadmissible for reasons of flagrant violations of the rights of Defence; (ii) order the hearing of witnesses and that Defence investigations be conducted; (iii) exclude from the proceedings, all indirect witnesses to the acts for which the Accused is charged; and (iv) order the release of the Accused pending the trial on the merits. During the oral presentation of the motion at the hearing of 26 September 1996, however, the Defence raised issues beyond the framework of the said motion by advancing complaints regarding, on the one hand, the detention conditions of the Accused during his imprisonment in Zambia and, on the other hand, the delay by the Prosecutor in disclosing the Indictment and supporting material. In its decision of 27 September 1996[16], the Chamber rejected the entire motion on the grounds that the objections raised by the Defence and the manner in which they were presented, did not provide sufficient basis for the Chamber to rule on the merits under Rule 73 of the Rules. That same day, the Chamber adjourned the trial as the request of the Defence and set 31 October 1996[17] as the official opening date of the trial on the merits.

15.   On 29 October 1996, the Chamber granted the Prosecutor's motion of 23 October 1996 for the transfer of a witness detained in Rwanda in order for him to testify before the Tribunal. **[page 25]** A similar motion by the Defence, filed on 30 October 1997, was granted by the Chamber, it being ordered that three witnesses then detained in Rwanda be transferred to the Tribunal's Detention Facilities for a period of not more than two months so as to testify in the trial[18]. However, two subsequent requests by the Defence for the transfer and appearance in court of five and thirteen witnesses detained in Rwanda respectively were rejected, on the basis, *inter alia*, that the Defence was unable to demonstrate how the appearance of each witness was undoubtedly material in the discovery of the truth or that the conditions stipulated in Rule 90*bis* (b) of the Rules had been met[19].

16.   Besides the above-mentioned motions, several pre-trial motions were filed by the Defence, including a motion for the defendant to sit at counsel table during trail, a motion for an expedited *in camera* hearing regarding Prosecutorial misconduct and a motion to compel the Prosecutor to conduct a fair and just investigation. These motions were not granted.

17.   The trial of the Accused on the merits opened on 9 January 1997 before Trial Chamber I, composed of Judge Laïty Kama, presiding, Judge Lennart Aspegren and Judge Navanethem Pillay. Pursuant to Rule 84 of the Rules, Honoré Rakotomanana and Yacob Haile-Mariam made the opening statement for the Prosecutor, which was followed by the opening statement for the Defence, made by Nicolas Tiangaye and Patrice Monthé. During the initial phase of the trial which took place over 26 trials days until 24 May 1997, 22 witnesses, including five expert witnesses, testified for the Prosecutor. Subsequent to the presentation of the Prosecutor's evidence, an *in camera* status conference was held after which the Chamber, at the request of the Defence, adjourned the trial until 29 September 1997. **[page 26]**

18.   All Prosecutor and Defence eye-witnesses requiring protection benefited from measures guaranteeing the confidentiality of their testimony[20]. No information which could in any way identify the witnesses was given. During the hearings, letters of the alphabet were used as pseudonyms to refer to

---

[15]   As adopted on 5 July 1995

[16]   Decision on the Preliminary Motion Submitted by the Defence on the Form of the Indictment and Exclusion of Evidence, *The Prosecutor v. Jean-Paul Akayesu*, Case No. ICTR-96-4-T, Trial Chamber I, 27 September 1996.

[17]   Decision on Postponement of the Trial, *The Prosecutor v. Jean-Paul Akayesu*, Case No. ICTR-96-4-T, Trial Chamber I, 27 September 1996. However, at the hearing of 31 October, the beginning of the trial was postponed to 9 January 1997 at the request of the Defence.

[18]   Order for Temporary Transfer of Three Detained Witnesses Pursuant to Rule 90*bis* of the Rules of Procedure and Evidence, *The Prosecutor v. Jean-Paul Akayesu*, Case No. ICTR-96-4-T, Trial Chamber I, 31 October 1997

[19]   Decision on a Motion for the Appearance and Protection of Witnesses Called by the Defence, *The Prosecutor v. Jean-Paul Akayesu*, Case No. ICTR-96-4-T, Trial Chamber I, 9 February 1998, & Decision on the Motion for the Transfer and Protection of Defence Witnesses, *The Prosecutor v. Jean-Paul Akayesu*, Case No. ICTR-96-4-T, Trial Chamber I, 26 February 1998

[20]   Decision on the preliminary motion submitted by the Prosecutor for protective measures for witnesses, *The Prosecutor v. Jean-Paul Akayesu*, Case No. ICTR-96-4-T, Trial Chamber I, 27 September 1996.

protected witnesses and screens isolated the said witnesses from the public, but not from the Accused and his counsel. One Defence witness was heard *in camera*.

19.   On 13 February 1997, as an interim measure pending a Chamber decision on a request by the Accused for the replacement of his counsel, Akayesu was authorized by the Chamber to cross-examine, along with his assigned counsel, prosecution witnesses. The pertinent decision was rendered on 16 January 1997[21], whereby the request for replacement of Counsel was dismissed and the interim measure terminated.

20.   Most of the Rwandan witnesses spoke in Kinyarwanda and their testimonies were interpreted into the two working languages of the Tribunal (French and English). By decision of 9 March 1998, the Chamber dismissed a Defence Motion, based on Rule 91 of the Rules, to direct the Prosecutor to investigate an alleged false testimony by prosecution witness "R". The Chamber found that for the Defence to raise doubts as to the reliability of statements made by a witness, was not by itself sufficient to establish strong grounds for believing that the witness may have knowingly and wilfully given false testimony[22].

21.   During the hearing of 23 January 1997, the Chamber requested the Prosecutor, in view of the exceptional nature of the offences, to submit all written witness statements already made **[page 27]** available by her in the Defence. The Prosecutor objected to the request; hence the Chamber, by a decision rendered on 28 January 1997, pursuant to Rules 89(A), 89(C) and 98 of the Rules, ordered the Prosecutor to submit all available written witness statements to the Chamber in the case and that all such statements to which reference had been made by either the Prosecutor or the Defence shall be admitted as evidence and form part of the record. However, this was subject to the caveat that disclosure of all the written statements did not necessarily entail their admissibility as evidence[23].

22.   On 4 February 1997, the Prosecutor, who had not yet complied with the order of 28 January 1997, filed a motion requesting the Chamber to reconsider and rescind the said order. The Prosecutor submitted, *inter alia*, that the order of 28 January 1997 represented an unjustified change in the established order for production of evidence and thus did not satisfy the provisions of Rule 85, that Rule 98 simply allows the Chamber to order the production of specific additional evidence and not the disclosure of all the evidence, that it involves the Chamber in the process of disclosure and, in actual fact, circumvents Rule 66(A), and that the order is prejudicial to the parties. On 6 March 1997, the Chamber declared the Prosecutor's motion groundless, and expressed surprise, in the circumstances, at receiving a motion asking it to reconsider and rescind its order, instead of a motion for clarification. The Chamber specified in its decision that the order of 28 January 1997 could only be interpreted with respect to the witness statements already communicated to the Defence[24]. On 16 April 1997, the Prosecutor filed a notice of intent to comply with the Chamber's order to submit witness statements.

23.   As stated above, 24 may 1997 marked the end of the first part of the trial of the Accused with the testimony of the last prosecution witness. However, on 16 June 1997, the Prosecutor submitted a request to bring an expedited oral motion before the Chamber seeking an amendment **[page 28]** of the Indictment. During the hearing held to that end on 17 June 1997 the Prosecutor sought leave to add three further Counts, namely, Count 13: rape, a Crime Against Humanity, punishable under Article 3 (g) of the Statute, Count 14: inhumane acts, a Crime Against Humanity, punishable under Article 3 (i) of the Statute, and Count 15: outrages on personal dignity, notably rape, degrading and humiliating treatment and indecent assault, a Violation of Article 3 Common to the Geneva Conventions and of Article 4(2)(e) of Additional Protocol II, as incorporated in Article 4(e) of the Statute. The Chamber granted leave to the

---

[21]   *Ibid 14*

[22]   Oral decision, *The Prosecutor v. Jean-Paul Akayesu*, Case No. ICTR-96-4-T, Trial Chamber I, 9 March 1998, written decision issued on 24 March 1998.

[23]   Decision by the Tribunal on its Request to the Prosecutor to Submit the Written Witness Statements, *The Prosecutor v. Jean-Paul Akayesu*, Case No. ICTR-96-4-T, Trial Chamber I, 28 January 1997.

[24]   Decision on the Prosecutor's Motion to Reconsider and Rescind the Order of 18 January 1997, *The Prosecutor v. Jean-Paul Akayesu*, Case No. ICTR-96-4-T, Trial Chamber I, 6 March 1997

Prosecutor to amend the Indictment and postponed the date for resumption of the trial to 23 October 1997[25].

24.   The second phase of the trial started on 23 October 1997 with the initial appearance of Akayesu for the new counts in a public session before the Chamber. The Accused pleaded not guilty to each of the new counts. The Prosecutor then proceeded to present six new witnesses, including an investigator with the Office of the Prosecutor. In all, the Prosecutor put 28 witnesses on the stand over 31 trial days. The Defence, for its part, presented its evidence over the course of 12 trial days between 4 November 1997 and 13 March 1998. It called 13 witnesses, including the Accused, to the stand. A total of 155 exhibits were submitted during the trial.

25.   During the second phase of the trial, the Defence requested and obtained the issuance of a subpoena for Major-General Roméo Dallaire, former force Commander of UNAMIR (United Nations Assistance Mission in Rwanda), whose immunity had been partially lifted by the UN Secretary-General, to appear as a witness for the Defence[26]. The Chamber also granted leave to a representative of the United Nations Secretariat to appear as an Amicus Curiae to make a statement on the lifting of the immunity Major-General Roméo Dallaire enjoys by virtue of his position as former force Commander of UNAMIR[27]. [page 29]

26.   However, the Chamber did not grant the Defence motion for the issuance of a subpoena for two persons accused before the Tribunal to appear as Defence witnesses, on the grounds that their fundamental rights, as recognized by Article 20(4)(g) of the Statute, would perhaps be violated, and that there would be a risk that their appearance as witnesses in the case could cause prejudice to them[28]. A further Defence motion for the appearance of another accused as an expert witness was similarly dismissed[29]. The Chamber held therein that the impartiality of the potential expert witness, who is accused by the Tribunal for crimes related to those with which Akayesu is charged, could not be assured and consequently that he did not fulfil the requisite conditions for appearing as an expert witness. Furthermore, the Chamber found that for this particular Accused to be compelled to appear as an expert witness in the case would be prejudicial to him and could possibly violate his fundamental rights, as recognized by the provisions of Article 20(4)(g) of the Statute and Article 14(3)(g) of the International Covenant of Civil and Political Rights of 1966.

27.   The Chamber dismissed a Defence motion for a site visit and the conduct of a forensic analysis of the remains of three alleged victims. The Chamber found that a new forensic analysis would not be appropriate nor, in any case, instrumental in the discovery of the truth, on the basis, *inter alia*, that a number of the purported mass graves, including, without a doubt, those supposedly in the vicinity of the Taba "bureau communal" had been subject of previous exhumations. Moreover, the Chamber felt that the arguments of the Defence Counsel in support of the motion were pertinent mainly to evaluating the credibility of certain witness statements [page 30] and not to showing the necessity for an exhumation and forensic analysis, as requested[30].

28.   None of the parties presented witnesses for rebuttal purposes. The Accused testified in his own defence on 12 March 1998 and was cross-examined the next day by the Prosecutor. The latter presented her final arguments on 19 and 23 March, and the Defence presented its closing arguments on 26 March

---

[25]   Leave to amend the Indictment, *The Prosecutor v. Jean-Paul Akayesu*, Case No. ICTR-96-4-T, Trial Chamber I, 17 June 1997.

[26]   Decision on the Motion to Subpoena a Witness, *The Prosecutor v. Jean-Paul Akayesu*, Case No. ICTR-94-T, Trial Chamber I, 19 November 1997.

[27]   Order Granting Leave for Amicus Curiae to Appear, *The Prosecutor v. Jean-Paul Akayesu*, Trial Chamber I, Case No. ITCR-96-4-T, 12 February 1998.

[28]   Oral decision on a Motion for Summonses and Protection of Witnesses Called by the Defence, *The Prosecutor v. Jean-Paul Akayesu*, Case No. ICTR-96-4-T, Trial Chamber I, 17 February 1998, written decision 23 February 1998.

[29]   Decision on a Defence Motion for the Appearance of an Accused as an Expert Witness, *The Prosecutor v. Jean-Paul Akayesu*, Case No. ICTR-96-4-T, Trial Chamber I, 9 March 1998.

[30]   Oral decision on the Defence Motion Requesting an Inspection of the Site and the Conduct of a Forensic Analysis, *The Prosecutor v. Jean-Paul Akayesu*, Case No. ICTR-96-4-T, Trial Chamber I, 17 February 1998, written decision 3 March 1998.

1998. The trial on the merits was held over a period of 60 days of hearings, since 9 January 1997. The case was adjourned on 26 March 1998 for deliberation on the Judgment by the Chamber.

1.4.2. The Accused's line of defence

29.   The Accused has pleaded not guilty to all counts of the Indictment, both at his initial appearance, held on 30 May 1996, and at the hearing of 23 October 1997 when he pleaded not guilty to each of the new counts which had been added to the Indictment when it was amended on 17 June 1997.

30.   In essence, the Defence case – insofar as the Chamber has been able to establish it – is that the Accused did not commit, order or participate in any of the killings, beatings or acts of sexual violence alleged in the Indictment. The Defence concedes that a genocide occurred in Rwanda and that massacres of Tutsi took place in Taba Commune, but it argues that the Accused was helpless to prevent them, being outnumbered and overpowered by one Silas Kubwimana and the Interahamwe. The Defence pointed out that, according to prosecution witness R, Akayesu had been so harassed by the Interahamwe that at one point he had had to flee Taba commune. Once the massacres had become widespread, the Accused was denuded of all authority and lacked the means to stop the killings. **[page 31]**

31.   The Defence claims that the Chamber should not require the Accused to be a hero, to have laid down his life – as, for example, did the bourgmestre of Mugina – in a futile attempt to prevent killings and beatings. The Defence alluded to the fact that General Dallaire, in charge of UNAMIR and 2,500 troops, was unable to prevent the genocide. How, then, was Akayesu, with 10 communal policemen at his disposal, to fare any better? Moreover, the Defence argue, no bourgmestre in the whole of Rwanda was able to prevent the massacres in his Commune, no matter how willing he was to do so.

32.   As for acts of sexual violence, the Defence case is somewhat different from that for killings and beatings, in that, whereas for the latter the Defence does not contest that there were killings and beatings, it does deny that there were acts of sexual violence committed, at least at the Bureau Communal. During his testimony the Accused emphatically denied that any rapes had taken place at the Bureau Communal, even when he was not there. The Chamber notes the Accused's emphatic denial of facts which are not entirely within his knowledge.

33.   As general remarks, the Defence alluded to the fragility of human testimony as opposed to documentary evidence, and specifically referred to the evidence of Dr. Mathias Ruzindana, who had testified about problems in relying on eye-witness accounts of Rwandans[31]. The Defence also raised problems associated with alleged "syndicates of informers", in which groups of Rwandans supposedly collaborated to concoct testimony against a person for revenge or other motives. This allegation is specifically dealt with below.

34.   As regards the Accused, the Defence pointed out that, though the Prosecutor admitted that the Accused had opposed massacres before 18 April 1994, the Prosecutor could not demonstrate that he was a "genocidal ideologue", since one did not adopt the ideology of genocide overnight. Hence, the Defence argued, he could not be convicted of genocide. **[page 32]**

35.   In general, the Defence argued that the Accused was a "scapegoat", who found himself Accused before the Chamber only because he was a Hutu and a bourgmestre at the time of the massacres.

36.   Turning to the specific allegations contained in the Indictment, the Defence case is that there was no change in Akayesu's attitude or behaviour before and after the Murambi meeting of 18 April 1998. Both before and after, he attempted to save Tutsi lives. Witness DBB testified that the Accused gave a Tutsi woman (witness DEEX) a laissez-passer, although he could not say whether the accused knew at the time that the woman was a Tutsi or not. Witness DEEX confirmed that she was given a laissez-passer by the accused. Witnesses DIX and DJX also heard that Akayesu had saved Tutsi lives.

---

[31]   See "Evidentiary Matters".

37.   The Defence also challenged the premise that the Murambi meeting of 18 April 1994 was the key event which led to a complete change in the accused's behaviour. Since, the Defence argued, it had not been shown that orders for the extermination of the Tutsi were given at the Murambi meeting by the interim government, it follows that the accused could not have returned to his Commune a changed man because of those non-existent orders. The Defence pointed out that only one prosecution witness and one Defence witness had attended the Murambi meeting, and that neither testified that an explicit message to kill the Tutsi had been given.

38.   Regarding the Gishyeshye meeting of 19 April 1994, the Defence argued that the accused was forced by the Interahamwe to read a document which allegedly mentioned the names of RPF accomplices, but that the accused tried to dissuade the population from being incited by the document, arguing that the mere appearance of names on a list did not mean that the persons named were accomplices of the RPF. The Defence also noted further "contradictions" in the accounts given by witnesses of the Gishyeshye meeting.

39.   As regards the killings of the eight Runda refugees and the five teachers, the Defence pointed out that the only witness to these killings was witness K, and that the accused had, at the **[page 33]** time of his interview by the OTP in Zambia, cited witness K as a possible *Defence* witness. It begged credulity that the accused would contemplate calling as a Defence witness a person whom he knew had seen him order such killings.

40.   Concerning the killings of the Karangwa brothers, the Defence argued that there was such uncertainty as to how they were killed, and by what instruments, that a conviction could not stand in the absence of these material averments. It was because of these inconsistencies and uncertainties that the Defence had asked for an exhumation of the bodies, which had not been granted.

41.   The charges of beatings the Defence contested on the grounds that no medical examination had been conducted on the alleged victims to verify that the injuries which they claimed were sustained as a result of the accused's actions could genuinely be so attributed.

42.   The charges of offences of sexual violence, the Defence argued, were added under the pressure of public opinion and were not credibly supported by the evidence. Witness J's account, for example, of living in a tree for one week after her family were killed and her sister raped, while several months pregnant, was simply not credible but rather the product of fantasy the Defence claimed – "of interest to psychiatrists, but not justice".[32]

43.   The Chamber has considered the Defence case extremely carefully and it will be treated here in the course of making the various factual and legal findings. There is one aspect which, however, should be dealt with here.

Putting the case to a witness

44.   In the Defence closing argument, Mr. Nicholas Tiangaye, made the suggestion that some, if not all, of the Prosecution witnesses who had testified against Jean-Paul Akayesu did so **[page 34]** because they were colluding in a "syndicate of informers" which would denounce a particular individual for political reasons or in order to take over his property. In this connection, Mr. Tiangaye quoted Rene Degni-Segui, the Special Rapporteur of the Commission on Human Rights on Rwanda, who recounted a story of a demonstrably innocent Rwandan who had been denounced by 15 witnesses as a participant in the genocide. Mr. Tiangaye concluded thus:

> "... there were cases of calumny which existed and which enabled people to denounce others regarding their participation in genocide in order to be able to take over their property."

Mr. Tiangaye then went on to say:

---

32   Hearing of 26 March 1998, p. 61 (French version)

"So, what do we do, Mr. President, ladies and gentlemen, when witnesses come to tell lies before the Chamber, what do we do?"[33]

45.   To the extent that Defence counsel invites the Chamber to disbelieve the testimony of Prosecution witnesses because they *may* belong to a syndicate of informers or that they *may* be denouncing. Akayesu in order to take over his property, and that they have therefore lied before the Chamber, it is to be noted this is a very serious allegation of false testimony or perjury, which is a criminal offence. Indeed, Defence counsel during the course of the trial made a motion for a certain prosecution witness to be investigated for false testimony; which motion was rejected in a Decision of this Trial Chamber in which it gave its reasons.[34] That matter does not concern the Chamber here. What *is* of concern is whether the Chamber should give any weight, in its deliberations, to the possibility raised by Defence counsel that prosecution witnesses may have been lying for one of the above-mentioned motives.

46.   The Chamber holds that, as a blanket allegation to undermine the credibility of **[page 35]** prosecution witnesses, this allegation can carry no weight, for two reasons. First, an attack on credibility which is not particularised with respect to individual witnesses is no attack at all on *those witnesses'* credibility; it is merely a generalised and unsubstantiated suspicion. Doubt can only arise where the criteria for doubt are fulfilled. To state that all prosecution witnesses should be disbelieved because some Rwandan witnesses elsewhere have lied is similar to saying, "some money is counterfeit, therefore all money might be counterfeit". If, and this is the second point, the Defence wish to challenge prosecution witnesses as members of an informer's syndicate, or to allege that they are lying in order to be able to confiscate the accused's property, then the Defence must *lay the foundations for that challenge and put the challenge to the witness in question during cross-examination.* This is both a matter of practicality and of principle. The practical matter is this: if the Defence does put to a witness the allegation that he is lying because he whishes to take the accused's property, then this may elicit a convincing admission or rebuttal. The witness may break down and reveal, by his words or demeanour, that he has indeed been lying for that purpose; alternatively, he may offer a convincing rebuttal, for example, by pointing out that the accused has no property which the witness could wish to misappropriate. Either way, the matter might be resolved. To never put the crucial question to the witness is to deprive the Chamber of such a possible resolution. As a matter of principle, it is only fair to a witness, whom the Defence wishes to accuse of lying, to give him or her an opportunity to hear that allegation and to respond to it. This is a rule in Common law,[35] but it is also simply a matter of justice and fairness to victims and witnesses, principles recognised in all legal systems throughout the world.

47.   It is to be noted that during the trial the Defence did not put, nor even suggest, to a single prosecution witness that he or she was lying because he or she had been drawn into a syndicate of informers and instructed as to how to testify against the accused, or that the witness was lying because he or she wished to take the accused's property. In these circumstances, Defence counsel's attempt in his closing arguments to tar all prosecution witnesses with the same broad **[page 36]** brush of suspicion cannot be accepted by the Chamber. Thus the credibility of each witness must be assessed on its merits, taking into account the witness's demeanour and the consistency and credibility or otherwise of the answers given by him or her under oath. **[page 37]**

1.5. The Accused and his functions in Taba (paragraphs 3-4 of the Indictment)

48.   Paragraphs 3 and 4 of the Indictment appear under the heading, "the Accused". Taking these paragraphs in turn, paragraph 3 reads as follows:

---

[33]   Transcript of hearing of 26 March 1998, p. 17.
[34]   See "Procedural Background" as relates to Decision on False Testimony.
[35]   See Adrian Keane, The Modern Law of Evidence, (Butterworths: 1989), p. 120: "A cross-examiner who whishes to suggest to the jury that the witness is not speaking the truth on a particular matter must lay a proper foundation by putting that matter to the witness so that he has an opportunity of giving any explanation which is open to him", noting, however, that this is not a "hard and fast" rule.

The Accused

3. **Jean Paul AKAYESU**, born in 1953 in Murehe sector, Taba commune, served as bourgmestre of that commune from April 1993 until June 1994. Prior to his appointment as bourgmestre, he was a teacher and school inspector in Taba.

49.   The Chamber confirms paragraph 3, which is common cause between the Prosecution and the Defence. On the basis of the evidence presented at trial, the Chamber finds the following facts have been established with regard to the Accused generally.

50.   The Accused, Akayesu was born in 1953 in Murehe sector, Taba commune in Rwanda, where he also grew up. He was an active athlete in Taba and a member of the local football team. In 1978 he married a local woman from the same commune, whom he had then known for ten years. They are still married and have five children together.

51.   Before being appointed bourgmestre in 1993, the Accused served as a teacher and was later promoted to Primary School Inspector in Taba. In this capacity he was in charge of inspecting the education in the commune and acted as head of the teachers. He would occasionally fill in as a substitute teacher and was popular among pupils and students of different educational levels in the commune. Generally speaking, the Accused was a well known and popular figure in the local community. **[page 38]**

52.   Akayesu became politically active within the commune in 1991 and on 1 July of the same year, following the transition into multipartyism, he was one of the signatories to the statute and a founding member of the new political party R called Mouvement Démocratique Républicain MDR Politically the goal of the MDR was not to be an extension of the traditional MDR Parmehutu, but rather an updated version thereof, diametrically opposed to the MRND. The MDR focused on pointing out the errors of the MRND such as delays in the provision of infrastructure, roads, schools, health facilities, lack of electricity, etc. Eventually, Akayesu was elected local president of the MDR in Taba commune. A sizeable proportion of the population in Taba became members of the MDR, and as the party grew, a certain animosity between members of the MDR and the MRND began to appear, resulting in several acts of violence. The other parties within the Commune, the Parti Social Démocratique, PSD and the Parti Libéral, PL cooperated with the MDR but, like the MDR, both parties experienced similar difficulties in cooperating with the MRND.

53.   On a personal level, Akayesu was considered a man of high morals, intelligence and integrity, possessing the qualities of a leader, who appeared to have the trust of the local community. These abilities were in all likelihood the main reasons why different groups in the commune, among others the leaders of the MDR, communal representatives and religious leaders, considered Akayesu a suitable candidate for bourgmestre in Taba for the 1993 elections. The Accused himself admits to having been reluctant to run for the post of bourgmestre, but was pressured into candidacy by the aforementioned groups, according to several witnesses, including Akayesu himself.

54.   In April 1993, Akayesu was elected bourgmestre after an election contested by four candidates. He then served as bourgmestre of Taba Commune from April 1993 until June 1994. According to the Accused, the duties of a bourgmestre were diverse. In short, he was in charge of the total life of the commune in terms of the economy, infrastructure, markets, medical care and the overall social life. Traditionally the role of the bourgmestre had always been to act as the representative of the President in the commune. Therefore the arrival of multipartyism did not particularly change the considerable amount of unofficial powers conferred upon the bourgmestre **[page 39]** by the people in the commune. The bourgmestre was the leader of the commune and commonly treated with great respect and deference by the population.

55.   In Taba Commune, Akayesu played a major role in leading the people. He would give advice on various matters concerning security, economics or on the social well-being of the citizens. His advice would generally be followed and he was considered a father-figure or parent of the commune, to whom people would also come for informal advice. After a period of economic difficulties in Taba Commune due to corruption under the previous administration, a clear difference could be detected when Akayesu

took office, as people would now settle their debts trusting the new administration. According to those of his colleagues appearing as witnesses before the Chamber, Akayesu was performing his task as bourgmestre well, prior to the period which is the subject of the Indictment.

56.   Paragraph 4 of the Indictment reads as follows:

> 4. As bourgmestre, **Jean Paul AKAYESU** was charged with the performance of executive functions and the maintenance of public order within his commune, subject to the authority of the prefect. He had exclusive control over the communal police, as well as any gendarmes put at the disposition of the commune. He was responsible for the execution of laws and regulations and the administration of justice, also subject only to the prefect's authority.

57.   The Chamber finds it necessary to explore in some detail the powers of the bourgmestre and, in particular, to distinguish between the *de facto* and *de jure* powers of a bourgmestre. In so doing, the Chamber will also deal with the allegation in paragraph 2 of the Indictment which reads, "In Rwanda, the bourgmestre is the most powerful figure in the commune. His *de facto* authority in the area is significantly greater than that which is conferred upon him *de jure*".

Background [page 40]

58.   A commune is governed by a bourgmestre in conjunction with the communal council which is composed of representatives of the different sectors in the commune. Below the sectors are the cellules and at the lowest level are the units of ten households. The latter two are really party structures, rather than administrative subdivisions.

59.   Before the advent of multi-partyism, appointment and removal of a bourgmestre was the prerogative of the State President, political loyalty being the criterion. The bourgmestre was the representative of the central government in the commune but embodied at the same time the commune as a semi-autonomous unit. In that capacity, he would, for example, arrange contracts of represent the commune in court. He also had the authority to allocate the resources of the commune, including the land. He had the sole responsibility and authority over the communal police and could call upon the national gendarmerie to restore order. In addition, he was a judicial officer. Moreover, as the trusted representative of the President, he had a series of unofficial powers and duties, to such an extent that he was the central person in the daily life of the ordinary people. Citizens needed his protection in order to function in society. The bourgmestre held considerable sway over the communal council. Although an elected body, the council was less a representative body of the interest of the population than it was simply a channel for passing orders down to the people.

60.   The introduction of multipartyism in 1991 had its effect on the local and national power structures from 1992 onwards. The MRND had to sacrifice the advantages which it enjoyed when it was the Siamese twin of the administration. A number of bourgmestres were removed on the advice of a pluralistic evaluation commission. The subsequent local elections were a clear victory for the opposition. Other bourgmestres were simply ousted by militia of an opposition party. Since then, the bourgmestres were no longer necessarily the representatives of the State President or of the central authority. Instead, they became primarily the representatives of their political party at the local level. But in any case, they would still remain the most important local representatives of power at the centre.

De *jure* powers [page 41]

61.   The office of bourgmestre in Rwanda is similar to the office of maire in France or bourgmestre in Belgium[36]. It is an executive civilian position in the territorial administrative subdivision of commune.

---

[36]   In France, Belgium and Rwanda, the bourgmestre has basically a threefold function: (1) head of the communal administration; (2) officier de l'état civil; and (3) maintaining and/or restoring the peace.

The primary function of the bourgmestre is to execute the laws adopted by the communal legislature, i.e., the elected communal council[37]. He "embodies the communal authority"[38].

The communal administration

62.   The relationship between a bourgmestre and the communal workforce is spelt out in the body of law which is called administrative law in Civil Law countries (as opposed to labour law which regulates employment in the private sector). The bourgmestre has the power to hire (appoint) and fire (remove) communal employees after advice from the communal council[39]. The President of the Republic decrees by law the legal status (rights and duties) of the communal personnel. Although the legal situation (administrative law) may be very different from the private sector (labour law), it is very much a relationship of employer and employee and, therefore, strictly limited to the scope of the employment. **[page 42]**

The communal police

63.   The bourgmestre, without being a part of the communal police, has ultimate authority over it and is entirely responsible for its organisation, functioning and control.[40]

64.   The communal police is a civilian police whose members do not fall under the military penal code. Sanctions and procedures for sanctions are the subject of administrative law. A bourgmestre has only disciplinary jurisdiction (e.g. blame, suspension) over his communal police.

65.   Although the law states that only the bourgmestre has authority over the police[41], he is, however, not its commander. Article 108 of the Loi sur l'organisation communales states, "Le commandement de la Police communale est assuré par un brigadier placé sous l'autorité du bourgmestre". Therefore, the relationship between the bourgmestre and the communal police is comparable to the relationship between a Minister of Defence and the High Command of the armed forces.

66.   In case of public disturbances, the prefect can assume direct control over the communal **[page 43]** police.[42]

Gendarmerie Nationale

67.   Paragraph 4 of the Indictment states that Akayesu as a bourgmestre had exclusive control over the communal police as well as any gendarmes put at the disposal of the commune.

---

[37]   Loi du 23 novembre 1963 sur l'organisation communale (reprinted in Codes et Lois du Rwanda, Reyntjes, F. et Gorus, J. (eds.), 1995).

Article 58: Le bourgmestre est, d'une manière générale, chargé d'exécuter les décisions du Conseil communal [...]

However, in case of urgency, the bourgmestre can issue police regulations and impose sanctions for violations (article 61). Furthermore, he always has the power to arrest, for a maximum of 48 hours, any person who breaches the peace (article 62).

[38]   Article 56: Le bourgmestre est à la foi représentant du pouvoir centrale dans la commune et personnification de l'autorité communale.

[39]   Article 93: Le pouvoir d'engagement, de suspension et de révocation appartient au bourgmestre après avis du Conseil communal conformément aux instructions du Ministre de l'intérieur.

[40]   Loi sur la police communale du 4 octobre 1977 (arrêté présidentiel n° 285/03) (reprinted in Codes et Lois du Rwanda, Reyntjes, F. et Gorus, J. (eds.), 1995)

Article 1: La Police communale est une force constituée au niveau de la commune. Elle est placée sous l'autorité du bourgmestre qui l'utilise dans sa tâche de maintien et de rétablissement de l'ordre public et d'exécution des lois et des règlements.

Article 4: Le bourgmestre assume l'entière responsabilité de l'organisation, du fonctionnement et du contrôle du corps de la Police communale. Il est aidé dans cette tâche par le brigadier.

[41]   Article 104 of the *Loi sur l'organisation communale*: Le bourgmestre a seul autorité sur les agents de la Police communale [...]

[42]   Article 104 [...] Toutefois, en cas de calamité publique ou lorsque des troubles menacent d'éclater ou ont éclaté, le préfet peut réquisitionner les agents de la Police communale et les placer sous son autorité directe.

68.   The Gendarmerie Nationale is a military force whose task it is to maintain public order when it is requested to do so[43].

69.   It is the prefect, not the bourgmestre who can request the intervention of the Gendarmerie[44]. The Gendarmes put at the disposal of the commune at the request of the prefect operate under the bourgmestre's authority[45]. It is far from clear, however, that in such circumstances a bourgmestre would have command authority over a military force.[46] **[page 44]**

Powers of a bourgmestre in times of war or national emergency

70.   Apart from asking the prefect to request the Gendarmerie to intervene (*supra*), there are few legal provisions on the powers of a bourgmestre in times of war or national emergency.

71.   A decree of 20 October 1959 (by the Belgian authorities) on the state of emergency is apparently still on the books. It gives the bourgmestre the power, once the the state of emergency has been declared, to order the evacuation, removal and internment of persons.[47]

De *facto* powers

72.   A number of witnesses testified before the Chamber as to the *de facto* powers of the bourgmestre and there is indeed evidence to support the Prosecutor's assertion that the bourgmestre enjoyed significant *de facto* authority. **[page 45]**

73.   The expert witness, Alison DesForges, testified that the bourgmestre was the most important authority for the ordinary citizens of a Commune, who in some sense exercised the powers of a chief in pre-colonial times.

74.   Witness E said that the bourgmestre was considered as the "parent" of all the population whose every order would be respected. Witness S went further and stated that the people would normally follow the orders of the administrative authority, i.e. the bourgmestre, even if those orders were illegal or wrongful. Witness V said that the people could not disobey the orders of the bourgmestre.

---

[43]   *Décret loi du 23 janvier 1974 sur la création de la Gendarmerie Nationale*
    Article 3: La Gendarmerie Nationale est une force armée instituée pour assurer le maintien de l'ordre et de l'exécution des loi.
    Article 4: les fonctions de la Gendarmerie Nationale ont un caractère à la fois préventif et répressif. Elles se divisent en fonctions ordinaires et fonctions extraordinaires. Les fonctions ordinaires sont celles que la Gendarmerie Nationale remplit en vertu de la loi sans réquisition préalable de l'autorité.
    Les fonctions extraordinaires sont celles que la Gendarmerie National ne peut remplir que sur réquisition de l'autorité compétente.
[44]   Article 103: [...] En outre, le préfet peut mettre à la disposition de la commune des éléments de la Police Nationale. [actuellement, il faut sans doute lire: la Gendarmerie Nationale]
[45]   Article 104: Le bourgmestre a seul autorité sur les agents de la Police communale et, par délégation de préfet, sur les éléments de la Police Nationale [lire: Gendarmerie Nationale] mis à la disposition de la commune.
[46]   Article 39 de la loi sur la Gendarmerie Nationale.
[47]   ETAT D'EXCEPTION – 20 octobre 1959 – Décret:
    Article 1: En cas de guerre, de mobilisation en Belgique ou au Congo, de troubles ou de circonstances graves menaçant la sécurité ou l'intérêts publics, le gouverneur général peut déclarer l'état d'exception.
    Article 4: Le gouverneur général, les autorités qu'il désigne et leurs délégués peuvent:
    (1) ordonner:
    a) des perquisitions de jour et de nuit dans les domiciles;
    b) l'évacution des personnes, leur éloignement, leur mise sous surveillance ou leur internement.
    (2) interdire:
    [...]
    MESURES D'EXCEPTION – 10 décembre 1959 – ordonnance n° 11/630
    Article 1:   Dans l'ensemble ou la partie du territoire déclarés en état d'exception:
        a) le gouverneur de province, le commissaire de district, le premier bourgmestre, ou leurs délégués exercent les pouvoirs prévus à l'article 4 du décret sur l'état d'exception.
        b) ...

75.   On the other hand, Witness DAAX, who was the prefect of the Gitarama prefecture in which the accused was bourgmestre – and hence the Accused's hierarchical superior – testified that the bourgmestre had to work within the ambit of the law and could not exceed his *de jure* powers, and that if he did so, the prefect would intervene.

76.   Witness R, himself a former bourgmestre, said that the duties and responsibilities of the bourgmestre were those prescribed and decreed by law, which the bourgmestre had to respect. The witness conceded, however, that the popularity of a bourgmestre might affect the extent to which his orders and advice were obeyed within the Commune. Witness R also admitted that, at least during the transitional period, certain bourgmestres exceeded their *de jure* powers with impunity, for example imprisoning their political rivals or embezzling from communal resources.

77.   In light of the above, the Chamber finds it proved beyond a reasonable doubt that, as paragraph 4 of the Indictment states, "As bourgmestre, Jean Paul AKAYESU was charged with the performance of executive functions and the maintenance of public order within his commune, subject to the authority of the prefect". The Chamber does find it proved that "[the bourgmestre] had exclusive control over the communal police, [...] [and authority over] any gendarmes put at the disposal of the commune". The Chamber does find it proved that "[the bourgmestre] was responsible for the execution of laws and regulations and the administration of justice, also subject only to the prefect's authority". The Chamber does find it proved that, "In Rwanda, the **[page 46]** bourgmestre is the most powerful figure in the commune. His *de facto* authority in the area is significantly greater than that which is conferred upon him *de jure*". **[page 47]**

2. HISTORICAL CONTEXT OF THE EVENTS IN RWANDA IN 1994

78.   It is the opinion of the Chamber that, in order to understand the events alleged in the Indictment, it is necessary to say, however briefly, something about the history of Rwanda, beginning from the pre-colonial period up to 1994.

79.   Rwanda is a small, very hilly country in the Great Lakes region of Central Africa. Before the events of 1994, it was the most densely populated country of the African continent (7.1 million inhabitants for 26,338 square kilometres). Ninety per cent of the population lives on agriculture. Its per capita income is among the lowest in the world, mainly because of a very high population pressure on land.

80.   Prior to and during colonial rule, first, under Germany, from about 1897, and then under Belgium which, after driving out Germany in 1917, was given a mandate by the League of Nations to administer it, Rwanda was a complex and an advances monarchy. The monarch ruled the country through his official representatives drawn from the Tutsi nobility. Thus, there emerged a highly sophisticated political culture which enabled the king to communicate with the people.

81.   Rwanda then, admittedly, had some eighteen clans defined primarily along lines of kinship. The terms Hutu and Tutsi were already in use but referred to individuals rather than to groups. In those days, the distinction between the Hutu and Tutsi was based on lineage rather than ethnicity. Indeed, the demarcation line was blurred: one could move from one status to another, as one became rich or poor, or even through marriage.

82.   Both German and Belgian colonial authorities, if only at the outset as far as the latter are concerned, relied on an elite essentially composed of people who referred to themselves as Tutsi, **[page 48]** a choice which, according to Dr. Alison Desforges, was born of racial or even racist considerations. In the minds of the colonizers, the Tutsi more like them, because of their height and colour, and were, therefore, more intelligent and better equipped to govern.

83.   In the early 1930s, Belgian authorities introduced a permanent distinction by dividing the population into three groups which they called ethnic groups, with the Hutu representing about 84 % of

the population, while the Tutsi (about 15 %) and Twa (about 1 %) accounted for the rest. In line with this division, it became mandatory for every Rwandan to carry an identity card mentioning his or her ethnicity. The Chamber notes that the reference to ethnic background on identity cards was maintained, even after Rwanda's independence and was, at last, abolished only after the tragic events the country experienced in 1994.

84.   According to the testimony of Dr. Alison Desforges, while the Catholic Church which arrived in the wake of European colonizers gave the monarch, his notables and the Tutsi population privileged access to education and training, it tried to convert them. However, in the face of some resistance, the missionaries for a while undertook to convert the Hutu instead. Yet, when the Belgians included being Christian among the criteria for determining the suitability of a candidate for employment in the civil service, the Tutsi, hitherto opposed to their conversion, became more willing to be converted to Christianity. Thus, they carried along most Hutu. Quoting a witness from whom she asked for an explanation for the massive conversion of Hutu to Christianity, Dr. Desforges testified that the reasons for the conversion were to be found in the cult of obedience to the chiefs which is highly developed in the Rwandan society. According to that witness, "you could not remain standing while your superiors were on their knees praying". For these reasons, therefore, it can be understood why at the time, that is, in the late 1920s and early 1930s, the church, like the colonizers, supported the Tutsi monopoly of power.

85.   From the late 1940s, at the dawn of the decolonization process, the Tutsi became aware of the benefits they could derive from the privileged status conferred on them by the Belgian colonizers and the Catholic church. They then attempted to free themselves somehow from Belgian political stewardship and to emancipate the Rwandan society from the grip of the **[page 49]** Catholic church. The desire for independence shown by the Tutsi elite certainly caused both the Belgians and the church to shift their alliances from the Tutsi to the Hutu, a shift rendered more radical by the change in the church's philosophy after the second world war, with the arrival of young priests from a more democratic and egalitarian trend of Christianity, who sought to develop political awareness among the Tutsi-dominated Hutu majority.

86.   Under pressure from the United Nations Trusteeship Council and following the shift in alliances just mentioned, Belgium changed its policy by granting more opportunities to the Hutu to acquire education and to hold senior positions in government services; This turn-about particularly angered the Tutsi, especially because, on the renewal of its mandate over Rwanda by the United Nations, Belgium was requested to establish representative organs in the Trust territory, so as to groom the natives for administration and, ultimately, grant independence to the country. The Tutsi therefore began the move to end Belgian domination, while the Hutu elite, for tactical reasons, favoured the continuation of the domination, hoping to make the Hutu masses aware of their political weight in Rwanda, in a bid to arrive at independence, which was unavoidable, at least on the basis of equality with the Tutsi. Belgium particularly appreciated this attitude as it gave it reason to believe that with the Hutu, independence would not spell a severance of ties.

87.   In 1956, in accordance with the directives of the United Nations Trusteeship Council, Belgium organized elections on the basis of universal suffrage in order to choose new members of local organs, such as the grassroots representative Councils. With the electorate voting on strictly ethnic lines, the Hutu of course obtained an overwhelming majority and thereby became aware of their political strength. The Tutsi, who were hoping to achieve independence while still holding the reins of power, came to the realization that universal suffrage meant the end of their supremacy; hence, confrontation with the Hutu became inevitable.

88.   Around 1957, the first political parties were formed and, as could be expected, they were ethnically rather than ideologically based. There were four political parties, namely the Mouvement démocratique républicain, Parmehuto ("MDR Parmehutu"), which clearly defined **[page 50]** itself as the Hutu grassroots movement; the Union Nationale Rwandaise ("UNAR"), the party of Tutsi monarchists; and, between the two extremes, the two others, Aprosoma, predominantly Hutu, and the Rassemblement démocratique rwandais ("RADER"), which brought together moderates from the Tutsi and Hutu elite.

89.   The dreaded political unrest broke out in November 1959, with increased bloody incidents, the first victims of which were the Hutu. In reprisal, the Hutu burnt down and looted Tutsi houses. Thus became embedded a cycle of violence which ended with the establishment on 18 October 1960, by the Belgian authorities, of an autonomous provisional Government headed by Grégoire Kayibanda, President of MDR Parmehutu, following the June 1960 communal elections that gave an overwhelming majority to Hutu parties. After the Tutsi monarch fled abroad, the Hutu opposition declared the Republic of Gitarama, on 28 January 1961, and set up a legislative assembly. On 6 February 1961, Belgium granted self-government to Rwanda. Independence was declared on 1 July 1962, with Grégoire Kayibanda at the helm of the new State, and, thus, President of the First Republic.

90.   The victory of Hutu parties increased the departure of Tutsi to neighbouring countries from where Tutsi exiles made incursions into Rwanda. The word Inyenzi, meaning cockroach, came to be used to refer to these assailants. Each attack was followed by reprisals against the Tutsi within the country and in 1963, such attacks caused the death of at least ten thousand of them, further increasing the number of those who went into exile. Concurrently, at the domestic level, the Hutu regime seized this opportunity to allocate to the Hutu the lands abandoned by Tutsi in exile and to redistribute posts within the Government and the civil service, in favour of the Hutu, on the basis of a quota system linked to the proportion of each ethnic group in the population.

91.   The dissensions that soon surfaced among the ruling Hutu led the regime to strengthen the primacy of the MDR Parmehutu party over all sectors of public life and institutions, thereby making it the *de facto* sole party. This consolidated the authority of President Grégoire Kayibanda as well as the influence of his entourage, most of who came from the same region as **[page 51]** he, that is the Gitarama region in the centre of the country. The drift towards ethnic and regional power became obvious. From then onwards, a rift took root within the Hutu political Establishment, between its key figures from the Centre and those from the North and South who showed great frustration. Increasingly isolated, President Kayibanda could not control the ethnic and regional dissensions. The disagreements within the regime resulted into anarchy, which enabled General Juvénal Habyarimana, Army Chief of Staff, to seize power through a coup on 5 July 1973. General Habyarimana dissolved the First Republic and established the Second Republic. Scores of political leaders were imprisoned and, later, executed or starved to death, as was the case with the former President, Grégoire Kayibanda.

92.   Following a trend then common in Africa, President Habyarimana, in 1975, instituted the one-party system with the creation of the Mouvement révolutionnaire national pour le développement (MRND), of which every Rwandan was a member *ipso facto*, including the newborn. Since the party encompassed everyone, there was no room for political pluralism. A law passed in 1978 made Rwanda officially a one-party State with the consequence that the MRND became a "State-party", as it formed one and the same entity with the Government. According to Dr. Desforges, the local administrative authority was, at the same time, the representative of the party within his administrative unit. There was therefore a single centralized organization, both for the State and the party, which stretched from the Head of State down to basic units known as cellules, with even smaller local organs, each comprising ten households, below the cellules. The cellules and local organs were, indeed, more of party organs, than administrative units. They were the agencies for the implementation of Umuganda, the mobilization programme which required people to allocate half a day's labour per week to some communal project, such as the construction of schools or road repairs.

93. According to testimonies given before the Chamber, particularly that of Dr. Desforges, Habyarimana's accession to power aroused a great deal of enthusiasm and hope, both inside and outside the country, and also among members of the Tutsi ethnic group. Indeed, the regime at the outset did guard against pursuing a clearly anti-Tutsi policy. Many Tutsi were then prepared to reach a compromise. However, as the years went by, power took its toll and Habyarimana's **[page 52]** policies became clearly anti-Tutsi. Like his predecessor, Grégoire Kayibanda, Habyarimana strengthened the policy of discrimination against the Tutsi by applying the same quota system in universities and government services. A policy of systematic discrimination was pursued even among the Hutu themselves, in favour of Hutu from Habyarimana's native region, namely Gisenyi and Ruhengeri in the north-west, to the

detriment of Hutu from other regions. This last aspect of Habyarimana's policy, considerably weakened his power: henceforth, he faced opposition not only from the Tutsi but also from the Hutu, who felt discriminated against and most of whom came from the central and southern regions. In the face of this situation, Habyarimana chose to relentlessly pursue the same policy like his predecessor who favoured his region, Gitarama. Like Kayibanda, he became increasingly isolated and the base of his regime narrowed down to a small intimate circle dubbed "Akazu", meaning the "President's household". This further radicalized the opposition whose ranks swelled more and more. On 1 October 1990, an attack was launched from Uganda by the Rwandan Patriotic Front (RPF) whose forebear, the Alliance rwandaise pour l'unité nationale ("ARUN"), was formed in 1979 by Tutsi exiles based in Uganda. The attack provided a pretext for the arrest of thousands of opposition members in Rwanda considered as supporters of the RPF.

94.   Faced with the worsening internal situation that attracted a growing number of Rwandans to the multi-party system, and pressured by foreign donors demanding not only economic but also political reforms in the form of much greater participation of the people in the country's management, President Habyarimana was compelled to accept the multi-party system in principle. On 28 December 1990, the preliminary draft of a political charter to establish a multi-party system was published. On 10 June 1991, the new constitution introducing the multi-party system was adopted, followed on 18 June by the promulgation of the law on political parties and the formation of the first parties, namely:

–   the Mouvement démocratique républicain (MDR), considered to be the biggest party in terms of membership and claiming historical links with the *MDR*-Parmehutu of Grégoire Kayibanda; its power-base was mainly the centre of the country, around Gitarama; **[page 53]**
–   the Parti social démocrate (PSD), whose membership included a good number of intellectuals, recruited its members mostly in the South, in Butare;
–   the Parti libéral (PL); and
–   the Parti démocrate chrétien (PDC).

95.   At the same time, Tutsi exiles, particularly those in Uganda organized themselves not only to launch incursions into Rwandan territory but also to form a political organization, the Rwandese Patriotic Front (RPF), with a military wing called the Rwandan Patriotic Army (RPA). The first objective of the exiles was to return to Rwanda. But they met with objection from the Rwandan authorities and President Habyarimana, who is alleged to have said that land in Rwanda would not be enough to feed all those who wanted to return. On these grounds, the exiles broadened their objectives to include the overthrow of Habyarimana.

96.   The above-mentioned RPF attack on 1 October 1991 sent shock waves throughout Rwanda. Members of the opposition parties formed in 1991, saw this as an opportunity to have an informal alliance with the RPF so as to further destabilize an already weakened regime. The regime finally accepted to share power between the MRND and the other political parties and, around March 1992, the Government and the opposition signed an agreement to set up a transitional coalition government headed by a Prime Minister from the MDR. Out of the nineteen ministries, the MRND obtained only nine. Pressured by the opposition, the MRND accepted that negotiations with the RPF be started. The negotiations led to the first cease-fire in July 1992 and the first part of the Arusha Accords[48]. The July 1992 cease-fire tacitly recognized RPF control over a portion of Rwandan territory in the north-east. The protocols signed following these accords included the October 1992 protocol establishing a transitional government and a transitional assembly and the participation of the RPF in both institutions. The political scene was now widened to comprise three blocs: the Habyarimana bloc, the internal opposition and the RPF. Experience showed that President Habyarimana accepted these accords only because he was compelled to do so, but had no intention of complying with what he himself **[page 54]** referred to as "un chiffon de papier", meaning a scrap of paper.

97.   Yet, the RPF did not drop its objective of seizing power. It therefore increased its military attacks. The massive attack of 8 February 1993 seriously undermined the relations between the RPF and the Hutu

---

[48]   Prosecution Exhibit No. 14

opposition parties, making it easy for Habyarimana supporters to convene an assembly of all Hutu. Thus, the bond built on Hutu kinship once again began to prevail over political differences. The three blocs mentioned earlier gave way to two ethnic- based opposing camps: on the one hand, the RPF, the supposed canopy of all Tutsi and, on the other hand, the other parties said to be composed essentially of the Hutu.

98.   In March 1992, a group of Hutu hard-liners founded a new radical political party, the Coalition pour la défense de la republique (CDR), or Coalition for the Defence of the Republic, which was more extremist than Habyarimana himself and opposed him on several occasions.

99.   To make the economic, social and political conflict look more like an ethnic conflict, the President's entourage, in particular, the army, persistently launched propaganda campaigns which often consisted of fabricating events. Dr. Alison Desforges in her testimony referred to this as "mirror politics", whereby a person accuses others of what he or she does or wants to do. In this regard, in the morning hours of 5 October 1990, the Rwandan army simulated an attack on Kigali and, immediately thereafter, the Government claimed that the city had just been infiltrated by the RPF, with the help of local Tutsi accomplices. Some eight thousand Tutsi and members of the Hutu opposition were arrested the next morning. Several dozens of them died in jail. Another example of mirror politics is the March 1992 killings in Bugesera which began a week after a propaganda agent working for the Habyarimana government distributed a tract claiming that the Tutsi of that region were preparing to kill many Hutu. The MRND militia, known as Interahamwe, participated in the Bugesera killings. It was the first time that this party's militia participated in killings of this scale. They were later joined by the militia of other parties or wings of Hutu extremist parties, including, in particular, the CDR militia known as the Impuzamugambi. **[page 55]**

100.   Mirror politics was also used in Kibulira, in the north-west, and in the Bagoguye region. In both cases, the population was goaded on to defend itself against fabricated attacks supposed to have been perpetrated by RPF infiltrators and to attack and kill their Tutsi neighbours. In passing, mention should be made of the role that Radio Rwanda and, later, the RTLM, founded in 1993 by people close to President Habyarimana, played in this anti-Tutsi propaganda. Besides the radio stations, there were other propaganda agents, the most notorious of whom was a certain Léon Mugesera, vice-president of the MRND in Gisenyi Préfecture and lecturer at the National University of Rwanda, who published two pamphlets accusing the Tutsi of planning a genocide of the Hutu[49]. During an MRND meeting in November 1992, the same Léon Mugesera called for the extermination of the Tutsi and the assassination of Hutu opposed to the President. He made reference to the idea that the Tutsi allegedly came from Ethiopia and, hence, that after they had been killed, they should be thrown into the Rwandan tributaries of the Nile, so that they should return to where they are supposed to have come from[50]. He exhorted his listeners to avoid the error of earlier massacres during which some Tutsi, particularly children, were spared.

101.   On the political front, a split was noticed in almost all the opposition parties on the issue of the proposed signing of a final peace agreement. This schismatic trend began with the MDR party, the main rival of the MRND, whose radical faction, later known as MDR Power, affiliated with the CDR and the MRND.

102.   On 4 August 1993, the Government of Rwanda and the RPF signed the final Arusha Accords and ended the war which started on 1 October 1990. The Accords provided, *inter alia*, for the establishment of a transitional government to include the RPF, the partial demobilization and integration of the two opposing armies (13,000 RPF and 35,000 FAR troops), the creation of a demilitarized zone between the RPF-controlled area in the north and the rest of the country, the stationing of an RPF battalion in the city of Kigali, and the deployment, in four phases, of a **[page 56]** UN peace-keeping force, the United Nations Assistance Mission for Rwanda (UNAMIR), with a two-year mandate.

---

[49]   Prosecution Exhitits Nos. 68 and 69.
[50]   Prosecution Exhibit No. 74.

103. On 23 October 1993, the President of Burundi, Melchior Ndadaye, a Hutu, was assassinated in the course of an attempted coup by Burundi Tutsi soldiers. Dr. Alison Desforges testified that in Rwanda, Hutu extremists exploited this assassination to prove that it was impossible to agree with the Tutsi, since they would always turn against their Hutu partners to kill them. A meeting held at the Kigali stadium at the end of October 1993 was entirely devoted to the discussion of the assassination of President Ndadaye, and in very virulent speech, Froduald Karamira, senior national vice-President of the Interahamwe, is alleged to have called for unreserved solidarity among all the Hutu, solidarity transcending the divide of political parties. He reportedly concluded his speech with a call for "Hutu-Power".

104. The assassination of President Ndadaye gave President Habyarimana and the CDR the opportunity to denounce, in a joint MRND – CDR statement issued at the end of 1993, the Arusha Accords, calling them treason. However, a few days later, pursuing his policy of prevarication towards the international community, Habyarimana signed another part of the peace accords. Indeed, the Arusha Accords no longer existed, except on paper. The President certainly did take the oath of office, but the installation of a transitional government was delayed, mainly by divisions within the political parties and the ensuing infightings.

105. The leaders of the CDR and the PSD were assassinated in February 1994. In Kigali, in the days that followed, the Interahamwe and the Impuzamugambi massacred Tutsi as well as Habyarimana's Hutu opponents. The Belgian Foreign Minister informed his representative at the UN of the worsening situation which "could result in an irreversible explosion of violence"[51]. At the same time, as he stated in his testimony before the Tribunal, UNAMIR commander, Major-General Dallaire, alerted the United Nations in New York of the discovery of arms caches and requested a charge in UNAMIR's engagement rules to enable him to seize the arms; but the **[page 57]** request was turned down. Meanwhile, anti-Tutsi propaganda on the media intensified. The RTLM constantly stepped up its attacks which became increasingly targeted and violent.

106. At the end of March 1994, the transitional government was still not set up and Rwanda was on the brink of bankruptcy. International donors and neighbouring countries put pressure on the Habyarimana government to implement the Arusha Accords.
On 6 April 1994, President Habyarimana and other heads of State of the region met in Dar-es-Salaam (Tanzania) to discuss the implementation of the peace accords. The aircraft carrying President Habyarimana and the Burundian President, Ntaryamirai, who were returning from the meeting, crashed around 8:30 pm near Kigali airport. All aboard were killed.

107. The Rwandan army and the militia immediately erected roadblocks around the city of Kigali. Before dawn on April 7 1994, in various parts of the country, the Presidential Guard and the militia started killing the Tutsi as well as Hutu known to be in favour of the Arusha Accords and power-sharing between the Tutsi and the Hutu. Among the first victims, were a number of ministers of the coalition government, including its Prime Minister, Agathe Uwilingiyimana (MDR), the president of the Supreme Court and virtually the entire leadership of the parti social démocrate (PSD). The constitutional vaccum thus created cleared the way for the establishment of the self-proclaimed Hutu-power interim government, mainly under the aegis of retired Colonel Théoneste Bagosora.

108. Soldiers of the Rwandan Armed Forces (FAR) executed ten Belgian blue helmets, thereby provoking the withdrawal of the Belgian contingent which formed the core of UNAMIR. On April 21 1994, the UN Security Council decided to reduce the peace-keepings force to 450 troops.

109. In the afternoon of 7 April 1994, RPF troops left their quarters in Kigali and their zone in the north, to resume open war against the Rwandan Armed Forces. Its troops from the north moved south, crossing the demilitarized zone, and entered the city of Kigali on April 12 1994, thus forcing the interim government to flee to Gitarama. **[page 58]**

---

[51]   Prosecution Exhibit No. 18

110. On April 12 1994, after public authorities announced over Radio Rwanda that "we need to unite against the enemy, the only enemy and this is the enemy that we have always known...it's the enemy who wants to reinstate the former feudal monarchy", it became clear that the Tutsi were the primary targets. During the week of 14 to 21 April 1994, the killing campaign reached it peak. The President of the interim government, the Prime Minister and some key ministers travelled to Butare and Gikongoro, and that marked the beginning of killings in these regions which had hitherto been peaceful. Thousands of people, sometimes encouraged or directed by local administrative officials, on the promise of safety, gathered unsuspectingly in churches, schools, hospitals and local government buildings. In reality, this was a trap intended to lead to the rapid extermination of a large number of people.

111. The killing of Tutsi which henceforth spared neither women nor children, continued up to 18 July 1994, when the RPF triumphantly entered Kigali. The estimated total number of victims in the conflict varies from 500,000 to 1,000,000 or more. **[page 59]**

3. GENOCIDE IN RWANDA IN 1994?

112. As regards the massacres which took place in Rwanda between April and July 1994, as detailed above in the chapter on this historical background to the Rwandan tragedy, the question before this Chamber is whether they constitute genocide. Indeed, if was felt in some quarters[52] that the tragic events which took place in Rwanda were only part of the war between the Rwandan Armed Forces (the RAF) and the Rwandan Patriotic Front (RPF). The answer to this question would allow a better understanding of the context within which the crimes with which the accused is charged are alleged to have been committed.

113. According to paragraph 2 of Article 2 of the Statute of the Tribunal, which reflects verbatim the definition of genocide as contained in the Convention on the Prevention and Punishment of the Crime of Genocide (hereinafter, "the Convention on Genocide")[53], genocide means any of the following acts referred to in said paragraph, committed with intent to destroy, in whole or in part, a national, ethnical, racial or religious group as such, namely, *inter alia*: killing members of the group; causing serious bodily or mental harm to members of the group.

114. Even though the number of victims is yet to be known with accuracy, no one can reasonably refute the fact that widespread killings were perpetrated throughout Rwanda in 1994.

115. Indeed, this is confirmed by the many testimonies heard by this Chamber. The testimony of Dr. Zachariah who appeared before this Chamber on 16 and 17 January 1997 is enlightening in this regard. Dr. Zachariah was a physician who at the time of the events was working for a non-governmental organisation, "Médecins sans frontières." In 1994 he was based in Butare and travelled over a good part of Rwanda upto its border with Burundi. He described in great detail **[page 60]** the heaps of bodies which he saw everywhere, on the roads, on the footpaths and in rivers and, particularly, the manner in which all these people had been killed. At the church in Butare, at the Gahidi mission, he saw many wounded persons in the hospital who, according to him, were all Tutsi and who, apparently, had sustained wounds inflicted with machetes to the face, the neck, and also to the ankle, at the Achilles' tendon, to prevent them from fleeing. The testimony given by Major-General Dallaire, former Commander of the United Nations Assistance Mission for Rwanda (UNAMIR) at the time of the events alleged in the Indictment, who was called by the defence, is of a similar vein. Major-General Dallaire spoke of troops of the Rwandan Armed Forces and of the Presidential Guard going into houses in Kigali that had been previously identified in order to kill. He also talked about the terrible murders in Kabgayi, very near Gitarama, where the interim Government was based and of the reports he received from observers throughout the country which mentioned killings in Gisenyi, Cyangugu and Kibongo.

---

[52] See the cross examination of Dr. Zachariah (witness) by one of the defence counsel.
[53] The Convention on the Prevention and Punishment of the Crime of Genocide, adopted by the United Nations General Assembly on 9 December 1948.

116. The British cameraman, Simon Cox, took photographs of bodies in many churches in Remera, Biambi, Shangi, between Cyangugu and Kibuye, and in Bisesero. He mentioned identity cards strewn on the ground, all of which ware marked "Tutsi". Consequently, in view of these widespread killings the victims of which were mainly Tutsi, the Chamber is of the opinion that the first requirement for there to be genocide has been met, the killing and causing serious bodily harm to members of a group.

117. The second requirement is that these killings and serious bodily harm, as is the case in this instance, be committed with the intent to destroy, in whole or in part, a particular group targeted as such.

118. In the opinion of the Chamber, there is no doubt that considering their undeniable scale, their systematic nature and their atrociousness, the massacres were aimed at exterminating the group that was targeted. Many facts show that the intention of the perpetrators of these killings was to cause the complete disappearance of the Tutsi. In this connection, Alison Deforges, an expert witness, in her testimony before this Chamber on 25 February 1997, stated as follows: "on the basis of the statements made by certain political leaders, on the basis of songs and **[page 61]** slogans popular among the Interahamwe, I believe that these people had the intention of completely wiping out the Tutsi from Rwanda so that-as they said on certain occasions – their children, later on, would not know what a Tutsi looked like, unless they referred to history books". Moreover, this testimony given by Dr. Desforges was confirmed by two prosecution witnesses, witness KK and witness OO, who testified separately before the Tribunal that one Silas Kubwimana had said during a public meeting chaired by the accused himself that all the Tutsi had to be killed so that someday Hutu children would not know what a Tutsi looked like.

119. Furthermore, as mentioned above, Dr. Zachariah also testified that the Achilles' tendons of many wounded persons were cut to prevent them from fleeing. In the opinion of the Chamber, this demonstrates the resolve of the perpetrators of these massacres not to spare any Tutsi. Their plan called for doing whatever was possible to prevent any Tutsi from escaping and, thus, to destroy the whole group. Witness OO further told the Chamber that during the same meeting, a certain Ruvugama, who was then a Member of Parliament, had stated that he would rest only when no single Tutsi is left in Rwanda".

120. Dr. Alison Desforges testified that many Tutsi bodies were often systematically thrown into the Nyabarongo river, a tributary of the Nile. Indeed, this has been corroborated by several images shown to the Chamber throughout the trial. She explained that the underlying intention of this act was to "send the Tutsi back to their place of origin", to "make them return to Abyssinia", in keeping with the allegation that the Tutsi are foreigners in Rwanda, where they are supposed to have settled following their arrival from the Nilotic regions.[54]

121. Other testimonies heard, especially that of Major-General Dallaire, also show that there was an intention to wipe out the Tutsi group in its entirety, since even newborn babies were not spared. Even pregnant women, including those of Hutu origin, were killed on the grounds that **[page 62]** the foetuses in their wombs were fathered by Tutsi men, for in a patrilineal society like Rwanda, the child belongs to the father's group of origin. In this regard, it is worthwhile noting the testimony of witness PP, heard by the Chamber on 11 April 1997, who mentioned a statement made publicly by the accused to the effect that if a Hutu woman were impregnated by a Tutsi man, the Hutu woman had to be found in order "for the pregnancy to be aborted". According to prosecution witnesses KK, PP and OO, the accused expressed this opinion on other occasions in the form of a Rwandese proverb according to which "if a snake wraps itself round a calabash, there is nothing that can be done, except to break the calabash" ("Iyo inzoka yiziritse ku gisabo, nta kundi bigenda barakimena)[55]. In the context of the period in question, this proverb meant that if a Hutu woman married to a Tutsi man was impregnated by him, the foetus had to be destroyed so that the Tutsi child which it would become should not survive. It should be noted in this regard that in Rwandese culture, breaking the "gisabo", which is a big calabash used as a churn was

---

54   See *supra*, in the chapter on the history of Rwanda, the statements made by Léon Mugesera during the meeting of the MRND held on 22 November 1992, referred to the fact that Tutsi had supposedly come from Ethiopia and that, after they were killed, their bodies should be thrown into the Rwandan tributaries of the Nile, so that they can go back to where they supposedly came. See Prosecution Exhibit tendered and recorded as No. 74.
55   These are the Kinyarwanda words used by witness PP

considered taboo. Yet, if a snake wraps itself round a *gisabo*, obviously, one has no choice but to ignore this taboo in order to kill the snake.

122. In light of the foregoing, it is now appropriate for the Chamber to consider the issue of specific intent that is required for genocide (*mens rea* or *dolus specialis*). In other words, it should be established that the above-mentioned acts were targeted at a particular group as such. In this respect also, many consistent and reliable testimonies, especially those of Major-General Dallaire, Dr. Zachariah, victim V, prosecution witness PP, defence witness DAAX, and particularly that of the accused himself unanimously agree on the fact that it was the Tutsi as members of an ethnic group which they formed in the context of the period[56] in question, who **[page 63]** were targeted during the massacres[57].

123. Two facts, in particular, which suggest that it was indeed the Tutsi who were targeted should be highlighted: Firstly, at the roadblocks which were erected in Kigali immediately after the crash of the President's plane on 6 April 1994 and, later on, in most of the country's localities, members of the Tutsi population were sorted out. Indeed, at these roadblocks which were manned, depending on the situation, either by soldiers, troops of the Presidential Guard and/or militiarnen, the systematic checking of identity cards indicating the ethnic group of their holders, allowed the separation of Hutu from Tutsi, with the latter being immediately apprehended and killed, sometimes on the spot. Secondly, the propaganda campaign conducted before and during the tragedy by the audiovisual media, for example, "Radio Television des Milles Collines" (RTLM), or the print media, like the Kangura[58] newspaper. These various news media overtly called for the killing of Tutsi, who were considered as the accomplices of the RPF and accused of plotting to take over the power lost during the revolution of 1959. Some articles and cartoons carried in the *Kangura* newspaper, entered in evidence, are unambiguous in this respect. In fact, even exhibit 25A could be added to this lot. Exhibit 25A is a letter from the "GZ" staff headquarters dated 21 September 1992 and signed by Deofratas Nsabimana, Colonel, BEM, to which is annexed a document prepared by a committee of ten officers and which deals with the definition of the term enemy. According to that document, which was intended for the widest possible dissemination, the enemy fell into two categories, namely: "the primary enemy" and the "enemy supporter". The primary enemy was defined as "the extremist Tutsi within the country or abroad who are nostalgic for power and who have NEVER acknowledge and STILL DO NOT acknowledge the realities of the Social Revolution of 1959, and who wish to regain power **[page 64]** in RWANDA by all possible means, including the use of weapons". On the other hand, the primary enemy supporter was "anyone who lent support in whatever form to the primary enemy". This document also stated that the primary enemy and their supporters came mostly from social groups comprising, in particular, "Tutsi refugees", "Tutsi within the country", "Hutu dissatisfied with the current regime", "Foreigners married to Tutsi women" and the "Nilotic-hamitic tribes in the region".

124. In the opinion of the Chamber, all this proves that it was indeed a particular group, the Tutsi ethnic group, which was targeted. Clearly, the victims were not chosen as individuals but, indeed, because they belonged to said group; and hence the victims were members of this group selected as such. According to Alison Desforges's testimony, the Tutsi were killed solely on account of having been born Tutsi.

---

[56]   The term *ethnic group* is, in general, used to refer to a group whose members speak the same language and/or have the same culture. Therefore, one can hardly talk of ethnic groups as regards Hutu and Tutsi, given that they share the same language and culture. However, in the context of the period in question, they were, in consonance with a distinction made by the colonizers, considered both by the authorities and themselves as belonging to two distinct ethnic groups; as such, their identity cards mentioned each holder's ethnic group. In its findings in chapter 7 of the judgment, the Chamber will come back to this issue.

[57]   However, the Tutsi were not the sole victims of the massacres. Many Hutu were also killed, though not because they were Hutu, but simply because they were, for one reason or another, viewed as having sided with the Tutsi.

[58]   It will be noted in this regard that in the *travaux preparatoires* of the Genocide Convention, the Yugoslav delegate indicated with regard to the genocide of Jews by the Nazis that the crimes began with the preparation and mobilization of the masses by means of the ideas spread by the necessary propaganda and in circles which financed this propaganda. See the Summary Records of the meetings of the Sixth Committee of the General Assembly, 21 September 1948-10 December 1948, Official Records of the General Assembly.

125. Clearly therefore, the massacres which occurred in Rwanda in 1994 had a specific objective, namely the extermination of the Tutsi, who were targeted especially because of their Tutsi origin and not because they were RPF fighters. In any case, the Tutsi children and pregnant women would, naturally, not have been among the fighters.

126. Consequently, the Chamber concludes from all the foregoing that genocide was, indeed, committed in Rwanda in 1994 against the Tutsi as a group. Furthermore, in the opinion of the Chamber, this genocide appears to have been meticulously organized. In fact, Dr. Alison Desforges testifying before the Chamber on 24 May 1997, talked of "centrally organized and supervised massacres". Indeed, some evidence supports this view that the genocide had been planned. First, the existence of lists of Tutsi to be eliminated is corroborated by many testimonies. In this respect, Dr. Zachariah mentioned the case of patients and nurses killed in a hospital because a soldier had a list including their names. There are also the arms caches in Kigali which Major-General Dallaire mentioned and regarding whose destruction he had sought the UN's authorization in vain. Lastly, there is the training of militiamen by the Rwandan Armed Forces and of course, the psychological preparation of the population to attack the Tutsi, which preparation was masterminded by some news media, with the RTLM at the forefront. **[page 65]**

127. Finally, in response to the question posed earlier in this chapter as to whether the tragic events that took place in Rwanda in 1994 occurred solely within the context of the conflict between the RAF and the RPF, the Chamber replies in the negative, since it holds that the genocide did indeed take place against the Tutsi group, alongside the conflict. The execution of this genocide was probably facilitated by the conflict, in the sens that the fighting against the RPF forces was used as a pretext for the propaganda inciting genocide against the Tutsi, by branding RPF fighters and Tutsi civilians together, through dissemination via the media of the idea that every Tutsi was allegedly an accomplice of the Inkotanyi. Very clearly, once the genocide got under way, the crime became one of the stakes in the conflict between the RPF and the RAF. In 1994, General Kagame, speaking on behalf of the RPF, declared that a cease fire could possibly not be implemented until the massacre of civilians by the government forces[59] had stopped.

128. In conclusion, it should be stressed that although the genocide against the Tutsi occurred concomitantly with the above-mentioned conflict, it was, evidently, fundamentally different from the conflict. The accused himself stated during his initial appearance before the Chamber, when recounting a conversation he had with one RAF officer and Silas Kubwimana, a leader of the Interahamwe, that the acts perpetrated by the Interahamwe against Tutsi civilians were not considered by the RAF officer to be of a nature to help the government armed forces in the conflict with the RPF[60]. Note is also taken of the testimony of witness KK which is in the same vein. This witness told the Chamber that while she and the children were taken away, an RAF soldier allegedly told persons who were persecuting her that "instead of going to confront the Inkotanyi at the war front, you are killing children, although children know nothing; they have never done politics". The Chamber's opinion is that the genocide was organized and planned not only by members of the RAF, but also by the political forces who were behind the "Hutu-power", **[page 66]** that it was executed essentially by civilians including the armed militia and even ordinary citizens, and above all, that the majority of the Tutsi victims were non-combatants, including thousands of women and children, even foetuses. The fact that the genocide took place while the RAF was in conflict with the RPF, can in no way be considered as an extenuating circumstance for it.

129. This being the case, the Chamber holds that the fact that genocide was indeed committed in Rwanda in 1994 and more particularly in Taba, cannot influence it in its decisions in the present case. Its sole task is to assess the individual criminal responsibility of the accused for the crimes with which he is

---

[59]   See the "Report of the United Nations High Commissioner for Human Rights on his mission to Rwanda, 11-12 May 1994" (E/CN.4?s-373, 19 May 1994), reproduced in annex "The United Nations and Rwanda, 1993-1996", Department of Public Information, United Nations, New York, 1996, p. 287.
[60]   See transcript of the hearing of 12 March 1998, p. 152

charged, the burden of proof being on the Prosecutor[61]. In spite of the irrefutable atrocities of the crimes committed in Rwanda, the judges must examine the facts adduced in a most dispassionate manner, bearing in mind that the accused is presumed innocent. Moreover, the seriousness of the charges brought against the accused makes it all the more necessary to examine scrupulously and meticulously all the inculpatory and exonerating evidence, in the context of a fair trial and in full resect of all the rights of the Accused. **[page 67]**

4. EVIDENTIARY MATTERS

130. The Chamber will address certain general evidentiary matters of concern which arose in relation to the evidence produced by the parties during this trial. These matters include the assessment of evidence, the impact of trauma on witnesses, questions of interpretation from Kinyarwanda into French and English, and cultural factors which might affect an understanding of the evidence presented.

Assessment of Evidence

131. In its assessment of the evidence, as a general principle, the Chamber has attached probative value to each testimony and each exhibit individually according to its credibility and relevance to the allegations at issue. As commonly provided for in most national criminal proceedings, the Chamber has considered the charges against the accused on the basis of the testimony and exhibits offered by the parties to support or challenge the allegations made in the Indictment. In seeking to establish the truth in its judgment, the Chamber has relied as well on indisputable facts and on other elements relevant to the case, such as constitutive documents pertaining to the establishment and jurisdiction of the Tribunal, even if these were not specifically tendered in evidence by the parties during trial. The Chamber notes that it is not restricted under the Statute of the Tribunal to apply any particular legal system and is not bound by any national rules of evidence. In accordance with Rule 89 of its Rules of Procedure and Evidence, the Chamber has applied the rules of evidence which in its view best favour a fair determination of the matter before it and are consonant with the spirit and general principles of law.

Unus Testis, Nullus Testis

132. The Chamber notes that during trial, only one testimony was presented in support of **[page 68]** certain facts alleged in the Indictment; hence the question arises as to the principle found in Civil Law systems: *unus testis, nullus testis* (one witness is no witness) whereby corroboration of evidence is required if it is to be admitted.

133. Without wishing to delve into a debate on the applicability of the rule of corroboration of evidence in this judgment, the Chamber recalls that the proceedings before it are conducted in accordance solely with the Statute of the Tribunal and its Rules and, as provided for by Rule 89(A), it shall not be bound by national rules of evidence. Furthermore, where evidentiary matters are concerned, the Chamber is bound only to the application of the provisions of its Statute and Rules, in particular Rule 89 of the Rules which sets out the general principle of the admissibility of any relevant evidence which has probative value, provided that it is in accordance with the requisites of a fair trial.

134. Rule 96(i) of the Rules alone specifically deals with the issue of corroboration of testimony required by the Chamber. The provisions of this Rule, which apply only to cases of testimony by victims of sexual assault, stipulate that no corroboration shall be required. In the Tadić judgment rendered by the

---

[61]   In the opinion of the Chamber, it is not only obvious that an accused person could be declared innocent of the crime of genocide even when it is established that genocide had indeed taken place, but also, in a case other than that of Rwanda, a person could be found guilty of genocide without necessarily having to establish that genocide had taken place throughout the country concerned.

ICTY, the Trial Chamber ruled that this "Sub-rule accords to the testimony of a victim of sexual assault the same presumption of reliability as the testimony of victims of other crimes, something which had long been denied to victims of sexual assault in common law [which] certainly does not [...] justify any inference that in cases of crimes other than sexual assault, corroboration is required. The proper inference is, in fact, directly to the contrary"[62].

135. In view of the above, the Chamber can rule on the basis of a single testimony provided such testimony is, in its opinion, relevant and credible.

136. The Chamber can freely assess the probative value of all relevant evidence. The Chamber had thus determined that in accordance with Rule 89, any relevant evidence having probative **[page 69]** value may be admitted into evidence, provided that it is being in accordance with the requisites of a fair trial. The Chamber finds that hearsay evidence is not inadmissible per se and has considered such evidence, with caution, in accordance with Rule 89.

Witness statements

137. During the trial, the Prosecutor and the Defence relied on pre-trial statements from witnesses for the purpose of cross-examination. The Chamber ordered that any such statements to which reference was made in the proceedings be submitted in evidence for consideration[63]. In many instances, the Defence has alleged inconsistencies and contradictions between the pre-trial statements of witnesses and their evidence at trial. The Chamber notes that these pre-trial statements were composed following interviews with witnesses by investigators of the Office of the Prosecution. These interviews were mostly conducted in Kinyarwanda, and the Chamber did not have access to transcripts of the interviews, but only translations thereof. It was therefore unable to consider the nature and form of the questions put to the witnesses, or the accuracy of interpretation at the time. The Chamber has considered inconsistencies and contradictions between these statements and testimony at trial with caution for these reasons, and in the light of the time lapse between the statements and the presentation of evidence at trial, the difficulties of recollecting precise details several years after the occurrence of the events, the difficulties of translation, and the fact that several witnesses were illiterate and stated that they had not read their written statements. Moreover, the statements were not made under solemn declaration and were not taken by judicial officers. In the circumstances, the probative value attached to the statements is, in the Chamber's view, considerably less than direct sworn testimony before the Chamber, the truth of which has been subjected to the test of cross-examination.

False testimony

138. Rule 91 of the Rules (False Testimony under Solemn Declaration) provides for, *iner alia*, **[page 70]** the investigation and possible prosecution of a witness whom the Chamber believes may have knowingly and wilfully given false testimony. As held by the Chamber in its decision rendered thereon in relation to a Defence motion requesting the Chamber to direct the Prosecutor to investigate the alleged false testimony by a witness[64], Rule 91(B) provides:

> *Either* the Chamber establishes *proprio motu* that strong grounds exist for believing that a witness has knowingly and wilfully given false testimony, and thence directs the Prosecutor to investigate the matter with a view to the preparation and submission of an Indictment for false testimony;

> *Or,* at the request of a party, it invites the Prosecutor to investigate the matter with a view to the preparation and submission of an Indictment for false testimony; and in this case, the onus is on

---

62   See ICTY Tadić Judgment, 7 May 1997, paras. 535 to 539
63   *Supra* "Procedural Background".
64   *Ibid*

the party to convince the Chamber that there exist strong grounds for believing that a witness has knowingly and wilfully given false testimony;

139. Further, the Chamber held in the decision, that the onus is on the party pleading a case of false testimony to prove that falsehoods of the witness statements, that they were made with harmful intent, or at least that they were made by a witness who was fully aware that they were false, and their possible bearing upon the judge's decisions. The Chamber found that for the Defence to raise only doubts as to the credibility of the statements made by the witness was not sufficient to establish strong grounds for believing that the witness may have knowingly and wilfully given false testimony, and that the assessment of credibility pertains to the rendering of the final judgment.

140. The majority of the witnesses who appeared before the Chamber were eye-witnesses, whose testimonies were based on events they had seen or heard in relation to the acts alleged in the Indictment. The Chamber noted that during the trial, for a number of these witnesses, there appeared to be contradictions or inaccuracies between, on the one hand, the content of their **[page 71]** testimonies under solemn declaration to the Chamber, and on the other, their earlier statements to the Prosecutor and the Defence. This alone is not a ground for believing that the witnesses gave false testimony. Indeed, an often levied criticism of testimony is its fallibility. Since testimony is based mainly on memory and sight, two human characteristics which often deceive the individual, this criticism is to be expected. Hence, testimony is rarely exact at to the events experienced. To deduce from any resultant contradictions and inaccuracies that there was false testimony, would be akin to criminalising frailties in human perceptions. Moreover, inaccuracies and contradictions between the said statements and the testimony given before the Court are also the result of the time lapse between the two. Memory over time naturally degenerates, hence it would be wrong and unjust for the Chamber to treat forgetfulness as being synonymous with giving false testimony. Moreover, false testimony requires the necessary *mens rea* and not a mere wrongful statement.

141. Were the Chamber to have strong grounds for believing that the witness had knowingly and wilfully given false testimony, with the intent to impede the due process of Justice, then Rule 91 of the Rules would be applied accordingly.

The impact of trauma on the testimony of witnesses

142. Many of the eye-witnesses who testified before the Chamber in this case have seen atrocities committed against their family members or close friends, and/or have themselves been the victims of such atrocities. The possible traumatism of these witnesses caused by their painful experience of violence during the conflict in Rwanda is a matter of particular concern to the Chamber. The recounting of this traumatic experience is likely to evoke memories of the fear and the pain once inflicted on the witness and thereby affects is or her ability fully or adequately to recount the sequence of events in a judicial context. The Chamber has considered the testimony of those witnesses in this light.

143. The Chamber is unable to exclude the possibility that some or all of these witnesses did actually suffer from post traumatic or extreme stress disorders, and has therefore carefully **[page 72]** perused the testimonies of these witnesses, those of the Prosecutor as well as those of the Defence, on the assumption that this might possibly have been the case. Inconsistencies or imprecisions in the testimonies, accordingly, have been assessed in the light of this assumption, personal background and the atrocities they have experienced or have been subjected to. Much as the Witness Protection Programme and the orders for protection of witnesses issued by the Chamber during this trial were designed primarily to reduce the danger for witnesses in coming to the Tribunal to testify, these measures may also have provided for some alleviation of stress. Reducing the physical danger to the witnesses in Rwanda, and ordering the non-disclosure of their identities to the media and the public, as well as accommodating them during their presence at the seat of the Tribunal in safe houses where medical and psychiatric assistance was available, are, in any event, measures conducive to easing the level of stress.

144. The Chamber has thanked each witness for his or her testimony during the trial proceedings and wishes to acknowledge in its judgement the strength and courage of survivors who have recounted their traumatic experiences, often reliving extremely painful emotions. Their testimony has been invaluable to the Chamber in its pursuit of truth regarding the events which took place in the commune of Taba in 1994.

Interpretation from Kinyarwanda into French and English

145. The majority of the witnesses in this trial testified in Kinyarwanda. The Chamber notes that the interpretation of oral testimony of witnesses from Kinyarwanda into one of the official languages of the Tribunal has been a particularly great challenge due to the fact that the syntax and everyday modes of expression in the Kinyarwanda language are complex and difficult to translate into French or English. These difficulties affected the pre-trial interviews carried out by investigators in the field, as well as the interpretation of examination and cross-examination during proceedings in Court. Most of the testimony of witnesses at trial was given in the language, Kinyarwanda, first interpreted into French, and then from French into English. This process entailed obvious risks of misunderstandings in the English version of words spoken in the source language by the witness in Kinyarwanda. For the reason, in cases where the [page 73] transcripts differ in English and French, the Chamber has relied on the French transcript for accuracy. In some cases, where the words spoken are central to the factual and legal findings of the Chamber, the words have been reproduced in this judgment in the original Kinyarwanda.

146. The words Inkotanyi, Inyenzi, Icyitso/Ibyitso, Interahamwe and the expressions used in Kinyarwanda for "rape", because of their significance to the findings of the Chamber, are considered particularly, as follows: The Chamber has relied substantially on the testimony of Dr. Mathias Ruzindana, an expert witness on linguistics, for its understanding of these terms. The Chamber notes that Dr. Ruzindana stated in his testimony that in ascertaining the specific meaning of certain words and expressions in Kinyarwanda, it is necessary to place them contextually, both in time and in space.

147. The origin of the term Inkotanyi can be tracked back to the 19th Century, at which time it was the name of one of the warrior groups of a Rwandese king, King Rwanbugiris. There is no evidence to suggest that this warrior group was monoethnic. Dr. Ruzindana suggested that the name Inkotanyi was borne with pride by these warriors. At the start of the war between the RPF and the Government of Rwanda, the RPF army wing was called Inkotanyi. As such, it should be assumed that the basic meaning of the term Inkotanyi is the RPF army. Based on the analysis of a number of Rwandan newspapers and RTLM cassettes, as well as his personal experiences during the conflict, Dr. Ruzindana believed the term Inkotanyi had a number of extended meanings, including RPF sympathizer or supporter, and, in some instances, it even seemed to make reference to Tutsi as an ethnic group.

148. The basic everyday meaning of the term *Inyenzi* is cockroach. Other meanings of the term stem from the history of Rwanda. During the "revolution" of 1959, refugees, mainly Tutsi, fled the country. Throughout the 1960's incursions on Rwandan soil were carried out by some of these refugees, who would enter and leave the country under the cover of the night, only rarely to be seen in the morning. This activity was likened to that of cockroaches, which are rarely seen during the day but often discovered at night, and accordingly these attackers were called Inyenzi. A similar comparison, between insurgent Tutsi refugees and cockroaches, was made when the [page 74] RPF army carried out a number of attacks in Rwanda in 1990. It was thought that the Inyenzi of 1990 were the children of the Inyenzi of the 1960's. "The cockroach begets another cockroach and not a butterfly" was an article heading in the magazine Kangura. Another article in this publication made the reference even more explicitly, saying "The war between us and the Inyenzi-Inkotanyi has lasted for too long. It is time we told the truth. The present war is a war between Hutu and Tutsi. It has not started today, it is an old one."[65]

149. Unlike the term Inkotanyi, the term Inyenzi had a negative, even abusive, connotation. The radio station RTLM broadcast on 20 April 1994, "They are a gang of Tutsi extremists who called themselves

---

[65]   Issue no. 10, page 10, 1993

Inkotanyi while they are no more than Inyenzi." and in a speech on 22 November 1992, Léon Mugesera said "Don't call them Inkotanyi, they are true Inyenzi". The term Inyenzi was widely used by extremist media, by those who had refused to accept the Arusha Peace Accords and those who wanted to exterminate the Tutsi, in whole or in part. It was often contained in RTLM broadcasts, a radio which, in the opinion of Dr. Ruzindana, was anti-Tutsi in its broadcastings.[66]

150. The term Icyitso, or Ibyitso in the plural, has been in usage in Kinyarwanda for quite some time. It is a common term which means accomplice. In ancient Rwandan history, a king wonting to launch an attack on neighbouring countries would send spies to the targeted country. These spies would recruit collaborators who would be known as Ibyitso. In Rwanda, the term has a negative connotation. Thus it should not be seen as being synonymous with "supporter", a term which can be viewed both positively and negatively, but perhaps rather "collaborator". The term evolved, as early as 1991, to include not only collaborators, but all Tutsi. The editor of Kangura stated in 1993, "When the war started, Hutu talked openly about the Tutsi, or they referred to **[page 75]** them, indirectly, calling them Ibyitso"[67].

151. The term Interahamwe derives from two words put together to make a noun, intera and hamwe. Intera comes from the verb "gutera" which can mean both to attack and to work. It was documented that in 1994, besides meaning to work or to attack, the word gutera could also mean to kill. Hamwe means together. Therefore Interahamwe could mean to attack or to work together, and, depending on the context, to kill together. The Interahamwe were the youth movement of the MRND. During the war, the term also covered anyone who had anti-Tutsi tendencies, irrespective of their political background, and who collaborated with the MRND youth.

152. The terms gusambanya, kurungora, kuryamana and gufata ku ngufu were used interchangeably by witnesses and translated by the interpreters as "rape". The Chamber has consulted its official trial interpreters to gain a precise understanding of these words and how they have been interpreted. The word gusambanya means "to bring (a person) to commit adultery or fornication". The word kurungora means "to have sexual intercourse with a woman". This term is used regardless of whether the woman is married or not, and regardless of whether she gives consent or not. The word kuryamana means "to share a bed" or "to have sexual intercourse", depending on the context. It seems similar to the colloquial usage in English and in French of the term "to sleep with". The term gufata ku ngufu means "to take (anything) by force" and also "to rape".

153. The context in which these terms are used is critical to an understanding of their meaning and their translation. The dictionary entry for kurungora[68], the most generic term for sexual intercourse, includes as an example of usage of this word, the sentence "Mukantwali yahuye n'abasore batatu baramwambura baramurongora," for which the dictionary translation into French is "Mukantwali a rencontré trois jeunes gens qui l'ont dévalisée et violée" (in English **[page 76]** "Mukantwali met three young men who robbed her of her belongings and raped her.")

154. The Chamber notes that the accused objected on one occasion to the translation of the words stated by Witness JJ ("Batangira kujya babafata ku ngufu babakoresha ibyo bashaka") as "They began to rape them." It was clarified that the witness said "they had their way with them." The Chamber notes that in this instance the term used, babafata ku ngufu, is the term which of the four terms identified in the paragraph above is the term most closely connected to the concept of force. Having reviewed in detail with the official trial interpreters the references to "rape" in the transcript, the Chamber is satisfied that the Kinyarwanda expressions have been accurately translated.

---

[66] Dr. Ruzindana believed that RTLM broadcasted somewhat extremist messages, abusive by their very nature, for instance "Well you will know those to kill because you will look at their noses...We will look at their nose, and so, we know which ones to kill"

[67] Issue no. 45, page 3, July 1993.

[68] Dictionnaire Rwandais-Français de l'Institut National de Recherche Scientifique (Three Volumes). Edition abrégée et adaptée par Irenéc JACOB.

Cultural Factors Affecting the Evidence of Witnesses

155. Dr. Mathias Ruzindana noted that most Rwandans live in an oral tradition in which facts are reported as they are perceived by the witness, often irrespective of whether the facts were personally witnessed or recounted by someone else. Since not many people are literate or own a radio, much of the information disseminated by the press in 1994 was transmitted to a larger number of secondary listeners by word of mouth, which inevitably carries the hazard of distortion of the information each time it is passed on to a new listener. Similarly, with regard to events in Taba, the Chamber noted that on examination it was at times clarified that evidence which had been reported as an eyewitness account was in fact a second-hand account of what was witnessed. Dr. Ruzindana explained this as a common phenomenon within the culture, but also confirmed that the Rwandan community was like any other and that a clear distinction could be articulated by the witnesses between what they had heard and what they had seen. The Chamber made a consistent effort to ensure that this distinction was drawn throughout the trial proceedings.

156. According to the testimony of Dr. Ruzindana, it is a particular feature of the Rwandan culture that people are not always direct in answering questions, especially if the question is delicate. In such cases, the answers given will very often have to be "decoded" in order to be **[page 77]** understood correctly. This interpretation will rely on the context, the particular speech community, the identity of and the relation between the orator and the listener, and the subject matter of the question. The Chamber noted this in the proceedings. For example, many witnesses when asked the ordinary meaning of the term Inyenzi were reluctant or unwilling to state that the word meant cockroach, although it became clear to the Chamber during the course of the proceedings that any Rwandan would know the ordinary meaning of the word. Similar cultural constraints were evident in their difficulty to be specific as to dates, times, distances, and locations. The Chamber also noted the inexperience of witnesses with maps, film and graphic representations of localities, in the light of this understanding, the Chamber did not draw any adverse conclusions regarding the credibility of witnesses based only on their reticence and their sometimes circuitous responses to questions. **[page 78]**

5. FACTUAL FINDINGS

5.1. General allegations (Paragraphs 5-11 of the Indictment)

Events Alleged

157. Paragraphs 5 to 11 of the indictment appear under the heading, "General Allegations". These general allegations are, for the most part, mixed questions of fact and law relating to the general elements of genocide, crimes against humanity, and violations of international humanitarian law, the crimes set forth in Articles 2, 3 and 4 of the Statute of the Tribunal, under which the Accused is charged. Several witnesses testified before the Chamber with regard to historical background and the general situation in Rwanda prior to and during 1994. The Chamber has substantially relied on the testimonies of Dr. Ronie Zachariah, Ms. Lindsey Hilson, Mr. Simon Cox, Dr. Alison Desforges, who testified as an expert witness, and General Romeo Dallaire, the force commander of UNAMIR at the time of these events as well as United Nations reports of which it takes judicial notice, for its general findings on the factual allegations set forth in paragraphs 5-11 of the indictment.

158. Dr. Zachariah, the Chief Medical and Field Coordinator for Medecins sans frontieres ("MSF"), based in the Butare region, testified that he witnessed widespread massacres of civilians in Rwanda from 13 to 24 April 1994. He stated that he travelled from Butare to Gitarama on 13 April 1994 in order to provide medical supplies to a hospital in Gitarama which had received 40 to 50 injured people. From 25 kilometres outside Gitarama, Dr. Zachariah said he and his team began to see refugees on the road, who reported the killings of civilians at roadblocks. At one of these barriers, Dr. Zachariah stated that his driver was treated aggressively by a guard manning the roadblock, because the driver was Tutsi and the Tutsi were accused of helping the RPF. Dr. Zachariah testified that it soon became apparent upon arrival

at Gitarama **[page 79]** Hospital that Tutsi civilians were being targeted for attack on a massive scale. Subsequently, Dr. Zachariah witnessed attacks on civilian populations, and killings of civilians. He recounted visiting Kibeho Church on 16 April 1994, where two to four thousand Tutsi civilians were apparently killed, and Butare on 17 April 1994, where a Burundian Tutsi was apparently beaten to death at a checkpoint, and where his purchase officer reported seeing the bodies of 5-10 dead civilians at every checkpoint on the road from Kigali. These checkpoints were apparently manned by well-armed, drunken soldiers and civilians. On the road from Butare to Burundi on 19 April 1994, Dr. Zachariah sated that saw civilians being massacred in villages throughout the countryside and at roadblocks. In his words:

> "All the way through we could see on the [...] hillside, where there were communities, people [...] being pulled out by people with machetes, and we could see piles of bodies. In fact the entire landscape was becoming spotted with corpses, with bodies, all the way from there until almost Burundi's border".
>
> (Hearing of 16 January 1997, pp 98-99)

159.   At the Rwanda-Burundi border, on the same day, Dr. Zachariah testified that he saw a group of 60 to 80 civilians fleeing towards the Burundian border, from men armed with machetes. He stated that most of these civilians were hacked to death before they reached the border. Returning form the Burundian border, on 21 April 1994, Dr. Zachariah stated that he had spoken to eye-witnesses who had informed him of the killings of approximately 40 Tutsi MSF personnel, in the Saga camps in Butare. He stated that his driver's entire family had been killed on the outskirts of Butare by *Interahamwe* and he had been informed of these killings by his driver who had managed to escape death. Dr. Zachariah testified that he had witnessed, on 22 April 1994, the aftermath of the massacre of the family of a moderate Hutu, Mr. Souphene, the sub-Prefect of Butare, by the Presidential Guard, and, on the same day, the killings of children in the Hotel Pascal in Butare and the executions of tens of Tutsi patients and nurses in Butare Hospital, including a Hutu nurse who was pregnant by a Tutsi man and whose child would therefore be Tutsi. Dr. Zachariah stated that he then decided to evacuate his team from Rwanda and he arrived at the Burundian border on 24 April 1994. On the way to the border and at the **[page 80]** border, he stated that he had crossed streams and rivers in which the mutilated corpses of men, women and children floated by at an estimated rate of five bodies every minute. Dr. Zachariah stated under cross-examination that in his opinion the attacks were both "organised and systematic".

160.   Lindsey Hilson, a journalist, testified that she was in Kigali from 7 February 1994 to mid-April 1994. Following the aeroplane crash of 6 April 1994 in which the Presidents of Rwanda and Burundi were killed, she said she heard from others and saw for herself the ensuing killings of Tutsi in the capital. On the third day after the aeroplane crash, she toured Kigali with aid workers and saw victims suffering from machete and gunshot wounds. In Kigali central hospital, where she described the situation as "absolutely terrible", wounded men, women and children of all ages were packed into the wards, and hospital gutters were "running red with blood". At the morgue she saw "a big pile like a mountain of bodies outside and these were bodies with slash wounds, with heads smashed in, many of them naked, men and women". She estimated that the pile outside the morgue contained about five hundred bodies, with more bodies being brought in all the time by pickup trucks. She stated that she also saw teams of convicts around Kigali collecting bodies in the backs of trucks for mass burial, as well as groups of armed men roaming the city with machetes, clubs and sticks.

161.   Simon Cox, a cameraman and photographer, testified that he was on an assignment in Rwanda during the time of the events set forth in the indictment. He said he entered Rwanda from Uganda, arriving in the border town of Mulindi, in the third week of April 1994. Thence he headed south with an RPF escort and found evidence of massacres of civilian men, women and children, whom it appeared from their identity cards were mostly Tutsi, in church compounds. En route to Rusumo, in the south-east of the country, he visited hospitals where Tutsi civilians suffering from machete wounds were being treated, some of whom he interviewed. At the Tanzanian border, near Rusumo, by the Kagera river which flows towards Lake Victoria, Mr. Cox saw and filmed corpses floating by at the rate of several corpses per minute. Later, at the beginning of May, he was in Kigali and saw more bodies of dead civilians on the roads. The Chamber viewed film footage taken by Mr. Cox. **[page 81]**

162. On a second trip, in June 1994, Mr. Cox visited the western part of Rwanda, arriving in Cyangugu from Zaire (now the Democratic Republic of Congo) and travelling north towards Kibuye. On that journey, he visited orphanages populated by Tutsi children whose parents had been massacred or disappeared. He visited a church in Shangi where a Priest described how the whole of his congregation who had been Tutsi had been hiding inside the church, because they had heard disturbances, and they were eventually all killed by large armed gangs of people, some of whom were equipped with hand grenades. The church had previously survived five repeated attacks. Mr. Cox himself examined the church and outbuildings and found graves, much blood and other evidence of killings. On the way to Kibuye, he saw further evidence of freshly dug mass graves in churchyards. Later, in the hills of Bisesero, he saw some 800 Tutsi civilians "in a desperate, desperate state", many apparently starving and with severe machete and bullet wounds, and with a great many corpses strewn all over the hills.

163. The testimony of an expert witness, Alison Desforges, which has been referred to and summarised above in the "Context of the conflict" section, also indicates that Tutsi and so-called moderate Hutu civilians were targeted for attacks on a massive scale in Rwanda at the time of the events which are the subject of this indictment.

164. In addition, the Chamber heard the testimony of General Romeo Dallaire, who was the force commander of UNAMIR in April 1994. General Dallaire described before the Chamber the massacres of civilian Tutsi which took place in Rwanda in 1994. He also testified in relation to the armed conflict which took place between the RPF and the FAR at the same time as the massacres. This conflict appeared to be a civil war between two well-organised armies. In this context, General Dallaire referred to the FAR and the RPF as "two armies", "two belligerents" or "two sides to the conflict". He noted that the mandate of the UNAMIR was to assist these two parties in implementing the Arusha Peace Accords which were signed on 4 October 1993. Subsequently, other military agreements were signed between the parties, including cease-fire agreements and agreements for arms-free zones. General Dallaire testified that the FAR was under the control of the government of Rwanda and that the RPF was under the control of Paul **[page 82]** Kagame. The FAR and RPF occupied different sides of a clearly demarcated demilitarised zone, and according to General Dallaire, the RPF comprised 12,000-13,000 soldiers deployed in three groups: two groups for reaction in the western flank of the demilitarised zone and another group in the eastern flank with six independent battalions. The RPF headquartered in Mulundi, and had a lightweight battalion stationed in Kigali. General Dallaire testified that the RPF troops were disciplined and possessed a well-structured leadership which was answerable to authority and which respected instruction.

165. In addition to the testimony of these witnesses, the Chamber takes judicial notice of the following United Nations reports, which extensively document the massacres which took place in Rwanda in 1994: notably, the *Final Report of the Commission of Experts Established Pursuant to Security Council Resolution 935 (1994)*. U.N. Doc. S/1994/1405 (1994); *Report of the Special Rapporteur of the Commission on Human Rights on Extrajudicial, Summary or Arbitrary Executions, Bacre Waly Ndiaye, on his mission to Rwanda from 8-17 April 1993*, U.N. Doc. E/CN.4/1994/7/Add.1 (1993); *Special Report of the Secretary-General on UNAMIR, containing a summary of the developing crisis in Rwanda and proposing three options for the role of the United Nations in Rwanda*, S/1994/470, 20 April 1994; *Report of the United Nations High Commissioner for Human Rights, Mr. José Ayala Lasso, on his mission to Rwanda 11-12 may 1994*, U.N. Doc. E/CN.4/S-3/3 (1994). See also, generally, the collection of United Nations documents in *The United Nations and Rwanda, 1993-1996*, The United Nations Blue Books Series, Volume X, Department of Public Information, United Nations, New York.

166. The Chamber notes that witnesses from Taba also attested to the mass killings which took place around the country.

Factual Findings

167. Paragraph 5 of the indictment alleges, "Unless otherwise specified, all acts and omissions set forth in this indictment took place between 1 January 1994 and 31 December 1994, in the commune of Taba,

prefecture of Gitarama, territory of Rwanda". This allegation, which supports **[page 83]** the legal finding that the Chamber has territorial and temporal jurisdiction over the crimes charged, is not contested, and the Chamber finds that it has been established by the evidence presented.

168. Paragraph 6 of the indictment alleges that the acts set forth in each paragraph of the indictment charging genocide, i.e. paragraphs 12-24, "were committed with intent to destroy, in whole or in part, a national, ethnic or racial group". That acts of violence committed in Rwanda during this time were committed with the intent to destroy the Tutsi population is evident not only from the testimony cited above of Dr. Zachariah, Ms. Hilson, Mr. Cox, Dr. Desforges and General Dallaire, but also from the witnesses who testified with regard to events in the commune of Taba. Witness JJ testified that she was driven away from her home, which was destroyed after a man came to the hill near where she lived and said that the bourgmestre had sent him so that no Tutsi would remain on the hill that night. At the meeting which was held on the morning of 19 April 1994, at which the Accused spoke, Witness OO testified that it was said by another speaker that all the Tutsi should be killed so that some day a child could be born who would have to ask what a Tutsi had looked like. She also quoted this speaker as saying "I will have peace when there will be no longer a Tutsi in Rwanda." Witness V testified that Tutsi were thrown into the Nyabarongo river, which flows towards the Nile, and told to "meet their parents in Abyssinia", signifying that the Tutsi came from Abyssinia (Ethiopia) and that they "should go back to where they came from" (hearing of 24 January 1997, p. 7)

169. In light of this evidence, the Chamber finds beyond a reasonable doubt that the acts of violence which took place in Rwanda during this time were committed with the intent to destroy the Tutsi population, and that the acts of violence which took place in Taba during this time were a part of this effort.

170. Paragraph 7 of the indictment alleges that the victims in each paragraph charging genocide were members of a national, ethnic, racial or religious group. The Chamber notes that the Tutsi population does not have its own language or a distinct culture from the rest of the Rwandan population. However, the Chamber finds that there are a number of objective indicators **[page 84]** of the group as a group with a distinct identity. Every Rwandan citizen was required before 1994 to carry an identity card which included an entry for ethnic group (ubwoko) in Kinyarawanda and *ethnie* in French), the ethnic group being Hutu, Tutsi or Twa. The Rwandan Constitution and laws in force in 1994 also identified Rwandans by reference to their ethnic group. Article 16 of the Constitution of the Rwandan Republic, of 10 June 1991, reads, "All citizens are equal before the law, without any discrimination, notably, on grounds of race, colour, origin, ethnicity, clan, sex, opinion, religion or social position". Article 57 of the Civil Code of 1988 provided that a person would be identified by "sex, ethnic group, name, residence and domicile." Article 118 of the Civil Code provided that birth certificates would include "the year, month, date and place of birth, the sex, the ethnic group, the first and last name of the infant." The Arusha Accords of 4 August 1993 in fact provided for the suppression of the mention of ethnicity on official documents (see Article 16 of the Protocol on diverse questions and final dispositions).

171. Moreover, customary rules existed in Rwanda governing the determination of ethnic group, which followed patrilineal lines of heredity. The identification of persons as belonging to the group of Hutu or Tutsi (or Twa) had thus become embedded in Rwandan culture. The Rwandan witnesses who testified before the Chamber identified themselves by ethnic group, and generally knew the ethnic group to which their friends and neighbours belonged. Moreover, the Tutsi were conceived of as an ethnic group by those who targeted them for killing.

172. As the expert witness, Alison Desforges, summarised:

"The primary criterion for [defining] an ethnic group is the sense of belonging to that ethnic group. It is a sense which can shift over time. In other words, the group, the definition of the group to which one feels allied may change over time. But, if you fix any given moment in time, and you say, how does this population divide itself, then you will see which ethnic groups are in existence in the minds of the participants at that time. The Rwandans currently, and for the last generation at least, have defined themselves in terms of these three ethnic groups. In addition reality is an interplay between the actual conditions and peoples' **[page 85]** subjective perception of those conditions. In Rwanda, the reality was shaped by the colonial experience which imposed a categorisation which was probably more fixed, and nor completely appropriate to the scene. But, the Belgians did impose this classification in the early 1930's when they required the population to be registered according to ethnic group. The categorisation imposed at that time is what people of the current generation have grown up with. They have always thought in terms of these categories, even if they did not, in their daily lives have to take cognizance of that. ... This practice was continued after independence by the First Republic and the Second Republic in Rwanda to such an extent that this division into three ethnic groups became an absolute reality".

173. Paragraph 8 of the indictment alleges that the acts set forth in each paragraph of the indictment charging crimes against humanity, i.e. paragraphs 12-24, "were committed as part of a widespread or systematic attack against a civilian population on national, political, ethnic or racial grounds". As set forth in the evidence, the scale of the attack was extraordinary. Defence counsel called the events which took place in Rwanda in 1994 "the greatest human tragedy" at the end of this century. Around the country, a massive number of killings took place within a very short time frame. Tutsi were clearly the target of the attack – at roadblocks, in shelters, and in their own homes. Hutu sympathetic to or supportive of Tutsi were also massacred. That the attack was systematic is evidenced by the unusually large shipments of machetes into the country shortly before it occurred. It is also evidenced by the structured manner in which the attack took place. Teachers and intellectuals were targeted first, in Taba as well as the rest of the country. Through the media and other propaganda, Hutu were encouraged systematically to attack Tutsi. For these reasons, the Chamber finds beyond a reasonable doubt that a widespread and systematic attack began in April 1994 in Rwanda, targeting the civilian Tutsi population and that the acts referred to in paragraphs 12-24 of the indictment were acts which formed part of this widespread and systematic attack.

174. Paragraph 9 of the indictment states, "At all times relevant to this indictment, a state of internal armed conflict existed in Rwanda". The Chamber notes the testimony of General **[page 86]** Dallaire, a witness called by the Defence, that the FAR was and the RPF were "two armies" engaged in hostilities, that the RPF had soldiers systematically deployed under a command structure headed by Paul Kagame, and that FAR and RPF forces occupied different sides of a clearly demarcated demilitarised zone. Based on the evidence presented, the Chamber finds beyond a reasonable doubt that armed conflict existed in Rwanda during the events alleged in the indictment, and that the RPF was an organised armed group, under responsible command, which exercised control over territory in Rwanda and was able to carry out sustained and concerted military operations.

175. Paragraph 10 of the indictment reads, "The victims referred to in this indictment were, at all relevant times, persons not taking an active part in the hostilities". The victims referred to in the indictment, several of whom testified before the Chamber, were farmers, teachers and refugees. The Chamber notes that the Defence did not challenge the civilian status of the victims by making any submissions or leading any evidence connecting any of the victims to the RPF or the hostilities that prevailed in 1994. Since the allegations in Paragraphs 13, 17 and those pertaining to Juvenal Rukundakuvuga and Emmanuel Sempabwa in paragraph 15 of the indictment have not been proved beyond a reasonable doubt, the Chamber finds that it is futile to determine whether these alleged victims were in fact civilians, taking no active part in the hostilities that prevailed in 1994. In light of the evidence presented by the Prosecutor, the Chamber finds beyond a reasonable doubt that all the other victims referred to in the indictment were civilians, not taking any active part in the hostilities that prevailed in 1994.

176. Paragraph 10A was added to the indictment when it was amended to include charges of sexual violence, set forth in Paragraphs 12A and 12B of the indictment. It is not an allegation of fact, rather it appears to be a definition of sexual violence proposed by the Prosecutor.

177. Paragraph 11 of the indictment sets forth the definition of individual criminal responsibility in Article 6(1) of the Statute of the Tribunal and alleges that the Accused is individually responsible for the crimes alleged in the indictment. The Chamber does not consider this to be a factual allegation but rather

a matter of legal issue, which is addressed in the legal **[page 87]** findings on each count. The Chamber notes that no general allegation has been made by the Prosecution in connection with Counts 13, 14 and 15, under which the Accused is charged with individual criminal responsibility under Article 6(3), as well as Article 6(1) of the Tribunal's Statute. **[page 88]**

5.2. Killings (Paragraphs 12, 13, 18, 19 & 20 of the Indictment)

5.2.1. Paragraph 12 of the Indictment

178. The Chamber now considers paragraph 12 of the Indictment, which alleges the responsibility of the Accused, his knowledge of the killings which took place in Taba between 7 April and the end of June 1994, and his failure to attempt to prevent these killings or to call for assistance from regional or national authorities.

179. Paragraph 12 of the Indictment reads as follows:

> 12. As bourgmestre, **Jean Paul AKAYESU** was responsible for maintaining law and public order in his commune. At least 2000 Tutsi were killed in Taba between April 7 and the end of June, 1994, while he was still in power. The killings in Taba were openly committed and so widespread that, as bourgmestre, **Jean Paul AKAYESU** must have know about them. Although he had the authority and responsibility to do so, **Jean Paul AKAYESU** never attempted to prevent the killing of Tutsi in the commune in any way or called for assistance from regional or national authorities to quell the violence.

180. Many witnesses testified regarding the responsibilities of the bourgmestre. Witness DZZ, a former police officer, testified that as bourgmestre, the Accused was responsible for maintaining law and public order in the commune. Witness R, a former bourgmestre, confirmed this testimony, as did Witness V and expert witness Alison Desforges. The responsibilities of the bourgmestre are set forth in Rwandese law, which provides in Article 108 of the Law on the Organization of the Commune that the brigadier has command of the communal police, under the authority of the bourgmestre. Moreover, according to the testimony of witness NN and others, the accused's authority over the communal police continued, and he continued to issue **[page 89]** them orders, throughout the period in question. Many witnesses testified as to their perception of the authority of the bourgmestre. Witness K and Witness NN both stated that as bourgmestre, the Accused was the leader of the commune, and Witness S, Witness V and Ephrem Karangwa, the current bourgmestre of Taba, all testified that the people of the commune respected and followed every order of the Accused, as bourgmestre. The bourgmestre was the most important person in the commune and its "parent" according to Ephrem Karangwa. He was "paramount for the life of the whole commune" and the representative of the executive power in the commune, according to Witness R, himself a former bourgmestre The Accused himself acknowledged that he was responsible for the maintenance of law and order in the commune. Accordingly, the Chamber finds that this proposition has been established.

181. With regard to the allegation that at least 2000 Tutsi were killed in Taba from 7 April to the end of June 1994, the Chamber notes that while many witnesses testified to widespread killings in Taba, very few witnesses were able to estimate numbers of people killed. Ephrem Karangwa, the present bourgmestre of Taba, testified that the population of Taba has decreased by 7,000 persons since April 1994, and he described mass graves in each sector of the commune. While some part of the population decrease may be attributed to refugees leaving the commune, it is clear from the testimony of many witnesses that a substantial number of people were killed in Taba. The number 2000 has not been contested by the Defence, and it seems to the Chamber, based on the evidence of killing and mass graves, a modest estimate of the number of people killed in Taba during this period. The testimony also uniformly establishes that virtually all of these people were Tutsi. Accordingly, the Chamber finds that it has been established beyond a reasonable doubt that at least 2000 Tutsi were killed in Taba from 7 April to the end of June 1994. It has also been established that the accused remained bourgmestre throughout this period.

182.   The Indictment alleges that the killings in Taba were openly committed and so widespread that the Accused must have known about them. A number of witnesses, including Witness PP and Witness V, testified that they informed the Accused of the killings which were taking place in Taba. Others, such as Witness NN, testified that the Accused was present at the bureau communal and elsewhere when killings took place, and that he witnessed these killings. **[page 90]** Others, including Witness KK, Witness NN, Witness G, Witness W, Witness J, Witness C, Witness JJ and Witness V, have testified that the Accused supervised and actively participated in the killings. The Accused himself acknowledged that he knew such killings were taking place. He testified that he was told that there were killings everywhere in Taba, and that it was the Tutsi who were being killed. He stated that on 19 April 1994, killings spread to most of the commune of Taba. The issue is not contested, and it has been established that the Accused knew that killings were taking place and were widespread in Taba during the period in question.

183.   The final allegation of paragraph 12 is that although he had the authority and responsibility to do so, Jean Paul Akayesu never attempted to prevent the killing of Tutsi in the commune in any way or called for assistance from regional or national authorities to quell the violence. The Accused contends that he did not have the power necessary to prevent the killings from taking place. The Chamber notes that the issue to be addressed is whether he ever attempted to do so. In the light of the evidence, the Chamber considers that it is necessary to distinguish between the period before 18 April 1994, when the key meeting between members of the interim government and the bourgmestres took place in Murambi, in Gitarama, and the period after 18 April 1994. Indeed, on the Prosecution's own case, a marked change in the accused's personality and behaviour took place after 18 April 1994.

184.   There is a substantial amount of evidence establishing that before 18 April 1994 the Accused did attempt to prevent violence from taking place in the commune of Taba. Many witnesses testified to the efforts of the Accused to maintain peace in the commune and that he opposed by force the Interahamwe's attempted incursions into the commune to ensure that the killings which had started in Kigali on 7 April 1994 did not spread to Taba. Witness W testified that on the order of the Accused to the population that they must resist these incursions, members of the Interahamwe were killed. Witness K testified that Taba commune was calm during the period when Akayesu wanted that there be calm. She said he would gather the population in a meeting and tell them that they had to be against the acts of violence in the commune. Witness A testified that when the Interahamwe tried to enter the commune of Taba, the bourgmestre did everything to fight against them, and called on the residents to go to the borders of the commune **[page 91]** to chase them away. The Accused testified that he intervened when refugees from Kigali were being shot at by the Interahamwe. The police returned fire and three Interahamwe were killed. The Accused testified that he confiscated their weapons and their vehicle.

185.   The Accused testified that he asked for three gendarmes at the meeting with the Prime Minister in Gitarama on 18 April 1994, to help him maintain order and security and to stop the killing of Tutsi. The only witnesses to attend the Murambi meeting were prosecution witness R, an MDR bourgmestre in Gitarama prefecture like the accused, and Defence witness DAAX, the former prefect of Gitarama. Witness R recalled three meetings of the bourgmestres in Gitarama prefecture convened by the prefect after 6 April 1994, and in his statement to the Office of the Prosecutor he said that the accused did ask for gendarmes at one of those meetings. When testifying before the Chamber, Witness R did not remember the accused having spoken at the Murambi meeting of 18 April 1994, although in his earlier statement to the Office of the Prosecutor, he stated that the accused had spoken at that meeting. Because of these inconsistencies, Defence counsel submitted a motion requesting the Chamber to consider a prosecution for false testimony, which this Chamber rejected in a Decision of 9 March 1998. As the Chamber stated in that Decision, it did not deem the matter appropriate for an investigation into false testimony, but rather it was a matter for the evaluation of the credibility of the witness in question. In this case, the Chamber considers that, despite discrepancies between Witness R's testimony and his prior statement to the Prosecutor relating to the sequence of the meetings addressed by the accused, if taken in the light most favourable to the accused, it corroborates the accused's account that at some point after 6 April 1994, and in all likelihood at the Murambi meeting of 18 April 1994, the accused asked for gendarmes to assist with the problems of security in his commune. Given the accused's testimony on this point, and its corroboration in part by the sole prosecution witness who was present at the Murambi

meeting, the accused's version of events – that he did call for assistance from the national and regional authorities – must be credited.

186. Moreover, Defence witness DAAX, the former prefect of Gitarama supports the accused's account. Witness DAAX testified that he convened three meetings of bourgmestres **[page 92]** between 6 April 1994 and 18 April 1994 – all of which were attended by the accused – the third meeting being the one which was moved from Gitarama to Murambi at the last minute at the request of the Prime Minister so that the Prime Minister and other Ministers could address the prefect and bourgmestres. At this third meeting, the prefect testified, the accused took the floor and complained of the problems of security in his commune, in common with the Prefect and other bourgmestres. Witness DAAX's testimony agrees with that of the accused that the Prime Minister did not reply directly to the bourgmestre's expressions of concern about security in their Communes, but that he rather read parts of a prepared policy speech and threatened the complaining bourgmestres with dismissal. Witness DAAX further testified that at least one bourgmestre, the bourgmestre of Mugina, was killed shortly after the meeting as a result. Witness DAAX also testified that the accused had to flee his commune due to pressure from the Interahamwe at some point between 6 April 1994 and 18 April 1994, and in any event after the first two meetings referred to above but before the third meeting. Witness DAAX said the Accused never officially requested gendarmes from him, unlike the bourgmestre of Mugina. Witness DAAX lost contact with the Accused after 18 April 1994. The Chamber notes that the Accused does not assert that he requested assistance from the prefect of Gitarama but rather from the Prime Minister, during the course of the meeting.

187. A substantial amount of evidence has been presented indicating that the conduct of the Accused did, however, change significantly after the meeting on 18 April 1994, and many witnesses, including Witnesses E, W, PP, V and G, testified to the collaboration of the Accused with the Interahamwe in Taba after this date. Witness A testified that he was surprised to see that the Accused had become a friend of the Interahamwe. The Accused contends that he was overwhelmed. Witness DAX and Witness DBB, both witnesses for the Defence, testified that the Interahamwe threatened to kill the Accused if he did not cooperate with them. The Accused testified that he was coerced by the Interahamwe and particularly by Silas Kubwimana, the head of the Interahamwe with whom he was seen quite frequently during this time. The Chamber notes that in his pre-trial written statement, the Accused gave a very different account of Silas Kubwimana, describing his mandate in the commune as that of a "peace-maker". **[page 93]**

188. The Chamber recognises the difficulties a bourgmestre encountered in attempting to save lives of Tutsi in the period in question. Prosecution witness R, who was the bourgmestre of another commune, in Gitarama prefecture, testified that there was very little he or other bourgmestres could do to prevent massacres in his commune once killings became widespread after 18 April 1994. He averred that a bourgmestre could do nothing openly to combat the killings after that date or he would risk being killed; what little he could do had to be done clandestinely. The Defence case is that this is precisely what the accused did.

189. Defence witnesses, DAAX, DAX, DCX, DBB and DCC confirm that the accused failed to prevent killings after 18 April 1994 and expressed the opinion that it was not possible for him to do anything with ten communal policemen at his disposal against more than a hundred Interahamwe.

190. The Defence contends that, despite pressure from the Interahamwe, the Accused continued to save lives after 18 April 1994. There is some evidence on this matter, referred to in the section on "the accused's line of Defence".

191. There is also evidence indicating that after 18 April 1994, there were people that came to the Accused for help, and he turned them away, and there is evidence that the Accused witnessed, participated in, supervised, and even ordered killings in Taba. Witness JJ testified that after her arrival at the bureau communal, where she came to seek refuge, she went to the Accused on behalf of a group of refugees, begging him to kill them with bullets so that they would not be hacked to death with machetes. She said he asked his police officers to chase them away and said that even if there were bullets he would not waste them on the refugees.

192.   The Chamber finds that the allegations set forth in paragraph 12 cannot be fully established. The Accused did take action between 7 April and 18 April to protect the citizens of his commune. It appears that he did also request assistance from national authorities at the meeting on 18 April 1994. Accordingly, the Accused did attempt to prevent the killing of Tutsi in his Commune, and it cannot be said that he never did so. **[page 94]**

193.   Nevertheless, the Chamber finds beyond a reasonable doubt that the conduct of the Accused changed after 18 April 1994 and that after this date the Accused did not attempt to prevent the killing of Tutsi in the commune of Taba. In fact, there is evidence that he not only knew of and witnessed killings, but that he participated in and even ordered killings. The fact that on one occasion he helped one Hutu woman protect her Tutsi children does not alter the Chamber's assessment that the Accused did not generally attempt to prevent the killings at all after 18 April. The Accused contends that he was subject to coercion, but the Chamber finds this contention greatly inconsistent with a substantial amount of concordant testimony from other witnesses. It is also inconsistent with his own pre-trial written statement. Witness C testified to having heard the accused say to an Interahamwe "I do not think that what we are doing is proper. We are going to have to pay for this blood that is being shed..", a statement which indicates the Accused's knowledge of the wrongfulness of his acts and his awareness of the consequences of his deeds. For these reasons, the Chamber does not accept the testimony of the Accused regarding his conduct after 18 April, and finds beyond a reasonable doubt that he did not attempt to prevent killings of Tutsi after this date. Whether he had the power to do so is not at issue, as he never even tried and as there is evidence establishing beyond a reasonable doubt that he consciously chose the course of collaboration with violence against Tutsi rather than shielding them from it.

5.2.2. Paragraph 13 of the Indictment

Alleged facts:

194.   Paragraph 13 of the Indictment is worded as follows:

> "On or about 19 April 1994, before dawn, in Gishyeshye sector, Taba commune, a group of men, one of whom was named François Ndimubanzi, killed a local teacher, Sylvère Karera, because he was accused of associating with the Rwandan **[page 95]** Patriotic Front ("RPF") and plotting to kill Hutu. Even though at least one of the perpetrators was turned over to **Jean-Paul Akayesu**, he failed to take measures to have him arrested".

195.   It is alleged that, by the acts with which he is charged in this paragraph, Akayesu is guilty of the offences which form the subject of three counts:

- Count 1 of the Indictment charges him with the crime of genocide, punishable under Article 2(3)(a) of the Statute;
- Count 2 charges him with the crime of complicity in genocide, punishable under Article 2(3)(e) of the Statute; and
- Count 3 charges him with the crime of extermination which is a Crime against Humanity, punishable under Article 3(b) of the Statute.

196.   In order to prove the acts alleged against Akayesu under paragraph 13 of the Indictment, it is necessary to first establish that Sylvère Karera, a teacher, was killed in the Gishyeshye sector, Taba commune, on 19 April 1994, before dawn, by a group of men, one of whom was named François Ndimubanzi and that he was killed because he was accused of associating with the RPF and plotting to kill Hutu. The Chamber must then be satisfied that at least one of the perpetrators of this killing was indeed turned over to Jean-Paul Akayesu, and that he failed to take measures to have him arrested.

With regard to the killing of Sylvère Karera in the Gishyeshye sector, Taba commune, on or about 19 April 1994, before dawn:

197.   Several Prosecution witnesses, particularly, those who appeared under the pseudonyms A, W, E and U, as well as Ephrem Karangwa, provided information on the killing of teacher Sylvère Karera in the night of 18 to 19 April 1994.

198.   Witness A, a Hutu man, testified that, during the night of 18 to 19 April 1994, he heard **[page 96]** people shouting that thieves had killed people at Remera school and calling on the population to stop them. Witness A affirmed that, on 19 April 1994, he had gone to Remara school. There he learnt from the headmaster that the prefect of studies, who turned out be Sylvère Karera, had been killed. The witness saw the body of the teacher before it was covered with a pink sheet at the request of the headmaster.

199.   Ephrem Karangwa, a Tutsi man, called by the Prosecutor as a witness who, at the material time, performed the functions of Inspecteur de police judiciaire of the Taba commune, stated before the Chamber that Sylvère Karera, a teacher at the Remera Rukoma school complex, was killed in the night of 18 to 19 April 1994 by members of the Interahamwe.

200.   Witness W, a Tutsi, who resided in Taba, where he worked as a teacher, testified that on returning from night patrols in which he had participated during the night of 18 to 19 April 1994, he learnt that the prefect of studies at the public school, Rukoma, had just been killed.

201.   Questioned on the death of Sylvère Karera, witness E stated that he had gone, in the night of 18 to 19 April 1994, to the entrance of Remera school. He did not directly see Karera's body, but had heard that the body was in the school premises. No one stopped him from entering the school, but he had preferred to go to the place from where the noise came which had brought him out if his home.

202.   Prosecution witness U also heard that a teacher, named Karera, had been killed. She stated that throughout the night, she had heard people shouting in the streets and announcing, particularly, that Karera had been killed.

203.   The Defence has never disputed the killing of Sylvère Karera in the night of 18 to 19 April 1994. The accused has himself confirmed, during his appearance as witness before the Chamber, that the teacher Sylvère Karera had been killed in the night of 18 to 19 April 1994.

Concerning the allegation that Sylvère Karera was killed by a group of men, one of whom [page 97] was named François Ndimubanzi, and that he was killed because he was accused of associating with the RPF and plotting to kill Hutu:

204.   The Chamber notes that though the Indictment alleges that Sylvère Karera was killed by a group of men, one of whom was named François Ndimubanzi, the Prosecutor has adduced no evidence to show number and identity of the perpetrators of the killing.

205.   As for the reasons alleged by the Prosecutor for the killing of Sylvère Karera, that is, associating with the RPF and plotting to kill Hutu, the Defence stated, in its concluding arguments, that they should be dismissed on the ground that Sylvère Karera was, according to the Defence, Hutu and that the Prosecutor's allegations that this teacher was killed because he was accused of plotting to kill Hutu were therefore without merit.

Concerning the allegation that at least one of the perpetrators of the killing of Sylvère Karera was turned over to Jean-Paul Akayesu and that he failed to take measures to have him arrested:

206.   Though the Indictment alleges that at least one of the perpetrators of the killing of Sylvère Karera was turned over to Akayesu, the Prosecutor has adduced no evidence to support this allegation.

207.   Witness E stated that, in the night of 18 to 19 April 1994, after going to the school entrance where Sylvère Karera had been killed, he went to the place from where came the noise which had brought him

out of his home. At Gishyeshye, from where came the noise, near a roadblock, he saw the body of another person who had been killed. A crowd gathered. It was said that teacher Karera was killed and that the remains near the roadblock were those of the Interahamwe who had just killed Karera. Apart from that dead Interahamwe, no other person was held responsible for killing Karera. Witness E specified that he had heard that Sylvère Karera had been killed by that Interahamwe alone. **[page 98]**

208. The witness called by the Prosecutor under the pseudonym Z, a Tutsi man, stated that, on or about 19 April 1994, in the early hours of the day following the killing of a Tutsi teacher in Remara and that of his murderer, who was killed by persons in charge of maintaining security, he and other persons stood near the body of the teacher's murderer. Akayesu, who was armed, separated members of the Interahamwe from the population. According to witness Z, Akayesu, in referring to the body on the spot, reportedly deplored the killing of this person.

209. Prosecution witness A testified that, in the night of 18 to 19 April 1994, an Interahamwe was killed. No investigation was conducted. He was simply buried immediately.

210. Prosecution witness U stated that some men told him, on 19 April 1994, that a person had been killed and that Akayesu had gone to where the body was and held a meeting there.

211. Several other witnesses indicated to the Chamber that a crowd had formed early in the morning of 19 April 1994, in Gishyeshye, around the body of a young member of the Interahamwe. That meeting is at the root of the allegations brought by the Prosecutor against Akayesu under paragraphs 14 and 15 of the Indictment. The factual findings of the Chamber on the holding of the said meeting are elaborated upon below.

212. The Prosecutor accepted this version of facts in her concluding arguments. She had then told the Chamber that, following the killing of the Tutsi teacher, Sylvère Karera, in the middle of the night of 18 to 19 April 1994, in Remera, by some members of the Interahamwe, the people of the commune had gone out into the streets to find out what was happening, wondering why a teacher had been killed. Later, according to the Prosecutor's statement, they caught one member of the Interahamwe in Gishyeshye and killed him.

213. In her concluding arguments, the Prosecutor did not mention any fact designed to show that one of the possible killers of Sylvère Karera was turned over to Jean-Paul Akayesu alive, contrary to what is alleged in paragraph 13 of the Indictment. **[page 99]**

214. During cross-examination of the accused appearing as witness in his own trial, the Prosecutor had him confirm that Sylvère Karera was killed in the night of 18 to 19 April 1994 and that later, one member of the Interahamwe, the person who had killed Karera, was also killed. The Prosecutor added that Prosecution witnesses had indeed testified to that.

215. During his appearance before the Chamber as witness, the accused argued that during the night of 18 to 19 April 1994, he was sleeping in the *Bureau Communal*, when towards 4 a.m., a certain Augustin Sebazungu, MDR treasurer at Taba, residing in the Gishyeshye sector, came to inform him that the situation in the sector was tense, following the killing of a young man, a member of the Interahamwe. The *Bourgmestre* then immediately alerted the police and went to the scene, accompanied by two policemen. There he found a body stretched out on the ground, covered with traces of blood, as if it had been hit. The accused affirmed before the Chamber that he seized the opportunity of this gathering which formed as people came to see what was happening, to address the population. He noted that members of the region's Interahamwe had rushed and surrounded the body of their young member. Akayesu told the Chamber that he had condemned the killing of the young man because he felt that it was not in that manner that law and order would be maintained, and that he had indicated that his arrest would simply have been enough.

Factual findings

216.   Prosecution witnesses appearing under the pseudonyms A, W, E and U, as well as Ephrem Karangwa, provided information which confirmed the Prosecutor's allegations as to the killing of teacher Sylvère Karera in the night of 18 to 19 April 1994. On the basis of such corroborative evidence, which was not substantially disputed by the Defence, the Chamber is satisfied that Sylvère Karera was actually killed, in Gishyeshye, in the night of 18 to 19 April 1994.

217.   The Chamber notes however that the Prosecutor has not adduced conclusive evidence to support her allegations relating to the number and identity of the perpetrators of the killing of **[page 100]** Sylvère Karera as well as the reasons for this murder.

218.   With regard to the allegation that at least one of the perpetrators of the killing of Sylvère Karera had been turned over to Jean-Paul Akayesu and that he failed to take any measures to have him arrested, for the reasons explained above and in the absence of pertinent evidence, the Chamber finds that the Prosecutor has not established beyond reasonable doubt that at least one of the perpetrators of the killing of Sylvère Karera was turned over alive to Akayesu, and that he failed to take any measures to have him arrested.

5.2.3. Paragraph 18 of the Indictment

219.   Paragraph 18 of the Indictment reads as follows:

> 18.   On or about April 19, 1994, the men who, on **Jean Paul AKAYESU**'s instructions, were searching for Ephrem Karangwa destroyed Ephrem Karangwa's house and burned down his mother's house. They then went to search the house of Ephrem Karangwa's brother-in-law in Musambira commune and found Ephrem Karangwa's three brothers there. The three brothers – Simon Mutijima, Thaddée Uwanyiligira and Jean Chrysostome Gakuba – tried to escape, but **Jean Paul AKAYESU** blew his whistle to alert local residents to the attempted escape and ordered the people to capture the brothers. After the brothers were captured, **Jean Paul AKAYESU** ordered and participated in the killing of the three brothers.

Events alleged

Testimony Of Ephrem Karangwa (witness d) [page 101]

220.   Ephrem Karangwa was assigned the pseudonym D and placed under the Tribunal's Witness Protection Unit, pursuant to an order of 26 September 1996, but he waived witness protection and elected to testify under his own name.

221.   Karangwa testified that he resided in Taba and in April 1994 he was the Inspecteur de Police Judiciaire (IPJ) in the Ministry of Justice for the Prosecutor in Taba commune having taken office in August 1984. As IPJ he investigated criminal complaints and transmitted case files to the Prosecutor. The witness's office was situated in the bureau communal in Taba. The witness testified that the head of any commune was the bourgmestre. The Accused who was the bourgmestre of Taba during the events of April 1994. The witness had known the Accused for about twenty years. The witness did not belong to any political party and he was not allowed to do so by the Minister of Justice. He testified that there was never any tension between him and the Accused and they had a good working relationship.

222.   Karangwa testified that in his role as IPJ he became aware that there were problems of a political nature between the political parties in Taba, especially the MDR and the MRND. The MDR had a greater following in Taba and this party was led by the Accused. On one occasion in 1992 there was a demonstration by the MDR which led to violence when the demonstrators tried to forcibly enter the bureau communal. The MDR wanted the bourgmestre at that time removed from office. The matter was investigated by the witness and referred to the Prosecutor for prosecution. The witness did not have any knowledge of the eventual out come of this matter, at the time of testifying. The witness said that he

knew of Silas Kubwimana and that he often complained about the Accused and the MDR officials. He said that there existed a file on this complaint at the Prosecutor's office. The witness said that he had become aware of the existence of this file in his official capacity as IPJ.

223. Karangwa testified that on the morning of 7 April 1994, while preparing to go to work he heard an announcement on the radio that the President had been killed. He also heard an announcement calling on people to remain wherever they ware and he therefore decided not to go to work. **[page 102]**

224. Karangwa testified that he had spoken to many people about the security situation in Taba. On 14 April 1994, he saw a blue Toyota Minibus pass him. He was informed that this motor vehicle and a white "pick up" were confiscated from the Interahamwe by the people of Kamembe. He was further informed that a police officer was killed and an Interahamwe wounded in this process.

225. Karangwa testified that on the night of 18 April 1994 he was outside his house because he had heard that Tutsi in Runda commune were being killed and since he was a tutsi he was afraid. He stated that Runda and Taba were neighbouring communes. At approximately 1 am on 19 April 1994, a person came to the witness's house and informed him that he had just attended a meeting led by the Accused where plans were being made to kill the witness and to commence killings in Taba in a similar manner to killings that were happening in Runda. This person advised the witness to flee with his family. The witness and his family hid on a hill and at dawn the witness's sisters, mother and wife went on foot to his wife's sisters house in Musambira and he and his brothers stayed behind because they wanted to verify the information that had been given to him. The witness said that he wondered why someone would want to kill him and his family, since they had no problem with anyone.

226. Karangwe testified that from his hiding place on the hill, he could see his house on the opposite hill about 150 metres away. The witness stated that he saw three vehicles drive up to his house between the hours of eight and nine o'clock in the morning. The Accused came in a blue Toyota mini bus, the one that the people had taken away from the Interahamwe. The witness was uncertain as to whether the Accused was driving the blue Toyota Hiace minibus. The witness described the other two vehicles as a white Toyota and a red Toyota. The witness could not see what the Accused had in his hands, but he did see the Accused wearing a military jacket. The Accused and the other people alighted from the motor vehicles and went down to the witness's house. The witness's dogs barked and someone in this group of people fired a round from a firearm and the dogs ran away. The witness stated that he saw this group of people then destroy his house and his mother's house. The witness stated that the houses were looted and burnt. The **[page 103]** witness identified prosecution exhibits 50 and 51 as being photographs of the remains of these houses.

227. Karangwa testified that this event confirmed the information that he had received and he then decided to join his family in Musambira. He arrived at Musambira at about 3 o'clock in the afternoon. He saw his family at the house of his brother in law, Laurent Kamondo and they immediately left for Kabgayi, whilst he awaited the arrival of his younger brothers. He stated that he could not stay in the house because he was afraid that the Accused would look for him there. Instead, he hid in an eucalyptus bush on the side of a hill approximately eighty metres from the house.

228. Karangwa testified that he saw two motor vehicles, a blue Toyota Hiace minibus and a red Toyota Hilux approach the house. These vehicles stopped approximately twenty five metres away from the house. This was the same minibus that was taken away from the Interahamwe and the Accused was using it at that time. Many people alighted from the vehicles and walked towards Laurent Kamondo's house. The witness recognised some of these people as the bourgmestre of Musambira, the Accused, a police officer named Emanuel Mushumba from the Taba commune, Mutiji Masivere, Winima Boniface and Munir Yarangaclaude who was the secretary of the MDR party in the commune of Taba (phonetic spelling). The Accused was wearing a military jacket and he had a gun in his hand.

229. Karangwa testified that he heard shouts and whistles as this group of people approached Laurent Kamondo's house. He saw people running and, thereafter, he saw his younger brothers in the court yard with these people. The witness stated that it was then that he realised that his brothers were in Musambira. The witness continued to hear shouts from these people and then he heard the Accused say

that his brothers must be shot. The witness heard gun shots and concluded that his brothers were killed and that the Accused had fired the gun. When asked by the Prosecutor whether he saw the gun that was used to kill his brothers, the witness replied that he saw the Accused carrying a gun when he arrived and that he heard the shots. **[page 104]**

230.   Karangwa testified that after the killing of his brothers, he fled to Kabgayi, and on arrival at the cathedral, the witness stated that he saw the Accused in a "pick up" drive up to the cathedral. The Accused was in the company of two police officers from the Taba commune named Emanuel Mushumba (phonetic spelling) and Ooli Musakarani (phonetic spelling) and a group of people. The witness said that he saw the Accused and these other people alight from the vehicle and look around the courtyard of the cathedral but they did not go inside. They then got back into the motor vehicle and left. The witness was informed by Witness V that the Accused was making enquiries about his whereabouts and he was advised to hide. The witness stayed in the seminary until the end of the war.

231.   Karangwa testified that he was not able to leave the seminary but that he heard from many people that the Accused was outside the seminary on many occasions. The Accused was able to come into the compound of the seminary from 30 May 1994. The witness recalled that he remembered that day clearly, because it was on that day that the Accused came to take him away, and he was saved by someone.

232.   Karangwa testified that he stayed in Kabgayi from 21 April 1994 to 2 June 1994. At the beginning of 1995 the witness went to work as IPJ in the public prosecutor's office in Gitarama and on 3 January 1996 became the bourgmestre of Taba. The witness said that at that time Tutsi were killed and the only reason the Accused looked for him was because he had worked in the commune and he was Tutsi.

233.   In response to a question from the bench, Karangwa stated that the fact that the Accused was present made him responsible for the death of his brothers. When asked for clarification as to whether the Accused ordered the shooting, the witness reaffirmed that the Accused ordered their shooting.

234.   Under cross examination, Karangwa testified that he had a very good working relationship with the Accused. The witness stated that the Accused dealt with civil disputes and he referred all criminal matters to the witness. The witness stated that he was generally invited **[page 105]** to meetings pertaining to security in Taba. He testified that he saw the Accused between 6 and 10 April 1994 in Kamembe. The Accused was there assessing the security situation, since there was an influx of people that were fleeing Kigali. The Accused sent commune police officers to ensure the security of these people. The Accused at this stage was opposed to any killing.

235.   In clarification of an averment in his written statement made to the Office of the Prosecutor (exhibit 105), the witness testified that the Accused held meetings on 18 and 19 April 1994 with a view to planning the genocide. The witness stated that he had not attended any of these meetings but he heard of them. The witness stated that at these meetings a decision was taken that the MDR and the MRND should not fight the Interahamwe and the CDR but they should fight the tutsi. This decision according to the witness, was taken at communal level by the bourgmestre. Although the bourgmestre belonged to the MDR all the political parties at communal level were under his authority. The witness did not go to work from 7 April 1994. The witness stated that he knew that there were major security problems in the commune and expressed the view that if the bourgmestre believed that the witness was competent to resolve these problems, the bourgmestre would have provided the witness with transport to go to work.

236.   The witness acknowledged the fact that the Accused fought against the Interahamwe after 6 April 1994 and went on to say that if the Accused had not done so the killing in Taba would have started much earlier. The Defence Counsel pointed out that in his written statement to the Office of the Prosecutor, the witness stated that he was about a kilometre away from his house when he saw the Accused come to his house with a group of people. The witness denied this and reaffirmed his testimony that he was 150 metres away from his house, on the opposite hill. According to the witness, he was able to identify the Accused by the way that he walked and the clothes that he was wearing. The witness could also hear what was spoken by the Accused and the group of people when they were at his house, although he was 150 metres away. The witness identified the people with the Accused as assistant bourgmestre Civil Mootijima (phonetic spelling), assistant bourgmestre Wimina Boniface (phonetic spelling), manager of a

popular bank Aloyce Kubunda (phonetic spelling), businessman Daniel Gasiba (phonetic spelling) and some communal police officers. **[page 106]**

237.   Karangwa testified under cross-examination, that when the Accused arrived at Laurent Kamondo's house at Musambira he immediately searched the house and found his three brothers. The Accused then killed the witness's three brothers by shooting them. The Defence Counsel pointed out that, in his written statement, the witness has stated that the Accused killed his brother, Jean Kististan (phonetic spelling), by shooting him and when his other two brothers tried to escape they were attacked and killed with machetes by the men who were with the Accused. The Defence Counsel requested an explanation from the witness in respect of this discrepancy. The witness denied that he stated this and maintained that all three of his brothers were shot.

238.   Karangwa testified under cross-examination, that he left Musambira immediately after his brothers were killed and when he was asked whether he buried is brothers, his response was that he did not have the time to do so. The Defence Counsel pointed out that the witness had stated in his written statement that he had buried his brothers near the house of Laurent Kamondo and requested the witness to explain this discrepancy. The witness denied this and maintained that his brothers were buried by Laurent Kamondo.

Testimony of Witness S

239.   Witness S testified that he is a Hutu farmer. In April 1994, he lived in the commune of Musambira. There was safety and security in Musumbira even after 6 April 1994 when the President's plane had crashed but this had changed on 19 April 1994. Witness S was in his house on 19 April 1994. In the morning of the same day, between 9am and 10 am, Ephrem Karangwa's wife, sisters and mother went to Witness S's home. Witness S spoke to these people on their arrival and they had informed him that killings had begun in the Taba commune and many people were leaving their homes and fleeing.

240.   Witness S testified that Ephrem Karangwa arrived at his home between 11 am and 12 noon on the same day. On his arrival, his wife, mother and sisters immediately left for Kabgayi. **[page 107]** Witness S spoke to Ephrem Karangwa who also informed him that killings had began in Taba. Witness S stepped out of his house and he stated that when he looked in the direction of Taba he could see columns of smoke. Witness S stated that Karangwa left saying that he was waiting for his brothers and on their arrival they would set off for Kabgayi to join the rest of their family.

241.   Witness S testified that Ephrem Karangwa's three brothers arrived at his house between 4 and 5 o'clock in the afternoon of 19 April 1994. The three brothers went into the witness's home and asked for their mother and sisters. Witness S informed them that they had already left. He also informed them that Ephrem Karangwa was waiting for them but that he did not know where. The witness said that the three brothers were wearing civilian clothes and they did not have any weapons in their possession. The three brothers together with Witness S went into the house. Whilst in the house, the witness heard the sound of cars. The three brothers went behind the house. Witness S went into the front court yard and he saw the motor vehicle that belonged to the commune of Musumbira. The witness described this motor vehicle as a red dual cab Hilux "pickup". Witness S then saw the bourgmestre of Musumbira, Justin Nyangwe and the assistant bourgmestre, Martin Kalisa, on the path that led to his house. He also saw the Accused with the assistant bourgmestre of Taba and a few police officers. Witness S did not know all the police officers that were in the group but he recognised them as police officers by the fact that they were wearing police uniforms and they were in possession of firearms. The witness recognised two of these police officers as being from the commune of Musambira. He did not know or recognise the other people in the group. These people were wearing civilian clothes.

242.   Witness S testified that he had known the Accused before the events of April 1994. When the witness visited Ephrem Karangwa at his office in the bureau communal, he often saw the Accused. According to Witness S, the Accused was wearing a long military jacket and he had a grenade in his hand. Witness S's father was also in the group of people that came to his house and the witness noticed

that his father was injured in his face and he was bleeding. By this time this group of people had arrived and were standing about three metres away from the house. Witness S's father said to him if Ephrem Karangwa was in the house he should hand him over **[page 108]** or else they will be killed by this group of people. The Accused at this time was standing next to the bourgmestre of Musambira. The bourgmestre of Musambira asked Witness S if Ephrem Karangwa was in the house. According to the witness he responded by saying that he was not in the house and invited the bourgmestre to search the house if he so wished. The assistant bourgmestre of Musumbira, Martin Kalisa, together with two police officers from Taba searched the house. Witness S was not allowed into the house whilst the search was being conducted and he stood outside. The Accused during this search ordered the police officers to surround the house, to prevent Ephrem Karangwa from running away. By this time many people from the general population of Musambira had gathered to see what was going on and they also acted on the Accused's instruction and surrounded the house.

243.   Witness S testified that the people searching the house did not find Ephrem Karangwa. Instead they came out with some cans of sardines and Accused the witness and his family of being "Inyenzi". At this time Ephrem Karangwa's brothers were behind the house with the witness's sister. The witness said he did not see this but he was informed by his sister that the brothers fled. The police officers blew their whistles and said stop these "Inyenzi" from running away and a group of people pursued the three brothers.

244.   Witness S testified that he heard people shouting "...stop that Inyenzi..." About ten minutes later, the mob of people returned with the three Karangwa brothers. According to Witness S, they had been beaten and although he did not see the beatings he saw the injuries sustained as a result of the beating. The brothers had certain open wounds that were bleeding and their clothes were torn. The three brothers were made to sit on the lawn about two metres from the entrance to the court yard, in the presence of the Accused. The bourgmestre of Musambira, Justin Nyangwe asked the Accused if he knew these three brothers. The Accused replied that they were from his commune. Justin Nyangwe then asked the Accused what must be done with them and the Accused responded by saying "we need to finish these people off..." and he confirmed this response by saying, they need to be shot. The police officers from Musambira made the three brothers lie on their stomachs. There was a crowd of people that had now gathered and they were asked to step back. All three brothers were shot at close range behind their heads, by two police **[page 109]** officers from Musambira. Monzatina (phonetic spelling) shot two of the brothers and Albert shot one of the brothers.

245.   Witness S testified that he and his family were told by Justin Nyangwe, the bourgmestre of Musambira, to get into the commune motor vehicle. Whilst they were being taken, Witness S heard people say that they were going to destroy his home because he and his family were "Inyenzi". The Accused and a group of people got into their motor vehicle and drove in the direction of Taba. The motor vehicle that Witness S was in started to move first and as it passed the motor vehicle of the Accused, the witness could see a person tied in the Accused's motor vehicle. Witness S and his family were taken to the bureau communal of Musambira where they were detained. He later managed to escape, but his three sisters were killed.

246.   Under cross-examination, Witness S testified that he met the Accused when he went to the bureau communal in Taba to visit Ephrem Karangwa who worked as an IPJ in the commune. He often visited Ephrem Karangwa at the bureau communal. Witness S also met the assistant bourgmestre of Taba, although he did not know his name.

247.   Witness S testified that before the Accused came to his house he went to his grand father's house and that was where he found Witness S's father. On arrival at Witness S's house, the Accused parked his motor vehicle on the tarred road and the bourgmestre of Musumbira parked his motor vehicle outside Witness S's house. Witness S was sitting inside his house at this time and he heard the sound of the engine of this motor vehicle the bourgmestre of Musambira travelled in, which was approximately 25 metres away from the house. The motor vehicle the Accused travelled in was approximately three to four hundred metres away on the tarred road. Witness S reiterated that he did not hear the sound of the engine of the Accused's motor vehicle but rather that of the motor vehicle the bourgmestre of Musumbira

travelled in. Witness S realised that the Accused was looking for Ephrem Karangwa when the bourgmestre of Musumbira asked if Ephrem Karangwa was there and also when his father asked him to hand over Ephrem Karangwa to the Accused if he was in the house. **[page 110]**

248. Under cross-examination Witness S confirmed that he had made a statement to the Prosecutor of Gitarama. This statement was tendered into evidence by the Defence as part of exhibit 104. Witness S stated that this statement did not pertain to the Accused but rather to the former bourgmestre of Musumbira, who was now in prison as a result of his conduct as mentioned in this statement. Witness S stated that he was asked specific questions about the bourgmestre of Musumbira. The Defence Counsel pointed out to Witness S that this statement mentioned that the Accused was with Kalisa Martin, the bourgmestre of Musambira and Justin Nyandwi. Witness S recalled that he had mentioned the Accused's involvement in respect of the killing of the Karangwa brothers to the Prosecutor of Gitarama but this was omitted from this statement.

249. Witness S testified under cross-examination that he saw the Accused with a grenade in his hand. He recognised this item in the Accused's hand as being a grenade because he saw soldiers with it before the war. Defence Counsel pointed out to Witness S that in his statement to the investigators at the Office of the Prosecutor he stated that the Accused came to his house with a gun and a grenade, whilst in his evidence in chief before the Chamber the witness testified that the Accused only had a grenade. Witness S denied making this statement to the investigators and maintained that he had only seen the Accused with a grenade.

250. Witness S testified that police officers in Musambira normally used whistles to indicate that the market was closing. Whistles were also used when there was a security problem in the region. He stated that the Karangwa brothers were chased by the people because at that time there was a search of homes for hidden people. The Police Officers blew whistles and shouted "catch these Inyenzi, don't let them get away". The people immediately chased after the Karangwa brothers. The witness stated that the people acted in this manner because it was an order from the authorities. The people generally followed orders given by the authorities even if the order leads to any wrongful conduct. Defence Counsel pointed out that the Karangwa brothers were not armed and they did not pose any threat to the people of Musambira and despite this they were assaulted by the mob of people chasing them, even though they were not ordered to do so. This illustrated that the people committed wrongful acts even if they were not ordered **[page 111]** to do so. Witness S did not tender an explanation in response to this issue raised by Defence Counsel.

The Testimony of Witness DAX

251. Witness DAX testified on behalf of the Defence. He stated that he knew Ephrem Karangwa and they are friends. He also knew Ephrem Karangwa's family. He stated that he did not hear anybody say that Ephrem Karangwa was to be killed or that someone was attempting to kill Ephrem Karangwa. Witness DAX testified that he had heard of the destruction of Ephrem Karangwa's house and the killing of his brothers. The witness had heard that Ephrem Karangwa's brothers were making their way to Kabgayi when they were killed in Kivumu in the Nyakabunda Commune (phonetic spelling). The witness stated that the Interahamwe were responsible for the deaths of the Karangwa brothers. The witness stated that he had since met Ephrem Karangwa several times in Kigali and although they did not discuss the details of his brothers death, the witness offered his condolences to Ephrem Karangwa.

252. Witness DAX testified that on 19 April 1994, Ephrem Karangwa's house was destroyed by neighbours. He stated that in a poor country like Rwanda it is difficult for a rich person to stay with poor neighbours. It was the Abaghi family, more specifically a person called Gahibi who destroyed the Karangwa house. A person named Gasimba Daniels, who was an enemy of Ephrem Karanga also participated in destroying the Karangwa house. Gasimba Daniels had purchased and distributed the petrol to the neighbours of Ephrem Karangwa, for the purpose of destroying Ephrem Karangwa's house. This petrol was used to set Ephrem Karangwa's house on fire. A certain person known as Usuri (phonetic spelling) also participated in destroying Ephrem Karangwa's house. The witness stated that he knew all

the people responsible for the destruction of Ephrem Karangwa's house and the Accused was not involved.

253. Witness DAX admitted under cross-examination that he did not see Ephrem Karangwa's house being destroyed but he had spoken to the people responsible for such destruction immediately after the house was set on fire. He observed that they were carrying doors that they **[page 112]** had removed from Ephrem Karangwa's house and they were boasting about their actions.

The Testimony of the Accused

254. The Accused testified that on 19 April 1994 at about 4 o'clock in the afternoon, he went to Musambira. He stated that the bourgmestre of Musambira promised to give him some fabric that he had intended to use to make a uniform for the new police officer he had employed. The Accused also stated that on 20 April 1994 he went to Kabgayi. He said that his reason for going to Kabyagi was to see one Kayibanda Alfred to ask him for shelter because he thought about fleeing. The Accused said that he saw Ephrem Karangwa's sister at Kabgayi. She greeted the Accused and he did the same. The Accused said that when he saw Karangwa's sister he realised that Karangwa was in Kabgayi. The Accused said that Karangwa abandoned him during the events of April 1994. He stated that he had written to Karangwa on two ocasions during the events of April 1994 and Karangwa had failed to respond. The Accused also stated that during the events of 1994 he saw Karangwa at Kamonyi. On this occasion he had spoken to Karangwa and asked Karangwa why he had abandoned him. That was all the Accused said in his testimony that was relevant to the allegations in paragraph 18 of the Indictment.

Factual Findings

255. The Chamber finds that on 19 April 1994, the Accused was searching for Ephrem Karangwa. At approximately 1 am, on that day, Karangwa received a report that at a meeting led by the Accused, plans were made to kill him and other Tutsi. Karangwa's evidence that the Accused was in pursuit of him and his family, is corroborated by many witnesses. Witnesses V, E and Z ware present at the meeting in the morning of 19 April 1994 at Gishyeshye, addressed by the Accused, when Karangwa's name was mentioned as being on a list of people to be killed; and the Accused named the IPJ as working with the RPF and told the people to look for him. Witness V reported this meeting to Karangwa, later in Kabgayi. Witness V saw the Accused in Kabgayi twice and on one of these times, on 20 April 1994, the Accused asked him to find Karangwa and bring Karangwa to him. Witness K, in the morning of 19 April 1994, saw the **[page 113]** Accused get into his vehicle at the Bureau Communal and instruct others to also get in so that Ephrem Karangwa would not escape them. Witness KK also heard the Accused refer to Tutsi and Ephrem Karangwa and say, "we now have to hunt them and kill all of them". Defence witness DCC confirmed under cross-examination that the Accused had wasted no time in pursuing Ephrem Karangwa.

256. Karangwa and his family left their house and went into hiding. His sisters, mother and wife went to his wife's sister's house in Musambira and he and his brothers hid on a hill opposite his house. Karangwa saw the Accused arrive at his house on the morning of 19 April 1994 in a blue Toyota Hiace mini bus, accompanied by men in two other Toyota vehicles, one red and the other white. The Accused was wearing a military jacket. A gun was fired which frightened the dogs away. The houses of Karangwa and his mother were burnt and looted. The Accused and the group of people then left. The fact that the Accused was wearing a military jacket during this time is corroborated by other witnesses. Witness S saw him in that military jacket later that day; Witness V saw him at Kabgayi on 20 April 1994 in the military uniform of the Rwandan army; defence Witness DAAX saw the Accused in a military jacket and warned him against it's use. Defence witness DFX confirmed that the Accused wore a soldier's shirt. The Accused testified that he wore a military jacket in May, given to him by a colonel of the Rwandan army.

257. Karangwa hid on a hill approximately 80 metres from the house of witness S in Musambira, to await his brothers. The Accused, together with the bourgmestre of Musambira, a police officer named Emanuel Musumba and others arrived in two motor vehicles that were blue and red in colour. Karangwa

heard shouts and whistles, and thereafter saw his brothers in the courtyard with these people. He heard the Accused say that his brothers must be shot and he heard gun-shots. His three brothers whom he names in his written statement to the prosecutor as; Simon Mutijima, Thadée Uwanyiligira, and Jean Chrysostome were shot dead.

258. Karangwa fled to Kabgayi where the Accused continued to look for him. Witness V told Karangwa that the Accused was looking for him in Kabgayi and he himself saw the Accused on [page 114] two occasions and evaded arrest. Karangwa remained in Kabgayi from 21 April to 21 June 1994. In cross-examination the witness denied various statements attributed to him in his written statement to the prosecutor and adhered to his testimony before the Chamber. He re-affirmed that he had not seen the shooting of his brothers but heard the Accused give the order that they be shot, and the fact that he was there made him responsible for their deaths.

259. The Defence Counsel submitted that because of the uncertainties and inconsistencies in the evidence before the Chamber on how the Karangwa brothers were killed and more specifically what weapons were used, material averments in respect of this allegation were not proved.

260. The Defence Counsel cross-examined Karangwa on the discrepancy between his evidence that his brothers were shot and his prior statement to the Office of the Prosecutor that two of his brothers died from injuries sustained from machete blows. Karangwa denied stating this to the Office of the Prosecutor and reaffirmed his testimony that all three of his brothers were shot. This explanation was not subjected to further cross-examination by Defence Counsel.

261. As noted else where, the Chamber places greater reliance on direct testimony rather than untested prior statements made under variable circumstances. The Chamber accepts Karangwa's explanation for the inconsistent prior statement and notes that his evidence that his brothers died of injuries inflicted by gun shots is consistent throughout his testimony and is corroborated by the testimony of witness S.

262. The Chamber finds that Karangwa gave a truthful account of events actually witnessed by him and that he did so without exaggeration or hostility. The Chamber is satisfied that the witness could reasonably have seen and heard the matters to which he testified. Witness S confirmed Karangwa's evidence in all material respects. Karangwa's three brothers came to Witness S's house on the afternoon of 19 April 1994. They were not armed and wore civilian clothes. They heard vehicles and the brothers hid behind the house. A red Hilux "pick-up" belonging to the commune of Musambira was outside his house. A group of people came to his [page 115] house; among them was the bourgmestre and assistant bourgmestre of Musambira, the Accused, whom he knew as the bourgmestre of Taba, the assistant bourgmestre of Taba, men in police uniforms carrying firearms, two of whom he knew as police from Musambira, and civilians.

263. The Accused held a grenade in his hand. The Chamber notes that this is in contradiction to Karangwa's observation that the Accused carried a gun. While it is clear from both their testimony that the Accused held a weapon in his hand, Witness S's identification thereof is more reliable, as he was in close proximity to the Accused in the courtyard of his house.

264. Witness S's house was searched by the assistant bourgmestre of Musambira and two policemen from Taba. During the search, the Accused ordered the police to surround the house to prevent Karangwa escaping. People from Musambira also acted on this instruction.

265. The brothers of Karangwa tried to flee, and the police officers blew their whistles and said stop those "Inyenzi" from running away. A mob of people took up the call, chased after the brothers and brought them back. The brothers were bleeding from open wounds and their clothing was torn. They were made to sit on the ground about 2 metres from the entrance to the courtyard. The bourgmestre of Musambira asked the Accused if he knew the men and what should be done with them. The Accused said they came from his commune and said we need to finish these people off-they need to be shot. All three brothers were then shot dead at close range in the back of their heads by two policemen from Musambira, in the Accused's presence.

266. After the killing, the Accused and his group drove off in the direction of Taba. Witness S saw a person tied up in the Accused's vehicle. Witness S and his family were detained at the bureau communal in Musambira, from where he later escaped. In cross-examination, the witness confirmed his direct testimony and he explained that he had omitted to give an account of the Accused's's involvement, in his statement to the prosecutor of Gitarama because he was asked specific questions related to the bourgmestre of Musambira. The chamber finds this to be a reasonable explanation and accepts the direct, eye-witness testimony of Witness S on these events and rejects the hearsay evidence of defence witness DXX. [page 116]

267. The Accused confirmed his presence in Musambira on the afternoon of 19 April 1994 and in Kabgayi on 20 April 1994, but offered explanations for his appearance that are beyond belief, in the light of overwhelming testimony to the effect that he was at that time in hot pursuit of Karangwa. The defence did not specifically address allegations, and failed to challenge the evidence of witnesses S, Karangwa and others on material issues, such as his hunt for Karangwa, orders to look for Karangwa and other tutsi to be killed, his presence at the houses of Karangwa and witness S, his carrying of a grenade and his participation in the killing of the Karangwa's brothers by ordering their deaths and being present when they were killed.

268. The Chamber has not found any evidence that the Accused blew the whistle to alert local residents to the attempted escape of the brothers but finds as proven beyond a reasonable doubt that the Accused was present at both houses, that he was searching for Karangwa, that the houses of Karangwa and his mother were destroyed in his presence by men under his control, that he went to search the house of Karangwa's brother-in-law in Musimbira and found Karangwa's brothers at this house, that he participated in the killings of the three brothers, named, Simon Mutijima, Thadee Uwanyiligira, and Jean Chrysostome Gakuba, by ordering their deaths and being present when they were killed by policemen, under the immediate authority of the Accused as bourgmestre of Taba commune and in response to his order made to the bourgmestre of Musambira.

5.2.4. Paragraph 19 and 20 of the Indictment

The Events Alleged

269. Paragraphs 19 and 20 of the Indictment read as follows:

19. On or about April 19, 1994, **Jean Paul Akayesu** took 8 detained men from [page 117] the Taba bureau communal and ordered militia members to kill them. The militia killed them with clubs, machetes, small axes and sticks. The victims had fled from Runda commune and had been held by **Jean Paul Akayesu**.

20. On or about April 19, 1994, **Jean Paul Akayesu** ordered the local people and militia to kill intellectual and influential people. Five teachers from the secondary school of Taba were killed on his instructions. The victims were Theogene, Phoebe Uwineze and her fiancé (whose name is unknown), Tharcisse Twizeyumuremye and Samuel. The local people and militia killed them with machetes and agricultural tools in front of the Taba bureau communal.

270. For his alleged participation in the acts described in paragraphs 19 and 20, Akayesu is charged under seven counts, namely:

- Count 1, Genocide, punishable by Article 2(3)(a) of the Statute of the Tribunal;
- Count 2, Complicity in Genocide, punishable by Article 2(3)(e) of the Statute of the Tribunal;
- Count 3, Crimes against Humanity (extermination), punishable by Article 3(b) of the Statute of the Tribunal;
- Count 7, Crimes against Humanity (murder), punishable by Article 3(a) of the Statute of the Tribunal;
- Count 8, Violations of Article 3 common to the Geneva Conventions, as incorporated by Article 4(a)(murder) of the Statute of the Tribunal;

- Count 9, Crimes against Humanity (murder) punishable by Article 3(a) of the Statute of the Tribunal; and
- Count 10, Violations of Article 3 common to the Geneva Conventions, as incorporated by Article 4(a)(murder) of the Statute of the Tribunal.

271. The Chamber noted, during the presentation of evidence in this case, that the events alleged occurred during a distinct period on or about 19 April 1994 at the bureau communal. **[page 118]** Consequently, both paragraphs will be treated together.

272. A number of specific acts can be identified in the events set out in paragraphs 19 and 20. It is alleged, as pertains to paragraph 19, firstly, that Akayesu took eight refugees from the bureau communal, secondly, that he ordered militia members to kill them, thirdly, that the refugees were consequently killed with clubs, machetes, small axes and sticks, and fourthly, that the victims had fled from Runda commune and had been held by Akayesu. As regards paragraph 20, firstly, Akayesu is accused of having ordered local people and militia to kill intellectual and influential people, and secondly, five teachers, named in the Indictment, from the secondary school of Taba were killed on his instructions by the local people and militia with machetes and agricultural tools in front of Taba bureau communal. With these specific allegations in mind, the Chamber shall proceed in determining whether the participation of the accused in the events enunciated in paragraphs 19 and 20 of the Indictment has been proved beyond reasonable doubt.

273. The first witness to appear for the Prosecutor to testify in relation to the events alleged in paragraphs 19 and 20 was Witness K, a Tutsi woman, married to a Hutu, who was an accountant/cashier at the bureau communal in Taba from 1990 until 1994. She had worked under the authority of Akayesu whilst he was bourgmestre of the commune at the time of the events alleged in the Indictment. Witness K testified as follows.

274. On 19 April 1994, between 9h00 and 10h00, she had gone to the bureau communal following a demand from Akayesu who requested her services as the account/cashier of the commune. On arriving that morning, she encountered the accused, whose mood appeared to have changed, outside the bureau communal. She said he spoke to her harshly, asking her why she was no longer coming to work. Witness K told him she was scared, and that she had come to the bureau communal on this occasion only because he had asked her. She said Akayesu then told her that she would know why she had come.

275. After this exchange, witness K, who was still standing next to the accused, testified that Akayesu called over a certain Etienne, and instructed him to bring the "youths". She saw Etienne **[page 119]** drive off in the direction of Remera, and return with a number of "youths" who were armed with traditional weapons, such as machetes and small axes[69]. Witness K said they all gathered close to Akayesu who told them "Messieurs, if you knew what the Tutsi who live with you are doing, I inform you that what I heard during the meeting is sufficient. Right now, I can no longer have pity for the Tutsi, especially the intellectuals. Even those who are with us, those we have kept here, I want to deliver them to you so that you can render a judgment unto them"[70]. The witness said Akayesu then proceeded to release the refugees from Runda held in the communal prison, and handed them – with the words "here they are" – to the Interahamwe, whom she also called the "killers".

276. Witness K affirmed that there were eight refugees, all men, three of whom she personally knew to be Tutsi. She explained that they did not have their hands tied and that they all looked fine. She said the Interahamwe escorted the eight refugees to the fence of the bureau communal, where they were made to sit on the ground, in a line, their backs to the fence and their legs straight out in front of them. According to the witness, the refugees pleaded for mercy as the Interahamwe prepared to kill them. Witness K

---

[69]   The witness identified Trial Exhibits 31, 33 & 37, as types of weapons carried by the "youths".
[70]   Kinyarwanda "Yarababwiye ngo: "Burya abatutsi mubana nabo, ngo ntabwo muzi ibyo bakora, ngo ibyo naraye menyeye mu nama I Gitarama birahagije. Ubu nta mpuhwe na nkeya nagirira abatutsi, cyane cyane abize. Ngo Nabariya bari hariya twari twarabitse, ngiye kubabaha mubacire urubanza"."

testified that Akayesu then said "Do it quickly", at which point they were killed rapidly by a large group of people who used whatever weapon they had on them.

277.   After the eight refugees had been killed, witness K said she heard Akayesu instruct a communal policeman to open the communal prison and release the persons who had been imprisoned for Common law offences so that they could bury the dead refugees. She said the persons who had been released from the prison by Akayesu put the bloody bodies of the victims onto a wheelbarrow and took them away to be buried. **[page 120]**

278.   Witness K testified she heard Akayesu tell those present to fetch the one who remained. She said this person was a professor by the name of Samuel. Witness K said that they fetched him and she saw him being killed with a machete blow to the neck.

279.   According to the witness, Akayesu then gave instructions for the release of all those who had broken the law, and told them to go into the hills with their whistles so as to sensitize the youth. Witness K understood this to mean go to your sectors, increase public awareness of the population and kill with them. Witness K testified she heard the accused tell the "killers" that she would be killed after she had been interrogated about the Inkotanyi secrets. She said Akayesu put her into her office, took her keys and locked her up. The witness said she saw Akayesu get into a car, instructing others to also get in so that Ephrem Karangwa wouldn't escape them.

280.   Witness K said she had other keys on her person, thus enabling her to access the meeting room in the bureau communal from where she was able to see the events occurring outside. She testified she saw many people being brought to the bureau communal and killed, some of the victims only making it as far as the front of the entrance of the bureau communal before being killed. According to the witness, amongst those killed were professors from Remera school. She said the bodies of the victims, even those still alive, were put into wheelbarrows and taken for burial.

281.   When questioned about the use of whistles, Witness K said she saw persons go behind the bureau communal to get a professor who lived there. She said that these persons used whistles so as to terrorize this professor, and to attract the attention of others nearby.

282.   Pursuant to a question from the Chamber as to the killing of teachers, witness K stated she was unsure how many were killed, but that she knew the names of some of them, Theogene, Tharcisse, a woman called Phoebe (the gérante of Remena secondary school), and her fiancé whose name she didn't know. She explained that the woman was killed because it was alleged a radio for communicating with the Inkotanyi had been found at her house. She further stated that the true reason for the killings of the teachers and the refugees was because they were Tutsi. **[page 121]**

283.   Under cross-examination, questioned about where the teachers she saw being killed had come from, witness K stated that some of the teachers had been brought from the direction of Remera and another from behind the bureau communal. Asked if Akayesu was then still present, she stated that she had explained that Akayesu wasn't present when the actual killings of the professors took place. She reasserted being next to Akayesu when he gave the order to kill the teachers.

284.   Under cross-examination, witness K further testified she had heard the refugees had been locked up in the prison of the bureau communal by Akayesu at the request of the bourgmestre of Runda, but that she hadn't heard whether this bourgmestre had asked for these refugees to be killed. She said she had found out the refugees were from Runda by speaking to at least two other individuals from Runda whom she knew. The witness testified not knowing why exactly the refugees had been locked up in the communal prison, but was adamant they had been killed because of their Tutsi ethnicity. Witness K also confirmed that she was next to Akayesu at the bureau communal when he gave the instructions to fetch the youths/Interahamwe and that she heard Akayesu order the killing of the refugees from Runda.

285.   Witness KK for the Prosecutor, a Hutu woman married to a Tutsi and residing in Taba commune in 1994, also testified in relation to the events alleged in paragraphs 19 and 20. She said that shortly after April 6, 1994, the houses of Tutsi including her own were pillaged, and that she sought refuge at the bureau communal with her Tutsi husband and nine children. She said many refugees came to the bureau

457

communal, but that they were treated differently depending on their ethnicity. According to the witness, the atmosphere changed a few days later with the arrival of a number of Interahamwe from Remera. She said the Interahamwe addressed the refugees in the presence of Akayesu in front of the bureau communal. According to witness KK, the Interahamwe stated that they had uncovered a Tutsi plan to kill the Hutu, but as their God was never far, and because they had discovered the plan, they were going to put the Tutsi where the Tutsi had planned to put the Hutu. **[page 122]**

286.   According to the testimony of witness KK, Akayesu then went to his Office. On his return, she asserted he was angry and brandished a document which he read to the refugees, by saying "We lived with Tutsi, there was a hatred between us. The IPJ, Karangwa Ephrem had planned to kill me so that he could replace me in my function as bourgmestre. We now have to hunt them and find all of them"[71]. The witness testified Akayesu continued by talking of a landmine planted by the Tutsi that had exploded at the primary school. This landmine, she heard the accused state, was the beginning of the planned killings of Hutu. She said the accused then stated that as schoolchildren of all ethnicities were in this school, when the explosion happened, it was aimed at all Rwandans.

287.   Witness KK testified Akayesu said further "there are many accomplices in our commune. There is an accomplice who is to be found behind the bureau communal, who is called Tharcisse. He was a professor"[72]. She said Akayesu then told the policemen and Interahamwe to fetch him. The witness saw Tharcisse and his wife being made to sit in the mud. She said the wife was undressed and told to go and die elsewhere. She also heard Akayesu ask Tharcisse for information on the Inkotanyi. She said Tharcisse replied "do what you will because I know no secrets". She testified Tharcisse was killed by the Interahamwe on the road outside the bureau communal. She testified Akayesu was standing near to where the victim was sitting.

288.   Witness KK said she also heard Akayesu order the Interahamwe to bring the teachers who taught in Remera, and say that the intellectuals were the source of all of the misery. She testified that she saw the Interahamwe return very angry with the teachers. She saw the teachers, the number of which she was unsure of being made to sit in the mud on the road outside the bureau communal, where Tharcisse had been killed. According to the witness, it was alleged that these teachers had communicated by radio with Inkotanyi. Witness KK said a young couple who **[page 123]** were soon to be married was killed first. She said that all the teachers were killed on the road in front of the bureau communal with little hoes and clubs and that she had heard it being stated that to kill them with a bullet or grenade would be inflicting a less atrocious death. The witness added that no one could ask for help because Tutsi were not allowed to live in Taba commune. She said the bodies of the teachers were then taken to makeshift ditches, and covered in earth and grass. According to witness KK, some of the teachers were still breathing when buried.

289.   Under cross-examination, witness KK asserted that no teachers had taken up refuge at the bureau communal, but that the massacres had started with the killing of the teachers. The Defence attempted to discredit the witness by raising doubts as to the various dates she spoke of during her testimony, however she explained that considering all that happened to her in April 1994, it was very difficult for her to remember with certainty the specific dates. She also confirmed never having seen Akayesu kill anyone himself, save that it was he who ordered the killings which took place before his eyes.

The case for the Defence

290.   Witness DCC for the Defence, detained in Rwanda at the time of his appearance before the Chamber, was a driver at the Taba bureau communal from 1 July 1993 until the events in 1994. During his examination-in-chief, he stated that he had not heard of Akayesu being an anti-Tutsi in the month of

---

[71]   Kinyarwanda: "Ngo twabanaga n'abatutsi ari inzigo. Ngo IPJ Karangwa Eprhem ngo yari yarateganyije kuzanyica; ngo kugira ngo ansimbure abe burugumesitiri; ngo none natwe tubahigirc kutababura."
[72]   Kinyarwanda: "Ibyitso tubifire ari byinshi muri Komini yacu. Ngo inyuma ya komini hari icyitso cyitwa Tharcisse. Ubwo yari umuprofeseri."

April, 1994. He also testified he came every day to the bureau communal during the massacres. During cross-examination, he added he had seen a substantial number of persons being killed at the bureau communal. According to the witness, the bodies of those killed were taken next to the primary school, however he said he never personally witnessed any burials of cadavers because he was not part of the people who took the bodies away. He maintained this statement even though he testified that he walked past the school every day on his way home. The Chamber notes thereupon, that in answer to questions put to him by the Chamber, pertaining to there being mass graves in the vicinity of the bureau communal, the witness said that he rarely went to the bureau communal during 1994 and that he had never seen any mass graves. **[page 124]**

291. Witness DCC testified that after 6 April 1994, refugees from Runda and Shyorongi started arriving at the bureau communal of Taba, where they were welcomed by the authorities and lodged in various premises. He said the refugees were all free and none were locked up in the prison. Witness DCC testified he saw Interahamwe on two occasions come to the bureau communal and kill people. On the first of these occasions, he said the Interahamwe were from Taba but that he did not personally see Akayesu. On the second of these occasions, he saw the Interahamwe from Runda with military personnel search the office of Akayesu after having forced him out of the bureau communal. He said the Interahamwe terrorised the people at the bureau communal and asked for identity cards. According to witness DCC, the Interahamwe took the Tutsi away to be killed. He also said that Akayesu did not have a good understanding with the Interahamwe who accused him at times of being an Inkotanyi as he was welcoming refugees at the bureau communal.

292. Reference was also made by the Defence to the statement given by witness DCC to the Prosecutor[73], in which he stated "What I know, Akayesu as only present at the commune office one time when four people were killed at the entrance of the office. Akayesu did not do anything about it. Akayesu knew that the killings of Tutsi took place in the commune. The killers were Interahamwe". According to the witness, Akayesu did nothing to stop the Interahamwe because he was powerless to do so.

293. During cross-examination, the witness asserted that he was 34 years old, that in 1994, he did not flee Taba or go to Uganda, and that he did not have knowledge of and never saw Akayesu searching for Karangwa. Witness DCC said he was arrested in Rwanda on 30 April 1996. The Prosecutor produced a report, "Witness to Genocide", of an interview given by witness DCC to an NGO named Africa Rights[74]. Witness DCC confirmed speaking to a Human Rights Organization in 1996. The Prosecutor summarized extracts of the said document which stated **[page 125]** that at the time of the interview, Witness DCC was 33 years old, that he had been recruited as the driver of the commune on 1 July 1993, that he had returned to Rwanda and was arrested on 30 April 1996. The Prosecutor read out another extract: "According to Akayesu's driver, [...] Akayesu lost no time in pursuing Ephrem. "On 19 April, Akayesu, assistant bourgmestre Mutijima and a communal policeman, Mushumba, went to Kamonyi to look for the IPJ of the commune, Ephrem Karangwa, saying that he was a great accomplice of the RPF. Akayesu and his team came back in the afternoon". Witness DCC confirmed that Akayesu had not wasted any time in pursuing Karangwa, but denied having spoken in Kamonyi, of Akayesu's return or that Akayesu had called Karangwa an accomplice of the RPF.

294. Witness DZZ for the Defence, a Hutu policeman in 1994 detained in Rwanda at the time of his appearance before the Chamber, testified manning barriers in the commune of Taba and guarding the bureau communal at the time of the events alleged. He said massacres had become widespread in the commune of Taba after 18 April 1994 and that he had heard of massacres at the bureau communal. He said he went to the bureau communal on a regular basis and manned a barrier nearby, but asserted that he did not personally witness any crimes at the bureau communal. He testified that he had not heard of Akayesu participating in the massacres, and that the accused had preached peace amongst the refugees. The witness said that Akayesu saved certain Tutsi, namely witness K and Karangwa, during the

---

[73]   See Exhibit 120
[74]   See Exhibit 134

massacres. In his mind, they had been saved because, had Akayesu supported the killings, Akayesu would also have targeted Karangwa and witness K.

295. Akayesu testified going to the bureau communal on 19 April 1994. On his arrival within the vicinity of the bureau communal, he said he saw the refugees running everywhere. In the courtyard of the bureau communal, according to Akayesu, the Interahamwe were killing the refugees who had fled from Runda and Shyorongi. He said he parked the car and saw the cashier, witness K. Akayesu said he was perplexed at seeing her and wondered from where she had come. He testified that he called out to her, ordering her to go into her office. He said he had to stop someone with a machete from attacking her and subsequently escorted her personally into the office of the bureau communal. According to Akayesu, he went back into the courtyard and saw **[page 126]** refugees who had been killed, and noted that others had managed to escape. However, at a later stage during his examination-in-chief, when asked whether anyone had ever been killed in the courtyard of the bureau communal, Akayesu stated that when he was at the bureau communal or when there had been Interahamwe attacks during his absence, no one had been killed in the courtyard. After these events, Akayesu said he departed with the communal police in the direction of Mbizi, consequent upon receiving information that some of the killers had gone to Mbizi.

296. During cross-examination, the Prosecutor presented tape recordings of interviews of Akayesu carried out by the Office of the Prosecutor on 10 and 11 April 1996 in Zambia[75]. The Prosecutor questioned the credibility of Akayesu's testimony before the Chamber regarding answers he had given about the refugees at the bureau communal on 18, 19 and 20 April 1994. During his testimony, Akayesu stated he was unable to distinguish intellectuals from the rest of the refugees on the basis that there was no criteria to make it possible to tell an intellectual apart from other persons. However, in the said interviews, the accused said he was surprised not to have seen intellectuals of the commune amongst the refugees who, in his opinion, appeared to be farmers, old women, children, and old people. The Chamber questioned Akayesu as to the differences in the answers given in court, on the one hand, and before the Office of the Prosecutor, of the other. Akayesu said he had not seen anyone who could be categorized as an intellectual/teacher, but that he was able to find out by speaking with the refugees whether or not there were any intellectuals/teachers amongst them.

297. Furthermore the accused confirmed that in the context of the events in 1994, had he hold the population to fight the enemy, this would have been understood as meaning fight the Tutsi. He also asserted not having control of the population after 18 April 1994. He said witness KK was at the bureau communal on 19 April 1994. Questioned as to the killings at the bureau communal on 19 April 1994, Akayesu said he did not see anyone killed with a machete because he was in the courtyard of the bureau communal attending to witness K. Akayesu added that he **[page 127]** never saw any bodies either outside or inside the perimeter of the bureau communal and never went behind the primary school. Further, Akayesu testified never personally seeing cadavers save for the bodies of two dead children in his sector. In answer to questions on the fate of the schoolteachers whom he said he knew, Akayesu stated only hearing of their killings near the bureau communal three days after their deaths.

298. In support of its case, the Defence recalled that at least 19 witnesses in this case had never seen Akayesu either personally kill or order killings, and that only one witness, witness K, had been called to testify in relation to the events in paragraphs 19 and 20 of the Indictment. The Defence questioned the credibility of witness K on the grounds that Akayesu, during the said interviews of 1996, had cited this particular witness as a potential defence witness. If witness K had really lived through all the events she testified on, argued the Defence, why would Akayesu have named her as a defence witness.

Factual Findings

299. The testimonies of witnesses K and KK evidenced, on the one hand, events which both K and KK witnessed, and on the other hand, events that only one of the two had witnessed. The Chamber recalls that the requirement of corroboration of a witness' testimony unique to certain events, i.e. the principle of

---

[75]   Exhibits 144, 144(a), 145 and 145(a)

unus testis nullus testis, is not applicable under the Rules of the Tribunal[76]. The Chamber found both witness K and witness KK to be credible. Their testimonies were not marked by hostility and were confirmed under cross-examination. The Defence attempted to discredit witness KK on the basis of her inability to remember specific dates and times. However, the Chamber considers that these lapes of memory were not significant and an inability to recall dates and times with specificity – particularly in the light of the traumatic experience of this witness – is not by itself a basis for discrediting the witness[77].

[page 128]

300. Further, the Defence contested the credibility of witness K on the premise that Akayesu had indicated to the Prosecutor in April 1996 that she was a potential defence witness. The Chamber finds this to be a mere affirmation by Akayesu of his intent to call a certain witness, and that it does not constitute a defence *per se* as to allegations contained in paragraphs 19 and 20 of the Indictment. Further the Defence claimed the Prosecutor had called only one witness in respect of the events alleged in the said paragraphs. In light of the testimonies of two witnesses, namely K and KK, the Chamber finds that latter to be an erroneous submission by the Defence.

301. In view of the aforementioned, the Chamber finds the testimonies of witnesses K and KK both to be credible on their own, and that when dealt with together they offer sufficient correlation as to events, dates and locations for the Chamber to base its findings thereon.

302. During their respective testimonies before the Chamber, both witnesses DCC and DZZ were evasive in answering questions in relation to the events alleged in paragraphs 19 and 20 of the Indictment. However, the Chamber notes that the reluctance of these witnesses in answering certain questions was limited either to their individual participation in the acts, or to events they had personally seen. The Chamber recalls that both witnesses DCC and DZZ were at the time of their testimonies, detained in prisons in Rwanda, hence it is understandable that neither wished to present self-incriminating evidence. The Chamber has considered the probative value of their testimonies in light of the above, and finds that the evasiveness and reluctance which punctuated their oral testimony reduced their credibility.

303. Witnesses K and KK for the Prosecution, testified that they witnessed massacres at the bureau communal. Witness K specified seeing the massacres on 19 April 1994 at the bureau communal, and witness KK testified that the massacres started with the killing of teachers.

304. Both witnesses presented by the Defence, witness DCC and DZZ, also testified that killings took place at the bureau communal. Witness DCC went to the bureau communal [page 129] everyday during the events. He saw people, mainly Tutsi, being massacred by the Interahamwe and taken to be buried behind the primary school. Furthermore, the Defence presented as evidence the statement given by witness DCC to the Prosecutor[78]. The section quoted by the Defence clearly indicates that Akayesu was at the bureau communal when four people were killed at the entrance of the office and that he knew the killing of Tutsi was taking place in the commune. Questioned as to why Akayesu did nothing to stop these acts perpetrated by the Interahamwe, witness DCC said Akayesu was powerless to do so. The Chamber notes that the testimony of witness DCC supports the prosecution's evidence that people were killed at the bureau communal, in the presence of the accused; and conflicts with Akayesu's testimony that no killings took place at the bureau communal and that the only dead bodies he saw were those of two children

305. Witness DZZ testified that he went regularly to the bureau communal but that he never personally saw any massacres or crimes he had heard of being perpetrated. He added that Akayesu never participated in the massacres and even preached peace amongst the refugees. He also affirmed that massacres in Taba had become widespread after 18 April 1994. However, the Chamber notes that for witness DZZ to stipulate on the occasions he went to the bureau communal he did not see any of the massacres, and further that he had not heard of Akayesu's participation in massacres, does not refute the

---

[76] See "Evidentiary Matters, *Unus testis nullus testis*".
[77] See further "Evidentiary Matters, assessment of evidence"
[78] Exhibit No. 120

specific allegations in paragraphs 19 and 20. Indeed, it is alleged killings occurred at the bureau communal in the presence and under the instructions of Akayesu. DZZ had heard there were massacres at the bureau communal but never personally witnessed any. The Chamber notes thereon that the defence presented by the testimony of witness DZZ supports the fact that there were massacres at the bureau communal but that it does not specifically address the events in the said paragraphs, as the witness was not present when the killings he had heard of took place.

306. Akayesu admitted during his examination-in-chief that he saw massacres of refugees at the bureau communal on 19 April 1994. This is corroborated by the testimonies of witnesses **[page 130]** DZZ, DCC, K and KK in relation to there being massacres at the bureau communal. The Chamber finds it has been proved beyond reasonable doubt that, firstly, there were refugees at the bureau communal and, secondly, that massacres did occur at the bureau communal on or about 19 April 1994.

307. Akayesu confirmed under cross-examination that he was able to identify intellectuals, teachers being an example he put to the Chamber, from the rest of the refugees. Witnesses K and KK both stated that Akayesu ordered the killing of certain intellectuals and other refugees. The Defence did not specifically address these allegations. Under cross-examination, questioned as to these allegations, Akayesu said he never saw anyone killed in the courtyard with a machete because he was attending to witness K, that he never saw any bodies inside or outside the courtyard of the bureau communal and that he heard of the deaths of the teachers three days after their killings. The Chamber finds that the veracity of these answers can be doubted. Indeed, Akayesu affirmed himself during his examination-in-chief that, on 19 April 1994, he saw refugees being attacked at the bureau communal, and that he saw some killed and others escape. Further, the Chamber finds implausible the assertion that he heard of the deaths of the Remera teachers three days later. Witnesses, including himself, have placed Akayesu at the bureau communal on 19 April 1994. Akayesu testified to seeing and hearing of searches of various intellectuals in Taba throughout the day of 19 April 1994, yet he somehow did not hear of killings that took place at the bureau communal the same day. The Chamber cannot accept Akayesu's assertion with regard to the killing of teachers. Further, the Chamber notes that Akayesu did not specifically contest the allegations that he ordered the militia and local population to kill intellectuals and influential people.

Paragraph 19

308. As pertains to the allegations in paragraph 19, evidence set out above has demonstrated that refugees from Runda had been held at the bureau communal by Akayesu. Evidence has established that Akayesu told the Interahamwe he had sent for that "[...] he could no longer have pity for the Tutsi. Even those who we have kept here, I want to deliver them to you so that you **[page 131]** can render a judgment unto them". It has been demonstrated that he then ordered the release of the refugees and handed them over to the Interahamwe with the words "here they are". Evidence has demonstrated that these refugees were made to sit next to the fence of the bureau communal and that when they begged for mercy, Akayesu said to the Interahamwe "do it quickly". It has been established that immediately after Akayesu had said this, the refugees were killed in his presence, by persons nearby who used whatever weapons they had on them. It has been established that the refugees were killed because they were Tutsi.

309. The Chamber finds that it has been proved beyond reasonable doubt that Akayesu released eight detained men of Runda commune whom he was holding in the bureau communal and handed them over to the Interahamwe. It has also been proved beyond reasonable doubt that Akayesu ordered the local militia to kill them. It has been proved beyond reasonable doubt that the eight refugees were killed by the Interahamwe in the presence of Akayesu. The Chamber also finds that it has been proved beyond reasonable doubt that traditional weapons, including machetes and small axes, were used in the killings, though it is has not been proved beyond reasonable doubt that sticks and clubs were used in the killings. It has been proved beyond reasonable doubt that the eight refugees were killed because they were Tutsi.

Paragraph 20

310. Evidence has demonstrated that after the killing of the refugees. Akayesu instructed people near him to "fetch the one who remained", and that consequent to this instruction, a certain professor by the name of Samuel was brought to the bureau communal. It has been established that Samuel was then killed with a machete blow to the neck.

311. Evidence has demonstrated that on or about 19 April 1994, Akayesu addressed refugees and Interahamwe in front of the bureau communal, calling for all Tutsi within the commune to be hunted and found. It has been established that Akayesu stated that there were accomplices in the commune, one of whom lived behind the bureau communal. It has been established that Akayesu cited a professor by the name of Tharcisse as the accomplice and ordered the **[page 132]** Interahamwe and communal policemen to fetch him. Evidence has established that persons using whistles fetched Tharcisse and his wife from behind the bureau communal. Tharcisse and his wife were made to sit in the mud on the road outside the bureau communal, whereupon his wife was undressed and told to leave. It has been established that Akayesu asked Tharcisse for information on the Inkotanyi, after which the Interahamwe killed Tharcisse in the presence of Akayesu.

312. Evidence has shown that Akayesu said to the Interahamwe that the intellectuals were the source of all the misery, and that he ordered the Interahamwe to bring the teachers from Remera. It has been demonstrated that a number of teachers from Remera school were brought to the road outside the bureau communal and killed with traditional weapons, including hoes and clubs. Evidence identified the victims to be Theogene and Phoebe Uwineze and her fiancé.

313. The Chamber finds that it has been proved beyond reasonable doubt that on or about 19 April 1994, Akayesu ordered the local people and Interahamwe to kill "intellectual people". It has been proved beyond reasonable doubt that, after the killing of the refugees, Akayesu instructed the local people and Interahamwe near him at the bureau communal to fetch "the one who remains", a professor by the name of Samuel, and that consequent to this instruction, a certain professor by the name of Samuel was brought to the bureau communal. It has been proved beyond reasonable doubt that Samuel was then killed by the local people and Interahamwe with a machete blow to the neck. The Chamber finds that it has been proved beyond reasonable doubt that teachers from the commune of Taba were killed pursuant to the instructions of Akayesu. The Chamber finds it has been proved beyond reasonable doubt that amongst the teachers who were killed were Tharcisse, Theogene, Phoebe Uwineze and her fiancé. It has been proved beyond reasonable doubt that Tharcisse was killed in the presence of Akayesu. The Chamber finds it has been proved beyond reasonable doubt that the victims were all killed by local people and Interahamwe using machetes and agricultural tools on the road in front of the bureau communal. The Chamber finds that it has not been proved beyond reasonable doubt that Akayesu ordered the killing of influential people, nor that the victims were teachers from the secondary school of Taba. **[page 133]**

314. The Chamber finds that it has been proved beyond reasonable doubt that the teachers were killed because they were Tutsi. **[page 134]**

5.3. Meeting

5.3.1. Paragraphs 14 and 15 of the Indictment

315. Paragraph 14 of the Indictment reads as follows: "The morning of April 19, 1994, following the murder of Sylvère Karera, Jean Paul Akayesu led a meeting in Gishyeshye sector at which he sanctioned the death of Sylvère Karera and urged the population to eliminate accomplices of the RPF, which was understood by those present to mean Tutsi. Over 100 people were present at the meeting. The killing of Tutsi in Taba began shortly after the meeting".

316. It is alleged that by the acts with which he is charged in this paragraph, the Accused is guilty of offences covered under four counts:

- Count 1 of the Indictment charges him with the crime of genocide, punishable under Article 2 (3)(a) of the Statute;

463

- Count 2 charges him with the crime of complicity in genocide, punishable under Article 2 (3)(e) of the Statute;

- Count 3 charges him with the crime of extermination which constitutes a crime against humanity, punishable under Article 3 (b) of the Statute; and

- Count 4 charges him with the crime of direct and public incitement to commit genocide, punishable under Article 2 (3)(c) of the Statute.

317. The Chamber deems that, in order to derive clear and articulate factual findings regarding the acts alleged in paragraph 14 if the Indictment, it is necessary to consider, separately, the facts relating to: **[page 135]**

firstly, the holding on the morning of 19 April 1994 of a meeting in Gishyeshye sector, alleged to have been attended by over 100 people and led by the Accused alone following the death of Mr. Karera;

secondly, the fact during that meeting, the Accused is alleged to have sanctioned the death of Sylvère Karera;

thirdly, the fact during that meeting, the Accused is alleged to have urged the population to eliminate the accomplices of the RPF, which was understood by those present to mean Tutsi; and

Fourthly, the killing of Tutsi in Taba is alleged to have begun shortly after the said meeting.

318. With regard to the facts in paragraph 14 of the Indictment detailed as follows:

"The morning of April 19, 1994, following the murder of Sylvère Karera, Jean Paul Akayesu led a meeting in Gishyeshye sector. (...) Over 100 people were present at the meeting."

319. The Chamber finds a substantial disparity between the French and English versions of paragraph 14 of the Indictment. While in the French version it is said that "Jean Paul Akayesu alone led a meeting," the English version only indicates that "Jean Paul Akayesu led a meeting," without specifying whether he led the meeting alone. The Chamber is of the opinion that the French version should be accepted in this particular case, because the Indictment was read to the Accused in French at his initial appearance, because the Accused and his counsel spoke French during the hearings and, above all, because the general principles of law stipulate that, in **[page 136]** criminal matters, the version favourable to the Accused should be selected. In the present case and in accordance with the French version of the Indictment, the Prosecution must not only establish that the Accused led the meeting, but also that he led it alone.

320. The murder of Sylvère Karera, a teacher killed on the night of 18 to 19 April 1994, and the subsequent events, alleged under paragraph 13 of the Indictment, have already been discussed *supra*.

321. Prosecution witness A testified that after he saw the remains of Sylvère Karera at the Remera school, he went to Gishyeshye on 19 April 1994, towards 6 or 7 o'clock in the morning, where he found a large gathering of 300 to 400 people at a crossroads. The witness stated that no one had convened the meeting but that it was rather a gathering of people attracted by the events. The crowd stood near to the body of a person identified as an Interahamwe from Gishyeshye, who was alleged to have killed Sylvère Karera. A small group of people, including the bourgmestre, the Accused, sector council members and four armed members of the Interahamwe, who could be identified by the MRND coat of arms on their caps, faced the crowd in such a way that enabled them to address it. The sector councillors called on the crowd to pay attention to the speech by the Witness A pointed out that the Interahamwe stood near a blue minibus in which the Accused had arrived, and that they seemed to have been escorting the latter, which was a surprise to the crowd.

322. A Tutsi man, appearing as a Prosecution witness under the pseudonym Z, testified that on or about 19 April 1994, in the early hours of the day following the murder of a Tutsi teacher in Remera, the murderer of this teacher was killed by persons responsible for maintaining law and order. Witness Z and other people gathered around the body of the teacher's murderer. The crowd Accused the Interahamwe

present of having caused the death of the teacher. The Accused, who was armed, separated the rest of the population from members of the Interahamwe and then addressed the crowd.

323. Prosecution witness V, a teacher in Taba for nearly 30 years, went to Gishyeshye sector [page 137] where he attended a meeting, at the place where the body of a Hutu man lay. He confirmed that a meeting was, then held on the road in Gishyeshye, in the presence of the Accused, who was carrying a gun, and who organized the said meeting. The witness estimated that it was attended by some 500 people. The people were standing in front of a house. The Accused himself stood in the middle of the road with the Interahamwe next to him, across the road from the people.

324. Ephrem Karangwa, a Tutsi man, called as witness for the Prosecution, who, at the time of the acts alleged in the Indictment, was the Inspecteur de police judiciaire (Senior law enforcement Officer, criminal investigation department) of the Taba commune, testified before the Chamber that on 19 April 1994, the Accused held a meeting in Gishyeshye sector.

325. Men, who had gone to inquire after Sylvère Karera, told witness U that a person had been killed following the murder of Karera and that the Accused himself had gone to where the body was and held a meeting there.

326. The holding of the said meeting was confirmed by the Accused himself, who told the Chamber during his testimony as witness, that at about 4 a.m., on the night of 18 to 19 April 1994, a certain Augustin Sebazungu, treasurer of the MDR in Taba and a resident of Gishyeshye sector, came to see him at the Bureau communal, where he had been sleeping, to inform him that the situation in Gishyeshye sector was tense, following the murder of a young man who was a member of the Interahamwe. The bourgmestre immediately alerted the police and went to the scene with two policemen, in a blue minibus. In Gishyeshye, he found a body stretched out on the ground, covered with traces of blood, as if it had been hit. The Accused affirmed before the Chamber that since people were coming to see what was happening, he took advantage of the fact that a crowd had gathered there to address the population. He noted that the Interahamwe of the region had flocked around the body of their young member. The Accused puts the crowd at the meeting at about 100 to 200 people, including Hutu and Tutsi, members of the Interahamwe, members of the MDR and probably other political parties. The Accused admitted before the Chamber that he asked the crowd to draw closer, and then addressed the crowd, while the two policemen accompanying him stood behind him. [page 138]

327. In his closing arguments, the Defence counsel underscored that the Accused never convened the Gishyeshye meeting, but that a crowd had spontaneously gathered after a man had been killed. The Accused, as bourgmestre, reportedly found himself among the crowd thus assembled which included members of the Interahamwe.

328. With regard to the facts in paragraph 14 of the Indictment detailed as follows:

"Jean Paul Akayesu (...) sanctioned the death of Sylvère Karera"

329. According to Prosecution witness V, the Accused stated that Sylvère Karera died because he was working with the Inkotanyi. The bourgmestre further stated that the person whose body lay at the meeting place had been wrongly killed, but that Sylvère Karera had been justly killed. Under cross-examination by the Defence, witness V reiterated that the Accused stated that Karera had been killed because he was working with the Inkotanyi.

330. Witness Z, a Tutsi man, testified that at the meeting which followed the murder of the Remera teacher, the Accused, who was armed, separated the rest of the population from the members of the Interahamwe and, speaking of the body on the ground, he reportedly deplored the murder of the person and stated that this person was dead and yet the enemy was still alive. According to witness Z, the Accused told the crowd that papers detailing Tutsi plans to exterminate the Hutu had been seized at the home of the teacher.

331. The Accused told the Chamber, during his testimony, that he had inquired of the crowd standing around the body of the young Interahamwe, why the young man had been killed. The people gathered

there, answered that he had looted and that he had been justly punished. The bourgmestre then stayed on to speak to the people, trying to explain the them that killing as a habit must stop and making them aware of the consequences. He condemned the murder of the young man because he felt that such was not a way of maintaining law and order, and explained that it would have been enough to arrest the young man. The Accused told the Chamber that he **[page 139]** had asked Augustin Sebazungu why he, as a prominent figure and an educated man, had failed to stop the population from killing the young man, to which Sebazungu reportedly replied that there was nothing he could do.

332. With regard to the facts in paragraph 14 of the Indictment detailed as follows:

> "Jean Paul Akayesu (...) urged the population to eliminate the accomplices of the RPF, which was understood by those present to mean Tutsi."

333. Prosecution witness A testified that, during the said meeting, the Accused held papers which he allegedly showed to the crowd saying that the papers had been seized at the home of an Inkotanyi accomplice. He also said the papers detailed what the Inkotanyi accomplices were to do. The Accused showed the papers to the public. He stated that things had changed and that the Inkotanyi and their accomplices wanted to seize power. According to witness A, the bourgmestre stated that everyone should do everything possible to fight against those people because they were seeking to restore the former regime. He said that he was personally going to search for some of the people. A teacher then told the Accused that he knew of an accomplice to which the Accused replied: "Go fetch this person". Witness A also stated that the Interahamwe allegedly told the Accused he was to put the people of the commune at their disposal. The bourgmestre then told the crowd to fight against the Inkotanyi and their accomplices. The witness stated that the crowd remained rather calm even though it was stunned by the unusual statement made by the Accused. Witness A was personally surprised, just as, in his words, the rest of the people present, to see that the bourgmestre had changed and that he seemed, among other things, to have become friends with the Interahamwe.

334. Prosecution witness V told the Chamber that at the Gishyeshye meeting of 19 April 1994, the Accused asked the population to collaborate with the Interahamwe in the fight against the Tutsi, the sole enemy of the Hutus. According to witness V, the Accused brandished documents which he said contained a list of names of Hutu that the Tutsi wanted to kill. He **[page 140]** read the papers and said that the Tutsi were holding meetings to exterminate the Hutu. Witness V felt that the bourgmestre wanted to make the population understand that the Tutsi were their enemies. The Accused said the Tutsi, the real and only enemies of the Hutu, must be killed. He called on the population to work with the Interahamwe to search for the sole enemy. He also said that there were well-known Tutsi people living in the commune, who were working with the RPF. Witness V stated that apart from the Accused, only a certain François took the floor, to state that a list of receipts for contributions, allegedly made by the Tutsi to the Inkotanyi, had been seized.

335. According to Prosecution witness C, during that meeting, showed the Accused the crowd documents which included a list of the names of Hutu whom the Inkotanyi and the Tutsi inhabitants of Taba wanted to kill and a list of the names of Tutsi who had paid their contributions to the RPF. The witness noted that, while the Interahamwe seemed to be happy, the crowd was stunned by the change in the behaviour of the bourgmestre. Witness C stated that the Accused said during the meeting that the Tutsi was the sole enemy of the Hutu. He confirmed that he did hear the Accused say the Tutsi must be killed.

336. Witness Z, a Tutsi man, testified that at the meeting which followed the murder of the Remera teacher, the Accused, who was armed, called on all those present to bury their political differences and unite to fight the enemy, the enemy being the Tutsi, the accomplices of the Inkotanyi. Witness Z stated that the Accused, speaking of the body of the young Interahamwe believed to have killed Sylvère Karera, deplored the murder of the person and said that he was dead whereas the enemy was still alive. Witness Z further testified that, at the meeting, the Accused had in his possession papers which included a list of names. The Accused read the papers and stated that the Tutsi were holding meetings to exterminate the Hutu. In addition to the Accused, a member of the Interahamwe, named François, also took the floor,

holding papers his hands. He showed the papers and said they had been seized at the home of the teacher killed in Remera. The documents included a list of the names of Tutsi who had paid their contributions to the Inkotanyi. The crowd was surprised to see that the Accused then seemed to be cooperating **[page 141]** with the Interahamwe. Witness Z felt that, during the said meeting, the Accused was addressing the Hutu and telling them to kill the Tutsi.

337. A certain Ephrem Karangwa, who was the Inspecteur de police judiciaire of Taba Commune at the time of the events, testified before the Chamber that at the Gishyeshye meeting, the Accused told the population to kill the Tutsi in Taba. The bourgmestre told the people that whether they supported the MDR, MRND or the PSD, they should unite and understand that there was only one enemy, namely the Tutsi. The Accused told the people not to fear the Interahamwe. According to the witness the people who attended the said meeting affirmed to him that, during the meeting, the Accused showed a list of people to be killed, which included the name of Ephrem Karangwa. Allegations that the Accused, *inter alia*, named Ephrem Karangwa during the said meeting, are included in paragraph 13 of the Indictment and elaborated upon here *infra*.

338. Men reportedly told Prosecution witness U that, at the meeting held by the Accused near the body of Sylvère Karera's murderer, it was said that the only enemy was the Tutsi and that all Tutsi must be killed. According to witness U, the crowd then allegedly said that the "plane" had been shot by the Inkotanyi, and that the Inkotanyi were the Tutsi.

339. Several Prosecution witnesses confirmed the Prosecution allegation that, when the Accused called on the people to fight against the enemy, the people present took it to mean that the Tutsi must be killed. Witness C, a male Hutu farmer like witness N, a female Hutu farmer, told the Chamber that, at the time of the alleged events, the "Inkotanyi" and the "Inyenzi" meant the Tutsi. Witness N specified that the Accused himself, as a leader, took the Tutsi to mean the Inkotanyi and the Inyenzi. Witness V also pointed out that, at the time of the events, the words Inkotanyi and Tutsi, were interchangeable in the countryside. He specified that, while all Inkotanyi were not Tutsi, everyone understood at the time that all Tutsi were Inkotanyi. Witness V also confirmed that the words Tutsi and Inkotanyi were synonymous and stated that the Tutsi had been pursued with such shouts as "There they are, those Inkotanyi, those Tutsi." He explained that the Tutsi were assimilated to the Inkotanyi. **[page 142]**

340. Dr. Mathias Ruzindana, Professor of Linguistics at the University of Rwanda, appearing as expert witness for the Prosecution, explained to the Chamber that, based on his own analyses of Rwandan publications and broadcasts by the RTLM and on his personal experience, he was of the opinion that, at the time of the events alleged in the Indictment, the term Inkotanyi had several extended meanings, from an RPF sympathizer to members of the Tutsi group, depending on the context.

341. According to witness DIX, a Hutu woman, appearing as a Defence witness, explained that in her opinion, the Interahamwe started to kill people because they thought that their neighbours had in their midst accomplices of enemies from outside the country.

342. A certain Joseph Matata, a Defence witness, testified before the Chamber that the contention that when the Accused called on the people to fight against the enemy, those present took it to mean that the Tutsi must be killed, had to rebutted. According to him, the latter's speech must be interpreted with two factors in mind, namely the context of RPF incursions into the Rwandan territory and the fact that people who knew the bourgmestre could not have construed his speech as a call to kill the Tutsi.

343. A Defence witness appearing under the pseudonym DZZ, denied that the Accused ever held a meeting in Taba commune at the time of the alleged acts.

344. During his testimony before the Chamber, the Accused stated that the Interahamwe began to shout when the crowd had gathered at Gishyeshye. He called on them to calm down, stating that it was necessary to work in an orderly fashion. The Interahamwe then reportedly informed the bourgmestre that soldiers, the Inkotanyi, were allegedly infiltrating the commune. The Accused maintained before the Chamber that he had replied that if they knew of a family harbouring an RPF militant, they could reveal such information to a councillor, an officer of the Cellule, a policeman or the bourgmestre, who would

then take up the case and follow it up. The Accused denied that he himself told the crowd that people, the accomplices of the Inkotanyi, **[page 143]** should be flushed out, but admitted that it was said in the crowd that certain families were harbouring RPF soldiers.

345. In response to Prosecution questions regarding the lists of names mentioned by several Prosecution witnesses, the Accused stated under cross-examination, that a certain François had given him papers he rapidly read through silently for his personal edification. Those papers included the names of people and their functions. The Accused testified that the Interahamwe ordered him twice to read out the list and he refused to do so. According to him, members of the Interahamwe then said that the list, which included the names of RPF soldiers and their supporters, had been seized in the office of an "Inspecteur de police judiciaire" in Runda, a member of the RPF, who had been killed while he was shooting at the soldiers and the communal police.

346. The Accused testified before the Chamber that he refused to read the list aloud to the crowd because he had time to recognize certain names on the list such as those of Karangwa, Charlotte, Rukundakuvuga and Mutabazi. According to the Accused, he allegedly explained to the assembled population that the list contained names which included that of Ephrem Karangwa, and that such a list constituted a real danger since anyone could someday find their name on such a list. Thus, he reportedly cautioned the people against such documents.

347. The Accused then specifically admitted before the Chamber that mentioning a name on such a list was seriously damaging to the person thus named and jeopardized their life. He also confirmed that made by a public official, such as the bourgmestre, such a statement would have so much more impact on the people, who would understand that the person was thus being denounced and that they would certainly be killed.

The position of the Defence as stated, particularly, during the closing arguments, regarding the documents read by the Accused, is that overexcited members of the Interahamwe allegedly forced the bourgmestre to read a document in their possession, which included the names of a certain number of people considered to be accomplices of the RPF. The Accused **[page 144]** allegedly tried to dissuade the demonstrators from denouncing anyone in such a manner, by explaining that there was no proof that the people whose names appeared on the list were indeed RPF supporters.

348. With regard to the facts in paragraph 14 of the Indictment detailed as follows:

"The killing of Tutsi in Taba began shortly after the meeting."

349. With regard to the allegation made in paragraph 14 of the Indictment, the Chamber feels that it is not sufficient to simply establish a possible coincidence between the Gishyeshye meeting and the beginning of the killing of Tutsi in Taba, but that there must be proof of a possible causal link between the statement made by the Accused during the said meeting and the beginning of the killings.

350. Witness Ephrem Karangwa, who was the "Inspecteur de police judiciaire" of Taba commune, at the time of the events testified that until 18 April 1994, the people of Taba were untited and there were no killings in Taba at that time.

351. According to Prosecution witness C, the Taba population followed the instructions given by the bourgmestre at the Gishyeshye meeting and began thereafter to destroy houses and to kill. The witness recalled that the people once again complied with the instructions of the Accused as they always had.

352. Prosecution witness W, a Tutsi, clearly stated that the attacks began on 19 April 1994. The first attack he witnessed took place on 19 April 1994 at about 2:00 p.m. Just before that, his younger brother, who had gone to find out what had happened in Rukoma, told him that a list of "Collaborators" had allegedly been discovered in the home of Sylvère Karera, and that the name of witness W was allegedly on the list. The witness then immediately went into hiding and later sought refuge in Kayenzi commune. **[page 145]**

353. Prosecution witness A, a Tutsi man, testified before the Chamber that five Tutsi were killed on the day of the meeting. From that date, witness A personally observed that the people were destroying

houses, taking away corrugated iron sheets, doors and anything they could carry, and killing cows which they ate. Some of the people tried to run away when the killings began. Most of the victims were Tutsi. Witness A said that in his opinion when the Accused began to have good relations with the Interahamwe, the latter did whatever they wanted with the commune. He felt that the people were thus subjected to propaganda designed to make one part of the population hate the other. The people were believed to have changed because of repeated statements and promises made to them and that, as a result, they allegedly began to kill.

354. Witness N, a 69-year old female Hutu farmer, also explained that the destruction of houses, the killing of cows and even the killings, began following said meeting. She attributed the scale of the killings to the Accused's fiery mood during said meeting and his urging to wage war against the Inkotanyi and the Tutsi. She felt that had the Accused not held the meeting in question, the killings would never have started at that very moment, even if the Interahamwe were more powerful than the bourgmestre.

355. The Accused himself confirmed to the Chamber that killings started in Taba on 19 April 1994. He said that, on that day, after addressing the crowd at Gishyeshye, he went to the Bureau communal where he noted that the Interahamwe had killed a good number of people, who had sought refuge there, including elderly people, women and children.

356. During its closing arguments, the Defence pointed out that Prosecution witness V had testified before the Chamber that many Tutsi had sought refuge at the Bureau communal on the night of 19 April 1994. It therefore expressed doubt as to the reliability of Prosecution Witness V who had also stated, during his testimony, that on the morning of the same 19 April 1994, the Accused had ordered the Tutsi to be killed.

357. A certain Joseph Matata, called as a Defence witness, explained to the Chamber that, in his opinion and according to testimonies he had allegedly collected in Taba, the militia began **[page 146]** to neutralize the Accused as from 19 April 1994. He therefore concluded that the beginning of the massacres was not linked to the Gishyeshye meeting, but that it was an unfortunate coincidence.

358. Factual findings:

359. On the basis of consist evidence and the facts confirmed by the Accused himself, the Chamber is satisfied beyond a reasonable doubt that the Accused was present in Gishyeshye, during the early hours of 19 April 1994, that he joined the crowd gathered around the body of a young member of the Interahamwe militia, and that he took the opportunity to address the people. The Chamber finds that the Accused did not convene the meeting, but that he joined an already formed gathering. Furthermore, on the basis of consistent evidence, the Chamber is satisfied beyond a reasonable doubt that on that occasion, the Accused, by virtue of his functions as bourgmestre and the authority he held over the population, did lead the crowd and the ensuing proceedings.

360. With regard to the Prosecution allegation that the Accused sanctioned the death of Sylvère Karera, the Chamber finds that the Accused himself admitted to having condemned the death of a young Interahamwe who had allegedly killed Karera, but failing to mention that he also condemned the death of Karera. The Chamber nevertheless points out that failure to condemn is not tantamount to approval in this case. However, on the basis of testimonies by witnesses V and Z, the Chamber finds that the Accused could very well have attributed the death of Sylvère Karera to his alleged complicity with the Inkotanyi and may have added that Karera had been justly killed. The Chamber however finds that no other evidence corroborated the testimony of witness V, whereas some ten witnesses had been questioned about facts relating to the murder of Sylvère Karera and the ensuing meeting at which the Accused spoke. Consequently, the Chamber holds that in the absence of conclusive evidence, the Prosecution has failed to establish beyond a reasonable doubt that the Accused publicly sanctioned the death of Sylvère Karera at the Gishyeshye gathering. **[page 147]**

361. With regard to the allegation that the Accused urged the population, during the said gathering, to eliminate the accomplices of the RPF, after considering the weight of all supporting and corroborative evidence, the Chamber is satisfied beyond a reasonable doubt that the Accused clearly called on the population to unite and eliminate the sole enemy: accomplices of the Inkotanyi. On the basis of

consistent evidence heard throughout the trial and the information provided by Dr. Ruzindana, appearing as an expert witness on linguistic issues, the Chamber is satisfied beyond a reasonable doubt that the population construed the Accused's call as a call to kill the Tutsi. The Chamber is satisfied beyond a reasonable doubt that the Accused was himself fully aware of the impact of his statement on the crowd and of the fact that his call to wage ware against Inkotanyi accomplices could be construed as one to kill the Tutsi in general.

362. Finally, relying on substantial evidence which was not essentially called into question by the Defence, and as it was confirmed by the Accused, the Chamber is satisfied beyond a reasonable doubt that there was a causal link between the statement of the Accused at the 19 April 1994 gathering and the ensuing widespread killings in Taba.

The events alleged

363. Paragraph 15 reads as follows:

> At the same meeting in Gishyeshye sector on April 19, 1994, **Jean Paul Akayesu** named at least three prominent Tutsis – Ephrem Karangwa, Juvénal Rukundakuvuga and Emmanuel Sempabwa – who had to be killed because of their alleged relationships with the RPF. Later that day, Juvénal Rukundakuvuga was killed in Kanyiya. Within the next few days, Emmanuel Sempabwa was clubbed to death in front of Taba *bureau communal*. **[page 148]**

It is the alleged that by his participation in relation to these acts the accused committed offences charged in six counts:

- Count 1, Genocide, punishable by Article 2(3)(a) of the Statute of the Tribunal;
- Count 2, Complicity in Genocide, punishable by Article 2(3)(e) of the Statute of the Tribunal;
- Count 3, Crimes against Humanity (extermination), punishable by Article 3(b) of the Statute of the Tribunal;
- Count 4, Direct and Public Incitement to Commit Genocide, punishable by virtue of Article 2(3)(c) of the Statute of the Tribunal;
- Count 5, Crimes against Humanity (murder), punishable by Article 3(a) of the Statute of the Tribunal; and
- Count 6, Violations of Article 3 common to the Geneva Conventions of 1949, as incorporated by Article 4(a)(murder) of the Statute of the Tribunal.

364. Paragraph 15 of the Indictment alleges that, at a meeting held on 19 April 1994 in Gishyeshye sector, the accused called for the killing of three prominent Tutsi due to their alleged relationships with the RPF. As a supposed consequence of being named, at least two of them, namely Juvénal Rukundakuvuga and Emmanuel Sempabwa, were subsequently killed. The acts which were allegedly further perpetrated as regards to Ephrem Karangwa are the subject of paragraphs 16, 17 and 18 of the Indictment.

365. It has already been established beyond reasonable doubt, as alleged in paragraph 14 of the Indictment, that Akayesu was present at an early morning gathering in Gishyeshye sector on April 19 1994. The Chamber found that Akayesu urged those present to unite to eliminate the only enemy, the accomplice of the Inkotanyi. The Chamber also found the terms Inkotanyi and accomplice during the said meeting to refer to Tutsi and that the accused was conscious that his utterances to the crowd would be understood as calls to kill the Tutsi in general.

366. It now needs to be established whether during this gathering. Akayesu specifically named Ephrem Karangwa, Juvénal Rukundakuvuga and Emmanuel Sempabwa who had to be killed because of their alleged relationships with the RPF. If it is proved beyond a reasonable that Akayesu named the said three, the Chamber will consider evidence presented in relation to their subsequent fates as alleged in the second and third sentences of paragraph 15 of the Indictment.

The Role, if any, of the Accused

367.   A number of the witnesses, namely witnesses V, C, A, Z and Akayesu, who testified in relation to the events alleged in paragraph 14 of the Indictment, also testified in relation to the specific allegations contained in paragraph 15 of the Indictment. Hence, the Chamber will limit itself to recalling the testimonies of these witnesses only as pertains to the paragraph 15 of the Indictment, i.e. the naming of three individuals and their subsequent fates, factual findings having already been made above to there having been a gathering in Gishyeshye and the pertinent general allegations.

368.   Witness Z, a Tutsi man, testified that on or about 19 April 1994, in the early hours of the morning, he was present at the Gishyeshye sector gathering, which was attended by Akayesu. He said Akayesu separated the crowd from the Interahamwe and called for all those present to forget their political differences until the enemy had been eliminated, the enemy being the Tutsi, the accomplices of the Inkotanyi.

369.   Witness Z said Akayesu, who was holding documents, cited Ephrem Karangwa as someone wanting to kill him and replace him as bourgmestre. He said the accused did not name anyone else in particular. According to witness Z, Akayesu said that he didn't want to give the names of the other persons because they lived nearby and someone might warn and help them escape. The witness said an Interahamwe by the name of François spoke about papers. According to the witness, the Interahamwe said the papers had been seized from the dead professor's house (see factual findings on paragraphs 13 and 14 of the Indictment) and contained details of monies paid by the Tutsi to the Inkotanyi. **[page 150]**

370.   Witness Z testified Akayesu announced on leaving that he was going so that those persons who are to be found between Taba and Kayenzi did not escape him. He said the accused left in a vehicle with the Interahamwe. Once back at his house which was on a neighbouring hill, the witness said he observed the persons who had been in the vehicle with Akayesu break down the door of Rukundakuvuga's house. He later heard that Rukundakuvuga was arrested. Under cross-examination, witness Z confirmed that Akayesu had not named Rukundakuvuga but added that Akayesu read from documents at the gathering.

371.   Witness V, a Tutsi teacher in Taba in Taba commune for nearly 28 years, testified he was present at the gathering at the Gishyeshye sector. He said that, during this gathering, Akayesu asked the population to collaborate with the Interahamwe in the fight against the only enemy of the Hutu, namely the Tutsi. The witness said Akayesu brandished documents on which there was a list of names of Hutu who were to be killed by the Inkotanyi and the Tutsi, and a list of RPF collaborators. The witness affirmed Akayesu said he knew of a number of people in the commune, namely three teachers, to be RPF collaborators who lived in Kanyenzi, and a fourth person, the "inspecteur de police judiciaire" who worked at the office of the commune. Witness V said the accused told the crowd that these people had to be sought to prevent them from escaping. The witness testified the accused named Ephrem Karangwa during the meeting, and by reference to where they lived also implicitly spoke of Juvénal Rukundakuvuga and Emmanuel Sempabwa, who were both Tutsi. According to the witness, the crowd understood that Akayesu was looking for these people as they were supposedly RPF accomplices.

372.   Witness V testified that of the four individuals spoken of by the accused, he saw two of the bodies at the bureau communal, and the body of Rukundakuvuga on the Kanyiya road as he fled the commune of Taba. The fourth person named at the meeting was able to escape.

373.   Under cross-examination, witness V asserted that Akayesu brandished three documents during the gathering. He said there was a list of people who were financing the RPF, a list of Hutu who had to be killed by the Tutsi, and a list of Tutsi RPF collaborators. The witness **[page 151]** testified that Akayesu only named Karangwa. Questioned as to the identification of other individuals, witness V said they weren't expressly cited, but Akayesu pointed to where they lived and said that they were teachers. According to witness V, as people immediately went to search for them it had been possible for individuals at the gathering to guess about whom Akayesu was speaking.

374.   Witness E, a Hutu man from Taba testified that he was present at the Gishyeshye gathering on the morning of 19 April 1994. He said Akayesu arrived in a car and addressed the crowd. According to the

witness, Akayesu, who was armed with a rifle, pointed to the Interahamwe who were alongside him and told the crowd that the Interahamwe and the MRND, the party to which belonged the Interahamwe, meant them no harm. Witness E said Akayesu told the crowd that all of the political parties were at present one and the same, and that the only enemy was the accomplice of the Inkotanyi. The witness said a certain François gave Akayesu some documents which had allegedly been found at the residence of a RPF accomplice. He said Akayesu told the crowd that all of the Inkotanyi accomplices had to be sought. Questioned as to any names being cited by Akayesu, the witness said only that of Ephrem Karangwa was mentioned.

375. Witness A, a Hutu man who worked with Akayesu from April 1993 up until 7 April 1994, testified that he attended the Gishyeshye gathering in the early hours of 19 April 1994. He said that on arriving, around 06h00 and 07h00 in the morning, he saw a crowd gathered around a body. According to the witness, amongst the people present were the bourgmestre, conseillers, the local population who had heard the noise the night before and Interahamwe. The witness said the members of the cellules and the conseillers asked the crowd to listen to the bourgmestre. Witness A declared Akayesu showed a number of documents to the people, and told the crowd that things had changed, that the Inkotanyi and their accomplices wanted to take power. Questioned as to the citing of names, the witness stated that Akayesu mentioned only Ephrem Karangwa, the "inspecteur de police judiciaire", as someone who had a plan to replace him. The witness added that Akayesu told the crowd that everyone had to do whatever they could to fight these people so as not to return to the previous regime, and that he too would personally search **[page 152]** for these people. Witness A testified that a teacher in the crowd informed Akayesu that he knew of another accomplice, in response to which Akayesu ordered that this person be found.

376. Under cross-examination, witness A affirmed that during the gathering in Gishyeshye, Akayesu named only Ephrem Karangwa, and mentioned no other names.

377. Witness C, a Hutu farmer, testified that he attended the Gishyeshye gathering. He said Akayesu addressed the crowd. According to the witness, the accused took documents from his jacket and stated that he was going to read the contents of the documents found at the Professor's house who had been killed in Remera. He said that Akayesu called for the crowd to listen attentively and to put into practice the contents of the documents. Witness C declared that thereafter Akayesu read out the documents.

378. Akayesu testified that on the morning of 19 April 1994 in Gishyeshye sector, a number of people, including Interahamwe, had assembled around the cadaver of an Interahamwe. Akayesu explained that during his discussions on commune security with the crowd at this gathering, a certain François, who had arrived with the Interahamwe, gave him a number of documents on which there figured names and occupations of supposed RPF accomplices and told him to read them. Though François told him to read out the names on the lists, the accused asserted that he did not do so, save for citing, reluctantly so, that of Ephrem Karangwa. In so doing he said he explained to those present at the gathering "there is on this list Ephrem Karangwa, tomorrow you may find yourselves on the list; will it then be said that you too are housing elements of the RPF, a soldier of the RPF?"

379. Under cross-examination, Akayesu declared that he did not read out any names but that he did cite that of Ephrem Karangwa. He added that he had summarized the contents of the documents in his possession by saying there was a list of names on which figured Ephrem Karangwa, tomorrow others could appear on the list, would it then be said that they too are hiding RPF soldiers. Akayesu said the Rukundakuvuga was also on the list, but denied having read it out. Akayesu stated it would be dangerous to publicly designate an individual as an **[page 153]** accomplice of the RPF

380. The Defence argued that Akayesu never convened the gathering at Gishyeshye. Instead, the accused was amongst a group of people who had gathered there after a man had been killed. The Defence submitted that Interahamwe were angry, and forced Akayesu to read a document, which contained the names of persons they believed to be accomplices of the RPF. The Defence averred that Akayesu tried to dissuade the Interahamwe from denouncing people in this manner as there was nothing to prove on the list that these people were accomplices of the RPF.

Findings of fact

381. The Chamber has already found beyond a reasonable doubt that Akayesu was present and did speak at the gathering in Gishyeshye sector on the morning of 19 April 1994. This has been developed in the factual findings pertaining to paragraph 14 of the Indictment.

382. Akayesu admitted to having been given a number of documents by the Interahamwe François, and that he did cite the name of Ephrem Karangwa during this gathering, as a forewarning to those present that they too could be deemed RPF accomplices if their names figured on the list. Akayesu also admitted it would be dangerous to cite the name of an individual as an RPF accomplice. However, he was adamant that at he did not read out the documents as such, but summarized them for the crowd. Akayesu confirmed names, save that of Ephrem Karangwa, also appeared on the list. Further, the Defence submitted in its closing arguments that Akayesu had been forced to read out the documents given to him by the Interahamwe.

383. Akayesu's testimony, as regards the naming of Ephrem Karangwa, is supported by the evidence presented by witnesses Z, V, E and A in this matter. All four affirmed that only the name of Ephrem Karangwa had been cited during the Gishyeshye gathering. Witnesses V and Z added that in their opinions it was possible to infer, from Akayesu's gestures and subsequent conduct, reference to Sempabwa and Rukundakuvuga. **[page 154]**

384. The Chamber finds that it has been proved beyond reasonable doubt that Akayesu did cite Ephrem Karangwa during the Gishyeshye meeting. It has also been established beyond a reasonable doubt he did so knowing of the consequences of naming someone as an RPF accomplice in the temporal context of the events alleged in the Indictment.

385. However, the Chamber is of the opinion that the evidence presented in this matter does not support the specific allegations that Akayesu named Juvénal Rukundakuvuga and Emmanuel Sempabwa. The evidence presented shows only an implicit, yet remote, allusion by Akayesu during the Gishyeshye gathering to these two individuals, and does not demonstrate that Akayesu expressly named them. Hence, the Chamber finds that it has not been proved beyond reasonable doubt that Akayesu named Juvénal Rukundakuvuga or Emmanuel Sempabwa during the Gishyeshye gathering on 19 April 1994, and that their fates were consequent upon the utterances of Akayesu at the Gishyeshye gathering. **[page 155]**

5.4. Beatings (Torture/Cruel Treatment) (Paragraphs 16, 17, 21, 22 & 23 of the Indictment)

Charges Set Forth in the Indictment

16. Jean Paul Akayesu, on or about April 19, 1994, conducted house-to-house searches in Taba. During these searches, residents, including Victim V, were interrogated and beaten with rifles and sticks in the presence of Jean Paul Akayesu. Jean Paul Akayesu personally threatened to kill the husband and child of Victim U if she did not provide him with information about the activities of the Tutsi he was seeking.

17. On or about April 19, 1994, Jean Paul Akayesu ordered the interrogation and beating of Victim X in an effort to learn the whereabouts of Ephrem Karangwa. During the beating, Victim X's fingers were broken as he tried to shield himself from blows with a metal stick.

21. On or about April 20, 1994, Jean Paul Akayesu and some communal police went to the house of Victim Y, a 68 year old woman. Jean Paul Akayesu interrogated her about the whereabouts of the wife of a university teacher. During the questioning, under Jean Paul Akayesu's supervision, the communal police hit Victim Y with a gun and sticks. They bound her arms and legs and repeatedly kicked her in the chest. Jean Paul Akayesu threatened to kill her if she failed to provide the information he sought.

22. Later that night, on or about April 20, 1994, Jean Paul Akayesu picked up Victim W in Taba and interrogated her also about the whereabouts of the wife of the university teacher. When she

stated she did not know, he forced her to lay on the road in front of his car and threatened to drive over her. **[page 156]**

23.   Thereafter, on or about April 20, 1994, Jean Paul Akayesu picked up Victim Z in Taba and interrogated him. During the interrogation, men under Jean Paul Akayesu's authority forced Victims Z and Y to beat each other and used a piece of Victim Y's dress to strangle Victim Z.

Events Alleged

386.   The Chamber notes that paragraph 16 of the Indictment includes allegations with respect to Victim V and Victim U. As the evidence which was given by and about Victim V (Witness A) relates to events which are described in paragraphs 21, 22 and 23 of the Indictment, the Chamber will consider this component of paragraph 16 together with the allegations set forth in paragraphs 21, 22 and 23.

387.   Witness K (Victim U), a Tutsi woman married to a Hutu man, was an accountant who worked for the Accused in the office of the bureau communal in Taba, during the events of April 1994. Witness K testified that on the morning of 19 April 1994 she went to the bureau communal at the request of the Accused and that she found him there outside the office with many people, changed in mood and in temper. She said he asked her why she had not been coming to work and she told him that she was afraid and had come only at his request. After then witnessing the killing of Tutsi at the bureau communal, which she said was ordered by the Accused. Witness K said the killers asked the Accused why she had not been killed as well. She said he told them that they were going to kill her after questioning her about the secrets of the Inkotanyi. According to Witness K, the Accused then took her keys, locked her in her office and left, saying he was going to search for Ephrem Karangwa, the Inspector of Judicial Police.

388.   The Accused returned, said Witness K, with other men whom she referred to as "killers", and they questioned her. She said they asked her to explain how she was cooperating with the Inkotanyi, which she denied. She said the Accused insisted and said that if she did not tell them how she worked with the Inkotanyi, they would kill her. After further discussion, she said the Accused again threatened her, saying she should tell them what she knew or they would kill her, **[page 157]** and then left. At this time she estimated it was about three o'clock in the afternoon. Witness K testified that the Accused returned at around midnight with a police officer and asked her whether she had decided to tell them what she knew. When she said she knew nothing, she said he told her, "I wash my hands of your blood." She said he then told her to leave the office and go home and when she expressed concern about the late hour, he asked the driver and the police to accompany her home.

389.   Under cross-examination, Witness K stated that her husband was a friend of the Accused. When asked why she was not killed, she said that Tutsi women married to Hutu men were not killed. In his testimony, the Accused confirmed that he saw Witness K at the bureau communal on 19 April 1994 and said that he had wondered why she was there. He said that he saw a man behind her with a machete and that he came between them and escorted her to the office, and told her to keep the door closed.

390.   Witness Q (Victim X), a Tutsi man who lived in Musambira, testified that on the same day, 19 April 1994, while he was there visiting, the Accused came to the home of his parents, looking for Ephrem Karangwa, the Inspector of Judicial Police for the commune of Taba. Witness Q told the Chamber that the four people who came – one of whom was a policeman armed with a gun, another armed with grenades and another with a small hatchet – made him, his brother, his sister and his brother-in-law sit down in the courtyard at the entrance of the house. He said they asked where Ephrem Karangwa was, and after a discussion in French, entered the house to search, leaving the policeman with them in the courtyard, his gun charged and ready to shoot. Witness Q said he recognized the policeman, who told his brother-in-law that it was Akayesu, the bourgmestre of Taba, who had come to his house. He said that Akayesu was wearing a long military jacket. Witness Q had not previously met the Accused but was able to identify him in court. He said the Accused and two other people came out of the house with boxes, papers and photographs, which they scattered in the courtyard, saying the photographs of

family members in Uganda had been sent by Inkotanyis. Witness Q said he and his relatives were then beaten and kicked by the two men who were with the Accused, and he was hit with a small axe on his right hand. He said his brother-in-law was hit and wounded in the head. The witness **[page 158]** displayed in court his right hand with a bent index finger, which he said had been broken from the beating when he raised his hand to ward off the blows. Witness Q testified that the Accused was present during this beating and watched it. He said the Accused was the one apparently responsible.

391. The other house-to-house searches referred to in the relevant paragraphs of the Indictment appear to have taken place on the next day and relate to the search by the Accused for Alexia, the wife of Pierre Ntereye, a university teacher. Witness N (Victim Y), a Hutu farmer, testified that she knew where Alexia was hiding. She said the Accused, whom she had known for two years, came to her house with three Interahamwe – Mugenzi, Francois and Singuranayo – at nine o'clock in the evening, the day after the meeting in the commune (i.e. 20 April), looking for Alexia. She said the Accused stayed in his vehicle, near the entrance of her home. The others broke down the door and pointed their guns at her, ordering her to show them the Inkotanyi hiding in her house. She said she told to search the house, and one of them went to search while the other one stayed at the door. Witness N testified that Mugenzi, who was a communal police officer, took her by the arm to the door and hit her on her head with the barrel of his rifle. She said Francois, who had gone into the house, found a young girl whom he told to open her mouth. According to Witness N, Singuranayo then forced open her mouth and struck her with the barrel of the gun.

392. Witness N said that when she told them that she did not know where Alexia was, she was lifted by her arms and legs by the three men and taken outside to the Accused. She said the Accused told her to lie down, which she did. She said Mugenzi then stepped on her neck and pushed the butt of his rifle into her neck. She said he stomped on her with a lot of force, and that the Accused then hit her with a club on her back. When she shouted, she said the Accused told her to be quiet, calling her the mother-in-law of the Inkotanyi and a "poisonous woman." Witness N testified that they then took her in the vehicle to a partially opened mine at a place called Buguli. She said the Accused ordered her to lie down in front of the vehicle, got into the driver's seat and told her that he was going to run her over. Mugenzi told her to tell them where the people she was hiding were or they would kill her. She said she told them that she did not **[page 159]** know and that they should kill her if they wanted. Witness N said Mugenzi then bound her arms and legs with a piece of cloth, pushed her to the ground and stomped on her with his foot. She said the others also joined in and stomped on her.

393. Witness N said she was then put in the vehicle and taken to the house of Ntereye's sisters. When they arrived, she said Francois called for Ntereye's niece Tabita (Victim W) and they questioned her. According to Witness N, the Accused remained in the vehicle and called Tabita from there. He asked her where Alexia was, and she said she did not know. Witness N testified that Tabita was then taken in the vehicle back to the mine. There, she said, they made her get out and told her to get in front of the vehicle. The Accused threatened to run her over and again asked her for the whereabouts of the people in question. She said Tabita was afraid and said that they had hidden in a sorghum field but that she did not know where they were. According to her testimony, Witness N was then told by the Accused that she was a "poisonous woman" and that she had hidden these people. She said they then began to strike her with their gun[s].

394. Witness N said that she and Tabita were then taken in the vehicle to a roadblock, where they picked up Victim Z, and they were then taken to Gishyeshye Sector. Witness N testified that she was at this time "almost dead" from the beating she had suffered. When they arrived, Witness N said she was thrown on the road, next to Victim Z, and they began to beat him with a club. She said the Accused then instructed Victim Z to beat her. She said Victim Z stood up and began to beat her, and that he beat her several times on her leg with a club. During this time, she testified that the Accused was standing next to them near the vehicle. Witness N said her hands were then tied in the back with a piece of cloth, the other end of which was used to strangle Victim Z. She said they tightened the cloth, and his eyes almost came out of their sockets. Victim Z then said that he thought he knew who had hidden Alexia. She said [they]

then started hitting him again, very hard, and the Accused asked [him] to hit her hard, to make her talk. Witness N said she threatened to bite [him] if [he] continued to hit her.

395. Witness N testified that she was then taken in the vehicle with Victim Z to a roadblock and there they picked up a person identified as Victim V (Witness A). She said they were taken **[page 160]** to Victim V's house, where they were taken out of the vehicle and thrown on the ground. According to the testimony, they started beating Victim Z again with the club and they also beat Victim V and told him to bring out the person he was hiding. Victim V said he was not hiding anybody. On direct examination, Witness N said the Accused told Victim V to raise his arms so that they could shoot him. On cross-examination, Witness N testified that Mugenzi told Victim V to raise his arms so that they could shoot him. She said they did not shoot him, and that the Accused told Victim V that they would continue searching for Alexia and that if they did not find her he would have to die.

396. Witness N testified that as a result of the beatings she received, her arm is limp. She said that she can no longer walk as she did before and that she needs help to get dressed. She testified that she can no longer work on the farm. The Trial Chamber notes that Witness N walked with difficulty, aided by a walking stick.

397. Witness C (Victim Z), a Hutu farmer, testified that he knew Alexia, that she was a Tutsi teacher and the wife of Ntereye. He said that she hid in his house during April 1994 and that she had come to his house because she realized that he had not participated in the killings. Witness C testified that some Interahamwe came to his house while he was out harvesting coffee. He said one of his children came to look for him after the child had been beaten and asked where Alexia was. Witness C returned to his house and found the Interahamwe at the entrance, carrying machetes and clubs. He said some also had grenades. According to the testimony, the Interahamwe surrounded Witness C and accused him of hiding Alexia. Witness C said that Alexia was not in his house, and one of them started beating him on his back with the blunt side of a machete. He said he then told them that Alexia sometimes hid in his house and sometimes in another person's house. They continued to beat him, and Witness C testified that when he realized that he was about to be killed he said that Alexia was in another [room]. He said the Interahamwe took him to Victim Y's house, and when they arrived they continued beating him. He said they asked Victim Y where Alexia was, and she said that Alexia had gone to her husband's relatives. Witness C said that the Interahamwe then left the house, taking him with them, and after a distance released him, saying that they had from him what they needed. **[page 161]**

398. Witness C (Victim Z) testified that one week after this incident, while participating in a night patrol, he saw the Accused, whom he had known for a long time, with three Interahamwes, Victim Y (Witness N) and Tabita, the niece of Ntereye, in a white twin cab. He said the Accused was driving and stopped at the roadblock, got out of his car and told the Interahamwe that they should bring Witness C to him. He said the Accused told him to get into the vehicle, which he did, and they drove to the forest. In the middle of the forest, Witness C said they stopped and asked him to get out and lie down in front of the vehicle. He said the Accused then stepped on his face, causing his lips to bleed, and kept his foot on Witness C's face while two of the Interahamwe – Francois and Mugenzi – began to beat him with the butt of their guns. During this time, he said he was asked repeatedly where Alexia was hiding.

399. Witness C said that during the beating, Victim Y (Witness N), who was in the vehicle, urged him to tell them where Alexia was, and when he realized that they were going to kill him, he told them that she was at his home. Concerned that they would find her there, Witness C said he then told them she was somewhere else and Victim Y told them that Victim V could advise them of her whereabouts. Witness C testified that he was then made to sit next to Victim Y and they were bound together, side by side, with a rope by the Interahamwe Mugenzi. He said the rope was put around his neck. Under cross-examination, Witness C clarified that the rope was in fact a piece of cloth that he had been wearing. When he began to vomit, Witness C said they were untied and the Accused then told them to get back into the vehicle. Witness C also testified on examination that he was asked by Francois to hit Victim Y and given a cudgel, with which he struck her once on the leg. He said he was told to tell Victim Y to tell them where Alexia was hiding. After this, Witness C testified that the Accused told them to get back into the vehicle and they were taken to the roadblock.

400.   At the roadblock, Witness C testified that they picked up Victim V and the Accused drove them to Victim V's house. When they arrived, he said the Accused asked his Interahamwes to search the house. He said two of them went in and came back, saying that Alexia was not in the house. According to Witness C, the Accused then told Victim V twice to **[page 162]** step aside and raise his arms in the air so that they could shoot at him. One of the Interahamwe told him a third time to raise his arms so that they could shoot him. Witness C said they did not shoot at Victim V, but they again beat him, Witness C, on the back with the blunt side of a machete. He said they were then asked to get back in the vehicle and went near the home of Victim Y, who was dropped off. They continued, he said, dropping one Interahamwe off at a roadblock and stopping at another roadblock, where the members of Ntereye's family had been arrested. Witness C testified that the Accused asked them to get in the vehicle – a woman, three children and three men. He said they then went to a commercial center near Remera Rukoma, and the people were taken to a prison there. Witness C and Victim V were left to wait in the vehicle while the Accused, Francois and Mugenzi went to drink beer at a place about fifteen feet from the vehicle. From the vehicle, Witness C testified that he heard the Accused say to the Interahamwe "I do not think that what we are doing is proper. We are going to have to pay for this blood that is being shed." After the Accused and the Interahamwe drank beer and returned to the vehicle, Witness C said they were taken near the school of Remera Rukoma, dropped off there and told to be at the office the next morning at 7:00.

401.   Witness C showed the Trial Chamber the scars he said he had from this beating, on the left side of his back. He said than he did not have scars on his lips but that he did have wounds on his head and a scar on his nose. He testified that he has continuing health problems such as a bleeding nose and pains in his head, and that his body is no longer what it was before.

402.   Witness A (Victim V), a Hutu man, testified that he knew Alexia and that he was the person who had found the hiding place for her. He said he saw the Accused, whom he had known for ten years and worked with, one night while he was on patrol, sometime between 7:00 and 9:00. He said the Accused was alone in a white pickup truck, and while they were talking, he saw people, including the Interahamwe Francois and a commune police officer, coming from the house of an elderly woman, who lived near him. He said they put this woman in the vehicle and took her to the forest, and shouts were heard as they beat her. Later, he said the Accused came back and took away another of his neighbours who was doing the night patrol, and he also heard this person crying out as he was being beaten. Witness A said they came back and picked **[page 163]** him up and went to his house. He said the Accused was driving the vehicle. He said they came into his house and searched for people they said were hiding there, in particular Alexia. Witness A said they had guns, and that after they searched the house they took him and the others to the gate of the house, and the commune police officer and Francois began to beat them with the butt of a rifle and a stick, asking them where Alexia was. At this time, he said the Accused was standing next to them and watching. He said when they discovered that Alexia was not in the house, they stopped the beating and put them in the vehicle. He said they released the elderly woman and sent her back to her house, and they continued to detain him and Victim Z.

403.   Witness A testified that near his house, they found nine people from families who had been stopped by night patrols. He said these people were presented to the Accused who put them in the vehicle and took them to a prison near Remera Hospital. He said the Accused and Francois went to have drinks and he was left in the vehicle with Victim Z and a young girl, guarded by the commune police officer. Afterwards, he said they went back to the bureau communal and on the way the Accused told them to go home but come back to the bureau communal early the next morning. At this time, he said it was approximately 2:00 in the morning. On cross-examination, Witness A said that he did not sustain serious injuries from the beatings apart from a broken rib which was treated.

404.   The Accused testified that after Ntereye was killed on 10 May 1994, people were saying that they still did not know where his wife was. The Accused said he knew that she was being sought, and he said he was determined to save her. He said that Ntereye had told him that she was going from house to house. He said he found an Interahamwe called Francois and told him that he had someone to save. He said he asked Francois to help him for a price and gave him twenty thousand. He said he then went to

Ntereye's sister's house and found his niece who told him that Alexia was living in the house of an elderly woman. He said he knew her to be a tough old lady and asked the niece to come with him to reassure her. He said they left – himself, a police officer and Francois. He said they called for the lady and she came, and he spoke to her. He said she told him that Alexia had been there but left and gone to Kayenzi. He said when he asked her whether she was telling the truth, she told him "I cannot lie because you are going to **[page 164]** do good for Alexia and then I have also heard that you tried to save Ntereye." He said he left with the niece and drove to Buguli and that he spoke to her and her sisters, warning them not to let the children go outside because they would be killed. In his testimony, the Accused then moved on to other events. The Accused later testified that when he went to look for Alexia, there were two or three people at the roadblock near the home of the old lady, but that neither Victim V nor Victim Z was there, and he did not see them on this occasion. He testified that Victim Y, Victim Z and Victim V were known to him. He also said there were no mines in Buguli.

Factual Findings

405. The Chamber finds that on 19 April 1994, Victim U (Witness K) was threatened by the Accused at the bureau communal. She went to the bureau communal because she had been summoned there by the Accused. She was questioned by the Accused in the presence of men whom she had just seen killing Tutsi at the bureau communal. In response to a question from the killers, Victim U heard the Accused tell them that she would be killed after she was questioned about the secrets of the Inkotanyi. The Accused then questioned Victim U and threatened that she would be killed if she did not divulge information about her cooperation with the Inkotanyi. The Accused then locked Victim U in her office and left. When he returned in the afternoon, he resumed questioning Victim U and again threatened that she would be killed if she did not provide information about the Inkotanyi. He left again and returned at midnight with a police officer. The Accused asked her whether she would tell them what she knew and when she said she knew nothing, he said "I wash my hands of your blood." He then asked the driver and the police to accompany her home.

406. The Chamber found Victim U to be a very credible witness whose testimony was not marked by anger or hostility and whose testimony was confirmed under cross-examination. The Chamber notes that the Accused in his testimony confirmed the presence of Victim U at the bureau communal on 19 April 1994. The Chamber does not accept his explanation of her presence there or his actions. If he intended to protect her, as he suggested, why did he take her key from her, why did he question her about the Inkotanyi, and why did he leave her there until **[page 165]** midnight? The Accused did not address any of these questions or specifically deny that he did any of these things. He did not even deny specifically that he told the others in her presence that she would be killed after questioning or that he threatened her when he questioned her. The Chamber notes that there is no evidence to suggest that the Accused threatened the husband or child of Victim U.

407. With regard to the allegations set forth in paragraph 17 of the Indictment, the Chamber is unable to find, beyond a reasonable doubt, that the Accused ordered the interrogation and beating of Victim X (Witness U) on 19 April 1994. The evidence presented in support of the allegation relies entirely on a single witness, the credibility of whom the Defence has successfully challenged. In cross-examination, the Defence questioned Witness Q regarding the details of the incident at his father's home, as they had been described by him in his pre-trial written statement. When asked about his prior statement that the Accused had been accompanied by two policemen rather than one, Witness Q explained that one of the policeman was from Taba and the other from Musambira. He said the second policeman had remained on the main road, and he had not actually seen this policeman which is why he did not mention him in his testimony. When asked about his prior statement that the Accused was armed rather than unarmed, Witness Q said that he had said that the Accused was wearing a military jacket and that he had heard that another policeman had a gun. When asked about his prior statement that he had been beaten by a policeman with a metal bar, Witness Q said that he was beaten by a man in civilian clothes, whom he assumed was a policeman because he was carrying a grenade. He said he was beaten with a metal instrument which had a pointed end. When asked about his prior statement that the Accused arrived in a

red Toyota and that he saw a man lying in the rear seat of the vehicle with his hands tied, Witness Q said that he did not see the man in the back seat but that he heard about him. He said he did not see the vehicle as it was 500 metres away, but that he had heard that it was red.

408. While the Chamber has been cautious in allowing the contents of pre-trial written statements to impeach the testimony of witnesses before it, in this case the inconsistencies between the testimony and the written statement of Victim X are many and too significant to **[page 166]** justify a finding of credibility without corroboration of other testimony. The Chamber notes that even if it were to accept the testimony of Victim X in full, it would not be able to find, beyond a reasonable doubt, that the Accused ordered the interrogation and beating of Victim X. The witness testified that the Accused was present and watched the beatings, but there is no evidence that he gave any orders. There is only evidence that words were spoken in French. No evidence has been presented as to what was said and by whom.

409. With regard to the search for Alexia, wife of Ntereye, the Chamber finds that at on the evening of 20 April 1994, the Accused went with two Interahamwe named Francois and Singuranayo and one communal police officer named Mugenzi to the house of Victim Y (Witness N), a [68] year old woman at the time. Mugenzi took her by the arm to the door and hit her on the head with the barrel of his rifle. Witness Y was then forcibly taken to the Accused, who ordered her to lie down. In the presence of the Accused, Victim Y was beaten by the communal police officer Mugenzi who stepped on her neck, pushed the butt of his rifle into her neck, and stomped on her. Victim Y was also beaten by the Accused, who hit her with a club on her back. She was interrogated by Mugenzi and the Accused about the whereabouts of Alexia, the wife of Ntereye, a university professor. She was then taken to Buguli, where the Accused made her lie down in front of the vehicle and threatened to run her over. At the mine, in the presence of the Accused, she was also threatened and interrogated by Mugenzi, who bound her arms and legs and stomped on her with his foot. The others stomped on her as well.

410. Later that night, the Accused picked up Tabita (Victim W) and interrogated her also about the whereabouts of Alexia, the wife of Ntereye. She was then taken in the vehicle back to the mine. She was asked to get in front of the vehicle, and the Accused threatened to run her over and again interrogated her about the whereabouts of Alexia.

411. Thereafter, on the same evening, the Accused picked up Victim Z (Witness C) and took him to a forrest in Gishyeshye Sector, where the Accused stepped on his face, causing his lips to bleed, and kept his foot on Victim Z's face while the Interahamwe Francois and the commune police officer Mugenzi beat him with the butt of their guns. Victim Z was tied to Victim Y with **[page 167]** a piece of cloth by Mugenzi, which was used to choke him. Victim Z was also forced by Francois to beat Victim Y with a cudgel he was given. During this time, Victim Z was interrogated, but it is unclear who actually did the interrogation.

412. Following the interrogation of Victim Y and Victim Z, the Accused picked up Victim V at a roadblock and took him, with Victim Y and Victim Z, to his house, which was searched by Interahamwe at the direction of the Accused. The Accused then told Victim V to raise his arms in the air and threatened to shoot him. In the presence of the Accused, Victim V was then beaten under interrogation by the Interahamwe Francois and the commune police officer Mugenzi with the butt of a rifle and a stick. Victim Z was beaten on the back with the blunt side of a machete. Victim Y, Victim Z and Victim V were then taken away in the vehicle and, after Victim Y was released near her home, Victim Z and Victim V were kept in the vehicle while the Accused and the others drank beer. Victim Z and Victim V were released at approximately 2:00 in the morning.

413. As a result of the beatings, Victim Y has trouble walking. Victim Z has scars on his back and continuing health problems. Victim V sustained a broken rib from the beatings.

414. The Chamber notes that the testimony of Witness N, Witness C and Witness A closely correlate in all material respects and even with regard to minor details. There were very few inconsistencies, of an extremely minor nature. Witness N said, for example, that Victim Z (Witness C) was beaten with a club. Victim Z testified that he was beaten with the butt of a gun. It is clear that there was a club, as it was

used by Victim Z to hit Victim Y (Witness N) when he was forced to do so. It is understandable that Victim Y may have therefore mistaken the instrument used on Victim Z. Victim Z initially testified that he was tied to Victim Y with a rope, whereas Victim Y testified that it was a piece of cloth. On cross-examination, however, Victim Z clarified that in fact it was a piece of cloth that was used.

415. The Chamber finds these facts have been established beyond a reasonable doubt. In making its factual findings, the Chamber has carefully considered the cross-examination by the **[page 168]** Defence of Prosecution witnesses and the evidence presented by the Defence in the form of testimony by the Accused. With regard to cross-examination, the Chamber notes that the Prosecution witnesses substantially confirmed their direct testimony. In his testimony, the Accused confirmed that he picked up the niece of Ntereye, with the Interahamwe Francois and his police officer, and went with her to the house of Victim Y. He confirmed that he drove with Ntereye's niece to Buguli, stating only that there were no mines in Buguli. The Accused also confirmed that he was looking for Alexia, the wife of Ntereye, but he maintained that he was determined to save her. He said that the paid Francois to help him in this effort. The Accused testified that he did not see Victim Z or Victim V at the roadblock near the home of Victim Y, although they all testified that they saw him and each other. According to the testimony of the Accused, the search for Alexia took place after the death of Ntereye on 10 May 1994. All the prosecution witnesses, however, date this search to 20 April 1994. The Defence in its cross-examination did not question the evidence given by the Prosecution witnesses about the date. The Accused also testified that when he spoke to Victim Y, she said "I cannot lie because you are going to do good for Alexia and then I have also heard that you tried to save Ntereye." Having heard Victim Y's (Witness N's) testimony, the Chamber finds it highly unlikely that she would have made such a statement and notes that the statement was not put to her by the Defence on cross-examination, in which the Accused himself participated. Moreover, the Accused's account of his efforts to find and save Alexia simply tapered off in his testimony, without any explanation as to whether he continued the search or gave it up and if so, why. The Chamber also notes the testimony of Witness PP, which it has accepted as credible, that when Alexia and her nieces were brought to the bureau communal, the Accused said to the Interahamwe, "Take them to Kinihira. Don't you know where killings take place, where the others have been killed?" The actions of the Accused were incompatible with a desire to save Alexia, and the Chamber does not accept the testimony of the Accused on these events as credible. **[page 169]**

5.5. Sexual Violence (Paragraphs 12A & 12B of the Indictment)

Charges Set Forth in the Indictment

12A. Between April 7 and the end of June, 1994, hundreds of civilians (hereinafter "displaced civilians") sought refuge at the bureau communal. The majority of these displaced civilians were Tutsi. While seeking refuge at the bureau communal, female displaced civilians were regularly taken by armed local militia and/or communal police and subjected to sexual violence, and/or beaten on or near the bureau communal premises. Displaced civilians were also murdered frequently on or near the bureau communal premises. Many women were forced to endure multiple acts of sexual violence which were at times committed by more than one assailant. These acts of sexual violence were generally accompanied by explicit threats of death or bodily harm. The female displaced civilians lived in constant fear and their physical and psychological health deteriorated as a result of the sexual violence and beatings and killings.

12B. Jean Paul Akayesu knew that the acts of sexual violence, beatings and murders were being committed and was at times present during their commission. Jean Paul Akayesu facilitated the commission of the sexual violence, beatings and murders by allowing the sexual violence and beatings and murders to occur on or near the bureau communal premises. By virtue of his presence during the commission of the sexual violence, beatings and murders and by failing to prevent the sexual violence, beatings and murders, Jean Paul Akayesu encouraged these activities.

Events Alleged

416. Allegations of sexual violence first came to the attention of the Chamber through the testimony of Witness J, a Tutsi woman, who stated that her six year-old daughter had been raped **[page 170]** by three Interahamwe when they came to kill her father. On examination by the Chamber, Witness J also testified that she had heard that young girls were raped at the bureau communal. Subsequently, Witness H, a Tutsi woman, testified that she herself was raped in a sorghum field and that, just outside the compound of the bureau communal, she personally saw other Tutsi women being raped and knew of at least three such cases of rape by Interahamwe. Witness H testified initially that the Accused, as well as commune police officers, were present while this was happening and did nothing to prevent the rapes. However, on examination by the Chamber as to whether Akayesu was aware that the rapes were going on, she responded that she didn't know, but that it happened at the bureau communal and he knew that the women were there. Witness H stated that some of the rapes occurred in the bush area nearby but that some of them occurred "on site". On examination by the Chamber, she said that the Accused was present during one of the rapes, but she could not confirm that he saw what was happening. While Witness H expressed the view that the Interahamwe acted with impunity and should have been prevented by the commune police and the Accused from committing abuses, she testified that no orders were given to the Interahamwe to rape. She also testified that she herself was beaten but not raped at the bureau communal.

417. On 17 June 1997, the Indictment was amended to include allegations of sexual violence and additional charges against the Accused under Article 3(g), Article 3(i) and Article 4(2)(e) of the ICTR Statute. In introducing this amendment, the Prosecution stated that the testimony of Witness H motivated them to renew their investigation of sexual violence in connection with events which took place in Taba at the bureau communal. The Prosecution stated that evidence previously available was not sufficient to link the Accused to acts of sexual violence and acknowledged that factors to explain this lack of evidence might include the shame that accompanies acts of sexual violence as well as insensitivity in the investigation of sexual violence. The Chamber notes that the Defence in its closing statement questioned whether the Indictment was amended in response to public pressure concerning the prosecution of sexual violence. The Chamber understands that the amendment of the Indictment resulted from the spontaneous testimony of sexual violence by Witness J and Witness H during the course of this trial and the subsequent investigation of the Prosecution, rather than from public pressure. **[page 171]** Nevertheless, the Chamber takes note of the interest shown in this issue by non-governmental organizations, which it considers as indicative of public concern over the historical exclusion of rape and other forms of sexual violence from the investigation and prosecution of war crimes. The investigation and presentation of evidence relating to sexual violence is in the interest of justice.

418. Following the amendment of the Indictment, Witness JJ, a Tutsi woman, testified about the events which took place in Taba after the plane crash. She that she was driven away from her home, which was destroyed by her Hutu neighbours who attacked her and her family after a man came to the hill near where she lived and said that the bourgmestre had sent him so that no Tutsi would remain on the hill that night. Witness JJ saw her Tutsi neighbours killed and she fled, seeking refuge in a nearby forest with her baby on her back and her younger sister, who had been wounded in the attack by a blow with an axe and two machete cuts. As she was being chased everywhere she went, Witness JJ said she went to the bureau communal. There she found more than sixty refugees down the road and on the field nearby. She testified that most of the refugees were women and children.

419. Witness JJ testified that the refugees at the bureau communal had been beaten by the Interahamwe and were lying on the ground when she arrived. Witness JJ encountered four Interahamwe outside the bureau communal, armed with knives, clubs, small axes and small hoes. That afternoon, she said, approximately forty more Interahamwe came and beat the refugees, including Witness JJ. At this time she said she saw the Accused, standing in the courtyard of the communal office, with two communal police officers who were armed with guns, one of whom was called Mushumba. Witness JJ said she was beaten on the head, the ribs and the right leg, which left her disabled. That evening, she said, the Accused came with a policeman to look for refugees and ordered the Interahamwe to beat them up, calling them "wicked, wicked people" and saying they "no longer had a right to shelter." The refugees were then

beaten and chased away. Witness JJ said she was beaten by the policeman Mushumna, who hit her with the butt of his gun just behind her ear. **[page 172]**

420.   Witness JJ testified that she spent the night in the rain in a field. The next day she said she returned to the bureau communal and went to the Accused, in a group of ten people representing the refugees, who asked that they be killed as the others had been because they were so tired of it all. She said the Accused told them that there were no more bullets and that he had gone to look for more in Gitarama but they had not yet been made available. He asked his police officers to chase them away and said that even if there were bullets they would not waste them on the refugees. As the refugees saw that death would be waiting for them anywhere else, Witness JJ testified they stayed at the bureau communal.

421.   Witness JJ testified that often the Interahamwe came to beat the refugees during the day, and that the policemen came to beat them at night. She also testified that the Interahamwe took young girls and women from their site of refuge near the bureau communal into a forest in the area and raped them. Witness JJ testified that this happened to her – that she was stripped of her clothing and raped in front of other people. At the request of the Prosecutor and with great embarrassment, she explicitly specified that the rapist, a young man armed with an axe and a long knife, penetrated her vagina with his penis. She stated that on this occasion she was raped twice. Subsequently, she told the Chamber, on a day when it was raining, she was taken by force from near the bureau communal into the cultural center within the compound of the bureau communal, in a group of approximately fifteen girls and women. In the cultural center, according to Witness JJ, they were raped. She was raped twice by one man. Then another man came to where she was lying and he also raped her. A third man then raped her, she said, at which point she described herself as feeling near dead. Witness JJ testified that she was at a later time dragged back to the cultural center in a group of approximately ten girls and women and they were raped. She was raped again, two times. Witness JJ testified that she could not count the total number of times she was raped. She said, "each time you encountered attackers they would rape you," – in the forest, in the sorghum fields. Witness JJ related to the Chamber the experience of finding her sister before she died, having been raped and cut with a machete.

422.   Witness JJ testified that when they arrived at the bureau communal the women were hoping the authorities would defend them but she was surprised to the contrary. In her testimony **[page 173]** she recalled lying in the cultural center, having been raped repeatedly by Interahamwe, and hearing the cries of young girls around her, girls as young as twelve or thirteen years old. On the way to the cultural center the first time she was raped, Witness JJ said that she and the others were taken past the Accused and that he was looking at them. The second time she was taken to the cultural center to be raped, Witness JJ recalled seeing the Accused standing at the entrance of the cultural center and hearing him say loudly to the Interahamwe, "Never ask me again what a Tutsi woman tastes like," and "Tomorrow they will be killed" (Ntihazagire umbaza uko umututsikazi yari ameze, ngo kandi mumenye ko ejo ngo nibabica nta kintu muzambaza. Ngo ejo bazabica). According to Witness JJ, most of the girls and women were subsequently killed, either brought to the river and killed there, after having returned to their houses, or killed at the bureau communal. Witness JJ testified that she never saw the Accused rape anyone, but she, like Witness H, believed that he had the means to prevent the rapes from taking place and never even tried to do so. In describing the Accused and the statement he made regarding the taste of Tutsi women, she said he was "talking as if someone were encouraging a player" (Yavugaga nk'ubwiriza umukinnyi) and suggested that he was the one "supervising" the acts of rape. Witness JJ said she did not witness any killings at the bureau communal, although she saw dead bodies there.

423.   Witness JJ fled from the bureau communal, she left her one year-old child with a Hutu man and woman, who said they had milk for the child and subsequently killed him. Witness JJ spoke of the heavy sorrow the war had caused her. She testified to the humiliation she felt as a mother, by the public nudity and being raped in the presence of children by young men. She said that just thinking about it made the war come alive inside of her. Witness JJ told the Chamber that she had remarried but that her life had never been the same because of the beatings and rapes she suffered. She said the pain in her ribs prevents her from farming because she can no longer use a hoe, and she used to live on the food that she could grow.

424. Witness OO, a young Tutsi woman, testified that she and her family sought refuge at the bureau communal in April 1994 and encountered many other Tutsi refugees there, on the road outside the compound. While she was there, she said, some Interahamwe arrived and started **[page 174]** killing people with machetes. She and two other girls tried to flee but were stopped by the Interahamwe who went back and told the Accused that they were taking the girls away to "sleep with" them. Witness OO told the Chamber that standing five metres away from the Accused, she heard him say in reply, "take them". She said she was then separated from the other girls and taken to a field by one Interahamwe called Antoine. When she refused to sit down, he pushed her to the ground and put his "sex" into hers, clarifying on examination that he penetrated her vagina with his penis. When she started to cry, she said he warned her that if she cried or shouted, others might come and kill her.

425. According to Witness OO, Antoine left her in the field and returned that night to take her to the house of a woman called Zimba, where she spent three nights. On the fourth night, she said Antoine returned and took her to another Interahamwe called Emanuel. She said that Antoine did the same thing he had done before to her, and that Emanuel followed him in turn. Witness OO told the Chamber she spent three days and nights at the house of Emanuel where every day she was sexually violated by both Antoine and Emanuel. Afterwards, she said she was chased away by them.

426. Witness OO returned to the bureau communal when she heard that an order had been given to stop the killing of women and children, but after hearing the Accused, Kubwimana and Ruvugama all call for the killing of Tutsi, she left and went back into hiding. Subsequently, she and her seven year-old sister were apprehended by Interahamwe and taken to a roadblock. Her sister and two other people were imprisoned overnight and killed in the morning. At the time of these events, Witness OO was fifteen years old. When asked how it was that the Accused had the authority to protect her from rape, Witness OO replied that if he had told the Interahamwe not to take her from the bureau communal, they would have listened to him because he was the bourgmestre. Witness OO was unable to identify the Accused in the courtroom. She told the Chamber that someone had pointed him out to her at the bureau communal as the bourgmestre but that she had not looked at him closely and that it had been a long time ago.

427. Witness KK, a Hutu woman married to a Tutsi man, also sought refuge at the bureau **[page 175]** communal in Taba after her home was destroyed. She testified that the Tutsi refugees there were beaten often by the police and the Accused, whom she described as "supervising." She recalled the Accused publicly name a teacher called Tharcisse as an accomplice and send the police to find him. They brought Tharcisse and his wife and make them sit in the mud. With the Accused standing nearby they then killed Tharcisse. They took off his wife's clothing and told her to go and die somewhere else. Witness KK testified that on the same day, on the orders of the Accused, the Interahamwe brought teachers from Remera, who were also forced to sit in the mud. She said they started by clubbing a young teacher who had been brought with his fiancee, and that during this time the Accused was walking around and supervising the police, who were beating refugees. The teachers were critically wounded with small hoes and taken in a wheelbarrow to a mass grave, many still breathing, left to die a slow death.

428. Witness KK testified that her husband was beaten at the bureau communal and injured on the head. After escaping, he was captured by Interahamwe, and Witness KK received a message from him requesting to speak to her before he died. She found him behind the bureau communal with Interahamwes armed with clubs and spears, who then took him away between the two buildings of the bureau communal. She learned later that he was killed. Witness KK later went to the Accused and asked him for an attestation to help her keep her children alive. She said he replied that it was not he who had made them be born Tutsi and that "when rats are killed you don't spare rats that are still in the form of fetus." Witness KK testified that she had been pregnant and miscarried after being beaten by police and Interahamwe. Of her nine children, only two survived the events of this period.

429. Witness KK also recalled seeing women and girls selected and taken away to the cultural center at the bureau communal by Interahamwes who said they were going to "sleep with" these women and girls. Witness KK testified regarding an incident in which the Accused told the Interahamwe to undress a young girl named Chantal, who he knew to be a gymnast, so that she could do gymnastics naked. The Accused told Chantal, who said she was Hutu, she must be a Tutsi because he knew her father to be a

Tutsi. As Chantal was forced to march around naked in front of many people, Witness KK testified that the Accused was laughing and happy with **[page 176]** this. Afterwards, she said he told the Interahamwes to take her away and said "you should first of all make sure that you sleep with this girl." (*Ngo kandi nababwiye ko muzajya mubanza mukirwanaho mukarongora abo bakobwa*) Witness KK also testified regarding the rape of Tutsi women married to Hutu men. She described, after leaving the bureau communal, encountering on the road a man and woman who had been killed. She said the woman, whom she knew to be a Tutsi married to a Hutu, was "not exactly dead" and still in agony. She described the Interahamwe forcing a piece of wood into the woman's sexual organs while she was still breathing, before she died. In most cases, Witness KK said that Tutsi women married to Hutu men "were left alone because it was said that these women deliver Hutu children." She said that there were Hutu men who married Tutsi women to save them, but that these women were sought, taken away forcibly and killed. She said that she never saw the Accused rape a woman.

430. Witness NN, a Tutsi woman and the younger sister of JJ, described being raped along with another sister by two men in the courtyard of their home, just after it was destroyed by their Hutu neighbours and her brother and father had been killed. Witness NN said one of the men told her that the girls had been spared so that they could be raped. She said her mother begged the men, who were armed with bludgeons and machetes, to kill her daughters rather than rape them in front of her, and the man replied that the "principle was to make them suffer" and the girls were then raped. Witness NN confirmed on examination that the man who raped her penetrated her vagina with his penis, saying he did it in an "atrocious" matter, mocking and taunting them. She said her sister was raped by the other man at the same time, near her, so that they could each see what was happening to the other. Afterwards, she said she begged for death.

431. According to the testimony of Witness NN, after these men left, two other men who were neighbours came and one of them raped her, while the other took her sister a little further away and raped her sister. She recalled that the neighbour said that marriage had been refused to them, but now they were going to sleep with the girls without penalty (peine). She said the men left afterwards, warning the girls that they would kill them if they did not stay where they were. That evening, she said two other younger men, around the age of 15 or 16, came and asked them to "teach them because they didn't know how it was done". After these two men raped the girls, **[page 177]** Witness NN said their mother asked her daughters to leave rather than continue to be tortured in front of her. The girls left and went into hiding with a relative.

432. After hiding for a week and one half, Witness NN said she heard that Akayesu had stopped the killings, and she went with her sister towards the bureau communal. On the way, having taken a different route from her sister, Witness NN said she met two men who said they would accompany her to the bureau communal and that they had been given orders by the bourgmestre. She said the two men then took her a short distance away and raped her, each of them in turn, leaving her there afterwards lying naked. Subsequently, she said four men herding cattle came upon her, and two of them raped her. These incidents took place in the countryside, not very far from the bureau communal, according to Witness NN. After the rapes, Witness NN said she could not move – she was unable to get up and unable to dress herself. She said her sister found her and brought her some ghee to put in her lower parts to relieve the muscles. When she was able to get up, Witness NN said she continued on her way to the bureau communal with her sister.

433. Witness NN estimated that she arrived at the bureau communal some time in the beginning of May, and she said she found about three hundred refugees there, mostly women and children. The morning after she arrived, she said she saw the Accused with a towel around his neck, moving to the place where two Interahamwes were driving a woman to rape her, between the bureau communal and the cultural center. She said she saw the Accused standing watching the men drag the woman and later on he entered the office. She said she saw the Interahamwe circle this woman and saw them on top of her but did not see them penetrate her. She also said there were many refugees watching while this was happening. During the rape, she said there were two commune policemen who were in front of the office of the bourgmestre, one called Mushumba and one called Nsengiyumva who was in plain clothes. She said they did nothing to prevent the rape from happening and that the Accused did nothing as well – only

watched and entered his office. She said after the rape she saw that the naked woman was hungry and cold, and the woman was pregnant. She said she was told by an Interahamwe that the woman died at the bureau communal. Witness NN said she did not see anyone raped inside the cultural center **[page 178]** but that the Interahamwe did come at night and take some girls away.

434.   Two days after arriving at the bureau communal, Witness NN recounted seeing an Interahamwe called Rafiki, whom she had known previously and who had previously told her that he wanted to live with her. When he saw her at the bureau communal, she said he told her that he was going to rape her and not marry her. She said Rafiki took her to his home not far from the bureau communal and locked her up there for two days, during which time he raped her repeatedly day and night, a total of approximately six times. She said often when he came to rape her, he had been smoking herbs or drinking alcohol. When she returned to the bureau communal, Witness NN said she found her sister, who told her that she also had been raped again, at the bureau communal. Witness NN testified that her sister was hungry and cold, and could not move. Her sister died and when they went to bury her, they found her body had been eaten by dogs.

435.   Witness NN said she saw the Accused often at the bureau communal and that she heard him tell police to remove the refugees, citing one occasion where a policeman named Mushuba beat and chased them away after receiving such an order from the Accused. She also recalled seeing the Accused when Ntereye was taken from the prison and killed. She did not witness this killing but heard a gunshot and later saw the corpse of Nteyere, his head crushed as if by a hammer. Subsequently, Witness NN said on two consecutive days she was taken with a group of several hundred people, mostly women and children, to a hole near the bureau communal where the Interahamwe were intending to kill them with a grenade. The first day they were apparently unable to find a grenade. On the second day, they were beaten and brought back to the hole. At that time Witness NN said Rafiki, the Interahamwe who had locked her in his house, took her out of the group and said that she was his wife. According to her testimony, the Interahamwe then started stabbing the group of people, beating them with machetes and throwing them into the hole while she was standing by. Witness NN said she closed her eyes but could hear people crying and shouting. She estimated that the killing of the group took twenty minutes, and recalled feeling as if she were dead, apart from the fact that she was still breathing.

436.   Witness NN said she was then taken by the younger brother of Rafiki back to his home **[page 179]** where she stayed for one week. While she was there, she said she was locked up by Rafiki, who gave the key to other young men who came and "slept with" her, which she explained meant that they took their "sex" and put it into hers. She did not recall how many times this happened, stating that they came every day but that sometimes they did not rape her. After a week, Witness NN told the Chamber that she ran away and hid in the bush. Witness NN expressed the opinion in her testimony that the Accused had the power to oppose the killings and rapes and that by not giving refuge to anybody at the bureau communal, he authorized the rapes which took place. She testified that as a result of the rapes she has had recurring vaginal discharge and pain which require treatment in hospital.

437.   Witness PP, a Tutsi woman married to a Hutu man, lived very near the bureau communal. Witness PP testified that she saw three women – Alexia, the wife of Ntereye, and her two nieces Nishimwe and Louise – raped and killed at Kinihira, a basin near the bureau communal. Witness PP said that the women were brought by the Interahamwe, at the direction of the Accused, in a vehicle of the bureau communal driven by Mutabaruka, the driver of the commune of Taba. She said the first saw the women in the vehicle at the bureau communal, where she heard the Accused say to the Interahamwe, "Take them to Kinihira. Don't you know where killings take place, where the others have been killed?" According to Witness PP, who then went to Kinihira herself, the three women were forced by the Interahamwe to undress and told to walk, run and perform exercises "so that they could display the tights of Tutsi women." At this took place, she said, in front of approximately two hundred people. After this, she said the women were raped. She described in particular detail the rape of Alexia by Interahamwe who threw her to the ground and climbed on top of her saying "Now, let's see what the vagina of a Tutsi woman feels like." According to Witness PP, Alexia gave the Interahamwe named Pierre her Bible before he raped her and told him, "Take this Bible because it's our memory, because you do not know

what you're doing." Then one person held her neck, others took her by the shoulders and others held her tights apart as numerous Interahamwe continued to rape her – Bongo after Pierre, and Habarurena after Bongo. According to the testimony, Alexia was pregnant. When she became weak she was turned over and lying on her stomach, she went into premature delivery during the rapes. Witness PP testified that the Interahamwe then went on to rape Nishimwe, a young girl, **[page 180]** and recalled lots of blood coming from her private parts after several men raped her. Louise was then raped by several Interahamwe while others held her down, and after the rapes, according to the testimony, all three women were placed on their stomachs and hit with sticks and killed.

438. Witness PP said that no one tried to rape her because they did not know which ethnic group she belonged to. She also said she was protected from rape by an Interahamwe named Bongo because she had given him a sandwich and tea, and he told the other Interahamwe not to harm her. Witness PP testified that some women and children were able to escape from the bureau communal in April 1994 but that they had to "sacrifice themselves" in order to survive. By sacrifice she said she meant that they submitted to rape and she said that she helped to care for one of these women who subsequently came to her house for a week. On cross-examination, Witness PP described her encounter with a woman called Vestine, whom she had rescued from the pit at Kinihira where people were being thrown and where Vestine had just given birth. Witness PP said she brought Vestine to stay in the house of Emmanuel, a man she knew, and when she went back two days later, he told her that Vestine had been taken by an Interahamwe called Habarurena to a sorghum field in a place known as Kanyinya. According to Witness PP, Habarurena kept Vestine in the sorghum field for a week and raped her repeatedly. When she next saw Vestine there was a liquid flowing from her private parts and Vestine told her, "I think it would be better to go Kinihira to be killed." The next day Witness PP said she saw Vestine being raped, together with other women, and there was nothing she could do. On the following day, from the church where she went to pray, Witness PP said she saw Vestine being killed with a machete, by an Interahamwe called Bongo, and thrown into the pit, having been brought back there by the Interahamwe Habarurena.

439. Defence Witness DBB, a former student of the Accused currently in detention in Rwanda, testified that he went to the bureau communal on the 17 April 1994. Thereafter he went into hiding during the massacres and did not go to the bureau communal at all. Witness DBB testified that he never heard of or saw violence perpetrated against women during the events which took place in 1994, and that no women in his sector were raped. Subsequently he did say that he heard people saying that women were being raped in the commune of Taba, outside of **[page 181]** his sector, but he said he did not witness this. Witness DBB said he did not hear the name of the Accused mentioned in connection with sexual violence and that it was being attributed to the people who were participating in the massacres and looting. Witness DBB expressed the view that these incidents were being done out of sight of the Accused. On cross-examination he said he did not know anything about the Accused allowing women to be taken away and raped at the bureau communal.

440. Defence Witness DCC, the driver of Taba commune, testified that he never heard about violence perpetrated against women in Taba commune, that the Accused perpetrated violence against women in the commune or that the Accused gave orders for women to be raped. He said that during the period he was at the bureau communal, in April and throughout May, there were refugees there and he was there every day. He said nothing happened to the women refugees, and that he did not witness any of them being beaten or taken away to be raped. He said he did not know Alexia, Ntereye's wife, and denied going to look for her, finding her, and driving her in the communal vehicle to the bureau communal and then to Kinihira. He said the bureau communal vehicle had broken down before the massacres started.

441. Defence Witness DZZ, a former Taba communal policeman currently in detention in Rwanda, testified that he went to the bureau communal every day and that incidents of sexual violence did not take place there. Witness DZZ also testified that he saw no crimes of any type being committed at the bureau communal. Witness DZZ was quite insistent that he heard of no cases of rape in the entire commune of Taba during this period. Defence Witness DCX in a similar statement said that when he was in Taba he heard no mention of sexual violence. He stated categorically that there was no rape. Defence Witness

DAX when asked whether he had heard that the Interahamwe had committed crimes of sexual violence against women stated that nobody talked about such things where he was. He said he could not affirm that elsewhere maybe such things were heard or took place.

442. Defence Witness Matata, called as an expert witness, noted only one case he had heard of in Taba, an attempted rape of two girls aged fourteen and fifteen. He expressed his opinion that [page 182] the bourgmestre would not have been aware of this case as it was in a region, Buguri sector, which the bourgmestre had never gone to. Witness Matata noted that there is a cultural factor which prevented people from talking about rape, but also suggested that the phenomenon of rape was introduced afterwards for purposes of blackmail. He said he had come across incidents of rape in other parts of the country but suggested that cases of rape were not frequent and not related to an ethnic group. Witness Matata expressed the opinion that rapists were more interested in satisfying their physical needs, that there were spontaneous acts of desire even in the context of killing. He noted that Tutsi women, in general, are quite beautiful and that raping them is not necessarily intended to destroy an ethnic group, but rather to have a beautiful woman.

443. Defence Witness DIX testified that her father lent his vehicle to the Accused and helped him ensure security in the commune during this period. Witness DIX testified that she was at home in Taba and heard all the news but that she did not hear anything about rape or sexual violence during the killings which took place. However, she said that she received all her information from her parents and neighbours and did not once go to the bureau communal after the killings started. She said that she herself saw the Accused just one time, in April. According to her testimony, she did not speak to him at that time, and has never spoken to him at any other time. Nevertheless, Witness DIX expressed the opinion that the Accused had committed no crime, and she was surprised that he was in prison. Defence witness DJX, a minor and the brother of Witness DIX, also testified that he did not hear anything about rape and he did not see any cases of rape. The Chamber notes that the written statements of these two witnesses, prepared and submitted by the Defence, are identical. Witness DJX was twelve years old at the time of the events, and like Witness DIX, he testified that he did not go to the bureau communal during this period. He said he saw the Accused two times.

444. Witness DFX testified that she was never a witness to acts of rape or sexual violence in Taba and that she never even heard anyone talk about them. The Chamber notes that this witness, who is a protected witness, has a close personal relationship to the Defendant. She testified, on examination by the Chamber, that the Accused did not tell her what was happening at the bureau communal, that she did not ask him, and that her source of information was from other people. [page 183] On cross-examination by the Prosecution, she testified that she herself never went to the bureau communal during this period for security reasons. On examination by the Chamber, the Witness acknowledged that in her written statement submitted by the Defence she had mentioned reports that the Interahamwe were abducting beautiful Tutsi girls and taking them home as mistresses. She conceded that such conduct could be considered sexual violence as it was not consensual.

445. Defence Witness DEEX, a Tutsi woman, testified that before killing women the Interahamwes raped them. Asked whether the Accused encouraged or authorized them in this sexual violence, she said she did not know. On cross-examination, she said that she did not personally witness sexual violence, although she heard that the girls at the house of the family where she had taken refuge were raped by the Interahamwe. Witness DEEX testified that she was given a laissez-passer by the Accused, which helped her to move around safely.

446. The Accused himself testified that he was completely surprised by the allegations of rape in Taba during the events which took place. He asserted that anyone saying that even a single woman was raped at the bureau communal was lying. While he acknowledged that some witnesses had testified that they were raped at the bureau communal, he swore, in the name of God, that the charge was made up. He said he never saw, and never heard from his policemen, that any woman was raped at the bureau communal. He said that he heard about rape accusations over Radio Rwanda and that women's associations had organized demonstrations and a march from Kigali to Taba. He suggested that perhaps this was intended to make the Chamber understand that in Taba women were raped at the bureau communal, but he insisted

that women were never raped within the premises of the bureau communal or on land belonging to the bureau communal or the commune.

447. In his testimony, the Accused recalled the allegation that he had forced a young girl, Chantal, to march naked. He said he did not know her and that it never took place. He said he would not do something like that. He referred to the account of a woman raped with a wooden stick as "savagery", questioning how a woman could witness such a thing, and he referred to the statement he had been accused of making at the entrance to the cultural center as "too much". He **[page 184]** also testified that the cultural center building is such that it would be difficult to see what was going on inside from the door and that it would be difficult for a woman lying down inside to know who is at the door. The Accused testified that there were women taking refuge all over and outside the bureau communal and that there were women in the cultural center. He denied that the Interahamwe brought women to the cultural center. He said that some of the women who look refuge at the bureau communal were killed and others escaped.

448. On examination by the Chamber, the Accused stated that he did hear about rapes in Kigali but only after he was out of the country. When asked by the Chamber for a reaction to the testimony of sexual violence, the Accused noted that rape was not mentioned in the pre-trial statements of Witness J and Witness H, although Witness H said on examination by the Chamber that she had mentioned her rape to investigators. The Accused suggested that his Indictment was amended because of pressure from the women's movement and women in Rwanda, whom he described as "worked up to agree that they have been raped." On examination by the Chamber, the Accused acknowledged that it was possible that rape might have taken place in the commune of Taba, but he insisted that no rape took place at the bureau communal. He said he first learned of the rape allegations in Taba at the Chamber and maintained that the charges were an "invented accusation.

Factual Findings

449. Having carefully reviewed the testimony of the Prosecution witnesses regarding sexual violence, the Chamber finds that there is sufficient credible evidence to establish beyond a reasonable doubt that during the events of 1994, Tutsi girls and women were subjected to sexual violence, beaten and killed on or near the bureau communal premises, as well as elsewhere in the commune of Taba. Witness H, Witness JJ, Witness OO, and Witness NN all testified that they themselves were raped, and all, with the exception of Witness OO, testified that they witnessed other girls and women being raped. Witness J, Witness KK and Witness PP also testified that they witnessed other girls and women being raped in the commune of Taba. Hundreds of Tutsi, mostly women and children, sought refuge at the bureau communal during this period and many rapes **[page 185]** took place on or near the premises of the bureau communal – Witness JJ was taken by Interahamwe from the refuge site near the bureau communal to a nearby forest area and raped there. She testified that this happened often to other young girls and women at the refuge site. Witness JJ was also raped repeatedly on two separate occasions in the cultural center on the premises of the bureau communal, once in a group of fifteen girls and women and once in a group of ten girls and women. Witness KK saw women and girls being selected and taken by the Interahamwe to the cultural center to be raped. Witness H saw women being raped outside the compound of the bureau communal, and Witness NN saw two Interahamwes take a woman and rape her between the bureau communal and the cultural center. Witness OO was taken from the bureau communal and raped in a nearby field. Witness PP saw three women being raped at Kinihira, the killing site near the bureau communal, and Witness NN found her younger sister, dying, after she had been raped at the bureau communal. Many other instances of rape in Taba outside the bureau communal – in fields, on the road, and in or just outside houses – were described by Witness J, Witness H, Witness OO, Witness KK, Witness NN and Witness PP. Witness KK and Witness PP also described other acts of sexual violence which took place on or near the premises of the bureau communal – the forced undressing and public humiliation of girls and women. The Chamber notes that much of the sexual violence took place in front of large number of people, and that all of it was directed against Tutsi women.

450. With a few exceptions, most of the rapes and all of the other acts of sexual violence described by the Prosecution witnesses were committed by Interahamwe. It was not been established that the perpetrator of the rape of Witness H in a sorghum field and six of the men who raped Witness NN were Interahamwe. In the case of Witness NN, two of her rapists were neighbours, two were teenage boys and two were herdsmen, and there is no evidence that any of these people were Interahamwe. Nevertheless, with regard to all evidence of rape and sexual violence which took place on or near the premises of the bureau communal, the perpetrators were all identified as Interahamwe. Interahamwe are also identified as the perpetrators of many rapes which took place outside the bureau communal, including the rapes of Witness H, Witness OO, Witness NN, Witness J's daughter, a woman near death seen by Witness KK and a woman called Vestine, seen by Witness PP. There is no suggestion in any of the evidence that the Accused or **[page 186]** any communal policemen perpetrated rape, and both Witness JJ and Witness KK affirmed that they never saw the Accused rape anyone.

451. In considering the role of the Accused in the sexual violence which took place and the extent of his direct knowledge of incidents of sexual violence, the Chamber has taken into account only evidence which is direct and unequivocal. Witness H testified that the Accused was present during the rape of Tutsi women outside the compound of the bureau communal, but as she could not confirm that he was aware that the rapes were taking place, the Chamber discounts this testimony in its assessment of the evidence. Witness PP recalled the Accused directing the Interahamwe to take Alexia and her two nieces to Kinihira, saying "Don't you know where killings take place, where the others have been killed?" The three women were raped before they were killed, but the statement of the Accused does not refer to sexual violence and there is no evidence that the Accused was present at Kinihira. For this reason, the Chamber also discounts this testimony in its assessment of the evidence.

452. On the basis of the evidence set forth herein, the Chamber finds beyond a reasonable doubt that the Accused had reason to know and in fact knew that sexual violence was taking place on or near the premises of the bureau communal, and that women were being taken away from the bureau communal and sexually violated. There is no evidence that the Accused took any measures to prevent acts of sexual violence or to punish the perpetrators of sexual violence. In fact there is evidence that the Accused ordered, instigated and otherwise aided and abetted sexual violence. The Accused watched two Interahamwe drag a woman to be raped between the bureau communal and the cultural center. The two commune policemen in front of his office witnessed the rape but did nothing to prevent it. On the two occasions Witness JJ was brought to the cultural center of the bureau communal to be raped, she and the group of girls and women with her were taken past the Accused, on the way. On the first occasion he was looking at them, and on the second occasion he was standing at the entrance to the cultural center. On this second occasion, he said, "Never ask me again what a Tutsi woman tastes like." Witness JJ described the Accused in making these statements as "talking as if someone were encouraging a player." More generally she stated that the Accused was the one "supervising" the acts of rape. When Witness OO and two **[page 187]** other girls were apprehended by Interahamwe in flight from the bureau communal, the Interahamwe went to the Accused and told him that they were taking the girls away to sleep with them. The Accused said "take them." The Accused told the Interahamwe to undress Chantal and march her around. He was laughing and happy to be watching and afterwards told the Interahamwe to take her away and said "you should first of all make sure that you sleep with this girl." The Chamber considers this statement as evidence that the Accused ordered and instigated sexual violence, although insufficient evidence was presented to establish beyond a reasonable doubt that Chantal was in fact raped.

453. In making its factual findings, the Chamber has carefully considered the cross-examination by the Defence of Prosecution witnesses and the evidence presented by the Defence. With regard to cross-examination, the Chamber notes that the Defence did not question the testimony of Witness J or Witness H on rape at all, although the Chamber itself questioned both witnesses on this testimony. Witness JJ, OO, KK, NN and PP were questioned by the Defence with regard to their testimony of sexual violence, but the testimony itself was never challenged. Details such as where the rapes took place, how many rapists there were, how old they were, whether the Accused participated in the rapes, who was raped and which rapists used condoms were all elicited by the Defence, but at no point did the Defence suggest to the witnesses that the rapes had not taken place. The main line of questioning by the Defence

with regard to the rapes and other sexual violence, other than to confirm the details of the testimony, related to whether the Accused had the authority to stop them. In cross-examination of the evidence presented by the Prosecution, specific incidents of sexual violence were never challenged by the Defence.

454. The Defence has raised discrepancies between the pre-trial written statements made by witnesses to the Office of the Prosecutor and their testimony before this Chamber, to challenge the credibility of these witnesses. The Chamber has considered the discrepancies which have been alleged with regard to the witnesses who testified on sexual violence and finds them to be unfounded or immaterial. For example, the Defence challenged Witness PP, quoting from her pre-trial statement that she stayed home during the genocide and recalling her testimony that she went out often as a contradiction. The Chamber pointed out to the Defence that elsewhere in her pre-**[page 188]** trial statement, Witness PP had also said "I went out of my house often." The Chamber established that during this period, Witness PP stayed, generally speaking, in the Taba commune, but that she went out of her house often. Selectively quoting from the pre-trial statements, the Defence often suggested inconsistencies which, upon examination or with further explanation, were found not to be inconsistencies.

455. With regard to the inconsistencies which were established by the Defence, the Chamber finds them to be immaterial. For example, Witness OO said in her pre-trial statement that she went to the bureau communal four days after the plane crash which killed President Habyarimana. In her testimony, she said she went to the bureau communal one week after the plane crash. Witness PP said in her pre-trial statement that when she rescued Vestine, Vestine was thereafter taken from her by Habarurena. In her testimony, Witness PP said she left Vestine at the house of Emmanuel, from which Vestine was taken by Habarurena. Whether Tutsi women were stripped on the way to or at Kinihira is the core of another discrepancy between the pre-trial statement and testimony of Witness PP. The Chamber considers that these inconsistencies are not of material consequence and that they are not substantial enough to impeach the credibility of the witnesses. The Chamber is of the view that the inconsistencies between pre-trial statements and witness testimony can be explained by the difficulties of recollecting precise details several years after the occurrence of the events, the trauma experienced by the witnesses to these events, the difficulties of translation, and the fact that several witnesses were illiterate and stated that they had not read their written statements.

456. The Defence in its closing argument used the example of Witness J to demonstrate the dishonesty of Prosecution witnesses. He recalled that Witness J testified that she was six months pregnant, and that when her brother was killed she climbed up a tree and stayed there for an entire week in her condition, without any food. In fact, the Defence is misrepresenting Witness J's testimony. She did not say that she stayed in a tree for a whole week without food. Witness J testified that when she got hungry she came down and went to a neighbour's house for food and that subsequently her neighbour brought food to her and then she would spend the night in the tree. Under cross-examination, Witness J testified that she came down from the tree every night. **[page 189]** What the Defence characterized as the "fantasy" of this witness, which may be "of interest to psychologists and not justice", the witness characterized as desperation, answering his challenge with the suggestion, "If somebody was chasing you, you would be able to climb a tree."

457. Of the twelve witnesses presented by the Defence, other than the Accused only two – DZZ and DCC – testified that they went regularly to the bureau communal after the killings began in Taba. These two witnesses contradicted each other on what they saw and heard. Witness DZZ, a former communal policeman currently contradicted each other on what they saw and heard. Witness DZZ, a former communal policeman currently in detention in Rwanda, testified that he heard of no cases of rape in the entire commune during this period. He testified that he was at the bureau communal every day and that no sexual violence took place there. He also testified that no crimes of any sort took place at the bureau communal – a categorical statement which, in the light of all the other witnesses who have testified that killings took place at the bureau communal, is highly implausible. The Accused himself testified that killings took place at the bureau communal. Witness DCC, who is currently in detention in Rwanda, also testified that killings took place at the bureau communal. Witness DCC was the driver of the commune

during this time, and he testified that he never heard that violence was perpetrated against women in Taba. He denied bringing Alexia, the wife of Ntereye, in the communal vehicle to the bureau communal and then to Kinihira, and he testified that this vehicle had broken down before the massacres started Yet Defence Witness DAX testified that the communal vehicle was in use between April and June. Witness PP also testified that she saw the driver in this vehicle within this time frame. For these reasons the Chamber does not accept the testimony of Witness DZZ and DCC with regard to sexual violence.

458. Most of the Defence witnesses did not go to the bureau communal during the period from 7 April 1994 to the end of June 1994. Witness DCX, who testified that he did not hear any mention of sexual violence, only went to the bureau communal two times during this period, for personal reasons, and passed by the bureau several times. Witness DEEX, a Tutsi woman, who testified that she went once to the bureau communal, did hear that woman were being raped by the Interahamwe before they were killed. The other Defence witnesses who testified that they had not heard any mention of sexual violence stated that they did not go to the bureau communal at **[page 190]** any time after the killings started. Witness DBB, Witness DAX, Witness DAAX, Witness DIX, Witness DJX, Witness DFX and Witness Matata never went to the bureau communal during this period. Witness DAAX and Witness Matata, who was called as an expert, were not in the commune of Taba during this period, and Witness DBB was in hiding after 17 April 1994. The Chamber considers that these witnesses were not in a position to know what occurred at the bureau communal. By their own accounts none of them, with the exception of Witness DAAX, had any conversation with the Accused regarding what was happening there. Witness DAAX, a prefet, testified that he lost contact with the Accused after 18 April 1994, before the killings began. The testimony of these witnesses therefore does not discredit the evidence presented by the Prosecution witnesses.

459. With regard to the testimony of the Accused, the Chamber finds very little concrete evidence or argument on sexual violence other than his bare denial that it occurred. The only specific incident referred to by the Accused on direct examination was the forced undressing and parading of Chantal, which he denied. On examination by the Chamber, the Accused subsequently referred to other incidents and a statement he was said to have made outside the cultural center, suggesting that it would be difficult for a person standing at the entrance to see what was happening inside, and that it would be difficult for a person inside lying down to see who was at the entrance. The Accused did not assert that this was impossible, and these comments were made in an offhand manner rather than as a serious defence. The Accused simply stated that there was very little to say about the allegations of sexual violence, that unlike the killings this was impossible and not even for discussion.

460. Faced with first-hand personal accounts form women who experienced and witnessed sexual violence in Taba and at the bureau communal, and who swore under oath that the Accused was present and saw what was happening, the Chamber does not accept the statement made by the Accused. The Accused insists that the charges are fabricated, but the Defence has offered the Chamber no evidence to support this assertion. There is overwhelming evidence to the contrary, and the Chamber does not accept the testimony of the Accused. The findings of the Chamber are based on the evidence which has been presented in this trial. As the Accused flatly denies the **[page 191]** occurrence of sexual violence at the bureau communal, he does not allow for the possibility that the sexual violence may have occurred but that he was unaware of it. **[page 192]**

6. THE LAW

6.1. Cumulative Charges

461. In the amended Indictment, the accused is charged cumulatively with more than one crime in relation to the same sets of facts, in all but count 4. For example the events described in paragraphs 12 to 23 of the Indictment are the subject of three counts of the Indictment – genocide (count 1), complicity in genocide (count 2) and crimes against humanity/extermination (count 3). Likewise, counts 5 and 6 of the Indictment charge murder as a crime against humanity and murder as a violation of common article 3 of

the Geneva Conventions, respectively, in relation to the same set of facts; the same is true of counts 7 and 8, and of counts 9 and 10, of the Indictment. Equally, counts 11 (crime against humanity/torture) and 12 (violation of common article 3/cruel treatment) relate to the same events. So do counts 13 (crime against humanity/rape), 14 (crimes against humanity/other inhumane acts) and 15 (violation of common article 3 and additional protocol II/rape).

462. The question which arises at this stage is whether, if the Chamber is convinced beyond a reasonable doubt that a given factual allegation set out in the Indictment has been established, it may find the accused guilty of all the crimes charged in relation to those facts or only one. The reason for posing this question is that it might be argued that the accumulation of criminal charges offends against the principle of double jeopardy or a substantive *non bis in idem* principle in criminal law. Thus an accused who is found guilty of both genocide and crimes against humanity in relation to the same set of facts may argue that he has been twice judged for the same offence, which is generally considered impermissible in criminal law.

463. The Chamber notes that this question has been posed, and answered, by the Trial Chamber of the ICTY in the first case before that Tribunal, *The Prosecutor v. Dusko Tadić* Trial Chamber II, confronted with this issue, stated: **[page 193]**

"In any event, since this is a matter that will only be relevant insofar as it might affect penalty, it can best be dealt with if and when matters of penalty fall for consideration. What can, however, be said with certainty is that penalty cannot be made to depend upon whether offences arising from the same conduct are alleged cumulatively or in the alternative. What is to be punished by penalty is proven criminal conduct and that will not depend upon technicalities of pleading". (Prosecutor v. Tadić, Decision on Defence Motion on Form of the Indictment at p. 10 (No. IT-94-1-T, T.Ch.II, 14 Nov, 1995)

464. In that case, when the matter reached the sentencing stage, the Trial Chamber dealt with the matter of cumulative criminal charges by imposing *concurrent* sentences for each cumulative charge. Thus, for example, in relation to one particular beating, the accused received 7 years' imprisonment for the beating as a crime against humanity, and a 6 year concurrent sentence for the same beating as a violation of the laws or customs of war.

465. The Chamber takes due note of the practice of the ICTY. This practice was also followed in the *Barbie* case, where the French *Cour de Cassation* held that a single event could be qualified both as a crime against humanity and as a war crime.[79]

466. It is clear that the practice of concurrent sentencing ensures that the accused is not twice punished for the same acts. Notwithstanding this absence of prejudice to the accused, it is still necessary to justify the prosecutorial practice of accumulating criminal charges.

467. The Chamber notes that in Civil Law systems, including that of Rwanda, there exists a principle known as *concours ideal d'infractions* which permits multiple convictions for the same act under certain circumstances. Rwandan law allows multiple convictions in the following circumstances: **[page 194]**

Code pénal du Rwanda: Chapitre VI – Du concours d'infractions:

Article 92.– Il y a concours d'infractions lorsque plusieurs infractions ont été commises par le même auteur sans qu'une condamnation soit intervenue entre ces infractions.
Article 93.– Il y concours idéal:
1° lorsque le fait unique au point de vue matériel est susceptible de plusieurs qualifications;
2° lorsque l'action comprend des faits qui, constituant des infractions distinctes, sont unis entre eux comme procédant d'une intention délictueuse unique ou comme étant les uns des circonstances aggravantes des autres.

---

[79]   Judgment of 20 December 1985, *Bulletin des arrets de la Cour de Cassation*, 1985, p. 1038, e.s)

Seront seules prononcées dans le premier cas les peines déterminées par la qualification la plus sévère, dans le second cas les peines prévues pour la répression de l'infraction la plus grave, mais dont le maximum pourra être alors élevé de moitié.

468.   On the basis of national and international law and jurisprudence, the Chamber concludes that it is acceptable to convict the accused of two offences in relation to the same set of facts in the following circumstances: (1) where the offences have different elements; or (2) where the provisions creating the offences protect different interests; or (3) where it is necessary to record a conviction for both offences in order fully to describe what the accused did. However, the Chamber finds that it is not justifiable to convict an accused of two offences in relation to the same set of facts where (a) one offence is a lesser included offence of the other, for example, murder and grievous bodily harm, robbery and theft, or rape and indecent assault; or (b) where one offence charges accomplice liability and the other offence charges liability as a principal, e.g. genocide and complicity in genocide.

469.   Having regard to its Statute, the Chamber believes that the offences under the Statute – genocide, crimes against humanity, and violations of article 3 common to the Geneva Conventions and of Additional Protocol II – have different elements and, moreover, are intended to protect **[page 195]** different interests. The crime of genocide exists to protect certain groups from extermination or attempted extermination. The concept of crimes against humanity exists to protect civilian populations from persecution. The idea of violations of article 3 common to the Geneva Conventions and of Additional Protocol II is to protect non-combatants from war crimes in civil war. These crimes have different purposes and are, therefore, never co-extensive. Thus it is legitimate to charge these crimes in relation to the same set of facts. It may, additionally, depending on the case, be necessary to record a conviction for more than one of these offences in order to reflect what crimes an accused committed. If, for example, a general ordered that all prisoners of war belonging to a particular ethnic group should be killed, with the intent thereby to eliminate the group, this would be both genocide and a violation of common article 3, although not necessarily a crime against humanity. Convictions for genocide and violations of common article 3 would accurately reflect the accused general's course of conduct.

470.   Conversely, the Chamber does not consider that any of genocide, crimes against humanity, and violations of article 3 common to the Geneva Conventions and of Additional Protocol II are lesser included forms of each other. The ICTR Statute does not establish a hierarchy of norms, but rather all three offences are presented on an equal footing. While genocide may be considered the gravest crime, there is no justification in the Statute for finding that crimes against humanity or violations of common article 3 and additional protocol II are in all circumstances alternative charges to genocide and thus lesser included offences. As stated, and it is a related point, these offences have different constituent elements. Again, this consideration renders multiple convictions for these offences in relation to the same set of facts permissible. **[page 196]**

6.2.   Individual criminal responsibility (Article 6 of the Statue)

471.   The Accused is charged under Article 6(1) of the Statute of the Tribunal with individual criminal responsibility for the crimes alleged in the Indictment. With regard to Counts 13, 14 and 15 on sexual violence, the Accused is charged additionally, or alternatively, under Article 6(3) of the Statute. In the opinion of the Tribunal, Articles 6(1) and 6(3) address distinct principles of criminal liability and should, therefore, be considered separately. Article 6(1) sets forth the basic principles of individual criminal liability, which are undoubtedly common to most national criminal jurisdictions. Article 6(3), by contrast, constitutes something of an exception to the principles articulated in Article 6(1), as it derives from military law, namely the principle of the liability of a commander for the acts of his subordinates or "command responsibility".

472. Article 6(1) provides that:

"A person who planned, instigated, ordered, committed or otherwise aided and abetted in the planning, preparation or execution of a crime referred to in articles 2 to 4 of the present Statute, shall be individually responsible for the crime".

Thus, in addition to responsibility as principal perpetrator, the Accused can be held responsible for the criminal acts of others where he plans with them, instigates them, orders them or aids and abets them to commit those acts.

473. Thus, Article 6(1) covers various stages of the commission of a crime, ranging from its initial planning to its execution, through its organization. However, the principle of individual criminal responsibility as provided for in Article 6(1) implies that the planning or preparation of the crime actually leads to its commission. Indeed, the principle of individual criminal **[page 197]** responsibility for an attempt to commit a crime obtained only in case of genocide[80]. Conversely, this would mean that with respect to any other form of criminal participation and, in particular, those referred to in Article 6(1), the perpetrator would incur criminal responsibility only if the offence were completed.

474. Article 6(1) thus appears to be in accord with the Judgments of the Nuremberg Tribunal which held that persons other than those who committed the crime, especially those who ordered it, could incur individual criminal responsibility.

475. The International Law Commission, in Article 2 (3) of the Draft Code of Crimes Against the Peace and Security of Mankind, reaffirmed the principle of individual responsibility for the five forms of participation deemed criminal referred to in Article 6 (1) and consistently included the phrase "which in fact occurs", with the exception of aiding and abetting, which is akin to complicity and therefore implies a principal offence.

476. The elements of the offences or, more specifically, the forms of participation in the commission of one of the crimes under Articles 2 to 4 of the Statute, as stipulated in Article 6 (1) of the said Statute, their elements are inherent in the forms of participation *per se* which render the perpetrators thereof individually responsible for such crimes. The moral element is reflected in the desire of the Accused that the crime be in fact committed.

477. In this respect, the International Criminal Tribunal for the former Yugoslavia found in the Tadić case that:

"a person may only be criminally responsible for conduct where it is determined that he knowingly participated in the commission of an offence" and that "his participation directly and substantially affected the commission of that offence through supporting the actual commission before, during, or after the incident."[81] **[page 198]**

478. This intent can be inferred from a certain number of facts, as concerns genocide, crimes against humanity and war crimes, for instance, from their massive and/or systematic nature or their atrocity, to be considered *infra* in the judgment, in the Tribunal's findings on the law applicable to each of the three crimes which constitute its *ratione materiae* jurisdiction.

479. Therefore, as can be seen, the forms of participation referred to in Article 6 (1), cannot render their perpetrator criminally liable where he did not act knowingly, and even where he should have had such knowledge. This greatly differs from Article 6 (3) analyzed here below, which does not necessarily require that the superior acted knowingly to render him criminally liable; it suffices that he had reason to know that his subordinates were about to commit or had committed a crime and failed to take the necessary or reasonable measures to prevent such acts or punish the perpetrators thereof. In a way, this is liability by omission or abstention.

---

[80]   See Virginia Morris & Michael P. Scharpf, Ibid., p. 235
[81]   Para. 692, page 270, The Prosecutor v. Dusko Tadić, Case No. IT-94-1-T, 7 May 1997, ICTY.

480. The first form of liability set forth in Article 6 (1) is **planning** of a crime. Such planning is similar to the notion of *complicity* in Civil law, or *conspiracy* under Common law, as stipulated in Article 2 (3) of the Statute. But the difference is that planning, unlike complicity or plotting, can be an act committed by one person. Planning can thus be defined as implying that one or several persons contemplate designing the commission of a crime at both the preparatory and execution phases.

481. The second form of liability is **"incitation"** (in the french version of the Statute) to commit a crime, reflected in the English version of Article 6 (1) by the word *instigated*. In English, it seems the words incitement and instigation are synonymous[82]. Furthermore, the word "instigated" or "instigation" is used to refer to incitation in several other instruments[83]. However, in certain **[page 199]** legal systems and, under Civil law, in particular, the two concepts are very different[84]. Furthermore, and even assuming that the two words were synonymous, the question would be to know whether instigation under Article 6 (1) must include the direct and public elements, required for incitement, particularly, incitement to commit genocide (Article 2 (3)(c) of the Statute) which, in this instance, translates *incitation* into English as "incitement" and no longer "instigation". Some people are of that opinion[85]. The Chamber also accepts this interpretation[86].

482. That said, the form of participation through instigation stipulated in Article 6 (1) of the Statute, involves prompting another to commit an offence; but this is different from incitement in that it is punishable only where it leads to the actual commission of an offence desired by the instigator[87].

483. By **ordering** the commission of one of the crimes referred to in Articles 2 to 4 of the Statute, a person also incurs individual criminal responsibility. Ordering implies a superior-subordinate relationship between the person giving the order and the one executing it. In other words, the person in a position of authority uses it to convince another to commit an offence. In certain legal systems, including that of Rwanda[88], ordering is a form of complicity through instructions given to the direct perpetrator of an offence. Regarding the position of authority, the Chamber considers that sometimes it can be just a question of fact. **[page 200]**

484. Article 6 (1) declares criminally responsible a person who "(...) or otherwise aided and abetted in the planning, preparation or execution of a crime referred to in Articles 2 to 4 (...)". **Aiding** and **Abetting**, which may appear to be synonymous, are indeed different. Aiding means giving assistance to someone. Abetting, on the other hand, would involve facilitating the commission of an act by being sympathetic thereto. The issue here is to whether the individual criminal responsibility provided for in Article 6(1) is incurred only where there was aiding and abetting at the same time. The Chamber is of the opinion that either aiding or abetting alone is sufficient to render the perpetrator criminally liable. In both instances, it is not necessary for the person aiding or abetting another to commit the offence to be present during the commission of the crime.

485. The Chamber finds that, in many legal systems, aiding and abetting constitute acts of complicity. However, though akin to the constituent elements of complicity, they themselves constitute one of the crimes referred to in Articles 2 to 4 of the Statute, particularly, genocide. The Chamber is consequently of the opinion that when dealing with a person Accused of having aided and abetted in the planning, preparation and execution of genocide, it must be proven that such a person did have the specific intent

---

[82] See, for example, the "Lexique Anglais-Français (principalement juridique) of the Council of Europe, Strasbourg, January 1997, which translates "incitement" by *incitation, instigation ou provocation* or the "Dictionnaire Français/ Anglais" Larousse, or the "Dictionnaire Français/ Anglais" Super Senior Robert Collins.

[83] Article 6 of the Nuremberg Charter, Article 7(1) of the ICTY Statute and Article 2(3)(b) of the Draft Code of Crimes Against the Peace and the Security of Mankind.

[84] See, for instance, Article 91 of the Rwandan Penal Code, quoted and analyzed above under Chapter 6.3.2.

[85] See Virginia Morris and Michael P. Scharpf, *Ibid.* p. 239. Comments on Article 2 (3)(f) of the Draft Code on Crimes Against the Peace and the Security of Mankind by the International Law Commission, which article considers incitement to commit a crime in the same way as Article 6(1) of the Tribunal's Statute.

[86] See *infra* the findings of the Chamber on the crime of direct and public incitement to commit genocide.

[87] On this issue, also see *infra* the findings of the Chamber on the crime of direct and public incitement to commit genocide.

[88] See Article 91 of the Penal Code, in "Codes et Lois du Rwanda", Université nationale du Rwanda, 31 December 1994 update, Volume I, 2nd edition; 1995, p. 395.

to commit genocide, namely that, he or she acted with the intent to destroy in whole or in part, a national, ethnical, racial or religious group, as such; whereas, as stated *supra*, the same requirement is not needed for complicity in genocide[89].

486.   Article 6(3) of the Statute deals with the responsibility of the superior, or command responsibility. This principle, which derives from the principle of individual criminal responsibility as applied in the Nuremberg and Tokyo trials, was subsequently codified in Article 86 of the Additional Protocol I to the Geneva Conventions of 8 June 1977.

487.   Article 6(3) stipulates that:

> "The fact that any of the acts referred to in Articles 2 to 4 of the present Statute was committed by a subordinate does not relieve his or her superior of criminal **[page 201]** responsibility if he or she knew or had reason to know that the subordinate was about to commit such acts or had done so and the superior failed to take the necessary and reasonable measures to prevent such acts or to punish the perpetrators thereof".

488.   There are varying views regarding the *Mens rea* required for command responsibility. According to one view it derives from a legal rule of strict liability, that is, the superior is criminally responsible for acts committed by his subordinate, without it being necessary to prove the criminal intent of the superior. Another view holds that negligence which is so serious as to be tantamount to consent or criminal intent, is a lesser requirement. Thus, the "Commentary on the Additional Protocols of 8 June 1977 to the Geneva Conventions of 12 August 1949" stated, in reference to Article 86 of the Additional Protocol I, and the *mens rea* requirement for command responsibility that:

> "[...] the negligence must be so serious that it is tantamount to malicious intent, apart from any link between the conduct in question and the damage that took place. This element in criminal law is far from being clarified, but it is essential, since it is precisely on the question of intent that the system of penal sanctions in the Conventions is based"[90].

489.   The Chamber holds that it is necessary to recall that criminal intent is the moral element required for any crime and that, where the objective is to ascertain the individual criminal responsibility of a person Accused of crimes falling within the jurisdiction of the Chamber, such as genocide, crimes against humanity and violations of Article 3 Common to the Geneva Conventions and of Additional Protocol II thereto, it is certainly proper to ensure that there has been malicious intent, or, at least, ensure that negligence was so serious as to be tantamount to acquiescence or even malicious intent. **[page 202]**

490.   As to whether the form of individual criminal responsibility referred to Article 6(3) of the Statute applies to persons in positions of both military and civilian authority, it should be noted that during the Tokyo trials, certain civilian authorities were convicted of war crimes under this principle. Hirota, former Foreign Minister of Japan, was convicted of atrocities – including mass rape – committed in the "rape of Nanking", under a count which charged that he had "recklessly disregarded their legal duty by virtue of their offices to take adequate steps to secure the observance and prevent breaches of the law and customs of war". The Tokyo Tribunal held that:

> "Hirota was derelict in his duty in not insisting before the Cabinet that immediate action be taken to put an end to the authorities, failing any other action open to him to bring about the same result. He was content to rely on assurances which he knew were not being implemented while hundreds of murders, violations of women, and other atrocities were being committed daily. His inaction amounted to criminal negligence".

It should, however, be noted that Judge Röling strongly dissented from this finding, and held that Hirota should have been acquitted. Concerning the principle of command responsibility as applied to a civilian leader, Judge Röling stated that:

---

89   See *infra* the findings of the Chamber on the crime of direct and public incitement to commit genocide.

90   Claude Pilloud et al., "Commentary on the Additional Protocols of 8 June 1977 to the Geneva Conventions of 12 August 1949", 1987, p. 1036.

"Generally speaking, a Tribunal should be very careful in holding civil government officials responsible for the behaviour of the army in the field. Moreover, the Tribunal is here to apply the general principles of law as they exist with relation to the responsibility for "omissions". Considerations of both law and policy, of both justice and expediency, indicate that this responsibility should only be recognized in a very restricted sense".

491. The Chamber therefore finds that in the case of civilians, the application of the principle of individual criminal responsibility, enshrined in Article 6 (3), to civilians remains contentious. Against this background, the Chamber holds that it is appropriate to assess on a case by case basis the power of authority actually devolved upon the Accused in order to determine whether or **[page 203]** not he had the power to take all necessary and reasonable measures to prevent the commission of the alleged crimes or to punish the perpetrators thereof. **[page 204]**

6.3. Genocide (Article 2 of the Statute)

6.3.1. Genocide

492. Article 2 of the Statute stipulates that the Tribunal shall have the power to prosecute persons responsible for genocide, complicity to commit genocide, direct and public incitement to commit genocide, attempt to commit genocide and complicity in genocide.

493. In accordance with the said provisions of the Statute, the Prosecutor has charged Akayesu with the crimes legally defined as genocide (count 1), complicity in genocide (count 2) and incitement to commit genocide (count 4).

Crime of Genocide, punishable under Article 2(3)(a) of the Statute

494. The definition of genocide, as given in Article 2 of the Tribunal's Statute, is taken verbatim from Articles 2 and 3 of the Convention on the Prevention and Punishment of the Crime of Genocide (the "Genocide Convention")[91]. It states:

"Genocide means any of the following acts committed with intent to destroy, in whole or in part, a national, ethnical, racial or religious group, as such:
(a) Killing members of the group;
(b) Causing serious bodily or mental harm to members of the group;
(c) Deliberately inflicting on the group conditions of life calculated to bring about its physical destruction in whole or in part;
(d) Imposing measures intended to prevent births within the group; **[page 205]**
(e) Forcibly transferring children of the group to another group."

495. The Genocide Convention is undeniably considered part of customary international law, as can be seen in the opinion of the International Court of Justice on the provisions of the Genocide Convention, and as was recalled by the United Nations' Secretary-General in his Report on the establishment of the International Criminal Tribunal for the former Yugoslavia[92].

496. The Chamber notes that Rwanda acceded, by legislative decree, to the Convention on Genocide on 12 February 1975[93]. Thus, punishment of the crime of genocide did exist in Rwanda in 1994, at the time of the acts alleged in the Indictment, and the perpetrator was liable to be brought before the competent courts of Rwanda to answer for this crime.

---

[91] The Convention on the Prevention and Punishment of the Crime of Genocide was adopted by the United Nations General Assembly, on 9 December 1948.
[92] Secretary General's Report to paragraph 2 of resolution 808 (1993) of the Security Council, 3 May 1993, S/25704.
[93] Legislative Decree of 12 February 1975, Official Gazette of the Republic of Rwanda, 1975, p. 230, Rwanda acceded to the Genocide Convention but stated that it shall not be bound by Article 9 of this Convention.

497. Contrary to popular belief, the crime of genocide does not imply the actual extermination of group in its entirety, but is understood as such once any one of the acts mentioned in Article 2(2)(a) through 2(2)(e) is committed with the specific intent to destroy "in whole or in part" a national, ethnical, racial or religious group.

498. Genocide is distinct from other crimes inasmuch as it embodies a special intent or *dolus specialis*. Special intent of a crime is the specific intention, required as a constitutive element of the crime, which demands that the perpetrator clearly seeks to produce the act charged. Thus, the special intent in the crime of genocide lies in "the intent to destroy, in whole or in part, a national, ethnical, racial or religious group, as such".

499. Thus, for a crime of genocide to have been committed, it is necessary that one of the acts **[page 206]** listed under Article 2(2) of the Statute be committed, that the particular act be committed against a specifically targeted group, it being a national, ethnical, racial or religious group. Consequently, in order to clarify the constitutive elements of the crime of genocide, the Chamber will first state its findings on the acts provided for under Article 2(2)(a) through Article 2(2)(e) of the Statute, the groups protected by the Genocide Convention, and the special intent or *dolus specialis* necessary for genocide to take place.

Killing members of the group (paragraph (a)):

500. With regard to Article 2(2)(a) of the Statute, like in the Genocide Convention, the Chamber notes that the said paragraph states "*meurtre*" in the French version while the English version states "killing". The Trial Chamber is of the opinion that the term "killing" used in the English version is too general, since it could very well include both intentional and unintentional homicides, whereas the term "*meurtre*", used in the French version, is more precise. It is accepted that there is murder when death has been caused with the intention to do so, as provided for, incidentally, in the Penal Code of Rwanda which stipulates in its Article 311 that "Homicide committed with intent to cause death shall be treated as murder".

501. Given the presumption of innocence of the accused, and pursuant to the general principles of criminal law, the Chamber holds that the version more favourable to the accused should be upheld and finds that Article 2(2)(a) of the Statute must be interpreted in accordance with the definition of murder given in the Penal Code of Rwanda, according to which "*meurtre*" (killing) is homicide committed with the intent to cause death. The Chamber notes in this regard that the *travaux préparatoires* of the Genocide Convention[94], show that the proposal by certain delegations that premeditation be made a necessary condition for there to be genocide, was rejected, because some delegates deemed it unnecessary for premeditation to be made a requirement; in their **[page 207]** opinion, by its constitutive physical elements, the very crime of genocide, necessarily entails premeditation.

Causing serious bodily or mental harm to members of the group (paragraph b)

502. Causing serious bodily or mental harm to members of the group does not necessarily mean that the harm is permanent and irremediable.

503. In the Adolf Eichmann case, who was convicted of crimes against the Jewish people, genocide under another legal definition, the District Court of Jerusalem stated in its judgment of 12 December 1961, that serious bodily or mental harm of members of the group can be caused

> "by the enslavement, starvation, deportation and persecution [...] and by their detention in ghettos, transit camps and concentration camps in conditions which were designed to cause their

---

[94]   Summary Records of the meetings of the Sixth Committee of the General Assembly, 21 September-10 December 1948, Official Records of the General Assembly.

degradation, deprivation of their rights as human beings, and to suppress them and cause them inhumane suffering and torture"[95].

504. For purposes of interpreting Article 2 (2)(b) of the Statute, the Chamber takes serious bodily or mental harm, without limiting itself thereto, to mean acts of torture, be they bodily or mental, inhumane or degrading treatment, persecution.

Deliberately inflicting on the group conditions of life calculated to bring about its physical destruction in whole or in part (paragraph c):

505. The Chamber holds that the expression deliberately inflicting on the group conditions of [page 208] life calculated to bring about its physical destruction in whole or in part, should be construed as the methods of destruction by which the perpetrator does not immediately kill the members of the group, but which, ultimately, seek their physical destruction.

506. For purposes of interpreting Article 2(2)(c) of the Statute, the Chamber is of the opinion that the means of deliberate inflicting on the group conditions of life calculated to bring about its physical destruction, in whole or part, include, *inter alia*, subjecting a group of people to a subsistence diet, systematic expulsion from homes and the reduction of essential medical services below minimum requirement.

Imposing measures intended to prevent births within the group (paragraph d):

507. For purposes of interpreting Article 2(2)(d) of the Statute, the Chamber holds that the measures intended to prevent births within the group, should be construed as sexual mutilation, the practice of sterilization, forced birth control, separation of the sexes and prohibition of marriages. In patriarchal societies, where membership of a group is determined by the identity of the father, an example of a measure intended to prevent births within a group is the case where, during rape, a woman of the said group is deliberately impregnated by a man of another group, with the intent to have her give birth to a child who will consequently not belong to its mother's group.

508. Furthermore, the Chamber notes that measures intended to prevent births within the group may be physical, but can also be mental. For instance, rape can be a measure intended to prevent births when the person raped refuses subsequently to procreate, in the same way that members of a group can be led, through threats or trauma, not to procreate.

Forcibly transferring children of the group to another group (paragraph e) [page 209]

509. With respect to forcibly transferring children of the group to another group, the Chamber is of the opinion that, as in the case of measures intended to prevent births, the objective is not only to sanction a direct act of forcible physical transfer, but also to sanction acts of threats or trauma which would lead to the forcible transfer of children from one group to another.

510. Since the special intent to commit genocide lies in the intent to "destroy, in whole or in part, a national, ethnical, racial or religious group, as such", it is necessary to consider a definition of the group as such. Article 2 of the Statute, just like the Genocide Convention, stipulates four types of victim groups, namely national, ethnical, racial or religious groups.

511. On reading through the *travaux préparatoires* of the Genocide Convention[96], it appears that the crime of genocide was allegedly perceived as targeting only "stable" groups, constituted in a permanent

---

[95]   "Attorney General of the Government of Israel vs. Adolph Eichmann", "District Court" of Jerusalem, 12 December 1961, quoted in the "The International Law Reports", vol. 36, 1968, p. 340.
[96]   Summary Records of the meetings of the Sixth Committee of the General Assembly, 21 September - 10 December 1948, Official Records of the General Assembly.

fashion and membership of which is determined by birth, with the exclusion of the more "mobile" groups which one joins through individual voluntary commitment, such as political and economic groups. Therefore, a common criterion in the four types of groups protected by the Genocide Convention is that membership in such groups would seem to be normally not challengeable by its members, who belong to it automatically, by birth, in a continuous and often irremediable manner.

512. Based on the *Nottebohm* decision[97] rendered by the International Court of Justice, the Chamber holds that a national group is defined as a collection of people who are perceived to share a legal bond based on common citizenship, coupled with reciprocity of rights and duties.

513. An ethnic group is generally defined as a group whose members share a common language or culture. **[page 210]**

514. The conventional definition of racial group is based on the hereditary physical traits often identified with a geographical region, irrespective of linguistic, cultural, national or religious factors.

515. The religious group is one whose members share the same religion, denomination or mode of worship.

516. Moreover, the Chamber considered whether the groups protected by the Genocide Convention, echoed in Article 2 of the Statute, should be limited to only the four groups expressly mentioned and whether they should not also include any group which is stable and permanent like the said four groups. In other words, the question that arises is whether it would be impossible to punish the physical destruction of a group as such under the Genocide Convention, if the said group, although stable and membership is by birth, does not meet the definition of any one of the four groups expressly protected by the Genocide Convention. In the opinion of the Chamber, it is particularly important to respect the intention of the drafters of the Genocide Convention, which according to the *travaux préparatoires*, was patently to ensure the protection of any stable and permanent group.

517. As stated above, the crime of genocide is characterized by its *dolus specialis*, or special intent, which lies in the fact that the acts charged, listed in Article 2 (2) of the Statute, must have been "committed with intent to destroy, in whole or in part, a national, ethnical, racial or religious group, as such".

518. Special intent is a well-known criminal law concept in the Roman-continental legal systems. It is required as a constituent element of certain offences and demands that the perpetrator have the clear intent to cause the offence charged. According to this meaning, special intent is the key element of an intentional offence, which offence is characterized by a **[page 211]** psychological relationship between the physical result and the mental state of the perpetrator[98].

519. As observed by the representative of Brazil during the *travaux préparatoires* of the Genocide Convention.

> "genocide [is] characterised by the factor of particular intent to destroy a group. In the absence of that factor, whatever the degree of atrocity of an act and however similar it might be on the acts described in the convention, that act could still not be called genocide."[99]

520. With regard to the crime of genocide, the offender is culpable only when he has committed one of the offences charged under Article 2(2) of the Statute with the clear intent to destroy, in whole or in part, a particular group. The offender is culpable because he knew or should have known that the act committed would destroy, in whole or in part, a group.

521. In concrete terms, for any of the acts charged under Article 2 (2) of the Statute to be a constitutive element of genocide, the act must have been committed against one or several individuals, because such

---

[97] International Court of Justice, 1995

[98] See in particular:Roger Merle et André Vitu, "Traité de droit criminel", Cujas, 1984, (first edition, 1967), p. 723 *et seg.*

[99] Summary Records of the meetings of the Sixth Committee of the General Assembly, 21 September - 10 December 1994, op. cit., p. 109.

individual or individuals were members of a specific group, and specifically because they belonged to this group. Thus, the victim is chosen not because of his individual identity, but rather on account of his membership of a national, ethnical, racial or religious group. The victim of the act is therefore a member of a group, chosen as such, which, hence, means that the victim of the crime of genocide is the group itself and not only the individual[100]. **[page 212]**

522. The perpetration of the act charged therefore extends beyond its actual commission, for example, the murder of a particular individual, for the realisation of an ulterior motive, which is to destroy, in whole or part, the group of which the individual is just one element.

523. On the issue of determining the offender's specific intent, the Chamber considers that intent is a mental factor which is difficult, even impossible, to determine. This is the reason why, in the absence of a confession from the accused, his intent can be inferred from a certain number of presumptions of fact. The Chamber considers that it is possible to deduce the genocidal intent inherent in a particular act charged from the general context of the perpetration of other culpable acts systematically directed against that same group, whether these acts were committed by the same offender or by others. Other factors, such as the scale of atrocities committed, their general nature, in a region or a country, or furthermore, the fact of deliberately and systematically targeting victims on account of their membership of a particular group, while excluding the members of other groups, can enable the Chamber to infer the genocidal intent of a particular act.

524. Trial Chamber I of the International Criminal Tribunal for the former Yugoslavia also stated that the specific intent of the crime of genocide

> "may be inferred from a number of facts such as the general political doctrine which gave rise to the acts possibly covered by the definition in Article 4, or the repetition of destructive and discriminatory acts. The intent may also be inferred from the perpetration of acts which violate, or which the perpetrators themselves consider to violate the very foundation of the group – acts which are not in themselves covered by the list in Article 4(2) but which are committed as part of the same pattern of conduct"[101]. **[page 213]**

Thus, in the matter brought before the International Criminal Tribunal for the former Yugoslavia, the Trial Chamber, in its findings, found that

> "this intent derives from the combined effect of speeches or projects laying the groundwork for and justifying the acts, from the massive scale of their destructive effect and from their specific nature, which aims at undermining what is considered to be the foundation of the group".[102]

6.3.2. Complicity in Genocide

The Crime of Complicity in Genocide, punishable under Article 2(3)e) of the Statute

525. Under Article 2(3)e) of the Statute, the Chamber shall have the power to prosecute persons who have committed complicity in genocide. The Prosecutor has charged Akayesu with such a crime under count 2 of the Indictment.

526. Principle VII of the "Nuremberg Principles"[103] reads

---

[100]   Concerning this issue, see in particular Nehemiah Robinson, "The Genocide Convention. Its Origins as Interpretation", p. 15, which states that victims as individuals *are important not per se but as members of the group to which they belong*.
[101]   International Criminal Tribunal for the former Yugoslavia, Decison of Trial Chamber I, Radovan Karadzic, Ratko Mladic case (Cases Nos. IT-95-5-R61 and IT-95-18-R61), Consideration of the Indictment within the framework of Rule 61 of the Rules of Procedure and Evidence, paragraph 94.
[102]   Ibid. Paragraph 95.
[103]   "Principles of International Law Recognized in the Charter of the Nuremberg Tribunal and in the Judgment of the Tribunal," adopted by the International Law Commission of the United Nations, 1950.

"complicity in the commission of a crime against peace, a war crime, or a crime against humanity as set forth in Principle VI is a crime under international law."

Thus, participation by complicity in the most serious violations of international humanitarian law was considered a crime as early as Nuremberg. **[page 214]**

527. The Chamber notes that complicity is viewed as a form of criminal participation by all criminal law systems, notably, under the Anglo-Saxon system (or Common Law) and the Roman-Continental system (or Civil Law). Since the accomplice to an offence may be defined as someone who associates himself in an offence committed by another[104], complicity necessarily implies the existence of a principal offence.[105]

528. According to one school of thought, complicity is "borrowed criminality" (criminalité d'emprunt). In other words, the accomplice borrows the criminality of the principal perpetrator. By borrowed criminality, it should be understood that the physical act which constitutes the act of complicity does not have its own inherent criminality, but rather it borrows the criminality of the act committed by the principal perpetrator of the criminal enterprise. Thus, the conduct of the accomplice emerges as a crime when the crime has been consummated by the principal perpetrator. The accomplice has not committed an autonomous crime, but has merely facilitated the criminal enterprise committed by another.

529. Therefore, the issue before the Chamber is whether genocide must actually be committed in order for any person to be found guilty of complicity in genocide. The Chamber notes that, as stated above, complicity can only exist when there is a punishable, principal act, in the commission of which the accomplice has associated himself. Complicity, therefore, implies a predicate offence committed by someone other than the accomplice.

530. Consequently, the Chamber is of the opinion that in order for an accused to be found guilty of complicity in genocide, it must, first of all, be proven beyond a reasonable doubt that the crime **[page 215]** of genocide has, indeed, been committed.

531. The issue thence is whether a person can be tried for complicity even where the perpetrator of the principal offence himself has not being tried. Under Article 89 of the Rwandan Penal Code, accomplices

"may be prosecuted even where the perpetrator may not face prosecution for personal reasons, such as double jeopardy, death, insanity or non-identification" [unofficial translation].

As far as the Chamber is aware, all criminal systems provide that an accomplice may also be tried, even where the principal perpetrator of the crime has not been identified, or where, for any other reasons, guilt could not be proven.

532. The Chamber notes that the logical inference from the foregoing is that an individual cannot thus be both the principal perpetrator of a particular act and the accomplice thereto. An act with which an accused is being charged cannot, therefore, be characterized both as an act of genocide and an act of complicity in genocide as pertains to this accused. Consequently, since the two are mutually exclusive, the same individual cannot be convicted of both crimes for the same act.

533. As regards the physical elements of complicity in genocide (*Actus Reus*), three forms of accomplice participation are recognized in most criminal Civil Law systems: complicity by instigation, complicity by aiding and abetting, and complicity by procuring means [106]. It should be noted that the Rwandan Penal Code includes two other forms of participation, namely, incitement to commit a crime through speeches, shouting or threats uttered in public places or at public gatherings, or through the sale

---

[104] The Osborn's Concise Law Dictionary defines an accomplice as: "any person who, either as a principal or as an accessory, has been associated with another person in the commission of any offence.", Sweet and Maxwell, 1993, p. 6.

[105] It appears from the *travaux préparations* of the Genocide Convention that only complicity in the completed offence of genocide was intended for punishment and not complicity in an attempt to commit genocide, complicity in incitement to commit genocide nor complicity in conspiracy to commit genocide, all of which were, in the eyes of some states, too vague to be punishable under the Convention.

[106] See, for example, Article 16 of the Senegalese Penal Code, Article 121-7 of the *Nouveau code pénal français* (New French Penal Code).

or dissemination, offer for sale or display of written material or **[page 216]** printed matter in public places or at public gatherings, or through the public display of placards or posters, and complicity by harbouring or aiding a criminal. Indeed, according to Article 91 of the Rwandan Penal Code:

> "An accomplice shall mean:
>
> 1. A person or persons who by means of gifts, promises, threats, abuse of authority or power, culpable machinations or artifice, directly incite(s) to commit such action or order(s) that such action be committed.
>
> 2. A person or persons who procure(s) weapons, instruments or any other means which are used in committing such action with the knowledge that they would be so used.
>
> 3. A person or persons who knowingly aid(s) or abet(s) the perpetrator or perpetrators of such action in the acts carried out in preparing or planning such action or in effectively committing it.
>
> 4. A person or persons who, whether through speeches, shouting or threats uttered in public places or at public gatherings, or through the sale or dissemination, offer for sale or display of written material or printed matter in public places or at public gatherings or through the public display of placards or posters, directly incite(s) the perpetrator or perpetrators to commit such an action without prejudice to the penalties applicable to those who incite others to commit offences, even where such incitement fails to produce results.
>
> 5. A person or persons who harbour(s) or aid(s) perpetrators under the circumstances provided for under Article 257 of this Code."[107] [unofficial translation]

534. The Chamber notes, first of all, that the said Article 91 of the Rwandan Penal Code draws **[page 217]** a distinction between "*instigation*" (instigation), on the one hand, as provided for by paragraph 1 of said Article, and "*incitation*" (incitement), on the other, which is referred to in paragraph 4 of the same Article. The Chamber notes in this respect that, as pertains to the crime of genocide, the latter form of complicity, i.e. by incitement, is the offence which under the Statute is given the specific legal definition of "direct and public incitement to commit genocide," punishable under Article 2(3)c), as distinguished from "complicity in genocide." The findings of the Chamber with respect to the crime of direct and public incitement to commit genocide will be detailed below. That said, instigation, which according to Article 91 of the Rwandan Penal Code, assumes the form of incitement or instruction to commit a crime, only constitutes complicity if it is accompanied by, "gift, promises, threats, abuse of authority or power, machinations or culpable artifice"[108]. In other words, under the Rwandan Penal Code, unless the instigation is accompanied by one of the aforesaid elements, the mere fact of prompting another to commit a crime is not punishable as complicity, even if such a person committed the crime as a result.

535. The ingredients of complicity under Common Law do not appear to be different from those under Civil Law. To a large extent, the forms of accomplice participation, namely "aid and abet, counsel and procure", mirror those conducts characterized under Civil Law as "l'aide et l'assistance, la fourniture des moyens".

536. Complicity by aiding or abetting implies a positive action which excludes, in principle, complicity by failure to act or omission. Procuring means is a very common form of complicity. It covers those persons who procured weapons, instruments or any other means to be used in the commission of an offence, with the full knowledge that they would be used for such purposes.

537. For the purposes of interpreting Article 2(3)e) of the Statute, which does not define the concept of complicity, the Chamber is of the opinion that it is necessary to define complicity as per the Rwandan Penal Code, and to consider the first three forms of criminal participation **[page 218]** referred to in Article 91 of the Rwandan Penal Code as being the elements of complicity in genocide, thus:

---

[107]   See Article 91 of the Penal Code in "Codes et lois du Rwanda", Université nationale du Rwanda, 31 December 1994 update, volume 1, 2nd edition: 1995, p. 395.

[108]   See especially *Cour de cassation française* (French Court of Cassation): Crim. 24 December 1942, JCP 19 944, ruling out prosecuting an individual as an accomplice who simply gave advice on committing a crime.

- complicity by <u>procuring means</u>, such as weapons, instruments or any other means, used to commit genocide, with the accomplice knowing that such means would be used for such a purpose;

- complicity by knowingly <u>aiding or abetting</u> a perpetrator of a genocide in the planning or enabling acts thereof;

- complicity by <u>instigation</u>, for which a person is liable who, though not directly participating in the crime of genocide crime, gave instructions to commit genocide, through gifts, promises, threats, abuse of authority or power, machinations or culpable artifice, or who directly incited to commit genocide.

538. The intent or mental element of complicity implies in general that, at the moment he acted, the accomplice knew of the assistance he was providing in the commission of the principal offence. In other words, the accomplice must have acted knowingly.

539. Moreover, as in all criminal Civil law systems, under Common law, notably English law, generally, the accomplice need not even wish that the principal offence be committed. In the case of <u>National Coal Board v. Gamble</u>[109], Justice Devlin stated

> "an indifference to the result of the crime does not of itself negate abetting. If one man deliberately sells to another a gun to be used for murdering a third, he may be indifferent about whether the third lives or dies and interested only the cash profit to be made out of the sale, but he can still be an aider and abettor." **[page 219]**

In 1975, the English House of Lords also upheld this definition of complicity, when it held that willingness to participate in the principal offence did not have to be established[110]. As a result, anyone who knowing of another's criminal purpose, voluntarily aids him or her in it, can be convicted of complicity even though he regretted the outcome of the offence.

540. As far as genocide is concerned, the intent of the accomplice is thus to knowingly aid or abet one or more persons to commit the crime of genocide. Therefore, the Chamber is of the opinion that an accomplice to genocide need not necessarily possess the *dolus specialis* of genocide, namely the specific intent to destroy, in whole or in part, a national, ethnic, racial or religious group, as such.

541. Thus, if for example, an accused knowingly aided or abetted another in the commission of a murder, while being unaware that the principal was committing such a murder, with the intent to destroy, in whole or in part, the group to which the murdered victim belonged, the accused could be prosecuted for complicity in murder, and certainly not for complicity in genocide. However, if the accused knowingly aided and abetted in the commission of such a murder while he knew or had reason to know that the principal was acting with genocidal intent, the accused would be an accomplice to genocide, even though he did not share the murderer's intent to destroy the group.

542. This finding by the Chamber comports with the decisions rendered by the District Court of Jerusalem on 12 December 1961 and the Supreme Court of Israel on 29 May 1962 in the case of Adolf Eichmann[111]. Since Eichmann raised the argument in his defence that he was a "small cog" in the Nazi machine, both the District Court and the Supreme Court dealt with accomplice liability and found that,

> "[...] even a small cog, even an insignificant operator, is under our criminal law **[page 220]** liable to be regarded as an accomplice in the commission of an offence, in which case he will be dealt with as if he were the actual murderer or destroyer".[112]

543. The District Court accepted that Eichmann did not personally devise the "Final Solution" himself, but nevertheless, as the head of those engaged in carrying out the "Final Solution" "acting in accordance with the directives of his superiors, but [with] wide discretionary powers in planning operations on his

---

[109]   *National Coal Board v. Gamble*, [1959] 1 QB 11.
[110]   *DPP for Northern Ireland v. Lynch*, [1975] AC 653.
[111]   Eichmann, *Op. Cit.*, p. 340.
[112]   *Ibid.*, p. 323.

own initiative," he incurred individual criminal liability for crimes against the Jewish people, as much as his superiors. Likewise, with respect to his subordinates who actually carried out the executions, "[...] the legal and moral responsibility of he who delivers up the victim to his death is, in our opinion, no smaller, and may be greater, than the responsibility of he who kills the victim with his own hands"[113]. The District Court found that participation in the extermination of all [...] victims from 1941 to 1945, irrespective of the extent of his participation"[114].

544. The findings of the Israeli courts in this case support the principle that the *mens rea*, or special intent, required for complicity in genocide is *knowledge* of the genocidal plan, coupled with the *actus reus* of participation in the execution of such plan. Crucially, then, it does not appear that the specific intent to commit the crime of genocide, as reflected in the phrase "with intent to destroy, in whole or in part, a national, ethnical, racial or religious group, as such," is required for complicity or accomplice liability.

545. In conclusion, the Chamber is of the opinion that an accused is liable as an accomplice to genocide if he knowingly aided or abetted or instigated one or more persons in the commission of genocide, while knowing that such a person or persons were committing genocide, even though the accused himself did not have the specific intent to destroy, in whole or in part, a national, **[page 221]** ethnical, racial or religious group, as such.

546. At this juncture, the Chamber will address another issue, namely that which, with respect to complicity in genocide covered under Article 2(3)(e) of the Statute, may arise from the forms of participation listed in Article 6 of the Statute entitled, "Individual Criminal Responsibility," and more specifically, those covered under paragraph 1 of the same Article. Indeed, under Article 6(1), "A person who planned, instigated, ordered, committed or otherwise aided and abetted in the planning, preparation or execution of a crime referred to in articles 2 to 4 of the present Statute, shall be individually responsible for the crime." Such forms of participation, which are summarized in the expression "[...] or otherwise aided or abetted [...]," are similar to the material elements of complicity, though they in and of themselves, characterize the crimes referred to in Articles 2 to 4 of the Statute, which include namely genocide.

547. Consequently, where a person is accused of aiding and abetting, planning, preparing or executing genocide, it must be proven that such a person acted with specific genocidal intent, i.e. the intent to destroy, in whole or in part, a national, ethnical, racial or religious group as such, whereas, as stated above, there is no such requirement to establish accomplice liability in genocide.

548. Another difference between complicity in genocide and the principle of abetting in the planning, preparation or execution a genocide as per Article 6(1), is that, in theory, complicity requires a positive act, i.e. an act of commission, whereas aiding and abetting may consist in failing to act or refraining from action. Thus, in the <u>Jefferson</u> and <u>Coney</u> cases, it was held that "The accused [...] only accidentally present [...] must know that his presence is actually encouraging the principal(s)"[115]. Similarly, the French Court of Cassation found that,

> "A person who, by his mere presence in a group of aggressors provided moral support to the assailants, and fully supported the criminal intent of the group, is **[page 222]** liable as an accomplice"[116] [unofficial translation].

The International Criminal Tribunal for the Former Yugoslavia also concluded in the Tadić judgment that:

[113]   District Court judgment, p. 179.
[114]   *Ibid.* p. 14.
[115]   *Jefferson* case (1994) 1 A11 ER 270 – *Coney* case (1882) 8 QDB 534; See Blackstone, A5.7, p. 72.
[116]   Crim, 20 January 1992: *Dr. pénal* 1992, 194.

"if the presence can be shown or inferred, by circumstantial or other evidence, to be knowing and to have a direct and substantial effect on the commission of the illegal act, then it is sufficient on which to base a finding of participation and assign the criminal culpability that accompanies it."[117]

6.3.3. Direct and Public Incitement to commit Genocide

THE CRIME OF DIRECT AND PUBLIC INCITEMENT TO COMMIT GENOCIDE, PUNISHABLE UNDER ARTICLE 2(3)(c) OF THE STATUTE

549. Under count 4, the Prosecutor charges Akayesu with direct and public incitement to commit genocide, a crime punishable under Article 2(3)(c) of the Statute.

550. Perhaps the most famous conviction for incitement to commit crimes of international dimension was that of Julius Streicher by the Nuremberg Tribunal for the virulently anti-Semitic articles which he had published in his weekly newspaper *Der Stürmer*. The Nuremberg Tribunal found that: "Streicher's incitement to murder and extermination, at the time when Jews in the East were being killed under the most horrible conditions, clearly constitutes persecution on political and racial grounds in connection with War Crimes, as defined by the Charter, and constitutes a **[page 223]** Crime against Humanity".[118]

551. At the time the Convention on Genocide was adopted, the delegates agreed to expressly spell out direct and public incitement to commit genocide as a specific crime, in particular, because of its critical role in the planning of a genocide, with the delegate from the USSR stating in this regard that, "It was impossible that hundreds of thousands of people should commit so many crimes unless they had been incited to do so and unless the crimes had been premeditated and carefully organized. He asked how in those circumstances, the inciters and organizers of the crime could be allowed to escape punishment, when they were the ones really responsible for the atrocities committed".[119]

552. Under Common law systems, incitement tends to be viewed as a particular form of criminal participation, punishable as such. Similarly, under the legislation of some Civil law countries, including Argentina, Bolivia, Chili, Peru, Spain, Uruguay and Venezuela, provocation, which is similar to incitement, is a specific form of participation in an offence[120]; but in most Civil law systems, incitement is most often treated as a form of complicity.

553. The Rwandan Penal Code is one such legislation. Indeed, as stated above, in the discussion on complicity in genocide, it does provide that direct and public incitement or provocation is a form of complicity. In fact, Article 91 subparagraph 4 provides that an accomplice shall mean "A person or persons who, whether through speeches, shouting or threats uttered in public places or at public gatherings, or through the sale or dissemination, offer for sale or display of written material or printed matter in public places or a public gatherings or through the public display of placards or posters, directly incite(s) the perpetrator or perpetrators to commit such an action without prejudice to the penalties applicable to those who incite others to commit offences, even **[page 224]** where such incitement fails to produce results".[121]

554. Under the Statute, direct and public incitement is expressly defined as a specific crime, punishable as such, by virtue of Article 2(3)(c). With respect to such a crime, the Chamber deems it appropriate to first define the three terms: incitement, direct and public.

---

[117] See Judgment of the International Criminal Tribunal for the Former Yugoslavia, Case No. IT-94-1-T, "The Prosecutor versus Dusko Tadić", 7 May 1997, paragraph 689.
[118] Nuremberg Proceedings, Vol. 22, p. 502.
[119] Summary Records of the meetings of the Sixt Committee of the General Assembly, 21 September – 10 December 1948, Official Records of the General Assembly, statements by Mr. Morozov, p. 241.
[120] Cf. Jean Pradel, *Droit pénal comparé* (Comparative Penal Law), Précis Dalloz: 1995, p. 277-278.
[121] Penal Code in, *"Codes et Lois du Rwanda"* (Codes and Laws of Rwanda), National University of Rwanda, 31 December 1994 update, Volume 1, 2nd Edition: 1995, p. 395. [*unofficial translation*]

555. Incitement is defined in Common law systems as encouraging or persuading another to commit an offence[122]. One line of authority in Common law would also view threats or other forms of pressure as a form of incitement[123]. As stated above, Civil law systems punish direct and public incitement assuming the form of provocation, which is defined as an act intended to directly provoke another to commit a crime or a misdemeanour through speeches, shouting or threats, or any other means of audiovisual communication[124]. Such a provocation, as defined under Civil law, is made up of the same elements as direct and public incitement to commit genocide covered by Article 2 of the Statute, that is to say it is both direct and public. **[page 225]**

556. The public element of incitement to commit genocide may be better appreciated in light of two factors: the place where the incitement occurred and whether or not assistance was selective or limited. A line of authority commonly followed in Civil law systems would regard words as being public where they were spoken aloud in a place that were public by definition[125]. According to the International Law Commission, public incitement is characterized by a call for criminal action to a number of individuals in a public place or to members of the general public at large by such means as the mass media, for example, radio or television[126]. It should be noted in this respect that at the time Convention on Genocide was adopted, the delegates specifically agreed to rule out the possibility of including private incitement to commit genocide as a crime, thereby underscoring their commitment to set aside for punishment only the truly public forms of incitement[127].

557. The "direct" element of incitement implies that the incitement assume a direct form and specifically provoke another to engage in a criminal act, and that more than mere vague or indirect suggestion goes to constitute direct incitement[128]. Under Civil law systems, provocation, the equivalent of incitement, is regarded as being direct where it is aimed at causing a specific offence to be committed. The prosecution must prove a definite causation between the act **[page 226]** characterized as incitement, or provocation in this case, and a specific offence[129]. However, the Chamber is of the opinion that the direct element of incitement should be viewed in the light of its cultural and linguistic content. Indeed, a particular speech may be perceived as "direct" in one country, and not so in another, depending on the audience[130]. The Chamber further recalls that incitement may be direct, and nonetheless implicit. Thus, at

---

[122]   "... someone who instigates or encourages another person to commit an offence should be liable to conviction for those acts of incitement, both because he is culpable for trying to cause a crime and because such liability is a step towards crime prevention." Andrew Ashworth, *Principles of Criminal Law*, Clarendon Press, Oxford: 1995, p. 462.

[123]   "The conduct required for incitement is some form of encouragement or persuasion to commit an offence, although there is authority which would regard threats or other forms of pressure as incitement." *Ibid,* p. 462.

[124]   See for example the French Penal Code, which defines provocation as follows: "Anyone, who whether through speeches, shouting or threats uttered in public places or at public gatherings or through the sale or dissemination, offer for sale or display of written material, printed matter, drawings, sketches, paintings, emblems, images or any other written or spoken medium or image in public places or at public gatherings, or through the public display of placards or posters, or through any other means of audiovisual communication" shall have directly provoked the perpetrator(s) to commit a crime or misdemeanour, shall be punished as an accomplice to such a crime or misdemeanour; L No. 72-546 of 1 July 1972 and L. No. 85-1317 of 13 December 1985. [*Unofficial translation*]

[125]   French Court of Cassation, Criminal Tribunal, 2 February 1950, Bull. crim., No. 38, p. 61.

[126]   The [...] Element of public incitement communicating the call for criminal action to a number of individuals in a public place or to members of the general public at large. Thus, an individual may communicate the call for criminal action in person in a public place or by technical means of mass communication, such as by radio or television.", Draft Code of Crimes Against the Peace and Security of Mankind, art. 2(3)(f); Report of the International Law Commission to the General Assembly, 51 U.N. ORGA Supp. (No. 10), at 26, U.N. Doc. A/51/10(1996).

[127]   See Yearbook of the United Nations, UN Fiftieth Edition, 1945-1995, Martinus Nijhoff Publishers, 1995 and the Summary Records of the Sixth Committee of the General Assembly, 21 September – 10 December 1948, Official Records of the General Assembly.

[128]   "The element of direct incitement requires specifically urging another individual to take immediate criminal action rather than merely making a vague or indirect suggestion." Draft Code of Crimes Against the Peace and Security of Mankind, art. 2(3)(I); Report of the International Law Commission to the General Assembly, 51 U.N. ORGA Supp. (No. 10), at 26, U.N. Doc. A/51/10(1996).

[129]   Article 23 of the French Law of 29 July 1881 on the provoking of crimes and offenses. See especially the analysis of André Vitu, *Traité de Droit criminel, Droit pénal spécial*, 1982.

[130]   On this subject, see above, in the findings of the Chamber on Evidentiary Matters, the developments pertaining to the analysis of the Kinyarwanda language presented by the expert witness Professor Mathis Ruzindana.

the time the Convention on Genocide was being drafted, the Polish delegate observed that is was sufficient to play skillfully on mob psychology by casting suspicion on certain groups, by insinuating that they were responsible for economic or other difficulties in order to create an atmosphere favourable to the perpetration of the crime.[131]

558.   The Chamber will therefore consider on a case-by-case basis whether, in light of the culture of Rwanda and the specific circumstances of the instant case, acts of incitement can be viewed as direct or not, by focusing mainly on the issue of whether the persons for whom the message was intended immediately grasped the implication thereof.

559.   In light of the foregoing, it can be noted in the final analysis that whatever the legal system, direct and public incitement must be defined for the purposes of interpreting Article 2(3)(c), as directly provoking the perpetrator(s) to commit genocide, whether through speeches, shouting or threats uttered in public places or at public gatherings, or through the sale or dissemination, offer for sale or display of written material or printed matter in public places or at public gatherings, or through the public display of placards or posters, or through any other means of audiovisual communication.

560.   The *mens rea* required for the crime of direct and public incitement to commit genocide **[page 227]** lies in the intent to directly prompt or provoke another to commit genocide. It implies a desire on the part of the perpetrator to create by his actions a particular state of mind necessary to commit such a crime in the minds of the person(s) he is so engaging. That is to say that the person who is inciting to commit genocide must have himself the specific intent to commit genocide, namely, to destroy, in whole or in part, a national, ethnical, racial or religious group, as such.

561.   Therefore, the issue before the Chamber is whether the crime of direct and public incitement to commit genocide can be punished even where such incitement was unsuccessful. It appears from the *travaux préparatoires* of the Convention on Genocide that the drafters of the Convention considered stating explicitly that incitement to commit genocide could be punished, whether or not it was successful. In the end, a majority decided against such an approach. Nevertheless, the Chamber is of the opinion that it cannot thereby be inferred that the intent of the drafters was not to punish unsuccessful acts of incitement. In light of the overall *travaux*, the Chamber holds the view that the drafters of the Convention simply decided not to specifically mention that such a form of incitement could be punished.

562.   There are under Common law so-called inchoate offences, which are punishable by virtue of the criminal act alone, irrespective of the result thereof, which may or may not have been achieved. The Civil law counterparts of inchoate offences are known as [*infractions formelles*] (acts constituting an offence per se irrespective of their results), as opposed to [*infractions matérielles*] (strict liability offences). Indeed, as is the case with inchoate offenses, in [*infractions formelles*], the method alone is punishable. Put another way, such offenses are "deemed to have been consummated regardless of the result archieved [*unofficial translation*]"[132] contrary to [*infractions matérielles*]. Indeed, Rwandan lawmakers appear to characterize the acts defined under Article 91(4) of the Rwandan Penal Code as so-called [*infractions formelles*], since provision is made for their punishment even where they proved unsuccessful. It should be noted, however, that such offences are the exception, the rule being that in theory, an offence can only be punished in relation to the result envisaged by the lawmakers. In the opinion of the Chamber, **[page 228]** the fact that such acts are in themselves particularly dangerous because of the high risk they carry for society, even if they fail to produce results, warrants that they be punished as an exceptional measure. The Chamber holds that genocide clearly falls within the category of crimes so serious that direct and public incitement to commit such a crime must be punished as such, even where such incitement failed to produce the result expected by the perpetrator. **[page 229]**

6.4.   Crimes against Humanity (Article 3 of the Statute)

---

[131]   Summary Records of the Sixth Committee of the General Assembly, 21 September – 10 December 1948, Official Records of the General Assembly.
[132]   Merle and Vitu, *Ibid*, p. 619

Crimes against Humanity – Historical development

563. Crimes against humanity were recognized in the Charter and Judgment of the Nuremberg Tribunal, as well as in Law No. 10 of the Control Council for Germany. Article 6(c) of the Charter of Nuremberg Tribunal defines crimes against humanity as

> "..murder, extermination, enslavement, deportation, and other inhumane acts committed against any civilian population, before or during the war, or persecutions on political, racial or religious grounds in execution of or in connexion with any crime within the jurisdiction of the Chamber, whether or not in violation of the domestic law of the country where perpetrated."

564. Article II of Law No. 10 of the Control Council Law defined crimes against humanity as:

> "Atrocities and Offenses, including but not limited to murder, extermination, enslavement, deportation, imprisonment, torture, rape, or other inhumane acts committed against any civilian population or persecution on political, racial or religious grounds, whether or not in violation of the domestic laws of the country where perpetrated."[133]

565. Crimes against humanity are aimed at any civilian population and are prohibited regardless of whether they are committed in an armed conflict, international or internal in character[134]. In fact, the concept of crimes against humanity had been recognised long before Nuremberg. On 28 **[page 230]** May 1915, the Governments of France, Great Britain and Russia made a declaration regarding the massacres of the Armenian population in Turkey, denouncing them as "crimes against humanity and civilisation for which all the members of the Turkish government will be held responsible together with its agents implicated in the massacres".[135] The 1919 Report of the Commission on the Responsibility of the Authors of the War and on Enforcement of Penalties formulated by representatives from several States and presented to the Paris Peace Conference also referred to "offences against ... the laws of humanity".[136]

566. These World War I notions derived, in part, from the Martens clause of the Hague Convention (IV) of 1907, which referred to "the usages established among civilised peoples, from the laws of humanity, and the dictates of the public conscience". In 1874, George Curtis called slavery a "crime against humanity". Other such phrases as "crimes against mankind" and "crimes against the human family" appear far earlier in human history (see 12 N.Y.L. Sch. J. Hum. Rts 545 (1995)).

567. The Chamber notes that, following the Nuremberg and Tokyo trials, the concept of crimes against humanity underwent a gradual evolution in the *Eichmann, Barbie, Touvier* and *Papon* cases.

568. In the *Eichmann* case, the accused, Otto Adolf Eichmann, was charged with offences under Nazi and Nazi Collaborators (punishment), Law, 5710/1950, for his participation in the implementation of the plan know as "the Final Solution of the Jewish problem". Pursuant to Section I (*b*) of the said law:

> "Crime against humanity means any of the following acts: murder, extermination, enslavement, starvation or deportation and other inhumane acts committed against **[page 231]** any civilian population, and persecution on national, racial, religious or political grounds."[137]

The district court in the Eichmann stated that crimes against humanity differs from genocide in that for the commission of genocide special intent is required. This special intent is not required for crimes against humanity[138]. Eichmann was convicted by the District court and sentenced to death. Eichmann appealed against his conviction and his appeal was dismissed by the supreme court.

569. In the *Barbie* case, the accused, Klaus Barbie, who was the head of the Gestapo in Lyons from November 1942 to August 1944, during the wartime occupation of France, was convicted in 1987 of

---

[133] International Law Reports, Volume 36, p. 31.
[134] Secretary General's Report on the ICTY Statute, (S/25704), paragraph 47.
[135] Roger Clark, Crimes against Humanity at Nuremberg, The Nuremberg and International Lawpage 177, Ginburgs and Kudriavtsev
[136] Id. p. 178
[137] International Law Report; volume 36; 1968 at p. 30
[138] *ILR*, Volume 36, Part 4, p. 5 at 41

crimes against humanity for his role in the deportation an extermination of civilians. Barbie appealed in cassation, but the appeal was dismissed. For the purposes of the present Judgment, what is of interest is the definition of crimes against humanity employed by the Court. The French Court of Cassation, in a Judgment rendered on 20 December 1985, stated:

> Crimes against humanity, within the meaning of Article 6(c) of the Charter of the International Military Tribunal annexed to the London Agreement of 8 August 1945, which were not subject to statutory limitation of the right of prosecution, even if they were crimes which could also be classified as war crimes within the meaning of Article 6(b) of the Charter, *were inhumane acts and persecution committed in a systematic manner in the name of a State practising a policy of ideological supremacy, not only against persons by reason of their membership of a racial or religious community, but also against the opponents of that policy, whatever the form of their opposition.* (Words italicized by the Court)[139] **[page 232]**

570. This was affirmed in a Judgment of the Court of Cassation of 3 June 1988, in which the Court held that:

> The fact that the accused, who had been found guilty of one of the crimes enumerated in Article 6(c) of the Charter of the Nuremberg Tribunal, in perpetrating that crime took part in the execution of a common plan to bring about the deportation or extermination of the civilian population during the war, or persecutions on political, racial or religious grounds, constituted not a distinct offence or an aggravating circumstance but rather *an essential element of the crime against humanity, consisting of the fact that the acts charged were performed in a systematic manner in the name of a State practising by those means a policy of ideological supremacy.*[140] (Emphasis added)

571. The definition of crimes against humanity developed in *Barbie* was further developed in the *Touvier* case. In that case, the accused, Paul Touvier, had been a high-ranking officer in the Militia (*Milice*) of Lyons, which operated in "Vichy" France during the German occupation. He was convicted of crimes against humanity for his role in the shooting of seven Jews at Rillieux on 29 June 1994 as a reprisal for the assassination by members of the Resistance, on the previous day, of the Minister for Propaganda of the "Vichy" Government.

572. The Court of Appeal applied the definition of crimes against humanity used in *Barbie*, stating that:

> The specific intent necessary to establish a crime against humanity was the intention to take part in the execution of a common plan by committing, in a systematic manner, inhuman acts or persecutions in the name of a State practising a policy of ideological supremacy.[141] **[page 233]**

573. Applying this definition, the Court of Appeal held that Touvier could not be guilty of crimes against humanity since he committed the acts in question in the name of the "Vichy" State, which was not a State practising a policy of ideological supremacy, although it collaborated with Nazi Germany, which clearly did practice such a policy.

574. The Court of Cassation allowed appeal from the decision of the Court of Appeal, on the grounds that the crimes committed by the accused had been committed at the instigation of a Gestapo officer, and to that extent were linked to Nazi Germany, a State practising a policy of ideological supremacy against persons by virtue of their membership of a racial or religious community. Therefore the crimes could be categorised as crimes against humanity. Touvier was eventually convicted of crimes against humanity by the *Cour d'Assises des Yvelines* on 20 April 1994.[142]

575. The definition of crimes against humanity used in *Barbie* was later affirmed by the ICTY in its *Vukovar* Rule 61 Decision of 3 April 1996 (IT-95-13-R61), to support its finding that crimes against

---

[139]   78 *ILR* 136 at 137
[140]   ILR pp. 332 and 336, *Gaz. Pal.* 1988, II, p. 745)
[141]   ILR, pp. 340 and 352-5.
[142]   *Le Monde*, 21 April 1994.

humanity applied equally where the victims of the acts were members of a resistance movement as to where the victims were civilians:

> "29. ... Although according to the terms of Article 5 of the Statute of this Tribunal ... combatants in the traditional sense of the term cannot be victims of a crime against humanity, this does not apply to individuals who, at one particular point in time, carried out acts of resistance. As the Commission of Experts, established pursuant to Security Council resolution 780, noted, "it seems obvious that Article 5 applies first and foremost to civilians, meaning people who are not combatants. This, however, should not lead to any quick conclusions concerning people who at one particular point in time did bear arms. ... Information of the overall circumstances is relevant for the interpretation of the provision in a spirit consistent with its purpose." (Doc S/1994/674, para. 78). **[page 234]**

576. This conclusion is supported by case law. In the Barbie case, the French Cour de Cassation said that:

> "inhumane acts and persecution which, in the name of a State practising a policy of ideological hegemony, were committed systematically or collectively not only against individuals because of their membership in a racial or religious group but also against the adversaries of that policy whatever the form of the opposition" could be considered a crime against humanity. (Cass. Crim. 20 December 1985).

577. Article 7 of the Statute of the International Criminal Court defines a crime against humanity as any of the enumerated acts committed as part of a widespread of systematic attack directed against any civilian population, with knowledge of the attack. These enumerated acts are murder; extermination; enslavement; deportation or forcible transfer of population; imprisonment or other severe deprivation of physical liberty in violation of fundamental rules of international law; torture; rape, sexual slavery, enforced prostitution, forces pregnancy, enforced sterilization, or any other form of sexual violence of comparable gravity; persecution against any identifiable group or collectively on political, racial, national, ethnic, cultural, religious, gender or other grounds that are universally recognised as impermissible under international law, in connection with any act referred to in this article or any other crime within the jurisdiction of the Court; enforced disappearance of persons; the crime of apartheid; other inhumane acts of a similar character intentionally causing great suffering, or serious injury to body or mental or physical health.[143]

Crimes against Humanity in Article 3 of the Statute of the Tribunal

578. The Chamber considers that Article 3 of the Statute confers on the Chamber the **[page 235]** jurisdiction to prosecute persons for various inhumane acts which constitute crimes against humanity. This category of crimes may be broadly broken down into four essential elements, namely:

(i)   the act must be inhumane in nature and character, causing great suffering, or serious injury to body or to mental or physical health;

(ii) the act must be committed as part of a wide spread or systematic attack;

(iii) the act must be committed against members of the civilian population;

(iv) the act must be committed on one or more discriminatory grounds, namely, national, political, ethnic, racial or religious grounds.

The act must be committed as part of a wide spread or systematic attack.

---

[143] Rome Statute of the International Criminal Court, adopted by the United Nations Diplomatic Conference of Plenipotentiaries on the Establishment of an International Court on 17 July 1998.

579. The Chamber considers that it is a prerequisite that the act must be committed as part of a wide spread or systematic attack and not just a random act of violence. The act can be part of a widespread or systematic attack and need not be a part of both.[144]

580. The concept of "widespread" may be defined as massive, frequent, large scale action, carried out collectively with considerable seriousness and directed against a multiplicity of victims. The concept of "systematic" may be defined as thoroughly organised and following a regular pattern on the basis of a common policy involving substantial public or private resources. There is no requirement that this policy must be adopted formally as the policy of a state. There **[page 236]** must however be some kind of preconceived plan or policy.[145]

581. The concept of "attack" maybe defined as a unlawful act of the kind enumerated in Article 3(a) to (I) of the Statute, like murder, extermination, enslavement etc. An attack may also be non violent in nature, like imposing a system of apartheid, which is declared a crime against humanity in Article 1 of the Apartheid Convention of 1973, or exerting pressure on the population to act in a particular manner, may come under the purview of an attack, if orchestrated on a massive scale or in a systematic manner.

The act must be directed against the civilian population

582. The Chamber considers that an act must be directed against the civilian population if it is to constitute a crime against humanity. Members of the civilian population are people who are not taking any active part in the hostilities, including members of the armed forces who laid down their arms and those persons placed *hors de combat* by sickness, wounds, detention or any other cause.[146] Where there are certain individuals within the civilian population who do not come within the definition of civilians, this does not deprive the population of its civilian character.[147]

The act must be committed on discriminatory grounds [page 237]

583. The Statute stipulates that inhumane acts committed against the civilian population must be committed on "national, political, ethnic, racial or religious grounds." Discrimination on the basis of a person's political ideology satisfies the requirement of "political" grounds as envisaged in Article 3 of the Statute. For definitions on national, ethnic, racial or religious grounds see supra.

584. Inhumane acts committed against persons not falling within any one of the discriminatory categories could constitute crimes against humanity if the perpetrator's intention was to further his attacks on the group discriminated against on one of the grounds mentioned in Article 3 of the Statute. The perpetrator must have the requisite intent for the commission of crimes against humanity.[148]

---

[144] In the original French version of the Statute, these requirements were worded cumulatively: "Dans le cadre dunc adieux generalise *et* systematic", thereby significantly increasing the threshold for application of this provision. Since Customary International Law requires only that the attack be either widespread or systematic, there are sufficient reasons to assume that the French version suffers from an error in translation.

[145] Report on the International Law Commission to the General Assembly, 51 U.N. GAOR Supp. (No 10) at 94 U.N.Doc. A/51/10 (1996)

[146] Note that this definition assimilates the definition of "civilian" to the categories of person protected by Common Article 3 of the Geneva Conventions; an assimilation which would not appear to be problematic. Note also that the ICTY *Vukovar* Rule 61 Decision, of 3 April 1996, recognised that crimes against humanity could be committed where the victims were captured members of a resistance movement who at one time had borne arms, who would thus qualify as persons placed *hors de combat* by detention.

[147] Protocol Additional to the Geneva Convention of 12 August 1949, and relating to the Protection of Victims of International Armed Conflict; Article 50.

[148] The Judgment of Prosecutor v. Duško Tadić, case no. IT94-I-T, addressed this issue, citing the case the Federation Nationale des Deportes et Internes Resistant et Patriot and Other v. Barbie 78 Int'L. Rep. 124, 125 (1995). On Appeal the Cour de Cassation quashed and annulled the judgment in part, holding that members of the resistance could be victims of crimes against humanity as long as the necessary intent for crimes against humanity was present. (Para. 641)

The enumerated acts

585. Article 3 of the Statute sets out various acts that constitute crimes against humanity, namely: murder; extermination; enslavement; deportation; imprisonment; torture; rape; persecution on political, racial and religious grounds; and; other inhumane acts. Although the category of acts that constitute crimes against humanity are set out in Article 3, this category is not exhaustive. Any act which is inhumane in nature and character may constitute a crime against humanity, provided the other elements are met. This is evident in (i) which caters for all other inhumane acts not stipulated in (a) to (h) of Article 3.

586. The Chamber notes that the accused is indicted for murder, extermination, torture, rape and other acts that constitute inhumane acts. The Chamber in interpreting Article 3 of the Statute, shall focus its discussion on these acts only. [page 238]

Murder

587. The Chamber considers that murder is a crime against humanity, pursuant to Article 3 (a) of the Statute. The International Law Commission discussed the inhumane act of murder in the context of the definition of crimes against humanity and concluded that the crime of murder is clearly understood and defined in the national law of every state and therefore there is no need to further explain this prohibited act.

588. The Chamber notes that article 3(a) of the English version of the Statute refers to "Murder", whilst the French version of the Statute refers to "Assassinat". Customary International Law dictates that it is the act of "Murder" that constitutes a crime against humanity and not "Assassinat". There are therefore sufficient reasons to assume that the French version of the Statute suffers from an error in translation.

589. The Chamber defines murder as the unlawful, intentional killing of a human being. The requisite elements of murder are:

1. the victim is dead;
2. the death resulted from an unlawful act or omission of the accused or a subordinate;
3. at the time of the killing the accused or a subordinate had the intention to kill or inflict grievous bodily harm on the deceased having known that such bodily harm is likely to cause the victim's death, and is reckless whether death ensures or not.

590. Murder must be committed as part of a widespread or systematic attack against a civilian population. The victim must be a member of this civilian population. The victim must have been murdered because he was discriminated against on national, ethnic, racial, political or religious grounds.

Extermination [page 239]

591. The Chamber considers that extermination is a crime against humanity, pursuant to Article 3 (c) of the Statute. Extermination is a crime which by its very nature is directed against a group of individuals. Extermination differs from murder in that it requires an element of mass destruction which is not required for murder.

592. The Chamber defines the essential elements of extermination as the following:

1. the accused or his subordinate participated in the killing of certain named or described persons;
2. the act or omission was unlawful and intentional.
3. the unlawful act or omission must be part of a widespread or systematic attack;
4. the attack must be against the civilian population;
5. the attack must be on discriminatory grounds, namely: national, political, ethnic, racial, or religious grounds.

513

Torture

593. The Chamber considers that torture is a crime against humanity pursuant to Article 3(f) of the Statute. Torture may be defined as:

> "..any act by which severe pain or suffering, whether physical or mental, is intentionally inflicted on a person for such purposes as obtaining from him or a third person information or a confession, punishing him for an act he or a third person has committed or is suspected of having committed, or intimidating or coercing him or a third person, or for any reason based on discrimination of any kind, when such pain or suffering is inflicted by or at the instigation of or with the consent or acquiescence of a public official or other person acting in an official **[page 240]** capacity."[149]

594. The Chamber defines the essential elements of torture as:

 (i) The perpetrator must intentionally inflict severe physical or mental pain or suffering upon the victim for one or more of the following purposes:

 (a) to obtain information or a confession from the victim or a third person;
 (b) to punish the victim or a third person for an act committed or suspected of having been committed by either of them;
 (c) for the purpose of intimidating or coercing the victim or the third person;
 (d) for any reason based on discrimination of any kind.

 (ii) The perpetrator was himself an official, or acted at the instigation of, or with the consent or acquiescence of, an official or person acting in an official capacity.

595. The Chamber finds that torture is a crime against humanity if the following further elements are satisfied:

 (a) Torture must be perpetrated as part of a widespread or systematic attack;
 (b) the attack must be against the civilian population;
 (c) the attack must be launched on discriminatory grounds, namely: national, ethnic, racial, religious and political grounds.

Rape

596. Considering the extent to which rape constitute crimes against humanity, pursuant to Article 3(g) of the Statute, the Chamber must define rape, as there is no commonly accepted **[page 241]** definition of this term in international law. While rape has been defined in certain national jurisdictions as non-consensual intercourse, variations on the act of rape may include acts which involve the insertion of objects and/or the use of bodily orifices not considered to be intrinsically sexual.

597. The Chamber considers that rape is a form of aggression and that the central elements of the crime of rape cannot be captured in a mechanical description of objects and body parts. The Convention against Torture and Other Cruel, Inhuman and Degrading Treatment or Punishment does not catalogue specific acts in its definition of torture, focusing rather on the conceptual frame work of state sanctioned violence. This approach is more useful in international law. Like torture, rape is used for such purposes as intimidation, degradation, humiliation, discrimination, punishment, control or destruction of a person. Like torture, rape is a violation of personal dignity, and rape in fact constitutes torture when inflicted by or at the instigation of or with the consent or acquiescence of a public official or other person acting in an official capacity.

598. The Chamber defines rape as a physical invasion of a sexual nature, committed on a person under circumstances which are coercive. Sexual violence which includes rape, is considered to be any act of a sexual nature which is committed on a person under circumstances which are coercive. This act must be committed:

---

[149] Convention against Torture and Other Cruel, Inhuman or Degrading Treatment or Punishment, Article 1

(a)   as part of a wide spread or systematic attack;

(b)   on a civilian population;

(c)   on certained catalogued discriminatory grounds, namely: national, ethnic, political, racial, or religious grounds. **[page 242]**

6.5.   Violations of Common Article 3 and Additional Protocol II (Article 4 of the Statute)

Article 4 of the Statute

599.   Pursuant to Article 4 of the Statute, the Chamber shall have the power to prosecute persons committing or ordering to be committed serious violations of Article 3 common to the four Geneva Conventions of 12 August 1949 for the Protection of War Victims, and of Additional Protocol II thereto of 8 June 1977. The violations shall include, but shall not be limited to:

a) violence to life, health and physical or mental well-being of persons, in particular murder as well as cruel treatment such as torture, mutilation or any form of corporal punishment;

b) collective punishments;

c) taking of hostages;

d) acts of terrorism;

e) outrages upon personal dignity, in particular humiliating and degrading treatment, rape, enforced prostitution and any form of indecent assault;

f) pillage;

g) the passing of sentences and the carrying out of executions without previous judgment pronounced by a regularly constituted court, affording all the judicial guarantees which are recognised as indispensable by civilised peoples; **[page 243]**

h) threats to commit any of the foregoing acts.

600.   Prior to developing the elements for the above cited offences contained within Article 4 of the Statute, the Chamber deems it necessary to comment upon the applicability of common Article 3 and Additional Protocol II as regards the situation which existed in Rwanda in 1994 at the time of the events contained in the Indictment.

Applicability of Common Article 3 and Additional Protocol II

601.   The four 1949 Geneva Conventions and the 1977 Additional Protocol I thereto generally apply to international armed conflicts only, whereas Article 3 common to the Geneva Conventions extends a minimum threshold of humanitarian protection as well to all persons affected by a non-international conflict, a protection which was further developed and enhanced in the 1977 Additional Protocol II. In the field of international humanitarian law, a clear distinction as to the thresholds of application has been made between situations of international armed conflicts, in which the law of armed conflicts is applicable as a whole, situations of non-international (internal) armed conflicts, where Common Article 3 and Additional Protocol II are applicable, and non-international armed conflicts where only Common Article 3 is applicable. Situations of internal disturbances are not covered by international humanitarian law.

602.   The distinction pertaining to situations of conflicts of a non-international character emanates from the differing intensity of the conflicts. Such distinction is inherent to the conditions of applicability specified for Common Article 3 or Additional Protocol II respectively. Common Article 3 applies to "armed conflicts not of an international character", whereas for a conflict to fall within the ambit of Additional Protocol II, it must "take place in the territory of a High Contracting Party between its armed forces and dissident armed forces or other organized armed groups which, under responsible command,

exercise such control over a part of its territory as to enable them to carry out sustained and concerted military operations and to implement this Protocol". Additional Protocol II does not in itself establish a criterion for a non-international **[page 244]** conflict, rather it merely develops and supplements the rules contained in Common Article 3 without modifying its conditions of application.[150]

603.   It should be stressed that the ascertainment of the intensity of a non-international conflict does not depend on the subjective judgment of the parties to the conflict. It should be recalled that the four Geneva Conventions, as well as the two Protocols, were adopted primarily to protect the victims, as well as potential victims, of armed conflicts. If the application of international humanitarian law depended solely on the discretionary judgment of the parties to the conflict, in most cases there would be a tendency for the conflict to be minimized by the parties thereto. Thus, on the basis of objective criteria, both Common Article 3 and Additional Protocol II will apply once it has been established there exists an internal armed conflict which fulfills their respective pre-determined criteria[151].

604.   The Security Council, when delimiting the subject-matter jurisdiction of the ICTR[152], incorporated violations of international humanitarian law which may be committed in the context of both an international and an internal armed conflict:

> " Given the nature of the conflict as non-international in character, the Council has incorporated within the subject-matter jurisdiction of the Tribunal violations of international humanitarian law which may either be committed in both international and internal armed conflicts, such as the crime of genocide and crimes against humanity, or may be committed only in internal armed conflicts, such as violations of article 3 common to the four Geneva Conventions, as more **[page 245]**fully elaborated in article 4 of Additional Protocol II.
>
> In that latter respect, the Security Council has elected to take a more expansive approach to the choice of the applicable law than the one underlying the Statute of the Yugoslav Tribunal, and included within the subject-matter jurisdiction of the Rwandan Tribunal international instruments regardless of whether they were considered part of customary international law or whether they have customarily entailed the individual criminal responsibility of the perpetrator of the crime. Article 4 of the Statute, accordingly, includes violations of Additional Protocol II, which, as a whole, has not yet been universally recognized as part of customary international law, for the first time criminalizes common article 3 of the four Geneva Conventions."[153]

605.   Although the Security Council elected to take a more expansive approach to the choice of the subject-matter jurisdiction of the Tribunal than that of the ICTY, by incorporating international instruments regardless of whether they were considered part of customary international law or whether they customarily entailed the individual criminal responsibility of the perpetrator of the crime, the Chamber believes, an essential question which should be addressed at this stage is whether Article 4 of the Statute includes norms which did not, at the time the crimes alleged in the Indictment were committed, form part of existing international customary law. Moreover, the Chamber recalls the establishment of the ICTY[154], during which the UN Secretary General asserted that in application of the principle of *nullum crimen sine lege* the International Tribunal should apply rules of International Humanitarian law which are <u>beyond any doubt part</u> of customary law.

606.   Notwithstanding the above, a possible approach would be for the Chamber not to look at the nature of the building blocks of Article 4 of the Statute nor for it to categorize the conflict as **[page 246]** such but, rather, to look only at the relevant parts of Common Article 3 and Additional Protocol II in the

---

[150]   See Article 1 (Material field of application) of Additional Protocol II;

[151]   *Ibid* and International Committee of the Red Cross Commentary on the Additional Protocols of 8 June 1977 to the Geneva Conventions of 12 August 1949, para. 4438, (hereinafter the "Commentary on Additional Protocol II").

[152]   See the Secretary General's Report on practical arrangements for the effective functioning of the International Tribunal for Rwanda, recommending Arusha as the seat of the Tribunal, UN Doc. S/1995/134, of 13 February 1995.

[153]   *Ibid* paragraphs 11 – 12

[154]   See the Secretary General's Report to the Security Council on establishment of the ICTY, UN Doc. S/25704, of 3 May 1993, para 34.

context of this trial. Indeed, the Security Council has itself never explicitly determined how an armed conflict should be characterised. Yet it would appear that, in the case of the ICTY, the Security Council, by making reference to the four Geneva Conventions, considered that the conflict in the former Yugoslavia was an international armed conflict, although it did not suggest the criteria by which it reached this finding. Similarly, when the Security Council added Additional Protocol II to the subject matter jurisdiction of the ICTR, this could suggest that the Security Council deemed the conflict in Rwanda as an Additional Protocol II conflict. Thus, it would not be necessary for the Chamber to determine the precise nature of the conflict, this having already been pre-determined by the Security Council. Article 4 of the Statute would be applicable irrespective of the "Additional Protocol II question", so long as the conflict were covered, at the very least, by the customary norms of Common Article 3. Findings would thus be made on the basis of whether or not it were proved beyond a reasonable doubt that there has been a serious violation in the form of one or more of the acts enumerated in Article 4 of the Statute.

607. However, the Chamber recalls the way in which the Prosecutor has brought some of the counts against the accused, namely counts 6, 8, 10, 12 and 15. For the first four of these, there is mention only of Common Article 3 as the subject matter jurisdiction of the particular alleged offences, whereas count 15 makes an additional reference to Additional Protocol II. To so add Additional Protocol II should not, in the opinion of the Chamber, be dealt with as a mere expansive enunciation of a *ratione materiae* which has been pre-determined by the Security Council. Rather, the Chamber finds it necessary and reasonable to establish the applicability of both Common Article 3 and Additional Protocol II individually. Thus, if an offence, as per count 15, is charged under both Common Article 3 and Additional Protocol II, it will not suffice to apply Common Article 3 and take for granted that Article 4 of the Statute, hence Additional Protocol II, is therefore automatically applicable.

608. It is today clear that the norms of Common Article 3 have acquired the status of customary law in that most States, by their domestic penal codes, have criminalized acts which if committed during internal armed conflict, would constitute violations of Common Article 3. It was also held **[page 247]** by the ICTY Trial Chamber in the Tadić judgment[155] that Article 3 of the ICTY Statute (Customs of War), being the body of customary international humanitarian law not covered by Articles 2, 4, and 5 of the ICTY Statute, included the regime of protection established under Common Article 3 applicable to armed conflicts not of an international character. This was in line with the view of the ICTY Appeals Chamber stipulating that Common Article 3 beyond doubt formed part of customary international law, and further that there exists a corpus of general principles and norms on internal armed conflict embracing Common Article 3 but having a much greater scope[156].

609. However, as aforesaid, Additional Protocol II as a whole was not deemed by the Secretary-General to have been universally recognized as part of customary international law. The Appeals Chamber concurred with this view inasmuch as "[m]any provisions of this Protocol [II] can now be regarded as declaratory of existing rules or as having crystallised in emerging rules of customary law[]", but not all.[157]

610. Whilst the Chamber is very much of the same view as pertains to Additional Protocol II as a whole, it should be recalled that the relevant Article in the context of the ICTR is Article 4(2) (Fundamental Guarantees) of Additional Protocol II[158]. All of the guarantees, as enumerated in Article 4 reaffirm and supplement Common Article 3[159] and, as discussed above, Common Article 3 being customary in nature, the Chamber is of the opinion that these guarantees did also at the time of the events alleged in the Indictment form part of existing international customary law. **[page 248]**

---

[155] See ICTY Tadić Judgment of 7 May 1997, paragraph 609
[156] Decision on the Defence Motion for Interlocutory Appeal on Jurisdiction of 2 October 1995, paragraphs 116 and 134.
[157] *Ibid* paragraph 117
[158] Save for 4(2)(f) slavery and the slave trade in all their forms
[159] As regards Collective Punishments'note should be taken of commentary thereon, para 4535 – 4536 Commentary on Additional Protocol II

Individual Criminal Responsibility

611. For the purposes of an international criminal Tribunal which is trying individuals, it is not sufficient merely to affirm that Common Article 3 and parts of Article 4 of Additional Protocol II – which comprise the subject-manner jurisdiction of Article 4 of the Statute – form part of international customary law. Even if Article 6 of the Statute provides for individual criminal responsibility as pertains to Articles 2, 3 and 4 of the Statute, it must also be shown that an individual committing serious violations of these customary norms incurs, as a matter of custom, individual criminal responsibility thereby. Otherwise, it might be argued that these instruments only state norms applicable to States and Parties to a conflict, and that they do not create crimes for which individuals may be tried.

612. As regards individual criminal responsibility for serious violations of Common Article 3, the ICTY has already affirmed this principle in the Tadić case. In the ICTY Appeals Chamber, the problem was posed thus:

" Even if customary international law includes certain basic principles applicable to both internal and international armed conflicts, Appellant argues that such provisions do not entail individual criminal responsibility when breaches are committed in internal armed conflicts; these provisions cannot, therefore, fall within the scope of the International Tribunal's jurisdiction.[160]"

613. Basing itself on rulings of the Nüremberg Tribunal, on "elements of international practice which show that States intend to criminalise serious breaches of customary rules and principles on internal conflicts", as well as on national legislation designed to implement the Geneva Conventions, the ICTY Appeals Chamber reached the conclusion: **[page 249]**

" All of these factors confirm that customary international law imposes criminal liability for serious violations of common Article 3, as supplemented by other general principles and rules on protection of victims of internal armed conflict, and for breaching certain fundamental principles and rules regarding means and methods of combat in civil strife.[161]"

614. This was affirmed by the ICTY Trial Chamber when it rendered in the Tadić judgment[162].

615. The Chamber considers this finding of the ICTY Appeals Chamber convincing and dispositive of the issue, both with respect to serious violations of Common Article 3 and of Additional Protocol II.

616. It should be noted, moreover, that Article 4 of the ICTR Statute states that, "The International Tribunal for Rwanda shall have the power to prosecute persons committing or ordering to be committed *serious violations* of Article 3 common to the Geneva Conventions of 12 August 1949 for the Protection of War Victims, and of Additional Protocol II thereto of 8 June 1977" (emphasis added). The Chamber understands the phrase "serious violation" to mean "a breach of a rule protecting important values [which] must involve grave consequences for the victim", in line with the above-mentioned Appeals Chamber Decision in Tadić paragraph 94. The list of serious violations which is provided in Article 4 of the Statute is taken from Common Article 3 – which contains fundamental prohibitions as a humanitarian minimum of protection for war victims – and Article 4 of Additional Protocol II, which equally outlines "Fundamental Guarantees". The list in Article 4 of the Statute thus comprises *serious* violations of the fundamental humanitarian guarantees which, as has been stated above, are recognized as part of international customary law. In the opinion of the Chamber, it is clear that the authors of such egregious violations must incur individual criminal responsibility for their deeds. **[page 250]**

617. The Chamber, therefore, concludes the violation of these norms entails, as a matter of customary international law, individual responsibility for the perpetrator. In addition to this argument from custom, there is the fact that the Geneva Conventions of 1949 (and thus Common Article 3) were ratified by Rwanda on 5 May 1964 and Additional Protocol II on 19 November 1984, and were therefore in force on the territory of Rwanda at the time of the alleged offences. Moreover, all the offences enumerated under

---

[160] Decision on the Defence Motion for Interlocutory Appeal on Jurisdiction of 2 October 1995, paragraph 128
[161] *Ibid* paragraph 134
[162] See ICTY Tadić Judgment of 7 May 1997, paragraph 613

Article 4 of the Statute constituted crimes under Rwandan law in 1994. Rwandan nationals were therefore aware, or should have been aware, in 1994 that they were amenable to the jurisdiction of Rwandan courts in case of commission of those offences falling under Article 4 of the Statute.

The nature of the conflict

618. As aforesaid, it will not suffice to establish that as the criteria of Common Article 3 have been met, the whole of Article 4 of the Statute, hence Additional Protocol II, will be applicable. Where alleged offences are charged under both Common Article 3 and Additional Protocol II, which has a higher threshold, the Prosecutor will need to prove that the criteria of applicability of, on the one hand, Common Article 3 and, on the other, Additional Protocol II have been met. This is so because Additional Protocol II is a legal instrument the overall sole purpose of which is to afford protection to victims in conflicts not of an international character. Hence, the Chamber deems it reasonable and necessary that, prior to deciding if there have been serious violations of the provisions of Article 4 of the Statute, where a specific reference has been made to Additional Protocol II in counts against an accused, it must be shown that the conflict is such as to satisfy the requirements of Additional Protocol II.

Common Article 3

619. The norms set by Common Article 3 apply to a conflict as soon as it is an "armed conflict not of an international character". An inherent question follows such a description, namely, what **[page 251]** constitutes an armed conflict? The Appeals Chamber in the Tadić decision on Jurisdiction[163] held "that an armed conflict exists whenever there is [...] protracted armed violence between governmental authorities and organized armed groups or between such groups within a State. International humanitarian law applies from the initiation of such armed conflicts and extends beyond the cessation of hostilities until [...] in the case of internal conflicts, a peaceful settlement is reached". Similarly, the Chamber notes that the ICRC commentary on Common Article 13[164] suggests useful criteria resulting from the various amendments discussed during the Diplomatic Conference of Geneva, 1949, *inter alia*:

- That the Party in revolt against the *de jure* Government possesses an organized military force, an authority responsible for its acts, acting within a determinate territory and having the means of respecting and ensuring the respect for the Convention.

- That the legal Government is obliged to have recourse to the regular military forces against insurgents organized as military in possession of a part of the national territory.

  (a) That the *de jure* Government has recognized the insurgents as belligerents; or

  (b) that it has claimed for itself the rights of a belligerent; or

  (c) that it has accorded the insurgents recognition as belligerents for the purposes only of the present Convention; or

  (d) that the dispute has been admitted to the agenda of the Security Council or the General Assembly of the United Nations as being a threat to international peace, a breach of peace, **[page 252]** or an act of aggression.

620. The above "reference" criteria were enunciated as a means of distinguishing genuine armed conflicts from mere acts of banditry or unorganized and short-lived insurrections[165]. The term, "armed conflict" in itself suggests the existence of hostilities between armed forces organized to a greater or

---

[163] See ICTY Decision on the Defence Motion for Interlocutory Appeal on Jurisdiction of 2 October 1995, para. 70
[164] See International Committee of the Red Cross, Commentary I Geneva Convention, Article 3, Paragraph 1 – Applicable Provisions
[165] *Ibid*

lesser extent[166]. This consequently rules out situations of internal disturbances and tensions. For a finding to be made on the existence of an internal armed conflict in the territory of Rwanda at the time of the events alleged, it will therefore be necessary to evaluate both the intensity and organization of the parties to the conflict.

621. Evidence presented in relation to paragraphs 5-11 of the Indictment[167], namely the testimony of Major-General Dallaire, has shown there to have been a civil war between two groups, being on the one side, the governmental forces, the FAR, and on the other side, the RPF. Both groups were well-organized and considered to be armies in their own right. Further, as pertains to the intensity of conflict, all observers to the events, including UNAMIR and UN Special rapporteurs, were unanimous in characterizing the confrontation between the two forces as a war, an internal armed conflict. Based on the foregoing, the Chamber finds there existed at the time of the events alleged in the Indictment an armed conflict not of an international character as covered by Common Article 3 of the 1949 Geneva Conventions.

Additional Protocol II

622. As stated above, Additional Protocol II applies to conflicts which "take place in the territory of a High Contracting Party between its armed forces and dissident armed forces or other organized armed groups which, under responsible command, exercise such control over a part of **[page 253]** its territory as to enable them to carry out sustained and concerted military operations and to implement this Protocol".

623. Thus, the conditions to be met to fulfil the material requirements of applicability of Additional Protocol II at the time of the events alleged in the Indictment would entail showing that:

(i)   an armed conflict took place in the territory of a High Contracting Party, namely Rwanda, between its armed forces and dissident armed forces or other organized armed groups;

(ii)   the dissident armed forces or other organized armed groups were under responsible command;

(iii)   the dissident armed forces or other organized armed groups were able to exercise such control over a part of their territory as to enable them to carry out sustained and concerted military operations; and

(iv)   the dissident armed forces or other organized armed groups were able to implement Additional Protocol II.

624. As per Common Article 3, these criteria have to be applied objectively, irrespective of the subjective conclusions of the parties involved in the conflict. A number of precisions need to be made about the said criteria prior to the Chamber making a finding thereon.[168]

625. The concept of armed conflict has already been discussed in the previous section pertaining to Common Article 3. It suffices to recall that an armed conflict is distinguished from internal disturbances by the level of intensity of the conflict and the degree of organization of the **[page 254]** parties to the conflict. Under Additional Protocol II, the parties to the conflict will usually either be the government confronting dissident armed forces, or the government fighting insurgent organized armed groups. The term, "armed forces" of the High Contracting Party is to be defined broadly, so as to cover all armed forces as described within national legislations.

626. The armed forces opposing the government must be under responsible command, which entails a degree of organization within the armed group or dissident armed forces. This degree of organization should be such so as to enable the armed group or dissident forces to plan and carry out concerted

---

[166]   See Commentary on Additional Protocol II, paras 4338-4341
[167]   See "Factual Findings – General Allegations (paragraphs 5-11 of the Indictment)"
[168]   See generally Commentary on Additional Protocol II, Article 1 (Material field of application)

military operations, and to impose disciple in the name of a *de facto* authority. Further, these armed forces must be able to dominate a sufficient part of the territory so as to maintain sustained and concerted military operations and to apply Additional Protocol II. In essence, the operations must be continuous and planned. The territory in their control is usually that which has eluded the control of the government forces.

627.   In the present case, evidence has been presented to the Chamber which showed there was at the least a conflict not of a international character in Rwanda at the time of the events alleged in the Indictment[169]. The Chamber, also taking judicial notice of a number of UN official documents dealing with the conflict in Rwanda in 1994, finds, in addition to the requirements of Common Article 3 being met, that the material conditions listed above relevant to Additional Protocol II have been fulfilled. It has been shown that there was a conflict between, on the one hand, the RPF, under the command of General Kagame, and, on the other, the governmental forces, the FAR. The RPF increased its control over the Rwandan territory from that agreed in the Arusha Accords to over half of the country by mid-May 1994, and carried out continuous and sustained military operations until the cease fire on 18 July 1994 which brought the war to an end. The RPF troops were disciplined and possessed a structured leadership which was answerable to authority. The RPF had also stated to the International Committee of the Red Cross that it was **[page 255]** bound by the rules of International Humanitarian law[170]. The Chamber finds the said conflict to have been an internal armed conflict within the meaning of Additional Protocol II. Further, the Chamber finds that conflict took place at the time of the events alleged in the Indictment.

Ratione personae

628.   Two distinct issues arise with respect to personal jurisdiction over serious violations of Common Article 3 and Additional Protocol II – the class of victims and the class of perpetrators.

The class of victims

629.   Paragraph 10 of the Indictment reads, "The victims referred to in this Indictment were, at all relevant times, persons not taking an active part in the hostilities". This is a material averment for charges involving Article 4 inasmuch as Common Article 3 is for the protection of "persons taking no active part in the hostilities" (Common Article 3(1)), and Article 4 of Additional Protocol II is for the protection of, "all persons who do not take a direct part or who have ceased to take part in hostilities". These phrases are so similar that, for the Chamber's purposes, they may be treated as synonymous. Whether the victims referred to in the Indictment are *indeed* persons not taking an active part in the hostilities is a factual question, which has been considered in the Factual Findings on the General Allegations (paragraphs 5-11 of the Indictment).

The class of perpetrators

630.   The four Geneva Conventions – as well as the two Additional Protocols – as stated above, were adopted primarily to protect the victims as well as potential victims of armed conflicts. This implies thus that the legal instruments are primarily addressed to persons who by virtue of their **[page 256]** authority, are responsible for the outbreak of, or are otherwise engaged in the conduct of hostilities. The category of persons to be held accountable in this respect then, would in most cases be limited to commanders, combatants and other members of the armed forces.

631.   Due to the overall protective and humanitarian purpose of these international legal instruments, however, the delimitation of this category of persons bound by the provisions in Common Article 3 and

---

[169]   See in particular documents referred to in "Factual Findings – General Allegations (paragraphs 5-11 of the Indictment)"
[170]   Report of the United Nations High Commissioner for Human Rights on his mission to Rwanda of 11-12 May 1994 (E/CN.4/S-3/3. 19 May 1994)

Additional Protocol II should not be too restricted. The duties and responsibilities of the Geneva Conventions and the Additional Protocols, hence, will normally apply only to individuals of all ranks belonging to the armed forces under the military command of either of the belligerent parties, or to individuals who were legitimately mandated and expected, as public officials or agents or persons otherwise holding public authority or *de facto* representing the Government, to support or fulfil the war efforts. The objective of this approach, thus, would be to apply the provisions of the Statute in a fashion which corresponds best with the underlying protective purpose of the Conventions and the Protocols.

632. However, the Indictment does not specifically aver that the accused falls in the class of persons who may be held responsible for serious violations of Common Article 3 and Additional Protocol II. It has not been alleged that the accused was officially a member of the Rwandan "armed forces" (in its broadest sense). It could, hence, be objected that, as a civilian, Article 4 of the Statute, which concerns the law of armed conflict, does not apply to him.

633. It is, in fact, well-established, at least since the Tokyo trials, that civilians may be held responsible for violations of international humanitarian law. Hirota, the former Foreign Minister of Japan, was convicted at Tokyo for crimes committed during the rape of Nanking[171]. Other post-World War II trials unequivocally support the imposition of individual criminal liability for war crimes on civilians where they have a link or connection with a party to the conflict[172] The **[page 257]** principle of holding civilians liable for breaches of the laws of war is, moreover, favored by a consideration of the humanitarian object and purpose of the Geneva Conventions and the Additional Protocols, which is to protect war victims from atrocities.

634. Thus it is clear from the above that the laws of war must apply equally to civilians as to combatants in the conventional sense. Further, the Chamber notes, in light of the above *dicta*, that the accused was not, at the time of the events in question, a mere civilian but a bourgmestre. The Chamber therefore concludes that, if so established factually, the accused could fall in the class of individuals who may be held responsible for serious violations of international humanitarian law, in particular serious violations of Common Article 3 and Additional Protocol II.

Ratione loci

635. There is no clear provision on applicability *ratione loci* either in Common Article 3 or Additional Protocol II. However, in this respect Additional Protocol II seems slightly clearer, in so far as it provides that the Protocol shall be applied "to all persons affected by an armed conflict as defined in Article 1". The commentary thereon[173] specifies that this applicability is irrespective of the exact location of the affected person in the territory of the State engaged in the conflict. The question of applicability *ratione loci* in non-international armed conflicts, when only Common Article 3 is of relevance should be approached the same way, i.e. the article must be applied in the whole territory of the State engaged in the conflict. This approach was followed by the Appeals **[page 258]** Chamber in its decision on jurisdiction in Tadić, wherein it was held that "the rules contained in [common] Article 3 also apply outside the narrow geographical context of the actual theatre of combat operations"[174].

---

[171]   See "General Legal Findings" – Individual Criminal Responsibility (Article 6 of the Statute)"

[172]   See *The Hadamar Trial*, Law Reports of Trials of War Criminals ("LRTWC"), Vol. I, pp. 53-54: "The accused were not members of the German armed forces, but personnel of a civilian institution. The decision of the Military Commission is, therefore, an application of the rule that the provisions of the laws or customs of war are addressed not only to combatants but also to civilians, and that civilians, by committing illegal acts against nationals of the opponent, may become guilty of war crimes"; *The Essen Lynching Case*, LRTWC, Vol. I, p. 88, in which, *inter alia*, three civilians were found guilty of the killing of unarmed prisoners of war; and *the Zyklon B Case*, LRTWC, Vol. I, p. 103: "The decision of the Military Court in the present case is a clear example of the application of the rule that the provisions of the laws and customs of war are addressed not only to combatants and to members of state and other public authorities, but to anybody who is in a position to assist in their violation. [...] The Military Court acted on the principle that any civilian who is an accessory to a violation of the laws and customs of war is himself also liable as a war criminal".

[173]   Commentary on Additional Protocol II, paragraph 4490

[174]   See ICTY Decision on the Defence Motion for Interlocutory Appeal on Jurisdiction of 2 October 1995, paragraph 69

636. Thus the mere fact that Rwanda was engaged in an armed conflict meeting the threshold requirements of Common Article 3 and Additional Protocol II means that these instruments would apply over the whole territory hence encompassing massacres which occurred away from the "war front". From this follows that it is not possible to apply rules in one part of the country (i.e. Common Article 3) and other rules in other parts of the country (i.e. Common Article 3 and Additional Protocol II). The aforesaid, however, is subject to the *caveat* that the crimes must not be committed by the perpetrator for purely personal motives.

Conclusion

637. The applicability of Common Article 3 and Additional Protocol II has been dealt with above and findings made thereon in the context of the temporal setting of events alleged in the Indictment. It remains for the Chamber to make its findings with regard the accused's culpability under Article 4 of the Statute. This will be dealt with in section 7 of the judgment. **[page 259]**

7. LEGAL FINDINGS

7.1. Counts 6, 8, 10 and 12 – Violations of Common Article 3 (murder and cruel treatment) and Count 15 – Violations of Common Article 3 and Additional Protocol II (outrages upon personal dignity, in particular rape...)

638. Counts 6, 8, 10 and 12 of the Indictment charge Akayesu with Violations of Common Article 3 of the 1949 Geneva Conventions, and Count 15 charges Akayesu of Violations of Common Article 3 of the 1949 Geneva Conventions and the 1977 Additional Protocol II thereto. All these counts are covered by Article 4 of the Statute.

639. It has already been proved beyond reasonable doubt that there was an armed conflict not of an international character between the Government of Rwanda and the RPF in 1994 at the time of the events alleged in the Indictment[175]. The Chamber found the conflict to meet the requirements of Common Article 3 as well as Additional Protocol II.

640. For Akayesu to be held criminally responsible under Article 4 of the Statute, it is incumbent on the Prosecutor to prove beyond a reasonable doubt that Akayesu acted for either the Government or the RPF in the execution of their respective conflict objectives. As stipulated earlier in this judgment, this implies that Akayesu would incur individual criminal responsibility for his acts if it were proved that by virtue of his authority, he is either responsible for the outbreak of, or is otherwise directly engaged in the conduct of hostilities. Hence, the Prosecutor will have to demonstrate to the Chamber and prove that Akayesu was either a member of the armed forces under the military command of either of the belligerent parties, or that he was legitimately mandated and expected, as a public official or agent or person otherwise holding public authority or *de facto* representing the Government, to support or fulfil the war efforts. Indeed, the Chamber **[page 260]** recalls that Article 4 of the Statute also applies to civilians.

641. Evidence presented during trial established that, at the time of the events alleged in the Indictment, Akayesu wore a military jacket, carried a rifle, he assisted the military on their arrival in Taba by undertaking a number of tasks, including reconnaissance and mapping of the commune, and the setting up of radio communications, and he allowed the military to use his office premises. The Prosecutor relied in part on these facts to demonstrate that there was a nexus between the actions of Akayesu and the conflict. Further the Prosecutor argued that reference by Akayesu to individuals as RPF accomplices was indicative of Akayesu connecting his actions to the conflict between the Government and the RPF.

642. It has been established in this judgement that Akayesu embodies the communal authority and that he held an executive civilian position in the territorial administrative subdivision of Commune. However,

---

[175]   *Supra* "Legal Findings on Article 4 of the Statute" and "Genocide in Rwanda in Rwanda in 1994"

the Prosecutor did not bring sufficient evidence to show how and in what capacity Akayesu was supporting the Government effort against the RPF. The evidence as pertains to the wearing of a military jacket and the carrying of a rifle, in the opinion of the Chamber, are not significant in demonstrating that Akayesu actively supported the war effort. Furthermore, the Chamber finds that the limited assistance given to the military by the accused in his role as the head of the commune does not suffice to establish that he actively supported the war effort. Moreover, the Chamber recalls it has been proved that references to RPF accomplices in the context of the events which occurred in Taba were to be understood as meaning Tutsi.[176]

643.   Considering the above, and based on all the evidence presented in this case, the Chamber finds that it has not been proved beyond reasonable doubt that the acts perpetrated by Akayesu in the commune of Taba at the time of the events alleged in the Indictment were committed in conjunction with the armed conflict. The Chamber further finds that it has not been proved beyond reasonable doubt that Akayesu was a member of the armed forces, or that he was legitimately mandated and expected, as a public official or agent or person otherwise holding public authority **[page 261]** or *de facto* representing the Government, to support or fulfil the war efforts.

644.   The Tribunal therefore finds that Jean-Paul Akayesu did not incur individual criminal responsibility under counts 6, 8, 10, 12 & 15 of the Indictment. **[page 262]**

7.2. Count 5 – Crimes against humanity (murder)

645.   Count 5 of the indictment charges the Accused with a crime against humanity (murder), pursuant to Article 3(a) of the Statute, for the acts alleged in paragraphs 15 and 18 of the indictment.

646.   The definition of crimes against humanity, including the various elements that comprise the enumerated offences under Article 3 of the Statute have already been discussed.

647.   The Chamber finds beyond a reasonable doubt that the Accused was present and addressed a gathering in Gishyeshye sector on the morning of 19 April 1994. The Chamber however finds that it has not been proven beyond a reasonable doubt that the Accused during this address, mentioned the names of Juvénal Rukundakuvuga or Emmanuel Sempabwa as Tutsi to be killed and as a result thereof they were subsequently killed.

648.   The Chamber finds beyond a reasonable doubt that during his search for Ephrem Karangwa, the Accused participated in the killing of Simon Mutijima, Thaddée Uwanyiligra and Jean Chrysostome, by ordering their deaths and being present when they were killed.

649.   The Chamber finds beyond a reasonable doubt that Simon Mutijima, Thaddée Uwanyiligra and Jean Chrysostome were civilians, taking no active part in the hostilities that prevailed in Rwanda in 1994 and the only reason they were killed in because they were Tutsi.

650.   The Chamber finds beyond a reasonable doubt that in ordering the killing of Simon Mutijima, Thaddée Uwanyiligra and Jean Chrysostome, the Accused had the requisite intent to kill them as part of a widespread or systematic attack against the civilian population of Rwanda on ethnic grounds. **[page 263]**

651.   The Chamber finds beyond a reasonable doubt that in ordering the killings of Simon Mutijima, Thaddée Uwanyiligra and Jean Chrysostome, the Accused is individually criminally responsible for the death of these victims, pursuant to Article 6(1) of the Statute.

652.   The Chamber finds beyond a reasonable doubt that there was a widespread and systematic attack against the civilian population in Rwanda on 19 April 1994 and the conduct of the Accused formed part of this attack.

653.   The Chamber finds beyond a reasonable doubt that the killing of Simon Mutijima, Thaddée Uwanyiligra and Jean Chrysostome constitutes murder committed, as part of a widespread or systematic

---

[176]   *Supra* "Factual findings on paragraphs 14 and 15 of the Indictment"

attack on the civilian population on ethnic grounds and as such constitutes a crime against humanity. Accordingly, the Chamber finds beyond a reasonable doubt that the Accused is guilty as charged in count 5 of the indictment. **[page 264]**

7.3. Count 7 – Crimes against Humanity (murder)

654. Count 7 of the indictment charges the Accused with a crime against humanity (murder), pursuant to Article 3(a) of the Statute, for the acts alleged in paragraph 19 of the indictment.

655. The definition of crimes against humanity, including the various elements that comprise the enumerated offences under Article 3 of the Statute have already been discussed.

656. The Chamber finds beyond a reasonable doubt that on 19 April 1994, the Accused took eight detained refugees who were civilians and who did not take any active part in the hostilities that prevailed in Rwanda in 1994 and handed them over to the local militia, known as the Interahamwe with orders that they be killed.

657. The Chamber finds beyond a reasonable doubt that the Interahamwe, acting on the orders from the Accused killed these eight refugees, at the bureau communal in the presence of the Accused.

658. The Chamber finds beyond a reasonable doubt that in ordering the killing of the eight refugees, the Accused had the requisite intent to kill them as part of a widespread or systematic attack against the civilian population of Rwanda on ethnic grounds and as such he is criminally responsible for the killing of these eight refugees.

659. The Chamber finds beyond a reasonable doubt that in ordering the killing of the eight refugees, the Accused is individually criminally responsible for the death of these victims, pursuant to Article 6(1) of the Statute.

660. The Chamber finds beyond a reasonable doubt that there was a widespread and systematic attack against the civilian population in Rwanda on 19 April 1994 and the conduct of the Accused **[page 265]** formed part of this attack.

661. The Chamber finds beyond a reasonable doubt that the killing of these eight refugees constitutes murder committed, as part of a widespread or systematic attack on the civilian population on ethnic grounds and as such constitutes a crime against humanity. Accordingly, the Chamber finds beyond a reasonable doubt that the Accused is guilty as charged in count 7 of the indictment. **[page 266]**

7.4. Count 9 – Crimes against Humanity (murder)

662. Count 9 of the indictment charges the Accused with a crime against humanity (murder), pursuant to Article 3(a) of the Statute, for the acts alleged in paragraph 20 of the indictment.

663. The definition of crimes against humanity, including the various elements that comprise the enumerated offences under Article 3 of the Statute have already been discussed.

664. The Chamber finds beyond a reasonable doubt that on 19 April 1994, the Accused ordered the local people and militia known as the Interahamwe to kill intellectual people.

665. The Chamber finds beyond a reasonable doubt that the Interahamwe and the local population, acting on the orders of the Accused killed five teachers namely; a professor known as Samuel; Tharcisse who was killed in the presence of the Accused; Theogene, Phoebe Uwineze and her fiancé.

666. The Chamber finds beyond a reasonable doubt that these five teachers were civilians and did not take any active part in the hostilities that prevailed in Rwanda in 1994.

667. The Chamber finds beyond a reasonable doubt that these five teachers were killed because they were Tutsi.

668.   The Chamber finds beyond a reasonable doubt that in ordering the killing of these five teachers, the Accused had the requisite intent to kill them as part of a widespread or systematic attack against the civilian population of Rwanda on ethnic grounds.

669.   The Chamber finds beyond a reasonable doubt that in ordering the killing of these five teachers, the Accused is individually criminally responsible for the death of these victims, **[page 267]** pursuant to Article 6(1) of the Statute.

670.   The Chamber finds beyond a reasonable doubt that there was a widespread and systematic attack against the civilian population in Rwanda on 19 April 1994 and the conduct of the Accused formed part of this attack.

671.   The Chamber finds, beyond a reasonable doubt that the killing of these five people constitute murder committed, as part of a widespread or systematic attack on the civilian population on ethnic grounds and as such constitutes a crime against humanity. Accordingly, the Chamber finds beyond a reasonable doubt that the Accused is guilty as charged in count 9 of the indictment. **[page 268]**

7.5. Count 4 – Direct and Public Incitement to commit Genocide

672.   Count 4 deals with the allegations described in paragraphs 14 and 15 of the Indictment, relating, essentially, to the speeches that Akayesu reportedly made at a meeting held in Gishyeshye on 19 April 1994. The Prosecutor alleges that, through his speeches, Akayesu committed the crime of direct and public incitement to commit genocide, a crime punishable under Article 2(3)(c) of the Statute.

673.   The Trial Chamber made the following factual findings on the events described in paragraphs 14 and 15 of the Indictment. The Chamber is satisfied beyond a reasonable doubt that:

(i)   Akayesu, in the early hours of 19 April 1994, joined a crowd of over 100 people which had gathered around the body of a young member of the Interahamwe in Gishyeshye.

(ii)   He seized that opportunity to address the people and, owing, particularly, to his functions as bourgmestre and his authority over the population, he led the gathering and the proceedings.

(iii)   It has been established that Akayesu then clearly urged the population to unite in order to eliminate what he termed the sole enemy; the accomplices of the Inkotanyi.

(iv)   On the basis of consistent testimonies heard throughout the proceedings and the evidence of Dr. Ruzindana, appearing as expert witness on linguistic matters, the Chamber is satisfied beyond a reasonable doubt that the population understood Akayesu's call as one to kill the Tutsi. Akayesu himself was fully aware of the impact of his speech on the crowd and of the fact that his call to fight against the accomplices of the Inkotanyi would be construed as a call to kill the Tutsi in general.

(v)   During the said meeting, Akayesu received from the Interahamwe documents which included lists of names, and read from the lists to the crowd by stating, in particular, that the names were those of RPF accomplices.

(vi)   Akayesu testified that the lists contained, especially, the name of Ephrem Karangwa, whom he named specifically, while being fully aware of the consequences of doing so. Indeed, he admitted before the Chamber that, at the time of the events alleged **[page 269]** in the Indictment, to label anyone in public as an accomplice of the RPF would put such a person in danger.

(vii)   The Chamber is of the opinion that there is a causal relationship between Akayesu's speeches at the gathering of 19 April 1994 and the ensuing widespread massacres of Tutsi in Taba.

674.   From the foregoing, the Chamber is satisfied beyond a reasonable doubt that, by the above-mentioned speeches made in public and in a public place, Akayesu had the intent to directly create a particular state of mind in his audience necessary to lead to the destruction of the Tutsi group, as such. Accordingly, the Chamber finds that the said acts constitute the crime of direct and public incitement to commit genocide, as defined above.

675.   In addition, the Chamber finds that the direct and public incitement to commit genocide as engaged in by Akayesu, was indeed successful and did lead to the destruction of a great number of Tutsi in the commune of Taba. **[page 270]]**

[page 270] 7.6. Count 11 – Crimes against Humanity (torture)

676.   In the light of its factual findings with regard to the allegations set forth in paragraphs 16, 17, 21, 22 and 23 of the Indictment, the Tribunal considers the criminal responsibility of the Accused on Count 11 for his acts in relation to the beatings of Victims U, V, W, X, Y and Z.

677.   The Tribunal notes that evidence has been presented at trial regarding the beating of victims not specifically named in paragraphs 16, 17, 21, 22 and 23 of the Indictment. Witness J, for example, testified that she was slapped and her brother was beaten by the Accused: As counts 11 and 12 are restricted to acts in relation to the beatings of Victims U, V, W, X, Y and Z, the Tribunal will restrict its legal findings to these acts.

678.   The Tribunal notes that paragraph 16 of the Indictment alleges that the Accused threatened to kill the husband and child of Victim U. The factual finding of the Tribunal is that the Accused threatened to kill Victim U, not her husband and child. The Tribunal considers that the allegations set forth in the Indictment sufficiently informed the Accused, in accordance with the requirements of due process, of the charge against him. The material allegation is that he threatened Victim U. Whether the threat was against her life or the life of her immediate family is not legally significant in the Tribunal's view.

679.   The Tribunal notes that Paragraph 21 of the Indictment refers to "communal police" without reference to the Interahamwe, although Paragraph 23 refers to "men under Jean Paul Akayesu's authority". In its factual findings, the Tribunal has determined that only Mugenzi was a communal police officer. The other person actively involved in the interrogation and beating of Victim Z and possibly the interrogation of Victim W was Francois, an Interahamwe. As Francois and Mugenzi were both acting in the presence of and under the immediate authority of the Accused, as bourgmestre, the Tribunal finds that in relation to the Accused the acts of Francois may be treated as equivalent to the acts of Mugenzi. **[page 271]**

680.   The Tribunal notes that the Accused himself participated in the beating of Victim Y by hitting her on the back with a club, and the beating of Victim Z by stepping on his face and holding his foot there while others beat him. It is alleged that he interrogated them but it is not specifically alleged in Paragraphs 21 and 23 of the Indictment that the Accused committed acts of physical violence. The Tribunal finds, however, that the allegations in the Indictment were sufficient notice to the Accused of the incidents in question, and that the exact role of the Accused in these incidents was a matter which was adjudicated at trial in accordance with the requirements of due process. For these reasons, the Tribunal finds that the Accused may be judged criminally responsible for his direct participation in these beatings, despite the absence of a specific allegation of direct participation by the Accused in the relevant paragraphs of the Indictment.

681.   The Tribunal interprets the word "torture", as set forth in Article 3(f) of its Statute, in accordance with the definition of torture set forth in the United Nations Convention Against Torture and Other Cruel, Inhuman or Degrading Treatment or Punishment, that is "any act by which severe pain or suffering, whether physical or mental, is intentionally inflicted on a person for such purposes as obtaining from him or a third person information or a confession, punishing him for an act he or a third person has committed or is suspected of having committed, or intimidating or coercing him or a third person, or for any reason based on discrimination of any kind, when such pain or suffering is inflicted by or at the instigation of or with the consent or acquiescence of a public official or other person acting in an official capacity."

682.   The Tribunal finds that the following acts committed by the Accused or by others in the presence of the Accused, at his instigation or with his consent or acquiescence, constitute torture;

(i)   the interrogation of Victim U, under threat to her life, by the Accused at the bureau communal, on 19 April 1994;

(ii)   the beating of Victim Y outside of her house by the Accused and Mugenzi on 20 April 1994;

(iii) the interrogation of Victim Y, under threat of her life, by the Accused, and the **[page 272]** beating of Victim Y under interrogation by Mugenzi, in the presence of the Accused, at a mine at Buguli on 20 April 1994;

(iv) the interrogation of Victim W, under threat to her life, a mine at Buguli by the Accused, on 20 April 1994;

(v)   the beating of Victim Z under interrogation by the Accused, and by Mugenzi and Francois in the presence of the Accused, in Gishyeshye Sector, on 20 April 1994;

(vi) the forcing of Victim Z to beat Victim Y under interrogation, by Francois in the presence of the Accused, in Gishyeshye Sector, on 20 April 1994;

(vii) the beating of Victim Z and Victim V by Mugenzi and Francois and the interrogation of Victim V, under threat to his life, by the Accused outside the house of Victim V, on 20 April 1994;

683. Accordingly, the Tribunal finds the Accused criminally responsible on Count 11 under Article 6(1) of its Statute for commission of the following acts of torture as crimes against humanity under Article 3(a) of its Statute:

(i)   his interrogation of Victim U, under threat to her life, at the bureau communal on 19 April 1994;

(ii)   his beating of Victim Y, outside of her house, on 20 April 1994;

(iii) his interrogation of Victim Y, under threat to her life, at a mine at Buguli on 20 April 1994;

(iv) his interrogation of Victim W, under threat to her life, at a mine at Buguli on 20 April 1994;

(v)   his beating of Victim Z in Gishyeshye Sector, on 20 April 1994;

(vi) his interrogation of Victim V, under threat to his life, outside of his house, on 20 April 1994.

648. The Tribunal finds the Accused criminally responsible on Count 11 under Article 6(1) of its Statute for implicitly ordering, as well as instigating, aiding and abetting, the following acts of torture, which were committed in his presence by men acting on his behalf, as crimes against **[page 273]** humanity under Article 3(a) of its Statute:

(i)   the beating of Victim Y outside of her house by Mugenzi on 20 April 1994;

(ii)   the beating of Victim Y, under interrogation, by Mugenzi, at a mine at Buguli on 20 April 1994;

(iii) the beating of Victim Z, under interrogation, by Mugenzi and Francois, in Gishyeshye Sector on 20 April 1994;

(iv) the forcing of Victim Z to beat Victim Y, under interrogation, by Francois, in Gishyeshye Sector on 20 April 1994. **[page 274]**

7.7. Count 13 (rape) and Count 14 (other inhumane acts) – Crimes against Humanity

685. In the light of its factual findings with regard to the allegations of sexual violence set forth in paragraphs 12A and 12B of the Indictment, the Tribunal considers the criminal responsibility of the Accused on Count 13, crimes against humanity (rape), punishable by Article 3(g) of the Statute of the Tribunal and Count 14, crimes against humanity (other inhumane acts), punishable by Article 3(i) of the Statute.

686. In considering the extent to which acts of sexual violence constitute crimes against humanity under Article 3(g) of its Statute, the Tribunal must define rape, as there is no commonly accepted definition of the term in international law. The Tribunal notes that many of the witnesses have used the term "rape" in their testimony. At times, the Prosecution and the Defence have also tried to elicit an explicit description of what happened in physical terms, to document what the witnesses mean by the term "rape". The Tribunal notes that while rape has been historically defined in national jurisdictions as non-consensual

sexual intercourse, variations on the form of rape may include acts which involve the insertion of objects and/or the use of bodily orifices not considered to be intrinsically sexual. An act such as that described by Witness KK in her testimony – the Interahamwes thrusting a piece of wood into the sexual organs of a woman as she lay dying – constitutes rape in the Tribunal's view.

687. The Tribunal considers that rape is a form of aggression and that the central elements of the crime of rape cannot be captured in a mechanical description of objects and body parts. The Tribunal also notes the cultural sensitivities involved in public discussion of intimate matters and recalls the painful reluctance and inability of witnesses to disclose graphic anatomical details of sexual violence they endured. The United Nations Convention Against Torture and Other Cruel, Inhuman and Degrading Treatment or Punishment does not catalogue specific acts in its definition of torture, focusing rather on the conceptual framework of state-sanctioned violence. The Tribunal **[page 275]** finds this approach more useful in the context of international law. Like torture, rape is used for such purposes as intimidation, degradation, humiliation, discrimination, punishment, control or destruction of a person. Like torture, rape is a violation of personal dignity, and rape in fact constitutes torture when it is inflicted by or at the instigation of or with the consent or acquiescence of a public official or other person acting in an official capacity.

688. The Tribunal defines rape as a physical invasion of a sexual nature, committed on a person under circumstances which are coercive. The Tribunal considers sexual violence, which includes rape, as any act of a sexual nature which is committed on a person under circumstances which are coercive. Sexual violence is not limited to physical invasion of the human body and may include acts which do not involve penetration or even physical contact. The incident described by Witness KK in which the Accused ordered the Interahamwe to undress a student and force her to do gymnastics naked in the public courtyard of the bureau communal, in front of a crowd, constitutes sexual violence. The Tribunal notes in this context that coercive circumstances need not be evidenced by a show of physical force. Threats, intimidation, extortion and other forms of duress which prey on fear or desperation may constitute coercion, and coercion may be inherent in certain circumstances, such as armed conflict or the military presence of Interahamwe among refugee Tutsi women at the bureau communal. Sexual violence falls within the scope of "other inhumane acts", set forth Article 3(i) of the Tribunal's Statute, "outrages upon personal dignity," set forth in Article 4(e) of the Statute, and "serious bodily or mental harm," set forth in Article 2(2)(b) of the Statute.

689. The Tribunal notes that as set forth by the Prosecution, Counts 13-15 are drawn on the basis of acts as described in paragraphs 12(A) and 12(B) of the Indictment. The allegations in these paragraphs of the Indictment are limited to events which took place "on or near the bureau communal premises." Many of the beatings, rapes and murders established by the evidence presented took place away from the bureau communal premises, and therefore the Tribunal does not make any legal findings with respect to these incidents pursuant to Counts 13, 14 and 15.

690. The Tribunal also notes that on the basis of acts described in paragraphs 12(A) and 12(B), **[page 276]** the Accused is charged only pursuant to Article 3(g) (rape) and 3(i) (other inhumane acts) of its Statute, but not Article 3(a)(murder) or Article 3(f)(torture). Similarly, on the basis of acts described in paragraphs 12(A) and 12(B), the Accused is charged only pursuant to Article 4(e)(outrages upon personal dignity) of its Statute, and not Article 4(a)(violence to life, health and physical or mental well-being of persons, in particular murder as well as cruel treatment such as torture, mutilation or any form of corporal punishment). As these paragraphs are not referenced elsewhere in the Indictment in connection with these other relevant Articles of the Statute of the Tribunal, the Tribunal concludes that the Accused has not been charged with the beatings and killings which have been established as Crimes Against Humanity or Violations of Article 3 Common to the Geneva Conventions. The Tribunal notes, however, that paragraphs 12(A) and 12(B) are referenced in Counts 1-3, Genocide and it considers the beatings and killings, as well as sexual violence, in connection with those counts.

691. The Tribunal has found that the Accused had reason to know and in fact knew that acts of sexual violence were occurring on or near the premises of the bureau communal and that he took no measures to prevent these acts or punish the perpetrators of them. The tribunal notes that it is only in consideration of

Counts 13, 14 and 15 that the Accused is charged with individual criminal responsibility under Section 6(3) of its Statute. As set forth in the Indictment, under Article 6(3) "an individual is criminally responsible as a superior for the acts of a subordinate if he or she knew or had reason to know that the subordinate was about to commit such acts or had done so and the superior failed to take the necessary and reasonable measures to prevent such acts or punish the perpetrators thereof." Although the evidence supports a finding that a superior/subordinate relationship existed between the Accused and the Interahamwe who were at the bureau communal, the Tribunal notes that there is no allegation in the Indictment that the Interahamwe, who are referred to as "armed local militia," were subordinates of the Accused. This relationship is a fundamental element of the criminal offence set forth in Article 6(3). The amendment of the Indictment with additional charges pursuant to Article 6(3) could arguably be interpreted as implying an allegation of the command responsibility required by Article 6(3). In fairness to the Accused, the Tribunal will not make this inference. Therefore, the Tribunal finds that it cannot consider the criminal responsibility of the Accused under Article 6(3). **[page 277]**

692. The Tribunal finds, under Article 6(1) of its Statute, that the Accused, by his own words, specifically ordered, instigated, aided and abetted the following acts of sexual violence:

   (i)   the multiple acts of rape of ten girls and women, including Witness JJ, by numerous Interahamwe in the cultural center of the bureau communal;
   (ii)   the rape of Witness OO by an Interahamwe named Antoine in a field near the bureau communal;
   (iii) the forced undressing and public marching of Chantal naked at the bureau communal.

693. The Tribunal finds, under Article 6(1) of its Statute, that the Accused aided and abetted the following acts of sexual violence, by allowing them to take place on or near the premises of the bureau communal, while he was present on the premises in respect of (i) and in his presence in respect of (ii) and (iii), and by facilitating the commission of these acts through his words of encouragement in other acts of sexual violence, which, by virtue of his authority, sent a clear signal of official tolerance for sexual violence, without which these acts would not have taken place:

   (i)   the multiple acts of rape of fifteen girls and women, including Witness JJ, by numerous Interahamwe in the cultural center of the bureau communal;
   (ii)   the rape of a woman by Interahamwe in between two buildings of the bureau communal, witnessed by Witness NN;
   (iii) the forced undressing of the wife of Tharcisse after making her sit in the mud outside the bureau communal, as witnessed by Witness KK;

694. The Tribunal finds, under Article 6(1) of its Statute, that the Accused, having had reason to know that sexual violence was occurring, aided and abetted the following acts of sexual violence, by allowing them to take place on or near the premises of the bureau communal and by facilitating the commission of such sexual violence through his words of encouragement in other **[page 278]** acts of sexual violence which, by virtue of his authority, sent a clear signal of official tolerance for sexual violence, without which these acts would not have taken place:

   (i)   the rape of Witness JJ by an Interahamwe who took her from outside the bureau communal and raped her in a nearby forest;
   (ii)   the rape of the younger sister of Witness NN by an Interahamwe at the bureau communal;
   (iii) the multiple rapes of Alexia, wife of Ntereye, and her two nieces Louise and Nishimwe by Interahamwe near the bureau communal;
   (iv)   the forced undressing of Alexia, wife of Ntereye, and her two nieces Louise and Nishimwe, and the forcing of the women to perform exercises naked in public near the bureau communal.

695. The Tribunal has established that a widespread and systematic attack against the civilian ethnic population of Tutsis took place in Taba, and more generally in Rwanda, between April 7 and the end of June, 1994. The Tribunal finds that the rape and other inhumane acts which took place on or near the bureau communal premises of Taba were committed as part of this attack.

COUNT 13

696.   The Accused is judged criminally responsible under Article 3(g) of the Statute for the following incidents of rape:

(i)   the rape of Witness JJ by an Interahamwe who took her from outside the bureau communal and raped her in a nearby forest;

(ii)   the multiple acts of rape of fifteen girls and women, including Witness JJ, by numerous Interahamwe in the cultural center of the bureau communal;

(iii) the multiple acts of rape of ten girls and women, including Witness JJ, by numerous Interahamwe in the cultural center of the bureau communal; **[page 279]**

(iv)   the rape of Witness OO by an Interahamwe named Antoine in a field near the bureau communal;

(v)   the rape of a woman by Interahamwe in between two buildings of the bureau communal, witnessed by Witness NN;

(vi)   the rape of the younger sister of Witness NN by an Interahamwe at the bureau communal;

(vii) the multiple rapes of Alexia, wife of Ntereye, and her two nieces Louise and Nishimwe by Interahamwe near the bureau communal.

COUNT 14

697.   The Accused is judged criminally responsible under Article 3(i) of the Statute for the following other inhumane acts:

(i)   the forced undressing of the wife of Tharcisse outside the bureau communal, after making her sit in the mud, as witnessed by Witness KK;

(ii)   the forces undressing and public marching of Chantal naked at the bureau communal;

(ii)   the forced undressing of Alexia, wife of Ntereye, and her two nieces Louise and Nishimwe, and the forcing of the women to perform exercises naked in public near the bureau communal. **[page 280]**

7.8. Count 1 – Genocide, Count 2 – Complicity in Genocide

698.   Count 1 relates to all the events described in the Indictment. The Prosecutor submits that by his acts alleged in paragraphs 12 to 23 of the Indictment, Akayesu committed the crime of genocide, punishable under Article 2(3)(a) of the Statute.

699.   Count 2 also relates to all the acts alleged in paragraphs 12 to 23 of the Indictment. The Prosecutor alleges that, by the said acts, the accused committed the crime of complicity in genocide, punishable under Article 2(3)(e) of the Statute.

700.   In its findings on the applicable law, the Chamber indicated *supra* that, in its opinion, the crime of genocide and that of complicity in genocide were two distinct crimes, and that the same person could certainly not be both the principal perpetrator of, and accomplice to, the same offence. Given that genocide and complicity in genocide are mutually exclusive by definition, the accused cannot obviously by found guilty of both these crimes for the same act. However, since the Prosecutor has charged the accused with both genocide and complicity in genocide for each of the alleged acts, the Chamber deems it necessary, in the instant case, to rule on counts 1 and 2 simultaneously, so as to determine, as far as each proven fact is concerned, whether it constituted genocide or complicity in genocide.

701.   Hence the question to be addressed is against which group the genocide was allegedly committed. Although the Prosecutor did not specifically state so in the Indictment, it is obvious, in the light of the context in which the alleged acts were committed, the testimonies presented and the Prosecutor's closing statement, that the genocide was committed against the Tutsi group. Article 2(2) of the Statute, like the Genocide Convention, provides that genocide may be committed against a national, ethnical, racial or

religious group. In its findings on the law applicable to the crime of genocide *supra*, the Chamber considered whether the protected groups should be limited to only the four groups specifically mentioned or whether any group, similar to **[page 281]** the four groups in terms of its stability and permanence, should also be included. The Chamber found that it was necessary, above all, to respect the intent of the drafters of the Genocide Convention which, according to the *travaux préparatoires*, was clearly to protect any stable and permanent group.

702.   In the light of the facts brought to its attention during the trial, the Chamber is of the opinion that, in Rwanda in 1994, the Tutsi constituted a group referred to as "ethnic" in official classifications. Thus, the identity cards at the time included a reference to "*ubwoko*" in Kinyarwanda or "*ethnie*" (ethnic group) in French which, depending on the case, referred to the designation Hutu or Tutsi, for example. The Chamber further noted that all the Rwandan witnesses who appeared before it invariably answered spontaneously and without hesitation the questions of the Prosecutor regarding their ethnic identity. Accordingly, the Chamber finds that, in any case, at the time of the alleged events, the Tutsi did indeed constitute a stable and permanent group and were identified as such by all.

703.   In the light of the foregoing, with respect to each of the acts alleged in the Indictment, the Chamber is satisfied beyond reasonable doubt, based on the factual findings it has rendered regarding each of the events described in paragraphs 12 to 23 of the Indictment, of the following:

704.   The Chamber finds that, as pertains to the acts alleged in **paragraph 12**, it has been established that, throughout the period covered in the Indictment, Akayesu, in his capacity as bourgmestre, was responsible for maintaining law and public order in the commune of Taba and that he had effective authority over the communal police. Moreover, as "leader" of Taba commune, of which he was one of the most prominent figures, the inhabitants respected him and followed his orders. Akayesu himself admitted before the Chamber that he had the power to assemble the population and that they obeyed his instructions. It has also been proven that a very large number of Tutsi were killed in Taba between 7 April and the end of June 1994, while Akayesu was bourgmestre of the Commune. Knowing of such killings, he opposed them and attempted to prevent them only until 18 April 1994, date after which he not only stopped trying to maintain law and order in his commune, but was also present during the acts of violence and **[page 282]** killings, and sometimes even gave orders himself for bodily or mental harm to be caused to certain Tutsi, and endorsed and even ordered the killing of several Tutsi.

705.   In the opinion of the Chamber, the said acts indeed incur the individual criminal responsibility of Akayesu for having ordered, committed, or otherwise aided and abetted in the preparation or execution of the killing of and causing serious bodily or mental harm to members of the Tutsi group. Indeed, the Chamber holds that the fact that Akayesu, as a local authority, failed to oppose such killings and serious bodily or mental harm constituted a form of tacit encouragement, which was compounded by being present to such criminal acts.

706.   With regard to the acts alleged in **paragraphs 12 (A) and 12 (B)** of the Indictment, the Prosecutor has shown beyond a reasonable doubt that between 7 April and the end of June 1994, numerous Tutsi who sought refuge at the Taba Bureau communal were frequently beaten by members of the Interahamwe on or near the premises of the Bureau communal. Some of them were killed. Numerous Tutsi women were forced to endure acts of sexual violence, mutilations and rape, often repeatedly, often publicly and often by more than one assailant. Tutsi women were systematically raped, as one female victim testified to by saying that "each time that you met assailants, they raped you". Numerous incidents of such rape and sexual violence against Tutsi women occurred inside or near the Bureau communal. It has been proven that some communal policemen armed with guns and the accused himself were present while some of these rapes and sexual violence were being committed. Furthermore, it is proven that on several occasions, by his presence, his attitude and his utterances, Akayesu encouraged such acts, one particular witness testifying that Akayesu, addressed the Interahamwe who were committing the rapes and said that "never ask me again what a Tutsi woman tastes like"[177]. In the opinion of the Chamber, this constitutes tacit encouragement to the rapes that were being committed.

---

[177]   "Nithazagirc umbaza uko umututsikazi yari ameze, ngo kandi mumenye ko ejo ngo nibabica nta kintu muzambaza."

707. In the opinion of the Chamber, the above-mentioned acts with which Akayesu is charged indeed render him individually criminally responsible for having abetted in the preparation or **[page 283]** execution of the killings of members of the Tutsi group and the infliction of serious bodily and mental harm on members of said group.

708. The Chamber found *supra*, with regard to the facts alleged in **paragraph 13** of the Indictment, that the Prosecutor failed to demonstrate beyond reasonable doubt that they are established.

709. As regards the facts alleged in **paragraphs 14 and 15** of the Indictment, it is established that in the early hours of 19 April 1994, Akayesu joined a gathering in Gishyeshye and took this opportunity to address the public; he led the meeting and conducted the proceedings. He then called on the population to unite in order to eliminate what he referred to as the sole enemy; the accomplices of the Inkotanyi; and the population understood that he was thus urging them to kill the Tutsi. Indeed, Akayesu himself knew of the impact of his statements on the crowd and of the fact that his call to fight against the accomplices of the Inkotanyi would be understood as exhortations to kill the Tutsi in general. Akayesu who had received from the Interahamwe documents containing lists of names did, in the course of the said gathering, summarize the contents of same to the crowd by pointing out in particular that the names were those of RPF accomplices. He specifically indicated to the participants that Ephrem Karangwa's name was on of the lists. Akayesu admitted before the Chamber that during the period in question, that to publicly label someone as an accomplice of the RPF would put such a person in danger. The statements thus made by Akayesu at that gathering immediately led to widespread killings of Tutsi in Taba.

710. Concerning the acts with which Akayesu is charged in paragraphs 14 and 15 of the Indictment, the Chamber recalls that it has found supra that they constitute direct and public incitement to commit genocide, a crime punishable under Article 2(3)(c) of the Statute as distinct from the crime of genocide[178]. **[page 284]**

711. With respect to the Prosecutor's allegations in **paragraph 16** of the Indictment, the Chamber is satisfied beyond a reasonable doubt that on 19 April 1994, Akayesu on two occasions threatened to kill victim U, a Tutsi woman, while she was being interrogated. He detained her for several hours at the Bureau communal, before allowing her to leave. In the evening of 20 April 1994, during a search conducted in the home of victim V, a Hutu man, Akayesu directly threatened to kill the latter. Victim V was thereafter beaten with a stick and the butt of a rifle by a communal policeman called Mugenzi and one Francois, a member of the Interahamwe militia, in the presence of the accused. One of Victim V's ribs was broken as a result of the beating.

712. In the opinion of the Chamber, the acts attributed to the accused in connection with victims U and V constitute serious bodily and mental harm inflicted on the two victims. However, while Akayesu does incur individual criminal responsibility by virtue of the acts committed against Victim U, a Tutsi, for having committed or otherwise aided and abetted in the infliction of serious bodily and mental harm on a member of the Tutsi group, such acts as committed against victim V were perpetrated against a Hutu and cannot, therefore, constitute a crime of genocide against the Tutsi group.

713. Regarding the acts alleged in **paragraph 17**, the Prosecutor has failed to satisfy the Chamber that they were proven beyond a reasonable doubt.

714. As for the allegations made in **paragraph 18** of the Indictment, it is established that on or about 19 April 1994, Akayesu and a group of men under his control were looking for Ephrem Karangwa and destroyed his house and that of his mother. They then went to search the house of Ephrem Karangwa's brother-in-law, in Musambira commune and found his three brothers there. When the three brothers, namely Simon Mutijima, Thaddee Uwanyiligira and Jean Chrysostome, tried to escape, Akayesu ordered that they be captured, and ordered that they be killed, and participated in their killing.

715. The Chamber holds that these acts indeed render Akayesu individually criminally responsible for having ordered, committed, aided and abetted in the preparation or execution of **[page 285]** the killings

---

[178]   See findings of the Chamber on Count 4.

of members of the Tutsi group and the infliction of serious bodily and mental harm on members of said group.

716. Regarding the allegations in **paragraph 19**, the Chamber is satisfied that it has been established that on or about 19 April 1994, Akayesu took from Taba communal prison eight refugees from Runda commune, handed them over to Interahamwe militiamen and ordered that they be killed. They were killed by the Interahamwe using various traditional weapons, including machetes and small axes, in front of the Bureau communal and in the presence of Akayesu who told the killers "do it quickly". The refugees were killed because they were Tutsi.

717. The Chamber holds that by virtue of such acts, Akayesu incurs individual criminal liability for having ordered, aided and abetted in the perpetration of the killings of members of the Tutsi group and in the infliction of serious bodily and mental harm on members of said group.

718. The Prosecutor has proved that, as alleged in **paragraph 20** of the Indictment, on that same day, Akayesu ordered the local people to kill intellectuals and to look for one Samuel, a professor who was then brought to the Bureau communal and killed with a machete blow to the neck. Teachers in Taba commune were killed later, on Akayesu's instructions. The victims included the following: Tharcisse Twizeyumuremye, Theogene, Phoebe Uwinzene and her fiancé whose name is unknown. They were killed on the road in front of the Bureau communal by the local people and the Interahamwe with machetes and agricultural tools. Akayesu personally witnessed the killings of Tharcisse.

719. In the opinion of the Chamber, Akayesu is indeed individually criminally responsible by virtue of such acts for having ordered, aided and abetted in the preparation or execution of the killings of members of the Tutsi group and in the infliction of serious bodily and mental harm on members of said group.

720. The Chamber finds that the acts alleged in **paragraph 21** have been proven. It has been established that on the evening of 20 April 1994, Akayesu, and two Interahamwe militiamen and **[page 286]** a communal policeman, one Mugenzi, who was armed at the time of the events in question, went to the house of Victim Y, a 69 year old Hutu woman, to interrogate her on the whereabouts of Alexia, the wife of Professor Ntereye. During the questioning which took place in the presence of Akayesu, the victim was hit and beaten several times. In particular, she was hit with the barrel of a rifle on the head by the communal policeman. She was forcibly taken away and ordered by Akayesu lie on the ground. Akayesu himself beat her on her back with a stick. Later on, he had her lie down in front of a vehicle and threatened to drive over her if she failed to give the information he sought.

721. Although the above constitute serious bodily and mental harm inflicted on the victim, the Chamber notes that they were committed against a Hutu woman. Consequently, they cannot constitute acts of genocide against the Tutsi group.

722. As regards the allegations in **paragraphs 22 and 23** of the Indictment, the Chamber is satisfied beyond reasonable doubt that on the evening of 20 April 1994, in the course of an interrogation, Akayesu forces Victim W to lay down in front of a vehicle and threatened to drive over her. That same evening, Akayesu, accompanied by Mugenzi, a communal policeman, and one Francois, an Interahamwe militiaman, interrogated victims Z and Y. The accused put his foot on the fact of victim Z, causing the said victim to bleed, while the police officer and the militiaman beat the victim with the butt of their rifles. The militiaman forced victim Z to beat victim Y with a stick. The two victims were tied together, causing victim Z to suffocate. Victim Z was also beaten on the back with the blade of a machete.

723. The Chamber holds that by virtue of the above-mentioned acts Akayesu is individually criminally responsible for having ordered, committed, aided and abetted in the preparation or infliction of serious bodily or mental harm on members of the Tutsi group.

724. From the foregoing, the Chamber is satisfied beyond a reasonable doubt, that Akayesu is individually criminally responsible, under Article 6(1) of the Statute, for having ordered, committed or otherwise aided and abetted in the commission of the acts described above in the **[page 287]** findings made by the Chamber on paragraphs 12, 12A, 12B, 16, 18, 19, 20, 22 and 23 of the Indictment, acts

which constitute the killing of members of the Tutsi group and the infliction of serious bodily and mental harm on members of said group.

725. Since the Prosecutor charged both genocide and complicity in genocide with respect to each of the above-mentioned acts, and since, as indicated *supra*, the Chamber is of the opinion that these charges are mutually exclusive, it must rule whether each of such acts constitutes genocide or complicity in genocide.

726. In this connection, the Chamber recalls that, in its findings on the applicable law, it held that an accused is an accomplice to genocide if he or she knowingly and wilfully aided or abetted or instigated another to commit a crime of genocide, while being aware of his genocidal plan, even where the accused had no specific intent to destroy, in whole or in part, a national, ethnical, racial or religious group, as such. It also found that Article 6(1) of the Statute provides for a form of participation through aiding and abetting which, though akin to the factual elements of complicity, nevertheless entails, in and of itself, the individual responsibility of the accused for the crime of genocide, in particular, where the accused had the specific intent to commit genocide, that is, the intent to destroy a particular group; this latter requirement is not needed where an accomplice to genocide is concerned.

727. Therefore, it is incumbent upon the Chamber to decide, in this instant case, whether or not Akayesu had a specific genocidal intent when he participated in the above-mentioned crimes, that is, the intent to destroy, in whole or in part, a group as such.

728. As stated in its findings on the law applicable to the crime of genocide, the Chamber holds the view that the intent underlying an act can be inferred from a number of facts[179]. The Chamber is of the opinion that it is possible to infer the genocidal intention that presided over the commission of a particular act, *inter alia*, from all acts or utterances of the accused, or from the **[page 288]** general context in which other culpable acts were perpetrated systematically against the same group, regardless of whether such other acts were committed by the same perpetrator or even by other perpetrators.

729. First of all, regarding Akayesu's acts and utterances during the period relating to the acts alleged in the Indictment, the Chamber is satisfied beyond reasonable doubt, on the basis of all evidence brought to its attention during the trial, that on several occasions the accused made speeches calling, more or less explicitly, for the commission of genocide. The Chamber, in particular, held in its findings on Count 4, that the accused incurred individual criminal responsibility for the crime of direct and public incitement to commit genocide. Yet, according to the Chamber, the crime of direct and public incitement to commit genocide lies in the intent to directly lead or provoke another to commit genocide, which implies that he who incites to commit genocide also has the specific intent to commit genocide: that is, to destroy, in whole or in part, a national, ethnical, racial or religious group, as such.

730. Furthermore, the Chamber has already established that genocide was committed against the Tutsi group in Rwanda in 1994, throughout the period covering the events alleged in the Indictment[180]. Owing to the very high number of atrocities committed against the Tutsi, their widespread nature not only in the commune of Taba, but also throughout Rwanda, and to the fact that the victims were systematically and deliberately selected because they belonged to the Tutsi group, with persons belonging to other groups being excluded, the Chamber is also able to infer, beyond reasonable doubt, the genocidal intent of the accused in the commission of the above-mentioned crimes.

731. With regard, particularly, to the acts described in paragraphs 12(A) and 12(B) of the Indictment, that is, rape and sexual violence, the Chamber wishes to underscore the fact that in its opinion, they constitute genocide in the same way as any other act as long as they were committed with the specific intent to destroy, in whole or in part, a particular group, targeted as **[page 289]** such. Indeed, rape and sexual violence certainly constitute infliction of serious bodily and mental harm on the victims[181] and are even, according to the Chamber, one of the worst ways of inflict harm on the victim as he or she suffers

---

179   See above the findings of the Trial Chamber on the law applicable to the crime of genocide.

180   See above, the findings of the Trial Chamber on the occurrence of genocide against the Tutsi group in Rwanda in 1994.

181   See above, the findings of the Trial Chamber on the Chapter relating to the law applicable to the crime of genocide, in particular, the definition of the constituent elements of genocide.

both bodily and mental harm. In light of all the evidence before it, the Chamber is satisfied that the acts of rape and sexual violence described above, were committed solely against Tutsi women, many of whom were subjected to the worst public humiliation, mutilated, and raped several times, often in public, in the Bureau communal premises or in other public places, and often by more than one assailant. These rapes resulted in physical and psychological destruction of Tutsi women, their families and their communities. Sexual violence was an integral part of the process of destruction, specifically targeting Tutsi women and specifically contributing to their destruction and to the destruction of the Tutsi group as a whole.

732. The rape of Tutsi women was systematic and was perpetrated against all Tutsi women and solely against them. A Tutsi woman, married to a Hutu, testified before the Chamber that she was not raped because her ethnic background was unknown. As part of the propaganda campaign geared to mobilizing the Hutu against the Tutsi, the Tutsi women were presented as sexual objects. Indeed, the Chamber was told, for an example, that before being raped and killed. Alexia, who was the wife of the Professor, Ntereye, and her two nieces, were forced by the Interahamwe to undress and ordered to run and do exercises "in order to display the thighs of Tutsi women". The Interahamwe who raped Alexia said, as he threw her on the ground and got on top of her, "let us now see what the vagina of a Tutsi woman takes like". As stated above, Akayesu himself, speaking to the Interahamwe who were committing the rapes, said to them: "don't ever ask again what a Tutsi woman tastes like". This sexualized representation of ethnic identity graphically illustrates that tutsi women were subjected to sexual violence because they were Tutsi. Sexual violence was a step in the process of destruction of the tutsi group – destruction of the spirit, of the will to live, and of life itself. **[page 290]**

733. On the basis of the substantial testimonies brought before it, the Chamber finds that in most cases, the rapes of Tutsi women in Taba, were accompanied with the intent to kill those women. Many rapes were perpetrated near mass graves where the women were taken to be killed. A victim testified that Tutsi women caught could be taken away by peasants and men with the promise that they would be collected later to be executed. Following an act of gang rape, a witness heard Akayesu say "tomorrow they will be killed" and they were actually killed. In this respect, it appears clearly to the Chamber that the acts of rape and sexual violence, as other acts of serious bodily and mental harm committed against the Tutsi, reflected the determination to make Tutsi women suffer and to mutilate them even before killing them, the intent being to destroy the Tutsi group while inflicting acute suffering on its members in the process.

734. In light of the foregoing, the Chamber finds firstly that the acts described *supra* are indeed acts as enumerated in Article 2 (2) of the Statute, which constitute the factual elements of the crime of genocide, namely the killings of Tutsi or the serious bodily and mental harm inflicted on the Tutsi. The Chamber is further satisfied beyond reasonable doubt that these various acts were committed by Akayesu with the specific intent to destroy the Tutsi group, as such. Consequently, the Chamber is of the opinion that the acts alleged in paragraphs 12, 12A, 12B, 16, 18, 19, 20, 22 and 23 of the Indictment and proven above, constitute the crime of genocide, but not the crime of complicity; hence, the Chamber finds Akayesu individually criminally responsible for genocide. **[page 291]**

7.9. Count 3 – Crimes against Humanity (extermination)

735. Count 3 of the indictment charges the Accused with crimes against humanity (extermination), pursuant to Article 3(b) of the Statute, for the acts alleged in paragraphs 12 to 23 of the indictment.

736. The definition of crimes against humanity, including the various elements that comprise the enumerated offences under Article 3 of the Statute have already been discussed.

737. The Chamber finds beyond a reasonable doubt that during his search for Ephrem Karangwa on 19 April 1994, the Accused participated in the killing of Simon Mutijima, Thaddée Uwanyiligra and Jean Chrysostome, by ordering their deaths and being present when they were killed.

738. The Chamber finds beyond a reasonable doubt that on 19 April 1994, the Accused took eight detained refugees and handed them over to the local militia, known as the Interahamwe with orders that they be killed.

739. The Chamber finds beyond a reasonable doubt that the Interahamwe and the local population, acting on the orders of the Accused killed five teachers namely: a professor known as Samuel; Tharcisse who was killed in the presence of the Accused; Theogene, Phoebe Uwineze and her fiancé.

740. The Chamber finds beyond a reasonable doubt that the eight refugees as well as Simon Mutijima, Thaddée Uwanyiligra, Jean Chrysostome, Samuel, Tharcisse, Theogene, Phoebe Uwineze and her fiancé were all civilians, taking no active part in the hostilities that prevailed in Rwanda in 1994 and the only reason they were killed is because they were Tutsi. **[page 292]**

741. The Chamber finds beyond a reasonable doubt that in ordering the killing of the eight refugees as well as Simon Mutijima, Thaddée Uwanyiligra, Jean Chrysostome, Samuel, Tharcisse, Theogene, Phoebe Uwineze and her fiancé, the Accused had the requisite intent to cause mass destruction, directed against certain groups of individuals, as part of a widespread or systematic attack against the civilian population of Rwanda on ethnic grounds.

742. The Chamber finds beyond a reasonable doubt that in ordering the killing of the eight refugees as well as Simon Mutijima, Thaddée Uwanyiligra, Jean Chrysostome, Samuel, Tharcisse, Theogene, Phoebe Uwineze and her fiancé, the Accused is individually criminally responsible for the death of these victims, pursuant to Article 6(1) of the Statute.

743. The Chamber finds beyond a reasonable doubt that there was a widespread and systematic attack against the civilian population in Rwanda on 19 April 1994 and the conduct of the Accused formed part of this attack.

744. Therefore the Chamber finds, beyond a reasonable doubt that the killing of the eight refugees as well as Simon Mutijima, Thaddée Uwanyiligra, Jean Chrysostome, Samuel, Tharcisse, Theogene, Phoebe Uwineze and her fiancé, constitute extermination committed, as part of a widespread or systematic attack on the civilian population on ethnic grounds and as such constitutes a crime against humanity. Accordingly, the Chamber finds beyond a reasonable doubt that the Accused is guilty as charged in count 3 of the indictment. **[page 293]**

8. VERDICT

FOR THE FOREGOING REASONS, having considered all of the evidence and the arguments, THE CHAMBER unanimously finds as follows:

Count 1: Guilty of Genocide

Count 2: Not guilty of Complicity in Genocide

Count 3: Guilty of Crime against Humanity (Extermination)

Count 4: Guilty of Direct and Public Incitement to Commit Genocide

Count 5: Guilty of Crime against Humanity (Murder)

Count 6: Not guilty of Violation of Article 3 common to the Geneva Conventions (Murder)

Count 7: Guilty of Crime against Humanity (Murder)

Count 8: Not guilty of Violation of Article 3 common to the Geneva Conventions (Murder)

Count 9: Guilty of Crime against Humanity (Murder)

Count 10: Not guilty of Violation of Article 3 common to the Geneva Conventions (Murder)

Count 11:   Guilty of Crime against Humanity (Torture) **[page 294]**

Count 12:   Not guilty of Violation of Article 3 common to the Geneva Conventions (Cruel Treatment)

Count 13:   Guilty of Crime against Humanity (Rape)

Count 14:   Guilty of Crime against Humanity (Other Inhumane Acts)

Count 15:   Not guilty of Violation of Article 3 common to the Geneva Conventions and of Article 4(2)(e) of Additional Protocol II (Outrage upon personal dignity, in particular Rape, Degrading and Humiliating Treatment and Indecent Assault)

Done in English and French,

Signed in Arusha, 2 September 1998

Laïty Kama   Lennart Aspegren   Navanethem Pillay

Presiding Judge   Judge   Judge

The International Criminal Tribunal for Rwanda, established by resolution of the United Nations Security Council on November 8, 1994, was created with the express purpose of prosecuting genocide. Like its Yugoslav counterpart, created eighteen months earlier, it had subject matter jurisdiction over the crime of genocide. But in addition, however, and in contrast with the Yugoslav tribunal, the text of the enabling resolution actually refers to genocide. The Council "express[es] once again its grave concern at the reports indicating that genocide and other systematic, widespread and flagrant violations of international humanitarian law have been committed in Rwanda". The first operative paragraph declares that the tribunal has "the sole purpose of prosecuting persons responsible for genocide and other serious violations of international humanitarian law".[1] The word genocide also figures in the Tribunal's full title: "The International Criminal Tribunal for the Prosecution of Persons Responsible for Genocide and Other Serious Violations of International Humanitarian Law Committed in the Territory of Rwanda and Rwandan citizens responsible for genocide and other such violations committed in the territory of neighbouring States, between 1 January 1994 and 31 December 1994".

Political charges of genocide are one thing, judicial determination following the production of evidence in an adversarial proceeding is another. The primordial achievement of Trial Chamber I of the International Criminal Tribunal for Rwanda in the September 2, 1998 judgment of Jean-Paul Akayesu is its conclusion that genocide, as defined in article 2 of the Tribunal's Statute and articles II and III of the 1948 Convention for the Prevention and Punishment of the Crime of Genocide,[2] in fact occurred during the months of April, May and June 1994. By contrast, the International Criminal Tribunal for the Former Yugoslavia has yet to convict an accused of genocide. Indeed, in a December 1999 judgment it acquitted an individual on the charge, stating that the Prosecutor had failed to prove that the crime of genocide had taken place during the Bosnian war.[3]

Akayesu was rendered by Trial Chamber I of the International Criminal Tribunal for Rwanda, composed of then-president Laity Kama and judges Lennart Aspegren and Navanethem Pillay. The massive decision[4] exhaustively analyses the facts in the case, and presents a lengthy discussion of many of the legal issues, including the definition of genocide, the nature of command responsibility and the threshold for non-international armed conflict. Indeed, although a few isolated domestic decisions – the Eichmann case being the most significant[5] – have endeavoured to interpret the definition of genocide found in articles II and III of the Convention, this is the first international decision to do so. It was rendered exactly fifty years after the adoption of the Convention by the General Assembly at its third session.

Akayesu was the *bourgmestre* or mayor of Taba commune, located a short drive from the outskirts of the capital of Rwanda, Kigali. A schoolteacher by profession, he had been appointed by President Juvénal Habyarimana in April 1993, and served until June 1994. According to the Tribunal, during the months of April, May and June of 1994 at least 2,000 Tutsi were killed in the commune. The evidence showed that in the early days of the genocide, Akayesu attempted to prevent violence in Taba commune. Witnesses described how he initially opposed efforts by the racist *interahamwe* militia to extend the scope of the genocidal massacres that had ravaged Kigali since the assassination of president Habyarimana on April 6, 1994. Akayesu attended a meeting on April 18 at which Prime Minister Jean Kambanda enlisted the support of Rwanda's *bourgmestres* in the ongoing genocide. Akayesu argued that from that point on, it was impossible to challenge the genocide openly, although he continued with clandestine attempts to resist the violence. But the Court rejects Akayesu's pretentions, concluding that from April 18 he participated actively and enthusiastically in the massacres, tolerating, ordering and, in some cases, directly engaging himself in killings, beatings and rapes.

---

[1]   U.N. Doc. S/RES/955 (1994).

[2]   *Convention on the Prevention and Punishment of the Crime of Genocide*, (1951) 78 U.N.T.S. 277.

[3]   ICTY, Judgment, *Prosecutor* v. *Jelesić*, Case No. IT-95-10-T, 14 December 1999.

[4]   The Akayesu judgment is just shy of 100,000 words. The May 7, 1997 judgment of the International Criminal Tribunal for the former Yugoslavia, in *Prosecutor* v. *Tadić* (IT-94-1-T), including the dissent, is about 127,000 words. The judgment of the International Military Tribunal of September 30-October 1, 1946 is about 89,000 words.

[5]   *A.-G. Israel* v. *Eichmann*, (1968) 36 International Law Reports 18 (District Court, Jerusalem); *A.G. Israel* v. *Eichmann*, (1968) 36 International Law Reports 277 (Supreme Court).

For example, on April 19, 1994, Akayesu was present at a public meeting attended by over 100 people. In its judgment, the Chamber accepts evidence that Akayesu had urged the population, during the gathering, to eliminate the accomplices of the rebel Rwandese Patriotic Front (RPF), which was associated with the Tutsi minority. It also says it is satisfied beyond a reasonable doubt that the population construed his remarks as a call to kill the Tutsi and, moreover, that Akayesu was himself fully aware of the impact his statement would have on the crowd. The Chamber finds there was a causal link between Akayesu's statement at the gathering and widespread killings of Tutsi in Taba that followed shortly afterwards.

The judgment presents a detailed review of Rwandan history, based largely on the testimony of expert witness Alison DesForges, a consultant to the non-governmental organization Human Rights Watch.[6] It notes the "policy of systematic discrimination" against not only the Tutsi minority but also against some regional Hutu groups by the regime of Juvénal Habyarimana, who ruled Rwanda from the early 1970s until his death in the airplane crash of April 7, 1994. The build-up to the events of 1994 is examined closely, including such incidents as the notorious November 1992 speech of Habyarimana henchman Leon Mugesera calling for the extermination of the Tutsi, and the hate mongering broadcasts of Radio Mille Collines. These elements are important in the Tribunal's conclusion that the massacres of 1994 were committed with the intent to destroy the Tutsi group.

Genocide

The major contribution of the decision is its analysis and application of the terms of articles II and III of the 1948 Convention for the Prevention and Punishment of the Crime of Genocide, which are repeated without change in article 2 of the Statute of the International Criminal Tribunal for Rwanda. Paragraph (2) corresponds to article II of the Convention, while paragraph (3) corresponds to article III.

Article 2. Genocide
1.   The International Tribunal for Rwanda shall have the power to prosecute persons committing genocide as defined in paragraph 2 of this article or of committing any of the other acts enumerated in paragraph 3 of this article.
2.   Genocide means any of the following acts committed with intent to destroy, in whole or in part, a national, ethnical, racial or religious group, as such:
      (a)   Killing members of the group;
      (b)   Causing serious bodily or mental harm to members of the group;
      (c)   Deliberately inflicting on the group conditions of life calculated to bring about its physical destruction in whole or in part;
      (d)   Imposing measures intended to prevent births within the group;
      (e)   Forcibly transferring children of the group to another group.
3.   The following acts shall be punishable:
      (a)   Genocide;
      (b)   Conspiracy to commit genocide;
      (c)   Direct and public incitement to commit genocide;
      (d)   Attempt to commit genocide;
      (e)   Complicity in genocide.

Thus, genocide consists of a series of enumerated acts, of which murder and causing serious bodily and mental harm are at the core, with the intent to destroy, in whole or in part, a national, ethnic, racial or religious group, "as such". The Trial Chamber in Akayesu proposes a general analysis of the elements of the provision. Much of what Trial Chamber I writes about the crime of genocide actually goes well beyond the factual requirements of the case and constitutes *obiter dicta.*

---

[6]   Judgment, par. 78-129. See: Alison des Forges, *Leave None to Tell the Story, Genocide in Rwanda*, New York/Washington/London/Brussels: Human Rights Watch, Paris: International Federation of Human Rights, 1999.

Protected Group

Article 2, paragraph 2 of the Statute indicates that genocide must be directed against a "national, ethnical, racial or religious group". The question of the existence of a protected group can be analysed from either an objective or a subjective standpoint. Taking an objective approach involves defining the group and then assessing whether the victims belong to it. A subjective standpoint, on the other hand, is unconcerned with whether the group really exists in an objective sense. Its analysis involves assessing the views and intentions of the perpetrator. In a 1999 judgment, a differently constituted Trial Chamber took the view that the Tutsi were an ethnic group because they had been so designated by the Rwandan authorities on their identity cards.[7] The Akayesu Trial Chamber, on the other hand, opts for an objective approach. This is where it gets into trouble, because for Trial Chamber I it is not at all clear that the Tutsi of Rwanda constitute a national, ethnical, racial or religious group.

To start with, the Tribunal attempts to define the scope of the four terms. Citing the Nottebohm decision of the International Court of Justice, the Tribunal defines a national group as "as a collection of people who are perceived to share a legal bond based on common citizenship, coupled with reciprocity of rights and duties".[8] The Tribunal's definition seems to link the concept of "national group" with that of the population of a nation state, thereby excluding most national minorities. It is interesting to note that the person who initially developed the concept of genocide, Raphael Lemkin, conceived of the crime of genocide as a continuation of the treaty regime established after World War I for the protection of national minorities.[9] As for racial groups, the Tribunal writes that "[t]he conventional definition of racial group is based on the hereditary physical traits often identified with a geographical region, irrespective of linguistic, cultural, national or religious factors". The judgment does not give a source for this "conventional" definition. But here too, the Tribunal definition seems unnecessarily narrow. In 1948, when the Convention was adopted, the term "racial group" was generally used to describe such entities as the "Jewish race", the "English race" and the "German race".[10] Although modern science now rejects the whole notion of the objective existence of "races",[11] for the purposes of the Convention the term ought to be construed not only to reflect the intent of the drafters but to ensure as large a protection of vulnerable groups as possible. In this respect, it may be useful to note that the International Convention for the Elimination of All Forms of Racial Discrimination does not limit the scope of "race" to hereditary physical traits, and defines racial discrimination as "any distinction, exclusion, restriction or preference based on race, colour, descent, or national or ethnic origin".[12] Thus, with respect to both national groups and racial groups, the Tribunal proposes an unduly restrictive definition, and one inconsistent with the use of these terms in 1948. This is an odd result for a human rights treaty, which ought to protect more people, not fewer, with the passage of time.

The term that seems closest to describing the Tutsi, at least intuitively, is "ethnical".[13] Indeed, elsewhere in the Akayesu judgment, when considering the provision on crimes against humanity, the Tribunal seems to concede without a second thought that the Tutsi are an ethnic group.[14] With respect to Article 2, paragraph 2 of the Statute, the Tribunal writes: "An ethnic group is generally defined as a group whose

---

[7]   ICTR, Judgment, *Prosecutor* v. *Kayishema and Ruzindana*, Case no. ICTR-95-1-T, T. Ch. II, 21 May 1999.

[8]   *Nottebohm (2nd phase) (Liechtenstein v. Guatemala)*, [1955] I.C.J. Reports 4. The Tribunal might have considered, as a more complete alternative, the definition of "communities" proposed by the Permanent Court of International Justice, and often associated with national minorities, in *Greco-Bulgarian Community*, 1930 P.C.I.J. (Ser. B) No. 17: "...a group of persons living in a given country or locality, having a race, religion, language and traditions of their own and united by this identity of race, religion, language and traditions in sentiment of solidarity, with a view to preserving their traditions, maintaining their form of worship, ensuring the instruction and upbringing of their children in accordance with the spirit and traditions of their race and rendering mutual assistance to each another."

[9]   Raphael Lemkin, Axis Rule in Occupied Europe, Analysis of Government, Proposals for Redress, Washington: Carnegie Endowment for World Peace, 1944, p. 79, 80-82, 85-87, 90-93.

[10]   For example: *United Kingdom* v. *Kramer* et al. ("Belsen trial"), (1947) 2 L.R.T.W.C. 1 (British Military Court), p. 106.

[11]   See Michael Banton, International Action Against Racial Discrimination, Oxford: Clarendon Press, 1996, p. 76-82.

[12]   (1969) 660 U.N.T.S. 195, art. 1(1).

[13]   The Convention, and by ricochet article 2 of the *Statute*, uses the word "ethnical", an antiquated term which means same as "ethnic". The Trial Chamber uses the word "ethnic" throughout the Akayesu judgment.

[14]   Judgment, par. 650, 653, 658, 668, 671. See also, at paragraph 124, "[i]n the opinion of the Chamber, all this proves that it was indeed a particular group, the Tutsi ethnic group, which was targeted."

members share a common language or culture."[15] But Rwanda's Tutsi and Hutu share the same language and culture, as the Tribunal observes, although it admits that other factors argue in favour of defining the Tutsi as an ethnic group. The Tribunal explains that Rwandan law, including the Constitution, identified citizens by ethnic group, although this was to be abolished as a result of the 1993 Arusha Peace Agreement.[16] But while the laws of Rwanda have specified since the time of the Belgian mandate that people are to be identified *inter alia* by membership in an ethnic group, there is no legal text to establish how ethnicity is determined. The Tribunal concludes, nevertheless, in the existence of "customary rules ... governing the determination of ethnic group, which followed patrilineal lines of heredity. The identification of persons as belonging to the group of Hutu or Tutsi (or Twa) had thus become embedded in Rwandan culture." The Tribunal adds that "[t]he Rwandan witnesses who testified before the Chamber identified themselves by ethnic group, and generally knew the ethnic group to which their friends and neighbours belonged. Moreover, the Tutsi were conceived of as an ethnic group by those who targeted them for killing."[17]

But the term "ethnic group" is a bone that sticks in the Tribunal's throat. Clearly vexed by the issue of classifying the Tutsi, and unsatisfied with its own observations on the existence of the Tutsi ethnic group within Rwandan society,[18] the Tribunal goes on to suggest that "the crime of genocide was allegedly perceived as targeting only 'stable' groups, constituted in a permanent fashion and membership of which is determined by birth, with the exclusion of the more 'mobile' groups which one joins through individual voluntary commitment, such as political and economic groups. Therefore, a common criterion in the four types of groups protected by the Genocide Convention is that membership in such groups would seem to be normally not challengeable by its members, who belong to it automatically, by birth, in a continuous and often irremediable manner."[19] It supports this very original interpretation with an inadequate general reference to the Sixth Committee debates in 1948.[20] The Tribunal indicates that the enumeration of the four groups found in article II of the Convention and article 2 of the Statute should be extended to "any group which is stable and permanent like the said four groups... In the opinion of the Chamber, it is particularly important to respect the intention of the drafters of the Genocide Convention which, according to the travaux préparatoires, was patently to ensure the protection of any stable and permanent group."[21]

This is a highly questionable proposition. It is true that one of the arguments invoked during the debates in 1948 in order to exclude "political" groups was the fact that they were not stable and permanent, in the sense of national, ethnic and racial groups, although this distinction was not nearly as helpful when it came to religious groups.[22] Yet political groups had been included in the definition of genocide adopted by the General Assembly in its 1946 resolution,[23] implying that as a customary principle, genocide clearly goes beyond groups that are "stable and permanent". The drafters of the Convention initially voted to include political groups within the enumeration,[24] only to drop them in an eleventh-hour compromise that had nothing to do with any general principle by which the instrument was to be restricted to stable and permanent groups.[25] It is a misreading of the *travaux* to conclude that the drafters'

---

[15]   Judgment, par. 513.

[16]   "Protocol of Agreement Between the Government of Rwanda and the Rwandese Patriotic Front on Miscellaneous Issues and Final Provisions," Aug. 3, 1993, art. 16, in William A. Schabas, Martin Imbleau, Introduction to Rwandan Law, Montreal: Editions Yvon Blais, 1997, p. 301.

[17]   Judgment, par. 171.

[18]   See, for example, Judgment, par. 702.

[19]   Judgment, par. 511.

[20]   *Ibid.*

[21]   Judgment, par. 516.

[22]   For example: U.N. Doc. E/AC.25/SR.4 (1948); U.N. Doc. A/C.6/SR.69 (1948); U.N. Doc. A/C.6/SR.74 (1948).

[23]   G.A. Res. 96(I).

[24]   U.N. Doc. A/C.6/SR.75 (1948). By twenty-nine votes to thirteen, with nine abstentions.

[25]   See the debates at U.N. Doc. A/C.6/SR.128 (1948). Egypt, which had abstained in the original vote, said it wanted to exclude political groups "primarily for practical reasons" because this could be an impediment to ratification. The United States, which had spearheaded efforts to include political groups, declared that it continued to think that its point of view was correct but, in a conciliatory spirit and in order to avoid the possibility that the application of the convention to political groups might prevent certain countries from acceding to it, would support the proposal to delete from article II the provisions relating to political groups.

intent "was patently to ensure the protection of any stable and permanent group".[26] Rather, they show a desire to restrict the scope of the term genocide to the narrow words of the Convention and to reject anything that might invite the interpreter to a liberal reading. In any case, the Tribunal's *ejusdem generis* approach to the enumeration can hardly be compatible with the principle of strict construction of penal law.

While noting that the Tutsi were identified as an ethnic group by all, the Tribunal refuses to classify them as an ethnic group in an objective sense. Here, then, its construct of "stable and permanent groups" comes to the rescue, because, "at the time of the alleged events, the Tutsi did indeed constitute a stable and permanent group".[27] The Tribunal suggests that there is a close relationship between subjective and objective conceptions. The fact that it was generally viewed that the Tutsi were an ethnic group is deemed to contribute to their stability and permanence. In fact, the opposite would seem to be the case. The more a group's existence is based on pure subjectivity, the more ephemeral its existence ought to be. If the existence of the Tutsi ethnic group depends upon a reference to this in an identity card, wouldn't the ethnicity tend to vanish once the reference on the identity card is suppressed, as was required by the 1993 Arusha Peace Agreement?

The Tribunal's interpretation of the groups contemplated by Article 2, paragraph 2 of the Statute is profoundly unsatisfactory. Although reference to the *travaux préparatoires* is recognized as a technique of treaty interpretation, can it be correct to conclude that while the drafters said one thing, they meant to say another, and that courts are entitled to correct the terms of the treaty accordingly? The alternative is the subjective analysis proposed by Trial Chamber II in Kayishema and Ruzindana some months later. But it too is not without serious flaws. Criminal law frequently defines crimes with reference to the status of the victim: child abuse and patricide are examples. It cannot be sufficient, in terms of the elements of the material acts of such crimes, for the perpetrator to believe that the victim is a child or a parent. There must be an objective reality to the status of the victim. And so it is with genocide. The problem with Trial Chamber I's analysis in Akayesu seems to be its desire to define rigidly the four groups listed within the Convention and the Statute, and to do so in light of politically correct 1990s conceptions that reject the validity of such notions as "racial groups". As the drafters conceived of the term in 1948, there can be no doubt that the Tutsi constituted and constitute a "racial group". Accordingly, the intentional destruction of the group in 1994 falls squarely within the parameters of the crime of genocide.

Special Intent and Motive

The Tribunal recalls that the crime of genocide is characterized by its "special intent" or *dolus specialis*, which is defined in the text of the provision: "the intent to destroy, in whole or in part, a national, ethnical, racial or religious group, as such". On the subject of premeditation, the Tribunal perpetuates the confusion in the *travaux préparatoires* on this subject, to which it refers. The judgment notes that the drafters of the Convention did not require that premeditation be an element of the offence of genocide, but that this was because some delegates considered this to be an unnecessary or redundant detail. In effect, by its very nature, which involves planning and preparation, the crime of genocide must be premeditated. The facts in Akayesu bear this out. While there is no really direct evidence of premeditation identified by the Tribunal, the circumstances of the offence, and the fact that it was committed over a period of several days, show that it was the result of premeditation.[28]

Intent can be inferred from presumptions of fact, the Tribunal explains. "[I]t is possible to deduce the genocidal intent inherent in a particular act charged from the general context of the perpetration of other culpable acts systematically directed against that same group, whether these acts were committed by the same offender or by others."[29] It may also be inferred, the Tribunal notes, from acts which violate "the very foundation of the group". Examples would be acts directed against cultural institutions. This was the

---

[26]   Judgment, par. 516.

[27]   Judgment, par. 702.

[28]   Blacks Law Dictionary (5th ed.) 1062 (1979), defines premeditation: "A prior determination to do an act, but such determination need not exist for any particular period before it is carried into effect. Term 'premeditation,' means 'thought of beforehand for any length of time, however short.'"

[29]   Judgment, par. 523.

approach of the International Criminal Tribunal for the Former Yugoslavia, in its Rule 61 hearing in the Karadžić and Mladić case.[30] Although "cultural genocide" as such was excluded from the 1948 Convention,[31] the Tribunals have introduced it indirectly, at least to the extent that cultural genocide provides the proof of circumstances that establish the genocidal intent of acts of physical genocide.

One important difficulty in interpretation which the Tribunal does not address directly is the issue of motive. There is no explicit reference to motive in Article II of the Genocide Convention, and the casual reader will be excused for failure to guess that the words "as such" are meant to express the concept. It is necessary to examine the *travaux préparatoires* in order to clarify the meaning to be given to the words "as such". It should be noted at the outset that intent and motive are not interchangeable notions. Several individuals may intend to commit the same crime, but for different motives. The original Secretariat draft of the Convention had omitted any reference to motive on the basis that it should be unnecessary to prove motive: "the minute the intention arose to destroy a human group, genocide was committed".[32] However, the *ad hoc* committee which met in early 1948 introduced the notion into its draft.[33] The matter was hotly debated in the Sixth Committee of the General Assembly in late 1948, where a compromise was proposed by Venezuela, eliminating any reference to motive, but including the words "as such".[34] Venezuela said that its amendment "should meet the views of those who wished to retain a statement of motives; indeed, the motives were implicitly included in the words 'as such'".[35] When the chair put the Venezuelan amendment to the vote, he said "its interpretation would rest with each Government when ratifying and applying the convention". The amendment was adopted by twenty-seven votes to twenty-two, with two abstentions.[36] In a subsequent comment, the United States said: "The judge who would have to apply the text would certainly tend to assume that the majority of the Committee had decided in favour of the interpretation given to the amendment by its author, since that interpretation had been known to the Committee before the amendment was voted upon."[37] But unfortunately, the first international judges to interpret the provision have passed completely over the issue of motive, which is not discussed at all in the judgment. In Akayesu's case, the motive can readily be deduced from the circumstances of the crime, namely, to destroy the Tutsi group. What the motive requirement really does is to open the door to a defence. Akayesu might have argued that his motive was to win the civil war rather than to destroy an ethnic group. But as he denied the facts altogether, Akayesu could hardly plead that he had committed the crimes with a non-genocidal motive.

Acts of Genocide

The Trial Chamber procedes to interpret the scope of the five "acts of genocide" listed in article II of the Convention, and repeated in paragraph 2 of article 2 of the Statute, although this is not always necessary in order to establish the crimes alleged in the indictment. The first, paragraph (a), consists of "killing members of the group". The Tribunal finds the term "killing" to be too general, in that it may include involuntary homicide as well as intentional killing. It notes that the French term *meurtre* is more precise, and opts for the latter[38]. The question is not a new one, and had been thoroughly canvassed at the time of the drafting of the Convention, when the United Kingdom made a similar observation.[39] But it was generally accepted then that within the context of the Convention as a whole, it could never refer to

---

[30]   ICTY, Review of the Indictments Pursuant to Rule 61 of the Rules of Procedure and Evidence, *Prosecutor* v. *Karadžić and Mladić,* Case Nos. IT-95-5-R61, IT-95-18-R61, T. Ch. I, 11 July 1996, ALC-I-679, par. 94.

[31]   U.N. Doc. A/C.6/SR.83 (1948).

[32]   U.N. Doc. E/AC.25/SR.11 (1948), p. 3.

[33]   U.N. Doc. E/794 (1948), p. 5.

[34]   U.N. Doc. A/C.6/SR.75 (1948). U.N. Doc. A/C.6/231 (1948).

[35]   U.N. Doc. A/C.6/SR.76 (1948).

[36]   U.N. Doc. A/C.6/SR.77 (1948).

[37]   *Ibid.* The United States was opposed to a motive requirement in the Convention. Fifty years later, it may have changed its mind. The "Annex on Definitional Elements" prepared by the United States of America for the 1998 Diplomatic Conference on the International Criminal Court specifies that genocide is committed "against a person in a national, ethnical, racial, or religious group, because of that person's membership in that group" (U.N. Doc. A/CONF.183/C.1/L.10 (1998), p. 1).

[38]   Judgment, par. 500.

[39]   U.N. Doc. A/C.6/SR.81.

involuntary killing, as "it had never been a question of defining unpremeditated killing as an act of genocide".[40]

Article 2, paragraph 3 specifies that the victims must be members of a protected group.[41] In Akayesu, the Trial Chamber considered whether murder of an individual who was not a member of the group, but who was killed within the context of genocide, could be considered an act of genocide. The Tribunal was convinced of Akayesu's presence and participation when Victim V was beaten with a stick and the butt of a rifle by a communal policeman called Mugenzi and by a member of the *interahamwe* militia. The Trial Chamber said that the act would have constituted genocide had Victim V been a Tutsi, but because Victim V was Hutu, Akayesu could not be convicted of genocide for this particular act.[42]

Causing serious bodily or mental harm to members of the group is the second act of genocide set out in paragraph 2(b) of the Statute (and article II(b) of the Convention). Referring to the Eichmann case,[43] the Tribunal states that "[c]ausing serious bodily or mental harm to members of the group does not necessarily mean that the harm is permanent and irremediable". There has been some controversy on this point in the past, with suggestions that harm must be permanent or irremediable. The United States, at the time of ratification of the Convention, formulated the following "understanding": "(2) That the term mental harm' in article II(b) means permanent impairment of mental faculties through drugs, torture or similar techniques." In the draft statute for an international criminal court, the Preparatory Committee noted that "[t]he reference to 'mental harm' is understood to mean more than the minor or temporary impairment of mental faculties".[44]

In one of its significant innovations, the Tribunal finds rape to be a form of genocide, in that it constitutes serious bodily or mental harm pursuant to paragraph (3)(b).[45] The Prosecutor had not included gender-based crimes in the initial indictment of Akayesu. It was only mid-way through the trial, after pressure from non-governmental organizations, that the indictment was amended. According to the Trial Chamber, "[R]ape and sexual violence certainly constitute infliction of serious bodily and mental harm on the victims ... and are even, according to the Chamber, one of the worst ways of [sic] inflict harm on the victim as he or she suffers both bodily and mental harm. In light of all the evidence before it, the Chamber is satisfied that the acts of rape and sexual violence described above, were committed solely against Tutsi women, many of whom were subjected to the worst public humiliation, mutilated, and raped several times, often in public, in the Bureau Communal premises or in other public places, and often by more than one assailant. These rapes resulted in physical and psychological destruction of Tutsi women, their families and their communities."[46]

One witness at the trial, identified only as "JJ" for the purposes of her own protection, recalled lying in the cultural centre of the commune, "having been raped repeatedly by *interahamwe*, and hearing the cries of young girls around her, girls as young as twelve or thirteen years old. On the way to the cultural centre the first time she was raped there, Witness JJ said that she and the others were taken past the Accused and that he was looking at them. The second time she was taken to the cultural centre to be raped, Witness JJ recalled seeing the Accused standing at the entrance of the cultural centre and hearing him say loudly to the *interahamwe*, 'Never ask me again what a Tutsi woman tastes like,' and 'Tomorrow they will be killed.'"[47] Akayesu denied that these events took place, claiming the indictment had been

---

[40]   U.N. Doc. A/C.6/SR.81 (Maktos, United States of America). See also: Nehemiah Robinson, The Genocide Convention: A Commentary, New York: Institute of Jewish Affairs, 1960, p. 63; Code of Crimes against the Peace and Security of Mankind, U.N. Doc. A/51/332 (1996).

[41]   Nothing prevents the offender from being a member of the targeted group, however: Benjamin Whitaker, "Revised and updated report on the question of the prevention and punishment of the crime of genocide", U.N. Doc. E/CN.4/Sub.2/1985/6, par. 31, p. 16.

[42]   Judgment, par. 710.

[43]   *A.-G. Israel* v. *Eichmann*, (1968) 36 International Law Reports. 5 (District Court, Jerusalem), p. 340.

[44]   U.N. Doc. A/AC.249/1998/CRP.8, p. 2.

[45]   On the historic issues relating to criminalization of rape, see: Theodor Meron, Rape as a Crime under International Law, 87 American Journal of International Law 1993, p. 424.

[46]   Judgment, par. 721.

[47]   Judgment, par. 422.

amended because of pressure from the women's movement and women in Rwanda, whom he described as "worked up to agree that they have been raped" and that the charges were an "invented accusation".[48]

The Trial Chamber also considered that rape could be subsumed within paragraph (d) of the definition of genocide:

> "For purposes of interpreting Article 2(2)(d) of the Statute [and article II(d) of the Convention], the Chamber holds that the measures intended to prevent births within the group, should be construed as sexual mutilation, the practice of sterilization, forced birth control, separation of the sexes and prohibition of marriages. In patriarchal societies, where membership of a group is determined by the identity of the father, an example of a measure intended to prevent births within a group is the case where, during rape, a woman of the said group is deliberately impregnated by a man of another group, with the intent to have her give birth to a child who will consequently not belong to its mother's group. Furthermore, the Chamber notes that measures intended to prevent births within the group may be physical, but can also be mental. For instance, rape can be a measure intended to prevent births when the person raped refuses subsequently to procreate, in the same way that members of a group can be led, through threats or trauma, not to procreate."[49]

Such views may seem exaggerated, because it is unrealistic and perhaps absurd to believe that a group can be destroyed in whole or in part by rape and similar crimes. In any case, this is not what the Convention provision demands. In contrast with paragraph (c), paragraph (d) does not require that the measures to restrict births be "calculated" to bring about the destruction of the group in whole or in part, only that they be intended to prevent births within the group. Such measures can be merely ancillary to a genocidal plan or programme, as they were, for example, in the case of the Nazis. Adolph Eichmann was tried on a charge of "devising measures intended to prevent child-bearing among the Jews". The Court said it did not regard prevention of child-bearing as an explicit part of the "final solution", concluding Eichmann's involvement in "imposing measures" had not been proven. Nevertheless, he was convicted for devising "measures the purpose of which was to prevent child-bearing among Jews by his instruction forbidding births and for the interruption of pregnancy of Jewish women in the Theresin Ghetto with intent to exterminate the Jewish people".[50]

"Other Acts" of Genocide

While genocide is defined in article II of the 1948 Convention, the forms of participation in genocide are enumerated in article III: murder, conspiracy, direct and public incitement, attempt and complicity. The provision concerning genocide in the Statute of the Tribunal, article 2, combines articles II and III. This is the source of potentially serious problems of interpretation, because article 6, paragraph 1 of the Statute also enumerates forms of participation applicable to all three categories of crimes, including genocide. It states: "A person who planned, instigated, ordered, committed or otherwise aided and abetted in the planning, perpetration or execution of a crime referred to in article 2 to 4 of the present Statute, shall be individually responsible for the crime." As a result, there is a degree of overlap between articles 2, paragraph 3 and 6, paragraph 1 of the Statute. For example, article 2, paragraph 3 (e) of the Statute establishes the crime of complicity to commit genocide, while article 6, paragraph 1 covers aiding and abetting. These are cognate if not totally identical concepts. Aware of this problem, the drafters of the Rome Statute of the International Criminal Court eliminated the enumeration in article III of the Convention and confined its definition of genocide to the text of article II,[51] leaving the question of forms of participation to a general provision applicable to all offences.

---

[48]   Judgment, par. 448.
[49]   Judgment, par. 507-508. Also: ICTR, Judgment, *Prosecutor* v. *Kayishema and Ruzindana*, Case No. ICTR-95-1-T, T. Ch. II, 21 May 1999, par. 117; ICTR, Judgment, *Prosecutor* v. *Rutaganda*, Case No. ICTR-96-3-T, T. Ch. I, 6 December 1999. Similar views are expressed in M. Cherif Bassiouni and Peter Manikas, The Law of the International Criminal Tribunal for the Former Yugoslavia, Irvington-on-Hudson, New York: Transnational Publishers, 1996, p. 588.
[50]   *A.-G. Israel* v. *Eichmann*, *supra* note 43, par. 199.
[51]   U.N. Doc. A/CONF.183/9 (1998), art. 6.

The issue arose with respect to speeches made by Akayesu on April 19, 1994 that constituted incitement of genocide, and that actually provoked killing and other crimes against the Tutsi in Taba commune. Article 2, paragraph 3 (c) of the Statute establishes the crime of direct and public incitement to commit genocide, and article 6, paragraph 1 speaks of instigation and abetting. The essential distinction between articles 2, paragraph 3 (c) and 6, paragraph 1 is that the former is an inchoate crime, one that may be committed even if the incitement does not actually result in the crime of genocide itself.[52] Because Akayesu's incitement actually resulted in crimes being committed, he could have been found guilty under article 6, paragraph 1 rather than 2, paragraph 3 (c). Nevertheless, the indictment referred to direct and public incitement as set out in article 2, paragraph 3 (c) of the Statute.

Interestingly, citing the common law, the Tribunal defines "incitement" as "instigation", and the word "instigation" appears in article 6, paragraph 1. But when it looks at Romano-Germanic law, it cites the French Penal Code and turns to the provisions dealing with provocation, suggesting that this must be both direct and public.[53] The Tribunal's references to French law are unnecessary if it is only intending to interpret article 2, paragraph 3 (c), because the words direct and public are already part of the text. But if the Tribunal means to suggest that instigation and abetting, as set out in article 6, paragraph 1, must also be direct and public, it unnecessarily restricts the scope of the Statute. Alternatively, the Trial Chamber may be implying that the incitement-related forms of participation in article 6, paragraph 1 are inoperative because "direct and public incitement" is specifically covered by article 2, paragraph 3 (c) of the Statute, which is consequently a form of *lex specialis*.

The Tribunal attempts to explain the distinctions between the different terminologies used to describe secondary participation. Discussing "planning", the Trial Chamber states:

> "Such planning is similar to the notion of complicity in Civil law, or conspiracy under Common law, as stipulated in Article 2(3) of the Statute. But the difference is that planning, unlike complicity or plotting, can be an act committed by one person. Planning can thus be defined as implying that one or several persons contemplate designing the commission of a crime at both the preparatory and execution phases."[54]

But it is inaccurate to associate "planning" with conspiracy as it is intended in the common law, because conspiracy is an inchoate crime. "Planning" within the meaning of the statutes of the *ad hoc* tribunals is only criminal if the underlying crime is committed. As for "instigation", the Rwanda Tribunal agrees it is synonymous with "incitement", at least in English law. According to the Tribunal, this involves "prompting another to commit an offence".[55] The third category is "ordering" the commission of an offence.

> "Ordering implies a superior-subordinate relationship between the person giving the order and the one executing it. In other words, the person in a position of authority uses it to convince another to commit an offence. In certain legal systems, including that of Rwanda, ordering is a form of complicity through instructions given to the direct perpetrator of an offence. Regarding the position of authority, the Chamber considers that sometimes it can be just a question of fact."[56]

The final form of criminal participation in article 6, paragraph 1 of the Statute is "aiding and abetting". This is a rather classic common law formulation of complicity. According to the Trial Chamber, aiding means giving assistance to someone, while abetting involves facilitating the commission of an act by

---

[52] For the debates, see: U.N. Doc. A/C.6/SR.85. An amendment by the United States aimed at removing inchoate incitement was defeated by twenty-seven to sixteen, with five abstentions.

[53] Gaston Stefani, Georges Levasseur, Bernard Bouloc, Droit pénal général, Paris: Dalloz, 1998, p. 263-265. This can also be seen in article 91, paragraph 1 of the Rwandan Penal Code, which is based on the French model. Actually, while the French *Code pénal* does require that incitement be direct, it imposes no requirement that it be public.

[54] Judgment, par. 480.

[55] *Ibid.*, par. 482.

[56] *Ibid.*, par. 483 (reference omitted).

being sympathetic thereto.[57] The two terms are disjunctive, and it is sufficient to prove one or the other form of participation, the Tribunal declares.[58] It asserts a distinction between "aiding and abetting", set out in article 6, paragraph 1, which is the general provision of the Statute applicable to all crimes covered by the Statute, and "complicity", which is in article 2, paragraph 3 and applies to genocide alone. This is hard to understand because in comparative criminal law the two mean essentially the same thing. Moreover, the drafters of the Genocide Convention intended "complicity", as used in article III(e), to embrace the familiar common law concept of "aiding and abetting". The Tribunal says that there are three forms of "complicity" in "civil law systems": complicity by instigation, complicity by aiding and abetting, and complicity by procuring.[59] But on closer examination, instigation is synonymous with abetting, and procuring is synonymous with aiding. The Trial Chamber adds that in Rwandan law there are two additional forms of complicity, namely incitement through speeches and harbouring or aiding a criminal. But once again, these concepts fit comfortably within the general terms of aiding and abetting. The Tribunal says that given the absence of a definition of complicity in the Statute, it will follow the approach of the Rwandan Penal Code.[60] All of this is quite contrived, and leads the Tribunal on some rather strange meanderings, particularly with respect to the *mens rea* of complicity. Why the Security Council would have created two different and at times contradictory concepts is never explained.

The confusion is aggravated when the Tribunal consideres the mental element *(mens rea)* of the different forms of complicity. In the case of complicity pursuant to article 2, paragraph 3 (e), it agrees that the accomplice must have knowledge of the circumstances and must have the specific intent for genocide. But in the case of complicity under article 6, paragraph 1, it claims that specific intent is not necessary. It reasons that an accomplice must act knowingly, but "need not even wish that the principal offence be committed". The Tribunal cites Lord Devlin, in an English case, stating that "an indifference to the result of the crime does not of itself negate abetting. If one man deliberately sells to another a gun to be used for murdering a third, he may be indifferent about whether the third lives or dies and interested only in the cash profit to be made out of the sale, but he can still be an aider and abettor."[61] According to the Tribunal:

> "Therefore, the Chamber is of the opinion that an accomplice to genocide need not necessarily possess the *dolus specialis* of genocide, namely the specific intent to destroy, in whole or in part, a national, ethnic, racial or religious group, as such. Thus, if for example, an accused knowingly aided or abetted another in the commission of a murder, while being unaware that the principal was committing such a murder, with the intent to destroy, in whole or in part, the group to which the murdered victim belonged, the accused could be prosecuted for complicity in murder, and certainly not for complicity in genocide. However, if the accused knowingly aided and abetted in the commission of such a murder while he knew or had reason to know that the principal was acting with genocidal intent, the accused would be an accomplice to genocide, even though he did not share the murderer's intent to destroy the group... In conclusion, the Chamber is of the opinion that an accused is liable as an accomplice to genocide if he knowingly aided or abetted or instigated one or more persons in the commission of genocide, while knowing that such a person or persons were committing genocide, even though the accused himself did not have the specific intent to destroy, in whole or in part, a national, ethnical, racial or religious group, as such."[62]

---

[57]   *Ibid.*, par. 484. According to Smith and Hogan, the words aiding and abetting connote different forms of activity. "The natural meaning of 'to aid' is 'to give help, support or assistance to'; and of 'to abet', 'to incite, instigate or encourage'": J.C. Smith, Brian Hogan, Criminal Law, 7th ed., London: Butterworths, 1992, p. 126.

[58]   ICTR, Judgment, *Prosecutor* v. *Kayishema and Ruzindana*, Case no. ICTR-95-1-T, T. Ch. II, 21 May 1999, par. 197.

[59]   It proposes more detailed definitions of some of these terms: Judgment, par. 538. Thus, "complicity by procuring means, such as weapons, instruments or any other means, used to commit genocide, with the accomplice knowing that such means would be used for such a purpose; complicity by knowingly aiding or abetting a perpetrator of a genocide in the planning or enabling acts thereof; complicity by instigation, for which a person is liable who, though not directly participating in the crime of genocide crime, gave instructions to commit genocide, through gifts, promises, threats, abuse of authority or power, machinations or culpable artifice, or who directly incited to commit genocide".

[60]   The Rwandan Penal Code was adopted in 1977, but is modelled on the nineteenth century codes of France and Belgium. See: William A. Schabas, Martin Imbleau, Introduction to Rwandan Law, Cowansville, Quebec: Editions Yvon Blais, 1998.

[61]   Judgment, par. 539. Citing: *National Coal Board* v. *Gamble*, [1959] 1 Q.B. 11, [1958] 3 All E.R. 203.

[62]   Judgment, par. 540, 541, 545.

The problem with this analysis is that the accomplice who knows of the principal offender's intent and who assists or encourages must necessarily share the genocidal intent. To say that the goal of the accomplice is to earn money by selling the weapon rather than to destroy a group in whole or in part is to confuse concepts of intent and motive. In any event, the Rwanda Tribunal's reference to English authority is incorrect, because the National Coal Board case, as well as subsequent judgments, actually confirm that the motive of the accomplice is irrelevant as long as knowledge and intent are present.[63]

The preoccupation of the Rwanda Tribunal with the *mens rea* of "aiding and abetting" is all the more unusual because the form of participation was "abetting" rather than "aiding". The accused was charged with inciting, instigating or encouraging, in other words abetting, rather than with providing material assistance, that is, aiding. It is often said that abetting relates to the *mens rea* of the principal offence whereas aiding relates to the *actus reus*.[64] The aider provides material help, and in this sense the *mens rea* is often unclear or equivocal, because the act is ostensibly innocent. The abettor, on the other hand, in effect provokes the crime with words and behaviour. If the acts of the abettor can be proved satisfactorily, it must be virtually self-evident that he or she had the *mens rea* to destroy, in whole or in part, a group protected by the Convention.

Complicity requires proof that the underlying or predicate crime has been committed by another person. However, the other person need not be charged or convicted in order for the liability of the accomplice to be established. In some cases, prosecution may be quite impossible, because the principal offender is dead or has disappeared, or because the principal offender is unfit to stand trial, or a minor, or immune from process. As the Trial Chamber notes, "[a]s far as the Chamber is aware, all criminal systems provide that an accomplice may also be tried, even where the principal perpetrator of the crime has not been identified, or where, for any other reasons, guilt could not be proven".[65]

Crimes Against Humanity

Akayesu was also charged with and convicted of several counts of crimes against humanity. Although perhaps less significant than its consideration of genocide, the Trial Chamber makes some important findings with respect to crimes against humanity. The enumeration of the acts constituting crimes against humanity in the Charter of the Nuremberg Tribunal did not include rape, although the omission was corrected in Control Council Law No. 10. Both statutes of the *ad hoc* tribunals include rape as a punishable act in the definition of crimes against humanity. Noting the lack of any commonly accepted definition of rape in international law, the Akayesu Trial Chamber proposes a definition. Accordingly: "The Chamber considers that rape is a form of aggression and that the central elements of the crime of rape cannot be captured in a mechanical description of objects and body parts. The Convention against Torture and Other Cruel, Inhuman and Degrading Treatment or Punishment does not catalogue specific acts in its definition of torture, focusing rather on the conceptual framework of state sanctioned violence. This approach is more useful in international law. Like torture, rape is used for such purposes as intimidation, degradation, humiliation, discrimination, punishment, control or destruction of a person. Like torture, rape is a violation of personal dignity, and rape in fact constitutes torture when inflicted by or at the instigation of or with the consent or acquiescence of a public official or other person acting in an official capacity. The Chamber defines rape as a physical invasion of a sexual nature, committed on a person under circumstances which are coercive. Sexual violence which includes rape, is considered to be any act of a sexual nature which is committed on a person under circumstances which are coercive."[66]

Shortly after Akayesu was rendered, a Trial Chamber of the International Criminal Tribunal for the Former Yugoslavia endorsed this approach in the "Celebici case".[67] But another Trial Chamber, in

---

[63]   *D.P.P. for Northern Ireland* v. *Lynch*, [1975] A.C. 653, [1975] 1 All E.R. 913 (H.L.). Also: J.C. Smith, Brian Hogan, Criminal Law, 7th ed., London: Butterworths, 1992, pp. 133-135.
[64]   *D.P.P. for Northern Ireland* v. *Lynch*, *ibid.*
[65]   Judgment, par. 531.
[66]   *Ibid.*, par. 597-599. Also, par. 687-688.
[67]   ICTY, Judgment, *Prosecutor* v. *Delalić* et al., Case No. IT-96-21-T, T. Ch. IIqtr, 16 November 1998, par. 1065-1066.

Furundžija, preferred a definition based on "a mechanical description of objects and body parts."[68] Some of the criminal acts of a sexual nature for which Akeyesu was found responsible did not meet the definition of rape adopted by the Trial Chamber. For example, Akayesu had ordered the *interahamwe* militia to undress a student and force her to do gymnastics naked in the public courtyard of the bureau communal. According to the Trial Chamber, this was a form of sexual violence that could be subsumed within the scope of "other inhumane acts", which operates as a kind of residual clause in the definition of crimes against humanity.[69]

The Akayesu Trial Chamber also considers the meaning to be given to the word torture, which is another of the enumerated acts within the definition of crimes against humanity. Here it opts for the definition found in article 1 of the Convention Against Torture and Other Cruel, Inhuman and Degrading Treatment or Punishment.[70] The Trial Chamber concludes that crimes against humanity must be committed on discriminatory grounds.[71] A Trial Chamber of the International Criminal Tribunal for the Former Yugoslavia had made a similar finding a year earlier in the Tadić case.[72] The Prosecutor's appeal on that point was granted in the July 15, 1999 decision of the Appeals Chamber.[73] However, there is a significant difference between the statutes of the two *ad hoc* tribunals which means the Appeals Chamber decision does not overrule Akayesu. The Statute of the Rwanda Tribunal stipulates that inhumane acts committed against the civilian population must be committed on "national, political, ethnic, racial or religious grounds". No similar formulation appears in article 5 of the Statute of the Yugoslav Tribunal, except with respect to persecutions.

War Crimes

Article 4 of the Statute gives the Tribunal jurisdiction over two categories of serious violations of the laws and customs of war committed during non-international armed conflict, as defined in common article 3 to the four Geneva Conventions of August 12, 1949 and in Protocol Additional II of 1977. But Akayesu was acquitted of charges based on the "war crimes" provision of the Statute. In its discussion, the Tribunal initially considers the legality of prosecution for such crimes, in light of the *nullum crimen sine lege* norm. Until adoption of Security Council resolution 955 creating the Rwanda Tribunal, it was widely believed among specialists in humanitarian law that the very concept of war crimes in non-international armed conflict did not exist. This view was strongly supported by the fact that the diplomatic conference of 1974-77 had specifically excluded the concept of grave breaches from Protocol Additional II because of a lack of acceptance of the notion of international criminality during non-international armed conflict. Moreover, the Security Council, in adopting the Statute of the International Criminal Tribunal for the Former Yugoslavia in 1993, had declared its intent to establish subject matter jurisdiction only over crimes that were unquestionably part of customary international law.[74] But in Akayesu, the Trial Chamber refers to a report from the Secretary-General of the United Nations that notes that when it created the Rwanda Tribunal, the Security Council "elected to take a more expansive approach to the choice of the subject-matter jurisdiction of the Tribunal than that of the ICTY, by incorporating international instruments regardless of whether they were considered part of customary international law or whether they customarily entailed the individual criminal responsibility of the perpetrator of the crime".[75]

---

[68]   ICTY, Judgment, *Prosecutor v. Furundžija*, Case no. IT-95-17/1-T, T. Ch. II, 10 December 1998, par. 185: "The objective elements of rape are: (i) the sexual penetration, however slight: (a) of the vagina or anus of the victim by the penis of the perpetrator or any other object used by the perpetrator; or (b) of the mouth of the victim by the penis of the perpetrator; (ii) by coercion or force or threat of force against the victim or a third person.

[69]   Judgment, par. 593, 695, 697.

[70]   *Ibid.*, par. 681.

[71]   *Ibid.*, par. 583-584.

[72]   ICTY, Opinion and Judgment, *Prosecutor v. Tadić*, IT-94-1-T, T. Ch. II, 7 May 1997, ALC-I-287, par. 650-652.

[73]   ICTY, Judgment, *Prosecutor v. Tadić*, IT-94-1-A, A. Ch., 15 July 1999, par. 298-305.

[74]   "Report of the Secretary-General Pursuant to Paragraph 2 of Security Council Resolution 808 (1993)", U.N. Doc. S/25704, para 34.

[75]   Judgment, par. 604. Citing U.N. Doc. S/1995/134.

With respect to common article 3 of the Geneva Conventions, there was already ample authority for its status as a customary norm, including a judgment of the International Court of Justice.[76] The Trial Chamber seems satisfied with a reference to that decision, although nowhere did the Court affirm that the customary status of common article 3 extends to individual criminal responsibility. As for Protocol Additional II to the Geneva Conventions, the Trial Chamber admits that probably "not all" of the instrument reflects customary law, although "the violations essentially complete and supplement common article 3, which it is conceded constitutes customary international law".[77] Here, the Trial Chamber of the Rwanda Tribunal relies largely on the jurisdictional decision of the Appeals Chamber of the Yugoslav Tribunal in Tadic finding that war crimes could indeed be committed in non-international armed conflict as a question of customary international law.[78]

Article 4 of the Statute criminalizes "serious violations of Article 3 common to the Geneva Conventions of 12 August 1949 for the Protection of War Victims, and of Additional Protocol II thereto of 8 June 1977", providing a non-exhaustive enumeration of such acts that is drawn from the text of common article 3. Protocol Additional II is rather less laconic than common article 3. But the Statute is silent as to the further violations of humanitarian law contained in the Protocol but not explicitly stated in common article 3. The Trial Chamber seems comfortable with the idea that these extend to the provisions of article 4 of Protocol Additional II, which deals with "Fundamental Guarantees", and which contains some rather detailed provisions dealing with protection of children that do not appear in common article 3.[79] The Trial Chamber is silent about breaches of articles 5 and 6, or of other provisions. Some of these are probably not *serious* violations, for example, denying the right of detainees to receive letters and cards.[80] But what is to be said, for example, of executing persons for crimes committed while under the age of eighteen?[81]

The second hurdle with respect to the war crimes charges is establishing the thresholds of applicability. Common article 3 and Protocol II have slightly different minimum conditions, the latter being somewhat more demanding in terms of organization of rebel forces and the control of their base areas. In any event, the Trial Chamber, accepts that the Rwanda conflict corresponds to the rather restrictive terms of article 1 of Protocol Additional II.[82] After satisfying itself on these preliminary questions, the Trial Chamber indicates that Akeyesu can only be convicted if he "acted for either the Government or the [Rwandese Patriotic Front] in the execution of their respective conflict objectives".[83] In this respect, the Prosecutor had relied on evidence showing that during the Rwandan genocide, "Akeyesu wore a military jacket, carried a rifle, he assisted the military on their arrival in Taba by undertaking a number of tasks, including reconnaissance and mapping of the commune, and the setting up of radio communications, and he allowed the military to use his office premises".[84] But for the Trial Chamber, these elements were not significant to show that Akayesu actively supported the war effort. He was a civilian official and not a member of the armed forces.[85] The result, then, is that Akayesu is acquitted of the war crimes charges.

Aside from the purely legal issues involved, from a policy standpoint some may consider this a rather troubling conclusion.[86] Generally, prosecutors will prefer war crimes charges because they do not involve the daunting thresholds of crimes against humanity and genocide, such as proof acts were widespread or systematic, that they were committed with specific intent or that they were committed with a discriminatory motive. With this in mind, and in order to equalize somewhat the prerequisites for

---

[76] *Military and Paramilitary Activities in and Against Nicaragua (Nicaragua v.United States)*, [1986] I.C.J. Reports 14.
[77] Judgment, par. 609-610.
[78] ICTY, Decision on the Defence Motion on Jurisdiction, *Prosecutor* v. *Tadić*, Case No. IT-94-1-AR72, A. Ch., 2 October 1995, ALC-I-33, par. 71-93.
[79] Judgment, par. 616.
[80] Protocol Additional II to the 1949 Geneva Conventions and Relating to The Protection of Victims of Non-International Armed Conflicts, (1979) 1125 U.N.T.S. 3, Article 5, paragraph 2 (b).
[81] Ibid., Article 6, paragraph 4.
[82] Judgment, par. 627. Also, par. 174.
[83] *Ibid.*, par. 640.
[84] *Ibid.*, par. 641.
[85] *Ibid.*, par. 643.
[86] See: Diane Marie Amann, Prosecutor v. Akayesu, 93 American Journal of International Law 1999, p. 199.

prosecution of war crimes, the Rome Statute of the International Criminal Court imposes a somewhat uncertain condition that war crimes "in particular [be] committed as a part of a plan or policy or as part of a large-scale commission of such crimes".[87] In practice, of course, international prosecution should rarely be unleashed in the case of isolated war crimes. Moreover, when war crimes reach the threshold established by the Rome Statute they will almost certainly overlap with crimes against humanity and genocide. In other words, Akayesu's acquittal for war crimes appears somewhat insignificant given that he was convicted of crimes against humanity and genocide. It can hardly be said that Akayesu has escaped international stigmatisation for his crimes even if the Office of the Prosecutor has failed on one count.

Cumulative Charges

Akayesu was charged with two or more offences with respect to various factual circumstances in the indictment. For example, he was charge cumulatively with genocide, complicity to commit genocide and crimes against humanity with respect to the same facts. The Tribunal considers whether this is inadmissible and may constitute a breach of the double jeopardy principle.[88] It finds support for the legitimacy of cumulative charging in the practice of the International Criminal Tribunal for the Former Yugoslavia, that of the French *Cour de Cassation* in the Barbie case,[89] and under criminal procedure as applied within Rwanda itself.[90] The Tribunal agrees that it is acceptable to convict for two crimes with respect to the same facts where the offences have different elements, where the provisions creating the offences protect different interests and where it is necessary to record a conviction for both offences in order fully to describe what the accused did. However, the Tribunal says it was not justifiable to convict an individual of offences where one offence is a lesser but included offence of the other, or where one offence charges accomplice liability and the other offence charges liability as a principal.

Accordingly, the Tribunal notes that the three categories of offences under the Statute protect different interests. Genocide protects groups from destruction, crimes against humanity protects civilian populations from persecution and the war crimes provisions protect non-combatants during civil war. "These crimes have different purposes and are, therefore, never co-extensive", says the Trial Chamber.[91] The Tribunal adds that none of the three crimes could be considered lesser and included offences of the other, adding that the Statute establishes no hierarchy of offences.

The issues raised in this portion of the judgment have given rise to varying views in judgments of the other Trial Chamber, as well as in those of the Chambers of the International Criminal Tribunal for the Former Yugoslavia. For example, in Kayishema, Trial Chamber II of the Rwanda Tribunal considered that there was a form of double jeopardy created by multiple accusations. In some circumstances, it said that crimes against humanity would indeed be a form of lesser and included offence of genocide.[92]

Similarly, the question of a hierarchy of offences has arisen frequently in matters of sentencing. Judges of the Yugoslav Tribunal appear to be divided as to whether or not there is a relative hierarchy among the offences. The Rome Statute suggests that war crimes are inherently less serious than genocide and crimes against humanity, because it allows certain defences to charges of war crimes but not to the other two categories of offence,[93] and it permits States to ratify or accede to the Statute without admitting subject matter jurisdiction over war crimes.[94]

Command Responsibility

Akayesu was charged under some of the counts in the indictment with criminal liability on the basis of command responsibility, as set out in article 6, paragraph 3 of the Statute. Command responsibility holds

---

[87]   Rome Statute of the International Criminal Court, U.N. Doc. A/CONF.183/9, Article 8, paragraph 1.
[88]   Judgment, par. 461-470.
[89]   *Barbie*, Crim., 20 déc. 1985, JCP, 1986, II, 20655, rapp. Le Gunehec, concl. Dontenwille.
[90]   *Code pénal*, Articles 92-93.
[91]   Judgment, par. 469.
[92]   ICTR, Judgment, *Prosecutor v. Kayishema and Ruzindana*, Case No. ICTR-95-1-T, T. Ch. II, 21 May 1999, par. 636.
[93]   Rome Statute, *supra* note 87, Articles 31, paragraph 1 (c) and 33.
[94]   *Ibid.*, Article 124.

an individual having superior authority criminally responsible for genocide, crimes against humanity or war crimes committed by a subordinate if the superior "knew or had reason to know that the subordinate was about to commit such acts or had done so and the superior failed to take the necessary and reasonable measures to prevent such acts or punish the perpetrators thereof". The Trial Chamber notes that while it had been established that a superior/subordinate relationship existed between Akayesu and the *interahamwe* located at the bureau communal, it had not been alleged in the indictment that the *interahamwe* were Akayesu's subordinates. The Trial Chamber seems overly technical on this point, but it says that "[i]n fairness to the Accused" it was not prepared to infer elements in the indictment.[95]

In the counts alleging command responsibility, Akayesu had also been charged under article 6, paragraph 1, that is, as a full participant in the crimes, either as principal perpetrator or accomplice. Thus, dismissal of the command responsibility charges did not result in his acquittal on these counts. This suggests a confusion as to the application of the principle of command responsibility. Historically, command responsibility has been used to obtain convictions of commanders when it was impossible to establish, whether by direct evidence, circumstantial evidence or legal presumption, that they had actually given the orders to commit the crimes or had in some other way, by act or omission, participated in their commission. Failing such proof, international prosecution fell back upon allegations of negligent command. In the counts alleging command responsibility, Akayesu was found guilty as a full-blown participant, indicating that the Trial Chamber was satisfied that he had both knowledge and intent. This degree of *mens rea* clearly rises above the negligence standard. Therefore, it would have amounted to double or cumulative charging to find Akayesu guilty as both a participant with full *mens rea* and a negligent commander. The Tribunal seems alive to the problem, and says that in the case of command responsibility, "it is certainly proper to ensure that there has been malicious intent, or, at least, ensure that negligence was so serious as to be tantamount to acquiescence or even malicious intent".[96] But either Akeyesu knowingly omitted to intervene to stop the *interahamwe* committing the crimes, or he did not know but "should have known" of the crimes. It cannot be both. The charges based on article 6, paragraph 3 should have been dismissed or at least stayed on this basis, and not, as the Tribunal has decided, because the indictment was insufficient. Even had the indictment been sufficient, Akayesu could not be convicted both on the basis of article 6, paragraph 3 and article 6, paragraph 1 on the same facts.

The Tribunal's reticence in dealing with command responsibility is reinforced by the civilian context. The Tribunal suggests that there is a precedent on this point, noting that a civilian, Hirota, was found guilty by the Tokyo Tribunal. But even the example cited in the judgment shows that Hirota's was not a case of mere negligence but rather one of criminal knowledge ("He was content to rely on assurances which he knew were not being implemented"). The Tribunal concludes that the application of command responsibility to civilians remains "contentious".[97] Although it makes no reference to the Rome Statute, adopted in July, 1998, the latter instrument contains a powerful supporting argument. The Rome Statute codifies the concept of command responsibility, but distinguishes between "military commanders" and "other superiors". Liability is limited to cases where a civilian superior "either knew, or consciously disregarded information which clearly indicated, that the subordinates were committing or about to commit such crimes".[98] The Rome Statute eliminates the pure negligence component of command responsibility in the case of civilian superiors, and as a minimum requires proof of "wilful blindness" which, in most national criminal justice systems, is deemed to constitute true criminal knowledge.[99]

Like Eichmann, the facts in Akayesu bear out Hannah Arendt's observation of the banality of evil.[100] A month after the conviction, the Trial Chamber sentenced Akayesu to a term of life imprisonment. The Akayesu judgment has its flaws, some of which are discussed above. At the same time, the findings of fact seem solid and well-reasoned, and it is unlikely the Appeal Chamber will dare to substitute a

---

[95] Judgment, par. 691.
[96] Judgment, par. 489.
[97] Judgment, par. 491.
[98] Rome Statute, *supra* note 88, Article 28, paragraph 2 (a).
[99] Glanville Williams, Criminal Law: The General Part, 2nd ed., London: Stevens & Sons Ltd., 1961, p. 159: "The rule that wilful blindness is equivalent to knowledge is essential, and is found throughout the criminal law."
[100] Hannah Arendt, Eichmann in Jerusalem, A Report on the Banality of Evil, New York: Penguin Books, 1994.

different assessment. Akayesu's initial notice of appeal focussed on ineffective representation, a sure sign that even he understands the weakness of the case and the compelling record upon which he has been condemned. Of course, Akayesu's defence was built not upon contesting the perpetration of genocide but on a claim that he was powerless to prevent it. As a first judgment interpreting articles II and II of the 1948 Genocide Convention, it clarifies some points but leaves several others unresolved.

William Schabas

International Criminal Tribunal for the Prosecution of Persons Responsible for Genocide and Other Serious Violations of International Humanitarian Law Committed in the Territory of Rwanda and Rwandan Citizens responsible for genocide and other such violations committed in the territory of neighbouring States between 1 January and 31 December 1994	Case No.	ICTR-95-1-T
	Date:	21 May 1999
	Original:	ENGLISH

TRIAL CHAMBER II

Before Judge(s):   **William H. Sekule, Presiding Judge**
  Yakov Ostrovsky
  Tafazzal Hossain Khan

Registry: **Mr. Agwu U. Okali**

Judgement: **21 May 1999**

THE PROSECUTOR

Vs.

CLÉMENT KAYISHEMA
and
OBED RUZINDANA

JUDGEMENT

Office of the Prosecutor:
  Mr. Jonah Rahetlah
  Ms. Brenda Sue Thornton
  Ms. Holo Makwaia

Counsel for the Defence for Clément Kayishema:
  Mr. André Ferran
  Mr. Philippe Moriceau

Counsel for the Defence for Obed Ruzindana:
  Mr. Pascal Besnier
  Mr. Willem Van der Griend

List of Contents

I. INTRODUCTION

1.1 The Tribunal and its Jurisdiction

1. This Judgement is rendered by Trial Chamber II of the International Tribunal for the prosecution of persons responsible for the serious violations of international humanitarian law committed in the territory of Rwanda and Rwandan citizens responsible for genocide and other such violations committed in the territory of neighbouring States, between 1 January and 31 December 1994 (the Tribunal). The Judgement follows the Indictment and the joint trial of Clement Kayishema and Obed Ruzindana.

2. The Tribunal was established by the United Nations Security Council's Resolution 955 of 8 November 1994.[1] After official investigations, the Security Council found indications of wide spread violations of international humanitarian law and concluded that the situation in that country in 1994 constituted a threat to international peace and security within the meaning of Chapter VII of the United Nations Charter, thus giving rise to the establishment of the Tribunal.

3. The Tribunal is governed by its Statute (the Statute), annexed to the Security Council Resolution 955, and by its Rules of Procedure and Evidence (the Rules), adopted by the Judges on 5 July 1995 and amended subsequently.[2] The Judges of the Tribunal, currently fourteen in all, are selected by the General Assembly and represent the principal legal systems of the world.

4. The *ratione materiae* jurisdiction of the Tribunal is set out in Articles 2, 3 and 4 of the Statute. Under the Statute, the Tribunal is empowered to prosecute persons who are alleged to have committed Genocide, as defined in Article 2, persons responsible for Crimes Against Humanity, as defined in Article 3 and persons responsible for serious violations of Article 3 Common to the Geneva Conventions of 12 August 1949 on the **[page 2]** Protection of Victims of War, and of Additional Protocol II thereto of 8 June 1977, a crime defined under Article 4 of the Tribunal's Statute.[3] Article 8 of the Statute provides that the Tribunal has concurrent jurisdiction with national courts over which, however, it has primacy. The temporal jurisdiction of the Tribunal is limited to acts committed from 1 January 1994 to 31 December 1994.

5. Finally, the Statute stipulates that the Prosecutor, who acts as a separate organ of the Tribunal, is responsible for the investigation and prosecution of the perpetrators of such violations. The Prosecutor is assisted by a Deputy Prosecutor, a team of senior trial attorneys, trial attorneys, and investigators based in Kigali, Rwanda. **[page 3]**

1.2 The Indictment

The amended Indictment, against the accused persons, is reproduced, in full, below.

**INTERNATIONAL CRIMINAL TRIBUNAL
FOR RWANDA**

CASE NO: ICTR-95-1-1 (sic)

**THE PROSECUTOR
OF THE TRIBUNAL**

AGAINST

---

[1] UN Doc. S/RES/955 of 8 Nov, 1994.
[2] The Rules were successively amended on 12 Jan. 1996, 15 May 1996, 4 Jul. 1996, 5 Jun. 1997 and 8 Jun. 1998.
[3] The provisions of these offences are detailed in Part IV of the Judgement, entitled The Law.

CLEMENT KAYISHEMA
OBED RUZINDANA

[Registry date stamped
11 April 1997]

First Amended Indictment

Richard J. Goldstone, Prosecutor of the International Criminal Tribunal for Rwanda, pursuant to his authority under Article 17 of the Statute of the International Criminal Tribunal for Rwanda (Tribunal Statute), charges:

1. This indictment charges persons responsible for the following massacres which occurred in the *Prefecture* of Kibuye, Republic of Rwanda:

   1.1 The massacre at the Catholic Church and the Home St. Jean complex in Kibuye town, where thousands of men, women and children were killed and numerous people injured around 17 April 1994.

   1.2 The massacre at the Stadium in Kibuye town, where thousands of men, women and children were killed and numerous people injured on about 18 and 19 April 1994. **[page 4]**

   1.3 The massacre at the Church in Mubuga, where thousands of men, women and children were killed and numerous people injured between about 14 and 17 April 1994.

   1.4 The massacres in the area of Bisesero, where thousands of men, women and children were killed and numerous people injured between about 10 April and 30 June 1994.

THE MASSACRES SITES

2. The Republic of Rwanda is divided into eleven *Prefectures*. These eleven *Prefectures* are further divided into communes. The *Prefecture* of Kibuye consists of nine communes. The massacres which form the basis of the charges in the indictment occurred in the *Prefecture* of Kibuye, in Gitesi, Gishyita and Gisovu communes.

3. The first massacre site addressed in this indictment, namely, the Catholic Church and Home St. Jean complex, is located in Kibuye town, Gitesi commune, on a piece of land which is surrounded on three sides by Lake Kivu. A road runs past the entrance to the catholic Church and Home St. Jean complex. The Catholic Church is visible from the road. The Home St. Jean is behind the Church and is not visible from the road.

4. The second massacre site addressed to in this indictment, the Stadium, is located near the main traffic circle in Kibuye town, Gitesi Commune. The town's main road runs past the Stadium. Immediately behind the Stadium is a high hill.

5. The third massacre site addressed in this indictment, the Church of Mubuga, is located in Gishyita Commune. Gishyita Commune is located in the southern part of Kibuye *Prefecture*. The Church in Mubuga is located approximately 20 kilometres from Kibuye town.

6. The fourth massacre site addressed in this indictment is the area of Bisesero. The area of Bisesero extends through two communes in the *Prefecture* of Kibuye: Gishyita and Gisovu. Bisesero is an area of high rolling hills, located in the southern portion of Kibuye *Prefecture*. The hills are very large, and are often separated by deep valleys.

BACKGROUND

7.   The structure of the executive branch, and the authority of the members therein, is set forth in the laws of Rwanda. In the *Prefecture*, the Prefect is the highest local representative of the government, and is the trustee of the State Authority. The Prefect has control over the government and its agencies throughout the *Prefecture*. **[page 5]**

8.   In each commune within a *Prefecture* there exists the council of the commune, which is led by the *Bourgmestre* of that Commune. The *Bourgmestre* of each commune is nominated by the Minister of the Interior and appointed by the President. As representative of the executive power, the *Bourgmestre* is subject to the hierarchical authority of the Prefect, but, subject to this authority, the Bourgmestre is in charge of governmental functions within his commune.

9.   The Prefect is responsible for maintaining the peace, public order, and security of persons and goods within the *Prefecture*. In fulfilling his duty to maintain peace, the Prefect can demand assistance from the army and the *Gendarmerie Nationale*. The *Bourgmestre* also has authority over those members of the *Gendarmerie Nationale* stationed in his *commune*.

10.   The *Gendarmerie Nationale* is an armed force established to maintain the public order and execute the laws. It is lead by the Minister of Defence, but can exercise its function of safeguarding the public order at the request of the competent national authority, which is the *Prefect*. The *Gendarmerie Nationale* has an affirmative duty to report to the *Prefect* information which has a bearing on the public order, as well as a duty to assist any person who, being in danger, requests its assistance. From January – July 1994, there were approximately 200 gendarmes in the *Prefecture* of Kibuye.

11.   The members of the executive branch also have control over the communal police. Each commune has Police Communale, who are engaged by the *Bourgmestre* of the commune. Normally the *Bourgmestre* has exclusive authority over the members of the Police Communale. In case of public calamities, however, the *Prefect* can claim the policemen of the Police Communale and place them under his direct control.

12.   The Interahamwe, an unofficial paramilitary group composed almost exclusively of extremist Hutus, had significant involvement in the events charged in this indictment. The National Revolutionary Movement for Development (MRND) party created the members of the Interahamwe as a military training organisation for MRND youth and based the members of the Interahamwe's leadership on the MRND's own structure, with leaders at the national, prefectoral, and communal levels. There was no official link between the Interahamwe and the Rwandan military, but members of the Army and Presidential Guard trained, guided and supported the Interahamwe. Occasionally, members of the Army or Presidential Guard participated in Interahamwe activities.

13.   On 6 April 1994, the airplane carrying then-president of Rwanda Juvenal Habyarimana crashed during its approach into Kigali airport in Rwanda. Almost immediately, the massacre of civilians began throughout Rwanda. During that time, individuals seeking Tutsis were able to focus their activities on specific locations because Tutsis, who believed themselves to be in danger, often fled in **[page 6]** large numbers to perceived safe areas such as churches and communal buildings. This practice, which was widely known, was based on the fact that in the past Tutsis who had sought refuge in such places had not been attacked. Thus, during the period of time relevant to this indictment, groups of people seeking refuge in the same area were most likely predominantly Tutsis.

14.   Also, during the times relevant to this indictment, the Rwandan government required all Rwandans to carry, at all times, identity cards that designated the bearer's status as Hutu, Tutsi, Twa or "naturalised". Individuals seeking Tutsis could identify their targets simply by asking individuals to show their identification card.

GENERAL ALLEGATIONS.

15.   All acts of (sic) omissions by the accused set forth in this indictment occurred during the period of 1 January 1994 to 31 December 1994 and in the territory of the Republic of Rwanda.

16. In each paragraph charging genocide, a crime recognised by Article 2 of the Tribunal Statute, the alleged acts or omissions were committed with intent to destroy, in whole or in part, an ethnic or racial group.

17. In each paragraph charging crimes against humanity, crimes recognised by Article 3 of the Tribunal Statute, the alleged acts or omissions, were part of a widespread or systematic attack against a civilian population on political, ethnic or racial grounds.

18. At all times relevant to this indictment, the victims, referred to in this indictment were protected under Article 3 common to the Geneva Conventions and by the Additional Protocol II thereto.

19. At all times relevant to this indictment, there was an internal armed conflict occurring within Rwanda.

20. At all times relevant to this indictment, Clement Kayishema was Prefect of Kibuye and exercised control over the *Prefecture* of Kibuye, including his subordinates in the executive branch and members of the Gendarmerie Nationale.

21. Each of the accused is individually responsible for the crimes alleged against him in this indictment, pursuant to Article 6 (1) of the Tribunal Statute. Individual responsibility includes planning, instigating, ordering, committing or otherwise aiding and abetting in the planning, preparation and execution of any of the crimes referred to in Articles 2 to 4 of the Tribunal Statute. **[page 7]**

22. In addition, Clement Kayishema is also or alternatively individually responsible as a superior for the criminal acts of his subordinates in the administration, the Gendarmerie Nationale, and the communal police with respect to each of the crimes charged, pursuant to Article 6 (3) of the Tribunal Statute. Superior individual responsibility is the responsibility of a superior for the acts of his subordinate if he knew or had reasons to know that his subordinate was about to commit such criminal acts or had done so and failed to take the necessary and reasonable measures to prevent such acts, or to punish the perpetrators thereof.

THE ACCUSED

23. **Clement Kayishema** was born in 1954 in Bwishyura Sector, Gitesi Commune, Kibuye *Prefecture*, Rwanda. Kayishema's father was Jean Baptiste Nabagiziki, and his mother was Anastasie Nyirabakunzi. He was appointed to the position of Prefect of Kibuye on 3 July 1992, and assumed his responsibility as Prefect soon after. **Clement Kayishema** acted as Prefect of Kibuye until his departure to Zaire in July 1994. He is believed to be currently in Bukavu, Zaire.

24. **Obed Ruzindana** is believed to have been borne around 1962 in Gisovu Sector, Gisovu Commune, Kibuye Prefecture, Rwanda. **Ruzindana's** father was Elie Murakaza. **Obed Ruzindana** was a commercial trader in Kigali during the time period in which the crimes alleged in this indictment occurred. He is believed to be currently somewhere in Zaire.

The Massacre at the Catholic Church and Home St. Jean

COUNTS 1-6

25. By about 17 April 1994, thousands of men, women and children from various locations had sought refuge in the Catholic Church and Home St. Jean complex (the Complex) located in Kibuye town. These men, women and children were unarmed and were predominantly Tutsis. They were in the complex seeking protection from attacks on Tutsis which had occurred throughout the *Prefecture* of Kibuye.

26. Some of the people who sought refuge in the Complex did so because Clement Kayishema ordered them to go there. When Clement Kayishema ordered people to the Complex, he knew or had reason to know that an attack on the complex was going to occur.

27.   After people gathered in the Complex, the Complex was surrounded by persons under Clement Kayishema's control, including members of the *Gendarmerie Nationale*. These persons prevented the men, women and children within the **[page 8]** Complex from leaving the Complex at a time when Clement Kayishema knew or had reason to know that an attack on the Complex was going to occur.

28.   On about 17 April 1994, Clement Kayishema ordered members of the Gendarmerie Nationale, communal police of Gitesi *commune*, members of the *Interahamwe* and armed civilians to attack the Complex, and personally participated in the attack. The attackers used guns, grenades, machetes, spears, cudgels and other weapons to kill the people in the Complex.

29.   The attack resulted in thousands of deaths and numerous injuries to the people within the complex. (Attachment A contains a list of some of the individuals killed in the attack, members of the Gendarmerie Nationale, the Interahamwe and armed civilians searched for and killed or injured survivors of the attack.

30.   Before the attack on the Complex, Clement Kayishema did not take measures to prevent an attack, and after the attack Clement Kayishema did not punish the perpetrators.

31.   By these acts and omissions, Clement Kayishema is criminally responsible for:

Count 1: GENOCIDE, a violation of Article 2 (3) (a) of the Tribunal Statute;

Count 2: CRIMES AGAINST HUMANITY, a violation of Article 3 (a) (murder) of the Tribunal Statute;

Count 3: CRIMES AGAINST HUMANITY, a violation of Article 3 (b) (extermination) of the Tribunal Statute;

Count 4: CRIMES AGAINST HUMANITY, a violation of Article 3 (i) (other inhumane acts) of the Tribunal Statute;

Count 5: A VIOLATION OF ARTICLE 3 COMMON TO THE GENEVA CONVENTIONS, a violation of Article 4 (a) of the Tribunal Statute; and

Count 6: A VIOLATION OF ADDITIONAL PROTOCOL II, a violation of Article 4 (a) of the Tribunal Statute.

The Massacre at the Stadium in Kibuye Town

COUNTS 7 – 12

32.   By about 18 April 1994, thousands of men, women and children from various locations had sought refuge in the Stadium located in Kibuye town. These men, women and children were unarmed and were predominantly Tutsis. They were in **[page 9]** the Stadium seeking refuge from attacks on Tutsis which had occurred throughout the *Prefecture* of Kibuye.

33.   Some of the people who sought refuge in the Stadium did so because Clement Kayishema ordered them to go there. When Clement Kayishema ordered people to go to the Stadium, he knew or had reason to know that an attack on the Stadium was going to occur.

34.   After people gathered in the Stadium, the Stadium was surrounded by persons under Clement Kayishema's control, including members of the Gendarmerie Nationale. These persons prevented the men, women and children within the Stadium from leaving the Stadium at a time when Clement Kayishema knew or had reason to know that an attack on the Complex (sic) was going to occur.

35.   On or about 18 April 1994, Clement Kayishema, went to Stadium and ordered the Gendarmerie Nationale, the communal police of Gitesi Commune, the members of the Interahamwe and armed civilians to attack the Stadium. Clement Kayishema initiated the attack himself by firing a gun into the air. In addition, Clement Kayishema personally participated in the attack. The attackers used guns, grenades, pangas, machetes, spears, cudgels and other weapons to kill the people in the Stadium. There were survivors of the attack on 18 April 1994. During the night of 18 April 1994 and the morning of 19 April 1994 gendarmes surrounding the Stadium prevented the survivors from leaving. The attack on

the Stadium continued on 19 April 1994. Throughout the attacks, men, women and children attempting to flee the attacks were killed.

36. The two days of attacks resulted in thousands of deaths and numerous injuries to the men, women and children within the Stadium (Attachment B contains a list of some of the individuals killed in the attacks).

37. Before the attacks on the Stadium Clement Kayishema did not take measures to prevent an attack from occurring, and after the attacks Clement Kayishema did not punish the perpetrators.

38. By these acts and omissions Clement Kayishema is criminally responsible for:

Count 7: GENOCIDE, a violation of Article 2 (3) (a) of the Tribunal Statute;

Count 8: CRIMES AGAINST HUMANITY, a violation of Article 3 (a) (murder) of the Tribunal Statute;

Count 9: CRIMES AGAINST HUMANITY, a violation of Article 3 (b) (extermination) of the Tribunal Statute;

Count 10: CRIMES AGAINST HUMANITY, a violation of Article 3 (i) (other inhumane acts) of the Tribunal Statute; **[page 10]**

Count 11: A VIOLATION OF ARTICLE 3 COMMON TO THE GENEVA CONVENTIONS, a violation of Article 4 (a) of the Tribunal Statute; and

Count 12: A VIOLATION OF ADDITIONAL PROTOCOL II, a violation of Article 4 (a) of the Tribunal Statute.

The Massacre at the Church in Mubuga
COUNTS 13 – 18

39. By about 14 April 1994, thousands of men, women and children congregated in the Church in Mubuga, Gishyita Commune. These men, women and children were predominantly Tutsis. They were in the church seeking refuge from attacks on Tutsis which had occurred throughout the *Prefecture* of Kibuye.

40. After the men, women and children began to congregate in the Church, Clement Kayishema visited the Church on several occasions. On or about 10 April Clement Kayishema brought gendarmes, under his control, to the Church. These gendarmes prevented the men, women and children within the church from leaving.

41. On or about 14 April 1994 individuals, including individuals under Clement Kayishema's control, directed members of the Gendarme Nationale, communal police of Gishyita commune, the Interahamwe and armed civilians to attack the Church. In addition, each of them personally participated in the attacks. The attackers used guns, grenades, machetes, spears, pangas, cudgels and other weapons to kill the people in the Church. Not all the people could be killed at once, so the attacks continued for several days. Both before and during these attacks persons under Clement Kayishema's control, including members of the Gendarmerie Nationale and communal police, prevented the men, women and children within the church from leaving.

42. The attacks resulted in thousands of deaths and numerous injuries to the men, women and children within the Church (Attachment C contains a list of some of the victims killed in the attacks).

43. Before the attacks on the Church in Mubuga, Clement Kayishema did not take measures to prevent the attacks, and after the attacks Clement Kayishema did not punish the perpetrators.

44. By these acts and omissions Clement Kayishema is criminally responsible for:

Count 13: GENOCIDE, a violation of Article 2 (3) (a) of the Tribunal Statute; **[page 11]**

Count 14: CRIMES AGAINST HUMANITY, a violation of Article 3 (a) (murder) of the Tribunal Statute;

Count 15: CRIMES AGAINST HUMANITY, a violation of Article 3 (b) (extermination) of the Tribunal Statute;

Count 16: CRIMES AGAINST HUMANITY, a violation of Article 3 (i) (other inhumane acts) of the Tribunal Statute;

Count 17: A VIOLATION OF ARTICLE 3 COMMON TO THE GENEVA CONVENTIONS, a violation of Article 4 (a) of the Tribunal Statute; and

Count 18: A VIOLATION OF ADDITIONAL PROTOCOL II, a violation of Article 4 (a) of the Tribunal Statute.

The Massacres in the Area of Bisesero

COUNTS 19-24

45.   The area of Bisesero spans over two communes of the Kibuye *Prefecture*. From about 9 April 1994 through 30 June 1994, thousands of men, women and children sought refuge in the area of Bisesero. These men, women and children were predominantly Tutsis and were seeking refuge from attacks on Tutsis which had occurred throughout the *Prefecture* of Kibuye.

46.   The area of Bisesero was regularly attacked, on almost a daily basis, throughout the period of about 9 April 1994 through about 30 June 1994. The attackers used guns, grenades, machetes, spears, pangas, cudgels and other weapons to kill the Tutsis in Bisesero. At various times the men, women and children seeking refuge in Bisesero attempted to defend themselves from these attacks with stones, sticks and other crude weapons.

47.   At various locations and times throughout April, May and June 1994, and often in concert, Clement Kayishema and Obed Ruzindana brought to the area of Bisesero members of the Gendarmerie Nationale, communal police of Gishyita and Gisovu communes, Interahamwe and armed civilians, and directed them to attack the people seeking refuge there. In addition, at various locations and times, and often in concert, Clement Kayishema and Obed Ruzindana personally attacked and killed persons seeking refuge in Bisesero.

48.   The attacks described above resulted in thousands of deaths and numerous injuries to the men, women and children within the area of Bisesero (Attachment D contains a list of some of the individuals killed in the attacks). **[page 12]**

49.   Throughout this time, Clement Kayishema did not take measures to prevent the attacks, and after the attacks Clement Kayishema did not punish the perpetrators

50.   By these acts and omissions Clement Kayishema and Obed Ruzindana are criminally responsible for:

Count 19: GENOCIDE, a violation of Article 2 (3) (a) of the Tribunal Statute;

Count 20: CRIMES AGAINST HUMANITY, a violation of Articles 3(a) (murder) of the Tribunal Statute;

Count 21: CRIMES AGAINST HUMANITY, a violation of Article 3(b) (extermination) of the Tribunal Statute;

Count 22: CRIMES AGAINST HUMANITY, a violation of Article 3(1) (other inhumane acts) of the Tribunal Statute;

Count 23: A VIOLATION OF ARTICLE 3 COMMON TO THE GENEVA CONVENTIONS, a violation of Article 4 (a) of the Tribunal Statute; and

Count 24: A VIOLATION OF ADDITIONAL PROTOCOL II, a violation of Article 4 (a) of the Tribunal Statute.

1996
Arusha, Tanzania

Signed
Richard J. Goldstone
Prosecutor

This rearranged version conforms to the Order of Trial Chamber II in its decision of 10 April 1997 on the indictment of 28 November 1995 confirmed by the Honourable Judge Pillay and amended on 29 April 1996, to serve as the Indictment for the accused Clement Kayishema and Obed Ruzindana in the case ICTR 95-1-I. **[page 13]**

1.3   The Accused

Clement Kayishema

6.   According to Clement Kayishema's (Kayishema), own testimony, he was born into a Hutu family in the Bwishyura Sector, Kibuye *Prefecture* in Rwanda, in 1954. His father was a teacher and later worked as a janitor in a hospital. Subsequently, he was hired as the commune secretary and was finally appointed judge at the Canton Tribunal. His mother and seven siblings were uneducated farmers.

7.   In 1974, Kayishema was appointed registrar in Kagnagare Canton Tribunal. The following year he was granted a scholarship to attend the faculty of medicine of the National University of Rwanda, in Butare. Upon graduation, he practiced general medicine and surgery. In 1984, he was sent by the Rwandan Government to work as a doctor in an Ugandan refugee camp. From 1986 to 1991, he held the position of medical director of the hospital of Nyanza. He was then transferred to the Kibuye hospital.

8.   Kayishema married a Rwandan woman by the name of Mukandoli, in 1987 with whom he had two children. Mukandoli holds a degree in education science from the National University of Rwanda, with a specialization in psychology.

9.   Kayishema joined the Christian Democratic Party (PDC), whose motto was "work, justice and fraternity," in April 1992. On 3 July 1992, Kayishema was appointed the *Prefect* of Kibuye *Prefecture*. This occurred at a time when the multiparty system came into effect in Rwanda. He was re-appointed to his post, after the death of the President in 1994, by the Interim Government.

Obed Ruzindana

10.   According to the testimony of witnesses; Obed Ruzindana (Ruzindana) was born in 1962 into a wealthy Hutu family in Gisovu Commune, Kibuye *Prefecture*, Rwanda. His father, Elie Murakaza, had been a *Bourgmestre* in the Mugonero Commune, where **[page 14]** the family resided. Murakaza and, by extension, his family were well known and respected in the community.

11.   Ruzindana left his home in Kibuye for Kigali in 1986-1987 and engaged in transporting merchandise out of Rwanda and importing goods into the country. He employed four drivers and by all accounts became a successful businessman in his own right.

12.   In 1991 he married a woman whom he had known since childhood. Mrs. Ruzindana testified that although both her parents were Tutsi, her father's identity card indicated that he was a Hutu. According to Mrs. Ruzindana it was possible to "pay" to change one's ethnicity on the identity card. Two children were born from this union in 1991 and 1993. Ruzindana and his family lived in Remera, Kigali until the tragic events of 1994 when they returned to Ruzindana's parents' home in Mugonero. **[page 15]**

1.4   Procedural Background of the Case

Pre-trial

13.   Kayishema and Ruzindana were initially charged in the original Indictment submitted by the Prosecutor, Richard Goldstone,[4] on 22 November 1995 together with six other suspects. The charges included conspiracy to commit genocide, Genocide and Crimes Against Humanity and violations of Common Article 3 and Additional Protocol II. The Indictment was confirmed by Judge Navanethem Pillay on 28 November 1995. Judge Pillay ordered that the Indictment be amended on 6 May 1996 to remove the conspiracy charges. It should be noted that a second Indictment was brought against Ruzindana on 17 June 1996, the trial of which is still pending. That Indictment was confirmed by Judge Tafazzal H. Khan on 21 June 1996.

14.   Kayishema was arrested on 2 May 1996 in Zambia and transferred to the United Nations Detention Unit Facility (the UNDF) in Arusha, on 26 May 1996. His initial appearance was held on 31 May 1996 before Trial Chamber I. Kayishema, represented by Mr. Andre Ferran, of the bar of Montpellier, France, and Philippe Moriceau of the bar of Montpellier, France, pleaded not guilty to all of the charges.

15.   Ruzindana was arrested on 20 September 1996 in Nairobi, Kenya and transferred to the UNDF on 22 September 1996. His initial appearance was held on 29 October 1996 before the Trial Chamber II. Ruzindana, represented by Mr. Pascal Besnier, of the bar of Paris, France, and Mr. Willem Van der Griend of the Bar of Rotterdam, the Netherlands, pleaded not guilty to all of the charges. The Chamber set a date for trial for 20 February 1997 while reserving the right to join with Kayishema.

16.   At the pretrial stage, the Trial Chamber received and decided many written motions from the Parties. Some of the more pertinent ones are detailed below. **[page 16]**

17.   Kayishema filed a preliminary Motion on 26 July 1996 in which he requested the annulment of the proceedings, and consequently, his provisional release. The Parties were heard on 5 November 1996 and the Defence request was rejected. Kayishema filed a further Motion on 23 October 1996 for postponement of the trial in order to enable him to prepare his case. The Prosecutor did not oppose the Motion but on 5 November 1996, filed a Motion for joinder of Kayishema and Ruzindana. The Tribunal ordered the joinder of the two accused. The trial date for Kayishema consequently was postponed to the trial date set for Ruzindana, which as mentioned above was 20 February 1997.[5]

18.   On 30 December 1996 Ruzindana filed a preliminary Motion objecting to the form of the Indictment and against joinder of his case with that of Kayishema based on various alleged procedural difficulties with the Indictment and the warrant of arrest. The request for annulment of the two Indictments and for his release was rejected as was the objection to the joinder.

19.   On 27 March 1997, the Prosecution brought a Motion for leave to sever and to join in a superseding Indictment and to amend the superseding Indictment in the cases against Kayishema, Gérard Ntakirutimana, and Ruzindana on the grounds of involvement in a same transaction. The Chamber rejected the Motion because the Prosecutor did not offer any evidence that demonstrated the nature of the common scheme.

20.   Kayishema brought another Motion on 7 March 1997 calling for the application of Article 20(2) and (4)(b) (Rights of the accused) of the Statute of the Tribunal by the Prosecution. The Defence further requested the Prosecution to divulge and limit its number of lawyers, consultants, assistants and investigators working on the case. The Chamber ruled[6] that the rights of the accused and equality between the parties should not be confused with the equality of means and resources. The Chamber

---

4   On 1 October 1996, Louise Arbour succeeded Richard Goldstone as Prosecutor of the Tribunal.

5   Decision on the joinder of the Accused and Setting the Date for Trial, the Prosecutor v. Clément Kayishema, Case No. ICTR-95-1-T, 6 November 1996.

6   Order on the Motion by the Defence Counsel for Application of Article 20 (2) and (4) (b) of the Statute of the International Tribunal for Rwanda, the Prosecutor v. Clément Kayishema, Case No. ICTR-95-1-T, Obed Ruzindana, Case No. ICTR-96-10-T; 5 May 1997.

concluded that the **[page 17]** Defence had not proved any violation of the rights of the accused as provided in Article 20(2) and (4)(b) of the Statute.

Trial

21.   On 11 April 1997 the trial of Kayishema and Ruzindana commenced before Trial Chamber II, composed of Judge William H. Sekule, presiding, Judge Yakov A. Ostrovsky and Judge Tafazzal H. Khan, based on the First Amended Indictment filed with the Registry on that day. The Prosecution team consisted of Mr. Jonah Rahetlah, Ms. Brenda Sue Thornton, and Ms. Holo Makwaia. Kayishema was represented by Mr. Andre Ferran and Mr. Philippe Moriceau. Mr. Pascal Besnier and Mr. Van der Griend formed the Defence team for Ruzindana. The Prosecution completed its. case on 13 March 1998, having called a total of 51 witnesses and having tendered into evidence over 350 exhibits.

22.   The Prosecution filed a Motion on 18 February 1998, pursuant to Rule 73 of the Rules, requesting the Trial Chamber to order the uninterrupted continuation of the trial of the accused and the consultation of both Parties in respect of the scheduling of this continuation. The Chamber was of the view that pursuant to Article 20(4)(b) of the Statute, the accused should be accorded adequate time and facilities for the preparation of their case.[7]

23.   The Defence commenced their case on 11 May 1998 and closed on 15 September 1998. It should be noted that at the conclusion of the Prosecution's case, the Defence requested an adjournment in order to prepare its case. In the interest of justice, the Trial Chamber granted the Defence Teams a generous two-month adjournment to prepare. The Defence presented a total of twenty-eight witnesses, sixteen of whom testified on behalf of accused, Ruzindana, seven for Kayishema and five for both accused persons. Kayishema testified on his own behalf. Over 59 Defence exhibits were admitted. **[page 18]**

24.   The Prosecutor presented closing argument from 21 October to 28 October 1998, Ruzindana's Defence from 28 October to 2 November 1998 and Kayishema's Defence from 3 to 16 November 1998. The Prosecutor presented the argument in rebuttal on 17 November 1998. The case was adjourned the same day for deliberation by the Trial Chamber.

25.   During the trial, numerous written and oral motions were heard. On 17 April 1997, the Defence challenged the credibility of a witness, where the oral testimony varied from the previous written statement taken by the prosecutor's investigators. The Chamber opined that variation may occur at times for appreciable reasons without giving cause to disregard the statement in whole or in part.[8] The Chamber ordered that when counsel perceives there to be a contradiction between the written and oral statement of a witness, Counsel should raise such question by putting to the witness the exact portion in issue to enable the witness to explain the discrepancy before the Tribunal. Counsels should then mark the relevant portion and submit it as an exhibit if they find that the contradiction or discrepancy raised was material to the credibility of the witness concerned.

26.   On 9 July 1997, Ruzindana filed a Motion pursuant to Rule 75 of the Rules seeking protective measures for potential witnesses noting that this protection should not extend to providing immunity from prosecution by an appropriate authority. The Trial Chamber[9] granted the Motion. A Motion filed by Kayishema seeking general **[page 19]** protective measures for witnesses who would testify on his behalf was also granted by the Chamber in its Decision on 23 March 1998.[10]

---

[7]   ecision on the Prosecution Motion for Directions for the Scheduling of the Continuation of the Trial of Clément Kayishema and Obed Ruzindana on the Charges as Contained in the Indictment No. ICTR-95-1-T, 12 March 1998.

[8]   Order on the Probative Value of Alleged Contradiction between the Oral and Written Statement of A Witness During Examination, the Prosecutor v. Clément Kayishema and Obed Ruzindana, Case No. ICTR95-I-T, 17 April 1997.

[9]   Decision on the Motion for the Protection of Defence Witnesses, the Prosecutor v. Clement Kayishema and Obed Ruzindana, Case No. ICTR-95-1-T, 6 October 1997.

[10]   Decision on the Motion for the Protection of Defence Witnesses, the Prosecutor v. Clément Kayishema and Obed Ruzindana, Case No. ICTR-95-1-T, 23 February 1998.

27.   On 12 March 1998 the Prosecutor filed a Motion requesting the Trial Chamber to order the Defence to comply with the provisions of rules 67(A)(ii) and 67(C) of the Rules of Procedure and Evidence. The Prosecutor submitted that if the Defence intended to offer the defence of alibi, it should notify the Prosecution as early as practicable but in any event prior to the commencement of the trial. The Chamber opined that Kayishema should make the necessary disclosure immediately if they intend to rely upon the defence of alibi or special defence. However, the Defence filed a joint Motion on 30 April 1998 requesting the Trial Chamber to interpret the notion of "defence of alibi" and "special defence" as stipulated in Rule 67 of the Rules of Procedure and Evidence. The Chamber dismissed the Defence Motion on the ground that it can not define rule 67 of the Rules in an abstract form without a specific problem to address.[11]

28.   Due to the Defence's continued non compliance with Rule 67(A)(ii) of the Rule of Procedure and Evidence, the Prosecution filed another Motion on 11 August 1998, seeking, *inter alia*, an order prohibiting the Defence of Kayishema from invoking the Defence of alibi or any special Defence. The Defence responded that, under Rule 67(B), failure of the Defence to notify the Prosecutor of the Defence of alibi or any special Defence as required by rule 67(A)(ii), does not limit the right of the accused to raise the Defence of alibi or special Defence. The Trial rejected the Defence's reasons for not providing details noting that the accused himself could have provided at least some details. The Chamber therefore reiterated its previous decision on this matter.[12] **[page 20]**

29.   On 22 June 1998, the Prosecution filed a Motion, seeking for a ruling that evidence of a Defence expert witness, a psychiatrist, be ruled inadmissible. The Chamber noted that it is important to observe the rights of the accused to a fair trial guaranteed under the provisions of Article 20 of the Statute in particular 20(4)(e) which provides that the accused shall have the rights to obtain the attendance of witnesses on his or her behalf. The expert was heard.[13]

30.   On 19 August 1998, the Chamber dismissed a Motion filed by the Defence requesting to re-examine witness DE. The Trial Chamber found that the case of Kayishema would not suffer prejudice in the absence of additional evidence from this witness and rejected the Motion.[14] **[page 21]**

II.   Historical Context of the 1994 Events in Rwanda

31.   It is necessary to address the historical context within which the events unfolded in Rwanda in 1994, in order to understand fully the events alleged in the Indictment and the evidence before the Trial Chamber. We will not engage in a lengthy examination of the geo-political or historical difficulties faced by Rwanda as a number of reports and other publications have been written on these issues to which interested persons can refer.

32.   The Trial Chamber is of the opinion that an attempt to explain the causal links between the history of Rwanda and the suffering endured by this nation in 1994 is not appropriate in this forum and may be futile. It is impossible to simplify all the ingredients that serve as a basis for killings on such a scale. Therefore, the account presented below is a brief explanation of issues related to the division of ethnic groups in Rwanda, a brief history of Rwanda's post-independence era, including a look at the 1991 Constitution, the Arusha Accords, and the creation of militias.

33.   The Trial Chamber has chosen to relay the events using neutral language and, where necessary, to discuss the cross-examination of the Prosecution witnesses. The summary is based exclusively on the

---

[11]   Decision on the Prosecution Motion for An Order Requesting Compliance by the Defence with Rules 67 (A)(ii) and 67(C) of the Rules, the Prosecutor v. Clément Kayishema and Obed Ruzindana, 15 June 1998.

[12]   Decision on the Prosecution Motion for A Ruling on the Defence Continued non Compliance with Rule 67 (A) (ii) and with the Written and Oral Orders of the Trial Chamber, the prosecutor v. Clément Kayishema and Obed Ruzindana, Case No. ICTR-95-1-T, 3 September 1998.

[13]   Decision on the Prosecution Motion Request to Rule Inadmissible the Evidence of Defence Expert Witness, Dr. Pouget, the Prosecutor v. Clément Kayishema and Obed Ruzindana, Case No. ICTR-95-1-T. 29 June 1998.

[14]   Decision on the Defence Motion for the Re-examination of Defence Witness DE, the Prosecutor v. Clément Kayishema and Obed Ruzindana, Case No. ICTR-95-1-T, 19 August 1998.

evidence presented to this Trial Chamber and no reference has been made to sources or materials that do not constitute a part of the record of the present case.

The Question of Ethnicity in Rwanda

34.   In 1994, apart from some foreign nationals, there were three officially recognised ethnic groups living in Rwanda, the Hutus, the Tutsis and the Twas. The Hutus constituted the overwhelming majority of the population. The Rwandan use of the term "ethnicity" requires some explanation because according to Prosecution witness, André Guichaoua, Professor of Sociology and Economics at the University of Lille, France, all Rwandans share the same national territory, speak the same language, believe in the same myths and share the same cultural traditions. The Trial Chamber opines that these shared [page 22] characteristics could be tantamount to a common ethnicity. Thus, it is recognised that prior to the colonisation of Rwanda, by Germany and later Belgium, the line separating the Hutus and Tutsis was permeable as the distinction was class-based. In other words, if a Hutu could acquire sufficient wealth, he would be considered a Tutsi.

35.   This begs the question-of how it became possible permanently to seal a person into one category after the Belgian colonisation. The Belgians instituted a system of national identification cards bearing the terms Hutu, Tutsi and Twa, under the category of ethnicity, which were used for administrative purposes in 1931. Although prior to the arrival of the European colonisers the Rwandans had referred to themselves as Hutus, Tutsis or Twas, it was after this point that the group identity solidified and this former sociological categorisation became a means of ethnic identification. From its inception, the identification card has been used to facilitate discrimination against one group or another in Rwanda, be it in the implementation of an ethnic based quota system in educational and employment opportunities or in implementing a policy of genocide as was done in 1994.

36.   For decades some claimed that Hutus and Twas were the original inhabitants of Rwanda and that Tutsis were "people from the Nile."[15] During cross-examination Guichaoua deposed that this idea has never been proven scientifically and that no one "category of occupants has more legitimacy than others."[16] Nonetheless, certain Hutu politicians have periodically used this concept to legitimise their call for "Hutu Power" and to incite hatred and division amongst the Rwandan population, as outlined below.

A Brief Glance at the Post-Independence Era

37.   In 1959, shortly prior to gaining independence, Rwanda witnessed the beginnings of intense ethnic tensions. During that year a number of Tutsi chiefs, farmers and other persons were massacred and their houses were set ablaze. Thousands of other Tutsis were forced to flee to neighbouring countries. Guichaoua stated that the deterioration of [page 23] ethnic relations could be attributed to the legacy of Tutsi favouritism by the colonial powers.

The First Republic

38. The country's first President, Gregoire Kayibanda, was elected in 1962 at which time the Hutu movements began to display their radicalisation more openly. Professor Guichaoua testified that anti-Tutsi movements had become so hostile that by 1963, 200,000 to 300,000 Tutsis sought refuge in neighbouring countries. Between 1962 and 1966 there were repeated attempts by armed Tutsi groups (labelled *Inyenzi* – cockroach) to regain power through incursions organised from neighbouring countries, mainly from Burundi. According to Professor Guichaoua, because an incursion in December 1963 reached the gates of Kigali, a hunt for Tutsis ensued throughout the country thereafter. The worsening tensions led to the consolidation of power by "the radical Hutu elements and helped to

---

[15]   Pros. exh. 103A, p. 8.
[16]   *Ibid.*

suppress the deep divisions within the regime in power which was increasingly marked by the personal and authoritarian style of government of President Kayibanda."[17]

39. President Kayibanda's attempt to maintain his hold on power is evident from the institution of a *de facto* single-party system in Rwanda in 1965. His party, the Republican Democratic Movement (MDR-PARMEHUTU) eliminated the Tutsi parties as well as other Hutu parties such as the Association for the Social Advancement of the Masses (APROSOMA). Factional political divisions, based on regions of origin from within the country, added further strain on the ethnic-base difficulties at that time. A new sense of supremacy, based on the existence of a legitimate majority population was fostered and contributed to the massacres of the Tutsis that occurred in Rwanda and Burundi in 1972-73. Thus, the inability of the First Republic to overcome ethnic tensions lead to its downfall and the assassination of President Kayibanda. **[page 24]**

The Second Republic

40. On 5 July 1973, the Chief of Staff, Major Juvenal Habyarimana, a native of Gisenyi *Prefecture*, seized power in a *coup d'etat*. His then Chief of Security, Alexis Kanyarengwe "implemented a strategy of political and ethnic tension, aimed at making the *coup d'etat*" seem necessary for restoring order to the country. Although the 1973 coup was interpreted as "simply settling scores between rival factions"[18] and having nothing to do with ethnic tensions, those in power encouraged the Hutus to chase away their Tutsi friends and colleagues from educational establishments and places of employment. Again, like in 1959, many Tutsis died at the hands of Hutu assailants and thousands of others fled the country. This brought about the advent of Rwanda's Second Republic.

41. Two years later, in 1975, the National Revolutionary Movement for Development (MRND) was created to replace the MDR. At its helm was President Habyarimana. This party controlled the country until the time of the tragic events in 1994. In 1978, President Habyarimana declared that the Hutu-Tutsi problem would be solved by ensuring that all Rwandans, from birth, were members of the MRND. Compulsory and exclusive membership in this party effectively erased any distinction between the party and the State. Habyarimana also promised that all segments of society would be ensured representation in high ranking government posts, taking into account its percentage in the total population. Of course this idea inherently contained a quota system that would further frustrate the efforts in reconciling ethnic difficulties.

42. For the next few years the Habyarimana government focused its efforts on issues of development. According to Professor Guichaoua, throughout the late 1970s and a part of the 1980s this government's efforts met with undeniable success in terms of low national debt, maintaining macroeconomic balances, monetary stability, food self-sufficiency, etc. Also during this time, the government re-introduced the system of *umuganda* — the Rwandan concept of communal work — meant to promote the value of organised or **[page 25]** spontaneous solidarity (mutual help among neighbours) among the people living in the hills.[19] Additionally, "the social cohesion of this peasant state and the submission of the peasantry to an extremely authoritarian and constraining order was due largely to a policy which succeeded in establishing a weakly differentiated social system."[20] Thus the misplaced belief and confidence the Rwandans had in their leadership, that existed during the colonial era, was put to use once again in 1994.

43. Despite this economic success and the government's ability to bring its citizens together to engage in community work, the largely agrarian population of Rwanda did not benefit. Rwandans began to protest the inequities, noticing the nepotism and widespread corruption in the government. The quota system mentioned above was another source of difficulties for the population. As gross social

---

[17] Pros. exh. 103A, p. 12.
[18] Ibid., p. 15. Professor Guichaoua cited to a proclamation following the coup by commander Theoneste Lizinde, which made no reference to the ethnic confrontations.
[19] *Ibid.*, p. 16.
[20] *Ibid.*, p. 18.

inequalities persisted and with other economic problems and food shortages that arose in 1988-89, the time was ripe for Tutsis outside the country to attempt to regain power once more.

44. On a number of occasions members of the Tutsi diaspora had attempted to return to Rwanda, only to be stopped at the boarder by claims that the small country could not absorb the returnees. For example, in 1982, when Uganda expelled various categories of refugees, Rwanda responded by closing its borders, refusing assistance to the thousands in need and only later allowing a small fraction of the Tutsi refugees to enter and resettle. Following these incidents, the thousands of Rwandans that remained in the neighbouring countries of Burundi, Tanzania, Uganda and Zaire began to pressure the world community and these governments to find a solution to their plight.

45. The Rwandan Patriotic Front (the RPF) was created as a response to the Tutsi Diaspora's frustration with the international community's minimal attention to the emotionally charged refugee problem. In October 1990, the RPF launched an attack into northeastern Rwanda from Uganda. This attack was supported by, *inter alia*, the majority of Tutsis living abroad and brought an intense period of diplomatic negotiations which **[page 26]** produced some noticeable results. For instance, by November 1990, the system of ethnic based scholastic and professional quotas was officially abolished and in December the Rwandan government declared an amnesty for certain prisoners. By March 1991 a cease-fire was called. Certain elements of the then Rwandan government however, were not eager to begin the process and therefore ensured that some of the more significant promises made were not implemented with due haste. Additionally, the extreme violence targeting the Tutsi population, especially in rural areas, continued unabated. Therefore, the RPF continued its strategy of a protracted war. Nevertheless, attempts were made at a democratic transition between 1991 and 1993.

The 1991 Constitution and Multi-Partism

46. Francois Nsanzuwera, a Rwandan scholar, testified that the 1991 Rwandan Constitution replaced the single party system with a multiparty system. It entrusted the National Assembly and the President of the Republic with legislative and executive power, respectively. The Constitution however did not render the President of the Republic accountable to the National Assembly.

47. The officially recognised parties were forbidden to use paramilitary forces (Article 26) and were granted access to the official media. Thereafter, the following parties were created: the *Mouvement Democratique République* (MDR), the *Parti Libéral* (PL), the *Parti Social-democrats* (PSD), the *Parti Democrate-chrétien* (PDC) and the *Coalition pour la Défense de la République* (CDR).

48. With the advent of multi-party politics, a very distinctive constitutional and administrative *status quo* would have purportedly manifested itself in Rwanda. This was the view of Professor Guibal, a titular Professor of constitutional and administrative law, Montpellier University, France. He was commissioned by the Defence to produce a report on the constitutional landscape of Rwanda, based upon the laws promulgated and in effect during and prior to the events of 1994.[21] **[page 27]**

49. It was Professor Guibal's opinion that as a result of the multi-partyism that emerged after the 1991 Constitution, the traditional delineation of the branches of Government was not discernible. Thus, there was no clear separation of powers between the executive, judiciary and central and regional administration. Rather, the witness testified, the constitutional framework that existed after 1991 was one that was delineated on a party-political basis also. Consequently, a dichotomy of hierarchies and relationships would have emerged throughout, and even transcended the branches of Government – one on an administrative level and one on a party political basis.

50. Professor Guibal then went on to describe the theoretical consequence of the system that existed in Rwanda, when faced with the events and turmoil of 1994. He was of the opinion that such a paradigm of multi-partyism, when confronted with these chaotic and unstable times, would have become a system of *crisis* multi-partyism. The Chamber was informed that such crisis multi-partyism would arise as pivotal

---

[21] What follows is a synopsis of this report and Professor Guibal's testimony on 27 and 28 May 1998.

governmental figures were moved to resolve the turmoil and conflicts upon partypolitical lines, rather than by the delineated constitutional means.

The Arusha Accords

51. Nsanzuwera testified that the Rwandan government and the RPF signed the Arusha Accords on 4 August 1993 in Arusha, Tanzania in order to bring about a peaceful settlement to the political and military crisis in Rwanda. The Accords constituted a compilation of several agreements and protocols previously signed, concerning notably cease-fire and power sharing between the warring factions. 47 articles of the 1991 Constitution were replaced by the provisions of the Arusha Accords, including articles on power sharing and the entrusting of additional power to the Prime Minister and certain organs of the government.

The Creation of Militias

52. While the negotiations for peace and power sharing were underway in Arusha, the MRND and the CDR stepped up their efforts to recruit members, especially from the **[page 28]** youth segment of the population. Both the MRND and the CDR, two Hutu based parties, intensified their efforts to fortify membership in their youth organisations known as the *Interahamwe* and the *Impuzamugambi*, respectively. Within a short period of time these recruits were converted to paramilitary forces. The parties ensured that the young recruits, made up mostly of former soldiers, gendarmes and prisoners, were militarily trained and indoctrinated. All these activities were carried out in direct violation of Article 26 of the 1991 Constitution and with the knowledge of the then Minister of Internal Affairs who was entrusted with the duty to suspend the activities of any political party for such activities.

53. By the end of 1993 CDR speeches, broadcast from government owned radio stations, referred to the Tutsis and Hutus from the opposition parties as collaborators of the RPF. These speeches encouraged the militias to target Tutsis in their daily acts of vandalism. Between 1992 and 1994 there were claims that the militias were supported by certain member of the military and the Presidential Guard. During this period many members of the judiciary were said to have turned a blind eye to the criminal acts of the militias either because they supported their activities or out of fear of reprisals. Assassination attempts, some of which were successful, were made on the lives of certain judges or magistrates who sought to carry out their duties faithfully. According to Nsanzuwera, by that time some claimed that members of the militias had become more powerful than members of the armed forces. As indicated in the parts that follow, the militias did in fact play a substantial role in the 1994 Genocide that occurred in this country.

Conclusion

54. The ethnic tensions were used by those in power in 1994 to carry out their plans to avoid power sharing. The responsible parties ignored the Arusha Accords and used the militias to carry out their genocidal plan and to incite the rest of the Hutu population into believing that all Tutsis and other persons who may not have supported the war against the RPF were in fact RPF supporters. It is against this backdrop that of thousands of people were slaughtered and mutilated in just three short months. **[page 29]**

III. EVIDENTIARY MATTERS

3.1 Equality of Arms

55. The notion of equality of arms is laid down in Article 20 of the Statute. Specifically, Article 20(2) states, ". . . the accused shall be entitled to a fair and public hearing . . . ." Article 20(4) also provides, ". . . the accused shall be entitled to the following minimum guarantees, in full equality. . . ," there then

follows a list of rights that must be respected, including the right to a legal counsel and the right to have adequate time and facilities to prepare his or her defence.

56.   Counsel for Kayishema filed a Motion, on 13 March 1997, calling for the application of Rule 20(2) and 20(4).[22] The Defence submitted that in order to conduct a fair trial, full equality should exist between the Prosecution and the Defence in terms of the means and facilities placed at their disposal. To this end, the Defence requested the Chamber to order the disclosure of the number of lawyers, consultants, assistants and investigators that had been at the disposal of the Prosecution since the beginning of the case. The Motion also requested the Chamber to order the Prosecutor to indicate the amount of time spent on the case and the various expenditures made. Finally, the Motion called upon the Chamber to restrict the number of assistants utilised by the Prosecution during trial to the same number as those authorised for the Defence.

57.   On the first two points raised by the Defence (request for information on the Prosecutor's resources), the Prosecution submitted that the information requested by Defence was not public and was intrinsically linked to the exercise of the Prosecutor's mandate, in accordance with Article 15 of the Statute.[23] **[page 30]**

58.   On the third point (request to limit the number of assistants to the Prosecutor), the Prosecution submitted that Article 20 of the Statute, establishes an equality of *rights*, rather than an equality of *means and resources*.

59.   The Chamber considered that the Defence did not prove any violation of the rights of the accused as laid down in Article 20(2) and 20(4).[24] The Chamber considered that the Defence should have addressed these issues under Article 17(C) of the Directive on Assignment of Defence Counsel (Defence Counsel Directive). This provision clearly states

> the costs and expenses of legal representation of the suspect or accused necessarily and reasonably incurred shall be covered by the Tribunal *to the extent that such expenses cannot be borne by the suspect or the accused because of his financial situation.* [emphasis added]

60.   This provision should be read in conjunction with Article 20(4)(d) of the Statute which stipulates that legal assistance shall be provided by the Tribunal, ". . . *if* he or she does not have sufficient means to pay for it." [emphasis added]. Therefore, at this juncture, the Trial Chamber would reiterate its earlier ruling on this Motion that the rights of the accused should not be interpreted to mean that the Defence is entitled to same means and resources as the Prosecution. Any other position would be contrary to the *status quo* that exists within jurisdictions throughout the world and would clearly not reflect the intentions of the drafters of this Tribunal's Statute.

61.   The question of equality of arms was verbally raised on other occasions. The Defence Counsel complained, for example, of the impossibility to verify the technical and material data about Kibuye *Prefecture* submitted by the Prosecution.[25] However, the Trial Chamber is aware that investigators, paid for by the Tribunal, was put at the disposal of the Defence. Furthermore, Article 17(C) establishes that any expenses incurred in the preparation of the Defence case relating, *inter alia*, to investigative costs are to be met by the Tribunal. The Trial Chamber is satisfied that all of the necessary **[page 31]** provisions for the preparation of a comprehensive defence were available, and were afforded to all Defence Counsel in this case. The utilisation of those resources is not a matter for the Trial Chamber.

---

[22]   Motion by the Defence Counsel for Kayishema Calling for the Application by the Prosecutor of Article 20(2) and 20(4)(b) of the Statute. Filed with the Registry, 13 March 1997. The issue was raised again by Mr. Ferran in his closing arguments, Trans., 3 Nov 1998, from p. 30.

[23]   The Prosecution's response to the Motion was filed with the Registry on 29 April 1997 and additional information was filed on 5 May 1997.

[24]   Order on the Motion by the Defence Counsel for Application of Article 20(2) and (4)(b) of the Statute, 5 May 1997.

[25]   Defence Closing Brief for Kayishema, 16 Oct. 1998, p. 3.

62.   Counsel for Kayishema also raised the issue of lack of time afforded to the Defence for the preparation of its case.[26] In this regard the Trial Chamber notes that Kayishema made his initial appearance before the Tribunal on 31 May 1996, Counsel having been assigned two days prior. The trial began on 11 April 1997 and the Defence did not commence its case until 11 May 1998, almost two years after the accused's initial appearance. As such, the Trial Chamber is satisfied that sufficient time was accorded to both Parties for the preparation of their respective cases.

63.   Specifically, on the time designated for the preparation of the closing arguments, the Defence expressed further dissatisfaction.[27] Having expressed his opinion that "the trial has been fair," Counsel for Kayishema however went on to submit that the eight days allowed him to prepare for his closing arguments was inequitable. in light of the one month time frame afforded to the Prosecution. However, the Chamber pronounced itself on this issue from the bench when it was declared,

> . . . for the record, I think the parties . . . agreed that the presentation of oral argument and filing of the relevant documents will be done within a time frame. . . So the concept of either one party being given one month does not arise . . [I]t was discussed openly with the understanding that each and every respective party had some work to do . . . That is the defence could prepare its own case . . . right from the word go . . . (President of the Chamber)[28]

64.   Moreover, were any particular issues of dispute or dissatisfaction to have arisen, the Trial Chamber should have been seized of these concerns in the appropriate manner and at the appropriate time. A cursory reference in the closing brief, and a desultory **[page 32]** allusion in Counsel's closing remarks is not an acceptable mode of raising the issue before the Chamber.

3.2   Reliability of Eyewitnesses

65.   Unlike the leaders of Nazi Germany, who meticulously documented their acts during World War II, the organisers and perpetrators of the massacres that occurred in Rwanda in 1994 left little documentation behind. Thus, both Parties relied predominantly upon the testimony of witnesses brought before this Chamber in order to establish their respective cases.

66.   A majority of the Prosecution witnesses were Tutsis who had survived attacks in Kibuye *Prefecture* (survivor witnesses), in which both accused allegedly participated. As such the Defence presented Dr. Régis Pouget to address the Trial Chamber on the credibility of eyewitness testimonies generally and, more specifically, upon the reliability of testimony from persons who had survived attacks having witnessed violent acts committed against their families, friends and neighbours.[29]

67.   The Prosecution contested the submission of the report, submitting that it was unnecessary and without probative value.[30] Nevertheless, the Trial Chamber, in exercising its discretion on this issue, received the report and heard the testimony of Dr. Pouget between 29 June and 2 July 1998.

Eyewitness Testimonies Generally

68.   The issue of identification is particularly pertinent in light of the defence of alibi advanced by the accused. The report prepared by Dr. Pouget and submitted on behalf of the Defence suggests that eyewitnesses often are not a reliable source of information. **[page 33]**

---

26   *Ibid.*, p. 2-3.

27   See Mr. Ferran's closing arguments, Trans., 3 Nov. 1998, pp. 54-55.

28   Trans., 3 Nov. 1998, pp. 55-56.

29   Def. exh. 59, Report on the Crowd Psychology. Dr. Pouget has been, *inter alia*, Professor of Psychiatry and Psychology, Director of Education, Montpellier University, France; and the appointed expert in psychology for Nimes and Montepellier Courts of Appeal, France.

30   Motion by the Prosecutor that Evidence of a Defence Expert Witness, Dr. Pouget, be Ruled Inadmissible Pursuant to Article l9(1) of the Statute and Rules 54 and 89 of the Rules.

69.   In order to support such a conclusion, Dr. Pouget proffered a number of reasons. It was his opinion, for example, that people do not pay attention to what they see yet, when uncertain about the answer to a question, they often give a definite answer nonetheless. He went on to describe various other, common-place factors that may affect the reliability of witness testimony generally. He observed, inter *alia*, that the passage of time often reduces the accuracy of recollection, and how this recollection may then be influenced either by the individual's own imperfect mental process of reconstructing past events, or by other external factors such as media reports or numerous conversations about the events.

70.   The Chamber does not consider that such general observations are in dispute. Equally, the Chamber concurs with Dr. Pouget's assertion that the corroboration of events, even by many witnesses, does not necessarily make the event and/or its details correct. However, the Trial Chamber is equally cognisant that, notwithstanding the foregoing analysis, all eyewitness testimony cannot be simply disregarded out-of-hand on, the premise that it *may* not be an exact recollection. Accordingly, it is for the Trial Chamber to decide upon the reliability of the witness testimony in light of its presentation in court and after its subjection to cross-examination. Thus, whilst corroboration of such testimony is not a guarantee of its accuracy, it is a factor that the Trial Chamber has taken into account when considering the testimonies.

71.   Similarly, prior knowledge of those identified is another factor that the Trial Chamber may take into account in considering the reliability of witness testimonies. For example, in the Tanzanian case of *Waziri Amani v. Republic*[31] the accused called into question his identification by witnesses. The Court of Appeals held that,

> if at the end of his (the witness') examination the judge is satisfied that the quality of identification is good, for example, when the identification was made by a witness after a long period of observation or in satisfactory conditions by a relative, a neighbour, a close friend, a workmate and the like, we think, he could in those circumstances safely convict on the evidence of identification. **[page 34]**

The case of *United States v. Telafaire*[32] also offers persuasive guidance on the other factors which may be taken into account. Firstly, the court in *Telafaire* held that the trier of fact must be convinced that the witness had the capacity and an adequate opportunity to observe the offender. Secondly, the identification of the accused by the witness should be the product of his own recollection and, thirdly, the trier of fact should take into consideration any inconsistency in the witness's identification of the accused at trial. Finally, it was held that the general credibility of the witness – his truthfulness and opportunity to make reliable observations – should also be borne in mind by the trier of fact.

72.   The Trial Chamber, in its examination of the evidence, has been alive to these various approaches and, where appropriate, has specifically delineated the salient considerations pertinent to its findings.

Survivors as Witnesses

73.   The report of Dr. Pouget, an expert in the field of psychology, address the reliability of testimony from those who, have witnessed traumatic events. It was his opinion that strong emotions experienced at the time of the events have a negative effect upon the quality of recollection. During traumatic events, he expounded, the natural defensive system either prevents the retention of those incidents or buries their memories so deep that they are not easily, if at all, accessible.

74.   This is the view of the expert Defence witness. However, as the Prosecutor highlighted, other views do exist. She produced, for example, other academic views which stated that stressful conditions

---

[31]   1980 TLR 250, 252.
[32]   469 F.2d 552 (D.C. Cir. 1972).

lead to an especially vivid and detailed recollection of events.[33] What is apparent to the Trial Chamber is that different witnesses, like different academics, think differently. **[page 35]**

75. The Chamber is aware of the impact of trauma on the testimony of witnesses. However, the testimonies cannot be simply disregarded because they describe traumatic and horrific realities. Some inconsistencies and imprecision in the testimonies are expected and were carefully considered in light of the circumstances faced by the witnesses. **[page 36]**

3.3. Witness Statements

76. The Parties raised apparent discrepancies or omissions that arose with regard to certain evidence when the witnesses' written statements were juxtaposed with their testimony given orally in Court. These written statements were drafted after the witnesses were interviewed by Prosecution investigators as part of the investigative process. Alleged inconsistencies were raised in relation to both Prosecution and Defence witnesses. The procedure adopted by the Trial Chamber for dealing with apparent inconsistencies was expounded during the hearing of evidence by Prosecution witness A. There, the Trial Chamber ordered that an alleged inconsistency be put to the witness and the witness be offered an opportunity to explain. In light of this explanation, if Counsel asserted that the inconsistency remained, the Counsel would mark the relevant portion of the witness statement and submit it as an exhibit for consideration by the Trial Chamber. Both Prosecution and Defence Counsel submitted such exhibits.[34]

77. The witness statements are not automatically evidence before the Trial Chamber *per se*. However, the statements may be used to impeach a witness. Where the relevant portion of the statement has been submitted as an exhibit, this portion will be considered by the Trial Chamber in light of the oral evidence and explanation offered by the witness. The Chamber is mindful that there was generally a considerable time lapse between the events to which the witnesses testified, the making of their prior statements, and their testimony before the Trial Chamber. However, notwithstanding the above, inconsistencies may raise doubt in relation to the particular piece of evidence in question or, where such inconsistencies are found to be material, to the witnesses' evidence as a whole.

78. Whether or not the explanation by the witness is enough to remove the doubt is determined on a case-by-case basis considering the circumstances surrounding the inconsistency and the subsequent explanation. However, to be released from doubt the **[page 37]** Trial Chamber generally demands an explanation of substance rather than mere procedure. For example, a common explanation provided by witnesses was that the interviewing investigator did not accurately reflect in the written statement what the witness said. Although such an explanation may well be true, particularly considering the translation difficulties, in the absence of evidence that corroborates the explanation, it is generally not enough to remove doubt. Indeed, it is not for the Trial Chamber to search for reasons to excuse inadequacies in the Prosecution's investigative process.

79. Conversely, where the witness provides a convincing explanation of substance, perhaps relating to the substance of the investigator's question, then this may be sufficient to remove the doubt raised.

80. Doubts about a testimony can be removed with the corroboration of other testimonies. However, corroboration of evidence is not a legal requirement to accept a testimony. This Chamber is nevertheless aware of the importance of corroboration and considered the testimonies in this light. This notion has been emphasised in the Factual Findings of this Judgement. **[page 38]**

3.4 Specificity of the Indictment

Introduction

---

[33]   An article by Ann Maass and Gautier Kohnken, in the Law and Human Behaviour Journal, vol. 13, no. 4, 1989, was shown to the witness and discussed in cross-examination. Trans., 2 Jul. 1998, p. 104.
[34]   See Pros. exh. 350A, 350B and 350C.

81.   The Indictment, in setting out the particulars of the charges against the accused, refers to events "around" and "about" a specific date, or between two specified dates. Kayishema is charged separately for massacres at the sites of the Catholic Church and Home St. Jean, the Stadium in Kibuye and Mubuga Church. Paragraphs 28, 35 and 41 of the Indictment detail these massacres as occurring on or about the 17, 18 and 14 April 1994 respectively. The fourth crime site for which both Kayishema and Ruzindana are charged is the Bisesero area between 9 April and 30 June. The question arises, therefore, as to whether sufficient certainty exists to enable an adequate defence to be advanced, thus to ensure the right of the accused to a fair trial.

The Allegations in Relation to the Massacres in the Bisesero Area

82.   The Trial Chamber considers it appropriate to distinguish between the first three sites in the Indictment, and the charges raised in respect of the Bisesero area. The exact dates on which massacres occurred at the Catholic Church and Home St. Jean, the Stadium and Mubuga Church were identified in the course of the trial by the Prosecution's case-in-chief. Accordingly, the findings made by this Chamber are set out below in the Factual Findings Part.

83.   The Chamber is aware of the difficulties of raising a defence where all of the elements of the offence are not precisely detailed in the Indictment. The difficulties are compounded because the alibi defence advanced by both accused persons does not remove them from the Bisesero vicinity at the time in question. The accused in the *Tadic* case faced similar difficulties.[35] In that instance the Trial Chamber observed the near impossibility of providing a 24-hour, day-by-day, and week-by-week account of the accused's whereabouts for an alibi defence which covers a duration of several months. The Trial Chamber is of the opinion that this is a substantive issue. **[page 39]**

84.   Nevertheless, it is important to note here that throughout the trial the burden of proving each material element of the offence, beyond a reasonable doubt, has remained firmly on the Prosecution. Whilst, *prima facie*, the accused should be informed in as greater detail as possible of the elements of the offence against them, such details will necessarily depend on the nature of the alleged crimes. The Trial Chamber finds that during its case-in-chief the Prosecution did focus upon various sites throughout the Bisesero region, but because of the wide-ranging nature of the attacks no further specificity was possible in the Indictment.

85.   It is unnecessary, however, for the Prosecution to prove an exact date of an offence where the date or time is not also a material element of the offence. Whilst it would be preferable to allege and prove an exact date of each offence, this can clearly not be demanded as a prerequisite for conviction where the time is not an essential element of that offence.[36] Furthermore, even where the date of the offence is an essential element, it is necessary to consider with what precision the timing of the offence must be detailed. It is not always possible to be precise as to exact events; this is especially true in light of the events that occurred in Rwanda in 1994 and in light of the evidence we have heard from witnesses. Consequently, the Chamber recognises that it has balanced the necessary practical considerations to enable the Prosecution to present its case, with the need to ensure sufficient specificity of location and matter of offence in order to allow a comprehensive defence to be raised.

86.   However, because of the foregoing observations, the Trial Chamber opines that where timing is of material importance to the charges, then the wording of the count should lift the offence from the general to the particular.[37] In this respect, the Trial Chamber notes that the *ratione temporis* of this Tribunal extends from 1 January 1994 to 31 December 1994, and the Indictment only refers only to events that occurred in the **[page 40]** Bisesero area between the 9 April and 30 June. In fact, during its case-in-chief,

---

[35]   *Prosecutor v. Dusko Tactić,* International Criminal Tribunal for the Former Yugoslavia, Case No. IT-94-1-T, 7 May 1997, para. 533. (Tactić Judgement.)
[36]   See, the *Tadić* Judgement, para. 534 and the cases cited therein.
[37]   See, for example, the Canadian cases of, *G.B., A.B. and C.S. v. R.* (1990) 2 S.C.R. 30, and *R v. Colgan* (1986) 30 C.C.C. (3d) 193 (Court of Appeal), where Monnin C.J.M. found an offence specified as occurring at some point within a six year period to be sufficiently precise.

and with the more precise definition of massacre sites within the Bisesero area, the Prosecution was able to pinpoint specific periods during which the alleged events occurred. Therefore, the date need only be identified where it is a material element of the offence and, where it is such a necessary element, the precision with which such dates need be identified varies from case to case. In light of this, the Trial Chamber opines that the lack of specificity does not have a bearing upon the otherwise proper and complete counts, and it did not prejudice the right of the accused to a fair trial. **[page 41]**

IV. THE LAW

4.1 GENOCIDE

87. Article 2(2) of the ICTR Statute reads:

Genocide means any of the following acts committed with intent to destroy, in whole or in part, a national, ethnical, racial or religious group, as such:

    a. Killing members of the group;

    b. Causing serious bodily or mental harm to members of the group;

    c. Deliberately inflicting on the group conditions of life calculated to bring about its physical destruction in whole or in part;

    d. Imposing measures intended to prevent births within the group;

    e. Forcibly transferring children of the group to another group.

The above definition reproduces Articles II and III of the Genocide Convention of 1948 and Article 17 of the International Law Commission Report 1996, Draft Code of Crimes Against the Peace and Security of Mankind (ILC Draft Code of Crimes).

88. The concept of genocide appeared first in the International Military Tribunal (Nuremberg) Judgement of 30 September and 1 October 1946, referring to the destruction of groups. The prohibition of genocide then was recognised by the General Assembly of the United Nations as a principle of international law. Resolution 260(A)(III) of 9 December 1948, adopting the Draft Genocide Convention, crystallised into international law the prohibition of that crime. The Genocide Convention became widely accepted as an international human rights instrument. Furthermore, the crime of genocide is considered part of international customary law and, moreover, a norm of *jus cogens*.

89. The definition of the crime of genocide was based upon that of crimes against humanity, that is, a combination of "extermination and persecutions on political, racial or religious grounds" and it was intended to cover "*the intentional destruction of groups in whole or in substantial part*" (emphasis added). The crime of genocide is a type of crime against humanity. Genocide, however, is different from other crimes against humanity. The **[page 42]** essential difference is that genocide requires the aforementioned specific intent to exterminate a protected group (in whole or in part) while crimes against humanity require the civilian population to be targeted as part of a widespread or systematic attack. There are instances where the discriminatory grounds coincide and overlap. This scenario is detailed in the present Judgement, in the Part VII on Cumulative Charges.

90. For the crime of genocide to be committed, two elements are required, namely, the *mens rea*, the requisite specific intent, and the *actus reus*, the prohibited act or omission.

4.1.1 The Mens Rea

91. A distinguishing aspect of the crime of genocide is the specific intent (*dolus specialis*) to destroy, a group in whole or in part. The *dolus specialis* applies to all acts of genocide mentioned in Article 2(a) to (e) of the Statute, that is, all the enumerated acts must be committed "with intent to destroy, in whole or in part, a national, ethnical, racial or religious group, as such." It is this specific intent that

distinguishes the crime of genocide from the ordinary crime of murder.[38] The Trial Chamber opines that for the crime of genocide to occur, the *mens rea* must be formed prior to the commission of the genocidal acts. The individual acts themselves, however, do not require premeditation; the only consideration is that the act should be done in furtherance of the genocidal intent.

92.   Under Article 6(3) of the Statute, the superior is criminally responsible for the acts committed by his subordinates if he or she knew or had reason to know that the subordinate was about to commit such acts or had done so and the superior failed to take the necessary and reasonable measures to prevent such acts or to punish the perpetrators thereof.

Proof of the Requisite Intent

93.   Regarding the assessment of the requisite intent, the Trial Chamber acknowledges that it may be difficult to find explicit manifestations of intent by the perpetrators. The perpetrator's actions, including circumstantial evidence, however may provide sufficient evidence of intent. The Commission of Experts in their Final Report on the situation in **[page 43]** Rwanda also noted this difficulty. Their Report suggested that the necessary element of intent can be inferred from sufficient facts, such as the number of group members affected.[39] The Chamber finds that the intent can be inferred either from words or deeds and may be demonstrated by a pattern of purposeful action.[40] In particular, the Chamber considers evidence such as the physical targeting of the group or their property; the use of derogatory language toward members of the targeted group; the weapons employed and the extent of bodily injury; the methodical way of planning, the systematic manner of killing. Furthermore, the number of victims from the group is also important. In the Report of the Sub-Commission on Genocide, the Special Rapporteur stated that "the relative proportionate scale of the actual or attempted destruction of a group, by any act listed in Articles II and III of the Genocide Convention, is strong evidence to prove the necessary intent to destroy a group in whole or in part."[41]

94.   It is also the view of the Chamber that although a specific plan to destroy does not a constitute an element of genocide, it would appear that it is not easy to carry out a genocide without such a plan, or organisation. Morris and Scharf note that "it is virtually impossible for the crime of genocide to be, committed without some or indirect involvement on the part of the State given the magnitude of this crime."[42] They suggested that "it is unnecessary for an individual to have knowledge of all details of the genocidal plan or policy." The Chamber concurs with this view.

Destruction of a Group

95.   The perpetrator must intend to destroy a group in whole or in part. This begs the question of what constitutes the "destruction of a group." The Prosecution suggests that the term should be broadly interpreted and encompass acts that are undertaken not only with the intent to cause death but also includes acts which may fall short of causing **[page 44]** death.[43] In the *Akayesu* Judgement, acts of sexual violence, which occurred in Taba Commune were found to form an integral part of the process of destruction, specifically, targeting Tutsi women and contributing to their destruction and the destruction of the Tutsi as a group.[44] The Trial Chamber concurs with this view and that of the International Law

---

[38]   Virginia Morris & Michael Scharf, THE INTERNATIONAL CRIMINAL TRIBUNAL FOR RWANDA, 167 (1998)
[39]   Cited in Bassiouni, in THE LAW OF THE INTERNATIONAL CRIMINAL TRIBUNAL FOR THE FORMER YUGOSLAVIA, p. 524, and UN AND RWANDA, 1993-6, p. 432, para. 166.
[40]   Wisconsin International Law Journal, 243 (1996).
[41]   UN Doc. E/CN.4/Sub.2/1985/6, p. 16, para. 29.
[42]   Morris & Scharf, *supra*, p. 168.
[43]   Prosecutor's Brief, 9 Oct. 1998, p. 30.
[44]   *Akayesu* Judgement, para. 731.

Commission (ILC) which stated that "it is not necessary to intend to achieve the complete annihilation of a group from every corner of the globe."[45]

Whole or in Part

96.   Another aspect for consideration is that the intent to destroy the group must be "in whole or in part." The ILC stated that "the crime of Genocide by its very nature requires the intention to destroy at least a substantial part of a particular group."[46] In the Report of the Sub-Commission on Genocide, the Special Rapporteur stated that "in part" would seem to imply a reasonably significant number, relative to the total of the group as a whole, or else a significant section of a group such as its leadership. Hence, both proportionate scale and total number are relevant.[47]

97. The Trial Chamber opines, therefore, that "in part" requires the intention to destroy a considerable number of individuals who are part of the group. Individuals must be targeted due to their membership of the group to satisfy this definition.

A National, Ethnical, Racial or Religious Group

98.   The intent must exist to "destroy a national, ethnical, racial or religious group, as such." Thus, the acts must be directed towards a specific group on these discriminatory grounds. An ethnic group is one whose members share a common language and culture; or, a group which distinguishes itself, as such (self identification); or, a group identified as such by others, including perpetrators of the crimes (identification by others). A racial **[page 45]** group is based on hereditary physical traits often identified with geography. A religious group includes denomination or mode of worship or a group sharing common beliefs.

Destroying in whole or in part a National, Ethnical, Racial or Religious Group as Such

99.   This phrase speaks to specific intent (the requisite *mens rea*). The "destroying" has to be directed at the group as such, that is, qua group, as stipulated in Article 2(2) of the Statute.

4.1.2 Actus Reus

100. Article 2(2)(a) to (e) of the ICTR Statute and Article II (a) to (e) of the Genocide Convention lists acts which, if committed with the specific intent, amount to genocide.

Killing Members of the Group

101. Article 2(2)(a) of the Statute, in the English language version, states that genocide means the act of "killing" committed with intent to destroy, in whole or in part, a national, ethnical, racial or religious group, as such. The French language version refers to *meurtre*, a term that requires the additional mental element of intent.

102. The Parties in their closing remarks addressed the differences between the English and French versions. The Prosecutor submitted that the term *meurtre* has a legal meaning in French law, that is, a deliberate homicide, whereas the term "killing" is merely the act of causing the death to another.[48] The

---

[45]   ILC Draft Code of Crimes, p. 42, para. 8. [Throughout the text, page citations to the International Law Commission (ILC) Report 1996 may refer to the Internet version at http://www.un.org/law/ilc/reports/1996/chapO2.htm.]

[46]   *Ibid.*

[47]   Mr. Whitaker, in UN Doc. E/CN.4/Sub.2/1985/6, p. 16, para. 29.

[48]   Trans., 21 Oct. 1998, p. 91.

Prosecutor contended that the language used in the English version is more flexible and would permit, if the need arises, a broadening of the meaning or interpretation.[49] The Defence teams submitted that "*meurtre*" should be applied, as it was in the *Akayesu* Judgement. The Defence submitted that where doubt exists then, as a general principle of criminal law, that doubt should be interpreted in favour of the accused.

103.   The Trial Chamber agrees that if a doubt exists, for a matter of statutory interpretation, that doubt must be interpreted in favour of the accused. Therefore, the **[page 46]** relevant act under Article 2(2)(a) is "*meurtre*," that is, unlawful and intentional killing. The Trial Chamber notes, however, that all the enumerated acts must be committed with intent to destroy a group in whole or in part. As stated by the ILC the enumerated acts "are by their very nature conscious, intentional or volitional acts which an individual could not usually commit without knowing that certain consequences were likely to result. They are not the type of acts that would normally occur by accident or even as a result of mere negligence . . . the definition of this crime requires a particular state of mind or a specific intent with respect to the overall consequences of the prohibited act."[50] Hence, there is virtually no difference between the two as the term "killing" is linked to the intent to destroy in whole or in part.

104.   The Chamber observes that the *Akayesu* Judgement does not fully define the term "killing."[51] It is the opinion of the Trial Chamber that there is virtually no difference between the term "killing" in the English version and "*meurtre*" in the French version of Article 2 (2)(a) of the Statute within the context of genocidal intent. Hence "killing" or "*meurtre*" should be considered along with the specific intent of genocide, that is, the intent to destroy in whole or in part, a national, ethnical, racial or religious group as such.

Causing Serious Bodily or Mental Harm to Members of the Group

105.   Pursuant to Article 2(2)(b) of the Statute states "causing serious bodily or mental harm to members of the group."

106.   This phrase, which is not defined by the Statute, was the subject of contention during the closing submissions of the Parties. The Prosecution submitted that "causing a bodily or a mental harm" means: to undertake an action that might cause injury to the physical and mental fullness, the total being of a person; that a human being is to be considered as a whole with structures and elements functioning in concert and harmony; that the term "serious" is applicable to both the bodily and the mental part of a person and is dependant upon the extent to which the physical body or mental well being is injured. **[page 47]**

107.   The Prosecution submitted that serious harm may include impact on one or more elements of the human structure, which disables the organs of the body and prevents them from functioning as normal. To this end, the harm caused need not bring about death but causes handicap such that the individual will be unable to be a socially useful unit or a socially existent unit of the group. The Prosecution submitted that blows and wounds inflicted would constitute serious harm when they are so violent or have such intensity that they immediately cause the malfunctioning of one or many essential mechanisms of the human body. The Prosecution also submits that non-physical aggressions such as the infliction of strong fear or strong terror, intimidation or threat are also serious mental harm.[52]

Serious Bodily Harm

108.   The phrase serious bodily harm should be determined on a case-by-case basis, using a common sense approach. In the *Akayesu* Judgement, it was held that serious bodily harm does not necessarily

---

49   *Ibid.*
50   ILC Draft Code of Crimes, p. 42, (commenting upon sub-paragraph (a) to (e) of Article 17).
51   Paras. 500 – 501, p. 206.
52   Rahetlah, submission, 21 October 1998, pp. 114 to 121.

mean harm that is permanent or irremediable.[53] The *Akayesu* Judgement further held that acts of sexual violence, rape, mutilations and interrogations combined with beatings, and/or threats of death, were all acts that amount to serious bodily harm.[54] The Trial Chamber concurs with these determinations.

109. It is the view of the Trial Chamber that, to large extent, "causing serious bodily harm" is self-explanatory. This phrase could be construed to mean harm that seriously injures the health, causes disfigurement or causes any serious injury to the external, internal organs or senses.

Serious Mental Harm

110. The phrase "serious mental harm" should also be determined on a case-by-case. The Prosecution submits that there is no prerequisite that mental suffering should be the result of physical harm. The Prosecution relies upon the commentary offered in the **[page 48]** Preparatory Committee's Definition of Crimes that suggests that serious mental harm should include "more than minor or temporary impairment on mental faculties."[55] The Prosecution suggested that the inflicting of strong fear or terror, intimidation or threat may amount to serious mental harm.

111. The Defence teams submitted that the serious bodily and mental harm alleged by the Prosecution was merely a consequence of attempts to kill and did not amount to genocidal offences in themselves. It argued that the Prosecution witnesses who had been wounded did not demonstrate that the perpetrators had intention to cause serious bodily or mental harm. The Defence contends therefore, that there was intention to cause murder and not to cause serious bodily or mental harm.

112. The Chamber considers that an accused may be held liable under these circumstances only where, at the time of the act, the accused had the intention to inflict serious mental harm in pursuit of the specific intention to destroy a group in whole or in part.

113. The Chamber opines that "causing serious mental harm" should be interpreted on a case-by-case basis in light of the relevant jurisprudence.

Deliberately Inflicting on the Group Conditions of Life Calculated to Bring About its Physical Destruction in Whole or in Part

114. Article 2(2)(c) of the Statute covers the act of "deliberately inflicting on the group conditions of life calculated to bring about its physical destruction in whole or in part." The Prosecution submits that Article 2(2)(c) applies to situations likely to cause death regardless of whether death actually occurs and allows for the punishment of the perpetrator for the infliction of substandard conditions of life which, if left to run their coarse, could bring about the physical destruction of the group.[56] **[page 49]**

115. The Trial Chamber concurs with the explanation within the Draft Convention, prepared by the U.N. Secretariat which interpreted this concept to include circumstances which will lead to a slow death, for example, lack of proper housing, clothing, hygiene and medical care or excessive work or physical exertion.[57]

116. It is the view of the Trial Chamber that "deliberately inflicting on the group conditions of life calculated to bring about its physical destruction in whole or in part," includes methods of destruction which do not immediately lead to the death of members of the group. The Chamber adopts the above interpretation.[58] Therefore the conditions of life envisaged include rape, the starving of a group of people,

---

[53]   *Akayesu* Judgement, para 502.
[54]   *Akayesu* Judgement, paras 706-07 and 711-12.
[55]   Prosecutor's Closing Brief, 9 Oct. 1998, p. 26.
[56]   Prosecutor's Closing Brief, 9 October 1998, p. 28.
[57]   Nehemiah Robinson, the Genocide Convention: A Commentary (1960), p. 123.
[58]   Robinson, supra, pp. 63-64.

reducing required medical services below a minimum, and withholding sufficient living accommodation for a reasonable period, provided the above would lead to the destruction of the group in whole or in part.

Imposing Measures Intended to Prevent Births Within the Group

117. Article 2(2)(d) of the Statute covers the act of imposing measures intended to prevent births within the group. The Trial Chamber concurs with the explanation provided in the *Akayesu* Judgement.

Forcibly Transferring Children of the Group to Another

118. Article 2(2)(e) of the Statute covers the act of forcibly transferring children of the group to another. The Trial Chamber concurs with the explanation provided in the *Akayesu* Judgement. **[page 50]**

4.2   Crimes Against Humanity

119.   Article 3 of the ICTR Statute states:

> The International Tribunal for Rwanda shall have the power to prosecute persons responsible for the following crimes when committed as part of a widespread or systematic attack against any civilian population on national, political, ethnic, racial or religious grounds:
>
> *a) Murder;*
>
> *b) Extermination;*
>
> *c) Enslavement;*
>
> *d) Deportation;*
>
> *e) Imprisonment;*
>
> *f) Torture;*
>
> *g) Rape;*
>
> *h) Prosecutions;*
>
> *i) Other inhumane acts.*

120.   Crimes against humanity were prosecuted at the Nuremberg trials. The Charter of the International Military Tribunal of Nuremberg[59] in its Article 6(c) (Annex to the Agreement for the Prosecution and Punishment of Major War Criminals of the European Axis (London Agreement)), describes the crimes against humanity as follows:

> ...namely murder, extermination, enslavement, deportation and other inhumane acts committed against any civilian populations, before or during the war; or persecutions on political, racial, or religious grounds in execution of or in connection with any crime within the jurisdiction of the Tribunal, whether or not in violation of the domestic law of the country where perpetrated.

121.   Crimes against humanity were also applied under Article II of Law No. 10 of the Control Council Law[60] and went through a gradual evolution in the domestic **[page 51]** cases of *Eichmann,*[61] *Barbie,*[62] and *Touvier.* More recently, crimes against humanity have been applied in the International Criminal Tribunals for both Rwanda and the Former Yugoslavia.

---

[59]   Law No. 10 of the Control Council for Germany.
[60]   International Law Reports (ILR), vol. 36, p. 31.
[61]   36 ILR.
[62]   125 ILR.

4.2.1 The Attack

122. The enumerated crimes must be committed as part of a widespread or systematic attack against any civilian population on national, political, ethnic, racial or religious grounds. The attack is the event in which the enumerated crimes must form part. Indeed, within a single attack, there may exist a combination of the enumerated crimes, for example murder, rape and deportation. The elements of the attack effectively exclude from crimes against humanity, acts carried out for purely personal motives and those outside of a broader policy or plan; a position which was adopted by the Defence.

Widespread or Systematic

123. The attack must contain one of the alternative conditions of being widespread or systematic.[63] A widespread attack is one that is directed against a multiplicity of victims.[64] A systematic attack means an attack carried out pursuant to a preconceived policy or plan. Either of these conditions will serve to exclude isolated or random inhumane acts committed for purely personal reasons.[65] **[page 52]**

The Policy Element

124. For an act of mass victimisation to be a crime against humanity, it must include a policy element. Either of the requirements of widespread or systematic are enough to exclude acts not committed as part of a broader policy or plan. Additionally, the requirement that the attack must be committed against a "civilian population" inevitably demands some kind of plan and, the discriminatory element of the attack is, by its very nature, only possible as a consequence of a policy.

125. Who or what must instigate the policy? Arguably, customary international law requires a showing that crimes against humanity are committed pursuant to an action or policy of a State. However, it is clear that the ICTR Statute does not demand the involvement of a State. Guidance on this issue may be gained from the ILC who, in the Draft Code of Crimes, stated that crimes against humanity are inhumane acts "instigated or directed by a Government or by any organisation or group."[66] The ILC explains that this requirement was,

> intended to exclude the situation in which an individual commits an inhumane act whilst acting on his own initiative pursuant to his own criminal plan in the absence of any encouragement or direction from either a Government or a group or an organisation ...The instigation or direction of a Government or any group, which may or may not be affiliated with a Government, gives the act its great dimension and makes it a crime against humanity imputable to private persons or agents of the State.[67]

126. The Trial Chamber concurs with the above view and finds that the Tribunal's jurisdiction covers both State and non-State actors. As *Prefect*, Kayishema was a State actor. As a businessman Ruzindana was a non-State actor. To have jurisdiction over either of the accused, the Chamber must be satisfied that their actions were instigated or directed by a Government or by any organisation or group. **[page 53]**

---

[63]   Despite the French text containing the conjunctive "and" instead of the disjunctive "or" between the terms widespread or systematic, the Trial Chamber is in no doubt that the correct interpretation is the disjunctive. The matter has already been settled in the *Akayesu* Judgement and needs no further debate here.

[64]   The ILC Draft Code of Crimes explained "large scale" (the term used in place of "widespread") to mean acts that are "directed against a multiplicity of victims." Article 18, para. 4 of commentary.

[65]   The ILC Draft Code of Crimes defines systematic as "meaning pursuant to a preconceived plan or policy. The implementation of this plan or policy could result in the repeated or continuous commission of inhumane acts. The thrust of this requirement is to exclude random acts that were not committed as part of a broader plan or policy." Article 18, para. 3 of commentary.

[66]   ILC Draft Code of Crimes Article 18.

[67]   ILC Draft Code of Crimes Art. 18 para. 5 of commentary.

Civilian Population

127. Traditionally, legal definitions of "civilian" or "civilian population" have been discussed within the context of armed conflict. However, under the Statute, crimes against humanity may be committed inside or outside the context of an armed conflict. Therefore, the term civilian must be understood within the context of war as well as relative peace. The Trial Chamber considers that a wide definition of civilian is applicable and, in the context of the situation of Kibuye *Prefecture* where there was no armed conflict, includes all persons *except* those who have the duty to maintain public order and have the legitimate means to exercise force. Non-civilians would include, for example, members of the FAR, the RPF, the police and the Gendarmerie Nationale.

128. With regard to the targeting of any civilian population, the Trial Chamber concurs with the finding in the *Tadic* decision that the targeted population must be predominantly civilian in nature but the presence of certain non-civilians in their midst does not change the character of that population.[68]

129. In any event, the Defence teams did not challenge the assertion that the victims of the alleged attacks were civilians. And, the Prosecution submitted that the victims in the four massacre sites were farmers, teachers and those seeking refuge from the attacks.

Discriminatory Grounds

130. The Statute contains a requirement additional to both the Nuremberg Charter and the ICTY Statute; that the attack be committed on national, political, ethnic, racial or religious grounds. The Prosecution submits that the discrimination at issue was based on ethnic or, alternatively, political grounds.[69] The Prosecution asserted that the discrimination was on ethnic grounds because the victims were Tutsis and political grounds because the Tutsis were accomplices or supporters of the RPF. The **[page 54]** Defence did not contest that the Tutsis were considered an ethnic group.[70] Political grounds include party political beliefs and political ideology.

131. The Prosecution submit that it is the intent of the perpetrator to discriminate against a group that is important rather than whether the victim was, in fact, a member of that targeted group. In this regard there are two issues for the Chamber to address. Firstly, in a scenario where the perpetrator's intention is to exterminate the Tutsi group and, in furtherance of this intent, he kills a Belgium Priest who is protecting the Tutsi, the Trial Chamber opines that such an act, would be based on discrimination against the Tutsi group.

132. The second relevant scenario is where the perpetrator attacks people on the grounds and in the *belief* that they are members of a group but, in fact, they are not, for example, where the perpetrator believes that a group of Tutsi are supporters of the RPF and therefore accomplices. In the scenario, the Trial Chamber opines that the Prosecution must show that the perpetrator's belief was objectively reasonable – based upon real facts – rather than being mere speculation or perverted deduction.

The Mental Element

133. The perpetrator must knowingly commit crimes against humanity in the sense that he must understand the overall context of his act. The Defence for Ruzindana submitted that to be guilty of crimes against humanity the perpetrator must know that there is an attack on a civilian population and that his act is part of the attack.[71] This issue has been addressed by the ICTY where it was stated that the

---

[68] *Tadić* Judgement, at para 638.
[69] Prosecutor's Closing Brief, p. 42.
[70] For detailed discussion regarding ethnicity see the Historical Context Part of the Judgement.
[71] Closing Arguments at p. 26.

accused must have acted with knowledge of the broader context of the attack;[72] a view which conforms to the wording of the Statute of the International Criminal Court (ICC) Article 7. **[page 55]**

134.   The Trial Chamber agrees with the Defence. Part of what transforms an individual's act(s) into a crime against humanity is the inclusion of the act within a greater dimension of criminal conduct; therefore an accused should be aware of this greater dimension in order to be culpable thereof. Accordingly, actual or constructive knowledge of the broader context of the attack, meaning that the accused must know that his act(s) is part of a widespread or systematic attack on a civilian population and pursuant to some kind of policy or plan, is necessary to satisfy the requisite *mens rea* element of the accused. This requirement further compliments the exclusion from crimes against humanity of isolated acts carried out for purely personal reasons.

4.2.2   The Crimes

135.   Article 3 entitles the International Criminal Tribunal for Rwanda to prosecute persons responsible for crimes enumerated within the Statute. The crimes must be committed as part of a widespread or systematic attack against any civilian population on national, political, ethnic, racial or religious grounds. The crimes themselves need not contain the three elements of the attack (i.e. widespread or systematic, against any civilian population, on discriminatory grounds), but must form *part of* such an attack. Indeed, the individual crimes contain their own specific elements. For an accused to be found guilty under crimes against humanity the Prosecution must prove that the accused is responsible for one of the crimes charged pursuant to Article 6(1) and/or 6(3) of the Statute. The following crimes are charged in the Indictment: murder, extermination and other inhumane acts.

Murder

136.   The Prosecution charges Kayishema with crimes against humanity for murder in Counts 2, 8, 14 and 20 of the Indictment, and Ruzindana with crimes against humanity for murder in Count 20 of the Indictment. **[page 56]**

137.   Article 3(a) of the English version of the Statute uses the term "murder," whilst the French version of the Statute uses the term "*assassinat*."[73] The use of these terms has been the subject of some debate because the *mens rea* for murder, as it is defined in most common law jurisdictions, includes but does not require premeditation; whereas, in most civil law systems; premeditation is always required for *assassinat*.[74] The *Akayesu* Judgement, which is the only case to have addressed the issue, stated that customary international law dictates that it is the act of murder that constitutes a crime against humanity and not *assassinat*. In *Akayesu*, the Chamber held that there were sufficient reasons to assume that the French version of the Statute suffers from an error in translation.[75] The Defence argued, *inter alia*, that the *Akayesu* solution of an error in translation was too simple and not convincing as both the French and the English versions of the Statute are originals. According to the Defence, murder was meant to be the equivalent of *assassinat*. However, the Prosecution argued that premeditation was not a necessary element and suggested, that the "unlawful killing of a human being as the result of the perpetrator engaging in conduct which was in reckless disregard for human life" is enough.

138.   The Trial Chamber agrees with the Defence. When interpreting a term from one language to another, one may find that there is no equivalent term that corresponds to all the subtleties and nuances.

---

[72]   *Tadić* Judgement, at para. 656, "therefore in addition to the intent to commit the underlying offence the perpetrator must know of the broader context in which his acts occur."

[73]   Indeed, the Statute, Article 2(2) (a) (Genocide) refers to "killing" – "*meurtre*" in French, while Article 4(a) refers to "murder" – "*meurtre*" in French.

[74]   Nouveau Code Pénal, Article 221-3 "Le meurtre commis avec préméditation constitue un assassinat. Il est puni de la récluson criminelle à perpetuité. [...]"

[75]   *Akayesu* Judgement, at para. 588.

This is particularly true with legal terms that represent jurisprudential concepts. Here, the *mens rea* for murder in common law overlaps with both *meurtre* and *assassinat* (that is, a *meurtre aggravé*) in civil systems.[76] The drafters chose to use the term *assassinat* rather than *meurtre*. As a matter of interpretation, the intention of the drafters should be followed so far as **[page 57]** possible and a statute should be given its plain meaning.[77] Since the concepts of murder and *assassinat* can correspond to one another, in the opinion of this Trial Chamber, there is no need to change the wording of the Statute. Although it may be argued that, under customary international law, it is murder rather than *assassinat* that constitutes the crime against humanity (a position asserted by the Chamber in the *Akayesu* Judgement), this court is bound by the wording of the ICTR Statute in particular. It is the ICTR Statute that reflects the intention of the international community for the purposes of trying those charged with violations of international law in Rwanda. Furthermore, the ICTR and ICTY Statutes did not reflect customary international law at the time of drafting. This is evident by the inclusion of the need for an armed conflict in the ICTY Statute and the inclusion of the requirement that the crimes be committed with discriminatory intent in the ICTR Statute. Accordingly, it may be presumed that the drafters intended to use *assassinat* alongside murder. Indeed, by using *assassinat* in French, the drafters may have intended that only the higher standards of *mens rea* for murder will suffice.[78]

139. If in doubt, a matter of interpretation should be decided in favour of the accused; in this case, the inclusion of premeditation is favourable to the accused. The Chamber finds, therefore, that murder and assassinat should be considered together in order to ascertain the standard of *mens rea* intended by the drafters and demanded by the ICTR Statute. When murder is considered along with *assassinat* the Chamber finds that the standard of *mens rea* required is intentional and premeditated killing. The result is premeditated when the actor formulated his intent to kill after a cool **[page 58]** moment of reflection.[79] The result is intended when it is the actor's purpose, or the actor is aware that it will occur in the ordinary course of events.

140. The accused is guilty of murder if the accused, engaging in conduct which is unlawful:

1. causes the death of another;

2. by a premeditated act or omission;

3. intending to kill any person or,

4. intending to cause grievous bodily harm to any person.

Thus, a premeditated murder that forms part of a widespread or systematic attack, against civilians, on discriminatory grounds will be a crime against humanity. Also included will be extrajudicial killings, that is "unlawful and deliberate killings carried out with the order of a Government or with its complicity or acquiescence."[80]

Extermination

---

[76] For example, at the high end of murder the *mens rea* corresponds to the *mens rea* of *assassinat*, i.e., unlawful killing with premeditation. Conversely, at the low end of murder where mere intention or recklessness is sufficient and premeditation is not required, the *mens rea* of murder corresponds to the *mens rea* of *meurtre*.

[77] Notably the text was drafted in English and French, both being original and authentic. The Statute was then translated into the four remaining official UN languages. Therefore, between English and French there was no translation. Accordingly, there can be no "error in translation" as such; there can only be a mistake in the drafting of an original text. Notably, the term used in the ICTY Statute is also *assassinat* (ICTY Statute Article 5(a)).

[78] Of course, in common law, there is no crime of unlawful killing that provides for a higher standard of *mens rea* than that of murder. Therefore, even if the drafters intended that only the standard of *mens rea* for assassinat would suffice, the drafters would still need to use the term murder in English.

[79] This explanation conforms to the French jurisprudence of the criminal court and to the United States Supreme Court case law.

[80] See Amnesty International's 14 Point Program for the Prevention of Extrajudicial Executions.

141. The Prosecution charges Kayishema with crimes against humanity for extermination in Counts 3, 9, 15 and 21 of the Indictment, and Ruzindana with crimes against humanity for extermination in Count 21 of the Indictment.

142. The crime of extermination was not specifically defined in the Statute or the Nuremberg Charter. Indeed, there is very little jurisprudence relating to the essential elements of extermination. In the *Akayesu* Judgement, Chamber I considered that extermination is a crime that by its very nature is directed against a group of individuals and differs from murder in that it requires an element of mass destruction that is not required for murder.[81] The Prosecution asserted that there is no need for a defined number of people to die for the killing to rise to an act of extermination; it is determined on a case-by-case basis even though there is the need for a numerical **[page 59]** requirement.[82] Notably, Akayesu was found guilty of extermination for ordering the killing of sixteen people.[83] The Chamber agrees that the difference between murder and extermination is the scale; extermination can be said to be murder on a massive scale. The Defence did not address the numerical question but argues that "the essence of extermination lies in the fact that it is an indiscriminate elimination."[84]

143. Cherif Bassiouni states that extermination is murder on a massive scale and may include unintentional killing:

> Extermination implies intentional and unintentional killing. The reason for the latter is that mass killing of a group of people involves planning and implementation by a number of persons who, though knowing and wanting the intended result, may not necessarily know their victims. Furthermore, such persons may not perform the *actus reus* that produced the deaths, nor have specific intent toward a particular victim.[85]

The ICC Statute (Article 7(2)(b)), offers an illustrative rather than definitive statement regarding extermination: "Extermination includes the intentional infliction of conditions of life, *inter alia* the deprivation of access to food and medicine, calculated to bring about the destruction of part of a population."

144. Having considered the above, the Chamber defines the requisite elements of extermination:

> The actor participates in the mass killing of others or in the creation of conditions of life that lead to the mass killing of others, through his act(s) or omission(s); having intended the killing, or being reckless, or grossly negligent as to whether the killing would result and; being aware that his act(s) or omission(s) forms part of a mass killing event; where, his act(s) or omission(s) forms part of a widespread or systematic attack against any civilian population on national, political, ethnic, racial or religious grounds.

145. The term "mass", which may be understood to mean "large scale," does not command a numerical imperative but may be determined on a case-by-case basis **[page 60]** using a common sense approach. The actor need not act with a specific individual(s) in mind.

146. The act(s) or omission(s) may be done with intention, recklessness, or gross negligence. The "creation of conditions of life that lead to mass killing" is the institution of circumstances that ultimately causes the mass death of others. For example: Imprisoning a large number of people and withholding the necessities of life which results in mass death; introducing a deadly virus into a population and preventing medical care which results in mass death. Extermination includes not only the implementation of mass killing or the creation of conditions of life that leads to mass killing, but also the planning thereof. In this event, the Prosecutor must prove a nexus between the planning and the actual killing.

---

[81] *Akayesu* Judgement, at para. 591.
[82] Prosecutor's Closing Brief, at p. 36.
[83] *Akayesu* Judgement, at para 735-744.
[84] Ruzindana Closing Argument, at p. 8.
[85] Cherif Bassiouni, Crimes Against Humanity in International Law (Martinus Nijhoff Publishers 1992).

147. An actor may be guilty of extermination if he kills, or creates the conditions of life that kills, a single person providing the actor is aware that his act(s) or omission(s) forms part of a mass killing event.[86] For a single killing to form part of extermination, the killing must actually form part of a mass killing event. An "event" exists when the (mass) killings have close proximity in time and place.

Other Inhumane Acts

148. The Prosecution charges Kayishema with crimes against humanity for other inhumane acts in Counts 4, 10, 16 and 22 of the Indictment, and Ruzindana with crimes against humanity for other inhumane acts in Count 22 of the Indictment.

149. Since the Nuremberg Charter, the category "other inhumane acts" has been maintained as a useful category for acts not specifically stated but which are of comparable gravity. The importance in maintaining such a category was elucidated **[page 61]** by the ICRC when commenting on inhumane treatment contained in Article 3 of the Geneva Conventions,

> It is always dangerous to try to go into too much detail – especially in this domain. However much care were taken in establishing a list of all the various forms of infliction, one would never be able to catch up with the imagination of future torturers who wished to satisfy their bestial instincts; and the more specific and complete a list tries to be, the more restrictive it becomes. The form of wording adopted is flexible and, at the same time, precise.[87]

150. Other inhumane acts include those crimes against humanity that are not otherwise specified in Article 3 of the Statute, but are of comparable seriousness. The ICC Statute (Article 7(k)), provides greater detail than the ICTR Statute to the meaning of other inhumane acts: "other inhumane acts of a similar character intentionally causing great suffering, or serious injury to body or to mental or physical health." The ILC commenting on Article 18 of its Draft Code of Crimes states

> The Commission recognized that it was impossible to establish an exhaustive list of the inhumane acts which may constitute crimes against humanity. First, this category of acts is intended to include only additional acts that are similar in gravity to those listed in the preceding subparagraphs. Second, the act must in fact cause injury to a human being in terms of physical or mental integrity, health or human dignity.

151. The Chamber notes the International Law Commission's commentary. In relation to the Statute, other inhumane acts include acts that are of similar gravity and seriousness to the enumerated acts of murder, extermination, enslavement, deportation, imprisonment, torture, rape, or persecution on political, racial and religious grounds. These will be acts or omissions that deliberately cause serious mental or physical suffering or injury or constitute a serious attack on human dignity. The Prosecution must prove a nexus between the inhumane act and the great suffering or serious injury to mental or physical health of the victim. The Chamber agrees with **[page 62]** the Prosecution submission that the acts that rise to the level of inhumane acts should be determined on a case-by-case basis.[88]

152. The Defence asserts that for an accused to be found guilty of mental harm, there must be a direct relation between the assailant and the victim.[89] The Prosecution on the other hand suggests that victims have suffered mental harm amounting to other inhumane acts due to them having witnessed atrocities for which the accused is responsible. For example, in relation to Count 4 the Prosecution submits,

> [w]ith respect to serious mental harm, six survivors testified (and the survivors of all the other massacres testified) that they witnessed family members and friends being killed. As established

---

[86]   For example, if ten FAR officers fire into a crowd of 200 Tutsis, killing them all. FAR officer X is a poor shot and kills only a single person, whereas officer Y kills 16. Because both X and Y participated in the mass killing and were both aware that their actions formed part of the mass killing event, they will both be guilty of extermination.

[87]   ICRC COMMENTARY ON THE GENEVA CONVENTIONS p. 54.

[88]   Prosecutor's Closing Brief, p. 37.

[89]   See, Ruzindana's Closing Arguments, pp. 38-41.

by the evidence, Tutsi civilians were placed in an environment of fear and desperation and were forced to witness the killing and the severe injuring of friends, family and other Tutsi civilians. The killings were brutal in manner. The people saw carnage and heard the people singing exterminate them, exterminate them .... The Prosecutor submits that such an environment inherently causes serious mental harm.[90]

153. The Chamber is in no doubt that a third party could suffer serious mental harm by witnessing acts committed against others, particularly against family or friends. However, to find an accused responsible for such harm under crimes against humanity, it is incumbent on the Prosecution to prove the *mens rea* on the part of the accused. Indeed, as stated above, inhumane acts are, *inter alia*, those which *deliberately* cause serious mental suffering. The Chamber considers that an accused may be held liable under these circumstances only where, at the time of the act, the accused had the intention to inflict serious mental suffering on the third party, or where the accused knew that his act was likely to cause serious mental suffering and was reckless as to whether such suffering would result. Accordingly, if at the time of the act, the accused was unaware of the third party bearing witness to his act, then he cannot be held responsible for the mental suffering of the third party. **[page 63]**

154. In summary, for an accused to be found guilty of crimes against humanity for other inhumane acts, he must commit an act of similar gravity and seriousness to the other enumerated crimes, with the intention to cause the other inhumane act, and with knowledge that the act is perpetrated within the overall context of the attack. **[page 64]**

4 .3   Violations of Article 3 Common to the Geneva Conventions and Additional Protocol II, thereto

155. Pursuant to Article 4 of the Statute; the Trial Chamber shall have the power to prosecute persons committing or ordering to be committed serious violations of Article 3 Common to the Four Geneva Conventions of 1949 (Common Article 3) for the protection of War Victims, and Additional Protocol II thereto of 1977 (Protocol II).

4.3.1 Customary Law

156. The Trial Chamber is cognisant of the ongoing discussions, in other forums, about whether the above-mentioned instruments should be considered customary international law that imposes criminal liability for their serious breaches. In the present case, such an analysis seems superfluous because the situation is rather clear. Rwanda became a party to the Conventions of 1949 on 5 May 1964 and to Protocol II on 19 November 1984. These instruments, therefore, were in force in the territory of Rwanda at the time when the tragic events took place within its borders.

157. Moreover, all the offences enumerated in Article 4 of the Statute, also constituted crimes under the laws of Rwanda. The other Party to the conflict, the RPF, also had stated to the International Committee of the Red Cross (ICRC) that it was bound by the rules of international humanitarian law. Therefore, there is no doubt that persons responsible for the breaches of these international instruments during the events in the Rwandan territories in 1994 could be subject to prosecution.

158. Thus, the question before the Trial Chamber, is not about the applicability of these instruments in a general sense, but to what extent they are applicable in the instant case. In order to answer this question, a more detailed legal analysis of these instruments as well as the historical background to their adoption is necessary. **[page 65]**

4 .3.2 Historical Background of Common Article 3

---

[90]   Prosecutor's Closing Brief, p. 80. See also pp. 93, 101, 105 and 134.

159. The Diplomatic Conference for the Establishment of International Conventions for the Protection of Victims of War, convened by the Swiss Federal Council, was held in Geneva from 21 April to 12 August 1949 (the Conference). The Conference was seized by the working documents that passed through the many preparatory stages. After four months of continuous debate, the Conference established the first, second, third and fourth Geneva Conventions.[91]

160. From the very beginning, it was understood that these four Conventions could be applicable only in international armed conflicts. However, the ICRC proposed at the Conference to apply these Conventions to non-international armed conflicts as well. The proposal of the ICRC was rejected as a result of almost universal opposition by the states.

161. During the debate on this issue, special attention was focused on the fourth Geneva Convention. For a long period, it was considered evident that civilians would remain outside hostilities. The ICRC recognised that "when the Second World War broke out, civilians were not provided with effective protection under any convention or treaty."[92]

162. It was emphasised by the ICRC that the Fourth Convention represented "an important step forward in written international law in the humanitarian field."[93] Therefore, in the opinion of the ICRC, it was necessary to apply it to internal armed conflicts as well. However, from the point of view of the delegations such an application could entail not only political but also technical difficulties.

163. Thus, the situation at the Conference was rather complicated. On the one hand, the idea of the ICRC to apply the four Geneva Conventions to internal armed conflicts had **[page 66]** been treated by many delegations as unfriendly attempts to interfere in the internal affairs of the states and to protect all forms of insurrections, rebellion, anarchy and the break-up of states and even plain brigandage. On the other hand, there was an understanding of the necessity to aid the victims of internal conflicts, the horrors of which sometimes surpass the horrors of international wars by reason of the fratricidal hatred they engender.[94]

164. The Conference rejected a considerable number of the alternative drafts on this issue and, as a result of lengthy and tremendous efforts, succeeded in approving Common Article 3 as it appears now in the four Geneva Conventions. Pursuant to this Article, each Party to a non-international conflict is bound to apply certain provisions as a minimum. The words "as a minimum" must be understood in the sense that the applicable provisions represent a compulsory minimum. At the same time, the Parties were encouraged not to limit themselves to the provided minimum. They were invited, in accordance with Common Article 3, "to endeavour to bring into force, by means of special agreements, all or part of the other provisions of the present Convention."

165. On this occasion, the ICRC pointed out: "To borrow the phrase of one of the delegates, Article 3 is like a "Convention in miniature." It applies to non-international conflicts only and will be the only Article applicable to them until such time as a special agreement between the Parties has brought into force between them all or part of the other provisions of the Convention."[95]

4.3.3 Historical Background of Additional Protocol II

---

[91] "First Convention," "second Convention," "third Convention" and "fourth Convention" mean, respectively, the Geneva Convention for the Amelioration of the Conditions of the Wounded and Sick in Armed Forces in the Field of 12 August 1949; the Geneva Convention for the Amelioration of the Conditions of the Wounded, Sick and Shipwrecked members of Armed Forces at Sea of 12 August 1949; the Geneva Convention Relative to the Treatment of Prisoners of War of 12 August 1949; the Geneva Convention relative to the Protection of Civilian Persons in Time of War of 12 August 1949.

[92] The Geneva Convention of 12 August 1949, Commentary, IV Geneva Convention, p. 3. (ICRC Pub., 1958). Hereafter, "Commentary on IV Geneva Convention, ICRC".

[93] *Ibid.*, p. 9.

[94] ICRC comments on Additional Protocol II. See the ICRC website, (visited 6 May. 1999) <http://www.icrc.org>.

[95] Commentary on IV Geneva Convention, p. 34.

166.   After the Conference in 1949, the idea to improve the situation with the protection of the victims of internal conflicts remained on the agenda. As a result of compromise, Common Article 3 was not drafted in a very clear way and there were practical difficulties with its application. Moreover, in light of the number and scale of armed conflicts that occurred in different parts of the world the need to improve the protection of the civilian population during armed conflicts became more urgent. In this respect, the **[page 67]** ICRC found it necessary to emphasise that "the development of arms and the increased radius of action given to armed forces by modern inventions have made it apparent that, notwithstanding the ruling theory, civilians were certainly "in the war", and exposed to the same dangers as the combatants – and sometimes worse."[96]

167.   In light of such circumstances, the ICRC began to prepare a new conference, which took place in 1977. One of the main purposes of this conference was to improve the protection of the civilian population during armed conflicts. Two Protocols additional to the Geneva Conventions of 1949 were adopted as a result of this conference. Protocol I deals with international armed conflict and Protocol II with non-international armed conflict. Commenting recently on the general problems in implementing the fourth Geneva Convention, the ICRC noted that this Convention "contains no detailed provisions for the protection of the civilian population against the dangers caused by military operations such as aerial bombardments and shelling. This gap was later filled by Protocol I Additional to the Geneva Conventions."[97] Similarly, Protocol II had to supplement Common Article 3 in order to improve the protection of civilians in internal armed conflicts.

168.   One of the very important supplements of Protocol II to Common Article 3 is Part IV entitled "Civilian Population." In this Part the Protocol provides not only for the protection of "individual civilians," but directly addresses the issue of the protection of the "civilian population." Article 13 of Additional Protocol II states, "the civilian population and individual civilians shall enjoy general protection against dangers arising from military operations." This part contains six detailed Articles providing for the protection of objects indispensable to the survival of the civilian population, protection of works and installations containing dangerous forces, protection of cultural objects and places of worship, prohibition of forced movement of civilians, activities of relief societies et cetera. **[page 68]**

4.3.4 The Test of Applicability of Common Article 3 and Additional Protocol II

Introduction

169.   The Trial Chamber is of the opinion that in order for an act to breach Common Article 3 and Protocol II, a number of elements must be shown. It must be established that the armed conflict in Rwanda in this period of time was of a non-international character. There must also be a link between the accused and the armed forces. Further, the crimes must be committed *ratione loci* and *ratione personae*. Finally, there must be a nexus between the crime and the armed conflict.

The Trial Chamber shall, therefore, consider each of these elements in turn.

The Nature of the Armed Conflict

170.   Both international instruments, Common Article 3 and Protocol II, were in force in 1994 in Rwanda. Therefore, it is proper to consider them together taking into account that Protocol II "develops and supplements Common Article 3 without modifying its existing conditions of application."[98] The general criteria in Protocol II for determining whether armed conflict is of a non-international character was one of the important supplements. An armed conflict which takes place in the territory of a High Contracting Party between its armed forces and dissident armed forces or other organised armed groups,

---

96   Preliminary remarks of the ICRC to the Geneva Conventions of August 12, 1949, p. 17.
97   Report by ICRC Meeting of Experts, Geneva, 27-29 October 1998, p. 2. See the ICRC website (visited 29 Dec. 1998) <http://www.icrc.org>.
98   See Art. 1 of Additional Protocol II.

in accordance with Protocol II, should be considered as a non-international armed conflict. This requirement reflects the essential distinction between an international armed conflict, conducted by two or more States, and non-international armed conflict conducted by a State and another armed force which does not qualify as a State.

171. Certain types of internal conflicts, which fall below a minimum threshold, are not recognised by Article 1(2) of Protocol II as non-international armed conflict, namely, "situations of internal disturbances and tensions, such as riots, isolated and sporadic acts of violence and other acts of a similar nature." The remaining criteria define the necessary characteristics of the dissident armed forces or other organised armed groups, which must: **[page 69]**

    1. be under responsible command;
    2. exercise control over part of the territory of the State;
    3. carry out sustained and concerted military operations, and
    4. be able to implement the Protocol.

172. Thus, in the present case, all material requirements existed to consider the situation in Rwanda, during April, May, June and July 1994, as an armed conflict, not of an international character. This conflict took place in the territory of Rwanda between governmental armed forces (Forces Armées Rwandaises – the FAR) and the dissident armed forces (Rwandese Patriotic Front – the RPF). These dissidents, under the responsible command of General Kagame, exercised control over part of the territory of Rwanda and were able to carry out sustained and concerted military operations as well as to implement Common Article 3 and Protocol II.

A Link Between the Accused and the Armed Forces

173. In accordance with Article 6 of the ICTR Statute, a person who "planned, instigated, ordered, committed or otherwise aided and abetted in the planning, preparation or execution of a crime referred to in Articles 2 to 4 of the present Statute, shall be individually responsible for the crime." Article 4 of the Statute especially provides for prosecuting persons for serious violations of Common Article 3 and Protocol II. Therefore, the question is whether the accused falls within the class of persons who may be held responsible for serious violations of these international instruments.

174. Violations of Common Article 3 and Protocol II could be committed during, or as a result of, military operations. This means that the Parties to an armed conflict should be responsible for such breaches. In the instant case, this would constitute the FAR and the RPF. The ability of the RPF as a dissident armed force to implement legally binding international instruments is considered in Protocol II as a fundamental criteria in order to recognise the non-international character of the armed conflict. The ability of the governmental armed forces to comply with the provisions of such instruments is axiomatic. In the instant case, the two armies were well organised and participated in the military operations under responsible military command. Therefore, based on Article 6(1) of the ICTR Statute, it could be concluded that the appropriate members of the FAR **[page 70]** and RPF shall be responsible individually for violations of Common Article 3 and Protocol II, if factually proven.

175. Thus, individuals of all ranks belonging to the armed forces under the military command of either of the belligerent Parties fall within the class of perpetrators. If individuals do not belong to the armed forces, they could bear the criminal responsibility only when there is a link between them and the armed forces. It cannot be disregarded that the governmental armed forces are under the permanent supervision of public officials representing the government who had to support the war efforts and fulfil a certain mandate. On this issue, in the *Akayesu* Judgement, Trial Chamber I was correct to include in the class of perpetrators, "individuals who were legitimately mandated and expected as public officials or agents or persons otherwise holding public authority or *de facto* representing the Government to support or fulfil the war efforts."[99]

---

[99]   *Akayesu* Judgement; para. 631.

176. Thus, the Trial Chamber is of the opinion that the laws of war apply not only to the members of the armed forces but, in certain cases, to civilians as well, if so established factually. In this case, the accused persons could fall within the class of individuals who may be held responsible for serious violations of Common Article 3 and Protocol II. Violations of these international instruments could be committed outside the theatre of combat. For example, the captured members of the RPF may be brought to any location within the territory of Rwanda and could be under the control or in the hands of persons who are not members of the armed forces. Therefore, every crime should be considered on a case-by-case basis taking into account the material evidence presented by the Prosecution. In other words, the evidence needs to show, beyond a reasonable doubt, that there was a link between the accused and the armed forces.

Ratione Personae

177. Two distinct issues arise with respect to personal jurisdiction over serious violations of Common Article 3 and Protocol II. In addition to the class of perpetrators, which has been considered above, the issue of the class of victims should be addressed. **[page 71]**

178. It is delineated in paragraph 1 of the Indictment that, "thousands of men, women, and children were killed and numerous people injured" at the four sites in the *Prefecture* of Kibuye between about 10 April and 30 June 1994. It was added in paragraphs 25, 32, 39 and 45 of the Indictment that "these men, women and children were unarmed and were predominantly Tutsis."

179. On the basis of the definition of the civilian population contained in Article 50 of Additional Protocol I, the conclusion could be made that the victims of the massacres which occurred at the four sites, referred to in the Indictment, qualify as the civilian population. This definition stipulates, "the civilian population comprises all persons who are civilians." The first paragraph of the same Article indicates that, "a civilian is any person who does not belong to one of the categories of persons referred to in Article 4(A)(1), (2), (3) and (6) of the Third Convention and in Article 43 of this Protocol." Each of these Articles enumerates the various types of combatants. Therefore, in accordance with this definition, for the purpose of protection of victims of armed conflict, all persons who are not combatants might be considered civilians.

180. On this basis, the ICRC comes to the following conclusion: "Thus the Protocol adopted the only satisfactory solution, which is that of a negative definition, namely, that the civilian population is made up of persons who are not members of the armed forces."[100] It should be noted that there is a certain distinction between the terms "civilians" and "civilian population." There are civilians who accompany the armed forces or are attached to them. Civilians could even be among combatants who take a direct part in the hostilities. There is clear confirmation of this fact in Protocol II which stipulates that, "civilians shall enjoy the protection afforded by this part unless and for such time as they take a direct part in the hostilities."[101] However, the civilian population as such does not participate in the armed conflict. Article 50 of Protocol I emphasises, **[page 72]** "the presence within the civilian population of individuals who do not come within the definition of civilian does not deprive the population of its civilian character."[102]

181. It is generally known that the civilian population is unarmed and is not in any way drawn into the armed conflict. The Chamber also takes into account the fact that the Defence did not challenge the civilian status of the victims. Whether there is a material averrment for charges involving Article 4 of the Statute is a question of findings which is addressed in Part VI of the Judgement.

---

[100]   COMMENTARY ON THE ADDITIONAL PROTOCOLS (Jean Pictet, ed.) (ICRC, Martinus Nijhoff Publishers, Geneva, 1987), p. 610, section 1913.
[101]   Additional Protocol II, Art. 13(3).
[102]   Additional Protocol 1, Article 50(3).

Ratione Loci

182. In spite of the fact that there is no clear provision on applicability *ratione loci* either in Common Article 3 or Protocol II, the juridical situation is rather clear. The Chamber has to recall that two Parties in the armed conflict were legally bound by the provisions of these international instruments. Therefore, in accordance, with requirements of international public law, these instruments should be applicable in the whole territory of Rwanda. Moreover, in Article 4 of Protocol II, which in principle reproduces Common Article 3, there is a clear indication that the enumerated criminal acts "shall remain prohibited at any time and in any place whatsoever." Therefore, it is unnecessary that serious violations of Common Article 3 and Protocol II occur in the actual theatre of operations. Captured persons, for example, could be brought to other locations of the territory, but despite this relocation, they should be treated humanely. The expression "at any time whatsoever" means that the temporal factor does not assume a narrow interpretation. This approach was confirmed by the ICTY Appeal Chamber in its decision on jurisdiction in the *Tadic* Judgement wherein it was held that,

> ... the geographical and temporal frame of reference for internal armed conflicts is similarly broad. This conception is reflected in the fact that beneficiaries of Common Article 3 of the Geneva Conventions are those taking no active part (or no longer taking an active part) in the hostilities. This indicates that the rules contained in Article 3 also apply outside the narrow geographical context of the actual theatre of combat operations.[103] **[page 73]**

183. The Appeal Chamber also remarked in this paragraph that "like Common Article 3, it explicitly protects all persons who do not take a direct part or who have ceased to take part in the hostilities ...Article 2(1) [of Protocol II] provides "this Protocol shall be applied [...] to all persons affected by an armed conflict as defined in Article 1"." After quoting Article 2(2) of Protocol II about persons who have been deprived of their liberty the Appeals Chamber noted that "under this last provision the temporal scope of the applicable rules clearly reaches beyond the actual hostilities. . . *The nexus required is only a relationship between the conflict and the deprivation of liberty*, not that the deprivation occurred in the midst of battle." [Emphasis added]. On the basis of the foregoing, the Appeal Chambers came to the conclusion that in case of internal conflict, until a peaceful settlement is achieved, international humanitarian law continues to apply in the whole territory under the control of a Party, whether or not actual combat takes place there and the crimes committed in these circumstances should be considered as crimes "in the context of an armed conflict."[104] Thus, the Appeals Chamber found that the alleged crimes should not be considered in the narrow geographical and temporal framework and should be understood as crimes committed in the context of an armed conflict if there is a relationship between this conflict and the offence.

Serious Violations

184. The competence of the Chamber is limited to serious violations of Common Article 3 and Protocol II. Article 4 of the ICTR Statute states that the persons committing or ordering to be committed *serious violations* of Common Article 3 and Protocol II should be prosecuted. The Chamber finds that this is a qualitative limitation of its competence and the phrase "serious violations" should be interpreted as breaches involving grave consequences. The list of prohibited acts, which is provided in Article 4 of the ICTR Statute, as well as in Common Article 3 and in Article 4 of Protocol II, undeniably should be recognised as serious violations entailing individual criminal responsibility. **[page 74]**

Nexus Requirement Between the Armed Conflict and the Crime

185. It is important to establish whether all the crimes committed during the non-international armed conflict should be considered as crimes connected with serious violations of Common Article 3 and

---

[103]   ICTY Decision on the Defence Motion for Interlocutory Appeal on Jurisdiction of 2 October 1995. para. 69.
[104]   Ibid. para. 70.

Protocol II. The Chamber is of the opinion that only offences, which have a nexus with the armed conflict, fall within this category. If there is not a direct link between the offences and the armed conflict there is no ground for the conclusion that Common Article 3 and Protocol II are violated.

186.   The jurisprudence in this area of the law requires such a link between the armed conflict and the offence. The ICTY Trial Chamber in the Judgement of *Prosecutor v. Zejnil Delalic, Zdravko Mucic, Hazim Delic and Esad Landzo* (*Celebici* Judgement) stated that "there must be an obvious link between the criminal act and the armed conflict."[105] The same point of view is reflected in the *Tadic* Judgement. In *Tadic*, the Trial Chamber remarked that "the only question to be determined in the circumstances of each individual case was whether the offences were closely related to the armed conflict as a whole."[106] In the *Akayesu* Judgement, the Trial Chamber found that ". . .it has not been proved beyond reasonable doubt that the acts perpetrated by Akayesu ...were committed in conjunction with the armed conflict." Such a conclusion means that, in the opinion of that Chamber, such a connection is necessary.

187.   This issue was discussed recently at the first session of the Preparatory Commission for the International Criminal Court (16 to 26 February 1999). From the point of view of the participants, war crimes would occur if the criminal conduct took place in the context of and was associated with the armed conflict.[107]

188.   Thus the term "nexus" should not be understood as something vague and indefinite. A direct connection between the alleged crimes, referred to in the Indictment, and the armed conflict should be established *factually*. No test, therefore, can be defined *in abstracto*. It is for the Trial Chamber, on a case-by-case basis, to adjudge on the facts **[page 75]** submitted as to whether a nexus existed. It is incumbent upon the Prosecution to present those facts and to prove, beyond a reasonable doubt, that such a nexus exists.

189.   The nexus requirement between the offence and the armed conflict is of crucial significance, taking into account that Common Article 3 and Protocol II are designed to protect the victims of the armed conflict. War crimes are inevitably connected with violations of Common Article 3 and Protocol II. Whether there is a nexus between the alleged crimes and the armed conflict in the instant case is an issue of legal findings which will be addressed in Part VI of the Judgement. At this stage it should be highlighted that the consideration of the applicability of the provisions of Common Article 3 and Protocol II would be proper if such a nexus is established.

Conclusion

190.   It remains for the Chamber to make a finding in the context of the events alleged in the Indictment with regard to the culpability of the accused under Article 4 of the ICTR Statute. This will be addressed in the Legal Findings Part of the Judgement. **[page 76]**

4.4   CRIMINAL RESPONSIBILITY, ARTICLES 6(1) AND 6(3)

4.4.1   Individual Responsibility – Article 6(1)

191.   The Indictment sets out in its General Allegations (paragraph 21) that both Kayishema and Ruzindana, pursuant to Article 6(1) of the Tribunal's Statute, are individually responsible for the execution of crimes referred to in Articles 2 to 4 of the same Statute. Whilst the Chamber will examine the specific charges raised in the Indictment below, it must first address the inherent requirement that the accused be individually responsible for the commission of these crimes. In this respect the Statute adopts a wide scope of inclusion. Article 6(l) states

---

[105]   *Prosecutor v. Zejnil Delalić, Zdravko Mucić, Hazim Delić and Esad Landzo*, Case No. IT-96-21-T, 16 Nov. 1998, para. 193.
[106]   *Tadić* Judgement, para. 573.
[107]   The Second Discussion Paper (PCNICC/ 1999/WGE/RT.2).

A person who planned, instigated, ordered, committed or otherwise aided and abetted in the planning, preparation and execution of the crime referred to in Articles 2 to 4 of the present Statute, shall be individually, responsible for the crime.

192. The Parties addressed the Chamber with regard to the interpretation and application of this paragraph to the events in question. Accordingly, it is necessary to consider the degree of participation required in the crimes delineated in Articles 2 to 4 of the Statute. Only then, and in light of the factual findings set out below, is it possible to identify whether either Ruzindana or Kayishema are individually criminally responsible pursuant to Article 6(1).

193. Before addressing the requisite elements necessary to find individual criminal responsibility under Article 6(1), the Trial Chamber will first examine the issue of statutory construction raised by Counsel for Ruzindana.

194. The Defence focused upon a very specific interpretation of Article 6(1). They contended that the modes of participation, "planning, instigation, ordering, committing", should be read cumulatively, but separately from, "aiding and abetting".[108] Only such a **[page 77]** position, it was submitted, would give full weight to the drafters use of "or" within the Article. Furthermore, because "abetting" and "instigating" have the same meaning, to avoid concurrence it was posited that "aiding and abetting" should also be read cumulatively despite the ruling in the *Akayesu* Judgement.

195. The Trial Chamber is of the opinion that the interpretation submitted by the Defence would not only offend common sense, but would also be contrary to the findings of the Chamber in the *Celebici* Judgement, where it stated categorically,

> . . . that individuals may be held criminally responsible for their participation in the commission of offences in *any* of the several capacities is in clear conformity with general principles of criminal law. As concluded by the Trial Chamber II in the *Tadic* Judgement, there can be no doubt that this corresponds to the position under customary international law.[109] [emphasis added]

196. Similar reasoning is found in the *Akayesu* Judgement where the Chamber remarked, "Article 6(1) covers *various* stages of the commission of a crime."[110] [emphasis added]. Trial Chamber I in the *Akayesu* Judgement also held that, "aiding and abetting" were not synonymous, thus could separately give rise to individual responsibility. After stating these principles the Chamber in *Akayesu* proceeded to find the accused guilty of nine counts pursuant to one or more of the modes of participation expressed in Article 6(1).

197. The Trial Chamber can see no reason to depart from these logical and well-founded expressions of international law. Therefore, if any of the modes of participation delineated in Article 6(1) can be shown, and the necessary *actus reus* and *mens rea* are evidenced, then that would suffice to adduce criminal responsibility under this Article. **[page 78]**

198. The Trial Chamber is of the opinion that, as was submitted by the Prosecution, there is a further two stage test which must be satisfied in order to establish individual criminal responsibility under Article 6(1). This test required the demonstration of (i) participation, that is that the accused's conduct contributed to the commission of an illegal act, and (ii) knowledge or intent, that is awareness by the actor of his participation in a crime.[111]

---

[108] Defence closing arguments, read from written brief submitted by Mr. Van der Griend on behalf of Ruzindana, on 28 October 1998 ("Closing Brief for Ruzindana"), p. 45. In the Closing Brief for Ruzindana, counsel at once urged this cumulative reading, and then endorsed its disjunctive formulation adopted by the *Akayesu* Judgement, p. 45. The Chamber enunciates its view here for the purpose of clarity.

[109] *Celebici* Judgement, para 321. See also the cases and conventions cited therein.

[110] Akayesu Judgement, para. 473. See also para. 484 where Trial Chamber I reads "aiding and abetting" disjunctively.

[111] Prosecution Closing Brief, p. 17. This test was drawn from the *Tadić* Judgement applying identical provisions in Article 7(1) of the ICTY Statute.

199. The first point of this test, the *actus reus* of participation, was considered in great detail by Trial Chamber I in the *Akayesu* Judgement and by the ICTY in the *Tadic* Judgement.[112] It is now firmly established that for the accused to be criminally culpable his conduct must have been proved, beyond a reasonable doubt, to have contributed to, or have had an effect on, the commission of the crime.[113] What constitutes the *actus reus* and the requisite contribution inevitably varies with each mode of participation set out in Article 6(1).[114] What is clear is that the contribution to the undertaking be a substantial one, and this is a question of fact for the Trial Chamber to consider.

200. It is not presupposed that the accused must be present at the scene of the crime, nor that his contribution be a direct one. That is to say, in light of the decision rendered in the *Furundzjia* Judgement and the jurisprudence set out therein, the role of the individual in the commission of the offence need not always be a tangible one. This is particularly pertinent where the accused is charged with the "aiding" or "abetting" of a crime. In *Furundzija* it was held, ". . . an approving spectator who is held in such respect by the other perpetrators that his presence encourages them in their conduct, may be guilty of complicity in a crime against humanity."[115] **[page 79]**

201. This Chamber concurs. The presence of such a spectator need not be a *conditio sine qua non* for the principal. Therefore, subject to the caveat that the accused knew the effect that his presence would have, he may be found responsible under Article 6(1) for such a contribution to the commission of any of the offences specified in the Tribunal's Statute.

202. This jurisprudence extends naturally to give rise to responsibility when the accused failed to act in breach of a clear duty to act. The question of responsibility arising from a duty to act, and any corresponding failure to execute such a duty is a question that is inextricably linked with the issue of command responsibility. This is because under Article 6(3) a clear duty is imposed upon those in authority, with the requisite means at their disposal, to prevent or punish the commission of a crime. However, individual responsibility pursuant to Article 6(1) is based, in this instance, not on the duty to act, but from the encouragement and support that might be afforded to the principals of the crime from such an omission.[116]

203. In view of such a broad scope of participation that may give rise to responsibility under Article 6(1), there must be a clear awareness that this participation will lead to the commission of a crime.[117] The Trial Chamber has set out, in Chapter 5.1 of this Judgement, that the clear objective of the atrocities occurring throughout Rwanda and the Kibuye *Prefecture*, in 1994, was to destroy the Tutsi population. The perpetrators of these crimes, therefore, were united in this common intention. On this point, the Chamber in the *Celebici* Judgement declared that where,

> . . . a plan exists, or where there otherwise is evidence that members of a group are acting with a common criminal purpose, all those who knowingly participate in, and directly and substantially contribute to, the realisation of this purpose may be held criminally responsible . . and . . .[d]epending upon the facts of a given situation, the culpable individual may, under such circumstances, be held **[page 80]** criminally responsible either as a direct perpetrator of, or as an aider and abettor to, the crime in question.[118]

---

[112] See, respectively, paras: 480-484, and paras. 673-674 and 688-692.

[113] See *Tadić* Judgement, para. 673-674; *Celebici* Judgement, para. 326; *Akayesu* Judgement, para. 473-475; *Furundzija* Judgement, para. 235; and the authorities cited therein.

[114] See *Akayesu* Judgement, paras. 480-485.

[115] *Furundzija* Judgement, para 207.

[116] See the *Akayesu* Judgement where the accused's failure to oppose the killings, in light of his authoritative position, was found to constitute a form of tacit encouragement, para. 705.

[117] What constitutes a crime is defined by the Tribunal's Statute. Therefore, only the actual commission of a crime will suffice, except for that of genocide where it is specifically stated that an "attempt" to commit genocide will give rise to criminal responsibility, Article 2(3)(d) of the Statute.

[118] *Celebici* Judgement, para. 328.

204. The Trial Chamber concludes, therefore, that the members of such a group would be responsible for the result of any acts done in furtherance of the common design where such furtherance would be probable from those acts.

205. Thus, the accused need not necessarily have the same *mens rea* as the principal offender. Whilst knowledge or intention will give rise to individual responsibility under Article 6(1), the distinction is only of importance in distinguishing whether the accused aids or abets a crime or is a co-perpetrator.[119]

206. Such a requirement of *mens rea* refutes the contention by Counsel for Kayishema that the burden of proof is reversed when the *actus reus* for responsibility, under this Article, arises through the failure to perform an act. The Prosecution must prove that the accused was aware that his failure to act would contribute to the commission of a crime.

207. In short, therefore, the Chamber finds that each of the modes of participation may, independently, give rise to criminal responsibility. The Prosecution must prove that through his mode of participation, whether it be by act(s) or omission(s), the accused contributed substantially to the commission of a crime and that, depending on the mode of participation in question, he was at least aware that his conduct would so contribute to the crime.

4.4.2 Command Responsibility – Article 6(3)

208. The Indictment further alleges that Kayishema was, "also or alternatively individually responsible for the criminal acts of his subordinates". In this respect, Article 6(3) is pertinent. It states, **[page 81]**

> The fact that any of the acts referred to in articles 2 to 4 of the present Statute was committed by a subordinate does not relieve his or her superior of criminal responsibility if he or she knew, or had reason to know that the subordinate was about to commit such acts or had done so and the superior failed to take the necessary and reasonable measures to prevent such acts or to punish the perpetrators thereof.[120]

Ruzindana is not charged under Article 6(3).

209. The principle of command responsibility is firmly established in international law, and its position as a principle of customary international law has recently been delineated by the ICTY in the *Celebici* Judgement.[121] The clear recognition of this doctrine is now reflected in Article 28 of the Rome Statute of the ICC.

210. The finding of responsibility under Article 6(1) of the Statute does not prevent the Chamber from finding responsibility additionally, or in the alternative, under Article 6(3). The two forms of responsibility are not mutually exclusive. The Chamber must, therefore, consider both forms of responsibility charged in order to fully reflect the culpability of the accused in light of the facts.

211. There were no submissions made by the Defence with regard to the legal underpinning of Article 6(3). As such, the Trial Chamber will consider the position advanced by the Prosecution concomitantly with its examination of the various elements that must be satisfied in order to establish criminal liability under the doctrine of command responsibility.

212. It is essential to consider first whether Kayishema, in his role as *Prefect*, is subject to the notion of command responsibility set out in Article 6(3). Secondly, it is incumbent upon the Chamber to consider who constitutes the subordinates over whom Kayishema would exercise command. In this respect it would also be necessary to clarify whether those subordinates must be under his *de jure* command, or if *de facto* subordination **[page 82]** would suffice. Thirdly, the requisite degree of knowledge of the subordinate's actions required to establish command responsibility must also be considered. Finally, the

---

[119] See *Furundzija* Judgement, paras. 250-257.
[120] Hereafter, responsibility arising under this Article shall be referred to as "command responsibility", or "superior responsibility". The terms will be used interchangeably.
[121] *Celebici* Judgement, paras. 333-343, in reference to the respective Article in the ICTY Statute.

Chamber must address the question of when an individual becomes responsible under this doctrine for failing to prevent a crime or punish the perpetration thereof.

Responsibility of a Non-Military Commander

213. The Prosecution submitted that the principle of superior responsibility applies not only to military commanders, but also extends to civilians in positions of authority.[122] The Chamber finds that the application of criminal responsibility to those civilians who wield the requisite authority is not a contentious one. There are a number of reasons for this.

214. The construction of the Statute itself is clear. It makes no limited reference to the responsibility to be incurred by military commanders alone.[123] Rather, the more generic term of "superior" is used. The Chamber concurs with the observation in the *Celebici* Judgement that this generic term, coupled with its juxtaposition to the individual criminal responsibility of "Head[s] of State or Government" or "responsible Government officials" in Article 6(2), clearly reflects the intention of the drafters to extend this provision of superior responsibility beyond military commanders, to also "encompass political leaders and other civilian superiors in positions of authority."[124]

215. The jurisprudence also supports this interpretation. Before Trial Chamber I of this Tribunal, the former Prime Minister, Jean Kambanda, pleaded guilty to crimes against humanity and genocide by virtue, *inter alia*, of Article 6(3).[125] Similarly, Omar Serushago, a prominent local civilian and leader of the members of the *Interahamwe* in Gisenyi *Prefecture*, also pleaded guilty to crimes against humanity and genocide and **[page 83]** acknowledged responsibility for these crimes pursuant to Article 6(3).[126] In addition, the *Celebici* Judgement, which addressed this issue in great detail, highlighted the practice of the Military Tribunal for the Far East (Tokyo Tribunal), and the Superior Military Government Court of the French Occupation Zone in Germany, where senior politicians and even leading industrialists were charged with the commission of war crimes committed by their subordinates.[127]

216. The crucial question in those cases was not the civilian status of the accused, but of the degree of authority he exercised over his subordinates.[128] Accordingly the Chamber accepts the submission made by the Prosecution that a civilian in a position of authority may be liable under the doctrine of command responsibility. The Chamber will turn, therefore, to consider in what instances a civilian can be considered a superior for the purposes of Article 6(3), and the requisite "degree of authority" necessary to establish individual criminal culpability pursuant to this doctrine of superior responsibility.

Concept of Superior: de Jure and de Facto Control

217. This superior-subordinate relationship lies at the heart of the concept of command responsibility. The basis under which he assumes responsibility is that, if he knew or had reason to know that a crime may or had been committed, then he must take all measures necessary to prevent the crime or punish the perpetrators. If he does not take such actions that are within his power then, accordingly, he is culpable for those crimes committed. The Trial Chamber in *Celebici* set out the guiding principle in this respect, when it stated that, "[T]he doctrine of command responsibility is ultimately predicated upon the power of the superior to control the acts of his subordinates".[129] The Chamber then elaborated upon this principle by warning that, "[We] must at all times be alive to the realities of any given situation and be prepared to

---

[122]   Closing Brief, p. 20.
[123]   *C.f.* the specification of the responsibility of "military commanders" in Article 87 of Protocol I Additional to the Geneva Conventions 1949, (Jean Pictet ed.).
[124]   *Celebici* Judgement, para. 356.
[125]   *Prosecutor v. Jean Kambanda*, Judgement and Sentence, Case No.: ICTR 97-23-S (Eng.).
[126]   *Prosecutor v. Omar Serushago*, Judgement and Sentence, Case No.: ICTR 98-39-S (Eng.).
[127]   *Ibid*, paras. 356-362.
[128]   See the opinion of Judge Röling in the "Rape of Nanking" case, and the *Akayesu* Judgement, para. 491.
[129]   *Celebici* Judgement, para. 376.

pierce such veils of formalism that may shield those individuals carrying the greatest responsibility for heinous acts."[130] **[page 84]**

218. In order to "pierce the veils of formalism" therefore, the Chamber must be prepared to look beyond the *de jure* powers enjoyed by the accused and consider the *de facto* authority he exercised within Kibuye during April to July 1994. The position expounded by the ILC that an individual should only be responsible for those crimes that were within his legitimate legal powers to prevent,[131] does not assist the Trial Chamber in tackling the, "realities of any given situation". Therefore, in view of the chaotic situation that which prevailed in Rwanda in these pivotal months of 1994, the Chamber must be free to consider whether Kayishema had the requisite control over those committing the atrocities to establish individual criminal liability under Article 6(3), whether by *de jure* or *de facto* command.

219. A concentration upon the *de jure* powers of the *prefect* would assist neither Party. For example, focussing upon the *de jure* power of the *prefect* under the 1991 Constitution would be to prevent proper consideration of the Defence's case that the climate in Rwanda and the practical realities at that time were such that the *prefect* not only had no control over certain *de jure* subordinates, but also that he had no means to effectively prevent the atrocities that were occurring. Equally, a restricted view of the concept of superior to those exercising *de jure* control would not enable the Chamber to adequately consider the arguments of the Prosecution. She submitted that Kayishema exercised both legal command over those committing the massacres and *de facto* authority over these and other assailants such as the members of the *Interahamwe*.

220. This approach is also congruent with the *Celebici* case and the authorities cited therein.[132] For example, having examined the Hostage and High Command cases the Chamber in *Celebici* concluded that they authoritatively asserted the principle that, "powers of influence not amounting to formal powers of command provide a sufficient basis for the imposition of command responsibility." This Trial Chamber concurs. **[page 85]**

221. Moreover, the Rome Statute for the ICC, having delineated the circumstances in which a military commander would incur responsibility as a superior, stipulates in Article 28(2) that all other superiors shall be criminally responsible for acts, "committed by subordinates under his or her *effective* control." [emphasis added].

222. Article 6 of this Tribunal's Statute is formulated in a broad manner. By including responsibility of all government officials, all superiors and all those acting pursuant to orders, it is clearly designed to ensure that those who are culpable for the commission of a crime under Articles 2 to 4 of the Statute cannot escape responsibility through legalistic formalities. Therefore, the Chamber is under a duty, pursuant to Article 6(3), to consider the responsibility of all individuals who exercised effective control, whether that control be *de jure* or *de facto*.

223. Where it can be shown that the accused was the *de jure* or *de facto* superior and that pursuant to his orders the atrocities were committed, then the Chamber considers that this must suffice to found command responsibility. The Chamber need only consider whether he knew or had reason to know and failed to prevent or punish the commission of the crimes if he did not in fact order them. If the Chamber is satisfied beyond a reasonable doubt that the accused ordered the alleged atrocities then it becomes unnecessary to consider whether he tried to prevent; and irrelevant whether he tried to punish.

224. However, in all other circumstances, the Chamber must give full consideration to the elements of "knowledge" and "failure to prevent and punish" that are set out in Article 6(3) of the Statute.

Knowledge of Subordinates' Actions

---

[130]   *Ibid.*, para. 377.
[131]   ILC Draft Code of Crimes.
[132]   *Celebici* Judgement, paras. 364-378.

225. The *mens rea* in Article 6(3) requires that for a superior to be held criminally responsible for the conduct of his subordinates he must have known, or had reason to know, of their criminal activities. If it can be proven beyond a reasonable doubt that the **[page 86]** superior knew of the crimes that were being committed by those over whom he exercised control then the requisite *mens rea* is clearly established.

226. However, when we consider that individual responsibility arises when the superior "had reason to know" that a crime had or was about to be committed, the requisite *mens rea* is not so clear. The expansive approach to apportioning command responsibility in the cases following the Second World War was observed by the Trial Chamber in the *Celebici* Judgement. These cases first imposed a duty for the commander to know everything that occurred within his ambit of jurisdiction, and then imposed responsibility upon the commander for failure to fulfil that duty.[133] The Chamber in the *Celebici* case did not follow this reasoning. Instead it preferred it be proven that some information be available that would put the accused on notice of an offence and require further investigation by him.

227. On this issue, the Chamber finds the distinction between military commanders and other superiors embodied in the Rome Statute an instructive one.[134] In the case of the former it imposes a more active duty upon the superior to inform himself of the activities of his subordinates when he, "knew or, owing to the circumstances at the time, should have known that the forces were committing or about to commit such, crimes." This is juxtaposed with the *mens rea* element demanded of all other superiors who must have, "[known], or consciously disregarded information which clearly indicated, that the subordinates were committing or about to commit such crimes."

228. The Trial Chamber agrees with this view insofar that it does not demand a *prima facie* duty upon a non-military commander to be seized of every activity of all persons under his or her control. In light of the objective of Article 6(3) which is to ascertain the individual criminal responsibility for crimes as serious as genocide, crimes against humanity and violations of Common Article 3 to the Geneva Conventions and Additional Protocol II thereto; the Chamber finds that the Prosecution must prove that the accused in **[page 87]** this case either knew, or consciously disregarded information which clearly indicated or put him on notice that his subordinates had committed, or were about to commit acts in breach of Articles 2 to 4 of this Tribunal's Statute.

Effective Control: Failure to Prevent or Punish a Crime

229. The principle of command responsibility must only apply to those superiors who exercise effective control over their subordinates. This material ability to control the actions of subordinates is the touchstone of individual responsibility under Article 6(3). The International Law Commission in its Draft Code went so far as to suggest that for a superior to incur criminal responsibility, he must have, "the legal competence to take measures to prevent or repress the crime *and* the material possibility to take such measures."[135] [emphasis added].

230. However, as the Chamber highlighted above, to give such prominence to the *de jure* power bestowed upon an individual is to provide justice to neither Party. There is a need to shed this legalistic formalism and to focus upon the situation which prevails in the given fact situation. Therefore, the Chamber prefers the position as set out in the *Celebici* Judgement where it was held that,

> . . . the superior have effective control over the persons committing the underlying violations of humanitarian law, in the sense of having the material ability to prevent and punish the commission of these offences. With the caveat that such authority can have a *de facto* as well as a *de jure* character. . . [136]

---

[133] See *Celebici* Judgement, para. 389, and the cases cited therein, particularly the *Hostage* case, the *Toyoda* case, and the *Pohl* case.
[134] Article 28(1)(a), and 28(2)(a).
[135] ILC Draft Code of Crimes, pp. 38-39.
[136] *Celebici* Judgement, para. 378.

231.   Accordingly, the ability to prevent and punish a crime is a question that is inherently linked with the given factual situation. Thus, only in light of the findings which follow and an examination of the overall conditions in which Kayishema had to operate as *Prefect*, can the Chamber consider who were the subordinates to Kayishema from April to July 1994 and whether he exercised the requisite degree of control over **[page 88]** them in order to conclude whether he is individually criminally responsible for the atrocities committed by them. **[page 89]**

V.   FACTUAL FINDINGS

5.1   Alibi

232.   Both Kayishema and Ruzindana raised the defence of alibi to the charges levied against them. Both accused assert that they were not at the sites when any of the massacres occurred. The Trial Chamber shall consider the arguments advanced by Kayishema and Ruzindana below. Before examining the specifics of the alibi defences, however, it is first necessary to consider the procedural concerns that have accompanied their invocation.

5.1.1 Alibi Defence and Rule 67 of the Rules

The salient provisions of Rule 67 of the Rules state that,

> (A) As early as reasonably possible and in any event prior to the commencement of the trial:

> (ii) the defence shall notify the Prosecutor of its intent to enter:

> > (a)   the defence of alibi; in which case the notification shall specify the place or places at which the accused claims to have been present at the time of the alleged crime and the names and addresses of witnesses and any other evidence upon which the accused intends to rely to establish the alibi

> (B)   Failure of the defence to provide such notice under this Rule shall not limit the right of the accused to rely on any of the above defences.

233.   The requirement upon the Defence to disclose its intention to rely upon the defence of alibi reflects the well-established practice in the common law jurisdictions around the world.[137] It is a requirement necessary in many jurisdictions, and in the jurisdiction of this Tribunal, in order to allow the Prosecution to adequately prepare its case. Once the accused has raised the defence of alibi, the burden to prove this defence may or may not rest upon him depending upon the jurisdiction concerned. In some jurisdictions such as **[page 90]** India, the burden of proof rests upon individuals, who plead the defence of alibi.[138] In several other jurisdictions as for example in South Africa, the burden of proof rests upon the Prosecution.[139]

234.   In the instant case, the Trial Chamber holds that the burden of proof rests upon the Prosecution to prove its case beyond a reasonable doubt in all aspects notwithstanding that the Defence raised alibi. After all, the accused is presumed innocent until the Prosecution has proved his guilt under Article 20(3) of the Statute. The accused is only required to raise the defence of alibi and fulfil the specific requirements of Rule 67(A)(ii) of the Rules, which stipulates the necessary information required about the defence of alibi.

235.   Under Rule 67 aforementioned, the Defence is required to notify the Prosecution about their intent to rely upon the defence of alibi. However, Counsel for Kayishema made absolutely no indication prior to the commencement of the trial of his intention to rely upon the defence of alibi, and Counsel for

---

[137]   In this respect see Criminal Justice Act 1967 s.ll of England which specifically legislates to require disclosure of alibi prior to trial. Similar legislation exists in Canada, as well as certain states of the United States and Australia.

[138]   Section 103 of the Indian Evidence Act. Refer to Sakar on Evidence, vol. 2 (1993), 14th Ed, p. 1341.

[139]   R v. Biya, (1952) 4 SA 514 (Appellate Division); Woolmington v. D.P.P (1935) A.C. 462 (H.L.) and R v. Wood, Cr. App. R. 74, at 78 (1968) (English Law); Sekitoleko v. Uganda [1967] E.A. 531 (U) (Ugandan Law).

Ruzindana only submitted limited information with regard to the witnesses that he intended to call. The Prosecution filed a formal complaint by Motion in which it requested the Trial Chamber to order compliance with Rule 67(A)(ii) of the Rules.[140]

236.   During the hearing, Kayishema was asked why, in light of the evidence he had heard against him, he had not raised his defence of alibi at an earlier stage. He stated that as far as the Office of the Prosecutor was concerned, the question was never asked of him. Furthermore, he raised the issue at the first opportunity with his Defence Counsel on 31 May 1996. **[page 91]**

237.   The Trial Chamber has considered the failure of both Defence Counsels to act in accordance with Rule 67(A)(ii). In its Decision on the above Prosecution Motion, the Chamber ruled,

> . . . that where good cause is not shown, for the application of Rule 67(B), the Trial Chamber is entitled to take into account this failure when weighing the credibility of the defence of alibi and/or any special defences presented.[141]

238.   The Trial Chamber notes that the Defence had ample time to prepare their client's defence and takes this on board in consideration of the timeliness of Counsel's notification of the Prosecution in accordance with Rule 67(A)(ii) of the Rules. This approach is congruent with those jurisdictions[142] facing similar difficulties in balancing the needs of the Prosecution with the Defendant's right to testify and present a defence.[143]

239.   Counsel for the Defence constantly advanced the argument that the Prosecution's concern over the continued violations of this rule was unjustified in light of the Prosecution's late disclosure of witness lists.[144] However, all Parties to the proceedings had the opportunity to raise such lack of disclosure in the appropriate manner before this Chamber. Therefore, the Defence's failure to follow the Rules of Procedure and Evidence is unacceptable and serves neither the interests of the accused nor of justice. Furthermore, the Defence's observation that under Rule 85 the Prosecution may bring evidence to rebut the alibi, does not mitigate the aforementioned duty upon the Defence under Rule 67.[145] Moreover, the mere fact that the Prosecutor did not utilise Rule 85 to bring evidence in rebuttal will not have any bearing upon the Trial Chamber's assessment of the evidence presented. Thus, this Chamber will accord no extra weight to the accused's defence of alibi merely because the Prosecution did not call witnesses in rebuttal. Considering the Decision on the above Motion, in which the Trial Chamber **[page 92]** ordered the compliance with Rules 67(A)(ii) and 67(B) and in light of the considerations discussed above, the Trial Chamber will, despite the non-compliance with its order and the defiance of the Defence Counsel, consider the defence of alibi advanced by both Kayishema and Ruzindana without prejudice to the accused.

5.1.2 Kayishema's Alibi Defence

240.   The essence of Kayishema's alibi is that he was in hiding from the morning of Saturday 16 April 1994, to the morning of Wednesday 20 April 1994. These dates purportedly removed him from the scene of the massacres at Catholic Church, Home St. Jean Complex and the Stadium that occurred on 16, 17, 18, 19 April. It would also remove him from Mubuga Church on the 16 April, the date that the Trial Chamber has found the major attack at this site occurred. It would not, however, account for his whereabouts in the days that preceded this attack. Kayishema also denies ever being present at any of the

---

[140]   In, Prosecutor v. Kayishema and Ruzindana, in the Decision on the Prosecution motion for a ruling on the Defence continued non compliance with Rule 67(A)(ii) and with the written and oral orders of the Trial Chamber, 3 Sept. 1998, Case No. International Criminal Tribunal for Rwanda-95-1-T.

[141]   Decision on non-compliance, *Ibid.*

[142]   For example, see Canada, R v. Dunbar and Logan, 68 C.C.C. (2d) 13 at pp. 62-3 (1982); R v. Cleghom 3 S.C.R. 175 (1995), and Australia, Petty and Maiden v. R, 173 CLR (1991) where, although no inference could be taken from the Defendant's prior silence, where a differing explanation had been given then inferences could be drawn.

[143]   Article 20 of the Statute.

[144]   This was reiterated once again even in Mr. Ferran's rejoinder, Trans., 17 Nov. 1998, pp. 133-139.

[145]   Rule 85(A)(iii) of the Rules.

massacre sites in the Bisesero area during the period set out in the Indictment, but provides no specific alibi.

241.   Kayishema testified before this Trial Chamber that in the early hours of Saturday 16 April, upon the departure of the commanding officer Major Jabo, the Tutsi gendarmes were mutinying and were looking for him with harmful intention. Upon receipt of this information he, with his wife and children, went into hiding. Kayishema stated in his testimony that between 9 and 10 a.m. he and his family left the *prefectorial* house and went into hiding. They sought refuge in the houses of white people in Kibuye because they had already been looted and no one was likely to return to them. The first house was that of Mr. Soufflet which lay along from the *Prefectorial* residence on Lake Kivu, approximately three kilometres from Home St. Jean and the Catholic Church. Kayishema stated that they remained there for the nights of 16 and 17 April. He and his family then moved next door, to the last house in that direction, for the remaining two nights. This was owned by a Swiss technical assistant who was working in the forestry department. Kayishema contended that he was absent from his family only when he would investigate **[page 93]** a noise outside or when his informant visited their hiding place. This absence was never in excess of 30 minutes.

242.   In an earlier account, Kayishema had volunteered details of this Prosecution period to the investigators, as shown in exhibit 350C, a transcript of the interview with investigators. On 6 November 1996, during the interview with investigators, Kayishema stated that he was in his own home during the period of the massacres at Home St. Jean, the Catholic Church, and the Stadium. Although at this time he could not remember the dates, or the days of the week that he was confined to his house, Kayishema identified individuals with whom he had hidden, namely Emmanuel Dusabimana, Alphonse Kayiranga, the wife of Lieutenant Charles Twagirayezu and the Tutsi wife of a Hutu named Francois. He did not, however, call any of these people to testify on his behalf. In this statement he also asserted that he would spend his nights, in the bush, hiding. During his cross-examination Kayishema explained the difference between his oral testimony and his statement to the investigators. He stated that his position in both was that he had been in hiding during the period of the massacres at the aforementioned sites and, therefore, could not have perpetrated the atrocities alleged.

243.   In his testimony, Kayishema went on to describe his activities after he came out of hiding. He talked of travelling around the *Prefecture*, burying bodies and taking wounded or malnourished children to the hospital, around 22 April. He met with the interim Prime Minister, Jean Kambanda, on 3 May and attended a public meeting with him. Kayishema also talked of going to Gitarama on 9 May in order to meet with the interim government that was based there at that time. His diary,[146] the personal diary of the *Prefect*, details meetings on 10, 11, and 13 May with his *sous prefects*. Kayishema referred to these meetings, as well as those on the 14 May with his prefectorial council and on 16 May with the interim president, in his testimony to the Trial Chamber. He also confirmed that he had gone into the Bisesero area throughout May, but only to conduct his prefectorial duties and to investigate the disparities between the information he had received and the actual situation in the area. Kayishema submitted, therefore, that **[page 94]** Defence witness DU, who testified that the defendant had not left his prefectorial office in this period, had been mistaken. Kayishema maintained, however, that he never visited any of the massacre sites in the Bisesero area during the months of April, May and June 1994 as charged in the Indictment. Moreover, when questioned in cross-examination about eye-witnesses who had identified him in the Bisesero area at specific sites such as Muyira Hill, and the Cave, Kayishema maintained that he did not know where such sites were even located. He asserted that those witnesses who identified him at various massacre sites either between 16 to 20 April, or in the Bisesero area during the massacres in April, May and June had erred.

Defence Witnesses in Support of Kayishema

---

[146]   Def. exh. 58.

244. In support of his alibi defence, the defendant called a number of witnesses, including his wife. In her first statement to investigators Mrs. Kayishema had stated that she, her husband and their children had gone into hiding in mid April. She also stated that on 13 May, the date of one of the major attacks in the Bisesero area, her husband had driven her to work in the morning and after dropping her at her work place, he went directly to his office. She arrived at work that Friday morning at 8 a.m., and returned home with her husband at 11 a.m.

245. In her testimony before the Chamber, however, Mrs. Kayishema, who holds a degree in education science and has served as a school inspector, clarified and elaborated upon her first statement. She contended that they had gone into hiding between 16 and 20 April 1994, following the departure of the commanding officer of the *gendarmerie nationale* in Kibuye Prefecture on 15 April. The corporal who remained was an RPF sympathiser and, she asserted, they had been informed that he had made various threats against the *prefect*. Although in her testimony Mrs. Kayishema referred to just female and sick gendarmes who had remained behind after the meeting on 15 April, she maintained that she and her husband had gone into hiding on 16 April for fear of their lives. They hid in the houses of those people who had been building the roads, staying in several houses and changing frequently. No more details about the houses were given. **[page 95]**

However, when questioned about her initial statement to investigators where she claimed to have gone into hiding in the bush for three days, she was able to clarify to this Chamber that she and her children had been hiding in the houses, and that her husband had spent the nights in the bush.

246. In her testimony, Kayishema's wife further elaborated upon the events of Friday 13 May 1994. In addition to the activities in the morning, she recalled that she had attended a public meeting chaired by her husband. The meeting, which began at 2 p.m., was to present the new *sous prefets*. Mrs. Kayishema did not offer any further testimony regarding her husband's whereabouts over the ensuing weeks, but simply stated that he continued with his duties as *Prefect* until their departure to Zaire on 16 July 1994.

247. Most witnesses for Kayishema had either not seen him at all during the period in question, such as witness DAC, or had seen him for very short periods of time on isolated occasions. Witness DN, for example, had seen him at a meeting in late April, witness DK saw him at a meeting to inaugurate a school in mid May, and witness DM had seen him briefly sometime in May at the roundabout at the centre of Kibuye Town. Consequently, although all Defence witnesses testified to never having heard of the participation of their *Prefect* in these massacres, very little specific evidence was proffered as to the accused's whereabouts during their execution. Only two other witnesses were able to provide further detailed insight into Kayishema's activities from 6 April 1994. With regard to the massacre at Mubuga Church, the only witness presented by the Defence was DV. The witness knew the accused by sight because he had seen him in Gitesi where he undertook his studies. He had not actually been present at the massacre and was unsure of the date it occurred. However, he lived only six to seven hundred meters from Mubuga Church and stated that he had not seen the defendant in the vicinity during the period of the massacres. In fact, witness DV testified that he did not see the defendant at all throughout April, May, June or July.

248. Witness DU testified as to Kayishema's whereabouts from 4 May to 16 July 1994. His testimony covered almost the entire period. He knew the defendant well and stayed **[page 96]** in Kayishema's house upon returning to Kibuye on 4 May. DU also worked in a canteen, just fifteen meters from the entrance of the *Prefecture* offices. Although he could not see Kayishema's office, he had a clear view of the entrance of these offices. He testified that he saw Kayishema every day over those two months. He ate breakfast, lunch and evening meals with Kayishema and his family, and often travelled to and from work with him. In the opinion of DU, Kayishema could not have visited the Bisesero area at any time from 4 May to 16 July because the defendant was never absent for periods in excess of 30 minutes. The witness felt able to state this with some certainty because of the proximity of the canteen to the defendant's offices and the fact that the noise of Kayishema's vehicle as he arrived at or departed from the offices made his whereabouts very obvious. The one exception that the witness could recall to these minimal absences was when Kayishema led a meeting and was gone for six hours. Mrs. Kayishema informed witness DU that Kayishema was at a meeting. Like the many other witnesses called for the

Defence, DU had never heard any reference to the participation in any massacres by his *Prefect*, Kayishema.

Examination of Kayishema's Alibi Defence

249. Having set out the defence propounded by Kayishema, the Trial Chamber has also given consideration to the various arguments raised by the Prosecution with regard to the issue of Kayishema's alibi. Particularly, the Chamber has taken note of the many contradictions in the defence raised by Kayishema. These are contradictions not only within his own testimony, but also contradictions between his testimony and the testimony of his wife and the other witnesses called on his behalf.

250. The Trial Chamber observes Kayishema's various statements to the investigators and to the Chamber do not correlate. For instance, in his first voluntary statement to investigators in July 1996 Kayishema made no reference to being in hiding or to the events which supposedly led to his being in hiding, namely the "mutiny" of the *gendarmerie nationale*. A number of observations may be made in this regard. In the first instance, the Trial Chamber does not make a negative finding due solely to Kayishema's non-disclosure of his alibi during the initial interviews with investigators. **[page 97]**

However, in addition to this non-disclosure within his interviews, in Kayishema's diary there was no mention of him either being in hiding or of the gendarme mutiny. The diary, Kayishema confirmed, was the personal diary of the *Prefect*. Whilst this Chamber appreciates that it is not possible to note every event which occurred, it is surprising that no mention was made of such major events, in particular those that precluded him from undertaking his official functions as *Prefect*.

251. The second statement given by Kayishema to investigators, on 6 November 1996, also differs in many respects from his testimony before this Chamber. In that interview, Kayishema did not remain silent, but gave specific details of his whereabouts during the massacres at the Home St. Jean complex, the Catholic Church and Gatwaro Stadium. He stated that he was in his home, the residence of the *Prefect*. When questioned specifically if he was in his home, for the whole time, Kayishema affirmed, "Home, in *my* house." Kayishema further provided the names of those individuals with whom he was hiding, as set out above. He also went on to describe how he would have to spend entire nights in the bush. Kayishema's statement that he was in his own home contradicts his testimony in court where he testified that he was in hiding in houses belonging to others. In his testimony, responding to a judicial question inquiring whether he was in *his* home or in hiding, Kayishema confirmed that he was hiding in the bush *at night*. This answer does not clear up the discrepancy. In his oral testimony Kayishema gave specific details of being in two houses for two nights each, moving from one to the other. Further, when questioned specifically as to why he had told investigators that he had been in *his* home, Kayishema referred to the need to protect the identity of those in whose houses he had occupied. Responding to another judicial question inquiring why, therefore, he had not told investigators that he had been in hiding could not reveal the identity of Kayishema simply asserted that he had not lied. Kayishema suggested that his response to investigators that he had been in his house had served its purpose, namely to protect the identity of those in the houses of whom he sought refuge.

252. One final point was raised with regard to Kayishema's presence at the sites of Home St. Jean, and the Stadium. In his statement to the investigators he was asked **[page 98]** specifically if he had ever visited any of these sites between 7 April and the end of May. He answered emphatically, no. Yet in cross-examination before this Chamber, he stated that he had been at the Catholic Church and Home St. Jean sometime between 13 April and the massacres. When questioned on this discrepancy, he answered that he understood that the investigator was asking whether he had been to these sites on a daily basis. This explanation is not entirely convincing.

Contradictions Between Kayishema's Evidence and the Evidence of his Wife and Others

253. The contradictions within this defence extend beyond the statements and testimonies of Kayishema alone. Discrepancies exist, for example, between his account and that of his wife's. In her statement to the investigators on 28 April 1998 Mrs. Kayishema maintained that she and her family were in hiding for three days in the bush, but she could not remember the days or dates. Almost two months later, before this Trial Chamber, she testified that they went into hiding on 15 April, and finally concluded under cross-examination that they had actually gone into hiding on 16 April. She made no mention of others being in their house prior to their departure. Whilst Mrs. Kayishema confirms that they were in hiding until 20 April, she talks of moving from house to house "frequently".[147] Her husband said that they were in just two houses. She testified that he spent the nights in the bush. He testified that for these four nights and days he did not leave her in excess of 30 minutes.

254. With respect to those dates outside of 16 to 20 April, Mrs. Kayishema's testimony offers little further insight. She does not provide any information of her husband's whereabouts on 15 April, during the massacres at Mubuga Church. Similarly, she provides little information on his movements after they came out of hiding. She does confirm that he continued his activities as *Prefect* and she also testified as to his activities on Friday 13 May 1994. It was on this date that one of the major attacks in the Bisesero area occurred. It was her testimony, however, that during that day Kayishema had driven her to work at around 8 a.m. They then returned home at approximately 11 a.m. that same morning where they stayed until she and her husband attended a public meeting **[page 99]** where the defendant presented the new *sous préfets* at 2 p.m. that afternoon. When asked why Mrs. Kayishema had not mentioned this meeting in the afternoon when speaking to investigators two months prior to her testimony she claimed that she had simply not remembered it. This meeting was entered in Kayishema's diary. However, whereas two previous meetings with regard to the new *sous prefects* had been written in French, this meeting was noted in another ink and written in Kinyarwanda. Furthermore, this note states that it was a meeting with all staff members to present the new *sous prefects*.[148] There is no mention of the meeting being a public one as Mrs. Kayishema had claimed. The Trial Chamber has some doubt whether the entry regarding this meeting was in fact entered at the time of events.

255. Beyond these specific days, and a few other notable days of interest such as when the Cardinal visited the region, the Mrs. Kayishema does not offer any further testimony as to her husband's actions during the remaining period when massacres were occurring in the Bisesero area. However, Witness DU, a friend of Kayishema who claims to have been resident in his house from 4 May, offers this alibi. He testified that apart from one day when the defendant was attending a meeting all morning, Kayishema never left his offices for more than half an hour. It is a testimony that is discredited initially by its improbability, especially in light of Kayishema's position as *Prefect* that demanded his presence over the whole *Prefecture*. It is also a testimony that is discredited by its contradictions with Mrs. Kayishema's and the defendant's own testimony before this Chamber. Kayishema gave detailed evidence of his continuing activities as *Prefect* throughout April, May and June. He specifically confirmed, contrary to the opinion of DU, that he had been to the Bisesero area. The testimony of witness DU, therefore, adds little weight to Kayishema's alibi defence for the massacres that occurred in the Bisesero region.

Kayishema's Elaboration

256. A further phenomenon highlighted by the Prosecution was the Kayishema's ability to recall exact dates, days and even times that he was in hiding during his testimony. It is **[page 100]** a matter of concern to this Trial Chamber because it is in sharp contrast to his interview, almost two years prior. In that interview in November 1996 Kayishema could not provide any dates or even days that he was in hiding. Kayishema was asked in cross-examination before this Trial Chamber why he had given the response to the investigators that he did not remember what days he was in hiding. His considered response was that, in the first place, he did not know what were going to be the key issues for his defence. Secondly, he asserted that he had the right to remain silent. However, this Chamber notes that

---

[147]   Trans., 24 June 1998, p. 121.
[148]   Def. exh. 58.

he did not remain silent. Rather, he specifically said that he did not remember.[149] The Chamber also notes that Kayishema could not have an answer what had aided his memory, in light of the absence of any entry in his diary, since that last interview. Although not conclusive in itself, the Trial Chamber has taken such elaboration into consideration.[150]

Finding

257.   In light of these contradictions, this Chamber does not find any merit in the defence advanced by Kayishema. Whilst the burden of proof rests upon the Prosecution to prove the case against Kayishema, the defence of alibi that has been raised on his behalf has not been sufficient to levy any doubt against that Prosecution case which is set out and considered below.

5.1.3 Ruzindana's Alibi Defence

258.   In total, 21 witnesses appeared on behalf of Ruzindana alone and gave testimony pertinent to his defence of alibi. Most of these witnesses did not give a comprehensive account of Ruzindana's whereabouts during the period when massacres were known to have occurred in the Bisesero region. Nevertheless, a picture was built by the Defence of a man continuing his business in the town of Mugonero. **[page 101]**

259.   After the death of President Habyarimana, on 6 April 1994, Ruzindana and his family left Remera, a neighbourhood of Kigali, where they had been living. They returned to Mugonero where Ruzindana's father continued to run a shop. Ruzindana was a businessman and a well-known figure in the area. A number of witnesses testified to having seen Ruzindana for varying periods of time between April and July 1994. Witnesses testified to having seen Ruzindana serving customers in his father's shop, others observed Ruzindana at the local market which was held every Wednesday, or noticed him on the roads between Kibuye, Cyangugu and Gisenyi.

260.   Specifically, witnesses such as DD testified to frequenting the store of Ruzindana's father "almost everyday" where, on most occasions, Ruzindana had served him.[151] Witness DD, a friend of Ruzindana's was not more specific but witness DAA apparently corroborated his account. Like DD, witness DAA worked in a store opposite the Ruzindana family shop and confirmed that Ruzindana was never away from Mugonero for more than a week. However, like all other witness who testified for the accused, he never accompanied Ruzindana on these business trips. Moreover, the only exact dates to which he could confirm that Ruzindana was present at Mugonero were the 12 to 14 April.

261.   Ruzindana was also seen regularly in the Mugonero market, which was held every Wednesday. Witnesses DB, DE, DF, DN, DQ, DS and DY identified Ruzindana in the market on numerous occasions throughout April, May and June. However, no exact dates were ever given by these witnesses. Witness DB, for example, saw the accused one Wednesday in early May; witness DF recollected seeing him four times in these three months; witness DQ saw him once in April and twice in May. Thus, it is possible to see that these sightings, which would last only a few minutes, are utilised by the Defence to reflect the activities of an individual continuing his normal course of business. They are not, and cannot, be offered as a comprehensive alibi for his whereabouts during the massacres in the Bisesero area. **[page 102]**

262.   Similarly, the Defence offered a number of examples where witnesses had seen Ruzindana on the roads in the conduct of his business. Other witnesses referred to Ruzindana driving one of his four trucks in the course of his trading, transporting beer or coffee to and from Mugonero. Witness DQ, for example, testified that Ruzindana passed by on the road to Kibuye on at least nine occasions in this period; witness

---

[149]   Pros. exh. 350CA.

[150]   Similar elaboration by the accused, central to the defence of alibi, were observed by the Trial Chamber in the *Tadic* Judgement, para. 502.

[151]   Trans., 20 May 1998, p.105.

DS saw him with empty beer bottles on the way to Kibuye; witness DD, who worked opposite the Ruzindana shop, talked of the accused leaving with empty beer bottles and returning, a few hours later, with full ones; and witness DR, who owned a kiosk near the roadside, testified that Ruzindana would often drive past with his driver in his green Toyota pickup truck – leaving at approximately 8 a.m. with empty beer bottles and returning around 4 p.m. with full ones. Although none of these witnesses were able to give the Trial Chamber any specific dates as to when they saw Ruzindana undertaking these trips, they were able to further elaborate upon the impression of an individual continuing his daily business activities. To this end, witnesses DB and DA also testified that Ruzindana was in the areas of Cyangugu and Gisenyi for business purposes. Once again, their information is very imprecise and relate his whereabouts for only very limited periods of time. For example, witness DB described how he met Ruzindana in Mugonero approximately one week after the President's death, in Cyangugu *Prefecture* on a Tuesday one month after that, and then in Mugonero on Wednesday of the next week.

263. The Chamber is cognisant of the difficulties often encountered by witnesses in recalling such details and we have, accordingly, set out our approach elsewhere.[152] However, the Trial Chamber observes that virtually none of the witnesses presented on behalf of the accused were able to give any substantial idea of his whereabouts in their testimony before this Tribunal. Beyond those already stipulated, only witness DH was, able to verify a certain date that Ruzindana was in Mugonero. He described how the accused was present when he arrived in Mugonero on the morning of Saturday 16 April. Witness DH, a relative of the accused, remained there until 3 p.m. and described how Ruzindana had also stayed in the town for the duration of his visit. Beyond that, like those witnesses set out above, witness DH simply describes how he had met Ruzindana **[page 103]** one day in mid May on the road to Kibuye, about twenty kilometres from Mugonero, and that Ruzindana had just bought supplies of beer.

264. Ruzindana's wife was one of the few who is able to give a more comprehensive picture of his movements. during this period. She testified that whilst he went to work, she would remain in the house during the day. However, because they shared a midday meal every day she could be certain that Ruzindana was within the vicinity of Mugonero on most days. Mrs. Ruzindana testified that the Ruzindana had only left for prolonged periods of time on four or five occasions. These periods could be either one or two days if Ruzindana had gone to Cyangugu or Gisenyi on business. Employees working in Ruzindana's house supported this testimony. The houseboy, DC, testified that Ruzindana would leave very early some mornings and would not return for up to two days. Although he had no personal knowledge of why Ruzindana was away, DC testified that on such occasions Ruzindana had instructed him to inform his family that he had gone for supplies. No clear indication of the days or dates that the accused would spend away from the home were offered. This is in common with those other witnesses set out above who corroborated the fact that Ruzindana would go away for either day trips or prolonged periods of time, but could also offer no certainty as to when those occasions were. Accordingly, as with sightings at the market and on the road, the Trial Chamber is unable to assess whether the sightings and trips away that have been alluded to were congruent or separate.

265. Each witness further testified that at no time did they see Ruzindana in the company of the militia or the armed forces or in the possession of any form of weapon during the period set out in the Indictment.

Examination of Ruzindana's Alibi Defence

266. The Prosecution questioned the reliability, credibility and relevance of various Defence witnesses. They raised the issue of reliability *vis-à-vis* the testimony of various witnesses who had close relationships with Ruzindana. Not only was there Ruzindana's **[page 104]** wife who testified, but also two other relations, a number of close friends, and two employees of Ruzindana. The Prosecution also raised the issue of credibility of a number of these witnesses. For example, witness DB states that he saw

---

[152]   Chapter 3.3

Ruzindana in Cyangugu on 26 June as Ruzindana headed for Zaire. The Prosecution noted, however, that DC also testified before the Chamber that Ruzindana was at home the entire day on 26 June.

267. The final point raised by the Prosecution is the pertinence of the testimony of many Defence witnesses. The majority of the witnesses were close relatives or former employees, who are likely to benefit from shielding Ruzindana from any criminal responsibility. Many individuals testified to having seen him on market day for various lengths of time between five minutes and one hour. Several more testified to having seen him on the road to Kibuye, even those who did not know Ruzindana nevertheless remembered his frequent journeys. However, even those who spent a great deal of time with Ruzindana: his wife, his sister, and his brother-in-law, as well as his servants, all testify that they did not travel with him on the frequent business trips that he supposedly made. They, like all of the other witnesses for the Defence, were not in a position to corroborate Ruzindana's location when he left on his "business trips."

268. These witnesses cannot account for the activities of Ruzindana even on a day-to-day basis, let alone 24-hours-a-day. His wife, after all, confirmed that Ruzindana was gone for two-day periods on a number of occasions. Furthermore, in cross-examination his wife conceded that the Defendant made many more daylong journeys to Kibuye although he did not spend the night.[153] The many witnesses who had seen him on the road to Kibuye confirmed these apparent trips. However, in cross-examination these witnesses also stated that this same road from Mugonero to Kibuye divided, branching off into the direction of Gishyita and the area of Bisesero.

269. Bisesero lies approximately twenty kilometres from Mugonero. Given the proximity, therefore, these day trips would have more than sufficed to enable Ruzindana **[page 105]** to reach the massacre sites and then return home. Accordingly, it is not sufficient for the purposes of his alibi defence, for witnesses to state that Ruzindana was the road from Mugonero or for Ruzindana's sister to state that whenever he was not on a business trip, that the accused would enjoy the family meal with them.

270. Furthermore, the Prosecution does not deny that Ruzindana continued trading throughout April, May and June, or that he made several other trips to locations such as Cyangugu. Rather, this supports the contention of Prosecution witnesses, X, FF and II who had not only heard reference to their attackers coming from Gisenyi, Gikongoro and Cyangugu, but had also noticed the accents peculiar to these regions.

Finding

271. The Chamber is cognisant of the difficulties raised in advancing this defence due to the time period covered in the Indictment. The legal issues that this gives rise to have already been considered.[154] At this juncture it is sufficient to note that, on a factual basis, many witnesses for the Defence were unable to provide specific dates as to when they had seen Ruzindana in Mugonero.

272. The burden of proof is, of course, on the Prosecution to prove their case beyond a reasonable doubt. In the opinion of the Trial Chamber, however, the alibi defence provided by Ruzindana does not diminish the Prosecution case. Even if the evidence proffered by the Defence in support of alibi is accepted in its entirety, it remains insufficient to raise doubt in relation to Ruzindana's presence in Bisesero at the times of the massacres. Accordingly, the Trial Chamber rejects the defence of alibi advanced by Ruzindana and has set out its factual findings below. **[page 106]**

5.2 Did Genocide Occur in Rwanda and Kibuye in 1994?

273. A question of general importance to this case is whether genocide took place in Rwanda in 1994, as the Prosecution has alleged. Considering the plethora of official reports, including United Nations

---

[153] This is a point corroborated by Defence witness DAA, who owned a shop opposite the Ruzindana family shop. See Trans., 18 and 19 Aug. 1998.
[154] See, chapter 3.4

documents,[155] which confirm that genocide occurred in Rwanda and the ab
argument to the contrary, one could consider this point, settled. Neverthele
fundamental to the case against the accused that the Trial Chamber feels obliged to
on this issue. The Trial Chamber underscores that a finding that genocide took p
dispositive of the question of the accused's innocence or guilt. It is the task of
findings of fact based on the Indictment against the accused and assess the evidenc
the possible responsibility of each person under the law only.

274. According to Article 2 of the Tribunal's Statute, genocide means various enumerated acts committed with intent to destroy in whole or in part, a national, ethnic, racial or religious group as such. The enumerated acts include, *inter alia*, killing members of a group and causing serious bodily or mental harm to members of the group. The purpose of this Chapter is not to decide whether specific acts by particular individuals amounted to genocidal acts, that is, acts committed with the special intent to destroy the Tutsi group in whole or in part. Rather, this Chapter assesses whether the events in Rwanda as a whole, reveal the existence of the elements of the crime of genocide. Such a finding allows for a better understanding of the context within which perpetrators may have committed the crimes alleged in the Indictment. Additionally, because the Indictment concerns events that took place in Kibuye, this Chapter of the Judgment includes a general examination of the events in that *prefecture*.

275. The Trial Chamber heard testimony from the United Nations Special Rapporteur of the Commission on Human Rights, Dr. René Degni-Segui, whose credentials qualified **[page 107]** him as an expert and whose testimony was convincing. The Trial Chamber is seized of his reports to the Security Council on the situation of human rights in Rwanda in 1994, which he submitted after conducting investigations throughout Cyangugu, Butare and Kibuye *prefectures*. *Inter alia*, Degni-Segui proffered evidence[156] before the Trial Chamber that perpetrators planned the genocide of the Tutsi population prior to 7 April 1994, and produced reports concerning the massacres, which occurred during hostilities. He testified that although to date no one has found any official written document outlining the genocidal plan, there exist sufficient indicators that a plan was in place prior to the crash of the President's plane on 7 April 1994. These indicators include (1) execution lists, which targeted the Tutsi elite, government ministers, leading businessmen, professors and high profile Hutus, who may have favoured the implementation of the Arusha Accords; (2) the spreading of extremist ideology through the Rwandan media which facilitated the campaign of incitement to exterminate the Tutsi population; (3) the use of the civil defence programme and the distribution of weapons to the civilian population; and, (4) the "screening" carried out at many roadblocks which were erected with great speed after the downing of the President's plane.[157] The outcome of the implementation of these indicators was the massacres carried out throughout the country.

276. It is the opinion of the Trial Chamber that the existence of such a plan would be strong evidence of the specific intent requirement for the crime of genocide. To make a finding on whether this plan existed, the Trial Chamber examines evidence presented regarding the more important indicators of the plan.

Background to the Events of 1994

277. The time was ripe in early 1994 for certain so-called Hutu extremists in power in Rwanda who opposed the Arusha Accords, to avoid having to share decision-making positions with opposition groups. After attending a meeting on the implementation of the Arusha Peace Accords, in Tanzania, President Juvénal Habyarimana was en route to **[page 108]** Rwanda when his plane was shot down over Kigali airport and crashed on 6 April 1994. Witness O testified that he on 8 April heard a broadcast on Radio France International (RFI) that the Rwandan People's Army (RPA or FAR) had announced the end of the cease-fire. The state of fear that ensued, caused by the rumours about the intentions of the RPF to

---

[155]   *See* Pros. exh. 328 – 331.
[156]   The witness produced seven reports for the Security Council. He relied most heavily on one Report, Pros. exh. 331, during his testimony before this Chamber (U.N. Doc. E/CN4/1995/71 1995).
[157]   See Pros. exh. 330B and 331B, p. 5.

611

xterminate the Hutus and the terror and insecurity that prevailed in Rwanda, served as a pretext for the execution of the genocidal plan and consequently the retention of power by the extremist Hutus. Based on eyewitness and expert testimony and reports, immediately after the plane crash, on 7 April 1994, massacres began throughout Rwanda.

278.   A radio announcement on the morning of 7 April, concerning the death of the President, ordered people to remain at home. This announcement was made in order to facilitate the movement of the soldiers and gendarmes from house to house to arrest and execute real and perceived enemies of the Hutu extremists, specifically those named on execution lists. Witnesses, including Degni-Segui and Prosecution witness RR, confirmed this fact.

The Effects of Extremist Ideology Disseminated Through the Mass Media

279.   Military and civilian official perpetuated ethnic tensions prior to 1994. *Kangura* newspaper, established after the 1990 RPF invasion, Radio Television Mille Colline (RTLM) arid other print and electronic media took an active part in the incitement of the Hutu population against the Tutsis. *Kangura* had published the "Ten Commandments" for the Hutus in 1991, which stated that the Tutsis were the enemy. In addition, according to witnesses, in 1991 ten military commanders produced a full report that answered the question how to defeat the enemy in the military, media and political domains. These witnesses also testified that in September 1992 the military issued a memorandum, based on, the 1991 report, which also defined the "enemy" as the Tutsi population, thereby transferring the hostile intentions of the RPF to all Tutsis. According to one report, prior to 6 April, the public authorities did not openly engage in inciting the Hutus to perpetrate massacres. On 19 April however, the President of the Interim **[page 109]** Government, told the people of Butare to "get to work" in the Rwandan sense of the term by using their machetes and axes.

280.   Several witnesses stated that during the atrocities "the Rwandese carried a radio set in one hand and a machete in the other."[158] This demonstrates that the radio was a powerful tool for the dissemination of ethnic hatred. Radio National and RTLM freely and regularly broadcasted ethnic hatred against the Tutsis. For example, a UNICEF report refers to an RTLM broadcast stating that "for babies who were still suckling . . . they [the assailants] had to cut the legs so that they would not be able to walk."[159] In 1992 Leon Mugesera, a professor turned propagandist for the MRND, declared in a public meeting "*nous ne commettrons pas l'erreur de '59 ou nous avons fait échoppé des plus jeunes*" (we will not make the 1959 mistake where we let the younger ones [Tutsis] escape.)[160] Mugusera also incited the Hutus by explaining that ". . . we must remove the entrails but there is shorter way, let us throw them into the river so they can go out of the country that way."[161] These speeches and reports became widely diffused through repetition in public meetings. and through the mass media.

281.   The dissemination and acceptance of such ideas was confirmed by a Hutu policeman to Prosecution witness Patrick de Saint-Exupery, a journalist reporting for the French newspaper *Le Figaro*. De Saint-Exupery remarked that the policeman had told him how they killed Tutsis "because they were the accomplices of the RPF" and that *no Tutsis should be left alive.*[162] (emphasis added.) This witness, who went to the Bisesero region late June 1994, described how "the hill was scattered, literally scattered with bodies, in small holes, in small ditches, on the foliage, along the ditches, there were bodies and there were many bodies."[163] **[page 110]**

282.   As a result of the diffusion of the anti-Tutsi propaganda, the, killings "started off like a little spark and then spread."[164] Degni-Segui stated that many communities were involved. Butare was an exception

---

[158]   Trans., 9 Mar. 1998, p. 47.
[159]   Trans., 5 Mar. 1998, at 112; Prosecution exh. 331 B.
[160]   Trans., 5 Mar. 1998, p. 98.
[161]   *Ibid.* p. 85.
[162]   Trans., 18 Nov. 1997, p. 136.
[163]   Trans., 18 Nov. 1997, p. 153.
[164]   Trans., 5 Mar. 1998, p. 110.

as there was resistance to carrying out the killings because the *prefect* was a Tutsi. The killings did not start in Butare until 19 April, after the Interim Government sacked the *prefect* and after a visit and an inciting speech by the interim President. The speech urged the inhabitants of Butare to engage in a murderous manhunt by appealing to the populace that "the enemies are among you, get rid of them."[165]

The Civil Defence Program and the Militias

283. In 1994, Rwandan officials controlled the militias and civil defence forces. The militias trained in military camps. During times of unrest or emergency states call such groups into duty to supplement its armed forces. The evidence before the Trial Chamber moreover reveals that both the militias and the civil defence forces programme became an integral part of the machinery carrying out the genocidal plan in 1994.

284. One of the means by which an ordinary Rwandan became involved in the genocide was through the civil defence programme. Initially both Hutus and Tutsis were involved in the civil defence programme. Authorities established the civil defence programme in 1990 for the security of the civilian population, whereby they could arm persons at all administrative levels, from the top of the *prefecture*, down to the cellule. Degni Segui confirmed this scheme during a conversation, with Bisimungu, the Chief of Staff of the Armed Forces, the chief of the police and the Commander of the Gendarmerie, during one of his visits to Rwanda. Unfortunately, the civil defence programme was used in 1994 to distribute weapons quickly and ultimately transformed into a mechanism to exterminate Tutsis. Numerous eyewitnesses such as Witnesses C and F confirmed this fact. They testified that they witnessed the distribution of machetes to civilians by the Prefectoral and Communal authorities in early April 1994. Other evidence before this Chamber shows that 50,000 machetes were ordered and distributed through this **[page 111]** programme shortly before the commencement of the 1994 massacres, to the militias of the MRND (members of the *Interahamwe*) and CDR (members of the *Impuzamugambi*), and the Hutu civilian population. Degni-Segui concluded that in the end this "system served to kill innocent people, namely Tutsis."[166]

285. Prosecution evidence, including letters from Rwandan authorities confirmed that "the population must remain watchful in order to unmask the enemy and his accomplices and hand them over to the authorities."[167] Witness R who was familiar with the administrative structure of Rwanda in 1994, affirmed that the people were told to "protect themselves within the Cellules and the Sectors," by organising patrols and erecting roadblocks.[168]

286. Other eyewitnesses recounted their versions of the occurrences at the massacre sites and almost all affirmed the presence of members of the *Interahamwe* and other armed civilians. In fact, several witnesses averred that the majority of the attackers were members of the militias and other civilians who were singing songs of extermination as they approached their victims. Several witnesses further stated that most of these attackers carried machetes and other traditional agricultural tools, as opposed to the gendarmes or police who were armed with guns and grenades.

Roadblocks and Identification Cards

287. The perpetrators of the genocide often employed roadblocks to identify their victims. Both Prosecution and Defence witnesses testified to this fact. Degni-Segui testified that within hours of the President's death, the military personnel, soldiers, the members of the *Interahamwe* and armed civilians erected and manned roadblocks. In fact, some roadblocks were erected within thirty to forty-five minutes

---

[165]   Pros. exh. 330B, p. 6.
[166]   Trans., 9 Mar. 1998, p. 101-102.
[167]   Pros. exh. 52, p. 4.
[168]   Trans., 2 Oct. 1997, p. 51.

after the crash of President's plane and remained throughout Rwanda for at least the following three months. According to this witness "what they had to do was to use identity cards to **[page 112]** separate the Tutsis from the Hutus. The Tutsis were arrested and thereafter executed, at times, on the spot."[169]

288. De Saint-Exupery confirmed the existence of roadblocks in Rwanda during the time in question. He testified that from Goma to Kibuye on 25 June 1994, "at the approach . . . to each locality, there was a roadblock."[170] Witness Sister Julianne Farrington stated that in May 1994 as she travelled from Butare to Kibuye, she went through 45 roadblocks. She further stated that at some roadblocks military personnel monitored movements, while others were manned by young Hutus in civilian dress. Other witnesses, including witnesses G, T, and Defence witness DA and DM, who travelled through various parts of Rwanda during the genocide, confirmed these facts before this Trial Chamber. The Trial Chamber notes that those who produced identity cards bearing the indication Hutu and those with travel documents were able to pass through these roadblocks without serious difficulties. Conversely, those identified as Tutsis were either arrested or killed. The Trial Chamber recognises that the erection of roadblocks is a natural phenomenon during times of war. However, the roadblocks in Rwanda were unrelated to the military operations. Sadly, they were used to identify the Tutsi victims of the genocide.

Conclusion

289. In summary, the Trial Chamber finds that the massacres of the Tutsi population indeed were "meticulously planned and systematically co-ordinated" by top level Hutu extremists in the former Rwandan government at the time in question.[171] The widespread nature of the attacks and the sheer number of those who perished within just three months is compelling evidence of this fact. This plan could not have been implemented without the participation of the militias and the Hutu population who had been convinced by these extremists that the Tutsi population, in fact, was the enemy and responsible for the downing of President Habyarimana's airplane. **[page 113]**

290. The cruelty with which the attackers killed, wounded and disfigured their victims indicates that the propaganda unleashed on Rwanda had the desired effect, namely the destruction of the Tutsi population. The involvement of the peasant population in the massacres was facilitated also by their misplaced belief and confidence in their leadership,[172] and an understanding that the encouragement of the authorities to guaranteed them impunity to kill the Tutsis and loot their property.

291. Final reports produced estimated the number of the victims of the genocide at approximately 800,000 to one million, nearly one-seventh of Rwanda's total population.[173] These facts combined prove the special intent requirement element of genocide. Moreover, there is ample evidence to find that the overwhelming majority of the victims of this tragedy were Tutsi civilians which leaves this Chamber satisfied that the targets of the massacres were "members of a group," in this case an ethnic group. In light of this evidence, the Trial Chamber finds a plan of genocide existed and perpetrators executed this plan in Rwanda between April and June 1994.

5.2.1 Genocide in Kibuye

292. Having determined that perpetrators carried out a genocidal plan in Rwanda in 1994, this Chamber now turns to assess the situation in Kibuye *Prefecture*. After the death of the President on 6 April 1994, the relatively calm co-existence of the Hutus and Tutsis came to a halt in Kibuye. According to the Prosecutor, Kibuye was among the first of the *prefectures* "to enter into this dance of death."[174] In Kibuye, the first incidents took place on 8 and 9 April 1994 in various *communes*. The Chamber heard

---

[169]   Trans., 5 Mar. 1998, p. 105.
[170]   Trans., 18 Nov. 1997, p. 118.
[171]   Trans., 5 Mar. 1998, 84.
[172]   See Part II, supra discussing the Historical Context of 1994 Events in Rwanda.
[173]   Pros. exh. 331 B, p. 5.
[174]   Trans., 11 Apr. 1997, at 34.

testimony and received documentary evidence that the perpetrators of the genocide in Kibuye acted with requisite intent to destroy the Tutsi population in whole or in part and that they in fact succeeded in achieving this goal. In this Chapter, this Chamber examines briefly the occurrences in Kibuye *Prefecture* from April to June 1994. **[page 114]**

Background

293.   The Chamber finds that events in Kibuye unfolded as follows. After the crash of the President's plane, the atmosphere quickly began to change. The Hutu population began openly to use accusatory or pejorative terms, such as *Inkotanyi* (Kinyarwanda for RPF accomplice/enemy)[175] and *Inyenzi* (Kinyarwanda for cockroach) when referring to the Tutsis. The members of the *Interahamwe* and other armed militant Hutus began a campaign of persecution against the Tutsis based on the victims' education and social prominence. Simultaneously, the Tutsi population, as a whole, suffered indiscriminate attacks in their homes. Perpetrators set on fire their houses and looted and killed their herds of cattle. Witness A testified that on the morning of 7 April 1994 his Hutu neighbours began to, engage in looting, attacking Tutsi-owned houses and slaughter Tutsi-owned livestock. Witnesses C, F, OO and E, corroborated these occurrences.

294.   On their way to the gathering places many witnesses saw roadblocks where the perpetrators separated Tutsis from the Hutus. Once the Tutsis reached these places they were injured, mutilated and some of the women were raped. In the end the Tutsis were massacred by Hutu assailants who sang songs whose lyrics exhorted extermination during the attacks. These attackers were armed and led by local government officials and other public figures. The fact that these massacres occurred is not in dispute. In fact, Kayishema testified that he and others engaged in a clean-up operation after the massacres.

295.   To illustrate implementation of the genocidal plan, the Trial Chamber now turns to examine the occurrences in the commune in Kibuye, immediately following the death of President Habyarimana, and other related issues which serve as further proof, such as meetings and documentary evidence, of the genocidal events in Kibuye. **[page 115]**

Initial Attacks at the Residences of the Tutsis

296.   There is sufficient evidence to find that in communes such as Gishyita Gitesi, Mabanza and Rutsiro the initial persecution of the Tutsis and individual attacks on their houses began almost immediately after the death of the President. The fact that killings took place throughout Kibuye is corroborated by a diary entry[176] which was tendered by Witness O. Witness O testified that initially after the President's death, in Gitesi Commune, there was relative calm. He also stated, however, that on 7 April "he saw wounded people everywhere, by the roadside, bushes and very close to the administrative headquarters of the *Prefecture*."[177] Witness O, under cross-examination, told the Trial Chamber that the first people to be killed were in Kigali and they were *alleged* to be RPF collaborators. Witness O testified there was a cause-and-effect relationship correlation between the 8 April radio announcement of the purported resumption of the war and the first deaths in Rwanda and, in particular, in Kibuye *Prefecture*.

297.   Witness F's testimony is illustrative of many other witnesses and of the situation as a whole. A resident of Gitesi commune, Witness F testified that he heard the news of the crash at 10 a.m. on 7 April and that as a result, the mood of the people changed to one of panic in his neighbourhood. On 7 or 8 April, a meeting took place at Mutekano Bar, situated some 400-500 meters from the Kibuye prison, along the road heading to the Kibuye *Prefecture* Office. Witness F testified during that period, he interacted with one Mathew, who was participating in the said meeting. Witness F observed the meeting,

---

[175]   *See* the testimonies of Witnesses G, U and Z explaining that *Inkotanyi* meant "all the Tutsis" or the „enemy".
[176]   Prosecution Exhibit 76E, as shown in the Trans., of 13 October 1997.
[177]   Trans., of 13 October 1997, p.149

the topic of which was security – addressing the "Tutsi problem" – from the roadside for about twenty minutes. Many local officials participated in the meeting.

298. Witness F testified that after the meeting of 8 April, he witnessed machetes being distributed by Ndida, the Commune Secretary. The machetes had been transported into the commune by Prefectoral trucks and the Secretary of Gitesi Commune supervised the unloading. They were taken towards the Petrol Rwanda fuel Station. About twenty **[page 116]** persons received a machete each including, Eriel Ndida, Rusigera, Siriaki, Emmanuel, the Headmaster and many others. On 9 April, the local officials departed to other commune after the distribution of machetes. That evening around his neighbourhood in Gitesi, Witness F noticed that the situation had changed and that militant Hutus openly were attacking the Tutsi. The proximity of the distribution of weapons to the massacres of Tutsi civilians is evidence of the genocidal plan. He noticed that militant Hutu had begun throwing rocks at Tutsis and throwing some persons into Lake Kivu. He also observed similar acts of violence in Gishyita commune. He stated that some persons from Gishyita crossed Lake Kivu to take refuge in the commune of Gitesi.[178]

299. On 12 April, the first person in Witness F's neighbourhood was killed. Munazi, who was with other militant Hutu and members of the Interahamwe killed Nyirakagando, an elderly Tutsi. Witness F and others saw her dead body in the morning of 13 April, as they were fleeing their homes. Witness F stated that "the Hutus killed her because she was Tutsi"[179]. Militant Hutus started by chasing Tutsi men. Witness F stated that "when the Tutsi realised that they were being pursued by the Hutus, they started to flee through the bushes."[180] Witness F's wife was gang-raped by the Hutus before her children's eyes on 13 April. Witness F's mother "was killed with the use of a spear to her neck" during the same attack.[181] Witness F left his wife who was no longer able to walk and first hid in the bush, within sight of his house and on 13 April fled to a Pentecostal church at Bukataye.

300. Witness F spent the night at the church parish at Bukataye. During the night, there was an attack on the church parish, led by the Headmaster of the Pentecostal school. People carrying clubs and spears accompanied the Headmaster of the school. He said, "the Tutsi who were in the Church should come out so that they could be killed."[182] Those who were unable to flee the Church were separated. Tutsi women separated from **[page 117]** the Hutu women. The latter remained and watched as the attackers killed the former. Witness F stated that the men, including him, then fled to the bushes.

Mass Movement of the Tutsi Population

301. Witness B testified that, when the attacks began in her commune, she and others decided to flee, stating "we did not want to be killed in our homes, and the people were saying that if you go to the Church no one could be killed there."[183] Witness B along with her mother, young sister and brother as well as four other Tutsis, left their village in Kabongo, Bishura sector, Gitesi commune, for the Catholic Church in Kibuye. As they fled, there were armed Hutus around their home.

302. Because the Tutsis were targets in their homes, they began to flee and seek refuge in traditional safety. Witness T, who worked at the Catholic Church and Home Saint Jean, (the Complex) testified that in the days following the President's death, a curfew was announced and people were told to stay at home. Tutsis, however, began to arrive on the peninsula, where the Complex is located, shortly thereafter. These Tutsis were from the hill of Bururga. Others came from Gitesi, Bishunda, Karongi and Kavi. They had converged at the communal office but they were not allowed to stay. Witness T stated that she helped lodge the thousands refugees, comprised of the elderly, women and children, in the dormitories at the Complex. Those seeking refuge were worried because their homes had been burnt. The

---

[178] Trans., 22 April 1997, p.36.
[179] Trans., 22 Apr. 1997, p. 46.
[180] Trans., 22 Apr. 1997, p. 47.
[181] Trans., 22 Apr. 1997, p. 49.
[182] Trans., 22 Apr. 1997, p. 51.
[183] Trans., 17 Apr. 1997, p. 8.

first incidents of burning homes started between 7 and 10 April in Burunga, the hill to the left of the Home St. Jean, and other hills nearby. Witness T stated that she saw the home of a friend aflame.

303. Explaining a diary entry from 14 April 1994 to the Trial Chamber, Witness O stated that those seeking refuge from Gitesi Commune, who were on their way to the Stadium, told him that they were fleeing massacres which had begun in their area. Witness O observed many massacres during that time and aided Tutsi survivors to reach Kibuye Hospital. **[page 118]**

304. Witness C testified that two days after the President's death people in Burunga, Mabanza commune started fleeing. She testified that attackers were attacking the Tutsi for being Tutsi and burning their houses. She explained that there was no apparent reason for these attacks besides these persons' ethnicity. Regarding the militant Hutu, she stated that "they themselves really could not find a reason for this because they would share everything on a day-to-day basis."[184] She saw, people fleeing from Mabanza, including a member of her extended family, and the family of Nyaribirangwe. Her relative had been dealt a machete blow to his head.

305. Witness B testified that they fled to the Catholic Church "because people like my father who had lived through other periods of unrest as in 1959, when there was an attack against the Tutsi, at that time people took refuge at the Church."[185] Witness T had a similar reason for going to a place of refuge. She testified that since the 1959 revolutions, whenever people felt insecure, they would go to churches, parishes and would be protected and be "respected in these places."[186] Additionally, witness F testified, that they arrived at the Catholic Church on 15 April at about 4 a.m. and found scores of other Tutsis who had come from other commune such as Mabanza, Rutsiro, Kaivere and Gishyita as well as Gisenyi *Prefecture*.

306. Witness A testified that on 7 April, militant Hutu began to attack Tutsi-owned houses, slaughtered Tutsi-owned livestock. The Abakiga (Hutus from the northern region of Rwanda) joined their fellow Hutu: On 12 April 1994, militant Abakiga Hutu identified the Tutsi by identification cards and massacres started in Gatunda shopping area. Witness A went to the Catholic Church, arrived 13 April between 6 and 7 a.m., and found numerous refugees gathered there.

307. Almost all Prosecution and Defence witness, including Mrs. Kayishema, who travelled throughout Kibuye *Prefecture*, testified that they encountered roadblocks. At **[page 119]** these roadblocks the attackers used identification cards to distinguish between and to separate Hutus from Tutsis.

Other Evidence of Intent to Commit Genocide

308. The record in the present case is replete with evidence that reveals the existence of a plan to destroy the Rwandan Tutsi population in 1994. The Trial Chamber explores briefly some of the more pertinent evidence relative to the acts demonstrating the intent to commit genocide that took place in Kibuye *Prefecture*.

309. Evidence presented to the Chamber shows that in Kibuye *Prefecture* the massacres were pre-arranged. For months before the commencement of the massacres, *bourgmestres* were communicating lists of suspected RPF members and supporters from their commune to the *Prefect*.[187] In addition, the Prosecutor produced a series of written communications between the Central Authorities,[188] Kayishema and the Communal Authorities that contain language regarding whether "work has begun" and whether more "workers" were needed in certain commune.[189] Another letter sent by Kayishema to the Minister of Defence requested military hardware and reinforcement to undertake clean-up efforts in Bisesero.[190]

---

[184]   Trans., 17 Apr. 1997, p. 116.
[185]   Trans., 17 April 1997, p. 11
[186]   Trans., 6 May 1997, p.24
[187]   Pros. exh. 55-58.
[188]   Pros. exh. 52, 54 and 296.
[189]   Pros. exh. 53. (Letter from Kayishema to all *Bourgmestres* in Kibuye.)
[190]   Pros. exh. 296.

310. Some of the most brutal massacres occurred after meetings organized by the *Prefectoral* authorities and attended by the heads of the Rwandan interim government and/or ordinary citizens of the *prefecture* to discuss matters of "security."[191] During one of these meetings Kayishema was heard requesting reinforcement from the central authorities to deal with the security problem in Bisesero. Witness O testified that on 3 May 1994, Interim Governmental Prime Minister Jean Kambanda visited Kibuye *prefecture* with a number of other officials, including Ministers of Interior, Information, and Finance, the *Prefect* of Kibuye, and the General Secretary of MDR party. Witness O **[page 120]** attended a meeting with these and other officials in his capacity as an official of Kibuye hospital and voiced his concern regarding seventy-two Tutsi children who survived the massacre at the Complex and were in poor physical condition at Kibuye hospital. Members of the *Interahamwe* had threatened these children, aged between 8 and 15 years. The Prime Minister did not personally respond to Witness O's concern, but asked the Minister of Information to do so. That minister rebuked Witness O, remarking that he should not protect people who don't want to be protected. He also declared that Witness O obviously did not approve of the politics of the Interim Government, and could not recognize the enemy. The Minister of Information gave the impression that the Interim Government recognized these infirm children as enemies. Later, these children were forcibly taken from the hospital and killed.

311. Sister Farrington testified to having witnessed the discriminatory attitude of various Kibuye authorities towards all Tutsis. During the occurrences Sister Farrington went to Kibuye Prefectoral offices to inquire about obtaining a *laissez-passer* that would allow some of the nuns from her convent to leave Rwanda. Over a period of three days she spoke with the Sous-*prefect*, Gashangore as well as Kayishema. Gashangore used hostile language when referring to Tutsis and accused specific people in the *Prefecture* of being "central to the activities of the *Inkotanyi*." During another attempt to obtain help, Sister Farrington spoke with Kayishema in his office where he spoke to her in an agitated and aggressive tone. Kayishema told her that there was a war prepared by the *Inkotanyi*, and the Tutsi people were collaborators of the enemy. As proof he showed her a list of names of people, maps and other documents allegedly preparing Tutsis to become revolutionaries.

Conclusion

312. Considering this evidence, the Trial Chamber finds that, in Kibuye *Prefecture*, the plan of genocide was implemented by the public officials. Persons in positions of authority used hate speech and mobilised their subordinates, such as the gendarmes the communal police, and the militias, who in turn assisted in the mobilisation of the Hutu population to the massacre sites where the killings took place. Tutsis were killed, based **[page 121]** on their ethnicity, first in their homes and when they attempted to flee to perceived safe havens they were stopped at roadblocks and some were killed on the spot. Those who arrived at churches and stadiums were attacked and as a result tens of thousands perished.

313. Having examined the reasons why Tutsis gathered at the four massacre sites, the Trial Chamber now examines the evidence specific to these sites and the role, if any, of the accused Kayishema, and his subordinates, as well as that of Ruzindana in the alleged crimes. **[page 122]**

5.3 An introduction: the Massacres at the Catholic Church and Home Saint-Jean Complex, Stadium in Kibuye Town and the Church in Mubuga

314. This Chapter addresses the occurences common to the first three massacre sites in the Indictment namely, the Catholic Church and Home Saint-Jean Complex (Complex), located in Kibuye, the Stadium in Kibuye (Stadium), and the Church in Mubuga (Mubuga Church), in Gishyita commune. This introduction does not include the fourth massacre site, Bisesero area, because the masscres in that area followed a slightly different pattern and took place over a much longer period of time than the first three sites. Additionally, under this Indictment, the Bisesro charges include both accused persons where as the first three sites concern Kayishema only. A summary of the witness testimonies for the first three sites paints the following picture.

---

[191] Meetings attended by Prime Minister Kambanda and/or his Ministers included that on 3 May 1994.

315.   In mid-April 1994, Tutsi seeking refuge from various communes converged on the three sites in order to escape atrocities perpetrated by the Hutus against the Tutsis. Throughout Kibuye *Prefecture*, Tutsis were being attacked, their houses set ablaze and cattle looted or slaughtered. Historically, community centres such as the Churches and the Stadium were regarded as safe havens where people gathered for protection in times of unrest; this was the case in April 1994. Many witnesses testified that they went to these sites with the belief that the prefectorial authorities would protect them. By the time some Tutsi reached the churches they were overflowing and these people continued on to the Stadium, often under the instruction of the gendarmes and local officials. By all accounts, very large numbers of Tutsis amassed in each of the three sites. Estimates varied from 4,000 to over 5,500 at Mubuga, about 8,000 at the Complex and, 5,000 to 27,000 at the Stadium.

316.   At all three sites, gendarmes guarded the entrances or completely surrounded the structure. The gendarmes controlled the congregation, maintaining order or preventing people from leaving. Witnesses testified that Tutsi who attempted to exit were killed by armed Hutu assailants. Conditions inside the massacre sites became desperate, particularly for the weak and wounded. The authorities did not provide food, water or **[page 123]** medical aid and, when supplies were offered, the Gendarmes prevented them from reaching the Tutsis.

317.   With thousands of internally displaced persons (hereinafter refugees)[192] effectively imprisoned at the three sites in Kibuye, five days of almost continuous massacres commenced. First, at Mubuga Church the major killing started on 15 April and continued on 16 April. On 15 and 16 April the Complex suffered preliminary attacks followed by a major slaughter on 17 April. On 18 April, the massacre at the Stadium began with the attackers returning on 19 April to complete the job. Evidence before the Trial Chamber suggests that thousands of Tutsi seeking refuge were killed during these few days.

318.   Testimony reveals striking similarities in the assailants' methods both during the initial gathering of Tutsis and later during the execution of the massacres. Some of those seeking refuge assembled at the three sites had done so owing to encouragement by Hutu officials. Initially, the gendarmes appeared merely to be maintaining order and allowed people to leave the Churches or Stadium to find food or water. Soon thereafter, however, authorities cut off supplies and prevented those seeking refuge from leaving. Those who attempted to leave were either chased back inside the structure or were killed by the armed attackers while the gendarmes watched. At this stage gendarmes and/or the members of the *Interahamwe* surrounded the Churches and at the Stadium gendarmes guarded the entrances. These conditions of siege soon turned into massive attacks by Gendarmes, communal police, prison wardens, the members of the *Interahamwe* and other armed civilians. Having surrounded the site, they usually waited for the order from an authority figure to begin the assault. The massacres started with the assailants throwing grenades, tear gas, flaming tires into the structure, or simply shooting into the crowds. Those who tried to escape were killed with traditional weapons. Following these hours of slaughter, the attackers would enter the building or Stadium carrying crude traditional weapons and kill those remaining alive. **[page 124]**

319.   The above background facts for the most part, are not refuted and the Trial Chamber finds ample evidence to support this general picture of events. The real issue for the Trial Chamber is the role, if any, played by Kayishema and/or those under his command or control, at the three crime sites. The Prosecution alleges that Kayishema was present, participated and led others at all three massacre sites. Kayishema admitted that he visited the sites when Tutsi were congregated but prior to the massacres to assess the situation. Kayishema, however, denies his presence during the days of attack. Indeed, Kayishema's alibi states that he was in hiding during the times of the massacres[193] because his life was under threat. He claims to have been hiding from 'the morning of 16 April through 20 April, coming out on the morning of 20 April.

---

[192]   Because the parties referred to the internally displaced persons as "those seeking refuge" throughout the trial, the Trial Chamber will remain consistent with this usage, noting however, that this use of the term in this context is inaccurate.
[193]   It should be noted that the massacre at Mubuga Church began on 15 April and that Kayishema's claim of alibi did not begin to until the morning of 16 April.

320. Evidence shows that others saw Kayishema at the three sites during the period of 14 to 18 April. On 14 April Kayishema stated that he visited Mubuga Church, but only to monitor the situation. Testimony, however, places Kayishema at Mubuga in the morning, of 15 April and at the Complex at 3 p.m. in the afternoon. The evidence suggests that the two churches are approximately 40 kilometres apart by road. Again, on 16 April, Kayishema was seen in the morning at Mubuga during the start of the attack and then at the Complex during the preliminary acts of violence. The following day, 17 April, witnesses testified that Kayishema was present at the Complex and played a pivotal role in the massive slaughter of that day. Lastly, Kayishema is said to have initiated the massacre at the Stadium on 18 April. The Trial Chamber now turns to separately assess the evidence for each of the four massacre sites enumerated in the Indictment.

5.3.1 The Massacre at the Catholic Church and Home St. Jean [page 125]

Background

321. According to the Indictment, the massacre site at the Home St. Jean Catholic Church Complex (Complex) is located in Kibuye, Gitesi commune, on the peninsula surrounded by Lake Kivu. A road runs perpendicular to the entrance to the Complex. One can see the Catholic Church but not Home Saint Jean from the road. The Complex, according to Expert witness Sjouke Eekma, is accessible by either the road from the roundabout or from the *Prefecture*. There were several doors to the Catholic Church.

322. During the unrest occurring in the commune soon after the crash of the President's plane, thousands of people sought refuge in places of worship such as the Complex. For instance, witness F testified, that he arrived at the Catholic Church on 15 April and found many other Tutsis who had arrived from other communes such as Mabanza, Rutsiro, Kaivere and Gishiyita as well as Gisenyi *Prefecture*. Witness B testified that she fled to the Catholic Church "because people like my father who had lived through other unrest as in 1959, when there was an attack against the Tutsi, at that time people took refuge at the (Catholic) Church."[194] Witness T corroborates other witnesses' reason for seeking refuge at the Church. She testified that since the 1959 revolutions, whenever people felt insecure, they would go to churches, parishes and would be protected; that is, they would be "respected in these places."[195]

323. The conditions inside these places of shelter worsened. In the Catholic Church people were crowded. Witness A testified that when a census was made for purposes of food distribution, the number of those seeking refuge was found to be 8,000 people of Tutsi ethnicity.[196] The census is corroborated by Witnesses T and F. The Tutsis seeking refuge received no assistance whatsoever from the *Prefectural* Authorities.

324. The major attack on the Complex took place on 17 April but prior to that attack, members of the *Interahamwe* and local officials launched several smaller attacks. Tutsi [page 126] seeking refuge threw stones and repulsed the smaller attacks. From about 15 April, the *gendarmerie nationale* surrounded and prevented the Tutsi from leaving.

325. Expert witnesses Dr. Haglund, a Forensic Anthropologist, and Dr. Peerwani a Pathologist, testified regarding the victims of the massacre. Both experts examined cadavers of thousands of people and described how they had been killed. Dr. Haglund testified that he had examined the large mass grave near the Catholic Church along with four additional areas that also contained human remains. Dr. Peerwani examined 122 cadavers during January and February 1996. Now part of the evidence, identification cards found on the victims indicated that they were all Tutsi.

326. Dr. Haglund's written report confirms that many people, men, women and children were killed at the Complex. Of the 493 dead examined by Dr. Haglund, only found one gunshot injury. He estimated that 36% of people in the grave had died from force trauma whereas 33% of the people died from an

---

[194]   Trans., 17 April 1997, p. 11.
[195]   ˙Trans., 6 May 1997, p. 24.
[196]   Trans., 15 Apr. 1997, p. 31.

undetermined cause. Dr. Haglund selected an individual as an example who he identified as a fifty year old man. The man's fibula had been completely severed by some sharp object,[197] which "would have severed the achilles" tendon rendering this individual partially crippled.[198] On the neck region "all the soft tissue from the right side of the neck towards the back would have been cut through"[199] and "a sharp cut mark in the tibia body, and in the inferior border of the scapular shoulder blade, another trauma caused by a blow of a sharp object."[200] Dr. Haglund concluded that the fifty-year old man was trying to protect himself by presenting different body aspects to the armed assailant. Dr. Peerwani, found stab wounds indicating the use of sharp force instruments and confirmed that many of the victims were young children and the old.

The Attacks [page 127]

15, 16 April 1994

327. Several witnesses testified about the minor attacks that occurred on 15 and 16 April. Witnesses T and A testified that an attack on the Complex occurred on 15 April at 3:00 p.m. During that attack, Witnesses A and D saw Kayishema snatching a child from its mother. Witness F testified that local officials participated in an attack on the Complex on 16 April. The gendarmes simply watched, but those seeking refuge repulsed the attack. After this event, witness F saw Kayishema and Mugambira, a prosperous Kibuye businessman, transporting weapons in their vehicles. A military pick-up also assisted in transporting weapons to the nearby Petrol Rwanda fuel station. Witness F saw the accused, Kayishema, hold a meeting with other assailants near the Petrol Rwanda fuel station.

17 April 1994 on Catholic Church

328. On 17 April, between 9 and 10 a.m., a major attack occurred at the Catholic Church, where thousands of Tutsi men, women and children had taken refuge. The attackers arrived from three directions, namely from the roundabout, the *Prefecture* and Lake Kivu. Witness F, who was standing in front of the Catholic Church, vividly described the various attackers. Witness F and others testified that the attackers were Hutu civilians; Twa civilians; communal police officers; prison guards and local officials such as the Communal Accountant; Rusizera, the Assistant *Bourgmestre*, Gahima, the Headmaster of the Pentecostal school, Emmanuel Kayihura and Siriaka Bigisimana. Other witnesses identified and corroborated the presence of the local officials. Witness E recognised the *conseillers* of Gishura Sector and witness C named particular officials such as *Conseiller* Ndambizimana; Calixte, the Prison Warden; and the *Bourgmestre* of Gitesi Commune. The attackers carried assorted weapons including machetes, swords, spears, small axes, clubs with nails, the "*impuzamugenzi*" and other agricultural tools. They were singing "let us exterminate them". Kayishema arrived with the attackers from the *Prefecture* Office in a white Toyota vehicle. Witnesses F, C, D, E and A clearly observed Kayishema's arrival. For example, witness F was sufficiently close to the accused to see that he was wearing a pair of white shorts. Witness A, D and F stated that Kayishema was carrying a sword. [page 128]

329. Witness F saw Kayishema arrive, get out of his vehicle along with the *gendarmes*, and receive applause as he walked towards the group of attackers. Witnesses F, D and E testified respectively that Kayishema ordered the assailants to "begin working, get down to work"[201] "go to work," or "start working."

330. They were all positioned so that they could hear Kayishema utter these words. According to witnesses E and F, the phrase "go to work" in the Rwandan context means "to kill Tutsis." At that point,

---

[197] Trans., 26 Nov. 1997, p. 29
[198] Trans.. 26 Nov. 1997, p. 30
[199] Trans., 26 Nov. 1997, p. 32
[200] Trans., 26 Nov. 1997, p. 33
[201] Trans., 22 Apr. 1997.

Witnesses E and F testified that after ordering attackers "to go to work," Kayishema climbed up the hill along the path near the Church, addressed the assembled attackers through a megaphone, informed them that he had received orders from Kigali to kill the Tutsis and commanded the *gendarmes* to shoot. Witness E said that Kayishema then fired three shots.

331.   Three witnesses saw Kayishema speak and give orders for the attackers to go to work. Only Witness E, however, claims to have seen Kayishema fire three signal shots. Witness A testified that it was the gendarmes opposite the Church who fired the shots. At that point some attackers began to throw stones at those seeking refuge and the *gendarmes* opened fire. The gendarmes shot the Tutsis who were in front of the Church. Soon thereafter the *gendarmes* and other Hutu assailants started to attack Tutsis inside the Church. They fired grenades and tear gas canisters inside the Church through the doors, and proceeded to fire their guns. Witness F who escaped by climbing a tree nearby, stated that "I could see quite clearly the square or the area in front of the Church. I could see him [Kayishema] with my own eyes."[202] Witness F saw Kayishema walk to the threshold of the Church and send an attacker to bring a jerrican of petrol. The petrol was poured on tires and the doors of the Church, and then set ablaze. According to witness A, the main door of the Church was burnt down. Witness C saw the attackers throw a tire which was doused with petrol, inside the Church. Many witnesses, including Witness F, testified that people were burnt. **[page 129]**

332.   At some point, Kayishema led the attackers who entered the Church and began to kill the survivors. Witness A, who had hidden under dead bodies and had smeared himself with blood, observed that Kayishema entered the Church with a young man and took steps to ensure that there were no survivors. Witness A stated that he could see Kayishema clearly since at that point the only attackers inside the Church were Kayishema and the young man. Witness A saw Kayishema use his sword to cut a person called Rutabana and a baby who was lying on top of witness A. With regard to this scene, witness A stated that he knew that it was a baby on top of him as he could feel the child's legs kicking him about the chest level.[203] Kayishema with his sword cut witness A, injuring him near his right clavicle, the right hand and the left elbow. The Trial Chamber was shown the scars of these injuries.

333.   Several witnesses, such as A, B, C, D and E managed to escape. Others, such as B, C, D fled to the Home St. Jean, whilst witness F fled to the Stadium.

17 April 1994 on Home St. Jean

334.   The attacks progressed from Catholic Church to the Home St. Jean when assailants descended upon the scene around 1 or 2 p.m., singing the lyrics "let's exterminate them." The assailants threw grenades inside the building and as a result, people suffocated. When the gendarmes broke the lock of the door, the fleeing Tutsis were faced with members of the *Interahamwe* wielding machetes and spears. Witnesses B and C survived by denouncing their Tutsi ethnicity to the attackers. Attackers allowed them to join a group of 15 to 20 Hutu who were being escorted to safety by the gendarmes and walked away from the Church. On their way, the two and others met Kayishema who asked the accompanying gendarmes "where are you taking these Tutsi?"[204] Notwithstanding that members of the group replied that they were all Hutu, Kayishema struck witness B with his machete. **[page 130]**

The Victims

335.   The attackers left thousands dead and many injured. Witness D estimated the number of those seeking refuge at the Complex prior to the major attack to be around 8,000. Witness A heard the same figure from Leonard Surasi, a man who had estimated the number in order to supply them with food. Witnesses A, B, C, D and F saw substantial numbers of dead bodies after the attack. Witness O, a local

---

202   *Ibid.*, p. 98.
203   Trans., 15 April 1997, p. 145.
204   Trans., 17 Apr. 1997, p.29.

Hutu who had recorded this massacre as an entry in his personal diary, testified that he had participated in burying the dead bodies. Witness E testified that one week after the massacre at the Church, he saw prisoners come to collect bodies for burial. They spent five days burying the dead. Witness G, a, Hutu, who had assisted in burying the dead, testified that at the Catholic Church, there were bodies along the road from the *Prefecture*, in front of the main door to the Church, inside the Church, in front of the Father's residence and also inside the Priests' house. He also stated that people assisting in the burial of the Tutsis were being threatened by Ruberanziza and Bisenyamana among other people.[205]

336.   At the Home St. Jean, in particular, Witness T, a person employed at Home St. Jean, testified that she lost nine staff members and their children. Witness G saw around 200 to 300 Tutsi corpses scattered in front, behind, in the cellar, on upper floors and around the Home St. Jean buildings. Further, many of the survivors were injured. Witness F observed about forty injured people, whose ankles had been cut.

Case for the Defence

337.   The defence for Kayishema offered a defence of alibi on the dates of the massacre, which appears above in Chapter 5.1 on Alibi. In cross-examination, the Defence challenged witness A's ability to having seen Kayishema when he entered the Church. They further questioned witness A's ability to have found space and time to smear himself with blood. This Chamber finds that although witness A's testimony may have lacked certain details, his testimony regarding Kayishema's presence and participation, on the whole, is credible. Moreover, witness A's description of Kayishema's attire and the weapon he carried conforms to the testimony of other witnesses, such as B, C and D. **[page 131]**

Further, witness A's identification of Kayishema is strengthened because he knew Kayishema prior to the events. Witness A first saw Kayishema in 1993 at the Kibuye Hospital (a friend pointed out Kayishema saying, "there is the *Prefect.*") This Chamber finds reliable witness A's deposition of Kayishema's presence and participation in the attacks of 17 April.

338.   Witness B testified regarding the encounter with Kayishema when she and others were being escorted as "Hutus" by *gendarmes*. Witness B affirmed that Kayishema wore white shorts and uttered "where are you taking these Tutsi?"[206] The *gendarmes* responded "these are not Tutsi but they are Hutus."[207] The Defence in their closing remarks did not deny the scene but claimed that Witness B was involuntarily wounded. The Defence suggested to the witness that the push was intended to put her back in line. The Trial Chamber finds witness B to be a credible witness who identified Kayishema during the attacks and heard him speak. Witness B met Kayishema in 1989 at the Kibuye hospital and thereafter had seen him from time to time. Witness C corroborated witness B's testimony regarding the attack. The Trial Chamber finds no material contradictions in witness B's story.

339.   Regarding witness C, the Trial Chamber notes that she knew Kayishema prior to the events. Witness C stated that she and the accused were from Bwishyura Sector and that she knew him and his father. She testified that she saw Kayishema cut the fingers of witness B with a machete. A list tendered into evidence by witness C shows the names of victims and attackers. The names of Kayishema and other local officials appear amongst the alleged attackers.

340.   The defence cross-examined witness D on his ability to hear Kayishema utter the words "go to work." Witness D stated that he heard Kayishema ordering the attackers to "go to work" from a distance of approximately ten to fifteen meters away, while standing **[page 132]** between the road which leads to the roundabout and to the *Prefecture*. The Defence also challenged witness D's account of his hiding in the ceiling of Home St. Jean. Witness D explained that he left the Church at 1 p.m. and stayed in the ceiling in Home St. Jean with five others, until 4 a.m. Witness T corroborates his account although she did not specifically single out witness A as being one of those in the ceiling.

---

[205]   Trans., 24 Apr. 1997, p.4.
[206]   Trans., 17 Apr. 1997, p. 93.
[207]   Trans., 17 Apr. 1997, p. 97.

341.   Witness D, identified Kayishema as one of the attackers. He knew Kayishema prior to the events because Kayishema attended meetings at the Home St. Jean in his capacity as the *Prefect* of Kibuye. Witness D saw Kayishema on 15 April in a white vehicle near the Home St. Jean. His account of Kayishema's arrival and description of the attack is corroborated by many witnesses including A, B, C and F. The Trial Chamber find's that witness D identified Kayishema and finds his account of Kayishema's participation credible.

342.   Witness F testified that he was in front of the Church when Kayishema arrived and that there was little distance between him and the attackers. Witness F confirmed seeing Kayishema and stated that he wore "white shorts" and carried a sword. Witness F's account of how Kayishema spoke through a megaphone was corroborated by witness E. Witness F knew Kayishema prior to the events and gave a detailed account of Kayishema's participation during the events of the attack. The Trial Chamber has considered witness F's testimony and finds his account of the events of 17 April is reliable and conforms to that of other witnesses.

343.   Witness E testified also that he heard Kayishema use a large megaphone to order attackers "to go to work."[208] According to this witness, Kayishema spoke using the megaphone to deliver a message from Kigali to exterminate the Tutsis, and fired gunshots. The Trial Chamber notes that witness E described Kayishema's arrival at the massacre site, identified Kayishema and described his participation. The Trial Chamber finds witness E's testimony regarding the events credible. Additionally, he knew Kayishema as the chief of Kibuye hospital prior to these events. His account of the **[page 133]** occurrences was corroborated by other witnesses. However, witness E was the sole eyewitness to testify that Kayishema fired the shot signaling the start of the massacre. Hence there exists some doubt as to whether Kayishema actually fired the shots, that sparked off the attack. This uncertainty is not surprising in light of the circumstances. Given the confusion of multiple shooters and the prevailing terror, this Chamber cannot find that Kayishema fired the shots. Nevertheless, the Trial Chamber finds that the shooting began following Kayishema's order. The Trial Chamber finds, beyond a reasonable doubt, that Kayishema ordered and instigated the attack upon the Catholic Church.

Conclusion

344.   The Trial Chamber finds that the witnesses' testimonies proved, beyond a reasonable doubt, that Kayishema was present at and participated in the 17 April 1994 massacres at the Complex. Witnesses, such as witness T and witness G, constituted "independent" witnesses, in the sense that they were not survivors as such, because they were not the target of the massacres. Their testimonies corroborated the events as recounted by those who survived the massacre. All the witnesses claimed that they previously knew Kayishema and they identified him at the trial. Moreover, the events occurred in broad daylight. The Hutu attackers killed with impunity as the local officials present not only refrained from preventing the massacre, but encouraged them.

345.   The defence failed to controvert the credibility of these witnesses or the reliability of the evidence on fundamental issues, in particular the identification of Kayishema during the attack. Minor discrepancies in testimony between witnesses did not raise a reasonable doubt as to the issue of Kayishema's participation.

Factual Findings

346.   With regard to Kayishema's participation in the Complex massacre, the Trial Chamber accepts the evidence of witnesses A, B, C, D, E, F, G and T. **[page 134]**

347.   Paragraph 25 of the Indictment alleges that by 17 April thousands of unarmed and predominantly Tutsi had gathered at the Complex. The Trial Chamber is satisfied from the evidence presented that there

---

[208]   Trans., 16 Apr., p. 156.

were indeed thousands of men, women and children who had sought refuge at the Complex. Further, the Trial Chamber finds that they were unarmed and predominantly Tutsi.

348. Paragraph 26 of the Indictment alleges that some Tutsis went to the Complex because Kayishema ordered them to do so at a time when Kayishema knew that an attack was going to occur. The Prosecution did not prove that the Tutsis were ordered to go to the Complex or that Kayishema ordered them to go there. Most of the witnesses went there on their own volition. Others such as witness B went there because in the past their parents had gone to such places for safety. It was only witness D, who testified that Kayishema ordered him to go to the Church.[209] This testimony while credible, does not satisfy this Chamber of the facts alleged in paragraph 26. Consequently, the Trial Chamber finds, beyond a reasonable doubt, that the Tutsi men, women and children went to the Complex on their own volition or because their parents had in the past found refuge in such places.

349. Paragraph 27 of the Indictment alleges that people under Kayishema's control, surrounded the Complex and prevented people from leaving at a time when Kayishema knew the attack was going to occur. This Chamber finds that the evidence of witnesses A, B, C, E and F shows that after those seeking refuge had gathered in the Complex it was surrounded by people under Kayishema's orders or control, including *gendarmes* and members of the *Interahamwe*. Witness D described how attackers in boats surrounded the peninsula on which the Complex is located. Witness B, described how the Complex was surrounded by members of the *Interahamwe* carrying machetes and spears. Witness C, testified that gendarmes prevented persons from leaving the Complex on 17 April 1994. **[page 135]**

350. The Trial Chamber finds, beyond a reasonable doubt that Kayishema knew or must have known that an attack was about to occur. This is because Kayishema stated that he had received orders from Kigali to kill Tutsis, he initiated the attack on 17 April, and he gave orders for the attack to begin. It follows, therefore, that Kayishema had the requisite knowledge. Kayishema was seen at the Complex twice before the attacks of 17 April and knew or must have known from the massive number of armed attackers that, in the circumstances of Kibuye *Prefecture* at the time, there was potential for a massacre to occur. Indeed, because smaller scale attacks had occurred there on the 15 and 16 April, Kayishema must have been aware of the potential for further attacks. Furthermore, as shown above in paragraph 28 of the Indictment, the Complex massacres followed the massacre at Mubuga Church where Kayishema had played a major role by initiating a systematic pattern of extermination within Kibuye. For these reasons, the Prosecution proved the allegations in paragraph 27.

351. Paragraph 28 of the Indictment alleges that on 17 April Kayishema went to the Complex, ordered the attackers to commence an attack and participated personally. Witnesses A, B, C, D, E and F testified that, notwithstanding the massive number of people seeking refuge at the Complex, they clearly saw Kayishema. The Trial Chamber finds the identification of Kayishema convincing. In making this finding the Trial Chamber is mindful that all the above-mentioned witnesses had known Kayishema prior to the events and successfully identified Kayishema at trial. In addition, the events occurred in broad daylight. The Trial Chamber finds, beyond a reasonable doubt, that on 15, 16 and 17 April, Kayishema went to the Complex, and that during the attacks it was not possible to leave the premises as those who attempted to flee were killed.

352. The Trial Chamber also finds, beyond a reasonable doubt that Kayishema participated in and played a leading role during the massacres at the Complex. Kayishema led the attackers from the *Prefecture* office to the massacre site at the Complex, he instigated and encouraged all the attackers by the message from Kigali to kill the Tutsis, which he delivered through the megaphone. Kayishema also orchestrated **[page 136]** the burning of the Church. Further, he cut one Rutabana inside the Church after the major offensive subsided.

353. Paragraph 29 of the Indictment alleges that the Complex attacks left thousands dead or injured. The Trial Chamber finds, beyond a reasonable doubt, that the single day of the major scale attack, as well as he smaller-scale sporadic attacks upon the Complex, resulted in the death of thousands of Tutsis whilst

---

[209]   Trans., 14 Apr. 1997, p. 12.

numerous others suffered injuries. This Chamber bases this finding primarily on the testimony of Dr. Haglund and Dr. Nizam Peerwani, Prosecution expert witnesses. Thus, the Prosecution has proved the facts alleged in paragraph 29.

354. In relation to paragraph 30 of the Indictment: The accusations in this paragraph are addressed in Chapter 6.1 *infra*.

5.3.2 The Massacre at the Stadium in Kibuye

Background

355. The witnesses presented a horrific account of the Kibuye Stadium massacre that occurred in mid-April 1994. Hutu military, police and the members of the *Interahamwe* conducted a massive, systematic, two-day slaughter of thousands of Tutsi civilians. Four witnesses were survivors of this massacre. Dr. Haglund, who visited the Stadium in September 1995, presented photographic slides. These slides depict a stadium with a field of grass about the size of a football pitch and additional side space for viewing; brick walls about eight foot high surround the Stadium on three sides and Gatwaro Hill flanks the fourth side. Spectator grandstands are located at one end. The road runs parallel to the side of the Stadium, facing Gatwaro Hill.

356. On Monday, 18 April 1994, at approximately 1 or 2 p.m., groups of gendarmes, communal police, prison wardens and members of the *Interahamwe* came from the direction of the roundabout in Kibuye town, surrounded the Stadium and started to massacre the Tutsi with tear gas, guns and grenades. The first attack of the massacre **[page 137]** finished at approximately 6 p.m. The next day, after celebrating in the local bar, attackers returned to kill survivors. The fact that the massacre at the Stadium occurred does not appear to be in dispute; Kayishema himself testified that a major attack at the Stadium took place on 18 April 1994[210] and witness DO estimated that about 4,000 of those seeking refuge were killed at the Stadium. Witness G, a local Hutu, who helped to bury bodies found in and near the Stadium, stated that dead bodies covered the entire ground of the Stadium and that bodies were buried using machinery over five days. Therefore, the issues for the Trial Chamber to consider here are whether Kayishema was present at the Stadium on 18 April 1994 and, if so, what was his role if any, and the role of anyone acting under Kayishema's orders or control.

The Role of Kayishema and His Subordinates

357. The Trial Chamber now assesses the evidence in relation to Kayishema's role at the Stadium massacre. In short, witnesses testified that Kayishema arrived in a white vehicle at the head of a column of attackers, ordered them to begin the killing and gave the signal by shooting a gun into a crowd of persons. The identification of Kayishema at the Stadium is strengthened by the witnesses' knowledge of the accused prior to the events in 1994. Witness I had known Kayishema since the accused was a child and had been the neighbour of Kayishema's parents. Indeed, Kayishema himself testified that witness I was a friend of his family. Witness K had known Kayishema before he was a *Prefect* and had seen him many times when he went for medical treatment. Witness M claimed to have known Kayishema all his life, but admitted that the accused did not know him well. Witness L had not known Kayishema before and testified that he only knew it was Kayishema at the Stadium because others had informed him so. With some variation in detail, witnesses I, K, L and M gave a similar account, both of the events and of Kayishema's role in particular. The testimony of witness I, the most lucid and complete is discussed thoroughly below, followed by the testimony of witnesses K, L, M, F, and NN.

Witnesses **[page 138]**

---

[210]   Trans., 10 Sept 1998, p. 24.

Witness I

358. Witness I is an elderly carpenter. In mid-April, sometime between 15, and 20 April 1994, witness I and seventeen other family members left their home in search of refuge and protection from massacres occurring throughout the *Prefecture* of Kibuye. Witness I testified that his *Conseiller* had told him to go to the Stadium where Tutsi would be safe. He explained that they arrived at the Stadium and stayed there for three or four days. When he arrived at the stadium no one was guarding the entrances but soon thereafter gendarmes started to control who could exit and, confiscated weapons from those who entered. Witness I testified that those attempting to leave were killed by members of the *Interahamwe* and, that he saw this happen. In the Stadium there was no firewood, the water had been cut off, and the Tutsi seeking refuge ate raw meat from cows. Sick and wounded were amongst them and those who attempted to seek help from the local hospital just yards from the Stadium were beaten back or killed. Those seeking refuge barely had room to sit down and there was no protection from sun or rain. The authorities provided no assistance. Soon after arrival the Tutsi heard from others about the massacres at Mubuga Church and Home St. John.

359. Witness I testified, describing his feelings, "For me I thought that no one would be able to kill off 15,000 people, and I thought that any authority who would represent so many people would not dare to kill them off, because these people worked for those persons in authority. They paid taxes and they provide assistance and they repair roads . . . . So I told myself that no one was going to be able to use firearms or machetes to kill us off. I said that no person in authority would be able to do such a thing."[211]

360. Witness I testified that at about 2 p.m. on 18 April armed civilians, soldiers, former soldiers and prison wardens armed with guns, clubs and machetes came from the direction of the roundabout in Kibuye. They divided into groups and surrounded the Stadium, taking position on the hills. From his viewpoint in the spectator grandstands witness I testified that he clearly observed Kayishema standing by the main entrance, near a house owned by the MRND. From this location, Kayishema could see into the **[page 139]** Stadium. Witness I saw Kayishema ask for a gun, shoot it toward the masses inside the Stadium as if to signal the attack to commence, and then give the gun back to the gendarme. Kayishema's two shots struck two people. At that point the massacre began. The attackers threw tear gas and grenades and fired guns into the Stadium. Witness I described the scene, "some were dead already, others were wounded in a way that they could no longer lift themselves from the ground. There were children who were crying because of the blows they had received. Others were bleeding or looking for water." The massacre stopped at approximately 6:00 or 6.30 p.m. After the attack ceased, witness I heard the attackers gathered in the bar next to the Stadium, drinking and dancing. On that first day witness I did not see attackers enter the Stadium. Those who tried to flee were killed with sharpened bamboo sticks. Witness I discovered that his two wives and fifteen children who accompanied him to the stadium had been killed on that day. During the night of 18 April he managed to escape and fled towards Karongi.

361. The Defence asserted that witness I did not mention to investigators in an interview prior to his testimony that he had seen two people killed by Kayishema's opening shots. Witness I admitted that, although he had seen two people hit by Kayishema's shots, he did not know whether the victims had died. The Trial Chamber accepts the evidence that Kayishema's shots struck two persons seeking refuge in the Stadium, an assertion that is corroborated by witness M.

Witnesses K, L, and M

362. Witnesses K, L and M are also Tutsis who had sought refuge inside the Stadium and survived the massacre of 18 April. Their testimony regarding the appalling conditions within the Stadium and the gendarmes preventing egress conforms to the evidence of witness I. In addition, the witnesses testified to an incident that occurred on the morning of 18 April; a white man started to count the people in the Stadium in order to bring aid but left when Kayishema, who arrived at the Stadium with gendarmes, threatened the same white man if he helped them. All three witnesses testified that they **[page 140]** did

---

[211] Trans., 28 April 1997, p. 49.

not understand the conversation between the white man and Kayishema in French, but that others translated the gist of it from French to Kinyarwanda.

363. Like witness I, witnesses K, L and M testifed that on 18 April at around 1 or 2 p.m., Kayishema came from the direction of the Kibuye roundabout accompanied by the members of the *Interahamwe*, gendarmes, communal police and prison wardens. The witnesses saw Kayishema walk to a position just outside the main gate, in front of the MRND building, and order the massacre to commence. Witnesses K and L added further that Kayishema was armed with a sword and that the attackers sere singing a song in Kinyarwanda with the lyrics, "exterminate them, exterminate them." These witnesses also testified that the attackers surrounded the Stadium, used tear gas, grenades and guns to kill those inside the Stadium, but did not enter.

364. Witness M gave nearly the same account as witness I with regard to Kayishema firing gunshots into the Stadium. M testified that Kayishema had taken a gun from a gendarme, fired it into the Stadium twice, hitting two people, and then fired once into the air, at which point the massacre started. Witnesses K and L, however, testified that they did not see Kayishema fire into the Stadium but heard him order the gendarmes to "fire on these Tutsi dogs." This difference in testimony is understandable considering that witnesses I and M were observing events from half way up the grandstands whereas witnesses K and L were positioned just inside the Stadium close to the main entrance. When considered together, the witness testimony shows that Kayishema first ordered the gendarmes to fire on the Tutsis and then grabbed a gun and personally fired twice into the Stadium, apparently to lead and set an example to start the massacre. It is reasonable that witnesses K and L did not see Kayishema shoot because, having heard Kayishema's orders to fire, they already were fleeing. Indeed, witness K testified that when he heard Kayishema give the order to shoot he immediately ran further back into the Stadium; witness L testified that when he heard Kayishema's order he ran to find his family and did not see Kayishema again. Witnesses K, L and M testified that the massacre continued until 6 or 6.30 p.m. Witness O, a Hutu doctor, testified that he heard the massacre start with firing and grenades at around 3 p.m. and continue until dark. **[page 141]**

365. There is less evidence relating to the massacres on the morning of 19 April. Witness K testified that at 6 a.m. he and others left the Stadium and fled up Gatwaro Hill when he saw the attackers returning to where they appeared to return in order to finish off any survivors with traditional weapons. As he fled, witness K saw the attackers going into the Stadium and heard shouts and screams. Their testimony did not place Kayishema at the Stadium on 19 April.

Witnesses F and NN

366. Witnesses F and NN observed events from hiding places outside the Stadium. The testimony of these witnesses conforms generally to that offered by witnesses I, K, L and M but also differs in some respects. Witness F testified that he survived the massacre at Catholic Church Home St. John and during the night of 17 April fled to Gatwaro Hill, from where he had a good view of the Stadium. He observed the events at the Stadium 18 April and Kayishema's participation, including the opening gunshots. Witness F, however, testified that Kayishema arrived with the attackers between 9.30 and 10 a.m. and estimated that they were there for approximately two hours before the massacre started. Contradicting the other witnesses, witness F testified that killers entered the Stadium on 18 April and began cutting up the Tutsis. The apparent confusion in witness F's account may be explained by the circumstances and the mental state in which he observed the events; responding to a question of what he did when the massacre started, witness F stated "I was astonished. I completely lost my head. I cannot even tell you what I witnessed as regards the massacres and this was because a lot of my family were inside the Stadium and they were being massacred."[212]

367. Witness NN testified that on 18 April he was hiding between two buildings about 40 metres from where Kayishema stopped by the Stadium's main entrance. Witness NN testified that, before shooting

---

[212]   Trans., 22 April 1997 p. 133.

into the Stadium, Kayishema murdered a Tutsi child and its mother. He stated that Kayishema then took the child from its mother, held it upside down by one leg, extended the other leg to a soldier and sliced it vertically with a sword. **[page 142]** According to NN, Kayishema shot the child's mother as she ran to the Stadium entrance. The Trial Chamber notes that NN observed the events from a different position, which could explain his divergent account. Furthermore, evidence suggests that Kayishema was surrounded by gendarme and members of the *Interahamwe* when he arrived at the main entrance and, therefore, the view of the other witnesses could have been obstructed at the time when Kayishema allegedly killed the child. However, the Stadium witnesses all testified that they had a clear view of Kayishema when he arrived and, that being so, it seems unlikely that they would omit an incident of such horror from their testimony. Furthermore, if Kayishema had first shot the child's mother before he moved to the main entrance from where he shot twice into the Stadium, the other witnesses likely would have observed this. According to their evidence, they did not. For all the above reasons, the Trial Chamber does not rely on the evidence proffered by witnesses F and NN pertaining to the Stadium massacre on 18 April 1994.

The Defence Case

368. In his defence, Kayishema testified that he was in hiding and did not go to the Stadium at the time of the massacres. However, Kayishema testified that he did visit the people seeking refuge at the Stadium sometime after 13 April but before they were killed; "Yes I went to the place but my CV is clear. I'm quite used to this sort of plague. When there are so, many people I know how to gather them together, how to seek solution to the problems, how to subdivide them according to their needs . . . ." In other words, Kayishema testified that he went to the Stadium in order to assess the situation. This, however, squarely contradicts his statement to Prosecution investigators. When asked by investigators if he ever went to the Stadium, Home St. John or Mubuga Church from 7 April 1994 until the end of the war, Kayishema gave a categorical "no". When questioned about this apparent contradiction during cross-examination Kayishema testified that he thought the investigator was asking him whether he had visited the sites *everyday* and therefore he answered in the negative.[213] With regard to gendarmes **[page 143]** guarding the gates of the Stadium and controlling the movement of people in and out, Kayishema testified that this was "true and normal."

369. The Defence raised further issues of detail. The Defence questioned why the huge number of Tutsis did not escape before the 18 April by overpowering the four or so gendarmes who were guarding the entrances. The witnesses were consistent in their responses, stating that the gendarmes were armed but those seeking refuge were powerless, therefore, those who tried to leave would have been killed. This fear seems reasonable particularly in light of the evidence that Tutsis had initially sought refuge in the Stadium as a means of escaping atrocities occurring throughout Kibuye. *Prefecture* and that Tutsis had been killed when they attempted to leave.

370. The Defence further asserts that there is no direct evidence that Kayishema ordered the water supply in the Stadium to be turned off as suggested by some Prosecution witnesses. The Trial Chamber agrees with the Defence; although it is clear that the taps in the Stadium did not supply water, there is no direct evidence that Kayishema was responsible.

Factual Findings

371. With regard to Kayishema's participation in the Stadium massacre, the Trial Chamber accepts the evidence of witnesses I, K, L and M. In cross-examination all four witnesses remained fundamentally faithful to the evidence proffered in chief.

372. Paragraph 32 of the Indictment alleges that by April 18 thousands of unarmed and predominantly Tutsis had gathered in the Stadium. The Defence pointed out that Prosecution witnesses did not give a consistent figure with regard to the number of Tutsi whom had gathered in the Stadium. Witness

---

[213]   See Prosecution exhibit 350c(b).

estimates varied from 5,000 to 27,000. The Trial Chamber does not consider this variation fatal to the reliability of the witness evidence. Mindful that the Indictment merely states "thousands of men, women and children had sought refuge in the Stadium located in Kibuye town," the Trial Chamber is satisfied from the evidence that there were indeed thousands of men, women and children **[page 144]** who had sought refuge at the Stadium. Further, the Trial Chamber finds that those seeking refuge were predominately Tutsi and, with the exception of a small number of machetes with which they slaughtered cows for food, they were unarmed.

373. Paragraph 33 of the Indictment alleges some refugees went to the Stadium because Kayishema ordered them to do at a time when Kayishema knew that an attack was going to occur. The Prosecution failed to prove this allegation. In fact, almost all witnesses testified to the contrary.

374. Paragraph 34 of the Indictment alleges that people under Kayishema's control, surrounded the Stadium and prevented people from leaving at a time when Kayishema knew the attack was going to occur. The evidence of Prosecution witnesses I, K, L and M, discussed above, is sufficient to show that after those seeking refuge had gathered in the Stadium, it was surrounded by people under Kayishema's control, including gendarmes. Witnesses I, K, L, M and O, testified that gendarmes prevented persons from leaving the Stadium from about 16 April 1994. Kayishema himself accepted that gendarmes were controlling the movement of people in and out of the Stadium. Furthermore, the Stadium massacre followed the massacres at Mubuga Church and Catholic Church, Home St. John. Indeed, a systematic pattern of extermination existed which is a clear demonstration of the specific intent to destroy Tutsis within Kibuye *Prefecture* in whole or in part. The evidence shows that Kayishema played a major role within this system. For these reasons, the Trial Chamber finds that at the time when the Tutsi were prevented from leaving, Kayishema knew or had reason to know that an attack on the Stadium was going to occur.

375. Paragraph 35 of the, Indictment alleges that on April 18 Kayishema went to the Stadium, initiated, ordered, and participated in the attack. It further alleges that during the night of April 18, attackers killed Tutsis if they tried to leave. Witnesses I, K, L and M notwithstanding the mass people, testified that they clearly saw and (in relation to K and L) heard Kayishema. The Trial Chamber finds the evidence of Kayishema's identification and participation convincing. In a scenario, such as the Stadium, it is not **[page 145]** surprising that those inside would strain to see and hear what was happening outside when a group of attackers arrived *en masse* at the main gate. The photographic exhibits indicate that witnesses I and M, positioned on the spectator stands, would be able to see over the Stadium wall to the main entrance. Witnesses K and L, positioned just inside the Stadium close to the main entrance, explained how, despite many people being between them and Kayishema, they wanted to see who had arrived and succeeded in doing so. All of the identification occurred in broad daylight. In making this finding the Trial Chamber is mindful that witnesses I, K and M had known Kayishema prior to the events and successfully identified Kayishema at the trial. Witness L, however, had not known Kayishema prior to the Stadium massacre, but others informed him that it was *Prefect* Kayishema at the time of the events. Therefore, the Trial Chamber must treat the identification of Kayishema by witness L with extra vigilance. The account of witness L is so similar to the other Prosecution witnesses, particularly K, such that the Trial Chamber accepts that his testimony related to the same man. Accordingly, the Trial Chamber considers that the testimony of L further corroborates the evidence of witnesses I, K, and M with regard to Kayishema's participation in the Stadium massacre.

376. The Trial Chamber finds beyond a reasonable doubt that on 18 April 1994 Kayishema went to the Stadium and ordered members of the *Gendarmerie Nationale*, communal police and members of the *Interahamwe* to attack the Stadium. Further, Kayishema initiated the attack by firing a gun into the Tutsi who had assembled in the Stadium and his shots struck two of them. The evidence indicates that the attackers tear gas, guns and grenades were used on 18 April and that the massacre continued on 19 April. However, the evidence relating to the 19 April is not sufficient to show which assailants were attacking the Stadium, or to prove Kayishema's presence. The Trial Chamber is also satisfied that during the attacks some of the Tutsis who attempted to flee were killed.

377. There is conflicting evidence pertaining to whether the Tutsis were prevented from leaving the Stadium during the night of April 18 and the morning of April 19. The Trial Chamber finds that the Prosecution has not proved their case on this issue. **[page 146]**

378. Paragraph 36 of the Indictment alleges that the Stadium attacks left thousands dead or injured. The Trial Chamber is convinced by the evidence that the two days of attacks on the Stadium resulted in thousands of deaths and numerous injuries to Tutsi men, women and children. Predominantly Hutu assailants perpetrated these acts.

379. In relation to paragraph 37 of the Indictment: The accusations in this paragraph are dealt with below in Part VI.

5.3.3 The Massacres at the Church in Mubuga

Background

380. The Church in Mubuga, like other places of worship in Rwanda, was regarded historically as a safe haven in times of unrest. This was also the case in 1994. The Prosecution alleges that by about 14 April 1994 thousands of unarmed men, women and children, most of whom were Tutsi, had gathered at the Church in Mubuga to escape ongoing and widespread violent attacks throughout Kibuye *Prefecture*. The Prosecution alleges that on 14 April the authorities of the *Prefecture*, including Kayishema and Bourgmestre Sikubwabo, came with gendarmes to the Church located in Gishyita Commune. According to one eyewitness,[214] Sikubwabo stated that he was going to exterminate the Tutsis. Over the next few days, attackers killed thousands of people. Only a handful of those who had sought refuge in the Church would survive this massacre, just one of many in Kibuye *Prefecture*.

381. The allegation that this appalling event occurred at Mubuga Church is not in dispute. In fact, an assortment of witnesses, including various eyewitnesses, Sister Julie Ann Farrington, Defence witness DP, and Kayishema, confirmed that after the massacre, corpses and/or human remains were found inside and/or in the immediate vicinity of Mubuga Church. Witnesses who visited this site shortly after the massacre remarked that the decomposing bodies caused a strong stench in the area. In addition, Dr. Haglund, **[page 147]** testified that he went to the Church grounds on 20 September 1995 to investigate two alleged graves sites there. He deposed that one grave had. been exhumed previously and the bodies had been reburied nearby. In the second area he found a depression in the ground and there were indications that this area had been disturbed. Upon an attempt to probe the second mass grave he found that the ground was too hard and therefore he did not conduct further investigations there. Due to uncontested evidence showing a massacre near the Church in Mubuga, the questions that remain relate to the presence and the participation of Kayishema and those under his control in this massacre.[215] The Trial Chamber examines the role Kayishema and his subordinates played at this massacre site, in detail, below.

Prosecution Case

382. Five Prosecution eyewitnesses, V, W, OO, PP and W appeared before the Trial Chamber to recount the events of prior to and during the massacre in mid-April 1994 at Mubuga Church.[216] With slight variations, these five eyewitnesses recounted the events in the following manner. While thousands of Tutsis congregated at this site, between 9 and 14 April 1994, witnesses heard that the *Prefect* had met with the Hutu priest and that the distribution of food to those seeking refuge was forbidden. The same

---

214   Trans., 3 Mar. 1998, p. 28.

215   The prosecutor presented witnesses who testified that Ruzindana was present and participated in the massacre at Mubuga Church. The Trial Chamber will not consider this evidence because the Indictment in question charges Clement Kayishema alone with crimes at this site.

216   Witness OO deposed that the massacres continued on 17 April 1994. There will be an examination of this potential discrepancy in the Analysis and Findings Chapter on the massacres at Mubuga Church below.

Hutu priest, who had replaced the Tutsi priest at Mubuga Church, refused water to those seeking refuge, and told them to "die, because your time has come."[217]

383. Paragraph 40 of the Indictment alleges that "[a]fter the men, women and children began to congregate in the Church, Clement Kayishema visited the Church on several occasions" and that on or about 10 April he brought gendarmes to this location who prevented those seeking refuge in the Church from leaving. All prosecution witnesses deposed that gendarmes had gathered on the Church grounds and patrolled the Church **[page 148]** complex to ensure that those who had sought shelter there would not leave. Witness V stated that gendarmes accompanied Kayishema before and during the attacks and witness PP stated that he saw gendarmes near the Church on 13 April. Witness UU stated that on the 15 April Kayishema arrived with "soldiers." The other three eyewitnesses stated that gendarmes were present throughout the congregation of those seeking refuge and during the massacres. For example; witness V stated that the gendarmes arrived on either the 9 or 10 April.

384. Witnesses V, OO and PP all confirmed the allegation that, prior to the attacks, the Tutsis could not leave the Church due to a fear of the gendarmes and other armed individuals patrolling the Church complex. According to one witness, this fear was founded upon the murder of individuals who had attempted to leave the Church building, to find food.

385. Paragraph 41 of the Indictment asserts that individuals under Kayishema's control "directed members of the *Gendarme* [sic] *Nationale*, communal police of Gishyita *commune*, members of the *Interahamwe* and armed civilians to attack the Church," and that these individuals directly participated in the events. What follows is how the events unfolded as recounted by Prosecution eyewitnesses before the Trial Chamber.

15 April 1994

386. A number of Prosecution eyewitnesses stated that after the Tutsis began to gather, the Church doors were kept locked from the inside in order to prevent the assailants, who previously had attempted to attack, from entering the Church. Therefore, on the morning of 15 April, the assailants began the attack by throwing tear gas grenades into the Church and shooting through the windows. Witnesses V, W and UU placed Kayishema and the local authorities at the Church on this day. According to witnesses OO and W, *Bourgmestre* Sikubwabo and *Conseillers* Mika Muhimana and Vincent Rutaganera led the attack. Witness V stated that he saw Kayishema arrive at the Church in the company of gendarmes on 15 April, while UU stated that he saw Kayishema in the company of **[page 149]** "soldiers" on this day. Witness V was the only witness that claimed that Kayishema had a gun and opened fire.

387. According to UU, on this day, Kayishema came to the Church and went to the home of the Hutu priest behind the Church. Witness OO confirmed the cooperation of the priest with Kayishema when he deposed that the priest instructed him to conduct a head count of the Tutsis in the Church for the *Prefect*. In addition, the Prosecution eyewitnesses confirmed the presence and/or participation of the communal police and civilians, such as local businessman Rundikayo, on this date. Witnesses indicated that although some people died from the effects of the tear gas, the number of Tutsis killed was relatively low on this day. By all accounts, the attackers left the Church in the afternoon of 15 April.

16 April 1994

388. On the morning of 16 April 1994 the Church doors were finally forced opened and the assailants entered the Church. Witness PP recalled that "we were hoping to be killed by bullets and not by machetes."[218] The attackers again used tear gas grenades, along with other traditional weapons and, during the ensuing panic some Tutsis were trampled to death.

---

[217]   Trans., 20 Nov. 1997, p. 16.
[218]   Trans., 3 Mar. 1998. p. 30.

389. Witness OO testified that, on the morning of 16 April, Kayishema came with soldiers of the National Army. Witness W was the other eyewitness who placed Kayishema at the Church on this date. It was claimed that in addition to Kayishema, local authorities such as *Bourgmestre* Sikubwabo and various *conseillers* were present at the Church on this date. Soldiers threw grenades and other armed attackers shot at and hacked with machetes the Tutsis inside the Church. After most people in the Church had been killed, witness OO, who hid under the corpses of fallen Tutsis, stated that he heard **[page 150]** the *Prefect* telling the local authorities "to come and collect the Caterpillar [bulldozer] to bury the dead."[219]

The Defence Case

390. The Defence conceded that Kayishema came to Mubuga Church on 14 April, but that he did so only to monitor the situation. In fact, during closing arguments, the Defence reminded the Trial Chamber that his visit to the Church is recorded in Kayishema's diary.[220] This was an obvious mistake as nothing is recorded in the said diary under this date.

391. The Defence also attempted to impeach Prosecution witnesses by stressing that some contradicted themselves, or each other, with regard to the exact hour of the commencement of the attacks or the varying dates of the end of the attacks. For example, the Chamber was asked to recall that witness OO deposed that the attacks did not end until 17 April while others claimed that the massacre, at this site, ended on 16 April. According to Kayishema's Defence Counsel the idea that "a witness can only identify Clement Kayishema if he knew him before" is incorrect."[221] In cross-examination issues of visibility were raised which will be analysed below.

Factual Findings

392. The allegations in paragraph 39 of the Indictment, that by about 14 April 1994 thousands of Tutsis congregated in Mubuga Church and that they were taking refuge from attacks which had occurred throughout Kibuye, are not in dispute. In addition all five Prosecution witnesses and at least one Defence witness confirmed that many Tutsis had come to the Church for protection. The witnesses gave slightly differing numbers about the persons that were gathered at the Church. Witness V estimated that about 4,000 people, mostly women and children had assembled there by 12 April, while witness W remarked that the number of persons taking shelter at this location was between 4,000 **[page 151]** to 5,000 by the time of the attacks. Witness OO stated that 5,565 were present at the Church according to ahead count he conducted on the instructions of the Hutu priest, who had told OO that this information was needed by the *Prefect* for humanitarian purposes. The Trial Chamber accepts that between 4,000 to 5,000 persons had taken refuge at Mubuga Church.

393. Paragraph 40 of the Indictment charges Kayishema with having visited the Church on several occasions before the attacks and having brought gendarmes to this location on or about 10 April. The gendarmes allegedly prevented the Tutsis within the Church from leaving. As discussed above, all Prosecution eyewitnesses affirmed having seen gendarmes at the Church while they were assembling there and during the attacks. With regard to Kayishema having brought the gendarmes two witnesses testified that prior to the attack they saw him at the Church either arriving with or in the company of gendarmes. Therefore, we find that whether these gendarmes came to this location with Kayishema or arrived without him is irrelevant as Kayishema knew or should have known of their activities, especially given the state of security in his *Prefecture*. The issue is the presence of the gendarmes and not whether they were physically transported to the crime site by Kayishema.

---

219   Trans., p. 39, 20 Nov. 1997. The Trial Chamber notes that the witness claimed this conversation took lace after the massacres, on 17 April, a date that was not corroborated by other witnesses.
220   Def. exh. 58.
221   Trans., 4 Nov. 1998, p. 148.

394.   Whether the gendarmes prevented the Tutsis from leaving the Church is the second question raised in paragraph 40 of the Indictment. The Defence contended that the gendarmes were present for the protection of the Tutsis. The Prosecution witnesses painted another picture. They stated that while the gendarmes were present before the attacks, armed assailants, including the members of the *Interahamwe*, surrounded the Church and attacked Tutsis attempting to exit, with impunity. Witnesses W and OO both affirmed that Tutsis who initially attempted to leave the Church for food or water were either chased back into the building or beaten to death by the armed assailants outside the Church. Witness OO stated that those seeking refuge could not even leave the Church to use the toilet. One Prosecution eyewitness testified that approximately, twelve to fifteen gendarmes were present at the Church. If this number was accurate, coupled with the fact that gendarmes are usually armed, then it would be conceivable that the gendarmes **[page 152]** could engage in the prevention of the departure of the Tutsi seeking refuge from this site. Moreover, during the attacks, the gendarmes were seen throwing grenades and shooting into the crowds of the unarmed civilians inside the Church. All these facts leave no doubt that the gendarmes were involved in the virtual imprisonment and later the massacre of the Tutsis in Mubuga Church until the attacks began inside the Church on the morning of 15 April.

395.   Paragraph 41 of the Indictment, surprisingly, does not charge Kayishema with having been present during the attacks. It states "on or about 14 April 1994 individuals, including individuals under Clement Kayishema's control, directed members of the *Gendarme* [sic] *Nationale*, communal police of Gishyita *commune*, members of the *Interahamwe* and armed civilians to attack the Church." The Indictment goes on to allege that the attacks continued for several days as not all the persons within the Church could be killed at one time. As aforementioned, all five Prosecution eyewitnesses to the events at Mubuga Church were there on the 14 and 15 April. Two witnesses deposed that they had been there on the 16 April and only one on 17 April 1994. These witnesses stated that they closed the doors to the Church to avoid being attacked by assailants. The Trial Chamber finds that, with regard to the date, there were no material contradictions in the oral testimonies of these five witnesses, as claimed by the Defence. The Trial Chamber further finds that the attackers, who surrounded the Church, began their attempts to kill the Tutsis before 15 April, but that the dates on which the massacres were carried out inside the Church were in fact 15 and 16 April in the presence, and at the direction of, local authorities.

396.   Because a number of eyewitnesses placed Kayishema at Mubuga Church during the attacks, at this juncture, it is appropriate to consider the identification of the accused at this location before and during the attacks. Preliminarily, we are cognizant of the fact that the events took place during the daytime, which renders visibility less problematic. Secondly, we note that because those seeking refuge were awaiting attacks, they must have been constantly seeking to know about the goings-on around the Church and were **[page 153]** therefore, as mentioned by some witnesses, such as W, looking outside through the windows and doors.

397.   Having observed the demeanor of the witnesses and listened closely to their oral testimony the Trial Chamber is satisfied that the eyewitnesses were credible and did not attempt to invent facts. This credibility was helpful in determining the reliability of the identification of the accused at the massacre site. Mubuga Church has three doors and several windows[222] and according to the eyewitnesses' accounts, the assailants, including Kayishema and his subordinates came close to the Church building at some point during the time in question. During cross-examination, some concerns of obstructed visibility were raised also in the case of OO, because he had placed Kayishema at the site by stating that while he (witness OO) was lying under the corpses of slaughtered Tutsis, he heard Kayishema speaking with other local authorities. The question then becomes one of voice recognition and not of visibility, as the Defence contend. The Trial Chamber is satisfied that the witnesses' prior familiarity with the accused – he had seen the *Prefect* at the installation of Sikubwabo as *Bourgmestre* and at local rallies – and having heard his voice at other meetings prior to the massacres would enable OO to recognise Kayishema's voice and render the identification of the accused a trustworthy one.

---

[222]   Pros. ex's. 37, 39 and 40.

398. The Defence contested the identification of the accused by witness W by pointing to the unfavorable visibility conditions caused by the tear gas released into the Church. Since there is both oral and pictorial[223] evidence of grenades having been used the Trial Chamber notes that this factor could have made for poor visibility. However, Mubuga Church covers a sizeable amount of space, capable of holding 4,000 to 5,000 persons. Witness W stated that he was not near the part of the Church where the grenade landed and was therefore able to view the persons outside. At any rate, it remains unclear whether the witness saw Kayishema prior to the launching of the tear gas grenade or after. Therefore, the Trial Chamber accepts the testimony of witness W.[224] **[page 154]**

399. Questions were also raised by the Defence regarding the reliability of witness UU's identification of the accused. UU testified that he was near the main entrance of Mubuga Church when Kayishema arrived in his vehicle. During cross-examination, however, he stated that he did not recognise Kayishema until he heard other people remark that the *Prefect* had arrived. The Trial Chamber observes that witness UU had met Kayishema on one occasion prior to April 1994, at Kayishema's grandfather's home, but may not have recognised him immediately upon his arrival at Mubuga Church on 15 April. However, the witness stated that after the declaration by others he did recall knowing Kayishema. The Trial Chamber finds this, in fact, to be the case.

400. Each one of these eyewitnesses, with the exception of PP, placed Kayishema at the site on at least one day either shortly before or during the attacks of 15 and 16 April. Witness PP's hearsay evidence also corroborated the accounts of other eyewitnesses. Additionally all eyewitnesses presented by the Prosecution for this site affirmed having seen at least one or more of the following outside the Church during the time in question: local authorities such as *Bourgmestre* Sikubwabo, *Conseillers* Muhimana and Rutagenera, Minister of Information Niyitegeka as well as gendarmes, members of the *Interahamwe*, communal police and other armed civilians. It is interesting to note that the Defence only contested the presence of local authorities during the cross-examination of Kayishema and not before.[225]

401. Paragraph 42 of the Indictment maintains that as a result of the attacks thousands of deaths and numerous injuries to men, women and children perished and numerous others sustained injuries.

402. The Trial Chamber has made a finding with regard to the number of the Tutsis present at the Church. Therefore, in light of the testimony that most of the persons assembled at the Church were slaughtered, the Trial Chamber deems it unnecessary to **[page 155]** focus on exact numbers. Suffices to say we find that thousands of persons were massacred at this site and therefore the Prosecution has met its burden beyond a reasonable doubt with regard to this allegation.

403. Paragraph 43 of the Indictment asserts the Kayishema did not attempt to prevent this massacre and failed to punish those responsible. This allegation is addressed in Chapter 6.1.

Conclusion

404. It is clear from the evidence presented to the Trial Chamber that of the thousands of Tutsis gathered at Mubuga Church, only a few survived this weekend massacre. The Trial Chamber is satisfied, beyond a reasonable doubt, that Kayishema and his subordinates, including local authorities, the gendarmes, the communal police and the members of the *Interahamwe* were present and participated at the attacks at Mubuga Church between 14 and 16 April. As aforementioned, Kayishema, is not charged with having been present during the attacks under paragraph 41 of the Indictment. In light of the testimony of the five witnesses the Chamber nevertheless finds that Kayishema was present during the actual attacks. We further find that his presence and the presence and the participation of other local authorities, encouraged the killings of the Tutsis who had assembled to seek refuge there. **[page 156]**

---

[223] Pros. exh. 47.

[224] It should be noted that witness W deposed that he had known Kayishema well before the attacks.

[225] When asked by Ms. Thornton about whom lead the massacres in Kibuye Prefecture, Kayishema stated that none of the local authorities had taken part and that trials were conducted after he fled the country, in July 1994, to find the culprits.

5.4 The Massacres in the Area of Bisesero

5.4.1 Introduction

405. The evidence before the Trial Chamber presents a picture of a massive, horrific assault on the Tutsis gathered in the Bisesero area by extremist Hutu military, communal police, members of the *Interahamwe* and armed civilians. These attacks continued throughout April, May and June 1994. The Bisesero area was home and area of refuge to many Tutsis during the genocide. Many Tutsis from other regions, hid in caves, scattered through woods and bushes, or gathered on the high hills in the area. Some Tutsis congregated in Bisesero because they had heard that they would be protected. This was not the case. Relentlessly, they were pursued by Hutus bent on genocide, who shot or hacked all the Tutsis they found.

406. The most severe attacks occurred in the Bisesero area on 13 and 14 May 1994, after an apparent two-week lull in the attacks. Some evidence asserted that this two-week pause in the attacks resulted from a resistance by the Tutsis assembled in Bisesero and attackers used this pause to regroup. Witness G attended a meeting, held on 3 May by Prime Minister Jean Kambanda at Kayishema's offices, in which Kayishema reported there was serious insecurity caused by those gathered in Bisesero and requested reinforcement to resolve the problem.[226] Soon after in mid May, the assailants again pursued those seeking refuge from place to place. At times, Hutu operations were conducted on a huge, organised scale with hundreds of assailants transported in buses to areas where Tutsi civilians had gathered. At other times, minor military or *Interahamwe* patrols throughout the region attacked Tutsis whenever they were found. The ultimate aim of these assaults appeared to be the complete annihilation of the entire Tutsi population. In pursuit of this objective, attackers killed thousands of Tutsi civilians. **[page 157]**

General Allegations

407. Paragraph 45 of the Indictment alleges, that the Bisesero area spans two communes, Gishyita and Gisovu, in Kibuye *Prefecture*. The Prosecution alleges that from about 9 April until 30 June 1994, thousands of men, women and children sought refuge in the area of Bisesero. Most were Tutsis seeking refuge from attacks that had occurred throughout the *Prefecture* of Kibuye.

408. Bisesero's geography is not in dispute. The Trial Chamber is seized of Prosecution exhibits, including maps and photographic slides, which depict the area of Bisesero.

409. Furthermore, the Defence did not contest the allegation that from about 9 April until 30 June 1994, Tutsis sought refuge in Bisesero from Hutu attacks that had occurred in other parts of Rwanda and, in particularly, other areas of Kibuye *Prefecture*. Many eyewitnesses confirmed having been amongst thousands of Tutsis fleeing other attacks within Kibuye *Prefecture*[227] and other witnesses confirmed having seen many Tutsis fleeing various areas in Kibuye to Bisesero. Kayishema testified: "I can tell you that the, [*sic*] aggressors were Hutu and the attacked were the Tutsis, some who came from Bisesero and others who had gathered in the hills of Bisesero. On both sides – on either side there were cases of mortality."[228] Numerous witnesses confirmed the mass murder of Tutsis in the Bisesero area. For instance, Chris McGreal, a journalist for the Londonbased *Guardian* newspaper, testified that he spoke to Tutsis seeking refuge on a hill in Bisesero in June 1994. While there, he saw evidence of mass killings in the area including human corpses. The Tutsis whom he interviewed told him that these bodies remained unburied because they (the Tutsis) feared attacks by the armed Hutus near the water. Patrick de Saint Exupery, a journalist for the Paris-based *Le Figaro*, visited Bisesero in June 1994. He confirmed that a "Bisesero Hill was scattered, literally scattered with bodies, in small holes, in small ditches, on the foliage, along the ditches, there were bodies and there were many bodies."[229] **[page 158]**

---

[226] Wimess G also testified that in the ensuing days he saw the members of the Interahamwe from Gisenyi *Prefecture*, armed with guns, going toward Bisesero.

[227] For example, witnesses OO, PP, W survived the massacres at Mubuga Church and took refuge in the Bisesero area.

[228] Trans., 4 Sept. 1998, p.59.

[229] Trans., 18 Nov. 1997, p.137.

410. Paragraph 46 of the Indictment, alleges that "the area of Bisesero was regularly attacked on almost a daily basis, throughout the period of about 9 April 1994 through 30 June 1994. The attackers used guns, grenades, machetes, spears, pangas, cudgels and other weapons to kill the Tutsis in Bisesero. At various times the men, women and children seeking refuge in Bisesero attempted to defend themselves from these attacks with stones, sticks and other crude weapons."

411. The above allegations were not contested. Most Prosecution witnesses, including survivors of attacks, confirmed that attacks took place on a regular basis, during the time in question. Witness OO testified that "the attacks were every day in Bisesero, but most frequent in Muyira and Gitwa. The attacks began at about 6 a.m. and would continue until about 4 to 5 p.m." Kayishema himself testified that "major attack"[230] and "massacres"[231] took place in Bisesero. There is sufficient evidence to show that attacks occurred at approximately twelve sites in the Bisesero area.[232] Dr. Haglund observed the aftermath of the massacres in September 1995 at various sites at Bisesero. Testifying about his visit to a hill on the border of Gishyita and Gisovu Commune, Dr. Haglund stated "[a]nd if one looks through field glasses or a magnifying instrument across . . . this hillside there were many white spots – it looks almost like strange mushrooms growing here and they represented skeletons, the heads of human bodies that were littered on this landscape . . . ."[233] and "in a brief walk around I observed a minimum of 40 to 50 individual skeletons lying about on the hill. These were skeletons on the surface. They represented men, women, children and adults."[234]

412. All types of weapons were used by the attackers, witness JJ confirmed that attackers were carrying "clubs, machetes and grenades." Witness HH also reported that **[page 159]** the assailants were armed with guns, machetes, swords and spears. The forensic evidence presented by Dr. Haglund confirmed that the victims were killed with such weapons during the massacres. Tutsis, who had gathered at Bisesero, also attempted to defend themselves with crude weapons. Witness X, along with other witnesses, confirmed this fact. Witness EE stated that the Tutsis threw rocks at the assailants to thwart attacks and escape.

5.4.2 Massacres Where Kayishema and Ruzindana Acted in Concert

413. The Prosecution alleges that at various massacre sites in Bisesero, Kayishema and Ruzindana often in concert, brought and directed groups of armed attackers. Moreover, the Prosecution accuses both of personally attacking and killing persons seeking refuge in Bisesero area. Evidence shows that assailants attacked the Tutsis seeking refuge over a vast area. For clarity, the Chamber discusses the evidence chronologically and site by site, with emphasis on the most severe attacks.

Bisesero Hill

414. Witness FF saw Kayishema, Ruzindana and Mika Muhimana, the *Conseiller* of the Gishyita sector, arriving at Bisesero in a white vehicle on 11 May. Kayishema was wearing a green shirt and carrying a megaphone. Ruzindana wore a white shirt and carried a weapon. Mika said through a megaphone that they were working for the Red Cross and that peace had returned. He urged people to bring the wounded and the handicapped to the Church in Mubuga where they would get blankets and beans. As those seeking refuge emerged from their hiding places Ruzindana stepped out of his vehicle and shot at a woman and two girls. Witness FF observed these events from a distance of approximately ten meters. This Chamber finds this uncontroverted testimony.

---

[230] Trans., 9 Sep. 1998, p. 37.
[231] Trans., 8 Sep. 1998, p. 117.
[232] The Trial Chamber notes that some witnesses used specific names of neighbourhoods when testifying about specific attacks. For the purpose of clarity however, we have grouped neighbouring localities together and described the attacks by date.
[233] Trans., 25 Nov. 1997, p. 65.
[234] Trans., 24 Nov. 1997, p. 82.

Attacks at Muyira Hill in May

415.   Muyira Hill is located in the Bisesero area on the border between Gishyita and Gisovu commune on the Gishyita side of the road that separates the two communes at this location. As Saint Exupery deposed, it was a manhunt for Tutsis. Many witnesses **[page 160]** identified Kayishema and/or Ruzindana at this massacre site including witnesses PP, OO, II, JJ, NN, HH, UU, FF, KK. Witnesses PP and OO were survivors of the Church in Mubuga massacres who then escaped to Bisesero. Witness PP testified that on 13 May Kayishema and Ruzindana were at the foot of Muyira Hill participating in the attacks. Witness PP clearly observed the attackers throwing grenades, chasing those seeking refuge and, before nightfall, Kayishema and Ruzindana shooting at the fleeing Tutsis. On 14 May, also at Muyira, PP heard Kayishema addressing a group of attackers who had come from other *prefectures*.

416.   Witness OO testified that the Muyira attacks were led by the *Bourgmestre*, the *Prefect, conseillers* and Ruzindana. The attackers separated into groups and encircled the Tutsis seeking refuge. According to OO, he stated that before the attacks, Ruzindana had distributed traditional weapons to the attackers. Witness OO stated that on 13 May Kayishema and Ruzindana came to Muyira Hill leading a convoy of vehicles, including buses, which were transporting soldiers. He testified that Kayishema signalled the start of the attack by firing a shot. Witness OO stated that he saw Kayishema clearly and described that Kayishema wore a green suit on that day. Witness OO saw Ruzindana who was armed, leading one of the group of attackers. Ruzindana shot witness OO, striking him in the foot that day. The Defence noted that the witness had told the Prosecution investigator he had been shot in the leg rather than foot. The witness explained that the Kinyarwanda word he had used on both occasions was "*ikirenge*," which means foot. The Trial Chamber is satisfied that, any discrepancy is not a material contradiction.

417.   With regard to the events of 14 May, OO saw Ruzindana and Kayishema arrive with members of the *Interahamwe*. From his hiding place that morning he heard Kayishema address the attackers who came from the other *prefectures* and remembered Kayishema saying "the dirt should be cleaned that day and that they should finish the job . . ." and that Kayishema and others would take care of what remained to be done.[235] **[page 161]**

418.   Witness II, testified that on 13 May he observed the government owned ONATRACOM buses arrive along with many other vehicles from which soldier exited. As the assailants began the attack, the Tutsis fled, after an initial attempt to defend themselves using stones. Witness II testified that he saw Ruzindana arrive with the soldiers and appear to lead them. Although during examination-in-chief II testified that he witnessed Ruzindana firing a gun at the Tutsis, in cross-examination, this statement proved to be based on an assumption rather than his direct observation. In addition, on the evening of 13 May, while he was hiding at Uwingabo Cellule, II observed the attackers regrouping. There he saw and heard Kayishema thanking those attackers from the surrounding commune and *prefectures*, including Ruzindana, for having shown such devotion to their work.

419.   On 14 May II observed the attackers as they again arrived in buses and cars. From a literal stone's throw away, II saw Kayishema and Ruzindana leading the group and observed both shoot at the Tutsis. Witness II fled in the direction of Karongi Hill and escaped. Witness II further claimed that he saw Ruzindana, on several occasions, giving money to several of the attackers.

420.   Witness JJ testified to the events at Muyira Hill on 13 May. He affirmed that Kayishema, dressed in a green civilian suit, arrived in a white vehicle with military escort and Ruzindana was seen to be transporting assailants. Kayishema held a short barrelled, black gun and a hand megaphone. He divided the attackers into groups, gave instructions and fired the first shot. Witness JJ recalled that at the end of the attack, Kayishema presided over the regrouped assailants. During the examination-in-chief, JJ initially stated that he was 300 meters away from Kayishema, but later approximated the distance to have been 120 meters.

421.   On 14 May, witness JJ again saw Kayishema between Gishyita Hill and Gisovu where the assailants parked their vehicles. At the end of the large-scale attack, **[page 162]** Kayishema brought

---

[235]   Trans., 20 Nov. 97, p. 86.

together and congratulated the assailants from other areas. Attackers shot witness JJ in the hand during the Muyira attacks.

422. Witness NN testified that on 13 May 1994, he recognised Kayishema, Ruzindana and *Bourgmestre* Ndimbati, among the attackers. Kayishema was waiting for those seeking refuge on the road and shot in the direction of three Tutsis named Mbunduye, Munyandamutsa and Hakizimana. The record is unclear whether the witness observed the death of any of these persons. Witness NN, who stated that Ruzindana transported members of the *Interahamwe* to the massacre site on 13 May. There he fired gunshots at two Tutsis named Ragasana and Birara and shot at OO, but missed. Witness NN, who lost an eye from a grenade explosion at this site recalled how the Hill was covered with dead at the end of the attack.

423. Witness HH testified that assailants during the attack of 13 May included Kayishema, Ruzindana, Musema, Ndimbati and Sikubwabo. As OO was hiding in the forest Kayishema and Ruzindana were quite close when OO saw them shoot at a group of Tutsis seeking refuge who were at the top of the hill. Witness HH remembered the attackers singing: "The Tutsis should be exterminated and thrown into the forest . . . don't spare the newly born baby, don't spare the elderly man, don't spare the elderly woman. Kagame left the country when he was a young baby."[236] In cross-examination, HH explained that he had not mentioned Ruzindana in his written statement because the Prosecution investigator had inquired only about the presence of responsible officials. Having reviewed the written statement, the Trial Chamber finds credible the witness's explanation.

424. Witness UU observed Kayishema at Mpura Hill, a 30-minute walk from Muyira Hill, on 14 May. There, he saw Kayishema near the top of Mpura, drinking beer with other assailants before the start of the attacks. He then saw Kayishema directing other leaders to the location of Tutsis nearby. Thereafter, the attackers began to pursue the Tutsis on Mpura Hill. Witness UU testified that he saw Ruzindana giving money to the [page 163] attackers on 15 May on Gitwa Hill in Mubuga and that he had heard a conversation between him and the attackers regarding additional payments. The witness's testimony clarified that he was able to observe the exchange of money. However, UU stated that he heard only the conversation between the attackers, and not that between Ruzindana and these assailants, who confirmed that they expected Ruzindana to pay them more in the following days. If the latter version of UU's testimony regarding additional payment is how the events unfolded, the evidence proffered amounts to hearsay. However, because other witnesses, such as II corroborate Ruzindana's disbursement of payments to the attackers at various sites, the Trial Chamber finds this discrepancy to be a minor one.

425. The witnesses above provide a thorough account of the role of Kayishema and Ruzindana in the Muyira attacks of 13 and 14 May 1994. The Trial Chamber need not detail the further evidence that supports the Prosecution's case. It suffices to say that the evidence of witnesses Z and AA affirms Ruzindana was participating in the Muyira Hill attacks.

Witnesses FF and KK

426. Witnesses FF and KK provided evidence that conforms generally to the accounts of the above witnesses. However, doubt exists as to the quality or reliability of their testimony. Witness FF stated that he observed the events from the peak of Gitwa Hill. The Defence proffered evidence that Gitwa Hill is about three kilometres from Muyira Hill and suggested that FF was testifying to events that were at least half that distance away. The Prosecution failed to prove otherwise. Accordingly, the Trial Chamber is not satisfied that FF had a clear view of events and deems his evidence unreliable.

427. Witness KK was a public official in Rwanda in 1994. He testified that on 13 May, he heard the attackers singing: "let's exterminate them, let's exterminate them, we must finish off these people who are hiding in bushes. Let's look for men, everywhere so that no one remains."[237] He further testified that on 14 May, Kayishema led the attackers, shot [page 164] at those seeking refuge as they descended Muyira

---

[236] Prosecution exh., 297.
[237] Trans., 26 Feb. 1998, pp. 33-34.

Hill, and addressed a crowd of assailants using a megaphone. In his written statements, however, KK had made no mention of Kayishema except in reference to a radio broadcast where the former Prime Minister had thanked Kayishema for being valiant. Witness KK explained this omission by stating that the Prosecution investigators had only asked him about those who came from his commune. A close review of his witness statement, however, reveals that this was not the case. The two statements made by witness KK to the investigating team, show that the investigators inquired about leaders of the attacks in general. They did not ask specific questions about the attackers' origins. For the above reasons, the Trial Chamber gives little weight to the evidence proffered by witness KK.

Attacks at Muyira Hill and Vicinity in June

428. The attacks in the Bisesero area continued into June 1994. A letter dated 12 June 1994 shows Kayishema's continued involvement in the massacres. In this letter, Kayishema requested from the Ministry of Defence a plethora of ammunition, such as "gun-propelled and hand grenades, bullets for R4 rifles and magazines for machine guns" to undertake a "clean-up operation" ("*ratissage*" in French) in Bisesero.[238]

429. Witness PP, who had seen Kayishema and Ruzindana at the attacks on Muyira Hill on 13 and 14 May, saw them again in June at Kucyapa. As PP was running through Kucyapa he saw Kayishema and Ruzindana who fired a gun at him and at the group with which he was fleeing. Later in June, PP saw Kayishema and Ruzindana for the last time near Kabanda's house. Here PP was with a group of unarmed Tutsis and saw both the accused and others fire guns and kill people. Witness PP also testified that Kabanda, a prominent businessman, was a particularly sought after target by both Kayishema and Ruzindana. Witness PP deposed that Kabanda was eventually shot by *Bourgmestre* Sikubwabo, decapitated and his head was delivered to Kayishema for reward. PP was hiding in a nearby bush when he saw Sikubwabo shoot Kabanda, but only heard about the beheading from others. The account of the beheading, given by PP, is not sufficient to prove particular direct acts of participation of the accused. However, with regard to the **[page 165]** acts of those under his control, in this instance *Bourgmestre* Sikubwabo, the Trial Chamber finds the evidence of this witness convincing.

430. In light of the above evidence, the Trial Chamber finds that Kayishema and Ruzindana were present at the massacres in Muyira Hill and its vicinity beginning on about 13 May 1994. Further, the Trial Chamber finds that Kayishema and Ruzindana helped transport other assailants to Muyira Hill and vicinity, instigated them to attack the Tutsis gathered there, orchestrated the method of attack, led the attacks, and personally participated in them. Additionally, with regard to Kayishema, this Chamber finds that the Prosecution has proved the participation in the massacres of his subordinates, including the gendarmes, communal police, members of the *Interahamwe*, and local officials, such as *Bourgmestre* Sikubwabo.

The Cave

431. One of the most horrific mass killings in Bisesero took place at a site simply called the "cave," located in Gishyita commune, Bisesero Sector, Kigarama cellule. Hutu assailants launched an attack on the cave where Tutsis sought refuge. The assailants came in the morning and fired guns and threw grenades into the crowd of Tutsis who sought refuge at this location. The attackers then fetched and piled wood at the entrance of the cave and set fire to it. The smoke killed hundreds of people inside. By all accounts, there was apparently only one survivor. The Prosecution asserts that Kayishema and Ruzindana were amongst those leading the attack.

432. Dr. Haglund visited the cave in September 1995 and described it by stating: "I went back perhaps 40 or 50 feet – about 10 metres. It got gradually smaller and smaller and narrower and it would make sharp turns and drops . . . ." Dr. Haglund took photographs from inside and outside the cave which the

---

[238]   Pros. exh., 296. 239 Pros. exh., 152-55.

Prosecution entered into evidence.[239] Dr. Haglund further stated "as I went [further back into the cave] . . . I did observe [the remains] of many individuals, men, women and children protruding from the mud that **[page 166]** had covered them up in the intervening rainy season, and at minimum, I observed at least 40 people in this area." Witness QQ, who's sister died at the cave, testified that he saw the smoke coming from the cave on the day of the attack, as he was fleeing from the hill. Later, when he went back to the cave, he discovered that the attackers had set the fire at the entrance.

433. Witness CC is the sole survivor of the massacre at the cave. On the day of the attack, in June 1994, witness CC was inside the cave. According to witness CC, the attack was launched at 9 a.m. when the attackers threw grenades into the cave that did not explode. Members of the *Interahamwe* then went to look for wood and dry grass and piled it and firewood and earth at the entrance of the cave and ignited. On several occasions, during the attack witness CC heard the members of the *Interahamwe* talking of Kayishema and Ruzindana in a manner that would suggest they orchestrated the attack.

Being inside the cave, however, CC never actually saw Kayishema or Ruzindana. CC claimed that he was able to stay alive by rubbing mud on his body and sipping dripping water. He did lose consciousness later but came to when cool air flowed into the cave after other Tutsis unblocked the entrance from outside.

434. Two witnesses, witness W and HH were hiding outside the cave and confirmed that Kayishema and Ruzindana were present and participated in the cave massacre. Witness W, who was hiding in a thorny bush less than five minutes walk from the cave entrance, testified that in May or June 1994, more than one hundred people, mostly the elderly, women and children took refuge in the cave. As the attackers arrived he heard them singing: "[w]e are going to exterminate them and put them in a hole." Kayishema, Ruzindana, *Bourgmestre* Sikubwabo and other local authorities were among the attackers. Witness W confirmed that the attack started in the morning when the attackers fired into the cave. Later they piled wood at the entrance of the cave and set the wood ablaze. Witness W further testified that Kayishema appeared to be leading a group of attackers and that Ruzindana was leading those attackers from Ruhengeri. After attackers departed at 5 or 6 p.m., Witness W and others re-opened the entrance to rescue any survivors. **[page 167]**

435. Witness HH testified that he fled to the cave after his wife and children were killed in another part of Kigarama. He remained outside watching the assailants in the nearby forest. He recognised Kayishema, Ruzindana, Sikubwabo, Ndimbati, and other civil authorities amongst the attackers. He recounted that the assailants fired into the cave, then closed the mouth of the cave, piled wood at the entrance and set the wood ablaze on the orders of Kayishema and Ruzindana. Witness HH confirmed W's account that Kayishema and Ruzindana were leading the groups of assailants and he saw the two men giving them instructions, "just like an overseer who is demonstrating to workers how the work should be done." After the attack, HH and others removed the earth from partially blocking the cave's entrance. Although his testimony is not completely clear on this point, it appears that when HH went into the cave he found no survivors, but later one person came out alive. Among the victims were HH's mother, sister, sister-in-law and her three children.

436. The Defence claims that there is a discrepancy between the testimony of witnesses CC, W and HH with regard to when CC was rescued from the cave. The Defence asserts that CC claimed to have stayed in the cave for three days and nights after the attack, while HH and W testified that after the departure of the assailants on the same evening, the cave entrance was opened and CC was rescued. The Trial Chamber does not find such a discrepancy. It is true that CC deposed that he remained in the cave for three days and nights after the attack. However, careful review of the transcript shows that HH stated that, although the rescuers opened the cave the same evening, they did not find any survivors on that day. HH testified that later one person came out alive. This conforms with CC's account. Witness W supported HH's account that the rescuers opened the cave on the same day and that they were able to save one survivor but did not mention the day that the survivor emerged from the cave. Witness HH and W both named the survivor as CC. It is also possible that CC lost track of time as he was unconscious for an

---

[239]   Pros. exh., 152-55.

unknown period of time. Whatever the exact day of CC's exit from the cave, the testimony of the three witnesses in relation to the presence and role of Kayishema, his subordinates and Ruzindana at the cave are a consistent and credible. **[page 168]**

437. The Chamber notes that no exact date of this event was established. Witness CC stated it was in June. Witness W indicated it happened in late May or June, but added that he was disoriented during this period due to starvation and other factors. According to witness HH, the massacre at the cave took place after French soldiers arrived, which he thought to be 30 June. The problem that witnesses have recollecting precise dates, and the consequential lack of specificity on when the events occurred, has been discussed above. In any event, the essential elements of the crimes depicting the location and nature of the atrocities correlate, thus clearly showing that the witnesses were testifying to the same massacre.

438. The Trial Chamber finds that an attack occurred at the cave and assailants killed scores of Tutsis. Further, both Kayishema and Ruzindana were present at the attack and played a leading role in directing the perpetrators of this massacre; Ruzindana of a particular group of attackers and Kayishema in general. This Chamber finds that gendarmes, members of the *Interahamwe* and various local officials were present and participated.

5.4.3 Massacres Where Kayishema and Ruzindana Acted Separately

439. There are a number of sites within the area of Bisesero area where the witnesses testified to having seen one of the two accused. The Trial Chamber first turns to evidence in relation to Kayishema, followed by that in relation to Ruzindana. Again, the evidence is presented and analysed chronologically and per site.

Attacks for Which Kayishema is Accused Separately

Karongi Hill

440. Testimony reveals that after the massacre at the Stadium, many Tutsi civilians fled to Karongi. Witness U testified that one morning in mid April Kayishema arrived with the *Conseiller* of Gitesi Commune, soldiers, gendarmes and Hutu civilians. Witness U was close to the arriving vehicles and observed Kayishema wearing a black, short sleeve **[page 169]** shirt and a pair of black trousers. They proceeded to attack Tutsis on Karongi Hill. During the siege, gendarmes and soldiers shot at the Tutsi crowd on the Hill while the Hutu civilians surrounded the Hill preventing escape. Witness U heard Kayishema, who was speaking through a megaphone, demand help for the attack. According to witnesses, the attack started around 10 a.m. and ended about 3 p.m.

441. After this attack at Karongi, witness U fled to Kigarama Hill (in the record transcribed as Muchigarama). Here, in late April, he witnessed another attack led by Kayishema. He stated that although Kayishema was not armed, "[i]t was as though he was a general of the army,"[240] and that thousands of Tutsis lost their lives during these attacks.

442. Witness DD testified that a large-scale attack took place at Karongi Hill towards the end of April. He saw, from a hiding place 30 to 35 meters away, that Kayishema arrived in a white car with other civic authorities, soldiers, gendarmes, communal police, members of the *Interahamwe* and civilians at about 9 a.m. Witness DD testified that Kayishema was wearing a white shirt, a black jacket and a pair of dark trousers and was carrying a long gun. After having given instructions to the attackers, Kayishema proceeded to the top of the Hill with other attackers. Kayishema shot at Rutazihana, a fleeing Tutsi refugee, and killed him instantaneously. The attack continued until the evening. Witness DD described how the slaughtered bodies on the Hill were like "small insects which had been killed off by

---

[240] Trans., 6 May 1997, p. 141.

insecticide."[241] On that day, DD lost many members of his family, including his mother, wife, nine children, four sisters and their children, five of his brother's children, two brothers and their wives.

443. During the cross-examination, the Defence Counsel stressed the difference between the written statement signed by DD and his oral testimony. In his statement to investigators the witness had described how his friend Rutazimana was killed by the bullet of a soldier, whereas in his testimony, he asserted that Kayishema had shot **[page 170]** Rutazimana. The doubt raised by this inconsistency, of which the accused is entitled to the benefit, was not dispelled by the explanation of the witness. With regard to prior inconsistent statements, the Trial Chamber is of the opinion that greater emphasis should be placed on direct testimony than on unchallenged prior statements. Although the witness's oral testimony was truthful overall and the accused bears responsibility for the acts of his subordinates at this site as one of the leaders of the attack, we find that with regard to the shooting incident a reasonable doubt has been raised.

Gitwa Cellule and Gitwa Hill

444. Yet another site where Kayishema allegedly led and participated in the attacks is Gitwa Cellule and Gitwa Hill. Witness MM, who lost his wife, four children, two brothers and one sister during the attacks, testified that he (the witness) saw Kayishema when he was hiding at Mukazirandimbwe. Kayishema came in a white double-cabin vehicle with soldiers and members of the *Interahamwe* who were carrying guns, clubs, machetes and spears. Kayishema ordered and urged the assailants to exterminate the Tutsis seeking refuge there. Witness MM saw Kayishema three times at Gitwa in similar circumstances during May. He testified that although he did not see Kayishema carry a weapon or observe any killing, he stated that, "wherever one went one saw nothing but bodies."[242]

Attacks for Which Ruzindana is Accused Separately

Mine at Nyiramuregro Hill

445. Nyiramurego Hill, where a mine is located, is in Bisesero sector. Witness RR testified that he saw Ruzindana arrive in a vehicle with members of the *Interahamwe*, park his car at the foot of the hill and distribute machetes and guns about 15 April. According to this witness Ruzindana told the attackers to "hurry up, I'm going to bring other people to help you. But each time bring me an identity card or a head and I will pay you." Although after cross-examination the exact distance at which RR observed Ruzindana remained unclear, RR maintained that he was close enough to hear and see Ruzindana on that occasion. **[page 171]**

446. Two witnesses gave specific accounts regarding another incident involving Ruzindana at Nyiramurego Hill. Witnesses II and EE stated that a group of Tutsis, who had taken refuge in the Mine, in this Hill, were killed by Ruzindana, members of the *Interahamwe* and soldiers. Both witnesses testified that a young Hutu boy who knew of these Tutsis hiding place brought the attackers to this site. Specifically, II testified that one morning after the Muyira attack on 14 May (either in May or June), while he was hiding near the road by this Hill, he saw Ruzindana arrive in a vehicle accompanied by the members of the *Interahamwe*. Ruzindana stayed by the roadside while the assailants began to uncover the mine entrances and kill those hiding within. Two young Tutsi women were discovered in the Mine by the members of the *Interahamwe* and Ruzindana ordered that they be brought to him. One of these young women, named Beatrice, a former schoolmate of II's, was approximately sixteen years old. Ruzindana tore open her blouse and then slowly cut off one of her breasts with a machete passed to him by an members of the *Interahamwe*. After he finished, Ruzindana cut off her other breast while mockingly telling her to look at the first breast as it lay on the ground. He then tore open her stomach. Beatrice died as a result of the assault. A member of the *Interahamwe*, following Ruzindana's lead, immediately

---

[241]   Trans., 25 Feb. 1998, p. 28.
[242]   Trans., 24 Feb. 1998, p. 27.

proceeded to kill the second young woman while Ruzindana watched. With some slight variation, witness EE confirmed this account. Both witnesses observed this event from hiding places alongside the road, adjacent to where Ruzindana and the assailants stopped to carryout the attack. Witness EE added that his family members were killed before his eyes as members of the *Interahamwe* and soldiers uncovered the holes in which the Tutsis were hiding and proceed to kill them and other Tutsis using firearms and machetes.

447.   The Trial Chamber is satisfied that both witnesses were able to observe the incident with sufficient visibility because the event occurred during the daytime and both were hiding within viewing distance. Furthermore, they both had known Ruzindana previously. Accordingly, the Trial Chamber is satisfied that the witnesses made proper identification of Ruzindana. **[page 172]**

Bisesero Hill

448.   During the second half of April 1994, witness Z observed regular attacks during which Ruzindana was present with members of the Presidential Guard and members of the *Interahamwe*. During these attacks Ruzindana would generally wait by his vehicle and give instructions to the attackers. At one of these attacks, on 14 April 1994, witness Z was hiding close to Ruzindana, on Bisesero Hill. Witness Z heard Ruzindana give orders to the assailants to surround the hill and begin the attack. This witness also claimed that Ruzindana was armed and shot at the Tutsis. However, the witness stated that "not many people died during this time period," but that there was pillaging of property that was distributed later amongst the attackers. The Trial Chamber is satisfied that Ruzindana was present and played a pivotal role in the massacres at this site by ordering the assailants to surround the Hill and kill the Tutsis hiding there.

Gitwa Cellule

449.   Another massacre site where Ruzindana was present was Gitwa Cellule. On 15 April 1994, witness KK saw Ruzindana transport assailants to this site in a vehicle, which he knew belonged to Ruzindana. Furthermore, witness KK was approximately 50 meters away when he saw Ruzindana shoot a Tutsi man named Ruzibiza in the leg. Ruzibiza fell to the ground.

450.   Later, in early May, witness MM observed Ruzindana leading members of the *Interahamwe* during a massacre at this location. The assailants began to chase MM and other Tutsis. MM's wife, who, was carrying their child on her back, was running behind MM when she was shot. As he was fleeing the scene, MM turned around to see the attackers, and claims to have seen Ruzindana aiming and firing at his wife. After the attack he returned to the place where his wife had fallen and saw that she had a bullet wound and had been mutilated by traditional weapons. Both his wife and baby were dead. When questioned by the Defence about the circumstances under which MM saw Ruzindana firing the gun, he admitted that he only saw Ruzindana for a short time and that he didn't know how a gun worked. **[page 173]**

451.   The Trial Chamber is satisfied that Ruzindana was amongst a group of attackers at the site who pursued the Tutsis hiding there in an attempt to kill them and that witness MM's wife and baby died as a result of this attack. The Trial Chamber is also satisfied that Ruzindana attempted to kill MM's wife because MM deposed that he saw Ruzindana aim in her direction. However, the Trial Chamber is not satisfied, beyond a reasonable doubt, that Ruzindana's gunshot actually struck MM's wife or that she in fact died from the bullet wound she received. The Prosecution did not establish that Ruzindana was the only assailant amongst the group who was firing into the fleeing Tutsis and the actual cause of her death remains unclear. The Defence challenged the credibility of MM on the ground that, in cross-examination, MM said that he had not met other Rwandans during his stay in Arusha. The Defence pointed out that it is well known that Prosecution witnesses are lodged together in the same house during their stay in Arusha. On reexamination, when asked why he refused to admit such a fact, MM claimed that he thought the question had referred to people with whom he was sharing his bed. Despite the confusion of this

response the Trial Chamber is satisfied that MM's testimony represented a strong and accurate account of the events in Bisesero.

The Vicinity of Muyira Hill

452. Attacks in the vicinity of Muyira Hill continued into June 1994. Witness II testified to one event at a hole formed by water running under the road in an area called Gahora in Gitwa Cellule. According to II, in early June many Tutsis children, as well as adults, were hiding in this hole; amongst them II's younger brother and sister. While hiding in the bush, just five meters away, witness II saw members of the *Interahamwe* coming down the valley to drink water from a tap near the hole. On discovering the Tutsis hiding there, the members of the *Interahamwe* informed Ruzindana that they had found "inyenzi." Ruzindana sent soldiers to monitor the hole and II heard him say that he was going to Gishyita to look for tools. Ruzindana returned with spades and a hose at about 1 p.m., at which time the soldiers and members of the *Interahamwe* began to unearth the Tutsis. The massacre started when Ruzindana and other soldiers opened fire. Many Tutsis died in the hole while others were shot or hacked to death near the roadside **[page 174]** as they tried to escape. After the attack, II found his brother and sister murdered in the nearby bushes. During cross-examination, II remained true to this account. The Trial Chamber finds beyond reasonable doubt that Ruzindana was present, participated and led the attack on the hole where an unknown number of Tutsi civilians were killed, including II's brother and sister.

5.4.4 Bisesero Analysis and Findings.

453. Paragraphs 45 and 46 of the Indictment have. been discussed above and the allegations therein, were not contested by the Defence.

454. Paragraph 47 of the Indictment directly implicates both the accused persons in the attacks at Bisesero. The most consequential evidence is the identification of the accused at the massacre sites by Prosecution witnesses. Also of grave importance in the case of Kayishema, is evidence of the participation of those under his control. The Trial Chamber is mindful of its obligation to vigorously analyse the evidence. Very pertinent is the witnesses' who knew the accused prior to the massacres; identification is far more reliable when it is based upon recognition of a person already known to the witness. Equally important are the conditions under which the witnesses identified the accused.[243] These issues are discussed below.

455. The Prosecution presented numerous eyewitnesses who testified that they saw Kayishema at various massacre sites in Bisesero. Most Prosecution witnesses claimed that they knew Kayishema before the events. Most commonly the witnesses recognised or knew Kayishema because he was the highest government official in Kibuye. For instance, OO and HH claimed to "know" Kayishema because he was the *Prefect* of Kibuye *Prefecture* and OO had met Kayishema at the installation of the *Bourgmestre* Sikubwabo. Witness OO added that all the inhabitants of Gishyita commune knew Kayishema because he was seen at civic rallies and meetings. In this regard, witness II stated that he saw Kayishema at the swearing ceremony of Sikubwabo. Witness DD had **[page 175]** seen Kayishema at meetings and recalled one such meeting at the Stadium. Witness HH testified that he used to see Kayishema at meetings and NN claimed to have participated in meetings organised by Kayishema. Witness KK had worked with Kayishema each time there was a meeting to organise. Witness PP knew Kayishema when the accused was a medical doctor at Kibuye hospital. A number of witnesses also knew Kayishema's family. For example, witness OO, knew Kayishema's grandfather and mother; witness JJ knew Kayishema's father; and witness UU greeted Kayishema in 1992 or 1993 when Kayishema came to visit his (Kayishema's) grandfather. Witness PP met Kayishema at Kibuye church when Kayishema had gone to see a priest there. All Prosecution survivor witnesses successfully identified of Kayishema in

---

[243]   See Part 3 on Evidentiary Matters, *supra.*

court. This prior familiarity with Kayishema enhanced the reliability of the witness's identification of Kayishema heard by the Trial Chamber.[244]

456. Similarly, most of the witnesses testified that they knew Ruzindana in some capacity prior to the massacres. Evidence suggests that Ruzindana was one of the most prominent traders in Kibuye and that his family was well known generally because his father had been the *Bourgmestre* of Gisovu. Some knew him personally, that is they had had contact with him previously or knew his family. For example, witness FF studied with Ruzindana. Ruzindana attended social functions at which witness OO was also present and had business dealings with him. Witness NN claimed to have been Ruzindana's friend and that he knew some members of his family. Witness RR had known Ruzindana since he was old enough to recognise people, and had been a fellow guest at the marriage of a local man named Antoine. Witness Z had known Ruzindana since at least 1986 and HH had known him long before 1994, having met him at the market and being a customer at his family's shop. Ruzindana was also a neighbour of witness BB's parents and they had played football together.

457. Other witnesses, knew Ruzindana by sight due to his reputation as a prominent businessman in their community and/or because of his father's standing in the **[page 176]** community.[245] Examples of such witnesses are II, KK, MM and PP. All Prosecution survivor witnesses successfully identified Ruzindana in court. This prior familiarity with the identity of Ruzindana enhanced the reliability of the identification evidence heard by the Trial Chamber.[246]

458. It is apparent that when the witnesses stated that they "knew" the accused they were not always referring to a personal acquaintance or friendship. Rather, the witnesses were sometimes referring to "knowing of" or "knowing who the accused was," due to his prominence in the community. The Trial Chamber is satisfied that the use of such phraseology was not an attempt by the witnesses to mislead the Trial Chamber. Indeed, it is consistent with common usage in much the same way as one would say that they "knew" President Nelson Mandela, even though they have never met him through his image in the media. In any event, for the purposes of identification, it is the physical recognition of the accused rather than personal acquaintance which is most pertinent. The above evidence suggests that most of the witnesses who identified Kayishema and/or Ruzindana, were aware of the physical appearance of the accused prior to seeing them at the massacre sites.

459. The conditions under which the witnesses saw the accused was closely scrutinised by the Defence teams. The Trial Chamber notes that all of the identifications at the massacre sites occurred in daylight. The witnesses were generally questioned about the distance from which they observed the accused. The evidence indicates that almost all of the witnesses were close enough to clearly observe the accused during the attacks and the level of detail provided by the witnesses supports this assertion. For example, at the Muyira Hill attack, where the witnesses were looking down at the accused from higher positions during daylight, the witnesses provided precise details regarding the accused participation. Witness PP saw both accused shooting at Tutsi; OO was close enough to see Kayishema wearing a green outfit and the following day recalled hearing specific words as Kayishema addressed the attackers; JJ also remembered Kayishema's green suit **[page 177]** on May 13 and added that Ruzindana was carrying a gun; II observed Kayishema thanking assailants on 13 May and saw both accused shoot at Tutsis on 14 May; NN testified that Ruzindana chased and shot at him; and HH, from his hiding place in the forest, observed both accused as they shot at those seeking refuge on top of the Hill.

460. A further example is the massacre at the cave; witnesses W and HH insisted that they had a clear view of the accused from their hiding places. Witness W stated that he was in bushes "less than five minutes walk away," whereas HH was concealed in the nearby forest. The ability of HH to see these events is supported by photographic exhibit 310, which represents HH's view of the cave from his hiding place. Lastly, witnesses EE and II identified Ruzindana as Beatrice's killer, at the Mine, from their respective hiding places alongside the road; both witnesses testified that they were close enough to hear

---

[244]   For a detailed explanation of the identification requirement see Chapter 3.2, *supra.*
[245]   Ruzindana's father, Murakaza was also a businessman and a former *Bourgmestre.*
[246]   *Ibid.*

Ruzindana. Prosecution photographic exhibits regarding these hiding places indicates that these witnesses could have clearly seen Ruzindana whist remaining concealed.

461. After reviewing the witness testimonies and Prosecution exhibits, the Trial Chamber is satisfied, beyond a reasonable doubt, that Kayishema was properly identified by prosecution witnesses FF, PP, OO, II, JJ, NN, HH, UU, W, U, DD and MM, as having participated in one or more of the assaults on the Tutsi population. And, that Ruzindana was properly identified by Prosecution witnesses FF, PP, OO, II, JJ, NN, HH, UU, W, EE, Z, KK, RR and MM, as having participated in one or more assaults.

462. Paragraph 47 of the Indictment alleges specifically that at various locations throughout April, May and June 1994, and often in concert, Clement Kayishema and Obed Ruzindana brought to the area of Bisesero members of the *gendarmerie nationale*, communal police, *Interahamwe* and armed civilians and directed them to attack people seeking refuge there. The Trial Chamber opines that bringing attackers to Bisesero could mean either personally transporting them in the same vehicle, or leading a convoy of vehicles. Furthermore, evidence to prove that the accused transported or lead the attackers from one area within Bisesero to another area within **[page 178]** Bisesero is enough to satisfy the wording of paragraph 47 of the Indictment. It is not incumbent on the Prosecution to prove from where the attackers came.

463. In relation to the 13 and 14 May assault at Muyira Hill, witnesses OO, II, JJ and NN testified that they had seen Kayishema and Ruzindana arrive at the head of the convoy of vehicles which transported the assailants to the massacre site. Testimony reveals that Ruzindana personally transported attackers. The witnesses confirmed that soldiers, members of, the *Interahamwe*, communal police and armed civilians, were amongst the attackers. Evidence provided by OO, JJ and UU proves how Kayishema directed the assaults, by splitting the assailants into groups, leading a group as it advanced up the Hill and indicating places where the Tutsis could be found. Indeed, PP, OO, II and JJ heard Kayishema address a group of attackers, encouraging them to "work" harder or thanking them for "work" done. Evidence shows that Kayishema used a megaphone to address the congregated attackers. Witness OO and JJ further testified that Kayishema signalled the start of the attacks by firing a shot into the air. Ruzindana also played a leadership role, heading a group of attackers up the Hill and shooting at those seeking refuge, as evidenced by II and OO. Witness OO also saw Ruzindana distributing traditional weapons prior to the attacks.

464. Evidence proffered in relation to other sites confirms the leadership role of both the accused. At the cave, W testified that Kayishema was directing the siege generally and Ruzindana was commanding the attackers from Ruhengeri; HH added that both the accused appeared to be giving instructions, as if demonstrating how the cave should be blocked, wood collected and fire built. At Karongi Hill, U saw Kayishema arrive with soldiers, gendarmes and Hutu civilians and use a megaphone to address the attackers; DD also observed Kayishema at this site giving instructions to soldiers, gendarmes, communal police and members of the *Interahamwe*. Ruzindana was also seen transporting members of the *Interahamwe* to the Mine at Nyiramurego Hill and then directing the attackers. At Bisesero Hill witness Z heard Ruzindana give orders to the assailants to surround the Hill and begin the assault. **[page 179]** Witness KK testified that Ruzindana transported attackers to Bisesero Hill and, in the following month, MM observed Ruzindana there leading members of the *Interahamwe*. Witness II testified that the massacre at the hole near Muyira Hill was orchestrated by Ruzindana and that it commenced on his instruction.

465. The strength and reliability of this evidence was not effectively challenged in Court. Accordingly, the Trial Chamber is satisfied that both Kayishema and Ruzindana brought members of the *gendarmerie nationals*, communal police, members of the *Interahamwe* and armed civilians to the area of Bisesero and directed them to attack those Tutsis seeking refuge.

466. Paragraph 47 of the Indictment further alleges that Kayishema and Ruzindana personally attacked and killed people seeking refuge in Bisesero. There is an abundance of evidence that reveals how Kayishema and Ruzindana participated in the attacks. Along with the evidence discussed in paragraphs above, many witnessed testified that they observed Kayishema and/or Ruzindana personally shoot at Tutsi those seeking refuge. At Bisesero Hill in April, Z recognised Ruzindana as he shot at those seeking

refuge. Later, at a similar spot in May, FF was just metres from Ruzindana when he observed him shooting at women and two girls. At Muyira Hill in May PP, II, NN and HH witnessed both the accused shooting at Tutsis as they fled. In June, PP was shot at by Kayishema and Ruzindana at Kucyapa. Two eyewitnesses testified that Ruzindana killed a young girl named Beatrice. At Gitwa Cellule in April, KK was approximately 50 metres from Ruzindana as he shot Ruzibiza, hitting him in the leg. And, MM testified that Ruzindana shot his wife in May.

467. The major contention of the reliability of witnesses, which was raised by the Defence, has been discussed within the analysis of evidence relating to the particular site. Defence challenges did not negate the quality and strength of the above evidence. The Trial Chamber is satisfied beyond reasonable doubt that Ruzindana and Kayishema personally attacked Tutsis seeking refuge during the assaults described in Bisesero. **[page 180]**

468. There is also strong evidence to show that both accused persons personally aided in the killings. The Trial Chamber is left with no doubt that Kayishema and Ruzindana aided and abetted, the killings through orchestration and direction.[247] Kayishema further abetted through his inciting speeches to assailants, and Ruzindana by his provision of transportation and weapons. The evidence proves that Kayishema and Ruzindana personally assisted in attacks that resulted in the killing of Tutsi civilians.

469. Cases of personal killing by Kayishema or Ruzindana relating to specific individuals is less certain. There is ample evidence to show that both the accused personally attempted to kill or injure those seeking refuge, generally by shooting at them. However, as discussed within the above text, in most instances where a witness testified to one or both of the accused shooting at a refugee, the Prosecution failed to establish a resulting death.[248] This is not surprising considering the circumstances under which the witnesses observed the events. One would not expect a fleeing refugee to risk his or her life in order to verify the death of a victim. Nonetheless, it is not for the Trial Chamber to speculate if Tutsis died as a direct consequence of shooting, or other acts, by an accused.

470. One instance where sufficient evidence has been proffered is the killing of Beatrice by Ruzindana. Witnesses II and EE both provided a horrific account of Ruzindana cutting off the breasts of Beatrice before killing her by slashing her stomach with a machete. The witnesses clearly observed Ruzindana mutilate and murder her, both heard him mock his victim in the process. Both witnesses recognised the victim, one of them as a former schoolmate and the other as a prominent person from the area. Both witnesses named the victim as Beatrice. Both witnesses deposed that Beatrice died as a result of Ruzindana's actions. For these reasons, the Trial Chamber is satisfied, beyond a reasonable doubt, that Ruzindana mutilated and personally killed Beatrice. **[page 181]**

471. In paragraph 48 of the Indictment the Prosecution alleges that the attacks resulted in the deaths of thousands men, women and children. All survivor witnesses attested to the fact that thousands were killed in the Bisesero area during April through June 1994. Witnesses, including Dr. Haglund and several journalists, confirmed this fact. Kayishema himself testified that massive burial efforts had taken place in this area.

472. Finally, in paragraph 49 of the Indictment it is alleged that Kayishema did not take measures to prevent the attacks or to punish the perpetrators is discussed in Chapter 6.1 of the Judgement, *infra.* **[page 182]**

VI. LEGAL FINDINGS

6.1 Kayishema's Command Responsibility

473. The Trial Chamber has made its findings as to fact. It is clear that Kayishema and Ruzindana either planned, instigated, ordered, committed or otherwise aided and abetted in the planning, preparation or

---

[247] See for example, the evidence relating to the massacres at Muyira Hill, the cave and the Mine at Nyiramuregra Hill.
[248] See the analysis of the evidence within the specific site Chapters above.

execution of many of the criminal acts prohibited by Articles 2 to 4 of this Statute, in relati[c] crime site. Their individual criminal responsibility under Article 6(1) has been proven [l] reasonable doubt and is set out by the Trial Chamber in its legal findings for the relevant cou   ...he factual findings which go to prove this individual criminal responsibility are also relevant to Kayishema's responsibility as a superior, in particular his knowledge and prevention of the attacks.

474. The extent of the liability to be incurred by Kayishema alone under the doctrine of command responsibility pursuant to Article 6(3) warrants further elaboration. In relation to the crime sites of the Complex, the Stadium, and Mubuga Church the Indictment asserts: "Before the attack on the [site] Clement Kayishema did not take measures to prevent the attack, and after the attack Clement Kayishema did not punish the perpetrators." See paragraphs 30, 37, and 43. In relation to the Bisesero Area the Indictment asserts: "Throughout this time, Clement Kayishema did not take measures to prevent the attack, and after the attack Clement Kayishema did not punish the perpetrators." See paragraph 49.

475. In relation to the extent of the liability to be incurred by Kayishema under the doctrine of command responsibility, the General Allegations of the Indictment assert, at paragraph 22, that Kayishema is responsible, as a superior, for the criminal acts of his subordinates in the administration, *gendarmerie nationale* and communal police. In relation to the specific sites it is alleged that Kayishema ordered these assailants and others such as the members of the *Interahamwe* and armed Hutu civilians to attack the Tutsi. As such, and in light of the proven facts, it is incumbent upon the Trial Chamber **[page 183]** to consider the degree of control exercised by Kayishema over the assailants, and his corresponding culpability for their criminal acts. The Chamber, where appropriate, will then proceed to examine[249] whether Kayishema took measures to prevent the attacks or punish the perpetrators, under each crime site.

The Assailants

476. *Bourgmestres* and other members of the administration, gendarmes, soldiers, communal police, prison wardens, members of the *Interahamwe* and armed civilians were identified at the massacre sites and the Trial Chamber has found that they participated in the atrocities at these sites. The question which the Trial Chamber must address, therefore, is whether Kayishema exercised *de jure* or *de facto* control over these assailants.

477. Both the Prosecution and Defence laid heavy emphasis upon whether Kayishema enjoyed *de jure* control over the appropriate administrative bodies and law enforcement agencies. Notably, both Parties also emphasised the turmoil that prevailed between April and July 1994. The Defence, for example, described, "a society that no longer recognised the rule of law"[250] and, in summarising the evidence of Professor Guibal, submitted that, "in common language, after the crash of the President's plane, the situation that occurred was such that a government had to be invented."[251]

478. The Chamber is mindful of the need, therefore, to view the *de jure* powers of Kayishema with an appreciation that, at the time, a chaotic situation that prevailed. Accordingly, any consideration as to the *de jure* powers exercised by Kayishema must be subject to an elucidation of the *de facto* power, or lack thereof, that he held over the assailants. **[page 184]**

De Jure Control

479. The Indictment states that the *Prefect* as trustee of the State Authority in the *Prefecture* had control over the *Prefectoral* administration and its agencies. The Chamber has found that, *inter alia Bourgmestre* Sikubwabo, a number of communal police, and members of the *gendarmerie nationale* were responsible for numerous deaths and injuries inflicted upon innocent Tutsis.

---

249   The law relating to this area has been discussed *supra* in Chapter 4.4.
250   Closing arguments, Mr. Ferran, Trans., p. 112, 3 Nov. 1998.
251   *Ibid.*, p. 90, 4 Nov 1998.

480. The Trial Chamber finds that it is beyond question that the *Prefect* exercised *de jure* authority over these assailants. The Rwandan law is very clear in this respect.

481. The *Prefects'* position *vis-à-vis* the *bourgmestre* is evidently one of hierarchical authority and supervisory jurisdiction. Two Rwandan statutes support this finding. The first, *Loi sur l'organisation de la commune*, 1963, clearly implies in Article 59 that the *bourgmestre* is under the hierarchical authority of the *Prefect*.[252] The same law provides at Article 85 that where a communal authority fails to execute measures prescribed by law or decree, then the *Prefect* may, ultimately, supplant this communal authority in order to remedy their inaction.[253] Moreover, at Articles 46 and 48, the *Loi sur L'organisation de la commune*, 1963, establishes the power of the *Prefect*, to take disciplinary sanctions against a *bourgmestre* and even to propose his dismissal to the Minister of the Interior. Coupled with this is the law as promulgated in the second statute submitted to this Trial Chamber, the *Décret-Loi organisation et fonctionnement de la préfecture*, 11 March 1975. Article 15 of this statute makes clear that, in addition to the hierarchical authority that the *Prefect* exercises over the *bourgmestres* and their services, he also has a general power of supervision over the acts of the communal authorities. Therefore, these provisions, coupled with the *Prefect's* overarching duty to maintain **[page 185]** public order and security, reflect the ultimate hierarchical authority enjoyed by the *Prefect* over the *bourgmestre*.[254]

482. The communal police are under the direct control over the *bourgmestre*. This matter was not disputed, and reflects the findings of the Trial Chamber in the *Akayesu* Judgement. Even if it is not axiomatic that the *Prefect* would hold the corresponding hierarchical *de jure* authority over the communal police, the law provides that in the situation which faced Rwanda and Kibuye *Prefecture* in 1994, it is the *Prefect* who retains ultimate control. To this end, the *Loi sur l'organisation de la commune*, 1963, allows the *Prefect* to requisition the communal police and place them under his direct authority in cases of grave public disorder or in times when unrest has occurred or is about to occur.[255]

483. Similarly, the *Prefect* exercises this ultimate authority of requisition over the *gendarmerie nationale*. The position set out in the *Décret-Loi sur la création de la Gendarmerie Nationale*, 1974, states that any competent administrative authority may requisition the *gendarmerie nationale*, that the advisability of the requisition cannot be questioned as long as it does not contravene any law or regulation, and that the requisition persists until the requisitioning authority informs the *gendarmerie* otherwise.[256] Moreover, the *gendarmerie nationale* may *only* execute certain functions, notably, ensuring the maintenance and restoration of public order, when it is legally requisitioned to do so.[257] The Trial Chamber recalls that Kayishema requisitioned the **[page 186]** *gendarmerie* both by telephone, and in writing, in the face of the public disorder that prevailed in Rwanda in the pivotal months of April to July 1994.

484. This *de jure* power of the *Prefect* was confirmed by the expert Defence witness, Professor Guibal. In his testimony to the Trial Chamber he opined that, even after the 1991 Constitution, in the advent of multiple party politics,

---

[252] Article 59: En tant que représentant du pouvoir exécutif, le *Bourgmestre* est soumis a l'autorité hiérarchique du préfet.

[253] Article 85: Lorsque les autorités communales font preuve de carence et n'exécutent pas des mesures prescrites par les lois ou règlements, le préfet pent après deux avertissements écrits restés sans effet se substituer à elles. Il peut prendre toutes les mesures appropriées pour parer à leur défaillance.

[254] Article 15: Le préfet, en plus du pouvoir hiérarchique qu'il a sur les Bourgmestres et leurs services administratifs, dispose sur les actes des autorités communales, du pouvoir général de tutelle, determiné par les dispositions de la loi communale.

[255] Article 104 (para. 2): Toutefois, en cas de calamité publique ou lorsque des troubles menacent déclater ou ont éclaté, le préfet peut réquisitionner les agents de la Police communale et les placer sous son autorité directe.

[256] Article 29: L'action des autorités administratives compétentes s'exerce a l'égard de la Gendarmerie Nationale par voie de réquisition; Article 33: L'autorité requise de la Gendarmerie Nationale ne peut discuter l'opportunité de la réquisition pour autant qu'elle n'aille pas à l'encontre d'une loi ou d'un règlement: Article 36: Les effets de la réquisition cessent lorsque l'autorité requérante signifie, par écrit ou verbalement, la levée de la requisition a l'autorité de Gendarmerie qui était chargée de son exécution.

[257] Décret-Loi sur la création de la Gendarmerie Nationale, reading Articles 4 and 24 in conjunction: Article 4 (para. 3): Les fonctions extraordinaires sont celles que la Gendarmerie Nationale ne peut remplir que sur réquisition de l'autorité compétente; Article 24 (Under section 23, Extraordinary functions): La Gendarmerie Nationale assure, le maintien et le rétablissement de l'ordre public lorsqu'elle en est le légalement requise.

the *Prefect* had considerable powers with regard to the *prefectorial* conference. The *Prefect*, according to the text of 1975, . . . could even requisition the intervention of the armed forces. The *Prefect* can define regulations for law and order and he can punish directly...[258]

485. Further, when Counsel for Kayishema asked whether, in light of the multi-party politics, it was, "a co-ordination role that the *Prefect* plays rather than the exercise of hierarchical power", Professor Guibal replied, "normally the relationships fall under the hierarchy rather than under co-ordination".[259]

486. Professor Guibal then proceeded to describe how the situation would have been very different in the tumultuous realities of Rwanda in 1994. The situation in the country and the peculiar nature of the party-orientated constitution would have led to what he described as "crisis multi-partyism". Although he did not examine the specific context of the Rwandan crisis, he explained that such a *status quo* would have arisen because each respective party would have felt that the situation should be resolved through them, not the constitution. A dichotomy between political and administrative hierarchy would have emerged. This led Professor Guibal to the conclusion that although the power of the *Prefect* over the forces of law and order existed formally in 1994, these powers were emptied of any real meaning when the ministers, the ultimate hierarchical superiors to the police, gendarmes and army, were of a different political persuasion. **[page 187]**

487. The Trial Chamber is of the opinion that such assertions clearly highlight the need to consider the *de facto* powers of the *Prefect* between April and July 1994. Such an examination will be conducted below. However, the delineation of power on party political grounds, whilst perhaps theoretically sound, should only be considered in light of the Trial Chambers findings that the administrative bodies, law enforcement agencies, and even armed civilians were engaged together in a common genocidal plan. The focus in these months was upon a unified, common intention to destroy the ethnic Tutsi population. Therefore, the question of political rivalries must have been, if it was at all salient, a secondary consideration.

488. The actions of Kayishema himself also appear to evidence a continued subordination of the *bourgmestres* to his *de jure* authority during the events of 1994 or, at least, an expectation of such subordination. Prosecution exhibit 51, for example, is a letter from Kayishema to the *bourgmestres* requesting that they recruit people to be "trained" for the civil defence programme. Prosecution exhibit 53 is another letter from Kayishema to the *bourgmestres*, dated 5 May 1994, which requests an urgent report on the security situation in their communes and to inform him of where "the works" had started. In addition, Kayishema testified to this Trial Chamber that in late May 1994, he went to the *Bourgmestres* in his *prefecture* and instructed them to disregard a letter that they had received directly from the Minister of Interior relating to the civil defence programme. His clear objective in doing so was to prevent the *Bourgmestres* from implementing the explicit instructions of the Minister.[260]

489. Even in the climate that prevailed, therefore, Kayishema clearly considered that this hierarchical relationship persisted and expected his "requests" to be executed. Accordingly, the Trial Chamber finds that it is beyond any doubt that Kayishema exercised *de jure* power over the *Bourgmestres*, communal police, gendarmes and other law enforcing agencies identified at the massacre sites. **[page 188]**

De Facto Control

490. However, the jurisprudence on this issue clearly reflects the need to look beyond simply the *de jure* authority enjoyed in a given situation and to consider the *de facto* power exercised. The Trial Chamber in the *Celebici* case stated that in the fact situation of the Former Yugoslavia, where the command structure was often ambiguous and illdefined,

---

[258] Trans., 27 May 1998, p.125.
[259] *Ibid.*
[260] Trans., 3 Sept. 1998, p. 113. The Trial Chamber was never seized of the details of these instructions. However, the contents of these instructions are only of secondary importance.

. . .persons effectively in command of such more informal structures, with power to prevent and punish the crimes of persons who are in fact under their control, may under certain circumstances be held responsible for their failure to do so. Thus the Trial Chamber accepts the . . . proposition that individuals in positions of authority, whether civilian or military structures, may incur criminal responsibility under the doctrine of command responsibility on the basis of their *de facto* as well as their *de jure* positions as superiors. *The mere absence of formal legal authority to control the actions of subordinates should therefore not be understood to preclude impositions of such responsibility.*[261] [emphasis added]

491. Thus, even where a clear hierarchy based upon *de jure* authority is not present, this does not prevent the finding of command responsibility. Equally, as we shall examine below, the mere existence of *de jure* power does not always necessitate the imposition of command responsibility. The culpability that this doctrine gives rise to must ultimately be predicated upon the power that the superior exercises over his subordinates in a given situation.

492. The Trial Chamber has found that acts or omissions of a *de facto* superior can give rise to individual criminal responsibility pursuant to Article 6(3) of the Statute. Thus, no legal or formal position of authority need exist between the accused and the perpetrators of the crimes. Rather, the influence that an individual exercises over the perpetrators of the crime may provide sufficient grounds for the imposition of command responsibility if it can be shown that such influence was used to order the commission of the crime or that, despite such *de facto* influence, the accused failed to prevent the crime. The *Celebici* case provides an exposition of the jurisprudence on this point.[262] One **[page 189]** particularly pertinent example is the *Roechling* case which the Trial Chamber in the *Celebici* Judgement summarised as,

> . . . an example of the imposition of superior responsibility on the basis of *de facto* power of control possessed by civilian leaders. While the accused in this case were found guilty, *inter alia*, of failing to take action against the abuse of forced labourers committed by members of the Gestapo, it is nowhere suggested that the accused had any formal authority to issue orders to personnel under Gestapo command.[263]

493. This passage is instructive not only when considering Kayishema's control over the less explicitly documented command structures which existed in Rwanda in 1994, such as the members of the *Interahamwe* and those armed civilians involved in the "civil defence programme"; but also when examining the realities of Kayishema's relationship with *bourgmestres*, communal police and the *gendarmerie nationale*.

494. Defence witnesses such as DN and DK testified to the lack of material means available for the *Prefect* to control the public disorder that ensued after the death of the President. Trial Chamber notes, however, that these witnesses did not actually contest the control that the *Prefect* exercised over the law enforcing and administrative bodies.

495. It was the Defence's position that the *Prefect* had insufficient means to prevent those assailants, including a few defecting members of the army and *gendarmerie nationale*, from committing the massacres of 1994. Kayishema himself testified that he had sent what gendarmes he had at his disposal to the area of Bisesero, but that there was little that could be done.

496. Professor Guibal, for the Defence, described how the *status quo* that emerged in 1994 after the death of the President would have been one where the traditional influence and power of the *Prefect* would have been greatly reduced. He was of the opinion that the authority the *Prefect*, as a member of a political party and in the climate of the "crisis multi-partyism", would have been diminished, both *de jure* and *de facto*. **[page 190]**

---

[261] *Celebici* Judgement, para. 354.
[262] *Ibid.*, paras. 375-376.
[263] *Ibid.*, para. 376.

497. In this respect, Professor Guibal referred to a "paralysis of power" suffered by the *Prefect*. Accordingly, it was submitted by the Defence, the political and administrative uncertainty that reigned between April and July 1994 was such as to curtail the *Prefect's* power of requisition and his influence over administrative bodies. This uncertainty, the Defence submitted, also manifested itself amongst the population as a whole. Professor Guibal opined that the citizens in such a climate of uncertainty would receive instructions and orders with difficulty.

498. In short, the Defence submitted that in the pivotal months of 1994, Kayishema was in not in a *de facto* position to control the actions of the assailants and that he was neither in a position to prevent nor to punish the commission of the massacres in his *Prefecture*.

499. Once again, however, the theoretical underpinning proffered by Professor Guibal does not reflect the reality that the Trial Chamber has found existed in Rwanda. The *Prefect* was a well-known, respected, and esteemed figure within his community.[264] The testimony of Kayishema provides an illustrative example of the influence that the *Prefect* enjoyed. He related to the Trial Chamber an instance in August 1992 when, soon after taking office, he was telephoned by the *Bourgmestre* of Gishyita Commune. The *Bourgmestre* reported that houses were being burnt down in his commune, people were fleeing and the situation was chaotic. Kayishema told the Trial Chamber that he was requested to go directly to the scene and intervene, that the *Bourgmestre* had said "I just want your presence here on the spot."[265]

500. The Trial Chamber draws three basic conclusions from this. Firstly, it is indicative of the effect that Kayishema's presence at a scene could have, thus is appurtenant to the responsibility he must bear in aiding and abetting the crimes pursuant to Article 6(1). Secondly, in times of crisis it was ultimately the *Prefect* that was called upon, with all the powers of influence that such a bearer of that title wielded. Finally, it also reflects the de **[page 191]** *facto* influence he had and the commensurate *de facto* authority he exercised as *Prefect* in such times. A clear parallel can be drawn with the climate that prevailed in Rwanda in 1994.

501. The facts of the case also reflect the *de facto* control that Kayishema exercised over *all* of the assailants participating in the massacres. Kayishema was often identified transporting or leading many of the assailants to the massacre sites. He was regularly identified, for example, in the company of members of the *Interahamwe* – transporting them, instructing them, rewarding them, as well as directing and leading their attacks. The Trial Chamber, therefore, is satisfied that Kayishema had strong affiliations with these assailants, and his command over them at each massacre site, as with the other assailants, was clearly established by witness testimony.

502. In the Bisesero area, for example, witness W testified that Kayishema was directing the massacre of those Tutsi who had sought refuge at the Cave. Witness U, at Karongi Hill, described to the Trial Chamber how Kayishema arrived at this location leading a number of soldiers, gendarmes, and armed civilians, addressed them by megaphone and then instructed them to attack. Upon these orders, the massacres began. These facts have been proven beyond a reasonable doubt.

503. The massacre that occurred at the Stadium provides a further striking example of the control exercised by Kayishema. The Trial Chamber has found that Kayishema transported gendarmes to the Stadium where, for two days, they simply stood guard and controlled the movement of persons in and out of the Stadium. Kayishema returned on 18 April leading more gendarmes, members of the *Interahamwe*, other armed civilians and prison wardens. Only then, when Kayishema ordered them to commence the attacks, firing into the crowd twice, did the guarding gendarmes begin their massacre. The onslaught by those who had been guarding the Stadium and those assailants who joined them were impromptu and unforeseen, but formed part of an attack that was clearly orchestrated and commanded by, *inter alia*, Kayishema. **[page 192]**

---

[264]   See Part II, Historical Context.
[265]   Trans., 3 Sept. 1998, p. 113.

504. All of the factual findings need not be recounted here. These examples are indicative of the pivotal role that Kayishema played in leading the execution of the massacres. It is clear that for all crime sites denoted in the Indictment, Kayishema had *de jure* authority over most of the assailants, and *de facto* control of them all. It has also been proved beyond reasonable doubt that the attacks that occurred were commenced upon his orders (Mubuga Church excepted). They were attacks clearly orchestrated by him, and only executed upon his direction.

505. Further, where the perpetrators of the massacres were found to be under the *de jure* or *de facto* control of Kayishema, and where the perpetrators committed the crimes pursuant to Kayishema's orders, the Trial Chamber is of the opinion that it is self-evident that the accused knew or had reason to know that the attacks were imminent and that he failed to take reasonable measures to prevent them. In such a case, the Trial Chamber need not examine further whether the accused failed to punish the perpetrators. Such an extended analysis would be superfluous.

506. The Trial Chamber finds, therefore, that Kayishema is individually criminally responsible, pursuant to Article 6(3) of the Statute, for the crimes committed by his *de jure* and *de facto* subordinates at the Home St. Jean and Catholic Church Complex, the Stadium and the Bisesero area.

507. It only remains for the Trial Chamber to consider whether Kayishema knew, or had reason to know, of those attacks at which he was not present. If he was so aware, or ought reasonably to have known of such impending attacks, then the Chamber must consider whether the accused attempted to prevent or punish the commission of those crimes.

Kayishema's Knowledge and Prevention of the Attack and Punishment of the Perpetrators

508. The Trial Chamber has not found that Kayishema, though present at Mubuga Church before and during the attacks there, specifically ordered the massacres. As such, **[page 193]** it is necessary to consider the remaining elements necessary to establish command responsibility under Article 6(3) of the Statute.

509. After examination of the facts presented, the Trial Chamber concludes that Kayishema knew or had reason to know that a large-scale massacre was imminent. The Trial Chamber is convinced of this fact for a number of reasons. First, the Tutsis were the subject of attacks throughout Rwanda by the date of the attack at Mubuga Church, and Kayishema was privy to this information. Second, following Kayishema's conversation with the Hutu priest, witnessed by a number of Tutsis at the Church, the priest refused the Tutsis access to water and informed them that they were about to die. Finally, the attackers included soldiers, gendarmes, and the members of the *Interahamwe*, all of whom he exercised either *de jure* or *de facto* control over.

510. In light of his duty to maintain public order, and seized of the fact that massacres were occurring elsewhere in Rwanda, the Trial Chamber is of the opinion that Kayishema was under a duty to ensure that these subordinates were not attacking those Tutsi seeking refuge in Mubuga Church. Moreover, his identification at the site both before and during the attacks leave the Trial Chamber in no doubt that Kayishema knew of the crimes that were being committed by his subordinates.

511. In order to establish responsibility of a superior under Article 6(3), it must also be shown that the accused was in a position to prevent or, alternatively, punish the subordinate perpetrators of those crimes. Clearly, the Trial Chamber cannot demand the impossible. Thus, any imposition of responsibility must be based upon a material ability of the accused to prevent or punish the crimes in question.

512. The accused, for instance, testified to the Trial Chamber that because the gendarmes had mutinied, he did not exercise the requisite control over their actions. However, not only did a number of the incursions upon Mubuga Church occur prior to the supposed mutiny (on the evening of 15 April), but the Trial Chamber has found this line of defence untenable in light of the overwhelming evidence presented by the **[page 194]** Prosecution that Kayishema was present at, instrumental in, and a participant of the

massacres delineated in the Indictment. Kayishema was in *de jure* and *de facto* control of the assailants and others, such as *Bourgmestre* Sikubwabo, identified as directing the attacks at Mubuga Church.

513. In light of this uncontestable control that Kayishema enjoyed, and his overarching duty as *Prefect* to maintain public order, the Trial Chamber, is of the opinion that a positive duty upon Kayishema existed to prevent the commission of the massacres. This point was enunciated succinctly by the United States Military Tribunal at Nuremberg in the *Hostage case* where it declared,

> [u]nder basic principles of command responsibility, an officer who merely stands by while his subordinates execute a criminal order of his superiors which he knows is criminal violates a moral obligation under international law. *By doing nothing he cannot wash his hands of international responsibility*"[266] [emphasis added]

No evidence was adduced that he attempted to prevent the atrocities that he knew were about to occur and which were within his power to prevent.

514. On the issue of Kayishema's failure to punish the perpetrators, the Defence submitted that the only power held by the *Prefect* in this respect was the ability to incarcerate for a period not exceeding 30 days. The Trial Chamber concurs with the Defence's submission that this would not be sufficient punishment for the perpetrators of the alleged crimes (though possibly sufficient as a short-term measure to help prevent further atrocities). However, the Trial Chamber is mindful that there is no evidence to suggest that in the 3 months between the start of these attacks and Kayishema's departure from Rwanda, no action was commenced which might ultimately have brought those responsible for these barbarous crimes to justice.

515. It is unnecessary to elaborate upon Kayishema's punishment of these perpetrators, or lack thereof, in any further detail. The task would be a superficial one in light of the **[page 195]** Trial Chamber's findings that Kayishema exercised clear, definitive control, both *de jure* and *de facto*, over the assailants at every massacre site set out in the Indictment. It has also been proved beyond a reasonable doubt that Kayishema ordered the attacks or, knowing of their imminence, failed to prevent them.

Conclusion

516. The inherent purpose of Article 6(3) is to ensure that a morally culpable individual is held responsible for those heinous acts committed under his command. Kayishema not only knew, and failed to prevent, those under his control from slaughtering thousands of innocent civilians; but he orchestrated and invariably led these bloody massacres. This Trial Chamber finds that in order to adequately reflect his culpability for these deaths, Kayishema he must be held responsible for the actions and atrocities committed. **[page 196]**

6.2   Genocide

517. Kayishema and Ruzindana both are charged with the crime of Genocide, under Article 2(3)(a) of the Statute. Kayishema is charged with Genocide under Counts 1, 7 and 13 for his responsibility for the crimes committed on 17 April 1994 at the Catholic Church and Home St. Jean (Complex), 18 April 1994 at Gatworo Stadium and 14 and 15 April 1994 at the Mubuga Church, respectively. Kayishema is also charged with Genocide under Count 19 for the crime of Genocide committed in the Bisesero area throughout April, May and June 1994. Kayishema is charged for his criminal responsibility under Articles 6(1) and 6(3) of the Statute.

518. Ruzindana is charged with Genocide under Count 19 for his role in the massacres that occurred in the Bisesero area. For his acts or omission Ruzindana is alleged to be criminally responsible under Article 6(1) of the Statute.

---

[266]   Cited, *Celebici* Judgement, para 338.

519. Genocide, in accordance with Article 2(2) of the Statute, means the commission of any of the acts enumerated in Article 2(2)(a) through to (e) of the Statute "with intent to destroy, in whole or in part, a national, ethnical, racial or religious group, as such." The components of the crime of genocide are discussed in the Chapter that examines the law relating to genocide.

520. In this Chapter, the Chamber first examines the accused persons' *mens rea* in order to determine whether they carried out acts with the specific intent to destroy the Tutsi group in whole or in part. In light of those findings, the Chamber examines the culpable genocidal acts for which the accused are responsible and determine their criminal responsibility under Articles 6(1) and 6(3) of the Statute.

6.2.1 The Components of Specific Intent [page 197]

521. In order to prove the commission of the crime of genocide the Prosecution must prove beyond a reasonable doubt, that the criminal acts were committed with the intent to destroy in whole or in part a national, ethnical, racial or religious group, as such.

The Targeted Group

522. The Prosecution submitted that the targeted group was the Tutsi population in Kibuye that was attacked on the grounds of ethnicity. The Chamber discusses the identity of the victims in detail within the Part on Factual Findings, addressing genocide in Kibuye generally and the massacres at the four crime sites in particular. The evidence proves, beyond a reasonable doubt, that the victims of the acts for which Kayishema and Ruzindana are charged were Tutsis.

523. The Chamber further accepts that the Tutsis were an ethnic group. In support of this contention the Prosecution provided evidence that since 1931, Rwandans were required to carry identification cards which indicated the ethnicity of the bearer as Hutu, Tutsi or Twa.[267] The government-issued identification cards specified the individual bearer's ethnicity. It should be noted that, in accordance with Rwandan custom, the ethnicity of a Rwandan child is derived from that of her or his father.

524. The Prosecution's expert witnesses, Professor Guichaoua and Mr. Nsanzuwera, also offered information on this issue. Through Mr. Nsanzuwera a copy of an identity card was tendered into evidence. He confirmed that all Rwandans were required to identify themselves by ethnicity on official documents. He added that identification based on ethnicity was a highly divisive issue in Rwanda. Therefore, the matter was addressed in the Arusha Peace Accords, which categorically resolved that there would be no mention of ethnicity on the identification cards of Rwandans from that period forth. Identification cards identifying the victims as Tutsis were found on those exhumed from mass graves in Kibuye. [page 198]

525. Additionally, the scores of survivors who testified before this Chamber stated that they were Tutsi and that those whom they saw massacred, during the time in question were also Tutsis.

526. In *Akayesu*, Trial Chamber I found that the Tutsis are an ethnic group, as such. Based on the evidence presented in the present case, this Trial Chamber concurs. The Trial Chamber finds beyond a reasonable doubt that the Tutsi victims of the massacres were an ethnical group as stipulated in Article 2(2) of the Statute, and were targeted as such.

Context of the Massacres

527. In the Law Part, the Trial Chamber acknowledges the difficulty in finding explicit manifestations of a perpetrator's intent. The Trial Chamber states that the specific intent can be inferred from words and

---

[267]   Prosecutor's Closing Brief, 9 October 1998, p. 28. See *supra* Part II, Historical Context.

deeds and may be demonstrated by a pattern of purposeful action. The evidence, in the present case, is considered in light of this reality.

Genocide ire Rwanda and Kibuye Generally

528. The Chamber examines the tragic events in Rwanda and in Kibuye in 1994 in Part V. The examination is useful here as it gives context to the crimes at the four crimes sites. The analysis shows that there indeed was a genocidal plan in place prior to the downing of the President's airplane in April 1994. This national plan to commit genocide was implemented at *prefecture* levels. For instance, Kayishema as the *Prefect*, disseminated information to the local officials above and below him using the established hierarchical lines of communications.[268]

529. The Prosecution submitted that the killings were planned and organised with a clear strategy, which was implemented by Kayishema and Ruzindana in Kibuye. The plan was executed efficiently and successfully in this *Prefecture*. Those who escaped the April massacres in and around Kibuye Town fled to Bisesero where they were relentlessly pursued and attacked. One witness described Bisesero Hill as strewn with **[page 199]** dead bodies "like small insects which had been killed off by insecticide."[269] There is documentary evidence that Kayishema requested reinforcement from the national authorities to attack the unarmed Tutsi population under the guise that there was a "security problem" in Bisesero.[270]

530. A letter dated 26 June 1994 written by the then *Bourgmestre* of Mabanza, Bagilishema to the *Prefect* of Kibuye, Kayishema, stated that there was no need for sending additional attackers to Mabanza because there were no Tutsis left in his commune.[271] The letter clearly indicates the knowledge and participation of the civilian authorities in the process of extermination.

Kayishema's Intent to Destroy in Whole or in Part the Tutsi Group, As Such

The Number of Victims

531. The number of Tutsis killed in the massacres, for which Kayishema is responsible, either individually or as a superior, provides evidence of Kayishema's intent. The Trial Chamber finds that enormous number of Tutsis were killed in each of the four crime sites. In the Complex, the number of Tutsis killed was estimated to be about 8,000; there were between 8,000 and 27,000 Tutsis massacred at the Stadium; and, at Mubuga Church between 4,000 and 5,500 Tutsi were massacred. The number killed in Bisesero is more difficult to estimate, however, evidence suggests that the number of those who perished was well into the tens of thousands.

532. Not only were Tutsis killed in tremendous numbers, but they were also killed regardless of gender or age. Men and women, old and young, were killed without mercy. Children were massacred before their parents' eyes, women raped in front of their families. No Tutsi was spared, neither the weak nor the pregnant. **[page 200]**

533. The number of the Tutsi victims is clear evidence of intent to destroy this ethnic group in whole or in part. The killers had the common intent to exterminate the ethnic group and Kayishema was instrumental in the realisation of that intent.

Methodology – Persistent Pattern of Conduct

534. The Trial Chamber finds compelling evidence that the attacks were carried out in a methodical manner. The Prosecution submitted that evidence of specific intent (*dolus specialis*) arises from the

---

[268]   See, for example, Pros exh's. 51 and 53.
[269]   See Chapter 5.4, *supra* (Bisesero Factual Findings.)
[270]   Pros. exh. 296.
[271]   Pros. exh. 59.

repetitive character of the planned and programmed massacres and the constant focus on the Tutsi members of the population. The perpetrators did not commit just one massacre but continually killed the Tutsi from April to June 1994.[272]

535. This consistent and methodical pattern of killing is further evidence of the specific intent. Kayishema was instrumental in executing this pattern of killing. Tutsi refugees gathered in places which had served historically as safe havens including the Complex, the Stadium and Mubuga Church. These places were surrounded by Hutu assailants, those inside the structure were not allowed to leave, and were denied food, medicine or sanitary facilities.[273] Eventually, the refugees were massacred. If there were too many Tutsis to kill in one day the killers would return to finish off their "work" the next morning. This Chamber finds that Kayishema instigated the attacks at the Complex and the Stadium.

536. In the area of Bisesero the attacks continued for several months; April, May and June of 1994. At Bisesero, evidence proves that Kayishema was leading and directing the attacks. The attackers were transported by government buses and other vehicles. This Chamber finds that Ruzindana brought the Hutu attackers in his personal vehicles and that Kayishema did the same in the trucks belonging to the *Prefecture*. The assailants included the local officials such as the *bourgmestres, counseillers*, communal police, the *gendarmerie nationale*, members of the *Interahamwe*, other soldiers as well as the accused themselves. **[page 201]**

537. The weapons used and the methods by which the Tutsis were killed are also consistent throughout the four crime sites. Generally, the witnesses testified that Kayishema and the gendarmes were armed with guns and grenades while other attackers used traditional farming instruments such as machetes and crude weapons such as bamboo spears. Grenades and guns were used at the crime sites where the Tutsis, were taking refuge in enclosed spaces to start the attack, and thereafter victims were hacked to death by machetes. Kayishema and Ruzindana both were seen carrying firearms at the crime sites.

Kayishema's Utterances

538. Kayishema's utterances, as well as utterances by other individuals under his direction before, during and after the massacres, also demonstrate the existence of his specific intent. Tutsis were called *Inkotanyi* meaning an RPF fighter or an enemy of Rwanda, *Inyenzi* meaning cockroach. They also were referred to as filth or dirt. Witness WW testified how she heard the Tutsi were being referred to as "dirt" when Kayishema told *Bourgmestre* Bagilishema that "all the dirt has to be removed,"[274] referring to the Tutsis who had sought shelter in the communal office. During the attacks at the Stadium, Kayishema called the Tutsi: "Tutsi dogs" and "Tutsi sons of bitches," when instigating the attackers to kill the Tutsi gathered there.

539. The Chamber also finds that Kayishema used a megaphone to relay a message from Kigali encouraging the extermination of the Tutsis during the attack at the Complex. Several witnesses who survived the massacres at the Complex heard Kayishema say "go to work" or "get down to work"[275] which, as many witnesses affirmed, meant to begin killing the Tutsis. Other witnesses testified to having heard the attackers, including members of the *Interahamwe*, who were *de facto* under Kayishema's control, sing songs about exterminating the Tutsi.[276] The Trial Chamber **[page 202]** accepts Prosecution exhibit 297, tendered through Witness HH, which was a transcription of the lyrics of one of these extermination songs. Essentially, the song urges attackers not to spare the elderly and even the babies because Kagame (the then RPF leader) left Rwanda as a child.[277] Again, the Chamber notes the common intention of the attackers with that of Kayishema.

---

272   Trans., 21 Oct. 1993, pp. 125 and 141.
273   See *supra* Chapter 5.3 (discussing safe places).
274   Trans., 19 Feb. 1998, p.34 and Chapter on Genocide in Kibuye
275   See *supra* (discussing Factual Findings).
276   See testimony of witnesses F, W, B, PP, NN.
277   See Chapter 5.4 , *supra* (Bisesero Factual Findings.).

540. In sum for all the reasons stated above the Chamber finds beyond a reasonable doubt that Kayishema had the intent to destroy the Tutsi group in whole or in part and, in pursuit of that intent, carried out the acts detailed below.

Ruzindana's Intent to Destroy in Whole or in Part the Tutsi Population, As Such

541. Ruzindana displayed his intent to rid the area of Tutsis by his words and deeds and through his persistent pattern of conduct throughout the Bisesero area.

Ruzindana's Utterances

542. Witnesses heard Ruzindana giving orders to the Hutu attackers in the Bisesero area. Specifically, some testified about Ruzindana's statements about not sparing babies whose mothers had been killed because those attacking the country initially left as children.[278] The Trial Chamber also heard evidence of Ruzindana's anti-Tutsi utterances to the assailants, saying that the Tutsi refugees were "the enemy."

Methodology – Persistent Pattern of Conduct

543. Ruzindana played a leadership role in the systematic patter of extermination of the Tutsis who had sought refuge in the area of Bisesero. Evidence proves that many of the Tutsis who had survived the massacres in and around Kibuye Town during April fled to Bisesero. Ruzindana was instrumental in the pursuit of these Tutsi persons, by transporting, encouraging, and leading the attacks. **[page 203]**

544. The Trial Chamber finds that at many of the crime sites within Bisesero, Ruzindana did bring Hutu assailants to the sites in his vehicles. Once at the site, Ruzindana directed attackers to kill and offered payment in exchange for the severed heads of well known Tutsis or identification cards of murdered Tutsis. Ruzindana was seen carrying firearms at many of the massacre sites. The Chamber accepted evidence from witnesses who testified about overhearing conversations between the Hutu assailants who referred to Ruzindana as their patron. Yet other witnesses affirmed that gendarmes, speaking among themselves, stated that they were not concerned about using too many bullets, because Ruzindana would purchase more for them. As a result of Ruzindana's consistent pattern of conduct, thousands of Tutsis were killed or seriously injured; men, women and children alike.

545. The Trial Chamber is satisfied, from all the evidence accepted, that the perpetrators of the culpable acts that occurred within Kibuye *Prefecture*, during the period in questions, were acting with a common intent and purpose. That intent was to destroy the Tutsi ethnic group within Kibuye. Both Kayishema and Ruzindana played pivotal roles in carrying out this common plan.

6.2.2 The Genocidal Acts of Kayishema and Ruzindana

546. The Prosecution alleges that the accused persons committed acts pursuant to Article 2(2). Although Article 2(2) includes a variety of acts, the Prosecution, during closing arguments, only addressed the Trial Chamber on killings (Article 2(2)(a)), causing serious bodily or mental harm (Article 2(2)(b)) to Tutsis, and deliberately inflicting on Tutsis conditions of life calculated to bring about their physical destruction (Article 2(2)(c)) in whole or in part.

547. As a preliminary matter, the Chamber finds that in implementing the policy of genocide, the intent of Kayishema, those under his control and Ruzindana, was to kill members of the Tutsi group at the four crime sites. Inherent in the act of mass killing is the infliction of serious bodily and mental harm. For example, the Trial Chamber was **[page 204]** presented with the opportunity to view numerous healing bullet and machete wounds. Furthermore, the Chamber heard the testimony of many witnesses who

---

[278] Trans., 14 Oct. 1997, p. 17.

recounted having watched their loved ones mutilated, raped or killed in a heinous manner. The evidence established that the genocidal act of the accused persons was killing. The Trial Chamber holds Kayishema and Ruzindana responsible for the results of the killings and serious bodily and mental harm to the Tutsi population in Kibuye.

548. No evidence was, proffered to show that the accused persons, or Kayishema's *de facto* and *de jure* subordinates, deliberately, inflicted, on the Tutsi group in Kibuye, conditions of life to bring about their physical destruction in whole or in part. The Chamber acknowledges the Prosecution argument that Tutsis seeking refuge at the four crime sites were deprived of food, water and adequate sanitary and medical facilities. These deprivations, however, were a result of the persecution of the Tutsis, with the intent to exterminate them within a short period of time thereafter. These deprivations were *not* the deliberate creation of conditions of life – as defined in Chapter 4.1 of this Judgement – intended to bring about their destruction. Additionally, the Chamber finds that the time periods during which these deprivation occurred were not of sufficient length or scale to bring about the destruction of the group. Therefore, the Trial Chamber only examines killings.

549. As stated above, the Chamber has found that Kayishema's and Ruzindana's culpable conduct was committed with the intent to destroy the Tutsi group in whole or in part. In relation to Kayishema this intent applies to all four massacre sites. For Ruzindana this intent relates, to Bisesero only.

550. Below, the Chamber addresses the evidence in relation to, Kayishema's and Ruzindana's genocidal acts. **[page 205]**

COUNT 1:

Charges Kayishema with Genocide in Violation of Article 2(3)(a) of the Statute for the Massacres at the Complex

551. With respect to the Complex, the Trial Chamber finds, *inter alia*, that by about 17 April 1994 thousands of Tutsis had gathered. Persons under Kayishema's control including gendarmes and members of the *Interahamwe* surrounded the Complex. There were also boats surrounding the peninsula on which the Complex was located. The attackers who had surrounded the Complex carried machetes, spears and other traditional weapons and prevented people from leaving. The Trial Chamber is satisfied that those attempting to flee were killed.

552. Kayishema led the attackers from the *Prefecture* office to the Complex. He then ordered them to begin the attack on the Tutsi by relaying a message from Kigali, through a megaphone, to, kill the Tutsis. Thus, Kayishema orchestrated and participated in the attack that lasted hours. As a result of the attack, thousands of Tutsis were killed.

553. The Trial Chamber finds that prior to the attack, Kayishema knew that it was imminent. Indeed, along with initiating the attack, he was seen at the Complex twice before the attacks of 17 April.

Kayishema's Criminal Responsibility

554. For the reasons stated above, pursuant to Article 6(1) of the Statute, Kayishema is individually responsible for instigating, ordering, committing or otherwise aiding and abetting in the planning, preparation and execution of genocide by the killing and causing of serious bodily harm to the Tutsis at the Complex on 17 April 1994.

555. Additionally, under Article 6(3) of the Statute, Kayishema is responsible, for genocide, as superior, for the mass killing and injuring of the Tutsi at the Complex on 17 April 1994, undertaken by his subordinates. The assailants at the Complex including gendarmes, members of the *Interahamwe*, local officials, including prison wardens, **[page 206]** *conseillers* and *bourgmestres*. The Trial Chamber finds that Kayishema had *de jure* control over most of the assailants and *de facto* control over all the attackers. The evidence proves that Kayishema was leading and directing the massacre. As stated in the Legal

Findings on Criminal Responsibility, because Kayishema himself participated in the massacres, it is self-evident that he knew that his subordinates were about to attack and failed to take reasonable and necessary measures to prevent them, when he had the material ability to do so.

COUNT 7:

Charges Kayishema with Genocide in Violation of Article 2(3)(a) of the Statute for the Massacres at the Stadium in Kibuye Town

556.   The Trial Chamber finds that by 18 April 1994, thousands of men, women and children, unarmed Tutsis, sought refuge in the Stadium located in Kibuye Town. Once the refugees had gathered, persons under Kayishema's control, including *gendarmes*, prevented refugees from leaving the Stadium and surrounded the Stadium. The Trial Chamber is satisfied that during the attacks, some of the Tutsi who attempted to flee were killed. Kayishema instigated the attacks by ordering the attackers to "shoot those Tutsi dogs" and by firing the first shot into the Stadium. As a result of the attack, thousands of people were killed and numerous sustained serious physical injuries.

557.   The Chamber finds beyond a reasonable doubt, that at the time when the Tutsi were prevented from leaving the Stadium, Kayishema knew or had reason to know that an attack was about to occur.

Kayishema 's Criminal Responsibility

558.   For the reasons stated above, Kayishema is individually criminally responsible under Article 6(1) of the Statute for instigating, ordering, committing or otherwise aiding and abetting in the planning, preparation and execution of genocide by killing and injuring Tutsis in the Stadium. **[page 207]**

559.   Under Article 6(3) of the Statute, Kayishema is responsible for genocide as a superior for the acts committed by his subordinates during the massacres at the Stadium on 18 April 1994. The assailants at the Stadium included gendarmes, soldiers, members of the *Interahamwe*, prison wardens and armed civilians. The Trial Chamber finds that Kayishema had *de jure* control over most of the assailants and *de facto* control over them all. The evidence proves that Kayishema ordered, led and directed the massacre. Accordingly, it is self-evident that he knew that his subordinates were about to commit the massacres and failed to take reasonable and necessary measures to prevent them, when he had the material ability to do so.

COUNT 13:

Charges Kayisherna with Genocide in Violation of Article 2(3)(a) of the Statute for the Massacres at the Church at Mubuga

560.   The Trial Chamber finds that, *inter alia*, thousands of Tutsis had gathered at Mubuga Church seeking refuge from attacks which were occurring throughout Kibuye *Prefecture*. Only a few of those seeking refuge survived the massacres that occurred on 15 and 16 April. Kayishema and his subordinates, including local officials, gendarmes, communal police and members of the *Interahamwe* were present and participated in the attacks. The Trial Chamber finds that those who initially attempted to leave the Church in search of food or water were forced to retreat or beaten to death by armed assailants outside the Church. Kayishema's presence prior and during the major attack and the participation of those under his control encouraged the killings of the Tutsi refugees assembled there. As a result of the attack, thousands of people were killed and numerous sustained serious physical injuries.

561.   The Chamber finds, beyond a reasonable doubt, that at the time when the Tutsis were prevented from leaving the Mubuga Church, Kayishema knew or had reason to know that an attack was about to occur. **[page 208]**

Kayishema's Criminal Responsibility

562. Under Article 6(1) of the Statute, Kayishema is individually responsible for genocide for the killing and serious injuring of Tutsis at the Mubuga Church on 15 and 16 April 1994. Kayishema visited the Church before the attacks and transported gendarmes. The Hutu Priest of this parish, who had been co-operating with Kayishema, specifically told the refugees that they were about to die, and asked that a headcount be done for the *Prefect*. The gendarmes eventually attacked the refugees. Kayishema also was present during the attacks. These findings prove beyond a reasonable doubt that Kayishema aided and abetted the preparation and execution of the massacre.

563. Additionally, under Article 6(3) of the Statute, Kayishema is responsible for genocide as a superior for the acts of his subordinates that took place at the Mubuga Church on 15 and 16 April 1994. The assailants at Mubuga included the *Bourgmestre* and the *conseillers* of the Commune, gendarmes, soldiers, members of the *Interahamwe*, communal police, other local officials and armed civilians. The Trial Chamber has found that Kayishema had *de jure* control over most of the assailants and *de facto* control over them all. It is clear that Kayishema knew that an attack was imminent by virtue of his presence before and during the massacre. Accordingly, the Trial Chamber finds, beyond a reasonable doubt, that Kayishema knew that his subordinates were about to attack the refugees in the Church and failed to take reasonable and necessary measures to prevent them, when he had the material ability to do so.

COUNT 19:

Charges Kayishema and Ruzindana with Genocide in Violation of Article 2(3)(a) of the Statute for the Massacres at the Area of Bisesero

564. The Trial Chamber finds that both Kayishema and Ruzindana brought the *gendarmerie nationale*, communal police, members of the *Interahamwe* and armed civilians to the area of Bisesero and directed them to attack the Tutsis. Both accused persons also personally participated in the attacks. Furthermore, the Trial Chamber found that Ruzindana mutilated and personally killed a sixteen-year-old girl named Beatrice at the Mine at Nyiramurego Hill. Accordingly, Kayishema and Ruzindana **[page 209]** were responsible for the killings at a number of massacre sites during April, May and June 1994. Hutu assailants during these attacks killed and injured thousands of Tutsis.

565. In relation to the 13 and 14 May assault at Muyira Hill, Kayishema and Ruzindana arrived at the head of the convoy of vehicles which transported soldiers, members of the *Interahamwe*, communal police and armed civilians. Some of the vehicles, in which the assailants arrived, belonged to the Rwandan Government. Kayishema signalled the start of the attacks by firing a shot into the air, directed the assaults by dividing the assailants into groups, and headed one group of them as it advanced up the Hill and verbally encouraged the attackers through a megaphone. Ruzindana also played a leadership role, distributing traditional weapons, leading a group of attackers up the Hill and shooting at the refugees.

566. The Trial Chamber finds that both accused persons also participated in other massacres. At the cave, Kayishema was directing the siege generally and Ruzindana was commanding the attackers from Ruhengeri; both were giving instructions to the attackers and orchestrating the attack. At Karonge Hill, Kayishema arrived with soldiers, gendarmes and Hutu civilians and used a megaphone to address the attackers, giving them instructions. Ruzindana was seen transporting members of the *Interahamwe* to the Mine at Nyiramurego Hill and then directing the attackers. At Bisesero Hill, Ruzindana was seen transporting attackers and giving orders to the assailants to surround the Hill and begin the assault. Ruzindana orchestrated the massacre at the Hole near Muyira Hill, and the assault commenced upon his instruction.

Kayishenia's Criminal Responsibility

567. In light of the factual findings outlined above, the Trial Chamber finds that the killings that took place in Bisesero during April, May and June 1994 were carried out with the intent to destroy the Tutsi group in whole or in part. Further, the Trial Chamber finds, beyond a reasonable doubt, that Kayishema caused the death of and serious bodily harm to Tutsis at numerous places in the Bisesero area including, Karonge Hill at the end **[page 210]** of April, Bisesero Hill on 11 May, Muyira Hill on 13 and 14 May, the Cave in Gishyita Commune, Gitwa Cellule in May and Kucyapa in June.

568. Under Article 6(1) of the Statute, Kayishema is individually responsible for genocide for killing and injuring the Tutsi at the attacks in the Bisesero area during April, May and June 1994 with the intent to destroy the Tutsi ethnic group. Kayishema's involvement varied from crime site to crime site within Bisesero. At the crime sites where he was found to have participated, Kayishema committed one or more of the following acts: headed the convoy of assailants; transported attackers in his vehicle; directed the initial positioning of the attackers; verbally encouraged them; initiated the attacks by orders or gunshots; lead the groups of attackers; shot at fleeing Tutsis; and, finally, thanked the Hutu attackers for their "work." These facts prove, beyond a reasonable doubt, that Kayishema, instigated, ordered, committed and otherwise aided and abetted in the preparation and execution of the massacre that resulted in thousands of deaths and serious bodily injuries with intent to destroy the Tutsi ethnic group.

569. Additionally, under Article 6(3) of the Statute; Kayishema is responsible for genocide, as superior, due to the killing and injuring that took place in Bisesero area in during April, May and June 1994 by his subordinates. The assailants in Bisesero were identified as gendarmes, soldiers, members of the *Interahamwe*, and armed civilians. The Trial Chamber finds that Kayishema had *de jure* control over most of the assailants and *de facto* control over them all. The evidence proves that Kayishema was leading and directing the massacres at numerous sites throughout the period.

Ruzindana's Criminal Responsibility

570. In light of the factual findings outlined above; the Trial Chamber finds that the killings that took which took place in Bisesero, during April, May and June 1994, were carried out with intent to destroy the Tutsi group in whole or in part. Further, the Trial Chamber finds beyond reasonable doubt that Ruzindana caused the death of Tutsis at numerous places in the Bisesero area including, the Mine at Nyiramurego Hill on 15 April, Gitwa Cellule in early May, Bisesero Hill on 11 May, Muyira Hill on 13 and 14 **[page 211]** May, the Cave, Kucyapa in June, the Hole near Muyira in early June. Ruzindana caused these deaths by premeditated acts or omissions, intending to do so.

571. In particular under Article 6(1) of the Statute, Ruzindana is individually responsible for the killings that took place within the attacks that the Trial Chamber has found he participated, in the Bisesero area during April, May and June 1994. Ruzindana's involvement varied from site to site and day to day. At the sites where he was found to have participated, Ruzindana committed one or more of the following acts: Headed the convoy of assailants; transported attackers in his vehicle; distributed weapons; orchestrated the assaults; lead the groups of attackers; shot at the Tutsi refugees; and, offered to reward the attackers with cash or beer. The Trial Chamber further found that Ruzindana personally mutilated and murdered individuals during the attack at the Mine at Nyiramuregra Hill. These findings prove beyond reasonable doubt that Ruzindana, instigated, ordered, committed and otherwise aided and abetted in the preparation and execution of the massacre that resulted in thousands of murders with the intent to destroy the Tutsi ethnic group. **[page 212]**

6.3 Crimes against Humanity

572. Counts 2, 8, 14, of the Indictment charge Kayishema with crimes against humanity for murder and Counts 3, 9, 15, charge him with crimes against humanity for extermination. Kayishema is charged also in Counts 4, 10, 16 with crimes against humanity other inhumane acts.

573. Count 20 charges both Kayishema and Ruzindana with crimes against humanity for murder, Count 21 charges them with crimes against humanity for extermination and Count 22 charges both accused with crimes against humanity for other inhumane acts.

574. Pursuant to Article 3 of the Statute, the Trial Chamber shall have the power to prosecute persons for a certain number of crimes committed as part of a widespread or systematic attack against any civilian population on national, political, ethnic; racial or religious grounds. The offences which constitute crimes against humanity when committed in such a context include, *inter alia*, murder, extermination, deportation, torture, rape, and other inhumane acts.

575. Under this Article the Prosecution charged the accused only for three crimes: murder, extermination and other inhumane acts committed as part of a widespread or systematic attack against the civilian population on discriminatory grounds.

Murder and Extermination

576. As far as murder and extermination are concerned indeed they took place in Kibuye *Prefecture* within the context of a widespread and systematic attack. The evidence produced proves that the attacks were aimed at the Tutsi civilian population as an ethnic group. Evidence also shows that the Tutsi victims were generally peasant farmers, refugees or persons of similar status, including the elderly, women and children. In light of the overwhelming testimony the Chamber finds, beyond a reasonable doubt, that the massacres were based on the grounds of ethnicity. **[page 213]**

577. Thus, all necessary elements exist for the conclusion that the accused could be convicted for crimes against humanity (murder) and crimes against humanity (extermination). However, in this particular case the crimes against humanity in question are completely absorbed by the crime of genocide. All counts for these crimes are based on the same facts and the same criminal conduct. These crimes were committed at the same massacre sites, against the same people, belonging to the Tutsi ethnic group with the same intent to destroy this group in whole or in part.

578. Considering the above and based on the facts the Trial Chamber finds that it will be improper to convict the accused persons for genocide as well as for crimes against humanity based on murder and extermination because the later two offences are subsumed fully by the counts of genocide as discussed in the Part of the Judgement entitled Cumulative Charges.

579. The responsibility of the accused persons for their criminal conduct is thus fully covered under those counts of genocide.

Other Inhumane Acts

580. As far as counts for other inhumane acts are concerned the accused could be found guilty of crimes against humanity based on other inhumane acts.

581. The crimes must be committed as part of a widespread or systematic attack against any civilian population on national, political, ethnic, racial or religious grounds. The accused must be aware that their crimes were committed in the context of such an attack. Furthermore, the policy element demands a showing that the crimes were instigated by a government or by an organisation or group. A detailed consideration of the elements of crimes against humanity can be found in the Part of the Judgement that addresses the Law.[279] **[page 214]**

582. As stated above, the Trial Chamber finds, beyond a reasonable doubt, the necessary elements of the attack exist to satisfy the crimes against humanity. The acts for which both accused are charged took place within the context of a widespread and systematic attack. Although only one of the alternative conditions must be proved by the Prosecution, the Trial Chamber finds that both conditions are satisfied.

---

[279]   *See* Crimes Against Humanity, Chapter 4.2.

Evidence before this Trial Chamber proves that the attacks in Rwanda generally, and in Kibuye *Prefecture* in particular, were carried out in a systematic manner, that, is, pursuant to a pre-arranged policy or plan.[280] The evidence of a policy or plan discussed in relation to the counts of genocide is applicable here. The evidence proves that the attacks in Rwanda generally, and in Kibuye *Prefecture* in particular, were aimed at the civilian population. Indeed, evidence shows that the victims in Kibuye were generally peasant farmers, those seeking refuge or persons of similar status, including the elderly, women and children. An abundance of evidence from witnesses, experts and Kayishema himself proves that the attacks in Kibuye *Prefecture* were carried out against Tutsis based on their ethnicity; again this issue is discussed in more detail in relation to the counts of genocide. Lastly, the Trial Chamber finds that the attack must have been part of a broader policy or plan that had been instigated or directed by any organisation or group and that the accused persons had knowledge that their conduct formed part of that attack.

583. For the accused to be found guilty of crimes against humanity for other inhumane acts they must, *inter alia*, commit an act of similar gravity and seriousness to the other enumerated crimes, with the intention to cause the other inhumane act. This important category of crimes is reserved for deliberate forms of infliction with (comparably serious) inhumane results that were intended or foreseeable and done with reckless disregard. Thus, the category of other inhumane acts demands a crime distinct from the other crimes against humanity, with its own culpable conduct and *mens rea*. The crime of other inhumane acts is not a lesser-included offence of the other enumerated crimes. In the opinion of the Trial Chamber, this category should not simply be utilised by the Prosecution as an all-encompassing, "catch all" category. **[page 215]**

584. In relation to all four sites the Indictment did not particularise the nature of the acts that the Prosecution relied upon for the charge of "other inhumane acts." Nor did the Indictment specify the nature and extent of the accused's responsibility for the other inhumane acts. This is true for both Kayishema and Ruzindana. In relation to the culpable acts, for each site the Indictment states little more than: The attackers used (specified) weapons to kill people at the site, the accused participated, and the attack resulted in thousands of deaths and numerous injuries. Not one act, allegedly perpetrated either by Ruzindana, Kayishema, or the other assailants, was specified as an "other inhumane act". Therefore, it was incumbent upon the Prosecution to rectify the vagueness of the counts during its presentation of evidence. Indeed, "the question of knowing whether the allegations appearing in the Indictment are vague will, in the final analysis, be settled at Trial."[281]

585. At trial, the Prosecution proffered evidence that the Hutu assailants, under Kayishema's and/or Ruzindana's control and direction, deliberately attempted to kill the Tutsi civilians at the sites for which they are respectively charged. As a result of the intent to massacre, most of the Tutsi were killed whilst others sustained injuries. The Prosecution presented its case on this basis. As such it was not difficult to identify the conduct and evidence that supported the charges of crimes against humanity for extermination and murder. However, the conduct to support the crimes of other inhumane acts was not so easily identified.

586. The Chamber heard horrific testimony of mutilation and other conduct by the Hutu assailants that could potentially amount to other inhumane acts. However, throughout trial the Prosecution failed to adequately particularise which pieces of evidence supported the other inhumane act charges. The most specific identification came in response to Defence objections. On a couple of occasions the Defence objected to the evidence of certain injuries proffered by the Prosecution, submitting that it was outside the nature and parameters of the charges. In response, the Prosecution identified the injuries as evidence of other inhumane acts. This method of using the crime as a "catch-all" - specifying **[page 216]** which acts support the count almost as a postscript – does not enable the counts of other inhumane acts to transcend from vagueness to reasonable precision. Further, the fact that some of the survivors displayed their injuries to the Trial Chamber did not mitigate the Prosecution's obligation to distinguish the specific

---

[280] *Ibid.*
[281] *The Prosecutor v. Tihomir Blaskic*, IT-95-14-PT, Decision on the Defence Motion Based Upon Defects.

ith the resultant injuries, as those that support the other inhumane act charges. Only in its :f did the Prosecution submit that the injuries sustained by the survivors amounted to other ιcts and, that the environment of fear and desperation where victims were forced to witness ; and severe injuring of friends, family, and other Tutsi inherently caused serious mental haɪι. Accordingly, the Defence teams were not properly seized of the acts that allegedly constituted the other inhumane acts charges until the end of the trial.

587. In interests of justice and a fair trial the Defence should be seized as promptly as possible, and at any event during the trial, of the conduct which allegedly offends each individual count of crimes against humanity for other inhumane acts. The Indictment did not identify the offending conduct or the nature and extent of the accused's responsibility. During trial, the Prosecution failed to rectify this imprecision. Accordingly, the fundamental rights of both the accused, namely to be informed of the charges against him and to be in a position to prepare his defence in due time with complete knowledge of the matter, has been disregarded in relation to all the counts of crimes against humanity for other inhumane acts. A right that is particularly important considering the gravity of the charges.

588. For all the above reasons, the Trial Chamber finds that the Prosecution has not proved its case against Kayishema pursuant to Counts 4, 10, 16, and 22 crimes against humanity for other inhumane acts.

589. For all the above reasons, the Trial Chamber finds that the Prosecution has not proved its case against Ruzindana pursuant to Count, 22, crimes against humanity for other inhumane acts. **[page 217]**

6.4   Common article 3 and Additional Protocol II

Counts 5, 11, 17, 23 – Violations of Common Article 3 (a violation of Article 4(a) of the ICTR Statute) and Counts 6, 12, 18, 24 – Violations of Protocol II (a violation of Article 4(a) of the ICTR Statute).

590. Counts 5, 11 and 17 of the Indictment charge Kayishema with violations of Common Article 3 and Counts 6, 12 and 18 charge Kayishema with violations of Protocol II.

591. Count 23 charges both Kayishema and Ruzindana with violations of Common Article 3 and count 24 charges them with violations of Protocol II. All these counts are covered by Article 4 of the ICTR Statute.

592. During the trial, evidence was produced that between about 10 April and 30 June 1994 thousands of men, women and children were killed and numerous persons injured as a result of massacres at the Catholic Church and Home St. Jean Complex, at the Stadium in Kibuye Town, at the Church in Mubuga and in the area of Bisesero in the *Prefecture* of Kibuye, Republic of Rwanda.

593. These men, women and children were unarmed and were predominantly Tutsis seeking protection from attacks that had occurred throughout various regions in Rwanda and Kibuye *Prefecture*. The Prosecution considers the massacred people as victims of the armed conflict and charges Kayishema and Ruzindana with serious violations of Common Article 3 and Protocol II.

594. From the point of view of the Prosecutor, under international law, in order to hold an individual liable for violations of Common Article 3 and/or Protocol II, the following five requirements must be met:

First, the alleged crime(s) must have been committed in the context of a non-international armed conflict. **[page 218]**

Second, temporal requirements for the applicability of the respective regime must be met.

Third, territorial requirements for the applicability of the respective regime must be met.

---

[282]   See, for example, Prosecutor's Closing Brief at p. 80.

Fourth, the individual(s) charged must be connected to a Party that was bound by the respective regime; and

Fifth, the victims(s) of the alleged crimes(s) must have been individual(s) that was (were) protected under the respective regime.[283]

595. The first requirement should be considered as a corner stone to clarify the situation in order to establish whether the alleged crimes referred to in the Indictment could be qualified as violations of Common Article 3 and Protocol II.

596. In order to hold Kayishema and Ruzindana criminally responsible for the above mentioned counts, from the point of view of the Prosecution, it must be proved that Common Article 3, as well as Protocol II applied to the situation in Rwanda in 1994.[284]

597. The Trial Chamber finds that this is not a question that need be addressed. It has been established, beyond a reasonable doubt, that there was an armed conflict, not of an international character, in Rwanda. This armed conflict took place between the governmental armed forces, the, FAR, and the dissident armed forces, the RPF, in the time of the events alleged in the Indictment, that is from April to July 1994. It has also been shown, beyond a reasonable doubt, that Rwanda was bound by Common Article 3 and Protocol II, which were applicable to "the situation in Rwanda in 1994." The Parties in this non-international conflict confirmed their readiness to comply with the rules of these international humanitarian instruments. As far as the second, temporal requirements, and the third, territorial requirements, are concerned, it should be added that these international instruments, as it was shown above, were applicable in the entire territory of Rwanda with the understanding that the alleged crimes should be considered **[page 219]** in the context of the armed conflict and interpreted in a broad territorial and temporal framework.

598. Therefore, the question which should be addressed is not whether Common Article 3 and Protocol II were applicable to "the situation in Rwanda in 1994," but whether these instruments were applicable to the alleged crimes at the four sites referred to in the Indictment. It is incumbent on the Prosecutor to prove the applicability of these international instruments to the above-mentioned crimes.

599. However, the Prosecution limited itself to state, "in order to hold Clement Kayishema and Obed Ruzindana criminally responsible for the above mentioned counts, the Prosecutor must prove that the alleged crimes must have been committed *in the context* of a non-international armed conflict."[285] [emphasis added]

600. The Prosecutor did not specify the meaning of the words "in the context." If she meant "during" an internal armed conflict, there is nothing to prove as it was recognised, and this matter was not in dispute, that in this period of time Rwanda was in a state of armed conflict not of international character. Therefore, in this case the words "in the context" are too general in character and do not clarify the situation in a proper way. When the country is in a state of armed conflict, crimes committed in this period of time could be considered as having been committed in the context of this conflict. However, it does not mean that all such crimes have a direct link with the armed conflict and all the victims of these crimes are victims of the armed conflict.

601. There is recognition, nevertheless, in the Prosecutor's Closing Brief that "the Prosecutor must also establish a nexus between the armed conflict and the alleged offence."[286] The following paragraph of this document was intended to prove such a nexus, **[page 220]**

In the present case, the Prosecutor submits that the evidence shows, beyond a reasonable doubt, that for each of the alleged violations there was a nexus between the crimes and the armed conflict

---

[283] Closing Brief of the Prosecutor, p. 45, para. 149-154 (Closing Brief).
[284] *Ibid*, p. 81, para. 306; p. 82, para. 312-33; p. 93, para. 370; p. 94, para. 377; p. 106, para. 436; p. 107, para. 142; p. 135, para. 559 and 565; p. 150, para. 75 and 82.
[285] *Ibid*, p. 81. para. 306; p. 93 para. 370; p. 106, para. 436; p. 135, para. 559; p. 150 para. 75.
[286] *Ibid*, p. 48, para. 163.

that was underway in Rwanda. The Tutsis who were massacred in Kibuye went to the four sites seeking refuge from attacks that were occurring on the Tutsis throughout Kibuye and Rwanda. These attacks were occurring because hostilities had broken out between the RPF and the FAR and the Tutsis were being sought out on the pretext that they were accomplices of the RPF, were "the enemy" and/or were responsible for the death of the President.[287]

602. It is true that "the Tutsis went to the four sites seeking refuge from attacks that were occurring on the Tutsis throughout Kibuye and Rwanda." However, the Tutsi were attacked by neither the RPF nor the FAR in the places where they sought refuge in Kibuye. It was proved through witness testimony that these attacks were undertaken by the civilian authorities as a result of a campaign to exterminate the Tutsi population in the country. Therefore, there is no ground to assert that there was a nexus between the committed crimes and the armed conflict, because "the Tutsis went to the four sites seeking refuge from attacks. . ." The Prosecutor's next allegation is that "these attacks were occurring because hostilities had broken out between the RPF and the FAR and the Tutsis were being sought out on the pretext that they were accomplices of the RPF, were "the enemy" and/or were responsible for the death of the President."

603. It is true that "hostilities had broken out between the RPF and the FAR" in this period of time. However, evidence was not produced that the military operations occurred in Kibuye *Prefecture* when the alleged crimes were committed. Furthermore, it was not shown that there was a direct link between crimes committed against these victims and the hostilities mentioned by the Prosecutor. It was also not proved that the victims were accomplices of the RPF and/or were responsible for the death of the President. The Prosecutor herself recognised that the Tutsis were being sought out *on the pretext* that they were accomplices etc. These allegations show only that the armed conflict had been used as pretext to unleash an official policy of genocide. Therefore, such allegations cannot be considered as evidence of a direct link between the alleged crimes and the armed conflict. **[page 221]**

604. The term "nexus" should not be understood as something vague and indefinite. A direct connection between the alleged crimes, referred to in the Indictment, and the armed conflict should be established factually. The Prosecutor must show that material provisions of Common Article 3 and Protocol II were violated and she has to produce the necessary evidence of these violations.

In this respect, the Prosecutor stated the following:

> A final requirement for the applicability of Common Article 3 and Additional Protocol II is that the victim be an individual that was protected by Common Article 3 and/or Additional Protocol II.

> Common Article 3 applies to persons taking no active part in the hostilities including members of the armed forces who have laid down their arms and those who are *hors de combat*.

> Additional Protocol II applies to all persons which do not take a direct part or who have ceased to take part in the hostilities (Article 4), persons whose liberty has been restricted (Article 5), the wounded, sick, and shipwrecked (Article 7), medical and religious personnel (Article 9) and the civilian population (Article 13).[288]

605. The Prosecutor did not specify whether she finds that all or only some of the enumerated Articles of Protocol II have been violated. In any case, Article 5 of Protocol II is not applicable to the alleged crimes because there is no evidence that the victims of these crimes were interned or detained persons, deprived of their liberty for reasons related to the armed conflict. It is sufficient to read all four paragraphs of this Article to realise its non-applicability to the crimes in question.

606. Again, no evidence was produced that Article 7 of Protocol II, which aims to protect the wounded, sick and shipwrecked persons, is applicable to the alleged crimes. It was not shown that the victims of the alleged crimes fall into this category. **[page 222]**

---

[287]   *Ibid*, p. 48, para. 165.
[288]   Closing Brief, p. 55, Paras. 188-190.

607. The Prosecutor raised also the question of applicability of Article 9 of Protocol II which deals with the protection of religious and medical personnel. In the instant case, pursuant to the evidence, the victims were not religious and medical personnel. Therefore, Article 9 cannot be applicable to the alleged crimes.

608. Article 13 of Protocol II is more pertinent to the case before the Trial Chamber, since it is devoted to the protection of the civilian population during armed conflicts. This Article, entitled "Protection of the Civilian Population" stipulates,

> 1. The civilian population and individual civilians shall enjoy general protection against the dangers arising from military operations. To give effect to this protection, the following rules shall be observed in all circumstances.

> 2. The civilian population as such, as well as individual civilians, shall not be the object of attack. Acts or threats of violence the primary purpose of which is to spread terror among the civilian population are prohibited.

609. From these two paragraphs of Article 13 it could be understood that military operations in all circumstances should be conducted in such a way not to create dangers for the civilian population, as well as individual civilians, and in any case this category of persons shall not be the object of attacks during military operations.

610. The Prosecutor emphasised that the attacks against the Tutsis at the four sites, referred to in the Indictment, "were occurring because hostilities had broken out between the RPF and the FAR."[289] It is true that such hostilities had broken out in different parts of the country. In accordance with Article 13, as well as Articles 14 to 18 of Protocol II, each Party in the conflict was obliged to conduct the hostilities without affecting the civilian population and individual civilians or creating dangers for them. The Prosecutor claimed,[290] and the witnesses confirmed, that there were no military operations in Kibuye Town nor in the area of Bisesero in this period of time. There is also no evidence that the civilian population, at the four sites in question, was affected by military operations which were under way in other regions of Rwanda. **[page 223]**

611. On the basis of the foregoing, it could not be asserted *pleno jure* that Articles 5, 7, 9 or 13 to 18 of Protocol II were violated in the case of the alleged crimes.

612. In charging Kayishema and Ruzindana with serious violations of Common Article 3 and Protocol II the Prosecutor specifically refers to Article 4(a) of the ICTR Statute. A separate analysis of Article 4(a) of the Statute is not merited, since this Article, Common Article 3 and Article 4 of Protocol II, are interconnected. Article 4(a) of the Statute coincides with Article 4(2)(a) of Protocol II which reproduces, without substantial changes, Common Article 3. These three Articles contain an enumeration of certain prohibited acts. Article 4(2) of Protocol II indicates that these acts are prohibited against persons refereed to in the first paragraph.[291] This category of persons is defined in this paragraph in the following way, "All persons who do not take a direct (active) part or who have ceased to take part in the hostilities."

613. In paragraph 192 of its Closing Brief the Prosecution pointed out that "in this case, the victims of the crimes *took no part* in the hostilities . . . they were unarmed and not affiliated with an armed force of any kind." [emphasis added]. In paragraph 193 and 194 the Prosecutor expressed her satisfaction that "the Defence did not challenge the civilian status of the victims by making any submissions or leading evidence connecting any victims to the RPF or hostilities that prevailed in 1994." However, in the next paragraph the Prosecution took another position by asserting that "the victims in this Indictment were civilians and *were taking no active part in the hostilities*" [emphasis added].[292]

---

[289] Closing Brief, p. 48, para. 165.
[290] See *Ibid*, p. 56, para. 195.
[291] The same indications are provided under Common Article 3.
[292] *Ibid*, p. 56, para. 196.

614. Thus, the position of the Prosecutor is not expressed *claris verbis*. If the victims "took no part in the hostilities" this is one situation, but if these persons "were *taking no active part* in the hostilities" this is another situation and in this case there is a need to prove that these men, women and children participated indirectly in the hostilities or at **[page 224]** least committed harmful acts against the Party in the conflict. If there is no such evidence of a nexus this statement sounds like *petitio principii*, and there is no legal ground for the conclusion that it met the fifth requirement established by the Prosecutor as necessary in order to hold individuals liable for violations of this treaty regime.[293]

615. Since the Prosecutor did not produce evidence of nexus between the alleged crimes and the armed conflict, the Trial Chamber is of the opinion that there is no ground to consider the applicability to the instant case of Article 4(a) of the Statute which covers Common Article 3 and Article 4(2)(a) of Protocol II.

616. It has already been illustrated that the FAR and the RPF were Parties in the internal armed conflict in Rwanda during the period of time in question. Pursuant to the above mentioned fourth requirement of the Prosecution, Kayishema and Ruzindana must be connected to one of these Parties and bound by the respective regime. In other words, to hold both accused criminally responsible for serious violations of Common Articles 3 and Protocol II it should be proved that there was some sort of a link between the armed forces and the accused.

617. It was shown that both accused were not members of the armed forces. However, it was recognised earlier in this Judgement that civilians could be connected with the armed forces if they are directly engaged in the conduct of hostilities or the alleged civilians were legitimately mandated and expected, as persons holding public authority or *de facto* representing the Government, to support or fulfil the war effort.

618. However, the Prosecution did not produce any evidence to show how and in what capacity Kayishema and in particular Ruzindana, who was not a public official, were supporting the Government efforts against the RPF. **[page 225]**

619. Presenting her case, the Prosecutor pointed out that Kayishema and Ruzindana carried rifles and participated in the massacres alleged in the Indictment. However, the Prosecutor herself recognised that the FAR or the RPF were not involved in these massacres, which were organised and directed by the civilian authorities of the country. She further recognised that the overwhelming majority of the attackers were civilians, armed with traditional weapons. This was proved through witness testimony, and also recognised by the Prosecutor in her Closing Brief, when she stated "the Hutu civilian population was mobilised to attack and kill the Tutsi population under the guise of the Civilian Defence Program."[294] Therefore, these men, women and children were killed not as a result of the military operations between the FAR and the RPF but because of the policy of extermination of the Tutsi, pursued by the official authorities of Rwanda. Therefore, it does not follow from the participation of the accused in these massacres that they were connected with the armed forces of the FAR or the RPF.

620. The struggle for power between the FAR and the RPF, which was underway in 1994, meant that each Party in this armed conflict, in all circumstances, had to treat humanely all persons belonging to the adverse Party. In this period of time, Rwanda had been invaded by the armed forces of the RPF and, in accordance with international law, the Government of this country was undoubtedly entitled to take all necessary measures to resist these attacks. But it does not follow that crimes could be committed against members of the RPF who were under the protection of Common Article 3 and Protocol II.

621. However, the crimes committed at the four sites, referred to in the Indictment, were not crimes against the RPF and its members. They were committed by the civilian authorities of this country against their own civilian population of a certain ethnicity and this fact was proven beyond a reasonable doubt

---

[293] During this analysis, the Prosecutor noted that it may appear that an expert witness, Professor Degni-Segui, took the position that the victims were not protected persons under the regimes. But the Trial Chamber, from point of the view of the Prosecutor, is free to reject or accept the testimony of experts. See Closing Brief. p. 56.
[294] *Ibid*, p. 49, para. 165.

during the trial. It is true that these atrocities were committed during the armed conflict. However, they were committed as part of a distinct policy of genocide; they were committed parallel to, and not as a result of, the armed conflict. Such crimes are undoubtedly the most serious of crimes which **[page 226]** could be committed during or in the absence of an armed conflict. In any event, however, these crimes are beyond the scope of Common Article 3 and Protocol II which aim to protect victims of armed conflict.

622.   In this respect, it is important to recall a recent statement of the ICRC that, "It should be stressed that in war time international humanitarian law coexists with human rights law, certain provisions of which cannot be derogated from. Protecting the individual *vis-à-vis* the enemy, (as opposed to protecting the individual *vis-à-vis* his own authorities) is one of the characteristics of the law of armed conflicts. A state at war cannot use the conflict as a pretext for ignoring the provisions of that law . . . ."[295] This is just what happened in Rwanda with only one clarification. The armed conflict there was used not only as a pretext for ignoring the provisions of human rights laws but, moreover, as a pretext for committing extremely serious crimes.

623.   Considering the above, and based on all the evidence presented in this case, the Trial Chamber finds that it has not been proved, beyond a reasonable doubt, that the crimes alleged in the Indictment were committed in direct conjunction with the armed conflict. The Trial Chamber further finds that the actions of Kayishema and Ruzindana, in the alleged period of time, had no direct connection with the military operations or with the victims of the armed conflict. It has not been shown that there was a direct link between the accused and the armed forces. Moreover, it cannot be concluded *pleno jure*, that the material provisions of Common Article 3 and Protocol II have been violated in this particular case. Thus both accused persons, *ipso facto et ipso jure*, cannot be individually responsible for violations of these international instruments.

624.   The Trial Chamber finds, therefore, that Kayishema did not incur individual criminal responsibility for breaches of Article 4 of the Statute under counts 5, 6, 11 ,12, 17 and 18, and neither Kayishema nor Ruzindana incurred liability under counts 23 and 24. **[page 227]**

VII.   CUMULATIVE CHARGES

Introduction

625.   The Indictment charges both accused persons cumulatively, *inter alia*, for Genocide, Crimes Against Humanity/Extermination (extermination) and Crimes Against Humanity/Murder (murder). Within each crime site, the three types of crimes in question[296] are based on the same conduct, and the Defence submits that these crimes amounts to the same offense. Therefore the Chamber must consider the facts of the present case as they apply to the charges. The focus of the analysis that follows therefore is whether the charges, as framed in the Indictment, are proper and sustainable. The issue is not one of concurrent sentencing.

Arguments of the Parties

626.   The Defence Teams submitted that the Trial Chamber should not convict for both genocide and Crimes Against Humanity because there is a *concur d'infraction* or concurrence of violations. The Defence for Ruzindana submitted that "Crimes Against Humanity have been largely absorbed by the Genocide Convention."[297] Furthermore, they argue that there is a partial overlap in the protected social interest of the two Articles of the Statute.[298] The Defence for Kayishema submitted that "The criterion

---

[295]   ICRC, Report of the Meeting of Experts, October 1998.

[296]   The Trial Chamber does not address the other three crimes charged in the present Indictment because, for various reasons outlined in the Legal Findings Part, the accused have not been found criminally responsible for each of these crimes.

[297]   Defence Closing Brief (Ruzindana), 29 Oct. 1998, at 6.

[298]   *Ibid.*

which makes it possible to give separate recognition to the two concepts in law (genocide and extermination) is that the special interests served by genocide are different from those served by extermination. In the instant case, the interests were the same, no convincing argument having been advanced to the contrary."[299] The Prosecution does not argue the **[page 228]** substantive issues involved in the possibility of a *concur d'infractions* or the overlapping elements of the crimes.

The Test of Concurrence of Crimes

627. It is only acceptable to convict an accused of two or more offences in relation to the same set of facts in the following circumstances: (1) where offences have differing elements, or (2) where the laws in question protect differing social interests. To address the issue of concurrence, that is whether two or more crimes charged in the Indictment could be considered the same offense, the Trial Chamber examines two factors: Firstly, whether the crimes as charged contain the same elements, and secondly, whether the laws in question protect the same social interests.[300] The Chamber first analyses the issue of concurrence as it applies to the laws of genocide and Crimes Against Humanity generally; that is, examine whether the violation of these laws *could* overlap? The Chamber will follow this analysis with an application to the case at bench; that is, ask whether the crimes *do* overlap given the factual circumstances of the present case?

General Analysis of Concurrence in Relation to Genocide and Crimes Against Humanity; Could the Violation of these Laws Overlap?

628. The Trial Chamber first examines concurrence as it relates to the umbrella laws of genocide and Crimes Against Humanity, addressing the elements that could be invoked when the laws are applied to different factual scenarios. This allows the Trial Chamber to determine whether concurrence *could* occur where genocide and one or more of the enumerated crimes within Crimes Against Humanity are charged in relation to the same set of facts.

629. In relation to the elements of the crimes in question, not all the elements of genocide or Crimes Against Humanity will be invoked in every case. Between the two crimes there are three elements that, if applied in a particular case, could be relied upon to prove one crime but not the others. In such a case there would be no overlap of elements. **[page 229]** In other circumstances however, the elements relied upon to prove each of the crimes could be the same.

630. Firstly, and most fundamentally, some of the enumerated crimes under Crimes Against Humanity would not be carried out with the objective to *destroy* a group in whole or in part; the primary requirement for genocide. For example, Crimes Against Humanity of deportation or imprisonment would not generally lead to the destruction of a protected group. Within Crimes Against Humanity, however, the enumerated crimes of murder (when carried out on a large scale) or extermination would, by their very nature, be committed with the objective to eliminate a part of the population based on discriminatory grounds. Indeed, the terms extermination and destroy are interchangeable in the context of these two crimes. Thus, the element could be the same, given the right factual circumstances.

631. Secondly, under Crimes Against Humanity all of the enumerated crimes must be committed specifically against a "civilian population"[301] where as to commit the crime of genocide one must commit acts to destroy "members of a group." The victims' civilian or military status has no bearing on proving an allegation of genocide. However, in some factual scenarios where the victims are members of the civilian population only, the element would be the same.

---

[299]   Defence Brief of Clement Kayishema at 7.
[300]   Many national jurisdictions have adopted such concepts in conducting criminal proceedings. *See* Blockburger v. United States, 284 U.S. 299 (1932).
[301]   For a detailed discussion on the definition of the civilian population, under Crimes Against Humanity, *see* Chapter 4.2, *supra*.

632.   Third, the discriminatory grounds under Crimes Against Humanity include a type of discrimination not included under genocide, that is political conviction. Where the Prosecution case is based on the same discriminatory grounds, the element would be the same.

633.   Fourthly, extermination requires a showing that at least one murder was a part of a mass killing event. Mass killing is not required for the crime of murder. Further, under the Statute, premeditation is required for murder but not for a killing that is a part of a **[page 230]** policy of extermination. However, as in the case before this Chamber, where all murders are premeditated and form a part of a mass killing event, the elements of the offences are the same.

634.   In sum, the Chamber finds that one may have the specific intent required to commit genocide and also to act pursuant to a policy that may fulfil the intent requirement for some Crimes Against Humanity, while carrying out acts that satisfy the material elements of both Crimes.

635.   Similarly, in relation to protecting differing "social interests," the elements of the two crimes may overlap when applied in some factual scenarios, but not in others. Under the crimes of genocide and Crimes Against Humanity the social interest protected is the prohibition of the killing of the protected class of persons. The class of persons is limited to the civilian population under Crimes Against Humanity whereas under genocide it is not limited to attacks against the civilian population. Where the status of the victims and the elements of the crimes are the same however, the laws may be said to protect the same social interests.

636.   Having examined the elements, both mental and physical, and the protected social interests, the Trial Chamber finds that genocide and Crimes Against Humanity may overlap in some factual scenarios, but not in others. This is not surprising. Both international crimes are offenses of mass victimization that may be invoked by a wide array of culpable conduct in connection with many, potentially different, factual situations. Accordingly, whether such overlap exists will depend on the specific facts of the case and the particular evidence relied upon by the Prosecution to prove the crimes.

Do the Crimes Overlap in the Present Case ?

637.   For his conduct at the Complex, Kayishema is charged cumulatively with Genocide (Count 1), Murder (Count 2) and Extermination (Count 3); for his conduct at the Stadium cumulatively with Genocide (Count 7), Murder (Count 8) and Extermination (Count 9); for his conduct at Mubuga Church cumulatively with Genocide (Count 13), Murder **[page 231]** (Count 14) and Extermination (Count 15); and, for his conduct in Bisesero cumulatively with Genocide (Count 19), Murder (Count 20) and Extermination (Count 21). Ruzindana is charged cumulatively for his conduct in Bisesero with Genocide (Count 19), Murder (Count 20) and Extermination (Count 21).

638.   In the instant case, both accused persons participated in the three-month long killing event that subsumed Rwanda, committing crimes in Kibuye *Prefecture*. In short, the Prosecution alleges and the Trial Chamber finds, that Kayishema and Ruzindana intended to kill vast numbers of Tutsis in Kibuye *Prefecture* and committed numerous acts, including aiding and abetting others, in pursuit of this objective. Evidence proves that the killings for which the accused were responsible were perpetrated against a civilian population. The Trial Chamber finds that the massacres were carried out solely on the basis of ethnicity. Moreover, in the present case the evidence produced indicates that the murders committed were part of the mass killing event. Each one of these issues is examined in detail below.

The Conduct Relied Upon to Prove All Three Crimes Was the Same – the Physical and Mental Elements

639.   The Prosecution case was based on the accused's objective to kill Tutsis in Kibuye *Prefecture*, or their aiding and abetting other Hutus to do so, over a three-month period. The policy of genocide in Kibuye, also served to prove the policy element for Crimes Against Humanity. With regard to the *actus reus* of both accused persons, the Trial Chamber finds that the attacks in which the accused participated and/or led resulted in thousands of deaths and numerous injuries. The same acts or omissions serve as the

basis for the Prosecution case in all three types of crimes in question. For example, the widespread or systematic element of the attack required for Crimes Against Humanity also served to prove that the acts perpetrated by the accused were genocidal acts namely, killings with intent to destroy the Tutsi ethnic group in whole or in part.

640. With regard to the *mens rea*, the Trial Chamber finds this case to be one of intentional extermination or destruction of the Tutsi population; all the killings and **[page 232]** serious injuries occurred as a result of this objective. It is the same intent that has served as the basis for all three types of crimes in question.

641. Therefore, the elements and the evidence used to prove these elements were the same for genocide and the crimes of extermination and murder, in the instant case.

The Protected Social Interest – The Victims Were the Same

642. The Trial Chamber finds that the victims of the massacres were Tutsi civilians.[302] The discriminatory ground upon which the attacks were based was solely one of ethnicity. Accordingly, the discriminatory element, which is a requirement for both genocide and Crimes Against Humanity, was the same. Furthermore, the Tutsi victims of the attacks were civilians; members of the civilian population in Kibuye *Prefecture*. The victims held the same status whether they were victims of the genocidal acts or the crimes of extermination or murder. Thus, in this case, the same evidence established that the acts of the accused were intended to destroy the Tutsi group, under genocide, and were equally part of a widespread or systematic attack against civilians on the grounds that they were Tutsis, under extermination and murder.

643. Therefore, in the instant case, the social interest protected, that is, the lives of Tutsi civilians, was the same for genocide and the crimes of extermination and murder under Crimes Against Humanity.

All Murders Were a Part of the Mass Killing Event

644. The Trial Chamber finds that the murders at each one of the crime sites took place as part of the policy of genocide and extermination within Kibuye *Prefecture*. All the killings were premeditated and were part of the overall plan to exterminate or destroy the Tutsi population. The killings go to prove the charges of Crimes Against Humanity for murder as well as extermination and genocide. None of the killings were presented to the Trial Chamber as a separate or detached incident from the massacres that occurred in the four crime sites in question. Therefore, the Trial Chamber finds that the elements of the **[page 233]** crimes are the same for all three types of crimes and that evidence used to prove one crime is used also prove the other two.

Findings

The Same Offence?

645. The Prosecution uses the same elements to show genocide, extermination and murder, and relies upon the same evidence to prove these elements. The evidence produced to prove one charge necessarily involved proof of the other. The culpable conduct that is, premeditated killing, relied upon to prove genocide, also satisfied the *actus reus* for extermination and murder. Additionally, all the murders were part of the extermination (the mass killing event) and were proved by relying on the same evidence. Indeed, extermination could only be established by proving killing on a massive scale.[303]

---

[302] See Legal Findings on Crimes Against Humanity.

[303] It is important to note that an accused may be guilty of extermination, under Crimes Against Humanity, when sufficient evidence is produced that he or she killed a single person as long as this killing was a part of a mass killing event.

646. The widespread or systematic nature of the attacks in Kibuye satisfied the required elements of Crimes Against Humanity, and also served as evidence of the requisite acts and Genocidal intent. The *mens rea* element in relation to all three crimes was also the same that is, to destroy or exterminate the Tutsi population. Therefore, the special intent required for genocide also satisfied the *mens rea* for extermination and murder. Finally, the protected social interest in the present case surely is the same. The class of protected persons, i.e., the victims of the attacks, for which Kayishema and Ruzindana were found responsible were Tutsi civilians. They were victims of a genocidal plan and a policy of extermination that involved mass murder. Finally, the Prosecutor failed to show that any of the murders alleged was outside the mass killing event, within each crime site. These collective murders all formed a part of the greater events occurring in Kibuye *Prefecture* during the time in question. **[page 234]**

647. Therefore, the Trial Chamber finds that, in the peculiar factual scenario in the present case, the crimes of genocide, extermination and murder overlap. Accordingly, there exists a *concur d'infractions par excellence* with regard to the three crimes within each of the four crime sites, that is to say these offenses were the same in the present case.

The Consequences of Concurrence

648. During the trial, the Prosecution used the same elements to prove all three types of crimes as they applied to the four crime sites. In the context of the present case the three laws in question protected the same social interests. Therefore, the counts of extermination and murder are subsumed fully by the counts of genocide. That is to say they are the same offence in this instance.

649. The Trial Chamber is therefore of the view that the circumstances in this case, as discussed above, do not give rise to the commission of more than one offence. The scenario only allows for a finding of either genocide or extermination and/or murder. Therefore because the crime of genocide is established against the accused persons, then they cannot simultaneously be convicted for murder and/or extermination, in this case. This would be improper as it would amount to convicting the accused persons twice for the same offence. This, the Trial Chamber deems to be highly prejudicial and untenable in law in the circumstances of this case. If the Prosecution intended to rely on the same elements and evidence to prove all three types of crimes, it should have charged in the alternative. As such, *these* cumulative charges are improper and untenable.

650. Further, even if the Trial Chamber was to find that the Counts of extermination and murder were tenable, the accused persons could not have been convicted for the collective murders, in this case, under Article 3(a) and extermination under Article 3(b) of the Statute, as charged. This is because, as stated above, the Prosecutor failed to prove that any of the murders alleged was outside the mass killing event, within each crime site. In this situation as well, the Prosecutor should have charged the accused in the alternative. **[page 235]**

VIII. THE VERDICT

FOR THE FORGOING REASONS, having considered all of the evidence and the arguments of the parties, THE TRIAL CHAMBER finds as follows:

(1)By a majority, Judge Khan dissenting,

Decides that the charges brought under Articles 3(a) and (b) of the Statute (Crimes Against Humanity (murder) and Crimes Against Humanity (extermination) respectively) were in the present case, fully subsumed by the counts brought under Article 2 of the Statute (Genocide), therefore finding the accused, Clement Kayishema, NOT GUILTY on counts 2, 3, 8, 9, 14, 15, and both accused persons, Clement Kayishema and Obed Ruzindana, NOT GUILTY on counts 20 and 21.

(2)Unanimously **finds** on the remaining charges as follows:

In the case against **Clement Kayishema**:

Count 1: Guilty of Genocide

Count 4: Not Guilty of Crimes Against Humanity/Other Inhumane Acts

Count 5: Not Guilty of a violation of Article 3 Common to the Geneva Conventions

Count 6: Not Guilty of a violation of Additional Protocol II

Count 7: Guilty of Genocide

Count 10: Not Guilty of Crimes Against Humanity/Other Inhumane Acts

Count 11: Not Guilty of a violation of Article 3 Common to the Geneva Conventions

Count 12: Not Guilty of a violation of Additional Protocol II

Count 13: Guilty of Genocide

Count 16: Not Guilty of Crimes Against Humanity/Other Inhumane Acts

Count 17: Not Guilty of a violation of Article 3 Common to the Geneva Conventions

Count 18: Not Guilty of a violation of Additional Protocol II **[page 236]**

Count 22: Not Guilty of Crimes Against Humanity/Other Inhumane Acts

Count 23: Not Guilty of a violation of Article 3 Common to the Geneva Conventions

Count 24: Not Guilty of a violation of Additional Protocol II

In the case against **Obed Ruzindana**:

Count 19: Guilty of Genocide

Count 22: Not Guilty of Crimes Against Humanity/Other Inhumane Acts

Count 23: Not Guilty of a violation of Article 3 Common to the Geneva Conventions

Count 24: Not Guilty of a violation of Additional Protocol II

Done in English and French, the English text being authoritative.

William H. Sekule
Presiding

Yakov A. Ostrovsky   Tafazzal Hossain Khan

Judge Khan appends a Separate and Dissenting Opinion to this Judgement.

Dated this twenty-first day of May 1999
Arusha
Tanzania

There was a joint trial against Kayishema and Ruzindana, who had co-operated in relation to some of the alleged crimes. Counsel for Kayishema complained at various stages during the proceedings, about not having adequate time and facilities for the preparation of the Defence. This concerned the right to a fair trial and the principle of equality of arms, as stipulated in Article 20 of the Statute.[1] In that context counsel requested that the Trial Chamber order the Prosecutor to indicate the amount of time spent on the case and the various expenditures made. The Trial Chamber denied the motion and held that equality of arms does not entitle the Defence to the same means and resources as the Prosecution. Yet it is interesting to note that the Registrar of the ICTY based the payment of Defence counsel on a similar method to that of the Prosecution calculated on what a senior attorney for the Prosecution would cost per hour.[2] That was then used as the sum payable to counsel for the Defence per hour.

Kayishema considered the indictment not specific enough given the references to events "around" or "about" a certain date. The Trial Chamber acknowledged that the defence of an alibi may, in particular, be frustrated by a wide range of time such as, in this case, a reference to events that took place between 9 April and 30 June. The Chamber did not require the Defence, in raising the alibi defence, to provide a 24-hour account of the accused's whereabouts over several months. On the other hand, it also did not require the Prosecution "to prove an exact date of an offence where the date or time is not also a material element of each offence." However, according to the Trial Chamber, "where timing is of material importance to the charges, then the wording of the count should lift the offence from the general to the particular."[3] What is considered to be a material element was not further specified. The Trial Chamber offered little more, than to say that a material element was a necessary element that may vary from case to case. Although the Trial Chamber concurred to a large extent with the reasoning of the Trial Chamber in the Tadić case, there were some differences. In particular, the Trial Chamber left out the more illustrative and explanatory parts of the Tadić Opinion and Judgment: "The date may be of the essence of an offence if an act is criminal only if done, or only if the consequences of the act manifest themselves, within a certain period of time, or if the date is an essential ingredient of the offence, or if a statute of limitations or its equivalent applies."[4] On the other hand, the case law of the ICTR provides an example of an even longer period in the Nsabimana case. The Trial Chamber in that case found: "With regard to the time periods mentioned in the concise statement of facts, we note that the period "1 January – 31 December 1994" is *ratione temporis* of the Tribunal's jurisdiction."[5]

In part V of the Judgement, which dealt with the Factual Findings, the Trial Chamber returned to the defence of alibi. Again, it mentioned that the Defence did not respect Rule 67 of the RPE by raising this defence only at a very late stage. The structure of the notice of alibi derives from United States' law. Following a United States Supreme Court decision in Williams v. Florida, the Defence was under the obligation to submit the notice of alibi at an early stage.[6] This was codified in Rule 12.1 of the Federal Rules of Criminal Procedure. However, the ICTR in Kayishema and Ruzindana was less stringent than the United States Supreme Court in Williams v. Florida to the extent that it did not make an early notice absolutely compulsory. Rule 67 (B) RPE already stipulates that there is no sanction to be imposed on the Defence for not respecting this rule. Any other view would have implications for the right to a fair trial.[7] It also does not change anything for the Prosecution. The burden of proof rests upon the Prosecution to

---

[1]   See ICTY, Judgement, *Prosecutor v. Tadić*, Case No. IT-94-1-A, 15 July 1999, par. 43-56.

[2]   See Dorothee de Sampaio Garrido-Nijgh, The Defence Unit of the Registry of the ICTY: Personal Recollections, in: Hans Bevers and Chantal Joubert, An Independent Defence before the International Criminal Court, Proceedings of the Conference held in The Hague, 1-2 November 1999, Amsterdam 2000, p.43-53.

[3]   Judgement, par. 85 and 86.

[4]   See ICTY, Opinion and Judgment, *Prosecutor v. Tadić*, Case No. IT-94-1-T, T.Ch.II, 7 May 1997, par. 534, ALC-I-392.

[5]   Decision on the Defence Motion for the Amendment of the Indictment, Withdrawal of Certain Charges and Protective Measures for Witnesses, *Prosecutor v. Nsabimana*, Case No. ICTR-97-29A-T, 24 September 1998, p. 7, in this volume at p. 27.

[6]   *Williams v. Florida*, 399 US 78.

[7]   Justice Black, Dissenting in *Williams v. Florida*, 399 US 479, held that "to require a defendant in an criminal case to disclose in advance the nature of his alibi defense" violates the Bill of Rights.

prove its case beyond reasonable doubt.[8] Both for Kayishema as for Ruzindana, the evidence proffered by the Defence in support of alibi was insufficient to raise doubt against the Prosecution case.[9]

Regarding the definition and requirements of the crime of genocide, the Trial Chamber fully concurred with the Akayesu Judgement except for the definition of the term "killing", which was not fully defined by the that judgement. The Trial Chamber, "is of the opinion that there is virtually no difference between the term "killing" in the English version and "meurtre" in the French version of Article 2 (2)(a) of the Statute with the context of genocidal intent." Killing/ meurtre should therefore be considered along with the specific intent of genocide to destroy a group as such.

One of the few issues in which the Trial Chamber did not completely follow the Akayesu Judgement related to the differences between the English term "murder" and the French "assassinat".[10] In Akayesu, the Trial Chamber held that there were sufficient reasons to assume that the French version of the Statute suffers from an error in translation in that it did not require premeditation. The Prosecution in this case concurred with the view of the Akayesu Chamber, which was opposed by the Defence. The Trial Chamber agreed with the Defence. It regarded itself bound by the Statute. If a matter of interpretation arises and there is doubt, it should be decided in favour of the accused. To require premeditation was favourable to the accused. Murder/ assassinat therefore requires that the actor formulated his intent to kill after a cool moment of reflection. To clarify things, the Trial Chamber stipulated four conditions before an accused could be held guilty of murder: 1 cause the death of another; 2 by a premeditated act or omission; 3 intending to kill any person or, 4 intending to cause grievous bodily harm to any person.[11]

As a consequence of the fact that the crimes for which the Tribunal is competent do not have a clear description as under national leading systems that have codified their substantive criminal law in a Penal Code, the Trial Chamber must begin by setting out the standards of the law. This technique is not new for this Trial Chamber and has been used by Trial Chamber I and by the ICTY Chambers as well. However, the case law of the two *ad hoc* Tribunals has gradually reached the stage where more and more standards of the law have been firmly established. The reasoning in the Kayishema and Ruzindana Judgement and even more so in the Rutaganda Judgement refer often to the Akayesu Judgement in particular, but also to the Tadic Judgement and the Furundzija Judgement of the ICTY. As such this is illustrative of the fact that the requirements of the law are less and less in dispute and that trials focus on the question of whether the accused has actually committed the alleged crimes.

Regarding the question as to who qualifies as a principal in relation to crimes against humanity, the Trial Chamber reiterated that such a crime may be committed by state officials, as well as by non-state officials. It regarded Kayishema, who was the prefect of Kibuye, as a State actor and businessman Ruzindana as a non-State actor.[12]

In Paragraph 134 the Trial Chamber discussed the requirements as to the mental element in relation of crimes against humanity. The accused must have knowledge of the broader context of the attack. This rules out incidental and isolated acts carried out for purely personal reasons. The case law of the ICTR and the ICTY is also of the utmost importance for the (still) very few prosecutions before national criminal courts for international crimes. This aspect, as well as the requirement as to the widespread or systematic nature of the attack, are of crucial importance to a case pending before the Amsterdam Court of Appeal in the fall of 2000. In that case the Court was asked to determine whether the killing of fifteen people in Suriname in 1982, by the then military leader of that country, Desi Bouterse, may be considered as a crime against humanity over which the Netherlands may have jurisdiction. Although a handful of other killings took place in the country, it seems that it does not fulfil the requirement that it is

---

[8]   See Judgement, par. 233-234.
[9]   See Judgement, par. 257 and 272.
[10]   Judgement, par. 137-139.
[11]   See Judgement, par.140.
[12]   Judgement, par. 126.

part of a widespread or systematic attack known to the accused.[13] On the contrary, no matter how systematic that individual attack might have been, it was an isolated incident. However, in the Expert Opinion requested by the Court, John Dugard held that the socalled "december murders of 1982" appear to fall within the definition of crimes against humanity.[14]

Only in her Closing Brief did the Prosecutor submit that the injuries sustained by the survivors of various attacks amounted to other inhuman acts and therefore could constitute a crime against humanity. In the interests of justice and a fair trial, the Trial Chamber held that the Prosecution had not proven the relevant count because the Defence had not been informed as promptly as possible of the conduct allegedly committed.[15]

In relation to the applicability of Common Article 3 and Additional Protocol II, the Trial Chamber also concurred with the Akayesu Judgement. It is interesting to see how the Trial Chamber established a distinction between "civilians" and "civilian population". Whereas the civilian population is made up of persons who are not members of the armed forces, civilians could be among the armed forces and take part in the hostilities. The civilian population as a whole does not participate in the armed conflict. Even the presence of non-civilians within the civilian population does not deprive it of its civilian character.

Since the Prosecutor did not produce evidence of a nexus between the alleged crimes and the armed conflict, the Trial Chamber saw no ground to consider the applicability of Common Article 3 and Additional Protocol II in the instant case.[16] It therefore held that both accused did not incur criminal responsibility.

In discussing the requirements of command responsibility, the Trial Chamber dealt with the concept of "superior". It thereby distinguished between *de jure* and *de facto* control.[17] Although the Trial Chamber did not regard *de jure* powers as completely irrelevant, it is clear that in the end *de facto* powers are of greater significance.[18] This is logical because it is linked to the concept of effective control. A commander is only responsible for acts over which he has effective control. This relates to *de jure* and *de facto* aspects.[19] In addition, the ability to prevent or punish a crime is a question that is inherently linked to the facts. The purpose of Article 6, paragraph 3 is to ensure that a morally culpable individual is held responsible for the heinous acts committed under his command.[20]

Another distinction made by the Trial Chamber was between military commanders and non-military commanders. When it comes to the knowledges of subordinates' actions, a more active attitude is expected from military commanders than of others to be informed of the activities of subordinates.[21] The Prosecution must prove that the non-military commander "either knew, or consciously disregarded information which clearly indicated or put him on notice that his subordinates had committed, or were about to commit acts in breach of Articles 2 to 4 of this Tribunals's Statute."[22]

The Trial Chamber specifically paid attention to the matter of cumulative charges in Part VII. The Defence had argued that the Trial Chamber could not convict for both genocide and crimes against humanity, because there was a concurrence of violations in relation to the same set of facts. The Trial Chamber accepted this in situations where offences have differing elements, or where the laws in question protect differing social interests. The Chamber first determined whether concurrence of

---

[13]   Of course this is an extra-judicial killing, which may as such also be included as a crime against humanity, see paragraph 140 of the Judgement. However, every crime that may qualify as a crime against humanity, does require more: the widespread or systematic nature of the attack.
[14]   C.J.R. Dugard, Opinion *In : Re Bouterse*, Leiden, 7 July 2000.
[15]   See Judgement, par. 587.
[16]   See Judgement, par. 615.
[17]   See Judgement, par. 217-224.
[18]   ICTY, Judgement, *Prosecutor v. Delalić/ Mucić/ Delić/ Landžo*, Case No. IT-96-21-T, T.Ch., 16 November 1998, par. 364-378.
[19]   See Judgement, par. 229-230.
[20]   See Judgement, par. 516.
[21]   See Judgement, par. 227.
[22]   See Judgement, par. 228.

genocide and crimes against humanity could occur.[23] On the basis of four examples, it found that one may at the same time have the specific intent required to commit genocide and also to act pursuant to a policy that may fulfil the intent requirements for some crimes against humanity. In addition, with regard to protected social interests, the Trial Chamber found that the two crimes may overlap in some scenarios, while not in others. The killings at each one of the crime sites took place as part of the policy of genocide, but might also prove the commission of crimes against humanity (murder/ extermination). "Therefore the Trial Chamber finds that the elements of the crimes are the same for all three types of crimes and that evidence used to prove one crime is used also to prove the other two."[24]

As a result no more than one offence was committed. Otherwise the accused would have been convicted twice for the same crime. "If the Prosecution intended to rely on the same elements and evidence to prove all three types of crimes, it should have charged in the alternative. As such, *these* cumulative charges are improper and untenable."[25] The Trial Chamber therefore regarded the relevant charges of crimes against humanity in the present case fully subsumed by the counts on genocide, and found both accused not guilty of the former. In his Dissenting Opinion, Judge Khan held that problems resulting from cumulative charging should be solved by concurrent sentencing.[26]

André Klip

---

[23]   See Judgement, par. 628.
[24]   See Judgement, par. 644.
[25]   See Judgement, par. 649.
[26]   See in this volume, par. 52, p. 691. For the opinion of another Trial Chamber of the ICTR in the Akayesu case. See Judgement, in this volume p. 399, as well as the comments by Ambos/ Wirth and Schabas respectively.

UNITED NATIONS   NATIONS UNIES

International Criminal Tribunal for Rwanda
Tribunal pénal international pour le Rwanda

Trial Chamber II – Chambre II

OR: ENG

Before:	**Judge William H. Sekule, Presiding** **Judge Yakov A. Ostrovsky** **Judge Tafazzal Hossain Khan**
Registry:	**Mr. Agwu U. Okali**
Decision of:	**21 May 1999**

THE PROSECUTOR
versus
CLEMENT KAYISHEMA
and
OBED RUZINDANA
Case No. ICTR-95-1-T

SEPARATE AND DISSENTING OPINION
OF JUDGE TAFAZZAL HOSSAIN KHAN REGARDING
THE VERDICTS UNDER THE CHARGES OF CRIMES AGAINST
HUMANITY/MURDER AND CRIMES AGAINST HUMANITY/EXTERMINATION

The Office of the Prosecutor:
    Mr. Jonah Rahetlah
    Ms. Brenda Sue Thornton
    Ms. Holo Makwaia

Counsel for Clement Kayishema:
    Mr. André Ferran
    Mr. Philippe Moriceau

Counsel for Obed Ruzindana:
    Mr. Pascal Besnier
    Mr. Willem van der Griend

[page 2] 1.   I fully agree with and share in the Judgment with the exception of the Majority's view that the charges of crimes against humanity/murder (hereinafter murder) and of crimes against humanity/extermination (hereinafter extermination) are improper and untenable. The Majority finds that there is no reason to enter a conviction under these counts. I respectfully **disagree**.

2.   The Majority's determination stems from the finding that *concur d'infractions par excellence* (hereinafter also referred to as concurrence) exists with regard to the three crimes of genocide, murder and extermination, within each of the four crime sites. The Majority thus determines that the three crimes amount to the same offence and pronounce verdicts of Not Guilty for all the counts of murder and of extermination, in relation to both accused persons. That is, Not Guilty under Counts 2, 3, 8, 9, 14, 15, 20 and 21 for Clement Kayishema and Counts 20 and 21 for Obed Ruzindana.

3.   I find that, notwithstanding the concurrence of crimes, the charges were proper and deserve full consideration. Having fully examined the criminal responsibility of the accused under the said charges, I Find Kayishema and Ruzindana Guilty for all the counts of murder and of extermination preferred against them.

Background

4.   In effect, the issue on which I dissent is the legal consequence of finding that concurrence exists between charges within the same indictment. That is, the effect of concurrence on the assessment of the guilt or innocence, the verdict pronounced (conviction) and the penalty imposed (sentence) in relation to those charges. In this case, concurrence is found on the basis that the same culpable conduct of the accused supports all three crimes, and that the three crimes, as proved, contain the same elements and protect the same social interest. I do not disagree with the finding that the charges, *as proved*, rely on the same evidence and the same culpable conduct. **[page 3]**

5.   However, I do not agree with the approach taken by the Majority with regard to the consequence of this concurrence. The Majority determines that the murder and extermination charges are "improper and untenable" and, consequently, do not fully address the criminal responsibility of the accused persons under those charges. The Majority opines,

> Therefore, the counts of extermination and murder are subsumed fully by the counts of genocide. That is to say they are the same offence in this instance.

> The Trial Chamber is therefore of the view that the circumstances in this case, as discussed above, do not give rise to the commission of more than one offence. The scenario only allows for a finding of either genocide or extermination and/or murder. Therefore because the crime of genocide is established against the accused persons, then they cannot simultaneously be convicted for murder and/or extermination, in this case. This would be improper as it would amount to convicting the accused persons twice for the same offence. This, the Trial Chamber deems to be highly prejudicial and untenable in law in the circumstances of this case. If the Prosecution intended to rely on the same elements and evidence to prove all three types of crimes, it should have charged in the alternative. As such, *these* cumulative charges are improper and untenable.[1]

6.   Ultimately, the Majority pronounces both the accused **Guilty** for the counts of genocide only but **Not Guilty** for the counts of murder and extermination under each crime site. I respectfully **disagree** with this approach. In my opinion, the consequence of concurrence should be dealt with at the penalty stage – by sentencing the accused concurrently for the cumulative charges – rather than at the *verdict*.

7.   In Part 1 of this Dissent I shall examine the submissions of the Parties, the relevant jurisprudence and its applicability to the case at Bench. In Part II, I shall address the criminal responsibility of the accused persons under the counts of murder and of extermination. **[page 4]**

---

[1]   Kayishema and Ruzindana Judgment at Part VII

PART 1
The Submissions of the Parties

8.   The Defence submitted that the Trial Chamber should not *convict* for both genocide and crimes, against humanity because there is a *concur d'infractions*. The Defence for Ruzindana submitted that "Crimes Against Humanity have been largely absorbed by the Genocide Convention"[2] and that there was a *partial* overlap in the protected social interest of the two Articles of the Statute.[3]

9.   The Prosecution, on the other hand, contended that it is permissible to convict the accused for all the established counts for which the accused persons were responsible and to impose multiple sentences. By issuing multiple sentences, the Prosecution submitted, the Chamber would adequately address the gravity of each crime, the role of the accused, and the totality of their, culpable conduct. The Prosecution further submitted that "multiple sentencing will not prejudice the convicted person. The Chamber may remedy any prejudicial effect by imposing concurrent sentences for offences which arise from the same factual circumstances."[4]

10.   I find that the substance of the Prosecution's submission is in line with the applicable jurisprudence from the International Criminal Tribunals.

The Jurisprudence

11.   The jurisprudence from national courts and the views of legal commentators on the issue of concurrence is mixed. Some argue that it is wrong to *convict* for two or more crimes that suffer from concurrence while others argue that an accused can be convicted for all the established crimes but; in order to avoid prejudice, *punished* for the established crimes concurrently (generally by imposing the sentence for the gravest crime).

12.   Notwithstanding this general lack of uniformity, the international criminal jurisprudence most relevant to this Tribunal has been consistent in its approach from the **[page 5]** very first case at the ICTY – *Prosecutor v. Dusko Tadic*. The ICTY and ICTR have consistently opined that the issue of cumulative charges should be addressed at the stage of penalty – by sentencing the accused concurrently for the established crimes that are supported by the same culpable conduct.

13.   In dealing with the issue of concurrence, it appears that the ICTY Chambers have limited their analysis to the overlap of the accused's *culpable conduct*. They have placed less emphasis on the overlapping *elements* of the cumulative crimes. I agree with this approach. What must be punished is culpable conduct; this principle applies to situations where the conduct offends two or more crimes, whether or not the factual situation also satisfies the distinct elements of the two or more crimes, as proven.

In *Prosecutor v. Dusko Tadic*, the Defence submitted that,

In the system of the amended indictment each event is composed of a general description of a vague behaviour of the accused and of a number of Counts, being multiple qualifications of the crimes arising from that behaviour.

Whereas the vague description of behaviour does not individualize specific behaviour per qualification, and where the multiple qualifications of each prosecuted behaviour in the sequential Counts are not individualized per victim nor indicted as alternatives or subsidiars to each other if resulting from the same behaviour, each charged event may result in a cumulation of Counts, being different qualified crimes, but resulting from the same alleged behaviour.

---

[2]   Defence Closing Brief (Ruzindana), p. 6, 29 Oct. 1998.
[3]   *Ibid.*
[4]   Prosecutor's Sentencing Brief at para 102.

683

> The present indictment is contrary to a fair administration of justice since it exposes the accused to the effect of a double jeopardy.[5]

14.   In its response to the above submission the Trial Chamber, in its Decision of 14 November 1995, ruled,

> In any event, since this is a matter that will only be at all relevant in so far as it might affect penalty, it can best be dealt with if and when matters of penalty fall for consideration. What can, however, be said with certainty is that penalty can **[page 6]** not be made to depend upon whether offences arising from the same conduct are alleged cumulatively or, in the alternative. *What is to be punished by penalty is proven criminal conduct* and that will not depend upon technicalities of pleading.[6] [Emphasis added]

The said Chamber fully addressed all the cumulative counts and, in July 1997, sentenced Tadic on findings of guilt for numerous counts which relied upon the same culpable conduct, stating that "[e]ach of the sentences is to be served concurrently."[7]

15.   Meanwhile, on 6 December 1996, the ICTY Appeals Chamber addressed the said issue in *Prosecutor v. Zejnil Delalic, et al.* (hereinafter *Celebici*), where it held,

> The accused also complains of being charged on multiple occasions throughout the Indictment with two differing crimes arising from one act or omission . . .

> On this matter, the Trial Chamber endorsed its reasoning on an identical issue in the *Tadic* case: [Quoting the text of the *Tadic* Decision as stated in paragraph 14 above]

> The Bench does not consider that the reasoning reveals an error, much less a grave one, justifying the granting of leave to appeal.[8]

16.   Following the above Appeals Chamber Decision, in the *Celebici* Judgment of 16 November 1998; the Trial Chamber held,

> The Trial Chamber . . . thus declined to evaluate this argument on the basis that the matter is only relevant to penalty considerations if the accused is *ultimately found guilty* of the charges in question. . . . It is in this context that the Trial Chamber here orders that each of the sentences is to be served concurrently. The sentence imposed shall not be consecutive.[9] [Emphasis added]

17.   Hence, the Appeals Chamber has clearly endorsed the view initially stated by the *Tadic* Trial Chamber and followed in several Tribunal cases; to wit, it is at the stage of **[page 7]** penalty (sentencing) where the issue of concurrence – and the contingent prejudice to the accused – should be addressed, rather than at the verdict.

18.   Notably, the Trial Chambers of the ICTR have dismissed defence preliminary motions where the defence argued that cumulative charging based upon the same culpable conduct is impermissible. For example, in *Prosecutor v. Nahimana*, dismissing the defence contentions, Trial Chamber I of the ICTR held,

> In any case and as far as the cumulation of charges is concerned, it is the highest penalty that should be imposed. However, it is evident that we are not at this stage yet.

> Finally, it should be pointed out in this regard that in the *Delalic* case, Trial Chamber I of the ICTY dismissed the objection raised by the Defence regarding the cumulation of charges on the

---

[5]   Prosecutor v. Dusko Tadić, Defence Motion on the Form of the Indictment. (4 September 1995), IT-94-I-T.
[6]   Prosecutor v. Dusko Tadić, Decision on the Defence Motion on the Form of the Indictment (14 November 1995) IT-94-I-T at p 6.
[7]   Prosecutor v. Dusko Tadić Sentencing Judgment at para 76.
[8]   Prosecutor v. Zejnil Delalić, *et al.*, Decision on Application for Leave to Appeal by Hazim Delić (Defects in the Form of the Indictment), IT-96-21-AR, Appeal Decision, at para IV.
[9]   Celebici Judgment, IT-96-21-T, at para 1286.

grounds that the question was only relevant to the penalty if the accused is ultimately found guilty.[10]

19.   The said issue was also raised in *Prosecutor v. Ntagerura*. On 28 November 1997, only four days later, Trial Chamber II of the ICTR fully endorsed the aforesaid view of Trial Chamber I, thus dismissing the defence contention.[11]

20.   In *Prosecutor v. Akayesu*, Chamber I of the ICTR again endorsed the principle pronounced in *Tadic* case and held,

> In that case, when the matter reached the sentencing stage, the Trial Chamber dealt with the matter of cumulative criminal charges by imposing concurrent sentences for each cumulative charge. Thus, for example, in relation to one particular beating, the accused received 7 years' imprisonment for the beating as a crime against humanity, and a 6 year concurrent sentence for the same beating as a violation of the laws or customs of war.

> The Chamber takes due note of the practice of the ICTY. This practice was also followed in the *Barbie* case, where the French *Cour de Cassation* held that a single event could be qualified both as a crime against humanity and as a war crime.[12] **[page 8]**

21.   More recently, on 24 February 1999, in the *Prosecutor v. Milorad Krnojelac*, Trial Chamber II of the ICTY held,

> This pleading issue has already been determined by the International Tribunal in favour of the prosecution: previous complaints that there has been an impermissible accumulation where the prosecution has charged such different offences based upon the same facts – as it is here – have been consistently dismissed by the Trial Chambers, upon the basis that the significance of that fact is relevant only to the question of penalty. More importantly, the **Appeals Chamber** has similarly dismissed such a complaint.

22.   In the same Decision, the Chamber further held,

> The Prosecution must be allowed to frame charges within the one indictment on the basis that the Tribunal of fact may not accept a particular element of one charge which does not have to be established for the other charges, and in any event in order to reflect the totality of the accused criminal conduct, so that the *punishment* imposed will do the same. Of course, great care must be taken in *sentencing* so that an offender *convicted* of different charges arising out of the same or substantially the same facts is not *punished* more than once for his commission of the individual act (or omissions) which are common to two or more of those charges. But there is no breach of the double jeopardy principle by the inclusion in the one indictment of the different charges arising out of the same or substantially the same facts.[13] (Emphasis added)

23.   Thus, the line of international jurisprudence has evolved to hold that where the prosecution has charged such different crimes based upon the same facts, the matter falls for consideration *once* an accused is ultimately found guilty. And, the consequence of cumulative charges can be suitably dealt with at the stage of sentencing, rather than at verdict. In my view, this approach applies equally well to matters where the elements of the crimes, as proved, also overlap.

24.   The jurisprudence in this area of international law is no doubt still fresh – the case at Bench is only the second trial wherein the accused have been prosecuted for the international crimes of genocide simultaneously with crimes against humanity. Although different approaches are conceivable, in my

---

[10]   Prosecutor v. Nahimana Decision on the Preliminary Motion Filed by the Defence Based on Defects in the Form of the Indictment, 24 November 1997, at para 37.

[11]   Prosecutor v. Ntagerura Decision on the Preliminary iviotion Filed by the Defence Based on Defects in the Form of the Indictment of 28 November 1997, at para 26.

[12]   Prosecutor v. Jean-Paul Akayesu, Judgement, ICTR-96-4-T (2 September 1998) at paras 464, 465.

[13]   Prosecutor v. Milorad Krnojelac, Decision on the Defence Preliminary Motion on the Form of the Indictment, at para 10.

view, it is important that the various **[page 9]** Chambers ensure that the jurisprudence ripens into a judicious, as well as a consistent, body of law.

25.   For the above reasons, and those that follow, I find no justification to depart from the approach employed by the Chambers in the aforementioned cases.

Were the Charges of Murder and of Extermination Improper and Untenable?

26.   The answer to this question, in my opinion, is an emphatic no.

27.   The Majority holds that if the Prosecution intended to rely on the same elements and evidence to prove all three types of crimes, it should have charged in the alternative and, that the cumulative charges are "improper and untenable."[14] Accordingly, the Majority does not fully address the accused's criminal responsibility under the charges of murder and extermination. I **disagree** with this approach.

28.   At the start of trial it was too early to assess concurrence. Whether the crimes *as proved* suffer from concurrence is a question that is best determined after a trial chamber has accepted or rejected the evidence adduced – only then will a chamber be fully seized of the culpable conduct and the elements applicable to the charges in question.[15] This much is accepted by the Majority in its determination,

> Having examined the elements, both mental and physical, and the protected social interests, the Trial Chamber finds that genocide and crimes against humanity may overlap in some factual scenarios, but not in others. This is not surprising. Both international crimes are offences of mass victimisation that may be invoked by a wide array of culpable conduct in connection with many, potentially different, factual situations. Accordingly, whether such overlap exists will depend on **[page 10]** the specific facts of the case and the particular evidence relied upon by the Prosecution to prove the crimes.[16]

29.   Not surprisingly, in *Prosecutor v. Milorad Krnojelac*, Trial Chamber II of the ICTY held that the Prosecution must be allowed to frame charges within the one indictment on the basis that the Tribunal may not accept a particular element of one charge and, in order to reflect the totality of the accused's conduct.[17]

30.   In the case at Bench, although Ruzindana filed a preliminary motion, pursuant to rule 72 (B)(ii) of the Rules, on defects in the form of the Indictment,[18] the cumulative nature of the charges was not challenged therein. Similarly, Kayishema filed preliminary motions, none of which addressed the cumulative charges. Therefore, it is reasonable to infer that the Defence teams did not raise the issue being mindful that the Tribunals had consistently dismissed such challenges. Nor did the Defence raise it during the presentation of evidence. Consequently, the Trial Chamber had no occasion to direct the Prosecution to amend the cumulative charges and the Prosecution had no reason to believe that they were improper and untenable.

31.   It is not fair on the Prosecution, nor does it serve the interests of justice, to find at this stage that the charges should have been in the alternative. Having regard to the jurisprudence referred to above, I hold that the charges are proper and tenable.

---

[14]   Kayishema and Ruzindana Judgment at Part VII

[15]   For example, in the present case, if the evidence to prove that the attacks were based on political grounds (one of the alleged discriminatory grounds for the crimes against humanity charges) had been accepted by the Chamber, then the crimes of extermination and murder would contain a different element from genocide. In this example, the elements of the charges would not completely overlap.

[16]   Kayishema and Ruzindana Judgment at Part VII

[17]   Prosecutor v. Milorad Krnojelac, *ibid.*

[18]   Preliminary Motions, filed by Ruzindana, (3 February 1997).

The Verdict Should Flow From the Chamber's Factual Findings Based Upon the Consideration of Proven Facts

32. Once the Prosecution has been permitted to proceed throughout trial with charges which, depending upon the Chamber's ultimate findings, may or may not overlap, the Trial Chamber is under the obligation to address the criminal responsibility on each charge. In my opinion, the verdict should be based upon the consideration of proven facts rather than the "technicalities of pleading." Here, this is particularly important since **[page 11]** the offences of genocide and crimes against humanity are intended to punish different evils and to protect different social interests. Indeed, finding as the Majority did that murder and extermination are subsumed by genocide and that they are the same offence. defeats the very scheme and object of the law.

33. Further, the full assessment of charges and the pronouncement of guilty verdicts are important in order to reflect the totality of the accused's culpable conduct. For crimes against humanity to be established, the Chamber must be satisfied that there was a widespread or systematic attack against a civilian population. These elements are not required for genocide. Genocide requires the specific intent to destroy a certain protected group, in whole or in part, and this destruction need not be part of a widespread or systematic attack, or targeted against a civilian population. Therefore, as in this case, where the culpable conduct was part of a widespread and systematic attack specifically against civilians, to record a conviction for genocide alone does not reflect the totality of the accused's culpable conduct. Similarly, if the Majority had chosen to convict for extermination alone instead of genocide, the verdict would still fail to adequately capture the totality of the accused's conduct.

The Approach Herein Does Not Prejudice the Accused

34. The concept of *concur d'infractions* is to protect an accused from prejudice where the same facts and conduct support a conviction for two or more crimes which rely upon the same elements. I fully endorse this principle. Indeed, it is unfair that an accused is punished more than once for one culpable conduct where the facts and victims are the same. However, any real prejudice in the instant case would arise from the *sentence* imposed rather than the *pronouncement of conviction*.

35. It is said that multiple convictions may unnecessarily tarnish the criminal record and image of the accused. I do not find this position convincing in the instant case. Here the realities that have emerged are so vast and complicated that they attract both the laws of genocide and crimes against humanity. Once the accused has been found guilty of the abominable crime of genocide, it is difficult to appreciate how the pronouncement of **[page 12]** additional guilty verdicts under the two crimes of murder and extermination would tarnish his image further or lead to other prejudice, when the sentences are ordered to run concurrently.

36. Further, as the Majority acknowledges, the Prosecution used the same elements to show the existence of the three crimes and, "relied upon the same evidence to prove these elements . . . [t]he evidence produced to prove one charge necessarily involved proof o f the other." Accordingly, during trial the accused persons were not prejudiced by having to refute any extra evidence due to the cumulative charges. On the other hand, had this been a case of double jeopardy (that is, where a person is prosecuted in *successive* trials for an offence for which he has already been acquitted or convicted), then the potential for prejudice would be obvious. Here, we are not concerned with successive trials.

37. Both Kayishema arid Ruzindana will be sentenced according to their culpable conduct which, in this case, is the leadership role they played in massacring thousands of Tutsi men, women and children, due purely to their ethnicity. Whether this conduct offends one or three crimes, the sentence imposed must be the same. In my opinion, a verdict that the accused persons are guilty for the counts of murder and of extermination, as well as genocide, will in no way prejudice the accused. Thus, concurrent sentencing based upon the proven criminal conduct is a satisfactory way of ensuring that the accused do not suffer prejudice.

PART II

The Criminal Responsibility Under the Counts of Murder and Extermination

38.   The Majority correctly determines that,

> The Prosecution uses the same elements to show genocide, extermination and murder, and relies upon the same evidence to prove these elements. The evidence produced to prove one charge necessarily involved proof of the other. The culpable conduct that is, premeditated killing, relied upon to prove genocide, also satisfied the *actus reus* for extermination and murder. Additionally, all the murders were part of the extermination (the mass killing event) arid were proved **[page 13]** by relying on the same evidence. Indeed, extermination could only be established by proving killing on a massive scale.

> The widespread or systematic nature of the attacks in Kibuye satisfied the required elements of crimes against humanity, and also served as evidence of the requisite acts and genocidal intent. The *mens rea* element in relation to all three crimes was also the same that is, to destroy or exterminate the Tutsi population. Therefore, the special intent required for genocide also satisfied the *mens rea* for extermination and murder. Finally, the protected social interest in the present case surely is the same. The class of protected persons, i.e., the victims of the attacks, for which Kayishema and Ruzindana were found responsible were Tutsi civilians. They were victims of a genocidal plan and a policy of extermination that involved mass murder. Finally, the Prosecutor failed to show that any of the murders alleged was outside the mass killing event, within each crime site. These collective murders all formed a part of the greater events occurring in Kibuye *Prefecture* during the time in question.[19]

39.   Thus, as is evident from the above, the Majority accepts the criminal responsibility of Kayishema and Ruzindana under the charges of murder and of extermination. The Trial Chamber's findings in relation to the evidence and the accused person's criminal responsibility pursuant to the charges of genocide will apply equally to murder and extermination under each crime site, respectively. However, for the sake of completeness, I am obliged to briefly address certain aspects of these counts.

The Attack

40.   The Trial Chamber has analysed the essential elements of the attack under crimes against humanity.[20] The analysis reveals that Kayishema's criminal conduct at the massacres at Mubuga Church, the Stadium, the Complex and Bisesero area was part of a widespread or systematic attack against a civilian population on ethnic grounds, and that Kayishema was aware that his acts formed part thereof. And, that Ruzindana's criminal conduct at Bisesero area was part of a widespread or systematic attack against a civilian population on ethnic grounds, and that Ruzindana was aware that his acts formed part thereof. The conduct of both accused was instigated or directed by a government or another organization or group. I concur with this analysis and shall not repeat it here. **[page 14]**

The Crimes

41.   The Majority did not specifically determine whether the evidence satisfies the distinct elements of the individual crimes of murder and extermination, at the four crime sites; an analysis that the Majority deems unnecessary due to the concurrence with genocide. Of course, a finding of guilt may, only be entered if the Prosecution has proved the requisite elements beyond all reasonable doubt. Therefore, below I shall apply the evidence to the distinct elements of murder and extermination bearing in mind that much of the evidence has already been discussed in detail pertaining to the genocide counts. The

---

19   Kayishema and Ruzindana Judgment at Part VII
20   Kayishema and Ruzindana Judgment Parts VI Chapter 3 and Part VII

criminal responsibility of the accused persons under each said count will be the same as that stated under the count of genocide, within the same crime site.

The massacres at the Catholic Church and Home St. John Complex

Count 2

42.　Count 2 charges Kayishema with crimes against humanity in violation of Article 3(a) (murder) of the Tribunal Statute. All the killings on 17 April 1994 at the Complex were murders, that is, premeditated and intentional killings. Further, Kayishema caused the death of Tutsis at the Complex massacre by premeditated acts or omissions, intending to do so. The criminal responsibility of Kayishema under Articles 6(1) and 6(3) for the massacres at the Complex has been established by the evidence, beyond all reasonable doubt, and accepted by this Chamber. Kayishema's criminal responsibility under Count 1 (genocide) is equally attracted and applicable to this Count 2 (murder).

Count 3

43.　Count 3 charges Kayishema with crimes against humanity in violation of Article 3(b) (extermination) of the Tribunal Statute. On 17 April 1994 at the Complex there was extermination, that is a mass killing event. Kayishema participated in the extermination, having intended the killings. The mass killing resulted in the death of thousands of Tutsis. The criminal responsibility of Kayishema under Articles 6(1) and 6(3) for the massacres at the Complex has been established by the evidence, beyond all reasonable **[page 15]** doubt, and accepted by this Chamber. Kayishema's criminal responsibility under Count 1 (genocide) is equally attracted and applicable to this Count 3 (extermination).

The massacres at the Stadium in Kibuye Town

Count 8

44.　Count 8 charges Kayishema with crimes against humanity in violation of Article 3(a) (murder) of the Tribunal Statute. All the killings on 18 April 1994 at the Stadium were murders, that is, premeditated and intentional killings. Kayishema caused the death of Tutsis in the Stadium massacre by premeditated acts or omissions, intending to do so. The criminal responsibility of Kayishema under Articles 6(1) and 6(3) for the massacres at the Stadium has been established by the evidence, beyond all reasonable doubt, and accepted by this Chamber. Kayishema's criminal responsibility under Count 7 (genocide) is equally attracted and applicable to this Count 8 (murder).

Count 9

45.　Count 9 charges Kayishema with crimes against humanity in violation of Article 3(b) (extermination) of the Tribunal Statute. On 18 April 1994 at the Stadium there was extermination, that is a mass killing event. Kayishema participated in the extermination, having intended the killings. The mass killing resulted in the death of thousands of Tutsis. The criminal responsibility of Kayishema under Articles 6(1) and 6(3) for the massacres at the Stadium has been established by the evidence, beyond all reasonable doubt, and accepted by this Chamber. Kayishema's criminal responsibility under Count 7 (genocide) is equally attracted and applicable to this Count 9 (extermination).

The massacres at the Church in Mubuga

Count 14

46.   Count 14 charges Kayishema with crimes against humanity in violation of Article 3(a) (murder) of the Tribunal Statute. All the killings on 15 and 16 April 1994 at the Mubuga Church were murders, that is, premeditated and intentional killings. Further, Kayishema caused the death of Tutsis at the Mubuga Church massacre by premeditated acts or omissions, intending to do so. The criminal responsibility of Kayishema under **[page 16]** Articles 6(1) and 6(3) for the massacres at Mubuga Church has been established by the evidence, beyond all reasonable doubt, and accepted by this Chamber. Kayishema's criminal responsibility under Count 13 (genocide) is equally attracted and applicable to this Count 14 (murder).

Count 15

47.   Count 15 charges Kayishema with crimes against humanity in violation of Article 3(b) (extermination) of the Tribunal Statute. On 15 and 16 April 1994 at Mubuga Church there was extermination, that is a mass killing event. Further Kayishema participated in the extermination; having intended the killings to take place. The mass killing resulted in the death of thousands of Tutsis. The criminal responsibility of Kayishema under Articles 6(1) and 6(3) for the massacres at Mubuga Church has been established by the evidence, beyond all reasonable doubt, and accepted by this Chamber. Kayishema's criminal responsibility under Count 13 (genocide) is equally attracted and applicable to this Count 15 (extermination).

The massacres in the Area of Bisesero – Kayishema

Count 20

48.   Count 20 charges Kayishema with crimes against humanity in violation of Article 3(a) (murder) of the Tribunal Statute. The killings that took place in Bisesero area during April, May and June 1994 that involved Kayishema were murders, that is, premeditated and intentional killings. Kayishema caused the death of Tutsis at numerous places, in the Bisesero area including, Karonge Hill at the end of April, Bisesero Hill on 11 May, Muyira Hill on 13 and 14 May, the Cave, Gitwa Cellule in May and Kucyapa in June. Kayishema caused these deaths by premeditated acts or omissions, intending to do so. The criminal responsibility of Kayishema under Articles 6(1) and 6(3) for the massacres at Bisesero area has been established by the evidence, beyond all reasonable doubt, and accepted by this Chamber. Kayishema's criminal responsibility under Count 19 (genocide) is equally attracted and applicable to this Count 20 (murder). **[page 17]**

Count 21

49.   Count 21 charges Kayishema with crimes against humanity in violation of Article 3(b) (extermination) of the Tribunal Statute. The killings in the Bisesero area during April, May and June 1994 amounted to an extermination, that is a mass killing event. Further, Kayishema participated in the extermination, having intended the killings. The mass killing resulted in the death of thousands of Tutsis. The criminal responsibility of Kayishema under Articles 6(1) and 6(3) for the massacres at Bisesero area has been established by the evidence, beyond all reasonable doubt, and accepted by this Chamber. Kayishema's criminal responsibility under Count 19 (genocide) is equally attracted and applicable to this Count 21 (extermination).

The massacres in the area of Bisesero – Ruzindana

Count 20

50.   Count 20 charges Ruzindana with crimes against humanity in violation of Article 3(a) (murder) of the Tribunal Statute. The killings that took place in Bisesero area during April, May and June 1994 that

involved Ruzindana were murders, that is, premeditated and intentional killings. Further, Ruzindana caused the death of Tutsis at numerous places in the Bisesero area including, the Mine on 15 April, Gitwa Cellule in early May, Bisesero Hill on 11 May, Muyira Hill on 13 and 14 May, the Cave, Kucyapa in June, the Hole near Muyira in early June. Ruzindana caused these deaths by premeditated acts or omissions, intending to do so. The criminal responsibility of Ruzindana under Articles 6(1) and 6(3) for the massacres at Bisesero area has been established by the evidence, beyond all reasonable doubt, and accepted by this Chamber. Ruzindana's criminal responsibility under Count 19 (genocide) is equally attracted and applicable to this Count 20 (murder).

Count 21

51.   Count 21 charges Ruzindana with crimes against humanity in violation of Article 3(b) (extermination) of the Tribunal Statute. The killings in the Bisesero area during April, May and June 1994 amounted to an extermination, that is a mass killing event. Further, Ruzindana participated in the extermination, having intended the killings. The **[page 18]** mass killing resulted in the death of thousands of Tutsis. The criminal responsibility of Ruzindana under Articles 6(1) and 6(3) for the massacres at Bisesero area has been established by the evidence, beyond all reasonable doubt; and accepted by this Chamber. Ruzindana's criminal responsibility under Count 19 (genocide), is equally attracted and applicable to this Count 21 (extermination).

Conclusion

52.   The relevant jurisprudence of the International Tribunals is well founded and applicable to this case. The approach employed therein properly avoids entering into the legal quagmire of overlapping acts, elements and social interests at the stage of *conviction*. Rather, it concentrates upon the criminal conduct at the stage of *sentencing*. In doing so, it ensures that the accused's culpable conduct is reflected in its totality and avoids prejudice through *concurrent sentencing*.

53.   In the case at Bench, the Trial Chamber finds that the same culpable conduct of the accused persons offends the crimes of genocide, murder and of extermination, within each crime site, on the facts and evidence of the case. In my opinion therefore, both accused persons should be found Guilty under each count of genocide; murder, and of extermination preferred against them, notwithstanding the finding that the crimes, *as proved*, suffer from *concur d'infractions*. **[page 19]**

Dissenting Verdict

Genocide

54.   Accordingly, I completely **agree** with and share in the verdict that Clement Kayishema is **Guilty** under Counts 1, 7, 13 and 19 for genocide. And, that Obed Ruzindana is **Guilty** under Count 19 for genocide.

Crimes against humanity/other inhumane acts

55.   Further, I completely **agree** with and share in the verdict that Clement Kayishema is **Not Guilty** under Counts 4, 10, 16 and 22 for crimes against humanity/other inhumane acts. And, that Obed Ruzindana is **Not Guilty** under Count 22 for crimes against humanity/other inhumane acts.

Violations of article 3 common to the Geneva Conventions and Additional Protocol II

56.   Further, I completely **agree** with and share in the verdict that Clement Kayishema is **Not Guilty** under Counts 5, 6, 11, 12, 17, 18, 23, and 24 for violations of article 3 common to the Geneva

Conventions and Additional Protocol II. And, that Obed Ruzindana is **Not Guilty** under Counts 23 and 24 violations of article 3 common to the Geneva Conventions and Additional Protocol II.

Crimes against humanity/murder and crimes against humanity/extermination -

Kayishema

57.   In light of the foregoing, **in addition** to the unanimous Guilty verdicts rendered by this Chamber for genocide, I would pronounce Clement Kayishema, **Guilty** under Counts 2, 8, 14, and 20 for crimes against humanity/murder and **Guilty** under Counts 3, 9, 15 and 21 for crimes against humanity/extermination. In order to ensure that Kayishema would not suffer prejudice due to the concurrence of his culpable conduct, I would order that the sentences imposed in relation to the said counts of murder and extermination be equal to, and served concurrently with, the sentences imposed for the **[page 20]** counts of genocide, under each of the four crime sites, respectively. I would not impose consecutive penalties.

Crimes against humanity/murder and crimes against humanity/extermination -

Ruzindana

58.   In light of the foregoing, **in addition** to the unanimous Guilty verdict rendered by this Chamber for genocide, I would pronounce Obed Ruzindana **Guilty** under Count 20 for crimes against humanity/murder and **Guilty** under Count 21 for crimes against humanity/extermination. In order to ensure that Ruzindana would not suffer, prejudice due to the concurrence of his culpable conduct, I would order that the sentences imposed in relation to the said counts of murder and extermination be equal to, and served concurrently with, the sentence imposed for the count of genocide, for his conduct within the Bisesero area. I would not impose consecutive penalties.

59.   For all the above reasons, I respectfully submit this Separate and Dissenting Opinion.

Done in English and French,
the English text being authoritative.

Judge Tafazzal Hossain Khan

Dated this twenty first day of May 1999
Arusha, Tanzania

International Criminal Tribunal for Rwanda
Tribunal Pénal International pour le Rwanda

OR: ENG

TRIAL CHAMBER II

Before: Judge William H. Sekule (Presiding)
Judge Yakov Ostrovsky
Judge Tafazzal Hossain Khan

Registry: Mr. Agwu U. Okali, Registrar

Decision of: 21 May 1999

THE PROSECUTOR

v.

CLÉMENT KAYISHEMA AND

OBED RUZINDANA

Case No. ICTR-95-1-T

SENTENCE

Office of the Prosecutor:
    Mr. Jonah Rahetlah
    Ms. Brenda Sue Thornton
    Ms. Holo Makwaia

Counsel for Clément Kayishema:
    Mr. André Ferran
    Mr. Philippe Moriceau

Counsel for Obed Ruzindana:
    Mr. Pascal Besnier
    Mr. Willem F. van der Griend

[page 1] SENTENCE

Background

1.   In determining the sentences, this Chamber is mindful that the Security Council, pursuant to Article 39 and Chapter VII of the United Nations Charter, established the Tribunal to ensure the effective redress of violations of international humanitarian law in Rwanda in 1994. The objective was to prosecute and punish the perpetrators of the atrocities in Rwanda in such a way as to put an end to impunity and promote national reconciliation and the restoration of peace.

2.   This Chamber must impose sentences on convicted persons for retribution,[1] deterrence,[2] rehabilitation[3] and to protect society[4]. As to deterrence, this Chamber seeks to dissuade for good those who will be tempted in the future to perpetrate such atrocities by showing them that the international community is no longer willing to tolerate serious violations of international humanitarian law and human rights.

General Principles of Sentencing and Applicable Law

3.   Article 23(2) of the Statute and Rule 101(B) oblige this Chamber, in determining sentences, to take into account a number of circumstances or factors. These circumstances include: the general practice regarding prison sentences in Rwanda; the gravity of the offences; the individual circumstances of the convicted persons, and; any aggravating or mitigating circumstances. These enumerated circumstances, however, are not necessarily mandatory or exhaustive. It is a matter of individualising the penalty considering the totality of the circumstances.

4.   Articles 22, 23, 26 and 27 of the Statute and Rules 86(C), 99, 100, 101, 102, 103 and 104 generally represent the applicable law for sentencing. Article 22(1) of the Statute specifically authorises a Trial Chamber to impose sentence and penalties on those persons convicted of crimes under the Statute. This Chamber also finds that it possesses **[page 2]** unfettered discretion[5] to go beyond the circumstances stated in the Statute and Rules to ensure justice in matters of sentencing. This Chamber now turns to analyse this law as it applies to the case at bench, impose sentences, and discuss the enforcement of sentences.

Discussion of Circumstances to Be Taken Into Account in Sentencing

General Practice Regarding Prison Sentences in Rwanda

5.   Article 23(1) of the Statute and Rule 101(B)(iii) provide that, in determining the term of sentences, the Trial Chamber shall have recourse to the general practice regarding prison sentences in Rwanda.

6.   Rwandan law empowers its courts to impose the <u>death penalty</u> for persons convicted of being " . . . planners organizers, instigators, supervisors and leaders of the crime of Genocide . . . [or] persons who acted in positions of authority at the national, prefectorial, communal, sector, or cell level . . . [or] notorious murders . . . by virtue of the zeal or excessive malice with which they committed atrocities . . .."[6] This Chamber notes that this law applies to acts committed after 1 October 1990. Rwandan law also

---

[1]   *See Prosecutor v. Serushago*, Case ICTR-98-39-S, at para. 20 (sentence of 5 Feb. 1999); *Prosecutor v. Kambunda.* Case ICTR-97-23-S, at para. 28 (judgment and sentencing of 4 Sept. 1998); *Prosecutor v. Akayesu*, Case ICTR-96-4-T, at para. 19 (sentence of 2 Oct. 1998); *Prosecutor v. Furundzija*, Case IT-9517/1-T-10. at para. 288 (judgment of 10 Dec. 1998); *Prosecutor v. Delalić.* Case IT-96=2I-T, at para. 1231 (judgment of 16 Nov. 1998).

[2]   *See Serushago*, at para. 20; *Kambanda*, at para. 28; *Akayesu*, at para. 19; *Furundzija.* at para. 288; *Delalic.* at para. 1234.

[3]   *See Serushago*, at para. 39; *Furundzija*, at para. 291; *Delalic*, at para. 1233; *Prosecutor v. Erdemovic.* Case IT-96-22, at para. 16.i (sentencing judgment of 5 Mar. 1998).

[4]   *See Delalic*, at para. 1232.

[5]   *See Serushago*, at para. 22; *Kambanda*, at para. 30; *Akayesu*, at para. 17.

[6]   Art. 2, Organic Law No. 08/96 of August 30, 1996 on the Organization of Prosecutions for Offences constituting the Crime of Genocide or Crimes against Humanity Committed since October 1, 1990 (Organic Law No. 08/96).

empowers its courts to impose a <u>life sentence</u> for persons convicted of being "persons whose criminal acts or whose acts of criminal participation place them among perpetrators, conspirators or accomplices of intentional homicide or of serious assault against the person causing death."[7]

7.   In light of the findings of the Judgement against Kayishema and Ruzindana, this Chamber finds that the general practice regarding prison sentences in Rwanda represents one factor supporting this Chamber's imposition of the maximum and very severe sentences, respectively.

Gravity of Offences

8.   Article 23(2) of the Statute provides that the Trial Chamber should take into account the gravity of the offences in determining the sentence.

9.   This Chamber finds that Kayishema and Ruzindana have committed genocide, an offence of the most extreme gravity, an offence that shocks the conscience of humanity. Trial Chamber I of this Tribunal has held that genocide constitutes the "crime of **[page 3]** crimes."[8] Article 2 of the Statute defines the crime of genocide and its unique element of special intent to "destroy in whole or in part, a national, ethnic, racial or religious group as such." For purposes of determining sentences, this Chamber finds that Kayishema's four convictions of genocide and Ruzindana's one conviction of genocide constitute offences beyond human comprehension and of the most extreme gravity.

Individual Circumstances of the Accused

10.   Article 23(2) of the Statute provides that the Trial Chamber should take into account the individual circumstances of the convicted person in determining the sentence. This Chamber addresses in turn the individual circumstances of Kayishema and Ruzindana; respectively.

Individual Circumstances of Kayishema

11.   Kayishema was born in 1954 in the Bwishyura Sector, Kibuye *Prefecture* in Rwanda. He is married and has two children. He graduated from the National University of Rwanda in medicine and practised general medicine and surgery. In 1992, he was appointed *Prefect* of Kibuye *Prefecture* and in 1994 re-appointed to this same post, after the death of the President. The Prosecution has not proved that Kayishema has any previous criminal convictions.[9]

Individual Circumstances of Ruzindana

12.   Ruzindana was born in 1962 in Gisovu Commune, Kibuye *Prefecture* in Rwanda. He is married and has two children. He was a successful businessman in the transport of merchandise and the import of goods. The Prosecution has not proved that Ruzindana has any previous criminal convictions. This Chamber considers the relatively young age of Ruzindana (thirty-two years old in 1994) and the possibility of his rehabilitation.

Aggravating Circumstances

13.   Rule 101(B)(i) requires that the Trial Chamber take into consideration any aggravating circumstances in determining sentence. Both Kayishema and Ruzindana voluntarily committed and

---

[7]   *Ibid.*

[8]   See *Serushago*, at para. 4; *Kambanda*, at para. 16; *Akayesu*, at para. 8.

[9]   See *Kambanda*, at para. 45'; *Akayesu*, at para. 35.iii; *Prosecutor v. Tadic*, Case IT-94-1, at para. 63 (sentencing judgment of 14 July 1997).

participated in the offences[10] and this represents one **[page 4]** aggravating circumstance. This Chamber now addresses in turn the particular aggravating circumstances for Kayishema and Ruzindana, respectively

Aggravating Circumstances for Kayishema

14.   The Prosecution cites four aggravating circumstances for Kayishema. First, the Prosecution cites Kayishema's disregard of his obligation, as a *Prefect*, to protect the Rwandan people and maintain peace and order, and the use of his position to effectuate the crimes in Kibuye. Second, the Prosecution cites the zeal with which Kayishema executed his crimes. Third, the Prosecution cites Kayishema's methodical and systematic execution of his crimes. Fourth, the Prosecution cites the behaviour of Kayishema after the criminal act, and notably his inaction to punish the perpetrators.

15.   This Chamber finds the presence of these four aggravating circumstances. This Chamber finds as an aggravating circumstance that Kayishema, as *Prefect*, held a position of authority.[11] This Chamber finds that Kayishema was a leader in the genocide in Kibuye *Prefecture*, and this abuse of power and betrayal of his high office constitutes the most significant aggravating circumstance.

16.   To give but one example of the zealousness of Kayishema's crimes, this Chamber recalls that Kayishema attacked places traditionally regarded as safe heavens, such as the Complex and Mubuga Church. The harm suffered by victims and their families represents an aggravating circumstance,[12] and this Chamber recalls the irreparable harm that Kayishema inflicted on his victims and their families. Kayishema asserted an alibi defence arid at all times denied his guilt.[13] This Chamber also finds that this fact, in light of the convictions, represents an additional aggravating circumstance.

Aggravating Circumstances for Ruzindana

17.   The Prosecution cited one aggravating factor, Ruzindana's behaviour after the criminal act, and notably the fact that Ruzindana smiled or laughed as survivors testified during trial.

18.   This Chamber finds the heinous means by which Ruzindana committed killings constitutes one aggravating circumstance. To give but one example, this Chamber recalls **[page 5]** the vicious nature of the murder of a sixteen-year old girl named Beatrice. Ruzindana ripped off her clothes and slowly cut off one of her breasts with a machete. When he finished, he cut off her other breast while mockingly telling her to look at the first one as it lay on the ground, and finally he tore open her stomach.

Mitigating Circumstances

19.   Rule 101(B)(ii) requires that the Trial Chamber take, into consideration any mitigating circumstances, in determining sentence. This Chamber addresses in turn the mitigating circumstances of Kayishema and Ruzindana, respectively.

20.   Before turning to the particulars in this case, this Chamber wishes to help define the term "mitigating circumstances" by noting some that were present in earlier cases. This Chamber is of the

---

[10]   See *Serushago*, at para. 30

[11]   See *Serushago*, at para. 28; *Kambanda*, at paras. 44, 60.viii; *Akayesu*; at para. 36.ii; *Delalic*, at para. 1220; *Cf. Tadic*, at para 60 (finding the lack of "an important leadership or organisational role" constituted a mitigating factor).

[12]   See *Delalic*, at para. 1225, *Tadic*, at para. 70.

[13]   See *Tadic*, at para. 58.

opinion that mitigating circumstances may include: cooperating with the Prosecutor;[14] surrendering to authorities;[15] admitting guilt,[16] and; demonstrating remorse for victims.[17]

Mitigating Circumstances for Kayishema

21.   Kayishema's Defence Counsel, in the portion of his closing argument dedicated to sentencing under Rule 86(C), proffered mitigating circumstances. First, he asked this Chamber to consider the explosion of the rule of law in Rwanda in 1994 (based on Professor Guibal's testimony). Second, he advanced the mitigating circumstance that his client was overwhelmed by the events and the mob or "crowd psychology" (based on Professor Pouget's testimony) that existed in Rwanda in 1994. Kayishema's Defence Counsel also asserts that this Chamber should take into account that Kayishema is a loyal and honest person. The Prosecution did not advance any mitigating circumstances for Kayishema. This Chamber notes that Kayishema voluntarily submitted to interviews by members of the Office of the Prosecutor.

22.   The Chamber gives very little weight to the mitigating circumstances for Kayishema. The two proposed mitigating circumstances rely on testimony that this Chamber finds not particularly probative. This Chamber also is not convinced of **[page 6]** Kayishema's qualities of loyalty and honesty in light of his convictions in this case. This Chamber finds the presence of some mitigating circumstances for Kayishema, but none of any significant weight in a case of this gravity. For Kayishema, the aggravating circumstances outweigh the mitigating circumstances.

Mitigating Circumstances for Ruzindana

23.   Ruzindana's Defence Counsel, in the portion of his closing argument dedicated to sentencing under Rule 86(C), implored this Chamber to consider mitigating circumstances, but did not mention any. The Prosecution did not suggest any mitigating circumstances for Ruzindana. This Chamber considers as a mitigating circumstance the fact that Ruzindana was not a *de jure* official. This Chamber finds the presence of some mitigating circumstances for Ruzindana, but none of any significant weight in a case of this gravity. For Ruzindana, the aggravating circumstances outweigh the mitigating circumstances.

Sentencing Recommendations

24.   Defence Counsel for Kayishema, in the alternative to acquittal, recommended that this Chamber impose a sentence with merely "symbolic implication." This Chamber takes this recommendation to mean a sentence of time already served in custody, or some similarly short sentence. Defence Counsel for Ruzindana, in the alternative to acquittal, declined to suggest any suitable sentence.

25.   The Prosedution, on the counts of which this Chamber finds Kayishema and Ruzindana guilty, recommends the following sentences. For Kayishema, the Prosecution recommends concurrent sentences of "life imprisonment" for each of the Counts 1, 7, 13 and 19. For Ruzindana, the Prosecution recommends a sentence of "life imprisonment" for Count 19.

26.   This Chamber notes the facts that distinguish between the different levels of culpability of Kayishema and Ruzindana for purposes of sentencing, including Count 19. Considering the totality of the circumstances, this Chamber finds that Kayishema deserves more punishment than Ruzindana. First and foremost, Kayishema held a position of high authority; Ruzindana did not. Second, Kayishema is guilty of four counts of genocide; Ruzindana is guilty of one. Third, this Chamber considers Ruzindana's relatively young age and the goal of rehabilitation in his case. Fourth, **[page 7]** evidence shows that with

---

[14]   See *Serushago*, at paras. 31-33,; *Kambanda*, at paras. 47, 60.i; *Erdemovic*, at para. 16.iv; *Tadic*, at para. 58.
[15]   See *Serushago*, at para. 34.
[16]   See *Serushago*, at para. 35; *Kambanda*, at para. 60.iii; *Erdemovic*, at para. 16.ii; *Tadic*, at para. 58.
[17]   See *Serushago*, at para. 40; *Kambanda*, at paras. 50-52; *Akayesu*, at para. 35; *Erdemovic*. at para. 16.iii.

regard to at least one criminal act, Kayishema instructed and praised Ruzindana, highlighting their different relative levels of criminal responsibility.

Fifth, Kayishema is an educated medical doctor who betrayed the ethical duty that he owed to his community. Sixth, this Chamber, in light of practical considerations, is of the opinion that a twenty-five year sentence represents a term of imprisonment just below that of imprisonment for the remainder of his life. Seventh, this Chamber finds these considerations and other interests of justice require that Kayishema and Ruzindana receive different sentences in regard to Count 19.

Imposition of Sentences

Sentence of Kayishema

27. This Chamber sentences Clement Kayishema to: Imprisonment for the remainder of his life for Count 1 (Genocide); Imprisonment for the remainder of his life for Count 7 (Genocide); Imprisonment for the remainder of his life for Count 13 (Genocide); Imprisonment for the remainder of his life for Count 19 (Genocide).

Sentence of Ruzindana

28. This Chamber sentences Obed Ruzindana to: Twenty-five years imprisonment for Count 19 (Genocide).

Enforcement of Sentences

Concurrent Terms of Sentences

29. Rule 101(C) provides that when the Trial Chamber imposes multiple sentences it shall indicate whether the convicted person shall serve the sentences consecutively or concurrently.[18] Here, this Chamber is imposing multiple sentences, namely four remainder-of-his-life sentences against Kayishema. Accordingly, this Chamber orders that Kayishema shall serve his four remainder-of-life sentences concurrently.

Custody Credit Under Rule 101 (D)

30. Rule 101(D) requires that the Tribunal give custody credit to the convicted person for the period of time during which he was detained.[19] This Chamber finds that Ruzindana, being in custody, has earned custody credit. This Chamber instructs the **[page 8]** Registrar to take the necessary steps to inform and ensure proper custody credit in the State imprisoning Ruzindana.

Remainder of His Life Sentence

31. Rule 101(A) authorises the Trial Chamber to sentence a convicted person "to imprisonment for a fixed term or the remainder of his life." This Chamber, in imposing four concurrent remainder-of-his-life sentences for Kayishema, finds that the "remainder of his life" sentence is distinct from a "life sentence" under the laws of most national jurisdictions. This Chamber gives the phrase "remainder of his life" under Rule 101(A) its plain meaning.

---

[18]   *Akayesu*, at para. 41; *Furundzija*; at paras. 292-96; *Delalic*, at para. 1286; *Tadic*, at para. 75.
[19]   See *Serushago*, at Part V; *Furundzija*, at Part IA; *Delalic*, at paras. 1287-89; *Erdemovic*, at Part VIII; *Tadic*, at para. 77.

DISPOSITION

32. TRIAL CHAMBER II

FOR THE FOREGOING REASONS;

DELIVERING its Judgement and sentence in public;

PURSUANT to the Articles of the Statute and the Rules;

CONSIDERING all of the evidence before it;

CONSIDERING general principles of sentencing and applicable law;

CONSIDERING the general practice regarding prison sentences in Rwanda;

CONSIDERING the gravity of the offences;

CONSIDERING the individual circumstances of Kayishema and Ruzindana;

CONSIDERING the aggravating and mitigating circumstances;

CONSIDERING the Prosecutor's Sentencing Brief;

HAVING heard from Kayishema and Ruzindana regarding sentencing;

HAVING heard the Prosecution and Kayishema and Ruzindana;

IN PUNISHMENT OF THE ABOVEMENTIONED CRIMES,

SENTENCES Clement Kayishema to:

COUNT 1 (Genocide): Imprisonment for the remainder of his life;

COUNT 7 (Genocide): Imprisonment for the remainder of his life;

COUNT 13 (Genocide): Imprisonment for the remainder of his life;

COUNT 19 (Genocide): Imprisonment for the remainder of his life;

SENTENTCES Obed Ruzindana to:

COUNT 19 (Genocide): Twenty-five (25) years imprisonment; **[page 9]**

DECIDES that the sentences shall begin to run from today, and shall run in accordance with Rule 102(A);

DECIDES that Kayishema shall serve his multiple sentences concurrently;

DECIDES that Kayishema and Ruzindana shall serve their sentences in a State designated by the President of the Tribunal, in consultation with this Chamber;

ORDERS the Registrar to convey via letter or note verbale information regarding the designation to the designated State and the Government of Rwanda;

ORDERS the Registrar to convey information to the designated State regarding the date of arrest and custody credits of Ruzindana in accordance with Rule 101(D);

ORDERS the Registrar to execute these sentences immediately, and;

ORDERS the Registrar in the event that Kayishema or Ruzindana appeals, to maintain the appellant in custody of the Tribunal until such a time as the Appeals Chamber has determined the appeal.

Arusha, 21 May 1999.

William H. Sekule	Yakov Ostrovsky	Tafazzal Hossain Khan
Presiding Judge	Judge	Judge

(Seal of the Tribunal)

The present note will mainly focus on the relationship between genocide and crimes against humanity, which are dealt with at the beginning. However, towards the end it will also turn to the purposes of sentencing and aggravating circumstances in the Kayishema Sentence.

Concurrence in the Dissenting Opinion of Judge Khan

The Dissenting Opinion of Judge Khan[1] is concerned with the *concours d'infractions* or "concurrence"[2] in relation to genocide and crimes against humanity. He disagrees with the majority views on two issues. His first point of concern is the majority's opinion that a "concurrence" of offences should result in an acquittal of a concurring offence that is "completely subsumed"[3] by the other. Judge Khan holds that such an acquittal is inappropriate and that the right of the accused not to be sentenced twice for the same conduct could be protected by imposing concurrent penalties instead of consecutive ones.[4]

The second issue on which Judge Khan dissents is the relationship between genocide and crimes against humanity. Judge Khan opposes the majority's finding, that genocide can overlap with crimes against humanity in certain cases and thereby completely subsume those latter crimes;[5] in his opinion, both forms of crime have a different scope.[6]

In our view, both questions are inherently linked since the consequences of "concurrence" depend on the type or kind of "concurrence" that exists between two or more alleged crimes. Thus, this comment must start with an examination of the structure of the concurrence of norms. Applying this structure to genocide and crimes against humanity will enable a more precise determination of the relation between these crimes. Finally, it is appropriate to more closely consider some consequences attached to the concurrence of offences for the sentencing judgement.

The basic structure of the concurrence of norms

Two basic possibilities exist for the relationship of two crimes which, according to their respective wording, are both applicable to the same conduct.[7]

a)   Merger

Firstly, two norms can relate to each other in the manner of a smaller circle that lies completely within a larger circle. In such a case every element of the crime that lies in the smaller circle (the "smaller" crime) is indispensable to meet the requirements of the other crime that lies in the larger circle (the "larger" crime).[8] The larger crime obviously requires further elements which are not part of the smaller crime. Think, for example, of the objective elements (actus reus) of theft and robbery. In many jurisdictions robbery is understood as *theft* plus the use of certain means of coercion.[9] Thus, the offence of theft is completely contained in the offence of robbery or – the other way round – robbery includes all elements of theft. Such a relationship between norms is referred to as merger (*Gesetzeskonkurrenz or Gesetzeseinheit*). In cases of merger several general principles of law apply. The most important is the

---

[1]   Please note that this comment refers only to the English version of these and other judgements even when the French texts are authoritative.

[2]   The word is used in a non-technical sense in the first few paragraphs. The precise meaning of "concurrence" will be developed *sub* 1.

[3]   Judgement, *Prosecutor v. Kayishema and Ruzindana,* Case No. ICTR-95-1-T, 21 May 1999, par. 648.

[4]   Separate and Dissenting Opinion of Judge Khan to the Judgement, *Prosecutor v. Kayishema and Ruzindana,* Case No. ICTR-95-1-T, 21 May 1999, par. 6.

[5]   *Kayishema, supra* note 3, par. 648.

[6]   *Kayishema,* Dissenting Opinion of Judge Khan, *supra* note 4, par. 32.

[7]   Apart from some minor differences (cf. *infra* note 15), the Chamber in *Prosecutor v. Kupreškić et al.* (Judgement, *Prosecutor v. Kupreškić et al.,* Case No. IT-95-16, 14 February 1999, par. 678 *et seq.*) takes a similar view to that expressed in this note.

[8]   Cf. *Kupreškić, supra* note 7 par. 683. The Chamber correctly points out that situations similar to merger may also occur if two crimes are interrelated, e.g., wounding and killing or, to use an example familiar to German lawyers, theft by means of housebreaking and damage to property (*ibid.* 686). For the purposes of this note, however, the explanation of the basic structure of concurrence is sufficient.

[9]   For example s. 322 (theft) and s. 342 (robbery) together with s. 2 "steal" Criminal Code of Canada (R.S., 1985, c C-46); §§ 242 (theft) and 249 (1) (robbery) of the German Criminal Code (Strafgesetzbuch – hereinafter StGB); art. 624 (theft) and 628 (1) (robbery) of the Italian Criminal Code (Codice Penale); cf. also Kupreškic, *supra* note 7, par. 694.

rule: *lex specialis derogat legi generali.*[10] Accordingly, the smaller crime will not be applied if the elements of the larger crime are met – the larger "consumes" the smaller crime. In fact, only one applicable norm exists.[11] Thus, merger could also be called "false" or "fake" concurrence. In this way the relationship between genocide and crimes against humanity is characterized in the Kayishema case by the majority of the Chamber. It takes the view that – at least in certain cases – the elements of the crime of genocide comprise completely the elements of the crimes against humanity.[12]

b)   Concurrence

The second possible relationship between two norms applicable to the same conduct may be symbolized by drawing two circles which are either completely separate or intersect. The two norms then each require at least one element that the other norm does not contain.[13] For example, as a consequence of a manipulation of his car, Tom is hurt in an accident and the car destroyed. The person responsible for the manipulation is liable to be punished for both bodily injury and damage to property. Although these offences apply to the same conduct, namely the manipulation of Tom's car, they remain punishable independent of each other. Here, we can speak of a case of "true" concurrence. Such cases in which the same conduct violates several norms (or the same norm more than once) are referred to as (ideal) concurrence of offences (*Idealkonkurrenz, concours idéal*).

It should be added that not only two different crimes, committed through the same conduct, can be related by way of concurrence, but also two infringements of the same provision. This is the case if certain fundamental legal values or interests – for example the right to life, health, freedom or honor – of two or more victims are violated. Because of the extraordinary personal nature of these values, each violation must be counted separately.[14] A classical example is the commission of murder or manslaughter. In most jurisdictions, murder includes all the elements of manslaughter and, therefore, is *lex specialis* to the latter.[15] However, if the same conduct causes several deaths, e.g. a terrorist attack, every death must be counted separately. If the conduct fulfills the requirements of murder only for some victims, whereas the rest of the killings only constitutes manslaughter, there can be no merger and the perpetrator is responsible for both (several cases of) murder and (several cases of) manslaughter. In other words, every killing requires a separate sentence.

Equally, the rules of concurrence apply if the offences in question protect different legal values.[16] The verdict must individualize the accused's conduct with regard to any legal value violated. According to Judge Khan genocide and crimes against humanity are "intended to punish different evils and to protect

---

[10]   Kupreškić, *supra* note 7, par. 683; Rissing-van Saan, in: Jähnke/Laufhütte/Odersky (eds.), StGB. Leipziger Kommentar. Großkommentar, Berlin 1992 *et seq.*, 28th supplement 1999, before §§ 53 et seq., margin note (mn) 73; Eser, in: Schönke-Schröder, Strafgesetzbuch Kommentar, 25th ed. 1997, § 249 mn 13. This principle was among the examples of general principles of law which were presented during the *travaux préparatoires* of art. 38 (1) (c) of the PCIJ Statute which is identical to the present art. 38 (1) (c) of the ICJ-Statute; cf. Cheng, General Principles of Law as Applied by International Courts and Tribunals, London 1953, 25 et seq.

[11]   Cf. Walther, Cumulation of Offenses, in: Cassese (ed), International Criminal Law and the ICC Statute, A Commentary, 3 vols, Oxford University Press, Oxford (forthcoming: 2001), mn. 11.6.17.

[12]   Kayishema, *supra* note 3, par. 627 *et seq.*

[13]   Cf. Kupreškić *supra* note 7, par. 679 *et seq.*

[14]   Kupreškić, *supra* note 7, par. 712; Rissing-van Saan, *supra* note 10, § 52 mn 36.; Gil Gil, Comentario a la primera sentencia del Tribunal Supremo Alemán condenando por el delito del genocidio, Revista de Derecho Penal y Criminología 4 (julio de 1999), 771, 788 *et seq.*

[15]   This is the almost unanimous opinion of German writers while the Supreme Court considers murder and manslaughter as two different offences (cf. Eser, *supra* note 10, before §§ 211 *et seq.*, mn 5-6).

[16]   Kayishema, *supra* note 3, para. 627; cf. also Judgement, *Prosecutor v. Akayesu*, Case No. ICTR-96-4-T, 2 September 1998, par. 468. The ICTY held in Kupreskić (*supra* note 7, par. 694 *et seq.*, 704, 711), however, that the criterion of different legal values or interests is of minor importance since in national jurisprudence it is usually only used to corroborate the result already achieved by a comparison of the elements of a crime (but see, on the other hand, the judgement of the German *Bundesgerichtshof* (hereinafter BGH), Neue Zeitschrift für Strafrecht 1999, p. 396, 402, which holds that the main difference between genocide and murder is the protected legal value). The Chamber's observation on the national jurisprudence is easily explained by the fact that a well structured national jurisdiction does not usually design two different crimes which contain exactly the same elements, but protect different values.

different social interests".[17] Thus, he considers that the relationship is one of (ideal) concurrence of offences.

c)   Accumulation of offences

If a criminal conduct takes place at several different times – i.e., the offences fulfilled are the results of several, separate acts – one speaks in the civil law systems of "real" concurrence (Realkonkurrenz, *concours réel*). In this case the common law speaks of an accumulation of offences, since the only link between the respective crimes is that they are tried together. While *Realkonkurrenz* accounts for a substantive approach, cumulation of offences reflects a rather procedural one.[18]

The relationship between genocide and crimes against humanity

The structure of concurrence developed above can be applied to the present case. The Chamber found that there was evidence of both genocide and crimes against humanity and it is important to understand how these counts relate to each other.

The majority states that at least in some cases (including the present one), genocide and crimes against humanity may "overlap", since the same facts may satisfy the elements of both crimes. The majority therefore held that crimes against humanity were "completely subsumed"[19] by the commission of an act of genocide.[20] It reached this conclusion after comparing the different elements of each of these crimes, concluding that the same facts may prove them both. Moreover, it held that both crimes protect the same values (or "social interest"), namely the "prohibition of the killing of the protected class of people".[21] This view was not shared by Judge *Khan*.[22]

a)   The legal values protected by the crime of genocide

The Chamber's reasoning overlooks the fact that the crime of genocide is the classical international "group crime". While there remains the controversial question as to whether the crime of genocide only protects the physical existence of a group[23] or whether the group as a social entity is protected,[24] it seems beyond doubt that the protection of the individual members of the group is only an indirect or secondary, albeit necessary, effect of the crime's collective protection approach. If one takes the view, however, that genocide "completely subsumes" crimes against humanity, one must demonstrate that the crime of genocide protects not only the group as such but also its individual members in a direct, parallel way.[25] The issue has recently been addressed by the Spanish scholar Alicia Gil Gil in her study on the elements of the crime of genocide[26] and her extensive comment on the first judgement on genocide delivered by the German *Bundesgerichtshof* ("BGH").[27] Starting from the assumption that genocide is a group crime i.e. the legal value protected is the existence of the group[28] she puts forward two arguments. First, as mentioned above,[29] the violation of certain fundamental legal values such as the right to life or health cannot be regarded as one single crime but must be regarded as several concurring crimes. Secondly, Gil

---

[17]   Kayishema, Dissenting Opinion of Judge Khan, *supra* note 4, par. 32.

[18]   However, under German law *Realkonkurrenz* can have a procedural impact as shown by §§ 460 *et seq.* Code of Criminal Procedure which regulate the formation of a unified sentence for different judgements.

[19]   Kayishema, *supra* note 3, par. 648.

[20]   However, Trial Chamber I in Akayesu (*supra* note 16, par. 470) did "not consider that any of genocide, crimes against humanity and [war crimes] are lesser included forms of each other".

[21]   Kayishema, *supra* note 3, par. 635.

[22]   Kayishema, Dissenting Opinion of Judge Khan, *supra* note 4, par. 32.

[23]   International Law Commission (ILC), Draft Code of Crimes against the Peace and Security of Mankind, <http://www.un.org/law/ilc/reports/1996/chap02.htm#doc13> Commentary on art. 17, par. 12.

[24]   See BGH *supra* note 16, 401; Jähnke in: Jähnke/Laufhütte/Odersky (eds.), StGB. Leipziger Kommentar. Großkommentar, Berlin 1992 *et seq.*, 31st supplement 1999, § 220a mn. 8; Ambos, Neue Zeitschrift für Strafrecht 1998, p.138.

[25]   Similar to the Kayishema Judgement the Akayesu Judgement (*supra* note 15, par. 521) held that the group *and* the individual are protected, but neither judgement sets out a substantive reason for this opinion.

[26]   Gil Gil, Derecho penal internacional, Madrid 1999, p. 159 *et seq.*, p. 201 *et seq.*

[27]   Gil Gil, *supra* note 14, 771.

[28]   Gil Gil, *supra* note 26, at 194-95 and passim. See also Robinson, the Genocide Convention. A Commentary, 2nd Ed. New York, 1960, p. 58 who states: "[T]he individuals are important not *per se* but only as members of the group" A similar formulation is used by the ILC (*supra* note 23, par. 6).

[29]   Supra Concurrence.

Gil shares the *BGH*'s view[30] that several attacks on a single group i.e. a single object of legal protection committed with the same intent to destroy this group, must be regarded as a single criminal act because the attacks are unified by this same intent.[31] Moreover, Gil Gil and the *BGH* consider that the different material elements of genocide suggest that the destruction of a group is typically achieved with multiple attacks since these elements are all formulated in a plural or collective form (for example "killing members of the group", "prevent births", article 2, paragraph 2 ICTR Statute).[32] This also follows from the plain meaning of the word "genocide" which means extinction or destruction of a group.[33] The crime of genocide is committed even when the destruction of a group is only attempted i.e. if the perpetrator started to commit genocidal acts by attacking members of the group with the intent that the destruction would be completed at some time in the future.[34] Subsequent acts committed in pursuance of this same intent cannot be separated from the first ones, since they are all aimed at the completion of the intended result – the destruction of the group.

Consequently, if multiple violations of the fundamental legal values of several individuals are considered as a multiplicity of crimes, while multiple attacks on a group pursuant to a genocidal intent cannot be regarded as separate acts, one must conclude that the same norm cannot address both situations.[35] Otherwise, the accumulation of several distinct crimes on the basis of a multiple violation of individual values would contradict the single violation of the rights of the group[36] and *vice versa*. In sum, the crime of genocide protects *only* the group as such but not the rights of the members of the group *as* individuals.

b)   The legal values protected by crimes against humanity

The Chamber held that the prohibition of crimes against humanity protects individuals.[37] This is a correct view. The prohibition of crimes against humanity protects the individual from violations of his most important rights[38] in situations where those rights are facing extreme danger, i.e. in cases of widespread or systematic attacks against civilians.[39] It follows for the reasons stated above that the prohibition of crimes against humanity cannot, protect a group and the members of this group at the same time. As a consequence, the prohibition of crimes against humanity protects only individuals a different object of protection than that of the prohibition of genocide, which primarily protects the existence of certain groups. A situation of merger as envisaged by the Chamber is impossible.

c)   Different elements between genocide and crimes against humanity

Judge Khan pointed out that the context elements of crimes against humanity – the requirement of a commission in the context of a widespread and systematic attack against a civilian population – does not constitute a part of the crime of genocide.[40] This view is corroborated by the ICTY, which has held that even a single perpetrator could meet the elements of genocide if he acts with the intent to extinguish an

---

[30]   BGH, *supra* note 16, p. 403.

[31]   Gil Gil, *supra* note 14, p. 779.

[32]   See also BGH *supra* note 16, p. 403.

[33]   *Genos* (gr.) = race, tribe and cide (from lat. caedere) = to kill.

[34]   Cf. Gil Gil, *supra* note 26, at p. 194-95 and passim. This is a common technique of which legislators of many jurisdictions avail themselves – for example, for the codification of the crime of theft. Theft is usually construed as the unlawful taking of an object with the specific *intent* to appropriate it or to deprive the lawful holder or proprietor of it (s. 322 Criminal Code of Canada (R.S., 1985, c C-46); § 242 StGB). There can be little doubt that the *actual* appropriation of the stolen object cannot constitute a separate (criminal) conduct which is distinct from the theft itself (Rissing-van Saan, *supra* note 10, before §§ 52 et seq., mn 21).

[35]   Gil Gil, *supra* note 14, p. 789.

[36]   A finding of multiple crimes against the group, which has been attacked only once by a single conduct, might even constitute a violation of *ne bis in idem* (Gil Gil, *supra* note 14, p. 790 footnote 62).

[37]   Kayishema, *supra* note 3, par. 635.

[38]   Becker, Der Tatbestand des Verbrechens gegen die Menschlichkeit, Berlin, 1996, at p. 118, holds that the most elementary human rights are protected. The ICTY held that human dignity is the legal value protected by crimes against humanity (Kupreskic, *supra* note 7, par. 694). Because human dignity is an individual right, this view is consistent with ours.

[39]   Cf. the chapeau of Article 2 ICTR Statute. The ICTY also regards a "widespread or systematic attack" a necessary element of crimes against humanity (Judgement, *Prosecutor v. Tadić*, Case No. IT-94-1, A. Ch., 15 June 1999, par. 248; cf. also Judgement, *Prosecutor v. Jelisić*, Case No. IT-95-10, 14 December 1999, par. 53).

[40]   Kayishema, Dissenting Opinion of Judge Khan, *supra* note 4, par. 33.

entire group.[41] The reason is that the "context" in genocide i.e. the destruction of a group is only required as a mental (subjective) element,[42] whereas the context element of in crimes against humanity is a material (objective) requirement of the offence. A similar argument could probably be made with regard to a state or organizational policy to commit an attack against civilians, considered to be a material requirement of crimes against humanity by both Tribunals[43] and the ICC Statute (article 7, paragraph 2 (a) ICC Statute), but which is not a material element of genocide.[44]

In our view, Judge Khan was correct. The accused was guilty of genocide *and* crimes against humanity and that the majority erred in law, when it held that crimes against humanity could be "completely subsumed" by genocide. Accordingly, the four counts of genocide and crimes against humanity with regard to Kayishema (and *mutatis mutandis,* for Ruzindana) should be seen as one single genocide – because all the four counts were attacks on the same group and motivated by the same genocidal intent[45] – and as several crimes against humanity (according to the number of victims). The question whether separate crimes against humanity concur or accumulate among each other or in relation to genocide is not relevant to the sentence (as discussed below) and will not be the subject of further consideration in this context.[46]

The consequences of merger, concurrence and accumulation of offences for the sentence

Judge Khan proposes concurrent penalties if there is a "concurrence" of offences, without distinguishing between merger and concurrence.[47] This approach is too simplistic since there is a fundamental difference between merger and concurrence: whereas in cases of merger one norm is sufficient to describe the unlawfulness of a conduct, in cases of concurrence (and accumulation), according to the very definition of the term, all the concurring norms are required to adequately describe the conduct. It clearly makes a difference whether a perpetrator commits one crime (for example one killing) or two or more crimes (two or more killings). This difference should also be reflected in the sentence.[48]

a)   Concurrence and accumulation of offences: a necessary distinction?

[41]   Jelisić *supra* note 39, par. 100; cf. also Akayesu *supra* note 16, par. 497.

[42]   Cf. also *supra* note 32. In the Preparatory Commission's draft of the Elements of Crimes for the ICC, a material context element was included following U.S. pressure. The compatibility of this element with the Statute is highly questionable, cf. Article 9, paragraph 3 ICC Statute. However, there is still a difference between the context element of crimes against humanity and the US-sponsored genocidal context element, since (unlike the former) the latter is drafted in such a way that, in principle, it requires no *mens rea*. The last element to all paragraphs of genocide reads: "The [genocidal] conduct took place in the context of a manifest pattern of similar conduct directed against that group or was conduct that could itself effect such destruction". The Introduction to the Elements of Genocide reads: "With respect to the last element listed for each crime: [...] - Notwithstanding the normal requirement for a mental element provided for in article 30, and recognizing that knowledge of the circumstances will usually be addressed in proving genocidal intent, the appropriate requirement, if any, for a mental element regarding this circumstance will need to be decided by the Court on a case by case basis." (see UN-Doc. PCNICC/2000/INF/3/Add.2; <http://www.un.org/law/icc/statute/elements/main.htm>).

[43]   E.g. Kayishema, *supra* note 3, par. 124 *et seq.* Judgement, *Prosecutor v. Kupreškić et. al.,* Case No. IT-95-16-T, 14 January 2000, par. 551. On the policy element see also Robinson, Defining crimes against humanity at the Rome conference, 93 American Journal of International Law 1999, p.43, 48 *et. seq.*; Swaak-Goldman, Crimes against humanity, in: McDonald/Swaak-Goldman (eds.), Substantive and procedural aspects of International Criminal Law. Volume I. The Hague et al. 2000, p. 141-168, at 158-9; McAuliffe de Guzman, The road from Rome: The developing law of crimes against humanity, 22 Human Rights Quarterly 2000, p.335, 368 *et seq*; on the history of the policy element see: Hwang, Defining crimes against humanity in the Rome Statute of the International Criminal Court, 22 Fordham International Law Journal 1998, p. 457 and *passim*.

[44]   The majority overlooks the fact that the policy element constitutes a material element rather than just being a special intent requirement; cf. Kayishema, *supra* note 3, par. 634.

[45]   The verdict as well as the opinion of Judge Khan (Kayishema, Dissenting Opinion of Judge Khan, *supra* note 4, par. 54 *et seq.*) list four counts of genocide and pronounces Kayishema guilty for all four counts.

[46]   Cf. on this question Gil Gil, *supra* note 14, p. 791 *et seq.*

[47]   Judge Khan uses the term "concurrence" not only when he develops his own opinion about the relationship between genocide and crimes against humanity (Kayishema, Dissenting Opinion of Judge Khan, *supra* note 4, par. 32 *et seq.*), but also when he addresses the Chamber's solution (*ibid.* par. 6 *et seq.*).

[48]   National jurisdictions tend to impose elevated penalties on perpetrators who have violated more than one crime by a single conduct (cf. *infra* note 14).

While the difference between merger and concurrence seems obvious, it is questionable whether there should be a distinction between concurrence (*Idealkonkurrenz*) and accumulation of offences (*Realkonkurrenz*). Both are similar in that they address a multitude of offences but differ in that concurrence deals with a single conduct whereas accumulation deals with multiple conduct.

A survey of national jurisdictions does not shed much light on the question since the existence of this distinction in many jurisdictions[49] does neither explain the way in which it is drawn[50] nor the consequences attached to it.

In German law, according to § 52 StGB (which contains the so called absorption principle), the concurrence of offences results in a punishment according to the statutory range (or sentencing tariff) of punishment provided for the gravest offence committed; however, the fact that the conduct violated several norms is taken into consideration for the determination of the actual sentence.[51] In cases of accumulation of offences, a "unified" or "comprehensive" sentence (Gesamtstrafe) is determined. It must be higher than the sentence incurred for the gravest offence but lower than the sum of all sentences (§ 54 StGB). In practice such sentences are usually much lower than the law allows. Italian law is stricter. In the case of concurrence of laws, the sentence can be tripled (art. 81 Italian Criminal Code). In the case of accumulation of offences the sentences are added (art. 72 *et seq.* Italian Criminal Code). Rwandan law allows in cases of concurrence, a 50%-increase of the maximum penalty provided for the gravest crime and in cases of accumulation for a doubling of this penalty (art. 93, 94 par. 2 Rwandan Criminal Code). British law, in principle, imposes concurrent penalties (i.e. the longest sentence governs) in cases of concurrence and cumulative penalties in cases of accumulation, but provides for many exceptions in which it treats concurrence like accumulation, imposing consecutive sentences.[52] On the other hand Anglo-American sentencing practice in cases of accumulation is characterised by extensive judicial discretion;[53] only recently have the U.S. Federal Sentencing Guidelines provided for a specific procedure to determine the sentences in cases of multiple convictions and endorsed unified "punishment" on the basis of a "combined" offence level.[54]

The only tendency that can be discerned from the practice of national jurisdictions is that accumulated crimes are often punished more severely than the same crimes in a case of concurrence. However, there are also several other jurisdictions, including Austria, Switzerland and Yugoslavia, that treat concurrence and accumulation identically.[55] As will be seen below, Article 78, paragraph 3 of the ICC Statute does not differentiate either.

In our view, it is difficult to argue convincingly for the distinction to be drawn between concurrence (*Idealkonkurrenz*) and accumulation of offences (*Realkonkurrenz*). No different conclusion should be drawn as to the guilt or danger of a perpetrator who has killed five people at the same time with a bomb or has killed each of them on five subsequent days with a gun.[56] In the latter case he may have been too

---

[49]   E.g. §§ 52, 53 StGB; art. 71 *et seq.* Italian Criminal Code; art. 39 *et seq.* Rwandan Criminal Code (Code Penal); British case law is not very clear on this issue but in general seems to draw the said distinction as well, applying a "single transaction" standard (A. Ashworth, Sentencing and criminal justice, 2nd ed. 1995, at p.205-206).

[50]   Italy, for example, treats the cases of concurrence of offences and the accumulated multiple violation of the same provision in the same way (art. 81 Italian Criminal Code) whereas the German StGB treats the multiple commission of the same crime in the same way as accumulation of different offences (§ 53 par. 1).

[51]   Cf. Stree, in: Schönke/Schröder, *supra* note 10, § 52 mn 47.

[52]   Ashworth, *supra* note 49, p. 204-05.

[53]   See A. Campell, Law of Sentencing, 2nd ed. 1991 (suppl. 1999), § 9: 10, 9: 12.

[54]   U.S. Sentencing Guidelines, reprinted in U.S. Code Annotated (1996 and subsequent supplements), in particular Part D, Introductory Commentary. Cf. also Jescheck/Weigend, Lehrbuch des Strafrechts. Allgemeiner Teil, 4th ed. Berlin, 1996, at 725.

[55]   § 28 Austrian Criminal Code; art. 68 Swiss Criminal Code; art. 48 SFRY Criminal Code (English translation in Kupreskić, *supra* note 7, note 992).

[56]   As has been shown, German law in principle, treats concurrence and accumulation differently. There are, however, several cases in which the courts and the jurisprudence have had recourse to exceptions to achieve more appropriate results (cf. Rissing-van Saan, *supra* note 10, before §§ 52 *et seq.*, mn 42 *et seq.* – *Fortsetzungszusammenhang*; *ibid.* § 52, mn 29 – exceptions from the so called *Klammerwirkung*). These exceptions show that the distinction between concurrence and accumulation is not an appropriate means to determine the sentence. Indeed, even in Austria, a state with a criminal law framework very similar to Germany, concurrence and accumulation are treated the same way (*supra* note 55).

scrupulous to make up his mind to kill all the five at once, whereas in the former case he could have coolly calculated the most efficient way to achieve his criminal purpose.

b)   Sentencing

The question as to what (elevated) penalties should be imposed in cases of concurrence or accumulation is difficult to answer on an abstract level because each national jurisdiction seems to treat this problem differently.[57] In any case, the inflexible all-or-nothing approach[58] that underlies the imposition of either concurrently or consecutively served sentences cannot be based on the Statutes of the *ad hoc* Tribunals, but is judge made law based on the Rules.[59]

In this sense the approach taken by the ICTY in Kupreškić is certainly preferable. The Trial Chamber ruled that the sentence incurred for the gravest crime could be increased if "the less serious offence committed by the same conduct significantly adds to the heinous nature of the prevailing offence."[60] However, this solution, which admittedly was determined only by considerations of fairness and soundness,[61] is itself not free from criticism. Firstly, the Chamber seems to apply it only to cases of concurrence (*Idealkonkurrenz*), thereby maintaining a differentiation between concurrence and accumulation (*Realkonkurrenz*). Secondly it is not clear why an elevation of the sentence should be dependent on whether the less serious offence significantly adds to the heinous nature of the prevailing offence. It seems more convincing to build the argument that the simple fact that the perpetrator has committed more than one crime, violating more than one legally protected value, is sufficient to consider him a more dangerous person than a perpetrator who commits only one crime.

Against this background Article 78, paragraph 3 of the ICC Statute[62] offers an even more convincing solution than Kupreškić, because it avoids both of these criticisms: It does not differentiate between concurrence and accumulation of offences since it refers (and is the only provision in the Statute to do so) to convictions for "more than one crime" i.e. the commission of multiple offences interrelated either by concurrence or accumulation. Moreover, this provision establishes "the highest individual sentence" as the minimum and thereby supports the argument that, as a rule, a sentence more severe than "the highest individual sentence" should be pronounced. Such an elevated sentence seems to be the most adequate answer to the multiple violation of legally protected values. As to the details of the formation of the penalty, the article provides for a solution very similar to the "comprehensive" sentence (*Gesamtstrafe*) imposed by German law in cases of accumulation (§ 54 StGB; see *supra* a.) without, however, attaching to this method of calculation the German distinction between *Ideal- und Realkonkurrenz*.

Some further remarks on the Kayishema Sentence

Purposes of sentencing

The Chamber considers retribution as one of the purposes of sentencing.[63] Although this reflects the general position of the *ad hoc* Tribunals, this appears problematic for at least two reasons. On the one hand, modern theories of punishment do not consider retribution as one of the purposes of punishment

---

[57]   Cf. *supra* notes 49-55; this is also observed by the Trial Chamber in Kupreškić, *supra* note 7, par. 717.

[58]   This approach goes back to the Common Law (cf. Ashworth *supra* note 49, p.204 *et seq.*) but, as mentioned, even this system now takes different concepts into consideration (*ibid.* p.209 *et seq.*). Moreover, to our knowledge there has been no judgement of the *ad hoc* Tribunals that has imposed consecutive penalties.

[59]   Cf. Rule 101 (c) which is common to both Tribunals' Rules of Procedure and Evidence.

[60]   Kupreškić, *supra* note 7, par. 718.

[61]   Kupreškić, *supra* note 7, par. 717-718.

[62]   The paragraph reads: "Art. 78 [...] (3) When a person has been convicted of more than one crime, the Court shall pronounce a sentence for each crime and a joint sentence specifying the total period of imprisonment. This period shall be no less than the highest individual sentence pronounced and shall not exceed 30 years imprisonment or a sentence of life imprisonment in conformity with article 77, paragraph 1 (b)." Art. 68 Swiss Criminal Code is very similar to this provision in that it also imposes an elevated penalty if multiple crimes are committed regardless of whether they concur or accumulate.

[63]   Sentencing Judgement, *Prosecutor v. Kayishema and Ruzindana,* Case No. ICTR-95-1-T, 21 May 1999, par. 2. – For a general view on the purposes of punishment in international criminal law see Ambos/ Steiner, Vom Sinn des Strafens auf innerstaatlicher und supranationaler Ebene, 40 Juristische Schulung 2000 (forthcoming).

since it has no preventive impact on the conduct of the perpetrator or of society as a whole. On the other hand, it is difficult to see how an organ established by the Security Council can invoke a purpose which does not fall within the mandate of the Security Council. The Security Council has the competence to carry out measures for the maintenance of international peace. The organ which is established by such a measure cannot have a different competence from the Security Council itself (*nemo dat quod non habet*). While other purposes of punishment, for example deterrence, rehabilitation and the protection of society, can certainly contribute to the protection of peace, it is inconceivable that retribution may assist this purpose.

Aggravating circumstances

Among the aggravating circumstances mentioned by the Chamber, two deserve special attention. First, the Chamber considers the voluntary commission of a crime – without giving any reasons[64] – as an aggravating circumstance.[65] However, every crime of which the accused can be found guilty in the present case must be committed with intent. According to legal doctrine and, in particular, the ICC Statute, a person has intent if he or she "means to engage in [a certain] conduct" (Article 30, paragraph 2 (a) ICC Statute) i.e. if he or she wants to commit this crime. Thus the Chamber seems to also use the mental element, necessary for the establishment of criminal responsibility on a substantive level, on the sentencing level to increase the average penalty. Such a "double use" is hardly compatible with the principle of guilt and is therefore prohibited under international, as well as most national criminal laws.[66]

Secondly, the Chamber considers Kayishema's denial of guilt as an aggravating circumstance,[67] quoting the Tadic sentencing judgement in support of its opinion. In that decision, however, it was stated that Tadic "has at all times denied his guilt [...]. Consequently, he is not entitled to any mitigation pursuant to the terms of Rule 101(B)(ii)".[68] Further, it must be recalled that the denial of guilt is a fundamental right of the accused known as the Latin maxim of *nemo tenetur se ipsum accusare*.[69] If the invocation of this right, however, gives rise to an aggravation of the sentence, the accused is effectively deprived of this right since he is left with the choice of confessing or facing a longer sentence.

Kai Ambos and Steffen Wirth

---

[64] The Chamber merely quotes another case (Sentencing Judgement, *Prosecutor v. Serushago*, Case No. ICTR-98-39-S, 5 February 1999, par. 30) where also without reasons the same assertion is made.

[65] Kayishema, Sentencing Judgement, *supra* note 63, par. 13.

[66] For the German law see Stree, in: Schönke/Schröder, *supra* note 10, § 46 mn 45.

[67] Kayishema, Sentencing Judgement, *supra* note 63, par. 16.

[68] Sentencing Judgement, *Prosecutor v. Tadić*, Case No. IT-94-1, 14 July 1997, par. 58 (emphasis added).

[69] See Article 14, paragraph 3 (g) of the International Covenant on Civil and Political Rights that reads that no one must be "compelled [...] to confess guilt".

International Criminal Tribunal for Rwanda
Tribunal Pénal International pour le Rwanda

Trial Chamber I

THE PROSECUTOR

VERSUS

GEORGES ANDERSON NDERUBUMWE RUTAGANDA

Case No. ICTR-96-3-T

JUDGEMENT AND SENTENCE

[page 1] **TABLE OF CONTENTS**

[page 3] 1. INTRODUCTION

1.1 The International Tribunal

1.   This Judgement is rendered by Trial Chamber 1 of the International Criminal Tribunal for Rwanda (the "Tribunal") composed of Judge Laïty Kama, presiding, Judge Lennart Aspegren, and Judge Navanethem Pillay, in the case of *The Prosecutor v. Georges Anderson Nderubumwe Rutaganda.*

2.   The Tribunal was established by the United Nations Security Council, pursuant to resolution 955 of 8 November 1994, after it had considered United Nations Reports[1] which indicated that genocide and systematic, widespread and flagrant violations of international humanitarian law had been committed in Rwanda. The Security Council determined that this situation constituted a threat to international peace and security, and was convinced that the prosecution of persons responsible for serious violations of international humanitarian law would contribute tot the process of national reconciliation and to the restoration and maintenance of peace in Rwanda. The Security Council established the Tribunal, under Chapter VII of the United Nations Charter.

3.   The Tribunal is governed by its Statute (the "Statute") annexed to Security Council Resolution 955, and by its Rules of Procedure and Evidence (the "Rules"), which were adopted by the Judges, on 5 July 1995 and subsequently amended.[2] **[page 4]**

1.2 The Indictment

4.   The Indictment (the "Indictment") against Georges Anderson Nderubumwe Rutaganda (the "Accused") was submitted by the Prosecutor on 13 February 1996 and was confirmed on 16 February 1996. The Indictment is set out here in full:

"The Prosecutor of the International Criminal Tribunal for Rwanda, pursuant to his authority under Article 17 of the Statute of the Tribunal charges:

GEORGES ANDERSON NDERUBUMWE RUTAGANDA

with **GENOCIDE, CRIMES AGAINST HUMANITY** and **VIOLATIONS OF ARTICLE 3 COMMON TO THE GENEVA CONVENTIONS,** as set forth below:

Background

1.   On April 6, 1994, a plane carrying President Juvenal Habyarimana of Rwanda and President Cyprien Ntaryamira of Burundi crashed at Kigali airport, killing all on board. Following the deaths of the two Presidents, widespread killings, having both political and ethnic dimensions, began in Kigali and spread to other parts of Rwanda.

The Accused

2.   Georges RUTAGANDA, born in 1958 in Masango commune, Gitarama prefecture, was an agricultural engineer and businessman; he was general manager and proprietor of Rutaganda SARL. Georges RUTAGANDA was also a member of the National and Prefectoral Committees of the

---

[1]   Preliminary Report of the Commission of Experts established pursuant to Security Council resolution 935 (1994), Final Report of the Commission of Experts established pursuant to Security Council resolution 935 (1994) (Document S/1994/1405) and Reports of the Special Rapporteur for Rwanda of the United Nations Commission on Human Rights (Document S/1994/1157, annexes I and II).

[2]   The Rules were successively amended on 12 January 1996, 15 May 1996, 4 July 1996, 5 June 1997, 8 June 1998, and 4 June 1999.

Mouvement Républicain National pour le Développement et la Démocratie (hereinafter, "MRND") and a shareholder of *Radio Télévision Libre des Mille Collines*. On April 6, 1994, he was serving as the second vice president of the National Committee of the **[page 5]** Interahamwe, the youth militia of the MRND.

General Allegations

3.   Unless otherwise specified, all acts set forth in this indictment took place between 1 January 1994 and 31 December 1994 in the prefectures of Kigali and Gitarama, territory of Rwanda.

4.   In each paragraph charging genocide, a crime recognized by Article 2 of the Statute of the Tribunal, the alleged acts were committed with intent to destroy, in whole or in part, a national, ethnical or racial group.

5.   The victims in each paragraph charging genocide were members of a national, ethnical, racial or religious group.

6.   In each paragraph charging crimes against humanity, crimes punishable by Article 3 of the Statute of the Tribunal, the alleged acts were committed as part of a widespread or systematic attack against a civilian population on political, ethnic or racial grounds.

7.   At all times relevant to this indictment, a state of internal armed conflict existed in Rwanda.

8.   The victims referred to in this indictment were, at all relevant times, persons taking no active part in the hostilities.

9.   The accused is individually responsible for the crimes alleged in this indictment. Under Article 6(1) of the Statute of the Tribunal, individual criminal responsibility is attributable to one who plans, instigates, orders, commits or otherwise aids and abets in the planning, preparation or execution of any of the crimes referred to in Articles 2 to 4 of the Statute of the Tribunal. **[page 6]**

Charges

10.   On or about April 6, 1994, Georges RUTAGANDA distributed guns and other weapons to Interahamwe members in Nyarugenge commune, Kigali.

11.   On or about April 10, 1994, Georges RUTAGANDA stationed Interahamwe members at a roadblock near his office at the "Amgar" garage in Kigali. Shortly after he left the area, the Interahamwe members started checking identity cards of people passing the roadblock. The Interahamwe members ordered persons with Tutsi identity cards to stand on one side of the road. Eight of the Tutsis were then killed. The victims included men, women and an infant who had been carried on the back of one of the women.

12.   In April 1994, on a date unknown, Tutsis who had been separated at a roadblock in front of the Amgar garage were taken to Georges RUTAGANDA and questioned by him. He thereafter directed that these Tutsis be detained with others at a nearby building. Later, Georges RUTAGANDA directed men under his control to take 10 Tutsi detainees to a deep, open hole near the Amgar garage. On Georges RUTAGANDA's orders, his men killed the 10 Tutsis with machetes and threw their bodies into the hole.

13.   From April 7 to April 11, 1994, thousands of unarmed Tutsi men, women and children and some unarmed Hutus sought refuge at the Ecole Technique Officielle ("ETO school") in Kicukiro sector, Kicukiro commune. The ETO school was considered a safe haven because Belgian soldiers, part of the United Nations Assistance Mission for Rwanda forces, were stationed there.

14.   On or about April 11, 1994, immediately after the Belgians withdrew from the ETO school, members of the Rwandan armed forces, the gendarmerie and militia, including the Interahamwe, attacked the ETO school and, using machetes, grenades and guns, killed the people who had sought refuge there. The Interahamwe separated Hutus from Tutsis during the attack, killing the **[page 7]** Tutsis. Georges RUTAGANDA participated in the attack at the ETO school, which resulted in the deaths of a large number of Tutsis.

15.   The men, women and children who survived the ETO school attack were forcibly transferred by Georges RUTAGANDA, members of the Interahamwe and soldiers to a gravel pit near the primary school of Nyanza. Presidential Guard members awaited their arrival. More Interahamwe members converged upon Nyanza from many directions and surrounded the group of survivors.

16.   On or about April 12, 1994, the survivors who were able to show that they were Hutu were permitted to leave the gravel pit. Tutsis who presented altered identity cards were immediately killed. Most of the remainder of the group were attacked and killed by grenades or shot to death. Those who tried to escape were attacked with machetes. Georges RUTAGANDA, among others, directed and participated in these attacks.

17.   In April of 1994, on dates unknown, in Masango commune, Georges RUTAGANDA and others known to the Prosecutor conducted house-to-house searches for Tutsis and their families. Throughout these searches, Tutsis were separated from Hutus and taken to a river. Georges RUTAGANDA instructed the Interahamwe to track all the Tutsis and throw them into the river.

18.   On or about April 28, 1994, Georges RUTAGANDA, together with Interahamwe members, collected residents from Kigali and detained them near the Amgar garage. Georges RUTAGANDA and the Interahamwe demanded identity cards from the detainees. A number of persons, including Emmanuel Kayitare, were forcibly separated from the group. Later that day, Emmanuel Kayitare attempted to flee from where he was being detained and Georges RUTAGANDA pursued him, caught him and struck him on the head with a machete and killed him.

19.   In June 1994, on a date unknown, Georges RUTAGANDA ordered people to bury the bodies of victims in order to conceal his crimes from the international community. **[page 8]**

Counts 1-2

(Genocide)

(Crimes Against Humanity)

By his acts in relation to the events described in paragraphs 10-19 Georges RUTAGANDA committed:

COUNT 1:   **GENOCIDE,** punishable by Article 2(3)(a) of the Statute of the Tribunal; and

COUNT 2:   **CRIMES AGAINST HUMANITY** (extermination) punishable by Article 3(b) of the Statute of the Tribunal.

Counts 3-4

(Crimes Against Humanity)

(Violations of Article 3 common to the Geneva Conventions)

By his acts in relation to the killings at the ETO school, as described in paragraph 14, Georges RUTAGANDA committed:

COUNT 3:   **CRIMES AGAINST HUMANITY** (murder) punishable by Article 3(a) of the Statute of the Tribunal; and

COUNT 4:   **VIOLATIONS OF ARTICLE 3 COMMON TO THE GENEVA CONVENTIONS,** as incorporated by Article 4(a) (murder) of the Statute of the Tribunal. **[page 9]**

Counts 5-6

(Crimes Against Humanity)

(Violations of Article 3 common to the Geneva Conventions)

By his acts in relation to the killings at the gravel pit in Nyanza, as described in paragraphs 15 and 16, Georges RUTAGANDA committed:

COUNT 5:   **CRIMES AGAINST HUMANITY** (murder) punishable by Article 3(a) of the Statute of the Tribunal; and

COUNT 6:   **VIOLATIONS OF ARTICLE 3 COMMON TO THE GENEVA CONVENTIONS,** as incorporated by Article 4(a) (murder) of the Statute of the Tribunal.

Counts 7-8

(Crime Against Humanity)

(Violation of Article 3 common to the Geneva Conventions)

By killing Emmanuel Kayitare, as described in paragraph 18, Georges RUTAGANDA committed:

COUNT 7:   **CRIME AGAINST HUMANITY** (murder) punishable by Article 3(a) of the Statute of the Tribunal; and **[page 10]**

COUNT 8:   **VIOLATION OF ARTICLE 3 COMMON TO THE GENEVA CONVENTIONS,** as incorporated by Article 4(a) (murder) of the Statute of the Tribunal. **[page 11]**

_____(Signed)

Richard J. Goldstone

Prosecutor; Kigali

12 February 1996"

1.3 Procedural Background

5.   On 13 February 1996 the Prosecutor submitted an Indictment against Georges Rutaganda for confirmation, pursuant to Article 17 of the Statute of the Tribunal.

6.   On 16 February 1996, Judge William H. Sekule, after having reviewed the Indictment and accompanying supporting material, confirmed the Indictment against the Accused, pursuant to Articles 18 of the Statute and Rule 47 of the Rules. On the same day the learned Judge issued a Warrant of Arrest for the Accused, which requested the Republic of Zambia to transfer the Accused to the custody of the Tribunal. The Accused was subsequently transferred to the Tribunal detention facility in Arusha, Tanzania, on 26 May 1996.

7.   The Accused made his initial appearance before the Tribunal on 30 May 1996, pursuant to Rule 62 of the Rules, and he was formally charged. At this hearing the Accused was represented by Counsel, and he pleaded not guilty to all the counts in the Indictment.

8.   On 8 September 1996, the Defence filed an extremely urgent motion requesting the postponement of all criminal proceedings against the Accused and the provisional release of the Accused, due to his state of health. The Chamber subsequently held that the Defence had not satisfied the provisions of

Rule 65 of the Rules and denied this motion. Due to the ill health of the Accused, the Chamber adjourned the commencement of trial to 6 March 1997.[3]

9.   On 6 December 1996, the Defence filed another motion requesting the provisional release of the Accused, on the grounds of the Accused's state of ill health and his need for medical treatment. The Chamber denied this motion and held that the Tribunal was able to provide adequate medical care to the Accused, and that there had been neither serious regression in his **[page 12]** medical condition nor had other exceptional circumstances arisen which justified his provisional release.

10.   The Accused requested the assignment of Counsel to represent him. The Registrar, after having established that the Accused was indigent, assigned Counsels Luc De Temmerman and Tiphaine Dickson to represent him. However, on 25 August 1997, the Accused requested the withdrawal of Mr. Luc De Temmerman, stating that he had lost confidence in the said Counsel because he had failed to provide sufficient legal and strategic support to his defence. Mr. De Temmerman Subsequently withdrew and the Accused was represented by Ms Tiphaine Dickson throughout the trial. The Prosecutor was represented during the trial by Mr. James Stewart, Mr. Udo Herbert Gehring and Ms Holo Makwaia.

11.   On 6 March 1997, the Chamber adjourned the trial for two weeks, following a request to this effect from the Prosecutor. The trial commenced on 18 March 1997. Twenty seven prosecution witnesses, including five experts, testified before the Prosecutor closed her case on 29 May 1998. The Defence case commenced on 8 February 1999. Fourteen witnesses, including three experts, testified on behalf of the Defence. The Defence closed its case on 23 April 1999. The Parties presented their closing submissions on 16 and 17 June 1999.

12.   During the course of the pre-trial and trial stages of the criminal proceeding, the Parties filed many motions on various procedural and substantive issues, including motions for disclosure of witness statements, a motion requesting that the deposition of sixteen witnesses be given by means of a video conference, pursuant to Rule 71 of the Rules, and a motion pertaining to the false testimony of a witness.

13.   Both Parties filed motions, requesting protective measures for their witnesses, pursuant to Article 19 and 21 of the Statute and Rule 69 an 75 of the Rules. The Chamber granted these motions and ordered *inter alia* that the names, addresses and other identifying information of the witnesses shall not be disclosed to the media and public, the witnesses will be assigned **[page 13]** pseudonyms and they will be referred to by these pseudonyms in all criminal proceedings before the Chamber and in discussions with the Parties. Therefore, most of the witnesses referred to in this Judgement are referred to by their assigned pseudonyms.

14.   In her closing arguments, the Prosecutor requested an amendment of the time periods alleged in paragraphs 10, 16 and 19 of the Indictment. The Chamber finds the Prosecutor's request inadmissable. **[page 14]**

1.4 Evidentiary Matters

15.   The Chamber finds that it is necessary to address certain issues relevant to the assessment of the evidence presented at trial.

16.   The Chamber notes that Rule 89(A) of the Rules provides that it is not bound by the rules of procedure and evidence of any particular national jurisdiction and concurs with the finding in the Judgement in *The Prosecutor v. Jean-Paul Akayesu* (the "*Akayesu Judgement*") which held:

"[...] the Chamber [...] is not restricted under the Statute of the Tribunal to apply any particular legal system and is not bound by any national rules of evidence"[4].

---

[3]   Decision on the Request Submitted by the Defence, *The Prosecutor v. Georges Rutaganda,* Case No. ICTR-96-3-T, 25 September 1996.
[4]   *The Prosecutor v. Jean-Paul Akayesu* (Case No. ICTR-96-4-T); Judgement of 2 September 1998, para. 131.

17.   In all pre-trial and trial proceedings and in the admission and evaluation of all evidence and exhibits presented at the trial, the Chamber has applied the Rules in a manner best favoured to a fair determination of the matter before it, and which is consonant with the spirit of the Statute and the general principles of law.

18.   The Chamber notes that, pursuant to Rule 96(i) of the Rules, no corroboration of the victim's testimony is required in the case of rape and sexual violence. The Chamber concurs with both the *Akayesu Judgement*[5] and the judgement of the International Criminal Tribunal for the former Yugoslavia in *The Prosecutor v. Dusko Tadić*, (the *"Tadić Judgement"*)[6], judgements which held that the fact that Rules stipulate that corroboration of the victims testimony is not required for crimes of sexual assault, does not justify the inference that corroboration of witnesses' testimony is, in fact, required, for other crimes. The Chamber's approach is that it will **[page 15]** rely on the evidence of a single witness, provided such evidence is relevant, admissible and credible. Pursuant to Rule 89 of the Rules, the Chamber may assess all relevant evidence which it deems to have probative value. The Rules do not exclude hearsay evidence, and the Chamber has the discretion to consider such evidence. Where the Chamber decides to consider such evidence, it is inclined to do so with caution.

19.   The Chamber notes that during the trial, the Prosecutor and the Defence relied on pre-trial statements from witnesses for the purposes of direct and cross-examination. In many instances, inconsistencies and contradictions between the pre-trial statements of witnesses and their testimonies at trial were pointed out by the Defence. The Chamber concurs with the reasoning in the *Akayesu Judgement*, which held:

> "[...]these pre-trial statements were composed following interviews with witnesses by investigators of the Office of the Prosecutor. These interviews were mostly conducted in Kinyarwanda, and the Chamber did not have access to transcripts of the interviews, but only translations thereof. It was therefore unable to consider the nature and form of the questions put to the witnesses, or the accuracy of interpretation at the time. The Chamber has considered inconsistencies and contradictions between these statements and testimony at trial with caution for these reasons, and in the light of the time lapse between the statements and the presentation of evidence at trial, the difficulties of recollecting precise details several years after the occurrence of the events, the difficulties of translation, and the fact that several witnesses were illiterate and stated that they had not read their written statements. Moreover, the statements were not made under solemn declaration and were not taken by judicial officers. In the circumstances, the probative value attached to the statements is, in the Chamber's view, considerably less than direct sworn testimony before the Chamber, the truth of which has been subjected to the test of **[page 16]** cross-examination."[7]

20.   During the trial proceedings, the Defence filed motions requesting investigations of alleged false testimony against two of the Prosecutor's witnesses. These motions were dismissed by the Chamber and this decision was appealed by the Defence. The Appeals Chamber dismissed these appeals. This Chamber reaffirms its position that false testimony is a deliberate offence which requires wilful intent on the part of the perpetrator to mislead the Judge and thus to cause harm[8]. The onus is on the party pleading a case of false testimony to prove the falsehood of the witness' statements and to establish that they were made with harmful intent, or, at least, that they were made by a witness who was fully aware that they were false. To only raise doubt as to the credibility of the statements made by the witness is not sufficient to reasonably demonstrate that the witness may have knowingly and wilfully given false testimony. In the Chamber's view, false testimony cannot be based solely on inaccurate statements made by the witness, but rather requires wilful intent to give false testimony. The Appeals Chamber pointed out that there is a clear distinction between the credibility of witness testimony and false testimony of a witness. The

---

[5]   *Akayesu Judgement*, para. 134.
[6]   *The Prosecutor v. Dusko Tadić* (Case No. IT-94-1-T) Judgement of 7 May 1997, para. 535 to 539.
[7]   *Akayesu Judgement*, para. 134.
[8]   *The Prosecutor v. Georges Anderson Nderubumwe Rutaganda*, (Case No. ICTR-96-3-T) Decision on the Defence Motion to Direct the Prosecutor to Investigate the Matter of False Testimony by Witness E.

testimony of a witness may lack credibility, but this does not necessarily mean that it amounts to false testimony falling within the ambit of Rule 91[9].

21.   The Chamber notes the Defence submission that some of the Prosecution witnesses are unreliable because they testified to events that they previously heard other people talk about, and that therefore the Prosecution's case is marred by "contamination". The Defence also submitted **[page 17]** that some of the evidence was obtained by illegal means, which rendered it inadmissible[10]. The Chamber finds that this is neither a matter of "contamination", nor of "illegal means of collecting information", but of hearsay.

22.   Many of the witnesses who testified before the Chamber in this case have seen atrocities committed against members of their families and close friends and/or have themselves been the victims of such atrocities. Some of these witnesses became very emotional and cried in the witnessbox, when they were questioned about certain events. A few witnesses displayed physical signs of fear and pain when they were asked about certain atrocities of which they were victims. The Chamber has taken into consideration these factors in assessing the evidence of such witnesses.

23.   The Chamber has also taken into consideration various social and cultural factors in assessing the testimony of some of the witnesses. Some of these witnesses were farmers and people who dit not have a high standard of education, and they had difficulty in identifying and testifying to some of the exhibits, such as photographs of various locations, maps etc. These witnesses also experienced difficulty in testifying as to dates, times, distances, colours and motor vehicles. In this regard, the Chamber also notes that many of the witnesses testified in Kinyarwanda and as such their testimonies were simultaneously translated into French and English. As a result, the essence of the witnesses' testimonies was at times lost. Counsel questioned witnesses in either English or French, and these questions were simultaneously translated to the witnesses in Kinyarwanda. In some instances it was evident, after translation, that the witnesses had not understood the questions. **[page 18]**

1.5 The Accused

24.   On 8 April 1999, the Accused testified that he was born on 28 November 1958 in Ngoma, in Gishyita *Commune*, Kibuye *Préfecture* in Rwanda. He grew up in Gitarama and Kibuye *Préfecture*, before studying and working in Butare and Kigali *Préfectures*.

25.   The Accused testified that his father, Esdras Mpamo, held many civil, public and political offices and government appointments, such as the Prefect of Kibuye, Cyangugu, and Butare *Préfectures*, the Rwandese Ambassador to Uganda and Germany and the Bourgmestre of Masango *Commune*, in the Gitarama *Préfecture*. The Accused testified that although he traveled a lot he considered his origin to be Masango *Commune* in the Gitarama *Préfecture* because his father was the Bourgmestre in this *Commune*, and he returned there throughout his youth. The Accused also testified that his father was a devout Seventh Day Adventist, and that his father's religious and political beliefs significantly influenced his upbringing and subsequent political decisions.

26.   The Accused testified that he is married and he is a father of three children. He stated that he received a degree in agricultural engineering in 1985, from National University of Rwanda and thereafter he was appointed agricultural engineer. He stated that as an agricultural engineer, he conducted agricultural research and he managed a farm which served as a model farm to the farmers of Huye *Commune*. According to the Accused, he was allowed to purchase this farm by virtue of a Presidential decree.

27.   The Accused testified that he applied to the Agricultural Ministry to be transferred from Butare in 1991, because of threats he had received from certain people in the Huye *Commune*, following his

---

[9]   *The Prosecutor v. Georges Anderson Nderubumwe Rutaganda*, (Case No. ICTR-96-3-T) Decision on Appeals against the Decisions by Trial Chamber I Rejecting the Defence Motions to Direct the Prosecutor to Investigate the Matter of False Testimony by witness "E" and "CC", 8 June 1998, para. 28.
[10]   See the Defence submissions, transcripts of 17 June 1996.

purchase of the farm that he managed. He stated that he was subsequently transferred to a post with the Rwandese Ministry of Agriculture in Kigali, although his family remained in Butare. **[page 19]**

28.   The Accused testified that, in June 1991, he commenced work as a business man in Kigali, dealing with import, under the name of Rutuganda SARL. He stated that Rutaganda SARL was a highly profitable enterprise, and maintained exclusive imports and distribution agreements with a number of European food and beverage producers, as well as exclusive supply agreements with smaller bars, distributors, and organizations in Rwanda.

29.   The Accused testified that he joined the MRND on or about September or October 1991. He stated that various political parties offered him membership, but he joined the MRND because he believed that this political party was in a position to provide the best economic and military protection, both of which were significant concerns for him as a business proprietor in Rwanda.

30.   The Accused testified that, after he joined the MRND party in 1991, he became the second vice president of its youth wing, the Interahamwe za MRND. He stated that he was involved in the creation of the Interahamwe za MRND and met regularly with its other leaders. **[page 20]**

2. THE APPLICABLE LAW

2.1 Individual Criminal Responsibility

31.   The Accused is charged under Article 6(1) of the Statute with individual criminal responsibility for the crimes alleged in the Indictment. Article 6(1) provides that:

"A person who planned, instigated, ordered, committed or otherwise aided and abetted in the planning, preparation or execution of a crime referred to in Articles 2 to 4 of the present Statute shall be individually responsible for the crime".

32.   In the *Akayesu Judgement* findings were made on the principle of individual criminal responsibility under Article 6(1) of the Statute. The Chamber notes that these findings are, in the main, the same as those made in the *Tadić Judgement* and in the judgements in *The Prosecutor v. Clément Kayishema and Obed Ruzindana* (the "*Kayishema and Ruzindana Judgement*")[11] and *The Prosecutor versus Zejnil Delalic, Zdravko Mucic, Hazim Delic, Esad Landzo*: '*The Celebici Case*', (the "*Celebici Judgement*")[12]. The Chamber is of the view that the position as derived from the afore-mentioned case law, with respect to the principle of individual criminal responsibility, and as articulated, notably, in the *Akayesu Judgement* is sufficiently established and is applicable in the instant case.

33.   The Chamber notes, that under Article 6(1), an accused person may incur individual criminal responsibility as a result of five forms of participation in the commission of one of the three crimes referred to in the Statute. Article 6(1) covers various stages in the commission **[page 21]** of a crime, ranging from its initial planning to its execution.

34.   The Chamber observes that the principle of individual criminal responsibility under Article 6(1) implies that the planning or preparation of a crime actually leads to its commission. However, the Chamber notes that Article 2(3) of the Statute, on the crime of genocide, provides for prosecution for attempted genocide, among other acts. However, attempt is by definition an inchoate crime, inherent in the criminal conduct *per se* irrespective of its result. Consequently, the Chamber holds that an accused may incur individual criminal responsibility for inchoate offences under Article 2(3) of the Statute and that, conversely, a person engaging in any form of participation in other crimes falling within the

---

[11]   Judgement of the International Criminal Tribunal for Rwanda, Trial Chamber II, *Prosecutor v. Clément Kayishema and Obed Ruzindana*, (Case No. ICTR-95-1-T) 21 May 1999.

[12]   Judgement of the International Criminal Tribunal for the Former Yugoslavia, (Case No. IT-96-21-T) *The Prosecutor v. Zejnil Delalic, Zdravko Mucic, Hazim Delic, Esad Landzo, "The Celebici Case"*, 16 November 1998.

jurisdiction of the Tribunal, such as those covered in Articles 3 and 4 of the Statute, could incur criminal responsibility only if the offence were consummated.

35.   The Chamber finds that in addition to incurring responsibility as a principal offender, the Accused may also be held criminally liable for criminal acts committed by others if, for example, he planned such acts, instigated another to commit them, ordered that they be committed or aided and abetted another in the commission of such acts.

36.   The Chamber defines the five forms of criminal participation under Article 6(1) as follows:

37.   Firstly, in the view of the Chamber, "planning" of a crime implies that one or more persons contemplate designing the commission of a crime at both its preparatory and execution phases.

38.   In the opinion of the Chamber, the second form of participation, that is, incitement to commit an offence, under Article 6(1), involves instigating another, directly and publicly, to commit an offence. Instigation is punishable only where it leads to the actual commission of an **[page 22]** offence desired by the instigator, except with genocide, where an accused may be held individually criminally liable for incitement to commit genocide under Article 2(3)(c) of the Statute, even where such incitement fails to produce a result.[13]

39.   In the opinion of the Chamber, ordering, which is a third form of participation, implies a superior-subordinate relationship between the person giving the order and the one executing it, with the person in a position of authority using such position to persuade another to commit an offence.

40.   Fourthly, an accused incurs criminal responsibility for the commission of a crime, under Article 6(1), where he actually "commits" one of the crimes within the jurisdiction *rationae materiae* of the Tribunal.

41.   The Chamber holds that an accused may participate in the commission of a crime either through direct commission of an unlawful act or by omission, where he has a duty to act.

42.   A fifth and last form of participation where individual criminal responsibility arises under Article 6(1), is "[...] otherwise aid[ing] and abett[ing] in the planning or execution of a crime referred to in Articles 2 to 4".

43.   The Chamber finds that aiding and abetting alone is sufficient to render the accused criminally liable. In both instances, it is not necessary that the person aiding and abetting another to commit an offence be present during the commission of the crime. The relevant act of assistance may be geographically and temporally unconnected to the actual commission of the offence. The Chamber holds that aiding and abetting include all acts of assistance in either physical form or in the form of moral support; nevertheless, it emphasizes that any act of **[page 23]** participation must substantially contribute to the commission of the crime. The aider and abettor assists or facilitates another in the accomplishment of a substantive offence. **[page 24]**

2.2 Genocide (Article 2 of the Statute)

44.   In accordance with the provisions of Article 2(3)(a) of the Statute, which stipulate that the Tribunal shall have the power to prosecute persons responsible for genocide, the Prosecutor has charged the Accused with genocide, Count 1 of the Indictment.

45.   The definition of genocide, as given in Article 2 of the Tribunal's Statute, is taken verbatim from Articles 2 and 3 of the Convention on the Prevention and Punishment of the Crime of Genocide (the "Genocide Convention")[14]. It reads as follows:

---

[13]   *Akayesu Judgement*, para. 562

[14]   The Convention on the Prevention and Punishment of the Crime of Genocide was adopted by the United Nations General Assembly on 9 December 1948.

"Genocide means any of the following acts committed with intent to destroy, in whole or in part, a national, ethnical, racial or religious group, as such:

(a) Killing members of the group;

(b) Causing serious bodily or mental harm to members of the group;

(c) Deliberately inflicting on the group conditions of life calculated to bring about its physical destruction in whole or in part;

(d) Imposing measures intended to prevent births within the group;

(e) Forcibly transferring children of the group to another group." **[page 25]**

46. The Genocide Convention is undeniably considered part of customary international law, as reflected in the advisory opinion issued in 1951 by the International Court of Justice on reservations to the Genocide Convention, and as noted by the United Nations Secretary-General in his Report on the establishment of the International Criminal Tribunal for the Former Yugoslavia[15].

47. The Chamber notes that Rwanda acceded, by legislative decree, to the Convention on Genocide on 12 February 1975[16]. Therefore the crime of genocide was punishable in Rwanda in 1994.

48. The Chamber adheres to the definition of the crime of genocide as it was defined in the *Akayesu Judgement*.

49. The Chamber accepts that the crime of genocide involves, firstly, that one of the acts listed under Article 2(2) of the Statute be committed; secondly, that such an act be committed against a national, ethnical, racial or religious group, specifically targeted as such; and, thirdly, that the "act be committed with the intent to destroy, in whole or in part, the targeted group".

The Acts Enumerated under Article 2(2)(a) to (e) of the Statute

50. Article 2(2)(a) of the Statute, like the corresponding provisions of the Genocide Convention, refers to "meurtre" in the French version and to "killing" in the English version. In the opinion of the Chamber, the term "killing" includes both intentional and unintentional **[page 26]** homicides, whereas the word "meurtre" covers homicide committed with the intent to cause death. Given the presumption of innocence, and pursuant to the general principles of criminal law, the Chamber holds that the version more favourable to the Accused should be adopted, and finds that Article 2(2)(a) of the Statute must be interpreted in accordance with the definition of murder in the Criminal Code of Rwanda, which provides, under Article 311, that "Homicide committed with intent to cause death shall be treated as murder".

51. For the purposes of interpreting Article 2(2)(b) of the Statute, the Chamber understands the words "serious bodily or mental harm" to include acts of bodily or mental torture, inhumane or degrading treatment, rape, sexual violence, and persecution. The Chamber is of the opinion that "serious harm" need not entail permanent or irremediable harm.

52. In the opinion of the Chamber, the words "deliberately inflicting on the group conditions of life calculated to bring about its physical destruction in whole or in part", as indicated in Article 2(2)(c) of the Statute, are to be construed "as methods of destruction by which the perpetrator does not necessarily intend to immediately kill the members of the group", but which are, ultimately, aimed at their physical destruction. The Chamber holds that the means of deliberately inflicting on the group conditions of life calculated to bring about its physical destruction, in whole or in part, include subjecting a group of people to a subsistence diet, systematic expulsion from their homes and deprivation of essential medical supplies below a minimum vital standard.

---

[15] Secretary-General's Report pursuant to para. 2 of Resolution 808 (1993) of the Security Council, 3 May 1993, S/25704.

[16] Legislative Decree of 12 February 1975, Official Gazette of the Republic of Rwanda, 1975, p. 230. Rwanda acceded to the Genocide Convention but stated that it shall not be bound by Article 9 of this Convention.

53.   For the purposes of interpreting Article 2(2)(d) of the Statute, the Chamber holds that the words "measures intended to prevent births within the group" should be construed as including sexual mutilation, enforced sterilization, forced birth control, forced separation of males and females, and prohibition of marriages. The Chamber notes that measures intended to prevent births within the group may be not only physical, but also mental. **[page 27]**

54.   The Chamber is of the opinion that the provisions of Article 2(2)(e) of the Statute, on the forcible transfer of children from one group to another, are aimed at sanctioning not only any direct act of forcible physical transfer, but also any acts of threats or trauma which would lead to the forcible transfer of children from one group to another group.

Potential Groups of Victims of the Crime of Genocide

55.   The Chamber is of the view that it is necessary to consider the issue of the potential groups of victims of genocide in light of the provisions of the Statute and the Genocide Convention, which stipulate that genocide aims at "destroy[ing], in whole or in part, a national, ethnical, racial or religious group, as such."

56.   The Chamber notes that the concepts of national, ethnical, racial and religious groups have been researched extensively and that, at present, there are no generally and internationally accepted precise definitions thereof. Each of these concepts must be assessed in the light of a particular political, social and cultural context. Moreover, the Chamber notes that for the purposes of applying the Genocide Convention, membership of a group is, in essence, a subjective rather than an objective concept. The victim is perceived by the perpetrator of genocide as belonging to a group slated for destruction. In some instances, the victim may perceive himself/herself as belonging to the said group.

57.   Nevertheless, the Chamber is of the view that a subjective definition alone is not enough to determine victim groups, as provided for in the Genocide Convention. It appears, from a reading of the *travaux préparatoires* of the Genocide Convention[17], that certain groups, such as political and economic groups, have been excluded from the protected groups, because they are considered to be "mobile groups" which one joins through individual, political commitment. **[page 28]** That would seem to suggest *a contrario* that the Convention was presumably intended to cover relatively stable and permanent groups.

58.   Therefore, the Chamber holds that in assessing whether a particular group may be considered as protected from the crime of genocide, it will proceed on a case-by-case basis, taking into account both the relevant evidence proffered and the political and cultural context as indicated *supra*.

The Special Intent of the Crime of Genocide.

59.   Genocide is distinct from other crimes because it requires *dolus specialis*, a special intent. Special intent of a crime is the specific intention which, as an element of the crime, requires that the perpetrator clearly intended the result charged. The *dolus specialis* of the crime of genocide lies in "the intent to destroy, in whole or in part, a national, ethnical, racial or religious group, as such". A person may be convicted of genocide only where it is established that he committed one of the acts referred to under Article 2(2) of the Statute with the specific intent to destroy, in whole or in part, a particular group.

60.   In concrete terms, for any of the acts charged to constitute genocide, the said acts must have been committed against one or more persons because such person or persons were members of a specific group, and specifically, because of their membership in this group. Thus, the victim is singled out not by reason of his individual identity, but rather on account of his being a member of a national, ethnical, racial or religious group. The victim of the act is, therefore, a member of a given group selected as such,

---

[17]   Summary Records of the meetings of the Sixth Committee of the General Assembly, 21 September – 10 December 1948, Official Records of the General Assembly.

which, ultimately, means the victim of the crime of genocide is the group itself and not the individual alone. The perpetration of the act charged, therefore, extends beyond its actual commission, for example, the murder of a particular person, to encompass the realization of the ulterior purpose to destroy, in whole or in part, the group of which the person is only a member. **[page 29]**

61.   The *dolus specialis* is a key element of an intentional offence, which offence is characterized by a psychological nexus between the physical result and the mental state of the perpetrator. With regard to the issue of determining the offender's specific intent, the Chamber applies the following reasoning, as held in the *Akayesu Judgement*:

> "[...] intent is a mental factor which is difficult, even impossible, to determine. This is the reason why, in the absence of a confession from the accused, his intent can be inferred from a certain number of presumptions of fact. The Chamber is of the view that the genocidal intent inherent in a particular act charged can be inferred from the general context of the perpetration of other culpable acts systematically directed against that same group, whether these acts were committed by the same offender or by others. Other factors, such as the scale of atrocities committed, their general nature, in a region or a country, or furthermore, the fact of deliberately and systematically targeting victims on account of their membership of a particular group, while excluding the members of other groups, can enable the Chamber to infer the genocidal intent of a particular act."[18]

62.   Similarly, in the *Kayishema and Ruzindana Judgement*, Trial Chamber II held that:

> "[...] The Chamber finds that the intent can be inferred either from words or deeds and may be determined by a pattern of purposeful action. In particular, the Chamber considers evidence such as [...] the methodical way of planning, the systematic manner of killing. [...]"[19] **[page 30]**

63.   Therefore, the Chamber is of the view that, in practice, intent can be, on a case-by-case basis, inferred from the material evidence submitted to the Chamber, including the evidence which demonstrates a consistent pattern of conduct by the Accused. **[page 31]**

2.3 Crimes against Humanity (Article 3 of the Statute)

64.   The Chamber notes that the *Akayesu Judgement* traced the historical development and evolution of crimes against humanity, as far back as the Charter of the International Military Tribunal of Nuremberg. The *Akayesu Judgement* also considered the gradual evolution of crimes against humanity in the cases of *Eichmann, Barbie, Touvier* and *Papon*[20]. The Chamber concurs with the historical development of crimes against humanity, as set forth in the *Akayesu Judgement*.

65.   The Chamber notes that Article 7 of the Statute of the International Criminal Court defines a crime against humanity as any of the enumerated acts committed as part of a widespread or systematic attack directed against any civilian population, with knowledge of the attack. These enumerated acts are murder; extermination; enslavement; deportation or forcible transfer of population; imprisonment or other severe deprivation of physical liberty in violation of fundamental rules of international law; torture; rape, sexual slavery, enforced prostitution, forced pregnancy, enforced sterilization, or any other form of sexual violence of comparable gravity; persecution against any identifiable group or collectivity on political, racial, national, ethnic, cultural, religious, gender or other grounds that are universally recognised as impermissible under international law, in connection with any act referred to in this paragraph or any other crime within the jurisdiction of the court; enforced disappearance of persons; the crime of apartheid; other inhumane acts of a similar character intentionally causing great suffering or serious injury to body or mental or physical health.[21] **[page 32]**

---

[18]   *Akayesu Judgement*, para. 523
[19]   *Kayishema and Ruzindana Judgement*, para. 93.
[20]   *Akayesu Judgement* para. 563 to 576
[21]   Rome Statute of the International Criminal Court, adopted by the United Nations Diplomatic Conference of Plenipotentiaries on the Establishment of an International Court on 17 July 1998.

Crimes against Humanity pursuant to Article 3 of the Statute of the Tribunal

66.   Article 3 of the Statute confers on the Tribunal the jurisdiction to prosecute persons for various inhumane acts which constitute crimes against humanity. The Chamber concurs with the reasoning in the *Akayesu Judgement* that offences falling within the ambit of crimes against humanity may be broadly broken down into four essential elements, namely:

   (a)   the *actus reus* must be inhumane in nature and character, causing great suffering, or serious injury to body or to mental or physical health

   (b)   the *actus reus* must be committed as part of a widespread or systematic attack

   (c)   the *actus reus* must be committed against members of the civilian population

   (d)   the *actus reus* must be committed on one or more discriminatory grounds, namely, national, political, ethnic, racial or religious grounds.[22]

The *Actus Reus* Must be Committed as Part of a Widespread or Systematic Attack

67.   The Chamber is of the opinion that the *actus reus* cannot be a random inhumane act, but rather an act committed as part of an attack. With regard to the nature of this attack, the Chamber notes that Article 3 of the English version of the Statute reads "[...] as part of a widespread or systematic attack. [...]" whilst the French version to the Statute reads "[...] dans le cadre d'une attaque généralisée et systématique [...]". The French version requires that the attack be both of a widespread *and* systematic nature, whilst the English version requires that the attack be of a widespread *or* systematic nature and need not be both. **[page 33]**

68.   The Chamber notes that customary international law requires that the attack be either of a widespread *or* systematic nature and need not be both. The English version of the Statute conforms more closely with customary international law and the Chamber therefore accepts the elements as set forth in Article 3 of the English version of the Statute and follows the interpretation in other ICTR judgements namely: that the "attack" under Article 3 of the Statute, must be either of a widespread or systematic nature and need not be both.[23]

69.   The Chamber notes that "widespread", as an element of crimes against humanity, was defined in the *Akayesu Judgement*, as massive, frequent, large scale action, carried out collectively with considerable seriousness and directed against a multiplicity of victims, whilst "systematic" was defined as thoroughly organised action, following a regular pattern on the basis of a common policy and involving substantial public or private resources[24]. The Chamber concurs with these definitions and finds that it is not essential for this policy to be adopted formally as a policy of a State. There must, however, be some kind of preconceived plan or policy[25].

70.   The Chamber notes that "attack", as an element of crimes against humanity, was defined in the *Akayesu Judgement*, as an unlawful act of the kind enumerated in Article 3(a) to (i) of the Statute, such as murder, extermination, enslavement etc. An attack may also be non-violent in nature, like imposing a system of apartheid, which is declared a crime against humanity in Article 1 of the Apartheid Convention of 1973, or exerting pressure on the population to act in **[page 34]** a particular manner may also come under the purview of an attack, if orchestrated on a massive scale or in a systematic manner[26]. The Chamber concurs with this definition.

71.   The Chamber considers that the perpetrator must have:

---

[22]   *Akayesu Judgement*, para. 578.
[23]   *Akayesu Judgement*, p. 235, fn 144; *Kayishema and Ruzindana Judgement*, p. 51, fn 63.
[24]   *Akayesu Judgement* para. 580.
[25]   Report on the International Law Commission to the General Assembly, 51 U.N. GAOR Supp. (No 10) at 94 U.N. Doc. A/51/10 (1996)
[26]   *Akayesu Judgement* para. 581.

"[...] actual or constructive knowledge of the broader context of the attack, meaning that the accused must know that his act(s) is part of a widespread or systematic attack on a civilian population and pursuant to some kind of policy or plan."[27]

The *Actus Reus* Must be Directed against the Civilian Population

72.   The Chamber notes that the *actus reus* must be directed against the civilian population, if it is to constitute a crime against humanity. In the *Akayesu Judgement*, the civilian population was defined as people who were not taking any active part in the hostilities[28]. The fact that there are certain individuals among the civilian population who are not civilians does not deprive the population of its civilian character[29]. The Chamber concurs with this definition.

The *Actus Reus* Must be Committed on Discriminatory Grounds

73.   The Statute stipulates that inhumane acts committed against the civilian population must be committed on "national, political, ethnic, racial or religious grounds." Discrimination on the [page 35] basis of a person's political ideology satisfies the requirement of 'political' grounds as envisaged in Article 3 of the Statute.

74.   Inhumane acts committed against persons not falling within any one of the discriminatory categories may constitute crimes against humanity if the perpetrator's intention in committing these acts, is to further his attack on the group discriminated against on one of the grounds specified in Article 3 of the Statute. The perpetrator must have the requisite intent for the commission of crimes against humanity.[30]

75.   The Chamber notes that the Appeals Chamber in the *Tadić* Appeal ruled that the Trial Chamber erred in finding that all crimes against humanity require a discriminatory intent. The Appeals Chamber stated that a discriminatory intent is an indispensable element of the offence only with regard to those crimes for which this is expressly required, that is the offence of persecution, pursuant to Article 5(h) of the Statute of the International Criminal Tribunal for the former Yugoslavia (the "ICTY").[31]

76.   The Chamber considers the provisions of Article 5 of the ICTY Statute, as compared to the provisions of Article 3 of the ICTR, Statute and notes that, although the provisions of both the aforementioned Articles pertain to crimes against humanity, except for persecution, there is a material and substantial difference in the elements of the offence that constitute crimes against humanity. This stems from the fact that Article 3 of the ICTR Statute expressly provides the enumerated discriminatory grounds of "national, political, ethnic, racial or religious", in respect of the offences of Murder; Extermination; Deportation; Imprisonment; Torture; Rape; and; Other Inhumane Acts, whilst the ICTY Statute does not stipulate any discriminatory grounds in respect of these offences. [page 36]

The Enumerated Acts

77.   Article 3 of the Statute sets out various acts that constitute crimes against humanity, namely; murder; extermination; enslavement; deportation; imprisonment; torture; rape; persecution on political, racial and religious grounds; and; other inhumane acts. Although the category of acts that constitute crimes against humanity are set out in Article 3, this category is not exhaustive. Any act which is

---

[27]   *Kayishema and Ruzindana Judgement* para. 134

[28]   *Akayesu Judgement*, para. 582. Note that this definition assimilates the definition of "civilian" to the categories of person protected by Common Article 3 of the Geneva Conventions.

[29]   *Ibid* para. 582, Protocol Additional to the Geneva Convention of 12 August 1949, and relating to the Protection of Victims of International Armed Conflict; Article 50.

[30]   *Akayesu Judgement*, para. 584.

[31]   *The Prosecutor v. Dusko Tadić*, Appeals Judgement of 15 July 1999; para. 305; p. 55.

inhumane in nature and character may constitute a crime against humanity, provided the other elements are satisfied. This is evident in (i) which caters for all other inhumane acts not stipulated in (a) to (h) of Article 3.

78.   The Chamber notes that in respect of crimes against humanity, the Accused is indicted for murder and extermination. The Chamber, in interpreting Article 3 of the Statute, will focus its discussion on these offences only.

Murder

79.   Pursuant to Article 3(a) of the Statute, murder constitutes a crime against humanity. The Chamber notes that Article 3(a) of the English version of the Statute refers to "Murder", whilst the French version of the Statute refers to "Assassinat". Customary International Law dictates that it is the offence of "Murder" that constitutes a crime against humanity and not "Assassinat".

80.   The *Akayesu Judgement* defined Murder as the unlawful, intentional killing of a human being. The requisite elements of murder are:

   (a)   The victim is dead;

   (b)   The death resulted from an unlawful act or omission of the accused or a subordinate; **[page 37]**

   (c)   At the time of the killing the accused or a subordinate had the intention to kill or inflict grievous bodily harm on the deceased having known that such bodily harm is likely to cause the victim's death, and is reckless as to whether or not death ensures;

   (d)   The victim was discriminated against on any one of the enumerated discriminatory grounds;

   (e)   The victim was a member of the civilian population; and

   (f)   The act or omission was part of a widespread or systematic attack on the civilian population.[32]

81.   The Chamber concurs with this definition of murder and is of the opinion that the act or omission that constitutes murder must be discriminatory in nature and directed against a member of the civilian population.

Extermination

82.   Pursuant to Article 3(c) of the Statute, extermination constitutes a crime against humanity. By its very nature, extermination is a crime which is directed against a group of individuals. Extermination differs from murder in that it requires an element of mass destruction which is not a pre-requisite for murder. **[page 38]**

83.   The *Akayesu Judgement*, defined the essential elements of extermination as follows:

   (a)   the accused or his subordinate participated in the killing of certain named or described persons;

   (b)   the act or omission was unlawful and intentional;

   (c)   the unlawful act or omission must be part of a widespread or systematic attack;

   (d)   the attack must be against the civilian population; and;

   (e)   the attack must be on discriminatory grounds, namely: national, political, ethnic, racial, or religious grounds.

---

[32]   *Akayesu Judgement*, para. 589 and 590.

84.   The Chamber concurs with this definition of extermination and is of the opinion that the act or omission that constitutes extermination must be discriminatory in nature and directed against members of the civilian population. Further, this act or omission includes, but is not limited to the direct act of killing. It can be any act or omission, or cumulative acts or omissions, that cause the death of the targeted group of individuals. **[page 39]**

2.4 Serious Violations of Common Article 3 of the Geneva Conventions and Additional Protocol II

Article 4 of the Statute

85.   Pursuant to Article 4 of the Statute, the Chamber shall have the power to prosecute persons committing or ordering to be committed serious violations of Article 3 common to the four Geneva Conventions of 12 August 1949 for the Protection of War Victims, and of Additional Protocol II thereto of 8 June 1977. These violations shall include, but shall not be limited to:

(a) violence to life, health and physical or mental well-being of persons, in particular murder as well as cruel treatment such as torture, mutilation or any form of corporal punishment;

(b) collective punishments;

(c) taking of hostages;

(d) acts of terrorism:

(e) outrages upon personal dignity, in particular humiliating and degrading treatment, rape, enforced prostitution and any form of indecent assault;

(f) pillage; **[page 40]**

(g) the passing of sentences and the carrying out of executions without previous judgment pronounced by a regularly constituted court, affording all the judicial guarantees which are recognised as indispensable by civilised peoples;

(h) threats to commit any of the foregoing acts.

Applicability of Common Article 3 and Additional Protocol II

86.   In applying Article 4 of the Statute, the Chamber must be satisfied that the principle of *nullum crimen sine lege* is not violated. Indeed, the creation of the Tribunal, in response to the alleged crimes perpetrated in Rwanda in 1994, raised the question all too familiar to the Nuremberg Tribunal and the ICTY, that of jurisdictions applying *ex post facto laws* in violation of this principle. In establishing the ICTY, the Secretary-General dealt with this issue by asserting that in the application of the principle of *nullum crimen sine lege* the International Tribunal should apply rules of international humanitarian law which are beyond any doubt part of customary law. However, in the case of this Tribunal, it was incumbent on the Chambers to decide whether or not the said principle had been adhered to[33], and whether individuals incurred individual criminal responsibility for violations of these international instruments.

87.   In the *Akayesu Judgement*, the Chamber expressed its opinion that the "norms of Common Article 3 had acquired the status of customary law in that most States, by their domestic penal codes, have criminalized acts which, if committed during internal armed conflict, would constitute violations of Common article 3". The finding of the Trial Chamber in this regard followed the precedents set by the ICTY[34], which established the customary nature of **[page 41]** Common Article 3. Moreover, the Chamber in the *Akayesu Judgement* held that, although not all of Additional Protocol II could be said to be

---

[33]   See *Akayesu Judgement*, para. 603 to 605.
[34]   See *Tadic Judgement* and Decision on the Defence Motion for Interlocutory Appeal on Jurisdiction of 2 October 1995.

customary law, the guarantees contained in Article 4(2) (Fundamental Guarantees) thereof, which reaffirm and supplement Common Article 3, form part of existing international law. All of the norms reproduced in Article 4 of the Statute are covered by Article 4(2) of Additional Protocol II.

88.   Furthermore, the Trial Chamber in the *Akayesu Judgement* concluded that violations of these norms would entail, as a matter of customary international law, individual responsibility for the perpetrator. It was also recalled that as Rwanda had become a party to the 1949 Geneva Conventions and their 1977 Additional Protocols, on 5 May 1964 and 19 November 1984, respectively, these instruments were in any case in force in the territory of Rwanda in 1994, and formed part of Rwandan law. Thus, Rwandan nationals who violated these international instruments incorporated into national law, including those offences as incorporated in Article 4 of the Statute, could be tried before the Rwandan national courts[35].

89.   In the *Kayishema and Ruzindana Judgement*, Trial Chamber II deemed it unnecessary to delve into the question as to whether the instruments incorporated in Article 4 of the Statute should be considered as customary international law. Rather the Trial Chamber found that the instruments were in force in the territory of Rwanda in 1994 and that persons could be prosecuted for breaches thereof on the basis that Rwanda had become a party to the Geneva Conventions and their Additional Protocols. The offences enumerated in Article 4 of the Statute, said the Trial Chamber, also constituted offences under Rwandan law[36]. **[page 42]**

90.   Thus it is clear that, at the time the crimes alleged in the Indictment were perpetrated, persons were bound to respect the guarantees provided for by the 1949 Geneva Conventions and their 1977 Additional Protocols, as incorporated in Article 4 of the Statute. Violations thereof, as a matter of custom and convention, incurred individual responsibility, and could result in the prosecution of the authors of the offences.

The Nature of the Conflict

91.   The 1949 Geneva Conventions and Additional Protocol I generally apply to international armed conflicts, whereas Common Article 3 extends a minimum threshold of humanitarian protection to persons affected by non-international armed conflicts. This protection has been enhanced and developed in the 1977 Additional Protocol II. Offences alleged to be covered by Article 4 of the Statute must, as a preliminary matter, have been committed in the context of a conflict of a non-international character satisfying the requirements of Common Article 3, which applies to "armed conflict not of an international character" and Additional Protocol II, applicable to conflicts which "take place in the territory of a High Contracting Party between its armed forces and dissident armed forces or other organized armed groups which, under responsible command, exercise such control over a part of its territory as to enable them to carry out sustained and concerted military operations and to implement this Protocol".

92.   First to be addressed is the question of what constitutes an armed conflict under Common Article 3. This issue was dealt with extensively during the 1949 Diplomatic Conference of Geneva leading to the adoption of the Conventions. Of concern to many participating States was the ambiguous and vague nature of the term "armed conflict". Although the Conference failed to provide a precise minimum threshold as to what constitutes an "armed conflict", it is clear that mere acts of banditry, internal disturbances and tensions, and unorganized and short-lived insurrections are to be ruled out. The International Committee of the Red Cross (the "ICRC"), **[page 43]** specifies further that conflicts referred to in Common Article 3 are armed conflicts with armed forces on either side engaged in hostilities: conflicts, in short, which are in many respects similar to an international conflict, but take place within the confines of a single country[37]. The ICTY Appeals Chamber offered guidance on the

---

[35]   See *Akayesu Judgement*, para. 616 and 617.
[36]   See *Kayishema and Ruzindana Judgement*, para. 156 and 157.
[37]   See generally ICRC Commentary IV Geneva Convention, para. 1 – Applicable Provisions.

matter by holding "that an armed conflict exists whenever there is [...]protracted armed violence between governmental authorities and organized armed groups or between such groups within a State. International humanitarian law applies from the initiation of such armed conflicts and extends beyond the cessation of hostilities until [...] in the case of internal conflicts, a peaceful settlement is reached"[38].

93.   It can thence be seen that the definition of an armed conflict *per se* termed in the abstract, and whether or not a situation can be described as an "armed conflict", meeting the criteria of Common Article 3, is to be decided upon on a case-by-case basis. Hence, in dealing with this issue, the *Akayesu Judgement* suggested an "evaluation test", whereby it is necessary to evaluate the intensity and the organization of the parties to the conflict to make a finding on the existence of an armed conflict. This approach also finds favour with the Trial Chamber in this instance.

94.   In addition to armed conflicts of a non-international character, satisfying the requirements of Common Article 3, under Article 4 of the Statute, the Tribunal has the power to prosecute persons responsible for serious violations of the 1977 Additional Protocol II, a legal instrument whose overall purpose is to afford protection to persons affected by non-international armed conflicts. As aforesaid, this instrument develops and supplements the rules contained in Common Article 3, without modifying its existing conditions of applicability. Additional Protocol II reaffirms Common Article 3, which, although it objectively characterized internal armed **[page 44]** conflicts, lacked clarity and enabled the States to have a wide area of discretion in its application. Thus the impetus behind the Conference of Government Experts and the Diplomatic Conference[39] in this regard was to improve the protection afforded to victims in non-international armed conflicts and to develop objective criteria which would not be dependent on the subjective judgements of the parties. The result is, on the one hand, that conflicts covered by Additional Protocol II have a higher intensity threshold than Common Article 3, and on the other, that Additional Protocol II is immediately applicable once the defined material conditions have been fulfilled. If an internal armed conflict meets the material conditions of Additional Protocol II, it then also automatically satisfies the threshold requirements of the broader Common Article 3.

95.   Pursuant to Article 1(1) of Additional Protocol II the material requirements to be satisfied for the applicability of Additional Protocol II are as follows:

> (i) an armed conflict takes place in the territory of a High Contracting Party, between its armed forces and dissident armed forces or other organized armed groups;

> (ii) the dissident armed forces or other organized armed groups are under responsible command;

> (iii) the dissident armed forces or other organized armed groups are able to exercise such control over a part of their territory as to enable them to carry out sustained and concerted military operations; and **[page 45]**

> (iv) the dissident armed forces or other organized armed groups are able to implement Additional Protocol II.

Ratione Personae

The Class of Perpetrator

96.   Under Common Article 3 of the Geneva Conventions, the perpetrator must belong to a "Party" to the conflict, whereas under Additional Protocol II[40] the perpetrator must be a member of the "armed forces" of either the Government or of the dissidents. There has been much discussion on the exact

---

38   *Ibid.* 34
39   Conference of Government Experts on the Reaffirmation and Development of International Humanitarian Law Applicable in Armed Conflicts, 24 May to 12 June 1971, and 3 May to 3 June 1972; Diplomatic Conference on the Reaffirmation and Development of International Humanitarian Law Applicable in Armed Conflicts, 20 February to 29 March 1974, 3 February to 18 April 1975, 21 April to 11 June 1976 and 17 March to 10 June 1977.
40   See Article 1(1) of Additional Protocol II

definition of "armed forces" and "Party", discussion, which in the opinion of the Chamber detracts from the overall protective purpose of these instruments. A too restrictive definition of these terms would likewise dilute the protection afforded by these instruments to the victims and potential victims of armed conflicts. Hence, the category of persons covered by these terms should not be limited to commanders and combatants but should be interpreted in their broadest sense.

97.   Moreover, it is well established from the jurisprudence of International Tribunals that civilians can be held as accountable as members of the armed forces or of a Party to the conflict. In this regard, reference should be made to the *Akayesu Judgement*, where it was held that:

> "It is, in fact, well-established, at least since the Tokyo trials, that civilians may be held responsible for violations of international humanitarian law. Hirota, the former Foreign Minister of Japan, was convicted at Tokyo for crimes committed during the rape of Nanking. Other post-World War II trials unequivocally support the imposition of **[page 46]** individual criminal liability for war crimes on civilians where they have a link or connection with a Party to the conflict. The principle of holding civilians liable for breaches of the laws of war is, moreover, favored by a consideration of the humanitarian object and purpose of the Geneva Conventions and the Additional Protocols, which is to protect war victims from atrocities."[41]

98.   Consequently, the duties and responsibilities of the Geneva Conventions and the Additional Protocols will normally apply to individuals of all ranks belonging to the armed forces under the military command of either of the belligerent parties, or to individuals who were legitimately mandated and expected, as public officials or agents or persons otherwise holding public authority or *de facto* representing the Government, to support or fulfil the war efforts. It will be a matter of evidence to establish if the accused falls into the category of persons who can be held individually criminally responsible for serious violations of these international instruments, and in this case, of the provisions of Article 4 of the Statute.

The Class of Victims

99.   Paragraph 8 of the Indictment states that the victims referred to in this Indictment were persons taking no active parte in the hostilities. This wording stems from the definitions to be found in Common Article 3(1) of the Geneva Conventions, which affords protection to "persons taking no active part in the hostilities, including members of the armed forces who have laid down their arms and those placed hors de combat", and is synonymous to Article 4 of Additional Protocol which refers to "all persons who do not take a direct part in the hostilities or who have ceased to take part in the hostilities". **[page 47]**

100.   From a reading of the Indictment, it can be adduced that the victims were all allegedly civilians. There is no concise definition of "civilian" in the Protocols. As such, a definition has evolved through a process of elimination, whereby the civilian population[42] is made up of persons who are not combatants or persons placed hors de combat, in other words, who are not members of the armed forces[43]. Pursuant to Article 13(2) of the Additional Protocol II, the civilian population, as well as individual civilians, shall not be the object of attack. However, if civilians take a direct part in the hostilities, they then lose their right to protection as civilians *per se* and could fall within the class of combatant. To take a "direct" part in the hostilities means acts of war which by their nature or purpose are likely to cause actual harm to the personnel and equipment of the enemy armed forces[44].

101.   It would be beyond the scope of the matter at hand for the Chamber to attempt to provide an exhaustive list of all categories of persons who are not considered civilians under the Geneva

---

[41]   *Akayesu Judgement*, para. 633
[42]   It should be noted that the civilian population comprises all persons who are civilians. (Article 50(2) of Additional Protocol II)
[43]   See ICRC Commentary on the Additional Protocols of 8 June 1977 to the Geneva Conventions of 12 August 1949, commentary on Protocol I, Article 50.
[44]   *Ibid.* Commentary on Additional Protocol II, Article 13.

Conventions and their Additional Protocols. Rather the Chamber considers that a civilian is anyone who falls outside the category of "perpetrator" developed *supra*, "perpetrators" being individuals of all ranks belonging to the armed forces under the military command of either of the belligerent parties, or to individuals who were legitimately mandated and expected, as public officials or agents or persons otherwise holding public authority or *de facto* representing the Government, to support or fulfil the war efforts. The class of civilians thus broadly defined, it will be a matter of evidence on a case-by-case basis to determine whether a victim has the status of civilian. **[page 48]**

Ratione Loci

102. The protection afforded to individuals under the Geneva Conventions and the Additional Protocols, extends throughout the territory of the State where the hostilities are occurring, once the objective material conditions for applicability of the said instruments have been satisfied.

103. This was affirmed in the *Akayesu Judgement*[45] and by the ICTY[46] (with regard in particular to Common Article 3), where it has been determined that the requirements of Common Article 3 and Additional Protocol II apply in the whole territory where the conflict is occurring and are not limited to the "war front" or to the "narrow geographical context of the actual theater of combat operations".

The Nexus between the Crime and the Armed Conflict

104. In addition to the offence being committed in the context of an armed conflict not of an international character satisfying the material requirements of Common Article 3 and Additional Protocol II, there must be a nexus between the offence and the armed conflict for Article 4 of the Statute to apply. By this it should be understood that the offence must be closely related to the hostilities or committed in conjunction with the armed conflict[47].

105. The Chamber notes the finding made in the *Kayishema and Ruzindana Judgement*, whereby the term nexus should not be defined *in abstracto*[48]. Rather, the evidence adduced in **[page 49]** support of the charges against the accused must satisfy the Chamber that such a nexus exists. Thus, the burden rests on the Prosecutor to prove beyond a reasonable doubt that, on the basis of the facts, such a nexus exists between the crime committed and the armed conflict.

The Specific Violation

106. The crime committed must represent a serious violation of Common Article 3 and Additional Protocol II, as incorporated in Article 4 of the Statute. A "serious violation" is one which breaches a rule protecting important values with grave consequences for the victim. The fundamental guarantees included in Article 4 of the Statute represent elementary considerations of humanity. Violations thereof would, by their very nature, be deemed serious.

107. The Accused is charged under Counts 4, 6 and 8 of the Indictment for violations of Article 3 common to the Geneva Conventions, as incorporated by Article 4(a) (murder) of the Statute of the Tribunal. If all the requirements of applicability of Article 4, as developed *supra* are met, the onus is on the Prosecutor to then prove that the alleged acts of the Accused constituted murder. The specific elements of murder are stated in Section 2.3 on Crimes against Humanity in the Applicable law. **[page 50]**

---

[45]   See *Akayesu Judgement* para. 635-636.
[46]   See ICTY *Tadić* decision on the Defence Motion for Interlocutory Appeal on Jurisdiction of 2 October 1995, para. 69.
[47]   See *Akayesu Judgement* para. 643 and *ibid*, para. 70.
[48]   See *Kayishema and Ruzindana Judgement* para. 188.

2.5 Cumulative Charges

108. In the indictment, the Accused, by his alleged acts in relation to the events described in paragraphs 10-19, is cumulatively charged with genocide (count 1) and crimes against humanity (extermination) (count 2). Moreover, by his alleged acts in relation to the killings at the *École Technique Officielle* described in paragraph 14, his acts at the gravel pit in Nyanza described in paragraphs 15 and 16, and for the alleged murder of Emmanuel Kayitare described in paragraph 18, Rutaganda is charged cumulatively with crimes against humanity (murder) (counts 3, 5 and 7) and violations of Article 3 common to the Geneva Conventions (murder) (counts 4, 6 and 8).

109. Therefore, the issue before the Chamber is whether, assuming that it is satisfied beyond a reasonable doubt that a particular act alleged in the indictment and given several legal characterizations under different counts has been established, it may adopt only one of the legal characterizations given to such act or whether it may find the Accused guilty on all the counts arising from the said act.

110. The Chamber notes, first of all, that the principle of cumulative charges was applied by the Nuremberg Tribunal, especially regarding war crimes and crimes against humanity[49]. **[page 51]**

111. Regarding especially the concurrence of the various crimes covered under the Statute, the Chamber, in the *Akayesu Judgement*, the first case brought before this Tribunal, considered the matter and held that:

> "[...] it is acceptable to convict the accused of two offences in relation to the same set of facts in the following circumstances: (1) where the offences have different elements; or (2) where the previous creating the offences protect different interests; or (3) where it is necessary to record a conviction for both offences in order fully to describe what the accused did. However, the Chamber finds that it is not justifiable to convict an accused of two offences in relation to the same set of facts where (a) one offence is a lesser included offence of the other, [...] or (b) where one offence charges accomplice liability and the other offence charges liability as [...]"[50].

112. Trial Chamber II of the Tribunal, in its *Kayishema and Ruzindana Judgement*, endorsed the afore-mentioned test of concurrence of crimes and found that it is only acceptable:

> "(1) where offences have differing elements, or (2) where the laws in question protect differing social interests."[51]

113. Trial Chamber II ruled that the cumulative charges in the *Kayishema and Ruzindana Judgement* in particular were legally improper and untenable. It found that all elements including the *mens rea* element requisite to show genocide, "extermination" and "murder" in the particular case were the same, and the evidence relied upon to prove the crimes were the same. **[page 52]** Furthermore, in the opinion of Trial Chamber II, the protected social interests were also the same. Therefore, it held that the Prosecutor should have charged the Accused in the alternative.[52]

---

[49] The indictment against the major German War Criminals presented to the International Military Tribunal stated that "the prosecution will rely upon the facts pleaded under Count Three (violations of the laws and customs of war) as also constituting crimes against humanity (Count Four)". Several accused persons were convicted of both war crimes and crimes against humanity. The judgement of the International Military Tribunal delivered at Nuremberg on 30 September and 1 October 1946 ruled that "[...] from the beginning of the war in 1939 war crimes were committed on a vast scale, which were also crimes against humanity." The commentary on *Justice* case held the same view: "It is clear that war crimes may also constitute crimes against humanity; the same offences may amount to both types of crimes." The trials on the basis of Control Council Law No. 10 followed the same approach. *Pohl, Heinz Karl Franslau, Hans Loerner*, and *Erwin Tschentscher* were all found to have committed war crimes and crimes against humanity. National cases, such as *Quinn v. Robinson*, the *Eichmann* case and the *Barbie* case also support this finding. In the *Tadić* case, the Trial Chamber II of ICTY, based on the above reasoning, ruled that "acts which are enumerated elsewhere in the Statute may also entail additional culpability if they meet the requirements of persecution." Thus, the same acts, which meet the requirements of other crimes-grave breaches of Geneva Conventions violation of the laws or customs of war and genocide, may also constitute the crimes against humanity for persecution.

[50] *Akayesu Judgement*, para. 468.

[51] *Kayishema and Ruzindana Judgement*, para. 627.

[52] *Kayishema and Ruzindana Judgement*, para. 645, 646 and 650.

114. Judge Tafazzal H. Khan, one of the Judges sitting in Trial Chamber II to consider the said case, dissented on the issue of cumulative charges. Relying on consistent jurisprudence he pointed out that the Chamber should have placed less emphasis on the overlapping elements of the cumulative crimes,

"What must be punished is culpable conduct; this principle applies to situations where the conduct offends two or more crimes, whether or not the factual situation also satisfies the distinct elements of the two or more crimes, as proven."[53]

115. In his dissenting opinion, the Judge goes on to emphasized that the full assessment of charges and the pronouncement of guilty verdicts are important in order to reflect the totality of the accused's culpable conduct.

"[...] where the culpable conduct was part of a widespread and systematic attack specifically against civilians, to record a conviction for genocide alone does not reflect the totality of the accused's culpable conduct. Similarly, if the Majority had chosen to convict for extermination alone instead of genocide, the verdict would still fail to adequately capture the totality of the accused's conduct."[54] **[page 53]**

116. This Chamber fully concurs with the dissenting opinion thus entered. It notes that this position, which endorses the principle of cumulative charges, also finds support in various decisions rendered by the ICTY. In the case of the *Prosecutor v. Zoran Kupreskic and others*, the Trial Chamber of ICTY in its decision on Defence challenges to form of the indictment held that:

"The Prosecutor may be justified in bringing cumulative charges when the articles of the Statute referred to are designed to protect different values and when each article requires proof of a legal element not required by the others."[55]

117. Furthermore, the Chamber holds that offences covered under the Statute - genocide, crimes against humanity and violations of Article 3 common to Geneva Conventions and of Additional Protocol II - have disparate ingredients and, especially, that their punishment is aimed at protecting discrete interests. As a result, multiple offenses may be charged on the basis of the same acts, in order to capture the full extent of the crimes committed by an accused.

118. Finally, the Chamber notes that in Civil Law systems, including that of Rwanda, there exists a so called doctrine of *concours idéal d'infractions* which allows multiple charges for the same act under certain circumstances. Rwandan law allows multiple charges in the following circumstances:

"Penal Code of Rwanda: Chapter VI - Concurrent offences:

Article 92: Where a person has committed several offences prior to a conviction on any such charges, such offences shall be concurrent. **[page 54]**

Article 93: Notional plurality of offences occurs:

1.   Where a single conduct may be characterized as constituting several offences;

2.   Where a conduct includes acts which, though constituting separate offences, are interrelated as deriving from the same criminal intent or as constituting lesser included offences of one another.

---

[53]   *Kayishema and Ruzindana Judgement*, Separate and Dissenting Opinion of Judge Tafazzal Hossain Khan Regarding the Verdicts Under the Charges of Crimes Against Humanity/Murder and Crimes Against Humanity/Extermination, para. 13.
[54]   *Ibid*, para. 33.
[55]   *The Prosecutor v. Zoran Kupreskić and others*, Decision on Defence Challenges to Form of the Indictment, IT-95-16-PT, 15 May 1998.

In the former case, only the sentence prescribed for the most serious offence shall be passed while, in the latter case, only the sentence provided for the most severely punished offence shall be passed, the maximum of which may be exceeded by half".[56]

119. Consequently, in light of the foregoing, the Chamber maintains that it is justified to convict an accused of two or more offences for the same act under certain circumstances and reiterates the above findings made in the *Akayesu Judgement*. **[page 55]**

3. THE DEFENCE CASE

120. The Accused pleaded not guilty to all counts of the Indictment at his initial appearance on 30 May 1996. The Defence case consisted of two main arguments. The first of these was a general defence. The second was a defence of alibi.

3.1 The Arguments of General Defence

121. The Defence developed several main lines of argument. The Defence argued that the political activity of the Accused was minimal. The Accused testified and, his Counsel argued, that his involvement in the *Interahamwe za MRND* was limited to participation in meetings of this organization in its earliest stage, which it was argued was as a "think tank" or "group of reflection"[57]. The Defence also argued that the meaning of *Interahamwe* changed significantly between 1991 and 1994. The Defence argued that the Accused was a member of the *Interahamwe za MRND* at its embryonic stage, and that the term *Interahamwe* later included people who were not all members of the *Interahamwe za MRND*.

122. The Defence Counsel questioned the credibility and reliability of several Prosecution witnesses. Counsel for the Defence submitted that the case file was "contaminated"[58] by virtue of testimony given concerning the "Hindi Mandal" building in the Amgar garage complex. The Defence further submitted that certain evidence gathered by Captain Luc Lemaire was illegally collected and thus could not be tendered as evidence by the Prosecutor. The Defence argued that **[page 56]** the United Nations Assistance Mission for Rwanda ("UNAMIR") contingent, of which Captain Lemaire was a part, had been prohibited from gathering intelligence[59].

123. The Defence called fourteen witnesses, including the Accused, who testified at length about the role of the Accused as second Vice-President of the *Interahamwe*. The Chamber notes that a number of Defence witnesses testified that the Accused took action to help others, including Tutsi refugees. The Defence further argued that, contrary to the allegations that the Accused detained Tutsi civilians in the "Hindi Mandal" building at the Amgar garage, that Tutsis actually sought refuge there and that the Accused permitted this and that he provided them with basic foodstuffs and medicine.

---

[56]   The English text quoted is an unofficial translation of the following "Code pénal du Rwanda: Chapitre VI – Du concours d'infractions":

Article 92 – Il y a concours d'infractions lorsque plusieurs infractions ont été commises par le même auteur sans qu'une condamnation soit intervenue entre ces infractions.

Article 93 – Il y a concours idéal:

1. Lorsque le fait unique au point de vue matériel est susceptible de plusieurs qualifications;

2. Lorsque l'action comprend des faits qui, constituant des infractions distinctes, sont unis entre eux comme procédant d'une intention délictueuse unique ou comme étant les uns des circonstances aggravantes des autres.

Seront seules prononcées dans le premier cas les peines déterminées par la qualification la plus sévère, dans le second cas les peines prévues pour la répression de l'infraction la plus grave, mais dont le maximum pourra être alors élevé de moitié".

[57]   See Testimony of Georges Rutaganda, transcript of 08, 09, 22 April 1999.

[58]   See Closing Argument of the Defence, transcript of 17 June 1999.

[59]   *Ibid.*

124. The Accused testified before the Chamber that prior to the advent of multiparty politics in Rwanda in 1991, he was a businessman with no interest in political participation. After being released from a presidentially assigned post in June 1991, he stated, he worked for himself, operating an import and distribution business registered as "Rutaganda SARL." The Accused testified that he focused on his business to the exclusion of any other civic, political, or administrative activities.

125. The Accused stated that he joined the MRND party in September or October 1991, in an atmosphere of increasing political tension in order to benefit from its protection and to safeguard his business interests. This tension was as a result of increasing competition between President Habyarimana's ruling MRND party and new opposition parties as they vied for members. It was in this context, the Accused testified, that he chose to join the MRND party because of the specific protections it afforded. He further submitted that although his father had been a member of the MDR, the strong regional affiliations which the MDR was reputed to have did not seem to him to be beneficial in light of the political climate in Kigali in 1991. It was at his father's **[page 57]** urging, he stated, that he joined the MRND party in 1991. The Accused was, he claimed, simply a member of the MRND party – with no time for, or interest in, wielding political influence within the party or among the general population.

126. Nonetheless, in November 1991, the Accused was invited to attend an initial meeting of intellectuals who sought to find ways to recruit for and promote the MRND party. The Accused told the Chamber that he was also to become an elected representative in the national committee of the MRND in April 1993, as a representative of Gitarama *Préfecture*.[60] As such, he was one among fifty-five representatives, five from each *Préfecture*, who met at National Assemblies and voted on party decisions and actions.

127. A select group of persons, whom the Accused referred to as intellectuals, convened in order to devise strategies for attracting new members and for furthering the MRND party's objectives in the new, multiparty political environment. This group was known as the *Interahamwe za MRND*. The Accused indicated to the court that this was an embryonic "think tank" for the MRND. The Accused testified that he dit not know when this initial "think tank" was organized, but that he was nonetheless involved in the initial impetus behind the creation of this committee. He participated in meetings of this group, he testified, in order to contribute his own ideas to the party. He stated that although more people joined this core group, they were all personally invited rather than publicly recruited. He stated that he attended one of their meetings for the first time in November 1991, at the invitation of Pheneas Ruhumuriza, who was later to become first Vice-President of the *Interahamwe za MRND*.[61]

128. According to the testimony given by the Accused, *Interahamwe* is a Kinyarwanda word that was used frequently by persons in political parties or other associations, which indicated a **[page 58]** close relationship between people who dit something together. This name was drawn, he explained, from a popular and patriotic song from the 1960s, which was associated with the MDR. Witness DNN gave a similar description of the source of the term Interahamwe.[62]

129. The Accused testified that the *Interahamwe za MRND* quickly grew from its embryonic form and gained both senior members and young recruits. The five members who were to compose the National Committee of the *Interahamwe za MRND* were selected by a larger assembly. The Accused was appointed as second vice president even though he declined to be a candidate in elections. He testified, however, that the five official positions comprising the National Committee, as those of ensuing committee heads and organizers were really only formalities, with no attached responsibility or authority.

130. The Accused stated that although the Committee had a clear structure and its members had titles which suggested a hierarchy of responsibility and authority; his position as second vice-president was a mere formality, and he dit not act in a capacity commensurate with the responsibility such a title might suggest. The Accused testified that there was no real leadership structure, budget, or autonomy – but that the titles, communiques, and meetings simply reflected a hope for future actions of the *Interahamwe za*

---

[60]   See *Testimony of Georges Rutaganda, transcript of 22 April 1999.*
[61]   See *Testimony of Georges Rutaganda, transcript of 08 April 1999.*
[62]   See *Testimony of Witness DNN, transcript of 16 February 1999.*

MRND. The Accused also testified that as second vice president and member of this National Committee, he acted as a mediator and liaison between the National Committee of the MRND party and the young members who joined the party, quite possibly as a response to the organization and initiative of the *Interahamwe za MRND*.

131.   According to the testimony of the Accused, the size and character of the *Interahamwe za MRND* changed significantly between its inception and the events which followed the death of President Habyarimana in April 1994. During his testimony, the Accused described a **[page 59]** transformation in the popular usage and understanding of the word Interahamwe, as well as an increase in the number of people who joined the MRND, and in particular the *Interahamwe za MRND*. The Accused testified that the *Interahamwe za MRND* was initially composed of a small number of men who were mostly between the ages of thirty and forty. The Accused later referred to the *Interahamwe* as "the youth", and also stated that increasing numbers of Rwandan youth were drawn to the party and were subsequently organized. The Accused testified that by 6 April 1994 the *Interahamwe* had become an entirely different organization than the one in which he was originally involved. The Accused stated that the organization had already changed by mid-1992, and continued its transformation through 1994.

132.   The Accused testified that the evolution of the *Interahamwe* as a youth wing of the party was an organic development, which he did not foresee when he joined this committee at its inception. Responding to questions concerning President Habyarimana's opinion of the *Interahamwe*, the Accused testified that in May 1992 President Habyarimana expressed his approval and encouraged "the youth" to join the organization.

133.   The Accused stated to the court that the *Interahamwe* was popularly understood to encompass many more people than the *Interahamwe za MRND*. The word *Interahamwe*, and even *Interahamwe za MRND*, gained a pejorative, or negative meaning in popular usage and was used to describe a large and loosely organized militia which is said to have fought against the RPF[63], as well as to connote certain persons who had committed acts of banditry and violence[64]. While stating that popular understanding of the word *Interahamwe* had changed, the Accused added that the way in which this term was used after 6 April 1994 had little to do with the MRND, and that he had little knowledge of the persons perpetrating such acts, much less any political, social, or ideological connection with them. **[page 60]**

134.   Testifying about roadblocks that *Interahamwe* members were alleged to have manned, and where the Accused was alleged to have been, the Accused stated that roadblocks were initially set up and manned by civilians, largely through efforts of the civil defence, which was a multi-ethnic corps of citizens rallying together against the Rwandan Patriotic Front (the "RPF") army. Some confusion may have arisen; he suggested, because some people wore clothing falsely said to be a uniform of the *Interahamwe*. He further testified that the *Interahamwe* did not create or monitor roadblocks, and was not officially or unofficially involved at the roadblock sites, or in criminal acts allegedly committed there and therefrom.

135.   Testifying about special clothing worn by *Interahamwe* and alleged Interahamwe members, the Accused submitted that there were both official and unofficial clothing and accessory items which were worn and promoted by the MRND. He also stated that there was no official uniform as such. He further stated that imposters wore clothing which had been associated with the MRND or *Interahamwe* when committing "evil" or criminal acts. This was the subject of a communiqué issued by the National Committee of the *Interahamwe za MRND*, addressed to the International Community and signed by the Accused, which discouraged members from wearing their "uniforms." According to the Accused, this communiqué was intended to dissociate the *Interahamwe* from Rwandan youths who were not members of, but who were publicly perceived as being members of and acting under the auspices of, the *Interahamwe za MRND* and who committed criminal or violent acts.

---

[63]   See *Testimony of Georges Rutaganda, transcript of 23 April 1999*.
[64]   See *Testimony of Georges Rutaganda, transcript of 22 April 1999*

136. Witness DNN testified, to the contrary, that *Interahamwe za MRND* members did have a uniform, made out of kitenge fabric in yellow, blue and black colours. However, some wore clothes of the same colour as the party flag, that is black, yellow and green. This uniform was needed to distinguish the members of *Interahamwe* from members of the youth wings of other political parties.[65] **[page 61]**

137. Finally, the Accused testified that although he did not officially resign after 6 April 1994, his position in the *Interahamwe za MRND* was effectively rendered irrelevant, in what he described as "chaos", both within the organization and throughout Rwanda.

3.2 Defence of Alibi

138. The Defence case included submission of a defence of alibi. In his testimony, the Accused stated that he was in locations other than those alleged to be crime sites, or involved in activities other than those alleged during the times at which the crimes enumerated in the indictment were allegedly committed.

139. In her closing argument, Defence Counsel stated that a notice of alibi. The Chamber notes that no record of a notice of alibi was filed at any time, and that there is no record of such a notice in the judicial archives or within the judicial record. Notwithstanding this, the Trial Chamber finds it appropriate and necessary to examine the defence of alibi, pursuant to Rule 67(B) of the Rules which states that "Failure of the defence to provide such notice under this Rule shall not limit the right of the Accused to rely on the above defences."[66]

140. The Accused, Witness DF, Witness DD, and Witness DDD testified regarding the whereabouts of the Accused between the evening of 6 April 1994 to 9 April 1994.

141. The Defence submitted that in the first days following the crash of the aeroplane carrying President Habyarimana, the Accused was busy seeking protection for his family, trying to obtain news, and searching for food and other goods. The Accused testified that on the night of 6 April 1994, he and his friends were taken out of a car at a location close to the Kimihurura roundabout. **[page 62]** They were first told to sit down and later they were told to lie down on the road. They were finally released, the Accused testified, at 3:00 a.m. on 7 April 1994. They were then stopped at another roadblock manned by gendarmes in Kicukiro. At that time, they were asked to get out of the car, to show their identity cards and to sit on a hill by the side of the road before being allowed to continue on their way. The Accused testified that he then passed "Sonatubes," the airport, Bugesera and the town before reaching his home. The Accused stated that he remained at home on 7 April 1994.[67]

142. Witness DF stated that he had a drink with the Accused on the evening of 6 April 1994, and that DF left the Accused at 9:00 p.m. that night.[68]

143. Witness DD testified that he had a drink with the Accused on the evening of 6 April 1994. Witness DD further testified that he and the Accused separated on the night of 6 April 1994. Witness DD stated that he telephoned the home of the Accused on the morning of 7 April 1994 and the Accused's wife told DD that the Accused had not yet returned. Witness DD stated that at about 1:00 p.m. he contacted the Accused. During this conversation, the Accused told DD that he had encountered problems at Kimihurura on the night of 6 April 1994. Witness DD testified that the Accused told him that members of the Presidential Guard had stopped him there, and that he had spent the night sleeping on the ground.[69]

144. Witness DDD testified that she saw the Accused at 3:00 am on 7 April 1994. At this time, the Accused told DDD that many roadblocks had been erected. Witness DDD testified that the Accused told her that he was stopped at a roadblock at Kimihurura roundabout at 9:00 p.m. **[page 63]** on 6 April 1994

---

[65]   See *Testimony of Witness DNN, 16 February 1999*

[66]   See *Rules of Procedure and Evidence*, Rule 67.

[67]   See *Testimony of Georges Rutaganda, transcripts of 21 and 22 April 1999.*

[68]   See *Testimony of Witness DF, transcript of 17 March 1999.*

[69]   See *Testimony of Witness DD, transcript of 16 March 1999.*

and left that roadblock after 12:00 a.m. on 7 April 1994. Witness DDD testified that she and the Accused stayed at home together on 7 April 1994.[70]

145. The Accused stated that on 8 April 1994, he walked towards the city from Kicukiro neighbourhood with a friend in order to find out whether his family should remain at home or leave. The Accused testified that he and his friend were shot at by the RPF as they neared a gendarmerie squad. After this, he decided to move his family. He stated that he took the road towards Rebero and left his family at the Rebero hotel. The Accused testified that he returned back in the evening and went to the parish mission by car. At the mission, he testified, he found a number of people whom he stated to the Chamber were seeking refuge from the RPF. The Accused proceeded, he testified, to visit the Conseiller to inquire where these refugees would spend the night. He testified that at his suggestion, some of these people followed him to his home where they spent the night.

146. The Accused testified that he went to the Rebero hotel on the morning of 9 April 1994, passing through roadblocks in front of the ETO school and around the air station. He testified that he returned with his family along the same route by which he had come. Arriving home, the Accused testified that he called his father, who informed him that his friend Jean Sebagenzi and his family had been killed. The Accused testified that he then went to see the Conseiller to get permission to move within the sector, in order to follow his father's wishes and bury the Sebagenzi family. The Accused testified that he was denied this permission by the Conseiller.

147. Witness DDD stated that she and the Accused went to the Rebero hotel, located on Rebero hill behind Kicukiro Sector on 8 April 1994. DDD testified that she next saw the Accused on 9 April 1994, at which time they left the Rebero hotel and returned to their house. Witness DDD stated that at that time a curfew had been imposed, and that the Accused went to the Sector **[page 64]** office seeking special permission to move freely. DDD further testified that the Accused was denied such permission at the Sector office.

148. The Accused, Witness DD, Witness DF, and Witness DDD testified as to the whereabouts of the Accused on 10 April 1994.

149. The Accused testified that he returned to see the Conseiller on Sunday 10 April 1994. At this time he was granted a permit allowing free movement and exempting him from the curfew which was in place. The Accused testified that he reached the home of a friend in Muyima, where caskets containing the bodies of the Sebagenzi family were being loaded into a pickup truck. The Accused stated to the Chamber that he continued along with these people as they made their way to Nyirambo to bury these people. En route, he testified, they passed through many roadblocks – where the caskets were even opened to verify that they contained only dead bodies.

150. Witness DDD testified that the Accused received permission to move on 10 April 1994. Witness DDD learned of this when the Accused returned home in order to take a vehicle to go to the abovementioned burial. DDD testified that the Accused returned at 7:00 p.m. on the evening of 10 April 1994. Upon his return he explained to DDD that it had taken a long time because they had been stopped at many roadblocks, they had been searched, and that the caskets were even searched at the Agakingiro roadblock, where also that there were six people to bury.

151. Witness DF stated that he saw the Accused at this burial, which DF thought took place on 10 April 1994. Witness DF further testified that people manning the roadblock at Agakingiro wanted to open the caskets being transported for burial, and that they were also stopped close to a mosque at Biryogo and at a roadblock close to St Andrews school in Nyirambo. **[page 65]**

152. Witness DD provided a detailed description of the day of the burial of 7 people in 5 coffins. He testified that they were detained at the Agakingiro roadblock, 10 metres from Amgar, while the coffins that he and the Accused were transporting were searched. Witness DD could not remember if the date was April 10; however, he thought that it took place on a Sunday afternoon.

---

[70]   See *Testimony of Witness DDD, transcript of 15 February 1999.*

153. The Accused, Witness DDD, Witness DF, and Witness DS gave testimony concerning the whereabouts of the Accused between 11 and 14 April 1994.

154. The Accused stated that at 7:30 a.m. on 11 April 1994, he left Kicukiro along with thirteen other people in a "505" sedan. They stopped at the house of an acquaintance where, the Accused testified, he wished to leave his family. Since this was not possible, they returned to his house. The Accused stated that they drove to Masango *Commune* instead, and that they arrived in Karambi in Masango at around 5:30 p.m. The Accused testified that he remained in his house in Karambi on the night of 11 April 1994. He stated that he had never been into the ETO compound, and was not near the premises on 11 April 1994. The Accused testified that early in the morning of 12 April 1994, he began thinking about how to finish construction of his house in Karambi. He testified that he drew up a contract with a trader and a mason for the construction work. He supervised the commencement of this work on 13 April 1994. The Accused stated that he returned to Kigali on the evening of 14 April 1994. He further testified that he could not reach Kicukiro because of the danger involved. Instead, he stated, he remained at the Amgar garage complex. The Accused testified that he found people hiding there. He stated to the Chamber that he took pity on these people and fed and cared for them. He also began to think of a strategy to evacuate them.

155. Witness DDD stated that she arrived in Kiyovu with the Accused at 9:00 a.m. on 11 April 1994 and stayed with a friend who was living there until about midday on that same day. DDD testified that they did not receive any special treatment at the roadblocks. Each of the adults had **[page 66]** to show their identity card at the roadblocks. Witness DDD stated that the officials manning the roadblocks did not have a special reaction to any of the occupants of the vehicle she traveled in. They crossed Nyabarongo and arrived in Masango at about 6:00 p.m. Witness DDD testified that the accused remained there for three days, departing for Kigali on 14 April 1994. Witness DDD testified that over the course of these three days, the Accused did not participate in any meetings.

156. Witness DF testified that the Accused left after the burial on 10 April 1994, and came back after two days. Witness DF stated that he saw the Accused at the Amgar garage. DF further stated that all of the people at the Amgar garage were there willingly, and had not been taken there by force.

157. The Accused, Witness DDD, Witness DEE, and Witness DS gave testimony concerning the whereabouts of the Accused from 15-18 April 1994.

158. The Accused testified that he arrived at the Amgar complex on 14 April 1994 and remained there on 15 April 1994. He also tried to collect money before returning to Masango *Commune*, where he told the Chamber he remained during the night of 16 April 1994. The Accused stated that he returned to Kigali early in the morning on 17 April 1994. The Defence Counsel submitted that the Accused organized the evacuation of vulnerable persons from the Amgar garage complex. The Chamber notes that the Accused did not specify a date on which the said evacuation occurred. The Accused stated that he met his mother and sister at the Red Cross in Kiyovu. He took them to the Amgar complex, he testified, and later a convoy was organized to move them. This was done with great difficulty. The Accused testified that they were sent back during their first attempt. The Accused testified that he remained in Kigali from 17 April 1994 until 29 April 1994.

159. Witness DEE testified that on 12 April 1994, she went to CHK hospital in Kigali. DEE stated that she then spent two days there and on the third she went to the Amgar complex. DEE **[page 67]** stated that she spent two days there, and that she saw the Accused there on both days. Witness DEE testified that when she saw the Accused there, he was wearing civilian clothing. DEE further testified that she never saw him enter the house carrying a weapon. DEE testified that she spent two days at the Amgar complex and that on the third day the Accused organized the departure for their respective *préfectures*.

160. Witness DEE testified that she, the Accused, and four other people, departed in a vehicle which the Accused drove. Witness DEE testified that they were stopped at roadblocks. On 9 February 1999, DEE stated to the Chamber that at the first roadblock everyone in the car, including the Accused, was asked to produce their identity cards. However, on 10 February 1999, during her second day of

testimony, she stated that they were not even asked for their identity cards[71]. This Witness testified that there was no special recognition or relationship between the Accused and the roadblock controller, and that this was evident because the Accused was asked to produce his identity card.

161. At a second roadblock which the witness stated was near the petrol station at Nyabugogo, the Accused was asked again to show his identity card. The people manning the roadblock also demanded the identity card of Witness DEE. Upon seeing it, these people told the witness that they should kill her. At this point, Witness DEE testified, the Accused begged them not to do so and gave them money. The Witness testified that the people at the roadblock did not know the Accused, which surprised her. DEE stated that she found this surprising because she thought that the Accused was well known throughout the country as he was an official of the MRND party.[72]

162. At a third roadblock, which was not far from the second, and was situated along the road, in the direction of the road to Gitarama, there were many people who had been stopped. DEE testified that on the evening before this trip, the RTLM had broadcast that the vehicle in which **[page 68]** they were traveling was being sought because the vehicle was said to have been used to find Tutsi and hide them. The witness testified, however, that the owner alleged by the RTLM was not the Accused, but was a person who was at the Amgar garage. This car was identified at the roadblock, but its passengers were not required to produce their identity cards. They turned around and went straight back to the Amgar complex. Witness DEE testified that the Accused organized another trip the next day. They traveled in a different car and reached Masango that night, 17 April 1994. They stayed in Masango at the house of the Accused's father.

163. Witness DDD stated that the Accused returned to Masango on 16 April 1994. DDD testified that the Accused left for Kigali again on the evening of 17 April 1994. Witness DDD further testified that the Accused dit not do anything special when he was at Masango, and that all he did was bring back food.

164. The Accused testified that he remained in Kigali without leaving between 17 April 1994 and 29 April 1994. He testified that he was very busy selling out his stocks of beer during this time. The Accused testified that he was approached by the Red Cross during the week of 17 to 24 April 1994. The Accused testified that the Red Cross asked him to draw up a communiqué appealing to MRND members, and in particular to members of the *Interahamwe za MRND*, if they were involved in killing, to stop, and to facilitate the transport of the wounded. The Accused stated that he left Kigali on 29 April 1994 and went to deposit his money at a bank in Gitarama. He then went to Masango to visit his family and stayed the night there. The Accused stated that he returned to Amgar on the following day and stayed there for about a week. On 8 May 1994, the Accused returned to Masango. He stated that he tried once again to deposit money in Gitarama before leaving. This did not work, so he asked his wife to deposit this money. He testified, without providing a date, that he went immediately back to Kigali and tried to shut down his business. The Accused testified that he could not state that he remained at Amgar permanently during the month of May 1994. Rather, he testified, he moved around a great deal and tried to attend to may matters. **[page 69]**

165. Witness DDD stated that the Accused went to Kigali from Masango on the evening of 17 April 1994 and did not return for a period of two to three weeks.

166. Witness DEE testified that she saw the Accused in Butare once but that they did not have any interaction. DEE stated that this was either at the end of April or the beginning of May 1994. DEE testified that Rutaganda did not stay in Butare for the month or so that followed. Witness DEE believed that the Accused was in Masango staying either with his parents or at his home. However, DEE never actually saw the Accused in Masango.

167. The Accused, Witness DDD, Witness DS, Witness DD, Witness DF, and Witness DEE gave testimony concerning the whereabouts of the Accused from the end of May 1994 to the beginning of July 1994.

---

[71]   See *Testimony of Witness DEE, transcripts of 9 & 10 February 1999.*
[72]   See *Testimony of Witness DEE, transcripts of 9 & 10 February 1999.*

168.   Defence Counsel submitted that the Accused left Kigali on 25 May 1994 and that he did not return there again. The Accused stated that he left the Amgar complex in Kigali on 27 May 1994. The Defence further stated that the Accused reached Cyangugu on 31 May 1994. The Accused testified that one week later, around 10 June 1994, he left Rwanda. He further testified that he returned to Rwanda twice to see his family. He stated that he did not return to Rwanda after the end of June 1994.

169.   Witness DDD testified that the Accused arrived at Masango on the evening of 27 May 1994. According to her testimony, DDD and the Accused departed for Gitarama together on 28 May 1994. DDD stated that they then went to Ngange, in Kivumu *Commune* before returning to Masango. According to the testimony of DDD they then departed for Cyangugu on the following day, 29 May 1994. They passed through roadblocks. At each one they had to present identity cards. DDD testified that the people manning the roadblocks did not recognize the Accused. DDD testified that they reached Cyangugu on the night of 31 May 1994. DDD **[page 70]** testified that they stayed there together for a month, before leaving on 1 July 1994, and that the Accused did not return to Kigali.

170.   Witness DS testified that he and the Accused left Kigali on 27 May 1994 and that they went to Gitarama.

171.   Witness DD testified to having left the Amgar complex in company of the Accused on 27 May 1994. They experienced difficulties crossing roadblocks, and had to pay people who were manning the roadblocks. Witness DD testified that their trip lasted three days, and that this was due to the difficulties they encountered trying to cross the roadblocks. DD stated that he saw the Accused often when the Accused came to visit his family in Cyangugu.

172.   Witness DF stated that DF and the Accused left the Amgar complex on the same day, on 27 May 1994. DF testified that the Accused was at first not allowed to pass through the Gikongoro roadblock, and that if he had been able to do so they would not have spent so many days there. DF stated that they reached Cyangugu on 31 May 1994. Witness DF stated that DF left Rwanda on 17 July. DF thought that the Accused departed two weeks earlier. DF testified that when the Accused reached Cyangugu, the Accused did not go to Kigali or Gikongoro.

173.   Witness DEE stated that around 17 to 19 June 1994, she left Gikongoro for Cyangugu with the Accused and others. At a roadblock the Accused's vehicle was searched. DEE testified that the Accused's attitude was not that of someone in control when they were at the roadblocks. DEE testified that other people were supervising and controlling the roadblocks. DEE testified that on the following day the Accused suggested that he should take them to Bukavu, Zaire. They went to Zaire at some point not later than 26 June 1994.[73] **[page 71]**

174.   The Chamber considers the defence of alibi, after having reviewed the Prosecutor's case in the factual findings on the relevant paragraphs of the Indictment.[74] **[page 72]**

4. FACTUAL FINDINGS

4.1 Paragraph 10 of the Indictment

175.   Paragraph 10 of the indictment reads as follows:

> "On or about April 6, 1994, Georges Rutaganda distributed guns and other weapons to *Interahamwe* members in Nyarugenge commune, Kigali."

---

[73]   See *Testimony of Witness DEE, transcripts of 09 & 10 February 1999.*
[74]   See Chapter 4 of this Judgement.

Events alleged

176.   Witness J, a Tutsi man who lived in the Cyahafi sector in the Nyarugenge *Commune*, testified that he had known the Accused since he was young because they were in neighboring *Communes*. He knew the Accused as the President of a sports team, as a Tuborg beer importer, and as someone he had seen leading several demonstrations of the *Interahamwe* of the MRND party. Witness J said that on 15 April, a policeman named Munyawara arrived in Cyahafi from Kimisagara and said that the *Inyenzi* had attacked and shot at the councillor of Cyahafi sector. The policeman gathered people together, including Witness J, and told them to follow him to go and fight the *Inyenzi* who were coming down.

177.   Witness J said the group stopped just below a bar called Mount Kigali by a public standpipe near Mr. Shyirakera's house. At 3:00 p.m., they saw a pick-up truck arrive and stop near the standpipe. They approached the truck and saw two people in front and two people in back in the open bed of the truck. The Accused got out on the passenger side, and went to the back of the truck. He opened the cab and they saw him distributing weapons to young people, some of whom Witness J said he recognized as *Interahamwe*. Among these he named Bizimungo, Ziad, Muzehe, Cyuma and Polisi and said they were *Interahamwe* who had gone for training in the *Commune* of Bicumbi. He said they were his neighbors and he knew them. **[page 73]** Witness J said that he was close to the vehicle, indicating the length of the courtroom as a measure. He clarified on examination that the Accused did not himself distribute the weapons but was standing next to the truck as they were distributed. After this distribution of weapons, according to Witness J, the shooting started. Witness J testified that Muzehe immediately shot someone called Rusagara, who was standint with them, and Rusagara died on the spot. He estimated that from the time of the arrival of the vehicle to the time of this first shot, less than ten minutes passed. When he heard the shot, Witness J immediately fled. The shooting continued, and Muzehe and Bizimungo shot at young people known to Witness J, whom he named as Kalinda Viater and Musoni Emmanuel. Witness J saw them fall immediately and jumped over their bodies as he fled home. He stated that all the men he saw shot were Tutsi.

178.   On cross-examination, the Defence produced two pre-trial written statements of Witness J. In the first statement, which was dated 5 December 1995, the witness said the event described had occurred on 6 April 1994. In the second statement, which was dated 3 May 1996, the witness had corrected this date to read 7 April 1994. Witness J maintained that it was either 15 or 16 April that Munyawera came to gather people together and stated that he had said it was 16 April at the time he made the statement. Witness J noted that it must have been 16 April, as on 6 April the plane had not yet been shot down. He said it was not possible that this happened on 7 April either because there was still calm on that date. He also stated that he did not remember saying to the Office of the Prosecutor that the event took place on 7 April.

179.   Witness J was also questioned as to whether the councillor of Cyahafi was shot before or after the distribution of arms. In his testimony he indicated the shooting was beforehand and in the pre-trial statement it was indicated as having happened afterwards. The witness stated that the councillor was shot during a meeting which took place before the firearms arrived. He suggested that what he said might not have been written down accurately. He explained that he had been in a hurry to get back to work when the interpreter translated the statement into Kinyarwanda. The interpreter had said he would come back to him with a revised statement but **[page 74]** Witness J said he never did. When asked whether he had not met with investigators again on 3 May 1996, he said he didn't really remember that.

180.   Witness J confirmed on cross-examination that the Accused did not distribute the weapons but that he got out and stood next to the vehicle while those in the back distributed the weapons. Witness J was also questioned as to when he fled – whether it was after Mr. Rusagara had been shot as he stated on direct examination, or as soon as people began getting out of the pickup truck, as reported in the pre-trial written statement. He responded that when the young men received weapons and approached them, they thought they were going to be defended. But then the firing began and at that time he fled.

181.   Witness M, a Tutsi man, testified that he was in Nyarugenge *Commune*, in the sector of Kimisagara, when he heard of the President's plane crash on RTLM radio. On the next day, 7 April, he

went to take refuge at the CHK hospital, which was 8 km from his house, after seeing people who had been killed by the *Interahamwe* and left strewn along the road, including neighbors he knew. On the way to the hospital he saw *Interahamwe* who were armed and bodies of people who had just been killed. He also saw two roadblocks, manned by soldiers and *Interahamwe*, with dead bodies lying nearby. He avoided these roadblocks for fear of being killed. At the hospital, Witness M saw many refugees and many dead bodies, three of which he recognized as Minister Zamubarumbao Fredrick and his daughter, and councillor Ngango Felistian. On 12 April, Witness M left the hospital and went to the Cyahafi sector, where he took refuge in the home of Nyamugambo, a Tutsi man, who told him that the sector was being protected by soldiers.

182.   Witness M said that the sector was peaceful until 15 April, when the Accused "had the killings started". He said he saw the Accused at 9:30 a.m. with six people inside a pick-up truck. They were armed with guns and wearing UNAMIR clothing and vests. Witness M was at a standpipe with other people, and had been there about one hour when the Accused arrived, **[page 75]** wearing a military uniform, and stopped in front of the house of Shirakara Nishon. After he arrived, Witness M saw the Accused giving the guns he had brought to the *Interahamwe*, and saw him give a gun to a man named Muzehe. Witness M said the Accused sent his driver, Francois, to look for *Interahamwe* to whom the guns would be distributed. He said the guns were short black rifles, which he saw himself, and he said he knew the men were *Interahamwe* because the person leading them was the vice-president of the *Interahamwe* and they were wearing the clothing of the MRND party. He said that the Accused told the *Interahamwe* to kill the Tutsi and if they did not, he would bring in a tank to exterminate them all. Witness M said he was eight to ten meters away from the vehicle and that the Accused, whom he identified in court, was speaking in a loud voice.

183.   Witness M said that the killing began that afternoon. After hearing the Accused say that the Tutsi should be killed, Witness M went back to where he was staying. In the afternoon, Muzehe shot Nyamugambo, the person who had provided refuge to Witness M, with the gun he had received from the Accused and then he came to loot the house. Witness M heard Muzehe say to an *Interahamwe* who was with him that he was going to tell the Accused that he had already started the job, and Muzehe left directly to go towards the Accused. Witness M was not able to hear what was said thereafter because he fled immediately. He stated that Muzehe did not kill him immediately because Muzehe was his friend and a taxi driver for whom he was a client. According to Witness M, of the 31 people who took refuge in Nyamugambo's house prior to the 15 April, the others were all killed by the *Interahamwe*. He said he knew they died because he hadn't seen them since. Witness M subsequently sought refuge with Alexander Murego, whose house was nearby, and he stayed in this house until the end of the war, during which his parents were killed.

184.   On cross-examination, Defence counsel questioned the circumstances in which Witness M went to the CHK. The witness stated that he went alone and that all those in the house with him separated when they fled. Defence counsel questioned the date on which Witness M saw the **[page 76]** Accused, which he testified had been 15 April. In the pre-trial written statement dated December 4, 1995, the date had been recorded as 16 April. The witness maintained that it was 15 April when he saw the Accused. The Defence pointed out to the witness that on direct examination he had testified that he was with five to ten people at the standpipe, whereas his written statement had indicated that eighty people were there, and that while he testified that the date on which he left his house for refuge was 7 April, the pre-trial written statement indicated this date as 9 April. Witness M affirmed that there were eighty people at the standpipe as he had said in the pre-trial statement. He maintained that he left his house on 7 April, suggesting that it may have been written down incorrectly.

185.   The Defence also challenged Witness M to explain why he had testified that he went to the standpipe to get water, while the pre-trial written statement indicates that he said he went to the standpipe to get guns, which he heard would be handed out for protection of the Tutsi. Witness M affirmed that he went to get guns as stated in his pre-trial statement and he said he thought he had testified to this on direct examination. Defence counsel pointed out that Witness M's statement says that when he reached the standpipe the Accused had already arrived, whereas in his testimony Witness M said that he had been

there for an hour when the Accused arrived. Defence counsel questioned Witness M as to how he knew that the people with the Accused were *Interahamwe*. He said he knew a number of them and that they were the ones carrying guns and killing. Witness M was also questioned on his testimony that they were wearing UNAMIR clothing, which he said he had heard had been taken from the Belgian soldiers who were killed.

186. Witness M reaffirmed on cross-examination that he heard the Accused say to the *Interahamwe* that they should go and kill the Tutsi or he would bring tanks to exterminate them. He was asked why he had not mentioned having heard this in his pre-trial statement, and he indicated that the statement he made at that time had been limited, whereas the Tribunal had not limited him and asked him for many more facts. He affirmed that the statement made by the **[page 77]** Accused was the immediate provocation to begin killings. When asked how he could have forgotten to mention such an important statement, he said his memory was not good.

187. Defence counsel questioned Witness M on a number of other details relating to the incident. In response to the question of whether or not Muzehe was armed before he received a weapon from the Accused, Witness M stated that he did not remember well, that he had given approximate dates and numbers, and that his statement had been made a long time ago. He again reviewed details of the event, stating that the eighty people present were crowded but not too closely, and reaffirming the details of his earlier testimony of the killing of Nyamugambo and that he witnessed this killing.

188. Witness U testified that after the death of the President, the *Interahamwe* began killing in Nyarugenge. After two days, he left his home because of the killing. He said the *Interahamwe* stopped him and others with him, arrested them and took them to a place where they were killing people. According to Witness U, soldiers from the Kigali camp arrived at around 2:30 p.m. to calm down the situation. They told the *Interahamwe* to stop killing, which they did briefly, and the soldiers went back to their camp. Afterwards, Witness U said that the Accused arrived, driving a pickup truck which was filled with firearms and machetes which he himself saw. Witness U stated that he knew the Accused because he had a shop in the business district which sold beer. Witness U said the Accused distributed the weapons to the *Interahamwe* and ordered them to work, and the Accused said there was a lot of dirt that needed to be cleaned up. The Accused remained there with a rifle which he had over his shoulder.

189. Seeing this, Witness U said he left the place because they had started killing the people who remained. He hid in bushes below a nearby garage, which appeared to the Chamber to be the Amgar garage. At this time it was 3:00 p.m. and there was no one at the garage. Witness U then saw the Accused arrive, with many other *Interahamwe* who seemed to be his guards. Witness U estimated that they were approximately thirty in number. Witness U was very near **[page 78]** the garage and said he could see clearly through the bush. He said the Accused spoke loudly as there were many people, and Witness U was able to hear. Witness U said this incident took place just below the garage. He said he did not know the name of the owner of the garage. Witness U left the bushes and went further down. When he turned around he saw that they were killing people with machetes and throwing them in the hole.

190. On cross examination, Witness U was asked how he knew the Accused, how often he had seen him and where. The Witness replied that he used to see the Accused in Kigali, in his shop or when he passed by on the way to meetings. He said he knew the Accused was President of the *Interahamwe* from the radio and from the meetings, and the fact that he took the floor at the meetings and spoke on the radio. On further questioning regarding how he knew the Accused to be President of the *Interahamwe* and the relationship between the MRND and the *Interahamwe*, Witness U said he had heard the Accused on the radio encouraging people to kill one another but that this was before the war.

191. When questioned on the distribution of weapons he witnessed, Witness U affirmed that this event took place two days after the President's plane was shot down. When confronted by Defence counsel with his pre-trial written statement, which recorded him as having said that the distribution took place on a Friday at the end of April 1994, he said he did not remember telling investigators that it was at the end of April. He said the day Agakingiro was attacked was the same day the weapons were distributed and the killings took place.

192. Witness U affirmed having said to investigators that he hid near the Accused's garage. When Defence counsel recalled that on direct examination he had said he did not know whose garage it was he hid near, he affirmed having said that he did not know the owner of the garage. Defence counsel elicited further detail from the witness on the circumstances prior to the arrival of the Accused in a pickup with weapons, and the witness affirmed that soldiers told the **[page 79]** *Interahamwe*, who he said were from Kimisagara and Cyahafi, to stop killing. He stated that the soldiers did not seize the weapons and left the *Interahamwe* armed.

193. Witness T testified that he was a neighbour of the Accused in Cyahafi sector, and that he knew him. He said that the killings that started after the death of the President on 6 April did not reach Cyahafi until late April because there was a group of Abakombozi, people from the Parti Social Democrate ("PSD"), defending the sector from *Interahamwe* from neighboring sectors. He said that around the time of 24 April, the *Interahamwe* attacked the Abakombozi and the killings started at around 5 p.m. He said the *Interahamwe* used guns in the attack. Witness T said that the Accused was present during the attack and had a red pick-up in which he brought weapons. He said that the Accused was standing in the vehicle and at that time the Tutsis and Hutus were separated and that when the killings were taking place, the Accused was sitting in the vehicle. He had an Uzzi gun, and Uzzi guns were being used for the killings. Witnes T said there were guns in the pick-up and that the Accused distributed some of them and the rest stayed in the pick-up. He said the Accused was assisted by the senior *Interahamwe* in the neighborhood, including Francois, the President of the *Interahamwe* in Cyahafi. He said the Accused gave the weapons to the President of the *Interahamwe*, who in turn distributed them. He said the *Interahamwe* gave weapons to those in the neighborhood who did not have any. On cross-examination, Witness T was asked about the weapons that he saw the Accused distribute, and specifically whether there pistols or only guns. He replied that the only type of weapon brought by the Accused was the Uzzi, although the *Interahamwe* may have gotten pistols from elsewhere.

194. Witness Q also stated that the Accused distributed firearms. Responding to questions from the Judges on the connection between the Accused and the *Interahamwe*, Witness Q testified that the Accused was a leader of the *Interahamwe* and cited the fact that he was the one who distributed firearms and ordered the distribution of firearms. Witness Q also stated that **[page 80]** everyone said that the Accused was distributing weapons at the *Commune* level. Witness Q was not cross-examined on this statement.

Factual Findings

195. Witness J and Witness M both testified about a distribution of firearms which took place in mid-April in Cyahafi Sector, Nyarugenge *Commune*. The Chamber found Witness J to be credible. He was consistent in his testimony on cross-examination and provided reasonable responses to the questions raised on cross-examination with regard to inconsistencies between his testimony and his pre-trial statement. Witness M, however, stated on cross-examination, that his memory had been affected by the events he had witnessed. The Chamber considers the testimony of Witness M to be unreliable with respect to details, particularly on dates, time, numbers and the sequence of events. The inconsistencies which arose in his testimony during cross-examination as well as the inconsistencies between his testimony and his pre-trial written statement are of a material nature in some cases. Although parts of his evidence are corroborated by the evidence of Witness J, other parts are materially inconsistent with the evidence of Witness J. Although the Chamber found Witness M to be a credible witness in that he made a sincere effort truthfully to recall what he saw and heard, and readily acknowledged his memory lapses, the Chamber considers that it cannot rely on the testimony of Witness M in its findings. The Chamber found Witness U, Witness T and Witness Q to be credible in their testimonies.

196. The Chamber notes that the testimony of the Accused and Witness DDD indicates that the Accused did leave his house on 8 April, and that he was in Kigali at the Amgar office on 15 April and on 24 April. His defence to the allegations set forth in paragraph 10 of the Indictment is a bare denial. The Chamber notes that under cross-examination, the Defence did not suggest to the Prosecution witnesses

that the Accused had not participated in the distribution of weapons, or that he was not present at Nyarugenge *Commune* on 8, 15 and 24 April 1994. Further the Defence did not produce any witnesses to confirm an alibi by testifying that the Accused was **[page 81]** elsewhere when the events described by the Prosecution witnesses took place, as he does in respect of other allegations in the Indictment. A number of Defence witnesses testified that the Accused was very busy selling beer after his return to Kigali on 14 April, but the Chamber considers that selling beer would not have precluded the Accused from also engaging in the distribution of guns as alleged by the Prosecutor. For these reasons, the Chamber considers that the Defence has not provided evidence which effectively refutes the evidence presented by the Prosecutor in support of the allegations set forth in paragraph 10 of the Indictment.

197. The Chamber finds that on 15 April 1994 in the afternoon, the Accused arrived in a pickup truck, with a driver and two men in the back, at a public standpipe in Cyahafi Sector, Nyarugenge *Commune*. In the back of the pickup truck were guns. The Accused got out of the vehicle, opened the back of the truck, and the men in the back distributed the guns to *Interahamwe*, including Bizimungo, Ziad, Muzehe, Cyuma and Polisi, while the Accused stood by. A crowd of people, including Witness J, had been gathered together at the standpipe by a policeman named Munyawara before the arrival of the Accused. Immediately following the distribution of the guns, Muzehe shot Rusagara, who died on the spot, and the shooting continued. Kalinda Viater and Musoni Emmanuel were shot by Muzehe and Bizimungo and fell immediately. All of the men shot were Tutsi. The crowd did not immediately disperse when the guns were distributed because they had been led to believe the *Interahamwe* who had received the weapons would protect them.

198. The Chamber finds that on the afternoon of 8 April 1994, the Accused arrived in a pickup truck at a place in Nyarugenge where the *Interahamwe* had been taking and killing people from the *Commune*. The pickup truck was filled with firearms and machetes, which the Accused distributed to the *Interahamwe*. He ordered them to work and said that there was a lot of dirt that needed to be cleaned up. The Accused was armed with a rifle slung over his shoulder and a machete hanging from his belt. **[page 82]**

199. The Chamber finds that on or about 24 April in Cyahafi sector, the Accused distributed Uzzi guns to the president of the *Interahamwe* of Cyahafi during an attack by the *Interahamwe* on the Abakombozi.

200. In its findings on these three incidents, the Chamber notes certain common features. In each case, the Accused arrived in a pick-up truck with guns, which he distributed or had distributed, to *Interahamwe* in Nyarugenge *Commune*. The distribution of these weapons was immediately followed by the killing of people who, in at least two of the incidents, had been gathered together at these places prior to the arrival of the Accused.

201. The Chamber notes that the dates of the three incidents – 8 April, 15 April, and 24 April – vary from the date on or about 6 April, which is set forth in paragraph 10 of the Indictment[75]. The phrase "on or about" indicates an approximate time frame, and the testimonies of the witnesses date the events within the month of April. The Chamber does not consider these variances to be material or to have prejudiced the Accused. The Accused had ample opportunity to cross-examine the witnesses. In reviewing the allegation set forth in this paragraph of the Indictment, the Chamber finds that the date is not of the essence. The essence of the allegation is that the Accused distributed weapons in this general time period. **[page 83]**

4.2 Paragraph 11 of the Indictment

202. Paragraph 11 of the Indictment reads as follows:

"On or about 11 April 1994, Georges Rutaganda stationed *Interahamwe* members at a roadblock near his office at the "Amgar" garage in Kigali. Shortly after he left the area, the *Interahamwe* members started checking identity cards of people passing the roadblock. The *Interahamwe*

---

[75] See Chapter I, Section 3 of this Judgement.

members ordered persons with Tutsi cards to stand on one side of the road. Eight of the Tutsis were then killed. The victims included men, women and an infant who had been carried on the back of one of the women".

203. The Chamber is of the opinion that for the sake of clarity with respect to its findings on the events alleged in paragraph 11 of the Indictment, it is necessary to discuss successively the events relating to:

- Firstly, the fact that Georges Rutaganda stationed *Interahamwe* members at a roadblock near the Amgar garage;

- Secondly, the fact that the *Interahamwe* members checked the identity cards of people passing the roadblock and ordered persons with Tutsi cards to stand on one side of the road; and

- Thirdly, the fact that eight Tutsis were then killed and the victims included men, women and an infant who had been carried on the back of one of the women. **[page 84]**

Regarding the fact that Georges Rutaganda stationed Interahamwe members at a roadblock near the "Amgar" garage:

204. The Chamber is of the opinion that as far as the above allegation is concerned, the Prosecutor must not only prove that a roadblock or a barrier was erected near the Amgar garage and manned by *Interahamwe* members but also that the Accused himself had stationed *Interahamwe* members there.

205. Prosecution Witnesses AA and HH identified in the slide tendered by the Prosecutor as exhibit 144, the location where the roadblock obstructing traffic was mounted, the location of the traffic lights and, on the left of the same slide, the wall of the Amgar Garage. According to the Prosecutor, the Amgar garage was located at the boundary of the Cyahafi *secteur*, in the Nyarugenge *Commune*, *Préfecture* of Kigali-*ville*. The main entrance to the garage opened onto the Avenue de la Justice where the said roadblock had allegedly been erected and which was indeed the location that witnesses AA and HH had identified as the location of the roadblock.

206. Witness HH, a Tutsi man, testified before the Chamber under direct examination that the roadblock near the Amgar garage was manned by members of the *Interahamwe* whom he could recognized by the *Interahamwe* uniform they wore, made out of red, yellow and green kitenge material, which was similar to the MRND party flag. During his cross-examination, the Defence asked Witness HH to explain the inconsistencies between his testimony and the statement he made to the investigators, as recorded in the transcripts of his questioning, to the effect that the roadblock was manned by soldiers. Witness HH replied that some *Interahamwe* dressed like soldiers.

207. Witness HH also testified before the Chamber that the young people manning the roadblock and with whom he had been in touch, had told him that the roadblock in front of Amgar was "Georges'". Witness HH, stated that he had been hiding near the Amgar garage and **[page 85]** as a result witnessed what took place at that roadblock. He testified that he saw the Accused come to the said roadblock many times, often in a Peugeot pick-up. According to Witness HH, the roadblock was the Accused's, indeed, like all roadblocks in Kigali and Rwanda, which were all under his control.

208. Witness HH also testified before the Tribunal that, on 20 May 1994, the *Interahamwe* had closed the road on which the said roadblock was erected. Witness HH asserted that he witnessed the arrival of the Accused at the roadblock around 9:00 a.m. According to HH, the Accused ordered the *Interahamwe* to open the road and they complied.

209. Prosecution Witness AA testified that, up until 18 April 1994, the road in front of Amgar Garage, like the neighbourhood, was controlled by the inhabitants of Agakingiro (Cyahafi). The people had erected a roadblock on that road which the *Interahamwe* destroyed on 18 April 1994. According to Witness AA, after the *Interahamwe* had attacked the neighbourhood and taken control of it, the Accused had a new roadblock erected in front of the gate to his garage. That roadblock was solidly built, with beer cases and wreckage from cars spanning the entire width of the road.

210. Witness AA stated that among the *Interahamwe* who used to come to the roadblocks, some were dressed in military uniforms while others wore *Interahamwe* uniforms.

211. According to Witness AA, the Accused was a famous man and the Amgar Garage, which belonged to him, was referred to at the time as a venue for the *Interahamwe*. According to the witness, people even spoke of "Rutaganda's soldiers" at that time.

212. Prosecution Witness T testified that soldiers of the Rwandan Armed Forces had erected a roadblock on the paved road, by a kiosk, near the Agakingiro market. Once resistance waned **[page 86]** in Cyahafi, towards the end of April, that roadblock was then controlled by the *Interahamwe*, who took over from the soldiers, who had gone to the frontline.

213. Prosecution Witness BB testified that he was arrested at the roadblock near the Accused's home. There were more than 10 people there, some of whom wore items of military uniform and others the *Interahamwe* uniform. BB explained, however, that none of those people was a real soldier. Some wore berets, with the sign of a pruning hook and a small hoe, identifying them as belonging to the *Interahamwe*. They were armed with guns, clubs, pangas, hammers, and knives. Witness BB stated that the *Interahamwe* had told him that their leaders were Robert Kajuga and Georges Rutaganda. The people manning the roadblocks said they would not kill anyone without prior instruction from Robert Kajuga or Georges Rutaganda.

214. Three defence witnesses confirmed that there was a roadblock in front of Amgar Garage. Witnesses DSS and DF stated that a roadblock had been mounted in front of Amgar Garage from 9 April 1994. According to Witness DD, the roadblock was erected from 7 April 1994 and was located about ten metres away from the garage, close to the traffic lights on Avenue de la Justice.

215. Witness DD testified that the people manning that roadblock were "bandits". He explained that some of them were armed, but that he saw neither uniforms nor any other signs suggesting that they were members of the *Interahamwe*. Witness DD also saw no distinctive signs or symbols that identified the people manning the roadblock with any political group whatsoever. **[page 87]**

Regarding the matter of the Interahamwe checking the identity cards of persons who passed through the roadblock and ordering persons whose identity cards indicated they were Tutsi to stand on one side of the road:

216. Prosecution Witness HH testified that he passed the roadblock on 8 April 1994. He stated that people crossing the roadblock had to show their identity cards and also raise their hands so that their pockets could be checked for grenades. According to Witness HH, the people manning the roadblock shot at persons whose identity cards indicated they were Tutsi. Witness HH testified before the Chamber that he managed to cross that roadblock despite the fact that he was Tutsi because he was in the middle of a crowd and he was carrying his identity card at arm's length so that his pockets could be searched.

217. During cross-examination, the Defence asked Witness HH to explain an apparent difference between his testimony and a pre-trial statement he made to the Prosecution investigators. Witness HH had told the investigators that he passed through the roadblock without showing his identity card because there was a crowd of people around.

218. Witness HH added that from the location where he was hiding near the roadblock, he had heard the Accused tell the *Interahamwe* manning the roadblock to check the identity cards very well. Witness HH specified that when the *Interahamwe* saw a card with the reference "Tutsi", they took the holder into a house nearby. According to HH, people were arrested in this way every day.

219. Prosecution Witness AA testified that, at the time of the alleged events, the roadblocks, including the one near Amgar Garage, were used by the *Interahamwe* to "do their job", which, according to AA, meant to arrest Tutsis or other persons and to strip them of their belongings. According to AA, to pass a roadblock, one had to show one's identity card or other document that indicated the holder's identity. **[page 88]**

220. Prosecution Witness BB testified that he was arrested at the roadblock near the residence of the Accused where he was asked to produce his identity card. According to BB, when the *Interahamwe* who manned the roadblock realized that he was Tutsi, they told him that they had received orders that very day to present anyone who had been apprehended at the roadblock to their president or vice-president. Two *Interahamwe*, one of whom carried a gun and the other grenades, removed his shoes and took him to the Accused at Amgar Garage. BB was then allegedly beaten by one of the *Interahamwe*. According to BB, the Accused then left and returned a little later and asked why BB who was Tutsi had not been killed. BB than held the Accused by the leg of his pants and asked him why he had not yet allowed the *Interahamwe* to kill him. BB testified that the Accused then kicked him and sent him away to do some work, gathering dirt in some area close by.

221. Under cross-examination, Witness BB acknowledged that upon his arrival at Amgar, when he was taken to the Accused, he was given tea because he was very weak. BB also admitted that a servant had brought him food. He then explained that it was indeed after he had been given the tea and food that the Accused had kicked him.

222. Defence Witness DD testifed that he could not confirm that the people manning the roadblock in front of Amgar Garage checked identity cards. He stated that he did not see anyone being taken aside and made to stand on one side of the road. Defence Witnesses DD, DDD and DNN testified that identity cards were checked at the roadblocks in order to identify RPF "infiltrators". **[page 89]**

Regarding the fact that eight Tutsis had been killed, including men, women and an infant on the back of one of the women:

223. Prosecution Witness HH testified that immediately after crossing the roadblock, he had heard the sound of gunfire as he ran away; he had turned around and seen dead bodies on the ground. Witness HH testified before the Chamber that they were eight of them including, children, men and women. One of the women who fell was carrying an infant on her back. Witness HH testified further that the youths manning the roadblock later gave him protection. They told him that they had killed men, women and children.

224. Under cross-examination, Witness HH initially testified that on crossing the roadblock, he had not paid attention to whether the identity cards of people in the crowd were being checked. In reply to the Judges' question as to the material discrepancy between his testimony under direct examination and his statement under cross-examination, Witness HH stated that Tutsis who appeared at the roadblock were detained there.

225. Prosecution Witness AA, after testifying that the *Interahamwe* stopped Tutsis or anyone else at roadblocks to strip them of their belongings, explained that when people were arrested, they were led away and the sound of gunfire could then be heard close to Amgar.

Factual Findings

226. Based on corroborated testimonies, the Chamber finds that as from an unspecified date in mid-April, a roadblock was erected by *Interahamwe* on the Avenue de la Justice near a traffic light not far from the entrance to the Amgar Garage at the Cyahafi Sector boundary, in Nyarugenge *Commune* of the Kigali-*ville Préfecture*. The Chamber holds that, at the said roadblock, the *Interahamwe* checked the identity cards of those who crossed it and detained those who carried identity cards bearing the "Tutsi" ethnic reference or were otherwise considered as **[page 90]** "Tutsi" because they had stated that they were not in possession of an identity card. However, the Chamber notes that the Prosecutor has not led evidence to the effect that the *Interahamwe* manning the roadblock had been stationed there by the Accused. Hence, the Chamber finds that it has not been proven beyond reasonable doubt that the Accused stationed *Interhamwe* members at the said roadblock.

227. With respect to the allegation regarding the killing of eight Tutsis, including men, women and an infant carried on her back by one of the women, the Chamber notes that just one witness – Witness HH – had testified to those specific events. However, it notes that the Prosecution Witness HH was unable to provide a convincing explanation of the material inconsistencies, identified by the Defence, in his

testimony before the Chamber and his earlier statement to the Prosecution investigators, as recorded. Accordingly, the Chamber has decided to disregard his testimony. Since the Prosecutor had not called any other witness, apart from Witness HH, to testify to such events, the Chamber finds that the allegation regarding the killing of eight Tutsis has not been proven beyond reasonable doubt. **[page 91]**

4.3 Paragraph 12 of the Indictment

228. Paragraph 12 of the Indictment reads as follows:

> "In April 1994, on a date unknown, Tutsis who had been separated at a roadblock in front of the Amgar garage were taken to Georges RUTAGANDA and questioned by him. He thereafter directed that these Tutsis be detained with others at a nearby building. Later, Georges RUTAGANDA directed men under his control to take 10 Tutsi detainees to a deep, open hole near the Amgar garage. On Georges RUTAGANDA's orders, his men killed the 10 Tutsis with machetes and threw their bodies into the hole."

Regarding the allegations that on a date unknown, in April 1994, Tutsis who had been separated at a roadblock in front of the Amgar garage were taken to Georges Rutaganda and questioned by him. He thereafter directed that they be detained with others at a nearby building:

229. The chamber notes that the said allegation follows the allegations contained in paragraph 11 of the Indictment. The Chamber, in its findings *supra* on the allegations set forth in paragraph 11, held that a roadblock had indeed been erected by the *Interahamwe* on Avenue de la Justice, near a traffic light, not far from the entrance to the Amgar Garage, at the Cyahafi sector boundary in Nyarugenge *Commune*.

230. Prosecution Witness BB testified before the Chamber that he was arrested at the roadblock near the residence of the Accused because he was a Tutsi. There were many people there, some of whom wore items of military uniform, while others were clad in *Interahamwe* uniform. According to Witness BB, the people at the roadblock said that they would kill no person without prior instruction from Robert Kajuga or Georges Rutaganda. When they realized that BB was Tutsi, the *Interahamwe* told him that they had received orders that very day to take **[page 92]** anyone apprehended at the roadblock to "the president or vice-president". Two *Interahamwe*, one of whom carried a gun and the other grenades, removed his shoes.

231. They took him to a location which Witness BB identified on the slide tendered by the Prosecutor as exhibit 145 as the Amgar garage. Witness BB was taken to the Accused in his office. An *Interahamwe* hit him. The Accused left the office and returned later. Witness BB testified that he held the Accused by the leg of his trousers and asked him why he had not yet allowed the *Interahamwe* to kill him. Witness BB testified that he begged for mercy but the Accused kicked him and sent him away to do some work, gathering dirt in a place where a cellar was under construction. Witness BB explained that the Accused had forced him to work on the cellar construction site without payment. In his opinion, he was therefore a slave of the Accused's. Witness BB testified that he stayed at Amgar until Kigali was captured by the RPF because he could no longer move about as he had thrown his identity card in some latrine.

232. Under cross-examination, Witness BB explained that the cellar was not under construction but that they were actually assigned to demolish part of a wall to create an entrance into the cellar from the Amgar garage. Witness BB also admitted that a mason had been hired to do the work and that the people, including himself, who were involved in such work were not prisoners, but mere workmen. Witness BB stated that there were no prisoners at that time and that, in fact, there were ordinary workmen who went home in the evenings.

233. Moreover, under cross-examination, when asked by the Defence to explain why, if the Accused had been the leader of a group of killers, BB had chosen to stay at the Accused's place rather than to move about and had found it safer to do so, Witness BB stated that he could not provide any explanation to that.

234. Prosecution Witness T who had testified that, at the time of the alleged events, he lived near Amgar garage, indicated that a neighbour of his, a Tutsi man, told him that, for a while, he **[page 93]** was forced to live inside Amgar garage. Around the end of May 1994, that man was killed. That same day, Witness T, his brother and their employee were arrested. The latter two men were also killed.

235. Prosecution Witness Q testified that, around 21 April 1994, he arrived at the Agakingiro roadblock where he was arrested because he did not have an identity card and because one of the people there, Vedaste Segatarama, had recognized him. Around 8 a.m., he was led into a garage, together with three other people who had also been detained at the roadblock because they had been identified as Tutsis on the basis of their identity cards.

236. Witness Q testified that he had not been to that garage before. He identified it before the Chamber on the slide which had been tendered by the Prosecutors as exhibit 145.

237. Witness Q stated that he was led, along with the three other Tutsis who had also been arrested, into the Chief's office. He testified before the Chamber that he recognized the office of the Accused to which he had been taken on the slide that had been filed as exhibit 149. They were introduced to the Accused, who ordered that they be locked up in the prison because they were *Inyenzi*. Witness Q explained that, in that office, the people who had been arrested were undergoing some kind of registration.

238. According to Witness Q, the prison where they were detained was in an Indian temple with the inscription "Hindi Mandal". He recognized it on a slide, tendered as exhibit 165. Witness Q stated that the temple was full, with about two hundred people. Only a small room, located behind the building and used for storage, was not full. Witness Q said that he was there for some three hours. The Accused then returned and said that 10 people should be taken out.

239. Defence Witnesses DD, DF and DDD testified before the Chamber that, in April, the Accused continued to sell beer within the premises of the Amgar garage. Witness DD stated that **[page 94]** he knew the people who had come to take refuge at Amgar. According to Witness DF people of various ethnic groups had been given refuge at Amgar, and no one was held against his or her will. Both Witnesses DD and DF testified that they saw no prisoners at Amgar. However, Witness DD explained that he did not go around the property to check.

240. Defence Witness DS testified that he remained with the Accused at Amgar from 14 April to 27 May 1994. Throughout that period, he never saw any prisoners or anyone being mistreated.

241. Defence Witness DEE stayed at Amgar from 14 to 17 April 1994. She explained that she was not the only Tutsi there. She knew some of the other Tutsis there. Of the Tutsis she did not know, she was told that they were hiding at Amgar. Witness DEE testified that she never saw any prisoners during her stay at Amgar, nor did she see anyone beaten, tortured or killed.

Regarding the allegations that Georges Rutaganda later directed men under his control to take 10 Tutsi detainees to a deep, open hole near the Amgar garage, and that upon his orders, his men had killed the 10 Tutsis with machetes and thrown their bodies into the hole:

242. Prosecution Witness BB identified on the slide tendered as exhibit 169, a site located between the ETM and the Accused's garage, where according to him the Tutsis were killed. According to Witness BB, at the time of the events referred to in the Indictment, there was a metal sheet wall near the blue fence located at the back to the right. It was at that spot that the Tutsis had been shot.

243. Prosecution Witness Q testified that after spending approximately three hours in the Indian temple, he was brought out, on the orders of the Accused, who had ordered that 10 people be taken outside. Witness Q stated that he himself, the three people who had been arrested with him at the roadblock and 10 other detainees were led away, around 10 or 11 a.m., to a pit, by men acting on the orders of the Accused. The pit was behind the garage, where there was a house with **[page 95]** a tiled roof and a fence. Witness Q identified the metal sheet fence on a slide tendered by the Prosecutor as exhibit 156. He recognized the location of the pit on the slide as exhibit 172, explaining that the metal item pictured on the slide was not there at the time of the events alleged.

751

244.   At the said pit, the 14 persons were made to sit down in a hole, the location of which Witness Q recognized on a slide, tendered as exhibit 168, and ordered to look down. The people who had taken them to the pit then asked the Accused, who was present at the site, whether to use guns or machetes to kill them. The Accused allegedly told them "to kill with guns, is a waste of bullets." Witness Q stated that the people who had taken them to the pit then started to kill with machetes. At that point he bowed his head and then he lost consciousness upon seeing two persons die.

245.   During cross-examination, the Defence asked Witness Q to explain why his statement to the investigators reflected that he had fainted after one man had killed three persons and a second person had killed three others. Witness Q confirmed before the Chamber that he fainted after two persons had been killed. He asserted that he had made the same statement to the investigators.

246.   According to Witness Q, after those two persons had been put to death, the other four persons still alive, including himself, were made to get up and bury them. Witness Q testified before the Chamber that at that point he had no strength left and the Accused spared him and another man. The Accused kicked Witness Q and told him to leave, and told him that he would be killed on the day of Habyarimana's burial.

247.   During cross-examination, the Defence asked Witness Q to explain the disparity between his testimony before the Tribunal and his earlier statement to the investigators. In the said statement, Witness Q had indicated that the Accused had ordered the four persons still alive to **[page 96]** throw the bodies of the victims into the pit and that, once they had finished doing that, the Accused kicked Witness Q who further explained that he then left with the four other persons.

248.   In reply to the question, Witness Q testified before the Chamber that he did not bury the people and that when the investigators had read out the statement to him before he signed it, it did not include any reference to the effect that he had buried the bodies.

249.   Defence Witness DD testified that he knew about the pit behind the Amgar garage and that around 26 April 1994, the Accused had a closed sheet metal fence built in front of the pit. Defence Witness DF also testified that the Accused had a metal fence built to protect his beer stocks. The said fence had no door. Witness DF explained that it was impossible to hear what was going on behind the fence from the garage. According to Witness DF, he was not aware that killings were going on at that location, but explained, however, that after the fence had been built, he could not know what was happening there. He did not hear any gunshots from the said location, but rather from the valley behind the "Hindi Mandal" temple.

250.   Defence Witness DEE testified that on 14 April 1994, the day he arrived at the Amgar garage, she saw a group of about 10 people including men, women and children there. She spoke to some of them and they told her that they had found refuge there. Witness DEE who was not sure where the others had come from, thought that they were the Accused's family members.

251.   During the time that she was at Amgar, from 14 to 17 April 1994, DEE heard gunshots and grenade explosions, but she was not sure where they came from. She explained that she was pregnant and sick at the time and was often lying down. **[page 97]**

Factual Findings

252.   The Chamber finds that all the Prosecutions witnesses who testified to the aforementioned allegations are credible, including Witnesses BB and Q, and consequently decides to admit their testimonies. Indeed, the Chamber is of the opinion that although under cross-examination the Defence pointed out some contradictions in the testimonies of Witnesses BB and Q, such contradictions are not of a material nature and do not vitiate the consistency of the substance of their testimonies, as to their account of the facts at issue in the instant case.

253.   With respect to Witness Q in particular, the Chamber holds that the said contradictions can probably be attributed to the trauma he may have suffered from having to recount the painful events he

witnessed and of which he was a victim. The Chamber stresses further that the time lapse between the events and the testimony of the witness must be taken into account in assessing the recollection of details.

254. Further, the Chamber recalls that the inconsistencies in the witnesses's testimonies and their pre-trial statements must be assessed in light of the difficulties inherent *inter alia* in interpreting the questions asked to the witnesses. It also important to note that these statements were not made under oath before a commissioner of oaths.

255. The Chamber notes that the testimonies of Defence Witnesses DD, DF, DS, DEE and DDD do not refute the fact that the Accused was in his office at the Amgar garage from 15 to 24 April 1994. Such testimonies were offered to prove that the Accused was transacting business at Amgar during that period. The Defence submitted that the Accused welcomed into Amgar refugees of diverse ethnic groups including Tutsis and that no one was held at Amgar against his or her will, nor mistreated, or tortured or killed. The Chamber considers that, in any case, these facts would not exclude the Accused's participation in the events alleged in paragraph 12 of the Indictment. **[page 98]**

256. The Chamber notes, furthermore, that Witness Q identified the hole where the ten persons were killed and where their bodies were thrown on the slide tendered by the Prosecutor as exhibit 168. The Chamber observes that the said slide shows the site identified as RUG-1 by Professor William Haglund, a forensic anthropologist, who appeared as an expert witness for the Prosecution. According to Professor Haglund, who exhumed several sites near Amgar garage, three bodies were exhumed from the hole identified as site "RUG-1". Dr. Nizam Peerwani, a pathologist, who had worked jointly with Professor Haglund and who also appeared as an expert witness for the Prosecutor submitted the following findings on the three exhumed bodies: the first body was that of a man aged between 35 and 45 at the time of death, the probable cause of which was homicide; the second body was that of a woman, aged between 30 and 39 at the time of death, the probable cause of which was homicide; and the third body was that of a man, aged between 35 and 45 at the time of death, the probable cause of which was blunt force trauma.

257. Firstly, the Chamber, on the basis of the testimony by Dr. Kathleen Reich, a forensic anthropologist, called by the Defence as an expert witness, is not satisfied that the scientific method used by Professor Haglund is such as to allow the Chamber to rely on his findings in the determination of the case.

258. Secondly, and above all, the Chamber notes that the Prosecutor failed to show a direct link between the findings of Professor Haglund and Dr. Peerwani and the specific allegations in the Indictment. Consequently, the Chamber holds that the findings of the said expert witnesses should not be admitted in the instant case.

259. Accordingly, the Chamber holds that the findings of the said expert witnesses do not help the Chamber determine the facts of the case. Moreover, the Chamber is not satisfied that the grave site referred to by Witness Q and the one exhumed by Professor Haglund are one and the same. **[page 99]**

260. Thus, on the basis of the corroborating testimonies of Witnesses Q and BB, the Chamber is satisfied beyond any reasonable doubt that, in April 1994, Tutsis who had been separated at a roadblock in front of Amgar garage were taken to the office of the Accused inside Amgar garage. Based on the corroborating testimonies of Witnesses Q and T, the Chamber is satisfied beyond reasonable doubt that the Accused ordered that the Tutsis thus brought to him be detained within the premises of the Amgar garage.

261. Based on the testimony of Witness Q, the Chamber is satisfied beyond any reasonable doubt that the Accused ordered men under his control to take fourteen detainees, including at least four Tutsis, to a deep hole located near Amgar garage and that on the orders of Georges Rutaganda and in his presence, his men killed ten of the said detainees with machetes. The bodies of the victims were thrown into the hole. **[page 100]**

4.4 Paragraphs 13, 14, 15 and 16 of the Indictment

262. The charges set forth in paragraphs 13, 14, 15 and 16 of the Indictment are as follows.

263. Paragraph 13 reads as follows:

"From April 7 to April 11, 1994, thousands of unarmed Tutsi men, women and children and some unarmed Hutus sought refuge at the *École Technique Officielle "ETO school"* in Kicukiro sector, Kicukiro *Commune*. The ETO school was considered a safe haven because Belgian soldiers, part of the United Nations Assistance Mission for Rwanda forces, were stationed there."

264. Paragraph 14 reads as follows:

"On or about April 11, 1994, immediately after the Belgians withdrew from the ETO school, members of the Rwandan armed forces, the *Gendarmerie* and militia, including the *Interahamwe*, attacked the ETO school and, using machetes, grenades and guns, killed the people who had sought refuge there. The *Interahamwe* separated Hutus from Tutsis during the attack, killing the Tutsis. Georges Rutaganda participated in the attack at the ETO school, which resulted in the deaths of a large number of Tutsis."

265. Paragraph 15 reads as follows:

"The men, women and children who survived the ETO school attack were forcibly transferred by Georges Rutaganda, members of the *Interahamwe* and soldiers to a gravel pit near the primary school of Nyanza. Presidential Guard members awaited their arrival. More *Interahamwe* members converged upon Nyanza from many directions and surrounded the group of survivors." **[page 101]**

266. Paragraph 16 reads as follows:

"On or about April 12, 1994, the survivors who were able to show that they were Hutu were permitted to leave the gravel pit. Tutsis who presented altered identity cards were immediately killed. Most of the remainder of the group were attacked and killed by grenades or shot to death. Those who tried to escape were attacked with machetes. Georges Rutaganda, among others, directed and participated in these attacks".

Events Alleged

267. Witness A, a Tutsi man who had worked for the Accused as a mason, testified that on 7 April 1994 he went with his wife and five children to the ETO, a kilometre away from his house, to seek refuge and protection because the UNAMIR troops were stationed there. Upon his arrival, he realized he had not brought any food or blankets and returned home for supplies, leaving his family in the ETO compound. According to Witness A, there were approximately six thousand refugees in the ETO compound, outside and inside the buildings. When Witness A returned that evening, after circumventing the *Interahamwe* he encountered outside, he was unable to re-enter the compound for there were too many people. He spent the night near the sports field of the ETO.

268. According to Witness A, the next day Colonel Leonides Rusatila arrived and asked the Hutus to separate themselves from the group. Thereafter approximately 600 to 1,000 Hutus left the compound. The witness testified that on 10 April 1994, UNAMIR troops left the compound, although the refugees begged them to stay, as the *Interahamwe* had already surrounded the ETO compound. The departure of the UNAMIR troops created panic among the refugees and caused many of them to leave the ETO entrance; as a result, Witness A was able to re-enter the compound where he was reunited with his family. The *Interahamwe* also came in at that time and **[page 102]** mixed in with the crowd of refugees inside the building. According to Witness A, the refugees then decided to proceed together to the Amahoro stadium. They therefore left the ETO and headed in that direction but were diverted en route by soldiers at a roadblock. They were gathered together with their arms up over their heads, and ordered to lie on the ground. A soldier with a megaphone then came to them and told them it was not a good idea to go to the stadium and suggested instead that they go to Nyanza, where he said they would be safe.

269. Thereupon, Witness A and his family headed for Nyanza in a group of approximately 4,500 persons, flanked on both sides by *Interahamwe*. According to the Witness, at this time the *Interahamwe*, armed with machetes, clubs, axes, spears, and nail studded metal sticks had started killing people along the way, threatening people, forcibly taking young girls, spitting on them and committing atrocities. Along the way, Witness A saw the Accused coming in the opposite direction from Nyanza in his vehicle. He pulled over to the side of the road, got out, and stood leaning against the vehicle. Witness A saw a mason who had worked for the Accused pleading him for help, but the Accused waved him away.

270. Upon arrival at Nyanza, Witness A saw the Accused again who was directing the *Interahamwe* into position to surround the refugees who had been gathered together in one spot. Armed soldiers had taken position on the hill overlooking this spot. A sack full of grenades was brought by a man, and Hutus were told to show their identity cards. These Hutus were allowed to leave. Some Tutsis who tried to pass for Hutus were killed on the spot by the *Interahamwe* who knew them, and others were forced back into the group. A grenade was then hurled into the crowd and the soldiers began to fire their guns. Those who tried to flee from the group were snatched back by the *Interahamwe* surrounding them. Witness A saw the child his wife was carrying on her back blown off by a grenade. He was shot and fell to the ground, still holding another of his children in his arms. Others fell on top of him. **[page 103]**

271. When the shooting stopped, Witness A heard the soldiers tell the *Interahamwe* to go to work, and the latter proceeded to kill people with clubs and other types of weapons. They also singled out some girls and put them aside. According to the witness they "had their way" with these girls and then killed them. Most of the women killed were stripped of their clothing, "so that Tutsi women could be seen naked." The *Interahamwe* continued to "have their way" until they left satisfied at around 11 p.m. Witness A's wife and four of his children were killed in this attack. His five year old child, whom he had shielded in his arms, sustained injuries from a grenade explosion. According to Witness A, when the *Interahamwe* returned the next day at dawn, he pretended to be dead. His injured arm was stepped on and he was hit on the head with a sharp object to see if he was alive, but he did not move. He spent that day, which he testified was Tuesday 12 April, at that spot, while the *Interahamwe* looted the bodies. In the morning of 13 April, RPF soldiers came and took him and other survivors away. Witness A testified that there were approximately two hundred survivors.

272. During the cross-examination, Defence counsel challenged the testimony of Witness A as being inconsistent with his prior statement dated 7 December 1995 made to OTP investigators. He had stated that he had three children, all of whom had died in the attack. When asked about his prior statement as to the number of children he had the witness maintained that four of his children had died in the attack and that only one had survived. He testified that he had no interest in saying there was a survivor among his children if they had all been killed.

273. Witness A was also asked about which radio station he was listening to on the morning of 7 April 1994. On direct examination he had testified that on that day he had tuned in to RTLM. The Witness explained that he generally listened to RTLM but that on that particular morning he had tuned in to Radio Rwanda. He further testified that RTLM broadcast only in the afternoon and that he had also learnt about the death of the President on RTLM on 7 April 1994 in the afternoon. Defence counsel also asked him how he had managed to listen to the radio, as **[page 104]** he had testified that he did not own a radio. The witness explained that he listened to the radio at his neighbour's house.

274. The Defence also asked the witness whether he knew the Accused well. The witness answered that he had never spoken to the Accused but had known him for six years, having seen him many times and having worked for him. Through further examination, Defence elicited additional details with respect to Witness A's earlier testimony regarding such matters as there being other persons with the Accused in his vehicle and the Accused positioning the *Interahamwe* at Nyanza.

275. Witness H, a Tutsi man from Kicukiro, testified that his house was attacked and searched in February 1994 by *Interahamwe*, armed with clubs, who had arrived shortly before a vehicle. Witness H was told that General Karangwa and the Accused, who owned the vehicle, were inside it. The Witness

said that the Accused was his neighbour and lived 600 metres from his house. He knew the Accused as a businessman who imported beer, and he also knew him as the vice-president of the *Interahamwe*. When the killings began after the plane crash on 6 April, Witness H took his family to the ETO school, for their protection, where UNAMIR troops told them to come inside the compound. He stated that there were 3,500 to 4,000 refugees at the ETO, some of whom were in buildings but most of whom were on the sports field where Witness H was. The witness testified that the *Interahamwe*, armed with guns, grenades and other weapons, came surrounded the ETO, but that they dit not attack because they were afraid of the UNAMIR troops.

276. On 11 April 1994, Witness H saw the UNAMIR troops packing up to leave. A group of refugees, including the Witness, positioned themselves in front of a UNAMIR vehicle and begged the troops to stay, but they would not. According to Witness H, once UNAMIR left the ETO compound, the *Interahamwe* immediately entered and proceeded to attack, firing guns and hurling grenades. At that time, Witness H saw the Accused with Gerard Karangwa, the President **[page 105]** of the *Interahamwe* at the *commune* level. According to the Witness, as an *Interahamwe* official at the national level, the Accused ranked higher than Karangwa. They were in the group in front of him, and the group began throwing grenades and firing. The Witness saw the Accused before the shots were fired.

277. Witness H testified that he left the ETO with others and headed for the Amahoro stadium which he thought would be safe as it was under RPF control. En route, they were stopped by the *Interahamwe* and led to a road where they found soldiers who ordered them to sit down on the road. Thereafter, a military commander came and told them that he was taking them to Nyanza where he could ensure their safety. Led by Colonel Rusatila and surrounded on both sides by soldiers and *Interahamwe*, the group of refugees was escorted to Nyanza. Along the way, the *Interahamwe*, who were armed with machetes, grenades, spears and other weapons, beat and threatened the refugees. Of the four thousand refugees, many were injured en route to Nyanza. Witness H saw the Accused on the way to Nyanza, at the Kicukiro centre. The Accused was in a separate group talking to a number of people, including Mr. Kagina, a teacher at the ETO school whom he knew to be a member of the *Interahamwe*. When they arrived at Nyanza, the *Interahamwe* and the soldiers ordered the refugees to stop and to sit down. The Hutus were told to identify themselves and to stand up. They showed their identity cards and were told to leave. Thereafter, grenades were thrown and shots fired at the group. Witness H managed to escape and hide under a small bush sixty metres away. From that location, the witness heard shots and cries of pain. When the soldiers ran out of grenades and bullets, they asked the *Interahamwe* to begin killing people with knives. The killing lasted for more than an hour. Witness H heard the soldiers tell the *Interahamwe* to look around for people who were not dead yet and finish them off. Witness H testified that he did not see the Accused at Nyanza. He had waited until nightfall, and then fled to Kicikuro.

278. Under cross-examination, Witness H confirmed that he had been at the ETO compound from 7 to 11 April. The Defence asked Witness H whether he had met *Interahamwe* on the way **[page 106]** to the ETO, to which he replied that he had seen several groups of *Interahamwe* carrying weapons, but that they had not prevented him from going to the ETO. The Defence also asked Witness H to state specifically where he was located on the ETO sports field, the number of UNAMIR troops and their location. Witness H stated that he had moved around on the sports field during his stay at the ETO. He testified that the UNAMIR troops were camped near the sports field. When questioned on the activities of the *Interahamwe* before the soldiers left, and the circumstances of his departure from the ETO, Witness H stated that while he was at the ETO the *Interahamwe* did launch small-scale attacks, which were repelled by the UNAMIR troops.

279. Defence counsel also asked Witness H how the refugees reacted to being diverted from the road to Amahoro stadium towards Nyanza, whether they believed what they had been told about their safety, how they felt, his location within the crowd of refugees, en route to Nyanza, and the location of the bush at Nyanza where he hid during the attack on the refugees as well as the location of the *Interahamwe* and the soldiers during that attack. To those and related questions from the Defence, Witness H replied by providing additional information that had remained unclear under direct examination.

280.   Witness DD, a Tutsi man who was a high school student in 1994, testified that he was a neighbour of the Accused and also knew him as the vice-president of the *Interahamwe*. When he learned of the death of the President, Witness DD and his family fled to the ETO for refuge because the UNAMIR troops were there and they thought their safety would be ensured. While at ETO, Witness DD saw the *Interahamwe*, some on foot and others in vehicles. They were armed, but Witness DD said they felt safe because of the UNAMIR presence. At the ETO, Witness DD stayed on the sports field, and had gone into one of the buildings only once. He estimated that there were approximately 5,000 refugees on the ETO premises. On 11 April, when the UNAMIR troops left, Witness DD saw the *Interahamwe* attack. He testified that *Interahamwe* leaders were present and named the Accused as well as the councillor of Kicukiro, who was also his neighbour, as having been among these leaders. He saw the Accused at about **[page 107]** fifty metres away from the ETO entrance, together with the councillor and many others he was unable to identify. According to Witness DD, all of them were armed, and the Accused had a gun. Witness DD fled the ETO when the *Interahamwe* attacked and was thus separated from his family.

281.   Witness DD went to the Sonatube factory, where he and other persons were stopped by soldiers who ordered them to sit on the ground, which they did. The soldiers said they would take them to Nyanza where they would provide them with assistance. According to Witness DD, the women with children were forcibly separated from the group and raped by the *Interahamwe*. Witness DD stated that he learned only later that the women had been raped, when he saw them again and they told him that the *Interahamwe* had made them their wives, raped them and impregnated them. When they arrived at Nyanza, the refugees were assembled and surrounded by soldiers and *Interahamwe*. The Hutus were then asked to show their identity cards and to separate themselves from the group, following which they were allowed to leave. Witness DD also saw a person who tried to pass for a Hutu, shot on the spot. Once the Hutus had been separated, the soldiers began to kill people and throw grenades. When they stopped throwing grenades, they asked the *Interahamwe* to check the bodies for any survivors and to finish them off. Witness DD testified that he did not see the Accused again after the ETO.

282.   During cross-examination, Defence counsel asked Witness DD about the circumstances in which he had seen the Accused at the ETO - where precisely it had been, and whether it was an open space with unobstructed view. The witness testified that he had been on the sports field when he saw the Accused. The Defence counsel submitted that in his pre-trial statement, Witness DD had stated that he had seen the Accused when he left the classroom with his family and that the Accused was in the school yard. The witness maintained that he had been on the sports field, and reiterated that he had come out of the classroom to see members of his family. He stated that the confusion stemmed from the fact that there was a basketball court near the entrance to the ETO. The Defence Counsel noted that there were several buildings between the **[page 108]** sports field and the ETO entrance and that the witness could have had an open, unobstructed view. The witness responded that he had been on the sports field and that there were no buildings there.

283.   Witness W, a Tutsi man, also a neighbour of the Accused's, testified that he knew the Accused as the vice-president of the *Interahamwe*, and also as an engineer and a business man. On the morning of 7 April, Witness W fled his home, for Luberizi. On the way, he met the Accused setting up a roadblock in the company of the *Interahamwe*.

284.   There were many people at that location and Witness W was able to return to his house, where he hid in the nearby bushes until nightfall, when he fled to the ETO together with four of his sister's children. He went to the ETO because the UNAMIR troops were there. Witness W testified that after the UNAMIR troops left, the *Interahamwe* and the Presidential Guard immediately entered the ETO compound, armed with grenades, machetes and clubs. He recognized some of the *Interahamwe* he had seen with the Accused at the roadblock on his way to the ETO but did not see the Accused. The *Interahamwe* then began to throw grenades onto the sports field and between the buildings where there were many people. His older brother's children and other people he knew were killed in that attack. Witness W also saw his mother die from a blow from a club. He himself was injured though not seriously and was able to flee through the back of the ETO compound to the house of a white person he knew. The latter who could not keep him in his house advised him to go to Sonatube.

285. Witness W walked towards Sonatube, together with others who had fled the ETO. They were stopped at Sonatube by soldiers who told them that Rusatila had ordered that they be sent to Nyanza where their security would be ensured. There were approximately 4,500 refugees at Sonatube. They sat on the ground for about 30 minutes, and were forced towards Nyanza by the *Interahamwe* and soldiers of the Presidential Guard. Along the way, the refugees, surrounded by the *Interahamwe*, were mistreated. Some were stripped off their clothing or money, and **[page 109]** others were killed by the *Interahamwe* and the Presidential Guards. Witness W recognized some of the *Interahamwe* on the road to Nyanza, and he observed the vehicle of the Accused bringing in *Interahamwe* as reinforcements. He testified that the Accused could have been in this vehicle, which he only saw from afar, but he did not actually see the Accused. As they approached Nyanza, Witness W realized that they would be killed rather than protected. He and about 150 of his companions broke away from the group and fled. Some of them were shot from behind by the *Interahamwe*. Witness W and his companions hid in the forest nearby waiting for nightfall, during which time they heard gunfire from the Nyanza hill. They then fled to an RPF zone, the group of 150 having been reduced to only 60 by the time they arrived.

286. During cross-examination, Defence counsel asked Witness W which members of his family arrived at the ETO school with him. The Witness stated that his father, the children of his elder brother and others living in the house were with him. When confronted with his testimony on direct examination, he explained that he had mistakenly said he was with the children of his sister but that he meant his brother. Most of the cross-examination of Witness W related to other events and not to his experience at the ETO and Nyanza.

287. Luc Lemaire, a captain in the Belgian army who served with UNAMIR, testified that he was stationed at the ETO school, until the departure of UNAMIR troops from ETO on 11 April. He testified that there were approximately 2,000 refugees in the ETO compound by the time UNAMIR left. Captain Lemaire testified that at that time there was increased aggression by the *Interahamwe* near the ETO and that the latter were gathering quite near the compound, and were seen sometimes with weapons. Under cross-examination, Captain Lemaire was questioned about the *Interahamwe*. He stated that he had not seen *Interahamwe* in uniform near the ETO, but that he knew that the people he had seen were *Interahamwe* for they were able to move about freely and he had been told so by those at the ETO compound who knew them. **[page 110]**

288. Defence Witness DZZ, a Hutu woman from Kicukiro, testified that she fled to a nearby church mission on 7 April, after hearing the sound of shooting. From there, on the same day she was taken by a Belgian priest to the ETO, about one and a half kilometres away, along with a group of 25 other refugees. She testified that when she arrived, there were about 2,000 refugees at the ETO. More people came subsequently, and Witness DZZ said she continued to hear gunshots. While she was at the ETO, she said that RPF soldiers in uniform came to take away some people who were Tutsi. On 9 April, the UNAMIR soldiers told Witness DZZ that they would be leaving, and she left the next day, on 10 April. Witness DZZ said that about 500 people remained at ETO by the time she left, and that many of those who left went to the Amahoro stadium. Witness DZZ returned home, which was approximately three kilometres away. She testified that she did not see any bodies or any roadblocks on the way. Under cross-examination, Witness DZZ stated that she could not testify to what happened at the ETO after she left on 10 April, or to what happened subsequently at Nyanza.

289. Defence Witness DPP testified that in April 1994 she was living in Kicukiro, approximately 400 to 500 metres from the ETO. She said that she saw the UNAMIR troops leave the ETO on 11 April on her way to get medicine for her sick child. After they left, she saw about fifty people including some people she knew go into ETO. She testified that they were not wearing uniforms and that some of them were armed. She heard gunshots, but from far away. Witness DPP saw people coming out of the ETO, carrying away school property, and then she saw men, women and children leaving the compound. She stated that they were not running and were unharmed. She testified that she did not see the Accused. In May 1994, Witness DPP sought refuge at the ETO. She said that at that time bullets were falling on the ETO, and she encountered some people who had taken refuge there after 6 April and stayed there throughout this period. She testified that there were mostly Tutsi but some Hutu refugees as well. After 11 May,

Witness DPP said that Government soldiers came to camp at the ETO as well, and that there was no problem between them and the Tutsis there. She testified that on 23 May everyone left the ETO, as the RPF were shooting. During cross-examination, Witness DPP stated that she **[page 111]** stayed by the ETO for two hours on 11 April. She said that she did not see people in the ETO being attacked and clarified that she saw people entering but could not see the place where the refugees were from where she was. She stated that one person she spoke to told her they were on the way to the stadium but had been stopped en route and forced back. This person also told her that when they reached where they were going some were killed by knives or shot dead.

290. The Accused testified that on the morning of 11 April, his neighbour woke him up to tell him that the RPF were already in the neighbourhood and that they had killed a child. The Accused decided that he and his family had to leave their house in Kicukiro. They left around 7:30 a.m., with 14 people in his vehicle, and they drove to the house of an acquaintance, passing through many roadblocks. He found his acquaintance about to leave for Kibuye with his family. They left the house of this acquaintance around noon, and after much trouble at the roadblocks, arrived around 5:30 p.m. in Masango, where the Accused had a house in Karambi. The Accused described a mass exodus from the city, with many people on foot and others in vehicles. The Accused said he was never in the ETO, at the entrance or in the compound, on 11 April or any other time. He said he knew of the buildings there only through the slides which had been presented during the trial proceedings and that he had had no reason to go to the ETO. The Accused said he remained in Masango *commune* until 14 April, when he returned to Kigali. During cross-examination, the Accused said that he had not been aware of the fact that there were refugees at the ETO.

291. Defence Witness DDD testified that she and the Accused and their family had left their home on the morning of 11 April and gone to the house of a family friend in Kiyovu, where they arrived at around 9 a.m. They found that this friend was leaving Kiyovu for security reasons. After managing to obtain petrol, Witness DDD said they left Kiyovu around mid-day for Masango, where they arrived at 6 p.m. She said that the Accused remained in Masango until 14 April. **[page 112]**

Factual Findings

292. Having heard and reviewed the testimony of the Prosecution witnesses regarding the allegations set forth in paragraphs 13, 14, 15 and 16 of the Indictment, the Trial Chamber finds Witness A, Witness H, Witness DD, Witness W and Captain Luc Lemaire all to be credible witnesses. They presented a similar account of the refugee situation at the ETO, the attack by the *Interahamwe* following the departure of UNAMIR troops, the diversion of refugees heading towards Amahoro stadium to Nyanza, and the massacre of refugees by soldiers and the *Interahamwe* which took place at Nyanza. Extensive cross-examination of the witnesses primarily elicited further details and background, without revealing any material inconsistencies. The Chamber considers that such inconsistencies as pointed out were not material and could for the most part be attributed to external factors relating to pre-trial statements and other language and translation issues. For example, the Defence highlighted the fact that the trial testimony of Witness A that he had four children who died and one who survived was inconsistent with the pre-trial statement he signed in 1995 stating that he had three children, all of whom died. The Chamber considers that the witness knew how many children he had and how many of them died, and that the error can be attributed to difficulties of transcription and translation, as addressed under the Evidentiary Matters.

293. Having heard and reviewed the testimony of the Defence witnesses, including the Accused, regarding the allegations set forth in paragraphs 13, 14, 15 and 16 of the Indictment, the Trial Chamber makes the following findings with regard to their evidence.

294. The Chamber notes that Witness DZZ was not, and did not claim to be, an eyewitness to the events at the ETO compound and at Nyanza on 11 April. Her testimony confirms that there were refugees at the ETO compound, but as she left prior to the events alleged in the Indictment, her testimony cannot challenge the eyewitness accounts of these events presented by the Prosecution. Her assertion that most refugees had left the compound and that only about 500 **[page 113]** remained there by the time she left

on 10 April, is inconsistent with the testimony of all the witnesses who were still there on 11 April when UNAMIR left, including Captain Luc Lemaire, who estimated – as they all did – that there were several thousand refugees at the ETO compound on 11 April.

295. Witness DPP was on the road in front of the ETO on 11 April, and she saw the UNAMIR troops leaving. She saw other people, including some armed, enter the compound, but she could not see inside the compound from where she was standing. She heard gunshots, although she said they were far away. She subsequently saw some people departing from the ETO but those people were not harmed and they were not running. The Chamber considers that much of this testimony is consistent with evidence provided by Prosecution witnesses, with regard to the departure of the UNAMIR troops and the subsequent incursion of others who were armed. Witness DPP concluded that these others went to loot the building, but testified that she was not in a position to see what was happening inside.

296. The Chamber accepts the evidence of Defence Witness DZZ and Defence Witness DPP but finds that this evidence does not refute the evidence presented by the Prosecution with respect to the allegations set forth in paragraphs 13, 14, 15 and 16 of the Indictment.

297. The Chamber has considered the testimony of the Accused and Witness DDD, jointly, as their testimony is consistent and puts forward a defence of alibi, claiming that the Accused was en route to Masango on 11 April and was not present at the ETO, at Nyanza, or at any of the locations on the way to the ETO from Nyanza where Witness A, Witness H, Witness DD and Witness W testified that they saw him on that day. The Chamber notes that the alibi defence was not introduced until near the end of the trial, after the Prosecution rested its case. Neither the Accused nor Witness DDD mentioned the alibi at the time of the arrest of the Accused or during any of the pre-trial proceedings. **[page 114]**

298. The Chamber particularly notes that Defence counsel did not mention the alibi of the Accused in her opening statement or in her cross-examination of any of the Prosecution witnesses who testified over a period of 18 months. Consequently, Witness A, Witness H, Witness DD and Witness W were never confronted with and given an opportunity to respond to the assertion that the Accused was not present on 11 April at the ETO or at Nyanza and that their testimony must therefore be false. The Chamber has found these Prosecution witnesses to be credible, and finds the extremely delayed revelation of an alibi defence to be suspect. The inference to be drawn is that this defence was an afterthought and that the account of dates was tailored by the Accused and Defense Witness DDD, following the conclusion of the Prosecution's case. The only witness to support the alibi of the Accused is Witness DDD, and the Chamber is mindful that she has a personal interest in his protection. For these reasons, the Chamber does not accept the testimony of the Accused and Witness DDD that they were on the way to Masango on 11 April.

299. On the basis of the testimony cited above, the Chamber finds it established beyond a reasonable doubt that from 7 April to 11 April 1994, several thousand people, primarily Tutsis, sought refuge at the ETO. As all of the witnesses testified, they went to the ETO because UNAMIR troops were stationed there and they thought they would find protection there. The *Interahamwe*, armed with guns, grenades, machetes and clubs, gathered outside the ETO compound, effectively surrounding it. Colonel Leonides Rusatila separated Hutus from Tutsis at the ETO, prior to the attack, and several hundred Hutus left the ETO compound. When the UNAMIR troops left the ETO on 11 April 1994, the *Interahamwe* and members of the Presidential Guard entered and attacked the compound, throwing grenades, firing guns and killing with machetes and clubs. A large number of Tutsis, including many family members and others known to the witnesses, were killed in this attack.

300. Witness H saw the Accused at the time of this attack on the ETO, just before shots were fired, together with Gerard Karangwa, the President of the *Interahamwe* at the *Commune* level, **[page 115]** in a group which began throwing grenades and firing. Witness DD also saw the Accused at the time of the attack, armed with a gun, about 50 metres away from the ETO entrance. Based on this evidence, the Chamber finds beyond a reasonable doubt that the Accused was present and participated in the attack on Tutsi refugees at the ETO school.

301.   Many of the refugees who escaped or survived the attack at ETO headed in groups towards the Amahoro Stadium, where they thought they would be safe as it was under RPF control. These groups were stopped en route by soldiers, gathered together near the Sonatube factory and diverted, having been told that Colonel Rusatila had ordered them to Nyanza where their safety would be ensured. Some women were taken forcibly from the group and subsequently raped. Flanked on both sides by *Interahamwe*, approximately 4,000 refugees were then forcibly marched to Nyanza. Along the way, these refugees were abused, threatened and killed by soldiers and by the *Interahamwe* surrounding them, who were armed with machetes, clubs, axes, and other weapons.

302.   When they arrived at Nyanza, the refugees were stopped by the *Interahamwe*, assembled together and made to sit down in one spot, below a hill on which there were armed soldiers. They were surrounded by *Interahamwe* and soldiers. Hutus were told to stand up and identify themselves and were allowed to leave. Some Tutsis who tried to leave, pretending they were Hutus, were killed on the spot by *Interahamwe* who knew them. Grenades were then thrown into the crowd by the *Interahamwe*, and the soldiers began to fire their guns from the hillside. Those who tried to flee were brought back by the *Interahamwe* surrounding them. This attack took place on 11 April, in the late afternoon and into the evening. Many were killed in this attack, including Witness A's wife and four of their five children. Following the shooting and grenades, the soldiers told the *Interahamwe* to begin killing people. The *Interahamwe* then began killing people with clubs and other weapons. Some girls were selected, put aside, and raped before they were killed. Clothing had been removed from many of the women who were killed. The killing lasted more than an hour. The soldiers then told the *Interahamwe* to look for those who were not **[page 116]** dead and finish them off. The *Interahamwe* left at approximately 11:00 p.m. and returned on the morning of 12 April, when they came back to loot and to kill all surviving refugees. Approximately 200 people survived the massacre.

303.   On the way to Nyanza, Witness A saw the Accused coming in a vehicle from the direction of Nyanza, pull over to the side of the road and get out. Thereafter, he saw the Accused wave away a person who had worked for him and approached him from the marching group of refugees for assistance. Witness H also saw the Accused on the way to Nyanza, standing in a group talking to a member of the *Interahamwe* whom he recognized and other people.

304.   Witness W saw a vehicle belonging to the Accused bringing in *Interahamwe* as reinforcements. At Nyanza, Witness A again saw the Accused, directing the *Interahamwe* who were armed with grenades, machetes and clubs – into position to surround the refugees just prior to the massacre. The Chamber finds beyond a reasonable doubt that the Accused was present and participated in the forced diversion of refugees to Nyanza and that he directed and participated in the attack at Nyanza. **[page 117]**

4.5 Paragraph 17 of the Indictment

305.   Paragraph 17 of the Indictment reads as follows:

"In April of 1994, on dates unknown, in Masango *Commune*, Georges Rutaganda and others known to the Prosecutor conducted house-to-house searches for Tutsis and their families. Throughout these searches, Tutsis were separated from Hutus and taken to a river. Georges Rutaganda instructed the *Interahamwe* to track all the Tutsis and throw them into the river".

Regarding allegations according to which in April of 1994, on dates unknown, in Masango Commune, Georges Rutaganda and others known to the Prosecutor conducted house-to-house searches for Tutsis and their families, and that throughout these searches, Tutsis were separated from Hutus and taken to a river:

306.   Prosecution Witness EE testified that he saw, on three occasions, the father of the accused and other *Interahamwe* go to pick up Tutsis in vehicles, telling them that they were taking them to a safe location. Witness EE testified that he had seen these vehicles go to the river. He also explained that other people were led on foot to the river. He testified that his neighbours had told him that the people taken to

the river had been thrown into it. Witness EE also stated that, from the window of his house, he heard people say they were returning from the river where they had just thrown Tutsis.

307.   Under cross-examination, in reply to the Defence, EE indicated that he could not see the river from his house.

308.   Prosecution Witness C also testified before the Chamber that, in Masango, the people who were tracking the Tutsis went to collect those who had sought refuge at the Bureau **[page 118]** communal in order to beat and kill them. Witness C testified that many Tutsis had therefore been killed in the Masango region. Those who sought refuge at the river were thrown into it while others were thrown into mass graves. In reply to questions from the Chamber, Witness C specified clearly that he did not see the Accused participate in the said massacres.

Regarding the allegations formulated as follows "Georges Rutaganda instructed the Interahamwe to track all the Tutsis and throw them into the river":

309.   Prosecution Witness O testified before the Chamber that he saw the accused, on 22 April 1994, at about 5 p.m., in Masango. According to Witness O, the Accused was in mufti, armed with a short firearm and was driving a white Toyota pick-up which he parked at some 15 metres from Witness O's shop. Witness O then stated that he saw at the rear of this vehicle, guns partially covered with a tarpaulin. Witness O also testified that the Accused was accompanied by Robert Kajuga, National President of the *Interahamwe* and some 10 other people including about four in military uniform and others in the distinctive green, red and yellow *Interahamwe* uniform. Witness O testified that some of the men accompanying the Accused carried grenades or firearms and that Kajuga was carrying grenades on his belt. Witness O further stated that he saw the Accused speak with a certain Karera, in charge of the Youth Wing of the local *Interahamwe za MRND*, in Masango, near a pole from which a flag flew.

310.   Prosecution Witness V testified before the Chamber that the Accused held a meeting at a place known as Gwanda (sic), located between Masango and Karambi, on a date he could not accurately recall. During the examination-in-chief, Witness V situated this meeting at the beginning of the month of May 1994 and, under cross-examination, he stated that it was rather in April 1994. Witness V stated that the Accused conducted this meeting in his capacity as Vice-President of the *Interahamwe*. Witness V testified that the Accused said during that meeting that it was necessary to stop eating the cows of Tutsis and to get rid of the Tutsis instead. Witness V, a Tutsi man, who attended the meeting, fled to safety. According to Witness V, the massacres **[page 119]** in Masango started after the Accused had held the said meeting. Witness V testified that prior to that there had been some looting but no killings.

311.   Prosecution Witness C saw the Accused attending an MRND meeting at Masango. According to the witness, the Accused was wearing the uniform of the *Interahamwe*. The father of the Accused, Esdras Mpamo, was also in attendance as well as a certain Jean-Marie Vianney Jyojyi. The two individuals who took the floor, Mwanafunzi Anteri and a Protestant pastor urged the gathering not to support the Arusha Accords and to fight the enemy. According to Witness C, the RPF and the Tutsis were referred to as "the enemy" at the time. The witness also testified that the proverbs used at the meeting were meant to convey the notion that Tutsis, their families and children were to be tracked. Witness C noted that the Accused was present throughout the meeting and did not object to the statements made there. He was seated with Mwananfuzi Anteri and Sebuhuro at the table facing the gathering. His father, Esdras Mpamo, a former *Bourgmestre* of Masango who at the time of the events alleged was an MRND parliamentarian was also seated at the table next to the speakers. Witness C testified that the attacks against the Tutsis started after that meting.

312.   Prosecution Witness EE, for his part, testified before the Chamber that he had attended a meeting, after 6 April 1994, at which the father of the Accused, Mpamo, who was chairing the meeting, had declared that Tutsis had to be killed to prevent them from taking over. The meeting was held near the Masango Communal Office. According to EE, the Accused was in attendance and was seated next to his father, at a table facing the audience. He explained that the Accused and his father were not the only ones seated at the table and that the Accused had not taken the floor.

313. Under cross-examination, Witness EE testified that he had attended that meeting because he had received a written invitation from Esdras Mpamo. He confirmed that he was personally surprised at the statements made at the meeting and that he had not reacted, nor had the **[page 120]** *bourgmestre*, Louis, who was also present. Witness EE then indicated that he was also seated at the table, next to the speakers, facing the audience.

Factual Findings

314. The Chamber notes that the Prosecutor had led no evidence in support of the allegations that in April 1994, the Accused had conducted house-to-house searches for Tutsis and their families in Masango *Commune* and that, throughout these searches, Tutsis were separated from Hutus and taken to a river.

315. Regarding the allegations that Georges Rutaganda had ordered the *Interahamwe* to track down all Tutsis and throw them into the river, the Chamber is satisfied, based on the testimonies of Witnesses C, V and EE, that the Accused had attended at least one meeting at which specific statements of incitement to kill Tutsis were made. The Chamber notes that the Accused did not object to such statements and that, in view of the authority he exercised over the population and the position he occupied during that meeting, being seated at the table of speakers next to his father, the former *bourgmestre* of the *Commune*, he had acquiesced to such statements. The Chamber notes however that only Prosecution Witness V had testified that the Accused had chaired the meeting and had taken the floor. The Chamber notes that V's testimony on this point is not corroborated by those of Witnesses C and EE, both of whom had declared that the Accused was indeed present at the meeting and had taken a seat at the table of speakers but had himself not taken the floor. Accordingly, the Chamber holds that, on the basis of uncorroborated testimonies presented to it, it has not been proven beyond a reasonable doubt that the Accused ordered that all Tutsis be tracked and thrown into the river. **[page 121]**

4.6 Paragraph 18 of the Indictment

316. Paragraph 18 of the Indictment reads as follows:

> "On or about April 28, 1994, Georges Rutaganda, together with *Interahamwe* members, collected residents from Kigali and detained them near the Amgar garage. Georges Rutaganda and the *Interahamwe* demanded identity cards from the detainees. A number of persons, including Emmanuel Kayitare, were forcibly separated from the group. Later that day, Emmanuel Kayitare attempted to flee from where he was being detained and Georges Rutaganda pursued him, caught him and struck him on the head with a machete and killed him."

Regarding the allegations that on or about April 28, 1994, the Accused, together with Interahamwe members, collected residents from Kigali and detained them near the Amgar garage and demanded identity cards from them:

317. Prosecution Witness U testified before the Chamber that, on a day, that he was unable to pin point but that he put after 6 April 1994, at about 3 p.m., he hid in a bush near a garage of which he knew neither the name nor the owner. Later, Witness U recognized the said garage on a slide tendered by the Prosecutor as Exhibit 143. The Chamber notes that the garage identified is Amgar.

318. The witness testified that he clearly saw the following events unfold near the garage from where he was hiding. The Accused and some 30 *Interahamwe*, some of whom were in military uniform and others in mufti, armed with tools such as machetes, took away some 30 people there to kill them. According to Witness U, the *Interahamwe* looked like the bodyguards of the Accused. **[page 122]**

319. Prosecution Witness AA testified that on 28 April 1994, around 10 a.m., *Interahamwe* conducted a house-to-house search in the Agakingiro neighbourhood asking the people to show their identity cards. They took away those they detained towards the "Hindi Mandal" temple, located near the Amgar garage and a mass grave, at a place now called Jango. According to Witness AA, streams of people who had

been forced out of their homes headed up towards that location. Witness AA was among the persons detained and led near the garage. He testified that the Accused was present at the location where the detainees were gathered. According to Witness AA, the Accused was the leader of those *Interahamwe*. He wore a military uniform, comprising a coat and trousers, and carried a rifle.

320. Under cross-examination, Witness AA reiterated his testimony that the Accused himself did not directly conduct searches, at least he did not see him do so. The Accused was present at the location where the detainees were gathered, near Amgar garage. The Accused was already there when AA arrived. Also under cross-examination, Witness AA testified that the Accused carried a pistol and not a rifle, and that he also carried grenades on his belt.

321. According to Witness AA, the persons who managed to leave this site where people had been assembled were Hutus. Those who were kept behind were either Tutsis or people from another ethnic group, known as member of political parties opposed to the government. According to Witness AA, those persons were later killed and buried on the spot.

Regarding the allegations that a number of persons, including Emmanuel Kayitare, were forcibly separated from the group and that when Emmanuel Kayitare attempted to flee, the Accused pursued him, caught him and struck him on the head with a machete and killed him:

322. Witness AA testified that the Accused was on the spot where the detainees including him were assembled. According to Witness AA, all the persons detained had their eyes riveted on the Accused in the hope that he would have mercy. Witness AA testified that the people were **[page 123]** afraid and that whenever the Accused looked at them they cast their eyes downwards. Witness AA was seated, crouching some 10 or 20 metres away from the Accused.

323. According to Witness AA, the detainees included Emmanuel Kayitare, nicknamed Rujindiri. Witness AA knew Emmanuel Kayitare's younger brother, Michel Kayitare very well. A man called Cekeri told Emmanuel that he knew him and that he was aware that he was going to the CND. Witness AA testified during the examination-in-chief that Emmanuel took fright and took off running. Witness AA saw the Accused grab Emmanuel by the collar to prevent him from escaping. The Accused seized a machete from Cekeri with which he struck Emmanuel on the neck.

324. In answer to questions from the Bench, Witness AA reiterated that the Accused did kill Emmanuel not with a bullet but rather with a machete. Witness AA then explained that the Accused was not carrying a gun but rather a pistol. When reminded by the Defence that he had testified before the Chamber, just as he had stated to the investigators of the Office of the Prosecutor that the Accused was carrying a gun, Witness AA replied that it was a pistol.

325. Under cross-examination, Witness AA testified that the Accused had grabbed Emmanuel by the collar of his shirt when the latter stood up to run and therefore had not chased after him. He further stated that the Accused had not even taken a step; he had merely turned around and grabbed Emmanuel. In answer to the Defence, Witness AA added that the Accused had seized Emmanuel with one hand while holding the weapon with the other hand. Witness AA confirmed that the Accused did not run after Emmanuel. Witness AA then stated that when he was called by Cekeri, Emmanuel stood up as if to walk towards him. Emmanuel walked by the Accused. That was when the Accused grabbed him by the neck. **[page 124]**

326. Witness AA then insisted on the fact that the Accused held Emmanuel by the collar of his shirt and not by the neck as he had previously stated to the investigators of the Office of the Prosecutor.

327. Under cross-examination, Witness AA reiterated his statement to the effect that the Accused had struck Emmanuel on the neck with a machete. In response to the Defence pointing out an inconsistency between his testimony and his statement to the investigators of the Office of the Prosecutor in which he had alleged that the Accused had split Emmanuel's skull, Witness AA stated that he had seen the Accused strike Emmanuel with a machete, that there had been a splash of blood and that he had covered his eyes with his hands.

328. In answer to the Bench which had asked whether the splash of blood was from the front or the back of the head, Witness AA stated that Emmanuel had fallen with his head to the ground and that there was so much blood that neither his face nor his hair could be seen.

329. Prosecution Witness U testified before the Chamber that Emmanuel and another person, nicknamed Venant, were among those arrested and taken near the garage close to where he was hiding. U knew Emmanuel very well. He stated that Emmanuel and Venant were tied together with their shirts lest they escaped. The Accused untied them.

330. Witness U testified that he had then heard the Accused, speaking out loud so as to be heard, telling those who were with him that he was going to show them how they should work. According to U, the Accused had a machete hanging from his belt with which he hit Emmanuel on the head. Witness U testified that Emmanuel's head was split in two. Emmanuel fell dead instantly. According to Witness U, Emmanuel was killed by machete in a single blow. **[page 125]**

331. Witness U testified further that when Emmanuel fell, the Accused then took the kalachnikov which he was carrying on his shoulder and shot Venant who also fell beside Emmanuel.

332. Again according to Witness U, the Accused then picked up their bodies and threw them into a pit with the help of those who were with him. Witness U identified the pit into which Emmanuel and Venant were thrown on the slide tendered as Prosecution Exhibit No. 169. According to U, Emmanuel was a Tutsi and Venant, a Hutu who did not approve of the killings.

333. Witness U also stated that as he attempted to flee, he saw the Accused engaged in killing with a machete assisted by *Interahamwe*. The bodies were then thrown into a pit. Witness U stated that there were two pits – a small one into which two bodies were thrown and a larger into which a lot of bodies were dumped.

Factual Findings

334. The Chamber is of the opinion that Witness AA is credible and, consequently, accepts his testimony. Although contradictions emerged under cross-examination in his testimony with regards to details, such contradictions are not material and do not impugn the substance of his testimony on the circumstances of the death of Emmanuel Kayitare. The Chamber finds that such contradictions may be attributed to the possible trauma caused to Witness AA as a result of recounting the painful events he had witnessed and the period of time between the said events and AA's appearance before the Chamber. Additionally, the Chamber recalls that the inconsistencies between the witness testimony and statements made before the trial must be analysed in the light of difficulties linked, particularly, to the interpretation of the questions asked and the fact that those were not solemn statements made before a commissioner of oaths. **[page 126]**

335. In the instant case, the Chamber notes, for instance, that the difficulties Witness AA faced in describing accurately the type of weapon carried by the Accused, that is, whether it was a rifle or a pistol, may be explained by lack of knowledge of weapons and by the fact that the witness is unable to tell apart the two types of weapons. Similarly, the Chamber is of the opinion that Witness AA's inability to indicate whether the blow unleashed by the Accused cut off the head or neck of the victim cannot call into question the reliability of his testimony since it is difficult for a lay person to ascertain the respective limits of the head and the neck.

336. Based on AA's testimony, as substantially corroborated by Witness U, the Chamber is satisfied beyond any reasonable doubt that, on 28 April 1994, the *Interahamwe* conducted a house-to-house search in the Agakingiro neighbourhood, asking people to show their identity cards. The Tutsi and people belonging to certain political parties were taken towards the "Hindi Mandal" temple, near the Amgar garage. The Accused was present at the location where the people caught were gathered. He wore a military uniform, comprising a coat and trousers, and carried a rifle.

337. Furthermore, after considering the respective testimonies of Witnesses AA and U, the Chamber is satisfied that they are corroborative as regards the circumstances surrounding the killing of Emmanuel Kayitare, a Tutsi, by the Accused.

338. The Chamber notes that Witness U identified the grave where Emmanuel and Venant were killed and into which their bodies were thrown on the slide tendered by the Prosecutor as exhibit 169.

339. The Chamber observes that said slide tendered as exhibit 169 shows the same view as the one tendered by the Prosecutor as exhibit 269, which has been referred to by Professor William Haglund, a forensic anthropologist, who had appeared as an expert witness for the Prosecutor, as an exhumation site identified as "RUG-1". **[page 127]**

340. According to Professor Haglund, three bodies were exhumed from the hole shown on the slide tendered as exhibit 269[76]. Dr. Nizam Peerwani, a pathologist, who had worked jointly with Professor Haglund and who had also appeared as an expert witness for the Prosecutor, submitted the following findings on the three bodies exhumed: The first body was that of a man aged between 35 and 45 years at the time of his death the probable cause of which, according to Dr. Peerwani, was homicide. The second body was that of a woman, aged between 30 and 39 years at the time of her death the probable cause of which was homicide. The third exhumed body was that of a man aged between 35 and 45 at the time of his death the probable cause of which, according to Dr. Peerwani, was blunt force trauma injuries.

341. Firstly, the Chamber, on the basis of the testimony by Dr. Kathleen Reich, a forensic anthropologist, called by the Defence as an expert witness, is not persuaded that the scientific method used by Professor Haglund is such as to allow the Chamber to rely on his conclusions in the determination of the case.

342. Secondly and, above all, the Chamber notes that the Prosecutor has failed to show a direct link between the findings of Professor Haglund and Dr. Peerwani and the specific allegations in the Indictment or even to call the attention of the Chamber to the fact that the slide tendered by the Prosecutor as exhibit 169, indentified by Witness U as showing the hole where Emmanuel and Venant were killed and into which their bodies were thrown shows the same view as the slide tendered as exhibit 269, featuring the exhumation site "RUG-1".

343. Consequently, the Chamber holds that the said findings are not helpful to the Chamber in determining the facts of the case. Moreover, the Chamber is not satisfied that the grave site **[page 128]** referred to by Witness U and Witness AA and that exhumed by Professor Haglund is one and the same.

344. Finally, on the basis of the testimonies of Witnesses AA and U, the Chamber finds that it has been established beyond any reasonable doubt that the Accused struck Emmanuel Kayitare with a machete and that the latter died instantly. **[page 129]**

4.7 Charges as set forth in Paragraph 19 of the Indictment.

345. Paragraph 19 of the Indictment reads as follows:

"In June 1994, on a date unknown, Georges RUTAGANDA ordered people to bury the bodies of victims in order to conceal his crimes from the international community."

Events Alleged

346. In respect of the aforementioned allegation, Witness Q testified in direct examination that he was hiding in the house that belonged to a person he identified as Thomas when an *Interahamwe* named Cyuma took him and a young girl to a hole behind the Technical school of Muhazi (École technique de

---

[76]   See Chapter 4, section 3 (of the present Judgement), factual findings on the allegations contained in paragraph 12 of the Indictment.

Muhazi). The Witness said that when he arrived at this hole he saw the corpse of this nephew lying inside. He said that the young girl was killed by an *Interahamwe* named Karangwa, on the orders of Cyuma and he was about to be killed when a woman he identified as Martha, who at that time was the head of the cell, stopped Cyuma and the others from killing him.

347. Witness Q testified in direct examination that, whilst at the hole behind the Technical school of Muhazi, he saw another hole that he referred to in his evidence as the third hole and he stated that he saw the Accused, in the company of others people, standing in the vicinity of this hole. The Witness stated that, from where he was, he could see this hole but he could not get to it. The Witness stated that the Accused thereafter called Martha who immediately went to him, whereupon the Accused ordered a stop to all killings during the day and the dead buried immediately, as the killings were badly perceived by the people the Witness described as "whites" and "foreigners". According to the Witness, the Accused further ordered that killing should only take place at night. **[page 130]**

348. Witness Q testified in direct examination that the Accused was addressing all those people in the vicinity of this third hole when he ordered that all killings be stopped and all corpses buried. The Witness stated that he did not hear the Accused give these orders but that he had learnt of these orders when Martha returned to the vicinity of the hole behind the Technical school and conveyed them to Cyuma, Karangwa and the others who had been participating in killings. When the Witness was asked by the Prosecutor to state what Martha said, in conveying the orders of the Accused, the Witness stated that Martha said that it was necessary to stop the killing. The remaining people will be killed after the burial of the Late President Juvenal Habyarimana.

349. Under cross examination Witness Q stated that Martha conveyed the orders of the Accused when she stated that the killing must stop and the dead must be buried immediately, because the foreigners were not in favour of the killing. In the tail end of his cross examination, the Witness stated that he saw and he heard the Accused give orders to Martha and the other people that were in the vicinity of the third hole. The Witness also testified that this incident took place at the end of April 1994.

350. Witness AA testified in chief, that on 28 April 1994 he saw the Accused kill Emmanuel behind the Amgar garage. The Witness also testified that there was a mass grave site at this location and many bodies, including that of Emmanuel were later exhumed from this mass grave.

351. Witness HH testified that he was hiding in a bush near a roadblock and he saw Prefect Renzaho telling people manning a roadblock to stop the killings during the day because there was a satellite that was monitoring their activities.

352. The Accused testified that he was taken by a member of UNAMIR to a roadblock where a UNAMIR convoy was stopped. He stated that there were 72 adults in the convoy. He stated that the roadblock was manned by angry people who were armed and soldiers. He stated that on **[page 131]** his arrival at the roadblock, people from the neighbourhood, some of whom were armed with sticks and machettes, gathered around. The Accused stated that the people at the roadblock were intent on killing those traveling in the convoy. The Accused said that when the people saw him alight the UNAMIR motor vehicle, they mocked him. The Accused stated that he spoke to some of the people at the roadblock and he told them that they were being monitored by satellite, in an attempt to persuade them to allow the convoy to pass.

353. Under cross-examination, the Accused confirmed saying to people that they were monitored by satellite and therefore people should not be killed. He stated that he made these statements to remind people of their responsibility. According to the Accused, he also used another argument to remind people of their responsibility. He would say that the International Community would not come to their assistance if they knew about any killings, but the Accused stated that he did not have any contact with anybody in the International Community.

Factual Findings

354. The Chamber considers that Witness Q identified the Accused in court, he knew of the Accused and of his father, before the events of 1994 and he described the Accused as a rich business man who lived in the neighbouring *Commune* of Masango. The Witness also testified that, after having been stopped at a roadblock at Agakingiro, he was taken by a person he identified as Vedaste Segatarama to the Accused. The Witness described how he was made to enter a little office and presented to the Accused. The Chamber is satisfied beyond a reasonable doubt that Witness Q is able to positively identify the Accused and that the Accused was present at this hole that served as a mass grave, as testified to by the Witness.

355. The Chamber notes that there are discrepancies in the testimony of Witness Q, such as his factual account of the exact words used by the Accused, in conveying his (the Accused's) orders. Despite these discrepancies, the Witness nevertheless conveyed clearly the crux of what **[page 132]** was ordered, that is the killing should stop and the bodies buried in order to conceal the dead from the foreigners.

356. It is clear from Witness Q's evidence that the Accused was present at this mass grave site and that he ordered the burial of bodies. However there is no evidence that the Accused gave these orders, in order to conceal his crimes from the International Community. The Chamber is satisfied beyond a reasonable doubt, that the Accused ordered the burial of bodies in order to conceal the dead from foreigners. The Chamber is however not satisfied beyond a reasonable doubt, that in giving the said order the Accused sought to conceal his crimes from the International Community. **[page 133]**

4.8 General allegations (Paragraphs 3-9 of the Indictment)

357. The Chamber now considers the general allegations in Paragraphs 5, 6, 7 and 8 of the Indictment.

Paragraph 6 alleges: *"In each paragraph charging crimes against humanity, crimes punishable by Article 3 of the Statute of the Tribunal, the alleged acts were committed as part of a widespread or systematic attack against a civilian population on political, ethnic or racial grounds"*;

Paragraph 7 alleges: *"At all times relevant to this Indictment, a state of internal armed conflict existed in Rwanda"*;

Paragraph 8 alleges: *"The victims referred to in this indictment were, at all relevant times, persons taking no active part in the hostilities"*:

358. In respect of the allegations in Paragraph 6 of the Indictment, Witness C testified that at a MNRD meeting held in April 1994, it was stated that Tutsis were the accomplices of the RPF. It was also stated that every Tutsi was the enemy[77]. Witness EE testified that a meeting was held at the *Commune* office, following the death of President Habyarimana. During this meeting the Accused's father stated that Tutsis had to be killed, to prevent them from assuming power[78]. Witness Hughes testified that, following radio announcements calling for the apprehension of Tutsis, people actively sought Tutsis at roadblocks and on the streets. Tutsis were terrified to walk the streets. Hughes stated that Tutsis were in hiding, even in areas where the killings had **[page 134]** not begun[79]. Witness W testified that following the death of the President, people in vehicles used megaphones to spread propaganda messages about the *Inkotanyi*. Following this announcement Tutsis were killed, their houses looted and burned, and their cattle killed.

359. The Chamber considers that Witnesses A, B, H, W, O, Z, BB and HH testified about the construction of roadblocks immediately after the death of President Habyarimana. People fleeing for

---

[77]   See Testimony of Witness C, transcript of 04 March, 1998
[78]   See Testimony of Witness EE, transcript of 04 March 1998
[79]   See Testimony of Witness Mr Hughes, transcripts of 25, 26 and 27 May 1998

safety, were intercepted at such roadblocks. Some people were selected to be killed, whilst others were allowed to proceed. Such selection and separation process began with the erection of such roadblocks.[80]

360. Witness W testified that the Accused ordered Councillors and heads of *cellules* to erect roadblocks. Roadblocks were immediately erected and all persons passing through these roadblocks, who produced identity cards indicating their Tutsi ethnicity, were apprehended and some were immediately killed.[81]

361. Witness A testified to having observed Tutsis separated from Hutus at the Nyanza crossroads[82]. Witness DD also testified that, at Nyanza, soldiers and members of the *Interahamwe* surrounded her group. According to the witness Hutus were asked to leave such group. Hutus were then asked to produce their identity cards. On producing their cards, a man who had lied about his ethnicity was immediately killed. The Tutsis were thereafter attacked by soldiers and members of the *Interahamwe*. The witness recalled that grenades were used in such attack[83]. Witness H also testified, that soldiers were everywhere. The soldiers asked them to sit **[page 135]** down and told Hutus to identify themselves and leave. They attacked the remaining group of people, by throwing grenades and firing guns into the group. The *Interahamwe* also participated killing people, with their knives[84]. Mr Hughes testified that a group of survivors from the Nyanza massacre were found with machete wounds to the back of their heads and limbs.[85]

362. Witness Z, a Hutu living in Kicukiro, testified that when he came out of his house, he observed corpses of men and women near a roadblock. He stated that he and others were divided into four groups to dig holes, collect and bury bodies[86].

363. An expert witness for the Prosecutor, Mr Nsanzuwera testified that the Accused held a high position within the *Interahamwe* and exercised authority over members of the *Interahamwe*. The witness also testified that the Accused was often present at roadblocks and barriers, issuing orders[87]. The Accused testified that after he joined the MRND party in 1991, he was involved in the creation of its youth wing, the *Interahamwe za MRND*, and was subsequently its second vice-president.

364. Defence witness DNN testified to hearing that the *Interahamwe* received military training. The witness also stated that such training commenced at the beginning of the war[88]. Witness DNN confirmed that they received this training[89]. **[page 136]**

365. Defence Witness DZZ stated that she had heard about the *Interahamwe* receiving military training, but only after the beginning of the war[90]. Defence Witness DNN confirmed that the *Interahamwe* received such training.[91]

366. Defence witnesses DDD[92], DD[93], DNN[94] and DZZ[95] testified that RPF infiltrators were identified at roadblocks, by virtue of their falsified identity cards. Defence Witness DEE testified that identity cards were verified at all roadblocks she passed through in Kigali, except the roadblock near the hospital. She

---

[80]   See supra, Chapter 4, part 2, on Factual Findings, para. 11
[81]   See Testimony of Witness W, transcript of 28 May 1997
[82]   See Testimony of Witness A, transcript of 24 March 1997
[83]   See Testimony of Witness DD, transcript of 27 May 1997
[84]   See Testimony of Witness H, transcript 26 March 1997
[85]   See Testimony of Witness Mr Hughes, transcript of 25 May 1998
[86]   See Testimony of Witness Z, transcript of 20 March 1998
[87]   See Testimony of expert witness Mr Nsanzuwera, transcript of 24 March 1998
[88]   See Testimony of Witness DZZ, transcript of 11 February 1999
[89]   See Testimony of Witness DNN, transcript of 16 February 1999
[90]   See Testimony of Witness DZZ, transcript of 11 February 1999
[91]   See Testimony of Witness DNN, transcript of 16 February 1999
[92]   See Testimony of Witness DDD, transcript of 16 February 1999
[93]   See Testimony of Witness DD, transcript of 17 March 1999
[94]   See Testimony of Witness DNN, transcript of 16 February 1999
[95]   See Testimony of Witness DZZ, transcript of 11 February 1999

stated that being in possession of an identity card, indicating Tutsi ethnicity, was justification enough to be killed.[96]

367. Witnesses H and DD testified to hiding in the house of a Burundian and survived house to house searches. Defence Witness DF testified to house to house searches conducted in Kigali. Witnesses U, T, J and Q testified that the Accused was present and participated in the distribution of weapons to the *Interahamwe*. It has been established that weapons were distributed to the *Interahamwe*. The Accused was present and participated in the distribution of weapons on at least three occasions. [page 137]

368. The Accused testified that:

"It developed a situation such that the people who were identified as RPF unfortunately I regret the fact and most of them were Tutsis. 90 percent were Tutsis and this led to a generalisation and excessive behaviour which also affected people who I – you know – old men, children and so on and so forth."[97]

"What happened in my country – in our country is an incident which I would call a tragedy, a tragedy. It's a series of massacres, of killings which affected people from the RPF and the Inkotanyi. Yesterday, I spoke about the generalisation of the Tutsis and this even affected children."[98]

369. According to Expert Witness Nsanzuwera, the Tutsi were systematically targeted as such, because they were considered to be opponents of the regime. Mr Nsanzuwera testified that, the militia, including the *Interahamwe*, killed Tutsis and Hutus who opposed the Hutu Regime, the [page 138] victims of these massacres being civilians. Mr Nsanzuwera also confirmed that the *Interahamwe*'s involvement in the killing of Tutsis was not spontaneous but well planned[99].

370. Professor Reyntjens, an expert witness for the Prosecution, testified to the existence of a plan formulated years prior to the events of 1994 in Rwanda, which suggests that the attacks were systematic[100]. Mr Hughes testified that the attacks appeared to be pre-planned due to their consistent pattern.[101]

371. The Chamber finds that there is sufficient evidence of meetings held to organise and encourage the targeting and killings of the Tutsi civilian population as such and not as "RPF Infiltrators", as testified to by Defence Witnesses DDD, DD, DNN and DZZ. The Chamber also finds that this organisation and encouragement took the form of radio broadcasts calling for the apprehension of Tutsi, the use of mobile announcement units to spread propaganda messages about the *Inkotanyi*, the distribution of weapons to the *Interahamwe* militia, the erection of roadblocks manned by soldiers and members of the *Interahamwe* to facilitate the identification, separation and subsequent killing of Tutsi civilians and, the house to house searches conducted to apprehend Tutsis, clearly suggest that a systematic attack on the Tutsi civilian population existed throughout Rwanda in 1994.

372. The Chamber accepts the testimony of expert Witnesses Mr Nsanzuwera and Professor Reyntjens that the attack on the Tutsi population was of a systematic character. The Chamber also accepts Mr. Nsanzuwera's evidence that the victims of the massacres were civilians. The Chamber finds that the

---

[96]   See Testimony of Witness DEE, transcript of 09 February 1999
[97]   See Testimony of the Accused, transcript of 21 April 1999. In French this reads:
       "Il a évolué, et une situation telle que les gens identifiés comme au FPR, malheureusement je regrette, étaient à plus de 90% Tutsi. Ce qui a conduit à une globalisation que je déplore – et même jusqu'à maintenant – à une globalisation et à un excès, un débordement... un débordement qui a touché également les personnes vraiment que moi je... des personnes, des vieillards, des enfants, tout ça."
[98]   See Testimony of the Accused, transcript of 22 April 1999. In French this reads:
       "Ce qui s'est passé dans notre pays c'est un incident, mais pas un incident, moi je le qualifie de drame, de drame. C'est une série de massacres, de tueries, qui ont gardé les gens du FPR et les Inkotanyi, j'ai expliqué hier dans la globalisation des Tutsis, qui a connu même des débordements jusqu'à atteindre les enfants."
[99]   See Testimony of expert Witness Mr Nsanzuwera, transcript of 23 April, 1998
[100] See Testimony of expert Witness Mr Reyntjens, transcript 13 October 1997
[101] See Testimony of Witness Mr Hughes, transcript of 25 May 1998

attack on the Tutsi population occurred in various parts of Rwanda, such as in Nyanza, Nyarugenge *Commune*, Kiemesakara Sector in the Kigali Prefecture, Nyamirambo, **[page 139]** Cyahafi, Kicukiro, Masango. The Chamber finds beyond a reasonable doubt that the attack on the Tutsi civilian population was of a widespread and systematic character.

With regard to the allegation in paragraph 5, which alleges that: "The victims in each paragraph charging genocide were members of a national, ethnical, racial or religious group".

373. As indicated *supra* in the discussion on the applicable law, the Chamber holds that in assessing whether a particular group may be considered as protected from the crime of genocide, it will proceed on a case-by-case basis, taking into account both the relevant evidence proffered and the political, social and cultural context.[102]

374. The Chamber concurs with the *Akayesu Judgement*[103], that the Tutsi population does not have its own language or a distinct culture from the rest of the Rwandan population. However, the Chamber finds that there are a number of objective indicators of the group as a group with a distinct identity. Every Rwandan citizen was, before 1994, required to carry an identity card which included an entry for ethnic group, the ethnic group being either Hutu, Tutsi or Twa. The Rwandan Constitution and laws in force in 1994 also identified Rwandans by reference to their ethnic group. Moreover, customary rules existed in Rwanda governing the determination of ethnic group, which followed patrilineal lines. The identification of persons as belonging to the group of Hutu or Tutsi or Twa had thus become embedded in Rwandan culture, and can, in the light of the *travaux préparatoires* of the Genocide Convention, qualify as a stable and permanent group, in the eyes of both the Rwandan society and the international community. In Rwanda in 1994, the Tutsi constituted an ethnic group. **[page 140]**

375. The reference to ethnic origin exists in the Rwandan life today as it did before 1994, although with different connotations, but still used by most Rwandans, inside and outside of the country. All witnesses heard referred to the Tutsi as a particular group and identified themselves before the Chamber by ethnicity.

376. The Chamber notes that the Defence did not challenge the fact that the Tutsi constitutes a group protected under the Genocide Convention, and further notes that the *Kayishema and Ruzindana Judgement*[104] and the *Akayesu Judgement*[105] establish that the Tutsi group is a group envisaged by the Genocide Convention.

377. Consequently, after having reviewed all the evidence presented, the Chamber finds that the Tutsi group is characterised by its stability and permanence and is generally accepted as a distinct group in Rwanda. Therefore, the Chamber considers that it constitutes a group protected by the Genocide Convention and, thence, by Article 2 of the Statute.

Regarding paragraph 7, which alleges that at all times relevant to this indictment, a state of internal armed conflict existed in Rwanda:

378. Paragraph 7 of the Indictment alleges that there existed in Rwanda at the time set out in the Indictment a state of internal armed conflict. According to the testimony of Professor Reyntjens, in the early 1990's Rwanda experienced a period of political turmoil while in transition to a multiparty political system. During this time several political parties were organised in opposition to the ruling party MRND. These parties included the *Mouvement Démocratique Républicain* (MDR), *Parti Social Démocrate* (PSD), *Parti Libéral* (PL), *Parti Démocrate Chrétien* (PDC) and the *Coalition pour la Défense de la République* (CDR). The **[page 141]** Accused testified that these political parties competed to recruit new members. Among the activities to attract newcomers was the creation of youth wings, and the Interahamwe was the youth wing of the MRND.

---

[102]   See Chapter 2, section 2 of this Judgement
[103]   *Akayesu Judgement*, para. 170
[104]   *Kayishema and Ruzindana Judgement* para. 291
[105]   *Akayesu Judgement* para. 170-172

379.   According to the Accused, the term *Interahamwe* attained a negative connotation and came to be used to describe in popular usage, after 6 April 1994, a large or loosely organized militia which is said to have fought against the RPF[106].

380.   Mr Nsanzuwera testified that the *Interahamwe* evolved from the youth wing of a political party into a militia[107]. Mr Nsanzuwera further testified that, on 5 January 1994, the President of Rwanda was sworn in but he did not swear in a government and the National Assembly as intended by the Arusha Peace Accords. Moreover certain obstacles remained that prevented the full participation of other political parties in the interim government. Consequently, widespread insecurity prevailed in Kigali. On 6 April 1994 the plane carrying President Habyarimana crashed. The interim government appealed to the population to join the civil defence and the RAF to fight against the RPF and eliminate the moderate wing within the government[108].

381.   The armed conflict between the government and the RPF resumed. The RPF battalion engaged in hostilities with the RAF, according to testimonies by Mr Reyntjens and Mr Nsanzuwera. Immediately, roadblocks were erected in and around Kigali and later extended to the rest of the country to prevent the penetration of RPF. However, according to testimonies of eyewitnesses heard by the Chamber, and of Mr Reyntjens as expert witness for the Prosecutor[109], **[page 142]** one only needed to be a suspected sympathiser of the RPF to be targeted. This resulted in a globalisation of crimes with Tutsis being systematically targeted and eliminated for representing the majority of RPF infiltrators. The Accused further testified that roadblocks were set up initially by civilians who, as the "civil defence" were rallying together against the RPF[110]. According to Mr Nsanzuwera, the civil defence was mainly composed of Interahamwe members and radical youth wings of other political parties like the CDR which aimed at the elimination of the Tutsi as a support for the RPF[111]. The Defence expert witness, Professor Mbonimpa, called the RPF a militia and agreed that militia also had a command structure, wore a different uniform, was armed, and capable of carrying out war. Both sides mobilised people for war through their radios, including the RTLM radio on the government's side. He stated that the RPF said that any force that intervened in the conflict was regarded as an enemy force[112].

382.   The Chamber notes the findings in the *Akayesu Judgement* and finds that the evidence establishes that there existed an internal armed conflict in Rwanda during the time period alleged in the Indictment. **[page 143]**

5. LEGAL FINDINGS

5.1 Count 1: Genocide

383.   Count 1 covers all the acts described in the Indictment. It is the Prosecutor's contention that, by his acts as alleged in paragraphs 10 to 19 of the Indictment, the Accused committed the crime of genocide punishable by Article 2(3)(a) of the Statute.

384.   In its findings *supra*[113] on the law applicable to the crime of genocide, the Chamber held that for the crime of genocide to be established, it was necessary, firstly, that one of the acts enumerated under Article 2(2) of the Statute be perpetrated; secondly, that such act be directed against a group specifically targeted as such on ethnic, racial or religious grounds; and thirdly, that such act be committed with intent to destroy the targeted group in whole or in part.

---

[106]   See Testimony of the Accused, transcript of 22 and 23 April 1999.
[107]   See Testimony of expert Witness Mr Nsanzuwera, transcript of 24 March 1998.
[108]   *Ibid.*
[109]   See Testimony of expert Witness Mr Reyntjens, transcript of 14 October 1997.
[110]   See Testimony of the Accused, transcript of 22 April 1999
[111]   See Testimony of expert Witness Mr Nsanzuwera, transcripts of 23, 24 and 27 March 1998
[112]   See Testimony of expert Witness Mr Mbonimpa, transcript of 6 April 1999
[113]   See Chapter 2, Section 2 of this Judgement.

Regarding the acts alleged in paragraphs 10 to 19 of the Indictment and based on its factual findings supra, the Chamber is satisfied beyond any reasonable doubt of the following:

385. Regarding the facts alleged in paragraph 10, the Chamber finds it is established beyond any reasonable doubt that, on the afternoon of 8 April 1994, the Accused arrived at Nyarugenge in a pick-up truck, filled with firearms and machetes. The Accused personally distributed weapons to the *Interahamwe* and ordered them to go to work stating that there was a lot of dirt that needed to be cleaned up. The Accused was carrying a rifle slung over his shoulder and a machete hanging from his belt. The Chamber also finds that it is established beyond any reasonable doubt that on 15 April 1994 in the afternoon, the Accused arrived at the Cyahafi Sector, Nyarugenge *Commune*, in a pick-up truck. The pick-up was parked near a public standpipe. The Accused got out of the vehicle, opened the back of the truck where the guns were **[page 144]** kept. The men who had come with him distributed the weapons to members of the *Interahamwe*. Immediately after the distribution of rifles, those who received them started shooting. Three persons were shot dead; all were Tutsis. The Chamber also finds that it is established beyond a reasonable doubt that on or about 24 April 1994, in the Cyahafi Sector, the Accused distributed Uzzi guns to the President of the *Interahamwe* of Cyahafi during an attack by the *Interahamwe* on the Abakombozi.

386. In the opinion of the Chamber, the Accused is individually criminally responsible by reason of such acts for having aided and abetted in the preparation for and perpetration of killings of members of the Tutsi group and for having caused serious bodily or mental harm to members of said group.

387. With respect to the acts alleged under paragraph 11 of the Indictment, the Prosecutor failed to satisfy the Chamber that such acts are proven beyond any reasonable doubt and that the Accused incurs criminal responsibility as a result.

388. Regarding the allegations included in paragraph 12 of the Indictment, the Chamber is satisfied beyond any reasonable doubt that in April 1994, Tutsis who had been separated at a roadblock in front of Amgar garage were taken to the office of the Accused inside Amgar garage and that the Accused thereafter directed that these Tutsis be detained within Amgar. The Accused subsequently directed men under his control to take fourteen detainees, at least four of whom were Tutsis, to a deep hole near Amgar garage. On the orders of the Accused and in his presence, his men killed ten of the detainees with machetes. The bodies of the victims were thrown into the hole.

389. In the opinion of the Chamber, the Accused is individually criminally responsible as charged for having ordered, committed, aided and abetted in the preparation and execution of **[page 145]** killings of members of the Tutsi group and caused serious bodily or mental harm to members of said group.

390. As concerns the acts alleged in paragraphs 13, 14, 15 and 16 of the Indictment, the Chamber finds that these have been established beyond any reasonable doubt. From 7 April to 11 April 1994, several thousand persons, most of them Tutsis, sought refuge at the ETO. Members of the *Interahamwe*, armed with rifles, grenades, machetes and cudgels gathered outside the ETO. Prior to the attack, the Hutus were separated from the Tutsis who were at the ETO, following which hundreds of Hutus then left the ETO compound. When UNAMIR troops withdrew from the ETO on 11 April 1994, members of the *Interahamwe* and of the Presidential Guard surrounded the compound and attacked the refugees, throwing grenades, firing shots and killing people with machetes and cudgels. The attack resulted in the deaths of a large number of Tutsis. The Accused was present during the ETO attack, armed with a rifle in the midst of a group of attackers who proceeded to throw grenades and fire shots. He was seen about fifty metres away from the entrance to the ETO. The Chamber finds that it is established beyond any reasonable doubt that the Accused was at the ETO and that he participated in the attack against the Tutsi refugees.

391. A large number of the refugees who managed to escape or survived the attack on the ETO then headed in groups for the Amahoro Stadium. On their way, they were intercepted by soldiers who assembled them close to the Sonatube factory and diverted them towards Nyanza. They were insulted, threatened and killed by soldiers and members of the *Interahamwe* who were escorting them and who were armed with machetes, cudgels, axes and other weapons. At Nyanza, the *Interahamwe* forced the

refugees to stop; they were assembled and made to sit at the foot of a hill where armed soldiers stood. The refugees were surrounded by *Interahamwe* and soldiers. The Hutus were asked to stand up and identify themselves and were subsequently allowed to leave. Some Tutsis who tried to leave pretending to be Hutus were killed on the spot by members of the *Interahamwe* who knew them. Grenades were then hurled into the crowd by the **[page 146]** *Interahamwe* and the soldiers on the hill started shooting. Those who tried to escape were escorted back by the *Interahamwe*. Many people were killed. After firing shots and throwing grenades at the refugees, the soldiers ordered the *Interahamwe* to start killing them. Thereupon the *Interahamwe* started killing, using cudgels and other weapons. Some young girls were singled out, taken aside and raped before being killed. Many of the women who were killed were stripped of their clothing. The soldiers then ordered the *Interahamwe* to check for survivors and to finish them off. The Accused directed the *Interahamwe* who were armed with grenades, machetes and clubs into position to surround the refugees just prior to the massacre. The Chamber finds that it has been established beyond any reasonable doubt that the Accused was present and participated in the Nyanza attack. Furthermore, it holds that by his presence, the Accused abetted in the perpetration of the crimes.

392. With respect to the acts alleged against the Accused, as described in paragraphs 13 to 16 of the Indictment, the Chamber finds that individual criminal responsibility attached to the Accused for having committed, aided and abetted in the killings of members of the Tutsi group and having caused serious bodily or mental harm to members of the Tutsi group.

393. With respect to the allegations made in paragraph 17 of the Indictment, the Chamber notes that the Prosecutor has failed to lead evidence in support of the allegations that, in April 1994, the Accused conducted searches in the Masango *Commune*. Nor has the Prosecutor satisfied the Chamber beyond any reasonable doubt that the Accused instructed that all Tutsis be tracked down and thrown into the river.

394. The Chamber finds, with regard to the events alleged in paragraph 18, that it is established beyond any reasonable doubt that, on 28 April 1994, *Interahamwe* conducted house-to-house searches in the Agakingiro neighbourhood demanding identity cards from people. Tutsis and people belonging to certain political parties were taken to the "Hindi Mandal" temple, near Amgar garage. The Accused was present at the location where the detainees had been gathered. **[page 147]** He was dressed in military uniform, including a coat and trousers, and was carrying a rifle. Among the detainees was Emmanuel Kayitare, alias Rujindiri, a Tutsi. A man called Cekeri told Emmanuel that he knew him and that he was aware that he was going to the National Development Council (CND). Emmanuel became frightened and took off running. The Accused caught Emmanuel by the collar of his shirt to prevent him from running away. He struck Emmanuel Kayitare on the head with a machete, killing him instantly.

395. The Chamber finds that the Accused incurs individual criminal responsibility for such acts for having personally killed a Tutsi and for having aided and abetted in the preparation or causing of serious bodily and mental harm on members of the Tutsi group.

396. Regarding the events alleged in paragraph 19 of the Indictment, the Chamber finds that, while it is established that the Accused ordered that the bodies of the victims be buried, the Prosecutor, however, failed to satisfy the Chamber beyond reasonable doubt that the Accused gave such orders in order to conceal his crimes from the international community.

397. In light of the foregoing, the Chamber is satisfied beyond reasonable doubt that the Accused incurs criminal responsibility, under Article 6(1) of the Statute, for having ordered, committed or otherwise aided and abetted in the preparation or execution of murders and the causing of serious bodily or mental harm on members of the Tutsi group. **[page 148]**

As to whether the above-mentioned acts were committed against the Tutsi group, specifically targeted, as such, and whether the Accused had the requisite intent in committing the above-mentioned acts for which he incurs criminal responsibility:

398. In its findings on the applicable law with respect to the crime of genocide[114], the Chamber held that, in practice, intent may be determined, on a case by case basis, through a logical inference from the material evidence submitted to it, and which establish a consistent pattern of conduct on the part of the Accused. Quoting a text from the findings in the *Akayesu Judgement*, it holds:

> "On the issue of determining the offender's specific intent, the Chamber considers that the intent is a mental factor which is difficult, even impossible, to determine. This is the reason why, in the absence of a confession from the Accused, his intent can be inferred from a certain number of presumptions of fact. The Chamber considers that it is possible to deduce the genocidal intent inherent in a particular act charged from the general context of the perpetration of other culpable acts systematically directed against that same group, whether these acts were committed by the same offender or by others. Other factors, such as the scale of atrocities committed, their general nature, in a region or a country, or furthermore, the fact of deliberately and systematically targeting victims on account of their membership of a particular group, while excluding the members of other groups, can enable the Chamber to infer the genocidal intent of a particular act".[115]

399. The Chamber notes that many corroborating testimonies presented at trial show that the Accused actively participated in the widespread attacks and killings committed against the Tutsi group. The Chamber is satisfied that the Accused, who held a position of authority because of his social standing, the reputation of his father and, above all, his position within the **[page 149]** *Interahamwe*, ordered and abetted in the commission of crimes against members of the Tutsi group. He also directly participated in committing crimes against Tutsis. The victims were systematically selected because they belonged to the Tutsi group and for the very fact that they belonged to the said group. As a result, the Chamber is satisfied beyond any reasonable doubt that, at the time of commission of all the above-mentioned acts which in its opinion are proven, the Accused had indeed the intent to destroy the Tutsi group as such.

400. Moreover, on the basis of evidence proffered at trial and discussed in this Judgement under the section on the general allegations,[116] the Chamber finds that, at the time of the events referred to in the Indictment, numerous atrocities were committed against Tutsis in Rwanda. From the widespread nature of such atrocities, throughout the Rwandan territory, and the fact that the victims were systematically and deliberately selected owing to their being members of the Tutsi group, to the exclusion of individuals who were not members of the said group, the Chamber is able to infer a general context within which acts aimed at destroying the Tutsi group were perpetrated. Consequently, the Chamber notes that such acts as are charged against the Accused were part of an overall context within which other criminal acts systematically directed against members of the Tutsi group, targeted as such, were committed.

401. The Chamber recalls that, in its findings on the general allegations, it also indicated that, in its opinion, the Tutsi group clearly constitutes a protected group, within the meaning of the Convention on genocide.

402. In light of the foregoing, the Chamber is satisfied beyond any reasonable doubt; **firstly**, that the above-mentioned acts for which the Accused incurs individual responsibility on the basis of the allegations under paragraphs 10, 12, 13, 14, 15, 16 and 18 of the Indictment, are constitutive of the material elements of the crime of genocide; **secondly**, that such acts were **[page 150]** committed by the Accused with the specific intent to destroy the Tutsi group as such; and **thirdly**, that the Tutsi group is a protected group under the Convention on genocide. Consequently, the Chamber finds that the Accused incurs individual criminal responsibility for the crime of genocide.

---

[114] See Chapter 2, Section 2 of this Judgement.
[115] *Akayesu Judgement*, para. 523.
[116] See Chapter 4, Section 8 of this Judgement.

5.2 Count 2: Crime Against Humanity (extermination)

403. Count 2 of the Indictment charges the Accused with crimes against humanity (extermination), pursuant to Article 3(b) and Article 6(1) of the Statute, for the acts alleged in paragraphs 10 to 19 of the Indictment.

404. In respect of paragraph 10 of the Indictment, the Chambers finds that on 8 April 1994, the Accused arrived at Nyarugenge *Commune* in a pick-up truck, carrying firearms and machetes. The Accused distributed weapons to the *Interahamwe* and ordered them to go to work, stating that there was a lot of dirt that needed to be cleaned up.

405. The Chamber finds that on the afternoon of 15 April 1994, the Accused went to Cyahafi Sector, Nyarugenge *Commune* in a pick-up truck. The Accused opened the back of the truck and the men who were with him distributed weapons to the *Interahamwe*. The Chamber also finds that on or about 24 April 1994 and in the Cyahafi sector, the Accused distributed fire arms to the President of the *Interahamwe* of Cyahafi, during an attack by the *Interahamwe* on the Abakombozi.

406. In respect of the allegations in paragraph 12 of the Indictment, the Chamber finds that in April 1994 Tutsis were singled out at a roadblock near the Amgar garage and taken to the Accused, who ordered the detention of these people. The Accused subsequently ordered that 14 detainees be taken to a hole near the Amgar garage. On the orders of the Accused and in his presence, ten of these detainees were killed and their bodies were thrown into the hole. **[page 151]**

407. In respect of the allegations in paragraphs 13 and 14 of the Indictment, the Chamber finds that several thousand people, mostly Tutsis, sought refuge at the ETO, from 7 to 11 April 1994. Following the departure of UNAMIR from the ETO, on 11 April 1994, Colonel Leonides Rusatila went into the ETO compound and separated Hutus from Tutsis and several hundred Hutus left the ETO. Thereafter the *Interahamwe*, together with the Presidential Guard attacked the people in the compound. The Accused was present and participated in this attack. A number of Tutsis, including many family members and others known to the witnesses were killed in the attack.

408. In respect of the allegations in paragraphs 15 and 16 of the Indictment, the Chamber finds that the Accused was present and participated in the forced diversion of refugees to Nyanza and that he directed and participated in the attack at Nyanza on 11 April 1994.

409. The Chamber notes that paragraph 16 of the Indictment alleges that certain events, namely the separation of Hutus and Tutsis refugees and the attack on the Tutsis refugees, took place on or about 12 April 1994. As noted by the Prosecutor, these events took place on 11 April 1994. The Chamber does not consider this variance to be material, particularly in light of the language "on or about". The sequence of events leading to the massacre is described in paragraphs 14, 15 and 16 of the Indictment as having commenced on 11 April 1994. Moreover, the killing at Nyanza was resumed on the morning of 12 April 1994. The Chamber considers that 11 April 1994 constitutes "on or about April 12, 1994".

410. The Chamber further notes that paragraphs 15 and 16 of the Indictment allege that refugees were transferred to a gravel pit near the primary school of Nyanza, where they were surrounded and attacked. As the Defence indicated in her closing statement, none of the witnesses described the site of the massacre as a gravel pit. The evidence establishes that the refugees were assembled and surrounded at a site at Nyanza, at the base of a nearby hill. The **[page 152]** Chamber does not consider the description of this site as a gravel pit in the allegation, to be of the essence to the charges set forth in the Indictment and finds that the allegations set forth in paragraph 15 and 16 of the Indictment have been proved, beyond a reasonable doubt.

411. In respect of the allegations in paragraph 18 of the Indictment, the Chamber finds beyond a reasonable doubt that on 28 April 1994, Emmanuel Kayitare, together with other people, were taken to the "Hindi Mandal" temple, near the Amgar Garage, where they were detained. The Accused was present at this location, and when Emmanuel Kayitare tried to escape by running off, the Accused grabbed him by his collar and struck him on his head with a machete, which resulted in his death.

412. The Chamber relies on this factual finding to hold the Accused criminally responsible for crimes against humanity (murder), as charged in Count 7 of the Indictment. The Chamber finds that the act of killing Emmanuel Kayitare, taken together with other proven acts, such as, the distribution of fire arms and machetes to the *Interahamwe* and the killings at ETO and Nyanza, cumulatively form the basis for crimes against humanity (extermination). The Chamber will therefore take into consideration the factual findings in paragraph 18, together with other proven acts, when assessing the responsibility of the Accused, in respect of Count 2.

413. In respect of the allegation in paragraph 19 of the Indictment, the Chamber finds that the accused ordered the burial of bodies, in order to conceal the dead from the "'foreigners". The Chamber finds that there is no evidence to suggest that the Accused ordered the burial of bodies to conceal his crimes from the international community. The allegation in paragraph 19 has therefore only been proved in part.

414. In respect of the allegations in paragraphs 11 and 17 of the Indictment, the Chamber finds that these allegations have not been proved, beyond a reasonable doubt. **[page 153]**

415. The Chamber notes that Article 6(1) of the Statute, provides that a person who "planned, instigated, ordered, committed or otherwise aided and abetted in the planning, preparation or execution of a crime referred to in Articles 2 to 4 of the present Statute, shall be individually responsible for the crime."

416. The Chamber finds beyond a reasonable doubt that the Accused: aided and abetted in the killings by distributing weapons to the *Interahamwe* on 8, 15 and 24 April 1994; ordered the killing of 10 people in April 1994 who were subsequently killed in his presence; participated in an attack on the people who sought refuge at the ETO; directed and participated in the attack at Nyanza; murdered Emmanuel Kayitare and by his conduct intended to cause the death of a large number of people belonging to the Tutsi ethnic group, because of their ethnicity.

417. The Chamber finds beyond a reasonable doubt that in the time periods referred to in the indictment there was a widespread and systematic attack on the Tutsi ethnic group, on ethnic grounds. The accused had knowledge of this attack, and he intended his conduct to be consistent with the pattern of this attack and to be a part of this attack.

418. The Chamber therefore finds beyond a reasonable doubt that the Accused is individually criminally responsible for crimes against humanity (extermination), pursuant to Articles 2(3)(b) and 6(1) of the Statute. **[page 154]**

5.3 Count 3: Crime Against Humanity (murder)

419. Count 3 of the Indictment charges the Accused with crimes against humanity (murder), pursuant to Articles 3(a) and 6(1) of the Statute, for the acts alleged in paragraph 14 of the Indictment.

420. The Chamber notes that pursuant to Count 2 of the Indictment, the Accused is charged for crimes against humanity (extermination), under Articles 3(b) and 6(1) of the Statute of the Tribunal, for the acts alleged in paragraphs 10-19 of the Indictment, which acts include the attack on the ETO compound, as alleged in paragraph 14. The allegations in paragraph 14 of the indictment also form the basis for Count 3, crimes against humanity (murder)

421. The Chamber concurs with the reasoning in the *Akayesu Judgement*[117] that:

> "[...] it is acceptable to convict the accused of two offences in relation to the same set of facts in the following circumstances: (1) where the offences have different elements; or (2) where the provisions creating the offences protect different interests; or (3) where it is necessary to record a conviction for both offences in order fully to describe what the accused did. However, the Chamber finds that it is not justifiable to convict an accused of two offences in relation to the same

---

[117] *Akayesu Judgement*, para. 468.

set of facts where (a) one offence is a lesser included offence of the other, for example, murder and grievous bodily harm, robbery and theft, or rape and indecent assault; or (b) where one offence charges accomplice liability and the other offence charges liability as a principal, e.g. genocide and complicity in genocide." **[page 155]**

422. As crimes against humanity, murder and extermination share the same constituent elements of the offence of a crime against humanity, that it is committed as part of a widespread or systematic attack against any civilian population on national, political, ethnic, racial or religious grounds. Both murder and extermination are constituted by unlawful, intentional killing. Murder is a the killing of one or more individuals, whereas extermination is a crime which is directed against a group of individuals.

423. The Chamber notes that in the *Akayesu Judgement*, a series of murder charges set forth in individual paragraphs of the Indictment were held collectively to constitute extermination. In that case the individual allegations which formed the basis for counts of murder and at the same time formed the basis for a collective count of extermination were incidents in which named persons had been murdered. In this case, the single allegation of the ETO attack, although charged as murder, is in itself an allegation of extermination, that is the killing of a collective group of individuals.

424. Having held the Accused criminally responsible for his conduct, as alleged in paragraph 14 of the Indictment, in respect of crimes against humanity (extermination), as charged in Count 2, the Chamber finds that he cannot also be held criminally responsible for crimes against humanity (murder), as charged in Count 3 of the Indictment on the basis of the same act. **[page 156]**

5.4 Count 5: Crime Against Humanity (murder)

425. Count 5 of the Indictment charges the Accused with crimes against humanity (murder), pursuant to Articles 3(a) and 6(1) of the Statute, for the acts alleged in paragraph 15 and 16 of the Indictment.

426. The Chamber notes that the Accused is charged, pursuant to Count 2 of the Indictment for crimes against humanity (extermination), under Articles 3(b) and 6(1) of the Statute, for the acts alleged in paragraphs 10-19 of the Indictment, which acts include the massacre of Tutsi refugees at Nyanza, as alleged in paragraphs 15 and 16. These allegations also support Count 5, crimes against humanity (murder).

427. For the reasons set forth in the legal findings pertaining to Count 3 above, the Chamber finds that the Accused cannot be held criminally responsible for crimes against humanity (murder), as charged in Count 5 of the Indictment. **[page 157]**

5.5 Count 7: Crime Against Humanity (murder)

428. Count 7 of the Indictment charges the Accused with crimes against humanity (murder), pursuant to Articles 3(a) and 6(1) of the Statute, for the acts alleged in paragraph 18 of the Indictment.

429. The Chamber finds beyond a reasonable doubt that on 28 April 1994, Emmanuel Kayitare together with other people were taken near the Amgar Garage, where they were detained. The Accused was present at this location and when Emmanuel Kayitare tried to escape by running off, the Accused grabbed hold of him by his collar and struck him on his head with a machette, which resulted in his death.

430. The Chamber notes that Article 6(1) of the Statute of the Tribunal provides that a person who "planned, instigated, ordered, committed or otherwise aided and abetted in the planning, preparation or execution of a crime referred to in articles 2 to 4 of the present Statute, shall be individually responsible for the crime." The Chamber finds beyond a reasonable doubt that the Accused detained or alternatively aided and abetted in the detention of Tutsis and other people belonging to certain political parties and that he murdered Emmanuel Kayitare when the said Kayitare attempted to escape.

431.   The Chamber finds beyond a reasonable doubt that Emmanuel Kayitare was a civilian belonging to the Tutsi ethnic group.

432.   The Chamber finds beyond a reasonable doubt that in April 1994 there was a widespread and systematic attack on the Tutsi ethnic group, because of their ethnicity. The accused had knowledge of this attack and he intended the murder of Kayitare to be consistent with the pattern of this attack and to be a part of this attack. **[page 158]**

433.   The Chamber finds beyond a reasonable doubt that the Accused is individually criminally responsible for crimes against humanity (murder), as charged in Count 7 of the Indictment. **[page 159]**

5.6 Counts 4, 6, and 8: Violation of Common Article 3 of the Geneva Conventions (murder)

434.   Counts 4, 6 and 8 of the Indictment charge the Accused with violations of Common Article 3 of the 1949 Geneva Conventions, as incorporated in Article 4 of the Statute. The Prosecutor has chosen to restrict the wording of these counts to violations of Common Article 3 only, even though Article 4 of the Statute covers both Common Article 3 and also Additional Protocol II of 1977 to the Geneva Conventions of 1949. As indicated *supra* by the Chamber[118], Additional Protocol II merely supplements and reaffirms Common Article 3, without modifying the article's field of applicability. The only true difference between the Article and the Protocol is the higher threshold to be met for internal conflicts to be characterized as meeting the requirements of the Additional Protocol.

435.   The Prosecutor, in her closing brief, outlined the elements of the offences and the burden of proof with which she was laden. In so doing, she developed not only the material requirements to be met for an offence to constitute a serious violation of Common Article 3, but also presented to the Chamber the material requirements to be met for Additional Protocol II to be applicable. It thus transpires from her argumentation that she intended to prove that the material requirements of both Common Article 3 and Additional Protocol II had to be met before any finding of guilt could be made with regard to counts 4, 6 and 8 of the Indictment. Moreover, were any doubt to remain as to whether the Prosecutor needs to demonstrate that Common Article 3 is applicable, or that both Common Article 3 and Additional Protocol II are applicable, the Chamber recalls that in criminal proceedings, matters in doubt should be interpreted in favour of the Accused. Furthermore, the Trial Chamber considers the material requirements of Article 4 of the Statute to be indivisible, in other words, that Common Article 3 and Additional Protocol II must be satisfied conjunctively, before an offence can be deemed to be covered by Article 4 of the Statute. Thus, it is the opinion of the Chamber that for a finding of guilt to be made for any **[page 160]** one of counts 4, 6 and 8 of the Indictment, the Chamber must be satisfied that the material requirements of Common Article 3 and Additional Protocol II have to be met. Consequently, the Prosecutor must prove that at the time of the events alleged in the Indictment there existed an internal armed conflict in the territory of Rwanda, which, at the very least, satisfied the material requirements of Additional Protocol II, as these requirements subsume those of Common Article 3.

436.   On the basis of evidence presented in this case by Professor Reyntjens, Mr. Nsanzuwera, Professor Mbonimpa and Captain Lemaire, the Chamber is satisfied that at the time of the events alleged in the Indictment, namely, in April, May and June 1994, there existed an internal armed conflict between, on the one hand, the government forces and, on the other, the dissident armed forces, the RPF. The RPF were under the responsible command of General Kagame and exercised such control over part of their territory as to enable them to carry on sustained and concerted military operations. The RPF also stated to the International Committee of the Red Cross that it considered itself bound by the rules of international humanitarian law[119]. Moreover, the theater of combat in April 1994 included the town of Kigali, as the opposing forces fought to gain control of the capital.

---

[118]   See section 2.4 of Applicable Law
[119]   See Report of the United Nations High Commissioner for Human Rights on his Mission to Rwanda 11-12 May 1994, paragraph 20.

437. Evidence adduced in support of the paragraphs contained in the general allegations, and more specifically paragraphs 7 and 8, and also the allegations set out in paragraphs 14, 15, 16 and 18 of the Indictment, demonstrate that the victims of the offences were unarmed civilians, men, women and children who had been identified as the "targets" on the basis of their ethnicity. Those persons who had carried weapons were disarmed by the UNAMIR troops on entering the ETO compound. The Chamber does not consider that the bearing of these weapons prior to being disarmed deprived the victims of the protection afforded to them by Common Article 3 of the Geneva Conventions and Additional Protocol II. Indeed, the Chamber is not of the opinion that **[page 161]** these "armed" civilians were taking a direct part in the hostilities, but rather finds that the bearing of these weapons was a desperate and futile attempt at survival against the thousands of armed assailants.

438. The Chamber is satisfied that the victims were persons taking no active part in the hostilities and were thus protected persons under Common Article 3 of the Geneva Conventions and Additional Protocol II.

439. The Accused was in a position of authority vis-à-vis the *Interahamwe* militia. Testimonies in this case have demonstrated that the Accused exerted control over the *Interahamwe*, that he distributed weapons to them during the events alleged in this Indictment, aiding and abetting in the commission of the crimes and directly participating in the massacres with the *Interahamwe*. The expert witness, Mr. Nsanzuwera, testified that the *Interahamwe* militia served two roles during April, May and June 1994, on the one hand, they supported the RAF war effort against the RPF, and on the other hand, they killed Tutsi and Hutu opponents.

440. Moreover, as testified by Mr. Nsanzuwera, there is merit in the submission of the Prosecutor that, considering the position of authority of the Accused over the *Interahamwe*, and the role that the *Interahamwe* served in supporting the RAF against the RPF, there is a nexus between the crimes committed and the armed conflict. In support thereof, the Prosecutor argues that the *Interahamwe* were the instrument of the military in extending the scope of the massacres.

441. Thus, the Chamber is also satisfied that the Accused, as second vice-president of the youth wing of the MRND, being known as the *Interahamwe za MRND* and being the youth wing of the political majority in the government in April 1994, falls within the category of persons who can be held individually responsible for serious violations of the provisions of Article 4 of the Statute. **[page 162]**

442. The Prosecutor argues that the *Interahamwe* orchestrated massacres as part of their support to the RAF in the conflict against the RPF, and as the Accused was in a position of authority over the *Interahamwe*, that, *ipso facto*, the acts of the Accused also formed part of that support. Such a conclusion, without being supported by the necessary evidence, is, in the opinion of the Chamber, insufficient to prove beyond reasonable doubt that the Accuses is individually criminally responsible for serious violations of Common Article 3 and Additional Protocol II. Consequently, the Chamber finds that the Prosecutor has not shown how the individual acts of the Accused, as alleged in the Indictment, during these massacres were committed in conjunction with the armed conflict.

443. Moreover, in the opinion of the Chamber, although the Genocide against the Tutsis and the conflict between the RAF and the RPF are undeniably linked, the Prosecutor cannot merely rely on a finding of Genocide and consider that, as such, serious violations of Common Article 3 and Additional Protocol II are thereby automatically established. Rather, the Prosecutor must discharge her burden by establishing that each material requirement of offences under Article 4 of the Statute are met.

444. The Chamber therefore finds that it has not been proved beyond reasonable doubt that there existed a nexus between the culpable acts committed by the Accused and the armed conflict.

445. Consequently, the Chamber finds the Accused not guilty of Counts 4, 6, and 8 of the Indictment, being serious violations of Common Article 3 of the Geneva Conventions (murder), as incorporated under Article 4(a) of the Statute. **[page 163]**

6. VERDICT

FOR THE FOREGOING REASONS, having considered all of the evidence and the arguments, THE CHAMBER unanimously finds as follows:

Count 1: Guilty of Genocide

Count 2: Guilty of Crime Against Humanity (Extermination)

Count 3: Not Guilty of Crime Against Humanity (Murder)

Count 4: Not Guilty of Violation of Article 3 Common to the Geneva Conventions (Murder)

Count 5: Not Guilty of Crime Against Humanity (Murder)

Count 6: Not Guilty of Violation of Article 3 Common to the Geneva Conventions (Murder)

Count 7: Guilty of Crime Against Humanity (Murder)

Count 8: Not Guilty of Violation of Article 3 Common to the Geneva Conventions (Murder) **[page 164]**

7. SENTENCE

446. The Chamber will now summarize the legal texts relating to sentences and penalties and their enforcement, before going on to specify the applicable scale of sentences, on the one hand, and the general principles governing the determination of penalties, on the other.

A. Applicable texts

447. The Chamber will apply the statutory and regulatory provisions hereafter. Article 22 of the Statute on judgement, Articles 23 and 26 dealing respectively with penalties and enforcement of sentences, Rules 101, 102, 103 and 104 of the Rules which cover respectively sentencing procedure on penalties, status of the convicted person, place and supervision of imprisonment.

B. Scale of sentences applicable to the Accused found guilty of one of the crimes listed in Articles 2, 3 or 4 of the Statute of the Tribunal

448. The Tribunal may impose on an accused who pleads guilty or is convicted as such, penalties ranging from prison terms up to and including life imprisonment. The Statute of the Tribunal excludes other forms of punishment such as the death sentence, penal servitude or a fine.

449. Whereas in most national systems the scale of penalties is determined in accordance with the gravity of the offence, the Chamber notes that the Statute does not rank the various crimes falling under the jurisdiction of the Tribunal and, thereby, the sentence to be handed down. In theory, the sentences are the same for each of the three crimes, namely a maximum term of life imprisonment. **[page 165]**

450. It should be noted, however, that in imposing the sentence, the Trial Chamber should take into account, in accordance with Article 23(2) of the Statute, such factors as the gravity of the offence. In the opinion of the Chamber, it is difficult to rank genocide and crimes against humanity as one being the lesser of the other in terms of their respective gravity. The Chamber holds that both crimes against humanity, already punished by the Nuremberg and Tokyo Tribunals, and genocide, a concept defined later, are crimes which are particularly shocking to the collective conscience.

451. Regarding the crime of genocide, in particular, the preamble to the Genocide Convention recognizes that at all periods of history, genocide has inflicted great losses on humanity and reiterates the

need for international cooperation to liberate humanity from such an odious scourge. The crime of genocide is unique because of its element of *dolus specialis*, (special intent) which requires that the crime be committed with the intent 'to destroy in whole or in part, a national, ethnic, racial or religious group as such', as stipulated in Article 2 of the Statute; hence the Chamber is of the opinion that genocide constitutes the "crime of crimes", which must be taken into account when deciding the sentence.

452. There is no argument that, precisely on account of their extreme gravity, crimes against humanity and genocide must be punished appropriately. Article 27 of the Charter of the Nuremberg Tribunal empowered that Tribunal, pursuant to Article 6(c) of the said Charter, to sentence any accused found guilty of crimes against humanity to death or such other punishment as shall be determined by it to be just.

453. Rwanda, like all the States which have incorporated crimes against humanity or genocide in their domestic legislation, provides the most severe penalties for such crimes under its criminal legislation. To this end, the Rwandan Organic Law on the Organization of Prosecutions for **[page 166]** Offences constituting Genocide or Crimes against Humanity, committed since 1 October 1990,[120], groups accused persons into four categories, according to their acts of criminal participation. Included in the first category are the masterminds of the crimes (planners, organizers), persons in positions of authority, and persons who have exhibited excessive cruelty and perpetrators of sexual violence. All such persons are punishable by the death penalty. The second category covers perpetrators, conspirators or accomplices in criminal acts, for whom the prescribed penalty is life imprisonment. Included in the third category are persons who, in addition to committing a substantive offence, are guilty of other serious assaults against the person. Such persons face a short-term imprisonment. The fourth category is that of persons who have committed offences against property.

454. Reference to the practice of sentencing in Rwanda and to the Organic law is for purposes of guidance. While referring as much as practicable to such practice of sentencing, the Chamber maintains its unfettered discretion to pass sentence on persons found guilty of crimes falling within its jurisdiction, taking into account the circumstances of the case and the individual circumstances of the accused persons.

C. General principles regarding the determination of sentences

455. In determining the sentence, the Chamber shall be mindful of the fact that this Tribunal was established by the Security Council pursuant to Chapter VII of the Charter of the United Nations within the context of measures the Council was empowered to take under Article 39 of the said Charter to ensure that violations of international humanitarian law in Rwanda in 1994 were halted and effectively redressed. The objective was to prosecute and punish the perpetrators of the atrocities in Rwanda in such a way as to put an end to impunity and thereby to promote national reconciliation and the restoration of peace. **[page 167]**

456. That said, it is clear that the penalties imposed on accused persons found guilty by the Tribunal must be directed, on the one hand, at retribution of the said accused, who must see their crimes punished, and over and above that, on other hand, at deterrence, namely to dissuade for ever, others who may be tempted in the future to perpetrate such atrocities by showing them that the international community shall not tolerate the serious violations of international humanitarian law and human rights.

457. The Chamber also recalls that, in the determination of sentences, it is required under Article 23(2) of the Statute and Rule 101(B) of the Rules to take into account a number of factors including the gravity of the offence, the individual circumstances of the convicted person, the existence of any aggravating or

---

[120]   Organic Law No. 8/96 of 30 August 1996, published in the Gazette of the Republic of Rwanda, 35th year. No. 17, 1 September 1996.

mitigating circumstances, including the substantial co-operation with the Prosecutor by the convicted person before or after his conviction. It is a matter, as it were, or individualizing the penalty.

458. Clearly, however, as far as the individualization of penalties is concerned, the judges of the Chamber cannot limit themselves to the factors mentioned in the Statute and the Rules. Here again, their unfettered discretion in assessing the facts and attendant circumstances should enable them to take into account any other factor that they deem pertinent.

459. Similarly, the factors referred to in the Statute and in the Rules cannot be interpreted as having to be applied cumulatively in the determination of the sentence. **[page 168]**

D. Submissions of the Parties

Prosecutor's submissions

460. In her final brief and in her closing argument made in open court on 16 June 1999, the Prosecutor submitted that the crimes committed by Rutaganda, in particular the crime of genocide and crimes against humanity, are of extremely serious offences calling for appropriate punishment. She submitted that the Chamber should take into account the status of Rutaganda in the society, his individual role in the execution of the crimes, his motivation, his mental disposition and his will, the attendant circumstances of his crimes and his behaviour after the criminal acts.

461. The Prosecutor submitted that the following aggravating circumstances are such as to justify a more severe sentence in this matter:

(i)   Rutaganda was known in society as the second vice-president of the *Interahamwe* at the national level. He also was a rich businessman;

(ii)   His criminal participation extended to all levels. He acted as a principal authority at Amgar garage, ETO and Nyanza massacres. He incited to kill and he also killed with his own hands. He provided logistical support in distributing weapons;

(iii)   He endorsed the genocidal plan of the interim government. At the same time, he seized the occasion for his personal gain;

(iv)   He played a leading role in the genocide. He killed or ordered his victims to be killed in cold blood; **[page 169]**

(v)   He ordered the *Interahamwe* to kill the victims with various blunt and sharp weapons in complete disregard for the suffering of the individual victim. The victims were placed in a world of total persecution which lasted for 100 days;

(vi)   In his capacity as direct supervisor of the *Interahamwe* at Amgar garage, he failed to punish the perpetrators. In fact, he was one of the principal offenders.

462. Furthermore, the Prosecutor submits that there are no mitigating circumstances. The Accused did not cooperate with the Prosecutor. He has shown no remorse for his crimes.

463. With regard to the issue of multiple sentences which could be imposed on Rutaganda as envisaged by Rule 101(c) of the Rules, the Prosecutor asked for separate sentences for each of the counts on which Rutaganda was found guilty while specifying that the Accused should serve the more severe sentence. The Prosecutor, submitted that the Chamber should impose a sentence for each offence committed in order to fully recognize the seriousness of each crime, and the particular role of the convicted person in its commission.

464. In conclusion, the Prosecutor recommends life imprisonment for each count for which the accused is convicted.

Defence's submissions

465.   During the final arguments hearing, the Defence submitted that Rutaganda is innocent and asked that he be acquitted of all eight counts charged. The Accused himself expressed his sorrow to the Rwandan population especially those who live in his native land. He called on **[page 170]** the Chamber to consider especially his health condition and though he did not feel he was guilty, he prayed that the Chamber afford him time to live with his children, should it find him guilty.

E. Personal circumstances of Georges Rutaganda

466.   Rutaganda was born on 28 November 1958. His father was a prominent person in Rwanda. Rutaganda is married and has three children. He was a rich businessman. He was a member of MRND at the national and prefectural levels. He served as the second vice-president of the *Interahamwe* at the national level.

467.   The Chamber has scrupulously examined all the submissions presented by the parties in determination of sentence; from which it derives the following:

F. Aggravating circumstances

(i)   Gravity of the Offences:

468.   The offences with which the accused Georges Rutaganda is charged are, indisputably, extremely serious, as the Trial Chamber already pointed out when it described genocide as the "crime of crimes".

(ii)   The position of authority of Georges Rutaganda in the *Interahamwe*

469.   Rutaganda was the second vice-president of the *Interahamwe* at the national level. The Chamber finds that the fact that a person in a high position abused his authority and committed crimes is to be viewed as an aggravating factor. **[page 171]**

(iii)   The role played by Rutaganda in the execution of the crimes

470.   The Chamber finds that Rutaganda played an important leading role in the execution of the crimes. He distributed weapons to the *Interahamwe* for the purpose of killing Tutsis. He positioned the *Interahamwe* at Nyanza and incited and ordered the killing of Tutsis on several occasions. As a second vice president of the *Interahamwe*, He killed Emmanuel Kayitare, alias Rujindiri, a Tutsi, by stricking him on the head with a machete.

G. Mitigating circumstances

(i)   Assistance given by Georges Rutaganda to certain people

471.   The Defence alleges that Georges Rutaganda, during the period of the commission of the crimes with which he is charged, helped people to evacuate to various destinations at various times and by various means. The Chamber accepts, as mitigating factors, the fact that Rutaganda had evacuated the families of witnesses DEE and DS and that he had used exceptional means to save witness DEE, the Tutsi wife of one of his friends and that he provided food and shelter to some refugees.

(ii)   Rutaganda's health condition

472. Rutaganda requested that the Chamber consider his present health condition. The Chamber notes that Rutaganda is in poor health and has had to seek medical help continously.

473. Having reviewed all the circumstances of the case, the Chamber is of the opinion that the aggravating factors outweigh the mitigating factors, especially as Rutaganda occupied a high position in the *Interahamwe* at the time the crimes were committed. He knowingly and **[page 172]** consciously participated in the commission of such crimes and never showed remorse for what he inflicted upon the victims.

TRIAL CHAMBER I

FOR THE FOREGOING REASONS;

DELIVERING its decision in public, *inter partes* and in the first instance;

PURSUANT to Articles 23, 26 and 27 of the Statute of the Tribunal and Rules 101, 102, 103 and 104 of the Rules of Procedure and Evidence;

Noting the general practice regarding sentencing in Rwanda;

Noting that Rutaganda has been found guilty of:

Genocide	– Count 1
Crime Against Humanity (extermination)	– Count 2
Crime Against Humanity (murder)	– Count 7

Noting the brief submitted by the Prosecutor;

Having heard the Prosecutor and the Defence;

IN PUNISHMENT OF THE ABOVE MENTIONED CRIMES, **[page 173]**

SENTENCES Georges Rutaganda to:

A SINGLE SENTENCE OF LIFE IMPRISONMENT

FOR ALL THE COUNTS ON WHICH HE HAS BEEN FOUND GUILTY

RULES that imprisonment shall be served in a State designated by the President of the Tribunal, in consultation with the Trial Chamber, the Government of Rwanda and the designated State shall be notified of such designation by the Registrar;

RULES that this judgement shall be enforced immediately, and that, however:

(i)   Until his transfer to the designated place of imprisonment, Georges Rutaganda shall be kept in detention under the present conditions;

(ii)   Upon notice of appeal, if any, the enforcement of the sentence shall be stayed until a decision has been rendered on the appeal, with the convicted person nevertheless remaining in detention.

Arusha, 6 December 1999,

Laïty Kama	Lennart Aspegren	Navanethem Pillay
Presiding Judge	Judge	Judge

This judgement was rendered by the same Trial Chamber as the Akayesu judgement : Judges Laïty Kama (Presiding), Aspegren and Pillay.[1] It relied heavily upon earlier judgements relating to genocide and crimes against humanity, the Akayesu case and the case against Kayishema and Ruzindana.[2] The major issues of those cases are dealt with by commentators Schabas and Ambos/ Wirth elsewhere in this book.[3] In addition to issues raised in those earlier decisions, two other issues are of particular interest in this decision : these involve both procedural and evidentiary matters, as well as aspects of substantive criminal law and jurisdiction.

Procedural and evidentiary matters

The Trial Chamber denied the Prosecutor's request, made during her closing arguments, to amend the time periods alleged in paragraphs 10, 16 and 19 of the indictment.[4] However, these time periods did not play a role in relation to those allegations that were not proven beyond a reasonable doubt. The ruling of the Trial Chamber is in sharp contrast with the acceptance of the defence notice of alibi which was presented in the closing argument of defence counsel. Pursuant to Rule 67 (B) of the Rules of Procedure and Evidence, the Trial Chamber found it appropriate and necessary to examine the notice of alibi.[5] However, in the end, defence arguments did not convince the Trial Chamber that an alibi existed.

The Trial Chamber accepted that the dates of the three incidents proven – 8 april, 15 april and 24 april – fulfilled the assertion made in the indictment that these events happened "on or about 6 april". This indicates an approximate time frame and the variances were not regarded as material or as having prejudiced the accused. In this respect, to accept that 24 april is still within "on or about 6 april" contrasts with a decision of the ICTY Trial Chamber in Tadić,[6] in which it granted leave to the prosecution to alter the long periods (a few months) specified in the indictment to a much shorter period.[7] With regard to the specific defence of an alibi, this reasoning is not convincing. A defendant who raises the defence of an alibi, will seek to prove that he was not there on or about 6 april, and not some 18 days later.

The Trial Chamber uses a rather broad test to determine whether evidence presented at trial should be admitted and how it should be evaluated. The Trial Chamber considered whether it was "best favoured to a fair determination of the matter before it, and (...) consonant with the spirit of the Statute and the general principles of law."[8] In this respect it uses the wide discretion, also accepted in the Akayesu and Tadic cases, not to require corroboration of evidence in the case of rape and sexual violence. The Trial Chamber was willing to rely on a single witness "provided such evidence is relevant, admissible and credible."[9]

Paragraph 22 of the Judgement is very unsatisfactory. The trial Chamber states : "Many of the witnesses who testified before the Chamber in this case have seen atrocities committed against members of their families and close friends and/ or have themselves been the victims of such atrocities. Some of these witnesses became very emotional and cried in the witness box, when they were questioned about certain events. A few witnesses displayed physical signs of fear and pain when they were asked about certain atrocities of which they were victims. The Chamber has taken into consideration these factors in assessing the evidence of such witnesses." What does the Trial Chamber mean when it takes such matters "into consideration" ? Are witnesses who show certain emotions to be regarded as reliable or unreliable ? The Trial Chamber raises important questions, but does not provide us with the answers.

---

[1]   See Judgement, *Prosecutor v. Akayesu*, Case No. ICTR-96-4-T, 2 september 1998, in this volume on p. 399
[2]   See in this volume, p. 399 and p. 555 respectively
[3]   See for their commentaries in this volume, p. 540 and p. 701 respectively.
[4]   See Judgement, par. 14.
[5]   See Judgement, par.139.
[6]   ICTY, Decision on the Defence Motion on the Form of the Indictment, *Prosecutor v. Tadić*, Case No. IT – 94-1-T, T.Ch.II, 14 november 1995. (Tadić (1995) I ICTY JR 293).
[7]   See ICTR, *Prosecutor v. Kayishema and Ruzindana*, par.85 and 86 : "where timing is of material importance to the charges, then the wording of the count should lift the offence from the general to the particular."
[8]   See Judgement, par. 17.
[9]   See Judgement, par. 18.

In addition, paragraph 23 is not clear where it deals with those aspects of the testimony in Kinyarwanda which were simultaneously translated into French and English. The Trial Chamber simply says : "As a result, the essence of the witnesses' testimonies was at times lost." This raises the question as to how the Trial Chamber knows that there were problems with the translation. Did the judges speak or understand Kinyarwanda ? And if they do, or are otherwise familiar with it, how did they react to it during trial ? It seems obvious that, should the court note that the interpreter is not doing his work correctly, he has to be replaced by a better qualified person. If the Trial Chamber had only taken this element into consideration when assessing the testimony of the witnesses, it may have been on the basis of other facts than presented by the parties, who will have pleaded their resepective cases relying upon the testimonies as interpreted in English and French. We do not know precisely how both the social and cultural factors and the translation problems influenced the Trial Chamber's evaluation of the evidence. Did it interpret the testimony more favourably towards the accused or towards the case of the Prosecutor ? These issues were dealt with extensively in the Akayesu Judgement.[10] However, the Trial Chamber does not refer to its earlier decision on this point.

With respect to the killing of people in a deep hole near Amgar garage and at the ETO compound the Trial Chamber accepted some inconsistencies between the various witness testimonies.[11] Some contradictions were pointed out by the defence, but these were not of a material nature and do no vitiate the consistency of the substance of these testimonies. With regard to witness Q, the Trial Chamber held that the contradictions "can probably be attributed to the trauma he may have suffered from having to recount the painful events he witnesses and of which he was a victim." Furthermore the lapse of time was considered as a factor to take into account in assessing the recollection of details. The Trial Chamber also noted that pre-trial statements were not made under oath before a commissioner of oaths. Again the Trial Chamber made reference to something that must be taken into account, but it does not say how. Is such a pre-trial statement less reliable and if so, why ? What has been stated is too implicit and leaves much room for interpretation.

A similar implicit decision was taken by the Trial Chamber regarding the witness who had signed a pre-trial statement in 1995 stating that he had three children, all of whom had died. At the trial he testified that he had four children and one survived. Although the Trial Chamber stated that it "considers that the witness knew how many children he had and how many of them died", it does not state specifically whether it took into account the testimony at trial or the pre-trial statement.[12] Neither did the Trial Chamber say that it allowed the number of children of the witness as evidence simply because it was not material to the case at hand. At paragraph 334 it held : "Additionally, the Chamber recalls that the inconsistencies between the witness testimony and statements made before the trial must be analysed in the light of difficulties linked, particularly, to the interpretation of the questions asked and the fact that those were not solemn statements made before a commissioner of oaths." Again, unlike the Akayesu judgement, the Trial Chamber failed to say what the result of this analysis is.

During the trial, both parties relied on pre-trial statements from witnesses. The Defence in particular was able to point to inconsistencies and contradictions between pre-trial statements and testimonies at trial. The Chamber followed the reasoning of the Akayesu Judgement by stating : "these pre-trial statements were composed following interviews with witnesses by investigators of the Office of the Prosecutor. These interviews were mostly conducted in Kinyarwanda, and the Chamber did not have access to transcripts of the interviews, but only translations thereof. It was therefore unable to consider the nature and form of the questions put to the witnesses, or the accuracy of interpretation at the time. The Chamber has considered inconsistencies and contradictions between these statements and testimony at trial with caution for these reasons, and in the light of the time lapse between the statements and the presentation of evidence at trial, the difficulties of recollecting precise details several years after the occurrence of the

---

[10]   Akayesu Judgement, p. 67. Interpretation from Kinyarwanda and cultural factors.

[11]   Paragraphs 252-255, 292 and 298.

[12]   This resembles the testimony of Dragan Opačić in the Tadić case before the ICTY. Opačić had, among other things, testified that his father had died. When confronted with his father later, the Prosecutor withdrew his testimony on suspicion of perjury committed by the witness. See also ALC-I-205.

events, the difficulties of translation, and the fact that several witnesses were illiterate and stated that they had not read their written statements. Moreover, the statements were not made under solemn declaration and were not taken by judicial officers. In the circumstances, the probative value attached to the statements is, in the Chamber's view, considerably less than direct sworn testimony before the Chamber, the truth of which has been subjected to the test of cross-examination."[13] This preference for testimony at trial was earlier expressed by the ICTY in the Tadić case.[14]

Substantive criminal law and jurisdiction

The Trial Chamber once again considered the overlap between Article 2, paragraph 3 and Article 6, paragraph 1 of the Statute. Article 6, paragraph 1 deals with various forms of participation and establishes individual responsibility. One of the categories is the planning or preparation of a crime. This could also fall under Article 2, paragraph 3, sub d of the Statute, which deals with an attempt to commit genocide. The Trial Chamber pointed out that Article 6 of the Statute may not be interpreted to form a general provision, similar to attempt, for all crimes. Only an attempt to genocide is to be regarded as an inchoate crime that could attract criminal responsibility. Any form of participation for crimes other than genocide require the offence to actually be consumated.[15]

The Chamber defined five forms of criminal participation which fall within Article 6, paragraph 1 :

1. Planning of a crime "implies that one or more persons contemplate designing the commission of a crime at both its preparatory and execution phases."
2. Incitement to commit an offence "involves instigating another, directly and publicly, to commit an offence."
3. Ordering "implies a superior-subordinate relationship between the person giving the order and the one executing it, with the person in a position of authority using such position to persuade another to commit an offence."
4. Committing "either through direct commission of an unlawful act or by omission. where there is a duty to act."
5. Aiding and abetting in the planning or execution of a crime referred to in Articles 2 – 4 of the Statute. "The Chamber finds that aiding and abetting alone is sufficient to render the accused criminally liable. In both instances, it is not necessary that the person aiding and abetting another to commit an offence be present during the commission of the crime. The relevant act of assistance may be geographically and temporally unconnected to the actual commission of the offence. The Chamber holds that aiding and abetting include all acts of assistance in either physical form or in the form of moral support; nevertheless, it emphasizes that any act of participation must substantially contribute to the commission of the crime. The aider and abettor assists or facilitates another in the accomplishment of a substantive offence."[16]

The fact that the Trial Chamber does not require that the aider and abettor is present during the commission of the crime and that he may also be temporally unconnected to the crime has serious implications for the jurisdiction of the Tribunal in general.[17] The Rwanda Tribunal has a rather limited jurisdiction as defined in Article 1 of the Statute, being limited to crimes committed in the year 1994. This excludes jurisdiction for crimes committed before 1 January 1994 or after 31 december 1994. If the aider and abettor may be temporally unconnected to the crime, does that mean that the activities of aiding and abetting can have taken place before 1994 ? The answer of the Trial Chamber seems to be in the affirmative. If that is so, the decision significantly extends the jurisdiction of the Rwanda Tribunal. Such a consequence is undesirable. It would place the principal in a more favourable position than those who aid or abet and thus play a minor role. Jurisdiction over the commission of the crime would remain limited to the year 1994, whilst an assistant to the crime may be held criminally responsible for his

---

13   See Akayesu Judgement, par. 134 and Rutaganda Judgement, par.19.
14   See Decision on the Defence Motion to Summon and Protect Defence Witnesses, and on the Giving of Evidence by Video-Link, *Prosecutor v. Tadić*, Case No. IT-94-1-T, T.Ch. II, 25 June 1996, ALC-I-217.
15   See Judgement, par. 34.
16   See Judgement, par. 43. See also Akayesu Judgement, par. 471-491. In this volume p. 493-497.
17   The facts of the case do not show any evidence of such implications.

behaviour in other years.[18] The fact that certain crimes do not fall within the jurisdiction of the Rwanda Tribunal does not mean that they are not crimes under international law. Since the two *ad hoc* tribunals only apply existing international law, their limitations must not be regarded as constitutive for criminal liability. Those who have committed similar crimes before or after 1994 may be prosecuted before national courts.

The geographical aspect is less controversial because the territorial jurisdiction (*ratione loci*) of the Rwanda Tribunal is already rather wide. However, it does raise the question as to over which territory the ICTR is competent. Article 1 speaks of "Rwanda and the territory of neighbouring states". Theoretically this leaves the question open as to whether an aider and abettor must perform his activities in Rwanda or neighbouring states, or that he may have assisted or facilitated from another country ? In addition, it is unclear what exactly is meant by neighbouring states. Does it require that Rwanda and the neighbouring country share a common border ? If that were the criterion, the Court's jurisdiction is limited to Uganda, Congo, Burundi and Tanzania.[19] If the common border is not the criterion, a certain distance to the border may be the relevant factor. Another possibility is that this would not be decided on the *locus delicti*, but on the relation to the conflict in Rwanda and whether the acts of such a person that resulted in any resultant in the Rwandan tragedy. The United Nations Secretary-General has stated that it was «mainly the refugee camps in Zaire and other neighbouring countries» which were envisaged.[20] Article 1 further combines a territorial principle with a nationality principle in the sense that, when considering the crimes committed in neighbouring countries, the Tribunal only has jurisdiction over Rwandan citizens. The present decision raises the question as to whether this applies to principals only.

For issues related to the definition of the crime of genocide,[21] there is an extensive commentary by Schabas in this volume. The Trial Chamber's reasoning in this case constitutes a summary of the more extensive reasoning in the Akayesu case.[22]

This Trial Chamber requires that the perpetrator must have the requisite intent for the commission of crimes against humanity.[23] In this respect it differs from the Appeals Chamber in the Tadić case, which stated that a discriminatory intent is an indispensable element of the offence only with regard to those crimes for which this is expressly required.[24] The Trial Chamber compares Articles 5 of the ICTY Statute and 3 of the ICTR Statute. The latter expressly provides for the requisite discriminatory grounds of «national, political, ethnic, racial or religious» whilst these are not stipulated in the ICTY Statute. It therefore requires the discriminatory intent not required by the ICTY Statute. The differences in the definitions of crimes against humanity in the Statutes of the two *ad hoc* Tribunals can be explained by the fact that they were both drawn with regard to the specific characteristics of the Yugoslav and the Rwandan conflicts respectively.[25]

The Prosecutor charged the accused cumulatively in the indictment. His overall activities were regarded as Genocide and Crimes against humanity. Three specific acts were characterised by the Prosecution as Crimes against humanity and Violations of common Article 3. With regard to the concurrence of various crimes under the Statute, the Trial Chamber fully concurred with the Dissenting Opinion of Judge Tafazzal H. Khan in the case against Kayishema and Ruzindana and cited the ICTY : "The Prosecutor may be justified in bringing cumulative charges when the articles of the Statute referred to are designed

---

[18]   See H.D. Wolswijk, *Locus delicti en rechtsmacht*, Utrecht 1998, p.195-272 for a discussion of the consequences that different jurisdictions over a principal and those who are complicit may have.

[19]   See the same four countries mentioned in the *Prosecutor v. Kayishema and Ruzindana* Judgement, par. 44. See also V. Morris and M. Scharf, The International Criminal Tribunal for Rwanda, Transnational Publishers 1998, p.291-297.

[20]   Report of the Secretary-General pursuant to paragraph 5 of Security Council Resolution 955 (1994), S/ 1995/134, p.4.

[21]   Judgement, par.44-63.

[22]   See ICTR, Judgement, *Prosecutor v. Akayesu*, Case No. ICTR-96-4-T, T.Ch.I, par. 525-548. In this volume p. 500-505

[23]   See an in depth discussion on crimes against humanity in : M. Cherif Bassiouni, Crimes Against Humanity in International Criminal Law, 2nd Edition, Dordrecht 1999 and Otto Triffterer (ed.) Commentary on the Rome Statute of the International Criminal Court, Baden-Baden 1999, p.117-172.

[24]   See Judgement, *Prosecutor v. Tadić*, Case No. IT-94-1-A, A.Ch., 15 July 1999, par.273-305. For a concurring decision see ICTY, Judgement, *Prosecutor v. Blaškić*, Case No. IT-95-14-T, T.Ch.I, 3 March 2000, par.260.

[25]   See also Larry D. Johnson, The International Tribunal for Rwanda, 67 International Review of Penal Law 1996, p.219; Kelly Dawn Askin, War Crimes Against Women, The Hague 1997, p.344-361.

to protect different values and when each article requires proof of a legal element not required by the others."[26] The Chamber held that the offences covered under the Statute (genocide/ crimes against humanity/ violations of common article 3) have disparate ingredients and the respective punishment for each is aimed at protecting discrete interests. It therefore allowed the claim of multiple offences for the same act "in order to capture the full extent of the crimes committed by an accused."[27]

The reasoning of the Trial Chamber is but a summary of the Akayesu case.[28] In that case it also referred to a decision of the ICTY in the Tadic case.[29] The Trial Chamber of the ICTY held that the emphasis was not on the cumulative charging as such, but on its relevance for the penalty : "In any event, since this is a matter that will only be at all relevant insofar as it might affect penalty, it can best be dealt with if and when matters of penalty fall for consideration. What can, however, be said with certainty is that penalty cannot be made to depend upon whether offences arising from the same conduct are alleged cumulatively or in the alternative. What is to be punished by penalty is proven criminal conduct and that will not depend upon technicalities of pleading."

However, the Trial Chamber in Akayesu then went on to refer not to issue of imposing concurrent sentences, but whether an accused may be convicted of two offences in relation to the same set of facts. This is a different matter. Even if the latter is accepted it does not tell us whether the sentences imposed shall be served concurrently or consecutively. Where the ICTY in Tadić and the ICTR in Kayishema imposed concurrent sentences, Rutaganda, Kambanda, Akayesu and Serushago were sentenced by the ICTR to a single sentence for all the counts on which they have been found guilty. This approach of the ICTR has now been followed by the ICTY in the Blaškić case. In that case, the Trial Chamber held that the crimes ascribed to the accused "form part of a single set of crimes committed in a given geographic region during a relatively extended time-span, the very length of which served to ground their characterisation as a crime against humanity, without its being possible to distinguish criminal intent from motive."[30]

I return to the question of whether it is acceptable to convict the accused of two offences in relation of the same set of facts. In the Akayesu case and cited in Rutaganda the Trial Chamber formulated three separate circumstances in which it would accept that this was possible : "(1) where the offences have different elements; or (2) where the provisions creating the offences protect different interests; or (3) where it is necessary to record a conviction for both offences in order to fully describe what the accused did. However the Chamber finds that it is not justifiable to convict an accused of two offences in relation to the same set of facts where (a) one offence is a lesser included offence of the other, for example, murder and grievous bodily harm, robbery and theft, or rape and indecent assault; or (b) where one offence charges accomplice liability and the other offence charges liability as a principal, e.g. genocide and complicity in genocide."[31]

In the case at hand the Trial Chamber also discussed whether the accused may be convicted of two offences in relation to the same set of facts (ie crimes against humanity (murder) and crimes against humanity (extermination)). In paragraph 422 it stated that "Both murder and extermination are constituted by unlawful, intentional killing. Murder is a (sic) the killing of one or more individuals, whereas extermination is a crime which is directed against a group of individuals." The Trial Chamber had already held Rutaganda criminally responsible for crimes against humanity (extermination). On the basis of the same facts it could not also hold him responsible for crimes against humanity (murder). The latter is already included in the finding of the former. In terms of a verdict the result is that the accused was declared "not guilty" of crimes against humanity (murder). This is strange because the Trial

---

[26]   See ICTY, Decision on Defence Challenges to Form of the Indictment, *Prosecutor v. Zoran Kupreškić, Mirjan Kupreškić, Vlatko Kupreškić, Santić, Alilović, Josipović, Katava, Papić*, Case No. IT-95-16-PT, 15 May 1998.

[27]   See further the commentary of Ambos and Wirth in this volume, p. 701.

[28]   See Akayesu, in this volume, p. 491-493, par. 461-470.

[29]   See Decision on Defence Motion on Form of the Indictment, *Prosecutor v. Tadić*, Case No. IT-94-1-T, T.Ch.II, 14 november 1995. (Tadic (1995) I ICTY JR 293 at p.303).

[30]   ICTY, Judgement, *Prosecutor v. Blaškić*, Case No. IT-95-14-T, T.Ch.I, 3 March 2000, par. 807.

[31]   Akayesu, par. 468 and Rutaganda Judgement, par. 421.

Chamber had established that he was guilty of the crime charged, but this crime was also part of an even more serious crime for which the accused was also found guilty. It would have been preferable had the Trial Chamber stated that the accused "cannot also be held criminally responsible" for the other crime.[32] This illustrates that this count had to be charged alternatively rather than cumulatively.

The Trial Chamber considered the material elements of Article 4 of the Statute to be indivisible in other words that Common Article 3 of the Geneva Conventions and Additional Protocol II must be satisfied conjunctively before an offence can be deemed to be covered by Article 4 of the Statute. In paragraph 437, the Chamber concluded that the bearing of weapons prior to being disarmed deprived the victims of the protection afforded to them by Common Article 3 and Additional Protocol II. The Trial Chamber held that the bearing of these weapons was a desparate and futile attempt at survival against thousands of armed assailants. It concluded that the victims were persons taking no active part in the hostilities and thus were protected persons. In this regard the Chamber concurred with case law of the ICTY.[33] However, the ICTY explicitly mentioned that the definition of civilians contained in Common Article 3 is not immediately applicable to crimes against humanity. It applied that definition only by analogy.[34] In contrast, the approach of the ICTR is rather poorly supported.

In the end the accused was found guilty of genocide, crimes against humanity (extermination) and crimes against humanity (murder). The Trial Chamber considered genocide to be the crime of the crimes. In determining the sentence the Trial Chamber had regard to the Nuremberg Charter and Rwandan law and found that these sources provided for the death penalty. However, the International Tribunal cannot impose the death penalty. It therefore sentenced Rutaganda to a single sentence of life imprisonment for all the counts on which he had been found guilty.

André Klip

---

[32]   See par. 424 and 427.

[33]   Individuals, who at one particular point in time carried out acts of resistance, may belong to the protected groups of crimes against humanity. ICTY, Review of Indictment Pursuant to Rule 61, Case IT-95-13-R61, *Prosecutor v. Mrkšić, Radić, Sljivancanin*, 3 april 1996, par. 29. See more recently ICTY, Judgement, *Prosecutor v. Blaškić*, Case No. IT-95-14-T, T.Ch. 3 March 2000, par.214.

[34]   ICTY, Opinion and Judgment, *Prosecutor v. Tadić*, Case No. IT-94-1-T, T.Ch.II, 7 May 1997, ALC-I-418.

UNITED NATIONS   NATIONS UNIES

International Criminal Tribunal for Rwanda
Tribunal pénal international pour le Rwanda

CHAMBER I – CHAMBRE I

OR: FR

Before: **Judge Laïty Kama, Presiding Judge**
               Judge Lennart Aspegren
               Judge Navanethem Pillay

Decision of: **4 September 1998**

Registry: **Mr. Agwu Okali**

THE PROSECUTOR

VERSUS

JEAN KAMBANDA

Case No. ICTR-97-23-S

JUDGEMENT and SENTENCE

Office of the Prosecutor:
    Mr. Bernard Muna
    Mr. Mohamed Othman
    Mr. James Stewart
    Mr. Udo Gehring

Counsel for the Defence:
    Mr. Oliver Michael Inglis

[page 1] I. The Proceedings

A. Background

1.   Jean Kambanda was arrested by the Kenyan authorities, on the basis of a formal request submitted to them by the Prosecutor on 9 July 1997, in accordance with the provisions of Rule 40 of the Rules of Procedure and Evidence (the "Rules"). On 16 July 1997, Judge Laïty Kama, ruling on the Prosecutor's motion of 9 July 1997, ordered the transfer and provisional detention of the suspect Jean Kambanda at the Detention Facility of the Tribunal for a period of thirty days, pursuant to Rule 40 *bis* of the Rules. The provisional detention of Jean Kambanda was extended twice for thirty days, the first time under the provisions of Rule 40 *bis* (F) and the second time under the provisions of Rule 40 *bis* (G).

2.   On 16 October 1997, an indictment against suspect Jean Kambanda, prepared by the Office of the Prosecutor, was submitted to Judge Yakov Ostrovsky, who confirmed it, issued a warrant of arrest against the accused and ordered his continued detention.

3.   On 1 May 1998, during his initial appearance before this Trial Chamber, the accused pleaded guilty to the six counts contained in the indictment, namely genocide, conspiracy to commit genocide, direct and public incitement to commit genocide, complicity in genocide, crimes against humanity (murder), punishable under Article 3 (a) of the Statute and crimes against humanity (extermination), punishable under Article 3 (b) of the Statute.

4.   After verifying the validity of his guilty plea, particularly in light of an agreement concluded between the Prosecutor, on the one hand, and the accused and his lawyer, on the other, an agreement which was signed by all parties,[1] the Chamber entered a plea of guilty against the accused on all the counts in the indictment. During a status conference held immediately after the initial appearance, the date for the pre-sentencing hearing, provided for under Rule 100 **[page 2]** of the Rules, was set for 31 August 1998. Later, at the request of the Prosecutor, this date was postponed to 3 September 1998. During that same status conference, the parties agreed to submit their respective briefs in advance of the above-mentioned pre-sentencing hearing. The submission date was later set for 15 August 1998. The Defence and the Prosecutor, in fact, filed their briefs before this date. The pre-sentencing hearing was held on 3 September 1998.

B. The guilty plea

5.   As indicated *supra*, Jean Kambanda pleaded guilty, pursuant to Rule 62 of the Rules, to all the six counts set forth in the indictment against him. As stated earlier, the accused confirmed that he had concluded an agreement with the Prosecutor, an agreement signed by his counsel and himself and placed under seal, in which he admitted having committed all the acts charged by the Prosecution.

6.   The Chamber, nevertheless, sought to verify the validity of the guilty plea. To this end, the Chamber asked the accused:

(i) if his guilty plea was entered voluntary, in other words, if he did so freely and knowingly, without pressure, threats, or promises;

(ii) if he clearly understood the charges against him as well as the consequences of his guilty plea; and

(iii) if his guilty plea was unequivocal, in other words, if he was aware that the said plea could not be refuted by any line of defence.

7.   The accused replied in the affirmative to all these questions. On the strength of these answers, the Chamber delivered its decision from the bench as follows:

---

[1]   See *infra*, section on guilty plea.

"Mr. Jean Kambanda, having deliberated and after verifying that your plea of guilty **[page 3]** is voluntary, unequivocal and that you clearly understand its terms and consequences,

Considering the factual and legal issues contained in the agreement concluded between you and the Office of the Prosecutor and that you have acknowledged that both you and your counsel have signed, the Tribunal finds you guilty on the six counts brought against you,

Orders your continued detention; and Rules that a status conference will be held immediately after this hearing, with the Registrar, to set a date for the pre-sentencing hearing [...]"[2]

II. Law and applicable principles

8.   The Chamber will now summarize the legal texts relating to sentences and penalties and their enforcement, before going on to specify the applicable scale of sentences, on the one hand, and the general principles on the determination of penalties, on the other.

A. Applicable texts

9.   The Chamber recalls below the statutory and regulatory provisions on sentencing, applicable to the accused.

Article 22 of the Statute: Judgment

"The Trial Chamber shall pronounce judgements and impose sentences and penalties on persons convicted of serious violations of international humanitarian law." **[page 4]**

Rule 100 of the Rules: Pre-sentencing procedure

"If the accused pleads guilty or if a Trial Chamber finds the accused guilty of a crime, the Prosecutor and the defence may submit any relevant information that may assist the Trial Chamber in determining an appropriate sentence."

Article 23 of the Statute: Penalties

"1.   The penalty imposed by the Trial Chamber shall be limited to imprisonment. In determining the terms of imprisonment, the Trial Chamber shall have recourse to the general practice regarding prison sentences in the courts of Rwanda.

2. In imposing the sentences, the Trial Chamber should take into account such factors as the gravity of the offence and the individual circumstances of the convicted person.

3. In addition to imprisonment, the Trial Chamber may order the return of any property and proceeds acquired by criminal conduct, including by means of duress, to their rightful owners."

Rule 101 of the Rules: Penalties

"(A) A person convicted by the Tribunal may be sentenced to imprisonment for a term up to and including the remainder of his life.

(B)   In determining the sentence, the Trial Chamber shall take into account the factors mentioned in Article 23 (2) of the Statute, as well as such factors as

---

[2]   See official transcript of hearing of 1 May 1998 before Trial Chamber I, International Criminal Tribunal for Rwanda, United Nations.

(i) any aggravating circumstances;

(ii) any mitigating circumstances including the substantial co-operation with **[page 5]** the Prosecutor by the convicted person before or after the conviction;

(iii) the general practice regarding prison sentences in the courts of Rwanda;

(v) the extent to which any penalty imposed by a court of any State on the convicted person for the same act has already been served, as referred to in Article 9 (3) of the Statute.

(C)   The Trial Chamber shall indicate whether multiple sentences shall be served consecutively or concurrently.

(D)   The sentence shall be pronounced in public and in the presence of the convicted person, subject to Rule 102 (B).

(E)   Credit shall be given to the convicted person for the period, if any, during which the convicted person was detained in custody pending his surrender to the Tribunal or pending trial or appeal."

Article 26 of the Statute: Enforcement of sentences

"Imprisonment shall be served in Rwanda or any of the States on a list of States which have indicated to the Security Council their willingness to accept convicted person. Such imprisonment shall be in accordance with the applicable law of the State concerned, subject to the supervision of the Tribunal."

Rule 102 of the Rules: Status of the convicted person

"(A) The sentence shall begin to run from the day it is pronounced under Rule 101(D). However, as soon as notice of appeal is given, the enforcement of the judgement shall thereupon be stayed until the decision on the appeal has been delivered, the convicted person meanwhile remaining in detention, as provided in Rule 64. **[page 6]**

(B)   If, by a previous decision of the Trial Chamber, the convicted person has been provisionally released, or is for any reason at liberty, and he is not present when the judgment is pronounced, the Trial Chamber shall issue a warrant for his arrest. On arrest, he shall be notified of the conviction and sentence, and the procedure provided in Rule 103 shall be followed."

Rule 103 of the Rules: Place of imprisonment

"(A) Imprisonment shall be served in Rwanda or any State designated by the Tribunal from a list of States which have indicated their willingness to accept convicted persons for the serving of sentences. Prior to a decision on the place of imprisonment, the Chamber shall notify the Government of Rwanda.

(B)   Transfer of the convicted person to that State shall be effected as soon as possible after the time-limit for appeal has elapsed."

Article 27 of the Statute: Pardon or commutation of sentences

"If, pursuant to the applicable law of the State in which the convicted person is imprisoned, he or she is eligible for pardon or commutation of sentence, the State concerned shall notify the International Tribunal for Rwanda accordingly. There shall only be pardon or commutation of sentence if the President of the International Tribunal for Rwanda, in consultation with the judges, so decides on the basis of the interests of justice and the general principles of law."

Rule 104 of the Rules: Supervision of imprisonment

> "All sentences of imprisonment shall be served under the supervision of the Tribunal or a body designated by it;" **[page 7]**

B. Scale of sentences applicable to the accused found guilty of one of the crimes listed in Articles 2, 3 or 4 of the Statute of the Tribunal.

10.   As noted from a reading of all the above provisions on penalties, the only penalties the Tribunal can impose on an accused who pleads guilty or is convicted as such are prison terms up to and including life imprisonment, pursuant in particular to Rule 101 (A) of the Rules, whose provisions apply to all crimes which fall within the jurisdiction of the Tribunal, namely genocide, (Article 2 of the Statute), crimes against humanity (Article 3) and violations of Article 3 common to the Geneva Conventions and of Additional Protocol II thereto (Article 4). The Statute of the Tribunal excludes other forms of punishment such as the death sentence, penal servitude or a fine.

11.   Neither Article 23 of the Statute nor Rule 101 of the Rules determine any specific penalty for each of the crimes falling under the jurisdiction of the Tribunal. The determination of sentences is left to the discretion of the Chamber, which should take into account, apart from the general practice regarding prison sentences in the courts of Rwanda, a number of other factors including the gravity of the crime, the personal circumstances of the convicted person, the existence of any aggravating or mitigating circumstances, including the substantial co-operation by the convicted person before or after conviction.

12.   Whereas in most national systems the scale of penalties is determined in accordance with the gravity of the offence, the Chamber notes that, as indicated *supra*, the Statute does not rank the various crimes falling under the jurisdiction of the Tribunal and , thereby, the sentence to be handed down. In theory, the sentences are the same for each of the three crimes, namely a maximum term of life imprisonment.

13.   It should be noted, however, that in imposing the sentence, the Trial Chamber should take into account, in accordance with Article 23 (2) of the Statute, such factors as the gravity of the offence. **[page 8]**

14.   As the Chamber has no doubt that despite the gravity of the violations of Article 3 common to the Geneva Conventions and of the Additional Protocol II thereto, they are considered as lesser crimes than genocide or crimes against humanity. On the other hand, it seems more difficult for the Chamber to rank genocide and crimes against humanity in terms of their respective gravity. The Chamber holds that crimes against humanity, already punished by the Nuremberg and Tokyo Tribunals, and genocide, a concept defined later, are crimes which particularly shock the collective conscience. The Chamber notes in this regard that the crimes prosecuted by the Nuremberg Tribunal, namely the holocaust of the Jews or the "Final Solution", were very much constitutive of genocide, but they could not be defined as such because the crime of genocide was not defined until later.

15.   The indictment setting forth the charges against the accused in the Nuremberg trial, stated, in regard to crimes against humanity that "these methods and crimes constituted violations of international law, domestic law as deriving from the criminal law of all civilised nations[3]. According to the International Criminal Tribunal for the former Yugoslavia ("ICTY"):

> "Crimes against humanity are serious acts of violence which harm human beings by striking what is most essential to them: their lives, liberty, physical welfare, health, and or dignity. They are inhumane acts that by their extent and gravity go beyond the limits tolerable to the international community, which must perforce demand their punishment. But crimes against humanity also transcend the individual because when the individual is assaulted, humanity comes under attack

---

[3]   Trial of the major war criminals before the International Military Tribunal, Nuremberg, 14 November 1945 – 1 October 1946, Vol. 1.

and is negated. It is therefore the concept of humanity as victim which essentially characterises crimes against humanity"[4].

16.   Regarding the crime of genocide, in particular, the preamble to the Genocide Convention **[page 9]** recognizes that at all periods of history, genocide has inflicted great losses on humanity and reiterates the need for international cooperation to liberate humanity from this scourge. The crime of genocide is unique because of its element of *dolus specialis* (special intent) which requires that the crime be committed with the intent "to destroy in whole or in part, a national, ethnic, racial or religious group as such", as stipulated in Article 2 of the Statute; hence the Chamber is of the opinion that genocide constitutes the crime of crimes, which must be taken into account when deciding the sentence.

17.   There is no argument that, precisely on account of their extreme gravity, crimes against humanity and genocide must be punished appropriately. Article 27 of the Charter of the Nuremberg Tribunal empowered that Tribunal, pursuant to Article 6 (c) of the said Charter, to sentence any accused found guilty of crimes against humanity to death or such other punishment as shall be determined by it to be just.

18.   Rwanda, like all the States which have incorporated crimes against humanity or genocide in their domestic legislation, has envisaged the most severe penalties in its criminal legislation for these crimes. To this end, the Rwandan Organic Law on the Organization of Prosecutions for Offences constituting the Crime of Genocide or Crimes against Humanity, committed since 1 October 1990, adopted in 1996[5], groups accused persons into four categories as follows:

"Category 1

a) persons whose criminal acts or those whose acts place them among planners, organizers, supervisors and leaders of crime of genocide or of a crime against humanity;

b) Persons who acted in positions of authority at the national, prefectural, communal, sector or cell, or in a political party, the army, religious organizations, or militia and **[page 10]** who perpetrated or fostered such crimes;

c) Notorious murders who by virtue of the zeal or excessive malice with which they committed atrocities, distinguished themselves in their areas of residence or where they passed;

d) Persons who committed acts of sexual violence.

Category 2

Persons whose criminal acts or whose acts of criminal participation place them among perpetrators, conspirators or accomplices of intentional homicide or of serious assault against the person causing death.

Category 3

Persons whose criminal acts or whose acts of criminal participation make them guilty of other serious assaults against the person.

Category 4

---

[4]   See International Criminal Tribunal for the former Yugoslavia, decision of Trial Chamber I of 1 November 1996, Drazen Erdemovic case.

[5]   Organic Law No. 8/96 of 30 August 1996, published in the Gazette of the Republic of Rwanda, 35th year, No. 17, 1 September 1996.

Persons who committed offences against property."

19. According to the list drawn up by the Attorney General of the Supreme Court of Rwanda, pursuant to the afore-mentioned Organic Law, and attached to the Prosecutor's brief, Jean Kambanda figures in Category 1. Article 14 of the Organic Law stipulates that:

"penalties imposed for the offences referred to in Article 1 shall be those provided for in the Penal Code, except that: **[page 11]**

a) persons in Category 1 are liable mandatorily to the death penalty;
b) for persons in Category 2, the death penalty is replaced by life imprisonment (...)"[6]

20. For persons in Category 3, the term of imprisonment shall be of shorter duration.

21. As indicated *supra*, in determining the sentence, the Chamber must, among other things, have recourse to the general practice regarding prison sentences in the courts of Rwanda (Article 23 of the Statute and Rule 101 of the Rules).

22. The Chamber notes that it is logical that in the determination of the sentence, it has recourse only to prison sentences applicable in Rwanda, to the exclusion of other sentences applicable in Rwanda, including the death sentence, since the Statute and the Rules provide that the Tribunal cannot impose this one type of sentence.

23. That said, the Chamber raises the question as to whether the scale of sentences applicable in Rwanda is mandatory or whether it is to be used only as a reference. The Chamber is of the opinion that such reference is but one of the factors that it has to take into account in determining the sentences. It also finds, as did Trial Chamber I of the ICTY in the Erdemovic case, that "the reference to this practice can be used for guidance, but is not binding"[7]. According to that Chamber, this opinion is supported by the interpretation of the United Nations Secretary-General, who in his report on the establishment of the ICTY stated that: "in determining the term of imprisonment, the Trial Chamber should have recourse to the general practice of prison sentences applicable in the courts of the former Yugoslavia."[8] **[page 12]**

24. Regarding the penalties, the Chamber notes that since the trials related to the events in 1994 began in this country, the death penalty and prison terms of up to life imprisonment have been passed on several occasions. However, the Chamber does not have information on the contents of these decisions, particularly their underlying reasons.

25. Also, while referring as much as practicable to the general practice regarding prison sentences in the courts of Rwanda, the Chamber will prefer, here too, to lean more on its unfettered discretion each time that it has to pass sentence on persons found guilty of crimes falling within its jurisdiction, taking into account the circumstances of the case and the standing of the accused persons.

C. General principles regarding the determination of sentences

26. In determining the sentence, the Chamber has to always have in mind that this Tribunal was established by the Security Council pursuant to Chapter VII of the Charter of the United Nations within the context of measures the Council was empowered to take under Article 39 of the said Charter to ensure that violations of international humanitarian law in Rwanda in 1994 were halted and effectively redressed. As required by the Charter in previous cases, the Council noted that the situation in Rwanda constituted a threat to international peace and security. And resolution 955 of 8 November 1994, which was passed by the Council in this connection, clearly indicates that the aim for the establishment of the

---

[6]   Ibid. p. 31
[7]   International Criminal Tribunal for the former Yugoslavia, decision of Trial Chamber I of first November 1996, Drazen Erdemovic case, paragraph 39.
[8]   Report of the Secretary-General prepared in accordance with paragraph 2 of Security Council resolution 808(1993), S/25704, 3 May 1993, paragraph 111.

Tribunal was to prosecute and punish the perpetrator of the atrocities in Rwanda in such a way as to put an end to impunity and thereby to promote national reconciliation and the restoration of peace.

27.   It will be noted that the preamble of Rwandan Organic Law, referred to above, states that:

"Considering that it is vital, in order to achieve national reconciliation, to forever eradicate the culture of impunity; **[page 13]**

Considering that the exceptional situation facing the country requires the adoption of adequate measures to meet the need of the Rwandan people for justice."

28.   That said, it is clear that the penalties imposed on accused persons found guilty by the Tribunal must be directed, on the one hand, at retribution of the said accused, who must see their crimes punished, and over and above that, on other hand, at deterrence, namely dissuading for good those who will attempt in future to perpetrate such atrocities by showing them that the international community was not ready to tolerate the serious violations of international humanitarian law and human rights.

29.   The Chamber recalls, however, that in the determination of sentences, it is required by Article 23 (2) of the Statute and Rule 101 (B) of the Rules to take into account a number of factors including the gravity of the offence, the individual circumstances of the accused, the existence of any aggravating or mitigating circumstances, including the substantial co-operation by the accused with the Prosecutor before or after his conviction. It is a matter, as it were, of individualising the penalty, for it is true that "among the joint perpetrators of an offence or among the persons guilty of the same type of offence, there is only one common element: the target offence which they committed with its inherent gravity. Apart from this common trait, there are, of necessity, fundamental differences in their respective personalities and responsibilities: their age, their background, their education, their intelligence, their mental structure.... It is not true that they are *a priori* subject to the same intensity of punishment" [unofficial translation][9]

30.   Clearly, however, as far as the individualisation of penalties is concerned, the judges of the Chamber cannot limit themselves to the factors mentioned in the Statute and the Rules. Here again, their unfettered discretion to evaluate the facts and attendant circumstances should enable them to take into account any other factor that they deem pertinent.

31.   Similarly, the factors at issue in the Statute and in the Rules cannot be interpreted as **[page 14]** having to be mandatorily cumulative in the determination of the sentence.

32.   Recalling these factors, the Chamber would like to emphasise three of them, in particular. These are aggravating circumstances, individual circumstances of Jean Kambanda[10] (Article 23 (2) of the Statute) and the mitigating circumstances.

33.   Regarding the aggravating circumstances, it will be noted that the gravity of crimes such as genocide and crimes against humanity which are particularly revolting to the collective conscience alone, is enough to merit lengthy elaboration. The Chamber will, however, come back to it when weighing the aggravating factors against the mitigating factor or factors in favour of the accused for the determination of the sentence.

34.   As far as the "individual circumstances of Jean Kambanda" are concerned, the individualisation of the sentence, as the expression itself seems to suggest, is not possible unless facts about his "personality" are known, including his background, his behaviour before, during and after the offence, his motives for the offence and demonstration of remorse thereafter.

35.   With regard to the mitigating circumstances, Article 6 (4) of the Statute states that the fact that an accused person acted pursuant to an order of a Government or of a superior shall not relieve him or her of criminal responsibility, but may be considered in mitigation of punishment if the Tribunal determines that justice so requires. The problem should not arise in the instant case, since the accused was the Prime

---

[9]   Merle and Virtu – Trait de Droit Criminal, Editions Culpas, paragraph 66, pages 115 and 116

[10]   The term "the accused" should rather be used since you don not pass sentence on a convicted person.

Minister. For its part, Rule 101 (B) (ii) of the Rules, as mentioned earlier stipulates as mitigating circumstances "the substantial co-operation by the convicted person with Prosecutor before or after the conviction." In this regard, when determining the sentence for Jean Kambanda, the Chamber will have to assess the extent of the co-operation by the accused referred to by the Prosecutor in the documents under seal entitled "Agreement on a guilty plea", signed by herself, the accused and his counsel. **[page 15]**

36.   However, the wording of above-mentioned Rule 101 (... any mitigating circumstances including the substantial ...) shows, in the opinion of the Chamber, that substantial co-operation by the accused with the Prosecutor could only be one mitigating circumstance, among others, when the accused pleads guilty plea or shows sincere repentance.

37.   Having said that, the Chamber should, nevertheless, stress that the principle must always remain that the reduction of the penalty stemming from the application of mitigating circumstances must not in any way diminish the gravity of the offence. The aforementioned Rwandan Organic Law No. 8/96 of 30/8/96 goes further because under the Law, persons falling under Category 1 cannot benefit from a reduction of sentences even after a guilty plea.

III. Case on Merits

38.   Having reviewed the principles set out above, the Trial Chamber proceeds to consider all relevant information submitted by both parties in order to determine an appropriate sentence in terms of Rule 100 of the Rules.

A.   **Facts of the Case**

39.   Together with his 'guilty' plea, Jean Kambanda submitted to the Chamber a document entitled "Plea Agreement between Jean Kambanda and the OTP", signed by Jean Kambanda and his defence counsel, Oliver Michael Inglis, on 28 April 1998, in which Jean Kambanda makes full admissions of all the relevant facts alleged in the indictment. In particular:

(i)   Jean Kambanda admits that there was in Rwanda in 1994 a widespread and systematic attack against the civilian population of Tutsi, the purpose of which was to exterminate them. Mass killings of hundreds of thousands of Tutsi occurred in Rwanda, including women and children, old and young who were pursued and killed at places where they had sought refuge i.e. prefectures, commune offices, schools, churches and **[page 16]** stadiums.

(ii)   Jean Kambanda acknowledges that as Prime Minister of the Interim Government of Rwanda from 8 April 1994 to 17 July 1994, he was head of the 20 member Council of Ministers and exercised *de jure* authority and control over the members of his government. The government determined and controlled national policy and had the administration and armed forces at its disposal. As Prime Minister, he also exercised de jure and *de facto* authority over senior civil servants and senior officers in the military.

(iii)   Jean Kambanda acknowledges that he participated in meetings of the Council of Ministers, cabinet meetings and meetings of *prefets* where the course of massacres were actively followed, but no action was taken to stop them. He was involved in the decision of the government for visits by designated ministers to prefectures as part of the government's security efforts and in order to call on the civilian population to be vigilant in detecting the enemy and its accomplices. Jean Kambanda also acknowledges participation in the dismissal of the *prefet* of Butare because the latter had opposed the massacres and the appointment of a new *prefet* to ensure the spread of massacre of Tutsi in Butare.

(iv)   Jean Kambanda acknowledges his participation in a high level security meeting at Gitarama in April 1994 between the President, T. Sindikubwabo, himself and the Chief of Staff of the Rwandan Armed Forces (FAR) and others, which discussed FAR's support in the fight against the

Rwandan Patriotic Front (RPF) and its "accomplices", understood to be the Tutsi and Moderate Hutu.

(v)   Jean Kambanda acknowledges that he issued the Directive on Civil Defence addressed to the *prefets* on 25 May 1994 (Directive No. 024-0273, disseminated on 8 June 1994). Jean Kambanda further admits that this directive encouraged and reinforced the *Interahamwe* who were committing mass killings of the Tutsi civilian population in the prefectures. Jean Kambanda further acknowledges that by this directive the Government, **[page 17]** assumed the responsibility for the actions of the Interahamwe.

(vi)   Jean Kambanda acknowledges that before 6 April 1994, political parties in concert with the Rwanda Armed Forces organized and began the military training of the youth wings of the MRND and CDR political parties (Interahamwe and Impuzamugambi respectively) with the intent to use them in the massacres that ensued. Furthermore, Jean Kambanda acknowledges that the Government headed by him distributed arms and ammunition to these groups. Additionally, Jean Kambanda confirms that roadblocks manned by mixed patrols of the Rwandan Armed Forces and the Interahamwe were set up in Kigali and elsewhere as soon as the death of President J.B. Habyarimana was announced on the Radio. Furthermore Jean Kambanda acknowledges the use of the media as part of the plan to mobilize and incite the population to commit massacres of the civilian Tutsi population. That apart, Jean Kambanda acknowledges the existence of groups within military, militia, and political structures which had planned the elimination of the Tutsi and Hutu political opponents.

(vii)   Jean Kambanda acknowledges that, on or about 21 June 1994, in his capacity as Prime Minister, he gave clear support to Radio Television Libre des Mille Collines (RTLM), with the knowledge that it was a radio station whose broadcasts incited killing, the commission of serious bodily or mental harm to, and persecution of Tutsi and moderate Hutu. On this occasion, speaking on this radio station, Jean Kambanda, as Prime Minister, encouraged the RTLM to continue to incite the massacres of the Tutsi civilian population, specifically stating that this radio station was "an indispensable weapon in the fight against the enemy".

(viii) Jean Kambanda acknowledges that following numerous meetings of the Council of Ministers between 8 April 1994 and 17 July 1994, he as Prime Minister, instigated, aided and abetted the *Prefets, Bourgmestres*, and members of the population to commit massacres and killings of civilians, in particular Tutsi and moderate Hutu. Furthermore, between 24 April 1994 and 17 July 1994, Jean Kambanda and Ministers of his **[page 18]** Government visited several prefectures, such as Butare, Gitarama (Nyabikenke), Gikongoro, Gisenyi and Kibuye to incite and encourage the population to commit these massacres including by congratulating the people who had committed these killings.

(ix)   Jean Kambanda acknowledges that on 3 May 1994, he was personally asked to take steps to protect children who had survived the massacre at a hospital and he did not respond. On the same day, after the meeting, the children were killed. He acknowledges that he failed in his duty to ensure the safety of the children and the population of Rwanda.

(x)   Jean Kambanda admits that in his particular role of making public engagements in the name of the government, he addressed public meetings, and the media, at various places in Rwanda directly and publicly inciting the population to commit acts of violence against Tutsi and moderate Hutu. He acknowledges uttering the incendiary phrase which was subsequently repeatedly broadcast, "you refuse to give your blood to your country and the dogs drink it for nothing." (Wima igihugu amaraso imbwa zikayanywera ubusa)

(xi)   Jean Kambanda acknowledges that he ordered the setting up of roadblocks with the knowledge that these roadblocks were used to identify Tutsi for elimination, and that as Prime Minister he participated in the distribution of arms and ammunition to members of political parties, militias and the population knowing that these weapons would be used in the perpetration of massacres of civilian Tutsi.

(xii) Jean Kambanda acknowledges that he knew or should have known that persons for whom he was responsible were committing crimes of massacre upon Tutsi and that he failed to prevent them or punish the perpetrators. Jean Kambanda admits that he was an eye witness to the massacres of Tutsi and also had knowledge of them from regular reports of prefets, and cabinet discussions. **[page 19]**

Judgement

40. In light of the admissions made by Jean Kambanda in amplification of his plea of guilty, the Trial Chamber, on 1st May 1998, accepted his plea and found him guilty on the following counts:

(1) By his acts or omissions described in paragraphs 3.12 to 3.15, and 3.17 to 3.19 of the indictment, Jean Kambanda is responsible for the killing of and the causing of serious bodily or mental harm to members of the Tutsi population with the intent to destroy, in whole or in part, an ethnic or racial group, as such, and has thereby committed **GENOCIDE**, stipulated in Article 2(3)(a) of the Statute as a crime, and attributed to him by virtue of Article 6(1) and 6(3), and punishable in reference to Articles 22 and 23 of the Statute of the Tribunal.

(2) By his acts or omissions described in paragraphs 3.8, 3.9, 3.13 to 3.15 and 3.19 of the indictment, Jean Kambanda did conspire with others, including Ministers of his Government, such as Pauline Nyiramasuhuko, Andre Ntagerura, Eliezer Niyitegeka and Edouard Karemera, to kill and to cause serious bodily or mental harm to members of the Tutsi population, with intent to destroy in whole or in part, an ethnic or racial group as such, and has thereby committed **CONSPIRACY TO COMMIT GENOCIDE**, stipulated in Articles 2(3)(b) of the Statute as a crime, and attributed to him by virtue of Article 6(1) and punishable in reference to Articles 22 and 23 of the Statute of the Tribunal.

(3) By his acts or omissions described in paragraphs 3.12 to 3.14 and 3.19 of the indictment, Jean Kambanda did directly and publicly incite to kill and to cause serious bodily or mental harm to members of the Tutsi population, with intent to destroy, in whole or in part, an ethnic group as such, and has thereby committed **DIRECT AND PUBLIC INCITEMENT TO COMMIT GENOCIDE**, stipulated in Articles 2(3)(c) of the Statute as a crime, and attributed to him by virtue of Article 6(1) and 6(3), which is punishable in **[page 20]** reference to Articles 22 and 23 of the Statute of the Tribunal.

(4) By his acts or omissions described in paragraphs 3.10, 3.12 to 3.15 and 3.17 to 3.19 of the indictment, which do not constitute the same acts relied on for counts 1, 2 and 3 Jean Kambanda was complicit in the killing and the causing of serious bodily or mental harm to members of the Tutsi population, and thereby committed **COMPLICITY IN GENOCIDE**, stipulated in Articles 2(3)(e) of the Statute as a crime, and attributed to him by virtue of Article 6(1) and 6(3), which is punishable in reference to Articles 22 and 23 of the Statute of the Tribunal.

(5) By his acts or omissions described in paragraphs 3.12 to 3.15 and 3.17 to 3.19 of the indictment, Jean Kambanda is responsible for the murder of civilians, as part of a widespread or systematic attack against a civilian population on ethnic or racial grounds, and has thereby committed a **CRIME AGAINST HUMANITY**, stipulated in Article 3(a) of the Statute as a crime, and attributed to him by virtue of Article 6(1) and 6(3), which is punishable in reference to Articles 22 and 23 of the Statute of the Tribunal.

(6) By his acts or omissions described in paragraphs 3.12 to 3.15, and 3.17 to 3.19 of the indictment, Jean Kambanda is responsible for the extermination of civilians, as part of a widespread or systematic attack against a civilian population on ethnic or racial grounds, and has thereby committed a **CRIME AGAINST HUMANITY**, stipulated in Article 3(b) of the Statute as a crime, and attributed to him by virtue of Article 6(1) and 6(3), which is punishable in reference to Articles 22 and 23 of the Statute of the Tribunal.

B.   Factors relating to Sentence

41.   Article 23(1) of the Statute stipulates that penalties imposed by the Trial Chamber shall be limited to imprisonment and that in the determination of imprisonment, the Trial Chamber shall have recourse to the general practice regarding prison sentences in the Courts of Rwanda. **[page 21]** The Trial Chamber notes that the Death sentence which is proscribed by the Statute of the ICTR is mandatory for crimes of this nature in Rwanda. Reference to the Rwandan sentencing practice is intended as a guide to determining an appropriate sentence and does not fetter the discretion of the judges of the Trial Chamber to determine the sentence. In determining the sentence, the Court shall, in accordance with the Rules of Procedure, take into account such factors as the gravity of the crime and the individual circumstances of Jean Kambanda.

(i)   Gravity of the Crime

42.   In the brief dated 10 August 1998 and in her closing argument at the hearing, the Prosecutor stressed the gravity of the crimes of genocide, and crimes against humanity. The heinous nature of the crime of genocide and its absolute prohibition makes its commission inherently aggravating. The magnitude of the crimes involving the killing of an estimated 500,000 civilians[11] in Rwanda, in a short span of 100 days constitutes an aggravating fact.

43.   Crimes against Humanity are as aforementioned conceived as offences of the gravest kind against the life and liberty of the human being.

44.   The crimes were committed during the time when Jean Kambanda was Prime Minister and he and his government were responsible for maintenance of peace and security. Jean Kambanda abused his authority and the trust of the civilian population. He personally participated in the genocide by distributing arms, making incendiary speeches and presiding over cabinet and other meetings where the massacres were planned and discussed. He failed to take necessary and reasonable measures to prevent his subordinates from committing crimes against the population. Abuse of positions of authority or trust is generally considered an aggravating factor. **[page 22]**

(ii)   Individual circumstances of Jean Kambanda

Personal particulars

45.   Jean Kambanda was born on 10 October 1955 at Mubumbano in the Prefecture of Butare. He has a wife and two children. He holds a Diploma d'Ingenieur Commercial and from May 1989 to April 1994, he worked in the Union des Banques Populaires du Rwanda rising to the position of Director of the network of those banks. He was Vice President of the Butare Section of the MDR and member of its Political Bureau. On 9 April 1994, he became Prime Minister of the Interim Government. The Prosecutor has not proved previous criminal convictions, if any, of Jean Kambanda.

(iii)   Mitigating Factors

46.   Defence Counsel has proffered three factors in mitigation: -Plea of guilty; remorse; which he claims is evident from the act of pleading guilty; and co-operation with the Prosecutor's office.

47.   The Prosecutor confirms that Jean Kambanda has extended substantial co-operation and invaluable information to the Prosecutor. The Prosecutor requests the Trial Chamber to regard as a significant mitigating factor, not only the substantial co-operation so far extended, but also the future co-operation when Jean Kambanda testifies for the prosecution in the trials of other accused.

---

[11]   U.N. Commission of Experts established pursuant to Security Council Resolution 935 (1994) Annex to UN Doc s/1994/1405, 9 December 1994, Paragraph 57)

48.   The Plea Agreement signed by the parties expressly records that no agreements, understandings or promises have been made between the parties with respect to sentence which, it is acknowledged, is at the discretion of the Trial Chamber.

49.   The Prosecutor however disclosed that Jean Kambanda's co-operation has been recognised by significant protection measures that have been put in place to alleviate any concerns that he **[page 23]** may have, about the security of his family.

50.   According to the Prosecutor, Jean Kambanda had expressed his intention to plead guilty immediately upon his arrest and transfer to the Tribunal, on 18 July 1997. Jean Kambanda declared in the Plea Agreement that he had resolved to plead guilty even before his arrest in Kenya and that his prime motivation for pleading guilty was the profound desire to tell the truth, as the truth was the only way to restoring national unity and reconciliation in Rwanda. Jean Kambanda condemned the massacres that occurred in Rwanda and considers his confession as a contribution towards the restoration of peace in Rwanda.

51.   The Chamber notes however that Jean Kambanda has offered no explanation for his voluntary participation in the genocide; nor has he expressed contrition, regret or sympathy for the victims in Rwanda, even when given the opportunity to do so by the Chamber, during the hearing of 3 September 1998.

52.   Both Counsel for Prosecution and Defence have urged the Chamber to interpret Jean Kambanda's guilty pleas as a signal of his remorse, repentance and acceptance of responsibility for his actions. The Chamber is mindful that remorse is not the only reasonable inference that can be drawn from a guilty plea; nevertheless it accepts that most national jurisdictions consider admissions of guilt as matters properly to be considered in mitigation of punishment.

"A prompt guilty plea is considered a major mitigating factor."[12]

53.   In civil criminal law systems, a guilt plea may be favourably considered as a mitigating factor, subject to the discretionary faculty of a judge.[13]

"An admission of guilt demonstrates honesty and it is important for the International **[page 24]** Tribunal to encourage people to come forth, whether already indicted or as unknown perpetrators."[14]

54.   The Chamber has furthermore been requested to take into account in favour of Jean Kambanda that his guilty plea has also occasioned judicial economy, saved victims the trauma and emotions of trial and enhanced the administration of justice.

55.   The Trial Chamber finds that the gravity of the crime has been established and the mitigatory impact on penalty has been characterised.

56.   The Trial Chamber holds the view that a finding of mitigating circumstances relates to assessment of sentence and in no way derogates from the gravity of the crime. It mitigates punishment, not the crime. In this respect the Trial Chamber adopts the reasoning of "Erdemovic" and the "Hostage" case cited therein.

"It must be observed however that mitigation of punishment does not in any sense of the word reduce the degree of crime. It is more a matter of grace than of defence. In other words, the punishment assessed is not a proper criterion to be considered in evaluating the findings of the court with reference to the degree of magnitude of the crime."[15]

57.   The degree of magnitude of the crime is still an essential criterion for evaluation of sentence.

---

12   R.V. Sandercock (1985); 22 C.C.C. (3d) 79 at p.86 C.R. (3d) 154 (1986) I.W.W.R. 291 (Alta CA.

13   Merle R & Vitu.A., Traite de Droit Criminel, les Circonstances Attenuantes, Ed. Cujas, 6eme ed., pp 946-954, 1984

14   Sentencing Judgement, P.V. Drazen Erdemovic, ICTY case No. IT96-22-Tbis, 5 March 1998, p. 16

15   Drazen Erdemovic Sentencing Judgment ICTY IT96-22 citing:- USA v Wilhelm List et al. (Hostage Case), XI T.W.C. 757,p. 1317 (1948)

58.   A sentence must reflect the predominant standard of proportionality between the gravity of the offence and the degree of responsibility of the offender. Just sentences contribute to respect for the law and the maintenance of a just, peaceful and safe society. **[page 25]**

59.   The Chamber recalls as aforementioned that the Tribunal was established at the request of the government of Rwanda; and the Tribunal was intended to enforce individual criminal accountability on behalf of the international community, contribute in ensuring the effective redress of violence and culture of impunity, and foster national reconciliation and peace in Rwanda. (Preamble, Security Council resolution 955(1994)).

60.   In her submissions, although the Prosecutor sought a term of life imprisonment for Jean Kambanda, she requested that the Tribunal, in the determination of the sentence, take into consideration the guilty plea and the cooperation of Jean Kambanda with her office. The Defence Counsel in his submissions emphasised that Jean Kambanda was only a puppet controlled by certain military authorities and that his power was consequently limited. He thus submitted that the Tribunal, taking into account the guilty plea, Jean Kambanda's cooperation and willingness to continue cooperating with the Prosecutor, and the role Jean Kambanda could play in the process of national reconciliation in Rwanda, sentence him for a term of imprisonment not exceeding two years.

61.   The Chamber has examined all the submissions presented by the Parties pertaining to the determination of sentence, from which it can be inferred:

(A)   (i)   Jean Kambanda has cooperated and is still willingly cooperating with the Office of the Prosecutor;

(ii)   the guilty plea of Jean Kambanda is likely to encourage other individuals to recognize their responsibilities during the tragic events which occurred in Rwanda in 1994;

(iii)   a guilty plea is generally considered, in most national jurisdictions, including Rwanda, as a mitigating circumstance; **[page 26]**

(B)   but that, however:

(v)   the crimes of which Jean Kambanda is responsible carry an intrinsic gravity, and their widespread, atrocious and systematic character is particularly shocking to the human conscience;

(vi)   Jean Kambanda committed the crimes knowingly and with premeditation;

(vii)   and, moreover, Jean Kambanda, as Prime Minister of Rwanda was entrusted with the duty and authority to protect the population and he abused this trust.

62.   On the basis of all of the above, the Chamber is of the opinion that the aggravating circumstances surrounding the crimes committed by Jean Kambanda negate the mitigating circumstances, especially since Jean Kambanda occupied a high ministerial post, at the time he committed the said crimes. **[page 27]**

IV. <u>VERDICT</u>

TRIAL CHAMBER I,

FOR THE FOREGOING REASONS,

DELIVERING its decision in public, inter partes and in the first instance;

PURSUANT to Articles 23, 26 and 27 of the Statute and Rules 100, 101, 102, 103 and 104 of the Rules of Procedure and Evidence;

NOTING the general practice of sentencing by the Courts of Rwanda;

NOTING the indictment as confirmed on 16 October 1997;

NOTING the Plea of guilty of Jean Kambanda on 1 May 1998 on the Counts of:

COUNT 1: Genocide (stipulated in Article 2(3)(a) of the Statute as a crime, and attributed to him by virtue of Article 6(1) and 6(3), and punishable in reference to Articles 22 and 23 of the Statute of the Tribunal);

COUNT 2: Conspiracy to commit genocide (stipulated in Article 2(3)(b) of the Statute as a crime, and attributed to him by virtue of Article 6(1) and punishable in reference to Articles 22 and 23 of the Statute of the Tribunal); **[page 28]**

COUNT 3: Direct and public incitement to commit genocide (stipulated in Article 2(3)(c) of the Statute as a crime, and attributed to him by virtue of Article 6(1) and 6(3), which is punishable in reference to Articles 22 and 23 of the Statute of the Tribunal);

COUNT 4: Complicity in genocide (stipulated in Article 2(3)(e) of the Statute as a crime, and attributed to him by virtue of Article 6(1) and 6(3), which is punishable in reference to Articles 22 and 23 of the Statute of the Tribunal);

COUNT 5: Crime against humanity (murder) (stipulated in Article 3(a) of the Statute as a crime, and attributed to him by virtue of Article 6(1) and 6(3), which is punishable in reference to Articles 22 and 23 of the Statute of the Tribunal);

COUNT 6: Crime against humanity (extermination) (stipulated in Article 3(b) of the Statute as a crime, and attributed to him by virtue of Article 6(1) and 6(3), which is punishable in reference to Articles 22 and 23 of the Statute of the Tribunal);

HAVING FOUND Jean Kambanda guilty on all six counts on 1 May 1998;

NOTING the briefs submitted by the parties;

HAVING HEARD the Closing Statements of the Prosecutor and the Defence Counsel;

IN PUNISHMENT OF THE ABOVEMENTIONED CRIMES,

SENTENCES Jean Kambanda,

born on 19 October 1955 in Gishamvu Commune, Butare Prefecture, Rwanda

TO   LIFE IMPRISONMENT **[page 29]**

RULES that imprisonment shall be served in a State designated by the President of the Tribunal, in consultation with the Trial Chamber and the said designation shall be conveyed to the government of Rwanda and the designated State by the Registry;

RULES that this judgement shall be enforced immediately, and that until his transfer to the said place of imprisonment, Jean Kambanda shall be kept in detention under the present conditions.

Arusha, 4 September 1998,

Laïty Kama	Lennart Aspegren	Navanethem Pillay
Presiding Judge	Judge	Judge

International Criminal Tribunal for Rwanda
Tribunal Pénal International pour le Rwanda

TRIAL CHAMBER I

OR: FR

Before:	Judge Laïty Kama, Presiding Judge
	Judge Lennart Aspegren
	Judge Navanethem Pillay
Registry:	Mr. Agwu U. Okali
	Ms. Prisca Nyambe
	Mr. Antoine Mindua
Decision of:	2 October 1998

THE PROSECUTOR

versus

JEAN PAUL AKAYESU

Case No. ICTR-96-4-T

SENTENCE

The Office of the Prosecutor:

Ms. Louise Arbour
Mr. Pierre-Richard Prosper

Jean Paul Akayesu in person

[page 2] THE INTERNATIONAL CRIMINAL TRIBUNAL FOR RWANDA ("the TRIBUNAL"),

SITTING AS Trial Chamber I composed of Judge Laïty Kama, presiding, Judge Lennart Aspegren and Judge Navanethem Pillay;

CONSIDERING that on 2 September 1998 a judgement was rendered by this Chamber in the matter of the Prosecutor versus Jean Paul Akayesu;

CONSIDERING that Jean Paul Akayesu was convicted of Genocide, Crime against Humanity (extermination), Direct and Public Incitement to commit Genocide, Crime against Humanity (torture), Crime against Humanity (rape), Crime against Humanity (other inhumane acts) and on three counts of Crimes against Humanity (murder);

CONSIDERING the written brief dated 21 September 1998 filed by the Prosecutor on the sentence and the points that she raised in support of the said brief at the pre-sentencing hearing of 28 September 1998;

CONSIDERING also the oral submission made by Jean Paul Akayesu at the said hearing of 28 September 1998, after having specifically renounced his right to be represented by counsel, despite having been informed of his right to counsel by the Chamber;

CONSIDERING Articles 22 and 27 of the Statute of the Tribunal (the "Statute") and Rules 100 to 104[1] of the Rules of Procedure and Evidence ("the Rules");

I. Applicable law and principles

1.   The Chamber will now summarize the legal provisions relating to sentences and their enforcement, before going on to specify the applicable scale of sentences, on the one hand, and the general principles on the determination of sentences, on the other.

A.   Applicable provisions

2.   The Chamber recalls below the provisions of the Statute and the Rules on sentencing, applicable to Akayesu.

Article 22 of the Statute: Judgement

"The Trial Chamber shall pronounce judgements and impose sentences and penalties on persons convicted of serious violations of international humanitarian law." **[page 3]**

Rule 100 of the Rules: Pre-sentencing procedure

"If the accused pleads guilty or if a Trial Chamber finds the accused guilty of a crime, the Prosecutor and the defence may submit any relevant information that may assist the Trial Chamber in determining an appropriate sentence."

Article 23 of the Statute: Penalties

"1.   The penalty imposed by the Trial Chamber shall be limited to imprisonment. In determining the terms of imprisonment, the Trial Chamber shall have recourse to the general practice regarding prison sentences in the courts of Rwanda.

---

[1]   Rules 100 to 102 are being applied as they were worded before 8 June 1998. (This footnote does not appear in the French version of this document.)

2. In imposing the sentences, the Trial Chambers should take into account such factors as the gravity of the offence and the individual circumstances of the convicted person.

3. In addition to imprisonment, the Trial Chambers may order the return of any property and proceeds acquired by criminal conduct, including by means of duress, to their rightful owners."

Rule 101 of the Rules: Penalties

"(A) A convicted person may be sentenced to imprisonment for a term up to and including the remainder of his life.

(B) In determining the sentence, the Trial Chamber shall take into account the factors mentioned in Article 23 (2) of the Statute, as well as such factors as:

> (i) any aggravating circumstances;

> (ii) any mitigating circumstances including the substantial co-operation with the Prosecutor by the convicted person before or after the conviction;

> (iii) the general practice regarding prison sentences in the courts of Rwanda;

> (iv) the extent to which any penalty imposed by a court of any State on the convicted person for the same act has already been served, as referred to in Article 9 (3) of the Statute.

(C) The Trial Chamber shall indicate whether multiple sentences shall be served consecutively or concurrently.

(D) The sentence shall be pronounced in public and in the presence of the convicted person, subject to Rule 102 (B).

(E) Credit shall be given to the convicted person for the period, if any, during **[page 4]** which the convicted person was detained in custody pending his surrender to the Tribunal or pending trial or appeal."

Article 26 of the Statute: Enforcement of sentences

"Imprisonment shall be served in Rwanda or any of the States on a list of States which have indicated to the Security Council their willingness to accept convicted persons, as designated by the International Tribunal for Rwanda. Such imprisonment shall be in accordance with the applicable law of the State concerned, subject to the supervision of the International Tribunal for Rwanda."

Rule 102 of the Rules: Status of the Convicted Person

"(A) The sentence shall begin to run from the day it is pronounced under Rule 101(D). However, as soon as notice of appeal is given, the enforcement of the judgement shall thereupon be stayed until the decision on the appeal has been delivered, the convicted person meanwhile remaining in detention, as provided in Rule 64.

(B) If, by a previous decision of the Trial Chamber, the convicted person has been provisionally released, or is for any reason at liberty, and he is not present when the judgement is pronounced, the Trial Chamber shall issue a warrant for his arrest. On arrest, he shall be notified of the conviction and sentence, and the procedure provided in Rule 103 shall be followed."

Rule 103 of the Rules: Place of imprisonment

"(A) Imprisonment shall be served in Rwanda or any State designated by the Tribunal from a list of States which have indicated their willingness to accept convicted persons for the serving of sentences. Prior to a decision on the place of imprisonment, the Chamber shall notify the Government of Rwanda.

(B) Transfer of the convicted person to that State shall be effected as soon as possible after the time-limit for appeal has elapsed."

Article 27 of the Statute: Pardon or commutation of sentences

"If, pursuant to the applicable law of the State in which the convicted person is imprisoned, he or she is eligible for pardon or commutation of sentence, the State concerned shall notify the International Tribunal for Rwanda accordingly. There shall only be pardon or commutation of sentence if the President of the International Tribunal for Rwanda, in consultation with the judges, so decides on the basis of the interests of justice and the general principles of law." **[page 5]**

Rule 104 of the Rules: Supervision of imprisonment

"All sentences of imprisonment shall be served under the supervision of the Tribunal or a body designated by it;"

B. Scale of sentences applicable to the accused found guilty of one of the crimes listed in Articles 2, 3 or 4 of the Statute of the Tribunal.

3. As noted from a reading of all the above provisions on sentences, the only penalties the Chamber can impose on an accused who pleads guilty or is convicted as such are prison terms up to and including life imprisonment, pursuant in particular to Rule 101 (A) of the Rules, whose provisions apply to all crimes which fall within the jurisdiction of the Tribunal, namely genocide, (Article 2 of the Statute), crimes against humanity (Article 3) and violations of Article 3 common to the Geneva Conventions and of Additional Protocol II thereto (Article 4). The Statute of the Tribunal excludes other forms of punishment such as the death sentence, penal servitude or a fine.

4. Neither Article 23 of the Statute nor Rule 101 of the Rules determine any specific penalty for each of the crimes falling under the jurisdiction of the Tribunal. The determination of sentences is left to the discretion of the Chamber, which shall take into account, apart from the general practice regarding prison sentences in the courts of Rwanda, a number of other factors, in particular the gravity of the crime, the personal circumstances of the convicted person, the existence of any aggravating or mitigating circumstances, including the substantial cooperation by the convicted person before or after conviction.

5. Whereas in most national criminal systems the scale of penalties is determined in accordance with the gravity of the offence, the Chamber notes that, as indicated *supra*, the Statute does not rank the various crimes falling under the jurisdiction of the Tribunal and , thereby, the sentence to be handed down. In theory, the sentences are the same for each of the three crimes, namely prison terms of up to life imprisonment.

6. It should be noted, however, that in imposing a sentence, the Trial Chamber shall take into account, in accordance with Article 23 (2) of the Statute, such factors as the gravity of the offence.

7. As the Chamber stated in the sentencing judgement handed down on 4 September 1998 in the matter of the "Prosecutor versus Jean Kambanda", it seems difficult for the Chamber to rank genocide and crimes against humanity in terms of their respective gravity. The Chamber held that crimes against humanity, already punished by the Nuremberg and Tokyo Tribunals, and genocide, a concept defined later, are crimes which particularly shock the collective conscience.

8.   Regarding the crime of genocide, in particular, the preamble to the Genocide Convention recognizes that at all periods of history, genocide has inflicted great losses on humanity and reiterates the need for international cooperation to liberate humanity from this scourge. The crime of genocide is unique because of its element of *dolus specialis* (special intent) which requires that the crime be committed with the intent "to destroy in whole or in part, a national, ethnic, racial **[page 6]** or religious group as such", as stipulated in Article 2 of the Statute; hence the Chamber is of the opinion that genocide constitutes the "crime of crimes", and will decide an appropriate sentence for this crime.

9.   With regard to crimes against humanity, the Chamber holds, like other courts before it, that such crimes are particularly shocking to the human conscience because they typify inhumane acts committed against civilians on a discriminatory basis.

10.   There is no argument that, precisely on account of their extreme gravity, genocide and crimes against humanity must be punished appropriately. Article 27 of the Charter of the Nuremberg Tribunal empowered that Tribunal, pursuant to Article 6 (c) of the said Charter, to sentence any accused found guilty of crimes against humanity to death or such other punishment as was determined by it to be just.

11.   Rwanda, like all the States which have incorporated genocide or crimes against humanity in their domestic legislation, has envisaged the most severe penalties in its criminal legislation for these crimes.

C.   General principles regarding the determination of sentences

12.   As indicated *supra*, in determining the sentence, the Chamber must, among other things, "have recourse to the general practice regarding prison sentences in the courts of Rwanda" (Article 23 of the Statute and Rule 101 of the Rules).

13.   The Chamber notes that it is logical that in the determination of the sentence, it has recourse only to prison sentences applicable in Rwanda, to the exclusion of other sentences applicable in that country, including the death sentence, since the Statute and the Rules provide that the Tribunal cannot impose this type of sentence.

14.   That said, the Chamber raises the question as to wether the scale of sentences applicable in Rwanda is mandatory or wether it is to be used only as a reference. The Chamber is of the opinion that such reference is but one of the factors that is has to take into account in determining sentences. Consequently, it holds, as in its sentencing judgement of 4 September 1998 in the case of the "Prosecutor versus Jean Kambanda" and as did Trial Chamber I of the International Criminal Tribunal for the former Yugoslavia (the "ICTY") in the Erdemovic case, that "reference to this practice can be used for guidance, but is not binding".[2] According to that Chamber, this opinion is supported by the interpretation of the Secretary-General of the United Nations, who in his report on the establishment of the ICTY stated that: "in determining the term of imprisonment, the Trial Chamber should have recourse to the general practice of prison sentences applicable in the courts of the former Yugoslavia."[3] **[page 7]**

15.   Regarding the penalties applicable in Rwanda, the Chamber notes that since the trials related to the events in 1994 began in this country, the death penalty and prison terms of up to life imprisonment have been passed on several occasions. However, the Chamber has not been able to have information on the contents of these decisions, particularly their underlying reasons.

16.   In this regard, the Chamber nevertheless recalls that by enabling legislation, Rwanda acceded to the Genocide Convention of 12 February 1975.[4] Therefore, as the Chamber stated in its judgement, criminal liability for the crime of genocide existed in Rwanda in 1994, when the crimes with which

---

[2]   International Criminal Tribunal for the former Yugoslavia decision of Trial Chamber I of 1 November 1996, Drazen Erdemovic case, paragraph 39.
[3]   Report of the Secretary-General prepared in accordance with paragraph 2 of Security Council resolution 808(1993), S/25704, 3 May 1993, paragraph 111.
[4]   Legislative Decree no. 8/75 of 12 February 1975, Official Gazette of the Republic of Rwanda, 1975, p. 230. Rwanda acceded to the Genocide Convention but stated that it was not bound by Article 9 of this Convention.

Akayesu is charged were committed and the perpetrators of such crimes could indeed be charged before the appropriate Rwandan courts.

17.	Therefore, while referring as much as practicable to "the general practice regarding prison sentences in the courts of Rwanda," the Chamber will prefer, in this instances, to learn more on its unfettered discretion each time that it has to pass sentence on persons found guilty of crimes falling within its jurisdiction, taking into account the circumstances of the case and the standing of the accused persons.

18.	In determining the sentence, the Chamber has to always bear in mind that this Tribunal was established by the Security Council pursuant to Chapter VII of the Charter of the United Nations within the context of measures the Council was empowered to take under Article 39 of the said Charter to ensure that violations of international humanitarian law in Rwanda in 1994 were halted and effectively redressed. As required by the Charter in such cases, the Council noted that the situation in Rwanda constituted a threat to international peace and security. Resolution 955 of 8 November 1994, which was adopted by the Council in this connection, clearly indicates that the establishment of the Tribunal was to prosecute and punish the perpetrators of the atrocities in Rwanda in such a way as to put an end to impunity and thereby to promote national reconciliation and the restoration of peace.

19.	It is therefore clear that the penalties imposed on convicted persons must be directed not only at retribution of the said persons, who must see their crimes punished, but also at deterrence, namely dissuading for good those who will be tempted in future to perpetrate such atrocities by showing them that the international community was no longer ready to tolerate serious violations of international humanitarian law and human rights.

20.	The Chamber recalls, however, that in the determination of sentences, it is required by Article 23 (2) of the Statute and Rule 101 (B) of the Rules to also take into account a number of factors including the gravity of the offence, the individual circumstances of the convicted person, the existence of any aggravating or mitigating circumstances, including the substantial cooperation by the convicted person with the Prosecutor before or after conviction. It is a matter, as it were, of individualizing the penalty.

21.	Clearly to the Chamber, however, as far as the individualization of penalties is concerned, **[page 8]** the judges cannot limit themselves to the factors mentioned in the Statute and the Rules. Here again, their unfettered discretion to evaluate the facts and attendant circumstances should enable them to take into account any other factor that they deem pertinent.

22.	Similarly, the factors at issue in the Statute and in the Rules cannot be interpreted as having to be mandatorily cumulative in the determination of the sentence.

23.	Recalling these factors, the Chamber would like to emphasize three of them, in particular. These are the aggravating circumstances, mitigating circumstances and the individual circumstances of the accused (Article 23 (2) of the Statute).

II. Case on Merits

24.	Having reviewed the principles set out above, the Trial Chamber proceeds to consider all relevant information submitted by both parties in order to determine an appropriate sentence in accordance with Rule 100 of the Rules.

## A.	Facts of the Case

25.	In rendering judgement on 2 September 1998 in the trial of Akayesu, the Trial Chamber found that it was established beyond a reasonable doubt that:

(i) Akayesu is individually criminally responsible for the killing of and causing serious bodily or mental harm to members of the Tutsi group;

(ii) Akayesu aided and abetted in the commission of acts of sexual violence by allowing such acts to take place on or near the premises of the *bureau communal*, while he was present on the said premises; he encouraged the commission of such acts through his words, which by virtue of his authority clearly suggested that acts of sexual violence were officially tolerated;

(iii) On 19 April 1994 Akayesu addressed a meeting at Gishyeshye and called on the population to fight against the accomplices of the *Inkotanyi*, knowing full well that his utterances would be construed by the people present as a call to kill the Tutsi; the widespread killing of Tutsi subsequently started in Taba;

(iv) At this meeting at Gishyeshye, Akayesu mentioned the name of Ephrem Karangwa and later that same day groups of people, acting on the orders of Akayesu and in his presence, destroyed Karangwa's house and Karangwa's mother's house and killed Karangwa's three brothers;

(v) Akayesu is individually criminally responsible for the death of eight refugees from Runda who were killed in his presence by the *Interahamwe*, acting on his orders;

vi) Akayesu is individually criminally responsible for the killing of five teachers, who were killed by the Interahamwe and local population, acting on his orders; **[page 9]**

(vii) Akayesu is individually criminally responsible for the torture of Victims U, V, W, X, Y, and Z.

B.   The Prosecutor's submissions on sentence

26.   In her brief and in her oral submissions made at the pre-sentencing hearing, the Prosecutor submitted that the crimes committed by Akayesu are of extreme gravity and that they deserve to be punished appropriately. She submitted that the Chamber should assess the personal role of Akayesu in the crimes as well as the attendant circumstances of those crimes. She recalled that Akayesu performed executive duties in Taba *commune*, that he was responsible for the enforcement of laws and regulations as well as for the administration of justice and that he also had absolute authority over the *communal* police.

27.   The Prosecutor stated that in her opinion, the following aggravating circumstances justify an enhancement in sentence in this matter:

(i)   Akayesu was in a position of authority and had the duty to protect the population and ensure their security;

(ii)   He betrayed the trust of the people and used his power as *bourgmestre* to commit crimes. He also used the *communal* police he was in charge of in commission of these crimes. He thus abused his powers;

(iii)   He possessed the specific intent to commit genocide and planned his actions accordingly, thus acting with premeditation;

(iv)   His criminal conduct was sustained and systematic and lasted for almost three months, becoming ever more intensive.

28.   Furthermore, the Prosecutor submits that in her opinion, on the basis of the information available there are no mitigating circumstances for Akayesu's conviction.

29.   With regard to the issue of multiple sentences which could be imposed on Akayesu as envisaged by Rule 101(C) of the Rules, the Prosecutor asked for separate sentences for each of the counts on which Akayesu was found guilty while specifying that the Chamber could impose concurrent sentences for offences arising from the same acts. In the opinion of the Prosecutor, the Chamber should impose a

sentence for each of the offences committed in order to reflect the gravity of each and every one of them and to properly assess the guilt of the accused.

30.   In the final analysis, the Prosecutor is asking for the following sentences for the crimes for which Akayesu was convicted:

Count 1 – Genocide: life imprisonment;

Count 3 – Crime against humanity (extermination): life imprisonment; **[page 10]**

Count 4 – Direct and public incitement to commit genocide: life imprisonment;

Count 5 – Crime against humanity (murder): life imprisonment or a minimum term of 30 years imprisonment;

Count 7 – Crime against humanity (murder): life imprisonment or a minimum of 30 years imprisonment;

Count 9 – Crime against humanity (murder): life imprisonment or a minimum term of 30 years imprisonment;

Count 11 – Crime against humanity (torture): minimum of 25 years imprisonment;

Count 13 – Crime against humanity (rape): life imprisonment;

Count 14 – Crime against humanity (inhumane acts): ten years imprisonment.

C.   Akayesu's Submissions

31   During the aforementioned pre-sentencing hearing, Akayesu told the Chamber that although he was innocent of the crimes of which he was convicted, he nevertheless intended to submit to the Chamber the following mitigating circumstances which according to him are in his favour:

(i)   Several testimonies submitted to the Chamber during the trial show that he was opposed to the killings and the violence. Akayesu argued that he even risked his own life in order to protect the population. He was pursued and one of the policemen responsible for his protection was killed and another policeman wounded.

(ii)   In his own words, as a "small *bourgmestre*" he had at his disposal only eight *communal* policemen. Akayesu compared his very limited powers and resources to those of Major General Dallaire, Commander of the United Nations Assistance Mission for Rwanda (UNAMIR), who, during his appearance before the Chamber, explained that even the international community itself was powerless in the face of the Rwandan tragedy.

(iii)   Akayesu submitted that he co-operated with the Prosecutor and the Tribunal in that he was available and disciplined and never obstructed the judicial process or sought to evade it.

32.   In fine, Akayesu also publicly paid tribute to all the victims of the tragic events which took place in Rwanda, be they Tutsi, Hutu or Twa. He asked for the forgiveness of the people of Rwanda and more specifically the people of Taba *commune*, not because he felt he was guilty of the crimes with which he was charged, but because he regretted that he was not able to carry out successfully his duty, namely the protection of the population of Taba. **[page 11]**

III. VERDICT

TRIAL CHAMBER I,

FOR THE FOREGOING REASONS,

DELIVERING its decision in public, *inter partes* and in the first instance;

PURSUANT to Articles 23, 26 and 27 of the Statute of the Tribunal and Rules 100, 101, 102, 103 and 104 of the Rules of Procedure and Evidence;

NOTING the general practice of sentencing by the courts of Rwanda;

NOTING that Akayesu was convicted on counts 1, 3, 4, 5, 7, 9, 11, 13 and 14 of the Indictment in the judgement of 2 September 1998;

NOTING the brief submitted by the Prosecutor;

HAVING HEARD the Prosecutor and Akayesu;

IN PUNISHMENT OF THE ABOVEMENTIONED CRIMES,

SENTENCES Jean Paul Akayesu,
born in 1953 in Murehe sector, Taba *commune*, Gitarama *prefecture*, Rwanda, to:

COUNT 1: life imprisonment for the crime of Genocide;

COUNT 3: life imprisonment for Crime against humanity (extermination);

COUNT 4: life imprisonment for the crime of Direct and Public incitement to commit genocide;

COUNT 5: fifteen years imprisonment for Crime against humanity (murder);

COUNT 7: fifteen years imprisonment for Crime against humanity (murder);

COUNT 9: fifteen years imprisonment for Crime against humanity (murder);

COUNT 11: ten years imprisonment for Crime against humanity (torture);

COUNT 13: fifteen years imprisonment for Crime against humanity (rape);

COUNT 14: ten years imprisonment for Crime against humanity (other in humane acts);

DECIDES that the above sentences shall be served concurrently and therefore directs that Akayesu serve:

A SINGLE SENTENCE OF LIFE IMPRISONMENT

International Criminal Tribunal for Rwanda
Tribunal Pénal International pour le Rwanda

TRIAL CHAMBER I

OR: ENG

Before: Judge Laïty Kama, Presiding Judge
            Judge Lennart Aspegren
            Judge Navanethem Pillay

Registry: Mr. John Kiyeyeu

Decision of: 14 December 1998

THE PROSECUTOR

versus

OMAR SERUSHAGO

Case No. ICTR-98-39-T

DECISION RELATING TO A PLEA OF GUILTY

<u>Office of the Prosecutor:</u>
        Mr. Bernard Muna, Deputy Prosecutor
        Mr. Mohamed Othman, Senior Legal Advisor
        Ms. Josée D'Aoust, Legal Adviser

<u>Defence counsel:</u>
        Mr. Mohamed Ismail

[page 2] THE TRIBUNAL,

Sitting as Trial Chamber I of the International Criminal Tribunal for Rwanda ("the Tribunal"), composed of Judge Laïty Kama, presiding, Judge Lennart Aspegren and Judge Navanethem Pillay;

WHEREAS the accused Omar Serushago appeared today before the Tribunal pursuant to the provisions of Rule 62 of the Rules of Procedure and Evidence ("the Rules"), assisted by his Counsel, Mr. Mohamed Ismail;

WHEREAS the indictment, dated 8 October 1998, filed by the Prosecutor against him and confirmed on 29 September 1998 by Judge Yakov Ostrovsky, was read out to him;

WHEREAS, during the hearing, the Tribunal took note of several modifications made in the said indictment in order to harmonize the English and French versions of the text;

TAKING NOTE of the Plea Agreement reached between the Prosecutor, on the one hand, and the accused and his Counsel, on the other hand, pertaining to a guilty plea, which Agreement was filed with the Registry of the Tribunal on 10 December 1998;

WHEREAS Omar Serushago has pleaded guilty to the first four counts preferred against him in the said indictment, namely:

(1) Genocide, a crime stipulated in Article 2(3)(a) of the Statute,
(2) Crime against humanity (murder), a crime stipulated in Article 3(a) of the Statute,
(3) Crime against humanity (extermination), a crime stipulated in Article 3(b) of the Statute,
(4) Crime against humanity (torture), a crime stipulated in Article 3(f) of the Statute;

WHEREAS the accused has pleaded not guilty to Count 5, namely, Crime against humanity (rape), a crime stipulated in Article 3(g) of the Statute;

WHEREAS, consequently during the hearing, the Prosecutor orally sought leave from the Chamber, pursuant to the provisions of Rules 73 and 51 of the Rules, to withdraw Count 5 relating to the crime of Crime against humanity (rape);

WHEREAS the Tribunal decided on the bench to grant leave to the Prosecutor to make the required modification in the indictment and to withdraw Count 5 relating to Crime against humanity (rape) and all the facts in the said indictment which exclusively substantiate this Count;

WHEREAS the Tribunal, during the said initial appearance hearing, verified the validity of the plea of guilty by asking the accused:

(i) whether his plea of guilty was voluntary, that is, whether he has entered the plea freely and consciously, without coercion, threats or promises; **[page 3]**

(ii) whether he fully understood the nature of the charges brought against him, as well as the consequences of his pleading guilty; and

(iii) whether his plea of guilty is unequivocal, that is, whether he is aware that the said plea is incompatible with any defence which could refute it;

WHEREAS the accused answered in the affirmative to each of the Tribunal's questions;

WHEREAS, additionally, the Tribunal notes, firstly, that there exist sufficient facts to substantiate the crimes brought against him in the first four counts to which he pleaded guilty and, secondly, that the participation of the accused in their commission is established considering the absence of any disagreement between the parties on the said facts;

FOR THESE REASONS,

THE TRIBUNAL

FINDS the accused Omar Serushago guilty of the charges preferred against him in the indictment, namely:

(1) Genocide, a crime stipulated in Article 2(3)(a) of the Statute,
(2) Crime against humanity (murder), a crime stipulated in Article 3(a) of the Statute,
(3) Crime against humanity (extermination), a crime stipulated in Article 3(b) of the Statute,
(4) Crime against humanity (torture), a crime stipulated in Article 3(f) of the Statute;

DECIDES that all relevant information that may assist in determining the appropriate sentence that the Parties may wish to submit to the Tribunal, pursuant to the provisions of Rule 100 (A) of the Rules, must be submitted to the Registry by the latest Friday 22 January 1999;

INSTRUCTS the Registrar to set the pre-sentencing hearing for Friday 29 January 1999 at 9.30 hrs;

ORDERS the continued detention of Omar Serushago under the same conditions as those which prevailed until his incarceration.

Arusha, 14 December 1998.

| Laïty Kama | Lennart Aspegren | Navanethem Pillay |
| Presiding Judge | Judge | Judge |

International Criminal Tribunal for Rwanda
Tribunal Pénal International pour le Rwanda

TRIAL CHAMBER I

OR: FR

Before: **Judge Laïty Kama, Président de Chambre**
Judge Lennart Aspegren
Judge Navanethem Pillay

Registry: **Mr. Agwu Okali**

Decision of: **5 February 1999**

THE PROSECUTOR

VERSUS

OMAR SERUSHAGO

Case No. ICTR-98-39-S

SENTENCE

Office of the Prosecutor:
   Mr. Bernard Muna, Deputy Prosecutor
   Mr. Mohamed Othman, Senior Legal Adviser
   Ms. Josée D'Aoust, Legal Adviser

Counsel for the Defence:
   Mr. Mohamed Ismail

[page 2] I. The Proceedings

A.   Background

1.   On 9 June 1998, Omar Serushago voluntarily surrendered himself to the authorities of the Côte d'Ivoire in Abidjan. Pursuant to a request of the Prosecutor dated 16 June 1998, President Laïty Kama ruling on the basis of Rule 40*bis* of the Rules of Procedure and Evidence (the "Rules") ordered on 30 June 1998 the transfer of Omar Serushago to the Detention Facility of the Tribunal where he was to be provisionally detained for a period of thirty days. The provisional detention of the suspect Omar Serushago was extended twice, firstly, under Rule 40*bis* (F), for a period of thirty days by Judge Kama, and secondly, under the provisions of Rule 40*bis* (G) by Judge Lennart Aspegren, for a further and final period of 20 days.

2.   On 24 September 1998, an indictment against the suspect Omar Serushago was filed by the Office of the Prosecutor for confirmation. The indictment was submitted to Judge Yakov Ostrovsky on 28 September 1998, and, pursuant to Rule 47(D) of the Rules, the Prosecutor was heard on 29 September 1998. The same day, Judge Yakov Ostrovsky confirmed counts 2, 3, 4, 5 and 6 of the said indictment, dismissing count 1 thereof. A warrant of arrest and order for continued detention were subsequently issued against Omar Serushago.

3.   In accordance with the terms of the abovementioned decision on the review of the indictment, the Prosecutor filed on 14 October 1998 an amended indictment against Omar Serushago.

4.   On 14 December 1998, during his initial appearance before this Trial Chamber, the accused pleaded guilty to four of the five counts in the modified indictment, namely, genocide, as stipulated in Article 2(3)(a) of the Statute of the Tribunal (the "Statute"), a crime against humanity (murder), as stipulated in Article 3(a) of the Statute, a crime against humanity (extermination), as stipulated in Article 3(b) of the Statute, and a crime against humanity, (torture), as stipulated in Article 3(f) of the Statute. Following a plea of not guilty by the accused to count 5 of the indictment, a crime against humanity (rape), as stipulated in Article 3(g) of the Statute, the Prosecutor was authorized by this Trial Chamber, on the basis of Rules 51 and 73 of the Rules, to withdraw the said count.

5.   After verifying the validity of his guilty plea, particularly in light of an agreement concluded between the Prosecutor, on the one hand, and the accused and his lawyer, on the other, an agreement which was signed by all the parties[1], the Chamber entered a plea of guilty against the accused on counts one to four in the indictment. Furthermore, it was decided, as provided for in Rule 100(A) of the Rules, that any relevant information that may assist the Chamber in determining an appropriate sentence which the Prosecutor and the Defence may wish to submit should be filed by the latest Friday 22 January 1999. In accordance with Rule 62(v) of the Rules, the Registrar was instructed to set the date of the pre-sentencing hearing for Friday [page 3] 29 January 1999, on which day it was held[2].

B.   The guilty plea

6.   As indicated *supra*, Omar Serushago pleaded guilty to four of the five counts set forth in the indictment against him. As stated earlier, the accused confirmed that he had concluded an agreement with the Prosecutor, an agreement signed by his counsel and himself and placed under seal, in which he admitted having committed all the acts to which he pleaded guilty to as charged by the Prosecutor.

7.   In accordance with sub-Rule 62(v) of the Rules, the Chamber sought to verify the validity of the guilty plea. To this end, the Chamber asked the accused:

(i) if his guilty plea was entered voluntarily, in other words, if he did so freely and knowingly, without pressure, threats, or promises;

---

[1]   See *infra*, section on guilty plea.
[2]   See Decision on Guilty Plea, issued on 14 December 1998.

(ii) if he clearly understood the charges against him as well as the consequences of his guilty plea; and

(iii) if his guilty plea was unequivocal, in other words, if he was aware that the said plea could not be refuted by any line of defence.

8.   The accused replied in the affirmative to all these questions. Furthermore, on the basis of lack of any material disagreement between the parties about the facts presented in support of counts one to four of the indictment, the Chamber found that the guilty plea was based on sufficient facts, firstly, for the crimes charged and, secondly, for the accused's participation therein.

9.   On the strength of the above, the Chamber found Omar Serushago guilty of genocide, as stipulated in Article 2(3)(a) of the Statute, a crime against humanity (murder), as stipulated in Article 3(a) of the Statute, a crime against humanity (extermination), as stipulated in Article 3(b) of the Statute, and a crime against humanity, (torture), as stipulated in Article 3(f) of the Statute.

II. Law and applicable principles

10.   The Chamber will now summarize the legal texts relating to sentences and penalties and their enforcement, before going on to specify the applicable scale of sentences, on the one hand, and the general principles on the determination of penalties, on the other.

A.   Applicable texts

11.   As it has previously done in the cases "The Prosecutor versus Jean Kambanda" and "The Prosecutor versus Jean Paul Akayesu", the Chamber will apply the statutory and regulatory **[page 4]** provisions hereafter. Article 22 of the Statute on judgement, Articles 23 and 26 dealing respectively with penalties and enforcement of sentences, Rules 100, 101, 102, 103 and 104 of the Rules which cover respectively sentencing procedure on a guilty plea, penalties, status of the convicted person, place and supervision of imprisonment.

B.   Scale of sentences applicable to the accused found guilty of one of the crimes listed in Articles 2, 3 or 4 of the Statute of the Tribunal

12.   As can be seen from a reading of all the above provisions on penalties, the only penalties the Tribunal can impose on an accused who pleads guilty or is convicted as such, are prison terms up to and including life imprisonment. The Statute of the Tribunal excludes other forms of punishment such as the death sentence, penal servitude or a fine.

13.   Whereas in most national systems the scale of penalties is determined in accordance with the gravity of the offence, the Chamber notes that, as indicated *supra*, the Statute does not rank the various crimes falling under the jurisdiction of the Tribunal and, thereby, the sentence to be handed down. In theory, the sentences are the same for each of the three crimes, namely a maximum term of life imprisonment.

14.   It should be noted, however, that in imposing the sentence, the Trial Chamber should take into account, in accordance with Article 23 (2) of the Statute, such factors as the gravity of the offence. As was held by the Chamber in the sentencing Judgements rendered on 2 October 1998 in the matter of "The Prosecutor versus Jean-Paul Akayesu" and on 4 September 1998 in the matter of "The Prosecutor versus Jean Kambanda", it is difficult to rank genocide and crimes against humanity as one being the lesser of the other in terms of their respective gravity. Therefore, the Chamber held in these two judgements that both crimes against humanity, already punished by the Nuremberg and Tokyo Tribunals, and genocide, a

concept defined later, are crimes which both particularly shock the collective conscience. In fact, they are inhumane acts committed against civilians on a discriminatory basis.

15.   Regarding the crime of genocide, in particular, the preamble to the Genocide Convention recognizes that at all periods of history, genocide has inflicted great losses on humanity and reiterates the need for international cooperation to liberate humanity from this scourge. The crime of genocide is unique because of its element of *dolus specialis* (special intent) which requires that the crime be committed with the intent 'to destroy in whole or in part, a national, ethnic, racial or religious group as such', as stipulated in Article 2 of the Statute; hence the Chamber is of the opinion that genocide constitutes the "crime of crimes", which must be taken into account when deciding the sentence.

16.   There is no argument that, precisely on account of their extreme gravity, crimes against humanity and genocide must be punished appropriately. Article 27 of the Charter of the Nuremberg Tribunal empowered that Tribunal, pursuant to Article 6 (c) of the said Charter, to sentence any accused found guilty of crimes against humanity to death or such other punishment as shall be determined by it to be just. **[page 5]**

17.   Rwanda, like all the States which have incorporated crimes against humanity or genocide in their domestic legislation, has envisaged the most severe penalties in the criminal legislation for these crimes. To this end, the Rwandan Organic Law on the Organization of Prosecutions for Offences constituting the Crime of Genocide or Crimes against Humanity, committed since 1 October 1990, adopted in 1996[3], groups accused persons into four categories, according to their acts of criminal participation. The first of these categories concerns the masterminds of the crimes (planners, organizers), persons in positions of authority, from persons who have exhibited excessive cruelty to perpetrators of sexual violence. All these people are punishable by a death penalty. The second category concerns perpetrators, conspirators or accomplices in criminal acts, who incur life imprisonment. The third category deals with persons who, in addition to committing a main crime, are guilty of other serious assaults against the person. Their sentence is short.The fourth and last category concerns persons who have committed offences against property.

18.   But as the Chamber had already stated in the afore-mentioned cases of "The Prosecutor versus Jean Kambanda" and "The Prosecutor versus Jean Paul Akayesu", reference to the practice of sentencing in Rwanda and to the Organic law is just an indication. Also, while referring as much as practicable to this general practice of sentencing, the Chamber will prefer, here too, to lean more on its unfettered discretion each time that it has to pass sentence on persons found guilty of crimes falling within its jurisdiction, taking into account the circumstances of the case and the standing of the accused persons.

C.   General principles regarding the determination of sentences

19.   In determining the sentence, the Chamber shall be mindful of the fact that this Tribunal was established by the Security Council pursuant to Chapter VII of the Charter of the United Nations within the context of measures the Council was empowered to take under Article 39 of the said Charter to ensure that violations of international humanitarian law in Rwanda in 1994 were halted and effectively redressed. The objective was to prosecute and punish the perpetrators of the atrocities in Rwanda in such a way as to put an end to impunity and thereby to promote national reconciliation and the restoration of peace.

20.   That said, it is clear that the penalties imposed on accused persons found guilty by the Tribunal must be directed, on the one hand, at retribution of the said accused, who must see their crimes punished, and over and above that, on other hand, at deterrence, namely to dissuade for good others who may be tempted in the future to perpetrate such atrocities by showing them that the international community shall not tolerate the serious violations of international humanitarian law and human rights.

---

[3]   Organic Law No. 8/96 of 30 August 1996, published in the Gazette of the Republic of Rwanda, 35th year, No. 17, 1 September 1996.

21.   However, the Chamber recalls that, in the determination of sentences, it is required by Article 23 (2) of the Statute and Rule 101 (B) of the Rules to take into account a number of factors including the gravity of the offence, the individual circumstances of the accused, the existence of any aggravating or mitigating circumstances, including the substantial co-operation **[page 6]** by the accused with the Prosecutor before or after his conviction. It is a matter, as it were, of individualizing the penalty.

22.   Clearly, however, as far as the individualization of penalties is concerned, the judges of the Chamber cannot limit themselves to the factors mentioned in the Statute and the Rules. Here again, their unfettered discretion to evaluate the facts and attendant circumstances should enable them to take into account any other factor that they deem pertinent.

23.   Similarly, the factors at issue in the Statute and in the Rules cannot be interpreted as having to be mandatorily cumulative in the determination of the sentence.

III. Case on Merits

24.   Having reviewed the principles set out above, the Trial Chamber proceeds to consider all relevant information submitted by both parties in order to determine an appropriate sentence in terms of Rule 101 of the Rules.

A.   Facts of the Case

25.   In addition to the guilty plea of Omar Serushago, the Prosecutor submitted to the Chamber a document entitled "Plea Agreement between Omar Serushago and the Office of the Prosecutor", signed by the representatives of the Prosecutor, on the one hand, and Omar Serushago and his defence counsel, Mohamed Ismail, on the other hand. In this document, Omar Serushago makes full of all the relevant facts alleged in counts one to four of the indictment, facts pertaining exclusively to count 5 of the indictment having been withdrawn by the Prosecutor with the permission of the Chamber. In particular:

(i)   Omar Serushago acknowledges that there was in Rwanda between 7 April-17 July 1994 a widespread or systematic attack against a civilian population, notably on civilian Tutsi and moderate Hutu, on political, ethnic or racial grounds, and which resulted in the death of hundreds of thousands of persons throughout Rwanda. Omar Serushago admits that the purpose of the mass killings of the Tutsi in Rwanda and those in Gisenyi between April and July 1994 was to exterminate them. Omar Serushago further recognizes that this is evidenced by the selective searching and targeting of Tutsi; the indiscriminate nature of the mass killings which victimized women and children, young people and old people alike, and the fact that they were pursued in the places where they had taken refuge, i.e. prefectures and communal offices, schools, churches and stadiums with the intent of exterminating them.

(ii)   Omar Serushago acknowledges that Gisenyi, the prefecture of origin of the deceased President, Juvénal Habyarimana, located in northwestern Rwanda, was the bastion of the *Mouvement républicain national pour la démocratie et le développement* (MRND) and the *Coalition pour la défense de la république* (CDR). He further declares that several prominent civil and military leaders who had espoused the extremist Hutu **[page 7]** ideology were from this prefecture and that after 1990, the prefecture was the theatre for much inter-ethnic tension and violence, causing the death of many Tutsi (e.g. the case with the *Bagogwe* in 1991). Omar Serushago additionally declares that the interim Government moved to Gisenyi in June 1994.

(iii)   Omar Serushago states that on the night of 6 to 7 April 1994, in Gisenyi prefecture, the military commander, Anatole Nsengiyumva ordered certain political leaders, local authorities and militiamen to assemble at the Gisenyi military camp. He declares that this meeting was attended by Bernard Munyagishari, Chairman of the Interahamwe for Gisenyi, Bamabé Samvura, Chairman of

CDR for Rubavu commune and Thomas Mugiraneza, Vice-Chairman of the Interahamwe for Gisenyi.

(iv)   Omar Serushago states that during this assembly, Anatole Nsengiyumva ordered the participants to kill all the RPF "accomplices"and all the Tutsi. Omar Serushago further declares that at the end of the meeting, Anatole Nsengiyumva ordered his subordinate, Lieutenant Bizumurenyi, to distribute weapons and grenades to the militiamen who were present.

(v)   Ofar Serushago admits that on 7 April 1994, he was informed by militiamen Thomas Mugirareza and Jumapiri Nyaribogi of the orders given by Lieutenant-Colonel Anatole Nsengiyumva during the night and the telegram he received from Kigali to start the massacres.

(vi)   Omar Serushago, acknowledges that as from 7 April 1994, the massacres of the Tutsi population and the killing of numerous Hutu political opponents were perpetrated in Gisenyi and in other localities throughout the territory of Rwanda. Omar Serushago admits that in Gisenyi prefecture the groups of militiamen most involved in the massacres were led, among others, by Bernard Munyagishari, Mabuye Twagirayesu, Hassan "Gitoki", Thomas Nugiraneza and himself.

(vii)   Omar Serushago, acknowledges that Barnabé Samvura, Damas Karikumutimana, Michel, Christophe Nizehimana, Thomas Mugiraneza, Hakiziman Faziri, Bernard Munyagishari, Hassan "Gitoki" and himself, among others, attended a meeting held in Gisenyi on or around 13 April, where he was assigned the supervision of one of the roadblocks located on the edge of Gisenyi town near the border with the Democratic Republic of Congo (former Zaïre), known as the "Corniche". Omar Serushago further admits that at that location, he searched for, identified and selected Tutsi and ordered militiamen, members of his group and his subordinates, including Thomas Mugiraneza, to take them to the "Commune Rouge"and execute them. Omar Serushago further acknowledges that his orders were followed and these persons were killed.

(viii)   Omar Serushago further acknowledges that as one of the leaders of the Interahamwe in Gisenyi, and as the head of a group of five militiamen, by virtue of the decisions he took and orders he gave Interahamwe assigned to operate under him at the road block called the "Corniche", he exercised authority and control over the group of militiamen, and other militiamen including, among others, Abuba, Thomas Mugiraneza, **[page 8]** Bahati, Gahutu. Gamisi-Pokou (alias 'Etranger'), Lionceau and Feruzi Ayabagabo. These militiamen committed massacres of the Tutsi population and moderate Hutus in Gisenyi prefecture with his knowledge and at his instigation.

(ix)   Omar Serushago acknowledges that on 20th April 1994, Thomas Mugiraneza, Hassan "Gitoki", Damas Kankumutimana, Michel, Abuba and himself, on the orders of Anatole Nsengiyumva, abducted about twenty Tutsi who had found refuge at the house of Bishop Aloys Bigirumwani in Gisenyi, in collusion with the soldiers who were present on the scene and were supposed to protect them. Omar Serushago further admits that they took them to a place known as "Commune Rouge" (Commune Rubavu) and executed them. Omar Serushago further admits that he personally killed four (one man and three women) of the twenty persons with a R4 rifle given to him at the Mukamira Camp, Ruhengeri, in 1993 by General Augustin Bizimungu, in order to combat the enemy – "*Inyenzi-Tutsi*".

(x)   Omar Serushago admits that at the end of April 1994, Thomas Mugiraneza, Bernard Munyagishari, Hassan "Gitoki", Damas Karikutimana, Michel, Abuba and himself on the orders of Appolinaire Bigamiro, the Gendarmerie commander for Gisenyi, went to the Gisenyi military camp to get several Tutsi and moderate Hutu detained in the Gendarmerie station jail. Omar Serushago further admits that in collusion with the guards present, they abducted them, brought them to "Commune Rouge", where they were killed by Interahamwe present on the site. Omar Serushago further admits that he gave his rifle to his younger brother and bodyguard, Feiruz Ayabagabo, who killed one of the Tutsi, who attempted to escape.

(xi)   Omar Serushago acknowledge that around 30 April 1994, Bernard Munyagishari, Thomas Mugiraneza, Damas Karikumutima, Michel, Abuba, Hassan "Gitoki", himself and others, on the orders of Appolinaire Bigamiro, went to the company Rwandex in Gisenyi to abduct and kill Tutsi who had sought refuge there. Upon their arrival, they beat to death a Tutsi guard who was trying to stop them. Afterwards, they abducted four persons of Tutsi origin who were identified by the gendarmes present at the scene. Omar Serushago further admits that they then brought them to "Commune Rouge", where they were killed by some members of the group.

(xii) Omar Serushago acknowledges that in June 1994, in Gisenyi, on the orders of Anatole Nsengiyumva, Thomas Mugiraneza and himself, abducted a Tutsi woman and brought her near "Commune Rouge" to execute her. This person was in fact killed by Lt. Rabuhihi, and ex-soldier of the 42nd Battalion, Force Armee Rwandaise (FAR).

(xiii) Omar Serushago acknowledges that at the end of June 1994, his brother Abbas Habyalimana, a Military Police Sergeant and himself, on the instigation of Félicien Nsengimana, a director in the President's Office, abducted and illegally confined a Tutsi man in order to obtain information and extort money from him. Omar Serushago admits that during this incident, they threatened, questioned, undressed, and repeatedly beat him in order to force him to divulge the information. The man was subsequently freed following a commotion on his ethnic identity which led the assailant to believe he was **[page 9]** Hutu.

(xiv) Omar Serushago acknowledges that between April and July 1994, roadblocks were set up by militiamen in Gisenyi préfecture, in order to identify the Tutsi and their "accomplices" and take them to "Commune Rouge" to execute them there. Omar Serushago further acknowledges that Anatole Nsengiyumva and himself distributed ammunition such as cartridges to the militiamen who manned them. Omar Serushago further admits that he distributed ammunition such as cartridges to the group of militiaman that manned the "Corniche" road block, which he was in charge of.

(xv) Omar Serushago acknowledges that between May and July 1994, he knew and participated in a number of meetings held by civil and military authorities that took place in Gisenyi. At these meetings, the progress and the smooth operation of the massacres were discussed and encouraged. Some of the meetings were intended to mobilize the Interahamwe to commit massacres in other prefectures. In particular, Omar Serushago admits that in May 1994, he attended a meeting held in Gisenyi, at which Anatole Nsengiyumva was present, where the fate of surviving Tutsi was discussed. Following this meeting, Anatole Nsengiyumva ordered Thomas Mugirareza, Mabuye Twagirayesu and Oman Serushago to kill the Bishop, Wenceslas Kalibushi. Before they executed the order, the group was informed by Bernard Munyagishari that instructions had come from Kigali to spare the Bishop.

(xvi) Omar Serushago further admits that in April 1994, he participated at a meeting held at Gisenyi Military Camp, and attended by Anatole Nsengiyumva, Bernard Munyagishari, Wellars Benzi, Appolinaire Biganiro and Hassan "Gitoki". The purpose of the meeting was to send militia reinforcements to Nyange, Kibuye Prefecture, in order to kill Tutsi who had organized resistance against Interahamwe attacks. During the meeting, ammunition and rocket launchers were distributed by Anatole Nsengiyumva to the militiamen. Following the meeting, around thirty militiamen were taken to Nyange in two pick ups, one driven by Safari Besesa. This operation which was led by Bernard Munyagishari from MRND and Mabuye Twagirayesu from CDR, lasted two days and led to numerous deaths.

(xvii) Omar Serushago further acknowledges that between May and June 1994, Anatole Nsengiyumva, Félicien Kabuga, Joseph Nzirorera, Secretary General of the MRND, and Juvénal Uwiligimana, Director of the *Office Rwandais du Tourisme et de Parcs Nationaux*, held a meeting in Gisenyi. During the meeting, Joseph Nzirorera and Juvénal Uwiligimana took note of the names of the Tutsi and moderate Hutu who had come from other préfectures and drew up a list of people to eliminate, which they handed over to him and to the other leaders of the Gisenyi militia groups. Omar Serushago admits that he executed the instructions and orders given to him by these civilian and military authorities.

(xiii) Omar Serushago acknowledges that in June 1994, he arrested at the Corniche road block, one of the people on that list, whose identity, collaboration with RPF and presence in Gisenyi was also broadcasted on RTLM. Omar Serushago further admits that the person was identified to him by Protais Zigiranyirazo, brother-in-law of the late President Habyariamana. Omar Serushago further admits that after arresting the person, he handed **[page 10]** him over to Thomas Mugiraneza a militiaman, who then took him to "Commune Rouge" where he was killed. Shortly thereafter, his subordinate reported that the person had in fact been killed by one of the Interahamwe, Kivenge, based at "Commune Rouge".

(xix) Omar Serushago admits that between 13 April to July 1994, he and his group travelled throughout the town of Gisenyi in search of Tutsi and moderate Hutu. On locating the victims his group of militiamen, including himself, either killed them on the spot or took them to "Commune Rouge", where they were executed.

(xx) Omar Serushago declares that since the massacres of the Bagogwe in 1991, Nyundo parish had been a place of refuge for Tutsi victims of ethnic violence. He further declares that as early as 7 April 1994, men, women and children, the majority of whom were Tutsi, sought refuge at that location.

(xxi) Omar Serushago further acknowledges that from 8 April to June 1994, the refugees at Nyundo parish were repeatedly attacked by soldiers and militiamen and that among those militiamen were his group of militiamen, including Damas Karikumutima. Omar Serushago further acknowledges that many people were killed during those attacks, and some three hundred people were abducted from Nyundo parish, paraded before the people of Gisenyi town by Bernard Munyagishari's group and then executed at "Commune Rouge" by militiamen.

(xxii) Omar Serushago declares that between 7 April to July 1994, many people were massacred in Gisenyi Prefecture and throughout Rwanda and that the majority of the victims were killed solely because they were Tutsi or appeared to be Tutsi. He further declares that the other victims, namely moderate Hutu, were killed because they were considered Tutsi accomplices, were linked to them through marriage or were opposed to the extremist Hutu ideology.

(xxiii) Omar Serushago further declares that from 7 April 1994 to July 1994, most of the massacres were perpetrated with the instigation, participation, assistance and encouragement of political leaders, civilian authorities, military personnel, gendarmes and Hutu militiamen.

(xxiv) Omar Serushago declares that Military officers, members of the Interim Government, militia leaders and Civilian authorities, planned, prepared, instigated, ordered, aided and abetted their subordinates and others in carrying out the massacres of the Tutsi population and their "accomplices". Omar Serushago further declares that without the assistance and complicity of the local and national civil and military authorities, the principal massacres would not have occurred.

B.   Judgement

26.   In light of the admissions made by Omar Serushago in amplification of his plea of guilty, the Trial Chamber, on 14 December 1998, accepted his plea and found him guilty on the following counts: **[page 11]**

(1) By the acts or omissions described in paragraphs 4.1 to 5.27 and more specifically in the paragraphs referred to below, Omar Serushago, pursuant to Article 6(1), according to paragraphs 3.2, 3.3, 4.1, 4.12, 4.15, 5.3, 5.7, to 5.16, 5.18, 5.19,5.27, and pursuant to Article 6(3), according to paragraphs 5.8 to 5.16, 5.18, 5.19, 5.21, is responsible for killing and causing serious bodily or mental harm to members of the Tutsi population with the intent to destroy, in whole or in part, a racial or ethnic group, and thereby committed **GENOCIDE**, a crime stipulated in Article 2(3)(a) of the Statute of the Tribunal, for which he is individually responsible pursuant to Article 6 of the Statute and which is punishable in reference to Articles 22 and 23 of the Statute.

(2) By the acts or omissions described in paragraphs 4.1 to 5.27 and more specifically in the paragraphs referred to below, Omar Serushago, pursuant to Article 6(1), according to paragraphs 3.2, 3.3, 4.1, 4.12, 4.15, 5.3, 5.7 to 5.16, 5.18, 5.19, 5.27, and pursuant to Article 6(3), according to paragraphs 5.8 to 5.16, 5.18, 5.19, 5.21, is responsible for the murder of persons as part of a widespread or systematic attack against a civilian population on political, ethnic or racial grounds, and thereby committed a **CRIME AGAINST HUMANITY**, a crime stipulated in Article 3(a) of the Statute of Tribunal, for which he is individually responsible pursuant to Article 6 of the Statute and which is punishable in reference to Articles 22 and 23 of the Statute.

(3) By the acts or omissions described in paragraphs 4.1 to 5.27 and more specifically in the paragraphs referred to below, Omar Serushago, pursuant to Article 6(1), according to paragraphs 3.2, 3.3, 4.1, 4.12, 4.15, 5.3, 5.7 to 5.16, 5.18, 5.19, 5.27, and pursuant to Article 6(3), according to paragraphs 5.8 to 5.16, 5:18, 5.19, 5.21 is responsible for the extermination of persons as part of a widespread or systematic attack against a civilian population on political, ethnic or racial grounds, and thereby committed a **CRIME AGAINST HUMANITY**, a crime stipulated in Article 3(b) of the Statute of Tribunal, for which he is individually responsible pursuant to Article 6 of the Statute and which is punishable in reference to Articles 22 and 23 of the Statute.

(4) By the acts or omissions described in paragraphs 4.1 to 5.27 and more specifically in the paragraphs referred to below, Omar Serushago, pursuant to Article 6(1), according to paragraphs 3.2, 3.3, 4.1, 4.12, 4.15, 5.3, 5.13, and pursuant to Article 6(3), according to paragraph 5.13, is responsible for torture as part of a widespread or systematic attack against a civilian population on political, ethnic or racial grounds, and thereby committed a **CRIME AGAINST HUMANITY**, a crime stipulated in Article 3(f) of Statute of the Tribunal, for which he is individually responsible pursuant to Article 6 of the Statute and which is punishable in reference to Articles 22 and 23 of the Statute.

C.   Facts related to the sentence

Aggravating circumstances

(i)   Gravity of the Offences:

27.   The offences with which the accused Omar Serushago is charged are, irrefutably, of **[page 12]** extreme gravity, as the Trial Chamber already pointed out when it described genocide as the "crime of crimes". Omar Serushago personally murdered four Tutsi, while thirty-three other people were killed by militiamen placed under his authority.

(ii)   Responsibility pursuant to Article 6(3) of the Statute

28.   It was submitted by the Prosecutor and admitted by the Defence, that Omar Serushago, in the commission of the crimes for which he has been found guilty, played a leading role and that he therefore incurs individual criminal responsibility under the provisions of Article 6 (3) of the Statute. At the time of commission of the offences for which he is held responsible, Omar Serushago enjoyed definite authority in his region. He participated in several meetings during which the fate of the Tutsi was decided.

29.   He was a *de facto* leader of the Interahamwe in Gisenyi. Within the scope of the activities of these militiamen, he gave orders which were followed. Omar Serushago admitted that several victims were executed on his orders while he was manning a roadblock erected near the border between Rwanda and the Democratic Republic of Congo. As stated *supra*, thirty-three persons were killed by people placed under his authority. The accused admitted that all these crimes were committed because their victims were Tutsi or because, being moderate Hutu, they were considered accomplices.

(iii)   Voluntary participation

30.   Omar Serushago committed the crimes knowingly and with premeditation.

Mitigating circumstances

    (i)   Cooperation with the Prosecutor:

31.   Omar Serushago's cooperation with the Prosecutor was substantial and ongoing.

32.   Even before his arrest, his cooperation enabled the Prosecutor to organize and above all to successfully carry out the "NAKI" (Nairobi-Kigali) operation, which resulted in the arrest of several high-ranking persons suspected of being responsible for the events of 1994 and who are now held in custody at the Detention Facility in Arusha awaiting trial.

33.   Furthermore, Omar Serushago has agreed to testify as a witness for the Prosecution in other trials pending before the Tribunal.

    (ii)   Voluntary surrender

34.   Omar Serushago voluntarily surrendered to the authorities of Côte d'Ivoire, although he had not yet been indicted by the Tribunal and was not included in the list of suspects wanted by Rwandan authorities. The Defence submits that when he surrendered he was fully aware that his surrender would lead to his indictment. **[page 13]**

    (iii)   Guilty plea

35.   It is important to recall that the accused pleaded guilty to four counts, namely genocide and three counts of crimes against humanity (murder, extermination, torture). As the Chamber established, his guilty plea was made voluntarily and was unequivocal. Omar Serushago clearly understood the nature of the charges against him and their consequences.

    (iv)   Family and social background

36.   Both the Prosecution and the Defence underscored that prior to the commission of the crimes of which he has been convicted, Omar Serushago lived in a highly politicized milieu. As the Defence Counsel stated, the political background of his family played a crucial role in his involvement with the Interahamwe militia. Indeed, the strong and old ties of friendship between his own father and President Juvenal Habyarimana led him to play a prominent role in Interahamwe circles in which he held a *de facto* position of authority.

37.   It should be noted that in spite of his activities with the Interahamwe, Omar Serushago never received military training. Without being contradicted by the Prosecutor, his counsel pointed out that he was therefore never truly positively involved. The weapon he used, an R4 gun, had been given to him in public by General Augustin Bizimungu in 1993.

    (v)   Assistance given by Omar Serushago to certain potential Tutsi victims during the Genocide

38.   The Defence alleges that Omar Serushago, during the period of the commission of the crimes with which he is charged, helped several Tutsi, including four Tutsi sisters whom he reportedly helped to cross the border between Rwanda and the Democratic Republic of Congo. The accused also hid a moderate Hutu and allowed many people who feared for their lives to cross this same border. This information not having been contradicted by the Prosecutor, the Trial Chamber holds that it is reasonable to consider that it is established.

    (vi)   Individual circumstances

39.   Both the Prosecutor and the Defence urged the Trial Chamber to take into account the family obligations of the accused who is a father of six children, two of whom are very young. The fact that Omar Serushago is only thirty-seven years old and that he had been very cooperative with the Prosecutor, in addition to showing remorse publicly, would suggest possible rehabilitation.

(vii)   Public expression of remorse and contrition

40.   During the pre-sentencing hearing, Omar Serushago expressed his remorse at length and openly. He asked for forgiveness from the victims of his crimes and the entire people of Rwanda. In addition to this act of contrition, he appealed for national reconciliation in Rwanda.

41.   The Trial Chamber endorses the opinion of Trial Chamber I of the International Criminal **[page 14]** Tribunal for the former Yugoslavia which in its decision of 29 November 1996 , in the matter of "The Prosecutor versus Drazen Erdemovic", held that "*it might take into account that the accused surrendered voluntarily to the International Tribunal, confessed, pleaded guilty, showed sincere and genuine remorse or contrition and stated his willingness to supply evidence with probative value against other individuals for crimes falling within the jurisdiction of the International Tribunal, if this manner of proceeding is beneficial to the administration of justice, fosters the co-operation of future witnesses, and is consistent with the requirements of a fair trial.*"

42.   Having reviewed all the circumstances of the case, the Trial Chamber is of the opinion that exceptional circumstances in mitigation surrounding the crimes committed by Omar Serushago may afford him some clemency.

V. VERDICT

TRIAL CHAMBER I,

FOR THE FOREGOING REASONS;

DELIVERING its decision in public;

PURSUANT to Articles 23, 26 and 27 of the Statute and Rules 100, 101, 102, 103 and 104 of the Rules of Procedure and Evidence;

NOTING the general practice of sentencing by the Courts of Rwanda;

NOTING the indictment confirmed on 28 September 1998;

NOTING the Plea of guilty of Omar Serushago on 14 December 1998 on the Counts of:

COUNT 1 genocide, as stipulated in Article 2(3)(a) of the Statute;

COUNT 2 a crime against humanity (murder), as stipulated in Article 3(a) of the Statute;

COUNT 3 a crime against humanity (extermination), as stipulated in Article 3(b) of the Statute;

COUNT 4 a crime against humanity (torture), as stipulated in Article 3(f) of the Statute;

HAVING FOUND Omar Serushago guilty on all four counts on 14 December 1998;

NOTING the briefs submitted by the parties;

HAVING HEARD the Closing Statements of the Prosecutor and the Defence Counsel; **[page 15]**

IN PUNISHMENT OF THE ABOVEMENTIONED CRIMES,

SENTENCES Omar Serushago;

born on 24 April 1961 in Rubavu Commune, Gisenyi Prefecture, Rwanda

To a single term of fifteen (15) years of imprisonment for all the crimes of which he has been convicted;

RULES that imprisonment shall be served in a State designated by the President of the Tribunal, in consultation with the Trial Chamber and the said designation shall be conveyed to the Government of Rwanda and the designated State by the Registry;

RULES that this judgement shall be enforced immediately, and that until his transfer to the said place of imprisonment, Omar Serushago shall be kept in detention under the present conditions;

RULES that credit shall be given to Omar Serushago for the period during which he has been detained as from 9 June 1998 pursuant to paragraph (D) of Rule 101 of the Rules of Procedure and Evidence which provides that credit shall be given to the convicted person for the period, if any, during which the convicted person was detained in custody pending his surrender to the Tribunal and for the period during which he was detained at the Detention Facility of the Tribunal;

Arusha, 5 February 1999.

Laïty Kama   Lennart Aspegren   Navanethem Pillay

Presiding judge   Judge   Judge

General Remarks

The Sentencing Judgments of Trial Chamber I in relation to Jean Kambanda, Jean Paul Akayesu, and Omar Serushago[1] are the first decisions on sentencing that address various legal issues of importance for both the Tribunal's jurisprudence and international criminal law as a whole. The following comment will focus on some of these issues, namely (1) the purposes of punishment, (2) the discretion of the Chamber in determining the sentence, (3) the ranking of crimes, (4) the admission of guilt as a mitigating factor, and (5) the passing of multiple sentences.

The Purposes of Punishment[2]

In the Blaškić case, a Trial Chamber of the ICTY held that "the determination of a 'fair' sentence, that is to say a sentence consonant with the interests of justice, depends on the objectives sought".[3] Thus, it is clear that the determination of the purposes of punishment may be of a practical importance with regard to the length of the sentence. If the sentence focuses on the rehabilitation of the offender, its length will differ according to the offender's social background: a person coming from a difficult social environment will certainly receive a harsher sentence than someone from a stable social group. On the other hand, if sentences are to be determined in accordance with repressive purposes, the circumstances of the offender's background will not be relevant in the determination of the length of imprisonment imposed.

Those sentencing decisions given so far both by the ICTR and the ICTY pursue both repressive and preventive objectives of sentencing.[4] Some decisions give preventive purposes of punishment – in their negative sense as a deterrent – the highest importance.[5] The three decisions discussed in this comment follow this approach. Taking account of Security Council Resolution 955 (1994), the Trial Chamber held in the Akayesu case that the imposition of penalties by the Tribunal is directed at retribution and deterrence.[6] Interestingly, despite the composition of the Tribunal being the same in all three cases,[7] the primary sentencing purpose in both the Kambanda case and in the Serushago case was just deterrence.[8] It is to be hoped further that subsequent sentencing decisions of the ICTR will shed further light on the prioritisation of sentencing purposes.

Apart from retribution and deterrence, aspects of positive general prevention in the form of national reconciliation and the (international) fight against impunity play an important role. Both purposes have been mentioned in Security Council Resolution 955 (1994) and referred to in the decisions under examination.[9] With regard to the promotion of national reconciliation, it is important to note that international criminal law often confronts situations in which people who have been fighting each other must attempt to live together peacefully after the termination of hostilities. Against this background, it becomes one of the most urgent tasks of international criminal tribunals to contribute to the challenging

---

[1]   Judge Laïty Kama, Presiding; Judge Lennart Aspegren; Judge Navanethem Pillay. Please note that this comment refers only to the English version of these and other judgments even when the French texts are authoritative.

[2]   For a rather detailed discussion of the sentencing purposes to be pursued by the ad hoc-Tribunals see Sentencing Judgement, *Prosecutor v. Erdemović*, Case No. IT-96- 22-T, 29 November 1996, par. 57-66, ALC-I-503. For a general view, starting from national criminal law see Ambos/ Steiner, Vom Sinn des Strafens auf innerstaatlicher und supranationaler Ebene, 40 Juristische Schulung 2000 (forthcoming).

[3]   Judgment, *Prosecutor v. Blaškić*, Case No. IT-95-14, 3 March 2000, par. 761.

[4]   Sentencing Judgement, *Prosecutor v. Erdemović*, Case No. IT-96-22-T, 29 November 1996, par. 64; Judgment, *Prosecutor v. Furundžija*, Case No. IT-95-17/1-T 10, 10 December 1998, par. 288; Sentencing Judgment, *Prosecutor v. Tadić*, Case No. IT-94-1-Tbis-R117, 11 November 1999, par. 9; Judgement, *Prosecutor v. Delalić et al.* ("Čelebići"), Case No. IT-96-21, 16 November 1998, par. 1203, 1231, 1234; Sentence, *Prosecutor v. Serushago*, Case No. ICTR 98-39-S, 5 February 1999, par. 20; Judgement, *Prosecutor v. Rutaganda*, Case No. ICTR 96-3, 6 December 1999, par 7.3.2; Sentence, *Prosecutor v. Kayishema and Ruzindana*, Case No. ICTR 95-1-T, 21 May 1999, par. 2.

[5]   Cf. Sentence, *Prosecutor v. Serushago*, Case No. ICTR 98-39-S, 5 February 1999, par. 20; Judgement, *Prosecutor v. Rutaganda*, Case No. ICTR 96-3, 6 December 1999, par. 7.3.2; Judgement, *Prosecutor v. Delalić et al.* ("Čelebići"), Case No. IT-96-21, 16 November 1998, par. 1203.

[6]   Akayesu case, par. 18 *et seq.*

[7]   See *supra* note 1.

[8]   Kambanda case, par. 28; Serushago case, par. 20: "[...] the penalties must be directed [...] at retribution [...] and *over and above that* [...] at deterrence" (emphasis added).

[9]   Kambanda case, par. 26 *et seq.*, 59 ; Akayesu case, par. 18 ; Serushago case, par. 19.

need to reunite and reconcile former warring parties. Public opinion must be reassured that the rules of international criminal law are applied and enforced. The perpetrators must be held responsible in trials that comply with international standards of due process. Such trials lead to the stabilisation of, and increase confidence towards the international legal order. The findings of the ICTR's Trial Chamber I on this matter are consistent with the judgements in Blaškić and Kupreškić et al of the ICTY.[10] In the latter, it was held that the sentencing decisions "create trust in and respect for the developing system of international justice".[11] This wording reminds one of wording included in the Preamble of the ICC Statute,[12] and indicates that the purposes of positive general prevention in sentencing are becoming increasingly important in international criminal law.

With respect to the fight against impunity, the judgments do not clarify in detail the meaning of this aim of punishment. However, it is clear from the international efforts to combat impunity[13] that this sentencing purpose addresses the world-wide phenomenon that crimes committed directly by, or with the acceptance by state- or non-state actors are not prosecuted, since these actors are typically powerful and influential enough to impede the proper and efficient activities of the responsible state organs. Thus, the sentencing purpose of fighting impunity stretches far beyond the responsibility of the individual perpetrator and pursues a more general preventive purpose of eradicating the "culture" of allowing human rights violators to go unpunished.

Finally, the sentencing purpose of *rehabilitation* was explicitly mentioned in Serushago. The Trial Chamber held that the age of the defendant, his co-operation with the Prosecutor, and his public showing of remorse "would suggest possible rehabilitation".[14] The significance of this sentencing purpose depends inter alia on the character of the armed conflict in which the crimes were committed. In international armed conflicts, perpetrators generally commit crimes against nationals of the other warring party. When the conflict ceases, most of the perpetrators will be reintegrated into their respective societies and live a law-abiding life. In these cases rehabilitation normally comes about "automatically" since there was never a split between these perpetrators and their society;[15] in fact they are normally received as patriotic war heroes and their crimes are not considered as such. The situation is radically different in a non-international armed conflict where members of the same country and society fight each other and later must search for reconciliation. This need of reconciliation entails the need of reintegration of the former fighters and their enemies and leads us to the sentencing purpose of rehabilitation. However, this purpose is regarded as less important than the "attempt to stigmatise the most serious violations of international humanitarian law."[16] This low "ranking" is also due to the fact that rehabilitative sentencing purposes are not referred to in Security Council Resolution 955 (1994).

The Discretion of the Chamber in Determining the Sentence

When determining the sentence, the Trial Chamber takes into account the gravity of the offence, the individual circumstances of the defendants, and any mitigating and/ or aggravating circumstances.[17] In all three judgments, the Trial Chamber takes the view that it is within its "unfettered discretion" to evaluate

---

[10] Judgment, *Prosecutor v. Blaškić*, Case No. IT-95-14, 3 March 2000, par. 763: "the International Tribunal [...]would thereby express its indignation over heinous crimes and denounce the perpetrators".

[11] Judgement, *Prosecutor v. Kupreškić et al.*, Case No. IT-95-16, 14 January 2000, par. 838.

[12] Cf. Preamble Rome Statute of the International Criminal Court, par. 11 (adopted by the United Nations Diplomatic Conference of Plenipotentiaries on the Establishment of an International Criminal Court on 17 July 1998, UN-Doc. A/Conf. 183/9 <www.un.org/law/icc>; hereinafter: "ICC Statute").

[13] See Ambos, Straflosigkeit von Menschenrechtsverletzungen, Freiburg i. Br. 1997, p. 7 et seq.; id., Impunidad y Derecho Penal Internacional, Buenos Aires (ad hoc) 1999, p. 33 et seq.

[14] Serushago case, par. 39.

[15] In contrast to the relationship between the perpetrator and her society with regard to "normal" crimes committed in peace time. In this case, the perpetrator stands outside her society.

[16] Sentencing Judgment, *Prosecutor v. Erdemović*, Case No. IT-96-22-T, 29 November 1996, par. 66.

[17] Cf. Article 23, paragraph 2 ICTR Statute.

all circumstances it considers to be important.[18] In accordance with the jurisprudence of the ICTY,[19] the Trial Chamber refers to, but is not bound by the general practice regarding prison sentences in the courts of Rwanda.[20] The Chamber holds that although it would refer "as much as practicable to this general practice of sentencing", it would prefer "to lean more on its unfettered discretion" when deciding upon the facts of the case and any other circumstance it deems important.[21] The term "unfettered discretion" must not, however, be misinterpreted as giving "carte blanche" to the Trial Chamber when deciding which factors must be taken into account in the determination of the sentence and to what extent. Although it cannot be doubted that a Trial Chamber possesses discretion with regard to sentencing and, in particular, is not directly bound by the sentencing practice in Rwanda or the former Yugoslavia, its discretion is bound by the applicable law.

The determination of the sentence and the evaluation of the factors upon which it is based are subject to appellate proceedings. According to Article 24 ICTR Statute, the Appeals Chamber shall rule on an appeal on both errors of law and fact which have invalidated the decision. In its judgment in Serushago, the Appeals Chamber held that the Trial Chamber's discretion ends if "it either took into account what it ought not to have, or failed to take into account what it ought to have taken into account in the weighing process involved in this exercise of discretion", provided "that this resulted in a miscarriage of justice".[22] Additionally, the discretion is limited by the principle of proportionality[23], and the sentencing decision must respect the sentencing purposes mentioned in Security Council Resolution 955 (1994). These legal limitations make it clear that the process of sentencing is not an intuitive one, but rather a legal exercise which – to a certain extent – is controlled and supervised by the Appeals Chamber. This guarantees the development of a consistent sentencing practice in international criminal law.

Similarly, the Appeals Chamber's decision in the Aleksovski case shows that the sentencing discretion of a Trial Chamber is not unlimited. The Appeals Chamber agreed with the Prosecutor's submission that the Trial Chamber had not given sufficient consideration to the gravity of the crimes committed by the defendant.[24] Furthermore, it held that the Trial Chamber erred by not having treated the defendant's position as a commander as an aggravating circumstance. For these reasons, the Appeals Chamber held that "the Trial Chamber's exercise of discretion in imposing sentence" constituted a "discernible error", necessitating for the imposition of a revised sentence by the Appeals Chamber.[25] Whilst this does not invalidate the principle that the determination of the sentence is the primary task of the Trial Chamber, if an error occurs that renders the sentence "manifestly inadequate", the sentencing decision can be revised upon appeal.[26]

Such an error may also exist if the Trial Chamber does not give due weight to the sentencing purposes as expressed in Security Council Resolution 955 (1994). The Resolution expresses the determination of the Security Council to *inter alia* "contribute to the process of national reconciliation and to the restoration and maintenance of peace". It follows that the Chambers of the Tribunal shall refrain from rendering sentences which might contradict purposes of sentencing applicable under international criminal law.[27] As mentioned above, the case law of the ICTR (and of the ICTY) has consistently demonstrated that

---

[18]   Kambanda case, par. 25, 30; Akayesu case, par. 17, 21; Serushago case, par. 18, 22.

[19]   Sentencing Judgment, *Prosecutor v. Erdemović*, Case No. IT-96-22-T, 29 November 1996, par. 39; Sentencing Judgment, *Prosecutor v. Tadić*, Case No. IT-94-1-Tbis-R117, 11 November 1999, par. 10 *et seq.*; Judgement, *Prosecutor v. Jelisić*, Case No. IT-95-10, 14 December 1999, par. 116 with further references. This practice has also been applied by the Appeals Chamber in Judgement in Sentencing, *Prosecutor v. Tadić*, Case No. IT-94-1-Abis, A. Ch., 26 January 2000, par. 73.

[20]   Article 23, paragraph 1 ICTR Statute.

[21]   Kambanda case, par. 23 *et seq.*; Akayesu case, par. 17 ; Serushago case, par. 18.

[22]   Reasons for Judgement, *Prosecutor v. Serushago*, Case No. ICTR 98-39-A, 6 April 2000, II. Discussion.

[23]   Judgement, *Prosecutor v. Blaškić*, Case No. IT-95-14, 3 March 2000, par. 796.

[24]   Cf. Article 81, paragraph 2 (a) ICC Statute that expressly provides that disproportionality between the crime and the sentence is to be regarded as a ground for appeal.

[25]   Judgement, *Prosecutor v. Aleksovski*, Case No. IT-95-14/1-A, A.Ch., 24 March 2000, par. 187.

[26]   *Ibid.*

[27]   In the Aleksovski case, the Appeals Chamber held that the sentences of the Tribunal shall reflect, not undermine the underlying purposes of sentencing: "[…] a sentence of the International Tribunal should make plain the condemnation of the international community of the behaviour in question" (*supra* note 25, par. 185).

retribution and deterrence are the most important purposes of punishment. Therefore, it is not within the discretion of a Trial Chamber to attribute to other sentencing purposes, for example rehabilitation, a degree of weight such that the sentence loses its deterrent effect or will no longer express the disapproval by the Tribunal and the international community. In sum, it is clear that the Tribunals' discretion is not unlimited but bound by the applicable law and subject to the supervision of the Appeals Chamber.

Ranking of Crimes

The fact that neither the ICTR Statute nor the ICTY Statute provide for specific penalties for the crimes within their respective scopes means that an important indicator for the ranking of these crimes is lacking. As a result, the Tribunals' task is not limited to the determination of sentences by taking into account the gravity of the offence and the individual circumstances of the defendant's conduct, but also encompasses – as a first step in the sentencing process – the establishment of a ranking of these crimes.[28] In the long run, this leads to a consistent sentencing practice that, in turn, contributes to the credibility and predictability of the Tribunals' sentences. ICTR's Trial Chamber I undertook the task of evaluating criteria for the establishment of such a gradation in the three decisons under examination.

When deciding on a ranking between the crime of genocide and a crime against humanity, the Trial Chamber admitted that "it seems difficult [...] to rank genocide and crimes against humanity in terms of their respective gravity", given the fact that these "are crimes which both particularly shock the collective conscience".[29] However, the Chamber found that genocide "is unique because of its element of dolus specialis (special intent) [...]; hence, the Chamber is of the opinion that genocide constitutes the 'crime of crimes'".[30] With regard to crimes against humanity, the Chamber referred to the Erdemović case and held that "crimes against humanity [...] transcend the individual because when the individual is assaulted, humanity comes under attack and is negated. It is therefore the concept of humanity as victim which essentially characterises crimes against humanity".[31] This reasoning also accounts for the view that crimes against humanity and genocide are more severe than war crimes (as violations of Art. 3 common to the Geneva Conventions and Additional Protocol II thereto).[32] However, the question whether or not crimes against humanity are intrinsically more serious than war crimes was not discussed in more detail since none of the three cases included counts of war crimes. Therefore, the finding of the Trial Chamber that violations of Art. 3 common to the Geneva Conventions and Additional Protocol II thereto are lesser crimes than genocide and crimes against humanity must be regarded as *obiter dictum*.[33]

While the Trial Chamber considered genocide as the "crime of crimes" that has to be punished with an appropriate sentence,[34] it did not impose a mandatory term of life imprisonment. In fact, the Chamber's sentence in the Serushago case indicates that it does not consider the imposition of a sentence of life imprisonment to be the general rule for genocide: while the Chamber issued two single sentences of life imprisonment for genocide and direct and public incitement to commit genocide in Akayesu,[35] Serushago received a sentence of 15 years imprisonment for *inter alia* a count of genocide. The Chamber found that

---

[28]   Cf. Judgement, *Prosecutor v. Aleksovski*, Case No. IT-95-14/1, 25 June 1999, par. 243: "[...] in order to implement the Tribunal's mandate, it is crucial to establish a gradation of sentences".

[29]   Kambanda case, par. 14; Akayesu case, par. 7; Serushago case, par. 14.

[30]   Kambanda case, par. 16.

[31]   Sentencing Judgement, *Prosecutor v. Erdemović*, Case No. IT-96-22-T, 29 November 1996, par. 28, ALC-I- 503.

[32]   Kambanda case, par. 14.

[33]   Whereas the majority of the Appeals Chamber in the Erdemovic case held that crimes against humanity "in their very nature [...] differ in principle from war crimes" and thus constituted more serious crimes (Judgement, *Prosecutor v. Erdemović*, Case No. IT-96-22-A, 7 October 1997, par. 21, 26, ALC-I-537; Judge Li dissenting), the majority of the Appeals Chamber in the Tadić case found "that there is in law no distinction between the seriousness of a crime against humanity and that of a war crime" (Judgement in Sentencing, *Prosecutor v. Tadić*, Case No. IT-94-1-Abis, A.Ch. 26 January 2000, par. 69; Judge Cassese dissenting). Therefore, the decision of the Trial Chamber in the three ICTR cases under examination follows the majority decision in the Erdemović case. However, it must be taken into consideration that the Appeals Decision in the Tadić case was rendered after the sentences in the cases of Kambanda, Akayesu, and Serushago had been handed down.

[34]   Kambanda case, par. 17.

[35]   Akayesu case, Sentence: The sentences for murder, torture, rape, and other inhumane acts as crimes against humanity were ten years (counts 11, 14) and fifteen years (counts 5, 7, 9 and 13) respectively. In the other two judgments, the Trial Chamber rendered a single sentence without passing single sentences for each count.

Serushago committed genocide and – as crimes against humanity – murder, extermination, and torture. According to his confession, he personally murdered four Tutsis, and 33 people were killed by militiamen who were placed under his authority.[36] In determining the sentence, a number of aggravating and mitigating circumstances were considered. Although the Chamber acknowledged that the crimes committed were "[…] irrefutably, of extreme gravity", it held that "exceptional circumstances in mitigation […] may afford him some clemency".[37] Against the background of the characterisation of genocide as the "crime of crimes" this sentence requires a closer examination.

Neither the Statute nor the Rules of the ICTR explain the term *"gravity of the offence"*. On the basis of national law and doctrine this term should be understood as referring to the harm or damage caused by the offence (objective element, actus reus) and the culpability of the offender as expressed in the commission of the act (subjective element, mens rea).[38] These two constituent elements of the gravity of the offence are influenced only by those aggravating and mitigating circumstances that directly affect the commission of the crime, including the personal motives of the perpetrator, the way in which she committed the act or her age at the time of the commission of the act.[39] The gravity of the offence provides for a range of punishment (for example from ten to fifteen years) within which the sentence must be determined for the individual perpetrator, after taking into account not only the nature of the crime, but also any aggravating and mitigating circumstances not contemporaneous with the commission of the crime – for example co-operation with the Prosecutor, the voluntary surrender to the Tribunal, a guilty plea, or a show of remorse. These factors do not affect the perpetrator's culpability[40] and, consequently, neither increase nor reduce the gravity of the crime.[41] Although they are important for the individualisation of the sentence, they should not be allowed to render the sentence disproportionate[42] to the gravity of the crime. Thus, this scheme also contributes to the difficult task of making the sentence commensurate with the gravity of the crime.

Another advantage of this approach is that it facilitates the comparability of the different crimes under the Tribunal's Statute since the particular factors mentioned above do not relate to the gravity of the crime but to the circumstances of the case before the Tribunal. This, in turn, facilitates the Appeals Chamber's task to review the sentencing decisions of the Trial Chambers. Finally, the establishment of a relationship between the gravity of the crimes and the various particular factors of any one case enhances the credibility of the Tribunal and the widespread acceptance of its sentences. On the basis of this approach, the punishment in Serushago appears to be particularly lenient. While the aggravating factors – the magnitude of the crime and the superior authority of the defendant – were contemporaneous with the commission of the crime, most of the mitigating factors – such as the co-operation with the Prosecutor, the voluntary surrender, and the guilty plea – were not. Thus, these factors could not reduce the

---

[36]   Serushago case, par. 27.
[37]   In addition to the "extreme gravity" of the crime, the Chamber held that he "played a leading role" in the commission of these crimes and, having been the *de facto* leader of the Interahamwe in Giseny, that he "enjoyed definite authority in his region" (Serushago case, par. 27 *et seq.*, 42). As mitigating circumstances, the Chamber considered the defendant's co-operation with the Prosecutor, his voluntary surrender, his guilty plea, his social background, his assistance given to certain potential Tutsi victims, his family obligations, and his show of remorse (*ibid.*, par. 31 *et seq.*).
[38]   Cf. Andrew Ashworth, Sentencing and Criminal Justice, 2nd ed., 1995, p. 134 (England); Nils Jareborg, Straffrättsideologiska Fragment, 1992, p. 156 (Sweden); Ángel Calderón Cerezo/José Antonio Choclán Montalvo, Derecho Penal-Parte General, tomo I, 1999, p. 504 (Spain); Günter Gribbohm, in: Burkhard Jähnke/Heinrich Wilhelm Laufhütte/Walter Odersky (eds.), Leipziger Kommentar zum StGB, 1994, § 46 mn 9 (Germany).
[39]   Similarly, a Trial Chamber in the Erdemović case distinguished between "circumstances contemporaneous with the carrying out of the criminal act", "circumstances following the commission of the acts", and "factors relating to personality" (Sentencing Judgment, *Prosecutor v. Erdemović*, Case No. IT-96-22-T, 29 November 1996, par. 86 *et seq.*, 102 *et seq.*, ALC-I-503).
[40]   Cf. Ashworth, *supra* note 38, at 135 (England); Jareborg, *supra* note 38, at 156 (Sweden); Calderón Cerezo/Choclán Montalvo, *supra* note 38, at 505 (Spain); Reinhart Maurach/Heinz Zipf, Strafrecht Allgemeiner Teil, Teilband 1, 8th ed., 1992, § 63 I A (Germany).
[41]   Cf. Judgment and Sentence, *Prosecutor v. Ruggiu*, Case No. ICTR 97-32-I, 1 June 2000, par. 80.
[42]   Kambanda case, par. 58: "A sentence must reflect the predominant standard of proportionality between the gravity of the offence and the degree of responsibility of the offender. Just sentences contribute to respect for the law and the maintenance of a just, peaceful and safe society."

"extreme" gravity of the crime and the Trial Chamber should have imposed a higher sentence to reflect the significance of the offence.

Guilty Plea[43]

An admission of guilt is an important mitigating factor that must be taken into account when determining the sentence. The extent to which it may be considered in mitigation of punishment is within the discretion of the sentencing judges. As previously mentioned, this discretion is not unlimited but the judges must bear in mind the purposes of punishment mentioned in Security Council Resolution 955 (1994). The assessment of the mitigation factors must not contradict these sentencing purposes. In concreto, the evaluation of the mitigating effect of a guilty plea is not an easy task. On the one hand, one may argue that the pursuit of national reconciliation calls for extensive mitigation because "the guilty plea [...] is likely to encourage other individuals to recognise their responsibilities [...]"[44] and to surrender to the Tribunal. This leads to further trials and the strengthening of the international legal order. On the other hand, extensive mitigation may have the opposite effect. If an admission of guilt leads to an excessively mitigated sentence, one could claim that the crimes were not properly addressed and, as a consequence, the rules of international criminal law were partially negated.

Although there are several reasons supporting the mitigating effect of a guilty plea – i.e. *inter alia* "keeping public expenditure in check, and minimising the stress on the victims and witnesses"[45] – it should not be forgotten that the ICTR deals with the most serious crimes. This must limit the discretion of the Tribunal to accord an admission of guilt a disproportionate weighting. It must also be recalled that a guilty plea does not reduce the gravity of the offence.

Single Sentence or Multiple Sentences?

There is no uniform sentencing practice of the ICTR with regard to the passing of a single sentence or multiple sentences. In the verdicts against Jean Kambanda, Omar Serushago, and Alfred Musema,[46] the Chambers rendered a single sentence for multiple counts. This approach has been adopted by the ICTY in Blaškić and Jelisić where it was held that the criminal acts "form[ed] part of a single set of crimes committed over a brief time span which does not allow for distinctions between their respective criminal intention and motives".[47] However, in all other cases decided by both the ICTR and the ICTY the Chambers passed multiple sentences for the counts on which the defendant was found guilty. In the words of Trial Chamber I of the ICTR, this was done "in order to reflect the gravity of each and every one of them and to properly assess the guilt of the accused".[48]

In order to protect the rights of the defendant, the latter approach should be uniformly adopted by both Tribunals. If the defendant does not know what impact each count has on the totality of the sentence, his right to appeal the sentence on the ground of disproportion between the crime and the sentence would be endangered. Further, it should be the aim of the ICTR to make the process of sentencing as transparent as possible. This will enhance trust in the court and its universal acceptance. Therefore, the Chamber should pass multiple sentences for those crimes for which the defendant has been convicted for.

Kai Ambos and Jan Christoph Nemitz

---

[43]   For general information on this issue cf. Sienho Yee, The Erdemović Sentencing Judgement: A questionable milestone for the International Criminal Tribunal for the former Yugoslavia, Georgia Journal of International and Comparative Law 1997, No. 2, p. 263 *et seq.*; Jan Christoph Nemitz/ Steffen Wirth, Legal Aspects of the Appeals Decision in the Erdemović-case: the Plea of Guilty and Duress in International Humanitarian Law, Humanitäres Völkerrecht – Informationsschriften 1998, No. 1, p. 43 *et seq.*

[44]   Kambanda case, par. 61.

[45]   Ashworth, *supra* note 38, p. 137.

[46]   Judgment, *Prosecutor v. Musema*, Case No. ICTR 96-13-T, 27 January 2000.

[47]   Judgment, *Prosecutor v. Jelisić*, Case No. IT-95-10, 14 December 1999, par. 137; cf. also Judgment, *Prosecutor v. Blaškić*, Case No. IT-95-14, 3 March 2000, par. 807.

[48]   Akayesu case, par. 29.

INDEX

CONTRIBUTORS AND EDITORS

Kai Ambos is an assessor (2nd state exam), Dr. iur. (Munich 1992) and since 1991, research fellow at the Max-Planck-Institute for Foreign and International Criminal Law, Freiburg im Breisgau, Germany. Since the beginning of 1996, he has been in charge of the "International Criminal Law" and "spanish-speaking Latin America" – sections (wiss. Referent) and scientific assistant (wiss. Assistent) at the University of Freiburg (Chair of Prof. Dr. Dr. as h.c. Albin Eser, M.C.J.). His main research areas are German and Latin American Criminal Law and Procedure, International Criminal Law and Drug Control (with an emphasis on the producing countries); His professorial thesis (Habilitation) at the University of Munich concerned the General Part of International Criminal Law. Among many other things, he has studied and researched at St. Anne's College, Oxford, UK (1986/87), Colombia, Peru and Bolivia (1990/1992) and the UN-Centre for Human Rights, Geneva (1994). He was a member of the German Delegation to the Diplomatic Conference on the Establishment of an International Criminal Court (Rome, 15 June – 17 July 1998).

John O'Dowd (B.C.L., Barrister at Law) is a College Lecturer in the Faculty of Law, University College Dublin, where he has taught since 1991. He has taught and published in the fields of constitutional and administrative law and media law. He is co-author, with Professor Finbar McAuley of the Irish chapter of van de Wyngaert (ed.), *Criminal procedure systems in the European Community* (1993). He has delivered a number of papers at academic seminars and symposia, dealing with international criminal co-operation from the perspective of the Irish legal system – most recently in relation to Irish ratification of the Statute of the International Criminal Court (*Irish Centre for Human Rights*, Galway, October 2000).

André Klip is a senior lecturer in international and European criminal law at Utrecht University. His dissertation on Witnesses Abroad in Criminal Matters, a comparison of the law of the United States, Germany and the Netherlands, was published in 1994. Since 1996 he has been a part-time judge at the Utrecht District Court (criminal division). He is co-author of International Criminal Law in the Netherlands, Freiburg im Breisgau 1997. He is vice-president of the Standing Committee of Experts on International Immigration, Refugee and Criminal Law, co-ordinator of the LL.M Specialisation on Internationalisation of Crime and Criminal Justice at Utrecht University and co-editor of the Commentary on Dutch law on International Co-operation in Criminal Matters.

Claus Kreß studied law at the Universities of Cologne, Geneva and Cambridge. His doctoral thesis deals with the legal regime of indirect aggression under the UN Charter. From 1996 to 2000 he held positions in the criminal law and in the international law departments of Germany's Federal Ministry of Justice. Recently, he has become senior research fellow in the international criminal law department at Cologne University to write his *Habilitation*. Hes was member to Gemany's delegation to the Rome conference and he is member of Germany's delegation to the Preparatory Commission of the ICC. He is senior honorary scholar of Gonville and Caius College, Cambridge, and correspondent to the Bochum Institute for International Peace and Armed Conflict.

Jan Christoph Nemitz, Master of International Law (Stockholm), is currently a research assistant at the Max-Planck-Institute for Foreign and International Criminal Law in Freiburg im Breisgau, Germany. He is Vice-President of the Committee for an Effective International Criminal Law (CoEICL) in Constance, Germany. From October 1996 until March 1997 he worked as a law clerk for the Office of the Prosecutor of the International Criminal Tribunal for the Former Yugoslavia. He is currently preparing a dissertation on the law of sentencing in international criminal law.

Tom Ongena is a research assistant at the University of Antwerp, Belgium. He is a member of the Research Group Criminal Law of Professor Christine Van den Wyngaert. His research is concentrated in the field of international criminal law. Since October 2000 he has been preparing a doctoral thesis on the *ne bis in idem* principle in national and international criminal law.

Alphons M. Orie graduated from Leyden University (1971) and worked at the Department of Criminal Law & Procedure of the Law Faculty of his alma mater until 1980. His research concentrated on international criminal law. He was co-author of a general introduction in International Criminal Law.

After being admitted to the Bar of the Hague, he specialised in Supreme Court cases but has also continued his specialist activities, both in research and practice, in the field of foreign and international criminal law. He acted as co-counsel in the first case heard by the ICTY, the Tadic case (1995-1997). He is chairman of the Dutch section of the Association Internationale de Droit Pénal. In 1997 he was appointed Judge in the Supreme Court of the Netherlands.

William A. Schabas studied history and international relations at the University of Toronto and law at the University of Montreal. He was dean of the law school at the University of Quebec at Montreal from 1994 to 1998. Since 2000, he is professor of human rights law at the National University of Ireland and Director of the Irish Centre for Human Rights. He is editor of Criminal Law Forum, and was a delegate to the 1998 Diplomatic Conference on the International Criminal Court for the International Centre for Criminal Law Reform. Professor Schabas is author of *Genocide in International Law, The Crime of Crimes*, published in 2000 by Cambridge University Press.

Michael P. Scharf is Professor of Law and Director of the Center for International Law and Policy at the New England School of Law in Boston, Massachusetts. From 1989-1993, Scharf worked in the Office of the Legal Adviser of the U.S. Department of State, where he served as Counsel to the Counter-Terrorism Bureau, Attorney-Adviser for Law Enforcement and Intelligence, Attorney-Adviser for United Nations Affairs, and as a member of the United States Delegations to the United Nations General Assembly and to the United Nations Human Rights Commission. Scharf is the author of dozens of articles and several books about the ad hoc war crimes tribunals and the International Criminal Court, including Balkan Justice, which was nominated for the Pulitzer Prize in 1998, and The International Criminal Tribunal for Rwanda (with Virginia Morris), which was awarded the 1999 American Society of International Law Certificate of Merit for the Outstanding book in International Law.

Elies van Sliedregt studied law at Utrecht University. She is currently working as a research assistant at the Law Faculty of Tilburg University and at the T.M.C. Asser Institute. As legal assistant she is involved in the case of one of the defendants in the 'Government case' before the ICTR. In June 2000 she attended the closing session of the Preparatory Committee for an International Criminal Court as a representative and member of the International Criminal Defence Attorney Association (ICDAA). She is correspondent to the Yearbook of International Humanitarian Law and is preparing a dissertation on the individual criminal responsibility for war crimes, in particular command responsibility.

Göran Sluiter is a lecturer in international law at Utrecht University. In the past, he has worked for the Netherlands Institute of Human Rights and the Willem Pompe Institute of Criminal Law and Criminology, both at Utrecht University. He is also affiliated with the Netherlands School of Human Rights. His research focuses on the relationship between national and international adjudication of international crimes, especially State co-operation in the field of evidence gathering. He has represented the Netherlands Institute of Human Rights at the December 1997 Session of the Preparatory Committee for an International Criminal Court and at the Rome Conference for the establishment of the ICC, in July 1998. From November 1998 until March 1999 he worked as a law clerk for the legal advisory section of the Office of the Prosecutor of the International Criminal Tribunal of the Former Yugoslavia.

Bert Swart studied law at Nijmegen University and at the University of Poitiers (France). His dissertation was on the admission and expulsion of aliens under Dutch law (1978). Other books include a study on Dutch extradition law (1986). From 1980 to 1996 he was professor of criminal law and criminal procedure at Utrecht University. In 1996, he became a judge at the Amsterdam Court of Appeal. He now holds the Van Hamel chair of international criminal law at the University of Amsterdam. He is co-author of International Criminal Law in the Netherlands, Freiburg im Breisgau 1997, and co-editor of the Commentary on Dutch law on International Co-operation in Criminal Matters. He is a member of the Royal Netherlands Academy of Arts and Sciences.

Tom Vander Beken studied law (1991) and criminology (1992) at Ghent University. His dissertation on the choice of the forum of an international criminal case was published in 1999. Currently he is lecturer in criminal law and co-director of the research group on drug policy, criminal policy and international crime of Ghent University, where he has been working since 1993. He has been an expert for the Belgian

Parliamentary Commission on Organised Crime (1996-1998). Most of his publications are on international criminal law and organised crime.

Steffen Wirth, Rechtsassessor (2nd state exam), is working as a research and teaching assistant at the Faculty of Public and International Law at the Albert-Ludwigs University in Freiburg im Breisgau, Germany. He is a Legal Expert for the Committee for an Effective International Criminal Law (CoEICL) in Constance, Germany, and has represented CoEICL at the fourth Session of the Preparatory Commission for the ICC in New York.